POCKET
DICTIONARY
OF WORDS
AND PHRASES

NTC's POCKET DICTIONARY OF WORDS AND PHRASES

12,000 Words, Idioms, and Phrasal Verbs for Travelers and Learners

EDITOR-IN-CHIEF

RICHARD A. SPEARS,

McGraw-Hill

icago New York San Francisco Lisbon London Madrid Mexico City
Milan New Delhi San Juan Seoul Singapore Sydney Toronto

Library of Congress Cataloging-in-Publication Data

Spears, Richard A.
  NTC's pocket dictionary of words and phrases / editor-in-chief, Richard A. Spears.
    p.   cm.
  ISBN 0-658-01700-4
  1. English language—Dictionaries.   2. English language—Terms and phrases.
I. Title: Pocket dictionary of words and phrases.   II. NTC Publishing Group.   III. Title.

PE1628 .S5827   2001
423'.1—dc21

2001030198

McGraw-Hill

A Division of The McGraw·Hill Companies

1 2 3 4 5 6 7 8 9 0   TCP/TCP   0 9 8 7 6 5 4 3 2 1

ISBN 0-658-01700-4

This book was set in Minion
Printed and bound by Transcontinental Printing

Cover design by Nick Panos
Interior design by Terry Stone

McGraw-Hill books are available at special quantity discounts to use as premiums and sales
promotions, or for use in corporate training programs. For more information, please write to the
Director of Special Sales, Professional Publishing, McGraw-Hill, Two Penn Plaza, New York, NY
10121-2298. Or contact your local bookstore.

DEC 1 1 2002

This book is printed on acid-free paper.

Contents

Introduction

NTC's Pocket Dictionary of Words and Phrases is for persons who are seeking to improve their ability to speak, read, write, and understand American English. It is a small, portable dictionary that will help learners with spelling, pronunciation, parts of speech, meaning, irregular forms, and the appropriate use of 12,000 common words and phrases.

This dictionary defines words using the smallest possible vocabulary, but when it is necessary, additional words are used to define difficult concepts. In many cases, more than one definition is given, so the learner has additional help in figuring out the meaning of a word or expression.

Phrases are entered in the dictionary in their normal alphabetical positions. Phrases are also indexed within the dictionary by means of cross-references. A cross-reference to each phrase is found at the entry of each non-initial, major word in the phrase. Thus, after **account** we find the cross-references:

→ COOK THE ACCOUNTS

→ GIVE A GOOD ACCOUNT OF ONESELF

→ SAVINGS ACCOUNT

→ TURN SOMETHING TO GOOD ACCOUNT

These cross-references enable a reader who can't remember an exact phrase to find it just by looking up one of the phrase's key words.

Poor Condition *Small*
Marks/Stains *Stains on*
GVK Date *the bottom Noted,*

How to Use This Dictionary

Many of the entry words in the dictionary have more than one sense. *Please study all the relevant senses* to make sure you have found the right one.

Nominals (*n.*) that do not follow the regular spelling or pronunciation rules in the formation of the plural are marked *irreg.*, and the form of the plural is given in the entry. Verbs (*tv., iv.*) that do not follow the regular rules for the formation of the past tense and past participle are marked *irreg.*, and the proper forms are given in the entry. The comparative and superlative forms of adjectives (*adj.*) and adverbs (*adv.*) are listed when there are forms—as with *red, redder, reddest*—that replace, or that exist in addition to, the comparatives and superlatives formed with *more* and *most*. After many of the definitions, you will find comments, enclosed in parentheses, containing further information about the entry word.

Keep in mind that the goal in using a monolingual learner's dictionary is not only to find the meanings of specific words, but also to develop the skills needed to acquire new words and senses of words from their actual use in context.

Useful Spelling Rules

The following basic spelling rules equip the learner to create and identify the most important derived and inflected forms of regular English nouns and verbs.

Words that have important irregular forms that do not follow these rules are identified in the dictionary.

Regular Verb Forms

Note: Many verbs that have irregular past-tense forms or irregular past participles nevertheless form the present tense and the present participle regularly.

For the third-person singular (the form used with *he*, *she*, *it*, and singular nouns) in the present tense:

■ Add *-s* to the bare verb. If the bare verb ends in *y* preceded by a consonant, change *y* to *ie* and then add *-s*. If the bare verb ends in *s*, *z*, *x*, *ch*, or *sh*, add *-es*.

like > *Bill likes*
cry > *the baby cries*
walk > *Anne walks*
buy > *the man buys*
carry > *a truck carries*
fix > *she fixes*
pass > *it passes*
notify > *he notifies*
catch > *she catches*

For the past tense and the past participle:

- ■ Add *-ed* to the bare verb. If the bare verb ends in *y* preceded by a consonant, change *y* to *i* before adding *-ed*. If the bare verb ends in *e*, just add *-d*.

  walk > walked
  like > liked
  judge > judged
  try > tried
  carry > carried
  measure > measured

For the present participle:

- ■ Add *-ing* to the bare verb. If the bare verb ends in a single *e* preceded either by a consonant or by *u*, drop the *e* before adding *-ing*. If the bare verb ends in *ie*, change *ie* to *y* before adding *-ing*.

  judge > judging
  take > taking
  ask > asking
  carry > carrying
  pay > paying
  pursue > pursuing
  hoe > hoeing
  see > seeing
  go > going
  lie > lying

Doubling of consonants in participles and past-tense forms:

■ When *-ed* or *-ing* is added to a word that ends in a consonant (other than *h*, *w*, *x*, or *y*) preceded by a single vowel, and the final syllable is stressed, then the consonant is normally doubled. Thus *commit* and *control*, which are accented on the last syllable, become *committed* and *controlling*, but *limit* and *cancel*, which are accented on the first syllable, become *limited* and *canceling*. Similarly, *stop* becomes *stopping*, but *look*, in which the consonant is preceded by two vowels, becomes *looking*.

Within the dictionary, forms that do not follow these doubling rules are noted in individual entries. The most typical exceptions to the doubling rules are words with a final *c* that becomes *ck* rather than doubling, e.g., *picnicking*, verbs that are compounds, and verbs with closely related noun senses or more than one pronunciation. Outside the dictionary, learners will encounter other exceptions, as well as some variation, because sometimes another option, although less familiar in American English, is also correct.

Regular Noun Plurals

To form the plural of a regular noun:

■ If the singular form ends in *s*, *z*, *x*, *ch*, or *sh*, add *-es*.

kiss > *kisses*
box > *boxes*
match > *matches*
dish > *dishes*
bus > *buses*

■ If the singular form ends in *y* preceded by a consonant, change *y* to *ie* and then add -*s*.

baby > babies
library > libraries
university > universities
butterfly > butterflies

■ For nouns ending in *o*, the regular plural form may be formed by adding -*es* or by adding -*s*. For some words, both spellings are possible. In this dictionary, each entry for a noun ending in *o* specifies the correct plural form or forms for that word.

radio > radios
potato > potatoes
tornado > tornados or *tornadoes*

■ For all other regular nouns, add -*s* to the singular form to make the plural.

table > tables
boy > boys
television > televisions
valley > valleys

An Important Note on the English Plural

The English plural is something that makes English very difficult for adults to learn. English nouns often cannot be made plural, unlike their counterparts in other languages. There is nothing that sounds more "non-English" than *advice, infor-*

mation, or *baggage* with the plural *s* on the end. There are many American English nouns in this dictionary that the learner should not attempt to make plural—ever! See a list of these nouns in List A on page xvii. In addition, there are many nouns in English that can be followed by the plural *s* that seem to be plural, but really refer to *kinds* or *types* of the noun in question. In the following entry, when the word *margarine* has an *s* on the end, it refers to different kinds, types, or varieties of *margarine.*

> **margarine** ['mɑr dʒə rɪn] *n.* a food made
> from animal or vegetable fats, used in
> place of butter; a spread for bread.
> (Plural only for types and instances.)

There are many American English nouns that can take the plural *s* while only referring to different kinds, types, instances, or varieties of the noun. See them in List B on page xx.

Lists of Words

These are important lists of words that can be consulted quickly. For further information, definitions, and examples, each word should be looked up in this dictionary.

List A

Nouns defined in this dictionary that never take the plural *s*. See the entry heads listed for details.

admiration	Catholicism	digestion	flesh
advice	cattle	diplomacy	former
anybody	chaos	dirt	freight
anyone	chatter	disgust	frostbite
anything	chess	dishwater	fun
applause	citizenship	distress	furniture
appreciation	clothing	distrust	fuzz
Arctic	common	drainage	glamour
arrogance	sense	dust	gloom
assistance	confusion	ease	golf
attendance	consent	east	gratitude
aviation	conservation	electricity	greed
awe	contempt	elegance	grief
baggage	courage	employment	grime
bathwater	cowardice	endurance	ground beef
blackness	cream cheese	equipment	guilt
bliss	dark	esteem	happiness
bloodshed	darkness	estimation	health
bookkeeping	daybreak	evidence	hockey
bowling	daylight	excellence	homework
bulk	decay	fame	housework
carelessness	destruction	few	hypnotism
cash	devout	filth	ill will

importance
independence
indigestion
information
insurance
intelligence
interference
isolation
jazz
jet propulsion
jewelry
knowledge
laughter
law of gravity
leakage
left
legislation
leisure
lighting
lightning
likelihood
lint
literacy
livestock
logic
loot
luck
luggage
machinery
magic
magnetism
maintenance
malice
mankind
math

mayonnaise
menstruation
merchandise
Midwest
might
mirth
misconduct
mistrust
moderation
moisture
molasses
moonlight
morale
morality
more
most
motherhood
much
mucus
nausea
needlework
neglect
nightlife
nonsense
north
northeast
northwest
nothing
now
nutrition
obedience
occult
offspring
old age
ooze

opposition
outer space
overkill
overtime
ownership
oxygen
ozone
pantyhose
paradise
parcel post
parsley
participation
patience
peace
pep
perfection
perjury
personnel
persuasion
petroleum
photography
pity
plenty
plumbing
poetry
police
poor
pork
postage
poultry
poverty
precision
preservation
prevention
prey

produce
progress
propaganda
prose
prosperity
prudence
psychiatry
psychology
publicity
punctuation
quickness
quiet
racism
rapidity
readiness
real estate
realism
reasoning
recklessness
recognition
recreation
redness
refuse
rejoicing
relief
research
revenge
ridicule
rot
rubbish
rudeness
running
rust
sadness
safekeeping

safety
salt water
sameness
sanitation
sanity
sarcasm
say
scenery
schoolwork
science
scrutiny
scuba
seafood
seaside
seclusion
secrecy
segregation
self-
   confidence
self-control
self-discipline
self-esteem
self-respect
self-service
selfishness
senility
seniority
serenity
seriousness
several
severity
sewage

sewing
sexual
   intercourse
shame
shelving
shipping
shopping
shrewdness
shrubbery
shyness
sightseeing
significance
silver
silverware
simplicity
sincerity
sizzle
skepticism
skiing
slander
slavery
sleep
sleet
slime
slow motion
slush
small talk
smuggling
soccer
social security
software
some

something
sorcery
south
southeast
southwest
spaghetti
starvation
static
stationery
storage
strife
stuff
stupidity
sunlight
sunshine
supervision
surf
suspense
tact
teamwork
tennis
terrorism
thunder
tourism
traction
traffic
transportation
trash
twilight
underclothing
underwear
undoing

unrest
upkeep
uranium
valor
vanilla
veal
vegetation
vigor
violence
vomit
warmth
wastepaper
wealth
wealthy
wear
weather
welfare
west
wetness
wilderness
willpower
wisdom
woodwork
worship
worth
wrath
wreckage
young
zeal
zest
zinc

List B

Nouns defined in this dictionary that can take the plural *s* resulting in the meaning "kinds, types, instances, or varieties of." See the entry heads listed for details.

action	caramel	cord	escape
addition	cardboard	cork	evaluation
adhesive	cargo	cost	evil
adoption	cement	cotton	examination
adventure	cereal	court	explanation
agony	chalk	crime	exposure
alcohol	champagne	cruelty	fabric
amputation	change	crystal	failure
appointment	charcoal	debt	fantasy
architecture	charm	defense	fashion
ash	cheese	denial	fat
bacon	cherry	depth	fate
bait	chocolate	destiny	fear
ballet	choice	detention	feed
bark	cider	dew	felt
beer	clay	difference	fiber
behavior	cleaner	difficulty	fiction
bleach	cloth	dip	film
blue	coal	disagreement	fire
brass	coffee	discipline	flight
bronze	combination	discomfort	flour
broth	comparison	disgrace	flu
brown	concern	division	foam
butter	confession	divorce	foil
buzz	conflict	dough	food
cake	conquest	duck	force
cancer	contraction	dynamite	friendship
candy	conversation	elm	frost
canvas	copulation	enjoyment	frosting

fruit	jelly	notepaper	posture
fur	juice	novelty	powder
future	ketchup	number	power
gas	landscape	oak	prejudice
gasoline	language	oil	primer
gauze	leather	opinion	privilege
glass	length	orange	prohibition
glue	liquor	pain	promotion
gold	lotion	paint	pronunciation
grain	loyalty	pardon	prophecy
grammar	lubrication	passion	protection
grass	luxury	pasta	pudding
gravel	marble	paste	purple
gravy	margarine	pastry	quarantine
gray	meal	payment	race
green	meat	pecan	reality
gum	meatloaf	pepper	rebellion
ham	medicine	performance	red
harmony	membership	perfume	redwood
honey	mesh	philosophy	regularity
horror	metal	pick	regulation
hurt	meter	pie	religion
identification	mileage	pigment	repetition
immersion	misfortune	pine	resignation
increase	mold	pink	responsibility
indentation	mortar	pitch	rhythm
infection	moss	pizza	rice
influence	motion	plaster	rope
injection	mousse	plastic	routine
ink	movement	pleasure	sacrifice
inspection	mulch	poison	salt
intensity	mustard	polish	sand
irritation	mystery	pollen	sandpaper
ivy	mythology	popcorn	satin
jam	noise	poplar	satisfaction

sauce	stock	theology	varnish
scripture	stone	theory	velocity
seaweed	stool	thread	velvet
separation	stress	tile	victory
shampoo	substitution	tissue	volume
sherbet	subtraction	tobacco	walnut
shortening	success	toil	war
silk	sugar	toothpaste	wax
sin	sunblock	torment	whiskey
skin	sunburn	tradition	white
smell	sunscreen	translation	wine
soap	syrup	triumph	wood
soil	tape	twine	wool
soup	taste	use	worry
speculation	tea	utterance	yeast
speed	technology	vacation	yellow
stain	tension	vaccination	
starch	terror	variation	
stew	theft	variety	

List C

Nouns defined in this dictionary that have irregular or variable plurals. Plural variants are separated by "/". The asterisk "*" means there is a unique feature of pronunciation. See the entry heads listed for details.

aircraft > aircraft	booth*
antenna > antennas/antennae	buffalo > buffalo/buffalos/
aquarium > aquaria/aquariums	buffaloes
basis > bases	cactus > cactuses/cacti
bath*	calf > calves
beaver > beaver/beavers	chairman > chairmen
bookshelf > bookshelves	child > children

cloth*

cod > cod

courthouse*

craftsman > craftsmen

crisis > crises

deer > deer

die > dice

doghouse*

dwarf > dwarves/dwarfs

elf > elves

elk > elk/elks

emphasis > emphases

fish > fish

fisherman > fishermen

focus > focuses/foci

foot > feet

footpath*

formula > formulae/formulas

fowl > fowl/fowls

fungus > funguses/fungi

gentleman > gentlemen

goldfish*

goose > geese

grandchild > grandchildren

greenhouse*

half > halves

hippopotamus >
   hippopotamuses/
   hippopotami

hoof > hooves

house*

index > indexes/indices

knife > knives

leaf > leaves

life > lives

lighthouse*

loaf > loaves

man > men

medium > mediums/media

mink > mink/minks

moose > moose

moth*

mouse > mice/(computer)
   mouses

mouth*

nucleus > nuclei

oasis > oases

oath*

octopus > octopuses/octopi

ox > oxen

parenthesis > parentheses

path*

penthouse*

perch > perch

policeman > policemen

policewoman > policewomen

radius > radiuses/radii

rhinoceros >
   rhinoceros/rhinoceroses

salesman > salesmen

salesperson >
   salespeople/salespersons

saleswoman > saleswomen

salmon > salmon

scarf > scarves

schoolchild > schoolchildren

sheath*

sheep > sheep

shelf > shelves

shellfish > shellfish

shrimp > shrimp/shrimps
sister-in-law > sisters-in-law
snowman > snowmen
sole > sole
sportsman > sportsmen
thief > thieves
tooth > teeth
tree house*
trout > trout
tuna > tuna/tunas
warehouse*

washcloth*
wharf > wharves
wife > wives
wolf > wolves
woman > women
wreath*
yen > yen
zebra > zebra/zebras

List D

Transitive verbs defined in this dictionary that can take a clause beginning with *that* as an object. (As with *I know that you can do it!*) These verbs can also take other forms of direct object. See the entry head listed for details.

accept
admit
advertise
advise
announce
answer
anticipate
appreciate
argue
ask
assume
believe
calculate
claim
confess

confirm
consider
decide
declare
demand
deny
determine
detest
discover
dream
establish
estimate
expect
explain
feel

find
foresee
forget
guarantee
guess
hear
imagine
indicate
know
learn
legislate
maintain
mention
murmur
note

notice
observe
ordain
parrot
petition
plead
pledge
preach
predict
prefer
prescribe
proclaim
profess
prophesy
propose
protest
prove
realize

recognize
recommend
regret
relate
remark
remember
report
request
require
resent
reveal
say
scream
scribble
see
sense
shout
show

signal
signify
state
stress
suggest
suspect
think
threaten
urge
vow
wail
whimper
whine
whisper
wire

List E

Transitive verbs defined in this dictionary that have a clause beginning with *that* as an object. (As with *I agree that you should go.*) See the entry heads listed for details.

agree
believe
bet
brag
comment
conclude
exclaim
fear

feel
figure
grant
guess
hint
hope
imagine
imply

indicate
joke
judge
move
note
observe
pray
pretend

promise

reason

reply

respond

rule

suppose

trust

understand

wager

wish

worry

List F

Verbs defined in this dictionary that have irregular past tenses or past participles. These are the principal parts of the verb. Commas separate the principal parts of the verbs. The present tense comes first, then the past, and then the past participle. Variants are separated by "/".

arise, arose, arisen

awake, awaked/awoke,
    awaked/awoke/awoken

babysit, babysat, babysat

bear, bore, borne/born

beat, beat, beat/beaten

become, became, become

begin, began, begun

bend, bent, bent

bet, bet, bet

bid, bid, bid

bind, bound, bound

bite, bit, bitten

bleed, bled, bled

blow, blew, blown

break, broke, broken

breed, bred, bred

bring, brought, brought

build, built, built

burn, burned/burnt,
    burned/burnt

burst, burst, burst

buy, bought, bought

catch, caught, caught

cut, cut, cut

deal, dealt, dealt

dig, dug, dug

dive, dived/dove, dived

do, did, done

draw, drew, drawn

dream, dreamed/dreamt,
    dreamed/dreamt

drink, drank, drunk

drive, drove, driven

dwell, dwelled/dwelt,
    dwelled/dwelt

eat, ate, eaten

fall, fell, fallen

feed, fed, fed

feel, felt, felt

fight, fought, fought

find, found, found

fit, fit/fitted, fit/fitted
flee, fled, fled
fly, flew, flown
forbid, forbad/forbade,
   forbidden
foresee, foresaw, foreseen
forget, forgot, forgot/forgotten
forgive, forgave, forgiven
freeze, froze, frozen
get, got, got/gotten
give, gave, given
go, went, gone
grind, ground, ground
grow, grew, grown
hang, hung, hung
hang, hanged, hanged
have, had, had
hear, heard, heard
hide, hid, hidden
hit, hit, hit
hold, held, held
housebreak, housebroke,
   housebroken
hurt, hurt, hurt
input, input/inputted,
   input/inputted
keep, kept, kept
kneel, knelt/kneeled,
   knelt/kneeled
know, knew, known
lay, laid, laid
lead, led, led
leap, leaped/leapt,
   leaped/leapt
leave, left, left

lend, lent, lent
let, let, let
lie, lay, lain
lie, lied, lied
light, lighted/lit, lighted/lit
lose, lost, lost
make, made, made
mean, meant, meant
meet, met, met
mislay, mislaid, mislaid
mistake, mistook, mistaken
misunderstand, misunderstood,
   misunderstood
mow, mowed, mowed/mown
outgrow, outgrew, outgrown
overcome, overcame, overcome
overeat, overate, overeaten
oversee, oversaw, overseen
oversleep, overslept, overslept
overthrow, overthrew,
   overthrown
panic, panicked, panicked
pay, paid, paid
picnic, picnicked, picnicked
plead, pleaded/pled,
   pleaded/pled
prepay, prepaid, prepaid
proofread, proofread,
   proofread
prove, proved, proved/proven
put, put, put
quit, quit, quit
read, read, read
rebuild, rebuilt, rebuilt
redo, redid, redone

repay, repaid, repaid
retake, retook, retaken
rewind, rewound, rewound
rewrite, rewrote, rewritten
ride, rode, ridden
rid, rid, rid
ring, rang, rung
rise, rose, risen
run, ran, run
saw, sawed, sawed/sawn
say, said, said
see, saw, seen
seek, sought, sought
sell, sold, sold
send, sent, sent
set, set, set
sew, sewed, sewed/sewn
shake, shook, shaken
shave, shaved, shaved/shaven
shear, sheared, sheared/shorn
shed, shed, shed
shine, shined/shone, shined/shone
shoot, shot, shot
show, showed, showed/shown
shrink, shrank/shrunk, shrunk/shrunken
shut, shut, shut
sing, sang, sung
sink, sank/sunk, sunk
sit, sat, sat
slay, slew, slain
sleep, slept, slept
slide, slid, slid

sling, slung, slung
slit, slit, slit
sneak, sneaked/snuck, sneaked/snuck
sow, sowed, sowed/sown
speak, spoke, spoken
speed, sped, sped
spell, spelled/spelt, spelled/spelt
spend, spent, spent
spill, spilled/spilt, spilled/spilt
spin, spun, spun
spit, spit/spat, spit/spat
split, split, split
spread, spread, spread
spring, sprang/sprung, sprung
stand, stood, stood
steal, stole, stolen
stick, stuck, stuck
sting, stung, stung
stink, stank/stunk, stunk
strike, struck, struck
string, strung, strung
swear, swore, sworn
sweat, sweat/sweated, sweat/sweated
sweep, swept, swept
swell, swelled, swelled/swollen
swim, swam, swum
swing, swung, swung
take, took, taken
teach, taught, taught
tear, tore, torn
tear, teared, teared
tell, told, told

think, thought, thought
thrive, thrived/throve,
  thrived/thriven
throw, threw, thrown
thrust, thrust, thrust
undergo, underwent,
  undergone
understand, understood,
  understood
undo, undid, undone
unwind, unwound, unwound
upset, upset, upset
wake, waked/woke,
  waked/woken

wear, wore, worn
weave, wove, woven
weave, wove/weaved, woven
wed, wedded/wed, wedded/wed
weep, wept, wept
wet, wetted/wet, wetted/wet
win, won, won
wind, wound, wound
wind, winded, winded
withhold, withheld, withheld
withstand, withstood,
  withstood
write, wrote, written

List G

Words defined in this dictionary having pronunciations that
vary from sense to sense.

a	consummate	estimate	midday
address	content	excess	minute
approximate	contest	excuse	misuse
arithmetic	contract	export	mobile
associate	contrary	graduate	moderate
bases	contrast	grease	mouth
bow	decrease	house	object
close	defect	impact	offense
combat	desert	import	offensive
complex	detail	incline	overhead
concrete	digest	increase	overlap
conduct	discharge	inside	overlook
conflict	dove	lead	overnight
construct	entrance	live	perfect

perfume
permit
present
proceed/
  proceeds
produce
progress
project
protest
read
rebel

rebound
recess
record
recount
refund
refuse
reject
replay
research
retake
rewrite

row
separate
sewer
sow
survey
suspect
tear
torment
upset
upstairs
use

used/used to
why
wind
wound

Abbreviations and Symbols

①, ②, ③, **etc.**   a number within a circle refers to the sense number of a word. The circled number by itself refers to a sense within the entry in which the circled number is found.

adj. adjective

adv. adverb

conj. conjunction

cont. contraction

interj. interjection

interrog. interrogative

irreg. irregular

iv. intransitive verb

n. noun; nominal

phr. phrase

prep. preposition

tv. transitive verb

Pronunciation

The symbols of the International Phonetic Alphabet are used to show the pronunciation of the words in this dictionary. The speech represented here is that of educated people, but it is not formal or overly precise. It is more representative of the West and the middle of the country than of the East, South, or upper Midwest.

Pronunciation of American English is variable in different regions of the country, but most native speakers of American English can understand one another quite well.

The goal of the pronunciation scheme is to provide the student with one acceptable model of pronunciation for each entry. Where the numbered senses of an entry are all pronounced the same way, the phonetic representation follows the main entry word. In entries where even one of the numbered senses is pronounced differently from the rest, all the senses are provided with a phonetic representation.

Sounds represented here as [or] are often pronounced as [ɔr] in some parts of the East. Similarly, the sequence [ɛr] is often pronounced [ær] in parts of the East. One heavy stress is marked for each word. The dictionary user should expect to hear variation in the pronunciation of most of the words listed in this or any dictionary, but should remain confident that the model provided here is understood and accepted in all parts of the country.

The chart on the next page shows the symbols used here and what they correspond to in some simple English words.

[ɑ]	stop top	[ʌ]	nut shut	[n]	new funny	[θ]	thin faith
[æ]	sat track	[ɚ]	bird turtle	[ŋ]	bring thing	[u]	food blue
[aʊ]	cow now	[f]	feel if	[o]	coat wrote	[ʊ]	put look
[aɪ]	bite my	[g]	get frog	[ɔɪ]	spoil boy	[v]	save van
[b]	beet bubble	[h]	hat who	[ɔ]	caught yawn	[w]	well wind
[d]	dead body	[i]	feet leak	[p]	tip pat	[ʌ]	wheel while
[ð]	that those	[ɪ]	bit hiss	[r]	rat berry	[z]	fuzzy zoo
[dʒ]	jail judge	[j]	yellow you	[s]	sun fast	[ʒ]	pleasure treasure
[e]	date sail	[k]	can keep	[ʃ]	fish sure	[']	'water ho'tel
[ɛ]	get set	[l]	lawn yellow	[t]	top pot		
[ə]	above around	[m]	family slam	[tʃ]	cheese pitcher		

a 1. [ˈe] *n.* the first in a series; the highest grade. (Capitalized. Note: Use A before words that begin with a consonant sound; use AN before words that begin with a vowel sound.) **2.** [ˈe, ə] *article* one; any. (See also AN.) **3.** [ˈe, ə] *prep.* each; every; per. (See also AN.)

an A for effort recognition for having tried to do something even if it was not successful.

abandon [ə ˈbæn dən] *tv.* to leave someone or something and not return; to desert someone or something.

abbreviation [ə bri vi ˈe ʃən] *n.* a shortened word or phrase that takes the place of a longer word or phrase.

ability [ə ˈbɪl ə ti] *n.* the power, capacity, or skill to do something.

able [ˈe bəl] *adj.* skilled; well qualified; capable. (Adv: *ably.*)

able to afford something AND **can afford** something […ə ˈford…] **1.** to have enough money to buy something; to be able to buy something. **2.** to endure the results of something.

able to do something **with** one's **eyes closed** able to do something very easily, even without having to think about it or look at it.

abode [ə ˈbod] *n.* the place where one lives.
→ TAKE UP ONE'S **ABODE** SOMEWHERE

about [ə ˈbaʊt] **1.** *prep.* regarding someone or something; concerning someone or something; having to do with someone or something.

2. *adv.* approximately; nearly.
3. *adv.* almost; not quite.

about to do something almost ready to do something.

above [ə ˈbʌv] **1.** *prep.* over—but not touching—someone or something. **2.** *prep.* greater than something; higher than something; more than something. **3.** *adv.* [written about or presented] previously [in the same written work or on the same page]. **4.** *adv.* in or at a higher place; over. **5.** *adv.* of a greater amount or quantity.

above average higher or better than the general level of quality.

above par better than average or normal.

above reproach not deserving of blame or criticism.

abroad [ə ˈbrɔd] *adv.* in another country; overseas.

absence [ˈæb səns] **1.** *n.* the quality of [someone's] not being present. (No plural.) **2.** *n.* a period of time when someone is not present. **3.** *n.* a lack; a deficiency. (No plural.)
→ CONSPICUOUS BY ONE'S ABSENCE

absent [ˈæb sənt] **1.** *adj.* not present at a place; away from a place. **2.** *adj.* not in existence; not evident; not present or visible. **3.** *adj.* [appearing] vague or not interested. (Adv: *absently.*)

absorb [əb ˈzɔrb] **1.** *tv.* to soak up a liquid. **2.** *tv.* to learn something; to take in new information; to learn something easily. (Figurative on ①.)

absorbent [əb 'zor bənt] *adj.* able to soak up liquids. (Adv: *absorbently.*)

accent ['æk sɛnt] **1.** *n.* the force or stress put on a word or a part of a word during speech. **2.** *n.* a mark written over a letter of the alphabet that gives the letter a special pronunciation or stress. **3.** *n.* a way of speaking a language, and especially of pronouncing a language. **4.** *tv.* to emphasize something, especially to put ① on a word or a part of a word during speech.

accept [æk 'sɛpt] *tv.* to take something that is offered. (Compare this with EXCEPT. The object can be a clause with THAT ⑦.)

acceptable [æk 'sɛp tə bəl] *adj.* worth accepting; satisfactory; good enough. (Adv: *acceptably.*)

accident ['æk sɪ dənt] *n.* an unexpected event, usually with harm to someone or something.

accidental [æk sɪ 'dɛn təl] *adj.* not on purpose; done or happening by mistake. (Adv: *accidentally.*)

accomplish [ə 'kɑm plɪʃ] *tv.* to finish something; to successfully complete something.

accomplishment [ə 'kɑm plɪʃ mənt] *n.* something that has been completed or achieved; a success.

according to someone or something as stated by someone; as indicated by something.

according to something in proportion to something; in relation to something.

account [ə 'kaʊnt] **1.** *n.* a report; a description; one's version of what happened in an event. **2.** *n.* a record of income [or money received] and expenses [or money paid out] assigned to a particular person, business, or class of transactions.
→ COOK THE ACCOUNTS
→ GIVE A GOOD ACCOUNT OF ONESELF
→ SAVINGS ACCOUNT
→ TURN SOMETHING TO GOOD ACCOUNT

accountant [ə 'kaʊnt nt] *n.* someone who is responsible for maintaining financial records or accounts; someone who prepares tax records.

accuracy ['æk jə rə si] *n.* correctness; the degree of freedom from errors. (No plural.)

accurate ['æk jə rət] *adj.* correct; exact; without error. (Adv: *accurately.*)

accuse [ə 'kjuz] *tv.* to claim or charge that someone has done something, usually something wrong or illegal.

ache ['ek] **1.** *n.* a pain; a soreness. **2.** *iv.* to hurt; to be sore.

Achilles' heel a weak point or fault in someone or something otherwise perfect or excellent. (From the Greek hero Achilles, who had only one vulnerable part of his body, his heel.)

an **aching heart** the feeling of pain because of love that is lost or has faded away, described as being in the heart, where love is said to reside.

the **acid test** a test whose findings are beyond doubt or dispute.

acknowledgment [æk 'nɑl ɪdʒ mənt] **1.** *n.* admission; stating that something is so. (No plural.) **2.** *n.* the recognition given to someone for doing something well. **3.** *n.* a report of having received something.

across [ə 'krɔs] **1.** *prep.* from one side of something to the other side. **2.** *prep.* on the other side of something. **3.** *adv.* to the other side of something.

act ['ækt] **1.** *n.* a division of a play or musical. **2.** *n.* one of many short performances within a longer program. **3.** *n.* something that is done; an instance of doing something. **4.** *n.* a law. **5.** *iv.* to perform in a play, film, TV program, or similar performance. **6.** *iv.* to behave in a certain way; to behave as if one is or feels a certain way.
→ CLEAN ONE'S ACT UP
→ READ SOMEONE THE RIOT ACT
→ A TOUGH ACT TO FOLLOW

act high-and-mighty to act proud and powerful; to act haughty.

an **act of God** an occurrence (usually an accident) for which no human is responsible, such as a storm, an earthquake, or a windstorm.

act one's **age** to behave more maturely; to act as grown-up as one really is.

act something **out 1.** to perform in real life a role that one has imagined in a fantasy. **2.** to demonstrate or communicate something through action rather than words.

act up [for a thing or a person] to behave badly.

act (up)on something **1.** to take action on a particular problem. **2.** to take action about something because of some special information.

action ['æk ʃən] **1.** *n.* activity; movement. (Plural only for types and instances.) **2.** *n.* the plot of a story; the events that happen in a story. (No plural. See also a COURSE OF ACTION.)

active ['æk tɪv] **1.** *adj.* moving; functioning; operating. (Adv: *actively.*) **2.** *adj.* lively; moving at a rapid, steady pace; busy. (Adv: *actively.*) **3.** *adj.* of or about sentences in which the subject does the action that is expressed in the verb. (The opposite of PASSIVE ②. Adv: *actively.*)
→ ON ACTIVE DUTY

activity [æk 'tɪv ə ti] *n.* action; movement; doing something.
→ A HIVE OF ACTIVITY

actor ['æk tɚ] *n.* a performer, male or female, in a play, musical, or movie. (See also ACTRESS.)

actress ['æk trəs] *n.* a female performer in a play, musical, or movie. (See also ACTOR.)

actual ['æk tʃu əl] *adj.* real; existing. (Adv: *actually.*)

actually ['æk tʃ(u)ə li] *adv.* in fact; really.

ad ['æd] *n.* an ADVERTISEMENT.

Adam ['æd əm] *n.* Eve's mate.
→ NOT KNOW SOMEONE FROM ADAM

add ['æd] *tv.* to join something to something else; to include something with something else.

add fuel to the fire AND **add fuel to the flame** to make a problem worse; to say or do something that makes a bad situation worse.

add fuel to the flame Go to ADD FUEL TO THE FIRE.

add insult to injury to make a bad situation worse; to hurt the feelings of a person who has already been hurt.

addition [ə 'dɪ ʃən] **1.** *n.* the adding together of two or more numbers. (Plural only for types and instances.) **2.** *n.* putting someone or something into something else. (Plural only for types and instances.)
→ IN ADDITION (TO SOMETHING)

additional [ə 'dɪʃ ə nəl] *adj.* extra; [something] further; more; added. (Adv: *additionally*.)

address 1. ['æ drɛs, ə 'drɛs] *n.* the street name and number, city, state, and other information telling the location of something, such as a building or house. **2.** [ə 'drɛs] *n.* a formal speech. **3.** [ə 'drɛs] *tv.* to write the street name, number, city, state, and other information on an envelope or package. **4.** [ə 'drɛs] *tv.* to speak directly to a person or a group of people. **5.** [ə 'drɛs] *tv.* to respond to a question; to say something about an issue or problem.

adequate ['æd ə kwɪt] *adj.* just enough but not more than enough; good enough. (Adv: *adequately*.)

adhesive [æd 'hi sɪv] **1.** *adj.* sticky; designed to stick to things. (Adv: *adhesively*.) **2.** *n.* glue; paste.

(Plural only for types and instances.)

adj. an abbreviation of ADJECTIVE.

adjective ['æ dʒɛk tɪv] *n.* a word that describes or modifies a noun or nominal.

adjust [ə 'dʒʌst] **1.** *tv.* to change something in a small way in order to try to make it work or fit better. **2.** *iv.* to become used to someone or something; to adapt to someone or something.

adjustable [ə 'dʒʌst ə bəl] *adj.* changeable; able to be changed in small amounts. (Adv: *adjustably*.)

administration [æd mɪn ɪ 'stre ʃən] **1.** *n.* the work of managing and directing. (No plural.) **2.** *n.* the office and staff of a high-ranking elected official, such as a president, governor, or mayor. **3.** *n.* a group of people who manage something.

admiration [æd mə 're ʃən] *n.* a feeling of pride, pleasure, and respect for someone or something. (No plural.)

admire [æd 'maɪ ɚ] *tv.* to regard someone or something with pride, pleasure, and respect.

admit [æd 'mɪt] **1.** *tv.* to allow someone or something to enter into someplace. **2.** *tv.* to allow someone to become a member of a club or organization. **3.** *tv.* to say that one has done something one is accused of; to say that something is true. (The object can be a clause with THAT ⑦.)

admit something **into** something to allow something to be introduced into something else.

adolescence [æd ə 'lɛs əns] *n.* the period of time between being a child and being an adult; the teenage years.

adolescent [æd ə 'lɛs ənt] **1.** *n.* a teenager; someone who is older than a child but not yet an adult. **2.** the *adj.* use of ①.

adopt [ə 'dɑpt] **1.** *iv.* to become the parent or parents of a child through legal proceedings. **2.** *tv.* to gain possession of and become responsible for the child of someone else, through the legal system. **3.** *tv.* to acquire a new practice, belief, or habit.

adoption [ə 'dɑp ʃən] **1.** *n.* acquiring and becoming responsible for the child of someone else, through the legal system. (Plural only for types and instances.) **2.** *n.* acquiring a new practice, belief, or habit. (No plural.)

adorable [ə 'dor ə bəl] *adj.* very cute; worthy of being adored. (Adv: *adorably.*)

adore [ə 'dor] *tv.* to admire and be fond of someone or something.

adult [ə 'dʌlt] **1.** *adj.* mature; fully grown; fully developed. **2.** *adj.* showing the behavior of a mature person. **3.** *adj.* intended for persons who are mature. (Often used referring to sex and violence in entertainment.) **4.** *n.* someone or something that is fully grown.

adv. an abbreviation of ADVERB.

advance [æd 'væns] **1.** *n.* a forward motion. **2.** *n.* money that is given to someone ahead of schedule or before it is earned; a loan taken against money that is to be paid at

a later time. **3.** *iv.* to progress or move forward; to move to a higher or better level. **4.** *tv.* to move someone or something forward or to a higher level. **5.** *tv.* to give someone money ahead of schedule or before it is earned. **6.** *adj.* prior; before the event. (Prenominal only.)
→ IN ADVANCE

advantage [æd 'væn tɪdʒ] *n.* something good or useful that will help someone with something; a benefit.
→ TAKE ADVANTAGE OF SOMEONE
→ TAKE ADVANTAGE OF SOMETHING
→ TURN SOMETHING TO ONE'S ADVANTAGE

adventure [æd 'vɛn tʃɚ] *n.* excitement; challenge. (Plural only for types and instances.)

adverb ['æd vɚb] *n.* a word that modifies or describes a verb, a verb phrase, an adjective, a sentence, or another adverb. (Abbreviated *adv.* here.)

advertise ['æd vɚ taɪz] **1.** *iv.* to make [something] known to the public, especially through signs, television, radio, newspapers, or magazines. **2.** *tv.* to make something known to the public through signs, television, radio, newspapers, magazines, or other means; to publicize something. (The object can be a clause with THAT ⑦.)

advertisement [æd vɚ 'taɪz mənt] *n.* a commercial; a notice about something, displayed to the public.

advice [æd 'vaɪs] *n.* recommendations or suggestions provided to help someone. (Compare this with

ADVISE. No plural. Number is expressed with *piece(s)* or *bit(s) of advice*.)
→ SAGE ADVICE

advise [æd 'vaɪz] *tv.* to give [someone] a particular kind of advice; to suggest doing something. (The object can be a clause with THAT ⑦.)

advise someone **against** someone or something to advise someone not to do something or not to choose someone or something.

advocate 1. ['æd vo ket] *tv.* to be in favor of something and argue for it. **2.** ['æd və kət] *n.* someone who does ①.
→ PLAY (THE) DEVIL'S ADVOCATE

affect [ə 'fɛkt] **1.** *tv.* to influence someone or something; to have an effect on someone or something. (Compare this with EFFECT.) **2.** *tv.* to display or exhibit a kind of behavior, especially by pretending or imitating.

affection [ə 'fɛk ʃən] *n.* love, caring, or fondness. (No plural. See also SOMEONE'S AFFECTIONS.)

affinity for someone or something a strong preference for someone or something; a strong liking for someone or something.

affirmative [ə 'fɜ mə tɪv] *adj.* meaning *yes*.
→ IN THE AFFIRMATIVE

afford [ə 'ford] *tv.* to be able to buy something.
→ ABLE TO AFFORD SOMETHING
→ CAN AFFORD SOMETHING

afraid [ə 'fred] *adj.* fearful of someone or something; scared of someone or something. (Not prenominal.)

afraid of one's **own shadow** easily frightened; always frightened, timid, or suspicious.

after ['æf tɚ] **1.** *conj.* later in time than when something happens; when something has finished happening. **2.** *prep.* at a later time than something; later in time than something. **3.** *prep.* further along in a sequence or series than someone or something. **4.** *prep.* in the name of someone; in honor of someone; for someone. **5.** *adv.* behind; to the rear; following.

afternoon [æf tɚ 'nun] **1.** *n.* the time of day from noon until the evening. **2.** the *adj.* use of ①.

afternoons [æf tɚ 'nunz] *adv.* every AFTERNOON.

again [ə 'gɛn] **1.** *adv.* once more; another time. **2.** *adv.* as [something was] before.

again and again repeatedly; again and even more.

against [ə 'gɛnst] **1.** *prep.* in opposition to someone or something; as an opponent of someone or something. **2.** *prep.* in a direction opposite to something. **3.** *prep.* coming toward and meeting someone or something. **4.** *prep.* [leaning or tilting and] in contact with someone or something.

against the clock in a race with time; in a great hurry to get something done before a particular time.

age ['edʒ] **1.** *n.* the amount of time that someone or something has been alive or in existence. (No plural.) **2.** *n.* advanced ①; evidence of much ①; oldness. (No

plural.) **3.** *n.* the specific ① of a person, usually given as a number of years; the specific ① of something. **4.** *n.* [for a person] the condition of having a certain ③; the time when a person has a certain ③. (The number comes after *age* and refers to years, unless some other measure is given, such as months, weeks, or days.) **5.** *n.* a period or stage of life. **6.** *n.* a period of history; a generation; an era. **7.** *iv.* to become old; to show increasing ①. **8.** *iv.* [for cheese, wine, whiskey, beef, etc.] to mature; to reach a peak of quality, taste, and strength. **9.** *tv.* to cause someone or something to grow old or appear old.
→ ACT ONE'S AGE
→ COME OF AGE
→ OLD AGE
→ RIPE OLD AGE

agent ['e dʒənt] **1.** *n.* someone who represents someone else; someone who sells certain things such as insurance, travel, tickets, land, buildings, etc. **2.** *n.* something that causes someone or something else to do something; something that causes some result to happen. **3.** *n.* a spy.

ago [ə 'go] *adj.* in the past; [time] already gone by. (After a noun that expresses a length of time.)
→ LONG AGO

agony ['æg ə ni] *n.* an intense, deep pain in the mind or the body; a deep suffering. (Plural only for types and instances.)

agree [ə 'gri] **1.** *iv.* [for people] to be in harmony or have the same opinion; [for people] to have no conflict of opinion or desire. **2.** *iv.* [for facts or things] to be consistent or to harmonize. **3.** *iv.* [for a form of a word] to match the form of another word grammatically. **4.** *tv.* to decide together that something is true or should happen; to accept someone's opinion that something is true or should happen. (The object can be a clause with THAT ⑦.)

agree to something to consent to something; to allow something to be done; to approve something.

agree (up)on someone or something to agree to the choice of someone or something.

agree with someone (**about** someone or something) AND **agree with** someone (**on** someone or something) to hold the same opinion as someone else about someone or something; to be of the same mind as someone else about someone or something.

agree with someone (**on** someone or something) Go to AGREE WITH SOMEONE (ABOUT SOMEONE OR SOMETHING).

agree with something **1.** [for something] to look good or go well with something else. **2.** [for something] to be in accord with something else.

agreement [ə 'gri mənt] *n.* a state of agreeing; holding the same opinion as someone else; a state of accepting a proposal.
→ IN AGREEMENT
→ REACH AN AGREEMENT

ahead [ə 'hɛd] **1.** *adv.* into the future; [preparing] for the future. **2.** *adv.* forward; continuing in the same direction. **3.** *adv.* into an

advanced position; into a better position.
→ COME OUT AHEAD
→ FULL STEAM AHEAD
→ PUSH AHEAD

ahead of one's **time** having ideas or attitudes that are too advanced to be acceptable to or appreciated by the society in which one is living.

ahead of schedule done before the time listed on the SCHEDULE ①.

ahead of someone or something at a place in front of or in advance of someone or something; at an earlier time than someone or something.

aid ['ed] **1.** *n.* help; assistance; support. (No plural.) **2.** *n.* something that helps someone or something else. **3.** *tv.* to provide someone or something with ①.

aim ['em] **1.** *tv.* to point something toward a target or a goal. **2.** *n.* a goal; a purpose; an intention. **3.** *n.* the pointing of something accurately. (No plural.)

aim something **at** someone or something to point or direct something at someone or something.

aim to please to really try to make people happy.

air ['er] **1.** *n.* the mixture of gases that surrounds the earth; the mixture of gases that people normally breathe. (No plural.) **2.** *n.* a mood or atmosphere. (No plural.) **3.** *tv.* to express a view or an opinion in public; to make something known.
→ BUILD CASTLES IN THE AIR
→ IN THE AIR
→ OFF THE AIR
→ ON THE AIR

→ OUT OF THIN AIR
→ UP IN THE AIR
→ VANISH INTO THIN AIR
→ WALK ON AIR

air one's **dirty linen in public** to discuss private or embarrassing matters in public, especially when quarreling.

air something **out** to allow fresh air to freshen something, such as clothing, a stale-smelling room, etc.

aircraft ['er kræft] *n., irreg.* a machine, such as an airplane or a helicopter, that flies in the air. (Plural: *aircraft.*)

airline ['er laɪn] *n.* a company that operates a number of aircraft for passengers or cargo.

airmail ['er mel] **1.** *n.* a system for sending international mail by airplane. (No plural.) **2.** *adv.* [sending mail] by ①. **3.** *tv.* to send something by ①.

airplane ['er plen] *n.* a heavier-than-air vehicle that flies through the air.

airport ['er port] *n.* a place where airplanes land and take off.

alarm [ə 'lɑrm] **1.** *n.* a warning sound or signal. **2.** *n.* a device that makes a warning sound or signal. **3.** *n.* excitement, anxiety, or shock. (No plural.) **4.** *n.* a clock that has a bell or other signal that is sounded to wake someone up. **5.** *tv.* to frighten or scare someone; to make someone afraid or fearful of danger.

alcohol ['æl kə hɔl] **1.** *n.* a liquid chemical used to make wounds and skin very clean or sterile or to dissolve substances. (Plural only for types and instances.) **2.** *n.* the substance found in beer, wine, and hard liquors that causes someone to be drunk. (Plural only for types and instances.) **3.** *n.* beer, wine, whiskey, spirits; drinks that contain ②. (No plural.)

alert [ə ˈlɚt] **1.** *adj.* wary; aware; watchful. (Adv: *alertly*.) **2.** *tv.* to warn someone about something, especially danger.

algebra [ˈæl dʒə brə] *n.* a branch of mathematics using letters and other symbols to represent numbers or sets of numbers in equations. (No plural.)

alike [ə ˈlaɪk] **1.** *adj.* similar; the same or almost the same. (Not prenominal.) **2.** *adv.* in the same way. **3.** *adv.* equally; in the same amount or degree.

alive [ə ˈlaɪv] **1.** *adj.* living; not dead. (Not prenominal.) **2.** *adj.* active, lively, or full of energy. (Figurative on ①. Not prenominal.)

all [ˈɔl] **1.** *adj.* each and every one [of the people or things]; the full amount [of something]; the whole extent of [something]. **2.** *adj.* the greatest amount possible [of something]. **3.** *pron.* everything or everyone mentioned earlier in the conversation or writing. (Treated as singular or plural.) **4.** *pron.* everything. (Treated as singular.) **5.** *adv.* completely.

all day long AND **all night long; all month long; all year long; all summer long** *adv.* throughout an entire period of time.

all in a day's work part of what is expected; typical or normal.

all joking aside being serious for a moment; in all seriousness.

all month long Go to ALL DAY LONG.

all night long Go to ALL DAY LONG.

(all) over again starting over completely again; going through something completely yet another time.

all over but the shouting decided and concluded; finished except for a celebration.

all skin and bones Go to NOTHING BUT SKIN AND BONES.

all summer long Go to ALL DAY LONG.

all thumbs very awkward and clumsy, especially with one's hands.

all walks of life all social, economic, and ethnic groups.

all year long Go to ALL DAY LONG.

alley [ˈæl i] **1.** *n.* a narrow road or pathway behind or between buildings. **2.** *n.* a BOWLING ALLEY. → UP A BLIND ALLEY

alligator [ˈæl ə get ɚ] *n.* a large reptile of the crocodile family.

allow [ə ˈlaʊ] *tv.* to make sure that there is a certain amount of time for something to be done.

allow for someone or something to make sure that there is enough of something for someone or something.

allow someone or something **in (something)** to permit someone or something to enter something or someplace.

allowance [ə 'laʊ əns] **1.** *n.* an amount of something, such as money, given to someone. **2.** *n.* an amount of something—time, forgiveness, tolerance—that is provided or allowed for someone or something.
→ MAKE ALLOWANCES FOR SOMETHING

almost ['ɔl most] *adv.* nearly, but not quite.

alone [ə 'lon] **1.** *adj.* by oneself; having no one else nearby. (Not prenominal.) **2.** *adv.* by oneself; with no help.

along [ə 'lɔŋ] *prep.* next to something for a distance; in a path next to something.

along with someone or something in addition to someone or something; together with someone or something.

aloof [ə 'luf] *adj.* unfriendly; reserved; unsympathetic. (Adv: *aloofly*.)

aloud [ə 'laʊd] *adv.* audibly; [of speech] spoken so that it can be heard.

alphabet ['æl fə bɛt] *n.* the list of letters—in proper order—used to write a language.

alphabetical [æl fə 'bɛt ɪ kəl] *adj.* arranged in the order of the letters in the alphabet. (Adv: *alphabetically* […ɪk li].)

alphabetize ['æl fə bə taɪz] *tv.* to place words in the same order as the letters of the alphabet.

already [ɔl 'rɛd i] *adv.* by now; by this point in time; previously. (This is different from *all ready*.)

also ['ɔl so] *adv.* as well; too; in addition.

although [ɔl 'ðo] *conj.* even though; despite; in spite of.

altogether ['ɔl tə gɛð ɚ] *adv.* completely. (Different from *all together*.)

aluminum [ə 'lum ə nəm] **1.** *n.* a metal that is lightweight and does not rust easily. (No plural.) **2.** *adj.* made of ①.

always ['ɔl wez] **1.** *adv.* every time; each time. **2.** *adv.* forever; without end.

am ['æm] *iv., irreg.* the first-person present singular form of BE. (Reduced to *'m* in the contraction I'M.)

amaze [ə 'mez] *tv.* to cause wonder in someone; to astound or astonish someone.

ambulance ['æm bjə ləns] *n.* a vehicle for taking sick or injured people to the hospital.

amend [ə 'mɛnd] *tv.* to change something; to modify something (especially laws).

amendment [ə 'mɛnd mənt] *n.* a change made by correcting or adding to something.

among [ə 'mʌŋ] **1.** *prep.* in the midst of people or things; surrounded by things or people. **2.** *prep.* within a group; within a set of choices. (Use BETWEEN with two people or things. Use AMONG with more than two.)

amount [ə 'maʊnt] **1.** *n.* how much there is of something; the quantity. **2.** *iv.* to be equal to a numerical figure; to total up to something.
→ DOWN BY SOME AMOUNT
→ GO FOR AN AMOUNT

→ LAY AN AMOUNT OF MONEY **OUT ON** SOMEONE OR SOMETHING
→ **RETAIL FOR** AN AMOUNT
→ **SELL FOR** SOME AMOUNT
→ **TALLY (WITH** AN AMOUNT)

amount to something **1.** [for someone or something] to become worthwhile or valuable. **2.** [for something] to be the equivalent of something.

amount to the same thing (as something) to be the same (as something); to be the equivalent of something.

amphibian [æm 'fɪb i ən] *n.* a kind of animal, such as a frog, that lives in water and on land.

ample ['æm pəl] *adj.* large enough; sufficient and adequate. (Adv: *amply.* Comp: *ampler;* sup: *amplest.*)

amputation [æm pjə 'te ʃən] *n.* the removal of all or part of an arm, a leg, a finger, or a toe. (Plural only for types and instances.)

amuse [ə 'mjuz] *tv.* to make someone laugh or smile; to give someone pleasure.

amusement [ə 'mjuz mənt] **1.** *n.* happiness; pleasure; enjoyment. (No plural.) **2.** *n.* something that makes someone happy; entertainment.

an ['æn] **1.** *article* one; any. (Note: Use A before words that begin with a consonant sound; use AN before words that begin with a vowel sound.) **2.** *prep.* each; per. (See note at ①.)

analyze ['æn ə laɪz] *tv.* to examine the details of something.

ancestor ['æn sɛs tɚ] *n.* a person, usually no longer living, from whom a person descends.

anchor ['æŋ kɚ] **1.** *n.* a heavy object, attached to a ship or boat, that catches on the sea bottom to keep the ship or boat from drifting away. **2.** *n.* something that holds something else in place. **3.** *n.* a newscaster; a central newscaster who introduces news reports from other people. **4.** *tv.* to keep a ship in place by lowering ① into the water. **5.** *tv.* to secure something; to hold something in place. **6.** *iv.* [for a ship] to remain in a place by dropping ①.

ancient ['en tʃənt] **1.** *adj.* from long ago in history. **2.** *adj.* very old. **3.** *n.* someone who lived long ago.

and ['ænd] **1.** *conj.* in addition to; plus; also. **2.** *conj.* then; as a result.

and so forth continuing talking in the same way; and so on.

and so on continuing on in the same way [without saying all the details]; continuing to talk, saying more and more.

and the like and similar people or things.

angel ['en dʒəl] **1.** *n.* a heavenly being; a messenger of God. **2.** *n.* a very kind, sweet person. (Figurative on ①.)

anger ['æŋ gɚ] **1.** *n.* strong feelings of annoyance and being upset. (No plural.) **2.** *tv.* to upset someone; to annoy someone very much.
→ **EXPRESS ONE'S ANGER**

angle ['æŋ gəl] **1.** *n.* a figure formed where two lines or sur-

faces come together. **2.** *n.* a point of view; a way of looking at an issue or idea. (Informal.) **3.** *tv.* to place two surfaces or lines so that they intersect. **4.** *iv.* to turn, perhaps sharply.
→ RIGHT ANGLE

angry ['æŋ gri] *adj.* irate; upset; annoyed. (Adv: *angrily.* Comp: *angrier*; sup: *angriest.*)

anguish ['æŋ gwɪʃ] *n.* mental pain or suffering; grief. (No plural.)

animal ['æn ə məl] **1.** *n.* a living creature that is not a plant. **2.** *adj.* from or containing ①. **3.** *adj.* relating to functions of the body instead of the mind.

ankle ['æŋ kəl] *n.* the joint that connects the foot with the leg.

anklebone ['æŋ kəl bon] *n.* the main bone of the ankle.

announce [ə 'naʊns] **1.** *tv.* to make something known to people. (The object can be a clause with THAT ⑦.) **2.** *tv.* to speak out the name of someone or something that is arriving.

announcement [ə 'naʊns mənt] *n.* a declaration; a public statement.

annoy [ə 'nɔɪ] *tv.* to bother or pester someone.

anonymous [ə 'nɑn ə məs] *adj.* unnamed; from an unknown source; created or done without revealing the name or identity of the creator or doer. (Adv: *anonymously.*)

another [ə 'nʌð ɚ] **1.** *pron.* an additional one; a different one. **2.** *adj.* consisting of one more of the same kind; [an] additional [one]. (Prenominal only.)

→ DANCE TO ANOTHER TUNE
→ A HORSE OF ANOTHER COLOR
→ NOT GIVE IT ANOTHER THOUGHT
→ ONE THING OR PERSON AFTER ANOTHER
→ ONE THING LEADS TO ANOTHER.

answer ['æn sɚ] **1.** *n.* a reply; a response to a question; a solution to a problem on a test. **2.** *n.* a response to a situation; way of solving a problem. **3.** *tv.* to give a response to something, such as a test question or a letter. **4.** *tv.* to reply to someone. (The object can be a clause with THAT ⑦.) **5.** *iv.* to give a reply.

answer for someone [for someone] to speak for someone else.

answer the door [after hearing the doorbell or a knock] to go to the door to see who is there.

ant ['ænt] *n.* a small insect that lives in a colony.

antenna [æn 'tɛn ə] **1.** *n.* a device that collects or receives electro-magnetic signals that have been broadcast, such as for radio or television. (Plural: *antennas.*) **2.** *n., irreg.* one of the sensitive feelers found in pairs on the heads of insects and some sea creatures. (Plural: ANTENNAE or *antennas.*)

antennae [æn 'tɛn i] a plural of ANTENNA ②.

antic ['æn tɪk] **1.** *n.* a playful or silly act. (Often plural.) **2.** *adj.* silly; playful. (Adv: *anticly* or *antically* [...ɪk li].)

anticipate [æn 'tɪs ə pet] *tv.* to expect something to happen; to prepare for something that is expected to happen. (The object can be a clause with THAT ⑦.)

antique [æn 'tik] **1.** *adj.* old, especially if valuable; belonging to a time long ago. **2.** *n.* an object that was made long ago.

antonym ['æn tə nɪm] *n.* a word that means the opposite of another word.

anxiety [æŋ 'zaɪ ə ti] *n.* nervousness; worry. (Singular or plural with the same meaning. Not countable.)

anxious ['æŋk ʃəs] **1.** *adj.* nervous; worried; troubled with a feeling of dread or concern. (Adv: *anxiously*.) **2.** *adj.* eager to do something; excited about doing something.

any ['ɛn i] **1.** *pron.* whichever one or ones. (To point out one from a group of two, use EITHER.) **2.** *pron.* even the smallest amount or number. (Always in the negative or questions. Use SOME in affirmative statements or commands.) **3.** *adj.* whichever [one or ones]. (To point out one from a group of two, use EITHER.) **4.** *adj.* even the smallest amount or number [of something]. (Always in the negative or questions. Use SOME in affirmative statements or commands.) **5.** *adv.* even the smallest amount.

anybody ['ɛn i bad i] **1.** *pron.* some person; any person; anyone; even one person. (Always in the negative or questions. Use SOMEBODY in affirmative statements or commands. No plural.) **2.** *n.* an important person. (Used in the negative or questions; use SOMEBODY in affirmative statements or commands. No plural.) **3.** *n.* any random person; whoever; no matter who. (No plural.)

anyhow ['ɛn i haʊ] *adv.* in any case; anyway; at any rate.

anymore [æn i 'mor] **1.** *adv.* at the present time in contrast to an earlier time. (This is different from *any more*. Usually in negative sentences.) **2.** *adv.* nowadays; recently. (This is different from *any more*. Colloquial. Common but not standard English when used in affirmative sentences.)

anyone ['ɛn i wən] **1.** *pron.* some person; any person; anybody. (Always in the negative or questions. Use SOMEONE in the affirmative. No plural.) **2.** *n.* just any person; whoever; no matter who. (No plural.)

anyplace ['ɛn i ples] **1.** *adv.* no matter where; in, at, or to a place; wherever. **2.** *adv.* [not] in, at, or to any place; [not] in, at, or to even one place. (Always in the negative or questions. Use SOMEPLACE in the affirmative.)

anything ['ɛn i θɪŋ] **1.** *n.* any thing, object, or event. (No plural.) **2.** *n.* [not] a single thing; [not] even one thing, object, or event. (Always in the negative or questions. Use SOMETHING in the affirmative. No plural.) **3.** *adv.* in any way. (Always in the negative or questions.)

anytime ['ɛn i taɪm] *adv.* whenever; at any time; no matter when.

anyway ['ɛn i we] *adv.* in any case; anyhow; nevertheless; at any rate.

anywhere ['ɛn i ʍɛr] **1.** *adv.* anyplace; wherever; in, at, or to any place; in, at, or to an unnamed

13

place; in, at, or to whatever place. **2.** *adv.* [not] somewhere; [not] in, at, or to even one place. (Always in the negative or questions. Use SOMEWHERE in affirmative statements and commands.)

apart [ə 'pɑrt] **1.** *adv.* not together; separately. **2.** *adv.* in pieces; into pieces.
→ BE POLES APART
→ COME APART AT THE SEAMS
→ FALL APART
→ TAKE SOMETHING APART

apartment [ə 'pɑrt mənt] *n.* a place to live within a large building; living quarters.

ape ['ep] **1.** *n.* a large monkeylike mammal without a tail. **2.** *tv.* to copy or mock someone or something; to imitate someone or something.

apologize [ə 'pɑl ə dʒɑɪz] *iv.* to make an apology; to say that one is sorry.

apology [ə 'pɑl ə dʒi] *n.* a statement of regret for having done something.

apostrophe [ə 'pɑs trə fi] **1.** *n.* the mark of punctuation (') showing where one or more letters have been omitted. **2.** *n.* the mark of punctuation (') used to show possession in nouns. (In regular singular nouns, add the apostrophe plus an *s*. In regular plural nouns, add the apostrophe after the plural *s*.)

appeal [ə 'pil] **1.** *n.* a plea for help; a request. **2.** *n.* a legal request that a court decision be examined by a higher judge or court. **3.** *n.* attraction; something that draws someone or something closer. (No

plural.) **4.** *tv.* to request that a court decision be examined by a higher judge or court. **5.** *iv.* to be attractive to someone.

appear [ə 'pɪr] **1.** *iv.* to become visible; to come into sight. **2.** *iv.* to seem to be a certain way; to look a certain way.

appear before someone **1.** to show up in the presence of someone, suddenly. **2.** to stand up in front of a particular judge in court.

applaud [ə 'plɔd] **1.** *iv.* to clap the hands together to show appreciation or approval. **2.** *tv.* to show appreciation for someone or something by clapping one's hands together.

applause [ə 'plɔz] *n.* a show of approval by clapping one's hands together. (No plural.)

apple ['æp əl] *n.* a firm, round fruit that has red, green, or yellow skin and is white inside.
→ (AS) EASY AS (APPLE) PIE

the **apple of** someone's **eye** someone's favorite person or thing; a boyfriend or a girlfriend; a person or a thing that someone wants.

appliance [ə 'plɑɪ əns] *n.* a machine, usually found in the home, with a specific function.

apply [ə 'plɑɪ] **1.** *tv.* to put or spread something on something else. **2.** *tv.* to use something; to make use of something. **3.** *tv.* to cause oneself to work or study hard. (Takes a reflexive object.) **4.** *iv.* to request something that requires approval—such as a loan, a job, or admission to a school—

usually in writing or through some other formal process. **5.** *iv.* to be appropriate or relevant to someone or something.

apply something **to** something **1.** to put something onto something. **2.** to use something, such as force, effort, etc., on something or in the performance of some task.

appoint [ə 'pɔɪnt] **1.** *tv.* to choose someone for a job or position; to assign someone to a position. **2.** *tv.* to fill a vacant office, position, or job; to determine who will serve in an office, position, or job. **3.** *tv.* to set a time.

appoint someone **to** something to select or assign someone to serve in a particular role.

appointment [ə 'pɔɪnt mənt] **1.** *n.* choosing someone to fill a position or to take a job. (Plural only for types and instances.) **2.** *n.* an arranged meeting; an agreement to meet at a specific time and place.

appreciate [ə 'pri ʃi et] **1.** *tv.* to be grateful for someone or something; to value someone or something. (The object can be a clause with THAT ⑦.) **2.** *iv.* to increase in value.

appreciation [ə pri ʃi 'e ʃən] **1.** *n.* a feeling of being grateful for someone or something. (No plural.) **2.** *n.* the recognition of the value of something. (No plural.) **3.** *n.* a rise in value; an increase in value. (No plural.)

approach [ə 'protʃ] **1.** *tv.* to go near someone or something; to get closer to someone or something in

time or space. **2.** *iv.* [for someone or something] to come closer in time or space. **3.** *n.* a way of solving a problem. **4.** *n.* an entrance; a path to something. **5.** *n.* an instance of [someone or something] coming closer.

approve [ə 'pruv] **1.** *iv.* to judge [someone or something] to be satisfactory or agreeable. **2.** *tv.* to grant approval of someone or something.

approximate 1. [ə 'prɑk sə mət] *adj.* estimated; not exact. (Adv: *approximately*.) **2.** [ə 'prɑk sə met] *tv.* to estimate something; to guess the amount of something. **3.** [ə 'prɑk sə met] *tv.* to be similar to someone or something; to appear to be almost the same as someone or something.

apricot ['e prə kɑt] **1.** *n.* a soft, fuzzy, yellowish fruit that is smaller than a peach and has a large pit. **2.** *adj.* made with ①.

April ['e prəl] Go to MONTH.

apron ['e prən] **1.** *n.* a protective skirt worn over one's clothing; a protective covering for the front of one's clothing. **2.** *n.* the part of a theater stage that is in front of where the curtain hangs.
→ TIED TO ONE'S MOTHER'S APRON STRINGS

apt ['æpt] **1.** *adj.* likely to do something; prone to doing something. **2.** *adj.* clever; easily taught. **3.** *adj.* suitable; appropriate; fitting. (Adv: *aptly*.)

aquaria [ə 'kwɛr i ə] a plural of AQUARIUM.

aquarium [ə ˈkwɛr i əm] **1.** *n.,*
irreg. a container for plants and
animals that live in the water.
(Plural: *aquariums* or AQUARIA.)
2. *n., irreg.* a public building containing ① for public viewing.

Arabic numeral [ˈɛr ə bɪk ˈnum ə
rəl] *n.* the most usual form of
number, such as 1, 2, 3, 4, 5.
(These forms come from Arabic
script.)

arc [ˈɑrk] **1.** *n.* a curve; a portion of
a circle. **2.** *iv.* to form a curve; to
take the shape of a curve.

arch [ˈɑrtʃ] **1.** *n.* a curved structure
over an opening, usually holding
the weight of the wall above it.
2. *n.* the curved part of the bottom of the foot. **3.** *iv.* to bend in
the shape of ①; to curve like ①.

archery [ˈɑrtʃ ə ri] *n.* the sport or
skill of shooting with a bow and
arrow. (No plural.)

architect [ˈɑrk ə tɛkt] *n.* someone
who designs buildings.

architecture [ˈɑrk ɪ tɛk tʃɚ] **1.** *n.*
the designing of buildings; the
study of building design. (Plural
only for types and instances.) **2.** *n.*
the particular design of a building.
(No plural.)

arctic [ˈɑrk tɪk] **1.** *adj.* relating to
the ARCTIC. (Sometimes capital-
ized.) **2.** *adj.* very cold; freezing.
(Adv: *arctically* […ɪk li].)

the **Arctic** *n.* the area around the
Arctic Ocean, near the North Pole.
(No plural. Treated as singular.)

are [ˈɑr] *iv., irreg.* a form of the verb
BE used in the second-person singular present and in all three
persons in the present-tense plu-

ral. (Reduced to *'re* in contractions.)

area [ˈɛr i ə] **1.** *n.* a space; a section.
2. *n.* a measure of a section of a
flat surface, determined, for
instance, by multiplying the length
of the surface by its width. **3.** *n.* a
subject; a field of interest or study.
(See also a GRAY AREA.)

area code [ˈɛr i ə kod] *n.* a series of
numbers, used especially when
making a long-distance phone call,
that identifies the general location
of the person being called.

aren't [ˈɑrnt] *cont.* are not.

aren't I *cont.* am I not. (Used in the
asking of certain questions.)

argue [ˈɑr gju] **1.** *iv.* to disagree
[with someone] verbally; to quar-
rel [with someone] verbally. **2.** *tv.*
to debate a point or issue by means
of an argument. (The object can
be a clause with THAT ⑦.)

argue against someone or something **1.** [for someone] to make a
case against someone or something; to oppose the choice of
someone or something in an argument. **2.** [for something, such as
facts] to support a case against
someone or something in an argument.

argue one's **way out (of** something) to talk and argue oneself
free of a problem.

argue someone **down** to defeat
someone in a debate.

argue something **down 1.** to defeat
a proposal or a motion in a meeting through discussion. **2.** to
reduce something, such as a bill or
a price, by arguing.

argument [ˈɑr gjə mənt] **1.** *n.* a quarrel, especially if spoken; a dispute. **2.** *n.* a debate or discussion of an issue on which people disagree.

arise [ə ˈraɪz] **1.** *iv., irreg.* to get up; to rise; to stand up. (Past tense: AROSE; past participle: ARISEN.) **2.** *iv., irreg.* to develop; to happen.

arise from something AND **arise out of** something **1.** to get up from something. **2.** to be due to something; to be caused by something.

arise out of something Go to ARISE FROM SOMETHING.

arisen [ə ˈrɪz ən] past participle of ARISE.

arithmetic 1. [ə ˈrɪθ mə tɪk] *n.* the part of mathematics using numbers to add, subtract, multiply, and divide. **2.** [ɛr ɪθ ˈmet ɪk] the *adj.* use of ①. (Adv: *arithmetically* [...ɪk li].)

arm [ˈɑrm] **1.** *n.* one of the upper limbs of a human being. **2.** *n.* one of the two parts of a chair that support the arms of someone who sits in the chair. **3.** *tv.* to equip someone or something with weapons.
→ COST AN ARM AND A LEG
→ FOLD ONE'S ARMS
→ GIVE ONE'S RIGHT ARM (FOR SOMEONE OR SOMETHING)
→ PAY AN ARM AND A LEG (FOR SOMETHING)
→ A SHOT IN THE ARM
→ TWIST SOMEONE'S ARM
→ UP IN ARMS

armchair [ˈɑrm tʃɛr] *n.* a seat, usually cushioned, with supports for the arms.

armed [ˈɑrmd] **1.** *adj.* carrying a gun or other weapons. **2.** *adj.* ready for war; prepared for battle.

armed to the teeth heavily armed with deadly weapons.

arm-in-arm [of persons] linked or hooked together by the arms.

armpit [ˈɑrm pɪt] *n.* the hollow underneath the place where the arm joins the shoulder.

armrest [ˈɑrm rɛst] *n.* the part of a chair or seat that supports someone's arm.

arms *n.* guns; weapons.

army [ˈɑrm i] *n.* a large group of land-based soldiers.

aroma [ə ˈrom ə] *n.* an odor, especially one that is pleasant or agreeable.

arose [ə ˈroz] past tense of ARISE.

around [ə ˈraʊnd] **1.** *prep.* enclosing someone or something all about; surrounding someone or something. **2.** *prep.* close to a certain time or location. **3.** *prep.* [traveling or touring] in various places in something; at different locations within something. (With verbs such as *run, walk, go, crawl, travel,* and *drive.*) **4.** *prep.* moving in a curved or circular pathway with relation to someone or something. **5.** *adv.* on every side; on all sides. **6.** *adv.* following a circle or a curve.

arouse [ə ˈraʊz] **1.** *tv.* to wake someone up. **2.** *tv.* to awaken someone's interest, causing curiosity, anger, sexual stimulation, or general interest.

arouse someone **from** something
to activate a person out of a state
of rest, sleep, or inaction.

arrange [ə 'rendʒ] **1.** *tv.* to put
things in a particular order; to put
things in specific locations. **2.** *tv.*
to prepare plans for something; to
plan details for something. **3.** *tv.*
to adapt a piece of music in a particular way.

arrange something **with** someone
or something to prepare or plan
something that will include someone or something.

arrangement [ə 'rendʒ mənt] **1.** *n.*
the order or positions in which
things have been put or placed.
2. *n.* a group of flowers arranged
in a pleasing way. **3.** *n.* a piece of
music that has been altered for a
particular purpose.

arrangements [ə 'rendʒ mənts] *n.*
plans; provisions for something.
→ MAKE ARRANGEMENTS

arrest [ə 'rɛst] **1.** *n.* the taking and
holding of someone using the
authority of the law. **2.** *tv.* to take
someone to the police station for
breaking a law. **3.** *tv.* to stop something from moving or working; to
bring something to an end.
→ UNDER ARREST

arrival [ə 'rɑɪ vəl] *n.* the reaching of
the place that one is going to;
coming to a place.

arrive [ə 'rɑɪv] *iv.* to reach the place
that one is going to.
→ HAVE ARRIVED

arrive at something **1.** to reach a
place. **2.** to reach a conclusion; to
make a decision.

arrive (up)on the scene (of
something**)** to reach the location
of an event in progress.

arrogance ['ɛr ə gəns] *n.* an
unpleasant attitude of superiority;
excessive pride. (No plural.)

arrogant ['ɛr ə gənt] *adj.* with an
unpleasant attitude of superiority;
showing arrogance. (Adv: *arrogantly.*)

arrow ['ɛr o] **1.** *n.* a thin, sharply
pointed stick that is shot from a
bow. **2.** *n.* a pointed symbol, indicating direction or position.

art ['ɑrt] **1.** *n.* the skilled creation of
things of beauty or significant
interest. (No plural. Typically
painting, drawing, sculpture, fic-
tion, poetry, theater, dance, music,
film, and photography.) **2.** *n.* the
product of ①, such as a painting,
drawing, or sculpture. (No plural.
Number is expressed with *work(s)
of art.*) **3.** *n.* the skill required to
do or to make something creative;
a creative craft.

article ['ɑr tɪ kəl] **1.** *n.* a small part
or section of a written document,
especially an official document
such as a contract. **2.** *n.* a specific
item; a piece of something. **3.** *n.* a
word like A, AN, and THE in English.
4. *n.* a small section of writing in a
larger work, as in a newspaper or
an encyclopedia.

artificial [ɑr tə 'fɪʃ əl] *adj.* not
authentic; not occurring in nature.
(Adv: *artificially.*)

artist ['ɑr tɪst] *n.* someone who
creates ART ② or practices ART ①.

artistic [ɑr 'tɪs tɪk] *adj.* creatively pleasing; showing creativity. (Adv: *artistically* [...ɪk li].)

the **arts** *n.* areas of activity associated with a kind of art. (Treated as plural.)

artwork ['ɑrt wɚk] **1.** *n.* one or more pieces of art, such as a painting or a sculpture. (No plural.) **2.** *n.* the pictures or illustrations that appear with written text. (No plural.)

as ['æz] **1.** *conj.* to the same amount or degree; equally; in the same way. **2.** *conj.* while; during; at the same time. **3.** *conj.* in the way that. **4.** *conj.* because; since. **5.** *prep.* in the role or function of something.

as a duck takes to water easily and naturally.

as an aside as a comment; as a comment that is not supposed to be heard by everyone.

(as) bad as all that as bad as reported; as bad as it seems.

(as) blind as a bat with imperfect sight; blind.

(as) busy as a beaver AND **(as) busy as a bee** very busy.

(as) busy as a bee Go to (AS) BUSY AS A BEAVER.

(as) busy as Grand Central Station very busy; crowded with customers or other people. (Grand Central Station is a large railroad station in New York City.)

(as) clear as mud not understandable.

(as) comfortable as an old shoe very comfortable; very comforting and familiar.

(as) cool as a cucumber calm and not agitated; with one's wits about one.

(as) dead as a dodo dead; no longer in existence. (*Dodo* = a large, extinct bird.)

(as) different as night and day completely different.

(as) easy as (apple) pie very easy.

(as) easy as duck soup very easy; requiring no effort.

as far as it goes as much as something does, categorizes, covers, or accomplishes.

as fast as one's **feet would carry** one as fast as possible.

(as) fit as a fiddle healthy and physically fit.

(as) flat as a pancake very flat.

as for someone or something in regard to someone or something; concerning someone or something.

(as) free as a bird carefree; completely free.

(as) full as a tick AND **(as) tight as a tick 1.** very tight. **2.** drunk.

(as) funny as a crutch not funny at all.

(as) good as done the same as being done; almost done. (Many different past participles can replace *done* in this phrase: *cooked, dead, finished, painted, typed,* etc.)

(as) good as gold genuine; authentic.

(as) happy as a clam happy and content.

(as) hard as nails very hard; cold and cruel.

(as) high as a kite AND **(as) high as the sky 1.** very high. **2.** drunk or drugged.

(as) high as the sky Go to (AS) HIGH AS A KITE.

(as) hungry as a bear very hungry.

as if *conj.* in the same way that it would be if [something were to happen].

(as) innocent as a lamb guiltless; naive.

as it were as one might say; in a way. (Sometimes used to qualify an assertion that may not sound reasonable or that is technically not true.)

(as) light as a feather of little weight.

(as) likely as not probably; with an even chance either way.

as long as AND **so long as 1.** provided that...; on the condition that.... **2.** since...; given the fact that.... **3.** during or throughout the period of time that....

as luck would have it by good or bad luck; as it turned out; by chance.

(as) mad as a hornet angry.

(as) mad as a March hare crazy. (Often associated with a character in Lewis Carroll's *Alice's Adventures in Wonderland,* though the phrase is actually older.)

(as) mad as a wet hen angry.

as one as if a group were one person. (Especially with *act, move,* or *speak.*)

(as) plain as day 1. very plain and simple. **2.** clear and understandable. (As transparent as daylight.)

as plain as the nose on one's **face** obvious; clearly evident.

(as) poor as a church mouse very poor.

(as) pretty as a picture very pretty.

(as) proud as a peacock very proud; haughty.

(as) quick as a wink very quickly.

(as) quiet as a mouse very quiet; shy and silent.

(as) regular as clockwork dependably regular.

(as) scarce as hens' teeth AND **scarcer than hens' teeth** very scarce or nonexistent.

(as) sick as a dog very sick; sick and vomiting.

(as) slippery as an eel devious; undependable.

(as) smart as a fox smart and clever.

(as) snug as a bug in a rug cozy and snug.

(as) sober as a judge 1. very formal, somber, or stuffy. **2.** not drunk; alert and completely sober.

(as) soft as a baby's bottom very soft and smooth to the touch.

as soon as at the moment that; at the time that; when.

(as) soon as possible at the earliest time.

(as) strong as an ox very strong.

(as) stubborn as a mule very stubborn.

as such considering the state something is in; as someone or something is.

as the crow flies straight across the land, as opposed to distances measured on a road, river, etc.

(as) thick as pea soup [of fog] very thick.

(as) thick as thieves very close-knit; friendly; allied.

as though *conj.* in the same way that it would be if [something were to happen].

(as) tight as a tick Go to (AS) FULL AS A TICK.

as to someone or something regarding someone or something; concerning someone or something; about someone or something.

as usual as is the normal or typical situation.

(as) weak as a kitten weak; weak and sickly.

as well also; in addition.

as well as in addition to [someone or something].

(as) white as the driven snow very white.

(as) wise as an owl very wise.

ash ['æʃ] **1.** *n.* what remains after matter has burned or exploded. (The plural form is used when referring to the individual particles and pieces.) **2.** *n.* a tree of the olive family. **3.** *n.* the wood of ②. (Plural only for types and instances.)

ashamed [ə 'ʃemd] *adj.* having shame [about something]. (Adv: *ashamedly* [ə 'ʃem əd li].)

aside [ə 'saɪd] **1.** *n.* something said that is not meant to be heard by all present; a remark made by an actor to the audience. **2.** *adv.* to the side; to one side; apart from someone or something. **3.** *adv.* away from oneself; to the side of oneself.
→ ALL JOKING ASIDE
→ AS AN ASIDE
→ ELBOW SOMEONE ASIDE
→ MOTION SOMEONE ASIDE
→ STAND ASIDE
→ STEP ASIDE

ask ['æsk] **1.** *tv.* to put a question to someone. **2.** *tv.* to request information by stating a question. (The object can be a clause with THAT ⑦.) **3.** *tv.* to request that someone do something or give one something. **4.** *tv.* to question someone about someone or something. **5.** *tv.* to invite someone to do something; to suggest that someone do something.

ask after someone to inquire about the health and well-being of someone.

ask for the moon to ask for too much; to make great demands; to ask for something that is difficult or impossible to obtain.

ask for trouble to do or say something that will cause trouble.

ask someone in((to) someplace) to invite someone inside someplace.

ask someone out (for something) Go to ASK SOMEONE OUT (TO SOMETHING).

ask someone out (to something) AND **ask someone out (for something)** to invite someone to go out to something or someplace [on a date].

ask someone **over** to invite someone who lives close by to come to one's home [for a visit].

ask someone **up** to ask someone to come to one's home for a visit. (Usually said when someone must travel north, up a hill, or to an upper-level apartment for the visit.)

asleep [ə 'slip] **1.** *adj.* sleeping; not awake. (Not prenominal.) **2.** *adj.* [of arms, legs, hands, feet] temporarily not feeling anything. (Not prenominal.)

asleep at the switch not attending to one's job; failing to do one's duty at the proper time.

aspersion [æs 'pɚ ʒən] *n.* a critical or derogatory remark.
→ CAST ASPERSIONS ON SOMEONE

aspirin ['æs prɪn] **1.** *n.* a medication for relieving pain, used especially for headaches. (No plural.) **2.** a tablet of ①. (Singular or plural with the same meaning.)

assail [ə 'sel] **1.** *tv.* to attack someone or something. **2.** *tv.* to criticize someone or something strongly.

asset ['æ sɛt] **1.** *n.* an item of value; an item of someone's property. **2.** *n.* a useful skill; a useful quality. (Figurative on ①.)

assign someone or something **to** someone or something to designate someone or something as belonging to someone or something.

assign something **to** someone to attribute something to someone; to blame something on someone.

assist [ə 'sɪst] **1.** *tv.* to help someone or something; to help

someone with something. **2.** *n.* an act of assistance.

assistance [ə 'sɪs təns] *n.* help; aid; cooperation. (No plural.)

assistant [ə 'sɪs tənt] *n.* someone who helps someone; someone whose job is to help someone.

associate **1.** [ə 'so si ət] *n.* a colleague; someone who works with someone else. **2.** [ə 'so si ət] *adj.* [of a job or position] not at the highest level, but typically at a higher level than an assistant. **3.** [ə 'so si et] *iv.* to make social contact with someone.

association [ə so si 'e ʃən] **1.** *n.* a connection or link between two things, people, or thoughts. **2.** *n.* a club, society, or organization; an alliance. **3.** *n.* a friendship; a relationship.

assume [ə 'sum] **1.** *tv.* to believe that something really is as one thinks it is; to suppose something is true. (The object can be a clause with THAT ⑦.) **2.** *tv.* to take control of something; to move into a role of leadership or responsibility for something.

assume liability (for something**)** to accept the responsibility for paying a cost.

assure [ə 'ʃʊr] *tv.* to promise someone something; to say something encouraging and positive to someone.

at ['æt] **1.** *prep.* located on a point or in a place. **2.** *prep.* in the direction of someone or something; toward someone or something. **3.** *prep.* engaged in something; being in a certain state or process.

4. *prep.* toward someone or something.

at a premium at a high price; priced high because of something special.

at a snail's pace very slowly.

at a stretch continuously; without stopping.

at bay at a distance.

at death's door near death.

at half-mast [of a flag] halfway up or down.

at last finally; after a long wait.

at loose ends restless and unsettled; unemployed.

at one fell swoop AND **in one fell swoop** in a single incident; as a single event. (*Fell* = terrible.)

at one's **wit's end** at the limits of one's mental resources.

at peace 1. peaceful; relaxed; happy. **2.** dead.

at random happening by chance; chosen for no special reason.

at regular intervals at points that are equal in distance apart.

at rest not moving; not active.

at risk in a situation where there is risk; in danger.

at sea on the sea; away on a voyage on the ocean.

at sea (about something**)** confused; lost and bewildered.

at sixes and sevens disorderly; lost and bewildered.

at someone's **doorstep** AND **on** someone's **doorstep** in someone's care; as someone's responsibility.

at the bottom of the ladder at the lowest level of pay and status.

at the drop of a hat immediately and without urging.

at the eleventh hour at the last possible moment.

at the end of one's **rope** at the limits of one's endurance.

at the forefront (of something**)** AND **in the forefront (of** something**)** the most important place; the place of greatest activity.

at the height of something at the most intense or forceful aspect of something.

at the helm (of something**)** in the position of being in control of something.

at the last minute at the last possible chance.

at the outside at the very most.

at the rear of something located at the back part of something.

at the top of one's **lungs** Go to AT THE TOP OF ONE'S VOICE.

at the top of one's **voice** AND **at the top of** one's **lungs** with a very loud voice; as loudly as is possible to speak or yell.

at the zenith of something [...'zi nıθ...] at the highest point of something; at the peak of something.

at this stage (of the game) at the current point in some event or situation; currently.

ate ['et] past tense of EAT.

athlete ['æθ lit] *n.* someone who participates in sports actively, especially a team member.

athletic [æθ 'lɛt ɪk] **1.** *adj.* strong; active; in good physical condition. (Adv: *athletically* […ɪk li].) **2.** *adj.* relating to athletes; in or for athletics. (Adv: *athletically* […ɪk li].)

athletics *n.* active sports; exercise and training for sports. (Treated as singular or plural. Not countable.)

atlas ['æt ləs] *n.* a book of maps.

atmosphere ['æt məs fɪr] **1.** *n.* the mixture of gases that surrounds a planet, especially the air that surrounds the earth. **2.** *n.* the air that is nearby; the air that one is breathing. (No plural.) **3.** *n.* the mood or feeling in a particular place. (No plural.)

atom ['æt əm] *n.* the smallest part of an element that has all the chemical properties of the element.

attach [ə 'tætʃ] **1.** *tv.* to fasten something to something else. **2.** *tv.* to associate a quality with someone or something; to think of a quality as belonging to someone or something.
→ WITH NO STRINGS ATTACHED
→ WITHOUT ANY STRINGS ATTACHED

attach oneself **to** someone **1.** to become emotionally attached to someone. **2.** to follow after someone; to become a constant companion to someone.

attach oneself **to** something to connect or secure oneself to something.

attack [ə 'tæk] **1.** *tv.* to try to harm someone or something, physically or verbally. **2.** *tv.* to begin work on a problem. (Figurative on ①.) **3.** *n.* an act of physical or verbal

violence against someone or something. **4.** *n.* a sudden period of sickness or disease.

attempt [ə 'tɛmpt] **1.** *n.* an effort to do something; a try at doing something. **2.** *tv.* to try to do something.

attend [ə 'tɛnd] **1.** *tv.* to be present at a place or event; to be present somewhere over a period of time. **2.** *iv.* to deal with someone or something; to manage something.

attendance [ə 'tɛn dəns] **1.** *n.* someone's presence at a location or event. (No plural.) **2.** *n.* the number of people present; the identity of the people attending something. (No plural.)
→ TAKE ATTENDANCE

attention [ə 'tɛn ʃən] *n.* care in doing something; careful and watchful awareness. (No plural.)
→ BRING SOMETHING TO SOMEONE'S ATTENTION
→ GRIP SOMEONE'S ATTENTION
→ HOLD SOMEONE'S ATTENTION
→ RIVET SOMEONE'S ATTENTION
→ SOMEONE'S ATTENTIONS

attic ['æt ɪk] *n.* the room at the top of a house, just under the roof.

attitude ['æt ə tud] **1.** *n.* a way of thinking, behaving, and feeling. **2.** *n.* a particular position or angle, especially of an aircraft.
→ WAIT-AND-SEE ATTITUDE

attractive [ə 'træk tɪv] *adj.* pretty; pleasing to the eye; handsome; creating interest. (Adv: *attractively*.)

auction ['ɔk ʃən] *n.* a sale where each item is sold to the person offering to pay the highest price.
→ DUTCH AUCTION

auction something **off** to sell something [to the highest bidder] at an auction.

audience ['ɔ di əns] **1.** *n.* a group of spectators who watch and listen to someone or something. **2.** *n.* the group of people who see a particular film, TV show, etc. **3.** *n.* a formal interview or meeting with a very important person.

audio ['ɔ di o] **1.** *n.* broadcast or recorded sound, not video; the part of television that can be heard. (No plural.) **2.** the *adj.* use of ①.

audition for something to try out for a part in something where one's singing, speaking, or playing is heard and judged.

audition someone **for** something to judge someone's singing, speaking, or playing potential for a part in a performance.

auditorium [ɔ dɪ 'tor i əm] **1.** *n.* the part of a performance hall where the audience sits. **2.** *n.* a large room or building used for public meetings, lectures, and similar things.

August ['ɔg əst] Go to MONTH.

aunt ['ænt] *n.* the sister of one's mother or father; the wife of the brother of one's mother or father; the wife of one's uncle.

authentic [ə 'θɛn tɪk] *adj.* real; genuine; known to be real or true. (Adv: *authentically* [...ɪk li].)

author ['ɔ θɚ] **1.** *n.* someone who writes books, poems, plays, articles, or similar compositions. **2.** *tv.* to write something; to compose something.

authorities *n.* members of a group who have the AUTHORITY ① to do something, such as to make rules; the police; the government.

authority [ə 'θɔr ə ti] **1.** *n.* the power and right to do something; control and managing in general. (No plural.) **2.** *n.* an expert.

auto ['ɔt o] *n.* a car; an AUTOMOBILE.

autograph ['ɔt ə græf] **1.** *n.* someone's signature, especially the signature of a famous person. **2.** the *adj.* use of ①. **3.** *tv.* to sign one's name on something.

automatic [ɔt ə 'mæt ɪk] **1.** *adj.* [of a machine] acting by itself; not needing outside help to perform a process. (Adv: *automatically* [...ɪk li].) **2.** *adj.* done without thinking; done out of habit or by instinct. (Adv: *automatically* [...ɪk li].)

automobile [ɔt ə mo 'bil] *n.* a car; a vehicle that can carry a small number of passengers.

autumn ['ɔt əm] *n.* fall; the season after summer and before winter.

aux. an abbreviation of AUXILIARY VERB.

auxiliary [ɔg 'zɪl jə ri] **1.** *adj.* secondary; supplementary; substitute. **2.** *n.* an AUXILIARY VERB. (Abbreviated *aux.* here.)

auxiliary verb AND **verbal auxiliary** [ɔg 'zɪl jə ri vɚb, 'vɚb əl ɔg 'zɪl jə ri] *n.* a word that is used before a verb to affect its tense, aspect, or mood.

avail oneself **of** something [ə 'vel...] to help oneself by making use of something that is available.

available [ə ˈvel ə bəl] *adj.* ready; accessible and not assigned or committed to something else.

avenue [ˈæv ə nu] **1.** *n.* a wide street in a city, sometimes lined with trees. **2.** *n.* a figurative pathway, representing a route to success.

avenue of escape the pathway or route along which someone or something escapes.

average [ˈæv (ə) rɪdʒ] **1.** *n.* an amount obtained by adding several numbers together and then dividing that total by the quantity of numbers that were added. **2.** *n.* something that is usual, typical, or normal. (No plural.) **3.** *tv.* to add several figures and then divide that total by the number of figures that were added. **4.** *adj.* usual; typical; normal; ordinary. (Adv: *averagely.*)
→ ABOVE AVERAGE
→ BELOW AVERAGE
→ ON THE AVERAGE

average out to even out ultimately; to be fair over the long term.

aviation [ev i ˈe ʃən] *n.* the flying of aircraft; the management of flying aircraft. (No plural.)

avocado [ɑv ə ˈkɑd o] **1.** *n.* a tropical fruit with rough green, black, or purple skin, soft green flesh, and a large pit. (Plural ends in -s.) **2.** *n.* the edible part of ①. (No plural.) **3.** *adj.* made from ②.

avoid [ə ˈvoɪd] **1.** *tv.* to elude contact with someone or something; to manage not to make contact with someone or something. **2.** *tv.* to prevent something from occurring.

await [ə ˈwet] *tv.* to expect someone or something to arrive; to wait for the arrival of someone or something.

awake [ə ˈwek] **1.** *adj.* not asleep; alert. (Not prenominal.) **2.** *iv.,* *irreg.* to stop sleeping; to wake. (Past tense: AWOKE; past participle: AWOKEN. See also AWAKEN.) **3.** *tv.,* *irreg.* to make someone or something stop sleeping; to wake someone or something up. (See also AWAKEN.) **4.** *tv., irreg.* to bring back memories of someone or something into one's thoughts.

awaken [ə ˈwek ən] **1.** *iv.* to stop sleeping; to wake. (See also AWAKE.) **2.** *tv.* to make someone or something stop sleeping; to wake someone or something up. (See also AWAKE.) **3.** *tv.* to bring back memories of someone or something into one's thoughts; to arouse in someone a new or hidden feeling, interest, talent, awareness, or emotion.

award [ə ˈword] **1.** *n.* something given to someone as repayment; something given to someone as a prize. **2.** *tv.* to give something to someone as the result of an official legal decision; to order the payment of money in a court of law. **3.** *tv.* to give a prize to someone; to give someone something as the result of an official decision.

aware [ə ˈwer] **1.** *adj.* alert; conscious; having control of one's senses. (Not usually prenominal.) **2.** *adj.* knowledgeable; in a state of knowing something. (Takes a clause with *that*.) **3.** *adj.* conscious of someone or something.

26

away [ə 'we] **1.** *adj.* at some distance; apart in distance. (Not prenominal.) **2.** *adj.* [of a game] not played on the home team's court or field. **3.** *adv.* at a distance from one position or direction to another; from one state or position to another. **4.** *adv.* without stopping; continuously.

away from one's **desk** not available for a telephone conversation; not available to be seen.

awe ['ɔ] **1.** *n.* a strong feeling of wonder and respect. (No plural.) **2.** *tv.* to fill someone with wonder and respect.

awful ['ɔ fʊl] *adj.* horrible; terrible; very bad. (Adv: AWFULLY.)

awfully ['ɔf (ə) li] **1.** *adv.* terribly; horribly; badly. **2.** *adv.* very; really.

awhile [ə 'ʍɑɪl] *adv.* for a short length of time; for a little bit of time.

awkward ['ɔk wɚd] **1.** *adj.* clumsy; not graceful. (Adv: *awkwardly.*)

2. *adj.* hard to manage; hard to control; not easily used. (Adv: *awkwardly.*) **3.** *adj.* embarrassing; embarrassed. (Adv: *awkwardly.*)

awning ['ɔ nɪŋ] *n.* a covering, extending over a walkway, door, or window.

awoke [ə 'wok] past tense of AWAKE.

awoken [ə 'wok ən] past participle of AWAKE.

ax(e) ['æks] *n.* a tool that consists of a heavy metal wedge attached to a handle, used to chop wood. (Plural: AXES.)
→ HAVE AN AX TO GRIND

axes 1. ['æk siz] plural of AXIS. **2.** ['æk sɪz] plural of AXE and AX.

axis ['æks ɪs] *n., irreg.* an imaginary line that goes through the center point of a sphere or a ball. (Plural: AXES.)

axle ['æk səl] *n.* the rod that connects a pair of wheels.

B

a **babe in the woods** a naive or innocent person; an inexperienced person.

baby ['be bi] **1.** *n.* an infant; a newly born child. **2.** *tv.* to treat someone or something like ①. **3.** the *adj.* use of ①.
→ (AS) SOFT AS A BABY'S BOTTOM
→ LEAVE SOMEONE HOLDING THE BABY

babysat ['beb i sæt] past tense and past participle of BABYSIT.

babysit ['be bi sɪt] **1.** *iv., irreg.* to care for someone's children. (Past tense and past participle: BABYSAT.) **2.** *tv., irreg.* to take care of children whose parents are away.

babysitter ['be bi sɪt ɚ] *n.* someone who takes care of children whose parents are away.

back ['bæk] **1.** *n.* the part of a body along the spine. **2.** *n.* the rear part of something. **3.** *n.* the part of a chair that supports ①. **4.** *iv.* to move backward out of something. **5.** *tv.* to support someone or something with money. **6.** *adj.* rear; opposite the front. (Prenominal only.) **7.** *adv.* to or toward the rear; backward. **8.** *adv.* earlier; in or to the past.

back and forth ['bæk ən 'forθ] *adv.* moving in one direction and then the other, over and over; moving from one to the other, again and again.

back away (from someone or something) AND **back off (from someone or something) 1.** to move backward from a person or thing; to withdraw physically from someone or something. **2.** to begin to appear uninterested in someone or something; to withdraw one's interest from someone or something.

back in circulation 1. [for something to be] available to the public again. (Said especially of things that are said to circulate, such as money, library books, and magazines.) **2.** [for a person to be] socially active again; dating again after a divorce or breakup with one's lover.

back off (from someone or something) Go to BACK AWAY (FROM SOMEONE OR SOMETHING).

back out (of something) 1. [for someone or something] to move backward out of something. **2.** [for someone] to withdraw from something.

back someone up to provide someone with some help; to support someone.

back to the drawing board time to start over again; it is time to plan something over again.

back to the salt mines time to return to work, school, or some other place that might be unpleasant.

backbone ['bæk bon] *n.* the spine.

background ['bæk graʊnd] **1.** *n.* [in a picture] the scene behind the main subject. **2.** *n.* the events leading up to something. (No plural.) **3.** *n.* the past training, education, and experience of someone.

backrest ['bæk rɛst] *n.* the vertical part of a chair that supports someone's back.

back-to-back 1. *adj.* adjacent and touching backs. **2.** *adj.* following immediately. (Said of things or events. In this case, the events are figuratively back-to-front.)

backup ['bæk əp] **1.** *n.* a substitute or replacement for someone or something. **2.** *n.* [in computers] a copy of a computer file or document. **3.** *adj.* spare; extra.

backward ['bæk wɚd] **1.** *adv.* toward the rear; with the back part going first. (Also **backwards**. See also FALL OVER BACKWARDS (TO DO SOMETHING).) **2.** *adv.* in a way that is the opposite of the normal way; in a way that reverses the order or direction of something. **3.** *adj.* directed toward the back or the starting point. **4.** *adj.* in a worse or earlier state; not modern. (Adv: *backwardly.*) **5.** *adj.* hesitant or shy. (Adv: *backwardly.*)

backyard ['bæk 'jɑrd] *n.* the lawn or area behind a house.

bacon ['bek ən] *n.* meat from the back and sides of a hog. (Plural only for types and instances.)

bacteria [bæk 'tɪr i ə] *n.* a group of tiny, one-celled organisms. (BACTE-RIA is plural. The singular is *bacterium.*)

bad ['bæd] **1.** *adj., irreg.* wicked; evil; not good. (Adv: *badly.* Comp: WORSE; sup: WORST.) **2.** *adj., irreg.* of poor quality; inferior; worthless; defective; not good. (Adv: *badly.* Comp: WORSE; sup: WORST.) **3.** *adj., irreg.* serious; severe. (Adv: *badly.* Comp: WORSE; sup: WORST.) **4.** *adj., irreg.* harmful; not healthful. (Adv: *badly.* Comp: WORSE; sup: WORST.) **5.** *adj., irreg.* [of a person, a creature, or a part of one's body feeling or appearing] sick, hurt, or unwell. **6.** *adj., irreg.* unpleasant; disagreeable; not nice. (Adv: *badly.* Comp: WORSE; sup: WORST.) **7.** *adj.* [of food] decayed or spoiled. **8.** *adv.* very much. (Colloquial.)
→ (AS) BAD AS ALL THAT
→ COME TO A BAD END
→ IN BAD FAITH
→ IN BAD TASTE
→ LEAVE A BAD TASTE IN SOMEONE'S MOUTH
→ THROW GOOD MONEY AFTER BAD

badge ['bædʒ] *n.* a pin or medal worn to show membership in an organization.

bag ['bæg] **1.** *n.* a sack; a pouchlike container. **2.** *n.* the contents of ①. **3.** *tv.* to put items into ①. **4.** *tv.* to kill wild game.
→ LEAVE SOMEONE HOLDING THE BAG
→ LET THE CAT OUT OF THE BAG
→ A MIXED BAG

bag and baggage *adv.* with one's luggage; with all one's possessions.

bag of tricks a collection of special techniques or methods.

baggage ['bæg ɪdʒ] *n.* luggage or suitcases. (No plural. Treated as singular. Number is expressed with *piece(s) of baggage.*)
→ BAG AND BAGGAGE

baggy ['bæg i] *adj.* puffy; having extra material that hangs in loose folds. (Adv: *baggily.* Comp: *baggier;* sup: *baggiest.*)

bail out (of something) 1. to parachute out of an airplane. **2.** to escape from or abandon something.

bail someone **out (of** something**)** to pay bail or bond money to get a person out of jail.

bait ['bet] **1.** *n.* someone or something used as a lure or temptation. (Plural only for types and instances.) **2.** *tv.* to put a worm or some kind of food on a hook in order to attract fish. **3.** *tv.* to put a lure into a trap.
→ FISH OR CUT BAIT

bake ['bek] **1.** *tv.* to cook something using dry heat, usually in an oven. **2.** *tv.* [for the sun or hot, dry weather] to make someone or something very hot. (Figurative on ①.) **3.** *iv.* to cook food by placing it in a hot oven.

baker ['bek ɚ] *n.* someone who bakes foods, usually breads or pastries.

bakery ['bek ri] *n.* a store or place where bread products and pastries are prepared and sold.

balance ['bæl əns] **1.** *n.* an even placement of weight; a stable position with weight placed evenly; the ability to stay in such a position. (No plural.) **2.** *n.* a device that compares the weights of two objects. **3.** *n.* an equality in weight, proportion, or value; harmony. (No plural.) **4.** *n.* the amount of money remaining on a bill after part of the bill has been paid; the amount of money remaining in an account after a transaction. **5.** *tv.* to place something in such a way that it is stable. **6.** *tv.* to apply credits and debits to an account to determine the correct amount of

money in the account. **7.** *tv.* to make something have symmetry in appearance or character.
→ CATCH SOMEONE OFF BALANCE
→ HANG IN THE BALANCE
→ STRIKE A BALANCE (BETWEEN TWO THINGS)

balcony ['bæl kə ni] **1.** *n.* a platform that extends outward from a room that is higher than ground level. **2.** *n.* [in a hall or auditorium] an upper level of seats that extends over the main floor.

bald ['bɔld] *adj.* having no hair on the head; without hair. (Comp: *balder*; sup: *baldest*.)

ball ['bɔl] **1.** *n.* a round object; a sphere. **2.** *n.* a toy that is a round object. **3.** *n.* an elegant dance or party.
→ the BALLS OF ONE'S FEET
→ CARRY THE BALL
→ DROP THE BALL
→ KEEP ONE'S EYE ON THE BALL
→ PLAY BALL (WITH SOMEONE)

ballet [bæ 'le] *n.* a form of graceful and precise dance that tells a story without using speech or singing. (Plural only for types and instances.)

balloon [bə 'lun] *n.* a container of rubber, fabric, or some other material that can be filled with air or gas.

ballot ['bæl ət] **1.** *n.* a method of voting involving pieces of paper or machines. **2.** *n.* a piece of paper on which one's vote is marked.
→ STUFF THE BALLOT BOX

the **balls of** one's **feet** the bottom part of the feet just under the toes.

bamboo [bæm 'bu] **1.** *n.* a type of very tall, woody grass typically found in warm countries. (No plural.) **2.** *adj.* made from the stems or wood of ①.

banana [bə 'næn ə] **1.** *n.* a long, tropical fruit with a yellow skin around a soft, white edible pulp. **2.** *adj.* made of or flavored with ①.

band ['bænd] **1.** *n.* a group of musicians, often including singers. **2.** *n.* a tribe; a group of people. **3.** *n.* a flat, thin strip of some material that is used to hold objects together. **4.** *n.* a stripe.
→ RUBBER BAND

band together (against someone or something**)** to unite in opposition to someone or something; to unite against someone or something.

bandage ['bæn dɪdʒ] **1.** *n.* a wrapping used to cover and protect a wound against dirt, germs, and infection. **2.** *tv.* to place ① on someone or something.

bandit ['bæn dɪt] *n.* a robber, especially one belonging to a band of outlaws.

bandwagon ['bænd wæg ən] **1.** *n.* a wagon or large cart that carries a band, as in a parade or circus. (Old.) **2.** *n.* [in idioms] an imaginary vehicle on which people following a particular trend or fad can ride.
→ CLIMB ON THE BANDWAGON
→ GET ON THE BANDWAGON
→ JUMP ON THE BANDWAGON

bang ['bæŋ] **1.** *n.* a sudden, loud noise; the sound of an explosion. **2.** *tv.* to hit something against something else, making a loud noise. **3.** *iv.* to hit [something]; to

make loud noises by striking something.
→ GO OVER WITH A BANG

bang into someone or something to knock or bump into someone or something.

bang one's **head against a brick wall** Go to BEAT ONE'S HEAD AGAINST THE WALL.

bangs *n.* hair that hangs down over the forehead or eyes rather than being combed back. (Treated as plural, but not countable.)

bank ['bæŋk] **1.** *n.* a corporation that lends, saves, and protects money. **2.** *n.* the building where money is loaned, saved, and protected. **3.** *n.* a place where certain objects are stored. **4.** *n.* the land along the side of a river, stream, or canal. **5.** *n.* a row or set of objects. **6.** *iv.* to do business with ①.
→ BREAK THE BANK

bank on something to count on something; to rely on something.

banker ['bæŋ kɚ] *n.* someone who is an owner of or an important officer in a bank.

banquet ['bæŋ kwɪt] **1.** *n.* a dinner and speeches, usually connected with a celebration or an event. **2.** *n.* a special dinner with a large menu; a feast.

bar ['bar] **1.** *n.* a counter or flat surface that someone stands behind to prepare and serve drinks or food to people. **2.** *n.* a counter or flat surface where different kinds of food items are kept, from which people choose whatever they would like to eat. **3.** *n.* a place where people can buy alcoholic drinks. **4.** *n.* a rigid rod of metal,

wood, or some other material.
5. *n.* a rectangular object made of certain kinds of material, such as soap or various metals. **6.** *n.* a measure in a piece of music. **7.** *tv.* to secure a door or window by placing ④ across it.

the **bar** *n.* the legal profession. (No plural. Treated as singular.)

barbecue AND **barbeque** ['bɑr bə kju] **1.** *n.* an outdoor grill used to cook food. **2.** *n.* a party or meal where people eat food cooked on a grill. **3.** *n.* the food that is prepared on an outdoor grill, especially food cooked with a spicy tomato sauce. **4.** *tv.* to cook food on a grill, often with a spicy tomato sauce. **5.** *iv.* [for food] to cook on an outdoor grill, often with a spicy tomato sauce.

barbeque ['bɑr bə kju] Go to BAR-BECUE.

barber ['bɑr bɚ] *n.* someone who cuts or styles hair, especially men's hair.

bare ['bɛr] **1.** *tv.* to uncover. **2.** *adj.* naked; exposed. (Adv: *barely.* Comp: *barer;* sup: *barest.*) **3.** *adj.* empty. (Adv: *barely.* Comp: *barer;* sup: *barest.*)

barefoot(ed) ['bɛr fʊt(əd)] **1.** *adv.* without shoes or socks; with nothing on the feet. **2.** *adj.* not wearing shoes or socks; having nothing on the feet.

barely ['bɛr li] *adv.* hardly; only just; not quite.

bargain ['bɑr gən] **1.** *n.* something that was bought for less money than it would normally cost. **2.** *n.* an agreement.

→ DRIVE A HARD BARGAIN
→ HOLD UP ONE'S END (OF THE BARGAIN)
→ IN THE BARGAIN
→ LIVE UP TO ONE'S END OF THE BARGAIN
→ THROW SOMETHING INTO THE BARGAIN

bargain for something to expect or anticipate something; to foresee something.

bargain with someone to set the terms of an agreement or a sale with someone.

barge in on someone or something to go or come rudely into a place and interrupt people or their activities.

barge into someone or something to bump or crash into someone or something, possibly on purpose.

bark ['bɑrk] **1.** *n.* the outer surface of a tree. (Plural only for types and instances.) **2.** *n.* the sound that is made by a dog. (See also ONE'S BARK IS WORSE THAN ONE'S BITE.) **3.** *iv.* to make the noise of a dog.

bark up the wrong tree to make the wrong choice; to ask the wrong person; to follow the wrong course.

barn ['bɑrn] **1.** *n.* a large farm building for keeping livestock and storing supplies and equipment. **2.** *n.* a large building where trucks and buses are kept and serviced.

barnyard ['bɑrn jɑrd] *n.* the fenced area surrounding a barn; a farmyard.

barometer [bə 'rɑm ə tɚ] **1.** *n.* a device that measures the air pressure that is all around us. **2.** *n.* something that indicates possible changes. (Figurative on ①.)

barrel ['bɛr əl] **1.** *n.* a large, rounded wooden container with a flat top and bottom. **2.** *n.* the contents of ①. **3.** *n.* the standard measurement of oil, equal to 42 U.S. gallons. **4.** *n.* the part of a gun through which the bullets travel.
→ GET SOMEONE OVER A BARREL
→ LOCK, STOCK, AND BARREL
→ SCRAPE THE BOTTOM OF THE BARREL

barricade ['bɛr ə ked] **1.** *n.* something that blocks the way. **2.** *tv.* to block off a passageway or a pathway.

barrier ['bɛr i ɚ] **1.** *n.* something that physically separates people or things. **2.** *n.* something that emotionally or spiritually separates people or things. (Figurative on ①.)

base ['bes] **1.** *n.* the bottom, supporting part of something. **2.** *n.* a starting point; the foundation from which other things develop. **3.** *n.* a center of operations; the main site of a business or organization. **4.** *n.* the center of operations and living quarters of a military unit. **5.** *n.* a chemical that is the opposite of an acid. **6.** *n.* [in baseball] one of the four "points" of the baseball diamond. **7.** *adj.* forming or serving as ① or ②; acting as a foundation.
→ GET TO FIRST BASE (WITH SOMEONE OR SOMETHING)
→ OFF BASE
→ REACH FIRST BASE (WITH SOMEONE OR SOMETHING)
→ STEAL A BASE

baseball ['bes bɔl] **1.** *n.* a team sport played with two teams of nine members each. (No plural.)
2. *n.* the white, leather-covered ball used in ①.

basement ['bes mənt] *n.* a space within the foundations of a building, tall enough to permit a person to stand.

bases **1.** ['be siz] plural of BASIS. **2.** ['be sɪz] plural of BASE.

basic ['bes ɪk] **1.** *adj.* fundamental; simple and required. (Adv: *basically* [...ɪk li].) **2.** *adj.* simple. (Adv: *basically* [...ɪk li].)

the **basics** *n.* the first principles of something on which other principles are built. (Treated as plural, but not countable.)

basin ['be sən] **1.** *n.* a large, shallow bowl or similar structure. **2.** *n.* the contents of ①. **3.** *n.* the area of land that is drained by a river or a system of rivers.

basis ['be sɪs] **1.** *n., irreg.* the foundation of something; the part of something from which other things develop. (Plural: BASES ['be siz].) **2.** *n., irreg.* an agreed-upon standard or status.

basket ['bæs kɪt] **1.** *n.* a container woven of strips of wood, twigs, or similar material. **2.** *n.* the contents of ①. **3.** *n.* [in basketball] the net, and the hoop to which it is attached, that are part of a basketball goal. **4.** *n.* a goal or score in the game of basketball.
→ PUT ALL ONE'S EGGS IN ONE BASKET
→ WASTEPAPER BASKET

basketball ['bæs kɪt bɔl] **1.** *n.* a team sport where points are scored by sending a ball through a BASKET ③. (No plural.) **2.** *n.* a ball used in ①.

bat [ˈbæt] **1.** *n.* a mouselike mammal that has large wings and usually flies at night. **2.** *n.* a wooden or metal club used in the game of baseball. **3.** *tv.* to hit a ball with ②. **4.** *tv.* to hit something; to slap at something.
→ (AS) BLIND AS A BAT
→ GO TO BAT FOR SOMEONE
→ LIKE A BAT OUT OF HELL
→ RIGHT OFF THE BAT
→ WITHOUT BATTING AN EYE

batch [ˈbætʃ] **1.** *n.* a group of things processed at the same time. **2.** *tv.* to group things together.

bath [ˈbæθ] **1.** *n., irreg.* the washing of someone or something. (Plural: [ˈbæðz] or [ˈbæθs].) **2.** *n., irreg.* water for bathing. **3.** *n., irreg.* a bathtub; a tub used for bathing. **4.** *n., irreg.* a bathroom; a room with a bathtub or shower.

bathe [ˈbeð] **1.** *iv.* to take a bath; to wash. (The present participle is *bathing* for all senses.) **2.** *tv.* to clean or wash someone; to give someone a bath. **3.** *tv.* to put water on something; to make something wet or moist.

bathrobe [ˈbæθ rob] *n.* a loose, coatlike garment worn before or after bathing or over pajamas. (See also ROBE.)

bathroom [ˈbæθ rum] *n.* a room having at least a toilet and a sink, and usually also a bathtub or a shower.
→ GO TO THE BATHROOM

bathtub [ˈbæθ təb] *n.* a large tub for bathing.

bathwater [ˈbæθ wɑt ɚ] *n.* water for bathing; the water contained in a bathtub. (No plural.)

battery [ˈbæt ə ri] **1.** *n.* a cylinder-shaped or square object inserted into flashlights, portable radios, cameras, etc., to provide electrical power. **2.** *n.* beating someone; striking and harming someone. (No plural.) **3.** *n.* a group of many large guns or other weapons. **4.** *n.* a series of tests or examinations.

battle [ˈbæt əl] **1.** *n.* a fight between two opposing forces during a war. **2.** *n.* a fight or crusade against someone or something. (Figurative on ①.) **3.** *tv.* to fight someone or something.

bawl [ˈbɔl] *iv.* to cry very loudly; to sob.

bawl someone **out** to scold someone.

bay [ˈbe] **1.** *n.* an opening in the shoreline of an ocean, sea, or lake, capable of sheltering ships. **2.** *iv.* to make a long, deep howl like a dog, wolf, etc.
→ AT BAY

be [ˈbi] **1.** *iv., irreg.* to exist in a certain way or as a certain thing; to exist in a certain state or condition. (Present tense: *I am, you are, he is, she is, it is, we are, you are, they are.* Past tense: *I was, you were, he was, she was, it was, we were, you were, they were.* Past participle: BEEN. Present participle: *being.*) **2.** *iv., irreg.* to occur; to happen. **3.** *iv., irreg.* to have a location; to exist at a specific place. **4.** *iv., irreg.* to exist. (Usually with THERE ③.) **5.** *iv., irreg.* to BE ① in the process of doing something.

be a fan of someone to be a follower of someone; to idolize someone.

be a heartbeat away from something to be the next ruler upon the final heartbeat of the current ruler.

be a marked man to be in danger of harm by someone else. (Usually with males.)

be a million miles away to be distracted and daydreaming; not to be paying attention.

be a slave to something someone who is under the control of something; someone who is controlled by something.

be a thorn in someone's **side** to be a constant bother or annoyance to someone.

be at someone to be argumentative or contentious with someone.

be behind (in something**)** to have failed to do one's work on time; to have failed to keep up with one's work.

be child's play [for a task] to be easy to do; [for a task] to be effortless.

be down 1. to be depressed or melancholy. **2.** [for a computer] to be inoperative.

be down (from someplace**)** to have come down from some higher place.

be down with something to be sick with some disease.

be from Missouri to require proof; to have to be shown [something]. (Missouri is "The Show Me State.")

be halfhearted (about someone or something**)** to be unenthusiastic about someone or something.

be in to be in attendance; to be available; to be in one's office.

be in on something to share in something; to be involved in something.

be into something **1.** to interfere or meddle with something. **2.** to be interested or involved in something.

be murder on something to be very destructive or harmful to something.

be of the persuasion that something is so to hold a belief that something is true or is in existence.

be off 1. [for one's plans or predictions] to be incorrect or inexact. **2.** not to be turned on. (As with electric switches or the things they control.) **3.** not to be at work or working.

be off on someone or something to be in a rage about someone or something; to be on a tirade about someone or something.

be off (on something**) 1.** to be incorrect in one's planning or prediction. **2.** to have started on something, such as a task or a journey.

be old hat to be old-fashioned; to be outmoded. (Refers to anything—except a hat—that is out of style.)

be on 1. to be turned on. (As with electric switches or the things they control.) **2.** [for some agreement or plan] to be confirmed and in effect. (Often used with a *for* phrase.)

be on something **1.** to be resting on something. **2.** to be taking medication. **3.** taking an illegal drug or controlled substance and acting strangely.

be on the safe side AND **be safe** to be safe; to be cautious; [to do something just] in case it is necessary; to be very well prepared.

be onto someone to have figured out what someone is doing; to have figured out that someone is being dishonest.

be onto something to have found something useful or promising; to be on the verge of discovering something.

be (out) in the open 1. to be visible in an open space; to be exposed in an open area. **2.** [for something] to be public knowledge.

be out (of something**) 1.** to be gone; to have left someplace; to be absent from a place. **2.** to have no more of something.

be (out) on strike Go to BE OUT (ON STRIKE).

be out (on strike) AND **be (out) on strike** to be away from one's job in a strike or protest.

be poles apart to be very different; to be far from coming to an agreement. (These *poles* are the extreme points, like the North Pole and the South Pole of the earth.)

be putty in someone's **hands** [for someone] to be easily influenced by someone else; excessively willing to do what someone else wishes.

be racked with pain suffering from severe pain.

be safe Go to BE ON THE SAFE SIDE.

be swimming in something to be engulfed by an excess of something, as if it were a flood.

be the death of one **(yet)** these kinds of problems will be one's ruin, death, or downfall.

be the death of someone or something to be the end of someone or something.

be the teacher's pet to be the teacher's favorite student. (To be treated like a pet, such as a cat or a dog.)

be through with someone or something to be finished with someone or something.

be up for something **1.** [for someone] to be mentally ready for something. **2.** [for something] to be available for something, such as auction, sale, etc.

be used to doing something [...'jus tə...] to be accustomed to doing something; [to be] comfortable with doing something because it is familiar.

be used to someone or something [...'jus tə...] to be familiar and comfortable with someone or something.

be with it to be up-to-date; to be knowledgeable about contemporary matters.

beach ['bitʃ] **1.** *n.* a shore covered with sand, pebbles, or stones. **2.** *tv.* to run or drive something onto the shore.

bead ['bid] **1.** *n.* a small piece of wood, metal, glass, plastic, stone, gemstone, or other material, usually with a hole through it for a string or a thread. **2.** *n.* a droplet of a liquid.

beak ['bik] *n.* the bill of a bird; the hard mouth structure of a bird or a turtle.

beam ['bim] **1.** *n.* a long, flat piece of wood, concrete, or metal. **2.** *n.* a ray of light; a stream of light; a stream of laser energy. **3.** *iv.* to radiate light; to make or give light. **4.** *iv.* to smile brightly; to look very happy.

bean ['bin] *n.* a seed of certain kinds of plants, and sometimes also the pod, used as food.
→ FULL OF BEANS
→ SPILL THE BEANS

bear ['bɛr] **1.** *n.* a powerful, furry animal with a short tail and claws. **2.** *n.* someone who believes that prices on stocks or bonds will fall. **3.** *tv., irreg.* to carry or transport something. (Past tense: BORE; past participle: BORNE.) **4.** *tv., irreg.* to accept the consequences of something; to take responsibility for something. **5.** *tv., irreg.* to manage to support someone or something; to carry the weight of someone or something. **6.** *tv., irreg.* to produce offspring; to give birth to a child. (When this sense is used in the passive voice and focuses on the child, as in *Jimmy was born in 1996*, the past participle is BORN; otherwise, the past participle is BORNE.) **7.** *tv., irreg.* [for a plant] to produce or yield something, such as fruit, flowers, or leaves.

→ (AS) HUNGRY AS A BEAR
→ GRIN AND BEAR IT
→ HAVE BEARING ON SOMETHING
→ MORE THAN ONE CAN BEAR

bear down (on someone or something**)** to put pressure or weight on someone or something.

bear one's **cross** AND **carry** one's **cross** to carry or bear one's burden; to endure one's difficulties. (This is a biblical theme.)

bear someone or something **in mind** Go to KEEP SOMEONE OR SOMETHING IN MIND.

bear someone or something **up** to hold someone or something up; to support someone or something.

bear someone **up** to sustain or encourage someone.

bear the brunt (of something**)** to withstand or endure the worst part or the strongest part of something, such as an attack.

bear up (under something**) 1.** to hold up under something; to sustain the weight of something. **2.** to remain brave under a mental or emotional burden.

bear (up)on something [for information or facts] to concern something or be relevant to something.

bear watching to need watching; to deserve observation or monitoring.

bear with someone or something to be patient with someone or something; to wait upon someone or something.

beard ['bɪrd] *n.* hair that grows on the side of the face, the chin, and the neck, usually of a male.

beard the lion in his den to face an adversary on the adversary's home ground.

beast ['bist] **1.** *n.* a monster; a scary creature. **2.** *n.* an animal, especially one with four feet.

beat ['bit] **1.** *n.* the rhythm of poetry or music. **2.** *n.* one unit of a musical measure. **3.** *n.* the area or route that someone, especially a police officer, walks on a regular basis. **4.** *tv., irreg.* to hit someone or something, especially repeatedly. (Past tense: *beat;* past participle: BEATEN.) **5.** *tv., irreg.* to mix food ingredients with a kitchen tool. **6.** *tv., irreg.* to win a game against someone or something; to triumph over someone or something in a competition. **7.** *iv., irreg.* to hit against someone or something again and again. **8.** *iv., irreg.* [for a heart] to throb; [for a heart] to pulse over and over. **9.** the past tense and a past participle of ④.
→ POUND A BEAT

beat a dead horse to continue fighting a battle that has been won; to continue to argue a point that is settled.

beat a path to someone's **door** [for people] to come to someone in great numbers.

beat about the bush Go to BEAT AROUND THE BUSH.

beat around the bush AND **beat about the bush** to avoid answering a question; to stall; to waste time.

beat down on someone or something [for rain or hail] to fall on someone or something.

beat one's **head against the wall** AND **bang** one's **head against a brick wall** to waste one's time trying to accomplish something that is completely hopeless.

beat someone **down** to defeat or demoralize someone.

beat someone **up** to strike someone as in BEAT ④; to hit someone repeatedly, typically with the fists.

beat something **down 1.** to break through something, such as a door or wall. **2.** to flatten something.

beat something **into** something to beat or whip something with a utensil, until it changes into something else.

beat something **up 1.** to beat something, such as an egg. **2.** to ruin something; to damage something.

beat the gun to manage to do something before the ending signal. (Originally from sports, referring to making a goal in the last seconds of a game.)

beaten ['bit n] Past participle of BEAT.

beautiful ['bju tə fʊl] *adj.* having great beauty; very pretty. (Adv: *beautifully* ['bju tə fli].)

beauty ['bju ti] **1.** *n.* the quality that makes someone or something very pleasing to look at; the quality that makes something very pleasing to hear or to think about. (No plural.) **2.** *n.* someone or something that is beautiful or excellent. **3.** *n.* excellence; suitability; cleverness. (No plural.)

beaver ['bi vɚ] *n., irreg.* a furry, plant-eating animal that dams up streams to form a pond in which it

builds its dwelling or lodge.
(Plural: *beaver* or *beavers*.)
→ (AS) BUSY AS A BEAVER
→ EAGER BEAVER

became [bɪ 'kem] past tense of
BECOME.

because [bɪ 'kɔz] *conj.* for the reason that.

because of someone or something
due to someone or something; on
account of someone or something.

become [bɪ 'kʌm] **1.** past participle of ②. **2.** *iv., irreg.* to come to
be something; to grow to be something. (Past tense: BECAME; past
participle: BECOME.) **3.** *iv., irreg.* to
turn into something; to change
into something. **4.** *tv., irreg.* [for
clothing, a haircut, etc.] to look
good on someone; to make someone look attractive.

bed [bɛd] **1.** *n.* a piece of furniture
used to sleep on, usually raised
and with a mattress, sheets, and
blankets. **2.** *n.* a flat base; a foundation; a bottom layer of support.
3. *n.* the soil at the bottom of a
body of water. **4.** *n.* an area of soil
where flowers and other plants
grow.
→ GET OUT OF THE WRONG SIDE OF THE
BED
→ GET UP ON THE WRONG SIDE OF THE
BED
→ GO TO BED
→ MAKE SOMEONE'S BED
→ MAKE A BED
→ PUT SOMEONE OR SOMETHING TO BED
→ SHOULD HAVE STOOD IN BED

bed down (for something**)** to lie
down to sleep for a period of time.

bedclothes ['bɛd kloʊ(ð)z] *n.* sheets
and a blanket; the cloth coverings

for a bed. (Treated as plural, but
not countable.)

bedding ['bɛd ɪŋ] *n.* the mattress
coverings, sheets, and blankets
used on a bed. (No plural.)

bedroom ['bɛd rum] *n.* a room in a
dwelling place where someone
sleeps.

bedside ['bɛd saɪd] *n.* the side of a
bed; the area beside a bed.

bedtime ['bɛd taɪm] *n.* the time
when someone usually goes to
bed.

bee ['bi] *n.* a small insect that can
sting and that makes honey.
→ (AS) BUSY AS A BEE
→ the BIRDS AND THE BEES
→ HAVE A BEE IN ONE'S BONNET
→ PUT A BEE IN SOMEONE'S BONNET

beef ['bif] *n.* the meat of a cow,
steer, or bull. (No plural.)
→ GROUND BEEF

beef something **up** to strengthen or
fortify something.

beefsteak ['bif stek] *n.* a slice of
the flesh of a cow, steer, or bull,
eaten as food. (Usually STEAK.)

beehive ['bi haɪv] *n.* a place where
bees live, reproduce, and make
honey.

beeline ['bi laɪn] *n.* the direct line
of flight that a bee follows
between its home and a food
source.
→ MAKE A BEELINE FOR SOMEONE OR SOMETHING

been [bɪn] past participle of BE.

been had been duped; been
cheated.

been through the mill been badly
treated; exhausted.

been to hell and back to have survived a great deal of trouble.

beer ['bɪr] **1.** *n.* a beverage (containing alcohol) made from grain and flavored with hops. (Plural only for types and instances.) **2.** *n.* a glass or can of ①; a serving of ①.

beet ['bit] *n.* a plant with a large, dark red root that is eaten as a vegetable.

beetle ['bit əl] *n.* a small insect whose wings are hard and protect its body.

before [bɪ 'fɔr] **1.** *conj.* at an earlier time than; previous to the time when [something happens]. **2.** *prep.* earlier than something; previous to something. **3.** *prep.* in front of someone or something. **4.** *adv.* earlier; previously. **5.** *adv.* until this moment in time; in the past.

beg ['bɛg] *iv.* to plead for something; to ask for something very humbly.

beg off ((on) something) to make excuses for not doing something.

beg the question 1. to evade the issue; to carry on a false argument where one assumes as proved the very point that is being argued. **2.** to invite the following question [question follows here]. (A completely incorrect reinterpretation of the phrase. Very popular in the last few years.)

began [bɪ 'gæn] past tense of BEGIN.

beggar ['bɛg ɚ] *n.* someone who asks for charity, especially money or food; a panhandler.

beggar description to be impossible to describe well enough to give an accurate picture; to be impossible to do justice to in words.

begin [bɪ 'gɪn] **1.** *iv., irreg.* [for something] to start [happening]; for someone or something to start [doing something]. (Past tense: BEGAN; past participle: BEGUN.) **2.** *iv., irreg.* to start to do something. **3.** *tv., irreg.* to start something; to commence something.

begin to see daylight to begin to see the end of a long task.

begin to see the light to begin to understand (something).

beginner [bɪ 'gɪn ɚ] *n.* someone just learning to do something; an amateur.

begun [bɪ 'gʌn] Past participle of BEGIN.

behavior [bɪ 'hev jɚ] *n.* the manner in which someone acts or behaves; conduct; manners. (Plural only for types and instances.)

behind [bɪ 'haɪnd] **1.** *prep.* in or to a place farther back than someone or something else; at the rear of someone or something. **2.** *prep.* later than someone or something; coming after someone or something; not current with something. **3.** *prep.* serving as the reason for something. **4.** *prep.* in support of someone or something. **5.** *adv.* toward the back; further back in place or time.

behind schedule not done by the time listed on the SCHEDULE ①.

being ['bi ɪŋ] *n.* a living thing; a living creature.
→ HUMAN BEING

belch 1. *n.* an audible release of stomach gas through the mouth. **2.** *n.* a puff of smoke or other vapors released or pushed out. **3.** *iv.* to make ①.

belch out [for smoke or steam] to burst, billow, or gush out.

belief [bɪ 'lif] **1.** *n.* something that is thought to be true; an opinion. **2.** *n.* a rule or principle of a religion or faith. (Often plural.)

believe [bɪ 'liv] **1.** *tv.* to accept that someone or something is true or real. (The object can be a clause with THAT ⑦.) **2.** *tv.* to have an opinion about something; to suppose something. (The object is a clause with THAT ⑦.)

believe in someone or something **1.** to accept that someone or something exists or is real. **2.** to have faith in someone or something; to trust someone or something.

believe it or not [one may choose to] believe this or not believe it since it seems surprising or unlikely.

bell ['bɛl] **1.** *n.* a cupped metal shell that makes a ringing sound when struck. **2.** *n.* the sound made by ① to mark the start or the finish of a period of time.
→ SAVED BY THE BELL

belly ['bɛl i] **1.** *n.* the stomach area of the body; a large, and sometimes rounded front part of the body. (Informal.) **2.** *n.* the inside

of certain things. **3.** *n.* the underside of certain things.

belong [bɪ 'lɔŋ] *iv.* [for someone or something] to have a proper or appropriate place or typical location.

belong to someone or something **1.** to be the property of someone or something. **2.** to be a member of something.

belongings [bɪ 'lɔŋ ɪŋz] *n.* the things that one owns; one's possessions. (Treated as plural, but not countable.)

below [bɪ 'lo] **1.** *prep.* beneath someone or something; under someone or something; lower than someone or something. **2.** *prep.* lower in status or rank than someone or something. **3.** *adv.* to a lower deck on a ship. **4.** *adv.* later [in a book or other written work]; after or following [on the same page or within the same written work].

below average lower or worse than the general level of quality.

below par not as good as average or normal.

belt ['bɛlt] **1.** *n.* a strip of leather or similar material fastened around the waist, to hold up trousers. **2.** *n.* a long, continuous loop of strong, flexible material used in machinery to transfer power. **3.** *n.* a SEAT BELT; a strap in a car that holds people securely in the seat.
→ GET SOMETHING UNDER ONE'S BELT
→ SAFETY BELT
→ TIGHTEN ONE'S BELT

belt up to secure oneself with a belt, usually a seat belt.

bench ['bɛntʃ] **1.** *n.* a seat—often unpadded—for two or more people. **2.** *n.* a place where players on a sports team sit when they are not playing. **3.** *n.* the seat a judge sits on. **4.** *n.* a judge or a group of judges in a court of law.
→ ON THE BENCH
→ WARM THE BENCH

bend ['bɛnd] **1.** *n.* a curve; a turn. **2.** *iv., irreg.* to become curved or crooked; to go in a direction away from a straight line. (Past tense and past participle: BENT.) **3.** *iv., irreg.* to change one's mind; to yield. **4.** *tv., irreg.* to cause an object to curve; to change the shape of a flexible object.
→ GO (A)ROUND THE BEND

bend down to curve downward; [for someone] to lean down.

bend over [for someone] to bend down at the waist.

bend someone's **ear** to talk to someone, perhaps annoyingly.

beneath [bɪ 'niθ] **1.** *prep.* under someone or something; below someone or something; lower than someone or something. **2.** *prep.* inferior to someone or something; worse than someone or something.

benefit ['bɛn ə fɪt] **1.** *n.* an advantage; something that is helpful or has a good effect. **2.** *n.* the sum of money paid to someone under the terms of an insurance or retirement contract. (Often plural.) **3.** *n.* something that one receives —in addition to a salary—for working, such as health insurance, life insurance, etc. **4.** *n.* an event with special entertainment, given to raise money for a worthy cause. **5.** *tv.* to serve to the good of someone or something.
→ GET THE BENEFIT OF THE DOUBT
→ GIVE SOMEONE THE BENEFIT OF THE DOUBT

benefit from something to improve or to profit from something; to be better because of something.

bent ['bɛnt] **1.** past tense and past participle of BEND. **2.** *adj.* crooked or curved; not straight.

berry ['bɛr i] *n.* the small, juicy fruit of a bush or shrub.

beside [bɪ 'saɪd] *prep.* at, by, or to the side of someone or something; next to someone or something.

besides [bɪ 'saɪdz] **1.** *prep.* in addition to someone or something; as well as someone or something. **2.** *adv.* also; furthermore; in any case; at any rate.

best ['bɛst] **1.** *adj.* the most excellent [thing]. (The superlative form of GOOD. See also BETTER.) **2.** *adv.* most excellently. (The superlative form of WELL. See also BETTER.) **3.** *tv.* to defeat someone; to do [something] much better than someone; to outwit someone.
→ COME OFF SECOND BEST
→ IN SOMEONE'S (OWN) (BEST) INTERESTS
→ PUT ONE'S BEST FOOT FORWARD
→ WITH THE BEST WILL IN THE WORLD
→ WORK OUT FOR THE BEST

the **best** *n.* someone or something that is better than anything else. (Stands for singular or plural nominals.)

bet ['bɛt] **1.** *n.* an amount of money gambled on something; a wager.

2. *tv., irreg.* to make a wager. (Past tense and past participle: **bet**.)

3. *tv., irreg.* to predict something; to make a guess that something will happen. (The object is a clause with THAT ⑦.)

bet on someone or something to gamble on the success of a participant in a contest.

betray [bɪ ˈtre] **1.** *tv.* to do something that shows that one is not loyal to a person; to be unfaithful to someone or something. **2.** *tv.* to show a sign of something; to reveal something.

better [ˈbɛt ɚ] **1.** *adj.* of more goodness; of greater benefit. (The comparative form of GOOD. See also BEST.) **2.** *adj.* healthier than before; improved in health; having recovered from an illness; in good health again. (Not prenominal.) **3.** *adv.* with more quality; with greater benefit. (The comparative form of WELL. See also BEST.) **4.** *tv.* to improve oneself; [for something] to improve itself.
→ HAD BETTER
→ KNOW BETTER
→ ONE'S BETTER HALF
→ THINK BETTER OF SOMETHING

the **better** *n.* [of a choice of two things] the one that is superior or more excellent. (No plural. Treated as singular.)

between [bɪ ˈtwin] **1.** *prep.* in the middle of two people or things; with something on both sides. **2.** *prep.* both together; in combination with the two. **3.** *prep.* in comparing two people or things.

between a rock and a hard place AND **between the devil and the deep blue sea** in a very difficult position; facing a hard decision.

between the devil and the deep blue sea Go to BETWEEN A ROCK AND A HARD PLACE.

beverage [ˈbɛv rɪdʒ] *n.* a drink other than water.

beware of someone or something [bɪ ˈwɛr...] *iv., irreg.* to use caution with someone or something. (Almost always a command.)

bewildered [bɪ ˈwɪl dɚd] *adj.* confused; puzzled; perplexed. (Adv: *bewilderedly*.)

beyond [bi ˈjɑnd] **1.** *prep.* farther than someone or something; on the other side of someone or something. **2.** *prep.* past someone's ability to understand or comprehend. **3.** *adv.* past; further; on the other side of someone or something.

beyond one's **depth 1.** [of someone] in water that is too deep; [of water] too deep for someone. **2.** [of someone] involved in something that is too difficult or advanced; [of something] beyond one's understanding or capabilities.

beyond one's **means** more than one can afford.

beyond the pale unacceptable; outlawed.

bias [ˈbaɪ əs] **1.** *n.* a prejudice. **2.** *tv.* to prejudice someone.
→ ON A BIAS
→ ON THE BIAS

biased [ˈbaɪ əst] *adj.* prejudiced; favoring one over another. (Adv: *biasedly*.)

bib ['bɪb] *n.* a napkin or piece of cloth worn around the neck.

bible ['baɪb əl] **1.** *n.* the holy writings of the Jewish religion; the Hebrew Scriptures. (Capitalized.) **2.** *n.* the holy writings of the Christian religion. (Capitalized.) **3.** *n.* a manual; a guidebook; a book of authority.

biblical ['bɪb lɪ kəl] *adj.* relating to the Bible. (Adv: *biblically* [...ɪk li].)

bicycle ['baɪ sɪ kəl] **1.** *n.* a vehicle with a metal frame and two wheels, operated by foot pedals. **2.** *iv.* to travel by ①.

bid ['bɪd] **1.** *n.* an offer of an amount of money for something for sale, especially at an auction. **2.** *n.* the presentation of the price for one's services, especially in a competition joined by others to do the same work. **3.** *n.* an attempt to seek or take power or control of something. **4.** *tv., irreg.* to offer an amount of money for something, especially at an auction. (Past tense and past participle: *bid*.)
→ DO SOMEONE'S BIDDING

big ['bɪg] **1.** *adj.* large; great in amount or size. (Comp: *bigger*; sup: *biggest*.) **2.** *adj.* important. (Comp: *bigger*; sup: *biggest*.) **3.** *adj.* adult; grown-up. (Comp: *bigger*; sup: *biggest*.)
→ HAVE A BIG MOUTH
→ HAVE EYES BIGGER THAN ONE'S STOMACH
→ ONE'S EYES ARE BIGGER THAN ONE'S STOMACH

a **big frog in a small pond** a relatively important person in the midst of less important people.

the **big moment** AND the **moment everyone has been waiting for** the special time that everyone has been waiting for.

bike ['baɪk] **1.** *n.* a bicycle. **2.** *n.* a motorcycle. **3.** *iv.* to ride a bicycle or motorcycle.

bilingual [baɪ 'lɪŋ gwəl] **1.** *adj.* [of a person] able to speak two languages. (Adv: *bilingually*.) **2.** *adj.* referring to two languages. (Adv: *bilingually*.)

bill ['bɪl] **1.** *n.* a written notice of money owed. **2.** *n.* a legal draft of a proposed law. **3.** *n.* a piece of printed money that is different from a coin. **4.** *n.* the hard part of a bird's mouth. **5.** *n.* the visor of a cap; the part of a cap that extends from the head and shields the eyes from the sun. **6.** *tv.* to present a notice of charges to someone or something.
→ FILL THE BILL
→ FIT THE BILL
→ FOOT THE BILL
→ GET A CLEAN BILL OF HEALTH
→ GIVE SOMEONE A CLEAN BILL OF HEALTH
→ PAD THE BILL
→ SELL SOMEONE A BILL OF GOODS

billion ['bɪl jən] **1.** *n.* 1,000,000,000; a thousand million of something, usually units of money. (A British *billion* is a million million.) **2.** *adj.* amounting to or equal to 1,000,000,000 of something.

bin ['bɪn] *n.* a container or enclosed space for storage.

bind ['baɪnd] *tv., irreg.* to secure something to something else with a tie or band; to tie something together with something else.

(Past tense and past participle: BOUND.)

binocular [bə 'nɑk jə lə·] *adj.* relating to both eyes; involving both eyes.

binoculars *n.* a viewing device made of two small telescopes, side by side. (Treated as a plural. Number is expressed with *pair(s) of binoculars*.)

biology [baɪ 'ɑl ə dʒi] *n.* the scientific study of living animals and plants. (No plural.)

bird ['bə·d] *n.* an animal that has feathers and wings.
→ (AS) FREE AS A BIRD
→ EARLY BIRD
→ EAT LIKE A BIRD
→ KILL TWO BIRDS WITH ONE STONE
→ a LITTLE BIRD TOLD ME

bird of prey ['bə·d əv 'pre] *n.* a bird that lives by killing and eating other animals. (Plural: *birds of prey*.)

the **birds and the bees** human reproduction.

a **bird's-eye view 1.** a view seen from high above. **2.** a brief survey of something; a hasty look at something.

birth ['bə·θ] **1.** *n.* the process of being born. **2.** *n.* the origin of something; the way something has come into being. (Figurative on ①.)
→ GIVE BIRTH TO SOMEONE OR SOME CREATURE
→ GIVE BIRTH TO SOMETHING

birthday ['bə·θ de] *n.* the date on which someone is born; a date of birth.
→ IN ONE'S BIRTHDAY SUIT

birthmark ['bə·θ mɑrk] *n.* a pigmented mark on the skin, usually red, brown, black, or purple, present from birth.

birthplace ['bə·θ ples] *n.* the city and country where someone was born; the place of someone's birth.

biscuit ['bɪs kɪt] *n.* a round, flat cake of bread, made with baking powder.

bit ['bɪt] **1.** past tense of BITE. **2.** *n.* a small amount of something; a tiny piece of something. **3.** *n.* the mouthpiece on a bridle, used to control a horse. **4.** *n.* the basic unit of information in a computer; a binary digit. **5.** *n.* the end of a drilling tool that bores or cuts holes.
→ CHAMP AT THE BIT
→ HAIR OF THE DOG THAT BIT ONE
→ IN A LITTLE BIT

bite ['baɪt] **1.** *n.* a mouthful of food; the amount of food taken in at one time. **2.** *n.* a light meal; a snack; a small amount of food. **3.** *n.* the mark or wound made on the skin when someone is BITTEN as in ⑤ by an animal or stung by an insect. **4.** *tv., irreg.* to grip or tear something with the teeth; to close the teeth around an object. (Past tense: BIT; past participle: BITTEN.) **5.** *iv., irreg.* [for a creature] to be able to pierce skin with its teeth; [for a creature] to have a habit of attacking people or other creatures with its teeth.
→ GRAB A BITE (TO EAT)
→ ONE'S BARK IS WORSE THAN ONE'S BITE.

bite off more than one **can chew** to take (on) more than one can deal with; to be overconfident.

45

bite on something **1.** to chew on something; to grasp something with the teeth. **2.** to respond to a lure.

bite one's **nails** to be nervous or anxious; to bite one's nails from nervousness or anxiety.

bite one's **tongue** to struggle not to say something that one really wants to say.

bite the dust to fall to defeat; to die.

bite the hand that feeds one to do harm to someone who does good things for one.

bitten ['bɪt n] Past participle of BITE.

bitter ['bɪt ɚ] **1.** adj. very sharp or harsh in taste; not sweet, salty, or sour. (Adv: bitterly.) **2.** adj. [of wind or weather] extremely cold. (Adv: bitterly.) **3.** adj. emotionally painful; distressful. (Adv: bitterly.) **4.** adj. resentful; hateful. (Adv: bitterly.)
→ TAKE THE BITTER WITH THE SWEET

bizarre [bɪ 'zɑr] adj. very strange; eccentric; weird. (Adv: bizarrely.)

black ['blæk] **1.** adj. the color of coal; the color of the darkest night; the opposite of white. (Comp: blacker; sup: blackest.) **2.** adj. [of coffee served] without cream or milk. **3.** adj. evil; wicked. (Adv: blackly. Comp: blacker; sup: blackest.) **4.** adj. [of people, usually of African descent] having dark-colored skin. (Occasionally capitalized.) **5.** adv. [of coffee served] without cream or milk. **6.** n. someone who is of African

descent having dark-colored skin. (Sometimes capitalized.)
→ GET A BLACK EYE
→ GIVE SOMEONE A BLACK EYE
→ IN BLACK AND WHITE
→ IN THE BLACK
→ PITCH BLACK
→ the POT CALLING THE KETTLE BLACK

black and blue bruised; showing signs of having been physically harmed.

black out 1. to pass out; to become unconscious. **2.** [for lights] to go out.

black something **out 1.** to cut or turn out the lights or electric power. **2.** to prevent the broadcast of a specific television or radio program in a specific area.

blacken ['blæk ən] **1.** tv. to make something black; to cause something to become black. **2.** iv. to become very dark or black; to turn black.

blackness ['blæk nəs] n. the state of being black. (No plural.)

blackout ['blæk aʊt] **1.** n. a complete loss of all electricity or power; a situation of complete darkness, especially caused by a loss of electrical power. **2.** n. a state of not being conscious.

blade ['bled] **1.** n. the flat, sharpened edge of a knife or tool. **2.** n. the flat, wide part of an oar or propeller. **3.** n. a long, flat leaf of grass or other plant. **4.** n. the metal part of an ice skate that makes contact with the ice.

blame ['blem] **1.** n. the responsibility for causing something that is bad or wrong. (No plural.) **2.** tv. to place the responsibility for doing something wrong on a person.

blame someone **for** something to hold someone responsible for something; to name someone as the cause of something.

blame something **on** someone to say that something is someone's fault; to place the guilt for something on someone.

blank ['blæŋk] **1.** *n.* an empty line or a space on a form. **2.** *adj.* without marks; having no writing. (Comp: *blanker;* sup: *blankest.*) **3.** *adj.* [of a facial expression] not showing recognition or response. (Adv: *blankly.* Comp: *blanker;* sup: *blankest.*)
→ DRAW A BLANK

a **blank check** freedom or permission to act as one wishes or thinks necessary.

blank something **out 1.** to forget something, perhaps on purpose; to blot something out of memory. **2.** to erase something, as on a computer screen.

blanket ['blæŋ kɪt] **1.** *n.* a piece of thick fabric, used to keep someone warm. **2.** *n.* a layer of something that covers something else. (Figurative on ①.) **3.** *tv.* [for something as in ②] to cover something.
→ a WET BLANKET

blare ['blɛr] **1.** *n.* a loud, harsh noise. **2.** *iv.* to make a loud, harsh noise.

blast ['blæst] **1.** *n.* a strong, sudden gust of air; a sudden, heavy wind. **2.** *n.* the noise and violent gust of air created by an explosion. **3.** *n.* an explosion. **4.** *tv.* to blow something up; to explode something.

blast off (for someplace) **1.** [for a rocket ship] to take off and head toward a destination. **2.** [for someone] to leave for a destination.

blaze ['blez] **1.** *n.* a fire; a flame. **2.** *iv.* to burn brightly; to burn with bright flames.

blaze down (on someone or something) [for the sun or other hot light] to burn down on someone or something.

blaze up 1. [for flames] to expand upward suddenly. **2.** [for trouble, especially violent trouble] to erupt suddenly.

bleach ['blitʃ] **1.** *n.* a substance that removes color or stains. (Plural only for types and instances.) **2.** *iv.* to become white or lighter; to turn white or lighter. **3.** *tv.* to turn something white or lighter; to cause something to become white or lighter.

bled ['blɛd] past tense and past participle of BLEED.

bleed ['blid] **1.** *iv., irreg.* to lose blood, as from a wound. (Past tense and past participle: BLED.) **2.** *iv., irreg.* [for color, ink, or dye] to seep or soak into other colors or dyes.

blend ['blɛnd] **1.** *n.* a mixture. **2.** *tv.* to combine something with something else. **3.** *iv.* to mix well or attractively with people or things.

blend in (with someone or something) to mix well with someone or something; to combine with someone or something.

blend in(to something**)** to combine nicely with something; to mix well with something.

blend something **in(to** something**)** to mix something evenly into something else.

blend something **together (with** something**)** to mix something evenly with something else.

bless ['blɛs] **1.** *tv.* to make someone or something holy through a religious ritual. **2.** *tv.* to ask God to place favor on the food that is to be eaten.

blessing ['blɛs ɪŋ] **1.** *n.* a prayer calling for God's favor or protection. **2.** *n.* God's favor or good fortune given to someone or something. **3.** *n.* approval.
→ THANKFUL FOR SMALL BLESSINGS

blew ['blu] past tense of BLOW.

blind ['blaɪnd] **1.** *adj.* unable to see; sightless. (Adv: *blindly.* Comp: *blinder;* sup: *blindest.*) **2.** *adj.* [of anger] irrational. (Adv: *blindly.* Comp: *blinder;* sup: *blindest.*) **3.** *tv.* to take away someone's or something's sight permanently or temporarily.
→ (AS) BLIND AS A BAT
→ TURN A BLIND EYE TO SOMEONE OR SOMETHING
→ UP A BLIND ALLEY

blinds *n.* a kind of window shade made of horizontal, or sometimes vertical, slats that can be tilted to block vision or shut out light. (Treated as plural.)

blink ['blɪŋk] **1.** *n.* [for an eye] to close and open quickly. **2.** *iv.* [for a light] to flash on and off quickly. **3.** *tv.* to close and open one's eyes quickly. **4.** *iv.* [for one's eyelids] to close and open quickly. **5.** *tv.* to turn a light on and off quickly; to flash a light.

blink back one's **tears** to fight back tears; to try to keep from crying.

bliss ['blɪs] *n.* complete happiness; joy. (No plural.)

blister ['blɪs tɚ] **1.** *n.* a bubble of fluid under the skin, formed by a burn or irritation. **2.** *iv.* [for a part of the skin] to raise up and fill with fluid in response to a burn or irritation. **3.** *tv.* to cause ① to form on someone or something.

blizzard ['blɪz ɚd] *n.* a snowstorm with strong winds, heavy snow, and possible thunder and lightning.

block ['blɑk] **1.** *n.* a solid piece of something, such as wood, stone, or ice. **2.** *n.* a large, flat piece of stone or wood on which items are cut, chopped, or split. **3.** *n.* the distance along a street from one intersection to the next. **4.** *n.* a group of seats or tickets for seats that are next to each other, as with the theater, an airline flight, or a sporting event. **5.** *tv.* to be or get in the way of something.
→ A CHIP OFF THE OLD BLOCK
→ ON THE BLOCK
→ STUMBLING BLOCK

block something **off** to prevent movement through something by putting up a barrier; to close a passageway.

block something **out 1.** to lay something out carefully; to map out the details of something. **2.** to obscure a clear view of something.

block something **(up)** to obstruct something; to stop the flow within a channel.

blond ['bland] **1.** *adj.* [of hair] fair or light in color. (Comp: *blonder*; sup: *blondest*.) **2.** *n.* someone with light-colored hair. (BLONDE is sometimes used for females.)

blonde ['bland] *n.* a woman or a girl with light-colored hair. (See also BLOND.)

blood ['blʌd] *n.* a red fluid moving through the bodies of animals. (No plural.)
→ BLUE BLOOD
→ CURDLE SOMEONE'S BLOOD
→ DRAW BLOOD
→ FLESH AND BLOOD
→ FRESH BLOOD
→ HAVE SOMEONE'S BLOOD ON ONE'S HANDS
→ IN ONE'S BLOOD
→ IN THE BLOOD
→ MAKE SOMEONE'S BLOOD BOIL
→ MAKE SOMEONE'S BLOOD RUN COLD
→ NEW BLOOD

blood vessel ['blʌd vɛs əl] *n.* a tube that carries blood through the bodies of living things.

bloodshed ['blʌd ʃɛd] *n.* injury or death caused by violence. (No plural.)

bloody *adj.* covered with blood.
→ CRY BLOODY MURDER
→ SCREAM BLOODY MURDER

bloom ['blum] **1.** *iv.* [for a plant] to produce flowers or blossoms. **2.** *iv.* [for a flower bud] to open.
→ IN BLOOM

blossom ['blas əm] **1.** *n.* a flower. **2.** *iv.* to produce flowers; to bloom. **3.** *iv.* [for a flower bud] to open.
→ IN BLOSSOM

blot ['blat] **1.** *n.* a spot or smeared area of ink. **2.** *tv.* to remove an excess amount of moisture by placing an absorbent paper over it and pressing. **3.** *tv.* to dry or clean something by placing an absorbent paper over it and pressing.

blot someone or something **out** to forget someone or something by covering up memories or by trying to forget.

blouse ['blaʊs] *n.* a woman's shirt.

blow ['blo] **1.** *iv., irreg.* [for wind or air] to be in motion. (Past tense: BLEW; past participle: BLOWN.) **2.** *iv., irreg.* [for something] to be lifted by or carried in the air or wind. **3.** *iv., irreg.* [for a sound-producing device, such as a horn] to make sound. **4.** *iv., irreg.* [for a fuse] to burn out. **5.** *tv., irreg.* to exhale air or smoke. **6.** *tv., irreg.* to sound a whistle or a horn, trumpet, or similar instrument. **7.** *n.* a hard hit or knock; a punch or sock.

blow a fuse to BURN OUT a fuse.

blow away [for something light] to be carried away by the wind.

blow in [for something] to cave in to the pressure of moving air.

blow itself out [for a storm or a tantrum] to lose strength and stop; to subside.

blow off 1. [for something] to be carried off of something by moving air. **2.** [for a valve or other pressure-maintaining device] to be forced off or away by high pressure.

blow off steam Go to LET OFF STEAM.

blow one's **nose** to drive mucus and other material from the nose using air pressure.

blow one's **own horn** Go to TOOT ONE'S OWN HORN.

blow over [for something, such as a storm] to diminish; to subside.

blow someone or something **away** [for the wind] to carry someone or something away.

blow someone or something **down** [for a rush of air] to knock someone or something over.

blow someone or something **over** [for the wind] to move strongly and upset someone or something.

blow someone or something **up 1.** to destroy someone or something by explosion. **2.** to exaggerate something [good or bad] about someone or something.

blow something **out** to extinguish a flame by blowing air on it.

blow something **out of (all) proportion** to cause something to be unrealistically proportioned relative to something else.

blow something **up 1.** to inflate something. **2.** to enlarge a photograph.

blow the whistle (on someone**)** to report someone's wrongdoing to someone (such as the police) who can stop the wrongdoing.

blow up 1. [for something] to explode. **2.** [for someone] to have an outburst of anger.

blown ['blon] Past participle of BLOW.

blue ['blu] **1.** *n.* the color of a clear sky on a bright day; the color of a deep, clear ocean. (Plural only for types and instances.) **2.** the *adj.* use of ①. (Comp: *bluer;* sup: *bluest.*) **3.** *adj.* sad. (Adv: *bluely.* Comp: *bluer;* sup: *bluest.*)
→ BETWEEN THE DEVIL AND THE DEEP BLUE SEA
→ BLACK AND BLUE
→ BURN WITH A LOW BLUE FLAME
→ LIKE A BOLT OUT OF THE BLUE
→ ONCE IN A BLUE MOON
→ OUT OF A CLEAR BLUE SKY
→ OUT OF THE BLUE
→ TALK A BLUE STREAK
→ TALK UNTIL ONE IS BLUE IN THE FACE

blue blood the blood (heredity) of a noble family; aristocratic ancestry.

the blues 1. *n.* sadness; depression. (Sometimes treated as singular. See also GET THE BLUES.) **2.** *n.* a type of music, similar to slow jazz. (Sometimes treated as singular.)

bluff ['blʌf] **1.** *n.* a steep hill or cliff with a wide front. **2.** *n.* a harmless deception; a trick that will not result in harm. **3.** *tv.* to deceive someone or some creature; to mislead someone or some creature into doing something.

blunder ['blʌn dɚ] **1.** *n.* a stupid mistake; a clumsy error. **2.** *iv.* to make a stupid mistake.

blunt ['blʌnt] **1.** *adj.* without a sharp edge or point. (Adv: *bluntly.* Comp: *blunter;* sup: *bluntest.*) **2.** *adj.* to the point; frank; not subtle. (Adv: *bluntly.* Comp: *blunter;* sup: *bluntest.*) **3.** *tv.* to make something dull; to make something less sharp.

board ['bord] **1.** *n.* a flat, thin piece of wood; a plank. **2.** *n.* a flat piece of wood or other rigid material,

used for a specific purpose. **3.** *n.* daily meals [when associated with one's lodging]. (No plural. Treated as singular.) **4.** *n.* a group of people who manage a company or other organization. **5.** *n.* a flat, sturdy piece of material on which a game is played. **6.** *tv.* to get on a ship, bus, train, or plane. **7.** *iv.* to receive meals and living space in exchange for money or work.
→ BACK TO THE DRAWING BOARD
→ BULLETIN BOARD

boast ['bost] **1.** *n.* a bragging statement. **2.** *iv.* to brag or exaggerate. **3.** *tv.* [for something] to offer or have a particular characteristic.

boat ['bot] *n.* a floating means of transportation, smaller than a ship, that carries people and cargo.
→ IN THE SAME BOAT
→ ROCK THE BOAT

bob ['bab] **1.** *n.* a quick up-and-down movement. **2.** *iv.* to move up and down quickly, as with something floating on water. **3.** *tv.* to cut something, especially hair, short.

body ['badi] **1.** *n.* the whole physical structure of a living creature or plant. **2.** *n.* a dead human or animal; a corpse. **3.** *n.* the main part of something. **4.** *n.* a collection of people or things taken as a group; a group; a collection. **5.** *n.* a large mass of something; an object.
→ KEEP BODY AND SOUL TOGETHER

bog down to become encumbered and slow down; to slow down.

boggle someone's **mind** to overwhelm someone; to mix up someone's thinking; to astound someone.

boil ['bɔɪl] **1.** *n.* a painful sore place surrounding an infection. **2.** *n.* the condition of something that BOILS as in ⑤. (No plural.) **3.** *tv.* to make a liquid so hot that it bubbles and turns into vapor. **4.** *tv.* to cook something by putting it in a liquid that is very hot as in ⑤. **5.** *iv.* [for a liquid] to become so hot that it bubbles and turns into vapor. **6.** *iv.* [for something] to cook in a liquid that is very hot as in ⑤.
→ HAVE A LOW BOILING POINT
→ MAKE SOMEONE'S BLOOD BOIL

boil down to something **1.** [for a liquid] to be condensed to something by boiling. **2.** [for a complex situation] to be reduced to its essentials.

boil over [for a liquid] to overflow while being boiled.

boil something **out (of** something**)** to remove something from something by boiling.

bold ['bold] **1.** *adj.* confident; sure of oneself; courageous. (Adv: *boldly.* Comp: *bolder;* sup: *boldest.*) **2.** *adj.* without shame; rude; not shy. (Adv: *boldly.* Comp: *bolder;* sup: *boldest.*) **3.** *adj.* [of printing] darker and thicker. (Comp: *bolder;* sup: *boldest.*)

bolt ['bolt] **1.** *n.* a metal pin or rod, with THREADS, used to connect or attach things. **2.** *n.* a rod that fastens a door, window, or gate. **3.** *n.* a flash or streak of lightning. **4.** *n.* a sudden, quick movement; an unexpected, quick movement. **5.** *n.* a roll of cloth. **6.** *tv.* to fasten two or more objects together with ①. **7.** *tv.* to lock a door, gate, or

window by sliding a metal ② into place. **8.** *iv.* to run away from someone or something; to move away from someone or something quickly and suddenly.
→ LIKE A BOLT OUT OF THE BLUE
→ NUTS AND BOLTS (OF SOMETHING)

bomb ['bɑm] **1.** *n.* an explosive weapon or device. **2.** *tv.* to attack an area by dropping ① on it from planes. **3.** *tv.* to use ① to cause damage or injury to someone or something.

bond ['bɑnd] **1.** *n.* a link or something in common that brings together two people or two groups of people. **2.** *n.* something that causes two objects to stick together. **3.** *n.* an agreement in which someone or a company promises, as an investment, to pay back a certain sum of money by a particular date. **4.** *iv.* [for an adhesive or paint] to become firmly attached.

bone ['bon] **1.** *n.* any one of the many parts of an animal's skeleton. **2.** *n.* the hard substance of which ① is made. (No plural.) **3.** *tv.* to remove ① from meat before cooking it.
→ ALL SKIN AND BONES
→ CHILLED TO THE BONE
→ CUT SOMETHING TO THE BONE
→ FEEL SOMETHING IN ONE'S BONES
→ HAVE A BONE TO PICK (WITH SOMEONE)
→ KNOW SOMETHING IN ONE'S BONES
→ NOTHING BUT SKIN AND BONES
→ WORK ONE'S FINGERS TO THE BONE

a **bone of contention** the subject or point of an argument; an unsettled point of disagreement.

bonfire ['bɑn faɪɚ] *n.* a large, controlled outdoor fire.

bonnet ['bɑn ət] *n.* a cloth hat for women or girls; any hat for women or girls.
→ HAVE A BEE IN ONE'S BONNET
→ PUT A BEE IN SOMEONE'S BONNET

bonus ['bon əs] **1.** *n.* something extra. **2.** the *adj.* use of ①.

book ['bʊk] **1.** *n.* a stack of pages, held within a cover. **2.** *n.* a subdivision of a longer written work. **3.** *n.* a set of objects that are held together under a cover. **4.** *tv.* to process a charge against someone who has been arrested for committing a crime. **5.** *tv.* to reserve space in advance for something, such as a play, an airplane flight, a room in a hotel, or a table in a restaurant. **6.** *tv.* to reserve the services of a performer in advance.
→ HAVE ONE'S NOSE IN A BOOK
→ KNOW SOMEONE OR SOMETHING LIKE A BOOK
→ an OPEN BOOK
→ READ SOMEONE LIKE A BOOK
→ TAKE A LEAF OUT OF SOMEONE'S BOOK
→ USE EVERY TRICK IN THE BOOK

book someone **through (to** someplace) to make transportation arrangements for someone that involve a number of changes and transfers.

bookcase ['bʊk kes] *n.* a set of shelves for books.

bookkeeper ['bʊk kip ɚ] *n.* someone who keeps track of the accounts of a company or an organization.

bookkeeping ['bʊk kip ɪŋ] *n.* the job of keeping track of the accounts of a company or an organization. (No plural.)

booklet ['bʊk lət] *n.* a thin book; a pamphlet.

bookmark ['bʊk mark] *n.* something placed between the pages of a book to keep the reader's place.

books *n.* the records of the money spent and earned by a company or organization. (Treated as plural, but not countable.)

bookshelf ['bʊk ʃɛlf] *n., irreg.* a horizontal board for holding and displaying books, as in a bookcase. (Plural: BOOKSHELVES.)

bookshelves ['bʊk ʃɛlvz] plural of BOOKSHELF.

bookshop ['bʊk ʃap] *n.* a store where books are sold.

bookstore ['bʊk stor] *n.* a store where books are sold.

boom ['bum] **1.** *n.* a large, echoing noise made when something explodes or crashes. **2.** *n.* a time of strong economic growth. **3.** *n.* a large, horizontal pole or beam used for support or in the lifting of a weight. **4.** *iv.* to make a large, echoing noise like an explosion or a crash.
→ LOWER THE BOOM ON SOMEONE

boom out [for a loud sound] to sound out like thunder.

boost ['bust] **1.** *n.* an upward push; an upward movement. **2.** *tv.* to push someone or something upward from beneath. **3.** *tv.* to increase something; to raise something.

boot ['but] **1.** *n.* a heavy shoe, often waterproof. **2.** *tv.* to kick someone or something. **3.** *tv.* to start a computer, causing it to make a series of

checks and set up its operating system.
→ QUAKE IN ONE'S BOOTS
→ SHAKE IN ONE'S BOOTS

boot someone **out (of** something**)** to force someone to leave someplace or someplace.

boot (something**) up** to start up a computer.

booth ['buθ] **1.** *n., irreg.* a seating area in a restaurant having bench seats with backs, placed on two sides of the table or around the table. (Plural: ['buðz] or ['buθs].) **2.** *n., irreg.* a small, enclosed space, such as the enclosure containing a public telephone. **3.** *n., irreg.* a display table or area—possibly enclosed—at a fair or a market.

border ['bor dɚ] **1.** *n.* a decorated area at the edge of something, and the edge itself. **2.** *n.* the dividing line between two countries, states, or other political units. **3.** *tv.* to adjoin or be next to a particular area.

border (up)on something **1.** [for something] to touch upon a boundary. **2.** [for some activity or idea] to be very similar to something else.

borderline ['bor dɚ laɪn] *n.* the line that marks a border—not clearly on either side of the border.
→ ON THE BORDERLINE

bore ['bor] **1.** past tense of BEAR. **2.** *tv.* to drill a hole in something. **3.** *tv.* to make someone tired by being dull. **4.** *iv.* to drill; to make a hole. **5.** *n.* someone or something that is boring; someone or something that is dull.

boredom ['bor dəm] *n.* a state or condition where one is bored and finds everything dull and uninteresting.
→ DIE OF BOREDOM

boring ['bor ɪŋ] *adj.* dull; not entertaining; causing people to lose interest and perhaps become sleepy. (Adv: *boringly.*)

born ['born] **1.** a past participle of BEAR. **2.** *adj.* possessing a certain quality or character since birth; by birth; natural. (Prenominal only.) **3.** *adj.* having a particular place of birth or national heritage. (Usually in hyphenated combinations.)
→ NOT BORN YESTERDAY

born with a silver spoon in one's **mouth** born with many advantages; born to a wealthy family; already showing the signs of great wealth at birth.

borne ['born] a past participle of BEAR.

borrow ['bar o] **1.** *tv.* to ask for, accept, and use something from someone with the intention of returning or replacing it. **2.** *tv.* to take something, such as a custom, trait, or idea, and use it as one's own.

boss ['bɔs] *n.* someone who is in charge of other people's work or of other workers.

boss someone **around** to order someone around.

botch something **up** to mess something up; to do a bad job of something.

both ['boθ] **1.** *adj.* one and one other; the two [people or things]. (See also EACH and EVERY.) **2.** *pron.* one thing or person and another thing or person; the two things or people.
→ BURN THE CANDLE AT BOTH ENDS
→ CUT BOTH WAYS
→ HAVE A FOOT IN BOTH CAMPS
→ PLAY BOTH ENDS (AGAINST THE MIDDLE)
→ WITH BOTH HANDS TIED BEHIND ONE'S BACK

bother ['bað ɚ] **1.** *n.* something that is time-consuming or annoying to do. **2.** *tv.* to annoy someone or something; to upset someone or something. **3.** *tv.* to interrupt or disturb someone.

bottle ['bɑt əl] **1.** *n.* a container, usually glass or plastic, with an opening at the end of a short or long neck. **2.** *n.* the contents of ①. **3.** *tv.* to put something in ①, usually for future use or sale.

bottle something **up (inside (someone))** [for someone] to keep serious emotions within and not express them.

bottleneck ['bɑt l nɛk] *n.* a narrow or crowded passage, like the neck of a bottle.

bottom ['bɑt əm] **1.** *n.* the lowest level of something; the deepest point of something. **2.** *n.* the underside of something; the lowest surface of something. **3.** *n.* land underneath water; the ground under a body of water. **4.** *n.* the part of the body on which one sits; the buttocks. **5.** *adj.* relating to the lowest part of something; relating to the underneath part of something.
→ (AS) SOFT AS A BABY'S BOTTOM
→ AT THE BOTTOM OF THE LADDER
→ FROM THE BOTTOM OF ONE'S HEART

→ FROM TOP TO BOTTOM
→ GET TO THE BOTTOM OF SOMETHING
→ HIT BOTTOM
→ LEARN SOMETHING FROM THE BOTTOM UP
→ SCRAPE THE BOTTOM OF THE BARREL

bottom out finally to reach the lowest or worst point.

bought ['bɔt] past tense and past participle of BUY.

boulder ['bol dɚ] *n.* a huge stone.

boulevard ['bʊl ə vard] *n.* a wide city street, usually lined with trees.

bounce ['baʊns] **1.** *n.* the return movement of an object when it hits a surface. **2.** *iv.* to spring up or away after hitting a surface. **3.** *tv.* to toss someone upward gently, causing an upward movement as in ②. **4.** *tv.* to cause something to hit against a surface and spring back.

bounce off ((of) something) to rebound from something.

bounce out (of something) to rebound out of or away from something.

bounce something off (of) someone or something 1. to make something rebound off someone or something. **2.** to try an idea or concept out on someone or a group. (Figurative.)

bound ['baʊnd] **1.** past tense and past participle of BIND. **2.** *adj.* tied up; fastened; glued into covers. **3.** *iv.* to jump; to leap forward; to bounce up. **4.** *n.* an upward jump; a forward jump.
→ BY LEAPS AND BOUNDS

bound hand and foot with hands and feet tied up.

boundary ['baʊn dri] *n.* a border; a line that marks the edge of a thing or a place.

bouquet [bo 'ke] *n.* an arrangement of cut flowers; a grouping of cut flowers that can be held in one hand.

bout ['baʊt] **1.** *n.* an attack of a disease. **2.** *n.* a specific contest or event, especially a boxing match.

bow 1. ['bo] *n.* a pretty knot, usually with two or more large loops. **2.** ['bo] *n.* a weapon that shoots arrows. **3.** ['bo] *n.* a stick with strings of hair stretched from end to end, used to play a stringed instrument, such as a violin. **4.** ['baʊ] *n.* an act of bending the body to show respect or in response to applause. **5.** ['baʊ] *n.* the front part of a ship or a boat. **6.** ['bo] *iv.* to bend into a curve, similar to ②; to form a curve. **7.** ['baʊ] *iv.* to bend the body when greeting or honoring someone. **8.** ['bo] *tv.* to cause something to bend into a curve, like the curve of ②; to cause something straight to form a curve.

bow and scrape ['baʊ...] to be very humble and subservient.

bow out (of something) ['baʊ...] to withdraw from something.

bowel ['baʊ əl] *n.* the upper or lower intestine; the upper and lower intestine.

bowel movement ['baʊl muv mənt] *n.* an act of expelling or getting rid of feces.

bowels *n.* the inner part of something; the inner workings of something.

bowl ['bol] **1.** *n.* a deep, rounded dish; a deep, rounded container. **2.** *n.* the contents of ①. **3.** *n.* the part of a pipe that holds the tobacco. **4.** *iv.* to play the game of bowling.

bowl someone **over 1.** to knock someone over. **2.** to astound someone. (Figurative.)

bowling ['bo lɪŋ] *n.* a game where a player rolls a large, hard ball along a narrow wooden floor in order to knock down as many as possible of the ten pins at the other end. (No plural.)

bowling alley [bo lɪŋ 'æl i] **1.** *n.* the path down which one rolls a large, hard ball in the game of bowling. **2.** *n.* the building containing a series of ①.

box ['bɑks] **1.** *n.* a rigid, cube-shaped container, used for storage or delivery. **2.** *n.* the contents of ①. **3.** *n.* a private seating area in a sports stadium, theater, etc. **4.** *n.* an empty square printed on a piece of paper or on a form. **5.** *n.* a square or rectangular container or receptacle designed for any of a number of special functions.
→ SAFE(TY)-DEPOSIT BOX
→ STUFF THE BALLOT BOX

box someone or something **in** to trap or confine someone or something.

boy ['bɔɪ] *n.* a male human, not yet fully matured.
→ SEPARATE THE MEN FROM THE BOYS

the **boys** a group of one's male friends.

brace ['bres] **1.** *n.* a support; something that holds something else in place. **2.** *tv.* to prepare oneself for an impact or some other strong force. **3.** *tv.* to prepare oneself for bad news.

brace someone or something **up** to prop up or add support to someone or something.

bracelet ['bres lɪt] *n.* a piece of jewelry worn around the wrist.

braces *n.* metal wires or bands attached to teeth to straighten them. (Treated as plural, but not countable.)

bracket ['bræk ɪt] **1.** *n.* an L-shaped object attached to a wall to support a shelf. **2.** *n.* a printed character used to set off items or to enclose a set of words. **3.** *tv.* to enclose words in ②, [such as these words].
→ TAX BRACKET

brag ['bræg] **1.** *iv.* to boast; to say too many good things about oneself. **2.** *tv.* to claim something in a boastful manner. (The object is a clause with THAT ⑦.)

braggart ['bræg ɚt] *n.* someone who brags; someone who boasts.

braid ['bred] **1.** *tv.* to interweave three or more strands of rope or bundles of hair, string, etc., into one ropelike band. **2.** *n.* a ropelike band made of woven strands.

brain ['bren] *n.* the part of the body inside the head that is the center of thinking and feeling and that controls the movement and operation of the body.
→ RACK ONE'S BRAIN(S)

brake ['brek] **1.** *n.* a device that slows or stops a machine or vehicle. (Often plural. Compare this with BRAKE.) **2.** *tv.* to cause something to stop or slow down. (Past tense and past participle: *braked*.) **3.** *iv.* to stop or slow down.

branch ['bræntʃ] **1.** *n.* a part of a tree that grows out of the trunk; an armlike part of a tree. **2.** *n.* a small stream or river that joins to a larger river. **3.** *n.* a division of a company; a smaller part of a larger organization or structure.
→ HOLD OUT THE OLIVE BRANCH

branch off (from something) to separate off from something; to divide away from something.

branch out to develop many branches, tributaries, or interests.

branch out (from something) **1.** [for a branch] to grow out of a tree branch or trunk. **2.** to expand away from something; to diversify away from narrower interests.

branch out (into something) to diversify and go into new areas.

brand ['brænd] **1.** *n.* a trade name; the name of a product by which the product is widely recognized. **2.** *n.* a special kind or type of something. **3.** *n.* a mark burned into the skin of cattle. **4.** *tv.* to mark cattle by burning a unique mark into their skin.

brass ['bræs] **1.** *n.* a metal made from copper and zinc. (Plural only for types and instances.) **2.** *n.* the family of wind instruments made of ① or some other metal, including the trumpet, trombone, and tuba. (Plural only for types and

instances.) **3.** the *adj.* use of ① or ②.
→ GET DOWN TO BRASS TACKS

brave ['brev] **1.** *tv.* to withstand something; to face something without fear. **2.** *adj.* showing courage; willing to face danger. (Adv: *bravely.* Comp: *braver;* sup: *bravest.*)
→ PUT ON A BRAVE FACE
→ PUT UP A (BRAVE) FRONT

bread ['brɛd] **1.** *n.* a type of food made by baking a mixture of flour, water, and other ingredients, often including yeast. (No plural. Treated as singular. Number is expressed with *piece(s)*, *slice(s)*, or *loaves of bread*.) **2.** *tv.* to cover food with crumbs or meal before cooking it.
→ KNOW WHICH SIDE ONE'S BREAD IS BUTTERED ON

bread and butter someone's livelihood or income. (The source of the money that buys food.)

breadth ['brɛdθ] **1.** *n.* width; the measurement of something from side to side. **2.** *n.* extent.
→ BY A HAIR'S BREADTH

break ['brek] **1.** *n.* a fracture; a place where something—especially a bone—has been broken. (Compare this with BRAKE.) **2.** *n.* a short period of rest from work. **3.** *n.* the period of time between school terms. **4.** *n.* an escape from jail or prison. **5.** *n.* the ending of a relationship with someone or something; the ending of an association with someone or something. **6.** *n.* a stop in a continuous action; an interruption. **7.** *n.* a chance to do something; an opportunity to do something.

8. *tv., irreg.* to cause something to fall apart; to crush something. (Past tense: BROKE; past participle: BROKEN.) **9.** *tv., irreg.* to damage something; to make something not work correctly; to make something unusable. **10.** *tv., irreg.* to crack something; to fracture something, especially a bone. **11.** *tv., irreg.* to violate an agreement or promise by failing to do what was promised. **12.** *tv., irreg.* to exchange a large unit of money for the same amount of money in smaller units. **13.** *iv., irreg.* to shatter; to smash; to fall apart. **14.** *iv., irreg.* to fail to operate; to stop functioning properly. **15.** *iv., irreg.* to crack; to fracture.
→ COFFEE BREAK

break a code to figure out a code; to decipher a code.

break a habit AND **break the habit; break** one's **habit** to end a habit.

break a law AND **break the law** to fail to obey a law; to act contrary to a law.

break a record to destroy a previously set high record by setting a new one.

break away (from someone) AND **break free (from** someone); **break loose (from** someone) **1.** to get free of the physical hold of someone. **2.** to sever or end a relationship with another person, especially the parent-child relationship.

break camp to close down a campsite; to pack up and move on.

break down 1. [for a mechanical device] to cease working. **2.** [for

someone] to have an emotional or mental collapse.

break down (and do something) to surrender to demands or emotions and agree to do something.

break free (from someone) Go to BREAK AWAY (FROM SOMEONE).

break in (on someone) **1.** to burst into a place and violate someone's privacy. **2.** to interrupt someone's conversation.

break in on something to interrupt something; to intrude upon something.

break into someplace to enter a closed area by force.

break into something Go to BREAK UP (INTO SOMETHING).

break into something **or** someplace) to force entry into a place criminally; to enter someplace forcibly for the purpose of robbery or other illegal acts.

break loose (from someone) Go to BREAK AWAY (FROM SOMEONE).

break new ground to begin to do something that no one else has done; to pioneer (in an enterprise).

break off (from something) [for a piece of something] to become separated from the whole.

break one's **back (to** do something) Go to BREAK ONE'S NECK (TO DO SOMETHING).

break one's **habit** Go to BREAK A HABIT.

break one's **neck (to** do something) AND **break** one's **back (to** do something) to work very hard to do something.

break one's **word** not to do what one said one would do; to fail to keep one's promise.

break out 1. [for widespread fighting] to emerge, erupt, or begin. **2.** [for a disease] to erupt and become epidemic.

break out in a cold sweat to perspire from fever, fear, or anxiety; to begin to sweat profusely and suddenly.

break out in tears Go to BREAK (OUT) INTO TEARS.

break (out) into tears AND **break out in tears** to start crying suddenly.

break out of something to get out of a confining place or situation; to escape from something or someplace.

break out (with something) [for the skin] to erupt with a specific disease such as measles, chicken pox, rubella, etc.

break someone **down** to cause a person to submit; to pressure a person to submit to something.

break someone **in** to train someone to do a new job; to supervise someone who is learning to do a new job.

break someone **up** to cause someone to begin laughing very hard.

break someone's **fall** to cushion a falling person; to lessen the impact of a falling person.

break someone's **heart** to cause someone emotional pain.

break something **down** to destroy a barrier.

break something **in 1.** to crush or batter something to pieces. **2.** to use a new device until it runs well and smoothly; to wear shoes, perhaps a little at a time, until they feel comfortable.

break something **off ((of)** something) to fracture or dislodge a piece off something.

break something **to** someone to tell bad news to someone.

break something **up** to end some kind of fighting or arguing.

break something **up (into** something) to break something into smaller pieces.

break the bank to leave someone without any money.

break the habit Go to BREAK A HABIT.

break the ice to initiate social interchanges and conversation; to get something started.

break the law Go to BREAK A LAW.

break the news (to someone) to tell someone some important news, usually bad news.

break through (something**)** to force [one's way] through an obstruction.

break up 1. [for something] to fall apart; to be broken to pieces. **2.** [for two people] to end a romance; [for lovers] to separate permanently. **3.** [for married persons] to divorce. **4.** [for a marriage] to dissolve in divorce. **5.** to begin laughing very hard.

break up (into something) AND **break into** something to divide or crumble into smaller parts.

break up (with someone) to end a romantic relationship with someone.

breakfast ['brɛk fəst] **1.** *n.* the first meal of the day. **2.** *iv.* to eat ① [somewhere or at some time].

breast ['brɛst] **1.** *n.* the chest; the part of the body between the neck and the stomach. **2.** *n.* the edible upper body of a fowl. **3.** *n.* one of the two milk-producing parts on the chest of the human female; a mammary gland.
→ MAKE A CLEAN BREAST OF SOMETHING

breath ['brɛθ] **1.** *n.* the air that moves in and out of the body when someone or something inhales or exhales. **2.** *n.* someone's exhaled air, especially if felt or smelled.
→ DON'T HOLD YOUR BREATH.
→ GET TIME TO CATCH ONE'S BREATH
→ IN THE SAME BREATH
→ TAKE SOMEONE'S BREATH AWAY
→ WASTE ONE'S BREATH
→ WITH EVERY (OTHER) BREATH

breathe ['brið] **1.** *iv.* to suck air into the lungs and push air out of the lungs. **2.** *tv.* to inhale or exhale something; to take something into the lungs or expel something from the lungs or throat.

breathe down someone's **neck 1.** to watch someone carefully; to watch someone's activities. **2.** to try to hurry someone along; to make someone get something done on time.

breathe one's **last** to die; to breathe one's last breath.

breathe something **in** to take something into the lungs, such as air, medicinal vapors, gas, etc.

breathe something **out** to exhale something.

bred ['brɛd] past tense and past participle of BREED.

breed ['brid] **1.** *n.* a group of creatures representing a unique or different kind or type; a subgroup of a certain species. **2.** *n.* a kind of something; a class of something. **3.** *iv., irreg.* to reproduce; to mate. (Past tense and past participle: BRED.) **4.** *tv., irreg.* to cause selected members of some kind of animal to reproduce, often for specific characteristics.

breeze ['briz] *n.* a light wind; a gentle wind.

a **breeze** *n.* something that is very easy; something that is easily done. (Informal. No plural.)

breeze along to travel along casually, rapidly, and happily; to go through life in a casual and carefree manner.

breeze in(to someplace) to enter a place quickly, in a happy and carefree manner.

breeze through (something) **1.** to complete some task rapidly and easily. **2.** to travel through a place rapidly.

brew ['bru] **1.** *n.* a liquid drink made by heating various ingredients in water. **2.** *tv.* to make a liquid drink by mixing and heating various ingredients in water. **3.** *tv.* to make beer or ale. **4.** *iv.* to develop; to gather; to form. (See also A STORM IS BREWING.) **5.** *iv.* [for a liquid drink] to develop into its final form.

brew a plot to plot something; to make a plot.

brew something **up 1.** to brew something, as in making coffee or tea. **2.** to cause something to happen; to foment something. (Figurative.)

brew up to build up; [for something, such as a storm] to begin to build and grow.

brick ['brɪk] **1.** *n.* a rectangular block—used in building things—made of cement or baked clay. **2.** the *adj.* use of ①.
→ BANG ONE'S HEAD AGAINST A BRICK WALL
→ HIT (SOMEONE) LIKE A TON OF BRICKS

bride ['braɪd] *n.* a woman who is about to be married or has just been married.
→ GIVE THE BRIDE AWAY

bridge ['brɪdʒ] **1.** *n.* a raised way over a river, street, train tracks, etc. **2.** *n.* something that links people or things. (Figurative on ①.) **3.** *n.* the navigation and control center of a ship. **4.** *n.* the upper part of the nose; the part of the nose between the eyes. **5.** *n.* the part of a pair of eyeglasses that rests on the nose. **6.** *n.* a type of card game for four people. (No plural.)
→ BURN ONE'S BRIDGES (BEHIND ONE)
→ CROSS A BRIDGE BEFORE ONE COMES TO IT
→ CROSS A BRIDGE WHEN ONE COMES TO IT
→ WATER UNDER THE BRIDGE

brief ['brif] **1.** *adj.* short in time; to the point. (Adv: *briefly.* Comp: *briefer;* sup: *briefest.*) **2.** *n.* [in law] a document that describes certain facts or information about a legal case. **3.** *tv.* to acquaint someone with certain facts or information.

briefs *n.* short and close-fitting underpants. (Treated as plural. Number can be expressed with *pair(s) of briefs.* Also countable.)

bright ['braɪt] **1.** *adj.* shiny; full of light; reflecting much light. (Adv: *brightly.* Comp: *brighter;* sup: *brightest.*) **2.** *adj.* smart; intelligent. (Adv: *brightly.* Comp: *brighter;* sup: *brightest.*) **3.** *adj.* vivid; brilliant. (Adv: *brightly.* Comp: *brighter;* sup: *brightest.*)

brim ['brɪm] **1.** *n.* the top edge of something, such as a cup. **2.** *n.* the circular, flat edge of a hat.

brimming with something **1.** full of some kind of happy behavior. **2.** full to the point of overflowing.

bring ['brɪŋ] **1.** *tv., irreg.* to carry or escort someone or something from a more distant place to a closer place. (Past tense and past participle: BROUGHT.) **2.** *tv., irreg.* to cause something to happen; to result in something. **3.** *tv., irreg.* to cause something to enter into a different state.

bring a verdict in [for a jury] to deliver its decision to the court.

bring down the curtain (on something**)** Go to RING DOWN THE CURTAIN (ON SOMETHING).

bring someone **down 1.** to assist or accompany someone from a higher place to a lower place. **2.** to bring someone to a place for a visit. **3.** to restore someone to a normal mood or attitude.

bring someone **in (on** something**)** to include someone in some deed or activity.

bring someone or something **up** **1.** to cause someone or something to go up with one from a lower place to a higher place. **2.** to mention someone or something. **3.** to raise someone or something; to care for someone or something up to adulthood.

bring someone **to** to help someone return to consciousness.

bring someone **up for** something to put someone's name up for promotion, review, discipline, etc.

bring someone **up on** something to provide something while raising a child to adulthood.

bring something **about** to make something happen.

bring something **back** to restore an earlier style or practice.

bring something **back (to** someone**)** to remind someone of something.

bring something **down 1.** to move something from a higher place to a lower place. **2.** to lower something, such as prices, profit, taxes, etc. **3.** to defeat or overcome something, such as an enemy, a government, etc.

bring something **in** to earn something, such as an amount of money; to draw or attract an amount of money.

bring something **on 1.** to cause something to happen; to cause a situation to occur. **2.** to cause a case of, or an attack of, a disease.

bring something **on** someone to cause something to go wrong for someone.

bring something **out** to issue something; to publish something; to present something [to the public].

bring something **out (in** someone**)** to cause a particular quality to be displayed by a person, such as virtue, courage, selfishness, etc.

bring something **to a head** to cause something to come to the point when a decision has to be made or action taken.

bring something **to light** to make something known; to discover something.

bring something **to** someone's **attention** to make someone aware of something; to mention or show something to someone.

bring the house down to excite a theatrical audience to laughter or applause or both.

bring up the rear to move along behind everyone else; to be at the end of a line.

brisk ['brɪsk] **1.** *adj.* [of movement, actions, activity, or rhythm] quick, rapid, or swift; [of rhythm, music, or activity] lively. (Adv: *briskly.* Comp: *brisker;* sup: *briskest.*) **2.** *adj.* stimulating, chilly. (Adv: *briskly.* Comp: *brisker;* sup: *briskest.*)

bristle ['brɪs əl] *n.* a short, stiff hair, as on a brush or on the back of a hog.

broad ['brɔd] **1.** *adj.* wide; vast; extensive; far-reaching. (Adv: *broadly.* Comp: *broader;* sup: *broadest.*) **2.** *adj.* main; general.

(Adv: *broadly.* Comp: *broader;* sup: *broadest.*
→ IN BROAD DAYLIGHT

broadcast ['brɔd kæst] **1.** *n.* a television or radio program. **2.** *tv.* to transmit a radio or television signal or program. **3.** *tv.* to make news widely known; to tell something to many people. **4.** *iv.* to transmit or send out radio waves.

broccoli ['brɑk ə li] *n.* a green vegetable that grows in branched stalks ending in clumps of buds. (No plural.)

broil ['brɔɪl] **1.** *tv.* to cook something by placing it over or under an open flame. **2.** *iv.* [for food] to cook over or under an open flame.

broke ['brok] **1.** past tense of BREAK. **2.** *adj.* having no money; completely without money; penniless.
→ FLAT BROKE
→ THAT'S THE STRAW THAT BROKE THE CAMEL'S BACK.

broken ['brok ən] **1.** Past participle of BREAK. **2.** *adj.* not working; not functioning; not operating; out of order.
→ DIE OF A BROKEN HEART

bronze ['brɑnz] **1.** *n.* a brownish metal made from copper and tin. (Plural only for types and instances.) **2.** *n.* a third-place medal; an award for coming in third place in a competition. **3.** *adj.* made from ①.

brook ['brʊk] *n.* a stream; a creek; a small river.

broom ['brum] *n.* a long-handled brush that is used to sweep floors.

broth ['brɔθ] *n.* the liquid part of soup. (Plural only for types and instances.)

brother ['brʌð ɚ] *n.* a male sibling.

brought ['brɔt] past tense and past participle of BRING.

brow ['braʊ] *n.* the forehead; the area around the eyebrows.
→ BY THE SWEAT OF ONE'S BROW
→ KNIT ONE'S BROW

brown ['braʊn] **1.** *n.* a deep, reddish tan color similar to the color of dirt or wood. (Plural only for types and instances.) **2.** *adj.* of the color of ①. (Comp: *browner;* sup: *brownest.*) **3.** *tv.* to cook something until it turns dark or gets crisp. **4.** *iv.* [for food] to cook until it becomes ②.

brown out [for the electricity] to decrease in power, causing electric lights to dim.

browse ['braʊz] *iv.* to look at goods casually when shopping.

browse through something to examine the contents of something, such as a book.

bruise ['bruz] **1.** *n.* a colored mark on the skin caused by being struck. **2.** *tv.* to cause ① by striking the body.

brunt ['brʌnt] *n.* the main force or impact of an attack.
→ BEAR THE BRUNT (OF SOMETHING)

brush ['brʌʃ] **1.** a device used for cleaning, combing, or painting—made of hard bristles attached to a handle. **2.** *tv.* to clean something, such as one's teeth, with ①. **3.** *tv.* to arrange or groom hair with ①.
→ HAVE A (CLOSE) BRUSH WITH SOMETHING

→ TARRED WITH THE SAME BRUSH

brush by someone or something AND **brush past** someone or something to push or move quickly past someone or something.

brush past someone or something Go to BRUSH BY SOMEONE OR SOMETHING.

brush someone **off 1.** to remove something, such as dust or lint, from someone by brushing. **2.** to reject someone; to dismiss someone.

brush something **away (from** something) to remove something from something by brushing; to get dirt or crumbs off something by brushing.

brush something **down** to clean and neaten fur or fabric by brushing.

brush something **off ((of)** someone or something) to remove something from someone or something by brushing.

brush something **under the carpet** Go to SWEEP SOMETHING UNDER THE CARPET.

brush (up) against someone or something to move past and touch someone or something.

brush up (on something) to improve one's knowledge of something or one's ability to do something.

bubble ['bʌb əl] **1.** *n.* a thin, spherical film of liquid that encloses a pocket of gas or air. **2.** *n.* a sphere of air within a solid or a liquid. **3.** *iv.* [for moving liquid] to make a sound that includes the popping or collapsing of ① or ②.

→ BURST SOMEONE'S BUBBLE

bubble over [for boiling or effervescent liquid] to spill or splatter over the edge of its container.

buck ['bʌk] **1.** *n.* the male of certain kinds of animals, such as deer and rabbits. **2.** *n.* one American dollar bill; a dollar. (Slang.) **3.** *iv.* [for an animal that is being ridden] to jump in an attempt to throw its rider.

→ PASS THE BUCK

bucket ['bʌk ɪt] **1.** *n.* a pail; an open-topped container with a curved wire handle. **2.** *n.* the contents of ①.

buckle ['bʌk əl] **1.** *n.* a fastener for securing a belt or strap. **2.** *tv.* to fasten a shoe, belt, etc., by using ①. **3.** *tv.* to cause pavement to bend and rise up. **4.** *iv.* [for pavement] to rise, fold, or break due to a force such as an earthquake or because of excessive heat. **5.** *iv.* [for someone's knees] to fold or collapse.

buckle someone **in** to attach someone securely with a vehicle's seat belt.

buckle someone or something **up** to attach someone or something securely with straps that buckle together.

buckle up to buckle one's seat belt, as in a car or plane.

bud ['bʌd] **1.** *n.* the part of a plant that becomes a leaf or a flower. **2.** *n.* a flower that has not opened all the way; a flower whose petals are still wrapped together. **3.** *iv.* [for a plant] to develop and open the parts that become leaves or flowers.

→ NIP SOMETHING IN THE BUD

buddy up (to someone**)** to become overly familiar or friendly with someone.

buddy up (with someone**)** to join with another person to form a pair that will do something together or share something.

budget ['bʌdʒ ət] **1.** *n.* a financial plan; an estimate of how much money will be earned and spent during a period of time. **2.** *n.* an amount of money allocated for a particular purpose. **3.** *tv.* to provide or reserve an amount of money for a particular purpose. **4.** *adj.* cheap; economical.

buffalo ['bʌf ə lo] *n.*, *irreg.* a type of wild ox native to Asia, Africa, and the Americas. (Plural: *buffalo*, *buffalos*, or *buffaloes*.)

buffet [bə 'fe] **1.** *n.* a large cabinet for holding utensils for serving and eating as well as tablecloths and napkins. **2.** *n.* a table or counter having bowls of food that diners can serve for themselves. **3.** the *adj.* use of ① or ②.

bug ['bʌg] **1.** *n.* any small insect or creature like an insect; any annoying insect. **2.** *n.* the flu; any minor sickness. (Informal.) **3.** *n.* an electronic device that permits someone to listen in secret to someone's private conversation. **4.** *n.* a problem; something that is wrong with a system, especially in a computer program. **5.** *tv.* to equip a room, telephone, etc., with ③. **6.** *iv.* [for someone's eyes] to open up wide and become very apparent.

→ (AS) SNUG AS A BUG IN A RUG
→ LIGHTNING BUG

build ['bɪld] **1.** *tv.*, *irreg.* to make something from separate pieces; to construct something. (Past tense and past participle: BUILT.) **2.** *tv.*, *irreg.* to develop something; to establish something a little bit at a time. **3.** *iv.*, *irreg.* [for something] to increase. **4.** *n.* the form of the body; the shape of the body; the muscle structure of the body.

build castles in Spain Go to BUILD CASTLES IN THE AIR.

build castles in the air AND **build castles in Spain** to daydream; to make plans that can never come true.

build on((to) something**)** to add to something by constructing an extension.

build someone **in(to** something**)** to make a person an integral part of an organization or a plan.

build someone **up 1.** to strengthen someone; to make someone healthier or stronger. **2.** to praise or exalt someone.

build someone **up (for** something**)** to prepare someone for something; to lead a person into a proper state of mind to receive some information.

build something **in(to** something**)** **1.** to make a piece of furniture or an appliance a part of a building's construction. **2.** to make a particular quality a basic part of something. **3.** to make a special restriction or specification a part of the plan of something.

build something **out of** something to construct something from parts or materials.

build something **up 1.** to add buildings to an area of land or a neighborhood. **2.** to develop, accumulate, or increase something, such as wealth, business, goodwill, etc. **3.** to praise or exalt something; to exaggerate the virtues of something.

build up to increase; to develop.

building ['bɪl dɪŋ] **1.** *n.* a structure where people live, work, or play. **2.** *n.* the business of constructing ①. (No plural.) **3.** the *adj.* use of ① or ②.

built ['bɪlt] past tense and past participle of BUILD.

bulb ['bʌlb] **1.** *n.* any rounded or globular-shaped object. **2.** *n.* a glass globe, with a special wire inside, that is used to create light from electricity. **3.** *n.* a swelling between the stem and roots of some plants, used for storing food for the plant.

bulk ['bʌlk] **1.** *n.* a great amount; a large amount of something. (No plural.) **2.** *n.* the major portion of something; the largest and most important part. (No plural.) **3.** *adj.* [containing] large [quantities or amounts].
→ IN BULK

bull ['bʊl] **1.** *n.* the male animal corresponding to a COW, if it is able to breed. **2.** *n.* someone who believes that prices on stocks or bonds will rise. **3.** *adj.* [of certain animals] male.
→ COCK-AND-BULL STORY
→ HIT THE BULL'S-EYE

→ TAKE THE BULL BY THE HORNS

a **bull in a china shop** a very clumsy person around breakable things.

bulldozer ['bʊl doz ɚ] *n.* a powerful tractor equipped with a strong blade that can push dirt and rocks.

bullet ['bʊl ɪt] *n.* a small piece of lead fired from a gun.

bulletin ['bʊl ə tən] **1.** *n.* a special news report; a piece of news; official information. **2.** *n.* a journal or newsletter published by a specific group.

bulletin board ['bʊl ə tən bord] *n.* a board where notices and signs can be posted.

bully ['bʊl i] **1.** *n.* someone, usually a male, who is mean or threatening. **2.** *tv.* to threaten someone; to be mean to someone.

bumblebee ['bʌm bəl bi] *n.* a large, hairy, black and yellow bee.

bump ['bʌmp] **1.** *n.* a lump or swelling in an otherwise flat area. **2.** *n.* a knock; a blow; a hit; a forceful contact. **3.** *tv.* to make forceful contact with someone or something. **4.** *tv.* [for an airline] to cancel someone's airplane reservation without warning.
→ GET GOOSE BUMPS
→ LIKE A BUMP ON A LOG

bump into someone to have a surprise meeting with someone.

bump into someone or something to make contact with someone or something; to run into someone or something.

bump (up) against someone or something to strike someone or something accidentally, usually relatively gently.

bumper ['bʌm pɚ] **1.** *n.* a strong, protective metal or fiberglass bar on the front and back of a vehicle. **2.** *n.* any device designed to protect someone or something from an impact. **3.** *adj.* large; abundant; plentiful.

bun ['bʌn] **1.** *n.* a bread product, such as that used to hold cooked hamburger meat or a wiener. **2.** *n.* a sweetened bread roll, sometimes with fruit or other fillings.

bunch ['bʌntʃ] **1.** *n.* a group of things that grow together or are placed together. **2.** *n.* a group of people or things; a large number of things or people.

bunch someone or something **up** to pack or cluster people or things together.

bunch up to pack or cluster together.

bundle ['bʌn dəl] **1.** *n.* a group of things gathered together. **2.** *tv.* to include a selection of software with the sale of computer hardware.

bundle off to leave in a hurry; to take all one's parcels and leave in a hurry.

bundle (oneself) **up** (against something) to wrap oneself up in protective clothing or bedding as protection against the cold.

bundle someone **in(to** something) **1.** to put someone, usually a child, into heavy outdoor clothing. **2.** to put someone, usually a child, into bed.

bundle someone or something **up** to wrap someone or something up; to wrap someone or something tightly.

bunny ['bʌn i] *n.* a rabbit; a hare.

buoy ['bɔɪ, 'bu i] **1.** *n.* a floating aid to navigation, used to display warnings or directions. **2.** *n.* a floating ring that can support a person in the water.

buoy someone or something **up** to prevent someone or something from sinking; to keep someone or something floating.

buoy someone **up** to make someone happy; to cheer someone up.

burden ['bɚd n] **1.** *n.* a heavy load. **2.** *n.* a heavy responsibility that strains a person. (Figurative on ①.) **3.** *tv.* to give someone or something a heavy load.

burglar ['bɚg lɚ] *n.* a criminal who enters someplace illegally to steal things.

burial ['bɛr i əl] *n.* the burying of something, especially a dead body.

burn ['bɚn] **1.** *n.* the mark caused by a flame or something that is very hot. **2.** *n.* an injury caused to someone who has been harmed by high heat. **3.** *tv., irreg.* to set fire to something; to destroy something by fire. (Past tense and past participle: usually *burned*, but sometimes BURNT.) **4.** *tv., irreg.* to damage someone or something with too much heat. **5.** *tv., irreg.* to consume a fuel or an energy source. **6.** *tv., irreg.* to sting something; to cause something to have a sharp feeling of heat. **7.** *iv., irreg.* to provide light; to give off light.

8. *iv., irreg.* [for an injury] to sting. **9.** *iv., irreg.* to be on fire. **10.** *iv., irreg.* [for food] to become scorched from overcooking.
→ FIDDLE WHILE ROME BURNS
→ GET ONE'S FINGERS BURNED
→ HAVE MONEY TO BURN
→ KEEP THE HOME FIRES BURNING
→ MONEY BURNS A HOLE IN SOMEONE'S POCKET.

burn away 1. [for something] to burn until there is no more of it. **2.** for something to keep on burning rapidly.

burn down 1. [for a building] to be destroyed by fire. **2.** [for a fire] to burn and dwindle away.

burn (itself) out 1. [for a flame or fire] to run out of fuel and go out. **2.** [for an electrical part] to fail and cease working or make a larger unit cease working.

burn off [for some excess volatile or flammable substance] to burn away or burn up.

burn one's bridges (behind one) 1. to make decisions that cannot be changed in the future. **2.** to be unpleasant in a situation that one is leaving, ensuring that one will never be welcome to return. **3.** to cut off the way back to where one came from, making it impossible to retreat.

burn someone at the stake 1. to set fire to a person tied to a post (as a form of execution). **2.** to chastise or denounce someone severely, but without violence.

burn someone or something to a crisp to burn someone or something totally or very badly.

burn someone out to wear someone out; to make someone ineffective through overuse.

burn someone up 1. to destroy someone by fire. **2.** to make someone very angry. (Figurative.)

burn something away to remove or destroy something by burning.

burn something down [for a fire] to destroy a building completely.

burn something off ((of) something) to cause excess volatile or flammable substance to burn until there is no more of it.

burn something out 1. to burn away the inside of something, getting rid of excess deposits. **2.** to wear out an electrical or electronic device through overuse.

burn something up to destroy something by fire.

burn the candle at both ends to work very hard and stay up very late at night.

burn the midnight oil to stay up working, especially studying, late at night.

burn up to be destroyed or consumed by fire.

burn with a low blue flame to be very angry, especially without displaying one's anger loudly.

burner ['bɚ nɚ] *n.* a device that makes a controlled flame for cooking or heating.
→ PUT SOMETHING ON THE BACK BURNER

burnt ['bɚnt] a past tense and past participle of BURN.

burrow ['bɚ o] **1.** *n.* a hole that an animal digs in the ground for a place to live. **2.** *iv.* [for a small animal] to work its way, digging, into soil, leaves, snow, etc.

burst ['bɚst] **1.** *tv., irreg.* to break something open; to cause something to explode. (Past tense and past participle: burst.) **2.** *iv., irreg.* to explode; to suddenly break open. **3.** *n.* a sudden outbreak; a violent outbreak; a barrage. **4.** *n.* a spurt; a quick, intense event.

burst at the seams 1. [for someone] to explode (figuratively) with pride or laughter. **2.** to explode from fullness.

burst in ((up)on someone or something**)** to intrude or come in thoughtlessly and suddenly and interrupt someone or something.

burst in (with something**)** to interrupt with some comment.

burst in(to someplace**)** to intrude or come into a place thoughtlessly and suddenly.

a **burst of energy** a sudden, powerful effort.

burst onto the scene to appear suddenly in a location.

burst out to explode outward; to break open under force.

burst out doing something to begin to do something suddenly, such as cry, laugh, shout, etc.

burst (out) into something **1.** [for plants or trees] to open their flowers seemingly suddenly and simultaneously. **2.** [for someone] to begin suddenly doing a particular activity, such as crying, laughing, or chattering; to begin producing the evidence of such activities as laughter, chatter, tears, etc.

burst out (of someplace**)** [for people] to come out of a place rapidly.

burst out with something to utter something loudly and suddenly.

burst someone's **bubble** to destroy someone's illusion or delusion; to destroy someone's fantasy.

burst (up)on the scene to appear suddenly somewhere; to enter or arrive suddenly some place.

burst with joy to be full to the bursting point with happiness.

bury ['ber i] **1.** *tv.* to put something in the ground, to cover something with dirt or soil. **2.** *tv.* to place a dead person or other creature in the ground. **3.** *tv.* to conceal someone or something; to hide someone or something.
→ DEAD AND BURIED

bury one's **head in the sand** AND **hide** one's **head in the sand** to ignore or hide from obvious signs of danger.

bury someone or something **away (**someplace**)** to bury or hide someone or something someplace.

bury the hatchet to stop fighting or arguing; to end old resentments.

bus ['bʌs] **1.** *n.* an enclosed motor vehicle that carries many passengers. **2.** *n.* [in a computer] a circuit that allows new devices and equipment to be connected to the main computer. **3.** *tv.* to transport someone using ①. **4.** *tv.* to remove dirty dishes from a table after a meal in a restaurant or cafeteria.

bush ['bʊʃ] *n.* a plant with several woody branches.
→ BEAT ABOUT THE BUSH

→ BEAT AROUND THE BUSH

bush out [for something] to develop many small branches or hairs. (Said of a plant, bush, beard, head of hair, etc.)

bushel ['bʊʃ əl] **1.** *n.* a unit of measurement of dry goods, especially crops, equal to 64 pints or 32 quarts. **2.** *adj.* holding or containing ①.
→ HIDE ONE'S LIGHT UNDER A BUSHEL

bushy ['bʊʃ i] *adj.* [of hair or fur] thick, dense, and shaggy. (Adv: *bushily.* Comp: *bushier;* sup: *bushiest.*)

business ['bɪz nəs] **1.** *n.* a profession; an occupation. **2.** *n.* buying, selling, or trading. (No plural.) **3.** *n.* a corporation; a company. **4.** *n.* affair; concern; a matter of interest. (No plural.)
→ DO A LAND-OFFICE BUSINESS
→ DRUM SOME BUSINESS UP
→ FUNNY BUSINESS
→ GET DOWN TO BUSINESS
→ GO ABOUT ONE'S BUSINESS
→ MIND ONE'S OWN BUSINESS
→ MONKEY BUSINESS
→ NONE OF SOMEONE'S BUSINESS
→ OPEN FOR BUSINESS
→ PLACE OF BUSINESS
→ SEND ONE ABOUT ONE'S BUSINESS

the **business end of** something the part or end of something that actually does the work or carries out the procedure.

busy ['bɪz i] **1.** *adj.* working; at work; having things to do. (Adv: *busily.* Comp: *busier;* sup: *busiest.*) **2.** *adj.* [of a telephone connection] in use. (Comp: *busier;* sup: *busiest.*) **3.** *adj.* occupied with something else at the time. (Comp: *busier;* sup: *busiest.*)

4. *adj.* distracting to look at because of clashing patterns; having too much detail. (Adv: *busily.* Comp: *busier;* sup: *busiest.*) **5.** *tv.* to make work for oneself; to occupy oneself with something.
→ (AS) BUSY AS A BEAVER
→ (AS) BUSY AS A BEE
→ (AS) BUSY AS GRAND CENTRAL STATION

but ['bʌt, bət] **1.** *conj.* on the contrary; however. **2.** *conj.* except. **3.** *prep.* except someone or something; except for someone or something; other than someone or something; besides someone or something. **4.** *adv.* only; merely; just.

butcher ['bʊtʃ ɚ] **1.** *n.* someone who kills animals that will be used for meat. **2.** *n.* someone who cuts up and sells the meat of animals. **3.** *tv.* to kill and cut up an animal for food. **4.** *tv.* to kill someone or something with great cruelty.

butt ['bʌt] **1.** *n.* the end or base of something. **2.** *n.* the leftover end of a cigar or cigarette. **3.** *n.* part of the body on which one sits; the buttocks. (Informal.) **4.** *n.* someone who is the victim of ridicule or the object of jokes or rudeness. **5.** *tv.* to strike or push hard against someone or something with the head. (Said especially of animals with horns.)

butt in (on someone or something**)** to interrupt someone or something.

butt into something to intrude upon something; to break into a conversation.

butt (up) against someone or something to press against someone or something firmly.

butter ['bʌt ɚ] **1.** *n.* the fatty part of milk left after it has been stirred and mixed over and over. (Plural only for types and instances.) **2.** *n.* certain foods mashed into a spreadable substance. (Plural only for types and instances.) **3.** *tv.* to put ① on something, usually bread.
→ BREAD AND BUTTER
→ KNOW WHICH SIDE ONE'S BREAD IS BUTTERED ON
→ LOOK AS IF BUTTER WOULDN'T MELT IN ONE'S MOUTH
→ PEANUT BUTTER

butter someone **up** AND **butter up to** someone to flatter someone; to treat someone especially nicely in hopes of special favors.

butter up to someone Go to BUTTER SOMEONE UP.

butterfly ['bʌt ɚ flaɪ] *n.* an insect with large, brightly colored wings.

buttermilk ['bʌt ɚ mɪlk] *n.* a drink made from milk to which certain kinds of bacteria have been added. (No plural.)

button ['bʌt n] **1.** *n.* a small, hard disc, used to fasten clothes or fabric. **2.** *n.* a small disc or similar device that is pressed to close an electrical circuit. **3.** *n.* a badge bearing a message, worn on the clothing. **4.** *tv.* to fasten or close two pieces of fabric together with ①.
→ ON THE BUTTON

button one's **lip** to get quiet and stay quiet.

button something **up** to fasten the edges of something with buttons.

button up to fasten one's buttons.

buttress something **up 1.** to brace something; to provide architectural support for something. **2.** to provide extra support, often financial support, for something. (Figurative.)

buy ['baɪ] **1.** *tv., irreg.* to purchase something; to pay money in exchange for something. (Past tense and past participle: BOUGHT.) **2.** *tv., irreg.* to acquire something, such as time. (Figurative on ①.) **3.** *tv., irreg.* to believe something. (Informal.) **4.** *n.* something that is offered for sale at a very good price.

buy in(to something**)** to purchase shares of something; to buy a part of something, sharing the ownership with other owners.

buy one's **way out (of** something**)** to get out of trouble by bribing someone to ignore what one has done wrong.

buy someone **off** to bribe someone to ignore what one is doing wrong.

buy someone or something **out** to purchase full ownership of something from someone or a group.

buy something to believe someone; to accept something to be a fact. (Also used literally.)

buy something **back (from** someone**)** to repurchase (from someone) something that one has previously sold.

buy something **for a song** to buy something cheaply.

71

buy something **out** to buy all of a particular item.

buy something **sight unseen** to buy something without seeing it first.

buy something **up** to buy all of something; to buy the entire supply of something.

buzz ['bʌz] **1.** *n.* the sound that bees make; a rapid humming sound. (Plural only for types and instances.) **2.** *iv.* to make a loud humming sound like bees do. **3.** *n.* a telephone call.
→ GIVE SOMEONE A BUZZ

buzz in(to someplace**)** to come into a place rapidly or unexpectedly.

by ['baɪ] **1.** *prep.* near someone or something; next to someone or something; alongside someone or something; beside someone or something. **2.** *prep.* [passing] near someone or something. **3.** *prep.* through the use of someone or something. **4.** *prep.* [done] through the process of doing something. **5.** *prep.* a word used in indicating the dimensions of something, especially the dimensions of a square area. (See also MULTIPLY ①.) **6.** *prep.* before some time; not later than some time. **7.** *prep.* [surpassing someone or something] according to a specific amount. **8.** *prep.* allotted according to something; in units of something. **9.** *adv.* past; beyond.

by a hair's breadth AND **by a whisker** just barely; by a very small distance.

by a show of hands a vote expressed by people raising their hands.

by a whisker Go to BY A HAIR'S BREADTH.

by chance accidentally; randomly; without planning.

by check by using a check.

by day AND **by night** during the day; during the night.

by herself 1. with the help of no one else. (Refers only to a female.) **2.** with no one else present; alone. (Refers only to a female.)

by himself 1. with the help of no one else. (Refers only to a male.) **2.** alone; with no one else present. (Refers only to a male.)

by itself with the help of nothing else; without the addition of anything else.

by leaps and bounds rapidly; by large movements forward.

by myself 1. without the help of anyone else. **2.** with no one else present; alone.

by night Go to BY DAY.

by ourselves 1. with the help of no one else but those present. **2.** with no one else other than those present.

by return mail by a subsequent mailing (back to the sender).

by the each; per. (Used to show a unit of measure, but not the rate of a measure.)

by the nape of the neck by the back of the neck.

by the same token in the same way; reciprocally.

by the seat of one's **pants** by sheer luck and very little skill; just barely.

by the skin of one's **teeth** just barely; by an amount equal to the thickness of the (imaginary) skin on one's teeth.

by the sweat of one's **brow** by one's efforts; by one's hard work.

by themselves 1. with help from no one else but those present. **2.** with no one else other than those present.

by virtue of something because of something; due to something.

by word of mouth by speaking rather than writing.

by yourself 1. with the help of no one else. **2.** with no one else present; alone.

by yourselves 1. with the help of no one else but those present. **2.** with no one else other than those present.

Bye(-bye) ['baɪ ('baɪ)] *interj.* Good-bye; Farewell.

byte ['baɪt] *n.* a unit of computer data, made up of eight bits.

C

cab ['kæb] *n.* a TAXI, a TAXICAB.

cabbage ['kæb ɪdʒ] *n.* a large, round vegetable with green or purple leaves. (Not usually plural unless referring to different kinds, types, or varieties. Number is expressed with *head(s) of cabbage*.)

cabin ['kæb ən] **1.** *n.* a small house made of wood, especially in a faraway area. **2.** *n.* a private room on a ship. **3.** *n.* the part of an airplane where the passengers sit.

cabinet ['kæb (ə) nət] **1.** *n.* a piece of furniture with shelves, used for storing or displaying something; a small storage unit with a door, as found in a kitchen. **2.** *n.* the group of people who advise a president, prime minister, etc.

cacti ['kæk taɪ] a plural of CACTUS.

cactus ['kæk təs] *n., irreg.* a desert plant with pulp on the inside and needles on the outside. (Plural: CACTI or *cactuses*.)

café [kæ 'fe] *n.* a place to buy simple meals; a small restaurant.

cafeteria [kæf ə 'tɪr i ə] *n.* a restaurant where one can choose from many selections, usually by passing by the items and placing one's choice of food on a tray.

cage ['kedʒ] **1.** *n.* an enclosure with bars or wires, where living creatures are kept. **2.** *tv.* to put someone or something in ①.

caged ['kedʒd] *adj.* enclosed; not free.

cake ['kek] **1.** *n.* a sweet, baked, breadlike food. (Plural only for types and instances.) **2.** *n.* a single, complete unit of ①.
→ EAT ONE'S CAKE AND HAVE IT TOO
→ HAVE ONE'S CAKE AND EAT IT TOO
→ LAYER CAKE
→ SELL LIKE HOT CAKES
→ A SLICE OF THE CAKE

calculate ['kæl kjə let] **1.** *iv.* to estimate; to figure out values. **2.** *tv.* to add, subtract, multiply, or divide numbers; to figure out the value of something. (The object can be a clause with THAT ⑦.)

calculator ['kæl kjə let ɚ] *n.* a machine that adds, subtracts, multiplies, and divides figures and performs other mathematical functions.

calculus ['kæl kjə ləs] *n.* a branch of higher mathematics using special symbols and operations. (No plural.)

calendar ['kæl ən dɚ] **1.** *n.* a system for keeping track of years and the divisions of years. **2.** *n.* a chart or table showing days, weeks, and months. **3.** *n.* a schedule of events; a list of events.

calf ['kæf] **1.** *n., irreg.* a young cow or bull. (Plural: CALVES.) **2.** *n., irreg.* the back of the leg from the knee to the ankle.
→ KILL THE FATTED CALF

call ['kɔl] **1.** *n.* a shout; a cry. **2.** *n.* an instance of someone contacting someone by telephone; a message or a conversation using the telephone; a TELEPHONE CALL; a PHONE CALL. **3.** *n.* a decision; a choice. **4.** *tv.* to try to contact someone by telephone; to telephone someone. **5.** *tv.* to demand someone's pres-

ence. **6.** *tv.* to name someone or something; to refer to or address someone or something as something. **7.** *tv.* [for an umpire] to make a decision in a ball game.
→ HAVE A CLOSE CALL
→ ISSUE A CALL FOR SOMETHING
→ PAY A CALL ON SOMEONE
→ PHONE CALL
→ the POT CALLING THE KETTLE BLACK
→ TELEPHONE CALL

call a meeting to order to announce that a meeting is about to begin.

call a spade a spade to call something by its right name; to speak frankly about something, even if it is unpleasant.

call back 1. to call [someone] again on the telephone at a later time. **2.** to return a telephone call received earlier.

call for someone or something to need, require, or demand something or the services of someone.

call in (to someplace**)** to telephone to some central place, such as one's place of work.

call it a day to quit work and go home; to say that the day's work has been completed.

call it quits to quit; to resign from something; to announce that one is quitting.

call of nature the need to go to the lavatory.

call on someone to visit someone.

call out (to someone**)** to call or shout to someone.

call someone **back 1.** to call someone again on the telephone. **2.** to

return a telephone call to a person who had called earlier.

call someone **down** to criticize or scold someone; to ask someone to behave better; to challenge someone's bad behavior.

call someone **in (for** something**)** **1.** to request that someone come to have a talk. **2.** to request a consultation with a specialist in some field.

call someone **on the carpet** to reprimand a person.

call someone or something **back** to call out that someone or something should come back.

call someone or something **up 1.** to request that someone or a group report for active military service. **2.** to call someone, a group, or a company on the telephone.

call someone **over (to** someplace**)** to request that someone come to where one is.

call something **(back) in** to order that something be returned.

call something **off** to cancel something, especially an event that has been planned for a certain date.

call something **out 1.** to draw on something, such as a particular quality or talent. **2.** to shout out something.

call the dogs off to stop threatening, chasing, or hounding (a person); (literally) to order dogs away from the chase.

call (the) roll AND **take (the) roll** to call the names of people on the roll, expecting them to reply if they are present.

call (up)on someone **1.** to visit someone. **2.** to choose someone to respond, as in a classroom.

call upon someone **(for** something**)** to choose someone to do or to help with some particular task.

caller ['kɔ lɚ] **1.** *n.* someone who makes a telephone call. **2.** *n.* a visitor.

calm ['kɑm] **1.** *adj.* quiet; serene; at peace. (Adv: *calmly.* Comp: *calmer;* sup: *calmest.*) **2.** *n.* a time or feeling of peace and quiet. (No plural.)

calm down to relax; to become less busy or active.

calm someone or some creature **(down)** to soothe someone or some creature; to cause someone or some creature to relax.

calorie ['kæl ə ri] *n.* a unit of energy supplied by food.

calves ['kævz] plural of CALF.

came ['kem] past tense of COME.

camel ['kæm əl] *n.* a large desert animal with one or two fatty humps on its back.
→ THAT'S THE STRAW THAT BROKE THE CAMEL'S BACK.

camera ['kæm (ə) rə] **1.** *n.* a device that takes pictures; a device that makes photographs. **2.** *n.* a device that records live action for television or movies.

camp ['kæmp] **1.** *n.* a remote or rural temporary residence, such as for soldiers, pioneers, refugees, people on vacation, etc. **2.** *n.* a remote or rural place where children are sent in the summer. **3.** *n.* a permanent living area for training and retraining members of

various military organizations. **4.** *iv.* to take a vacation in a natural setting; to stay outside in a remote or rural area, sleeping in a tent or a camper instead of a hotel.
→ BREAK CAMP
→ HAVE A FOOT IN BOTH CAMPS
→ PITCH CAMP

camp out to live out of doors temporarily in a tent or camping vehicle, as on a vacation or special camping trip.

campaign [kæm 'pen] **1.** *n.* the period of time before an election when the candidates try to persuade people to vote for them. **2.** *n.* a coordinated series of events with a specific goal or purpose. (See also a SMEAR CAMPAIGN (AGAINST SOMEONE).)

camper ['kæm pɚ] **1.** *n.* someone who CAMPS ④; someone who takes a vacation in a rural or remote area. **2.** *n.* a special vehicle, designed for camping.

campfire ['kæmp faɪɚ] *n.* a fire that campers cook on and sit around at night to keep warm while telling stories and enjoying the outdoors.

campsite ['kæmp saɪt] *n.* the area where campers set up their tents.

campus ['kæmp əs] **1.** *n.* the buildings, lawns, and other areas of a school, college, or university. **2.** *n.* the buildings and surrounding areas of a large company. **3.** the *adj.* use of ① or ②.
→ OFF CAMPUS
→ ON CAMPUS

can ['kæn, kən] **1.** *aux.* a word indicating ability to do something. (See also COULD.) **2.** *aux.* a form indicating permission to do something. (In general use but considered informal. In more formal English, MAY is used for this function. See also COULD.) **3.** *tv.* to preserve food by sealing it in an airtight container. (Past tense and past participle: *canned.*) **4.** *n.* a container shaped like a tube with a top and a bottom, usually made of metal. **5.** *n.* the contents of ④.

can afford something Go to ABLE TO AFFORD SOMETHING.

canal [kə'næl] *n.* a long waterway—usually man-made—that is not a river.

canary [kə'nɛr i] *n.* a small, yellow bird that sings.
→ LOOK LIKE THE CAT THAT SWALLOWED THE CANARY

cancel ['kæn səl] **1.** *tv.* to end or stop something that is occurring or planned. **2.** *tv.* to place a mark on a postage stamp, check, ticket, etc., so that it cannot be used again.

cancel out (of something**)** to withdraw from something.

cancer ['kæn sɚ] **1.** *n.* a disease characterized by a tumor or tumors growing and spreading throughout the body. (Plural only for types and instances.) **2.** *n.* something evil or horrible that spreads out over an area. (Figurative on ①.)

candidate ['kæn dɪ det] **1.** *n.* someone who is seeking a public office or other job. **2.** *n.* a recommended or possible choice of a thing or person.

candle ['kæn dəl] *n.* an object made of wax molded around a

string or wick. (The wick burns and gives off light.)
→ BURN THE CANDLE AT BOTH ENDS
→ CAN'T HOLD A CANDLE TO SOMEONE

candy ['kæn di] **1.** *n.* a sweet food made with sugar and additional flavors. (Plural only for types and instances. Number is expressed by *piece(s) of candy.*) **2.** *n.* a piece or a serving of ①.

cane ['ken] *n.* a stick used as an aid in walking.

cannot [kə 'nɑt] *aux.* the negative form of CAN. (See also CAN'T.)

cannot help doing something not able to refrain from doing something; not able not to do something.

cannot stomach someone or something Go to NOT ABLE TO STOMACH SOMEONE OR SOMETHING.

canoe [kə 'nu] **1.** *n.* a small boat that is moved by paddling. **2.** *iv.* to travel by ①.
→ PADDLE ONE'S OWN CANOE

can't [kænt] *cont.* cannot.

can't carry a tune unable to sing a simple melody; lacking musical ability.

can't hold a candle to someone not equal to someone; not worthy to associate with someone; unable to measure up to someone.

can't make heads or tails (out) of someone or something unable to understand someone or something; unable to tell one end of someone or something from the other.

can't see beyond the end of one's **nose** unaware of the things that might happen in the future; not farsighted; self-centered.

can't see one's **hand in front of** one's **face** unable to see very far, usually due to darkness or fog.

can't wait (for something **to happen)** [to be very eager and] to be unable to endure the wait for something to happen.

can't wait (to do something) [to be very eager and] unable to endure the wait until it is possible to do something.

canvas ['kæn vəs] **1.** *n.* a heavy, sturdy fabric made from cotton or another strong fiber. (Plural only for types and instances.) **2.** *n.* a panel of fabric—usually stretched on a frame—that painters paint on. **3.** *n.* a painting that has been painted on ②.

canyon ['kæn jən] *n.* a deep, narrow valley, often with a river running through it.

cap ['kæp] **1.** *n.* a (round) cover for the head, often with a shade for the eyes. **2.** *n.* the cover or the top of a bottle or small jar; a small lid. **3.** *tv.* to close something with ②; to put ② on something. **4.** *tv.* to limit something at a specific point.
→ a FEATHER IN ONE'S CAP
→ PUT A CAP ON SOMETHING
→ PUT ON ONE'S THINKING CAP

capable ['ke pə bəl] *adj.* able; having the power or ability to do something. (Adv: *capably*.)

capable of (doing) something having the ability to do something or the capacity for doing something.

capacity [kə 'pæs ə ti] **1.** *n.* the amount of something that a space

or container will hold; the amount of space in something. **2.** *n.* the ability to do something. (No plural.) **3.** *n.* a job, role, or function; a set of responsibilities.

cape ['kep] **1.** *n.* a long, sleeveless garment worn over clothes. **2.** *n.* a piece of land that sticks out into a body of water.

capital ['kæp ɪ təl] **1.** *n.* a city that is the center of a government. (Compare this with CAPITOL.) **2.** *n.* any special or central city, with reference to a certain feature or attribute. **3.** *n.* an uppercase letter of the alphabet. **4.** *n.* money that is invested with the hope that it will earn more money. (No plural.) **5.** *adj.* [of a crime] punishable by death.

capitol ['kæp ɪ təl] *n.* the building where legislators do their work. (Compare this with CAPITAL.)

captain ['kæp tən] **1.** *n.* someone in charge of a ship, boat, or airplane. **2.** *n.* an officer in the military or the police. **3.** *n.* the leader of a team.

capture ['kæp tʃɚ] **1.** *tv.* to catch someone or something; to make someone or something a captive. **2.** *tv.* to take something by force; to take control of something. **3.** *tv.* to accurately show a feeling or atmosphere through artistic expression.

car ['kɑr] **1.** *n.* an automobile; a vehicle that can carry a small number of passengers. **2.** *n.* one unit of a train. **3.** *n.* any of a number of different structures used to carry goods or people.

caramel ['kær ə məl, 'kar məl] **1.** *n.* a kind of candy made by heating sugar. (Plural only for types and instances.) **2.** *adj.* made with or flavored with ①.

carbon ['kar bən] **1.** *n.* a chemical element occurring in nature as coal, graphite, and diamonds. (No plural.) **2.** *n.* a CARBON COPY.

carbon copy ['kar bən 'kap i] **1.** *n.* a copy of a document made by placing a special kind of carbon-coated paper between two other sheets of paper while one types the document on a typewriter. **2.** *n.* someone or something that is almost identical to someone or something else. (Figurative on ①.)

card ['kard] **1.** *n.* a stiff, rectangular piece of paper. **2.** *n.* a rectangle of stiff paper used in games, such as bridge or poker.
→ CREDIT CARD
→ IN THE CARDS
→ LAY ONE'S CARDS ON THE TABLE
→ PLAY ONE'S CARDS CLOSE TO ONE'S VEST
→ PLAY ONE'S CARDS CLOSE TO THE CHEST
→ PUT ONE'S CARDS ON THE TABLE

cardboard ['kard bord] **1.** *n.* a kind of heavy, thick, stiff paper. (Plural only for types and instances.) **2.** *adj.* made of ①.

cardinal ['kard nəl] **1.** *n.* a bird—the males of which are bright red—with a crest on its head. **2.** *n.* a high-ranking official of the Roman Catholic Church.

cardinal number Go to CARDINAL NUMERAL.

cardinal numeral AND **cardinal number** ['kard (ə) nəl 'num ə rəl, 'kard (ə) nəl 'nʌm bɚ] *n.* a number

used in counting, such as one, two, three. (Can be shortened to CARDINAL. See also ORDINAL NUMBER.)

care ['kɛr] **1.** *n.* serious attention; focused thought; caution. (No plural.) **2.** *n.* the responsibility of providing for, protecting, or medically treating someone. (No plural.) **3.** *n.* a worry; a source of anxiety; a concern.
→ TAKE CARE OF SOMEONE OR SOMETHING
→ THAT TAKES CARE OF THAT.

care (about someone or something**)** to have concern for someone or something; to show serious interest in the welfare of someone or something.

care for someone or something **1.** to be responsible for someone or something; to watch over someone or something. **2.** to like someone or something; to want someone or something. (Usually in the negative or in questions.)

career [kə 'rɪr] **1.** *n.* one's chosen work; what one does to earn money. **2.** the *adj.* use of ①.

careful ['kɛr fʊl] **1.** *adj.* cautious; avoiding danger or damage. (Adv: *carefully*.) **2.** *adj.* detailed; thorough. (Adv: *carefully*.)

careless ['kɛr ləs] *adj.* without care; clumsy; done without thought. (Adv: *carelessly*.)

carelessness ['kɛr ləs nəs] *n.* a lack of concern; a lack of care. (No plural.)

cargo ['kar go] *n.* goods being carried by a vehicle; freight. (Plural only for types and instances. Plural: *cargoes* or *cargos*.)

carnival ['kɑr nə vəl] *n.* a circus; a traveling amusement show having RIDES ④.

carol ['kɛr əl] *n.* a song of joy, especially a Christmas song.

carpenter ['kɑr pən tɚ] *n.* someone who builds things with wood.

carpet ['kɑr pɪt] **1.** *n.* a rug; a thick floor covering made out of fabric. **2.** *tv.* to cover a floor with ①.
→ BRUSH SOMETHING UNDER THE CARPET
→ CALL SOMEONE ON THE CARPET
→ GET THE RED-CARPET TREATMENT
→ GIVE SOMEONE THE RED-CARPET TREATMENT
→ ROLL OUT THE RED CARPET FOR SOMEONE
→ SWEEP SOMETHING UNDER THE CARPET

carriage ['kɛr ɪdʒ] *n.* a car or vehicle pulled by horses.

carrot ['kɛr ət] *n.* a vegetable with a long, thin, edible orange root.

carry ['kɛr i] **1.** *tv.* to pick up and take someone or something somewhere. **2.** *tv.* to support the weight of something. **3.** *tv.* to spread a disease or sickness. **4.** *tv.* to win the vote of a state or district. **5.** *tv.* [when adding a column of numbers, if the result is greater than 9] to transfer units of ten to the next column to the left as units of one. **6.** *tv.* [for a store] to have an item available for sale. **7.** *iv.* [for a voice or sound] to travel far.
→ (AS) FAST AS ONE'S FEET WOULD CARRY ONE
→ CAN'T CARRY A TUNE
→ LETTER CARRIER
→ MAIL CARRIER
→ NOT CARRY WEIGHT (WITH SOMEONE)

carry a secret to the grave AND **carry a secret to** one's **grave; take a secret to** one's **grave** to avoid telling a secret, even to the day of one's death.

carry a torch (for someone**)** AND **carry the torch** to be in love with someone who does not love one in return; to brood over a hopeless love affair.

carry on (about someone or something**) 1.** to talk excitedly or at length about someone or something. **2.** to have an emotional display of distress about someone or something; to behave badly or wildly about someone or something.

carry on (with someone**)** to flirt with someone; to have a love affair with someone.

carry on (with something**)** to continue doing something.

carry one's **cross** Go to BEAR ONE'S CROSS.

carry over (to something**) 1.** [for a sum or other figure] to be taken to another column of figures. **2.** to last or continue until another time.

carry someone or something **about** to carry someone or something with one; to carry someone or something from place to place.

carry someone or something **away** to take or steal someone or something.

carry someone or something **off** to take or steal someone or something.

carry something **off 1.** to make something happen; to accomplish something. **2.** to make some sort of deception believable and successful.

carry something **on 1.** to do something over a period of time. **2.** to continue to do something as a tradition.

carry something **on(to** something**)** to take something onto a vehicle.

carry something **out** to complete, accomplish, or execute a task, order, or assignment.

carry the ball 1. to be the player holding the ball, especially in football when a goal is made. **2.** to be in charge; to make sure that a job gets done.

carry the torch Go to CARRY A TORCH (FOR SOMEONE).

carry the weight of the world on one's **shoulders** to appear to be burdened by all the problems in the whole world.

carry through (on something**)** to carry something out satisfactorily; to complete some act as promised.

cart ['kɑrt] **1.** *n.* a vehicle pulled by a horse, mule, dog, etc. **2.** *n.* a large basket on wheels, such as those found in grocery stores and other shops.
→ PUT THE CART BEFORE THE HORSE

cart someone or something **off** to take or haul someone or something away. (When used with *someone* the person is treated like an object.)

carte blanche complete freedom to act or proceed as one pleases. (Literally, a blank card.)

carton ['kɑrt n] **1.** *n.* a cardboard or plastic container or package. **2.** *n.* ① considered as a measurement of something.

cartoon [kɑr 'tun] **1.** *n.* a drawing or series of drawings that is usually intended to be funny. **2.** *n.* a film in which each frame is a drawing. (Also an *animated cartoon*.)

carve ['kɑrv] **1.** *tv.* to cut or sculpt wood, ivory, soap, or some other substance into a shape. **2.** *tv.* to slice or cut up cooked meat for serving at a meal.

carve something **in(to** something**)** to cut letters or symbols into something.

carve something **into** something to create a carved object by sculpturing raw material.

carve something **out (of** something**)** to remove something from the inside of something else by carving or cutting.

carve something **up** to divide something up, perhaps carelessly.

case ['kes] **1.** *n.* a crate; a box. **2.** *n.* an instance; an occurrence. **3.** *n.* a legal action or lawsuit.
→ IN CASE
→ an OPEN-AND-SHUT CASE
→ PROVIDED THAT SOMETHING IS THE CASE
→ SEEING THAT SOMETHING IS THE CASE
→ SOMETHING IS THE CASE

case in point an example of what one is talking about.

a **case of mistaken identity** the incorrect identification of someone.

cash ['kæʃ] **1.** *n.* money; currency, but not a check or a credit card. (No plural.) **2.** *tv.* to exchange a check for currency. **3.** *tv.* to give money in exchange for a check.

cash in (on something) to earn a lot of money at something; to make a profit at something.

cash (one's **chips) in 1.** to turn in one's gaming tokens or poker chips when one quits playing. **2.** to quit [anything], as if one were cashing in gaming tokens. **3.** to die. (Slang. Using the same metaphor as ②.)

cash-and-carry having to do with a sale of goods or a way of selling that requires that the buyer pay for the goods and take them at the time of purchase.

cashier [kæ 'ʃɪr] *n.* someone who handles the paying out and taking in of money, especially at a store or bank.

cassette [kə 'sɛt] *n.* a plastic case containing a pair of reels of magnetic audiotape or videotape.

cassette player [kə 'sɛt ple ɚ] *n.* a device that plays back sound recorded on a cassette.

cassette recorder [kə 'sɛt rɪ 'kor dɚ] *n.* a device that records sound onto a cassette and plays it back.

cast ['kæst] **1.** *n.* all of the performers in a play, musical, opera, TV show, or movie. **2.** *n.* a protective support for a broken bone, often made from plaster. **3.** *tv., irreg.* to throw something. (Past tense and past participle: *cast.*) **4.** *tv., irreg.* to throw a fishing lure into the water; to drop a fishing net into the water. **5.** *tv., irreg.* to create a shadow on something. **6.** *tv., irreg.* to move and aim one's eyes or line of sight at someone or something. **7.** *tv., irreg.* to select the performers for a play, film, opera, etc. **8.** *tv., irreg.* to create an object by pouring a soft substance into a mold and letting it harden into the shape of the mold.

cast aspersions on someone to make a rude and insulting remark.

cast in the same mold very similar.

cast off (from something) [for the crew of a boat or ship] to push away from the dock or pier; to begin the process of undocking a boat or ship.

cast (one's **) pearls before swine** to waste something good on someone who doesn't care about it. (As if throwing something of great value under the feet of pigs. From a biblical quotation.)

cast one's **vote** to vote; to place one's ballot in the ballot box.

cast someone or something **off** to dispose of someone or something; to throw someone or something aside or away.

cast someone or something **out** to throw someone or something out. (Stilted.)

cast someone or something **up** [for the waves] to bring up and deposit someone or something on the shore.

cast the first stone to make the first criticism; to be the first to attack.

castle ['kæs əl] **1.** *n.* a large fortress where a country's king and queen live. **2.** *n.* a game piece in chess, usually shaped like ①.
→ BUILD CASTLES IN SPAIN
→ BUILD CASTLES IN THE AIR

casual ['kæʒ ju əl] **1.** *adj.* [of someone] relaxed and free; [of an event] not formal. (Adv: *casually*.) **2.** *adj.* done without thought or planning. (Adv: *casually*.)

cat ['kæt] **1.** *n.* one of a member of the family of mammals that includes ②, lions, leopards, tigers, jaguars, and lynxes. **2.** *n.* a small mammal, with claws, sharp teeth, whiskers, often kept as a pet.
→ LET THE CAT OUT OF THE BAG
→ LOOK LIKE THE CAT THAT SWALLOWED THE CANARY
→ PLAY CAT AND MOUSE (WITH SOMEONE)
→ RAIN CATS AND DOGS

catch ['kætʃ] **1.** *tv., irreg.* to seize and hold someone or something. (Past tense and past participle: CAUGHT.) **2.** *tv., irreg.* to find someone in the act of doing something. **3.** *tv., irreg.* to get a disease caused by bacteria or viruses. **4.** *tv., irreg.* to reach or make contact with someone or something just in time. **5.** *tv., irreg.* to experience something through one of the senses; to understand someone or something. **6.** *tv., irreg.* [for something] to snare or entangle someone or something. **7.** *n.* a game or pastime where people throw and receive a ball back and forth. **8.** *n.* an act of grasping or receiving something as in ①. **9.** *n.* a fastener; a locking or latching device.
→ GET TIME TO CATCH ONE'S BREATH

catch a whiff of something Go to GET A WHIFF OF SOMETHING.

catch cold AND **take cold** to contract a cold (the disease).

catch fire to begin to burn; to ignite.

catch on (with someone) [for something] to become popular with someone.

catch one's **death (of cold)** AND **take** one's **death (of cold)** to contract a cold; to catch a serious cold.

catch on (to someone or something) to figure out someone or something.

catch someone **napping** to find someone unprepared.

catch someone **off balance** to encounter a person who is not prepared; to surprise someone. (Also used literally.)

catch someone **up in** something [for excitement or interest] to extend to and engross someone.

catch someone **up (on** someone or something) to tell someone the news of someone or something.

catch someone's **eye** AND **get** someone's **eye**; **have** someone's **eye** to establish eye contact with someone; to attract someone's attention.

catch up (on someone or something) to learn the news of someone or something.

catch up (on something) to bring one's efforts with something up-to-date; to do the work that one should have done.

catch up (to someone or something) to get even with or equal to someone or something.

catch up (with someone or something) to increase the rate of movement or growth to become even with or equal to someone or something.

catcher ['kætʃ ɚ] *n.* [in baseball] the player who is behind the batter.

caterpillar ['kæt ə pɪl ɚ] *n.* the creature, somewhat like a worm, that is the young form of a butterfly or a moth.

cathedral [kə 'θi drəl] *n.* a large, important church, especially a major, ancient church.

catholic ['kæθ (ə) lɪk] **1.** *adj.* universal; wide ranging. (Adv: *catholically* [...ɪk li].) **2.** *adj.* of or about the Roman Catholic Church or religion. (Capitalized.) **3.** *n.* a member of the Roman Catholic Church. (Capitalized.)

Catholicism [kə 'θɑl ə sɪz əm] *n.* the religion and teachings of the Roman Catholic Church. (No plural.)

catsup ['kæt səp] Go to KETCHUP.

cattle ['kæt əl] *n.* cows and bulls in general. (No plural. Treated as plural, but not countable. Number is expressed with *head of cattle*, as in *10 head of cattle*.)

Caucasian [kɔ 'ke ʒən] **1.** *adj.* [of a person, usually of European descent] having light-colored skin; WHITE ⑥. (In common, but not technical, use.) **2.** *n.* a CAUCASIAN as in ① person; a person having WHITE ⑥ skin.

caught ['kɔt] past tense and past participle of the CATCH.

caught in the cross fire trapped between two fighting people or groups. (As if one were stranded between two opposing armies who are firing bullets at each other.)

caught short to be without something one needs, especially money.

caught unaware(s) surprised and unprepared.

cause ['kɔz] **1.** *tv.* to make something happen. **2.** *n.* someone or something that makes something happen; someone or something that produces an effect. **3.** *n.* a philosophy or a charity; a political or social movement.

cause (some) eyebrows to raise to shock people; to surprise and dismay people.

cause (some) tongues to wag to cause people to gossip; to give people something to gossip about.

caution ['kɔʃn] *n.* care; being careful.
→ THROW CAUTION TO THE WIND

cave ['kev] *n.* a natural chamber or tunnel inside a mountain or under the earth.

cave in (on someone or something**)** [for a roof or ceiling] to collapse on someone or something.

cave in (to someone or something**)** to give in to someone or something; to yield to someone or something.

cavern ['kæv ən] *n.* a large cave; a large chamber in a cave.

cavity ['kæv ɪ ti] **1.** *n.* a hole; a hollow, enclosed space. **2.** *n.* a rotten place on a tooth.

cease ['sis] **1.** *tv.* to stop doing something; to quit doing something. **2.** *iv.* to stop; to finish.

ceiling ['si lɪŋ] **1.** *n.* the underside of a roof; a surface that forms the overhead part of a room. **2.** *n.* the upper limit of something, especially of costs. (Figurative on ①.)

celebrate ['sɛl ə bret] **1.** *tv.* to have a festive event or a party on a special day or for a special season. **2.** *tv.* to perform a specific procedure or a ritual. **3.** *tv.* to praise someone or something. **4.** *iv.* to be festive for a certain reason.

celebration [sɛl ə 'bre ʃən] *n.* a festival; a festive event.

celery ['sɛl (ə) ri] *n.* a light-green vegetable with long, crisp stalks and leafy ends. (No plural. Number is expressed with *stick(s)* or *stalk(s) of celery*.)

cell ['sɛl] **1.** *n.* the basic biological unit of living tissue. **2.** *n.* a subdivision of certain things, such as in a beehive or as with zones for portable wireless telephones. **3.** *n.* a cagelike room for keeping prisoners. **4.** *n.* a battery; one of the sections of a battery.

cellar ['sɛl ɚ] *n.* a basement; an underground room.

cello ['tʃɛl o] *n.* a stringed instrument, similar to a violin but larger. (It stands on the floor between the player's knees. Plural ends in *-s*.)

cellular ['sɛl jə lɚ] the *adj.* form of CELL ① or ②. (Adv: *cellularly.*)

cell(ular) telephone ['sɛl (jə lɚ) 'tɛl ə fon] *n.* a portable telephone using radio-wave transmission within a large area that is divided into smaller cells, allowing the same radio frequency to be used

in different cells by different users. (Often shortened to *cell phone*.)

cement [sɪ 'mɛnt] **1.** *n.* a gluelike substance that joins things together. (Plural only for types and instances.) **2.** *n.* a gray powder made of clay and limestone that hardens when mixed with water. (No plural.) **3.** *tv.* to join two things together.

cemetery ['sɛm ə tɛr i] *n.* a graveyard; a place where dead people are buried.

censor ['sɛn sɚ] **1.** *n.* someone who seeks to remove offensive words and pictures from material seen by the public. **2.** *tv.* to suppress the publication or performance of offensive material.

census ['sɛn səs] **1.** *n.* the process of counting the number of people who live in an area. **2.** *n.* the official number of people who live in an area; a report of what was found in collecting information for ①.

cent ['sɛnt] *n.* a penny; one one-hundredth of a dollar.
→ PUT IN ONE'S TWO CENTS(' WORTH)

center ['sɛn tɚ] **1.** *n.* the point in the middle of a circle or sphere that is the same distance from all points on the circle or on the surface of the sphere; a place that is in the middle of something. **2.** *n.* a major site or focus of an activity. **3.** *adj.* middle. (Prenominal only.) **4.** *tv.* to place someone or something in the middle of something.

center something **on** someone or something to base something on someone or something.

Centigrade ['sɛn ə gred] *n.* the metric system of measuring temperature. (No plural. The same as *Celsius.* Abbreviated *C.*)

centimeter ['sɛn ə mit ɚ] *n.* a measure of length, equal to one one-hundredth of a meter. (An inch is 2.54 centimeters.)

central ['sɛn trəl] **1.** *adj.* near the center. (Adv: *centrally.*) **2.** *adj.* primary; essential. (Adv: *centrally.*)
→ (AS) BUSY AS GRAND CENTRAL STATION

century ['sɛn tʃə ri] **1.** *n.* one hundred years. **2.** *n.* a block of time that begins every one hundred years, starting sometime close to the birth of Jesus Christ or some other specific event.

ceramic [sə 'ræm ɪk] *adj.* made of hard, baked clay, able to withstand great heat.

ceramics *n.* the making of pottery by shaping clay and baking it until it hardens. (Treated as singular.)

cereal ['sɪr i əl] **1.** *n.* one of a number of plants that provide grain. (Plural only for types and instances.) **2.** *n.* a food product made from grains, usually served at breakfast with milk. (Plural only for types and instances.)

ceremony ['sɛr ə mon i] **1.** *n.* a tradition or ritual associated with a particular event. **2.** *n.* the formal behavior seen in certain religious, social, or political events. (No plural.)

certain ['sɚt n] **1.** *adj.* definite or known, but not stated; particular and specific, but not identified. (Prenominal only.) **2.** *adj.* sure; confident; having no doubt (about something).

certain to do something sure to do something.

certainly ['sɚt n li] **1.** *adv.* definitely; surely; positively. **2.** *adv.* yes, by all means. (An answer to a question.)

certainty ['sɚt n ti] **1.** *n.* the state of being sure or certain. (No plural.) **2.** *n.* something that is known to be true.

chain ['tʃen] **1.** *n.* links or rings, especially made of metal, that are joined together in a row. **2.** *n.* a group of stores or businesses with the same name, owned by the same company or person. (A *chain store.*) **3.** *tv.* to bind someone or something with ①.

chair ['tʃɛr] **1.** *n.* a piece of furniture for sitting, sometimes with arms; a piece of furniture for one person to sit on. **2.** *n.* a person who presides over a committee or a meeting. **3.** *n.* the head of a department, especially in a university. **4.** *tv.* to lead or preside over a meeting, department, or committee.
→ ARMCHAIR
→ ROCKING CHAIR

chairman ['tʃɛr mən] *n., irreg.* the head of a department or committee; the person in charge of a meeting. (Either male or female. See also CHAIR. Plural: CHAIRMEN.)

chairmen ['tʃɛr mən] plural of CHAIRMAN.

chalk ['tʃɔk] **1.** *n.* a soft, white limestone. (Plural only for types and instances.) **2.** *n.* a stick of ① used for writing, as on a chalkboard. (No plural. Number is expressed with *piece(s)* or *stick(s) of chalk*.)

chalk something **out 1.** to draw a picture of something in chalk, especially to illustrate a plan of some type. **2.** to explain something carefully to someone, as if one were talking about a chalk drawing. (Often figurative.)

chalk something **up 1.** to write something on a chalkboard. **2.** to add a mark or point to one's score.

chalk something **up to** something to account for something with something else; to blame something on something else.

challenge ['tʃæl ɪndʒ] **1.** *n.* a dare; an invitation to a competition. **2.** *n.* a difficult task. **3.** *tv.* [for a difficult task] to test someone or something.

chamber ['tʃem bɚ] **1.** *n.* a room. **2.** *n.* a division of government, such as the House of Representatives or the Senate of the United States Congress, separately; certain organizations, such as the chamber of commerce of an area. **3.** *n.* a compartment within something; an enclosed space inside the body.

chameleon [kə 'mil (i)jən] **1.** *n.* a lizard that changes the color of its skin to match its surroundings. **2.** *n.* someone who is very changeable.

champ ['tʃæmp] *n.* a champion; a winner.

champ at the bit to be ready and anxious to do something. (Originally said about horses.)

champagne [ʃæm 'pen] *n.* a sparkling white wine made in the Champagne area of France, or similar wines made elsewhere. (Plural only for types and instances.)

champion ['tʃæmp i ən] **1.** *n.* a winner; someone who has won a contest or competition. **2.** *n.* someone who supports or argues in favor of someone or something; someone who advocates something. **3.** *tv.* to support someone or something; to speak in favor of someone or something.

chance ['tʃæns] **1.** *n.* fate; fortune. (No plural.) **2.** *n.* the probability that something might happen. (No plural.) **3.** *n.* an opportunity. **4.** *tv.* to risk something.
→ BY CHANCE
→ FAT CHANCE
→ FIGHTING CHANCE
→ LET THE CHANCE SLIP BY
→ ON THE OFF CHANCE
→ a SPORTING CHANCE

chance (up)on someone or something to find someone or something by accident; to happen upon someone or something.

change ['tʃendʒ] **1.** *n.* the process of becoming something different. (Plural only for types and instances.) **2.** *n.* something new or different; something that replaces something else. **3.** *n.* bills or coins of lower value given in exchange for bills or coins of a higher value; the money returned to someone who has paid a sum higher than the price. (No plural. Treated as singular.) **4.** *n.* loose coins. (No plural. Treated as singular.) **5.** *tv.* to replace something. **6.** *tv.* to cause something to become different. **7.** *tv.* to remove clothing and put on different clothing. **8.** *tv.* to replace a baby's dirty diaper with a clean one. **9.** *iv.* to become different. **10.** *iv.* to take off one set of clothes and put on another.

a **change of pace** a change of activity; a change.

a **change of scenery** a move to a different place, where the scenery is different or where things in general are different.

change out of something to take off a set of clothing and put on another.

change the subject to begin talking about something different.

channel ['tʃæn əl] **1.** *n.* a deeper passage through a harbor, where vessels can sail safely; the deepest part of a river or stream. **2.** *n.* the frequencies assigned to a particular television station.
→ GO THROUGH CHANNELS

chaos ['ke ɑs] *n.* complete confusion; complete disorder; anarchy. (No plural.)

chapel ['tʃæp əl] *n.* a place of worship that is smaller than a sanctuary.

chapter ['tʃæp tɚ] **1.** *n.* a division within a book; a section of a book. **2.** *n.* a division of an organization or society.
→ RECITE SOMETHING CHAPTER AND VERSE

character ['kɛr ɪk tɚ] **1.** *n.* a person in a book, movie, play, television show, etc. **2.** *n.* the nature of someone or something; the essential qualities of someone or something, especially someone's moral qualities. **3.** *n.* high personal quality; integrity; moral goodness. (No plural.) **4.** *n.* an unusual or eccentric person. **5.** *n.* a symbol used in writing, such as a letter, number, or other symbol.

characteristic [kɛr ɪk tə 'rɪs tɪk] **1.** *n.* a single feature; a special quality of someone or something. **2.** *adj.* relating to the features or qualities of something. (Adv: *characteristically* [...ɪk li].)

charcoal ['tʃɑr kol] *n.* a carbon-based fuel made by burning wood partially. (Plural only for types and instances.)

charge ['tʃɑɚdʒ] **1.** *n.* the cost of something; the amount of money needed to pay for something. (Often plural.) **2.** *n.* control [of someone or something]. (No plural.) **3.** *n.* someone or something that must be watched over. **4.** *n.* an accusation; a statement that someone has done something criminal. **5.** *n.* a sudden, moving attack. **6.** *n.* the amount of electrical energy stored in a battery or a particle of matter. **7.** *n.* the explosive material used in one explosion. **8.** *tv.* to present a claim of a sum of money for goods or services. **9.** *tv.* to place ① on an account instead of paying cash. **10.** *tv.* to rush toward and attack someone or something. **11.** *tv.* to provide a battery with energy; to send electricity through something, such as a circuit. **12.** *tv.* to ask for pay at a certain rate.
→ LODGE A CHARGE AGAINST SOMEONE

charge in(to someplace) to bolt or run wildly into a place.

charge off to bolt or run away.

charge out of someplace [for someone] to bolt or burst out of someplace.

charge someone **up** to excite someone; to make a person enthusiastic about something.

charge something **up 1.** to apply an electrical charge to a battery. **2.** to load or fill something, such as a fire extinguisher. **3.** to reinvigorate something.

charge something **(up) to** someone or something to place the cost of something on the account of someone or a group.

charity ['tʃɛr ɪ ti] **1.** *n.* love, kindness, and generosity shown toward other people. (No plural.) **2.** *n.* an organization that helps people in need.

charm ['tʃɑrm] **1.** *n.* a pleasing, attractive personality trait. (Plural only for types and instances.) **2.** *n.* a small toy or trinket worn on a necklace or bracelet. **3.** *n.* something that has magical powers. **4.** *tv.* to influence someone by using ①.

chart something **out (for** someone or something) to lay out a plan or course for someone or something.

chase ['tʃes] **1.** *n.* an act of running after someone or something. **2.** *tv.* to run after someone or something.
→ CUT TO THE CHASE
→ LEAD SOMEONE ON A MERRY CHASE
→ WILD-GOOSE CHASE

chase someone or something **down** to track down and seize someone or something.

chat ['tʃæt] **1.** *iv.* to talk; to have a friendly talk. **2.** *n.* a pleasant conversation; a friendly talk.

chatter ['tʃæt ɚ] **1.** *iv.* to talk about unimportant things. **2.** *iv.* [for one's teeth] to click together because of fear or coldness. **3.** *n.* unimportant talk. (No plural.)

cheap ['tʃip] **1.** *adj.* inexpensive; not costing a lot of money. (Adv: *cheaply.* Comp: *cheaper;* sup: *cheapest.*) **2.** *adj.* poorly made; of poor quality; of poor value. (Adv: *cheaply.* Comp: *cheaper;* sup: *cheapest.*)
→ DIRT CHEAP

cheat ['tʃit] **1.** *tv.* to deceive someone in a game or in commerce, as a means of gaining money or some other advantage. **2.** *iv.* to succeed by doing something that is not fair or honest. **3.** *n.* someone who CHEATS as in ① or ②; someone who does not play fairly.

cheat someone **out of** something to get something from someone by deception.

check ['tʃɛk] **1.** *n.* a written order to a bank to pay an amount of money to someone or something. **2.** *n.* the mark (✓). **3.** *n.* the bill for a meal in a restaurant. **4.** *n.* something that stops or restrains someone or something. **5.** *n.* a brief look at someone or something; an inspection of someone or something. **6.** *tv.* to examine something; to look at something closely but quickly. **7.** *tv.* to put one's belongings into the care of

someone and receive a receipt for the property. **8.** *tv.* to restrain someone or something; to stop someone or something.
→ a BLANK CHECK
→ BY CHECK
→ HONOR SOMEONE'S CHECK
→ MAKE A CHECK OUT (TO SOMEONE OR SOMETHING)

check back (on someone or something) to look into the state of someone or something again at a later time.

check back (with someone) to inquire of someone again at a later time.

check in (at something) to go to a place and record one's arrival.

check in on someone or something to go into a place and make sure that someone or something is all right.

check into something 1. to investigate a matter. **2.** to sign oneself into a place to stay, such as a hotel, hospital, motel, etc.

check on someone or something to investigate someone or something; to seek out the facts about someone or something.

check out [for someone or something] to prove to be correctly represented.

check out (from something) to do the paperwork necessary to leave a place and then leave.

check out (of something) to do the paperwork necessary to leave a place, such as a hotel.

check someone in to record the arrival of someone.

check someone or something off to mark or cross out the name of a person or thing on a list.

check someone or something out to evaluate someone or something.

check someone or something over to examine someone or something closely.

check something in 1. to record that someone has returned something. **2.** to take something to a place, return it, and make sure that its return has been recorded. **3.** to examine a shipment or an order received and make certain that everything ordered was received.

check something off to place a (✓) by an item on a list after it has been looked at, examined, or accounted for.

check up (on someone or something) to determine the state of someone or something.

cheek ['tʃik] *n.* the part of the face below the eye.
→ TURN THE OTHER CHEEK

cheekbone ['tʃik bon] *n.* the bone just below the eye.

cheer ['tʃɪr] **1.** *n.* an encouraging yell; some applause and shouting meant to encourage someone. **2.** *n.* happiness; a good state of mind. (No plural.) **3.** *iv.* to yell and shout in support of someone or something; to yell in encouragement. **4.** *tv.* to encourage someone by shouts of support.

cheer someone (up) to make a sad person happy.

cheer up [for a sad person] to become happy.

cheerful ['tʃɪr fʊl] **1.** *adj.* in good spirits; full of cheer; happy. (Adv: *cheerfully.*) **2.** *adj.* pleasant; [of something] bright and pleasing. (Adv: *cheerfully.*)

cheery ['tʃɪr i] **1.** *adj.* full of cheer; showing cheer. (Adv: *cheerily.* Comp: *cheerier;* sup: *cheeriest.*) **2.** *adj.* bright and cheerful; causing cheer. (Adv: *cheerily.* Comp: *cheerier;* sup: *cheeriest.*)

cheese ['tʃiz] **1.** *n.* a food made from the solid parts of processed milk. (Plural only for types and instances.) **2.** the *adj.* use of ①.
→ CREAM CHEESE

chef ['ʃɛf] **1.** *n.* a professional cook. **2.** *n.* any cook; whoever is doing the cooking.

chemical ['kɛm ɪ kəl] **1.** *n.* an element or a mixture of basic elements. **2.** the *adj.* use of ①. (Adv: *chemically* [...ɪk li].)

chemist ['kɛm ɪst] *n.* a scientist whose specialty is the theory and use of substances.

cherish ['tʃɛr ɪʃ] **1.** *tv.* to treat someone or something very lovingly; to have great fondness for someone or something. **2.** *tv.* to keep the idea of someone or something in one's mind.

cherry ['tʃɛr i] **1.** *n.* a tree that produces small, round, bright red fruits with one pit. **2.** *n.* wood from ①. (Plural only for types and instances.) **3.** *n.* the fruit of ①. **4.** *adj.* made with or flavored with ③. **5.** *adj.* made from ②.

chess ['tʃɛs] *n.* a game played by two people on a special board, with 32 pieces. (No plural.)

chest ['tʃɛst] **1.** *n.* the upper front part of the body. **2.** *n.* a piece of furniture with drawers, used to store clothes, linen, and other items. (Often *chest of drawers.*) **3.** *n.* a large, wooden storage box.
→ GET SOMETHING OFF ONE'S CHEST
→ PLAY ONE'S CARDS CLOSE TO THE CHEST

chew ['tʃu] **1.** *tv.* to crush food with the teeth before swallowing it. **2.** *iv.* to bite down with the teeth.
→ BITE OFF MORE THAN ONE CAN CHEW

chew something **off ((of)** something) to bite or gnaw something off something.

chew something **up** to grind food with the teeth until it can be swallowed.

chick ['tʃɪk] *n.* a baby chicken or other baby bird.

chicken ['tʃɪk ən] **1.** *n.* a bird raised on a farm for meat and eggs; a hen or a rooster. **2.** *n.* the meat of ①. (No plural.) **3.** *adj.* made with or flavored with ②.
→ COUNT ONE'S CHICKENS BEFORE THEY HATCH
→ NO SPRING CHICKEN

chickens have come home to roost all the problems have returned to the person who caused the problems and that person must now solve them or take the blame.

chief ['tʃif] **1.** *n.* the head of an organization or group; the leader. **2.** *adj.* most important; principal; main. (Adv: *chiefly.*)

child ['tʃaɪld] *n., irreg.* a young person; a boy or a girl; someone's son or daughter. (Plural: CHILDREN.)

→ BE CHILD'S PLAY
→ EXPECTING (A CHILD)

childhood ['tʃaɪlfhʊd] *n.* the time period during which one is a child. (See also IN ONE'S SECOND CHILDHOOD.)

children ['tʃɪl drɪn] plural of CHILD.

chill ['tʃɪl] **1.** *n.* a coldness, especially a damp coldness. **2.** *n.* a cold feeling; a lasting cold feeling caused by being in the cold too long. **3.** *n.* a coldness of manner; an unpleasant attitude; an unfriendly attitude. (Figurative on ①. No plural.) **4.** *n.* a sense of severe fright, possibly accompanied by the feeling of ②. **5.** *tv.* to cool something. **6.** *iv.* to become cool or cold.

chilled to the bone very cold.

chime in (with something**)** to add a comment to the discussion.

chimney ['tʃɪm ni] *n.* the structure that carries smoke to the outside and above a building.

chimpanzee [tʃɪm 'pæn zi] *n.* an African ape, closely related to humans.

chin ['tʃɪn] *n.* the part of the face below the lower lip.
→ TAKE SOMETHING ON THE CHIN

china ['tʃaɪn ə] *n.* high-quality dishes, cups, and saucers made of fine, thin ceramic material. (No plural.)
→ A BULL IN A CHINA SHOP

chip ['tʃɪp] **1.** *n.* a small piece that has broken off a larger object. **2.** *n.* the dent that is left where a small piece of something has broken off. **3.** *n.* a flat, crunchy, fried or baked snack made of starch. (Usually made from potatoes or corn. Also short for POTATO CHIP.) **4.** *tv.* to break off a small piece of something. **5.** *tv.* to shape something by picking away or cutting away at it piece by piece. **6.** *iv.* [for something] to lose a small bit, through CHIPPING as in ④.
→ CASH (ONE'S CHIPS) IN
→ HAVE A CHIP ON ONE'S SHOULDER
→ POTATO CHIP

chip away [for something] to break off or break away in small chips.

chip in (on something**) (for** someone**)** to contribute money toward something for someone.

a **chip off the old block** a person (usually a male) who behaves in the same way as his father or resembles his father. (The father is the "old block.")

chocolate ['tʃak (ə) lət] **1.** *n.* a tasty, sweet food made from roasted cacao beans, usually in the form of candy, syrup, a brewed beverage, or a flavor in cooking. (Plural only for types and instances.) **2.** *n.* a piece of ①. **3.** *adj.* made with or flavored with ①.

choice ['tʃɔɪs] **1.** *n.* a selection from which one can choose. (Plural only for types and instances.) **2.** *n.* the actual selection; someone or something chosen or selected. **3.** *adj.* of very high quality; excellent; best; optimal. (Adv: *choicely.*)
→ HOBSON'S CHOICE

choir ['kwaɪɚ] *n.* a singing group, especially one in a church.

choke ['tʃok] **1.** *n.* the part of an engine that controls the amount of air that goes into the engine. **2.** *tv.* to cut off someone's or some creature's air supply. **3.** *iv.* to react to having one's air supply cut off.

choke on something to begin to gag and cough on something stuck in the throat.

choke someone **up** to cause someone to feel like sobbing.

choke something **back** to fight hard to keep something from coming out of one's mouth, such as sobs, the truth, angry words, vomit, etc.

choke something **down** to work hard to swallow something, usually because it tastes bad.

choke something **up 1.** to clog something up; to fill up and block something. **2.** to cough or choke until something that has blocked one's windpipe is brought up.

choke up 1. to feel like sobbing. **2.** to become frightened or saddened so that one cannot speak.

choke up (about someone or something**)** to become very emotional about someone or something.

choose ['tʃuz] **1.** *tv., irreg.* to pick or select someone or something from a group. (Past tense: CHOSE; past participle: CHOSEN.) **2.** *iv., irreg.* to do the process of selection.
→ PICK AND CHOOSE

choose up sides to select opposing sides for a debate, fight, or game.

choosy ['tʃu zi] *adj.* hard to please; hard to make happy; particular. (Adv: *choosily.* Comp: *choosier;* sup: *choosiest.*)

chop ['tʃap] **1.** *n.* a movement with an axe or blade that cuts into something; a blow that cuts into something. **2.** *n.* a slice of meat, including some bone, especially lamb or pork. **3.** *tv.* to cut something by hitting it with something sharp.

chop someone **off** to stop someone in the middle of a sentence or speech.

chop something **down** to fell a tree or a pole; to fell a person by cutting with a sword or something similar.

chop something **off** to cut something off, perhaps with an axe.

chord ['kord] *n.* two or more musical tones played at the same time.
→ STRIKE A CHORD (WITH SOMEONE)

chore ['tʃor] *n.* a regular task; a duty.

chorus ['kor əs] **1.** *n.* a group of people who sing together; a choir. **2.** *n.* the part of a song that is repeated after each song. **3.** *n.* words or noises that are said together or at the same time.

chose ['tʃoz] past tense of CHOOSE.

chosen ['tʃo zən] Past participle of CHOOSE.

Christian ['krɪs tʃən] *n.* a member of the CHRISTIAN RELIGION.

Christian religion AND **Christianity** ['krɪs tʃən rɪ 'lɪdʒ ən, krɪs tʃi 'æn ə ti] *n.* a religion whose basis is in the teachings of Jesus Christ.

Christianity [krɪs tʃi 'æn ə ti] Go to CHRISTIAN RELIGION.

Christmas ['krɪs məs] *n.* December 25; the day on which the birth of Christ is celebrated by many Christians.

chromosome ['krom ə som] *n.* one of many very tiny cellular structures containing genes.

chum ['tʃʌm] *n.* a good friend; a buddy.

chunk ['tʃʌŋk] *n.* a thick, irregularly shaped piece of something.

church ['tʃɚtʃ] **1.** *n.* a building where Christians gather to worship. **2.** *n.* the worship service celebrated within ①. (No plural.) **3.** *n.* the members of a particular religious organization. **4.** *n.* the institutional organization of a religious body, its policies, and its practices. (No plural.)
→ (AS) POOR AS A CHURCH MOUSE

cider ['saɪ dɚ] *n.* apple juice; juice pressed from apples. (Plural only for types and instances.)

cigar [sɪ 'gɑr] *n.* a carefully packed roll of dried tobacco leaves, used for smoking.

cigarette [sɪg ə 'rɛt] *n.* a small roll of cut tobacco wrapped in paper, used for smoking.

circle ['sɚ kəl] **1.** *n.* a curved line where every point on the line is the same distance from a center point. **2.** *n.* anything shaped like ①; a ring. **3.** *n.* a group of people with related interests. **4.** *tv.* to form a ring around someone or something. **5.** *tv.* to draw a ring around something that is written or printed.
→ COME FULL CIRCLE
→ GO (A)ROUND IN CIRCLES
→ IN A VICIOUS CIRCLE
→ RUN (AROUND) IN CIRCLES
→ TALK IN CIRCLES

circuit ['sɚ kɪt] **1.** *n.* a complete trip around something. **2.** *n.* the path that the flow of electricity follows.
→ SHORT CIRCUIT

circular ['sɚ kjə lɚ] **1.** *n.* a printed sheet that is sent to many people. **2.** *adj.* in the shape of a circle; round; ringlike. (Adv: *circularly*.)

circulate ['sɚ kjə let] **1.** *tv.* to send something from person to person; to send something from place to place. **2.** *tv.* to carry something, such as medicine, by way of the circulation of blood. **3.** *iv.* to go around from person to person. **4.** *iv.* [for blood] to flow from the heart through the body and back to the heart.

circulate something **through** something to route something through something; to make something travel through something.

circulate through something **1.** [for a fluid in a closed system of pipes or tubes] to flow through the various pathways of pipes and tubes. **2.** to travel through something; to make the rounds through something.

circulation [sɚk jə 'le ʃən] *n.* the process of circulating.
→ BACK IN CIRCULATION
→ OUT OF CIRCULATION

circus ['sɚ kəs] *n.* a traveling show featuring clowns, acrobats, ani-

mals, magicians, and other similar acts.
→ LIKE A THREE-RING CIRCUS

cite ['saɪt] **1.** *tv.* to use someone or something as a reference to support a claim or statement of fact. **2.** *tv.* to refer to or list a citation. **3.** *tv.* to recognize someone for having done an exceptional deed. **4.** *tv.* to give someone an order to appear in court.

citizen ['sɪt ə zən] *n.* someone who is a legal resident of a specific political region; someone who has full rights of membership in a state or country.
→ SENIOR CITIZEN

citizenship ['sɪt ə zən ʃɪp] **1.** *n.* the state of being an official citizen. (No plural.) **2.** *n.* the behavior expected of a citizen. (No plural.)

citrus ['sɪ trəs] **1.** *n.* a family of fruit including oranges, tangerines, grapefruit, limes, lemons, etc. (No plural.) **2.** the *adj.* use of ①.

city ['sɪt i] **1.** *n.* a large town; a large residential and business center. **2.** the *adj.* use of ①.

city hall ['sɪt i 'hɔl] **1.** *n.* the administrative building for a city government. (Sometimes capitalized.) **2.** *n.* a city government or administration; the offices in ① and the government leaders working in ①. (Sometimes capitalized.)

civil ['sɪv əl] **1.** *adj.* of or about citizens and their government, activities, rights, and responsibilities. **2.** *adj.* polite; courteous; behaving properly. (Adv: *civilly*.) **3.** *adj.* relating to a legal action that does not deal with criminal law.

→ KEEP A CIVIL TONGUE (IN ONE'S HEAD)

civilian [sɪ 'vɪl jən] *n.* a citizen who is not in the military.

civilize ['sɪv ə laɪz] *tv.* to make someone or a culture more organized and less primitive.

claim ['klem] **1.** *n.* a document or statement requesting that a payment be made. **2.** *n.* a statement presented as fact; a statement that something is true. **3.** *tv.* to assert one's right to own something. **4.** *tv.* to say a statement as fact; to state that something is true. (The object can be a clause with THAT ⑦.)

claim a life [for something] to take the life of someone.

clam ['klæm] **1.** *n.* an edible marine animal having a pair of shells that open like a book. **2.** the *adj.* use of ①.
→ (AS) HAPPY AS A CLAM

clamp ['klæmp] **1.** *n.* a device that holds things together with pressure. **2.** *tv.* to hold things together with pressure.

clamp down (on someone or something) to restrain or limit someone or someone's actions.

clap ['klæp] **1.** *n.* the sound made when one brings one's palms together, as in applause. **2.** *n.* a loud burst of thunder. **3.** *iv.* to make applause.

clarinet [klɛr ə 'nɛt] *n.* a tube-shaped musical instrument of the woodwind family.

class ['klæs] **1.** *n.* a group of similar things. **2.** *n.* someone's social and economic ranking. **3.** *n.* a

course that is taught; a subject that is taught. **4.** *n.* a specific session of learning; a period of time spent in instruction. **5.** *n.* all the people in a certain grade or year of schooling. **6.** *n.* a term of address for a group of students in a classroom. (No plural.) **7.** *n.* the ability to behave properly, politely, or elegantly. (No plural.)
→ CUT CLASS

class roll *n.* a list of the names of people, especially those who are enrolled in school.

classic ['klæs ɪk] **1.** *n.* something, especially art, music, or writing, that is of very high quality and will be or is remembered through history. **2.** *adj.* of high quality; the best; of great and lasting importance; serving as a standard for others of its kind. **3.** *adj.* typical; just as one would anticipate.

classical ['klæs ɪ kəl] **1.** *adj.* of or about ancient Greece and Rome. (Adv: *classically* [...ɪk li].) **2.** *adj.* [of music, such as symphonies and operas, dance, and other art forms] serious and requiring a high degree of training and skill.

classmate ['klæs met] *n.* someone in the same class at school.

classroom ['klæs rum] *n.* a room in a school or building where classes are held.

clause ['klɔz] **1.** *n.* a phrase that has a subject and a verb. **2.** *n.* a single provision in a legal document.
→ RELATIVE CLAUSE

claw ['klɔ] **1.** *n.* a sharp, hard, curved nail on the foot of an animal or a bird. **2.** *n.* the pinchers of

a lobster, crab, or other shellfish. **3.** *n.* the part of the hammer that is used for removing nails. **4.** *tv.* to scratch or tear someone or something with ①.

claw something **off ((of)** someone or something**)** to rip or tear something off from someone or something.

clay ['kle] **1.** *n.* a kind of sticky soil, used for pottery. (Plural only for types and instances.) **2.** *adj.* made of or concerning ①.
→ HAVE FEET OF CLAY

clean ['klin] **1.** *adj.* tidy; not dirty. (Adv: *cleanly.*) **2.** *adj.* new; fresh; unused. **3.** *adj.* morally pure; not DIRTY ②. (Adv: *cleanly.*) **4.** *adj.* smooth; even; not rough. (Adv: *cleanly.*) **5.** *tv.* to make something ①. **6.** *tv.* to prepare an animal for cooking and eating by removing the parts that cannot be eaten.
→ GET A CLEAN BILL OF HEALTH
→ GIVE SOMEONE A CLEAN BILL OF HEALTH
→ HAVE CLEAN HANDS
→ MAKE A CLEAN BREAST OF SOMETHING
→ START (OFF) WITH A CLEAN SLATE

clean one's **act up** to start behaving better.

clean someone or something **down** to clean someone or something by brushing or with flowing water.

clean someone or something **out (of** something**)** to remove people or things from something or some place.

clean someone or something **up** to get someone or something clean.

clean something **off** to take something off something; to remove something such as dirt or dirty dishes.

clean something **off ((of)** something) to remove something from something.

clean something **out** to remove dirt or unwanted things from the inside of something.

clean up (on someone or something) to make a large profit from someone or some business activity.

cleaner ['kli nɚ] **1.** *n.* soap, bleach, or some other product that cleans. (Plural only for types and instances.) **2.** *n.* someone who cleans clothing and fabric for a living.
→ VACUUM CLEANER

cleaners *n.* a business that launders or cleans clothing and other items. (Treated as singular or plural.)

cleanse ['klɛnz] *tv.* to clean something well; to make something more pure.

clear ['klɪr] **1.** *adj.* transparent; allowing light through. (Adv: *clearly.* Comp: *clearer;* sup: *clearest.*) **2.** *adj.* bright; free from clouds or fog. (Adv: *clearly.* Comp: *clearer;* sup: *clearest.*) **3.** *adj.* without marks or blemishes; without defects. (Comp: *clearer;* sup: *clearest.*) **4.** *adj.* easy to understand; making perfect sense. (Adv: *clearly.* Comp: *clearer;* sup: *clearest.*) **5.** *adj.* easy to hear or see. (Adv: *clearly.* Comp: *clearer;* sup: *clearest.*) **6.** *adj.* certain; easy to understand. (Adv: *clearly.* Comp: *clearer;* sup: *clearest.*) **7.** *adj.* without anything in the way. (Comp: *clearer;* sup: *clearest.*) **8.** *adv.* com-

pletely; all the way. **9.** *tv.* to move someone or something so that the way is open. **10.** *tv.* to make an area empty by removing people or things. **11.** *tv.* to chop down trees and remove stones from the land. **12.** *tv.* to remove blame or guilt from someone or something. **13.** *tv.* [for a bank] to send a check successfully through procedures necessary to have the check paid. **14.** *iv.* [for a check] to successfully travel through the procedures necessary to assure payment. **15.** *iv.* [for the sky] to become free of clouds.
→ (AS) CLEAR AS MUD
→ THE COAST IS CLEAR.
→ MAKE ONESELF CLEAR
→ OUT OF A CLEAR BLUE SKY

clear of something without touching something; away from something.

clear out (of someplace) to get out of someplace.

clear something **away** to take something away.

clear something **off ((of)** something) to take something off something.

clear something **up 1.** to clarify something; to take away the confusion about something. **2.** to cure a disease.

clear the table to remove the dishes and other eating utensils from the table after a meal.

clear up 1. [for something] to become more understandable. **2.** [for a disease] to improve or become cured. **3.** [for the sky] to become clearer.

clergy [ˈklɚ dʒi] *n.* ministers; priests; pastors. (No plural. Number is expressed by the phrase *member(s) of the clergy.*)

clerk [ˈklɚk] **1.** *n.* an office worker, especially one who keeps track of records, files, and information. **2.** *n.* someone who helps customers with goods and sales; someone who works behind a counter and helps customers.

clever [ˈklɛv ɚ] *adj.* [of someone or a creature] capable of interesting, creative activities. (Adv: *cleverly.* Comp: *cleverer;* sup: *cleverest.*)

cliché [kli ˈʃe] *n.* an expression that is trite and tiresome and is used too often.

click [ˈklɪk] **1.** *n.* a short, quick noise; a snapping sound. **2.** *tv.* to make a noise by snapping things together. **3.** *iv.* to snap; to make a snapping noise.

client [ˈklaɪ ənt] *n.* someone served by a company or by a professional such as a lawyer.

cliff [ˈklɪf] *n.* a high, steep wall of rock or earth.

climate [ˈklaɪ mət] **1.** *n.* the typical weather conditions of a certain area. **2.** *n.* the general atmosphere, mood, attitude, or feeling.

climax [ˈklaɪ mæks] **1.** *n.* the most exciting point in an event; the most intense part of an event; the most dramatic point of a story. **2.** *iv.* to reach the most exciting point in an event.

climb [ˈklaɪm] **1.** *n.* the process of going up something, especially through much effort or using the hands and feet. **2.** *tv.* to go up something, especially through much effort or using the hands and feet. **3.** *iv.* to go to a higher level.

climb on the bandwagon Go to GET ON THE BANDWAGON.

climber [ˈklaɪm ɚ] **1.** *n.* someone who hikes or climbs up mountains, cliffs, slopes, etc. **2.** *n.* a plant that grows up something.

clinic [ˈklɪn ɪk] *n.* a medical office where minor medical problems are treated.

clip [ˈklɪp] **1.** *n.* a device that holds sheets of paper together; a small device for gripping or holding things together. **2.** *n.* a brief part of a film, book, magazine, or newspaper. **3.** *tv.* to hold things together with ①.
→ PAPER CLIP

clip someone's wings to restrain someone; to reduce or put an end to a child's or teenager's privileges. (As with birds or fowl whose wings are clipped to keep them at home.)

clip something on((to) someone or something) to attach something to someone or something with a clip.

clip something out (of something) to remove something from something by clipping or cutting.

cloak [ˈklok] **1.** *n.* a long coat without sleeves; an outer garment like a cape. **2.** *tv.* to cover something up; to obscure something.

cloak-and-dagger involving secrecy and plotting.

clock [ˈklɑk] **1.** *n.* a machine that keeps track of the time of day; a timepiece. **2.** *tv.* to measure the

length of time it takes for someone or something to do something; to measure a rate of speed.
→ AGAINST THE CLOCK

clock in to record one's time of arrival, usually by punching a time clock.

clock out to record one's time of departure, usually by punching a time clock.

clock someone **in** to observe and record someone's time of arrival.

clock someone **out** to observe and record someone's time of departure.

clockwork ['klɑk wɚk] *n.* the moving parts inside a clock or mechanical device, such as a wind-up toy.
→ (AS) REGULAR AS CLOCKWORK
→ GO LIKE CLOCKWORK

clog something **up** [for something] to obstruct a channel or conduit.

clog up [for a channel or conduit] to become blocked.

close 1. ['klos] *adj.* near in space or time. (Adv: *closely.* Comp: *closer;* sup: *closest.*) **2.** ['klos] *adj.* near in spirit; dear; intimate; confidential. (Adv: *closely.* Comp: *closer;* sup: *closest.*) **3.** ['klos] *adj.* careful; strict. (Adv: *closely.* Comp: *closer;* sup: *closest.*) **4.** ['klos] *adj.* almost equal; almost the same. (Adv: *closely.* Comp: *closer;* sup: *closest.*) **5.** ['klos] *adv.* near in space or time. **6.** ['kloz] *tv.* to shut something. **7.** ['kloz] *tv.* to bring something to an end; to conclude something. **8.** ['kloz] *tv.* to complete an electrical circuit. **9.** ['kloz] *iv.* to shut. **10.** ['kloz] *iv.* to end; to finish; to bring to an

end; to conclude. **11.** ['kloz] *n.* the end; the finish; the conclusion.
→ ABLE TO DO SOMETHING WITH ONE'S EYES CLOSED
→ HAVE A (CLOSE) BRUSH WITH SOMETHING
→ HAVE A CLOSE CALL
→ HAVE A CLOSE SHAVE
→ KEEP A CLOSE REIN ON SOMEONE OR SOMETHING
→ PLAY ONE'S CARDS CLOSE TO ONE'S VEST
→ PLAY ONE'S CARDS CLOSE TO THE CHEST

close at hand within reach; handy.

close down [for a business, office, shop, etc.] to close permanently or temporarily.

close in (on someone or something**)** to move in on someone or something.

close ranks 1. to move closer together in a military formation. **2.** to join (with someone**).**

close someone or something **down** to force someone or someone's business, office, shop, etc., to close permanently or temporarily.

close someone or something **up** **1.** to close someone or someone's business, office, shop, etc., temporarily or permanently. **2.** to close someone or something completely. (Said of a person being stitched up at the end of a surgical procedure.)

close someone **out of** something to prevent someone from getting into something, such as a class, a room, a privilege, etc.

close something **out 1.** to sell off a particular kind of merchandise with the intention of not selling it in the future. **2.** to prevent further registration in something.

close up [for an opening] to close completely.

closed ['klozd] *adj.* not open; shut.

closet ['klɔz ɪt] **1.** *n.* a small room where clothing and personal objects are kept. **2.** *adj.* secret; hiding; covert.
→ COME OUT OF THE CLOSET
→ SKELETON IN THE CLOSET

cloth ['klɔθ] **1.** *n.* woven material; woven fabric. (Plural only for types and instances.) **2.** *n., irreg.* a piece of woven material or fabric. (Plural: [klɔðz].)
→ CUT FROM THE SAME CLOTH
→ MAKE SOMETHING UP OUT OF WHOLE CLOTH

clothe ['kloð] *tv.* to put garments on someone or something; to dress someone or something.

clothes ['klo(ð)z] *n.* clothing; garments; something to wear, such as a shirt, a sweater, pants, or socks. (Treated as plural, but not countable.)

clothesline ['kloz laɪn] *n.* a length of rope on which clothes and other laundry can be hung to dry.

clothespin ['kloz pɪn] *n.* a wooden or plastic clip used to attach damp clothes to a clothesline.

clothing ['klo ðɪŋ] *n.* clothes; garments. (No plural. Treated as singular. See also a WOLF IN SHEEP'S CLOTHING.)

cloud ['klaʊd] **1.** *n.* a large white or gray mass in the sky, made of water vapor. **2.** *n.* a large puff of smoke or dust; a visible mass of gas or particles that is still or

moves in the air. **3.** *tv.* to obscure something; to hide something.
→ HAVE ONE'S HEAD IN THE CLOUDS
→ ON CLOUD NINE
→ UNDER A CLOUD (OF SUSPICION)

cloud up [for the sky] to fill with clouds.

cloudy ['klaʊ di] **1.** *adj.* [of sky] having clouds. (Adv: *cloudily.* Comp: *cloudier;* sup: *cloudiest.*) **2.** *adj.* not able to be seen through clearly. (Figurative on ①. Adv: *cloudily.* Comp: *cloudier;* sup: *cloudiest.*)

clown ['klaʊn] **1.** *n.* a performer who wears a funny costume and makeup and tries to make people laugh. **2.** *n.* someone who is always making jokes and trying to make other people laugh.

clown around (with someone**)** to join with someone in acting silly; [for two or more people] to act silly together.

club ['klʌb] **1.** *n.* a large, thick, blunt wooden stick. **2.** *n.* a nightclub; a place where liquor is served or where people can dance. **3.** *n.* an organization or group of people who meet to pursue a specific activity. **4.** *n.* one of four different symbols found in a deck of playing cards; the symbol (♣). **5.** *n.* the stick with a metal end used to hit a golf ball. (Short for GOLF CLUB.) **6.** *tv.* to beat someone or something with ①.
→ GOLF CLUB
→ JOIN THE CLUB!

clue ['klu] *n.* a hint; some information that will help to solve a problem.

clue someone **in (on** something) to inform someone about something.

clump ['klʌmp] **1.** *n.* a group of something; a mass of something. **2.** *tv.* to group things together; to gather something into ①.

clumsy ['klʌm zi] *adj.* awkward; likely to trip or stumble on something. (Adv: *clumsily.* Comp: *clumsier;* sup: *clumsiest.*)

clutch ['klətʃ] *tv.* to grasp something; to hold onto something.

clutches ['klətʃ əz] *n.* one's grasp; a person's holding onto someone or something.
→ IN(TO) SOMEONE'S CLUTCHES

clutter something **up** to mess something up; to fill something or someplace up with too many things.

coach ['kotʃ] **1.** *n.* someone who is in charge of a team; someone who trains players on a team. **2.** *n.* someone who trains someone else. **3.** *n.* an enclosed carriage, typically pulled by horses. **4.** *n.* a railway car where passengers ride in seats. (As opposed to railway cars where people can eat or can lie down to sleep.) **5.** *n.* a cross-country bus; a bus used for touring or carrying people over a long distance. **6.** *n.* the tourist section of an airplane; the cheapest kind of air travel. (No plural.) **7.** *adv.* [traveling] in or by ⑥. **8.** *tv.* to instruct someone in a sport, skill, or craft.

coal ['kol] **1.** *n.* a black mineral made of carbon, used as fuel. (Plural only for types and instances.) **2.** *n.* a hot, glowing chunk of burning ① or charcoal.

→ HAUL SOMEONE OVER THE COALS
→ RAKE SOMEONE OVER THE COALS

coarse ['kors] **1.** *adj.* having a rough texture; not smooth. (Adv: *coarsely.* Comp: *coarser;* sup: *coarsest.*) **2.** *adj.* vulgar; crude. (Adv: *coarsely.* Comp: *coarser;* sup: *coarsest.*)

coast ['kost] **1.** *n.* land along and beside the sea. **2.** *iv.* to glide without using energy.

The **coast is clear.** There is no visible danger.

coastal ['kos təl] *adj.* along the coast; on the coast. (Adv: *coastally.*)

coast-to-coast from the Atlantic Ocean to the Pacific Ocean (in North America); all the land between the Atlantic and Pacific Oceans.

coat ['kot] **1.** *n.* a heavy item of clothing, worn over one's other clothes during cold weather. **2.** *n.* the fur of an animal; the pelt of an animal. **3.** *n.* a layer of something, such as paint, that covers a surface. **4.** *tv.* to cover the surface of something with a layer of something.

cob ['kɑb] *n.* the central core of an ear of corn. (Short for CORNCOB.)

cock of the walk someone who acts more important than others in a group.

cock-and-bull story a silly, made-up story; a story that is a lie.

cocoon [kə 'kun] *n.* the protective shell in which a caterpillar wraps itself while it transforms into a butterfly or a moth.

cod ['kɑd] **1.** *n., irreg.* a kind of edible fish that lives in cold water. (Plural: *cod*.) **2.** *n.* the flesh of ①, eaten as food. (No plural.)

code ['kod] **1.** *n.* a secret writing system; a system of symbols used for communication. **2.** *n.* a set of laws; a set of rules. **3.** *tv.* to translate a message into ①. **4.** *tv.* to mark an object with a special number or symbol.
→ AREA CODE
→ BREAK A CODE
→ ZIP CODE

coffee ['kɔf i] **1.** *n.* the roasted beans of a kind of tree. (Either whole or ground. Plural only for types and instances.) **2.** *n.* a drink made from roasted, ground ①. (No plural.)

coffee break ['kɔf i brek] *n.* a rest period during which coffee or some other refreshment is enjoyed.

coffeepot ['kɔf i pɑt] *n.* a pot used to brew and serve coffee.

coffin ['kɔf ən] *n.* a box in which the body of a dead person is placed for burial.
→ NAIL IN SOMEONE'S OR SOMETHING'S COFFIN

coil ['kɔil] **1.** *n.* a length of something, such as rope, wound into a stack of circular loops. **2.** *n.* a circular loop. **3.** *tv.* to wrap something around and around into a circle. **4.** *iv.* to form into a circular loop.

coil something up to roll or twist something into a coil.

coin ['kɔin] **1.** *n.* a piece of money made from metal. **2.** *tv.* to press metal into ①; to make money

from metal. **3.** *tv.* to invent a new word; to make up a new word.

cold ['kold] **1.** *n.* a physical state or property of something having relatively less heat. (No plural.) **2.** *n.* weather that is characterized by ①; a lack of warmth in the outside temperature. (No plural.) **3.** *n.* a common illness that causes sneezing, a runny nose, a sore throat, etc. **4.** *adj.* not hot; not having heat. (Comp: *colder;* sup: *coldest.*) **5.** *adj.* [of a living creature] uncomfortable from not having heat. (Adv: *coldly.* Comp: *colder;* sup: *coldest.*) **6.** *adj.* mean; unfriendly; unpleasant. (Adv: *coldly.* Comp: *colder;* sup: *coldest.*)
→ BREAK OUT IN A COLD SWEAT
→ CATCH COLD
→ CATCH ONE'S DEATH (OF COLD)
→ DASH COLD WATER ON SOMETHING
→ GET COLD FEET
→ KNOCK SOMEONE COLD
→ MAKE SOMEONE'S BLOOD RUN COLD
→ OUT COLD
→ POUR COLD WATER ON SOMETHING
→ TAKE COLD
→ TAKE ONE'S DEATH (OF COLD)
→ THROW COLD WATER ON SOMETHING

cold comfort no comfort or consolation at all.

collapse [kə 'læps] **1.** *n.* an instance of falling down; a loss of the air contained in something. (No plural.) **2.** *n.* the total ruin of something. **3.** *iv.* to fall down; to become ruined. **4.** *iv.* to fail; to break down completely.

collapse into something **1.** to fall down into something. **2.** [for someone] to fall into a particular kind of despair.

collapse under someone or something to cave in under the weight of someone or something.

collar ['kɑl ɚ] **1.** *n.* the part of a piece of clothing that wraps around the neck. **2.** *n.* a band around the neck of an animal.
→ HOT UNDER THE COLLAR

collect [kə 'lɛkt] **1.** *tv.* to ask for or to receive money that is owed. **2.** *tv.* to gather items together; to bring items together. **3.** *tv.* to find and take, get, or buy something or a class of things as a hobby. **4.** *adj.* [of a telephone call] charged to the person or number called. **5.** *adv.* charging a telephone call to the person or telephone number called.

college ['kɑl ɪdʒ] *n.* a school of higher education; an undergraduate division within a university.

colonial [kə 'lon i əl] **1.** *adj.* of or about a colony. (Adv: *colonially.*) **2.** *adj.* of or about the original thirteen colonies of the United States. (Adv: *colonially.*) **3.** *n.* a person who lives or lived in a colony.

colony ['kɑl ə ni] **1.** *n.* an area that is settled and ruled by a country but is located apart from it. **2.** *n.* the place where a social group of ants or termites lives and breeds.

color ['kʌl ɚ] **1.** *n.* the quality of light that causes people to see the differences among red, orange, yellow, blue, green, purple, etc.; a hue; a tint. **2.** *tv.* to give something ①; to paint or draw with something that has ①. **3.** *tv.* to affect something; to influence something. (Figurative on ②.) **4.** *iv.* to

draw with crayons or markers. **5.** *adj.* [of film or video recording] using all the colors, not just black and white.
→ A HORSE OF A DIFFERENT COLOR
→ A HORSE OF ANOTHER COLOR
→ PRIMARY COLOR
→ SHOW ONE'S (TRUE) COLORS
→ WITH FLYING COLORS

colt ['kolt] *n.* a young male horse.

column ['kɑl əm] **1.** *n.* a supporting pillar or a thick post. **2.** *n.* a series of words or symbols arranged in a line from top to bottom. **3.** *n.* a newspaper article, especially one written by a columnist.

coma ['ko mə] *n.* a state of complete unconsciousness, often due to illness.
→ LAPSE INTO A COMA

comb ['kom] **1.** *n.* a toothed strip of plastic or something similar, used for arranging hair. **2.** *n.* the red growth on top of the heads of chickens and turkeys. **3.** *tv.* to arrange one's hair with ①. **4.** *tv.* to thoroughly look through an area for something; to search a place for something.
→ GO OVER SOMETHING WITH A FINE-TOOTH COMB
→ SEARCH SOMETHING WITH A FINE-TOOTH COMB

comb something **out** to comb something and make it straight or neat.

comb something **out (of** something) to remove knots and snarls from something by combing.

combat 1. ['kɑm bæt] *n.* war; conflict; battle. (No plural.) **2.** ['kɑm bæt] the *adj.* use of ①. **3.** [kəm 'bæt] *tv.* to fight someone or something; to battle someone or

103

something. (Past tense and past participle: *combated*.)

combination [kɑm bɪ 'ne ʃən] **1.** *n.* the process of combining. (Plural only for types and instances.) **2.** *n.* something that is made by an act of combining. **3.** *n.* the sequence of numbers needed to open a COM-BINATION LOCK.

combination lock [kɑm bɪ 'ne ʃən lɑk] *n.* a lock that is opened by turning a dial to a secret COMBINA-TION ③ of numbers or by pressing numbered buttons in the proper sequence, instead of with a key.

combine [kəm 'baɪn] **1.** *tv.* to join two or more things together. **2.** *iv.* to unite; to join.

come ['kʌm] **1.** *iv., irreg.* to move toward someone or something; to move toward the location of the person who is speaking. (Past tense: CAME; past participle: *come*.) **2.** *iv., irreg.* to arrive; to get somewhere. **3.** *iv., irreg.* [for goods that have been purchased] to arrive or be available equipped in a certain way.
  → CHICKENS HAVE COME HOME TO ROOST
  → CROSS A BRIDGE BEFORE ONE COMES TO IT
  → CROSS A BRIDGE WHEN ONE COMES TO IT
  → a DREAM COME TRUE
  → EASY COME, EASY GO
  → FIRST COME, FIRST SERVED
  → (HAD) KNOWN IT WAS COMING
  → IF WORST COMES TO WORST
  → NOT KNOW ENOUGH TO COME IN OUT OF THE RAIN

come about [for a boat] to change its angle against the wind; [for a boat] to change tack.

come across someone or something AND **run across** someone or something to find someone or something; to discover someone or something.

come apart at the seams to lose one's emotional self-control suddenly. (From the literal sense, referring to a garment falling apart.)

come around 1. to agree in the end; to agree finally. **2.** to return to consciousness.

come as no surprise will not be surprising [for someone] to learn [something].

come away empty-handed to return without anything.

come away (from someone or something**)** to move away from someone or something.

come back to return to an advantageous or favorable state or condition.

come back (to someone or something**)** to return to someone or something.

come by something **1.** to travel by a specific carrier, such as a plane, a boat, or a car. (The literal sense.) **2.** to find or get something.

come down in the world to lose one's social position or financial standing.

come down with something to catch a disease.

come from nowhere to come as a surprise with no warning.

come full circle to return to the original position or state of affairs.

come home (to roost) to return to cause trouble (for someone). (As chickens or other birds return home to roost.)

come in 1. to enter. (Often a command or polite request.) **2.** to arrive; [for a shipment of something] to arrive.

come in out of the rain to become alert and sensible. (Also used literally.)

come into its own [for something] to achieve its proper recognition.

come into one's own [for someone] to achieve one's proper recognition.

come of age to reach an age when one is old enough to own property, get married, and sign legal contracts.

come off to happen as planned; to come to fruition; to succeed. (Colloquial.)

come off ((of) something) [for something] to become detached from something else.

come off second best to win second place or worse; to lose out to someone else.

come on 1. to hurry along after someone. (Usually a command.) **2.** [for electricity or some other device] to start operating. **3.** to walk out and appear on stage. **4.** [for a pain] to begin hurting; [for a disease] to attack someone. **5.** to yield; to agree. (Usually a command.) **6.** [for a program] to be broadcast on radio or television.

come on((to) someone or something) to find someone or something by accident; to happen onto someone or something.

come out 1. to exit; to leave the inside of a place. **2.** to result; to succeed; to happen. **3.** to come before the public; to be published; to be made public. **4.** to become visible or evident.

come out ahead to end up with a profit; to improve one's situation.

come out in the wash to work out all right. (This means that problems or difficulties will go away as dirt goes away in the process of washing.)

come out of left field [for a problem or dilemma] to come from a place that would not be expected.

come out of the closet 1. to reveal one's secret interests. **2.** to reveal that one is a homosexual.

come out with something 1. to publish something. **2.** to express or utter something. **3.** to say or shout something.

come over to come for a visit.

come over someone [for something] to affect a person, perhaps suddenly.

come over someone or something to move over and above someone or something.

come over (to our side) to join up with our side; to become one of our group, party, etc.

come over to something to change to something; to convert to something.

come through to be approved; to be sanctioned.

come through (for someone or something) to produce or perform as promised for someone or a group.

come through (something**) 1.** to survive something. **2.** to pass through something.

come through (with something) to produce or deliver something as promised.

come to to become conscious; to return to consciousness.

come to a bad end to have a disaster, perhaps one that is deserved or expected; to die an unfortunate death.

come to a dead end to arrive at an absolute stopping point.

come to a head to come to a crucial point; to reach a point where a problem must be solved.

come to a standstill to stop, temporarily or permanently.

come to a stop [for someone or something] to stop moving or happening.

come to an end to stop; to finish.

come to an untimely end to die an early death.

come to grief to fail; to suffer trouble or bad luck.

come to grips with something to face something; to comprehend something.

come to light to become known.

come to one's **senses** to wake up; to become conscious; to start thinking clearly.

come to pass to happen. (Literary.)

come to terms with someone or something to face someone or something and deal with the person or thing as a problem that needs to be dealt with.

come to the point AND **get to the point** to get to the important part (of something).

come to think of it I just remembered something about . . .; now that I think about it . . .

come true to become real; [for a dream or a wish] actually to happen.

come up 1. to come from a lower place to a higher one. **2.** to come near; to approach. **3.** to come to someone's attention.

come up against someone or something to reach an obstacle in the form of someone or something.

come up in the world to improve one's status or situation in life.

come up something [for a tossed coin] to turn out to be either heads or tails.

come what may no matter what might happen.

comedy ['kɑm ə di] **1.** *n.* a funny play or movie; the opposite of a tragedy. **2.** *n.* the element of movies or plays that makes people laugh; the opposite of tragedy. (No plural.)

comfort ['kʌm fɚt] *n.* the quality of relief, ease, satisfaction.
→ COLD COMFORT

comfortable [ˈkʌm fɚ tə bəl] *adj.*
giving comfort, ease, or rest.
→ (AS) COMFORTABLE AS AN OLD SHOE

comic [ˈkɑm ɪk] **1.** *adj.* funny;
humorous. (Adv: *comically* [...ɪk
li].) **2.** *n.* a pamphlet printed in
color on cheap paper where stories
are told in COMIC STRIPS. (From
comic book.) **3.** *n.* someone who
tells jokes and funny stories.

comic strip [ˈkɑm ɪk strɪp] *n.* a
series of several cartoons printed
in a row; a cartoon series that
appears daily or weekly, usually in
newspapers.

comics *n.* the newspaper pages containing cartoons and COMIC STRIPS.
(Treated as plural.)

command [kə ˈmænd] **1.** *n.* an
order; a statement that tells someone what to do; a direction; an
instruction. **2.** *tv.* to give an order
to someone. **3.** *tv.* to control someone or something. **4.** *tv.* [for
someone or someone's character]
to deserve and receive respect and
attention.

comment [ˈkɑm ɛnt] **1.** *n.* a remark
about something; a statement
about something. **2.** *tv.* to state an
opinion; to make a remark. (The
object is a clause with THAT (7).)

comment on something to make a
statement about something; to
remark about something.

commit [kə ˈmɪt] **1.** *tv.* to do a
crime; to do something illegal. **2.**
tv. to place someone [in a mental
institution].

commit oneself **to** something to
pledge oneself to do something.

commit someone **to** something to
place someone under the control
or authority of a hospital, institution, or prison.

committee [kə ˈmɪt i] *n.* a group of
people who meet to perform a
specific duty, usually as part of a
larger organization.

common [ˈkɑm ən] **1.** *adj.* usual;
typical; frequently encountered;
widespread. (Adv: *commonly*.
Comp: *commoner*; sup: *common-
est*.) **2.** *adj.* shared or used by two
or more people. (Adv: *commonly*.)
3. *adj.* without distinction; ordinary. (Adv: *commonly*. Comp:
commoner; sup: *commonest*.)

common sense [ˈkɑm ən ˈsɛns] *n.*
basic reasonable and practical
thinking. (No plural.)

communication [kə mjun ɪ ˈke
ʃən] **1.** *n.* sending and receiving
information. (No plural.) **2.** *n.* an
announcement or statement in
written or spoken form.

communications *n.* the means or
media for communication.

community [kə ˈmjun ə ti] **1.** *n.* an
area or region where people live
and communicate with each other;
a neighborhood or town. **2.** *n.* a
group of people who have a common interest, occupation, or
background. **3.** the *adj.* use of (1)
or (2).

companion [kəm ˈpæn jən] **1.** *n.*
someone with whom time is spent.
2. *n.* something that matches
something else; something that is
part of a set.

company [ˈkʌm pə ni] **1.** *n.* a business organization; a business. **2.** *n.*

guests; visitors. (No plural. Treated as singular.)
→ TWO'S COMPANY(, THREE'S A CROWD).

comparative [kəm 'pɛr ə tɪv] **1.** *adj.* of or about studies based on comparison. (Adv: *comparatively.*) **2.** *adj.* of or about a form of an adverb or adjective that typically has an *-er* suffix or is a combination of the adverb or adjective and the word *more.* (Some adverbs and adjectives have irregular COMPARATIVES ④, however.) **3.** *adj.* as compared with others. (Adv: *comparatively.*) **4.** *n.* a form of an adjective or adverb as described in ②. (Abbreviated *comp.* here.)

compare [kəm 'pɛr] *tv.* to determine or show how two things are the same or different.

compare someone or something **to** someone or something to point out the similarities between a person or thing and another person or thing.

compare someone or something **with** someone or something to determine or show how a person or thing resembles, or differs from, another person or thing.

comparison [kəm 'pɛr ə sən] *n.* showing how things are the same or different. (Plural only for types and instances.)

compass ['kʌm pəs] **1.** *n.* a device that points to the north and indicates direction for the purposes of travel or finding out where one is located. **2.** *n.* a simple device used to draw circles or parts of circles.

compete [kəm 'pit] *iv.* to participate in a game, contest, or rivalry, with the hope of winning; to take part in a game or contest.

competition [kʌm pɪ 'tɪ ʃən] **1.** *n.* a contest. **2.** *n.* the state that exists between rivals. (No plural.) **3.** *n.* a rival or a group of rivals. (No plural.)

competitive [kəm 'pɛt ɪ tɪv] **1.** *adj.* eager to compete; aggressive in competition. (Adv: *competitively.*) **2.** *adj.* low in price; [of a low price] able to compete. (Adv: *competitively.*) **3.** *adj.* involving competition. (Adv: *competitively.*)

complain [kəm 'plen] *iv.* to say that one is unhappy, angry, or annoyed.

complaint [kəm 'plent] **1.** *n.* a statement expressing annoyance or anger about something. **2.** *n.* a statement that a crime has been committed. **3.** *n.* a sickness; an illness.

complete [kəm 'plit] **1.** *adj.* entire; whole; with all the necessary parts. (Adv: *completely.*) **2.** *tv.* to finish something; to end something; to do something until it is done. **3.** *tv.* to make something whole; to fill in all the parts of something.

complex 1. ['kɑm plɛks] *n.* a set of related buildings. **2.** ['kɑm plɛks] *n.* a psychological condition. **3.** [kəm 'plɛks, 'kɑm plɛks] *adj.* difficult; complicated; hard to understand. (Adv: *complexly.*)

compliment ['kɑm plɪ mənt] *n.* a statement of praise.
→ FISH FOR A COMPLIMENT

composition [kɑm pə 'zɪ ʃən] **1.** *n.* the process of putting things together to form one whole thing. (No plural.) **2.** *n.* the arrangement of the parts of something. (No plural.) **3.** *n.* a piece of music, a symphony; a piece of writing, such as an essay or a poem. **4.** *n.* the process of writing a piece of music or an essay, narrative, research paper, etc. (No plural.) **5.** *n.* the things that make up something; the ingredients of something; the parts of something. (No plural.)

comprehend [kɑm prɪ 'hend] *tv.* to understand something.

compromise ['kɑm prə maɪz] **1.** *n.* an agreement to settle an argument where both sides yield a little. **2.** *iv.* to come to an agreement by which both sides yield a little. **3.** *tv.* to endanger someone's reputation, position, or morals.
→ REACH A COMPROMISE

computer [kəm 'pjut ɚ] **1.** *n.* an electronic machine that processes data at high speeds. **2.** the *adj.* use of ①.

computer file [kəm 'pjut ɚ 'faɪl] *n.* a unit of data or information in digital form, stored on a floppy disk or hard drive.

comrade ['kɑm ræd] *n.* a friend; a companion.

con someone **out of something** to trick someone out of money or something of value.

conceal [kən 'sil] *tv.* to hide someone or something.

concept ['kɑn sept] *n.* a thought; an idea; a notion.

concern [kən 'sɚn] **1.** *tv.* to matter to someone; to be important to someone; to worry someone. **2.** *tv.* to be about something; to have to do with something; to deal with something. **3.** *n.* a matter of interest; a matter of importance; something that is of interest. **4.** *n.* care; worry; anxiety. (Plural only for types and instances.)

concert ['kɑn sɚt] **1.** *n.* a musical performance by one or more musicians. **2.** the *adj.* use of ①.

conclude [kən 'klud] **1.** *tv.* to finish something; to come to the end of something. **2.** *tv.* to reach an opinion by thinking about something. (The object is a clause with THAT ⑦.) **3.** *iv.* [for a process or activity] to finish or end.

conclusion [kən 'klu ʒən] **1.** *n.* the end of something. **2.** *n.* the final decision reached by thinking about something.
→ a FOREGONE CONCLUSION
→ JUMP TO CONCLUSIONS

concrete 1. ['kɑn krit] *n.* a stone-like material made from cement, sand, gravel, and water, used in construction and paving. (No plural.) **2.** ['kɑn krit] *adj.* made from ①. **3.** [kɑn 'krit] *adj.* actual; existing; real; definite; not abstract. (Adv: *concretely.*)

condition [kən 'dɪ ʃən] **1.** *n.* a state of being; a situation that someone or something is in. (No plural.) **2. conditions** *n.* a group of related states or situations, as with the weather or the state of the economy. **3.** *n.* the state of someone's health. (No plural.) **4.** *n.* something that is necessary before

something else can happen. **5.** *tv.* to shape someone's or something's behavior; to train someone or something. **6.** *tv.* to cause someone to become more physically fit.
→ IN GOOD CONDITION
→ IN MINT CONDITION
→ IN THE PINK (OF CONDITION)

conduct 1. ['kan dəkt] *n.* behavior; the way someone behaves. (No plural.) **2.** [kən 'dʌkt] *tv.* to lead someone or something; to guide someone or something. **3.** [kən 'dʌkt] *tv.* to behave [oneself] in a particular manner. (Takes a reflexive object.) **4.** [kən 'dʌkt] *tv.* to provide a path for electricity or heat to travel.

conductor [kən 'dʌk tɚ] **1.** *n.* someone who directs an orchestra, band, choir, or other musical group. **2.** *n.* someone who checks tickets and collects fares on a train. **3.** *n.* a substance electricity or heat can travel through.

cone ['kon] **1.** *n.* a solid form that changes from a circle at one end to a point at the other end. **2.** *n.* a crisp, thin, ①-shaped pastry, used for holding ice cream. **3.** *n.* the seed-bearing fruit of a pine tree.

conference ['kan frəns] *n.* a meeting to discuss a specific topic.

confess [kən 'fɛs] *tv.* to admit something; to state that one has done something wrong. (The object can be a clause with THAT ⑦.)

confess to something to admit doing something; to state that one has done something wrong.

confession [kən 'fɛ ʃən] *n.* the process or activity of confessing or admitting something. (Plural only for types and instances.)

confidence ['kan fɪ dəns] **1.** *n.* a strong trust in someone or something; a strong belief in someone or something. (No plural.) **2.** *n.* a feeling of assurance; a belief in oneself and one's abilities. (No plural.)
→ a VOTE OF CONFIDENCE

confidential [kan fɪ 'dɛn ʃəl] **1.** *adj.* secret; kept as secret. (Adv: *confidentially*.) **2.** *adj.* [of someone] trusted with secrets.

confine [kən 'faɪn] **1.** *tv.* to keep someone or a creature in a small space; to enclose someone or some creature in a small space. **2.** *tv.* to restrict or limit conversation or statements to a particular subject.

confirm [kən 'fɚm] **1.** *tv.* to check something to make certain it is true, accurate, complete, or still in effect. (The object can be a clause with THAT ⑦.) **2.** *tv.* to approve and agree that someone should be officially chosen for office. (The object can be a clause with THAT ⑦.)

confirmed [kən 'fɚmd] **1.** *adj.* shown to be true, accurate, complete, or still in effect. **2.** *adj.* determined to remain in a particular state.

conflict 1. ['kan flɪkt] *n.* disagreement; fighting. (Plural only for types and instances.) **2.** [kən 'flɪkt] *iv.* [for things] to differ or disagree.

confuse [kən 'fjuz] *tv.* to puzzle someone; to make someone wonder about something.

confuse someone or something **with** someone or something to mistake someone or something for someone or something else.

confusion [kən'fju ʒən] **1.** *n.* a feeling of being confused or puzzled. (No plural.) **2.** *n.* a noisy lack of order. (No plural.)

congratulate [kən'grætʃ ə let] *tv.* to extend one's good wishes to someone.

congregation [kaŋ grə 'ge ʃən] *n.* a group of people, especially in a church service.

congress ['kaŋ grəs] **1.** *n.* the group of people elected to make laws. **2.** *n.* a meeting of representatives to or members of an organization. **3.** *n.* the House of Representatives and the Senate of the United States. (Capitalized. No plural.)

conj. an abbreviation of CONJUNC-TION.

conjugate ['kan dʒə get] *tv.* to tell the forms of a verb in a language.

conjunction [kən 'dʒʌŋk ʃən] *n.* a part of speech that connects words, phrases, and clauses. (Abbreviated *conj.* here.)

connect [kə 'nɛkt] **1.** *tv.* to serve as a link between two things. **2.** *tv.* to join or attach certain electronic devices. **3.** *tv.* to link someone to someone or something through an electronic means. **4.** *tv.* to relate something to something else; to associate one thought with another. **5.** *iv.* to link with something; to link to something.

connect (up) to something to attach to something; to attach something to some electrical device.

connection [kə 'nɛk ʃən] **1.** *n.* the physical link among or between things. **2.** *n.* the relationship among or between thoughts. **3.** *n.* the electronic link that connects two people by telephone. **4.** *n.* an airplane flight that one boards at an intermediate stop. **5.** *n.* someone who is a social or business contact.

conquer ['kaŋ kɚ] **1.** *tv.* to defeat someone in war; to subdue a people, army, or land. **2.** *tv.* to overcome a difficulty.

conquest ['kaŋ kwɛst] **1.** *n.* the attempt to subdue, defeat, or conquer a people or a country. (Plural only for types and instances.) **2.** *n.* the object or target of ①. (Figurative on ①.) **3.** *n.* someone who is the target of a romantic or sexual quest.

conscious ['kan ʃəs] **1.** *adj.* awake, alert, and aware of immediate surroundings. (Adv: *consciously.*) **2.** *adj.* intentional; intended. (Adv: *consciously.*)

conscious of something aware of or knowledgeable about something.

consent [kən 'sɛnt] *n.* permission; approval. (No plural.)

consent (to (do) something) to agree to something; to permit something.

conservation [kan sɚ 've ʃən] *n.* the practice of conserving, protecting, or preserving something, such as water, the state of the land, or other resources. (No plural.)

consider [kən 'sɪd ɚ] **1.** *tv.* to think carefully about something. (The object can be a clause with THAT ⑦.) **2.** *tv.* to think of someone or something in a certain way. (The object can be a clause with THAT ⑦.) **3.** *tv.* to take something into account. (The object can be a clause with THAT ⑦.)

consignment [kən 'saɪn mənt] *n.* a shipment of goods.
→ ON CONSIGNMENT

consist of something [kən 'sɪst...] to be made of something.

consonant ['kɑn sə nənt] **1.** *n.* a speech sound that is made by restricting the flow of sound or air in the vocal tract; a speech sound that is not a vowel. (The word has different meanings depending on whether one is talking about sounds or spelling letters. These are the IPA symbols for the American English consonants: p, t, k, b, d, g, f, h, s, m, n, ŋ, v, z, ʒ, ʃ, θ, ð, l, r, w, j.) **2.** *n.* a letter of an alphabet that represents ①. (These are the individual letters that represent American English consonants: p, t, k, b, d, g, f, h, s, m, n, v, z, i, r, w, j, y, c, q, x.)

conspicuous by one's **absence** to have one's absence (from an event) noticed.

constant ['kɑn stənt] **1.** *adj.* continuous; continuing without stopping. (Adv: *constantly.*) **2.** *adj.* loyal; faithful; unchanging. (Adv: *constantly.*) **3.** *n.* a figure, quality, or measurement that stays the same.

constellation [kɑn stə 'le ʃən] *n.* a particular group of stars.

constrict [kən 'strɪkt] *tv.* to tighten something; to make something narrower; to make something contract.

construct 1. [kən 'strʌkt] *tv.* to build something; to put something together. **2.** ['kɑn strʌkt] *n.* a theory; a made-up idea.

construction [kən 'strʌk ʃən] **1.** *n.* the process of building. (No plural.) **2.** *n.* the business of building buildings; the business of constructing buildings. (No plural.)
→ UNDER CONSTRUCTION

consult [kən 'sʌlt] **1.** *tv.* to seek advice or information from someone or something. **2.** *iv.* to offer and supply technical business advice as a profession.

consult with someone to discuss something with someone, seeking advice.

consultant [kən 'sʌl tənt] *n.* someone who consults; someone who is hired by a company to give advice.

consume [kən 'sum] **1.** *tv.* to eat or drink something. **2.** *tv.* to use something; to use all of something.

consumer [kən 'su mɚ] *n.* someone who buys a product or a service.

consummate 1. ['kɑn sə mət] *adj.* perfect; total and ideal. (Adv: *consummately.*) **2.** ['kɑn sə met] *tv.* to fulfill something; to complete something; to make something complete.

cont. an abbreviation of CONTRACTION ③.

contact ['kɑn tækt] **1.** *tv.* to communicate with someone; to get in touch with someone. **2.** *tv.* to touch someone or something. **3.** *n.* touching; coming together. (No plural.) **4.** *n.* a person inside an organization through whom one can get needed information or favors. **5.** *n.* a metal part that touches another metal part, closing an electrical circuit.

contagious [kən 'te dʒəs] *adj.* [of a disease] easily passed from person to person. (Adv: *contagiously.*)

contain [kən 'ten] **1.** *tv.* to hold someone or something; to have, hold, or include someone or something as a part of a larger thing. **2.** *tv.* to hold back something; to restrain something; to keep something under control.

container [kən 'te nɚ] *n.* something that contains something.

contamination [kən tæm ə 'ne ʃən] **1.** *n.* making something impure; polluting something. (No plural.) **2.** *n.* a substance that causes ①. (No plural.)

contemplation [kɑn təm 'ple ʃən] *n.* serious thought. (No plural.)

contempt [kən 'tempt] *n.* hatred; loathing. (No plural.)
→ IN CONTEMPT (OF COURT)

content 1. [kən 'tɛnt] *adj.* satisfied; pleased. (Adv: *contently.*) **2.** ['kɑn tɛnt] *n.* something that is contained within something, such as the text of a book or the ingredients of food. (No plural.)
→ ONE'S HEART'S CONTENT

contention [kən 'tɛn ʃən] **1.** *n.* a claim. **2.** *n.* struggling together; competition. (No plural form.)
→ a BONE OF CONTENTION

contents *n.* the ingredients that make up something; everything that is contained within something. (Treated as plural. Sometimes singular.)
→ TABLE OF CONTENTS

contest 1. ['kɑn tɛst] *n.* a competition that will determine a winner. **2.** [kən 'tɛst] *tv.* to challenge something, especially in a court of law.

contestant [kən 'tɛs tənt] *n.* someone who competes in a contest; a competitor.

context ['kɑn tɛkst] *n.* the words before and after another word that help determine its meaning.
→ IN THE CONTEXT OF SOMETHING

continent ['kɑn tə nənt] *n.* one of the large landmasses of earth: Africa, Australia, North America, South America, Antarctica, Europe, and Asia.

continental [kɑn tə 'nɛn təl] **1.** *adj.* of or about a continent; contained within a continent. (Adv: *continentally.*) **2.** *adj.* of or about the continent of Europe and the cultures and people found there. (England is sometimes included.)

continual [kən 'tɪn ju əl] *adj.* happening again and again; repeated; over and over. (Compare this with CONTINUOUS. Adv: *continually.*)

continue [kən 'tɪn ju] **1.** *tv.* to make something keep on happening. (Takes a gerund as an object.) **2.** *tv.* to resume something after an interruption. **3.** *tv.* to postpone a trial until a later time. **4.** *iv.* to go on happening; to remain the same way. **5.** *iv.* to resume after being stopped.

continue to do something to do something again and again.

continuous [kən 'tɪn ju əs] *adj.* without stopping; without an interruption; ongoing. (See also CONTINUAL. Adv: *continuously*.)

contract 1. ['kɑn trækt] *n.* a legal document that describes an agreement between two or more people or companies. **2.** [kən 'trækt] *tv.* to hire someone under a contract for a specific project. **3.** [kən 'trækt] *tv.* to catch a disease. **4.** [kən 'trækt] *iv.* to enter into an agreement with someone; to agree to do something by contract. **5.** [kən 'trækt] *iv.* to shrink; to shorten; to come together; to become narrow.

contract something **out** to make an agreement with someone to do a specific amount of work.

contraction [kən 'træk ʃən] **1.** *n.* an amount of shrinking. (Plural only for types and instances.) **2.** *n.* the tensing of a muscle, especially of the uterus during childbirth. **3.** *n.* a shortened word, made by replacing a letter or letters with an apostrophe ('); the shortening of one or more spoken words by removing a sound or sounds. (Abbreviated CONT. here.)

contradiction [kɑn trə 'dɪk ʃən] *n.* a statement that is the opposite of something that has been said.
→ a CONTRADICTION IN TERMS

a **contradiction in terms** a phrase or statement containing a contradiction.

contrary 1. ['kɑn trer i] *adj.* completely opposite; opposed. (Adv: *contrarily* [kɑn 'trer ə li].) **2.** [kɑn 'trer i, 'kɑn trer i] *adj.* stubborn; refusing to do what is wanted. (Adv: *contrarily* [kɑn 'trer ə li].)
→ ON THE CONTRARY

contrary to something in spite of something; regardless of something.

contrast 1. ['kɑn træst] *n.* a noticeable difference; an obvious difference. **2.** ['kɑn træst] *n.* noticeable differences between the light and dark parts of an image. (No plural.) **3.** [kən 'træst] *tv.* to compare the differences found in two or more things. **4.** [kən 'træst] *iv.* to be noticeably different.

control [kən 'trol] **1.** *n.* authority; the power to direct someone or something. **2.** *n.* a lever or other device used to operate machinery or something like a radio or television set. (Often plural.) **3.** *tv.* to have power over something; to have authority over something; to direct someone or something; to rule someone or something. **4.** *tv.* to exercise the power to restrain, regulate, steer, guide, or command someone or something.

control the purse strings to be in charge of the money in a business or a household.

convenient [kən 'vin jənt] **1.** *adj.* suitable. (Adv: *conveniently*.) **2.** *adj.* available; within reach. (Adv: *conveniently*.)

convention [kən 'ven ʃən] **1.** *n.* a large meeting; a group of people gathered together for a specific purpose. **2.** *n.* a formal agreement between countries. **3.** *n.* the way things are typically done; the way things are expected to be done.

conventional [kən 'vɛn ʃə nəl] *adj.* usual and typical; basic and standard. (Adv: *conventionally.*)

conversation [kɑn və 'se ʃən] *n.* discussion; talk between people. (Plural only for types and instances.)
→ OPEN A CONVERSATION

convey [kən 've] **1.** *tv.* to take someone or something from one place to another. **2.** *tv.* to express something; to communicate something. (Figurative on ①.)

convince [kən 'vɪns] *tv.* to persuade someone about something; to persuade someone that something is true.

convincing [kən 'vɪn sɪŋ] **1.** *adj.* acting to persuade someone of something. (Adv: *convincingly.*) **2.** *adj.* realistic; like the real thing. (Adv: *convincingly.*)

convulsion [kən 'vʌl ʃən] *n.* an uncontrollable, violent jerking of muscles.

cook ['kʊk] **1.** *n.* someone who prepares food to be eaten. **2.** *tv.* to prepare food for eating by heating it. **3.** *iv.* to prepare food; to work as ①.

cook someone's **goose** to damage or ruin someone; to do something that cannot be undone.

cook (something**) out** to cook food out of doors.

cook something **to perfection** to cook something perfectly.

cook something **up (with** someone**)** to arrange or plan to do something with someone.

cook the accounts to cheat in bookkeeping; to make the accounts appear to balance when they do not.

cookbook ['kʊk bʊk] *n.* a book that gives detailed instructions on how to prepare different kinds of food; a book of recipes.

cookie ['kʊk i] *n.* a small, hard, sweet cake made of flour, sugar, eggs, and other ingredients.

cool ['kul] **1.** *adj.* between warm and cold; somewhat cold but not very cold. (Adv: *coolly.* Comp: *cooler;* sup: *coolest.*) **2.** *adj.* calm, not excited; relaxed. (Informal. Adv: *coolly.* Comp: *cooler;* sup: *coolest.*) **3.** *adj.* less than friendly; unfriendly; reserved. (Adv: *coolly.* Comp: *cooler;* sup: *coolest.*) **4.** *adj.* admirable; very good. (Informal. Comp: *cooler;* sup: *coolest.*) **5.** *tv.* to make something less warm. **6.** *iv.* to become less warm.
→ (AS) COOL AS A CUCUMBER

cool down AND **cool off 1.** to become cooler. **2.** [for someone] to become less angry.

cool off Go to COOL DOWN.

cool one's **heels** to wait (for someone).

cool someone **down** AND **cool** someone **off** to make someone less angry.

cool someone **off** Go to COOL SOMEONE DOWN.

cool someone or something **down** AND **cool** someone or something **off** to make someone or something less hot.

cool someone or something **off** Go to COOL SOMEONE OR SOMETHING DOWN.

115

cooperate [ko 'ap ə ret] *iv.* to work together with someone to get something done; to unite in order to get something done more easily.

cop ['kap] *n.* a police officer. (Informal.)

copier ['kap i ɚ] *n.* a machine that makes copies of documents.

copper ['kap ɚ] *n.* a soft, reddish-tan metallic element. (No plural.)

copulate ['kap jə let] *iv.* [for two creatures] to join together sexually, usually in order to breed.

copulation [kap jə 'le ʃən] *n.* sexual intercourse; joining together sexually. (Plural only for types and instances.)

copy ['kap i] **1.** *n.* one item made to look like or work like another item; a duplicate; a replica. **2.** *n.* a single issue of a newspaper, book, or magazine. **3.** *n.* written material that is ready to be edited or rewritten. (No plural.) **4.** *tv.* to make a duplicate of something. **5.** *tv.* to imitate someone's actions. **6.** *tv.* to reproduce written material by writing it by hand. **7.** *tv.* to cheat on a test by writing the answers from someone else's paper.
→ CARBON COPY

copyright ['kap i raɪt] **1.** *n.* the legal right to produce, publish, or sell a book, play, song, movie, or other work of music or literature. **2.** *tv.* to protect one's exclusive right to publish a work of music or literature by registering one's ownership with the government copyright office.

cord ['kord] **1.** *n.* a thick string; a thin rope. (Plural only for types and instances.) **2.** *n.* a wire with a protective covering, especially those that connect an electrical appliance to an electrical outlet. (The same as EXTENSION CORD.)

cordless ['kord ləs] *adj.* not having or needing an electrical power cord; operated by battery. (Adv: *cordlessly*.)

core ['kor] **1.** *n.* the center of something; the heart of something; the important part. **2.** *n.* the hard part of the inside of a fruit, especially of an apple or a pear. **3.** *tv.* to cut ② from a piece of fruit.

cork ['kork] **1.** *n.* the light, soft bark of the cork oak tree, used in many products. (Plural only for types and instances.) **2.** *n.* the piece of shaped ① that fits in the neck of a bottle. **3.** *adj.* made of ①. **4.** *tv.* to seal a bottle by putting ② into the neck of the bottle.

corn ['korn] **1.** *n.* a tall cereal plant producing large grains on corncobs, sometimes called *maize*. (No plural. Number is expressed with *corn stalk(s)*.) **2.** *n.* the soft and tender young grains of corn eaten by humans as a vegetable. (No plural. Number is expressed with *kernel(s) of corn* for the individual grains. *Ear(s) of corn* refers to grains of ① still attached to the CORNCOB they grow on.) **3.** *n.* hard grains of ①, eaten by livestock or processed into other foods. (No plural. Number is expressed with *ear(s) of corn* or *kernel(s) of corn* as in ②.) **4.** *n.* a hard, painful patch of skin on the foot or toe. **5.** *adj.* made from ③; having ③ as an ingredient.

corncob ['korn kɑb] *n.* the cylinder of fiber that corn grows on.

corner ['kor nɚ] **1.** *n.* the point where two lines meet; the line formed where two surfaces meet. **2.** *n.* the space where two walls meet. **3.** *n.* one of the four squared areas nearest to the intersection of two streets. **4.** *tv.* to trap someone or some creature in a place or situation from which it is difficult or impossible to escape.
→ OUT OF THE CORNER OF ONE'S EYE

cornfield ['korn fild] *n.* a field where corn is grown; a field of corn plants.

cornflakes ['korn fleks] *n.* a breakfast cereal of toasted flakes of corn. (Treated as singular or plural.)

corporation [kor pə 're ʃən] *n.* a business, firm, or company.

corpse ['korps] *n.* a dead body.

corral [kə 'ræl] **1.** *n.* a fenced area where horses and cattle are kept. **2.** *tv.* to put livestock into ①.

correct [kə 'rɛkt] **1.** *adj.* right; without error; true. (Adv: *correctly.*) **2.** *adj.* proper; acceptable. (Adv: *correctly.*) **3.** *tv.* to mark answers on a test as right or wrong; to point out the mistakes. **4.** *tv.* to fix a mistake; to change a wrong answer to the right answer; to make something right.
→ STAND CORRECTED

correction [kə 'rɛkt ʃən] *n.* a change that is made when something wrong is replaced with something right.

correspond (to something) [kor ə 'spɑnd...] to match (with some-

thing else); to follow the pattern (of something).

correspond (with someone) [kor ə 'spɑnd...] to exchange letters (with someone).

corrupt [kə 'rʌpt] **1.** *adj.* not honest; [of politicians] easily influenced by the payment of money. (Adv: *corruptly.*) **2.** *tv.* to make someone become bad; to make a good person become bad; to make a moral person become immoral. **3.** *tv.* to ruin something in the execution of a process.

cost ['kɔst] **1.** *n.* the price of something; the amount of money that one must pay to buy something. (Plural only for types and instances.) **2.** *n.* a sacrifice; the loss of something in order to achieve something. **3.** *tv., irreg.* to require a specific amount of money for purchase. (Past tense and past participle: *cost.*) **4.** *tv., irreg.* to cause the loss of something; to sacrifice something. **5.** *tv., irreg.* to require the expenditure of time, work, or energy.

cost a pretty penny to cost a lot of money.

cost an arm and a leg to cost too much.

costly ['kɔst li] **1.** *adj.* costing a lot of money; expensive. (Comp: *costlier;* sup: *costliest.*) **2.** *adj.* serious; troublesome; unfortunate. (Comp: *costlier;* sup: *costliest.*)

costume ['kɑs tum] *n.* clothes that are worn when someone is pretending to be someone else or from another time or place; clothes that represent another culture, time period, or person, as used in the theater.

cot ['kɑt] *n.* a narrow bed made of a piece of canvas stretched over a frame, used especially for camping.

cottage ['kɑt ɪdʒ] *n.* a small house, especially a small home in the country; a vacation house.

cotton ['kɑt n] **1.** *n.* a soft white fiber used to make yarn, thread, and fabric. (No plural. Number is expressed with *bale(s) of cotton.*) **2.** *n.* cloth woven of ①. (Plural only for types and instances.) **3.** *n.* the plant that produces ①. (Plural only for types and instances.) **4.** *adj.* made out of ① or ②.

couch ['kɑʊtʃ] *n.* a long piece of furniture that two or more people can sit on or that someone can lie down on; a sofa.

cougar ['ku gɚ] *n.* a large, tan, wild cat; a mountain lion.

cough ['kɔf] **1.** *n.* the act or sound of forcing air from the lungs quickly and with force, making a dry, rough noise through the throat. **2.** *iv.* to force air out of the lungs as in ①.

cough drop ['kɔf drɑp] *n.* a piece of medicated material—often like candy—that is held in the mouth to soothe a sore throat and prevent coughing.

could ['kʊd] **1.** *aux.* the past form of CAN ①, expressing ability. **2.** *aux.* the past form of CAN ②, expressing permission. **3.** *aux.* a form of CAN ②, used in making polite requests. **4.** *aux.* a form of

CAN ①, expressing possibility or an explanation.

couldn't ['kʊd nt] **1.** *cont.* could not; was not able [to do something]. **2.** *cont.* could not?; wouldn't you please?

could've ['kʊd əv] *cont.* could have. (Where HAVE is an auxiliary.)

council ['kɑʊn səl] *n.* a group of people who are appointed or elected to make laws for a city, school, church, or other organization. (Compare this with COUNSEL.)

counsel ['kɑʊn səl] **1.** *tv.* to advise someone; to give someone advice. (Compare this with COUNCIL.) **2.** *n.* advice; a piece of advice. (No plural.)

counselor ['kɑʊn sə lɚ] **1.** *n.* someone who advises people; someone who gives advice. **2.** *n.* someone who is in charge of children at a camp. **3.** *n.* a lawyer. (Also a term of address for a lawyer.)

count ['kɑʊnt] **1.** *n.* the total of people or things obtained after one has figured out how many there are. **2.** *tv.* to figure out how many; to determine how many.
→ EVERY MINUTE COUNTS
→ EVERY MOMENT COUNTS
→ STAND UP AND BE COUNTED

count down to count backwards to an event that will start when zero is reached.

count heads Go to COUNT NOSES.

count noses AND **count heads** to count people.

count off [for a series of people, one by one] to say aloud the next number in a fixed sequence.

count on someone or something to rely on someone or something; to depend on someone or something.

count one's **chickens before they hatch** to plan how to utilize the benefits of something before those benefits are available. (Frequently used in the negative.)

count someone or something **off** to count people or things, to see if they are all there.

count someone **out (for** something) to exclude someone from something.

count something **in** to include something in a count of something.

count something **out** to give out things, counting them, one by one.

count (up)on someone or something to rely on someone or something.

countable ['kaʊnt ə bəl] *adj.* able to be counted or enumerated; subject to being counted.

counter ['kaʊn tɚ] **1.** *n.* a flat surface at which customers sit or stand to be served in a fast-food store, bank, or other establishment. **2.** *n.* [in a kitchen] a flat surface where food is prepared. **3.** *n.* a device that is used to count objects or people; a device that keeps track of the number of objects or people.
→ UNDER THE COUNTER

counterfeit ['kaʊn tɚ fɪt] **1.** *adj.* fake; imitation; not genuine. **2.** *n.* an illegal copy; a fake. **3.** *tv.* to make an illegal copy of something, especially money.

country ['kʌn tri] **1.** *n.* a nation, including its land and its people; a political subdivision. **2.** *n.* land without many people or buildings; the opposite of *city*. (No plural.) **3.** the *adj.* use of ① or ②.

county ['kaʊn ti] *n.* a political division of most U.S. states.

couple ['kʌp əl] *n.* two people, usually male and female who share a romantic interest. (Treated as singular when referring to a unit and plural when referring to the individuals.)

a **couple of** people or things two; two or three; a few; some; not many. (COUPLE is treated as plural, but not countable.)

couple up (with someone) [for one person] to join another person.

coupon ['ku pan, 'kju pan] *n.* a printed form that offers a discount for a product or service.

courage ['kɚ ɪdʒ] *n.* bravery; a lack of fear. (No plural.)
→ DUTCH COURAGE
→ MUSTER (UP) ONE'S COURAGE
→ PLUCK UP SOMEONE'S COURAGE
→ SCREW UP ONE'S COURAGE

courageous [kə 're dʒəs] *adj.* fearless; facing danger in spite of fear. (Adv: *courageously*.)

courier ['kɚ i ɚ] *n.* a messenger; someone who transports documents or other valuable items.

course ['kors] **1.** *n.* the pathway or route of someone or something. **2.** *n.* a sequence of actions. **3.** *n.* a class offered by a school or an instructor. **4.** *n.* one of the parts of a meal in which parts are served

separately. **5.** *iv.* [for water] to flow in a river; [for tears] to run down one's face.
→ TAKE A COURSE (IN SOMETHING)

a **course of action** the procedures or sequence of actions that someone will follow to accomplish a goal.

court ['kort] **1.** *n.* the place where legal matters are decided and the people who are present there, such as a judge and other officials. (Plural only for types and instances.) **2.** *n.* the space where certain games such as basketball and tennis are played.
→ IN CONTEMPT (OF COURT)
→ LAUGH SOMETHING OUT OF COURT
→ SETTLE (SOMETHING) (OUT OF COURT)
→ THROW ONESELF AT THE MERCY OF THE COURT
→ THROW ONESELF ON THE MERCY OF THE COURT

the **court** *n.* the judge, often speaking for the entire COURT ①. (No plural. Treated as singular.)

courteous ['kɚ ti əs] *adj.* showing courtesy; polite; well mannered. (Adv: *courteously.*)

courtesy ['kɚ tɪs i] **1.** *n.* a state of being polite and showing good manners. (No plural.) **2.** *n.* an act of kindness; a favor; a thoughtful act.

courthouse ['kort haʊs] **1.** *n.,* *irreg.* a building containing the rooms where court is held. (Plural: [...haʊ zəz].) **2.** *n.* the building that houses the government offices—including the county court—of a particular county.

courtroom ['kort rum] *n.* a room where a session of court is held.

cousin ['kʌz ən] *n.* the child of one's aunt or uncle; the nephew or niece of one's parent.

cove ['kov] *n.* a small bay along the coast.

cover ['kʌv ɚ] **1.** *n.* the protective top—like a lid—for something. **2.** *n.* the front and back of a book or magazine. **3.** *n.* a blanket. **4.** *n.* something that is hiding a secret; a legal business that is operating as a disguise for an illegal business. **5.** *tv.* to place something on top of something else to protect or hide it; to spread something on top of something else to protect or hide it. **6.** *tv.* to coat the surface of something; to spread over something. **7.** *tv.* to amount to enough money to pay for something. **8.** *tv.* to include something; to discuss or reveal something. **9.** *tv.* to travel a certain distance. **10.** *tv.* to occupy a certain area; to extend over a certain area. **11.** *tv.* to shelter someone or something; to provide shelter for someone or something.

cover a lot of ground **1.** to travel over a great distance; to investigate a wide expanse of land. **2.** to deal with much information and many facts.

cover for someone **1.** to make excuses for someone; to conceal someone's errors. **2.** to handle someone else's work.

cover someone or something **up** to place something on someone or something for protection or concealment.

cover something **up** to conceal a wrongdoing; to conceal evidence.

cover (up) for someone to conceal someone's wrongdoing by lying or working in someone's place.

cow ['kaʊ] **1.** *n.* an adult female of a kind of very large animal that provides milk and is eaten for meat. **2.** *n.* the female of certain animals, including the elephant.
→ SACRED COW

coward ['kaʊ ə·d] *n.* someone who has no courage; someone who runs away from danger.

cowardice ['kaʊ ə· dɪs] *n.* lack of courage. (No plural.)

cowboy ['kaʊ bɔɪ] *n.* someone, usually a male, who works on a cattle ranch.

coworker ['ko wə· kə·] *n.* a fellow worker; someone with whom one works.

coyote [kaɪ 'ot (i)] *n.* an animal, similar to a large, skinny dog, that lives in western North America.

cozy ['ko zi] *adj.* snug; warm and comfortable. (Adv: *cozily.* Comp: *cozier;* sup: *coziest.*)

crab ['kræb] **1.** *n.* an edible sea creature with a hard shell, four pairs of legs, and one pair of claws. **2.** *n.* the meat of ① eaten as food. (No plural.) **3.** *n.* an unhappy person who complains a lot.

crabby ['kræb i] *adj.* unhappy and making complaints. (Adv: *crabbily.* Comp: *crabbier;* sup: *crabbiest.*)

crack ['kræk] **1.** *n.* the line that is made in something when it splits or breaks; a narrow opening in something or between two things. **2.** *n.* a short, sharp noise like the noise of a powerful slap. **3.** *n.* a remark that is intended to hurt or make someone feel bad. **4.** *tv.* to break something without separating it into pieces; to fracture something. **5.** *tv.* to strike someone; to hit someone somewhere. **6.** *iv.* [for something] to break without separating into pieces.
→ MAKE CRACKS (ABOUT SOMEONE OR SOMETHING)

crack a joke to tell a joke.

crack a smile to smile a little, perhaps reluctantly.

crack down (on someone or something**)** to put limits on someone or something; to become strict about enforcing rules about someone or something.

crack someone or something **up** to damage someone or something.

cracker ['kræk ə·] *n.* a flat, thin, square, unsweetened biscuit, often salted.

cradle ['kred l] **1.** *n.* a small, rocking bed for a baby or a doll. **2.** *n.* the place where something begins; the origin of something. **3.** *tv.* to hold a baby in one's arms while rocking it back and forth; to hold something carefully.
→ ROB THE CRADLE

craft ['kræft] **1.** *n.* a special skill for creating something; a special talent. **2.** *n., irreg.* a boat, especially a small one. (Plural: *craft.*) **3.** *tv.* to build or create something that requires skill or talent.

craftsman ['kræfts mən] *n., irreg.* someone who builds something by hand. (Plural: CRAFTSMEN.)

craftsmen ['kræfts mən] plural of CRAFTSMAN.

cram [ˈkræm] **1.** *tv.* to force someone or something into a small space. **2.** *tv.* to fill a space too full; to put too many people or things into a space.

cramp someone's **style** to limit someone in some way.

crane [ˈkren] **1.** *n.* a bird with long legs and a long neck—usually feeding on fish, frogs, etc. **2.** *n.* a large machine with a movable arm that lifts and moves very heavy things.

crank [ˈkræŋk] **1.** *n.* an arm or lever that transfers rotating motion to a shaft or axle. **2.** *tv.* to make something work by turning ①.

crash [ˈkræʃ] **1.** *n.* the loud sound of something hitting something else. **2.** *n.* a sudden economic disaster; a time when the stock market falls rapidly. **3.** *n.* a vehicle accident; a loud collision of vehicles. **4.** *tv.* to cause a loud collision of a vehicle and something else. **5.** *iv.* to make a sudden, loud noise. **6.** *iv.* [for a computer] to stop working.

crash into someone or something to bump or ram into someone or something.

crash through something to break through something.

crate [ˈkret] *n.* a rough wooden or plastic shipping box.

crate something **(up)** to pack something in a crate.

crave [ˈkrev] *tv.* to have a very strong desire for something; to want something very badly.

crawl [ˈkrɔl] **1.** *iv.* to move on one's hands and knees; to move forward

in a horizontal position. **2.** *iv.* [for something] to move very slowly. (Figurative on ①.)

crayon [ˈkre ɑn] *n.* a colored stick of wax, used for drawing on paper or making pictures.

crazy [ˈkrez i] **1.** *adj.* insane; mentally ill. (Adv: *crazily.* Comp: *crazier;* sup: *craziest.*) **2.** *adj.* stupid; foolish. (Adv: *crazily.* Comp: *crazier;* sup: *craziest.*) **3.** *adj.* wild; bizarre. (Adv: *crazily.* Comp: *crazier;* sup: *craziest.*)
→ GO CRAZY

cream [ˈkrim] **1.** *n.* the fatty part of cow's milk that rises to the top. (No plural.) **2.** *n.* a soft, thick substance used to benefit or carry medicine to the skin. **3.** *tv.* to mash something to a creamy texture.

cream cheese [ˈkrim tʃiz] *n.* a soft, thick, white cheese made from cream and milk. (No plural.)

cream of the crop the best of all.

creamy [ˈkrim i] *adj.* containing a lot of cream; as smooth as cream. (Adv: *creamily.* Comp: *creamier;* sup: *creamiest.*)

crease [ˈkris] **1.** *n.* a deep fold; a line made in something by folding it and pressing down along the fold. **2.** *tv.* to make a line in something, such as paper or fabric, by folding it and pressing down.

create [kri ˈet] **1.** *tv.* to bring something new into being; to invent something. **2.** *tv.* to cause something to happen; to bring about something.

creation [kri ˈe ʃən] **1.** *n.* bringing something new into being. (No

plural.) **2.** *n.* the process of bringing the universe into being. (No plural.) **3.** *n.* the universe; everything created by God. (No plural. Often capitalized.) **4.** *n.* something that is invented; something that is produced or made for the first time.
→ IN CREATION

creative [kri 'e tɪv] *adj.* able to think of new ideas or new ways to solve problems; able to develop works of art. (Adv: *creatively.*)

creature ['kri tʃɚ] *n.* a living animal; a living being.

credible ['krɛd ə bəl] *adj.* believable; worthy of belief; worthy of trust. (Adv: *credibly.*)

credit ['krɛd ɪt] **1.** *n.* an arrangement allowing a person to purchase goods or services now and pay later, or to borrow money now and pay it back later. (No plural.) **2.** *n.* the amount of money in an account; an account balance greater than zero. **3.** *n.* an amount of money that is added to an account. **4.** *n.* recognition given to someone for having done something. (No plural.) **5.** *n.* mention of someone's work on a book, movie, or performance appearing in a list of similar writers, artists, or technicians.
→ GIVE CREDIT WHERE CREDIT IS DUE
→ ON CREDIT

credit card ['krɛd ɪt 'kɑrd] *n.* a plastic card that allows someone to use CREDIT ① extended by a bank.

creek ['krik] *n.* a small, narrow river; a small stream.

creep ['krip] **1.** *iv., irreg.* to move slowly, with the body close to the ground. (Past tense and past participle: *creeped* or CREPT.) **2.** *iv., irreg.* to grow along a surface; to grow up a wall. **3.** *n.* a very slow movement. (No plural.)

creep by [for time] to pass slowly.

crept ['krɛpt] a past tense and past participle of CREEP.

crew ['kru] **1.** *n.* a group of people who work together, especially on a ship, a plane, at a theater, etc. **2.** *n.* the people on a team that competes in boat races.

crib ['krɪb] **1.** *n.* a baby's bed that has sides so the baby can't fall out. **2.** *n.* a storage shed for grain.

cricket ['krɪk ɪt] **1.** *n.* a small, long-legged insect, the male of which makes a chirping noise by rubbing his front wings together. **2.** *n.* an outdoor sport played in England with a (flat) bat and a ball. (No plural.)

crime ['kraɪm] *n.* the breaking of laws in general. (Plural only for types and instances.)

criminal ['krɪm ə nəl] *n.* someone who commits a crime; someone who breaks a law.

crises ['kraɪ siz] plural of CRISIS.

crisis ['kraɪ sɪs] *n., irreg.* a serious and threatening situation, the resolution of which will determine the future. (Plural: CRISES.)

crisp ['krɪsp] **1.** *adj.* easily broken; easily snapped into parts. (Adv: *crisply.* Comp: *crisper;* sup: *crispest.*) **2.** *adj.* fresh; firm. (Adv: *crisply.* Comp: *crisper;* sup: *crispest.*) **3.** *adj.* [of air] cool and refreshing. (Adv: *crisply.* Comp: *crisper;* sup: *crispest.*)

→ **BURN** SOMEONE OR SOMETHING **TO A CRISP**

critic ['krɪt ɪk] **1.** *n.* someone who writes evaluations of artistic works or performances. **2.** *n.* someone who finds fault with people or things.

criticism ['krɪt ə sɪz əm] **1.** *n.* the process of evaluating and presenting statements that analyze and make judgments about something or someone's performance. (No plural.) **2.** *n.* a critical remark or statement. (Usually negative unless specifically positive.)

criticize ['krɪt ə saɪz] **1.** *tv.* to find fault with someone or something. **2.** *iv.* to judge the good and bad points of something. (Usually negative unless specifically positive.)

croak ['krok] **1.** *n.* the noise that a frog makes. **2.** *iv.* to make the characteristic sound of a frog. **3.** *iv.* to make a noise like ①.

crocodile ['krɑk ə daɪl] **1.** *n.* a large, dangerous reptile with many teeth and a powerful tail. **2.** *adj.* made from the skin of ①.
→ **SHED CROCODILE TEARS**

crook ['krʊk] **1.** *n.* a criminal; a thief. **2.** *n.* a bent part of something; a hooked part of something. **3.** *tv.* to bend something; to make a bend or a hook in something. **4.** *iv.* to bend.

crooked ['krʊk əd] **1.** *adj.* bent; not straight; twisted. (Adv: *crookedly.*) **2.** *adj.* not honest; thieving; criminal. (Adv: *crookedly.*)

crop ['krɑp] **1.** *n.* a plant or food product grown and harvested by a farmer. **2.** *tv.* to cut or trim something.

→ **CREAM OF THE CROP**

crop out to appear on the surface; [for something] to reveal itself in the open; to begin to show above the surface.

crop up to appear without warning; to happen suddenly; [for something] to begin to reveal itself in the open.

cross ['krɔs] **1.** *n.* a sign or structure in a form similar to an X. **2.** *n.* a vertical post with a horizontal post attached to it near the top that people were hung on as a punishment in ancient times. **3.** *n.* the shape of the Christian symbol on which Jesus died. **4.** *n.* a combination or blend; a hybrid. **5.** *tv.* to move from one side of something to the other; to go across something. **6.** *tv.* to form an intersection with something else. **7.** *tv.* to anger someone; to upset someone. **8.** *tv.* to breed species or varieties of animals in such a way as to give yet a different creature. **9.** *iv.* to make an intersection; to form the shape of ②.
→ **BEAR** ONE'S **CROSS**
→ **CARRY** ONE'S **CROSS**
→ **CAUGHT IN THE CROSS FIRE**

cross a bridge before one **comes to it** to worry excessively about something before it happens.

cross a bridge when one **comes to it** to deal with a problem only when one is faced with the problem.

cross one's **heart (and hope to die)** to make a pledge or vow that the truth is being told.

cross someone or something **off ((of)** something) to eliminate a name from a list or record.

cross someone or something **out** to draw a line through the name of someone or something on a list or record.

cross swords (with someone) to enter into an argument with someone.

cross-examine someone to ask someone questions in great detail; to question a suspect or a witness closely.

crouch down to stoop or huddle down.

crow ['kro] **1.** *n.* a large, black bird. **2.** *iv.* [for a rooster] to make its loud noise.
→ AS THE CROW FLIES

crowd ['kraʊd] **1.** *n.* a large group of people; a gathering of people. **2.** *iv.* [for many people or creatures] to gather closely together.
→ Two's COMPANY(, THREE'S A CROWD).

crowd in (on someone or something) to press or crush around someone or something.

crowd in(to someplace) to push or squeeze into someplace.

crowd together to pack tightly together.

crown ['kraʊn] **1.** *n.* the circular metal object worn on the heads of royal persons. **2.** *n.* something that is worn around the head like ①. **3.** *n.* the office or authority of a monarch. (No plural.) **4.** *n.* the top part of something, especially a tooth, a hat, or a mountain.

5. *tv.* to make someone king or queen.

crude ['krud] **1.** *adj.* in a natural state; not refined; raw. (Adv: *crudely.* Comp: *cruder;* sup: *crudest.*) **2.** *adj.* vulgar; without manners. (Adv: *crudely.* Comp: *cruder;* sup: *crudest.*) **3.** *adj.* not expertly done; rough; awkward. (Adv: *crudely.* Comp: *cruder;* sup: *crudest.*)

cruel ['kru əl] **1.** *adj.* evil; wicked; fond of causing pain. (Adv: *cruelly.* Comp: *crueler;* sup: *cruelest.*) **2.** *adj.* causing pain; causing suffering. (Adv: *cruelly.* Comp: *crueler;* sup: *cruelest.*)

cruelty ['kru əl ti] *n.* harshness; the quality of causing pain and distress. (Plural only for types and instances.)

cruise ['kruz] **1.** *n.* a trip on a boat for pleasure; a vacation on a boat or ship. **2.** *iv.* to travel at a constant speed.

crumb ['krʌm] *n.* a particle of bread or cake.

crumble something **(up) (into** something) to crunch up or break up something into pieces.

crumple someone or something **up** to fold up or crush someone or something.

crunch ['krʌntʃ] **1.** *n.* the sound of something snapping and breaking, especially of something being chewed. **2.** *n.* the pressure felt when many deadlines happen at the same time.

crunch someone or something **up** to break someone or something up into pieces.

crunchy ['krʌn tʃi] *adj.* making a breaking noise when chewed. (Adv: *crunchily.* Comp: *crunchier;* sup: *crunchiest.*)

crusade [kru 'sed] **1.** *n.* a fight against something bad; a fight for something good. **2.** *iv.* to fight against something bad; to fight for something good.

the **Crusades** *n.* the religious expeditions of the Christians against the Muslims in the twelfth and thirteenth centuries. (Treated as plural.)

crush ['krʌʃ] **1.** *tv.* to squeeze or press on something with great force and collapse it. **2.** *tv.* to break something into small pieces by pressing or pounding. **3.** *tv.* to force juice out of fruit by squeezing it. **4.** *n.* a strong desire for someone; an infatuation with someone.

crush something **out** to put out a fire or flame by crushing.

crush something **up** to reduce the mass of something by crushing.

crush something **up (into** something) **1.** to press something with great force until it is reduced to something smaller. **2.** to break something up into small pieces.

crush (up) against someone or something to press hard against someone or something.

crust ['krʌst] *n.* the hard outside layer of something, including the earth, a pie, a loaf of bread, etc. (See also the UPPER CRUST.)

crutch ['krʌtʃ] *n.* a support under the arms that helps a lame person walk.

→ (AS) FUNNY AS A CRUTCH

the **crux of the matter** the central issue of the matter. (*Crux* is an old word meaning "cross.")

cry ['kraɪ] **1.** *n.* an expression of pain or anger; a loud expression of emotion. **2.** *n.* a shout; a call. **3.** *n.* a period of weeping. **4.** *iv.* to weep; to sob; to shed tears.
→ HUE AND CRY

cry before one **is hurt** to cry or complain upon the threat of harm.

cry bloody murder AND **scream bloody murder** to scream as if something very serious has happened. (As if one has found the result of a bloody act of murder.)

cry one's **eyes out** to cry very hard.

cry over spilled milk to be unhappy about something that cannot be undone.

cry wolf to cry or complain about something when nothing is really wrong.

crystal ['krɪs təl] **1.** *n.* a solid chemical compound occurring in a regular shape, such as a square or rectangle. **2.** *n.* a hard, clear substance like glass that contains a lot of lead. (Plural only for types and instances.) **3.** *n.* clear, expensive drinking vessels made of ②. (No plural.) **4.** *n.* the clear cover over the face of a watch. **5.** *adj.* made from ②. **6.** *adj.* clear; transparent.

cub ['kʌb] *n.* one of the young of certain animals, including bears, lions, and foxes.

cube ['kjub] **1.** *n.* a solid object having six square sides all the

same size. **2.** *n.* the number that is the result of multiplying some other number by itself two times. **3.** *tv.* to multiply a number by itself two times, that is, number × number × number. **4.** *tv.* to cut up food into little cubes as in ①.
→ ICE CUBE

cucumber ['kju kəm bɚ] *n.* a long, green vegetable, eaten raw in salads or pickled.
→ (AS) COOL AS A CUCUMBER

cud ['kʌd] *n.* a lump of chewed food that an animal, such as a cow, brings back into its mouth from its stomach in order to chew on it some more.

cuddle ['kʌd l] *tv.* to hold someone with love and affection; to hug someone for a while.

cuddle up (to someone or something**)** to nestle or snuggle close to someone or something to get warm or to be intimate.

cue ['kju] **1.** *n.* a long, narrow stick used to hit balls in billiards and similar games. **2.** *n.* something that is a signal for someone to do or say something; a line that prompts an actor to say the next line or do the next action. **3.** *tv.* to signal something to do or say something; to give someone ②.
→ TAKE ONE'S CUE FROM SOMEONE

cue someone **in** to give a signal or cue to someone at the right time, usually in a performance of some kind.

cuff ['kʌf] **1.** *n.* the turned-up edge of cloth near the ankles on trousers; the thicker material near the wrists on shirts. **2.** *tv.* to hit someone with one's hand.
→ PUT SOMETHING ON THE CUFF

cuisine [kwɪ 'zin] **1.** *n.* a particular way—usually national and cultural—of preparing food. **2.** *n.* food, especially the food of a particular country or region.

cult ['kʌlt] **1.** *n.* members of a strange or radical system of worship or admiration. **2.** *adj.* attracting a small number of fans, who seem like ①.

culture ['kʌl tʃɚ] **1.** *n.* the social patterns of the people in a particular domain. **2.** *n.* the artistic and social tastes of a society. (No plural.) **3.** *n.* a growth of bacteria in a container in a laboratory.

cup ['kʌp] **1.** *n.* a drinking container having a loop-shaped handle. **2.** *n.* the contents of ①. **3.** *n.* a standard unit of measurement equal to eight ounces. **4.** *n.* an award; a trophy. (Often shaped like ① or a larger vessel.)
→ NOT SOMEONE'S CUP OF TEA

cupboard ['kʌb ɚd] *n.* a cabinet lined with shelves, used to store plates, cups, food, or kitchen supplies.

cupcake ['kʌp kek] *n.* a small cake, shaped as if it had been cooked in a cup.

curb ['kɚb] **1.** *n.* the raised edge or rim of a road. **2.** *n.* a restraint; a control. **3.** *tv.* to restrain something; to control something; to keep something back.

curdle someone's **blood** to frighten or disgust someone severely.

cure [ˈkjʊr] **1.** *n.* a medicine that will make a sick person better; a remedy. **2.** *tv.* to make someone well again; to get rid of a disease or a bad habit. **3.** *tv.* to preserve meat by salting, smoking, or drying it.

curiosity [kjʊr i ˈɑs ə ti] *n.* the quality of wanting to know something; wondering about something.
→ PIQUE SOMEONE'S CURIOSITY

curious [ˈkjʊr i əs] **1.** *adj.* inquisitive; wanting to learn about something. (Adv: *curiously*.) **2.** *adj.* weird; odd; strange; unusual. (Adv: *curiously*.)

curl [ˈkɚl] **1.** *n.* a group of hairs that are looped or twisted. **2.** *n.* twist; an amount of twisting. (No plural.) **3.** *n.* something that is shaped like a loop or a spiral. **4.** *tv.* to cause a bunch of hairs to twist into loops or coils. **5.** *tv.* to cause something to wind around an object; to wind something around an object. **6.** *iv.* to twist into loops or coils.

curl someone's **hair** to frighten or alarm someone severely; to shock someone with sight, sound, or taste.

curl something **up** to roll something up into a coil.

curl up and die to retreat and die.

curl up (in(to) something) **1.** to roll into a coil. **2.** to roll into a coil in a resting place, such as a chair or a bed.

currency [ˈkɚ ən si] **1.** *n.* the kind of money that is used in a particular country. **2.** *n.* the quality of being in general use. (No plural.)

current [ˈkɚ ənt] **1.** *adj.* up-to-date; recent; of or about the present time. (Adv: *currently*.) **2.** *n.* a moving stream of air or water; a flow. **3.** *n.* the flow of electricity; the rate of the flow of electricity.
→ SWIM AGAINST THE CURRENT

curse [ˈkɚs] **1.** *n.* a word or statement asking a powerful being to bring evil or harm to someone or something. **2.** *n.* a word used when saying ①. **3.** *tv.* to utter ② against someone or something. (Past tense and past participle: *cursed* [ˈkɚst].) **4.** *iv.* to utter ②.

curt [ˈkɚt] *adj.* rudely brief; short (with someone or something) in a rude way. (Adv: *curtly*.)

curtain [ˈkɚt n] *n.* a piece of fabric hung as a barrier to sight.
→ BRING DOWN THE CURTAIN (ON SOMETHING)
→ RING DOWN THE CURTAIN (ON SOMETHING)

curve [ˈkɚv] **1.** *n.* a smooth bend; a continuously bending line. **2.** *tv.* to make something bend; to bend something into ①. **3.** *iv.* to bend in the shape of ①.
→ PITCH SOMEONE A CURVE
→ THROW SOMEONE A CURVE

cushion [ˈkʊʃ ən] **1.** *n.* a padded pillow for sitting. **2.** *tv.* to soften something from shock or impact.

custodian [kə ˈstod i ən] **1.** *n.* someone who has custody over someone else; someone who is in charge of someone or something. **2.** *n.* a janitor; someone who keeps someplace clean and makes small repairs.

custody ['kʌs tə di] *n.* care; guardianship.
→ IN SOMEONE'S OR SOMETHING'S CUSTODY
→ IN CUSTODY (OF SOMEONE OR SOMETHING)

custom ['kʌs təm] **1.** *n.* a tradition; a social tradition; a socially expected practice. **2.** *n.* a habit; a regular practice; a usual event. **3.** *adj.* made to order; specially made for a customer.

customer ['kʌs tə mɚ] *n.* someone who buys a product or a service from a person or a business.

cut ['kʌt] **1.** *n.* an opening made in the skin accidentally. **2.** *n.* a reduction in an amount of money; the taking away of funds for something. **3.** *n.* a piece of something that has been cut as in ④ from something; a piece [of meat]. **4.** *tv., irreg.* to separate something from something else with a sharp object; to sever something from something else. (Past tense and past participle: *cut*.) **5.** *tv., irreg.* to make an opening in something with a sharp object. **6.** *tv., irreg.* to shorten something with a sharp object; to trim something with a sharp object. **7.** *tv., irreg.* to reduce something; to decrease something. **8.** *tv., irreg.* to dissolve something; to dilute something. **9.** *iv., irreg.* to slice into something.
→ FISH OR CUT BAIT

cut back (on something**)** to reduce the use, amount, or cost of something.

cut both ways to affect both sides of an issue equally.

cut class to skip going to (a school) class.

cut down (on something**)** to reduce the amount of something or of doing something; to use or buy less of something.

cut from the same cloth sharing a lot of similarities; seeming to have been created, reared, or fashioned in the same way.

cut in (on someone**) 1.** [for someone] to ask to replace one member of a dancing couple. **2.** [for someone] to interrupt someone who is talking.

cut in (on something**) 1.** to interrupt something, especially some sort of electronic transmission. **2.** to join others who are doing something even when not invited.

cut in (with something**)** to interrupt [someone] with a comment; to speak abruptly, interrupting what someone else is saying.

cut off to turn off of a road, path, highway, etc.

cut off one's **nose to spite** one's **face** to harm oneself as a result of trying to punish another person.

cut one's **losses** to reduce one's losses of money, goods, or other things of value.

cut one's **(own) throat** to cause certain failure for oneself; to do damage to oneself.

cut someone or something **off from** something to isolate someone or something from someplace or something.

cut someone or something **(off) short** to end something before it is finished; to end one's speaking before one is finished.

cut someone **to the quick** to hurt someone's feelings very badly. (Can be used literally when *quick* refers to the tender flesh at the base of fingernails and toenails.)

cut something **away (from** something**)** to separate something from something by cutting.

cut something **back** to prune plants; to reduce the size of plants, bushes, etc.

cut something **down 1.** to chop something down; to saw or cut at something until it falls down. **2.** to destroy someone's argument; to destroy someone's position or standing. **3.** to reduce the price of something.

cut something **in(to** something**)** to mix something into something else.

cut something **off 1.** to shorten something. **2.** to turn something off, such as power, electricity, water, an engine, etc.

cut something **out 1.** to cut something, such as a piece of paper, loose so it can be removed. **2.** to stop doing something. (Colloquial. Usually a command. Typically: **Cut that out!**)

cut something **out (from** something**)** Go to CUT SOMETHING OUT (OF SOMETHING).

cut something **out (of** something**)** AND **cut** something **out (from** something**)** to cut a pattern or shape from cloth, paper, sheet metal, etc.; to remove something

from something by cutting; to excise something from something.

cut something **to the bone 1.** to slice flesh deeply to the bone. **2.** to cut down severely (on something).

cut something **(too) fine** to allow scarcely enough time, money, etc., in order to accomplish something.

cut the ground out from under someone to destroy the foundation of someone's plan or argument.

cut to the chase to get to the important matters.

cut-and-dried ['kʌt æn 'draɪd] *adj.* routine; not requiring much thought or effort.

cute ['kjut] *adj.* clever and pretty; simple and attractive. (Adv: *cutely.* Comp: *cuter;* sup: *cutest.*)

cycle ['saɪ kəl] **1.** *n.* one instance of a process that repeats over and over. **2.** *iv.* to ride a bicycle.

cyclist ['saɪ klɪst] *n.* someone who rides a bicycle or motorcycle, especially as a regular activity.

cyclone ['saɪ klon] *n.* a tornado; a strong, violent wind that moves in a circle.

cylinder ['sɪl ən dɚ] **1.** *n.* a tube; a solid or hollow object with a circular top and bottom and long, curved sides. **2.** *n.* the part of a car engine in which a piston moves back and forth.
→ FIRING ON ALL CYLINDERS

cymbal ['sɪm bəl] *n.* one of a pair of brass discs that are struck together to make a loud, ringing noise in orchestras and bands.

cynic ['sɪn ɪk] *n.* someone who believes the worst about everything and everybody.

cynical ['sɪn ɪ kəl] *adj.* believing the worst about everything and everybody. (Adv: *cynically* [...ɪk li].)

czar AND **tsar** ['zɑr] **1.** *n.* the male leader of Russia; a Russian king. (Until 1917.) **2.** *n.* a leader; someone who is in charge of something. (Figurative on ①.)

D

dab something **on((to)** something) to pat or paint carefully something onto something else.

dad ['dæd] *n.* a father. (Also a term of address.)

daddy ['dæd i] *n.* a familiar nickname for a father. (Capitalized when written as a proper noun.)

dagger ['dæg ɚ] *n.* a short, sharp knife carried as a weapon.
→ LOOK DAGGERS AT SOMEONE

daily ['de li] **1.** *adj.* done or occurring every day. **2.** *adj.* suitable for a single day. **3.** *adv.* on every day.

daily dozen physical exercises done every day. (Informal.)

dairy ['dɛr i] **1.** *n.* a company that processes milk products. **2.** the *adj.* use of ①.

daisy ['de zi] *n.* a long-stemmed plant bearing circular flowers, typically white with yellow centers.

dam ['dæm] *n.* a solid barrier in a river or stream that holds back the flow of water.

dam something **(up)** to build a solid barrier in a river or a stream to hold back the flow of water.

damage ['dæm ɪdʒ] **1.** *n.* harm; an act that causes loss or pain. (No plural.) **2.** *tv.* to harm something.

damages *n.* charges or costs for harm or loss, usually considered to be a punishment.

damn ['dæm] **1.** *adj.* cursed; declared to be bad as in ③. (Prenominal only. A curse word. Use only with caution.) **2.** *interj.* I am angry!; I am frustrated! (A curse word. Use only with caution.) **3.** *tv.* to declare something to be bad.

damn someone or something **with faint praise** to criticize someone or something indirectly by not praising enthusiastically.

damp ['dæmp] *adj.* moist; slightly wet. (Adv: *damply.* Comp: *damper;* sup: *dampest.*)

dance ['dæns] **1.** *tv.* to perform a type of movement of the body, usually with music. **2.** *iv.* to move one's body in a rhythm, usually to music, usually with another person. **3.** *n.* the art and study of the movement of the body, in rhythm, especially to music. (No plural.) **4.** *n.* a set series of body movements done to music. **5.** *n.* an act or session of ②. **6.** *n.* a social event where music is played and people DANCE as in ②.
→ GO INTO ONE'S SONG AND DANCE ABOUT SOMETHING

dance to another tune to shift quickly to different behavior; to change one's behavior or attitude.

danger ['den dʒɚ] **1.** *n.* the possibility of harm. (No plural.) **2.** *n.* someone or something that could cause harm, injury, or death.
→ FRAUGHT WITH DANGER

dangerous ['den dʒɚ əs] *adj.* risky; having the potential for causing harm. (Adv: *dangerously.*)

dare ['dɛr] **1.** *n.* a challenge; a statement that challenges someone to take a risk. **2.** *aux.* to have enough courage or boldness [to do something]. (Usually used in negative sentences and questions.)

dare someone **to** do something to challenge someone to do something risky.

dark ['dɑrk] **1.** *adj.* without light. (Adv: *darkly.* Comp: *darker;* sup: *darkest.*) **2.** *adj.* not light in color; having little brightness or color. (Adv: *darkly.* Comp: *darker;* sup: *darkest.*) **3.** *n.* the absence of light; darkness; nighttime. (No plural.) → PITCH-DARK

dark horse someone whose abilities, plans, or feelings are little known to others.

darken ['dɑr kən] **1.** *tv.* to make something darker. **2.** *iv.* to become darker.
→ GO AND NEVER DARKEN ONE'S DOOR AGAIN

darkness ['dɑrk nəs] *n.* the quality of having no light. (No plural.)

dart in and out [for something moving] to dart quickly between two things, or into a number of things, and move away again.

dash cold water on something Go to POUR COLD WATER ON SOMETHING.

dash off [for someone] to leave in a hurry.

dash out (for something**)** [for someone] to leave a place in a hurry to get something.

dash something **off 1.** to make or do something quickly. **2.** to write a note or letter quickly and send it off.

data ['det ə, 'dæt ə] *n.* information; pieces of information; facts; a set of facts. (The Latin plural of

datum. Treated as singular or plural in English.)

date ['det] **1.** *n.* the number of the day of a month, often including the name of the month or the name of the month and the year; the name of a month and the year; the year. (① refers to the number of the day of a month; the day of the week is called the DAY.) **2.** *n.* a brown, fleshy fruit with a long pit, grown on certain palm trees. **3.** *n.* a social meeting between two people, typically male and female, who have planned to go somewhere or do something together. **4.** *n.* a person with whom one has a DATE as in ③. **5.** *tv.* to mark something with ①; to show the ① of something. **6.** *tv.* to show or signal that someone or something is out-of-date or old-fashioned. **7.** *tv.* to have DATES as in ③ with a particular person. **8.** *iv.* to go out on DATES as in ③ frequently or habitually.

date back (to someone or something**)** to have origins that extend back to the time of someone or something.

daughter ['dɔ tɚ] *n.* a female child.

Davy Jones's locker the bottom of the sea, especially when it is a grave. (From the seamen's name for the spirit of the sea.)

dawn ['dɔn] **1.** *n.* the period of morning when light is first seen in the eastern sky; sunrise. **2.** *n.* the beginning of something. (Figurative on ①.) **3.** *iv.* [for the day] to become bright or light.
→ FROM DAWN TO DUSK

dawn (up)on someone [for a fact] to become apparent to someone; [for something] to be realized by someone.

day ['de] **1.** *n.* a period of 24 hours, especially from midnight to midnight; one of the seven divisions of the week. (The days of the week, in order, are MONDAY, TUESDAY, WEDNESDAY, THURSDAY, FRIDAY, SATURDAY, SUNDAY.) **2.** *n.* the period of time between sunrise and sunset; the opposite of night. **3.** *n.* the time spent at work; the hours of work. **4.** *n.* a time; a period.
→ ALL DAY LONG
→ ALL IN A DAY'S WORK
→ (AS) DIFFERENT AS NIGHT AND DAY
→ (AS) PLAIN AS DAY
→ BY DAY
→ CALL IT A DAY
→ the GOOD OLD DAYS
→ HAVE HAD ITS DAY
→ LATE IN THE DAY
→ NINE DAYS' WONDER
→ ONE'S DAYS ARE NUMBERED
→ the ORDER OF THE DAY
→ SAVE SOMETHING FOR A RAINY DAY
→ SAVE THE DAY
→ SEE THE LIGHT (OF DAY)

daybreak ['de brek] *n.* dawn; the first light of day. (No plural.)

daylight ['de laɪt] *n.* the light of day. (No plural.)
→ BEGIN TO SEE DAYLIGHT
→ IN BROAD DAYLIGHT

daylight robbery the practice of blatantly or grossly overcharging.

days *adv.* during the daytime; during each day.

days running AND **weeks running; months running; years running** days in a series; months in a series; etc. (Follows a number.)

day-to-day ['de tə 'de] *adj.* daily; happening every day.

dead ['dɛd] **1.** *adj.* no longer living. **2.** *adj.* not having the electrical energy to work. (Figurative on ①.) **3.** *adj.* not active; dull. (Figurative on ①. Comp: *deader;* sup: *deadest.*) **4.** *adv.* completely; exactly; absolutely. **5.** *n.* the time when it is the darkest, coldest, etc. (No plural.)
→ (AS) DEAD AS A DODO
→ BEAT A DEAD HORSE
→ COME TO A DEAD END
→ HAVE SOMEONE DEAD TO RIGHTS
→ IN A DEAD HEAT
→ LEAVE SOMEONE FOR DEAD
→ WAKE THE DEAD

the **dead** *n.* dead people; people who have died. (No plural. Treated as plural, but not countable.)

dead and buried gone forever. (Refers literally to persons and figuratively to ideas and other things.)

dead to the world tired; exhausted; sleeping soundly. (Asleep and oblivious to what is going on in the rest of the world.)

deadline ['dɛd laɪn] *n.* the date when something is due; the time by which something must be finished.

deaf ['dɛf] **1.** *adj.* not able to hear. (Adv: *deafly.* Comp: *deafer;* sup: *deafest.*) **2.** *adj.* unwilling to hear; heedless. (Figurative on ①. Adv: *deafly.* Comp: *deafer;* sup: *deafest.*)
→ TURN A DEAF EAR (TO SOMETHING)

the **deaf** *n.* people who are DEAF ①. (No plural. Treated as plural, but not countable.)

deal ['dil] **1.** *tv., irreg.* to pass out cards in a card game. (Past tense and past participle: DEALT.) **2.** *tv., irreg.* to deliver something, such as a blow. **3.** *iv., irreg.* to pass out cards in a card game. **4.** *n.* a bargain; an agreement for the purchase of goods or services, especially if at a cost lower than expected.
→ a GREAT DEAL
→ SQUARE DEAL

deal something **out** to pass something out piece by piece, giving everyone equal shares.

deal with someone or something to do business with someone or some entity.

deal with something **1.** [for something, such as a book, essay, article, explanation, etc.] to tell about, discuss, or concern something. **2.** to cope with something; to manage to handle something; to have control of something.

dealer ['di lɚ] **1.** *n.* someone who passes out cards in a card game. **2.** *n.* someone who is in the business of trade; someone who buys and sells certain products. (Usually a RETAIL merchant.)

dealt ['dɛlt] past tense and past participle of DEAL.

dean ['din] *n.* the head of a teaching division within a university, a college, or a private school.

dear ['dɪr] **1.** *adj.* loved very much. (Adv: *dearly*. Comp: *dearer*; sup: *dearest*.) **2.** *adj.* a form of address used at the beginning of a letter. **3.** *n.* a treasured person; a person who is loved very much. (Also a term of address.)

death ['dɛθ] **1.** *n.* the state of being dead. (No plural.) **2.** *n.* the act of dying; the end of life.
→ AT DEATH'S DOOR
→ BE THE DEATH OF SOMEONE OR SOMETHING
→ BE THE DEATH OF ONE (YET)
→ CATCH ONE'S DEATH (OF COLD)
→ the KISS of DEATH
→ a MATTER OF LIFE AND DEATH
→ MEET ONE'S DEATH
→ SIGN ONE'S OWN DEATH WARRANT
→ TAKE ONE'S DEATH (OF COLD)

death on someone or something **1.** very effective in acting against someone or something. **2.** [with *something*] accurate or deadly at doing something requiring skill or great effort.

debate [dɪ 'bet] **1.** *n.* an event where two or more people with different points of view talk about an issue. **2.** *n.* a formal, structured argument where the two sides of an issue are presented in an orderly fashion by opposing speakers. **3.** *n.* formal, structured arguing done as a school activity. (No plural.) **4.** *tv.* to discuss and argue something with someone. **5.** *iv.* [for two people or groups] to speak for the opposite sides of an issue.

debit ['dɛb ɪt] **1.** *n.* a record of an amount that is owed or must be subtracted from the balance in an account. (Compare this with DEBT.) **2.** *tv.* to charge an amount of money against someone's account. **3.** *tv.* to charge someone's account for a sum of money.

debt ['dɛt] *n.* the condition of owing something to someone. (Plural only for types and instances.)

→ IN DEBT
→ PAY ONE'S DEBT (TO SOCIETY)

decade ['dɛk ed] **1.** *n.* a period of ten years. **2.** *n.* one of the ten equal divisions of a century, such as 1950–1959.

decay [dɪ 'ke] **1.** *n.* rot; the rotting of something. (No plural.) **2.** *iv.* to rot. **3.** *tv.* to cause something to rot.

deceive [dɪ 'siv] *tv.* to make someone believe something that is not true.

December [dɪ 'sɛm bɚ] Go to MONTH.

deception [dɪ 'sɛp ʃən] *n.* deceiving, cheating, or defrauding. (No plural form in this sense.)

decide [dɪ 'saɪd] **1.** *tv.* to determine the outcome of something. **2.** *tv.* to make a choice; to reach a decision about something. (The object can be a clause with THAT ⑦.)

decide on to choose something; to pick something out.

decide (up)on someone or something to choose someone or something; to make a judgment about some aspect of someone or something.

decimal point ['dɛs (ə) məl pɔɪnt] *n.* a period (.) that separates whole numbers from fractions.

decision [dɪ 'sɪ ʒən] *n.* a choice; a selection; a judgment; a resolution.

deck ['dɛk] **1.** *n.* a set of cards; a pack of cards. **2.** *n.* the floor of a ship. **3.** *n.* a raised wooden patio, attached to the back door of a house.

deck someone or something **out (in** something) AND **deck** someone or something **out (with** something) to decorate someone or something with something.

deck someone or something **out (with** something) Go to DECK SOMEONE OR SOMETHING OUT (IN SOMETHING).

declare [dɪ 'klɛr] *tv.* to proclaim something; to make something known; to say something publicly. (The object can be a clause with THAT ⑦.)

decline [dɪ 'klaɪn] **1.** *iv.* to move from good to bad; to move from high to low; to go from better to worse. **2.** *iv.* to turn [something] down; to refuse [something]. **3.** *tv.* to list the different case endings of a noun or adjective. (Compare this with CONJUGATE.) **4.** *tv.* to turn something down; to refuse an offer. **5.** *n.* the gradual change from high to low; the loss of power, strength, or health.

decorate ['dɛk ə ret] **1.** *tv.* to put up decorations. **2.** *tv.* to honor a soldier with a medal. **3.** *iv.* to paint a room, put up wallpaper, hang drapes, lay carpet, or add furniture to a room.

decoration [dɛk ə 're ʃən] **1.** *n.* an object or things used to make something or a place look pretty. **2.** *n.* an award or honor given to a soldier.

decorative ['dɛk ə rə tɪv] *adj.* pretty; used for decorating. (Adv: *decoratively.*)

decrease 1. ['di kris] *n.* a drop; a fall; a lessening; a reduction. **2.** ['di kris] *n.* the amount that something has been reduced or lessened. **3.** [dɪ 'krɪs] *iv.* to become less; to become smaller in size or strength. **4.** [dɪ 'krɪs] *tv.* to cause something to become less; to cause something to become smaller in size or strength.

deed ['did] **1.** *n.* something that is performed; an act; an action. **2.** *n.* a legal document that officially transfers the ownership of land or buildings to someone. (Compare this with TITLE ④.)

deem it (to be) necessary AND **deem that it is necessary** to believe that something is necessary.

deem that it is necessary Go to DEEM IT (TO BE) NECESSARY.

deep ['dip] **1.** *adj.* extending far down from the top or far back from the front. (Adv: *deeply.* Comp: *deeper;* sup: *deepest.*) **2.** *adj.* reaching a certain depth; extending a certain distance down, in, or back. (Follows a measure of depth. Comp: *deeper.*) **3.** *adj.* [of a sound] low-pitched and strong. (Adv: *deeply.* Comp: *deeper;* sup: *deepest.*) **4.** *adj.* [of a color] intense or strong. (Adv: *deeply.* Comp: *deeper;* sup: *deepest.*) **5.** *adj.* intense; strong; extreme. (Adv: *deeply.* Comp: *deeper;* sup: *deepest.*) **6.** *adj.* difficult to understand; past one's understanding. (Comp: *deeper;* sup: *deepest.*)
→ BETWEEN THE DEVIL AND THE DEEP BLUE SEA
→ GO OFF THE DEEP END
→ IN DEEP WATER
→ JUMP OFF THE DEEP END

→ JUMP OFF THE DEEP END (OVER SOMEONE OR SOMETHING)
→ ONE'S DEEPEST SYMPATHY

deer ['dɪr] *n., irreg.* a fast, hoofed animal, the males of which have antlers. (Plural: *deer.*)

defeat [dɪ 'fit] **1.** *tv.* to cause someone to lose; to beat someone in a contest. **2.** *n.* loss [of a contest]; failure to win. (No plural.) **3.** *n.* an instance of winning as in ①. **4.** *n.* a loss of a contest.

defect 1. ['di fɛkt, dɪ 'fɛkt] *n.* a flaw. **2.** [dɪ 'fɛkt] *iv.* to go over to the other side of a conflict; to join up with one's enemies.

defend [dɪ 'fɛnd] *tv.* to fight for someone or something physically or verbally; to protect someone or something.

defendant [dɪ 'fɛn dənt] *n.* someone who is the target of legal action in a court of law.

defense [dɪ 'fɛns] **1.** *n.* protection against someone or something; defending someone or something; preparation to defend against someone or something. (Plural only for types and instances.) **2.** *n.* the skill of a sports team in protecting its goal or in preventing the other team from scoring points. (Plural only for types and instances.) **3.** *n.* the lawyer or lawyers who defend someone in court. (No plural.) **4.** *n.* the way that a lawyer argues a case in favor of a defendant; an argument used to defend oneself. (No plural.)

defensive [dɪ 'fɛn sɪv] *adj.* protective; used for defense. (Adv: *defensively.*)
→ ON THE DEFENSIVE

define [dɪ 'faɪn] *tv.* to explain the meaning of a word or expression.

defy [dɪ 'faɪ] *tv.* to resist authority; to go against a rule or a regulation.

degree [dɪ 'gri] **1.** *n.* a unit of measurement, as used for measuring temperature or angles. **2.** *n.* the extent of something; the level of something. **3.** *n.* a title awarded by a university or college to a student who has met certain requirements. **4.** *n.* a level in the comparison of adjectives or adverbs.

delete [dɪ 'lit] *tv.* to remove something from something, especially from a list or a piece of writing.

delicate ['dɛl ə kɪt] **1.** *adj.* fragile; easily damaged. (Adv: *delicately.*) **2.** *adj.* subtly flavored. (Adv: *delicately.*)

delicious [dɪ 'lɪʃ əs] *adj.* pleasing to the senses, especially taste and smell. (Adv: *deliciously.*)

delight [dɪ 'laɪt] **1.** *n.* pleasure; joy. **2.** *n.* something that is pleasing; something that causes joy. **3.** *tv.* to give someone pleasure; to cause someone joy; to please someone.
→ RAVISHED WITH DELIGHT

deliver [dɪ 'lɪv ɚ] **1.** *tv.* to take something [to someone or someplace]. **2.** *tv.* [for a woman] to give birth to a baby. **3.** *tv.* [for a doctor or someone else] to assist a baby in being born. **4.** *tv.* to give a speech; to read something out loud.
→ SIGNED, SEALED, AND DELIVERED

delivery [dɪ 'lɪv ə ri] **1.** *n.* the act of taking something to someone. **2.** *n.* something that is taken to someone. **3.** *n.* the process of giving birth. **4.** *n.* the style or manner of speaking; the style used when giving a speech. (No plural.)

deluxe [də 'lʌks] *adj.* of very good quality; of great luxury. (Adv: *deluxely.*)

demand [dɪ 'mænd] **1.** *n.* an urgent request; a strong order. **2.** *n.* [buyers'] strength of desire for a product or service. (No plural.) **3.** *tv.* to ask urgently for something; [for an authority] to request something firmly. (The object can be a clause with THAT ⑦.) **4.** *tv.* to require something; to need something. (The object can be a clause with THAT ⑦.)

democracy [dɪ 'mɑ krə si] **1.** *n.* the system of government ultimately controlled by the people who are governed. (No plural.) **2.** *n.* a country whose system of government is ①.

demon ['di mən] *n.* an evil spirit; a devil.

den ['dɛn] **1.** *n.* the lair or home of a wild animal. **2.** *n.* a center of bad or illegal activities. **3.** *n.* a room in a house used for studying or working.
→ BEARD THE LION IN HIS DEN

denial [dɪ 'naɪ əl] *n.* insisting that something does not exist or is not true; denying that something exists or is true. (Plural only for types and instances.)
→ IN DENIAL

dense ['dɛns] *adj.* thick; tightly packed together. (Adv: *densely.* Comp: *denser;* sup: *densest.*)

dent ['dɛnt] **1.** *n.* a shallow hollow in a surface; an indentation; a place where a small part of a surface has been pressed down or pressed inward. **2.** *tv.* to make a small hollow in something.

dent something **up** to mar or make depressions in something.

dental ['dɛn təl] *adj.* of or about the teeth or their care. (Adv: *dentally*.)

dentist ['dɛn tɪst] *n.* a health-care professional who specializes in the care of the teeth.

deny [dɪ 'naɪ] **1.** *tv.* to declare that something is not true. (The object can be a clause with THAT ⑦.) **2.** *tv.* to refuse to grant someone or something permission to do something; to refuse to allow someone or something to have something.

depart [dɪ 'pɑrt] **1.** *iv.* to go away; to start a journey by leaving a place. **2.** *tv.* to go away from a place; to leave a state or status.

department [dɪ 'pɑrt mənt] **1.** *n.* a unit within an organization. **2.** the *adj.* use of ①.

department store [dɪ 'pɑrt mənt stor] *n.* a large store where merchandise is sold in various departments.

dependent [dɪ 'pɛn dənt] **1.** *adj.* relying on someone else for support or care. (Adv: *dependently*.) **2.** *n.* someone who relies on someone else for support. **3.** *n.* someone who can be listed on a wage earner's income-tax form as ② and thereby reduce the wage earner's taxes.

deposit [dɪ 'pɑz ɪt] **1.** *n.* an amount of money paid toward a product or service. **2.** *n.* an amount of

money paid as security on a rented dwelling. **3.** *n.* something that is put down; something that is laid down. **4.** *n.* money that is put in a monetary account. **5.** *tv.* to place money in a monetary account. **6.** *tv.* to put something down in a specific place.
→ SAFE(TY)-DEPOSIT BOX

deposit something **in(to)** something to put something into something.

depository [dɪ 'pɑz ɪ tor i] **1.** *n.* a place where things are kept safe; a place where things are deposited and kept safe. **2.** *n.* a warehouse.

depth ['dɛpθ] *n.* the distance from top to bottom or front to back. (Plural only for types and instances.)
→ BEYOND ONE'S DEPTH

derogatory [dɪ 'rɑg ə tor i] *adj.* showing contempt; rude; very negative and critical. (Adv: *derogatorily* [dɪ rɑg ə 'tor ə li].)

descend [dɪ 'sɛnd] **1.** *tv.* to move from a higher part to a lower part on or along something; to climb down something. **2.** *iv.* to go down; to go from a high place to a lower place; to move downward. **3.** *iv.* to come from an earlier time.

describe [dɪ 'skraɪb] *tv.* to tell about someone or something in written or spoken words.

description [dɪ 'skrɪp ʃən] *n.* a statement that describes someone or something.
→ BEGGAR DESCRIPTION

desert 1. ['dɛz ərt] *n.* an area of land with little rainfall and little or no human population. (Compare this with DESSERT.) **2.** ['dɛz ərt] the *adj.* use of ①. **3.** [dɪ 'zɚt] *tv.* to abandon someone or something; to go away and leave someone or something behind. **4.** [dɪ 'zɚt] *tv.* to leave a place and make it empty. **5.** [dɪ 'zɚt] *iv.* to be absent from military duty without permission.

desert a sinking ship AND **leave a sinking ship** to leave a place, a person, or a situation when things become difficult or unpleasant. (Rats are said to be the first to leave a ship that is sinking.)

desert island ['dɛz ɚt 'aɪ lənd] *n.* a remote island, usually small and uninhabited, and typically having the features of a desert.

deserve [dɪ 'zɚv] *tv.* to be worthy of something; to merit something.

design [dɪ 'zaɪn] **1.** *n.* a plan showing how something will be made; the way something is arranged; the layout of something. **2.** *n.* a (visual) pattern; drawings or markings. **3.** *tv.* to make the plans for building or decorating something. **4.** *tv.* to plan and execute an arrangement of pictures, images, diagrams, lines, circles, etc.

designer [dɪ 'zaɪ nɚ] *n.* someone who makes designs; someone who plans how buildings, clothing, rooms, or works of graphic art will look.

desire [dɪ 'zaɪɚ] **1.** *n.* a strong wish for something; a request for something. **2.** *n.* someone or something that is wished for. **3.** *tv.* to want something very much.

desire to do something to want to do something very much.

desk ['dɛsk] *n.* a piece of furniture with a flat top—often with drawers on the lower part.
→ AWAY FROM ONE'S DESK

dessert [dɪ 'zɚt] *n.* a special, often sweet, food served at the end of a meal. (Compare this with DESERT.)

destiny ['dɛs tə ni] *n.* the force that determines future events. (Plural only for types and instances.)

destroy [dɪ 'strɔɪ] *tv.* to make someone or something completely useless; to do away with someone or something.

destruction [dɪ 'strʌk ʃən] **1.** *n.* ruining or destroying something. (No plural.) **2.** *n.* ruins; the result of destroying. (No plural.)

detail 1. ['di tel, dɪ 'tel] *n.* a small fact about something. **2.** ['di tel] *n.* a drawing that shows all of the fine or small parts of something. **3.** [dɪ 'tel] *tv.* to give all the facts of a story or issue.
→ GO INTO DETAIL
→ IN DETAIL

detain [dɪ 'ten] **1.** *tv.* to delay someone or something; to keep someone or something from leaving. **2.** *tv.* [for the police] to keep or hold someone.

detective [dɪ 'tɛk tɪv] *n.* a police officer or other licensed person who searches for information about crimes.

detention [dɪ 'tɛn ʃən] *n.* keeping someone from leaving; holding someone in a place such as a jail or a classroom. (Plural only for types and instances.)

determine [dɪ 'tɚ mɪn] *tv.* to figure something out. (The object can be a clause with THAT ⑦.)

deterrent [dɪ 'tɚ ənt] *n.* something that keeps someone or something from doing something; something that encourages someone or something not to do something.

detest [dɪ 'tɛst] *tv.* to hate someone or something very much. (The object can be a clause with THAT ⑦.)

detour ['di tu ɚ] **1.** *n.* a route that turns away from the regular route and is taken to avoid someone or something. **2.** *iv.* to use ①; to travel the long way around something.

develop [dɪ 'vɛl əp] **1.** *tv.* to create something and attempt to cause it to flourish. **2.** *tv.* [in photography] to cause images to appear on film through chemical processes. **3.** *tv.* [for someone or some creature] to begin to show signs of something or experience something. **4.** *tv.* to build houses, buildings, and stores on empty land. **5.** *iv.* to grow and mature. **6.** *iv.* to grow and prosper; to strengthen; to mature.

device [dɪ 'vaɪs] *n.* a tool or machine meant to be used for a specific purpose.

devil ['dɛv əl] **1.** *n.* an evil spirit; a demon. **2.** *n.* Satan; the supreme spirit of evil. (Sometimes capitalized.) **3.** *n.* someone who is mischievous.
→ BETWEEN THE DEVIL AND THE DEEP BLUE SEA
→ FOR THE DEVIL OF IT
→ GIVE THE DEVIL HER DUE
→ GIVE THE DEVIL HIS DUE
→ PLAY (THE) DEVIL'S ADVOCATE
→ SPEAK OF THE DEVIL
→ THERE WILL BE THE DEVIL TO PAY.

devote something **to** something [dɪ 'vot...] to give or allot something to something.

devout [dɪ 'vaut] **1.** *adj.* actively religious. (Adv: *devoutly.*) **2.** *adj.* sincere; deeply committed to someone or something. (Figurative on ①. Adv: *devoutly.*)

the **devout** *n.* religious people. (No plural. Treated as plural, but not countable.)

dew ['du] *n.* tiny drops of water that have fallen from cooling, moist air. (Plural only for types and instances.)

diabetes [daɪ ə 'bit ɪs] *n.* a disease where there is too much sugar in the blood and urine. (Treated as singular.)

diagram ['daɪ ə græm] **1.** *n.* a drawing that helps explain something. **2.** *tv.* to make a drawing to help explain something. **3.** *tv.* to make a drawing that shows the relationships between the parts of a sentence.

dial ['daɪl] **1.** *n.* on an older telephone, the wheel—with holes for one's finger—that is turned in order to make a telephone call. **2.** *n.* the part of a watch or a clock that has the numbers on it; the face of a watch or clock. **3.** *tv.* to place a telephone call to someone or to some number, either by rotating ① of a telephone or by pushing the buttons of a telephone. **4.** *iv.* to operate a telephone by turning ① or pushing buttons.

dial tone [ˈdaɪl ton] *n.* the sound heard when one picks up a telephone receiver, indicating that a telephone call can be made.

dialect [ˈdaɪ ə lɛkt] *n.* a variety of a language.

dialogue AND **dialog** [ˈdaɪ ə lɔg] **1.** *n.* speech between two or more people. (No plural.) **2.** *n.* a discussion between two or more people who express differences of opinion.

diameter [daɪ ˈæm ɪ tɚ] *n.* the length of a straight line within a circle and going through the center of the circle.

diamond [ˈdaɪ (ə) mənd] **1.** *n.* a figure with four sides of equal length that is viewed as standing on one of its points. **2.** *n.* a playing card that has one or more shapes like (♦) on it. **3.** *n.* a clear gem formed from carbon. **4.** *n.* [in baseball] the space defined by the four bases.

a **diamond in the rough** a valuable or potentially excellent person or thing hidden by an unpolished or rough exterior.

diaper [ˈdaɪ (ə) pɚ] **1.** *n.* a piece of cloth or other fiber that a baby wears between its legs before the baby has learned to use a toilet. **2.** *tv.* to put ① on a baby.
→ SOIL ONE'S DIAPER(S)

diary [ˈdaɪ (ə) ri] *n.* a journal; a book in which one records the events in one's life.

dice [ˈdaɪs] **1.** plural of DIE ③. **2.** *tv.* to chop a food up into tiny cubes.

dictionary [ˈdɪk ʃə ner i] *n.* a book that explains the meanings of words.

did [dɪd] past tense of DO.

didn't [ˈdɪd nt] *cont.* did not.

die [ˈdaɪ] **1.** *iv.* to stop living; to become dead. (Present participle: DYING.) **2.** *iv.* [for a machine] to stop working. (Figurative on ①.) **3.** *n., irreg.* a small cube that has a different number of spots on each side. (Plural: DICE. Usually plural.)
→ CROSS ONE'S HEART (AND HOPE TO DIE)
→ CURL UP AND DIE

die away AND **die down** to fade away. (See also DIE OUT.)

die back [for vegetation] to die part way back to the roots.

die down Go to DIE AWAY.

die of a broken heart 1. to die of emotional distress. **2.** to suffer from emotional distress, especially from a failed romance.

die of boredom to suffer from boredom; to be very bored.

die off [for living things] to perish one by one until there are no more.

die on someone to perish while in someone's care.

die on the vine Go to WITHER ON THE VINE.

die out 1. [for a species or family] to perish totally because of the failure to produce offspring. **2.** [for an idea, practice, style, etc.] to fade away through time.

diet [ˈdaɪ ɪt] **1.** *n.* the food that a person or an animal usually and typically eats. **2.** *n.* a controlled or prescribed selection of foods. **3.** *iv.* to control one's choice of foods for the purpose of losing weight.

difference ['dɪf rəns] **1.** *n.* a way that two people or things are not alike. (Plural only for types and instances.) **2.** *n.* the amount remaining when one amount is subtracted from another. (No plural.)
→ SPLIT THE DIFFERENCE

different ['dɪf rənt] *adj.* not the same. (Adv: *differently*.)
→ (AS) DIFFERENT AS NIGHT AND DAY
→ a HORSE OF A DIFFERENT COLOR
→ MARCH TO A DIFFERENT DRUMMER

different from someone or something not like someone or something; not the same as someone or something. (Also with THAN. Adv: *differently*.)

difficult ['dɪf ə kəlt] *adj.* hard to do; hard to understand. (Adv: *difficulty*.)

difficulty ['dɪf ə kəl ti] *n.* the quality of being hard to do or understand. (Plural only for types and instances.)

dig ['dɪg] *tv., irreg.* to make a hole in something by removing part of it, as with removing soil with a shovel. (Past tense and past participle: DUG.)

dig down 1. to excavate deeply. **2.** to be generous, as if one were reaching deeply into one's pocket for lots of money.

dig in one's **heels** to refuse to alter one's course of action or opinions; to be obstinate or determined.

dig in(to something) **1.** to use a shovel to penetrate a mass of

something. **2.** to begin to process something; to go to work on something. **3.** to begin to eat food. (Slang.)

dig one's **own grave** to be responsible for one's own downfall or ruin.

dig out (of something) to channel or excavate one's way out of something.

dig someone or something **out (of** something) to excavate in order to get someone or something out of something; to dig about in order to get someone or something out of something.

dig something **in(to** something) to stab or jab something into something.

dig up some dirt on someone to find out something bad about someone. (The *dirt* is gossip.)

digest 1. ['daɪ dʒɛst] *n.* a short version of a long piece of writing; a summary or a collection of summaries. **2.** [dɪ 'dʒɛst] *tv.* to dissolve food in the stomach so that it can be changed into a form that the body can use. **3.** [dɪ 'dʒɛst] *tv.* to take thoughts into the mind; to think about something very deeply and make it part of one's thinking. (Figurative on ②.)

digestion [dɪ 'dʒɛs tʃən] *n.* the process of breaking down food in the stomach so that it can be changed into a form that will give nourishment to the rest of the body. (No plural.)

digit ['dɪdʒ ɪt] **1.** *n.* a number from 0 through 9. **2.** *n.* a finger or a toe.

digital ['dɪdʒ ɪ təl] **1.** *adj.* [of a clock or watch] using numbers rather than hands. (*Adv:* *digitally*.) **2.** *adj.* of or about storing, retrieving, and working with information that is stored electronically using the digits 0 and 1. (*Adv:* *digitally*.)

dignity ['dɪg nə ti] *n.* self-respect; personal worth. (No plural.)

dilemma [dɪ 'lɛm ə] *n.* a difficult choice between two options.
→ ON THE HORNS OF A DILEMMA

dilute [dɪ 'lut] **1.** *tv.* to weaken something by the addition of a fluid. **2.** *tv.* to make something weaker; to make something less severe. (Figurative on ①.)

dim ['dɪm] **1.** *adj.* barely lit; not bright. (*Adv:* *dimly.* Comp: *dimmer;* sup: *dimmest.*) **2.** *adj.* vague; unclear in the mind; hard to remember. (*Adv:* *dimly.* Comp: *dimmer;* sup: *dimmest.*)

dim out [for a light] to grow dim and go out altogether.

dim something **down** to make lights dim.

dime ['daɪm] *n.* a coin worth 10 U.S. cents.
→ TURN ON A DIME

dimension [dɪ 'mɛn ʃən] *n.* the measurement of something in one direction; the length, the width, or the depth of something.

diminish [dɪ 'mɪn ɪʃ] **1.** *tv.* to cause something to become smaller; to cause something to become less important; to reduce something. **2.** *iv.* to become smaller; to become less important; to decrease.

din something **in(to** someone) to repeat something over and over to someone.

dine ['daɪn] *iv.* to eat a meal, especially to eat dinner.

dine in to eat at home rather than at a restaurant.

dine off something to make a meal of something; to make many meals of something. (Formal.)

dine out to eat away from home.

dining room ['daɪn ɪŋ rum] *n.* in a house, building, or apartment, the room where meals are served.

dinner ['dɪn ɚ] **1.** *n.* the main meal of the day; either a large midday meal or a large evening meal. **2.** *n.* a formal event where an evening meal is served.

dinosaur ['daɪ nə sor] *n.* a large, prehistoric reptile that is now extinct.

dip ['dɪp] **1.** *n.* a sharp slope downward. **2.** *n.* a quick plunge into water or other liquid; a quick swim in water. **3.** *n.* a creamy mixture of foods or a thick sauce that is eaten with crackers, potato chips, or vegetables. (Plural only for types and instances.) **4.** *tv.* to lower and raise something quickly.

dip in((to) something) **1.** to reach into a liquid. **2.** to reach into a substance, usually to remove some of the substance. **3.** to take out part of something one has been saving. (Figurative.)

dip something **in((to)** something) to put something into a substance in order to take some of it.

diplomacy [dɪ 'plo mə si] **1.** *n.* tact; skill used in dealing with people. (No plural.) **2.** *n.* the business of maintaining good relationships between countries. (No plural.)

direct [dɪ 'rɛkt] **1.** *adj.* going from one place to another place without leaving the path; going the straightest or shortest way. (Adv: *directly.*) **2.** *adj.* exact; to the point; forthright. (Adv: *directly.*) **3.** *tv.* to guide someone or something; to be in charge of someone or something. **4.** *tv.* to establish and oversee the design and execution of a play or a film, particularly overseeing the actors' performances; to instruct actors how to perform in a particular play, opera, film, etc.

direct object [də 'rɛkt 'ɑb dʒɛkt] *n.* a noun, pronoun, or phrase that receives the action of a TRANSITIVE VERB; a noun, pronoun, or phrase on which the verb operates.

direction [dɪ 'rɛk ʃən] **1.** *n.* the guidance or control of something. (No plural.) **2.** *n.* the path taken by something that moves; movement. **3.** *n.* the way that someone or something faces, such as to the north, south, east, or west.

directions 1. *n.* instructions. **2.** *n.* a statement of how to get to a place.

director [dɪ 'rɛk tə·] **1.** *n.* someone who leads a group of musicians as they perform; a conductor; someone who DIRECTS ④ actors, films, plays, etc. **2.** *n.* someone who is in charge of an institution, company, school, or department.

directory [dɪ 'rɛk tə ri] **1.** *n.* a list of names arranged in the order of the alphabet, usually including addresses and telephone numbers. **2.** *n.* any list that shows where to find someone or something.

dirt [ˈdɚt] **1.** *n.* soil; earth. (No plural.) **2.** *n.* dust, grime, mud; filth. (No plural.)
→ DIG UP SOME DIRT ON SOMEONE

dirt cheap extremely cheap. (Informal.)

dirty [ˈdɚ ti] **1.** *adj.* not clean. (Adv: *dirtily.* Comp: *dirtier;* sup: *dirtiest.*) **2.** *adj.* of or about sex or excrement in a crude way. (Adv: *dirtily.* Comp: *dirtier;* sup: *dirtiest.*) **3.** *tv.* to cause something to become unclean.
→ AIR ONE'S DIRTY LINEN IN PUBLIC
→ GET ONE'S HANDS DIRTY
→ WASH ONE'S DIRTY LINEN IN PUBLIC

dirty one's **hands** Go to GET ONE'S HANDS DIRTY.

dirty something **up** to get something dirty.

dirty work 1. unpleasant or uninteresting work. **2.** dishonest or underhanded actions; treachery.

disagree [dɪs ə 'gri] *iv.* not to agree with someone; to have an opinion different from someone else's opinion.

disagree with someone [for food] to cause someone to have an upset stomach.

disagreeable [dɪs ə 'gri ə bəl] *adj.* not pleasant; unpleasant. (Adv: *disagreeably.*)

disagreement [dɪs ə 'gri mənt] *n.* a difference in opinion; a failure to agree. (Plural only for types and instances.)

disappear [dɪs ə 'piɚ] **1.** *iv.* to vanish; to cease to appear; to go out of sight. **2.** *iv.* to cease to exist in a place; to be no longer in a place.

disappoint [dɪs ə 'pɔɪnt] *tv.* to fail to please someone; to make someone unhappy by not doing something that was expected or desired; to make someone unhappy by not being or happening as expected or desired.

disapproval [dɪs ə 'pruv əl] *n.* rejection; the failure to give approval to someone or something; unfavorable opinion. (No plural.)

disapprove (of someone or something**)** [dɪs ə 'pruv...] not to approve of someone or something; to have a bad opinion of someone or something.

disc Go to DISK.

discharge 1. ['dɪs tʃɑrdʒ] *n.* the sound of an explosion; the firing of a gun. **2.** ['dɪs tʃɑrdʒ] *n.* the release of someone or something, especially when this requires official approval. **3.** ['dɪs tʃɑrdʒ] *n.* the carrying out of one's duties; the performance of one's duties. (No plural.) **4.** ['dɪs tʃɑrdʒ] *n.* giving something off; releasing something. **5.** ['dɪs tʃɑrdʒ] *n.* something that is given off; something that is let out. **6.** [dɪs 'tʃɑrdʒ] *tv.* to fire a gun; to cause an explosion. **7.** [dɪs 'tʃɑrdʒ] *tv.* to dismiss someone from employment. **8.** [dɪs 'tʃɑrdʒ] *tv.* to let something out; to pour something out. **9.** [dɪs 'tʃɑrdʒ] *tv.* to do one's duty; to keep a promise; to repay a debt.

discipline ['dɪs ə plɪn] **1.** *n.* controlled behavior achieved as the result of training; order. (Plural only for types and instances.) **2.** *n.* a field or branch of learning. **3.** *tv.* to punish someone. **4.** *tv.* to train someone or something to behave properly; to train someone or something to be obedient.

discomfort [dɪs 'kʌm fɚt] **1.** *n.* an uncomfortable feeling. (Plural only for types and instances.) **2.** *n.* something that causes an uncomfortable feeling.

discover [dɪ 'skʌv ɚ] *tv.* to find something for the first time; to become aware of something for the first time; to find out for the first time how something functions or happens. (The object can be a clause with THAT ⑦.)

discovery [dɪ 'skʌv ə ri] **1.** *n.* an instance of discovering something. **2.** *n.* someone or something that has been discovered; something not known of before.

discreet [dɪ 'skrit] *adj.* very cautious, so as not to draw anyone's attention; keeping something a secret; able to keep a secret. (Adv: *discreetly.*)

discuss [dɪ 'skʌs] *tv.* to talk about something; to have a conversation about something.

disease [dɪ 'ziz] *n.* an illness; a sickness.
→ HAVE FOOT-IN-MOUTH DISEASE

disgrace [dɪs 'gres] **1.** *n.* shame; the loss of honor. (Plural only for types and instances.) **2.** *tv.* to bring shame upon someone.

disguise [dɪs 'gaɪz] **1.** *n.* something that conceals who someone really is; something that conceals what something really is. **2.** *tv.* to change the appearance of a thing or a person to make identification difficult.

disgust [dɪs 'gʌst] **1.** *n.* a strong feeling of dislike; a loathing for someone or something. (No plural.) **2.** *tv.* to revolt someone; to offend someone.

dish ['dɪʃ] **1.** *n.* a plate; a flat, circular object used to serve food or to eat from. **2.** *n.* a particular food that is served at a meal.
→ DO THE DISHES

dish something **out (to** someone**) 1.** AND **dish** something **up (for** someone**)** to place food onto dishes for someone. **2.** to give out criticism or punishment to someone.

dish something **up (for** someone**)** Go to DISH SOMETHING OUT (TO SOMEONE).

dishonest [dɪs 'an ɪst] *adj.* not honest. (Adv: *dishonestly.*)

dishwater ['dɪʃ wɑt ɚ] *n.* the water that dishes are to be washed in; water that dishes have been washed in. (No plural.)

disillusioned [dɪs ə 'lu ʒənd] *adj.* freed from illusion.

disk AND **disc** ['dɪsk] *n.* a thin, flat, and circular object.
→ FLOPPY DISK

disk drive ['dɪsk draɪv] *n.* a device inside a computer, used for reading and storing digital information on a spinning disk. (Can be shortened to DRIVE.)

diskette [dɪ 'sket] *n.* a device—usually held in a square of plastic—for storing digital computer information. (Can be shortened to DISK.)

dismal ['dɪz məl] *adj.* dull and filled with gloom. (Adv: *dismally.*)

dismiss [dɪs 'mɪs] **1.** *tv.* to allow people to leave; to send people away. **2.** *tv.* to end someone's employment. **3.** *tv.* to refuse to consider something; to refuse to listen to someone or something.

display [dɪ 'sple] **1.** *tv.* to show something; to exhibit something. **2.** *n.* something that is shown; something that is exhibited.

dispose of something [dɪ 'spoz...] to get rid of something; to throw something away.

dissolve [dɪ 'zalv] **1.** *tv.* to melt a solid, such as sugar, into a liquid. **2.** *tv.* to break up a union or a bond; to end an association. **3.** *iv.* [for a solid] to become mixed in a liquid.

distance ['dɪs təns] *n.* the length of the space between two things.
→ GO THE DISTANCE
→ LONG DISTANCE
→ WITHIN WALKING DISTANCE

distant ['dɪs tənt] **1.** *adj.* far away; not near in space or time. (Adv: *distantly.*) **2.** *adj.* not very friendly; aloof. (Adv: *distantly.*)

distinct [dɪ 'stɪŋkt] **1.** *adj.* different; separate; able to be seen as unique. (Adv: *distinctly.*) **2.** *adj.* obvious; easy to notice. (Adv: *distinctly.*)

distress [dɪ 'stres] **1.** *n.* grief; anxiety. (No plural.) **2.** *tv.* to trouble someone; to cause someone to feel anxiety, discomfort, or suffering.

district ['dɪs trɪkt] *n.* an area; a region; a part of a country, state, county, or city.

distrust [dɪs 'trʌst] **1.** *n.* a lack of trust. (No plural.) **2.** *tv.* not to trust someone or something; not to put one's trust in someone or something.

disturb [dɪ 'stɚb] **1.** *tv.* to bother or annoy someone or something; to interrupt someone or something. **2.** *tv.* to change, handle, or move something.

ditch ['dɪtʃ] **1.** *n.* a long, low, narrow deep place in the ground, where water can flow. **2.** *tv.* to land an airplane in the water and abandon it. **3.** *tv.* to abandon or get rid of someone or something.

dive ['daɪv] **1.** *n.* a jump into something, especially water, usually with one's hands or head first. **2.** *n.* an underwater swim, as with scuba diving; time spent underwater. **3.** *n.* a plunge; a quick movement down. **4.** *iv., irreg.* to jump into deep water, entering smoothly, leading with the feet or with the hands raised above the head. (Past tense: *dived* or *DOVE*; past participle: *dived.*) **5.** *iv., irreg.* to spend time underwater, as with scuba diving. **6.** *iv., irreg.* to go down quickly; to plunge down. **7.** *iv., irreg.* to move away and hide quickly.
→ SCUBA (DIVING)

dive in(to something) 1. to plunge into something; to jump into something head first. **2.** to plunge

into some business or activity. (Figurative.)

diver ['daɪ vɚ] **1.** *n.* someone who dives into water, especially in a contest with other divers. **2.** *n.* someone who swims underwater, as with scuba diving.
→ SCUBA DIVER

divide [dɪ 'vaɪd] **1.** *tv.* to split something into smaller portions. **2.** *iv.* to separate; to split up.

divide a number **by** a number to split an amount (or a number) into a stated number of equal parts.

divide a number **into** a number to determine what a number must be multiplied by to result in a given number; to determine how many times a number goes into a given number.

divide by a number to split [the amount represented by a number] into a given number of equal parts.

divide something **in** something Go TO DIVIDE SOMETHING INTO SOMETHING.

divide something **into** something **1.** AND **divide** something **in** something to separate something into parts. **2.** to do mathematical division so that the divisor goes into the number that is to be divided.

divine [dɪ 'vaɪn] **1.** *adj.* of or about God; holy; sacred. (Adv: *divinely.*) **2.** *adj.* fabulous; excellent; wonderful. (Figurative on ①. Adv: *divinely.*)

division [dɪ 'vɪ ʒən] **1.** *n.* the process of dividing one number by another number. (No plural.) **2.** *n.*

a split; a dividing line. **3.** *n.* a major part of a very large company. **4.** *n.* dividing into portions. (Plural only for types and instances.)

divorce [dɪ'vors] **1.** *n.* the legal ending of a marriage. (Plural only for types and instances.) **2.** *tv.* to end one's marriage to someone. **3.** *tv.* to grant ① to a husband and wife.

dizzy ['dɪz i] **1.** *adj.* feeling like everything is spinning around; not steady. (Adv: *dizzily.* Comp: *dizzier;* sup: *dizziest.*) **2.** *adj.* confusing; hectic. (Informal. Adv: *dizzily.* Comp: *dizzier;* sup: *dizziest.*)

do ['du] **1.** *tv.* to perform an action; to finish an action; to end an action. (Past tense: DID; past participle: DONE. See also DOES.) **2.** *tv.* to solve something; to find an answer. **3.** *tv.* to cover a distance; to go at a certain speed. **4.** *iv.* to be OK; to suit one's needs. **5.** *iv.* to get along; to function or exist. (Used to ask if someone is feeling all right, to inquire of someone's health.) **6.** *aux.* a question word in the present and past tenses. (In the future tense, *will* is used.) **7.** *aux.* a form used to make negative constructions. **8.** *aux.* a form used to emphasize a verb. **9.** *aux.* a particle used to repeat a verb that has already been said or written.

do a land-office business to do a large amount of business in a short period of time. (As if selling land during a land rush.)

do someone **a good turn** to do something that is helpful to someone.

do someone **a kindness** to do a kind deed for a person.

do someone or something **in 1.** to wear someone or some creature out. **2.** to destroy or ruin someone or something. **3.** to kill someone or some creature.

do someone or something **over** to remodel or redecorate something; to redo someone's appearance.

do someone or something **up** to make someone or something attractive; to decorate or ornament someone or something.

do someone's **bidding** to do what is requested.

do someone's **heart good** to make someone feel good emotionally. (Also used literally.)

do something by hand to do something with one's hands rather than using a machine.

do something for a living to do some kind of work to earn enough money to live.

do something in a heartbeat to do something almost immediately.

do something up 1. to fasten, zip, hook, or button some item of clothing. **2.** to wrap up something, such as a package, gift, etc. **3.** to arrange, fix, repair, cook, clean, etc., something.

do the dishes to wash the dishes; to wash and dry the dishes.

do the honors to act as host or hostess and serve one's guests by pouring drinks, slicing meat, making (drinking) toasts, etc.

do without (someone or something) to manage or get along without someone or something that is usually needed.

dock ['dɑk] **1.** *n.* a pier; a platform built for moving things and people on and off boats and ships. **2.** *n.* a platform for loading and unloading goods. **3.** *tv.* to bring a ship or boat up to ①. **4.** *iv.* [for a boat or ship] to arrive at ①; [for a boat or ship] to tie up to ①.

doctor ['dɑk tɚ] **1.** *n.* someone who has received the highest degree from a university. (Abbreviated *Dr.*) **2.** *n.* someone who is licensed to practice medicine; a medical doctor. (Abbreviated *Dr.* when used as a title.)
→ JUST WHAT THE DOCTOR ORDERED

document ['dɑk jə mənt] **1.** *n.* a piece of paper or an electronic file with information (usually writing or printing) on it; a text. **2.** *tv.* to make and keep written records about something. **3.** *tv.* to list the evidence that will support what one has written. **4.** *tv.* to record something in detail over time.

doe ['do] *n.* a female of certain animals, such as the deer.

does ['dʌz] *aux.* the third-person present singular of DO.

doesn't ['dʌz ənt] *cont.* does not.

dog ['dɔg] **1.** *n.* a common pet found in many homes and sometimes used in hunting. **2.** *tv.* to follow someone closely; to pursue someone eagerly.
→ (AS) SICK AS A DOG
→ CALL THE DOGS OFF
→ GO TO THE DOGS
→ HAIR OF THE DOG THAT BIT ONE
→ LEAD A DOG'S LIFE
→ LIVE A DOG'S LIFE
→ RAIN CATS AND DOGS
→ SHAGGY-DOG STORY
→ the TAIL WAGGING THE DOG

dog eat dog a situation in which one has to act ruthlessly in order to survive or succeed; ruthless competition.

dog in the manger one who prevents other people from doing or having what one does not wish them to do or have.

doghouse ['dɔg haʊs] *n., irreg.* a small outdoor shelter for a dog to sleep in. (Plural: [...haʊ zəz].)
→ IN THE DOGHOUSE

doldrums ['dol drəmz] **1.** *n.* an area of light winds, at sea, north of the equator. (Treated as plural.) **2.** *n.* inactivity; gloominess; boredom. (Treated as plural.)
→ IN THE DOLDRUMS

dole something **out (to** someone**)** to distribute something to someone.

doll ['dɑl] **1.** *n.* a figure of a human or animal, often a baby, used as a toy. **2.** *n.* an attractive or cute male or female of any age. (Informal.)

doll someone **up** to dress someone up in fancy clothes. (See also GET (ALL) DOLLED UP.)

dollar ['dɑl ɚ] *n.* the main unit of money in the United States; 100 cents; $1. (The dollar is also the name of the main unit of money in several other countries, but each is worth a value different from that of the U.S. dollar.)
→ FEEL LIKE A MILLION (DOLLARS)
→ LOOK LIKE A MILLION DOLLARS

dollar for dollar considering the amount of money involved; considering the cost. (Often seen in advertising.)

domain [do 'men] **1.** *n.* the area where someone or something is typically found. **2.** *n.* the area under the control of a ruler.

dome ['dom] *n.* a rounded roof; the top of a building shaped like an upside-down bowl.

domestic [də 'mɛs tɪk] **1.** *adj.* of or about the home; of, about, or within the family. (Adv: *domestically* [...ɪk li].) **2.** *adj.* not imported; not foreign. (Adv: *domestically* [...ɪk li].) **3.** *adj.* tame; not wild. (Adv: *domestically* [...ɪk li].)

dominate ['dɑm ə net] *tv.* to control someone or something; to be the most important person or thing among certain other people or things.

donate ['do net] *tv.* to give something to a charity or other organization.

done ['dʌn] **1.** past participle of DO. **2.** *adj.* completed; finished. (Not compared. Not prenominal.) **3.** *adj.* [of food] having been cooked fully or enough. (Can be compared.)

donkey ['dɔŋ ki] *n.* an animal that has four feet and hooves, is smaller than a horse, and is used to carry people or things.

don't ['dont] *cont.* do not.

Don't hold your breath. Do not stop breathing (while waiting for something to happen), because the wait will be very long.

Don't let someone or something **get you down.** Do not allow yourself to be overcome by someone or something.

doom ['dum] **1.** *n.* a horrible fate; a death that cannot be avoided. (No plural.) **2.** *tv.* to cause someone or something to fail; to cause something to be ruined or destroyed. **3.** *tv.* [for something] to condemn someone to an unpleasant future.

door ['dor] **1.** *n.* a movable panel of wood, glass, or metal that fits into an opening through which someone or something may pass. **2.** *n.* the opening into which ① fits. **3.** *n.* the (figurative) route or pathway to something, such as opportunity. (Figurative on ②.)
→ ANSWER THE DOOR
→ AT DEATH'S DOOR
→ BEAT A PATH TO SOMEONE'S DOOR
→ GET ONE'S FOOT IN THE DOOR
→ GO AND NEVER DARKEN ONE'S DOOR AGAIN
→ KEEP THE WOLF FROM THE DOOR
→ NEXT DOOR
→ NEXT-DOOR NEIGHBOR
→ STORM DOOR

doorstep ['dor stɛp] *n.* a step just outside a door.
→ AT SOMEONE'S DOORSTEP
→ ON SOMEONE'S DOORSTEP

dorm ['dorm] *n.* a DORMITORY; a building in which students live on a college campus.

dormitory ['dorm ɪ tor i] **1.** *n.* a building or room containing beds for a number of people, especially on a college campus. (Abbreviated as DORM.) **2.** *n.* a room housing sleeping facilities for a number of people.

dose ['dos] **1.** *n.* the amount of medicine that is to be taken at one time. **2.** *tv.* to give someone or something a specific amount of medicine.

a **dose of** one's **own medicine** the same kind of treatment that one gives to other people. (Often with *give, get,* or *have.*)

dot ['dɑt] *n.* a small spot; a small, round mark.
→ ON THE DOT
→ SIGN ON THE DOTTED LINE

double ['dʌb əl] **1.** *adj.* having twice the amount as something else. (Adv: *doubly.*) **2.** *tv.* to cause something to become twice the amount that it previously was. **3.** *iv.* to become twice the amount that something was previously.
→ SEE DOUBLE

double back (on someone**)** to follow one's own pathway back toward a pursuer.

double back (on something**)** to follow one's own pathway back toward where one started.

double over to bend in the middle.

double something **over** to fold something over.

double up (on someone or something**)** [for people] to deal with someone or something in pairs.

double up (with someone**)** to share something with someone.

double up (with something**)** to bend in the middle with something such as laughter, howls, pain, etc.

doubt ['daʊt] **1.** *n.* lack of belief; a state of not being certain. (No plural.) **2.** *n.* a feeling of disbelief about something; a feeling of not being certain about something. (Often plural.) **3.** *tv.* not to believe or trust something; to be uncertain about something; to consider something unlikely.
→ GET THE BENEFIT OF THE DOUBT
→ GIVE SOMEONE THE BENEFIT OF THE DOUBT

doubting Thomas someone who will not easily believe something without strong proof or evidence.

dough ['do] *n.* a soft mixture of flour, water, and possibly other ingredients. (Plural only for types and instances.)

dove 1. ['dov] a past tense of DIVE. **2.** ['dʌv] *n.* a gray or white bird, a little smaller than a pigeon. (Often thought of as a symbol of peace.)

down ['daʊn] **1.** *adj.* aimed toward a lower place or level; associated with a place or area that is lower than where one is at the moment. **2.** *adj.* sad; unhappy. **3.** *adj.* finished; completed. (Not prenominal.) **4.** *adv.* from a higher place to a lower place; in a direction from a higher place to a lower place. **5.** *adv.* from an earlier time to a later time. **6.** *adv.* [moving] toward the south; [moving] to a place that corresponds to south on a map. **7.** *adv.* onto paper; into writing. **8.** *adv.* as an advance payment against the purchase price. **9.** *adv.* toward having less energy, strength, production, volume, or intensity. **10.** *adv.* over [to someplace]; in a specific direction. (Informal.) **11.** *prep.* on or along something to a lower place. **12.** *prep.* to the end of something; along the length of something.

13. *tv.* to make someone fall to the ground; to knock someone over. (Informal.) **14.** *tv.* to eat or swallow something very quickly and without much chewing. **15.** *n.* soft feathers, used inside pillows, quilts, etc. (No plural.)

down and out having no money or means of support.

down by some amount having a score that is lower, by the specified amount, than someone else's score or the other team's score.

down in the mouth sad-faced; depressed and unsmiling. (Refers to a frown or sagging mouth.)

down the drain lost forever; wasted. (Also used literally.)

down the tube ruined; wasted. (Slang.)

down to the wire at the very last minute; up to the very last instant. (Refers to a wire that marks the end of a horse race.)

downpour ['daʊn pɔr] *n.* a very heavy rainfall.

down-to-earth practical; not fanciful; realistic.

downtown ['daʊn 'taʊn] **1.** *adv.* [moving] toward the center of a town or city; [moving] into the center of a town or city. **2.** *adv.* at the center of a town or city. **3.** *adj.* in the center of a town or city; in the business district of a town or city. **4.** *n.* the center of a town or city; the business district of a town or city. (No plural.)

downward ['daʊn wɚd] *adj.* moving or directed toward a lower position; moving toward a lower level. (Adv: *downwardly.*)

downward(s) *adv.* toward a lower position; toward a lower level.

doze ['doz] **1.** *n.* a nap; a small amount of sleep. **2.** *iv.* to take a nap; to sleep for a short period of time.

doze off (to sleep) to slip away into sleep.

dozen ['dʌz ən] **1.** *n.* a set of twelve things. **2.** *adj.* twelve; a set or total of twelve.
→ DAILY DOZEN
→ SIX OF ONE AND HALF A DOZEN OF THE OTHER

drab ['dræb] *adj.* dull; gray; boring; not exciting. (Adv: *drably.* Comp: *drabber;* sup: *drabbest.*)

draft ['dræft] **1.** *n.* a current of air—usually cold—inside an enclosed space. **2.** *n.* a roughly drawn plan; an early version of a document before the final copy is written. **3.** *tv.* to force someone to serve in the military. **4.** *tv.* to choose someone to do a job or a task. (Figurative on ③.)

drag ['dræg] **1.** *tv.* to pull someone or something along on the ground. **2.** *tv.* to force someone or something to come along. **3.** *iv.* [for someone or something] to touch the ground while being moved.

drag behind to follow along behind someone.

drag on to go on slowly for a very long time; to last a very long time.

drag one's **feet** to act very slowly, often deliberately.

drag out to last for a long time.

drag someone or something **in(to something)** **1.** to haul or pull someone or something into something or some place. **2.** to involve someone or a group in something.

drag someone or something **off (to** someone or something) to haul someone or something away to someone, something, or some place.

drag someone **up** to force someone to come up or to come and stand nearby.

drag something **behind** one to pull something that is behind one.

drag something **out** to make something last for a long time.

drag something **out of** someone to force someone to reveal something; to pull an answer or information out of someone laboriously.

drain ['dren] **1.** *n.* a pipe or ditch that takes liquids away from an area. **2.** *n.* something that takes away something else a little bit at a time; something that slowly takes something else away. **3.** *tv.* to draw liquid away from a place. **4.** *tv.* to empty a container of a liquid. **5.** *tv.* to take something away slowly, a bit at a time. (Figurative on ④.) **6.** *tv.* to drink all the contents of a glass or container. **7.** *tv.* to empty something by drinking all the liquid from it. (Informal.) **8.** *tv.* to remove someone's energy, endurance, or other quality. **9.** *iv.* [for something] to lose liquid slowly.
→ DOWN THE DRAIN
→ POUR MONEY DOWN THE DRAIN

drain away [for something] to flow away.

drain out to flow out or empty.

drain something **away (from** something) to channel some liquid away from something.

drain something **off (from** something) to cause or permit something to flow out of something.

drain something **off (of** something) to cause or permit something to flow from the surface or top of something.

drain something **out of** something to cause something to flow from something; to empty all of some liquid out of something.

drainage ['dren ɪdʒ] **1.** *n.* removing liquid from something or someplace. (No plural.) **2.** *n.* the ability of an area to drain properly. (No plural.)

drama ['drɑm ə] **1.** *n.* the study of plays and the theater. (No plural.) **2.** *n.* a serious play or movie; a play or movie that is not a comedy. **3.** *n.* emotional, exciting, or thrilling events. (No plural. Treated as singular.)

drank ['dræŋk] past tense of DRINK.

drape ['drep] **1.** *n.* a heavy curtain. (Often plural.) **2.** *n.* the particular way that fabric hangs. (No plural.) **3.** *tv.* to cover someone or something with fabric that hangs down in a decorative way.

draw ['drɔ] **1.** *n.* an attraction; a reason people go to a particular place. **2.** *iv., irreg.* to make pictures using pen, pencil, crayon, etc. (Past tense: DREW; past participle: DRAWN.) **3.** *tv., irreg.* to make a picture of something with a pen, pencil, crayon, marker, etc. **4.** *tv., irreg.* to attract someone or some-

thing. **5.** *tv., irreg.* to take a breath; to take in air.
→ BACK TO THE DRAWING BOARD
→ QUICK ON THE DRAW

a **draw** *n.* a tie; a game where both teams have the same score.

draw a blank 1. to get no response; to find nothing. **2.** to fail to remember (something).

draw a line between something **and** something **else** AND **draw the line between** something **and** something else to separate two things; to distinguish or differentiate between two things.

draw away (from someone or something**)** to pull back or away from someone or something.

draw back to pull back; to respond to being pulled back.

draw back (from someone or something**)** to pull back from someone or something; to recoil from someone or something.

draw blood 1. to hit or bite (a person or an animal) and make a wound that bleeds. **2.** to anger or insult a person.

draw lots to choose from a group of things to determine who will do something. (Typically, to choose a straw from a bundle of straws. The person with the shortest straw is selected.)

draw near [for a particular time] to approach.

draw near (to someone or something**)** to come near to someone or something.

draw on someone or something to use someone or something in some beneficial way.

draw oneself **up (to** something**)** to stand up straight and reach a certain height.

draw some people **together** to make people seek one another for emotional support.

draw someone or something **in(to** something**) 1.** to pull someone or something into something; to attract someone or something in. **2.** to sketch a picture, adding someone or something into the picture. **3.** to involve someone or something in something.

draw someone or something **out (of** something**) 1.** to lure someone or some creature out of something or someplace. **2.** to pull someone or something out of something or someplace.

draw someone or something **to(ward)** someone or something to pull someone or something to someone or something.

draw someone **out (about** someone or something**)** Go to DRAW SOMEONE OUT (ON SOMEONE OR SOMETHING).

draw someone **out (on** someone or something**)** AND **draw** someone **out (about** someone or something**)** to find out someone's private thoughts about someone or something.

draw something **off (from** something**)** to remove a portion of a liquid from something; to cause something to flow from something.

draw something **out 1.** to extend something in time. **2.** to lengthen something.

draw something **out (of** someone) to encourage someone to say or tell something; to get some information from someone, with difficulty.

draw something **up 1.** to pull something close by, such as a chair, stool, etc. **2.** to draft a document; to prepare a document.

draw the line between something **and** something else Go to DRAW A LINE BETWEEN SOMETHING AND SOMETHING ELSE.

draw up to pull up; to shrink up.

draw (up) alongside ((of) someone or something) to move up even with someone or something in motion.

drawer ['drɔr] *n.* a storage box or compartment that slides in and out of a desk, dresser, etc.

drawn ['drɔn] Past participle of DRAW.

dread ['drɛd] **1.** *n.* strong fear that something [bad] might happen or fear of something that is going to happen. (No plural.) **2.** *tv.* to approach something in the future with fear, wishing that it would not happen.

dream ['drim] **1.** *iv., irreg.* to have thoughts and images while one sleeps. (Past tense and past participle: *dreamed* or DREAMT.) **2.** *tv., irreg.* to see something in one's DREAMS as in ③. (The object can be a clause with THAT ⑦.) **3.** *n.* the thoughts and images one has while sleeping. **4.** *n.* a desire; a wish.
→ PIPE DREAM

a **dream** *n.* a very beautiful person or thing; something excellent; something that is of high quality. (No plural.)

dream about someone or something AND **dream of** someone or something to have mental pictures about someone or something, especially in one's sleep.

a **dream come true** a wish or a dream that has become real.

dream of someone or something Go to DREAM ABOUT SOMEONE OR SOMETHING.

dream something **up** to invent something; to fabricate something. (The *something* can be the word *something*.)

dreamt ['drɛmt] a past tense and past participle of DREAM.

dredge someone or something **up 1.** to scoop or rake someone or something up from underwater. **2.** to seek and find someone or something. (Slang.)

drench ['drɛntʃ] *tv.* to cover someone or something with liquid— water unless some other liquid is mentioned.

dress ['drɛs] **1.** *n.* an item of women's clothing covering an area from the shoulders to somewhere along the legs. **2.** *n.* clothing in general. (No plural.) **3.** *adj.* [of clothing, shoes, etc.] formal. (Prenominal only.) **4.** *tv.* to put clothes on someone. **5.** *tv.* to bandage a wound or cut. **6.** *tv.* to prepare an animal's body for cooking or for market. **7.** *iv.* to put clothes on oneself or someone else as in ④.

dress someone **down** to scold someone.

dress someone or something **up** to make someone or something appear fancier than is actually so.

dress someone or something **(up) (in** something**)** to clothe, decorate, or ornament someone or something in something.

dress (up) as someone or something to dress in the manner of someone or something or to look like someone or something.

dresser ['drɛs ɚ] *n.* a piece of furniture with several drawers that clothes are kept in; a chest of drawers.

dressing-down a scolding.

drew ['dru] past tense of DRAW.

drift ['drɪft] **1.** *n.* a mass of snow or sand that is moved by the wind. **2.** *n.* a gradual movement toward someone or something, especially in air or water. (No plural.) **3.** *iv.* to move toward something or away from something gradually; to move gradually in some direction. **4.** *iv.* [for someone] to move from place to place without a purpose or established plan.
→ GET THE DRIFT OF SOMETHING

drift back (to someone or something**)** to move back to someone or something slowly, on the surface of water.

drift in(to something**)** to move slowly and gradually into something.

drift off to move slowly away.

drift out to move out of a place slowly.

drift to(ward) someone or something to move slowly and gradually toward someone or something.

drill ['drɪl] **1.** *n.* a machine that is used to make a hole in something. **2.** *n.* a classroom practice exercise. **3.** *n.* an event where people practice what they would do in a real emergency. **4.** *tv.* to make a hole in something with ①. **5.** *tv.* to train people by having them practice. **6.** *iv.* to make holes with ①.

drill into something to bore into or penetrate something.

drill something **in(to** someone or something**)** to force knowledge into someone or something. (Figurative.)

drink ['drɪŋk] **1.** *tv., irreg.* to swallow a liquid. (Past tense: DRANK; past participle: DRUNK.) **2.** *iv., irreg.* to use or consume [alcohol]. **3.** *n.* a liquid meant to be swallowed. **4.** *n.* a container filled with a liquid that is meant to be swallowed. **5.** *n.* a kind of drink that contains alcohol.
→ SOFT DRINK

drink something **down** to drink something; to consume all of something by drinking it.

drink something **in** to absorb something; to take in information, sights, a story, etc. (Figurative.)

drink something **up** to drink all of something.

drink to excess to drink too much alcohol; to drink alcohol continually.

drink up to drink something; to drink all of something.

drip ['drɪp] **1.** *n.* the action of liquid falling one drop at a time. **2.** *n.* the sound of a liquid falling one drop at a time. **3.** *tv.* to cause something to fall one drop at a time. **4.** *iv.* to fall one drop at a time; to leak; to release one drop at a time.

drip something **in(to** something) to make something fall into something drop by drop.

drive ['drɑɪv] **1.** *tv., irreg.* to cause a car or other vehicle to move, and to direct its movement. (Past tense: DROVE; past participle: DRIVEN.) **2.** *tv., irreg.* to take someone in a vehicle to someplace. **3.** *tv., irreg.* to ram or force something into or through something else. **4.** *iv., irreg.* to ride in and steer or direct [a vehicle]. **5.** *n.* a trip in a car or other vehicle; the act of traveling as in ④. **6.** *n.* the energy and desire to do something. (No plural.) **7.** *n.* a place to guide or park a car between a road and a house or garage. **8.** *n.* an electronic device inside a computer, used for storing and reading computer files and programs. (Short for DISK DRIVE.)

drive a hard bargain to work hard to negotiate prices or agreements in one's own favor.

drive a price **up** AND **force** a price **up** to cause the price of something to increase.

drive away to leave someplace driving a vehicle.

drive back to propel a vehicle back to where it started.

drive down (to someplace) to run a vehicle to a relatively lower place or to a place in the south.

drive off to leave somewhere, driving a vehicle.

drive on to continue driving; to continue with one's journey.

drive out (to someplace) to propel a vehicle to a place that is away from the center of things.

drive over (to someplace) to go in a car to someplace that is neither close by nor far away.

drive someone **down (to** someplace) to transport someone to a relatively lower place or to a place in the south.

drive someone **on (to** something) to make someone move onward toward some kind of success.

drive someone or something **(away) (from** someplace) to repel someone or some creature from someplace.

drive someone or something **back** to force someone or something away; to force someone or something to retreat.

drive someone or something **off** to repel or chase away someone or something.

drive someone or something **out (of** something) to force or chase someone or some creature out of something or someplace.

drive someone **to the wall** Go to FORCE SOMEONE TO THE WALL.

drive someone **up (to** someplace) to transport someone to a place on a higher level or to a place in the north.

drive something **down** to force the price of something down.

drive something **down (to** someplace) to transport a vehicle to a place by driving it there.

drive through (something**)** to motor from one side of something to the other; to pass through something while driving.

drive up to something to drive a car up close to something; to pull a car up to something.

driven ['drɪv ən] Past participle of DRIVE.
→ (AS) WHITE AS THE DRIVEN SNOW

driver ['draɪ vɚ] *n.* someone who drives a car or other vehicle.

driveway ['draɪv we] *n.* a short length of road from the street to a house or garage.

drizzle down (on someone or something**)** to rain on someone or something.

drone on to continue to make a low-pitched noise or to speak in a dull and boring voice.

drone on (about someone or something**)** to lecture or narrate in a low-pitched, dull, and boring manner.

drop ['drɑp] **1.** *n.* a small ball of liquid; a small amount of liquid. **2.** *n.* a sudden fall; a sudden downward movement. **3.** *n.* the length of a fall; the distance between something and the ground. **4.** *tv.* to let someone or something fall, either by accident or on purpose. **5.** *tv.* to leave something out; to omit something. **6.** *tv.* to stop something; to end something; to stop talking about something. **7.** *iv.* to fall; to go lower; to sink.
→ AT THE DROP OF A HAT
→ COUGH DROP
→ SO QUIET YOU COULD HEAR A PIN DROP

→ SO STILL YOU COULD HEAR A PIN DROP

drop away 1. to fall off; to fall away. **2.** to reduce in number over time.

drop back 1. to fall back to an original position. **2.** to go slowly and lose one's position in a march or procession.

drop behind (in something**)** to fail to keep up with a schedule.

drop behind (someone or something**) 1.** to reduce speed and end up after someone or a group, at the back of a moving line. **2.** to fail to keep up with the schedule being followed by someone or a group.

drop below someone or something to fall to a point lower than someone or something.

drop by (someplace**)** AND **go by (**someplace**)** to stop for a casual visit.

drop by the wayside AND **fall by the wayside 1.** to leave a march or procession to rest beside the pathway. (The origin of the figurative usage in ②.) **2.** to fail to keep up with others. (Figurative.)

drop down 1. [for someone] to fall down or stoop down. **2.** [for something] to fall from above.

drop everything to stop doing whatever you are doing.

drop in to come for a casual visit.

drop in (on someone**)** to come for an unexpected, casual visit.

drop in one's **tracks** to stop or collapse from exhaustion; to die suddenly.

drop in (to say hello) to come for a brief, friendly visit.

drop names to mention the names of important or famous people as if they were personal friends.

drop off 1. [for someone or something] to fall off something. **2.** [for a part of something] to break away and fall off. **3.** to decrease or decline. (Figurative.)

drop out (of something**) 1.** [for someone] to resign from or cease being a member of something; [for someone] to leave school. **2.** to fall out of something. **3.** [for the bottom of something] to break loose and drop.

drop over to come for a casual visit.

drop someone **a few lines** Go to DROP SOMEONE A LINE.

drop someone **a line** AND **drop** someone **a few lines** to write a letter or a note to someone. (The *line* refers to lines of writing.)

drop someone or something **down** to let someone or something fall.

drop someone or something **in(to** something**)** to let someone or something fall into something.

drop someone or something **off ((at)** someplace**) 1.** to let someone or a group out of a vehicle at a particular place; to deliver someone or something to someplace. **2.** to give someone or a group a ride to someplace.

drop someone or something **off (of** something**)** to let someone or something fall from something; to make someone or something fall from something.

drop someone's **name** AND **drop the name of** someone to mention the name of an important or famous person as if that person were a personal friend.

drop the ball to make a blunder; to fail in some way.

drop the name of someone Go to DROP SOMEONE'S NAME.

drop the subject to stop talking about whatever is being talked about.

drop up (someplace**)** to come for a visit to a place that is relatively higher or in the north.

drove ['drov] past tense of DRIVE.

drown ['draʊn] **1.** *tv.* to kill someone or something by suffocating the person or thing underwater. **2.** *tv.* to flood an area with a liquid. **3.** *iv.* to die underwater as in ①.

drown one's **sorrows** Go to DROWN ONE'S TROUBLES.

drown one's **troubles** AND **drown** one's **sorrows** to try to forget one's problems by drinking a lot of alcohol.

drown someone or something **out 1.** [for a flood] to drive someone or some creature away from home. **2.** to make more noise than someone or something.

drowsy ['draʊ zi] *adj.* tired; sleepy. (Adv: *drowsily*. Comp: *drowsier*; sup: *drowsiest*.)

drug ['drʌg] **1.** *n.* a medicine. **2.** *n.* a substance used illegally for the pleasure it creates. **3.** *tv.* to give someone ①.

a **drug on the market** something that is for sale everywhere in great abundance; a glut on the market.

druggist ['drʌg ɪst] *n.* someone who is licensed to package and sell medicine.

drugstore ['drʌg stor] *n.* a place where medicine is sold, along with makeup, toothpaste, and many other items.

drum ['drʌm] **1.** *n.* a musical instrument, usually shaped like a cylinder, with a flexible cover stretched over one or both ends. **2.** *n.* a container shaped like ①.

drum some business up to create business or commerce.

drum someone **out of** something to expel or send someone away from something, especially in a formal or public fashion. (From the military use of drums on such occasions.)

drum something **in(to someone)** AND **drum** something **in(to someone's head)** to teach someone something intensely. (Figurative.)

drum something **in(to someone's head)** Go to DRUM SOMETHING IN(TO SOMEONE).

drum something **out** to beat a rhythm, loudly and clearly, as if teaching it to someone.

drummer ['drʌm ɚ] *n.* someone who plays a drum or a number of them.
→ MARCH TO A DIFFERENT DRUMMER

drunk ['drʌŋk] **1.** Past participle of DRINK. **2.** *n.* a person who has taken too much alcohol. **3.** *adj.* concerning a person who has taken too much alcohol. (Also

drunken. Comp: *drunker*; sup: *drunkest*.)

drunken ['drʌŋk ən] DRUNK ③.

dry ['draɪ] **1.** *adj.* not wet; not moist; without water. (Adv: *dryly*. Comp: *drier*; sup: *driest*.) **2.** *adj.* not allowing alcohol to be sold; without alcohol. **3.** *adj.* boring; not interesting. (Adv: *dryly*. Comp: *drier*; sup: *driest*.) **4.** *tv.* to cause something to be ①; to remove all the moisture from something. **5.** *iv.* to become ①; to completely lose moisture.
→ LEAVE SOMEONE HIGH AND DRY

dry behind the ears mature and grown up. (Usually expressed as a negative. See also WET BEHIND THE EARS.)

dry out 1. [for someone or something wet] to become dry. **2.** to recover from too much alcohol and the effects of drunkenness.

dry run an attempt; a rehearsal.

dry someone or something **off** to remove the moisture from the surface of someone or something.

dry someone **out** to cause someone to become sober; to cause someone to stop drinking alcohol to excess. (Informal.)

dry something **out** to make something become dry.

dry something **up 1.** to cause moisture to dry away to nothing. **2.** to cure a skin rash by the use of medicine that dries.

dry up 1. [for something] to become dry; [for something] to dry away to nothing. **2.** [for someone] to be quiet or go away. (Slang.)

dryer ['draɪ ɚ] *n.* a machine that dries clothes.

dual ['du əl] *adj.* having two parts; having two purposes. (Adv: *dually.*)

dub something **in** to mix a new sound recording into an old one.

duck ['dʌk] **1.** *n.* a kind of fowl that lives near water, has a bill, and has webbed feet for swimming. **2.** *n.* the meat of ①. (No plural.) **3.** *n.* a sturdy kind of cotton cloth. (Plural only for types and instances.) **4.** *iv.* to stoop down so that one doesn't get hit by something; to dip one's head so one doesn't bump it into something. **5.** *iv.* to avoid being seen by moving quickly somewhere. **6.** *tv.* to dip one's head down so that it is not hit against something.
  → AS A DUCK TAKES TO WATER
  → (AS) EASY AS DUCK SOUP
  → GET ONE'S DUCKS IN A ROW
  → LIKE SITTING DUCKS
  → LIKE WATER OFF A DUCK'S BACK
  → LOVELY WEATHER FOR DUCKS

duck down to stoop down quickly, as if to avoid being hit.

duck out (of someplace**)** to sneak out of someplace.

duck out of something to evade something; to escape doing something.

due ['du] **1.** *adj.* owing; having to be paid. (Not prenominal.) **2.** *adv.* directly; in the exact direction; straight.
  → GIVE CREDIT WHERE CREDIT IS DUE
  → GIVE THE DEVIL HER DUE
  → GIVE THE DEVIL HIS DUE
  → PAY ONE'S DUES

due to someone or something owing to someone or something; because of someone or something. (This use is objected to by some.)

dues *n.* a sum of money owed by each member of an organization. (Treated as plural. Rarely countable.)

duet [du 'ɛt] *n.* music to be performed by two people.

dug ['dʌg] past tense and past participle of DIG.

dull ['dʌl] **1.** *adj.* not sharp; blunt. (Adv: *dully.* Comp: *duller;* sup: *dullest.*) **2.** *adj.* not exciting; boring. (Adv: *dully.* Comp: *duller;* sup: *dullest.*) **3.** *adj.* not shiny. (Adv: *dully.* Comp: *duller;* sup: *dullest.*) **4.** *adj.* not smart; somewhat stupid. (Adv: *dully.* Comp: *duller;* sup: *dullest.*) **5.** *tv.* to make something less sharp. **6.** *tv.* to lessen physical or emotional pain.

dumb ['dʌm] **1.** *adj.* stupid; foolish; not smart. (Adv: *dumbly.* Comp: *dumber;* sup: *dumbest.*) **2.** *adj.* [of animals] not able to speak. (Can be offensive when applied to humans. Adv: *dumbly.* Comp: *dumber;* sup: *dumbest.*)

dump ['dʌmp] **1.** *n.* a place where trash is taken. **2.** *tv.* to unload something into a pile; to empty something into a pile.

dunce ['dʌns] *n.* a stupid-acting person; someone who learns things slowly.

dung ['dʌŋ] *n.* feces, especially from animals. (No plural.)

dunk ['dʌŋk] *tv.* to push someone or something underwater for a few moments.

duration [dəˈeʃən] *n.* the amount of time that something lasts. (No plural form.)
→ FOR THE DURATION

during [ˈdɜrɪŋ] **1.** *prep.* throughout an event that lasts a period of time; all through a period of time. **2.** *prep.* at some point in a period of time; at some time within a period of time.

dusk [ˈdʌsk] *n.* the period of the day after the sun sets but before it is completely dark; twilight.
→ FROM DAWN TO DUSK

dust [ˈdʌst] **1.** *n.* a fine powder of dried earth. (No plural.) **2.** *n.* a fine powder, especially particles that settle from the air and coat indoor surfaces. (No plural.) **3.** *tv.* to clean a surface or a place by removing ②. **4.** *tv.* to cover something with ① or ②. **5.** *tv.* to spray crops with an insect killer or a weed-killer. (Referred originally to powdered chemicals.) **6.** *iv.* to remove ② from something or from a place as a part of cleaning.
→ BITE THE DUST

dust someone or something **off** to wipe or brush the dust off someone or something.

dust something **out** to brush the dust out of something.

dusty [ˈdʌs ti] **1.** *adj.* covered with dust; full of dust. (Adv: *dustily.* Comp: *dustier;* sup: *dustiest.*) **2.** *adj.* like dust; [of a color] somewhat gray, as if mixed with dust. (Comp: *dustier;* sup: *dustiest.*)

Dutch auction an auction or sale that starts off with a high asking price, which is then reduced until a buyer is found.

Dutch courage unusual or artificial courage arising from the influence of alcohol. (Potentially offensive.)

Dutch treat a social occasion where one pays for oneself. (See also GO DUTCH.)

Dutch uncle a man who gives frank and direct advice to someone in the manner of a parent or relative.

duty [ˈdu ti] **1.** *n.* a task; an obligation; a responsibility. **2.** *n.* a tax placed on products from another country.
→ IN THE LINE OF DUTY
→ OFF DUTY
→ ON ACTIVE DUTY
→ ON DUTY

dwarf [ˈdwɔrf] **1.** *n., irreg.* someone or something that is smaller than normal or typical. (Plural: DWARVES or *dwarfs.*) **2.** *adj.* smaller than expected; smaller than normally found. (Prenominal only.) **3.** *tv.* [for someone or something large] to make someone or something appear even smaller in a comparison.

dwarves [ˈdwɔrvz] a plural of DWARF.

dwell [ˈdwɛl] *iv., irreg.* to live someplace; to live in a place. (Past tense and past participle: *dwelled* or DWELT.)

dwell on something to linger on something; to keep thinking about an idea.

dwelling [ˈdwɛl ɪŋ] *n.* a residence; a place where someone lives.

dwelt [ˈdwɛlt] a past tense and past participle of DWELL.

dye ['daɪ] **1.** *n.* a liquid that is used to color fabric or hair. **2.** *tv.* to color something by placing it in ①; to color something with ①. (Present participle: *dyeing*.)

dying ['daɪ ɪŋ] **1.** the present participle of DIE. **2.** *adj.* in the process of becoming dead.

dynamite ['daɪ nə maɪt] **1.** *n.* a chemical that is meant to explode, usually ammonium nitrate. (Plural only for types and instances.) **2.** *n.* someone or something that causes a great shock or surprise; someone or something exciting that attracts a lot of attention or interest. (Figurative on ①. Informal.) **3.** *tv.* to destroy something by an explosion with ①.

E

each ['itʃ] **1.** *adj.* every [one].
2. *pron.* every one [of those mentioned before]; every individual person or thing [of those mentioned before]. **3.** *adv.* for every one.

eager ['i gɚ] *adj.* acting very willing and ready to do something. (Adv: *eagerly.*)

eager beaver someone who is very enthusiastic; someone who works very hard.

eager to do something having a strong desire to do something and being very willing to do it.

eagle ['i gəl] *n.* a strong bird of prey of the hawk family, having excellent vision.

eagle eye careful attention; an intently watchful gaze. (From the sharp eyesight of the eagle.)

ear ['ɪr] **1.** *n.* the organ of hearing, one of which is located on either side of the head. **2.** *n.* the external, visible part of the organ of hearing. **3.** *n.* a CORNCOB and the corn growing on it. (Short for EAR OF CORN.)
→ BEND SOMEONE'S EAR
→ DRY BEHIND THE EARS
→ GET SOMEONE'S EAR
→ GO IN ONE EAR AND OUT THE OTHER
→ HAVE AN EAR FOR SOMETHING
→ HAVE ONE'S EAR TO THE GROUND
→ IN ONE EAR AND OUT THE OTHER
→ KEEP ONE'S EAR TO THE GROUND
→ LEND AN EAR (TO SOMEONE)
→ MAKE A SILK PURSE OUT OF A SOW'S EAR
→ PLAY SOMETHING BY EAR
→ ONE'S EARS ARE RED
→ PLAY BY EAR
→ PRICK UP ONE'S EARS

→ TURN A DEAF EAR (TO SOMETHING)
→ UP TO ONE'S EARS (IN SOMETHING)
→ WALLS HAVE EARS.
→ WET BEHIND THE EARS

ear of corn ['ɪr əv 'kɔrn] *n.* the rodlike, fibrous core on which grains of corn grow. (Plural: *ears of corn.*)

eardrum ['ɪr drəm] *n.* a very thin bit of tissue inside the ear that vibrates when struck by sound waves.

early ['ɚ li] **1.** *adj.* happening toward the first part of something; happening toward the beginning of something. (Comp: *earlier*; sup: *earliest.*) **2.** *adj.* arriving before the expected time. (Comp: *earlier*; sup: *earliest.*) **3.** *adj.* ancient; happening long ago in time. (Comp: *earlier*; sup: *earliest.*) **4.** *adv.* during or toward the first part of something. (Comp: *earlier*; sup: *earliest.*) **5.** *adv.* before the expected time. (Comp: *earlier*; sup: *earliest.*)

early bird someone who gets up or arrives early; someone who starts something very promptly, especially someone who gains an advantage of some kind by so doing.

earn ['ɚn] **1.** *tv.* to gain a sum of money or something else of value, especially by working. **2.** *tv.* to merit something; to deserve something. (Figurative on ①.)

earn one's **keep** to help out with chores in return for food and a place to live; to earn one's pay by doing what is expected.

earnest ['ɚ nəst] *adj.* very serious; wishing to do [something] very well. (Adv: *earnestly.*)
→ IN EARNEST

ears are ringing [for someone's ears] to have a ringing sound because they have been exposed to an explosion, very loud music, or some other very loud sound.

earth ['ɚθ] **1.** *n.* the planet we live on; the third planet from the sun. (Often capitalized. No plural.) **2.** *n.* soil; land. (No plural.) **3.** *n.* the surface of ①. (No plural.)
→ LIKE NOTHING ON EARTH
→ MOVE HEAVEN AND EARTH TO DO SOMETHING
→ ON EARTH
→ a PARADISE ON EARTH
→ RUN SOMEONE OR SOMETHING TO EARTH
→ SALT OF THE EARTH
→ TO THE ENDS OF THE EARTH

earthly ['ɚθ li] *adj.* of or on the earth; of a part of life on earth rather than in heaven.

earthquake AND **quake** ['ɚθ kwek, 'kwek] *n.* a violent shaking of the ground by natural forces.

earthworm ['ɚθ wɚm] *n.* a worm that lives in the soil.

ease ['iz] **1.** *tv.* to make something less hard to do; to make something easier. **2.** *tv.* to make something become less strong or have less pain. **3.** *tv.* to move something [somewhere] gently and carefully. **4.** *iv.* to become less hard or less difficult. **5.** *n.* freedom from problems or bother; peaceful rest. (No plural.)
→ WITH EASE

ease away (from someone or something**)** to pull away from someone or something slowly and carefully.

ease back on something to move something back slowly and carefully. (Usually refers to a throttle or some other control on an airplane or other vehicle.)

ease off [for something] to diminish.

ease off (from someone or something**)** to move away from someone or something, slowly and carefully.

ease off (on someone or something**)** to let up doing something to someone or something; to diminish one's pressure or demands on someone or something.

ease out (of something**)** to move out of something, slowly and carefully; to retreat from something.

ease someone **out (of** something**) 1.** to get someone out of something carefully. **2.** to get someone out of an office or position quietly and without much embarrassment.

ease up (on someone or something**)** to treat someone or something more gently.

east ['ist] **1.** *n.* the direction to the right of someone or something facing north; the direction where the sun appears to rise. (No plural.) **2.** *n.* the eastern region of a country. (Capitalized when referring to a specific region of the United States.) **3.** *adj.* in ①; from ①; toward ①; of or about ①. (Prenominal only.) **4.** *adv.* at, facing, or toward ①.

easy ['i zi] **1.** *adj.* simple; not hard; not difficult. (Adv: *easily.* Comp: *easier;* sup: *easiest.*) **2.** *adv.* without stress; without worry; relaxed. Comp: *easier;* sup: *easiest.*)
→ (AS) EASY AS (APPLE) PIE
→ (AS) EASY AS DUCK SOUP
→ FREE AND EASY
→ GET OFF EASY

easy come, easy go said to explain the loss of something that required only a small amount of effort to get in the first place.

Easy does it. Act with care.

eat ['it] **1.** *tv., irreg.* to put food in one's mouth, chew, and swallow it. (Past tense: ATE; past participle: EATEN.) **2.** *tv., irreg.* to create a hole by chewing or wearing something away. **3.** *iv., irreg.* to take food into the body.
→ DOG EAT DOG
→ GRAB A BITE (TO EAT)
→ HAVE ONE'S CAKE AND EAT IT TOO

eat (away) at someone [for a problem] to trouble someone constantly. (Figurative.)

eat (away) at something **1.** to eat something eagerly and rapidly. **2.** to erode something.

eat humble pie 1. to act very humbly when one is shown to be wrong. **2.** to accept insults and humiliation.

eat in to eat a meal at home.

eat in(to something) to erode something; to etch something.

eat like a bird to eat only small amounts of food; to peck at one's food.

eat like a horse to eat large amounts of food.

eat one's **cake and have it too**
Go to HAVE ONE'S CAKE AND EAT IT TOO.

eat one's **hat** something that one says one will do if a certain very unlikely event really happens. (Used to express the belief that the event will not occur. Always used with a phrase beginning with *if*.)

eat one's **heart out 1.** to be very sad (about someone or something). **2.** to be envious (of someone or something).

eat one's **words** to have to take back one's statements; to confess that one's predictions were wrong.

eat out to eat a meal away from home.

eat out of someone's **hand** to do exactly as someone says; to grovel to someone.

eat someone **out of house and home** to eat a lot of food (in someone's home); to eat all the food in the house.

eat someone **up 1.** to consume a person. (Figurative.) **2.** [for insects] to bite a person all over. (Figurative.)

eat something **away** to erode something; to consume something bit by bit.

eat something **off ((of) something)** to erode something off a larger part.

eat something **out 1.** to eat a meal or a particular food away from home. **2.** [for something or some creature] to consume the inside of something.

eat (something**) out of** something to eat food directly from a container, such as a bag, box, can, etc.

eat something **up 1.** to devour all of some food or some creature. **2.** [for someone] to believe something completely.

eat up to eat everything; to eat eagerly. (Usually a command to begin eating.)

eaten ['it n] Past participle of EAT.

echo ['ɛk o] **1.** *n.* a sound that is heard twice because the sound waves have bounced off a surface and returned. (Plural ends in -*es*.) **2.** *iv.* [for a sound] to reflect back. **3.** *tv.* to reflect sound; to repeat a sound. **4.** *tv.* to repeat something that someone has said.

echo back to something [for something] to recall something similar in the past.

economic [ɛk ə 'nɑm ɪk] **1.** *adj.* of or about ECONOMICS. (Adv: *economically* [...ɪk li].) **2.** *adj.* saving money; using money wisely. (Also **economical**. Adv: *economically* [...ɪk li].)

economics 1. *n.* financial matters or issues. (Usually treated as singular.) **2.** *n.* the study of the production and use of goods and services in a society. (Treated as singular.)

edge ['ɛdʒ] **1.** *n.* the rim of something; the outer border of something. **2.** *n.* the cutting part of a cutting tool or instrument. **3.** *n.* an advantage. (No plural.) **4.** *tv.* to provide something with a border.
→ SET SOMEONE'S TEETH ON EDGE

edge away (from someone or something**)** to move cautiously away from someone or something.

edgewise ['ɛdʒ waɪz] *adv.* leading with an edge; with the edge going first.
→ GET A WORD IN EDGEWISE

edible ['ɛd ə bəl] *adj.* able to be eaten. (Adv: *edibly*.)

edit ['ɛd ɪt] *tv.* to prepare text, video, or audio for publication or production.

edition [ɪ 'dɪ ʃən] *n.* the copies of one book made in one printing or series of printings until the text is changed or revised.

editor ['ɛd ɪ tɚ] **1.** *n.* someone who prepares text for publication; someone who prepares film, video, or audio for production. **2.** *n.* someone who works for a newspaper, a magazine, or a book publisher, arranging for new material, editing, and production.

educate ['ɛdʒ ə ket] *tv.* to teach someone something; to instruct someone how to do something.

education [ɛdʒ ə 'ke ʃən] **1.** *n.* the teaching of knowledge and skills; a system for teaching knowledge and skills. (No plural.) **2.** *n.* the learning or knowledge that is obtained by studying or being taught. (No plural.)

eel ['il] **1.** *n.* a long, snakelike fish not having fins. **2.** *n.* the edible flesh of ①. (No plural.)
→ (AS) SLIPPERY AS AN EEL

effect [ɪ 'fɛkt] **1.** *n.* a result; something that happens because of something else. (Compare this

with AFFECT.) **2.** *tv.* to cause a result; to produce a result.
→ IN EFFECT

effective [ɪ ˈfɛk tɪv] *adj.* good at producing or causing results. (Adv: *effectively*.)

efficient [ɪ ˈfɪ ʃənt] *adj.* organized; using time, energy, and money without waste. (Adv: *efficiently*.)

effigy [ˈɛf ə dʒi] *n.* a crude representation of a disliked person, usually made for ridicule or mocking.
→ HANG SOMEONE IN EFFIGY

effort [ˈɛf ɚt] *n.* the use of physical or mental energy to do hard work.
→ an A FOR EFFORT

egg [ˈɛg] **1.** *n.* the female reproductive cell. **2.** *n.* a round object, containing ①, covered with a shell, produced by a female bird or reptile and often used for food. **3.** *n.* the edible part of ②. **4.** *n.* some amount of ③. (No plural. Treated as singular.)
→ HAVE EGG ON ONE'S FACE
→ KILL THE GOOSE THAT LAID THE GOLDEN EGG
→ LAY AN EGG
→ PUT ALL ONE'S EGGS IN ONE BASKET
→ TEACH ONE'S GRANDMOTHER TO SUCK EGGS
→ WALK ON EGGS

egg someone on to incite someone to do something; to encourage someone to do something.

eggshell [ˈɛg ʃɛl] *n.* the hard, protective outside layer of a bird's egg.

ego [ˈi go] **1.** *n.* one's sense of oneself and one's value. (Plural ends in -s.) **2.** *n.* an overly large sense of self-esteem; a view of oneself that makes one seem far more impor-

tant than one really is. (Plural ends in -s.)

eight [ˈet] 8. (See FOUR for more information.)

eighteen [ˈet tin] 18. (See FOUR for more information.)

eighteenth [et ˈtinθ] 18th. (See FOURTH for more information.)

eighth [ˈetθ] 8th. (See FOURTH for more information.)

eightieth [ˈet i əθ] 80th. (See FOURTH for more information.)

eighty [ˈet i] 80. (See FORTY for further information.)

either [ˈi ðɚ] **1.** *adj.* one or the other [choosing between two people or things]; no matter which [of two]. **2.** *adj.* both; each of two; one and the other. **3.** *pron.* one person or thing, or the other person or thing; one person or thing from a choice of two people or things. (Treated as singular.) **4.** *adv.* as well; in addition; also. (Only in negative constructions. Use TOO in the affirmative.)

either....or *conj.* one or the other from a choice of two things.

eke something out to extend something; to add to something.

elastic [ə ˈlæs tɪk] **1.** *adj.* [of something that is] able to return to its original shape after being stretched. (Adv: *elastically* […ɪk li].) **2.** *n.* [in clothing] a band of fabric and rubber that can stretch.

elbow [ˈɛl bo] **1.** *n.* the joint where the arm bends in the middle. **2.** *n.* a pipe that is bent, curved, or shaped like the angle of ①.
→ RUB ELBOWS WITH SOMEONE

elbow (one's way) through something to push or drive oneself through something, such as a crowd, perhaps using one's elbows or arms to move people out of the way.

elbow someone **aside** to push someone aside with one's arm.

elect [ɪ 'lɛkt] *tv.* [for a group of voters] to choose someone by voting.

election [ɪ 'lɛk ʃən] *n.* the process of voting to choose between two or more options.

electric [ɪ 'lɛk trɪk] **1.** *adj.* carrying electricity; of or about electricity. (Also *electrical. Adv: electrically* [...ɪk li].) **2.** *adj.* producing electricity. (*Adv: electrically* [...ɪk li].) **3.** *adj.* powered by electricity. (*Adv: electrically* [...ɪk li].) **4.** *adj.* exciting; full of excitement; thrilling. (*Adv: electrically* [...ɪk li].)

electric plug [ɪ 'lɛk trɪk 'plʌg] **1.** *n.* a device used to attach a lamp or appliance to an electrical outlet. (Can be shortened to PLUG.) **2.** *n.* an electrical outlet or receptacle. (Informal. Can be shortened to PLUG.)

electric receptacle [ɪ 'lɛk trɪk rɪ 'sɛp tɪ kəl] *n.* an electric outlet; a connection, usually in the wall, to which lamps and appliances can be attached. (Can be shortened to RECEPTACLE.)

electricity [ɪ lɛk 'trɪs ə ti] *n.* a source of power that comes from batteries, electric companies, and natural occurrences like friction and lightning. (No plural.)

electromagnetic [ɛ lɛk tro mæg 'nɛt ɪk] *adj.* concerning electric and magnetic waves, especially as used in broadcasting. (Adv: *electromagnetically* [...ɪk li].)

electron [ɪ 'lɛk trɑn] *n.* a negatively charged particle, smaller than an atom.

electronic [ɪ lɛk 'trɑn ɪk] *adj.* of or about modern electrical circuits as found in radios and television sets. (Adv: *electronically* [...ɪk li].)

electronics *n.* the study and design of the electrical circuits used in computers, radios, televisions, etc. (Treated as singular.)

elegance ['ɛl ə gəns] *n.* fine style, grace, and beauty. (No plural.)

elegant ['ɛl ə gənt] *adj.* beautiful; having or showing good taste. (Adv: *elegantly.*)

element ['ɛl ə mənt] **1.** *n.* one of several kinds of basic matter that cannot be broken down further into other kinds of basic matter. **2.** *n.* a piece of a larger theme.
→ OUT OF ONE'S ELEMENT

elementary [ɛl ə 'mɛn tri] *adj.* basic; introductory.

the **elements** *n.* the weather; air, wind, rain, and sunlight. (Treated as plural, but not countable.)

elephant ['ɛl ə fənt] *n.* a large land mammal of Africa and Asia, with tough gray skin, large ears, and a long trunk.
→ WHITE ELEPHANT

elevator ['ɛl ə ve tɚ] *n.* a moving cage or chamber that carries people and things from floor to floor in a building with more than one story.

eleven [ɪ ˈlɛv ən] 11. (See FOUR for more information.)

eleventh [ɪ ˈlɛv əntθ] 11th. (See FOURTH for more information.)

elf [ˈɛlf] *n., irreg.* a small humanlike creature—full of mischief—of fairy tales and myths. (Plural: ELVES.)

elk [ˈɛlk] **1.** *n., irreg.* [in North America] a large deer, the males of which have large, spreading horns. (Plural: *elk* or *elks.*) **2.** *n., irreg.* [in Europe] a moose.

elm [ˈɛlm] **1.** *n.* a large tree that loses its leaves each fall and is planted to make shade. **2.** *n.* wood from ①. (Plural only for types and instances.) **3.** *adj.* made of ②.

else [ˈɛls] **1.** *adj.* otherwise; apart from someone or something; instead. **2.** *adj.* in addition to someone or something; as well.

elsewhere [ˈɛls ʍɛr] *adv.* in some other place.

elude [ɪ ˈlud] **1.** *tv.* to evade or avoid capture, often by being clever. **2.** *tv.* [for a concept] to be hard to remember or understand.

elusive [ɪ ˈlu sɪv] *adj.* [of someone or something that is] hard to find or hard to catch. (Adv: *elusively.*)

elves [ˈɛlvz] plural of ELF.

embarrass [ɛm ˈbɛr əs] *tv.* to make someone feel ashamed or uncomfortable by making something visible or known in public.

emblazon something **on(to)** something [ɛm ˈble zən…] **1.** to decorate something with something. **2.** to mark something with writing or symbols that proclaim something.

emergency [ɪ ˈmɚ dʒən si] **1.** *n.* a time when urgent action is needed; a dangerous situation that must be taken care of at once. **2.** the *adj.* use of ①.

emergency room [ɪ ˈmɚ dʒən si rum] *n.* the place in a hospital where injuries and sudden illnesses are cared for.

emotion [ɪ ˈmo ʃən] **1.** *n.* feeling—other than with the physical senses—or a show of feeling. (No plural.) **2.** *n.* a feeling, such as sadness, joy, anxiety, etc.
→ LET ONE'S EMOTIONS SHOW

emperor [ˈɛmp ɚ rɚ] *n.* someone, especially a male, who rules an EMPIRE.

emphases [ˈɛm fə siz] plural of EMPHASIS.

emphasis [ˈɛm fə sɪs] **1.** *n.* importance that is placed on or given to something. (No plural.) **2.** *n., irreg.* something that has received or should receive ①. (Plural: EMPHASES.) **3.** *n.* increased loudness or (voice) stress given to particular syllables, words, or phrases. (No plural.)

emphasize [ˈɛm fə saɪz] **1.** *tv.* to place special importance on something. **2.** *tv.* to stress something, especially a syllable, word, or phrase.

empire [ˈɛm paɪr] *n.* a group of countries ruled by an EMPEROR or EMPRESS.

employ [ɛm ˈplɔɪ] **1.** *tv.* to hire someone to do work for pay. **2.** *tv.* to use something for a particular purpose.

employable [ɛm 'plɔɪ ə bəl] *adj.*
suitable for employment. (Adv:
employably.)

employee [ɛm 'plɔɪ i] *n.* someone
who works for a company or a
person for pay.

employer [ɛm 'plɔɪ ɚ] *n.* a person
or company that employs people.

employment [ɛm 'plɔɪ mənt] **1.** *n.*
the condition of holding a job. (No
plural.) **2.** *n.* the work that one
does; one's job. (No plural.)

empress ['ɛm prəs] *n.* a woman
who rules an EMPIRE.

empty ['ɛmp ti] **1.** *adj.* having
nothing or no one within; vacant.
(Comp: *emptier;* sup: *emptiest.*)
2. *adj.* without meaning; without
purpose; senseless. (Figurative on
①. Adv: *emptily.* Comp: *emptier;*
sup: *emptiest.*) **3.** *tv.* to cause
something to be ① by removing
all the contents. **4.** *iv.* [for some-
thing] to become ①.
→ COME AWAY EMPTY-HANDED
→ GO AWAY EMPTY-HANDED

empty something **out** to remove or
pour out all of the contents from
something.

enact [ɛn 'ækt] **1.** *tv.* to make a bill
into a law; to pass a law. **2.** *tv.* to
perform a part in a play or a
movie; to act something out.

enclose [ɛn 'kloz] **1.** *tv.* to put
something in an envelope, box,
etc. **2.** *tv.* to close something in on
all sides; to put walls up around
something.

enclosed [ɛn 'klozd] **1.** *adj.*
included in an envelope or a package. **2.** *adj.* shut in on all sides;
surrounded; having walls around
on all sides.

encore ['ɑŋ kor] **1.** *n.* the performance of an additional piece of
music, or a repeat of a piece of
music, after the end of a concert,
at the demand of the audience.
2. *adj.* repeated.

encounter [ɛn 'kɑun tɚ] **1.** *tv.* to
meet someone or something by
chance. **2.** *n.* a meeting, especially
by chance.

encourage [ɛn 'kɚ ɪdʒ] *tv.* to give
someone the courage or confidence to do something.

encouragement [ɛn 'kɚ ɪdʒ mənt]
n. words or actions that encourage
someone. (No plural.)

end ['ɛnd] **1.** *n.* the final stopping
point of a continuing process. (No
plural.) **2.** *n.* the last part of some-
thing. **3.** *n.* death. (A euphemism.)
4. *n.* a purpose; an intended out-
come; a result. **5.** *iv.* to stop; to fin-
ish; to exist no longer. **6.** *tv.* to
stop something; to finish some-
thing.
→ AT ONE'S WIT'S END
→ AT THE END OF ONE'S ROPE
→ AT LOOSE ENDS
→ BURN THE CANDLE AT BOTH ENDS
→ the BUSINESS END OF SOMETHING
→ CAN'T SEE BEYOND THE END OF ONE'S
    NOSE
→ COME TO A BAD END
→ COME TO A DEAD END
→ COME TO AN END
→ COME TO AN UNTIMELY END
→ GET THE SHORT END OF THE STICK
→ GO OFF THE DEEP END
→ HOLD UP ONE'S END (OF THE BAR-
    GAIN)
→ JUMP OFF THE DEEP END
→ JUMP OFF THE DEEP END (OVER
    SOMEONE OR SOMETHING)

→ LIVE UP TO ONE'S END OF THE BAR-
 GAIN
→ MAKE SOMEONE'S HAIR STAND ON END
→ MEET ONE'S END
→ NOT SEE FURTHER THAN THE END OF
 ONE'S NOSE
→ PLAY BOTH ENDS (AGAINST THE MID-
 DLE)
→ SEE THE LIGHT (AT THE END OF THE
 TUNNEL)
→ TO THE ENDS OF THE EARTH

an **end in itself** something done
 for its own sake; something that
 needs no additional purpose for it
 to be worthwhile.

the **end of the line** Go to the END
 OF THE ROAD.

the **end of the road** and the **end
 of the line 1.** the end; the end of
 the whole process. **2.** death.

end something **up** to terminate
 something; to bring something to
 an end.

end up to come to an end.

end up at something to be at something or someplace at the end.

end up doing something to have to
 do something one has tried to get
 out of doing.

end up somehow to come to the
 end of something in a particular
 way.

end up something to become something at the end of everything.

**end up with the short end of
 the stick** Go to GET THE SHORT END
 OF THE STICK.

endless ['ɛnd ləs] *adj.* without end;
 continuous; without stopping.
 (Adv: *endlessly.*)

endurance [ɛn 'dur əns] *n.* the
 ability to keep going; the ability to
 endure. (No plural.)

endure [ɛn 'dur] **1.** *tv.* to withstand
 something; to put up with some-
 thing; to tolerate something. **2.** *iv.*
 to last; to keep going.

enemy ['ɛn ə mi] **1.** *n.* an opponent
 of someone or something; some-
 one who fights against someone or
 something. **2.** *n.* a country that
 another country fights against
 during a war; an army that
 another army fights against during
 a war.

energy ['ɛn ɚ dʒi] *n.* the power
 needed to do something; the force
 that powers people or machines.
 (No plural.)

engage [ɛn 'gedʒ] **1.** *tv.* to take up
 someone's time; to keep someone
 busy. **2.** *tv.* to obtain the services
 of someone. **3.** *tv.* to rent something or a place. **4.** *iv.* [for mechanical parts] to move into
 operating position with one
 another.

engine ['ɛn dʒən] **1.** *n.* a machine
 that uses power from gas, electricity, water pressure, steam, etc., to
 create power or motion. **2.** *n.* a
 powered train car that pulls or
 pushes the other train cars; a locomotive.
→ FIRE ENGINE
→ JET ENGINE

engineer [ɛn dʒə 'nɪr] **1.** *n.* someone who drives a locomotive. **2.** *n.*
 someone who has training in a
 branch of engineering. **3.** *tv.* [for
 ②] to do the designing and planning of something, such as a
 building, bridge, computer, automobile, etc.

engrave something **on(to)** something to cut symbols into the surface of something.

engrave something **(up)on** something **1.** to cut letters or a design into the surface of something. **2.** to imprint something firmly on someone's mind.

enjoy [ɛn 'dʒɔɪ] *tv.* to have something that is good; to feel fortunate to have something; to take pleasure in something.

enjoyment [ɛn 'dʒɔɪ mənt] *n.* joy; pleasure; happiness. (Plural only for types and instances.)

enlarge **(up)on** something to add details to a report about something.

enlist someone **in** something to recruit someone into something; to recruit someone into the armed services.

enormous [ɪ 'nɔr məs] *adj.* huge; large; very big. (Adv: *enormously.*)

enough [ɪ 'nʌf] **1.** *adj.* as much as is needed; as much as is necessary; adequate. **2.** *pron.* a necessary amount; an adequate amount. **3.** *adv.* to an adequate degree. (Follows an adjective or a verb.)
→ GET UP ENOUGH NERVE (TO DO SOMETHING)
→ NOT KNOW ENOUGH TO COME IN OUT OF THE RAIN

Enough is enough. That is enough, and there should be no more.

enough to go around enough to serve all who have a need.

enroll AND **enrol** [ɛn 'rol] *tv.* to sign someone up for a club, school, or other group.

enrol(l) **(in** something**)** to become a member of a club, school, or other group.

ensure [ɛn 'ʃʊr] *tv.* to make sure that something happens; to make something certain to happen. (Compare this with INSURE.)

enter ['ɛn tɚ] **1.** *tv.* to go into a place; to come into a place. **2.** *tv.* to join something; to begin a career or course of study. **3.** *tv.* to write down something in a journal, log, or record book. **4.** *tv.* to type data or other information into a computer. **5.** *n.* the key labeled *enter* on a computer keyboard.

enter in something to enroll as a participant in something, such as a contest, competition, etc.

enter into something **1.** to get into something. **2.** to join in something.

enter one's **mind** to come to one's mind; [for an idea or memory] to come into one's consciousness; to be thought of.

enter someone or something **in((to)** something**)** to enroll someone or something in something; to make someone or something a competitor in something.

enter (up)on something **1.** to come in at a particular point as marked by something. **2.** to begin something.

entertain [ɛn tɚ 'ten] **1.** *tv.* to amuse someone; to provide an audience with amusement. **2.** *tv.* to provide guests or associates with food, amusement, and hospitality. **3.** *tv.* to consider something; to think about something.

entertainment [ɛn tɚ 'ten mənt] *n.* amusement; an entertaining performance. (A plural form is rare.)

entire [ɛn 'taɪɚ] *adj.* whole; including everyone or everything. (Adv: *entirely.*)

entirety [ɛn 'taɪr ə ti] *n.* a state of completeness.
→ IN ITS ENTIRETY
→ IN THEIR ENTIRETY

entomb someone or something **in** something **1.** to place someone or something in a tomb. **2.** to imprison someone or some creature in a tomblike enclosure.

entrance 1. ['ɛn trəns] *n.* the right to go into a place; the right to enter a place. (No plural.) **2.** ['ɛn trəns] *n.* an instance of entering. **3.** ['ɛn trəns] *n.* the way into a room or place; the door to a room or other place. **4.** [ɛn 'træns] *tv.* to charm someone.

entrust someone or something **with** someone or something [ɛn 'trʌst] **1.** to charge someone or some group with the care of someone or something. **2.** to place someone or something in the care of someone or something.

entry ['ɛn tri] **1.** *n.* going into a place or a room. **2.** *n.* an entrance; the way into a room or a place. **3.** *n.* a piece of information or data that is put into a computer, journal, database, dictionary, encyclopedia, or record book, or is put on a list.

envelop [ɛn 'vɛl əp] *tv.* to wrap around someone or something; to completely cover someone or something.

envelope ['ɛn və lop] *n.* a paper cover that letters and documents are placed in for mailing.

environment [ɛn 'vaɪ ən mənt] *n.* the state and nature of the immediate area.

the **environment** *n.* nature, including the atmosphere, oceans, lands, and all creatures. (No plural. Treated as singular.)

envy ['ɛn vi] **1.** *n.* a negative, greedy feeling toward someone who has someone or something that one wants. (No plural.) **2.** *tv.* to have a negative feeling toward someone who has someone or something that one wants.
→ GREEN WITH ENVY

equal ['i kwəl] **1.** *adj.* the same as someone or something; in the same amount or degree. (Adv: *equally.*) **2.** *tv.* to be the same as someone or something else; to have the same amount or degree of something as someone or something else. **3.** *n.* a person who is on the same level as someone else—in social standing, ability, rank, etc.

equality [ɪ 'kwɑl ə ti] *n.* the condition of having the same amount or degree of something as someone or something else. (No plural.)

equalize ['i kwə laɪz] *tv.* to cause something to equal something else.

equation [ɪ 'kwe ʒən] *n.* a statement showing that two amounts are equal.

equator [ɪ ˈkwet ɚ] *n.* the imaginary line around the middle of the earth (or any planet) halfway between the north and south poles.

equip someone **with** something [ɪ ˈkwɪp…] to provide someone with the necessary supplies or tools.

equip something **with** something to provide something with additional or needed parts or devices.

equipment [ɪ ˈkwɪp mənt] *n.* things that are furnished or supplied, especially the tools and supplies needed to do a job. (No plural. Number is expressed with *piece(s) of equipment*.)

equivalent [ɪ ˈkwɪv ə lənt] *adj.* same; equal in level or degree. (Adv: *equivalently*.)

erase [ɪ ˈres] **1.** *tv.* to remove something written or drawn in pencil, ink, or chalk by rubbing it with an eraser. **2.** *tv.* to wipe something clean by removing the writing—especially chalk or pencil writing—on it. **3.** *tv.* to remove something completely. (Figurative on ①.)

erase something **from** something to delete or wipe something from something.

eraser [ɪ ˈres ɚ] *n.* a small rubber object that erases pencil markings; a rectangular block of felt that rubs out chalk markings.

erect [ɪ ˈrɛkt] **1.** *adj.* standing straight up in a vertical position. (Adv: *erectly*.) **2.** *adj.* upright; straight up. **3.** *tv.* to build something. **4.** *tv.* to cause something to stand in a vertical position.

err [ɛr, ɚ] *iv.* to make a mistake; to be wrong.

errand [ˈɛr ənd] *n.* a short trip to do something useful or helpful.
→ ON A FOOL'S ERRAND
→ RUN AN ERRAND

error [ˈɛr ɚ] **1.** *n.* a mistake; something that is wrong. **2.** *n.* a bad play by someone on a baseball team.

erupt [ɪ ˈrʌpt] **1.** *iv.* [for a volcano] to explode. **2.** *iv.* [for anger, violence, arguments, etc.] to be released suddenly.

erupt from something to burst out of something or someplace.

erupt in something AND **erupt with** something to develop a rash on the skin.

erupt into something to become a serious problem suddenly; to blow up into something.

erupt with something Go to ERUPT IN SOMETHING.

eruption [ɪ ˈrʌp ʃən] **1.** *n.* an explosion of a volcano; a flowing out of material from a volcano. **2.** *n.* a bursting forth of anger, violence, fighting, etc.

escalate into something to intensify into something; to increase gradually into something.

escalator [ˈɛs kə le tɚ] *n.* a moving staircase that carries people to a higher or lower floor of a building.

escape [ɛ ˈskep] **1.** *n.* fleeing a dangerous place, an enclosed place, or a bad situation. (Plural only for types and instances.) **2.** *iv.* to become free; to get away. **3.** *iv.* to leak from a container. **4.** *iv.* to elude being caught; to avoid being

caught. **5.** *tv.* to (seem to) avoid being seen, heard, remembered, etc.
→ AVENUE OF ESCAPE
→ FIRE ESCAPE

especially [ɛ 'spɛʃ ə li] *adv.* mainly; primarily; particularly.

essay ['ɛs e] *n.* a written work about a specific topic.

essence ['ɛs əns] **1.** *n.* the most important part of something; the important features that make up someone or something. **2.** *n.* a perfume or similar substance.
→ IN ESSENCE

establish [ɛ 'stæb lɪʃ] **1.** *tv.* to start an organization; to found an organization. **2.** *tv.* to start something, such as a policy or plan. **3.** *tv.* to place oneself or itself as something or in a specific role. (Takes a reflexive object.) **4.** *tv.* to prove something; to determine the truth of something. (The object can be a clause with THAT ⑦.)

establishment [ɛ 'stæb lɪʃ mənt] **1.** *n.* establishing something. (No plural.) **2.** *n.* a company or organization.

estate [ɛ 'stet] **1.** *n.* everything that someone owns; the property of someone who has just died. **2.** *n.* a house and related buildings set on a large piece of property.
→ REAL ESTATE

esteem [ɛ 'stim] *n.* opinion or regard, favorable unless indicated otherwise. (No plural.)

estimate 1. ['ɛst ə mət] *n.* a statement that shows about how much someone will charge to do a certain amount of work; an approximate calculation of an amount of

money, intended to represent the final cost fairly closely. **2.** *n.* ['ɛst ə mət] a guess or projection. **3.** ['ɛst ə met] *tv.* to calculate how much something will cost; to determine an approximate amount of money. (The object can be a clause with THAT ⑦.) **4.** ['ɛst ə met] *tv.* to guess or project an outcome.

estimation [est ə 'me ʃən] *n.* one's opinion or judgment. (No plural.)

et cetera ['ɛt 'sɛt ə rə] and other similar things; and so forth; and other things like those just named. (Abbreviated as ETC.)

etc. an abbreviation of ET CETERA.

eternal [ɪ 'tɚ nəl] *adj.* without ending; existing forever. (Adv: *eternally.*)

eternity [ɪ 'tɚ nə ti] *n.* time without beginning or ending. (No plural.)

ethic ['ɛθ ɪk] *n.* the body of morals governing a person or a group. (No plural.)

ethics 1. *n.* standards of right and wrong within a society. (Treated as plural, but not countable.) **2.** *n.* the study of the standards of right and wrong; the study of morals. (Treated as singular.)

ethnic ['ɛθ nɪk] *adj.* of or about a particular variety, group, or subgroup of people, such as divisions according to race, language, country, etc. (Adv: *ethnically* […ɪk li].)

euphemism ['ju fə mɪz əm] *n.* a word or phrase that replaces a less polite or more harsh word or expression.

evade [ɪ 'ved] *tv.* to avoid doing something; to avoid the consequences of something.

evaluate [ɪ 'væl ju et] *tv.* to study and make a judgment about the value of someone or something.

evaluation [ɪ væl ju 'e ʃən] **1.** *n.* studying the worth, value, or status of something. (Plural only for types and instances.) **2.** *n.* a judgment or statement about the status or quality of someone or something.

eve ['iv] *n.* the night or day before an important day.

even ['i vən] **1.** *adj.* smooth; not rough; level; on the same level; uniform. (Adv: *evenly.*) **2.** *adj.* [of a number] able to be divided by 2 with nothing left over. (Adv: *evenly.*) **3.** *adj.* equal. (Adv: *evenly.*) **4.** *adv.* still more; yet more. (Used to make a comparison stronger.) **5.** *adv.* more than expected; in a way that would not be expected. **6.** *tv.* to smooth something out; to make something smooth; to make something level.
→ KEEP ON AN EVEN KEEL
→ KEEP SOMETHING ON AN EVEN KEEL

even something **off** to make something even or smooth.

even something **out** to make something even or level.

even something **up** to make something even, square, level, equal, balanced, etc.

evening ['iv nɪŋ] **1.** *n.* the last part of the day; the period of the day after the afternoon and before the night. **2.** the *adj.* use of ①.

evenings *adv.* every evening; happening every ①.

event [ə 'vɛnt] *n.* something that happens; an occurrence.

eventual [ə 'vɛn tʃu əl] *adj.* at some time in the future. (Adv: *eventually.*)

ever ['ɛv ɚ] **1.** *adv.* at any time. (Used especially in negative sentences, questions, and sentences with *if,* and after comparatives with *than,* after superlatives, or after *as.*) **2.** *adv.* always; forever.

every ['ɛv ri] **1.** *adj.* all; each. (For two people or things, use BOTH.) **2.** *adj.* per; once during each unit. **3.** *adj.* all possible.
→ HANG ON SOMEONE'S EVERY WORD
→ USE EVERY TRICK IN THE BOOK
→ WITH EVERY (OTHER) BREATH

every inch a something AND **every inch the** something completely; in every way.

every inch the something Go to EVERY INCH A SOMETHING.

every living soul every person.

every minute counts AND **every moment counts** time is very important.

every moment counts Go to EVERY MINUTE COUNTS.

every other person or thing every second person or thing; alternating.

every Tom, Dick, and Harry everyone, without discrimination; ordinary people. (Not necessarily males.)

everybody ['ɛv ri bad i] *pron.* every person; everyone.

everyday ['ɛv ri de] **1.** *adj.* happening every day. (Prenominal only.) **2.** *adj.* common; ordinary; not special. (Compare this with *every day* (adv.), meaning "each day.")

everyone ['ɛv ri wən] *pron.* every person; all; everybody. (Treated as singular.)
→ the MOMENT EVERYONE HAS BEEN WAITING FOR

everything ['ɛv ri θɪŋ] **1.** *pron.* each thing. **2.** *pron.* the only thing that is important; the only goal or value.
→ DROP EVERYTHING
→ WITH EVERYTHING (ON IT)

everything but the kitchen sink almost everything one can think of.

everything from A to Z Go to EVERYTHING FROM SOUP TO NUTS.

everything from soup to nuts AND **everything from A to Z** almost everything one can think of. (The main entry is used especially when describing the many things served at a meal.)

everything humanly possible everything that is in the range of human powers.

everywhere ['ɛv ri mɛr] *adv.* in all places; in every location; at every point.

evidence ['ɛv ə dəns] *n.* something that proves a claim or statement. (No plural.)

evil ['i vəl] **1.** *adj.* very bad; capable of doing very bad things. (Adv: *evilly.*) **2.** *n.* badness. (Plural only for types and instances.)
→ the LESSER OF TWO EVILS

evolution [ɛv ə 'lu ʃən] **1.** *n.* the changes of something from an early stage to a more advanced stage. (No plural.) **2.** *n.* the scientific theory that all living creatures developed from simpler forms of life over millions of years. (No plural.)

exact [ɪg 'zækt] *adj.* without mistakes; precise; completely correct. (Adv: *exactly.*)

exact something **from** someone to demand something from someone; to take something from someone.

exactly [ɪg 'zækt li] **1.** *adv.* precisely; accurately; only as requested or ordered. **2.** *interj.* That is quite right!

exam [ɪg 'zæm] *n.* an EXAMINATION.

examination [ɪg zæm ɪ 'ne ʃən] **1.** *n.* examining, studying, or observing someone or something. (Plural only for types and instances.) **2.** *n.* a test; a series of questions given to test someone's knowledge of a certain topic.
→ PHYSICAL EXAMINATION

examine [ɪg 'zæm ɪn] **1.** *tv.* to look at someone or something very closely. **2.** *tv.* to make a medical study of the state of someone's body.
→ CROSS-EXAMINE SOMEONE

example [ɪg 'zæm pəl] **1.** *n.* something that clarifies what one is talking about; a sample of what is being talked about. **2.** *n.* someone or something that should be imitated; a model.

exceed [ɛk 'sid] **1.** *tv.* to go beyond the limits of something; to surpass the upper boundary of something. **2.** *tv.* to surpass something.

excel [ɛk 'sɛl] *iv.* to do very well at something; to be outstanding at something.

excellence ['ɛk sə ləns] *n.* a superior quality; the best quality possible; an extremely good quality. (No plural.)

excellent ['ɛk sə lənt] *adj.* superior; extremely good; outstanding; of very high quality. (Adv: *excellently*.)

except [ɛk 'sɛpt] *tv.* to exclude someone or something; to omit someone or something. (Compare this with ACCEPT.)

except for someone or something **1.** other than someone or something; besides someone or something; not including someone or something. **2.** were it not for someone or something; if someone or something were different.

excess 1. ['ɛk sɛs] *n.* the amount that is over a certain limit or boundary; the part of something that is too much. (No plural.) **2.** ['ɛk sɛs] *adj.* extra; beyond the proper limit; beyond what is needed.
→ DRINK TO EXCESS

excesses [ɛk 'sɛs əs] *n.* spending for expensive things; wasting money by spending it on things that cost a lot of money.

excessive [ɛk 'sɛs ɪv] *adj.* extra; beyond the proper limit; beyond what is needed; too much. (Adv: *excessively*.)

exchange [ɛks 'tʃendʒ] **1.** *tv.* to trade something for something else; to trade someone for someone else. **2.** *n.* an instance of giving someone something for something else; an instance of trading something for something else. **3.** *n.* a conversation; a short dialogue. **4.** *n.* a place where things, such as stocks, are bought and sold. **5.** *n.* a particular part of the telephone switching system, represented in the United States by the first three digits of a local telephone number.

excite [ɛk 'saɪt] *tv.* to interest or stimulate someone or something.

excitement [ɛk 'saɪt mənt] *n.* the feeling of great interest, eagerness, and stimulation. (A plural form is rare and is not countable.)
→ a RIPPLE OF EXCITEMENT

exciting [ɛk 'saɪ tɪŋ] *adj.* causing excitement; very interesting; stimulating. (Adv: *excitingly*.)

exclaim [ɛk 'sklem] *tv.* to shout something; to say something with strong feeling. (The object is a clause with THAT ⑦.)

exclamation [ɛk sklə 'me ʃən] *n.* a loud statement; a statement made with strong feeling or emotion.

exclamation point [ɛk sklə 'me ʃən pɔɪnt] *n.* a punctuation mark (!) written at the end of a word, phrase, or sentence that is an exclamation.

exclude someone or something **from** something to leave someone or something out of something; to leave someone or something off a list.

excrement ['ɛk skrə mənt] *n.* feces; solid waste from the bowels. (No plural.)

excuse 1. [ɛk 'skjus] *n.* a reason that attempts to explain or justify something that is wrong. **2.** [ɛk 'skjuz] *tv.* to forgive someone for bad manners; to pardon someone.

3. [ɛk 'skjuz] *tv.* to give someone permission to leave.

excuse oneself to make polite apologies or explanations before leaving a place.

execute ['ɛks ə kjut] **1.** *tv.* to do something as ordered; to carry out something; to perform an act. **2.** *tv.* to kill someone as a punishment; to punish someone with death. **3.** *tv.* to make a document effective as of a certain date by signing it.

execution [ɛks ə 'kju ʃən] **1.** *n.* the doing of something; the carrying out of an order. (No plural.) **2.** *n.* the killing of someone as a punishment.

executive [ɛg 'zɛk jə tiv] **1.** *n.* someone who manages an organization in business or government. **2.** *adj.* in the manner of ①; firm and authoritative. **3.** *adj.* of or about the branch of government that manages, but not the branches that make laws and run the courts.

exempt [ɛg 'zɛmpt] **1.** *tv.* to free someone from a duty or obligation. **2.** *adj.* free from a duty or obligation.

exempt someone **from** something to release someone from the obligation to do something; to allow a person not to be affected by a rule or law.

exercise ['ɛk sɚ saiz] **1.** *n.* active use of the muscles of the body. (No plural form in this sense.) **2.** *n.* a specific act of ①. **3.** *n.* a question or problem designed to train someone in problem solving.

4. *n.* an activity designed to train someone for a military task. **5.** *tv.* to actively use one or more muscles or areas of the body. **6.** *tv.* to actively use something, such as a power, right, privilege, or option. **7.** *iv.* to be physically active in order to strengthen the heart and muscles or to lose weight.

exhale [ɛks 'hel] **1.** *iv.* to breathe out; to push air out from the lungs. **2.** *tv.* to breathe air or smoke out of the body.

exhaust [ɛg 'zɔst] **1.** *n.* steam, gas, or vapor that is the waste product of burning. (No plural.) **2.** *tv.* to use up all of someone's or something's resources or energy. **3.** *tv.* to cause someone to become very tired.

exist [ɛg 'zist] **1.** *iv.* to be; to be in reality. **2.** *iv.* to last through time; to continue to be. **3.** *iv.* to manage to live with only the minimum of physical needs met.

existence [ɛg 'zis təns] **1.** *n.* being; the condition of actually being or existing. (No plural.) **2.** *n.* living; continuing to be; a way of living. (No plural.)
→ IN EXISTENCE

exit ['ɛg zit] **1.** *n.* the way out, especially from a place or room. **2.** *n.* the roadway leading off a highway. **3.** *n.* leaving someplace, especially a stage. **4.** *iv.* to leave [a place, such as a stage or a highway]. **5.** *tv.* to leave a place.

expand into something to grow into something; to enlarge into something.

expand something **into** something to enlarge something into something; to make something grow into something.

expand (up)on something to add detail to a report about something.

expect [ɛk 'spɛkt] *tv.* to anticipate the arrival of something; to anticipate the birth of a baby; to anticipate that something will happen. (The object can be a clause with THAT ⑦.)

expect to do something to think that one will do something.

expecting (a child) pregnant.

expedition [ɛk spɪ 'dɪ ʃən] *n.* a trip; a journey; a specific course of travel to a certain place.
→ GO ON A FISHING EXPEDITION

expel [ɛk 'spɛl] **1.** *tv.* to force someone or something out of a place. **2.** *tv.* to order that someone not attend a school, usually because of bad behavior or bad grades; to end someone's membership in an organization.

expense [ɛk 'spɛns] *n.* the amount of money that a product or service costs; an item of cost, as in a budget.

expensive [ɛk 'spɛn sɪv] *adj.* costing a lot of money; high-priced; costly. (Adv: *expensively.*)

experience [ɛk 'spɪr i əns] **1.** *n.* knowledge gained from remembering past events and the results of one's actions during those events; skills gained from living one's life. (No plural.) **2.** *n.* something that happens to someone; an event that gives someone ①. **3.** *tv.* to learn about something by being involved in it when it happens; to feel or encounter something.

experiment [ɛk 'spɛr ə mənt] **1.** *n.* a test that is carried out to prove an idea or theory or show that it is wrong. **2.** *iv.* to try something in order to find out about it.

experiment (up)on someone or something to use someone or something as the subject of an experiment.

expert ['ɛk spɚt] **1.** *n.* someone who is an authority on something; someone who knows a lot about a certain topic. **2.** *adj.* having a lot of knowledge or skill. (Adv: *expertly.*)

explain [ɛk 'splen] **1.** *tv.* to make something easier to understand; to talk in detail about something; to make something clear. **2.** *tv.* to give an excuse for something. (The object can be a clause with THAT ⑦.)

explain something **away** to explain something so that it is no longer a problem.

explanation [ɛk splə 'ne ʃən] *n.* information that makes something easier to understand; a description. (Plural only for types and instances.)

explode [ɛk 'splod] **1.** *iv.* to blow up, as with a bomb; to burst. **2.** *iv.* to get very angry. (Figurative on ①.) **3.** *tv.* to cause something to EXPLODE as in ①.

explore [ɛk 'splor] **1.** *tv.* to study and examine a place that has not been examined before. **2.** *tv.* to examine or consider a plan or idea carefully. (Figurative on ①.)

explosion [ɛk 'splo ʒən] *n.* a loud, violent burst; an act of exploding; the blowing up of something.

export 1. ['ɛk sport] *n.* a product that is shipped to another country; a product that is sold to another country. **2.** ['ɛk sport] the *adj.* use of ①. **3.** [ɛk 'sport] *tv.* to ship a product to another country for sale; to sell a product in another country.

exposure [ɛk 'spo ʒɚ] **1.** *n.* showing something to the public; showing something that was hidden. (Plural only for types and instances.) **2.** *n.* attention given to someone or something by newspapers, television, magazines, etc. (No plural.) **3.** *n.* a section of film [used in photography] that will produce a single image.

express [ɛk 'sprɛs] **1.** *tv.* [for someone] to put a thought or idea into words; to speak about an idea. **2.** *tv.* [for someone] to convey a feeling or emotion through words, signs, gestures, or writing. **3.** *tv.* [for something] to indicate something; to show something. **4.** *adj.* [of transportation] traveling without stopping or with fewer stops. **5.** *adj.* of or about a rapid means of shipment or delivery.

express one's **anger** to allow a release or expression of anger, such as through angry words, violence, or talk.

expression [ɛk 'sprɛ ʃən] **1.** *n.* the look on one's face that indicates how one feels. **2.** *n.* the process

of expressing oneself in some way. **3.** *n.* a phrase or clause that is used to express an idea; an idiom.

extend [ɛk 'stɛnd] **1.** *tv.* to stretch something, making it longer. **2.** *tv.* to make something last longer in time. (Figurative on ①.) **3.** *tv.* to present an offer; to utter an offer or a wish. **4.** *iv.* to increase in length. **5.** *iv.* to spread out in all directions. **6.** *iv.* to continue in space or time.

extend across something to spread across something.

extension [ɛk 'stɛn ʃən] **1.** *n.* something that is added to something to make it longer or larger; an additional part. **2.** *n.* extra time given beyond a deadline. **3.** *n.* an electric cord that acts to extend the distance between an electric receptacle and the device that needs to be plugged in. (Short for EXTENSION CORD.)

extension cord [ɛk 'stɛn ʃən 'kord] *n.* a length of electrical cord with a plug on one end and a receptacle on the other. (Can be shortened to EXTENSION.)

extent [ɛk 'stɛnt] *n.* the distance or degree to which something extends or reaches; the degree to which something is covered or accounted for.

exterior [ɛk 'stɪr i ɚ] **1.** *n.* the outside of something. **2.** the *adj.* use of ①.

external [ɛk 'stɚ nəl] **1.** *adj.* outside; outer. (Adv: *externally.*) **2.** *adj.* coming from the outside; being affected by someone or

183

something on the outside. (Adv: *externally*.)

extinct [ɛk 'stɪŋkt] **1.** *adj.* [of a plant or animal species that is] no longer in existence. **2.** *adj.* [of a volcano] no longer capable of erupting.

extra ['ɛk strə] **1.** *adj.* more or greater than is expected; more or greater than usual; additional. **2.** *adv.* more than usual; additionally. **3.** *n.* an actor who is hired to be part of the background or part of a crowd.
→ GO THE EXTRA MILE

extreme [ɛk 'strim] **1.** *adj.* to the greatest degree; to the furthest point possible in any direction; furthest. (Adv: *extremely*.) **2.** *n.* one of two things that are as far apart from each other as possible.

eye ['aɪ] **1.** *n.* one of the two organs of sight; an EYEBALL. **2.** *n.* the ring of color on someone's eye; the iris. **3.** *tv.* to glance at or look at someone or something; to watch someone or something. (The present participle is *eying* or *eyeing*.)
→ ABLE TO DO SOMETHING WITH ONE'S EYES CLOSED
→ the APPLE OF SOMEONE'S EYE
→ a BIRD'S-EYE VIEW
→ CATCH SOMEONE'S EYE
→ CRY ONE'S EYES OUT
→ EAGLE EYE
→ FEAST ONE'S EYES (ON SOMEONE OR SOMETHING)
→ GET A BLACK EYE
→ GET SOMEONE'S EYE
→ GET STARS IN ONE'S EYES
→ GIVE SOMEONE A BLACK EYE
→ GIVE SOMEONE THE EYE
→ HAVE EYES BIGGER THAN ONE'S STOMACH
→ HAVE EYES IN THE BACK OF ONE'S HEAD
→ HAVE SOMEONE'S EYE
→ HIT SOMEONE (RIGHT) BETWEEN THE EYES
→ HIT THE BULL'S-EYE
→ IN ONE'S MIND'S EYE
→ IN THE PUBLIC EYE
→ IN THE TWINKLING OF AN EYE
→ KEEP AN EYE OUT (FOR SOMEONE OR SOMETHING)
→ KEEP ONE'S EYE ON THE BALL
→ KEEP ONE'S WEATHER EYE OPEN
→ ONE'S EYES ARE BIGGER THAN ONE'S STOMACH.
→ OUT OF THE CORNER OF ONE'S EYE
→ PULL THE WOOL OVER SOMEONE'S EYES
→ PUT SOMEONE'S EYE OUT
→ SEE EYE TO EYE (ABOUT SOMETHING)
→ SEE EYE TO EYE ON SOMETHING
→ TURN A BLIND EYE TO SOMEONE OR SOMETHING
→ WITH THE NAKED EYE
→ WITHOUT BATTING AN EYE

eye of the storm 1. the center of a hurricane or other major storm. **2.** the center of a problem; the center of a commotion or a disturbance.

eyeball ['aɪ bɔl] *n.* the round part of the eye that sits in the socket. (The same as EYE ①.)

eyeball-to-eyeball person-to-person; face-to-face.

eyebrow ['aɪ braʊ] *n.* the curved ridge of hair on one's forehead, just above the eye.
→ CAUSE (SOME) EYEBROWS TO RAISE
→ RAISE SOME EYEBROWS

eyeful ['aɪ fʊl] the full vision of a shocking or surprising sight.
→ GET AN EYEFUL (OF SOMEONE OR SOMETHING)

eyeglasses ['aɪ glæs əz] *n.* two lenses held together by a frame and worn in front of the eyes to improve vision. (Treated as plural. Usually shortened to GLASSES.)

eyelash ['aɪ læʃ] *n.* one of the many small, thin hairs that grow on the edge of the eyelid.

eyelid ['aɪ lɪd] *n.* the fold of skin that moves over the eye.

eyewitness ['aɪ 'wɪt nəs] *n.* someone who sees an event happen; someone who sees an accident or crime take place.

F Go to FAHRENHEIT.

fable ['fe bəl] **1.** *n.* a story that teaches a lesson, often using animals as the characters of the story. **2.** *n.* a lie; a story about an event that did not really happen.

fabric ['fæb rɪk] *n.* material or cloth made by weaving threads together. (Plural only for types and instances.)

fabricate ['fæb rɪ ket] **1.** *tv.* to build something. **2.** *tv.* to make up a story or a lie; to invent an excuse. (Figurative on ①.)

face ['fes] **1.** *n.* the front part of the head from the hair to the chin. **2.** *n.* a look; an expression; the way someone's ① looks. **3.** *n.* the front part or surface of something. **4.** *tv.* to look at someone or something or toward a particular direction. **5.** *tv.* to deal with someone or something. **6.** *tv.* to cover the front part of something or the edges of something with a decoration.
→ (AS) PLAIN AS THE NOSE ON ONE'S FACE
→ CAN'T SEE ONE'S HAND IN FRONT OF ONE'S FACE
→ CUT OFF ONE'S NOSE TO SPITE ONE'S FACE
→ FALL FLAT (ON ONE'S FACE)
→ FLY IN THE FACE OF SOMEONE OR SOMETHING
→ HAVE EGG ON ONE'S FACE
→ KEEP A STRAIGHT FACE
→ LOSE FACE
→ MAKE A FACE
→ NOT SHOW ONE'S FACE
→ PUT ON A BRAVE FACE
→ SLAP IN THE FACE
→ STARE SOMEONE IN THE FACE
→ TAKE SOMEONE OR SOMETHING AT FACE VALUE
→ TALK UNTIL ONE IS BLUE IN THE FACE
→ TELL ONE TO ONE'S FACE

face off 1. to begin a hockey game with two players facing one another. **2.** to prepare for a confrontation.

face someone **down** to make a face-to-face stand with someone who eventually backs down.

face the music to receive punishment; to accept the unpleasant results of one's actions.

face toward someone or something to look toward someone or something or toward a particular direction; to be directed toward a particular direction.

face up (to someone or something**)** to confront with courage someone or something representing a threat or an unpleasantness.

facilities *n.* a bathroom; a restroom. (Euphemistic. Treated as plural, but not countable.)

facility [fə 'sɪl ə ti] *n.* something—especially a building or equipment—built, provided, or established for a specific purpose; a building or site used by a company for its business, especially for a factory or offices. (Often plural.)

fact ['fækt] *n.* something that is true; something that really happened.
→ GET THE FACTS STRAIGHT
→ GROUNDED IN FACT
→ IN FACT
→ KNOWN FACT

factor ['fæk tɚ] *n.* one of a number of elements that contribute to a result.

factory ['fæk tə ri] *n.* a building where products are made, usually with machines.

faculty ['fæk əl ti] **1.** *n.* the teachers at a school, college, or university, as a group. **2.** *n.* a skill; an ability, especially a mental ability. **3.** the *adj.* use of ①.

fad ['fæd] *n.* a very popular thing that everyone does or has for a short period of time.

fade ['fed] **1.** *iv.* to lose color; to become pale; to become less bright. **2.** *iv.* to become weak; to lose energy. (Figurative on ①.) **3.** *tv.* to cause something to lose color or become pale as in ①.

fade away into something to diminish into something.

fade down [for sound] to diminish.

Fahrenheit ['fɛr ən haɪt] **1.** *n.* a system of measuring temperature that is not metric. (No plural. From Gabriel Fahrenheit, a German physicist who invented the Fahrenheit scale.) **2.** the *adj.* use of ①. (Follows DEGREE(S). Abbreviated *F.*)

fail ['fel] **1.** *tv.* not to succeed at something, especially a course or an examination in school. **2.** *tv.* to give a student a grade that means failure. **3.** *tv.* not to help someone; to let someone down. **4.** *iv.* [for part of a person's body] to become weak; [for something] to stop working; [for something] not to succeed. **5.** *iv.* [for a business] not to succeed. **6.** *iv.* not to succeed in a task that one has tried to do; not to pass a school course.

failure ['fel jɚ] **1.** *n.* failing; not succeeding. (Plural only for types and instances.) **2.** *n.* someone whose life has had almost no success.

faint ['fent] **1.** *adj.* barely noticeable; dim; not clear. (Adv: *faintly.* Comp: *fainter;* sup: *faintest.*) **2.** *adj.* [of someone] temporarily weak or dizzy; [of someone] about to pass out. (Adv: *faintly.* Comp: *fainter;* sup: *faintest.*) **3.** *iv.* to pass out; to lose consciousness.
→ DAMN SOMEONE OR SOMETHING WITH FAINT PRAISE

fair ['fɛr] **1.** *n.* a yearly event held in a town, state, or county. **2.** *adj.* just; honest; giving good judgments; not favoring one thing or person over another. (Adv: *fairly.* Comp: *fairer;* sup: *fairest.*) **3.** *adj.* [of skin or hair] very light in color. (Adv: *fairly.* Comp: *fairer;* sup: *fairest.*) **4.** *adj.* [of someone] having light hair or skin as in ③. (Comp: *fairer;* sup: *fairest.*) **5.** *adj.* considerable; ample. (Adv: *fairly.*) **6.** *adj.* not too bad; pretty good; adequate. (Adv: *fairly.* Comp: *fairer;* sup: *fairest.*)
→ ONE'S FAIR SHARE

fair game someone or something that it is quite permissible to attack.

fair-weather friend a person who is one's friend only when things are going well for one. (When things go badly, this person will desert one.)

fairy ['fɛr i] *n.* a small mythical being that looks human, does magic, and sometimes has wings.

faith ['feθ] **1.** *n.* a strong belief in something that cannot be proved; a strong belief in someone or in a god. (No plural.) **2.** *n.* a particular religion. **3.** *n.* loyalty; trust. (No plural.)
→ IN BAD FAITH
→ TAKE SOMETHING ON FAITH

faithful ['feθ fʊl] *adj.* loyal.

fake ['fek] **1.** *tv.* to make a copy of something with the purpose of deceiving someone. **2.** *tv.* to pretend to do something or have something in order to deceive someone. **3.** *n.* something that is made to take the place of an original in order to deceive someone. **4.** *n.* someone who is a fraud. **5.** *adj.* false; not genuine; made in order to deceive someone.

fall ['fɔl] **1.** *iv., irreg.* to drop to a lower level from a higher level. (Past tense: FELL; past participle: FALLEN.) **2.** *iv., irreg.* to lose power; to be defeated. (Figurative on ①.) **3.** *iv., irreg.* [for vision] to aim downward. **4.** *iv., irreg.* to go from a standing position to a lying position in one quick movement; to collapse. **5.** *iv., irreg.* [for an event] to happen on a particular day of the week or in a particular month of the year. **6.** *n.* the autumn; the season between summer and winter. **7.** *n.* suddenly going from a standing position to a lying position. **8.** *n.* a decrease; a drop; a lowering. **9.** *n.* the collapse of a political unit; a defeat, especially when at war.
→ BREAK SOMEONE'S FALL
→ RIDING FOR A FALL

fall apart to break into pieces; to disassemble. (Both literal and figurative uses.)

fall back to move back from something; to retreat from something.

fall back on(to) someone or something **1.** to fall backwards onto someone or something. **2.** to begin to use someone or something held in reserve. (Figurative.)

fall behind (in something**)** AND **fall behind (on** something**); fall behind (with** something**); get behind (in** something**); get behind (on** something**); get behind (with** something**)** to lag behind schedule in some kind of work or some other scheduled activity.

fall behind (on something**)** Go to FALL BEHIND (IN SOMETHING).

fall behind (with something**)** Go to FALL BEHIND (IN SOMETHING).

fall between two stools to come somewhere between two possibilities and so fail to meet the requirements of either.

fall by the wayside Go to DROP BY THE WAYSIDE.

fall down to drop or topple.

fall down on the job to fail to do something properly; to fail to do one's job adequately.

fall (down) to something to fall or drop to something below.

fall flat (on one's **face)** AND **fall flat (on** its **face)** to be completely unsuccessful.

fall foul of someone or something to do something that annoys or offends someone or something; to do something that is contrary to the rules.

fall from grace to cease to be held in favor, especially because of some wrong or foolish action.

fall ill to become ill.

fall in to form a line and stand at attention. (Military. Often a command.)

fall in love (with someone or something**)** to become enamored of someone or something.

fall in(to) line (with someone or something**) 1.** to get into a line with other people or a group. **2.** to behave in a manner similar to someone or something. (Figurative.)

fall in(to) place to fit together; to become organized.

fall in(to step) to get into the same marching pattern as everyone else as regards which foot moves forward. (Everyone should be moving the same foot forward at the same time.)

fall off to decline.

fall off ((of) something**)** to drop or slip off of something.

fall outside something to be beyond someone's power, responsibility, or jurisdiction.

fall over to topple over and fall down.

fall over backwards (to do something**)** to go to great extremes to do something; to endure all sorts of trouble to do something. (Figurative.)

fall over someone or something to stumble over someone or something.

fall short (of something**) 1.** to lack something; to lack enough of something. **2.** to fail to achieve a goal.

fall through [for something, such as plans] to fail.

fall to to begin doing something.

fall to pieces 1. to break into pieces. **2.** to become emotionally upset. (Figurative.)

fall to someone or something to become the responsibility of someone or a group.

fall upon someone **(to** do something**)** to become someone's responsibility to do something.

fallen ['fɔl ən] past participle of FALL.

fallow ['fæl o] adj. [of land] not farmed for a period of time, usually in order to help replenish the soil with nutrients.
→ LIE FALLOW

falls n. a waterfall. (Treated as plural.)

false ['fɔls] **1.** adj. not true; wrong; incorrect. (Adv: falsely. Comp: falser; sup: falsest.) **2.** adj. not loyal; not faithful. (Adv: falsely. Comp: falser; sup: falsest.) **3.** adj. not real; artificial; fake. (Comp: falser; sup: falsest.)
→ LULL SOMEONE INTO A FALSE SENSE OF SECURITY

fame ['fem] n. the quality of being very well known. (No plural.)

familiar [fə 'mɪl jɚ] **1.** adj. known; well known; common. (Adv:

familiarly.) **2.** *adj.* friendly; overly friendly. (Adv: *familiarly.*)
→ HAVE A FAMILIAR RING

familiar with someone or something having a good knowledge of someone or something.

family ['fæm (ə) li] **1.** *n.* a group of people related to each other. **2.** *n.* a mother, father, and one child or more; a parent and one child or more. **3.** *n.* a group of things that are related in some way or share common features, such as animals, plants, languages, etc. **4.** the *adj.* use of ①, ②, or ③.
→ RUN IN THE FAMILY

famine ['fæm ən] *n.* a period of time when there is little or no food.

famous ['fe məs] *adj.* very well known.

fan ['fæn] **1.** *n.* someone who admires someone or something very much. (A shortening of FANATIC.) **2.** *n.* a device or machine used to move air in order to cool someone or something. **3.** *tv.* to move air onto something.
→ BE A FAN OF SOMEONE

fan out (from someplace) to spread or move outward from a particular area in the shape of a fan.

fan something **out** to spread something out so that all parts can be seen better.

fan the flames (of something) to make something more intense; to make a situation worse.

fanatic [fə 'næt ɪk] *n.* someone who is too eager about and devoted to someone or something.

fancy ['fæn si] **1.** *adj.* elegant; stylish; nicely decorated. (Adv: *fancily.* Comp: *fancier;* sup: *fanciest.*) **2.** *n.* the imagination; the ability to create imaginative ideas or images. **3.** *n.* something that is imagined; a notion.
→ FLIGHT OF FANCY
→ FOOTLOOSE AND FANCY-FREE
→ STRIKE SOMEONE'S FANCY
→ TICKLE SOMEONE'S FANCY

fang ['fæŋ] *n.* a long, sharp tooth.

fantasy ['fæn tə si] *n.* interesting thoughts and visions in the mind, somewhat like a dream. (Plural only for types and instances.)

far ['fɑr] **1.** *adj., irreg.* more distant; not as close as something else. (Comp: FARTHER OR FURTHER; sup: FARTHEST OR FURTHEST.) **2.** *adv., irreg.* at or to a distant time or place; a long way away in time or space. (Comp: FARTHER OR FURTHER; sup: FARTHEST OR FURTHEST.) **3.** *adv.* much; many; a lot. (Used before a comparative such as *more, less,* or *longer.*)
→ AS FAR AS IT GOES

faraway look AND **far-off look** an appearance on one's face of having one's mind in another place.

fare ['fɛr] **1.** *n.* the amount of money required to ride a bus, train, plane, subway, taxi, etc. **2.** *n.* the food that is served at a meal. (No plural.)

farewell [fɛr 'wɛl] **1.** *n.* an act of leaving and saying good-bye. **2.** the *adj.* use of ①. **3.** *interj.* good-bye.

farm ['fɑrm] **1.** *n.* a parcel of land used to grow crops or to raise animals. **2.** *tv.* to work on the land to make it grow plants, especially food; to plow land. **3.** *iv.* to grow crops and raise animals as a living. **4.** the *adj.* use of ①.

farm someone **out** to send someone (somewhere) for care or development.

farm something **out 1.** to deplete the fertility of land by farming too intensely. **2.** to make money by renting out land or buildings. **3.** to send work to someone to be done away from one's normal place of business; to subcontract work.

farmer ['fɑr mɚ] *n.* someone who grows crops and raises animals on a farm.

far-off look Go to FARAWAY LOOK.

fart ['fɑrt] **1.** *iv.* to release gas from the bowels through the anus. (Potentially offensive. The topic and the word are not heard in polite company. Use with caution.) **2.** *n.* the sound or odor of the release of gas from the bowels. **3.** *n.* a stupid and annoying person.

farther ['fɑr ðɚ] **1.** *adj.* more distant in space or time. (One of the comparative forms of FAR, along with FURTHER.) **2.** *adv.* more distant in space or time. (One of the comparative forms of FAR, along with FURTHER.)

farthest ['fɑr ðəst] *adj.* the most distant in space or time. (One of the superlative forms of FAR, along with FURTHEST.)

fashion ['fæ ʃən] **1.** *n.* the current, typical styles of dress or behavior within a society. (Plural only for types and instances.) **2.** *n.* the

manner or way in which something is done; a method. (No plural.) **3.** *tv.* to form or shape something; to form something by hand.
→ IN FASHION

fast ['fæst] **1.** *adv.* quickly; rapidly. (Comp: *faster*; sup: *fastest*.) **2.** *adv.* tight(ly); without moving; securely. **3.** *adj.* quick; rapid; speedy; not slow. (Comp: *faster*; sup: *fastest*.) **4.** *adj.* [of a clock or watch] showing a time that is later than the real time. (Comp: *faster*; sup: *fastest*.) **5.** *iv.* to go without food. **6.** *n.* a period of time when someone does not eat, for religious, health, or political reasons.
→ (AS) FAST AS ONE'S FEET WOULD CARRY ONE
→ a HARD-AND-FAST RULE
→ MAKE FAST WORK OF SOMEONE OR SOMETHING
→ PLAY FAST AND LOOSE (WITH SOMEONE OR SOMETHING)
→ THICK AND FAST

fasten ['fæs ən] **1.** *tv.* to tie, lock, or hook something closed. **2.** *tv.* to attach something to someone or something.

fasten something **up** to close something up, using buttons, a zipper, snaps, hooks, a clasp, or other things meant to hold something closed.

fasten (up)on someone or something **1.** to take firm hold of someone or something. **2.** to fix one's attention on someone or something. (Figurative.)

fastener ['fæs ən ɚ] *n.* a device that secures or fastens something shut.

faster and faster at an increasing rate of speed; fast and then even faster.

fastidious [fæ 'stɪd i əs] **1.** *adj.* hard to please; choosing carefully. (Adv: *fastidiously*.) **2.** *adj.* preferring cleanliness and orderliness. (Adv: *fastidiously*.)

fat ['fæt] **1.** *n.* animal tissue filled with oil. (Plural only for types and instances.) **2.** *n.* loose flesh filled with ①. (No plural.) **3.** *adj.* overweight; having too much ②. (Adv: *fatly*. Comp: *fatter*; sup: *fattest*.)
→ KILL THE FATTED CALF
→ LIVE OFF THE FAT OF THE LAND

fat chance very little likelihood. (Informal.)

fate ['fet] **1.** *n.* a force that is said to control what happens. (Plural only for types and instances.) **2.** *n.* the destiny of someone or something; what will happen to someone or something. **3.** *tv.* [for ①] to determine what happens to someone or something. (Usually passive.)
→ LEAVE ONE TO ONE'S FATE

father ['fɑ ðɚ] **1.** *n.* the male parent of a child. (Also a term of address. Capitalized when written as a proper noun.) **2.** *n.* the inventor of something; the founder of something; the leader of something. (Figurative on ①.) **3.** *tv.* [for a male creature] to fertilize an egg, which will lead to the development of a child.

fatigue [fə 'tig] **1.** *n.* a state of being very tired from too much mental or physical work. (No plural.) **2.** *tv.* to tire someone or something; to make someone or something tired.

fatten ['fæt n] **1.** *tv.* to cause someone or something to grow larger. **2.** *tv.* to increase the size or value of an offer. (Figurative on ①.)

fatten someone or something up (with something) to use something to make someone or some creature fat.

fatty ['fæt i] *adj.* full of or containing fat. (Comp: *fattier*; sup: *fattiest*.)

faucet ['fɔs ɪt] *n.* a device that controls the flow of water or some other liquid from a pipe or container; a tap.

fault ['fɔlt] **1.** *n.* a personal shortcoming; a flaw in someone's personality. **2.** *n.* the responsibility for causing something bad to happen. (No plural.) **3.** *n.* a crack in the surface of the earth.

faulty ['fɔl ti] *adj.* flawed; incorrect; having an error or mistake. (Adv: *faultily*. Comp: *faultier*; sup: *faultiest*.)

favor ['fe vɚ] **1.** *n.* a state of being valuable or worthy in someone else's view. (No plural.) **2.** *n.* an act of kindness; something nice that is done for someone else. **3.** *tv.* to prefer someone or something; to like someone or something at the expense of someone or something else. **4.** *tv.* to support someone or something; to support an issue, a plan, a theory, an option, etc. **5.** *tv.* to expect someone or something to win.
→ RULE IN FAVOR OF SOMEONE OR SOMETHING

favor someone or something **with** something to provide someone or something with something beneficial or special.

favorite ['fev (ə) rɪt] **1.** *adj.* preferred over every other choice; liked better than everything or everyone else. **2.** *n.* someone or something that is preferred over every other choice; someone or something that is liked better than everyone or everything else.

fax ['fæks] **1.** *n.* a machine that sends an exact copy of a piece of paper to another machine, over telephone lines. **2.** *n.* something that has been sent or received by way of ①. **3.** the *adj.* use of ① or ②. **4.** *tv.* to send a document to someone by using ①.

fear ['fɪr] **1.** *n.* the feeling of being afraid; the feeling of being in danger. (Plural only for types and instances.) **2.** *n.* a specific source of ① and the feeling caused by that source. **3.** *tv.* to be afraid of someone or something. **4.** *tv.* to feel that something unpleasant is the case or may happen. (Often used as a polite way of expressing regret that one must say something unpleasant. The object is a clause with THAT ⑦.)
→ FOR FEAR OF SOMETHING

feast ['fist] **1.** *n.* a large meal, especially one for a special occasion; a banquet. **2.** *iv.* to eat a lot of food, often in the company of others, especially as part of a celebration.

feast one's **eyes (on** someone or something**)** to look at someone or something with pleasure, envy, or admiration. (As if such visions provided a feast of visual delight for one's eyes.)

feat ['fit] *n.* a remarkable accomplishment; an act or deed that shows skill or talent.

feather ['fɛð ɚ] *n.* one of many hard stems bearing soft fibers that cover the body of a bird.
→ (AS) LIGHT AS A FEATHER
→ IN FINE FEATHER
→ MAKE THE FEATHERS FLY
→ RUFFLE ITS FEATHERS
→ RUFFLE SOMEONE'S FEATHERS

a **feather in** one's **cap** an honor; a reward for something.

feather one's **(own) nest 1.** to decorate and furnish one's home in style and comfort. (Birds line their nests with feathers to make them warm and comfortable.) **2.** to use power and prestige to provide for oneself selfishly.

feature ['fi tʃɚ] **1.** *n.* an important aspect of something; a quality of something that stands out. **2.** *n.* a part of the face. **3.** *n.* a special article in a newspaper; an important news story. **4.** *tv.* to present or focus on an important element of something. **5.** *tv.* to present someone special as an actor in a movie, play, or television show.

February ['fɛb ru ɛr ɪ] Go to MONTH.

feces ['fi siz] *n.* excrement; animal waste. (From Latin. Treated as plural, but not countable.)

fed ['fɛd] past tense and past participle of FEED.

federal ['fɛd (ə) rəl] **1.** *adj.* of or about the organization of a group of states. (Adv: *federally.*) **2.** *adj.* of or about the United States government. (Adv: *federally.*)

fee ['fi] *n.* money that is paid in exchange for a service or privilege.

feeble ['fi bəl] *adj.* weak; frail; lacking force; lacking strength. (Adv: *feebly.* Comp: *feebler;* sup: *feeblest.*)

feed ['fid] **1.** *tv., irreg.* to nourish someone or something with food; to give food to someone or something. (Past tense and past participle: FED.) **2.** *tv., irreg.* to supply something without stopping; to provide something without stopping. (Figurative on ①.) **3.** *n.* food that is given to animals, especially on a farm. (Plural only for types and instances.)
→ BITE THE HAND THAT FEEDS ONE
→ SPOON-FEED SOMEONE

feed off (of) something to eat something in particular customarily.

feed (up)on someone or something to eat someone or something.

feel ['fil] **1.** *tv., irreg.* to touch someone or something. (Past tense and past participle: FELT.) **2.** *tv., irreg.* to experience or sense being touched by someone or something. **3.** *tv., irreg.* to receive information by touching. **4.** *tv., irreg.* to experience an emotion; to experience something in one's mind. (The object can be a clause with THAT ⑦.) **5.** *tv., irreg.* to consider something; to have an opinion about something. (The object is a clause with THAT ⑦.) **6.** *iv., irreg.* to experience [an emotion]; to experience [something in one's mind]. **7.** *n.* a kind of shape or texture that is sensed by touching. (No plural.)

→ GET THE FEEL OF SOMETHING

feel a glow of something a feeling of contentment, happiness, satisfaction, peace, etc.

feel for someone to feel the emotional pain that someone else is feeling; to empathize or sympathize with someone.

feel like a million (dollars) to feel well and healthy, both physically and mentally; to feel like something unbelievably good.

feel like a new person to feel refreshed and renewed, especially after getting well or getting dressed up.

feel like doing something to want to do something; to be in the mood to do something.

feel out of place to feel that one does not belong in someplace or situation.

feel out of something to feel alienated from something.

feel someone **out (about** someone or something**)** to find out what someone thinks about someone or something.

feel something **in** one's **bones** AND **know** something **in** one's **bones** to sense something; to have an intuition about something.

feel the pinch to have money problems; to experience hardship because of having too little money. (Informal.)

feel up to something to feel like doing something; to feel well enough to do something.

feeler ['fi lɚ] **1.** *n.* an antenna; a part of the body of an insect or shellfish that is used for touching or sensing. **2.** *n.* an inquiry or suggestion that is made to determine what other people are thinking or feeling.

feeling ['fi lɪŋ] **1.** *n.* sensation produced by touching something or by being touched by something; the ability to feel things. (No plural.) **2.** *n.* a sensation that is a response to touch, pressure, heat, cold, or pain. **3.** *n.* an emotion. **4.** *n.* an idea based on what one feels or suspects.
→ GUT FEELING
→ HAVE MIXED FEELINGS (ABOUT SOMEONE OR SOMETHING)

feet ['fit] plural of FOOT.
→ (AS) FAST AS ONE'S FEET WOULD CARRY ONE
→ the BALLS OF ONE'S FEET
→ DRAG ONE'S FEET
→ FIND ONE'S FEET
→ GET A LOAD OFF ONE'S FEET
→ GET BACK ON ONE'S FEET
→ GET COLD FEET
→ GET ONE'S FEET ON THE GROUND
→ GET ONE'S FEET WET
→ GET TO ONE'S FEET
→ HAVE FEET OF CLAY
→ KEEP ONE'S FEET ON THE GROUND
→ LET GRASS GROW UNDER ONE'S FEET
→ ON ONE'S FEET
→ SET ONE (BACK) ON ONE'S FEET
→ SET ONE ON ONE'S FEET AGAIN
→ SIT AT SOMEONE'S FEET
→ STAND ON ONE'S OWN TWO FEET
→ TAKE A LOAD OFF ONE'S FEET
→ THINK ON ONE'S FEET
→ THROW ONESELF AT SOMEONE'S FEET

fell ['fɛl] past tense of FALL.
→ AT ONE FELL SWOOP
→ IN ONE FELL SWOOP

fellow ['fɛl o] **1.** *n.* a man; a male. **2.** *n.* a position of rank or status at a school or university, usually without teaching responsibilities.

(For either sex.) **3.** *adj.* similar; alike; sharing a common interest or occupation. (For either sex. Prenominal only.)

fellowship ['fɛl o ʃɪp] **1.** *n.* a group; a social organization. (Not restricted to males.) **2.** *n.* friendly discussion and activity with other people; friendship. (No plural.) **3.** *n.* money that is given to an advanced student to pay for schooling.

felt ['fɛlt] **1.** past tense and past participle of FEEL. **2.** *n.* a thick cloth made of pressed fibers. (Plural only for types and instances.) **3.** *adj.* made of ②.

female ['fi mel] **1.** *adj.* of or about women or girls; of or about animals of the sex that can bear young or lay eggs. **2.** *n.* a woman; a girl; an animal of the sex that bears young or lays eggs.

feminine ['fɛm ə nɪn] **1.** *adj.* of or about the characteristics of women; of or about the qualities of women. (Adv: *femininely.*) **2.** *adj.* of or about the one of the three grammatical genders that is neither masculine nor neuter.

fence ['fɛns] *n.* a barrier that encloses a space to keep people or things from coming into or leaving that space.
→ MEND (ONE'S) FENCES
→ SIT ON THE FENCE

fence someone or something **off (from** something**)** to separate someone or something from something with a fence or barrier.

fence something **in** to enclose some creature or something within a fence or barrier.

fend someone or something **off** to hold someone or something off; to fight someone or something off.

fender ['fɛn dɚ] *n.* a part of a vehicle's body that forms a protective shield over a wheel.

ferryboat ['fɛr i 'bot] *n.* a boat that takes cars and people across a river or a lake.

fertile ['fɚt əl] **1.** *adj.* able to reproduce or develop new life easily. (Adv: *fertilely.*) **2.** *adj.* [of soil] rich in (plant) food that helps reproduction and growth. (Adv: *fertilely.*) **3.** *adj.* creative; able to produce good ideas. (Figurative on ①. Adv: *fertilely.*)

fertilize ['fɚ tə laɪz] **1.** *tv.* to provide nutrients to the land so that crops will grow well. **2.** *tv.* [for a male reproductive cell] to join with a female reproductive cell; [for a male's sperm] to join with a female's ovum (egg). **3.** *tv.* to cause a male reproductive cell to join with a female reproductive cell, as in ②.

fervor ['fɚ vɚ] *n.* passion; excitement; strong emotion. (No plural.)

festive ['fɛs tɪv] *adj.* merry; exciting; like a celebration; joyous. (Adv: *festively.*)

fetch ['fɛtʃ] **1.** *tv.* to bring something to someone; to go somewhere and get something for someone. **2.** *tv.* [for something] to bring in a certain amount of money when sold.

fever ['fi vɚ] *n.* a state of sickness where the temperature of the body rises above normal.
→ RUN A FEVER

feverish ['fi vɚ ɪʃ] **1.** *adj.* having a higher body temperature than normal. (Adv: *feverishly.*) **2.** *adj.* excited and fast; restless. (Figurative on ①. Adv: *feverishly.*)

few ['fju] *adj.* not many; a smaller number than expected. (Used with items that can be counted. Compare this with LITTLE. Used without *a.* Comp: *fewer;* sup: *fewest.*)
→ DROP SOMEONE A FEW LINES
→ PRECIOUS FEW

a **few** *n.* a small number [of those items previously mentioned]. (Treated as plural. Use *a little* for things that cannot be counted.)

fiber ['faɪ bɚ] **1.** *n.* one of many threads, strands, or rigid cellular structures that form many plant, animal, and artificial substances. **2.** *n.* edible plant FIBERS as in ①. (Plural only for types and instances.)

fiction ['fɪk ʃən] **1.** *n.* literature that is written about imaginary events and not about real events. (No plural.) **2.** *n.* information that is not true but instead has been created by someone. (Plural only for types and instances.)

fiddle ['fɪd l] **1.** *n.* a violin. (Informal.) **2.** *iv.* to play ①.
→ (AS) FIT AS A FIDDLE
→ PLAY SECOND FIDDLE (TO SOMEONE)

fiddle around (with SOMEONE OR SOMETHING**)** to toy with or play around with someone or something.

fiddle while Rome burns to do something trivial or nothing at all while something disastrous happens. (From a legend that the emperor Nero played the lyre while Rome was burning.)

field ['fild] **1.** *n.* a large area of land used for a specific purpose, such as growing crops, raising cattle, playing certain sports, fighting a battle, landing airplanes, etc. **2.** *n.* an area of knowledge; an area of study.
→ COME OUT OF LEFT FIELD
→ OUT IN LEFT FIELD
→ PLAY THE FIELD

field questions to answer a series of questions, especially from reporters.

fierce ['firs] *adj.* violent; cruel; untamed; wild. (Adv: *fiercely.* Comp: *fiercer;* sup: *fiercest.*)

fifteen ['fif 'tin] 15. Go to FOUR.

fifteenth ['fif 'tinθ] 15th. Go to FOURTH.

fifth ['fifθ] **1.** 5th. Go to FOURTH. **2.** *n.* 20 percent of a full gallon of liquor.

fiftieth ['fif ti əθ] 50th. Go to FOURTH.

fifty ['fif ti] 50. Go to FORTY.

fig ['fig] *n.* a soft, sweet fruit with many seeds.

fight ['fait] **1.** *n.* a struggle; a battle. **2.** *tv., irreg.* to battle someone; to make combat against someone. (Past tense and past participle: FOUGHT.) **3.** *iv., irreg.* to do battle; to argue.

fight against someone or something to battle against someone or something.

fight back (at someone or something**)** to defend oneself against someone or something; to retaliate against someone or something.

fight (one's**) way) back to** something to struggle to return to something or someplace.

fight one's **way out of** something to struggle to get out of something or someplace.

fight (one's**) way) through** something **1.** to struggle to get through something; to struggle to penetrate something. **2.** to struggle to work through all of something.

fight someone or something **down** to fight against and defeat someone or something.

fight someone or something **hammer and tongs** AND **fight** someone or something **tooth and nail; go at it hammer and tongs; go at it tooth and nail** to fight against someone or something energetically and with great determination. (These phrases are old and refer to fighting with and without weapons.)

fight someone or something **tooth and nail** Go to FIGHT SOMEONE OR SOMETHING HAMMER AND TONGS.

fight something **down 1.** to struggle to hold something back; to struggle to keep from being overwhelmed by something. **2.** to struggle to swallow something; to fight to get something down one's throat.

fight something **through (**something**)** to force something through some sort of procedure or process.

fighting chance a good possibility of success, especially if every effort is made.

figurative on [of a word or phrase] based on some other, more literal, word or phrase.

figure ['fɪg jɚ] **1.** *n.* a human body; the form of a human body. **2.** *n.* a person, usually well known or important. **3.** *n.* a digit; one of the numbers from 0 to 9. **4.** *n.* a total; a sum; an amount. **5.** *n.* a chart or diagram in a book that explains information in the text. **6.** *tv.* to consider something; to believe something. (The object is a clause with THAT ⑦.)
→ IN ROUND FIGURES

figure on something to plan on something; to count on doing something.

figure someone or something **in((to)** something) to include someone or something into the total.

figure someone or something **out** to come to understand someone or something; to solve something such as a puzzle, a riddle, or a mystery.

figure something **up** to add up the amount of something.

file ['faɪl] **1.** *n.* a metal tool that is scraped over rough surfaces to make them smooth and even. **2.** *n.* a folder or other container used for holding and storing papers in an organized way. **3.** *n.* the papers within ②; the information contained in ②. **4.** *n.* a COMPUTER FILE; a unit of data or information in digital form, such as is stored on a floppy disk or disk drive. **5.** *tv.* to smooth something with ①. **6.** *tv.* to organize papers by putting them into the appropriate ②; to

put a piece of paper in the appropriate ②. **7.** *iv.* to move in a line, going into or out of a place.
→ COMPUTER FILE

file in((to) something) [for a line of people] to move into something or someplace.

file out (of something) [for a line of people] to move out of something or someplace.

file something **away** to put something away, usually in a file folder or file cabinet; to keep something in one's memory.

fill ['fɪl] **1.** *tv.* to provide what is requested; to supply a product when it is requested; to meet someone's demand for something. **2.** *iv.* to become full.
→ GET ONE'S FILL OF SOMEONE OR SOMETHING

fill in (for someone or something) to substitute for someone or something; to take the place of someone or something.

fill out to become full; to gain weight.

fill someone **in (on** someone or something) to tell someone the details about someone or something.

fill someone's **shoes** to take the place of some other person and do that person's work satisfactorily.

fill something **in 1.** to add material to an indentation, hole, etc., to make it full. **2.** to write in the blank spaces on a paper; to write on a form.

fill something **out** to complete a form by writing in the blank spaces.

fill something **(up) 1.** to put something into a container or a place until there is no more room to put anything else in. **2.** to take up all available space or time; to occupy all available space or time.

fill the bill AND **fit the bill** to be exactly the thing that is needed.

fill up 1. to become full. **2.** to fill one's gas tank. (Informal.)

film ['fɪlm] **1.** *n.* the material that photographs or movies are recorded on. (Plural only for types and instances.) **2.** *n.* a movie; a motion picture. **3.** *n.* a thin layer of something; a coating. **4.** *tv.* to record someone or something on ① in a particular place or manner.

filter ['fɪl tɚ] **1.** *n.* a device that strains fluids or gases to separate solids from them; a device that cleans a fluid or gas that passes through it. **2.** *tv.* to pass a substance through ①.

filth ['fɪlθ] *n.* grime; dirt that is difficult to clean off. (No plural.)

filthy ['fɪl θi] the *adj.* form of FILTH; dirt and grime.

fin ['fɪn] **1.** *n.* a flat organ—like a small fan—on a fish that allows it to control its movement in the water. **2.** *n.* one of a pair of rubber or plastic shoes with flat projections, used by divers to move themselves through the water.

final ['faɪ nəl] **1.** *adj.* last; at the end; ultimate. (Adv: *finally*.) **2.** *n.* the last examination in a school course. (Often plural, referring to the last examinations in all of one's courses for the term or semester.)

→ GET THE FINAL WORD

final fling the last act or period of enjoyment before a change in one's circumstances or lifestyle.

find ['faɪnd] **1.** *tv., irreg.* to discover or locate someone or something that one was looking for. (Past tense and past participle: FOUND.) **2.** *tv., irreg.* to recover something; to discover something. **3.** *tv., irreg.* to decide that someone or something has a certain quality; to consider someone or something to be a certain way. (The object can be a clause with THAT ⑦.)

find for someone or something [for a jury or a judge] to announce a decision in favor of one side of a case.

find it in one's **heart (to** do something**)** to have the courage or compassion to do something.

find one's **feet** to become used to a new situation or experience.

find one's or its **way** somewhere **1.** [with *one's*; for someone] to discover the route to a place. **2.** [with *its*; for something] to end up in a place. (This expression avoids accusing someone of moving the thing or things to the place. In the plural, *their way* is used.)

find one's **own level** to find the position or rank to which one is best suited.

find someone **guilty** AND **find** someone **innocent** to decide guilt or innocence and deliver a verdict in a court of law.

find someone **innocent** Go to FIND SOMEONE GUILTY.

find something **out** to learn something; to learn information.

fine ['faɪn] **1.** *n.* an amount of money that must be paid as a punishment; a penalty. **2.** *adj.* acceptable or suitable; very good; excellent. (Adv: *finely.* Comp: *finer;* sup: *finest.*) **3.** *adj.* of high quality; very delicate and of high quality. (Adv: *finely.* Comp: *finer;* sup: *finest.*) **4.** *adj.* not coarse; consisting of small particles; in the form of a powder. (Adv: *finely.* Comp: *finer;* sup: *finest.*) **5.** *adj.* very thin; very small. (Adv: *finely.* Comp: *finer;* sup: *finest.*) **6.** *adv.* well; nicely; excellently. **7.** *tv.* to charge someone or something an amount of money as a punishment or penalty.
→ CUT SOMETHING (TOO) FINE
→ GO OVER SOMETHING WITH A FINE-TOOTH COMB
→ IN FINE FEATHER
→ SEARCH SOMETHING WITH A FINE-TOOTH COMB

a **fine kettle of fish** a real mess; an unsatisfactory situation.

finger ['fɪŋ gɚ] *n.* one of the five extensions or digits at the end of the hand.
→ GET ONE'S FINGERS BURNED
→ HAVE ONE'S FINGER IN THE PIE
→ HAVE ONE'S FINGER IN TOO MANY PIES
→ LAY A FINGER ON SOMEONE OR SOMETHING
→ POINT THE FINGER AT SOMEONE
→ TWIST SOMEONE AROUND ONE'S LITTLE FINGER
→ SLIP THROUGH SOMEONE'S FINGERS
→ WORK ONE'S FINGERS TO THE BONE

fingernail ['fɪŋ gɚ nel] *n.* the hard, flat covering at the end of each finger.

fingerprint ['fɪŋ gɚ prɪnt] *n.* the light, oily mark left by the ridges on the skin of one's fingers.

fingertip ['fɪŋ gɚ tɪp] *n.* the end of a finger.
→ HAVE SOMETHING AT ONE'S FINGERTIPS

finish ['fɪn ɪʃ] **1.** *tv.* to bring something to an end; to complete or conclude something. **2.** *tv.* to use all of something; to eat or drink all of something. **3.** *tv.* to cover something made out of wood with a protective coat of varnish, paint, or something similar. **4.** *iv.* [for someone] to reach the end of doing something. **5.** *n.* the end; the conclusion; the final part of something. **6.** *n.* a protective coating of paint, varnish, lacquer, or stain on a wooden surface; a protective coating on any surface.

finish someone or something **up** to finish doing something to someone or something.

finish something **off** to eat or drink up all of something; to eat or drink up the last portion of something.

finish up to complete the doing of something.

fire ['faɪɚ] **1.** *n.* heat, flames, and light made by burning something. (Plural only for types and instances.) **2.** *n.* an area of burning with ①. **3.** *n.* passion; strong emotion; fervor. (Figurative on ①. No plural.) **4.** *n.* the shooting of weapons; the noise made by shooting guns. (No plural.) **5.** *tv.* to get rid of an employee; to end someone's employment.
→ ADD FUEL TO THE FIRE
→ CATCH FIRE

→ CAUGHT IN THE CROSS FIRE
→ HANG FIRE
→ HAVE TOO MANY IRONS IN THE FIRE
→ KEEP THE HOME FIRES BURNING
→ ON FIRE
→ OUT OF THE FRYING PAN INTO THE FIRE
→ PLAY WITH FIRE
→ SET THE WORLD ON FIRE
→ UNDER FIRE

fire a gun to shoot a gun; to discharge a gun.

Fire away! Begin to do something. (Often refers to speaking or asking questions.)

fire engine ['faɪɚ ɛn dʒɪn] *n.* a truck that carries water and hoses to put out fires.

fire escape ['faɪɚ ə skep] **1.** *n.* a special exit from a building in case the building catches fire. **2.** *n.* a special metal staircase attached to the outside of a building, used as an escape route in case of FIRE ①.

fire (something) back at someone or something to shoot a gun back at someone or something.

firecracker ['faɪɚ kræk ɚ] *n.* a small device that explodes when set afire, making a lot of noise.

firefighter ['faɪɚ faɪt ɚ] *n.* someone who is trained to put out fires and rescue people.

firefly Go to LIGHTNING BUG.

fireplace ['faɪɚ ples] *n.* a place in a house or building where a fire can be built to provide heat.

fireproof ['faɪɚ pruf] **1.** *adj.* not able to catch fire; hard to burn. **2.** *tv.* to make something so it is able to resist to fire.

firing on all cylinders working at full strength; making every possible effort. (From an internal combustion engine.)

firm ['fɚm] **1.** *adj.* solid; hard. (Adv: *firmly.* Comp: *firmer;* sup: *firmest.*) **2.** *adj.* not easily moved; steady. (Adv: *firmly.* Comp: *firmer;* sup: *firmest.*) **3.** *adj.* final and not to be changed. (Adv: *firmly.* Comp: *firmer;* sup: *firmest.*) **4.** *n.* a company; a business.

firm something **up 1.** to make something more stable or firm. **2.** to make a monetary offer for something more appealing and definite.

firm up 1. to become more stable or viable; to recover from or stop a decline. (Figurative.) **2.** to develop better muscle tone; to become less flabby.

first ['fɚst] **1.** *adj.* before everything or everyone else; at the beginning. (The ordinal number for ONE. Adv: *firstly.*) **2.** *adv.* before anything else; before another event. **3.** *adv.* never having happened before. **4.** *n.* someone or something that is the ① thing or person. (No plural.)
→ CAST THE FIRST STONE
→ GET TO FIRST BASE (WITH SOMEONE OR SOMETHING)
→ LOVE AT FIRST SIGHT
→ OF THE FIRST WATER
→ REACH FIRST BASE (WITH SOMEONE OR SOMETHING)

first and foremost first and most important.

first come, first served [of a situation in which] the first people to arrive will be served first.

first name ['fɚst 'nem] *n.* one's name, given at birth and—in English—placed before one's surname.

first of all the very first thing; before anything else. (Similar expressions, *second of all* or *third of all*, are said but do not make a lot of sense.)

first thing (in the morning) before anything else in the morning.

First things first. The most important things must be taken care of first.

first-aid kit ['fɚst 'ed kɪt] *n.* a box that holds medicine, bandages, and other useful things to take care of someone in an emergency.

firsthand ['fɚst 'hænd] **1.** *adj.* direct; coming from the source directly; witnessed. **2.** *adv.* directly; from the source.

fish ['fɪʃ] **1.** *n., irreg.* any of various animals without legs that live underwater and typically have fins and scales. (Plural: *fish* unless referring to a number of species.) **2.** *n.* the meat of ① used as food. (No plural.) **3.** *iv.* to try to catch ①.
→ A FINE KETTLE OF FISH
→ GO ON A FISHING EXPEDITION
→ HAVE OTHER FISH TO FRY
→ LIKE A FISH OUT OF WATER
→ NEITHER FISH NOR FOWL
→ THERE ARE PLENTY OF OTHER FISH IN THE SEA.
→ TUNA (FISH)

fish for a compliment to try to get someone to pay one a compliment. (As if one were tempting someone to utter a compliment.)

fish in troubled waters to involve oneself in a difficult, confused, or dangerous situation, especially with a view to gaining an advantage.

fish or cut bait either do the job you are supposed to be doing or quit and let someone else do it. (Refers to fishing or moving aside and preparing the bait for others more active in the task of fishing to use.)

fish someone or something **out (of something)** to pull someone or something out of something or someplace.

fish something **up (out of** something**)** to pull or hoist something out of something.

fish tank ['fɪʃ tæŋk] *n.* an aquarium; a container for holding fish or other creatures, usually with water.

fishbowl ['fɪʃ bol] *n.* a container that fish are kept in; a small aquarium. (See also FISH TANK.)

fisherman ['fɪʃ ɚ mən] *n., irreg.* someone who catches fish for a living; a man who fishes. (Plural: FISHERMEN.)

fishermen ['fɪʃ ɚ mən] plural of FISHERMAN.

fishhook ['fɪʃ hʊk] *n.* a sharp hook used to catch fish.

fist ['fɪst] *n.* the hand with the fingers closed tightly.
→ HAND OVER FIST

fit ['fɪt] **1.** *iv., irreg.* to be the right size for something. (Past tense and past participle: *fit* or *fitted*.) **2.** *tv., irreg.* to suit something or someone; to be matched to someone

or something. **3.** *tv., irreg.* [for something] to be the right size for someone or something. **4.** *tv., irreg.* to make something match something else in some way. **5.** *adj.* suitable; having the things that are needed. (Adv: *fitly.* Comp: *fitter;* sup: *fittest.*) **6.** *adj.* healthy; in good condition. (Comp: *fitter;* sup: *fittest.*) **7.** *n.* the way that something FITS as in ①.
→ (AS) FIT AS A FIDDLE

fit for a king totally suitable; suitable for royalty.

fit in((to) something) [for something] to be a suitable size to go into something.

fit like a glove to fit very well; to fit tightly or snugly.

fit someone or something in((to) something) to manage to place someone or something into something.

fit someone or something out (for something) to equip someone or something for something; to outfit someone or something for something.

fit someone to a T Go to SUIT SOMEONE TO A T.

fit something on((to) something) to manage to place something onto something.

fit the bill Go to FILL THE BILL.

five [ˈfaɪv] **1.** 5. (See FOUR for more information.) **2.** *n.* a BILL ③ or NOTE ③ worth 5 dollars.

fix [ˈfɪks] **1.** *tv.* to repair something; to make something work again. **2.** *tv.* to make something firm; to place something firmly into something. **3.** *tv.* to prepare food or

drink. **4.** *tv.* to choose a date and time; to determine a date, time, or place.

fix someone or something up to rehabilitate someone or something.

fix someone's wagon to punish someone; to get even with someone; to plot against someone.

fix something over to redo something; to redecorate something.

fixings [ˈfɪks ɪŋz] all the condiments that accompany a certain kind of food.
→ WITH ALL THE FIXINGS

flag [ˈflæg] **1.** *n.* a piece of cloth of a certain color pattern that represents a country, state, city, school, or organization, or is used as a signal. **2.** *iv.* to become tired; to weaken.

flag someone or something down to show a signal or wave, indicating that someone or something should stop.

flagpole [ˈflæg pol] *n.* a pole on which a flag is mounted or attached.

flake [ˈflek] *n.* a loose piece of something; a bit of something; a thin, light piece of something.

flake off to fall off in thin, loose pieces.

flame [ˈflem] **1.** *n.* a tongue of fire; a segment of yellow, white, blue, or red light that shoots out from a fire. **2.** *n.* an angry e-mail message. **3.** *tv.* to criticize someone sharply in a message on the Internet. (Slang.)
→ ADD FUEL TO THE FLAME
→ BURN WITH A LOW BLUE FLAME

→ FAN THE FLAMES (OF SOMETHING)
→ GO UP IN FLAMES

flame up 1. [for something] to catch fire and burst into flames. **2.** [for a fire] to expand and send out larger flames.

flammable ['flæm ə bəl] *adj.* INFLAMMABLE; likely to catch fire; easily set on fire. (Adv: *flammably.*)

flap ['flæp] **1.** *n.* a cover, placed over an opening, that is hinged or attached at one end. **2.** *iv.* to move back and forth, as with the movement of birds' wings. **3.** *tv.* to move something back and forth, as with the movement of birds' wings.

flare ['flɛr] **1.** *n.* a bright flame. **2.** *n.* something that provides a bright light, used as a signal or as a warning of danger.

flare up 1. [for something] to ignite and burn. **2.** [for a fire] to expand rapidly. **3.** [for a disease] to get worse suddenly. **4.** [for a dispute] to break out or escalate into a battle.

flare up (at someone or something) to lose one's temper at someone or something.

flash ['flæʃ] **1.** *n.* a quick, strong burst of light. **2.** *iv.* to give off a burst of light for a brief moment. **3.** *tv.* to make something give off a burst of light for a brief moment.
→ IN A FLASH

flash back (on someone or something) to provide a glimpse of someone or something in the past. (In films, literature, and television.)

a **flash in the pan** someone or something that draws a lot of attention for a very brief time.

flashlight ['flæʃ laɪt] *n.* a small, portable light that typically uses batteries for power.

flat ['flæt] **1.** *adj.* [of a surface] level, even, and smooth. (Adv: *flatly.* Comp: *flatter;* sup: *flattest.*) **2.** *adj.* having lost air; not filled with air. (Adv: *flatly.* Comp: *flatter;* sup: *flattest.*) **3.** *adj.* stable; not moving higher or lower. (Comp: *flatter;* sup: *flattest.*) **4.** *adj.* dull; not exciting. (Adv: *flatly.* Comp: *flatter;* sup: *flattest.*) **5.** *adj.* [sounding a musical sound] lower in pitch than what something is supposed to be. (Adv: *flatly.* Comp: *flatter;* sup: *flattest.*) **6.** *n.* an apartment. **7.** *n.* a note that is one-half step lower in pitch than a natural note. **8.** *n.* a tire with no air in it. (Short for FLAT TIRE.)
→ (AS) FLAT AS A PANCAKE
→ FALL FLAT (ON ONE'S FACE)
→ IN NOTHING FLAT

flat broke completely broke; with no money at all.

flat tire ['flæt 'taɪɚ] *n.* a tire that does not have enough air. (Can be shortened to FLAT.)

flatten someone or something (out) to make someone or something flat.

flavor ['fle vɚ] **1.** *n.* a specific taste; the way something tastes. **2.** *n.* something that is added to a food to give it a specific taste. **3.** *n.* a special quality or characteristic.

flaw ['flɔ] *n.* a fault; a defect; an indication of damage.

flea ['fli] *n.* a tiny insect that lives on an animal's skin, sucking blood and eating dead skin.

fled ['flɛd] past tense and past participle of FLEE.

flee ['fli] **1.** *tv., irreg.* to escape from danger. (Past tense and past participle: FLED.) **2.** *iv., irreg.* to run quickly away from something or toward something.

flesh ['flɛʃ] **1.** *n.* the soft part of the body covered by skin; meat. (No plural.) **2.** *n.* the soft part of a fruit or vegetable that can be eaten. (No plural.)
→ IN THE FLESH

flesh and blood 1. a living human body, especially with reference to its natural limitations; a human being. **2.** the quality of being alive. **3.** one's own relatives; one's own kin.

flesh out to become more fleshy.

flesh something **out (with** something) to make the frame or skeleton of something complete; to add detail to the basic framework of something.

flew ['flu] past tense of FLY.

flexible ['flɛk sə bəl] **1.** *adj.* able to bend easily; not rigid. (Adv: *flexibly*.) **2.** *adj.* able to be changed; able to serve a number of purposes. (Figurative on ①. Adv: *flexibly*.)

flick something **off** to turn something off, using a switch.

flick something **off ((of)** someone or something) to brush or knock a speck of something off of someone or something.

flick something **on** to turn something on, using a switch.

flicker ['flɪk ɚ] **1.** *n.* a light or flame that is not steady; a light or flame that wavers. **2.** *n.* a short burst of energy or excitement that dies out quickly. (Figurative on ①.) **3.** *iv.* to burn unsteadily; to burn as a flame.

flicker out [for a flame] to dwindle, little by little, until it goes out.

flight ['flaɪt] **1.** *n.* flying; flying through the air. (Plural only for types and instances.) **2.** *n.* running away from someone or something; an escape from danger. (No plural.) **3.** *n.* a set of stairs.
→ IN FLIGHT

flight of fancy an idea or suggestion that is out of touch with reality or possibility.

fling ['flɪŋ] *n.* a throw; a toss, especially to get rid of something.
→ FINAL FLING

fling something **off (of** oneself) **1.** to yank something off of oneself hastily. **2.** to pull or take off an article of clothing.

flip ['flɪp] **1.** *n.* a throw that tosses something into the air; a tossing action that moves something. **2.** *n.* a kind of jump where one turns one's body in the air. **3.** *tv.* to cause something to turn about or spin through the air.

flip through something to go quickly through the leaves of a book, magazine, etc., page by page.

flirt ['flɚt] *n.* someone who tries to attract someone's attention romantically or sexually.

flirt (with someone) to behave in a way that gets someone's attention—with romance in mind.

flirt with the idea of doing something to think about doing something; to toy with an idea; to consider something, but not too seriously.

float ['flot] **1.** *iv.* to remain on top of water or a liquid; to stay above water. **2.** *iv.* to hover; to remain in the air. (Figurative on ①.) **3.** *tv.* to release something so it can move as in ①.

float a loan to get a loan; to arrange for a loan.

flock in((to) someplace) to move into someplace in crowds.

flock together to gather together in great numbers. (Typically said of birds and sheep.)

flood ['flʌd] **1.** *n.* a large amount of water lying on land that is normally dry. **2.** *n.* a powerful surge of water moving over the land. **3.** *n.* a large amount of something. (Figurative on ②.) **4.** *tv.* to cover an area with water; to cover something with water. **5.** *iv.* to spill or overflow with great volumes of water; to become covered with a great amount of water.

flood in(to something) to pour into something. (Both literally, with water, and figuratively.)

flood out (of something) to pour out of something or someplace.

flood someone or something out (of something) [for too much water] to force someone or something to leave something or someplace.

floor ['flor] **1.** *n.* the surface of a room that is walked on; the inside bottom surface of a room. **2.** *n.* one level of a building; a story.
→ WALK THE FLOOR

floppy disk ['flɑp i 'dɪsk] *n.* a round, flat, magnetic computer storage device that can be moved from computer to computer.

florist ['flor ɪst] *n.* someone who arranges and sells flowers for a living.

flour ['flaʊ ɚ] *n.* a powder made from grinding wheat, corn, or other grain, used in cooking. (Compare this with FLOWER. Plural only for types and instances.)

flow ['flo] **1.** *n.* the movement of running water; the movement of a fluid. (No plural.) **2.** *n.* the even and ordered movement of things in a series. (No plural. Figurative on ①.) **3.** *iv.* to move like running water; to move smoothly along a route. **4.** *iv.* to move easily and in an orderly fashion.

flow in(to something) to course into something; to pour into something. (Both literal and figurative.)

flow out (of something) 1. to course or pour out of something. **2.** to issue forth from something.

flower ['flaʊ ɚ] **1.** *n.* a plant that produces blossoms. **2.** *n.* a blossom; the brightly colored petals of a plant. **3.** *iv.* to bloom; [for a plant] to produce ②.

flown ['flon] past participle of FLY.

the flu [...'flu] *n.* influenza; a disease like a very bad cold. (Plural only for types and instances.)

fluent ['flu ənt] *adj.* able to speak, read, write, or understand a language as well as a native speaker of that language. (Adv: *fluently*.)

fluffy ['flʌf i] *adj.* soft, light, and airy. (Adv: *fluffily*. Comp: *fluffier*; sup: *fluffiest*.)

fluid ['flu ɪd] **1.** *n.* a liquid or a gas; a substance that can flow. (Technically, a gas is a fluid.) **2.** *adj.* moving freely; flowing freely as with a liquid or a gas. (Adv: *fluidly*.)

flush ['flʌʃ] **1.** *n.* an act of releasing water to cleanse a toilet bowl. **2.** *tv.* to clean something, especially a toilet bowl, with a stream of water.

flush something **away** to wash something unwanted away.

flush with something **1.** even with something; sharing a surface with something. **2.** having lots of something.

flute ['flut] *n.* a musical instrument that is shaped like a long, thin pipe.

fly ['flaɪ] **1.** *tv., irreg.* to "drive" an airplane; to guide something that moves through the air. (Past tense: FLEW; past participle: FLOWN.) **2.** *tv., irreg.* to raise or otherwise display a flag. **3.** *iv., irreg.* to move through the air; to move in the air. **4.** *iv., irreg.* to travel by airplane. **5.** *iv., irreg.* [for time] to pass quickly. (Figurative on ③.) **6.** *n.* a small insect; a bug; a mosquito. **7.** *n.* the flap of material that covers a zipper in trousers.
→ AS THE CROW FLIES
→ GET OFF TO A FLYING START
→ MAKE THE FEATHERS FLY
→ MAKE THE FUR FLY
→ TIME FLIES
→ WITH FLYING COLORS

fly by 1. to soar past. **2.** [for time] to go quickly. (Figurative.)

fly in the face of someone or something AND **fly in the teeth of** someone or something to disregard, defy, or show disrespect for someone or something.

fly in the ointment a small, unpleasant matter that spoils something; a drawback.

fly in the teeth of someone or something Go to FLY IN THE FACE OF SOMEONE OR SOMETHING.

fly in(to something) to arrive in an airplane at something or someplace.

fly off 1. to take to flight quickly. **2.** to leave in a hurry. (Figurative.)

fly off the handle to lose one's temper.

foam ['fom] *n.* a mass of small bubbles; froth. (Plural only for types and instances.)

foam at the mouth to be very angry. (Related to a "mad dog"—a dog with rabies—that foams at the mouth.)

fob someone or something **off (on(to)** someone) to get rid of someone or something by transferring that someone or something to someone else.

foci ['fo saɪ] a plural of FOCUS.

focus ['fok əs] **1.** *n.* the position or setting of a lens that provides the clearest image. (No plural.) **2.** *n., irreg.* the center of attention; the center of interest. (Figurative on ①. Plural: *focuses* or FOCI.) **3.** *tv.* to adjust a lens, or the eyes, so that the image that passes through them is sharp and clear.

focus on someone or something [for a lens] to cause light rays or lines of sight to converge on a particular point or person.

foe ['fo] *n.* the enemy in general; an enemy.

fog ['fɔg] *n.* water vapor suspended in the air; a heavy mist. (No plural.)

fog over [for something made of glass] to become covered over with water vapor.

fog something **up** to make something made of glass become covered with a film of water vapor.

fog up [for something made of glass] to become partially or completely obscured by a film of water vapor.

foggy ['fɔg i] *adj.* covered or filled with fog; [of weather] having much fog. (Adv: *foggily.* Comp: *foggier;* sup: *foggiest.*)

foil ['fɔɪl] **1.** *n.* a very thin, light sheet of metal, usually aluminum, used to wrap food or as a decoration. (Plural only for types and instances.) **2.** *tv.* to spoil someone's plans; to prevent something from happening.

foist something **(off) on** someone to force someone to take something that they don't want.

fold ['fold] *tv.* to bend something so that part of it lies on top of the rest of it; to double something over onto itself.

fold one's **arms** to cross one's arms and bring them close to one's body.

fold one's **hands** to bring one's hands together, palm to palm, with the fingers interlocking; to grasp one's hands together, palm to palm, perpendicular to one another.

fold something **back** to bend a sheet or flap of something back.

fold something **in(to** something**)** to blend something, such as eggs, into batter.

fold something **over** to double something over; to make a fold in something.

fold something **up** to double something over into its original folded position.

fold up 1. [for something] to close by folding. **2.** [for a business] to cease operating. **3.** [for someone] to faint.

folder ['fol dɚ] *n.* a holder made of heavy paper used for filing, organizing, or storing papers.

folk ['fok] **1.** *n.* a group of people. (No plural. Treated as plural. See also FOLKS.) **2.** *adj.* of or about the common people; traditional.

folk song ['fok sɔŋ] *n.* a song that is in the traditional style of a country or group of people.

folklore ['fok lor] *n.* traditions, stories, customs, and beliefs that are passed down from generation to generation within a culture. (No plural.)

folks *n.* people in general, often relatives. (Treated as plural. Informal.)
→ ONE'S FOLKS

follow ['fɑl o] **1.** *tv.* to come after someone or something in space or time. **2.** *tv.* to pursue someone or something; to go after someone or something. **3.** *tv.* to obey a set of rules or instructions. **4.** *tv.* to understand a person who is leading one through an explanation; to understand an explanation as someone explains it. **5.** *tv.* to study or pay attention to or have a continuing interest in something, such as a sport. **6.** *iv.* [for something] to happen as a logical or typical result of something.
→ A TOUGH ACT TO FOLLOW

follow one's **heart** to act according to one's feelings; to obey one's sympathetic or compassionate inclinations.

follow orders to do as one has been instructed.

follow someone **up** AND **follow up (on** someone**)** to check on the work that someone has done.

follow someone's **lead** to do something the way another person is doing it.

follow something **through** Go to FOLLOW THROUGH (WITH SOMETHING).

follow something **up** AND **follow up (on** something**) 1.** to check something out. **2.** to make sure that something was done the way it was intended.

follow through (on something**)** to supervise something to its com-

pletion; to oversee something to make sure it gets done properly.

follow through (with something**)** AND **follow** something **through** to complete an activity, doing what was promised.

follow up (on someone**)** Go to FOLLOW SOMEONE UP.

follow up (on something**)** Go to FOLLOW SOMETHING UP.

fond ['fɑnd] *adj.* loving; tender. (Adv: *fondly.* Comp: *fonder;* sup: *fondest.*)

fond of someone or something liking someone or something; having a desire for someone or something. (Comp: *fonder;* sup: *fondest.*)

food ['fud] *n.* something that is eaten by animals and plants. (Plural only for types and instances.)

food for thought something to think about.

fool ['ful] **1.** *n.* an idiot; a stupid person; someone who has no common sense. **2.** *tv.* to trick someone; to play a joke on someone.
→ ON A FOOL'S ERRAND

fool around to waste time doing something unnecessary or doing something amateurishly.

foolish ['ful ɪʃ] *adj.* silly; lacking sense; stupid; ridiculous. (Adv: *foolishly.*)

foolproof ['ful pruf] *adj.* not capable of failing; so simple that a fool could use it without problems.

a **fool's paradise** a condition of seeming happiness that is based on false assumptions and will not last. (Treated as a place grammatically.)

foot ['fʊt] **1.** *n.*, *irreg.* the end of a leg; the part of a human or animal body that touches the ground and supports the body. (Plural: FEET.) **2.** *n.* the bottom or lower end of a bed, mountain, cliff, ladder, hill, page, etc. (No plural.) **3.** *n.*, *irreg.* a unit of measurement equal to 12 inches or just over 30 centimeters.
→ BOUND HAND AND FOOT
→ GET ONE'S FOOT IN THE DOOR
→ HAVE A FOOT IN BOTH CAMPS
→ HAVE FOOT-IN-MOUTH DISEASE
→ NOT SET FOOT SOMEWHERE
→ ON FOOT
→ PUT ONE'S BEST FOOT FORWARD
→ PUT ONE'S FOOT IN IT
→ PUT ONE'S FOOT IN ONE'S MOUTH
→ SET FOOT SOMEWHERE
→ STICK ONE'S FOOT IN ONE'S MOUTH
→ WAIT ON SOMEONE HAND AND FOOT

foot the bill to pay the bill; to pay (for something).

football ['fʊt bɔl] **1.** *n.* a sport played between two teams of eleven players each, on a field having a goal on each end, using ②. (No plural. Compare this with SOCCER.) **2.** *n.* the leather, oval ball used in ①. **3.** the *adj.* use of ① or ②.

foothold ['fʊt hold] *n.* a space for one's foot that helps one climb up or down something. (Plural: *footholds.*)
→ GET A FOOTHOLD (SOMEWHERE)

footloose and fancy-free without responsibilities or commitments.

footnote ['fʊt not] **1.** *n.* a note at the bottom of a page that clarifies

or provides a source for something that appears higher on the page. **2.** *tv.* to provide ① for a piece of information.

footpath ['fʊt pæθ] *n.*, *irreg.* a path that is made for walking. (Plural: ['fʊt pæðz].)

footprint ['fʊt prɪnt] **1.** *n.* the mark made by pressing a foot in soft earth or snow. **2.** *n.* the mark made by tracking dirt from a muddy area onto a clean floor.

for [for] **1.** *prep.* meant to be used by someone or something; meant to belong to someone; meant to be given to someone. (Indicates who or what will benefit.) **2.** *prep.* meant to be used in doing something; with a function or purpose connected with something. **3.** *prep.* instead of someone or something; in place of someone or something. **4.** *prep.* in favor of someone or something; in support of someone or something. **5.** *prep.* in search of someone or something. (Indicates the target of the search.) **6.** *prep.* in a certain amount; by the exchange of a certain amount. **7.** *prep.* during something; throughout a period of time. **8.** *conj.* because; since; as. (Formal.)

for fear of something out of fear for something; because of fear of something.

for free for no charge or cost; free of any cost.

for instance for example.

for safekeeping for the purpose of keeping someone or something safe.

for sale available to be sold.

for someone's or something's **sake** AND **for the sake of** someone or something [...'sek] for the purpose or benefit of someone or something; to satisfy the demands of someone or something.

for the devil of it AND **for the hell of it** just for fun; because it is slightly evil; for no good reason. (Some people may object to the word *hell*.)

for the duration for the whole time that something continues.

for the good of someone or something for the benefit, profit, or advantage of someone or something.

for the hell of it Go to FOR THE DEVIL OF IT.

for the record so that (one's own version of) the facts will be known; so there will be a record of a particular fact.

for the sake of someone or something Go to FOR SOMEONE'S OR SOMETHING'S SAKE.

forbade AND **forbad** [for 'bed, for 'bæd] past tense of FORBID.

forbid [for 'bɪd] **1.** *tv., irreg.* to prohibit something. (Past tense: FORBAD or FORBADE; past participle: FORBIDDEN.) **2.** *tv., irreg.* to state that someone must not do something; to prohibit someone from doing something.

forbidden [for 'bɪd n] **1.** Past participle of FORBID. **2.** *adj.* prohibited; banned; not allowed.

forbidden fruit someone or something that one finds attractive or desirable partly because the person or thing is unobtainable.

force ['fors] **1.** *n.* power; physical strength. (Plural only for types and instances.) **2.** *n.* military strength. (No plural.) **3.** *n.* an influence; someone or something that is an influence. **4.** *n.* a group of soldiers, police officers, etc. **5.** *tv.* to push or move something using ①. **6.** *tv.* to make someone do something, especially by the use of ①.
→ TASK FORCE

force a price **up** Go to DRIVE A PRICE UP.

force someone or something **out (of** something) to drive someone or something out of something or someplace.

force someone **to the wall** AND **drive** someone **to the wall** to push someone to an extreme position; to put someone into an awkward position.

force someone's **hand** to force a person to reveal plans, strategies, or secrets. (Refers to a handful of cards in card playing.)

force something **down** to force oneself to swallow something.

force something **through** something to press or drive something through resistance.

forefront ['for frənt] in the place of greatest activity and visibility.
→ AT THE FOREFRONT (OF SOMETHING)
→ IN THE FOREFRONT (OF SOMETHING)

a **foregone conclusion** a conclusion already reached; an inevitable result.

forehead ['for hɛd] *n.* the part of the face between the eyebrows and the hair.

foreign ['for ɪn] *adj.* not native to one's country; of or about a country other than one's own. (Adv: *foreignly.*)

foreigner ['for ən ɚ] *n.* someone who comes from another country; someone who was born in another country.

foremost ['for most] **1.** *adj.* first; most important. **2.** *adv.* first; most importantly.
→ FIRST AND FOREMOST

foresaw [for 'sɔ] past tense of FORESEE.

foresee [for 'si] *tv., irreg.* to be aware of something before it happens; to imagine or predict that something will happen. (Past tense: FORESAW; past participle: FORESEEN. The object can be a clause with THAT ⑦.)

foreseen [for 'sin] past participle of FORESEE.

forest ['for əst] *n.* a large area of land covered with trees.
→ NOT ABLE TO SEE THE FOREST FOR THE TREES

forever [for 'ɛv ɚ] *adv.* always; with no beginning and no end; throughout all time.

forfeit ['for fɪt] *tv.* to give up something; to lose something as a punishment.

forgave [for 'gev] past tense of FORGIVE.

forget [for 'gɛt] **1.** *tv., irreg.* to lose a piece of information from one's memory. (Past tense: FORGOT; past participle: FORGOT or FORGOTTEN.)

The object can be a clause with THAT ⑦.) **2.** *tv., irreg.* to leave someone or something behind; not to take someone or something with oneself.

forget to do something to fail to remember to do something.

forgive [for 'gɪv] **1.** *tv., irreg.* to pardon someone for an error or wrongdoing. (Past tense: FORGAVE; past participle: FORGIVEN.) **2.** *tv., irreg.* to cancel payment of a debt; to relieve someone of a debt before it is paid back.

forgive and forget to forgive someone (for something) and forget that it ever happened.

forgiven [for 'gɪv ən] past participle of FORGIVE.

forgot [for 'gɑt] past tense of FORGET; a past participle of FORGET.

forgotten [for 'gɑt n] a past participle of FORGET.

fork ['fork] **1.** *n.* an eating tool with a handle and two, three, or four spikes, used to gather and hold food when eating. **2.** *n.* the place where something splits into two branches. **3.** *n.* one of the two branches that something splits into. **4.** *iv.* to split into two branches.
→ SPEAK WITH A FORKED TONGUE

fork money out (for something**)** to pay (perhaps unwillingly) for something.

fork something **over (to** someone**)** to give something to someone. (Slang. Usually refers to money.)

form ['form] **1.** *n.* a shape; the shape of someone or something; the way someone or something is

shaped. **2.** *n.* a kind; a sort; a type. **3.** *n.* a document that has blank spaces on it that need to be filled with information. **4.** *n.* a word or part of a word. **5.** *iv.* to come into being; to be created. **6.** *tv.* to develop something; to develop into something; to cause something to come into being. **7.** *tv.* to make up something; to be a part of something.
→ IN TOP FORM
→ INFINITIVE FORM

form an opinion to think up or decide on an opinion.

formal ['form əl] **1.** *adj.* according to custom; according to rules. (Adv: *formally*.) **2.** *adj.* [of behavior, language use, clothes, etc.] serious and proper; [of a person or situation] having serious and proper behavior, dress, etc. (Adv: *formally*. See also INFORMAL.) **3.** *adj.* [of clothing] of the highest level or style prescribed by the rules of manners. (Adv: *formally*.) **4.** *adj.* [of an event] where fancy clothing as in ③ is expected or required. (Adv: *formally*.) **5.** *n.* a woman's (usually long) gown suitable for an event that is ④.

format ['for mæt] **1.** *n.* the way events are ordered or arranged; the way things are placed on a page. **2.** *tv.* to arrange something to look a certain way, as with the order and arrangement in the pages of a book or other document. (Past tense and past participle: *format-ted*. Present participle: *format-ting*.) **3.** *tv.* to make a computer disk ready to accept information. (Past tense and past participle: *for-matted*. Present participle: *format-ting*.)

former ['for mɚ] *adj.* past; previous. (Prenominal only. Adv: *for-merly*.)

the **former** *n.* the first of two things mentioned. (No plural. Treated as singular or plural, but not countable.)

formula ['form jə lə] **1.** *n., irreg.* a series of symbols that show the chemical ingredients of a substance. (Plural: *formulas* or FORMU-LAE.) **2.** *n., irreg.* a mathematical rule that is expressed with numbers or symbols. (Plural: *formulas* or FORMULAE.) **3.** *n.* a pattern or a standard set of parts or actions. (Figurative on ②.) **4.** *n.* animal milk or another milk substitute for feeding babies. (No plural.)

formulae ['form jə laɪ] a plural of FORMULA.

fort ['fort] **1.** *n.* a structure or building used for defense that can withstand enemy attack; a number of strong buildings behind a barrier. **2.** *n.* a permanent military base.
→ HOLD THE FORT

forth ['forθ] *adv.* forward; onward; outward.
→ AND SO FORTH
→ BACK AND FORTH
→ HOLD FORTH (ON SOMEONE OR SOMETHING)

forties *n.* the decade beginning in 1940; the 1940s. (Similar definitions for *twenties, thirties, fifties, sixties, seventies, eighties, nineties*.)

fortieth ['for ti əθ] 40th. Go to FOURTH.

fortress ['for trɪs] *n.* a very strong building built to resist attacks. (See also FORT.)

fortunate ['for tʃə nɪt] **1.** *adj.* lucky; bringing good results; representing good fortune. (Adv: *fortunately.*) **2.** *adj.* having had good luck. (Adv: *fortunately.*)

fortune ['for tʃən] **1.** *n.* good luck; success. (No plural.) **2.** *n.* everything that will happen to someone in the future. **3.** *n.* a lot of money and property that someone owns.

forty ['for ti] **1.** *n.* the cardinal number 40; the number between 39 and 41. (No plural. Similar definitions for TWENTY, THIRTY, FIFTY, SIXTY, SEVENTY, EIGHTY, NINETY.) **2.** *adj.* 40; consisting of 40 things; having 40 things. (Similar definitions for TWENTY, THIRTY, FIFTY, SIXTY, SEVENTY, EIGHTY, NINETY.) **3.** *pron.* 40 people or things already mentioned or able to be determined by context. (Similar definitions for TWENTY, THIRTY, FIFTY, SIXTY, SEVENTY, EIGHTY, NINETY.)
→ TAKE FORTY WINKS

forum ['for əm] *n.* a meeting where someone can discuss something; a place where someone can talk about something, especially items of public interest.

forward ['for wə-d] **1.** *adv.* ahead; toward the front; into the future. (Also **forwards**.) **2.** *adj.* [moving] toward the front; [looking] into the future. **3.** *tv.* to have mail sent onward to a new address when one moves.
→ PUT ONE'S BEST FOOT FORWARD

fought ['fɔt] past tense and past participle of FIGHT.

foul ['faʊl] **1.** *adj.* dirty; nasty and rotten. (Adv: *foully.* Comp: *fouler;* sup: *foulest.*) **2.** *adj.* nasty; rude and unpleasant. (Adv: *foully.* Comp: *fouler;* sup: *foulest.*) **3.** *adj.* evil; really bad. (Figurative on ①. Adv: *foully.* Comp: *fouler;* sup: *foulest.*) **4.** *adj.* [of a ball] going outside the proper playing area. (Sports.) **5.** *adj.* [of weather] bad. (Adv: *foully.* Comp: *fouler;* sup: *foulest.*) **6.** *tv.* to make something dirty. **7.** *n.* an action in a game that is against the rules. **8.** *n.* [in baseball] a ball that is hit outside the proper playing area.
→ FALL FOUL OF SOMEONE OR SOMETHING

foul one's **own nest** to harm one's own interests; to bring disadvantage upon oneself.

foul play illegal activity; bad practices.

foul someone or something **up** to make errors concerning someone or something; to mess someone or something up. (Informal.)

foul up to make an error. (Informal.)

found ['faʊnd] **1.** past tense and past participle of FIND. **2.** *tv.* to establish an organization; to provide money or support to help start an organization. (Past tense and past participle: *founded.*)

foundation [faʊn 'de ʃən] **1.** *n.* the base of a building. (Rarely plural.) **2.** *n.* the base of a custom or tradition; a basis. (Figurative on ①.) **3.** *n.* an institution that gives out money or grants to special causes.

fountain ['faʊn tn] **1.** *n.* a stream of water that sprays up into the air. **2.** *n.* a structure—designed and built by humans—that sprays a stream of water into the air.

four ['for] **1.** *n.* the cardinal number 4; the number between 3 and 5. (No plural. The ordinal form is FOURTH. Similar definitions for ONE, TWO, THREE, FIVE, SIX, SEVEN, EIGHT, NINE, TEN, ELEVEN, TWELVE, THIRTEEN, FOURTEEN, FIFTEEN, SIXTEEN, SEVENTEEN, EIGHTEEN, NINETEEN.) **2.** *adj.* 4; consisting of 4 things; having 4 things. (The ordinal form is FOURTH. This covers other terms as in ①.) **3.** *pron.* 4 people or things already mentioned or able to be determined by context. (The ordinal form is FOURTH. This covers other terms as in ①.)
→ ON ALL FOURS

fourteen ['fort 'tin] 14. Go to FOUR.

fourteenth ['fort 'tinθ] **1.** *n.* one of 14 equal parts. **2.** *adj.* of the 14th item in a series of things; of the item between the 13th and 15th in a series; between the 13th and 15th. **3.** *pron.* the 14th item in a series of people or things already mentioned or able to be determined by context.

fourth ['forθ] **1.** *n.* 4th; one of 4 equal parts; a quarter; a half of a half. (Similar definitions for THIRD, FIFTH, SIXTH, SEVENTH, EIGHTH, NINTH, TENTH, ELEVENTH, TWELFTH, THIRTEENTH, FOURTEENTH, FIFTEENTH, SIXTEENTH, SEVENTEENTH, EIGHTEENTH, NINETEENTH, TWENTIETH, THIRTIETH, FORTIETH, FIFTIETH, SIXTIETH, SEVENTIETH, EIGHTIETH, NINETIETH, [ONE] HUNDREDTH, [ONE] THOUSANDTH, [ONE] MILLIONTH, [ONE] BILLIONTH, and [ONE] TRILLIONTH. See also FIRST, SECOND.) **2.** *n.* the 4th item in a series

of people or things already mentioned or able to be determined by context. (This covers other terms as in ①. See also FIRST, SECOND.) **3.** *adj.* of the 4th item in a series of things; of the item between the 3rd and 5th in a series. (This covers other terms as in ①. See also FIRST, SECOND.) **4.** *adv.* in the 4th position or rank. (This covers other terms as in ①. See also FIRST, SECOND.)

Fourth of July [forθ əv dʒə 'laɪ] *n.* an American holiday celebrating independence from Great Britain on July 4, 1776.

fowl ['faʊl] **1.** *n.*, *irreg.* one of a number of various kinds of birds of limited flight, kept for their eggs or meat, such as the chicken, duck, turkey, etc. (Plural: *fowl* or *fowls*.) **2.** *n.* the meat of ①. (No plural.)
→ NEITHER FISH NOR FOWL

fox ['faks] **1.** *n.* a wild animal related to the dog, having a bushy tail. **2.** *n.* the fur or pelt of ①. (No plural.) **3.** *adj.* made of ②.
→ (AS) SMART AS A FOX

fraction ['fræk ʃən] **1.** *n.* a part of a whole number. **2.** *n.* a small piece or portion of something. (No plural.)

fracture ['fræk tʃɚ] **1.** *n.* a break or crack, especially a break in a bone. **2.** *tv.* to break something by creating a crack in it. **3.** *iv.* to break; to crack.

fragile ['frædʒ əl] *adj.* easily broken; delicate. (Adv: *fragilely.*)

fragment ['fræg mənt] **1.** *n.* a small piece of something. **2.** *iv.* to break into pieces or sections. **3.** *tv.* to

fragrance ['fre grəns] *n.* a smell or scent that is pleasant.

fragrant ['fre grənt] *adj.* smelling good; having a nice smell. (Adv: *fragrantly.*)

frail ['frel] *adj.* thin and weak; not strong; easily hurt. (Adv: *fraily.*)

frame ['frem] **1.** *n.* a structure that provides support for something. **2.** *n.* a firm border that something, such as a door, a window, or a picture, is set into. **3.** *n.* the shape or form of a human body; the structure of the body. **4.** *tv.* to place something in ②; to build ② for something. **5.** *tv.* to cause someone to appear guilty of a crime by manipulating evidence or lying.

frank ['fræŋk] *adj.* straightforward; truthful; honest; [of someone] speaking the truth even if it "hurts." (Adv: *frankly.* Comp: *franker;* sup: *frankest.*)

frantic ['fræn tɪk] *adj.* very excited; wild with emotion. (Adv: *frantically* […ɪk li].)

fraud ['frɔd] **1.** *n.* cheating; something done to deceive someone. (No plural.) **2.** *n.* a false or deceiving thing or act. **3.** *n.* someone who pretends to be someone or something else.

fraught with danger [of something] full of something dangerous or unpleasant.

fray ['fre] **1.** *tv.* to cause a rope or string to unravel; to separate the threads that make up string or rope. **2.** *iv.* to unravel; to become worn at the edges. **3.** *n.* an argument; a brawl.
→ JOIN THE FRAY
→ JUMP INTO THE FRAY

freak ['frik] **1.** *n.* someone or something that is not normally developed. (Not polite for humans.) **2.** *adj.* very unusual. (Prenominal only.)

freckle ['frɛk əl] **1.** *n.* one of many small dark dots on the skin. **2.** *iv.* to become covered with ①, usually because of exposure to the sun.

free ['fri] **1.** *adj.* independent; not someone's slave; not ruled by a bad ruler. (Adv: *freely.* Comp: *freer;* sup: *freest.*) **2.** *adj.* costing no money; without cost. **3.** *adj.* not limited; not restricted; not bound by rules. (Adv: *freely.* Comp: *freer;* sup: *freest.*) **4.** *adj.* not busy; available. (Comp: *freer;* sup: *freest.*) **5.** *adj.* generous; lavish; giving. (Adv: *freely.* Comp: *freer;* sup: *freest.*) **6.** *adj.* having an open path; having nothing in one's way. **7.** *adv.* without cost; without having to pay money. **8.** *tv.* to release someone or something.
→ (AS) FREE AS A BIRD
→ BREAK FREE (FROM SOMEONE)
→ FOOTLOOSE AND FANCY-FREE
→ FOR FREE
→ SET SOMEONE OR SOMETHING FREE

free and easy casual.

free translation a translation that is not completely accurate and not well thought out.

freedom ['fri dəm] **1.** *n.* liberty; a state where one is free from constraint. (No plural.) **2.** *n.* a right.
→ GIVE ONE ONE'S FREEDOM

free-for-all a disorganized fight or contest involving everyone; a brawl.

freeze ['friz] **1.** *iv., irreg.* to become solid as the temperature gets colder. (Past tense: FROZE; past participle: FROZEN.) **2.** *iv., irreg.* [for someone or some creature] to become very cold in cold weather. **3.** *iv., irreg.* to become completely still; to stop all movement. (Figurative on ①.) **4.** *tv., irreg.* to turn something into ice; to cause something to harden as the temperature gets colder. **5.** *tv., irreg.* to place food in a freezer so that it stays fresh; to preserve something at an extremely low temperature. **6.** *tv., irreg.* to cause someone or something to become completely still. **7.** *tv., irreg.* to keep the price of something at a certain level; not to allow an amount to change. **8.** *n.* a time when the temperature is 32 degrees FAHRENHEIT, 0 degrees CENTIGRADE, or below.

freeze over [for a body of water] to get cold and form a layer of ice on top.

freeze up 1. [for something] to freeze and stop functioning. **2.** [for someone] to become frightened and anxious, and be unable to continue with something.

freezer ['friz ɚ] *n.* an appliance that remains at a temperature below 32 degrees Fahrenheit in order to store and preserve food and other things.

freight ['fret] **1.** *n.* cargo; products that are carried by truck, plane, train, etc. (No plural.) **2.** *n.* the

cost of shipping something as ①. **3.** the *adj.* use of ① or ②.

French fry ['frɛntʃ fraɪ] *n.* a long, narrow piece of potato that has been fried in deep fat. (Usually plural. Can be shortened to FRIES.)

frenzy ['frɛn zi] *n.* a wild fury; an excited state.

frequency ['fri kwən si] **1.** *n.* the rate of [something] happening; how often an event occurs. (No plural.) **2.** *n.* the number of times that something occurs within a given period of time.

frequent ['fri kwənt] **1.** *adj.* happening often; occurring often; common. (Adv: *frequently.*) **2.** *tv.* to go to a certain place often.

fresh ['frɛʃ] **1.** *adj.* new; newly or recently made, done, obtained, etc., especially if not yet used or changed. (Adv: *freshly.* Comp: *fresher;* sup: *freshest.*) **2.** *adj.* not stale; not spoiled; [of foods] not canned, frozen, dried, or preserved in another way; [of fruits or vegetables] recently picked or harvested. (Adv: *freshly.* Comp: *fresher;* sup: *freshest.*)

fresh blood AND **new blood** new personnel; new members brought into a group to revive it.

freshen someone or something **up** to revive or restore the appearance or vitality of someone or something.

fret ['frɛt] *iv.* to worry about something; to be upset.

friction ['frɪk ʃən] **1.** *n.* rubbing against something that resists the rubbing. (No plural.) **2.** *n.* the resistance that prevents one object from easily sliding over another object. (No plural.) **3.** *n.* a disagreement because of differences in opinions.

Friday [ˈfraɪ de] Go to DAY.

friend [ˈfrɛnd] **1.** *n.* someone whom someone else knows well and likes. **2.** *n.* someone or something that supports or helps someone or something.
→ FAIR-WEATHER FRIEND
→ MAKE A FRIEND
→ MAKE FRIENDS

friendly [ˈfrɛnd li] *adj.* like a friend; nice, kind, or pleasant. (Comp: *friendlier;* sup: *friendliest.*)

friendship [ˈfrɛnd ʃɪp] *n.* being friends with someone. (Plural only for types and instances.)
→ STRIKE UP A FRIENDSHIP

fries [ˈfraɪz] *n.* FRENCH FRIES. (Treated as plural.)

fright [ˈfraɪt] *n.* fear; terror; the condition of being scared. (No plural.)

frighten someone or something **away** AND **frighten** someone or something **off** to scare someone or something away.

frighten someone or something **off** Go to FRIGHTEN SOMEONE OR SOMETHING AWAY.

frill [ˈfrɪl] **1.** *n.* a decorative edge on cloth. **2.** *n.* something that is an added bonus but is not necessary. (Usually plural.)

fringe [ˈfrɪndʒ] **1.** *n.* a border for clothing or material, made of a row of threads or strings hanging loose. **2.** *n.* the edge of something; something that is far away from the center. (Figurative on ①.

Sometimes plural with the same meaning.) **3.** *tv.* to enclose something and serve as its border.
→ LUNATIC FRINGE

frisk [ˈfrɪsk] *tv.* to pat and press on the body in a search for weapons, drugs, evidence, or stolen property.

frog [ˈfrɔg] *n.* a small creature, living in water and on land, that hops and has special feet for swimming.
→ A BIG FROG IN A SMALL POND
→ HAVE A FROG IN ONE'S THROAT

from [ˈfrʌm] **1.** *prep.* starting at a particular time or place; originating at a particular time or place. **2.** *prep.* a word indicating separation or difference. **3.** *prep.* out of someone or something. **4.** *prep.* sent by someone or something; given by someone or something. **5.** *prep.* because of something; owing to something.

from dawn to dusk during the period of the day when there is light; from the rising of the sun to the setting of the sun.

from hand to hand from one person to a series of other persons; from one person's hand to another person's hand, and so forth.

from pillar to post from one place to a series of other places; (figuratively) from person to person, as with gossip.

from rags to riches from poverty to wealth; from modesty to elegance.

from side to side moving first to one side and then to the other, repeatedly.

from start to finish from the beginning to the end; throughout.

from stem to stern from one end to another. (Refers to the front and back ends of a ship. Also used literally in reference to ships.)

from the bottom of one's **heart** sincerely.

from the ground up from the beginning; from start to finish.

from the old school holding attitudes or ideas that were popular and important in the past, but that are no longer considered relevant or in line with modern trends.

from the top from the beginning of something, such as a song or a script.

from the word go from the beginning; from the very start of things. (Actually from the uttering of the word *go*.)

from top to bottom from the highest point to the lowest point; throughout.

front ['frʌnt] **1.** *n.* the part of something that faces forward. **2.** *n.* a border between two masses of air of different temperatures or pressures. **3.** *n.* the way one appears to other people; the way one seems to be when around other people; an outward appearance. **4.** *iv.* to face in a certain direction. **5.** *adj.* closest to ①. (Prenominal only.)
→ CAN'T SEE ONE'S HAND IN FRONT OF ONE'S FACE
→ PUT UP A (BRAVE) FRONT

frost ['frɔst] **1.** *n.* frozen moisture on the surface of something, especially the ground; small ice crystals on the surface of something. (Plural only for types and instances.) **2.** *iv.* to be covered with small ice crystals; to be covered with frozen moisture. **3.** *tv.* to put frosting on a cake or dessert.

frostbite ['frɔst baɪt] *n.* an injury caused by exposing skin to extremely cold weather without protection. (No plural.)

frosting ['frɔs tɪŋ] *n.* a mixture of sugar and other things that is spread on top of a cake or pastry. (Plural only for types and instances.)

froth ['frɔθ] *n.* foam; a mass of white bubbles that forms on top of liquids or around the mouth. (No plural.)

frown ['fraʊn] **1.** *n.* the opposite of a smile; the look on one's face made by pulling the eyebrows together and squinting the eyes. **2.** *iv.* to pull one's eyebrows together and squint the eyes; to scowl; to look angry.

froze ['froz] past tense of FREEZE.

frozen ['froz ən] Past participle of FREEZE.

fruit ['frut] *n.* the part of a plant that contains seeds and can be eaten as food. (Plural only for types and instances. Number is expressed with *piece(s) of fruit*.)
→ FORBIDDEN FRUIT

fruitcake ['frut kek] *n.* a cake that has dried fruit and spices in it.

the fruits of one's **labor(s)** the results of one's work.

fry ['fraɪ] *tv.* to cook something in hot fat.
→ FRENCH FRY

→ HAVE OTHER FISH TO FRY
→ OUT OF THE FRYING PAN INTO THE
   FIRE
→ SMALL FRY

fuck ['fʌk] **1.** *tv.* to copulate [with] someone or some creature. (Taboo. Potentially offensive. Use only with discretion. A highly offensive word to many people. There are many additional meanings and constructions with the word.) **2.** *iv.* to copulate. (Comments as with ①.)

fudge ['fʌdʒ] **1.** *n.* a thick, rich chocolate candy. (No plural.) **2.** *iv.* to attempt to lie to or deceive someone. (Informal.)

fuel ['fjul] **1.** *n.* material that is burned to make heat or energy. **2.** *tv.* to supply something with ①. **3.** *tv.* to provide someone or something with energy or encouragement. (Figurative on ②.)
→ ADD FUEL TO THE FIRE
→ ADD FUEL TO THE FLAME

fuel up to fill one's tank with fuel.

full ['fʊl] **1.** *adj.* completely filled; having no empty space. (Adv: *fully.* Comp: *fuller;* sup: *fullest.*) **2.** *adj.* entire; complete; whole. (Adv: *fully.*) **3.** *adj.* at the highest or greatest extent or amount possible.
→ (AS) FULL AS A TICK
→ COME FULL CIRCLE
→ HAVE ONE'S HANDS FULL (WITH SOME-
   ONE OR SOMETHING)
→ IN FULL SWING

full of beans very lively and cheerful; healthy and energetic.

full of oneself conceited; self-important.

full steam ahead forward at the greatest speed possible; with as much energy and enthusiasm as possible. (From an instruction given to steamships.)

full-time ['fʊl 'taɪm] **1.** *adj.* all the time; 24 hours a day. **2.** *adj.* [of a job that] takes up the working day, usually 8 hours a day, 5 days a week. **3.** *adv.* throughout the normal workweek.

fun ['fʌn] **1.** *n.* enjoyment, especially from play or amusement. (No plural.) **2.** *adj.* entertaining; playful. (Colloquial.)
→ POKE FUN (AT SOMEONE)

fun and games playing around; doing worthless things; activities that are a waste of time.

function ['fʌŋk ʃən] **1.** *n.* the proper use of something; the purpose of something. **2.** *n.* a social gathering; an event where people get together and do things such as talk, drink, or celebrate. **3.** *iv.* to work properly; to operate; to be in proper use.

fund ['fʌnd] **1.** *n.* an amount of money that is reserved for a specific reason. **2.** *n.* an investment that is really a combination of other investments, such as stocks and bonds. (Short for MUTUAL FUND.) **3.** *tv.* to provide someone or something with money; to provide money for something.
→ MUTUAL FUND

funds *n.* money; an amount or supply of money. (Treated as plural, but not countable.)

funeral ['fjun (ə) rəl] **1.** *n.* a ceremony performed when someone is buried. **2.** the *adj.* use of ①.

funeral home ['fjun (ə) rəl 'hom] the place where a funeral is held;

the place of business of an undertaker.

fungi ['fʌn dʒaɪ] a plural of FUNGUS.

fungus ['fʌŋ gəs] *n.*, *irreg.* a plant that does not have leaves and is not green, such as the mushroom. (Plural: FUNGI or *funguses*.)

funnel ['fʌn əl] *n.* a cone-shaped device with a wide mouth and a narrow spout on the bottom, used when pouring liquids from one container into another.

funny ['fʌn i] **1.** *adj.* amusing; causing laughter. (Comp: *funnier*; sup: *funniest*.) **2.** *adj.* strange; weird; unusual; odd. (Comp: *funnier*; sup: *funniest*.)
→ (AS) FUNNY AS A CRUTCH
→ STRIKE SOMEONE FUNNY

funny business trickery or deception; illegal activity. (Informal.)

fur ['fɚ] **1.** *n.* the short, soft hair that grows on many mammals. (Plural only for types and instances.) **2.** *n.* a coat or other garment made from animal skin covered with ①. **3.** *adj.* made from animal skin covered with ①.
→ MAKE THE FUR FLY
→ RUB SOMEONE'S FUR THE WRONG WAY

furnace ['fɚ nəs] *n.* an oven that can be heated at very high temperatures to melt metal, heat a building, etc.

furnish ['fɚ nɪʃ] **1.** *tv.* to provide something; to supply something. **2.** *tv.* to supply and arrange furniture in a place.

furniture ['fɚ nɪ tʃɚ] *n.* the objects in a house, apartment, or office that can be moved, such as tables, chairs, desks, etc. (No plural.

Number is expressed with *piece(s) of furniture*.)

furry ['fɚ i] *adj.* covered with fur; having fur. (Adv: *furrily*. Comp: *furrier*; sup: *furriest*.)

further ['fɚ ðɚ] **1.** *adj.* more distant in space or time. (One of the comparative forms of FAR, along with FARTHER.) **2.** *adv.* more distant in space or time. (One of the comparative forms of FAR, along with FARTHER.) **3.** *adv.* to a greater degree or extent; to a more advanced level. (One of the comparative forms of FAR, along with FARTHER.) **4.** *tv.* to advance or promote someone or something.
→ NOT SEE FURTHER THAN THE END OF ONE'S NOSE

furthermore ['fɚ ðɚ mor] *adv.* also; in addition to what has been said or stated.

furthest ['fɚ ðəst] *adj.* the most distant in space or time. (One of the superlative forms of FAR, along with FARTHEST.)

fury ['fjʊr i] **1.** *n.* violent anger; rage. (No plural.) **2.** *n.* power or force.

fuse ['fjuz] **1.** *tv.* to melt something together with something else; to melt two things together. **2.** *iv.* [for two or more things] to melt together. **3.** *n.* a part of an electrical circuit that melts and stops the flow of electricity when there is a dangerous amount of electricity flowing through the circuit.
→ BLOW A FUSE

fuss ['fʌs] **1.** *iv.* to whine and cry. **2.** *n.* argument; complaining. (Informal.)
→ KICK UP A FUSS

fuss (around) with someone or something to keep bothering with someone or something; to fiddle, mess, or tinker with someone or something.

fussy ['fʌs i] *adj.* hard to please; likely to complain about everything. (Adv: *fussily.* Comp: *fussier;* sup: *fussiest.*)

futile ['fjut əl] *adj.* hopeless; useless; worthless. (Adv: *futilely.*)

future ['fju tʃɚ] **1.** *adj.* coming; yet to come; later. (Prenominal only.) **2.** *n.* the time that is to come; events that will happen. (No plural.) **3.** *n.* the things that are planned for one's life. (Plural only for types and instances.) **4.** *n.* the tense of verbs that describe actions that are to happen or actions that will happen.

fuzz ['fʌz] *n.* short, soft, light hairs. (No plural.)

fuzzy ['fʌz i] *adj.* having fuzz; covered with fuzz. (Adv: *fuzzily.* Comp: *fuzzier;* sup: *fuzziest.*)

G

gadget ['gædʒ ɪt] *n.* any small, practical device, tool, or appliance.

gain ['gen] **1.** *tv.* to get something; to obtain something; to acquire something. **2.** *tv.* [for a clock or watch] to reach a later time than it should have. **3.** *tv.* to earn or save time. **4.** *iv.* to earn, get, or acquire something of value. **5.** *n.* a profit. (Often plural.) **6.** *n.* an increase in something.
→ ILL-GOTTEN GAINS

gain ground to make progress; to advance; to become more important or popular.

galaxy ['gæl ək si] *n.* a large mass or cluster of stars and their solar systems in space.

gale ['gel] **1.** *n.* a very strong wind. **2.** *n.* an outburst, especially of laughter. (Often plural.)

gall ['gɔl] **1.** *n.* bile, a bitter liquid made by the liver. (Especially of animals. No plural form.) **2.** *n.* a sore spot on the hide of an animal, usually caused by rubbing or chafing. **3.** *n.* rudeness; impudence. (No plural form.) **4.** *tv.* to cause a sore to develop by rubbing or chafing. **5.** *tv.* to annoy or bother someone severely; to irritate someone. (Figurative on ④.)
→ HAVE THE GALL TO DO SOMETHING

gallant ['gæl ənt] *adj.* honorable and brave; very polite. (Refers especially to men who are very polite toward women. Adv: *gallantly*.)

gallery ['gæl ə ri] **1.** *n.* a balcony, often running along a wall or out-side a window. **2.** *n.* a room or building where art is displayed.
→ PLAY TO THE GALLERY

gallon ['gæl ən] *n.* a unit of liquid measure, equal to 4 quarts, 8 pints, or almost 3.8 liters.

gallop ['gæl əp] **1.** *n.* a fast way that a horse runs. (In a GALLOP, all four of the horse's feet are off the ground at once during each stride.) **2.** *iv.* to move quickly; [for a horse] to run fast.

gambit ['gæm bɪt] an initial movement or statement made to secure a position that is to one's advantage.
→ OPENING GAMBIT

gamble on someone or something **1.** to make a wager on something concerning someone or something. **2.** to run a risk by choosing or depending on someone or something.

game ['gem] **1.** *n.* a kind of contest, sporting event, or pastime played according to a set of rules. **2.** *n.* an instance of playing ①. **3.** *n.* wild animals that are hunted for sport or food. (No plural. Treated as a singular.)
→ AT THIS STAGE (OF THE GAME)
→ FAIR GAME
→ FUN AND GAMES

game warden ['gem 'word n] *n.* someone who enforces laws of or about hunting and fishing.

gamut ['gæm ət] *n.* the entire range of something from one extreme to the other. (No plural form.)
→ RUN THE GAMUT

gang ['gæŋ] **1.** *n.* a group of people who work, play, or do things together. **2.** *n.* a group of young criminals.

gang up (on someone or something) [for a group] to make an assault on someone or something.

gap ['gæp] **1.** *n.* an opening created by a crack; an opening created where two objects or structures do not meet. **2.** *n.* an interruption in time; a period of time between two events or the parts of an event. **3.** *n.* an easily seen difference between two things or groups of people.

garage [gə 'rɑʒ] *n.* a building, or a part of a building, used to store a car or other motor vehicle.

garbage ['gɑr bɪdʒ] *n.* trash; rubbish; useless things that are thrown away. (No plural.)

the **garbage** *n.* the container that holds trash and the trash that it holds. (No plural in this sense.)

garden ['gɑrd n] **1.** *n.* a piece of land where plants, flowers, or vegetables are grown. **2.** *iv.* to raise and take care of plants grown in ①.
→ LEAD SOMEONE DOWN THE GARDEN PATH

gardener ['gɑrd nɚ] *n.* someone who takes care of a garden; someone who plants and nourishes plants in a garden.

garment ['gɑr mənt] *n.* an article of clothing; a piece of clothing.

gas ['gæs] **1.** *n.* vapor; a substance that is not in a liquid or solid state at a temperature that is comfortable for people. (Plural only for types and instances.) **2.** *n.* a naturally occurring vapor that will burn and is used for cooking and heating. (No plural.) **3.** *n.* GASOLINE, the liquid made from petroleum that is used to operate motors and engines. (Plural only for types and instances.)
→ OUT OF GAS
→ RUN OUT OF GAS
→ STEP ON THE GAS

gash ['gæʃ] **1.** *n.* a large or deep cut or wound; a slash. **2.** *tv.* to slash or cut something.

gasoline [gæs ə 'lin] *n.* a liquid that is made from oil and is used to operate motors and engines. (Plural only for types and instances.)

gasp ['gæsp] **1.** *n.* a quick, short inward breath; a quick breathing in of air. **2.** *iv.* to breathe in suddenly as in surprise, shock, fear, etc.

gate ['get] **1.** *n.* a barrier that can be opened or closed at an opening in a fence or wall. **2.** *n.* a decorative structure, including ①, serving as a formal entrance to a park, cemetery, street, etc. **3.** *n.* the place where people enter a stadium, arena, etc. **4.** *n.* the entrance to the passage to an airplane in an airport.

gather ['gæð ɚ] **1.** *tv.* to bring something together; to collect something together; to bring people together. **2.** *tv.* to gain or increase in something, especially speed or intensity. **3.** *iv.* to come together into a big group.

gather something **in 1.** to collect something and bring it in; to harvest something. **2.** to fold or bunch cloth together when sewing or fitting clothing.

gather something **up** to collect something; to pick something up.

gathering ['gæð ɚ ɪŋ] *n.* a group of people; a group of people who have come together for a specific purpose.

gauze ['gɔz] *n.* a thin, loosely woven cloth. (Plural only for types and instances.)

gave ['gev] past tense of GIVE.

gay ['ge] **1.** *adj.* happy; cheerful; brightly colored. (Adv: *gaily.* Comp: *gayer;* sup: *gayest.*) **2.** *adj.* [of someone, usually a male] attracted to people of the same sex. (Comp: *gayer;* sup: *gayest.*) **3.** *n.* a person who is ②, usually a male.

gaze ['gez] *n.* an intent stare.

gaze at someone or something to stare at someone or something intently; to look at someone or something for a long time in admiration or wonder.

gaze out on something to look out on something, such as a lovely view, from inside a building.

gear ['gɪr] **1.** *n.* a wheel, with teeth along its edge, that moves similar wheels of differing diameters. **2.** *n.* equipment; tools; the things required to do a certain activity. (No plural. Treated as singular.)

gear something **to** someone or something to cause something to match someone or something else;

to create or adapt something for someone or a specific purpose.

geese ['gis] plural of GOOSE.

gem ['dʒɛm] **1.** *n.* a jewel; a precious stone, especially one used in jewelry. **2.** *n.* someone or something that is very beautiful or wonderful; a perfect example of someone or something. (Figurative on ①.)

gender ['dʒɛn dɚ] **1.** *n.* [in grammar] a subdivision of nouns into masculine, feminine, and, sometimes, neuter categories. **2.** *n.* SEX ③; the condition of being male or female.

gene ['dʒin] *n.* a part of a chromosome within every living cell that determines a characteristic of a plant or animal.

general ['dʒɛn ə rəl] **1.** *adj.* widespread; commonly known, understood, believed, or experienced. (Adv: *generally.*) **2.** *adj.* not specific; not specialized. (Adv: *generally.*) **3.** *adj.* usual; regular; appropriate to most situations. (Adv: *generally.*) **4.** *n.* a high-ranking army or air force officer. → IN GENERAL

generation [dʒɛn ə 're ʃən] **1.** *n.* producing or creating something. (No plural.) **2.** *n.* one stage in the history of a family. **3.** *n.* all the people of the same culture who were born around the same time, taken as a group.

generous ['dʒɛn ə rəs] **1.** *adj.* not selfish; giving freely. (Adv: *generously.*) **2.** *adj.* [of an amount] more than is needed; [of an amount] large. (Adv: *generously.*)

gentle ['dʒɛn təl] *adj.* pleasantly mild; not rough; tame; kind. (Adv: *gently* ['dʒɛnt li]. Comp: *gentler*; sup: *gentlest*.)

gentleman ['dʒɛn tl mən] **1.** *n.*, *irreg.* a man who is refined, polite, and well mannered. (The male counterpart of LADY. Plural: GENTLE-MEN.) **2.** *n.*, *irreg.* a polite term for MAN ①.

gentlemen ['dʒɛn tl mən] plural of GENTLEMAN.

gently ['dʒɛnt li] **1.** *adv.* in a kind way; in a way that does not cause pain or worry. **2.** *adv.* smoothly; mildly; not roughly.

genuine ['dʒɛn ju ɪn] **1.** *adj.* real; actual; not fake; not artificial. (Adv: *genuinely*.) **2.** *adj.* sincere. (Adv: *genuinely*.)

geography [dʒi 'ɑ grə fi] *n.* the study of the features of the surface of earth, including the land and climate, countries, and the people and cultures of the countries. (No plural.)

geology [dʒi 'ɑl ə dʒi] *n.* the study of the origin and the structure of earth. (No plural.)

geometry [dʒi 'ɑm ɪ tri] **1.** *n.* the part of mathematics that deals with the relationships and properties of points, lines, curves, angles, surfaces, and solids. (No plural.) **2.** the *adj.* use of ①.

germ ['dʒɚm] *n.* a very small organism that causes disease.

gesture ['dʒɛs tʃɚ] **1.** *n.* a movement made with a part of the body to communicate or to emphasize a statement, emotion, or feeling. **2.** *n.* an act of kindness or cour-tesy; an act that demonstrates friendship. **3.** *iv.* to use hand motions and facial movements when communicating; to make ①.

get ['gɛt] **1.** *tv., irreg.* to obtain something; to receive something. (Past tense: GOT; past participle: GOT or GOTTEN.) **2.** *tv., irreg.* to bring something; to fetch some-thing. **3.** *tv., irreg.* to understand something; to comprehend some-thing. **4.** *tv., irreg.* to cause some-thing to happen to someone or something; to cause someone or something to be a certain way. **5.** *iv., irreg.* to become. **6.** *iv., irreg.* to arrive somewhere; to reach a certain point or place. (Followed by an adverb such as HOME, THERE, or SOMEWHERE or by a prepositional phrase.)
→ DON'T LET SOMEONE OR SOMETHING GET YOU DOWN.
→ GIVE AS GOOD AS ONE GETS

get a black eye 1. to get a bruise near the eye from being struck. (Note: *Get* usually means to become, to acquire, or to cause. *Have* usually means to possess, to be, or to have resulted in.) **2.** to have one's character or reputation harmed.

get a clean bill of health [for someone] to be pronounced healthy by a physician. (Also with *have*. See the note at GET A BLACK EYE.)

get a foothold (somewhere) an initial position of support; a start-ing point.

get a handle on something Go to HAVE A HANDLE ON SOMETHING.

get a load off one's **feet** AND **take a load off** one's **feet** to sit down; to enjoy the results of sitting down.

get a load off one's **mind** to say what one is thinking.

get a lot of mileage out of something to get a lot of use from something, as if it were a car.

get a lump in one's **throat** to have the feeling of something in one's throat—as if one were going to cry. (Also with *have*. See the note at GET A BLACK EYE.)

get a whiff of something AND **catch a whiff of** something **1.** to smell the odor of something. **2.** to learn about someone almost accidentally.

get a word in edgewise to manage to say something when other people are talking and ignoring one. (Usually negative.)

get about AND **get around** to move around freely.

get above oneself to behave as though one is better or more important than one is.

get across (something) to manage to cross something.

get after someone **1.** to bother or nag someone about doing something. **2.** to begin to chase someone.

get ahead of oneself [for someone] to do or say something sooner than it ought to be done so that the proper explanation or preparations have not been made.

get (all) dolled up to dress (oneself) up. (Usually used for females, but not necessarily.)

get along (on a shoestring) to be able to afford to live on very little money.

get along with someone or something to manage with someone or something; to manage with only something.

get along without someone or something to manage without someone or something.

get an eyeful (of someone or something**)** to see everything; to see a shocking or surprising sight.

get around Go to GET ABOUT.

get at someone or something **1.** to manage to lay hands on someone or something; to get someone or something. **2.** to manage to attack someone or something.

get at something to arrive at a point of discussion; to work toward stating a point of discussion or an accusation.

get away (from someone or something**) 1.** to go away from someone or something. **2.** to escape from someone, something, or someplace.

get back (at someone**)** to get revenge on someone.

get back on one's **feet 1.** to recover from an illness and leave one's sickbed. (Both literal and figurative.) **2.** to recover from anything, especially financial problems. (Figurative.)

get back (someplace**)** to manage to return to someplace.

get back to someone or something to return to dealing with someone or something.

get behind (in something) Go to FALL BEHIND (IN SOMETHING).

get behind (on something) Go to FALL BEHIND (IN SOMETHING).

get behind someone or something to back or support someone or something; to put oneself into a position to "push" or promote someone or something.

get behind (with something) Go to FALL BEHIND (IN SOMETHING).

get by (on something) to survive with only something; to survive by relying on something.

get by without someone or something to survive without someone or something.

get cold feet to become timid or frightened; to have one's feet seem to freeze with fear. (Also with *have*. See the note at GET A BLACK EYE.)

get down to brass tacks to begin to talk about important things.

get down to business AND **get down to work** to begin to get serious; to begin to negotiate or conduct business.

get down to something to reach the point of dealing with something; to begin to work on something seriously. (Especially with *business, brass tacks, work, cases*.)

get down to work Go to GET DOWN TO BUSINESS.

get goose bumps AND **get goose pimples** [for someone's skin] to feel prickly or become bumpy due to fear or excitement. (Also with *have*. See the note at GET A BLACK EYE.)

get goose pimples Go to GET GOOSE BUMPS.

get in someone's **hair** to bother or irritate someone.

get into the swing of things to join into the routine or the activities. (Refers to the rhythm of routinized activity.)

get married to become united as husband and wife.

get off easy AND **get off lightly** to receive little or no punishment for doing something wrong.

get off lightly Go to GET OFF EASY.

get off ((of) something) to stop discussing the topic that one is supposed to be discussing [and start discussing something else]; to stray from the topic at hand.

get off the hook to free oneself from an obligation.

get off to a flying start to have a very successful beginning.

get on to get along; to thrive.

get on someone's **nerves** to irritate someone.

get on the bandwagon AND **climb on the bandwagon; jump on the bandwagon** to join the popular side (of an issue); to take a popular position.

get on with someone to get along with someone; to be friendly with someone.

get on with something to continue doing something.

get on without someone or something to survive and carry on without someone or something.

get one's ducks in a row to put one's affairs in order; to get things ready.

get one's feet on the ground to get firmly established or reestablished. (Also with *have*. See the note at GET A BLACK EYE.)

get one's feet wet to begin something; to have one's first experience of something.

get one's fill of someone or something to receive enough of someone or something. (Also with *have*. See the note at GET A BLACK EYE.)

get one's fingers burned to have a bad experience.

get one's foot in the door to achieve a favorable position (for further action); to take the first step in a process. (Also with *have*. See the note at GET A BLACK EYE.)

get one's hands dirty AND **dirty one's hands; soil one's hands** to become involved with something illegal; to do a shameful thing; to do something that is beneath one.

get one's head above water to get ahead of one's problems; to catch up with one's work or responsibilities. (Also used literally. Also with *have*. See the note at GET A BLACK EYE.)

get one's just deserts to get what one deserves. (Here, DESERTS = what one deserves.)

get one's just reward(s) to get something as bad as one deserves.

get one's second wind (Also with *have*. See the note at GET A BLACK EYE.) **1.** [for someone] to achieve stability in breathing after brief exertion. **2.** to become more active or productive (after starting off slowly).

get one's teeth into something to start on something seriously, especially a difficult task.

get onto someone **(about** something**)** to remind someone about something.

get out [for something] to become publicly known.

get out (of something**) 1.** to escape from something. **2.** to get free of the responsibility of doing something.

get out of the wrong side of the bed Go to GET UP ON THE WRONG SIDE OF THE BED.

get over someone or something **1.** to move or climb over someone or something. **2.** to recover from difficulties regarding someone or something.

get over something to recover from a disease.

get rid of someone or something to make oneself free of someone or something; to remove someone or something and be free of the person or thing.

get right on something to do something immediately.

get second thoughts about someone or something to form doubts about someone or something. (Also with *have*. See the note at GET A BLACK EYE.)

get sidetracked to become diverted from one's task; to start off on a second task before the first one is finished.

get someone **down** to make someone depressed or sad.

get someone **in(to something)** to manage to get someone enrolled into something; to manage to get someone accepted into something.

get (someone) off the hook to free someone from an obligation; to help someone out of an awkward situation.

get someone **on(to)** someone or something to assign someone to attend to someone or something.

get someone **over a barrel** AND **get** someone **under** one's **thumb** to put someone at one's mercy; to get control over someone. (Also with *have*. See the note at GET A BLACK EYE.)

get someone **to** do something to persuade someone to do something; to convince someone to do something.

get someone **under** one's **thumb** Go to GET SOMEONE OVER A BARREL.

get someone **up (for something)** to get someone into peak condition for something; to prepare someone for something.

get someone's **ear** to get someone to listen (to one); to hold someone's attention. (Also with *have*. See the note at GET A BLACK EYE.)

get someone's **eye** Go to CATCH SOMEONE'S EYE.

get something **across (to** someone**)** to make someone understand something.

get something **down (on paper)** to write some information down on paper; to capture some information in writing.

get something **into** someone's **thick head** Go to GET SOMETHING THROUGH SOMEONE'S THICK SKULL.

get something **off** one's **chest** to tell something that has been bothering one. (Also with *have*. See the note at GET A BLACK EYE.)

get something **off (the ground)** to get something started.

get something **off (to** someone or something**)** to send something to someone or something.

get something **out 1.** to remove or extricate something. **2.** to manage to get something said.

get something **out of** someone to cause or force someone to give specific information.

get something **out of** someone or something to remove something from someone or something.

get something **over (to** someone**) 1.** to deliver something to someone. **2.** to make someone understand something; to succeed in explaining something to someone.

get something **sewed up 1.** to get something stitched together (by someone). (Also with *have*. See the note at GET A BLACK EYE.) **2.** AND **get** something **wrapped up** to get something settled or finished.

get something **straight** to understand something clearly. (Also with *have*. See the note at GET A BLACK EYE.)

get something **through** someone's **thick skull** AND **get** something **into** someone's **thick head** to make someone understand something; to put some information into someone's mind.

get something **under** one's **belt** (Also with *have*. See the note at GET A BLACK EYE.) **1.** to eat or drink something. (This means the food goes into one's stomach and is under one's belt.) **2.** to learn something well; to assimilate some information.

get something **under way** to get something started. (Also with *have*. See the note at GET A BLACK EYE. Originally nautical.)

get something **up** to organize, plan, and assemble something.

get something **wrapped up** Go to GET SOMETHING SEWED UP.

get stars in one's **eyes** to be obsessed with show business; to be fascinated with the stage. (Also with *have*. See the note at GET A BLACK EYE. Refers to stardom, as in the stars of Hollywood or New York.)

get the benefit of the doubt to receive a judgment in one's favor when the evidence is neither for one nor against one. (Also with *have*. See the note at GET A BLACK EYE.)

get the blues to become sad or depressed; to become melancholy. (Also with *have*. See the note at GET A BLACK EYE.)

get the drift of something to understand the general idea of something.

get the facts straight to get a good understanding of the facts; to make sure that all the facts are accurate and properly stated.

get the feel of something to acquire the ability to do something; to develop the skill or talent for doing something.

get the final word Go to GET THE LAST WORD.

get the hang of something to learn how to do something; to learn how something works. (Also with *have*. See the note at GET A BLACK EYE.)

get the inside track to get the advantage (over someone) because of special connections, special knowledge, or favoritism. (Also with *have*. See the note at GET A BLACK EYE.)

get the jump on someone to do something before someone; to get ahead of someone. (Also with *have*. See the note at GET A BLACK EYE.)

get the last laugh to laugh at or ridicule someone who has laughed at or ridiculed one; to put someone in the same bad position that one was once in. (Also with *have*. See the note at GET A BLACK EYE.)

get the last word AND **get the final word** to make the final point (in an argument); to make the final decision (in some matter). (Also with *have*. See the note at GET A BLACK EYE.)

get the message Go to GET THE WORD.

get the nod to be chosen. (Also with *have*. See the note at GET A BLACK EYE.)

get the red-carpet treatment to receive very special treatment; to receive royal treatment; to be treated like royalty.

get the runaround to receive a series of excuses, delays, and referrals.

get the shock of one's **life** to receive a serious (emotional) shock. (Also with *have*. See the note at GET A BLACK EYE.)

get the short end of the stick AND **end up with the short end of the stick** to get less (than someone else); to be cheated or deceived. (Also with *have*. See the note at GET A BLACK EYE.)

get the upper hand (on someone**)** to get into a position superior to someone; to gain an advantage over someone. (Also with *have*. See the note at GET A BLACK EYE.)

get the word AND **get the message** to receive an explanation; to receive the final and authoritative explanation. (Also with *have*. See the note at GET A BLACK EYE.)

get through (something**) 1.** to complete something; to manage to finish something. **2.** to penetrate something.

get through to someone or something **1.** to make contact, usually on the telephone, with someone or a group. **2.** to manage to get one's message, feelings, desires, etc., understood by someone or a group.

get through with someone or something **1.** to finish with someone or something. **2.** to manage to transport someone or something through difficulties or barriers.

get time to catch one's **breath** to find enough time to relax or behave normally. (Also with *have*. See the note at GET A BLACK EYE.)

get to do something to be allowed to do something; to be permitted to do something.

get to first base (with someone or something**)** AND **reach first base (with** someone or something**)** to make a major advance with someone or something. (*First base* refers to baseball.)

get to one's **feet** to stand up.

get to someone to affect someone emotionally in a bad way; to bother someone.

get to the bottom of something to reach an understanding of the causes of something.

get to the heart of the matter to focus on the essentials of a matter.

get to the point Go to COME TO THE POINT.

get two strikes against one to get several factors against one; to be at a disadvantage; to get into a position where success is unlikely. (From baseball, where a player is "out" after three strikes. Also with *have*. See the note at GET A BLACK EYE.)

get under someone's **skin** to bother or irritate someone. (Refers to an irritant such as an insect or chemical that penetrates the skin.)

get up enough nerve (to do something) to become brave enough to do something.

get up on the wrong side of the bed AND **get out of the wrong side of the bed** to get up in the morning in a bad mood; to start the day in a bad mood.

get wind of something to hear about something; to receive information about something.

get worked up about something Go to GET WORKED UP (OVER SOMETHING).

get worked up (over something) AND **get worked up about something** to become excited or emotionally distressed about something.

ghost ['gost] *n.* an apparent image of a dead person, moving among the living.
→ GIVE UP THE GHOST

giant ['dʒaɪ ənt] **1.** *n.* a fictional or mythical humanlike creature who is very, very large. **2.** *n.* an unusually large person or animal. **3.** *n.* a person who is very important or known to be excellent at something. **4.** *adj.* very large; enormous. (Prenominal only.)

gift ['gɪft] **1.** *n.* a present; something that is given to someone without expecting anything in return. **2.** *n.* a special skill or talent.

gild the lily to add ornament or decoration to something that is pleasing in its original state; to

attempt to improve something that is already fine the way it is.

giraffe [dʒə 'ræf] *n.* an African animal that has long legs and a very long neck.

girl ['gɚl] **1.** *n.* a female child. **2.** *n.* a woman. (Informal. Considered derogatory by some.) **3.** *n.* a man's girlfriend. (Informal.)

girlfriend ['gɚl frɛnd] **1.** *n.* a woman with whom someone is romantically involved. **2.** *n.* a female friend.

give ['gɪv] **1.** *tv., irreg.* to cause someone or something to have or receive something; to cause something to become owned by someone. (Past tense: GAVE; past participle: GIVEN.) **2.** *tv., irreg.* to supply something; to provide something. **3.** *tv., irreg.* to make some sort of a sound with the mouth. **4.** *iv., irreg.* to be flexible; to be elastic; not to break when pushed or pulled.
→ NOT GIVE IT ANOTHER THOUGHT

give a good account of oneself to do something well or thoroughly.

give as good as one **gets** to give as much as one receives. (Usually in the present tense.)

give birth to someone or some creature to bring a baby or other offspring into the world through birth.

give birth to something to develop, invent, or start something.

give credit where credit is due to give credit to someone who deserves it; to acknowledge or thank someone who deserves it.

give in [for something] to cave in; to push in or collapse.

give in (to someone or something**)** to give up to someone or something; to capitulate to someone or something.

give one one's **freedom** to set someone free; to divorce someone.

give one's **right arm (for** someone or something**)** to be willing to give something of great value for someone or something.

give out 1. to wear out and stop; to quit operating. **2.** to be depleted.

give someone **a black eye 1.** to hit someone near the eye so that a dark bruise appears. (See also GET A BLACK EYE.) **2.** to harm the character or reputation of someone.

give someone **a buzz** Go to GIVE SOMEONE A RING.

give someone **a clean bill of health** [for a physician] to pronounce someone healthy.

give someone **a piece of** one's **mind** to bawl someone out; to scold someone. (Actually to give someone a helping of what one is thinking about.)

give someone **a ring** AND **give** someone **a buzz** to call someone on the telephone. (*Ring* and *buzz* refer to the bell of a telephone.)

give someone or something **back (to** someone or something**)** to return someone or something to someone or something.

give someone or something **up (to** someone**)** to hand someone or something over to someone; to relinquish claims on someone or

something in favor of someone else.

give someone **the benefit of the doubt** to pass judgment in someone's favor when the evidence is neither for nor against that person.

give someone **the eye** to look at someone in a way that communicates romantic interest.

give someone **the red-carpet treatment** to treat someone royally.

give someone **the runaround** to give someone a series of excuses, delays, or referrals.

give someone **the shirt off** one's **back** to be very generous or solicitous of someone.

give someone **what for** to scold or rebuke someone strongly. (Informal.)

give something **a lick and a promise** to do something poorly—quickly and carelessly.

give something **a shot** AND **take a shot at** something to try something.

give something **a whirl** make a try at something. (Here WHIRL = a try.)

give something **away (to** someone**)** **1.** to donate to, or bestow something upon, someone. **2.** to tell a secret to someone. **3.** to reveal the answer to a question, riddle, or problem to someone.

give something **off** to release or send out something; to emit or exude something.

give something **out 1.** to distribute something; to pass something out.

2. to make something known to the public.

give something **over (to** someone or something**)** to hand something over to someone or something.

give something **up** to yield something or someone.

give the bride away [for a bride's father] to accompany the bride to the groom in a wedding ceremony.

give the devil her due Go to GIVE THE DEVIL HIS DUE.

give the devil his due AND **give the devil her due** to give one's foe proper credit (for something).

give up (on someone or something**)** to give up trying to do something with someone or something, such as being friendly, managing, etc., giving advice, managing, etc.

give up the ghost to die; to release one's spirit.

given ['gɪv ən] Past participle of GIVE.

a **given** a fact that is taken for granted; a fact that is assumed.

given to doing something likely to do something; inclined to do something habitually.

glad ['glæd] **1.** *adj.* happy; content; pleased; joyful. (Adv: *gladly.* Comp: *gladder;* sup: *gladdest.*) **2.** *adj.* causing happiness, pleasure, or joy. (Adv: *gladly.* Comp: *gladder;* sup: *gladdest.*)

glamour ['glæm ər] *n.* charm and beauty. (No plural.)

glance ['glæns] *n.* a brief look toward someone or something.

glance at something AND **glance through** something; **glance over** something to quickly look at or over someone or something; to read something quickly.

glance back (at someone**) 1.** to look quickly again at someone. **2.** to look quickly at someone who is behind you.

glance down (at something**)** to look quickly downward at something.

glance off ((of) someone or something**)** to bounce off someone or something.

glance over something Go to GLANCE AT SOMETHING.

glance through something Go to GLANCE AT SOMETHING.

glare ['glɛər] **1.** *n.* a harsh, angry stare. **2.** *n.* strong, bright light. (No plural.) **3.** *iv.* to stare angrily.

glass ['glæs] **1.** *n.* a hard, stiff, easily broken, usually clear substance, used to make windows, drinking GLASSES as in ②, eyeglasses, etc. (Plural only for types and instances.) **2.** *n.* a container that is used to drink from, usually made of ①. (The GLASS for drinking does not have a handle.) **3.** *n.* the contents of ②.

glasses *n.* EYEGLASSES. (Treated as plural. Short for EYEGLASSES. (Number is expressed with *pair(s)* of *glasses.*)

glee ['gli] *n.* great happiness. (No plural.)

gleeful ['gli fʊl] *adj.* very happy; joyful. (Adv: *gleefully.*)

glide ['glaɪd] **1.** *iv.* to move smoothly. **2.** *iv.* to move through the air without engine power.

global [ˈglob əl] *adj.* of or about the whole world; worldwide. (Adv: *globally.*)

globe [ˈglob] **1.** *n.* a ball; a sphere. **2.** *n.* a ball or sphere with a map of the world on it. **3.** *n.* the earth; the world.

gloom [ˈglum] *n.* the feeling of sadness and dullness. (No plural.)

glorify [ˈglor ə faɪ] **1.** *tv.* to honor or worship someone; to praise someone or something. **2.** *tv.* to exaggerate the importance of someone or something.

glorious [ˈglor i əs] *adj.* beautiful; splendid; wonderful. (Adv: *gloriously.*)

glory [ˈglor i] **1.** *n.* praise and honor. (No plural.) **2.** *n.* something of great beauty or wonder.

glossary [ˈglɔs ə ri] *n.* a list of words and their definitions, as used within a particular book or article.

glove [ˈglʌv] *n.* one of a pair of fitted coverings for the hand, typically made of fabric or leather and having individual "pockets" for each finger and thumb.
→ FIT LIKE A GLOVE
→ HAND IN GLOVE (WITH SOMEONE)
→ HANDLE SOMEONE WITH KID GLOVES

glow [ˈglo] **1.** *iv.* to shine; to give off a weak light. **2.** *iv.* to be very hot; to be so hot as to be red, yellow, or white with heat. **3.** *iv.* to be very excited with emotion or energy. **4.** *iv.* to show a healthy appearance; to have bright red cheeks. **5.** *n.* a weak light.
→ FEEL A GLOW OF SOMETHING

glue [ˈglu] **1.** *n.* a thick, sticky liquid that is used to make something stick to something else; an adhesive. (Plural only for types and instances.) **2.** *tv.* to stick something to something else using ①.

glum [ˈglʌm] *adj.* sad; disappointed. (Adv: *glumly.* Comp: *glummer;* sup: *glummest.*)

glut [ˈglʌt] **1.** *n.* too much of something. **2.** *tv.* to supply someone or something with too much of something.

glutton [ˈglʌt n] *n.* someone who eats or drinks too much.

a **glutton for punishment** someone who seems to like doing or seeking out difficult, unpleasant, or badly paid tasks.

gnash one's **teeth** to slash and chop with the teeth.

gnat [ˈnæt] *n.* a small fly that bites.

gnaw (away) at someone to worry someone; to create constant anxiety in someone.

gnaw (away) at someone or something to chew at someone or something.

gnaw on something to chew on something. (Usually said of an animal.)

go [ˈgo] **1.** *iv., irreg.* to move from one place to another; [for time] to progress or pass. **2.** *tv., irreg.* to practice or perform certain sports activities, such as running, swimming, canoeing, fencing, jogging, skiing, walking, or other activities expressed with words ending in -*ing*. (Past tense: WENT; past participle: GONE. The third-person

singular present tense is GOES.)
3. *iv., irreg.* to leave. **4.** *iv., irreg.* to reach a certain time or place; to extend to a certain time or place. **5.** *iv., irreg.* to work; to function. **6.** *iv., irreg.* to become. **7.** *iv., irreg.* to become worn-out; to weaken. **8.** *iv., irreg.* to belong in a certain place. **9.** *iv., irreg.* [for the activities in a period of time] to unfold in some way, good or bad. **10.** *iv., irreg.* to progress through a series of words or musical notes.
→ EASY COME, EASY GO
→ FROM THE WORD GO

go about one's **business** to mind one's business; to move elsewhere and mind one's own business; to focus on one's own tasks.

go after someone or something **1.** to pursue someone or something. **2.** to charge or attack someone or some creature.

go against someone or something to turn against someone or something; to oppose someone or something.

go against the grain to go against one's natural inclination; to be contrary to one's nature. (Refers to the lay of the grain of wood. Against the grain = perpendicular to the direction of the grain.)

go along for the ride to accompany (someone) for the pleasure of riding along; to accompany someone for no special reason. (Also with *come*.)

go along with someone or something to agree with someone or agree to something.

go and never darken one's **door again** to go away and not come back.

go (a)round in circles to keep going over the same ideas or repeating the same actions, often resulting in confusion and without reaching a satisfactory decision or conclusion.

go around someone to avoid dealing with someone. (Figurative.)

go (a)round the bend 1. to travel around a turn or a curve; to make a turn or a curve. **2.** to go crazy; to lose one's mind.

go at it hammer and tongs Go to FIGHT SOMEONE OR SOMETHING HAMMER AND TONGS.

go at it tooth and nail Go to FIGHT SOMEONE OR SOMETHING HAMMER AND TONGS.

go away to leave. (Often a command.)

go away empty-handed to depart with nothing.

go away with someone or something **1.** to leave in the company of someone or something. **2.** to take someone, some creature, or a group away with one.

go back to return to the place of origin.

go back on one's **word** to break a promise that one has made.

go back on something to reverse one's position on something, especially one's word or a promise.

go behind someone's **back 1.** to move behind someone; to locate oneself at someone's back. **2.** to do

237

something that is kept a secret from someone. (Figurative.)

go below to go beneath the main deck of a ship. (Nautical.)

go by (someplace) Go to DROP BY (SOMEPLACE).

go crazy to become crazy, disoriented, or frustrated.

go down 1. to sink below a normal or expected level or height. **2.** to descend to a lower measurement. **3.** to be swallowed. **4.** to fall or drop down, as when struck or injured.

go down in history to be remembered as historically important.

go Dutch to share the cost of a meal or some other event.

go for an amount [for something] to sell for or be sold at a certain price.

go in for something to enjoy doing something; to be fond of something.

go in one ear and out the other [for something] to be heard and then forgotten.

go in with someone **(on** something**)** to join efforts with someone on a project; to pool financial resources with someone to buy something.

go into a nosedive AND **take a nosedive 1.** [for an airplane] to dive suddenly toward the ground, nose first. **2.** [for one's health or one's emotional or financial situation] to decline rapidly.

go into a number [for a number] to divide into another number.

go into a tailspin 1. [for an airplane] to lose control and spin to the earth, nose first. **2.** [for someone] to become disoriented or panicked; [for someone's life] to fall apart.

go into detail to give all the details; to present and discuss the details.

go into hiding to conceal oneself in a hidden place for a period of time.

go into one's **song and dance about** something to start giving one's usual or typical explanations or excuses about something.

go in((to) something) to enter something; to penetrate something.

go like clockwork to progress with regularity and dependability.

go off 1. [for an explosive device] to explode. **2.** [for a sound-creating device] to make its noise. **3.** [for an event] to happen or take place.

go off (by oneself**)** to go into seclusion; to isolate oneself.

go off on a tangent suddenly to go in another direction; suddenly to change one's line of thought, course of action, etc. (A reference to geometry. The plural is *go off on tangents*.)

go off the deep end AND **jump off the deep end** to become deeply involved (with someone or something) before one is ready; to follow one's emotions into a difficult situation. (Refers to going into a swimming pool at the deep end.)

go off with someone to go away with someone.

go on 1. to continue. **2.** to hush up; to stop acting silly. (Always a command. No tenses.) **3.** to happen.

go on a fishing expedition to attempt to discover information.

go on a rampage to have a rampage.

go on (and on) about someone or something to talk endlessly about someone or something.

go on at someone to yell at and criticize someone.

go (on) before (someone**) 1.** to precede someone. **2.** to die before someone. (Euphemism.)

go out 1. to leave one's house. **2.** to become extinguished.

go out for someone or something to leave in order to bring back someone or something.

go out (for something**)** to try out for a sports team.

go (out) on strike [for a group of people] to quit working at their jobs until certain demands are met.

go out with someone to go on a date with someone; to date someone on a regular basis.

go over someone**'s head** [for the intellectual content of something] to be too difficult for someone to understand. (As if it flew over one's head rather than entering into one's store of knowledge.)

go over something **with a fine-tooth comb** AND **search** something **with a fine-tooth comb** to search through something very carefully.

go over with a bang [for something] to be funny or entertaining. (Refers chiefly to jokes or stage performances.)

go overboard 1. to fall off or out of a boat or ship. **2.** to do too much; to be extravagant.

go the distance to do the whole amount; to play the entire game; to run the whole race.

go the extra mile to try harder to please someone or to get the task done correctly; to do more than one is required to do to reach a goal.

go the limit to do or have as much as possible.

go through to be approved; to pass examination; to be ratified.

go through channels to proceed by consulting the proper persons or offices.

go through someone to consult someone as a necessary step in doing something.

go through something **1.** to search through something. **2.** to use up all of something rapidly. **3.** [for something] to pass through an opening. **4.** to pass through various stages or processes. **5.** to work through something, such as an explanation or story. **6.** to experience or endure something. **7.** to rehearse something; to practice something for performance.

go through the motions to make a feeble effort to do something; to do something insincerely.

go through the roof to go very high; to reach a very high degree (of something).

go to bat for someone to support or help someone. (From the use of a substitute batter in baseball.)

go to bed to go to where one's bed is, get into it, and go to sleep.

go to Davy Jones's locker to go to the bottom of the sea. (Thought of as a nautical expression.)

go to pot AND **go to the dogs** to go to ruin; to become ruined; to deteriorate.

go to rack and ruin AND **go to wrack and ruin** to become ruined. (The words *rack* and *wrack* mean "wreckage" and are found only in this expression.)

go to seed Go to RUN TO SEED.

go to someone's **head** to make someone conceited; to make someone overly proud.

go to the bathroom to use the toilet; to urinate; to defecate.

go to the dogs Go to GO TO POT.

go to the lavatory to go somewhere and use a toilet.

go to the toilet to use the toilet.

go to the wall to fail or be defeated after being pushed to the extreme.

go to town to work hard or fast. (Also used literally.)

go to wrack and ruin Go to GO TO RACK AND RUIN.

go under 1. to sink beneath the surface of the water. **2.** [for something] to fail. **3.** to become unconscious from anesthesia.

go up in flames AND **go up in smoke** to burn up; to be consumed in flames.

go up in smoke Go to GO UP IN FLAMES.

go with something to match something; to look good with something.

go without (someone**)** to manage without a particular type of person.

go without (something**)** to manage without something.

goal ['gol] **1.** *n.* an aim; a purpose; a result that one would like to achieve from doing something. **2.** *n.* [in sports] a place where players try to send a ball in order to score points. **3.** *n.* [in sports] an instance of sending a ball through or past (2), and the points earned by doing this. **4.** *n.* the finish line; the end point of a race.

goalie ['go li] *n.* a GOALKEEPER. (A shortening of GOALKEEPER.)

goalkeeper ['gol kip ɚ] *n.* [in sports] the player whose position is in front of the team's goal and who tries to prevent players on the other team from scoring.

goat ['got] *n.* an animal with horns, similar to a sheep.
→ SEPARATE THE SHEEP FROM THE GOATS

god ['gɑd] **1.** *n.* a male spiritual being who is worshiped. (Compare this with GODDESS.) **2.** *n.* someone or something admired as ①. **3.** *n.* [in religions such as Christianity, Islam, and Judaism] the one spiritual being that is worshiped as the creator and ruler of

everything. (Capitalized. No plural.)
→ an ACT of GOD

goddess ['gɑd əs] *n.* a female spiritual being who is worshiped.

goes ['goz] the third-person singular, present tense of GO.
→ AS FAR AS IT GOES

goggles ['gɑg əlz] *n.* a pair of protective lenses that are worn during swimming, skiing, biking, and other activities. (Treated as plural. Number is expressed with *pair(s) of goggles*.)

going to do something planning to do something; intending or meaning to do something. (A form of the future tense in English.)

gold ['gold] **1.** *n.* a chemical element that is a soft, yellow metal, is very valuable, and is the standard for money in many countries. (No plural.) **2.** *n.* coins or jewelry made of ①. (No plural.) **3.** *n.* a deep yellow color. (Plural only for types and instances.) **4.** *adj.* made of ①. **5.** *adj.* deep yellow in color. (Comp: *golder*; sup: *goldest*.)
→ (AS) GOOD AS GOLD
→ HAVE A HEART OF GOLD
→ WORTH ITS WEIGHT IN GOLD

golden ['gol dən] **1.** *adj.* made from gold; yellowish as if made from gold. **2.** *adj.* [of anniversaries] the fiftieth.
→ KILL THE GOOSE THAT LAID THE GOLDEN EGG

golden rule ['gol dən 'rul] *n.* the principle that one should treat other people the way one would like to be treated. (From the Bible.)

goldfish ['gold fɪʃ] *n., irreg.* a kind of small fish, typically orange or gold, commonly kept as a pet. (Plural: *goldfish*.)

golf ['gɔlf] **1.** *n.* a game played on a large area of land, where players use a club to hit a small ball into a hole, using as few strokes as possible. (No plural.) **2.** *iv.* to play ①.

golf club ['gɔlf kləb] *n.* a long, metal mallet used in the game of golf. (Can be shortened to CLUB.)

gone ['gɔn] Past participle of GO.

good ['gʊd] **1.** *adj., irreg.* having positive qualities; satisfactory; suitable; not negative. (Adv: WELL. Comp: BETTER; sup: BEST.) **2.** *adj., irreg.* having proper morals; moral; not evil. **3.** *adj., irreg.* enjoyable; pleasant; satisfying. (Adv: *well*. Comp: BETTER; sup: BEST.) **4.** *adj., irreg.* complete; thorough; full. (Adv: WELL. Comp: BETTER; sup: BEST) **5.** *adj., irreg.* skillful; talented; able to do something right. (Adv: WELL. Comp: BETTER; sup: BEST) **6.** *adj., irreg.* properly behaved; obedient. (Comp: BETTER; sup: BEST.) **7.** *adj.* ripe; edible; not spoiled; not rotten. **8.** *n.* excellence; virtue; goodness. (No plural.)
→ (AS) GOOD AS DONE
→ (AS) GOOD AS GOLD
→ DO SOMEONE A GOOD TURN
→ DO SOMEONE'S HEART GOOD
→ FOR THE GOOD OF SOMEONE OR SOMETHING
→ GIVE A GOOD ACCOUNT OF ONESELF
→ GIVE AS GOOD AS ONE GETS
→ HAVE A GOOD HEAD ON ONE'S SHOULDERS
→ IN GOOD CONDITION
→ IN GOOD SHAPE
→ IN THE PICTURE OF (GOOD) HEALTH

→ KISS SOMETHING GOOD-BYE
→ LOOK GOOD ON PAPER
→ MAKE GOOD MONEY
→ PUT IN A GOOD WORD (FOR SOMEONE)
→ THROW GOOD MONEY AFTER BAD
→ TOO GOOD TO BE TRUE
→ TURN SOMETHING TO GOOD ACCOUNT
→ YOUR GUESS IS AS GOOD AS MINE.

the **good old days** back in an earlier time that everyone remembers as a better time, even if it really wasn't.

good to go all ready to go; all checked and pronounced ready to go.

good-bye [gʊd 'baɪ] **1.** *interj.* farewell, as said when someone leaves. **2.** *adj.* of or about leaving; of or about a departure.

goods *n.* items for sale; products that are made to be sold. (Treated as plural, but not countable.)
→ SELL SOMEONE A BILL OF GOODS

goose ['gus] *n., irreg.* a bird having a long neck and similar to a large duck. (Plural: GEESE.)
→ COOK SOMEONE'S GOOSE
→ GET GOOSE BUMPS
→ GET GOOSE PIMPLES
→ KILL THE GOOSE THAT LAID THE GOLDEN EGG
→ WILD-GOOSE CHASE

gorilla [gə 'rɪl ə] *n.* the largest kind of ape.

gospel ['gas pəl] *n.* one of the first four books of the New Testament of the Bible. (Capitalized.)

the **gospel truth** [of truth] undeniable.

gossip ['gas əp] **1.** *n.* talk about other people, which may or may not be true; rumors about other people. (No plural.) **2.** *n.* someone who often talks about other people

and other people's private lives. **3.** *iv.* to talk about other people and their private lives; to spread rumors about other people.

got ['gat] past tense and a past participle of GET.

gotten ['gat n] a past participle of GET.
→ ILL-GOTTEN GAINS

gourmet [gor 'me] **1.** *n.* someone who enjoys fine foods and wine. **2.** *adj.* [of food and drink] produced according to the highest cooking standards.

govern ['gʌv ɚn] **1.** *iv.* to rule [over someone or something]; to be the leader of a group of people. **2.** *tv.* to rule or lead a group of people. **3.** *tv.* to guide, control, or regulate something.

government ['gʌv ɚn mənt] **1.** *n.* the system of rule over a country and its people. (No plural.) **2.** *n.* the political organization ruling in a particular area. **3.** the *adj.* use of ① or ②. (Also *governmental*.)

governor ['gʌv ɚ nɚ] **1.** *n.* the title of the executive officer of each state of the United States. **2.** *n.* someone who governs or rules certain organizations. **3.** *n.* a device that controls the speed of a car or other vehicle, either keeping it at a constant speed or not allowing it to go over a certain speed.

gown ['gaʊn] **1.** *n.* a formal dress for a woman. **2.** *n.* a NIGHTGOWN. **3.** *n.* a type of loose ceremonial covering or robe such as is worn at graduation ceremonies.

grab ['græb] **1.** *tv.* to seize and hold someone or something; to snatch someone or something; to take something rudely. **2.** *tv.* to get and bring something; to fetch something. (Informal.) **3.** *n.* an act of seizing as in ①.

grab a bite (to eat) to get something to eat; to get food that can be eaten quickly.

grab on(to someone or something) to grasp someone or something; to hold on to someone or something.

grace ['gres] **1.** *n.* elegance, smoothness, or attractiveness of form or motion. (No plural.) **2.** *n.* calm and tolerant elegance. (No plural.) **3.** *n.* favor; mercy; favorable regard. (No plural.) **4.** *n.* a prayer said before eating. (No plural.) **5.** *tv.* to make something more beautiful or elegant; to add beauty or elegance to something.
→ FALL FROM GRACE
→ SAY GRACE

grace someone or something with one's presence to honor someone or something with one's presence.

graced with something made elegant by means of some ornament or decoration.

grade ['gred] **1.** *n.* a level in school corresponding to a year of study. **2.** *n.* a mark, given to a student for a class, test, paper, or assignment, that shows how well or how poorly the student did. **3.** *n.* a degree of quality. **4.** *n.* the slope of a road, roof, terrace, etc. **5.** *tv.* to give ② for the work of a student.

grade someone or something down to lower the ranking, rating, or score of someone or something.

graduate 1. ['græ dʒu ət] *n.* someone who has completed high school, college, or university. **2.** ['græ dʒu et] *tv.* to depart from a school, college, or university with a degree.

graduate from something to earn and receive a degree from an educational institution.

graduation [græ dʒu 'e ʃən] **1.** *n.* the ceremony where students become GRADUATES ①. **2.** *n.* one of a series of marks on something showing the units of measurement.

grain ['gren] **1.** *n.* grass or cereal plants grown for their edible seeds. (Plural only for types and instances.) **2.** *n.* seeds of ①. (Plural only for types and instances.) **3.** *n.* an individual seed of ①. **4.** *n.* a tiny particle of something, such as sand or salt. **5.** *n.* a very small unit of weight, equal to about 64.8 milligrams. **6.** *n.* the pattern or direction of the fibers of wood. (Plural only for types and instances.)
→ GO AGAINST THE GRAIN
→ TAKE SOMETHING WITH A GRAIN OF SALT

a grain of truth even the smallest amount of truth.

gram ['græm] *n.* the basic unit for measuring weight in the metric system, equal to ¹⁄₁₀₀₀ of a kilogram or about ¹⁄₂₈ of an ounce.

grammar ['græm ɚ] **1.** *n.* a system of rules and principles in a language that determines how sentences are formed; the study of sentence structure and the relationships between words within sentences. (Plural only for types and instances.) **2.** *n.* a statement of the rules of a language that accounts for how sentences are formed, especially the description of what the standard form of the language is like. **3.** *n.* following the rules of ② in the use of written and spoken language. (No plural.)

grammar school ['græm ɚ 'skul] *n.* a school at the elementary level.

grand ['grænd] **1.** *adj.* impressive; magnificent. (Adv: *grandly.* Comp: *grander;* sup: *grandest.*) **2.** *n.* a thousand dollars. (Slang. No plural.)
→ (AS) BUSY AS GRAND CENTRAL STATION

grand total ['grænd 'tot əl] *n.* the complete total; the final total.

grandchild ['græn(d) tʃaɪld] *n., irreg.* a child of one's child. (Plural: GRANDCHILDREN.)

grandchildren ['græn(d) tʃɪl drən] plural of GRANDCHILD.

granddad ['græn dæd] *n.* grandfather; the father of one's mother or father. (Also a term of address. Capitalized when written as a proper noun.)

granddaughter ['græn dɔt ɚ] *n.* the daughter of one's son or daughter.

grandfather ['græn(d) fɑ ðɚ] *n.* the father of one's mother or father. (Also a term of address. Capitalized when written as a proper noun.)

grandma ['græm mɑ] *n.* grandmother; the mother of one's mother or father. (Also a term of address. Capitalized when written as a proper noun.)

grandmother ['græn(d) məð ɚ] *n.* the mother of one's mother or father. (Also a term of address. Capitalized when written as a proper noun.)
→ TEACH ONE'S GRANDMOTHER TO SUCK EGGS

grandpa ['græm pɑ] *n.* grandfather; the father of one's mother or father. (Also a term of address. Capitalized when written as a proper noun.)

grandparent ['græn(d) per ənt] *n.* a grandmother or a grandfather; the parent of one's parent. (The plural usually refers to one or more pairs consisting of a GRANDMOTHER and a GRANDFATHER.)

grandson ['græn(d) sən] *n.* the son of one's child.

grant ['grænt] **1.** *n.* money that is given by a government or a private agency for a worthy purpose. **2.** *tv.* to give something formally to someone. **3.** *tv.* to give permission for something to someone; to give someone permission for something. **4.** *tv.* to concede that something is true; to admit to someone that something is true. (The object is a clause with THAT ⑦.)
→ TAKE SOMEONE OR SOMETHING FOR GRANTED

grape ['grep] **1.** *n.* a red, green, or purple fruit that grows in bunches on vines. **2.** *adj.* made of or flavored with ①.

graph ['græf] **1.** *n.* a drawing that shows the difference between two or more amounts or the changes in amounts through time. **2.** *tv.* to place information on ①; to make ①.

grass ['græs] *n.* a plant with thin blades instead of leaves. (Plural only for types and instances.)
→ LET GRASS GROW UNDER ONE'S FEET

grate on someone('s **nerves**) to annoy someone; to bother someone.

gratitude ['græt ə tud] *n.* the quality of being thankful; a feeling or expression of thanks. (No plural.)

grave ['grev] **1.** *n.* the place where someone is buried; a burial site. **2.** *n.* the actual hole that someone is buried in. **3.** *adj.* very serious; dire. (Adv: *gravely*.)
→ CARRY A SECRET TO THE GRAVE
→ DIG ONE'S OWN GRAVE
→ TAKE A SECRET TO ONE'S GRAVE
→ TURN OVER IN ONE'S GRAVE

the **grave** *n.* death. (No plural. Treated as singular.)

gravel ['græv əl] *n.* crushed rock; pebbles about the size of peas. (Plural only for types and instances.)

graveyard ['grev jɑrd] *n.* a cemetery; a place where dead people are buried.

gravity ['græv ə ti] **1.** *n.* the force that pulls things toward the center of planets, stars, moons, etc.; the force that pulls things toward the center of the earth. (No plural.) **2.** *n.* seriousness; importance. (No plural.)
→ LAW OF GRAVITY

gravy ['gre vi] **1.** *n.* the juice that drips from meat when it cooks. (Plural only for types and instances.) **2.** *n.* a sauce made from ①, often thickened with flour or something similar. (Plural only for types and instances.)

→ RIDE THE GRAVY TRAIN

gray ['gre] **1.** *n.* the color made when white is mixed with black. (Plural only for types and instances.) **2.** *n.* the color GRAY as in ①, when found in the hair. (No plural.) **3.** *adj.* (Adv: *grayly.* Comp: *grayer;* sup: *grayest.*) **4.** *iv.* [for hair] to become ③; [for someone] to develop ②.

a **gray area** an area of a subject, etc., that is difficult to put into a particular category, as it is not clearly defined and may have connections or associations with more than one category.

gray matter intelligence; brains; power of thought.

graze on something **1.** [for animals] to browse or forage in a particular location. **2.** [for animals] to browse or forage, eating something in particular.

grease 1. ['gris] *n.* melted animal fat or any similarly oily substance. (No plural.) **2.** ['gris, 'griz] *tv.* to coat something with ①.

great ['gret] **1.** *adj.* large in size or importance. (Adv: *greatly.* Comp: *greater;* sup: *greatest.*) **2.** *adj.* good; very good. (Adv: *greatly.* Comp: *greater;* sup: *greatest.*) **3.** *interj.* Super!; Wonderful! (Sometimes used sarcastically.)
→ MAKE A GREAT SHOW OF SOMETHING
→ SET GREAT STORE BY SOMEONE OR SOMETHING

a **great deal** much; a lot.

greatly ['gret li] *adv.* very much.

greed ['grid] *n.* a strong desire for money, possessions, or power. (No plural.)

greedy ['gri di] *adj.* showing greed; desiring money, possessions, or power too strongly. (Adv: *greedily.* Comp: *greedier*; sup: *greediest*.)

green ['grin] **1.** *n.* the color of grass or of the leaves of trees in the summer; the color made when blue and yellow are mixed together. (Plural only for types and instances.) **2.** *n.* a grassy area. **3.** *adj.* of the color of grass. (Comp: *greener*; sup: *greenest*.) **4.** *adj.* unripe; not yet ripe or mature. (Comp: *greener*; sup: *greenest*.) **5.** *adj.* without experience; young. (Figurative on ④. Comp: *greener*; sup: *greenest*.)
→ HAVE A GREEN THUMB

green with envy envious; jealous.

greenhouse ['grin haʊs] *n., irreg.* a building with a glass roof and glass walls where the temperature is controlled so that plants can grow inside all year round. (Plural: [...haʊ zəz].)

greens *n.* the leaves of certain plants eaten as food. (Treated as plural.)

greet ['grit] *tv.* to welcome someone; to address someone, especially upon meeting or arrival.

greeting ['gri tɪŋ] *n.* a word, phrase, or action—such as *Hello*—said or done when meeting someone or when answering the telephone.

grew ['gru] past tense of GROW.

grid ['grɪd] **1.** *n.* a series of lines arranged vertically and horizontally forming squares, especially as found on maps or graphs. **2.** *n.* a series of rods, bars, or wires arranged as in ①. **3.** *n.* a network of electrical lines spread over a large area; a network of roads.

grief ['grif] *n.* sorrow; distress. (No plural.)
→ COME TO GRIEF

grill ['grɪl] **1.** *n.* a grid of metal rods set over a fire, on which food is placed to cook; a BARBECUE ①. **2.** *n.* an outdoor stove that cooks food placed on a framework of rows of metal bars. **3.** *tv.* to cook food on ① or ②. **4.** *tv.* to question someone forcefully and thoroughly. **5.** *iv.* [for food] to be cooked on ① or ②.

grille ['grɪl] **1.** *n.* a grate above the front bumper of a car in front of the radiator. (Compare this with GRILL.) **2.** *n.* a grid of metal bars placed in a door or window.

grim ['grɪm] **1.** *adj.* not likely to turn out well. (Adv: *grimly.* Comp: *grimmer*; sup: *grimmest*.) **2.** *adj.* [looking] stern and harsh. (Adv: *grimly.* Comp: *grimmer*; sup: *grimmest*.)

grime ['graɪm] *n.* thick, oily dirt. (No plural.)

grin ['grɪn] **1.** *n.* a big smile. **2.** *iv.* to smile widely so that one's teeth show.

grin and bear it to endure something unpleasant in good humor.

grind ['graɪnd] **1.** *tv., irreg.* to make something into a powder or tiny chunks, by crushing or pounding it. (Past tense and past participle: GROUND.) **2.** *tv., irreg.* to rub things together with force.

grind someone **down** to wear someone down by constant

requests; to wear someone down by constant nagging.

grind something **away** to remove something by grinding.

grind something **down** to make something smooth or even by grinding.

grind something **out 1.** to produce something by grinding. **2.** to produce something in a mechanical or perfunctory manner.
→ HAVE AN AX TO GRIND

grind something **up** to pulverize or break something up by crushing, rubbing, or abrasion.

grind to a halt to slow to a stop; to run down.

grindstone ['graɪnd ston] n. a thick, round wheel of stone that is used to sharpen knives.
→ KEEP ONE'S NOSE TO THE GRINDSTONE
→ PUT ONE'S NOSE TO THE GRINDSTONE

grip ['grɪp] **1.** tv. to hold someone or something tightly with one's hands. **2.** n. a tight hold on someone or something.
→ COME TO GRIPS WITH SOMETHING
→ LOSE ONE'S GRIP

grip SOMEONE'S ATTENTION to attract and hold someone's attention.

gripe ['graɪp] n. a complaint.

gripe (about someone or something**)** to complain about someone or something; to whine about someone or something.

grit one's **teeth** to grind one's teeth together in anger or determination.

groan ['gron] **1.** n. a loud, deep noise of pain, disappointment, or disapproval. **2.** iv. to make a loud, deep noise of pain, disappoint-

ment, or disapproval. **3.** iv. [for an enormous bulk] to make a deep noise or creak.

groan under the weight of something to suffer under the burden or domination of something.

grocer ['gro sɚ] n. someone who owns or runs a GROCERY STORE; someone who sells food and basic supplies.

groceries ['gros riz...] n. items bought at a GROCERY STORE. (Treated as plural, but not countable.)

grocery (store) ['gros ri...] n. a store where food can be bought.

groom ['grum] **1.** n. a man who is getting married. **2.** tv. to clean and comb a horse. **3.** tv. to make someone's hair neat. **4.** tv. to prepare someone for a specific duty.

ground ['graʊnd] **1.** past tense and past participle of GRIND. **2.** adj. broken or chopped into powder or into tiny chunks by grinding. **3.** n. the surface of the earth. (No plural.) **4.** tv. to cause a pilot, airplane, or bird to stay on the surface of the earth. (Past tense and past participle: grounded.) **5.** tv. to make someone stay in a certain place as punishment. (Figurative on ④. Past tense and past participle: grounded.) **6.** tv. to make an electrical device safer by extending a wire into ③. (Past tense and past participle: grounded.)
→ BREAK NEW GROUND
→ COVER A LOT OF GROUND
→ CUT THE GROUND OUT FROM UNDER SOMEONE
→ FROM THE GROUND UP

→ GAIN GROUND
→ GET ONE'S FEET ON THE GROUND
→ GET SOMETHING OFF (THE GROUND)
→ HAVE ONE'S EAR TO THE GROUND
→ HOLD ONE'S GROUND
→ KEEP ONE'S EAR TO THE GROUND
→ KEEP ONE'S FEET ON THE GROUND
→ STAND ONE'S GROUND

ground beef ['graʊnd 'bif] *n.* beef that has been chopped or ground fine; hamburger. (No plural.)

grounded in fact based on facts.

grounds *n.* the remains of powdered coffee beans after coffee has been made from them. (Treated as plural, but not countable.)

grounds for something a basis or cause for legal action such as a lawsuit.

group ['grup] **1.** *n.* a number of people or things considered as a unit; a category. **2.** *tv.* to arrange people or things into categories; to place things or people together in ①.

grow ['gro] **1.** *tv., irreg.* to care for plants, causing them to mature. (Past tense: GREW; past participle: GROWN.) **2.** *iv., irreg.* to become bigger, larger, or more powerful; to increase. **3.** *iv., irreg.* to become a certain way.

grow into something to develop into something.

grow to do something to gradually begin to do certain things, using verbs such as *feel, know, like, need, respect, sense, suspect, think, want, wonder,* etc.

growl ['graʊl] **1.** *n.* a deep, threatening sound, especially one made in anger. **2.** *iv.* to make a deep, threatening sound; to say some-

thing in a deep, threatening way, especially when angry or irritated.

grown ['gron] **1.** Past participle of GROW. **2.** *adj.* fully developed; adult; mature; ripe.

growth ['groθ] **1.** *n.* development; the amount someone or something develops in a certain period of time. (No plural.) **2.** *n.* an increase; the process of becoming bigger, larger, or more powerful. (No plural.) **3.** *n.* an unnatural or unhealthy lump of tissue; a tumor.

guarantee [gɛr ən 'ti] **1.** *n.* a written document that promises that a certain product will operate properly for a certain amount of time. **2.** *n.* a written or verbal promise that one will be responsible for something, especially for certain debts or actions. **3.** *tv.* to promise that something will be done. (The object can be a clause with THAT ⑦.) **4.** *tv.* to promise to be responsible for certain debts, actions, or results. **5.** *tv.* to provide ①, promising that a product will work properly for a period of time.

guard ['gɑrd] **1.** *n.* someone or some creature that watches and protects someone or something. **2.** the *adj.* use of ①. **3.** *tv.* to protect someone or something; to keep someone or something from escaping.

guess ['gɛs] **1.** *n.* an opinion or statement that is given without really knowing what is true. **2.** *tv.* to make a successful try at figuring out the right answer to a question. (The object can be a clause with THAT ⑦.) **3.** *tv.* to think that something will probably happen; to

suppose that something will happen. (The object is a clause with THAT ⑦.)
→ HAZARD A GUESS
→ YOUR GUESS IS AS GOOD AS MINE.

guess at SOMETHING to make a guess at getting the right answer to a question.

guest ['gɛst] **1.** *n.* someone who visits another person's home because of an invitation. **2.** *n.* someone who is taken to dinner or to a place of entertainment by someone else, who is paying for it. **3.** *n.* someone who is invited by an organization or government to make a visit. **4.** *n.* a customer of a hotel, motel, etc.

guest of honor a guest who gets special attention from everyone; the person for whom a party, celebration, or ceremony is given.

guide ['gaɪd] **1.** *n.* someone who shows someone else the way. **2.** *n.* someone who leads tours. **3.** *n.* a book or chart of information about a thing or a place. **4.** *tv.* to lead someone to the right place. **5.** *tv.* to lead a tour. **6.** *tv.* to direct the business of something; to control something. **7.** *tv.* to advise someone.

guilt ['gɪlt] **1.** *n.* the feeling that one has done something wrong or bad. (No plural.) **2.** *n.* the burden or responsibility of having done something wrong or bad. (No plural.)

guilty ['gɪl ti] *adj.* having broken a rule or done something wrong; judged in a court to have done a crime; not innocent. (Adv: *guiltily.* Comp: *guiltier;* sup: *guiltiest.*)

→ FIND SOMEONE GUILTY

guinea pig ['gɪn i pɪg] **1.** *n.* a small rodent, often kept as a pet or used in medical and scientific experiments. **2.** *n.* someone who is being used in an experiment. (Figurative on ①.)
→ SERVE AS A GUINEA PIG

gulf ['gʌlf] **1.** *n.* an area of sea, larger than a bay, surrounded by land on two or three sides. **2.** *n.* a large or wide separation. (Figurative on ①.)

gum ['gʌm] **1.** *n.* a soft, sticky, flavored substance that people chew. (Plural only for types and instances.) **2.** *n.* the upper or lower ridge of flesh that covers the jaw bones and surrounds the bases of the teeth.

gun ['gʌn] **1.** *n.* a weapon that shoots bullets. **2.** *n.* a device or tool that has a handle and trigger like ①, used for applying or installing something.
→ BEAT THE GUN
→ FIRE A GUN
→ JUMP THE GUN
→ STICK TO ONE'S GUNS

gun for someone to be looking for someone, presumably to harm that person, as with a gun.

gush ['gʌʃ] **1.** *n.* a large flow of a fluid. **2.** *iv.* to flow out rapidly and in large amounts. **3.** *tv.* to allow a fluid to flow; to make fluid flow.

gust ['gʌst] **1.** *n.* a strong rush of wind or smoke. **2.** *iv.* [for the wind] to move in short, strong bursts.

gut ['gʌt] **1.** *n.* the area of the intestines or stomach. (No plural.)

2. *tv.* to take the intestines and organs out of an animal.

gut feeling AND **gut reaction; gut response** a personal, intuitive feeling or response.

gut reaction Go to GUT FEELING.

gut response Go to GUT FEELING.

guts 1. *n.* the intestines. (Treated as plural, but not countable. Colloquial.) **2.** *n.* courage. (Treated as plural, but not countable. Colloquial.)
→ HATE SOMEONE'S GUTS

gutter ['gʌt ɚ] **1.** *n.* a metal channel hanging on the edge of a roof to carry away water when it rains. **2.** *n.* the wide, wooden channel on either side of a bowling lane. **3.** *n.*

on a street, a lower, formed channel that leads water and other waste to the entrance of a sewer.
→ IN THE GUTTER

guy ['gaɪ] **1.** *n.* a man; a boy. (Informal.) **2.** *n.* a person, male or female, especially in the plural. (Informal.)

gym ['dʒɪm] **1.** *n.* a gymnasium. **2.** the *adj.* use of ①.

gymnasium [dʒɪm 'nez i əm] *n.* a large room or building for physical education, physical training, or certain sports events such as basketball and wrestling. (Can be shortened to GYM.)

gyp someone **out of** something to deceive someone in order to get something of value.

H

habit [ˈhæb ɪt] **1.** *n.* an action that is done over and over, usually without thinking about it. **2.** *n.* an addiction; a strong need for drugs, tobacco, alcohol, etc. **3.** *n.* the uniform worn by a monk or a nun.
→ BREAK A HABIT
→ BREAK ONE'S HABIT
→ BREAK THE HABIT

hack something **down** to chop something down.

hack something **up 1.** to chop something up into pieces. **2.** to damage or mangle something.

had [ˈhæd] **1.** past tense and past participle of HAVE. **2.** *aux.* the past-tense form of HAVE ⑤, used in forming the past PERFECT verb form. (Used before the past participle of a verb. Reduced to 'd in contractions. See also HAS.)
→ BEEN HAD
→ HAVE HAD ITS DAY

had better is obliged to; should. (Often -'d better.)

(had) known it was coming Go to KNEW IT WAS COMING.

hadn't [ˈhæd nt] *cont.* had not.

hag [ˈhæg] *n.* an ugly old woman; a witch.

hail [ˈhel] **1.** *n.* round pellets of ice that fall from the sky like rain. (No plural. Number is expressed with HAILSTONE(S).) **2.** *n.* a group of things that come in small, sharp units. **3.** *n.* a continual series of demands, objections, questions, etc. **4.** *tv.* to greet or welcome someone with cheers, joy, and approval. **5.** *tv.* to honor and praise someone or something; to praise and approve something eagerly. **6.** *iv.* [for ①] to fall from the sky.

hail-fellow-well-met friendly to everyone; falsely friendly to everyone. (Usually said of males.)

hailstone [ˈhel ston] *n.* a small, round ball of ice that falls from the sky like rain.

hailstorm [ˈhel storm] *n.* a storm that produces or includes hail.

hair [ˈhɛr] **1.** *n.* the strands or fibers that grow on the body of an animal, especially the ones that grow on top of the heads of humans. (No plural. Treated as singular.) **2.** *n.* one of the strands or fibers that grow on the body of an animal as in ①.
→ BY A HAIR'S BREADTH
→ CURL SOMEONE'S HAIR
→ GET IN SOMEONE'S HAIR
→ HANG BY A HAIR
→ LET ONE'S HAIR DOWN
→ MAKE SOMEONE'S HAIR STAND ON END
→ NEITHER HIDE NOR HAIR
→ PART SOMEONE'S HAIR
→ TEAR ONE'S HAIR (OUT)

hair of the dog that bit one a drink of liquor taken when one has a hangover; a drink of liquor taken when one is recovering from drinking too much liquor.

hairbrush [ˈhɛr brəʃ] *n.* a brush used for smoothing hair and making it look orderly.

haircut [ˈhɛr kət] **1.** *n.* an act or instance of cutting hair, especially the hair on top of someone's head. **2.** *n.* the particular way that one's hair has been cut; a hairstyle.

hairy ['hɛr i] *adj.* covered with hair; having a lot of hair. (Comp: *hairier;* sup: *hairiest.*)

hale and hearty well and healthy.

half ['hæf] **1.** *n., irreg.* either of two equal parts that form a complete thing. (Plural: HALVES.) **2.** *n.* a portion—as described in ① —of the amount of people or things already mentioned or referred to. (Treated as singular or plural.) **3.** *adj.* being ① of an amount; being one of two equal parts. **4.** *adv.* part of the way; not completely.
→ AT HALF-MAST
→ ONE'S BETTER HALF
→ SIX OF ONE AND HALF A DOZEN OF THE OTHER

halfhearted ['hæf 'hɑrt ɪd] *adj.* not too enthusiastic; without excitement. (Adv: *halfheartedly.*)
→ BE HALFHEARTED (ABOUT SOMEONE OR SOMETHING)

halfway ['hæf 'we] **1.** *adj.* at the middle; in the middle. **2.** *adv.* to the point that is ①.
→ MEET SOMEONE HALFWAY

hall ['hɔl] **1.** *n.* a passage that connects rooms and stairways inside a house or building. (See also HALLWAY.) **2.** *n.* a large room for big meetings, lectures, dances, etc. **3.** *n.* a building where college students live, sleep, study, or have classes.
→ CITY HALL

hallway ['hɔl we] *n.* a HALL; a passage that connects rooms and stairways inside a house or building.

halt ['hɔlt] **1.** *iv.* to stop. **2.** *tv.* to cause someone or something to stop.

→ GRIND TO A HALT

halves ['hævz] plural of HALF.

ham ['hæm] **1.** *n.* the upper part of a hog's rear hip and thigh, preserved by salt and a special kind of wood smoke. **2.** *n.* ① eaten as food. (Plural only for types and instances.)

ham something **up** to perform in something in an exaggerated and exhibitionist manner.

hamburger ['hæm bɚ gɚ] **1.** *n.* beef that has been ground into tiny bits. (No plural.) **2.** *n.* a sandwich made of cooked ground beef and a specially shaped bun.

hammer ['hæm ɚ] **1.** *n.* a tool with a heavy metal head that is used to pound nails or to break things. **2.** *tv.* to hit something with ①.
→ FIGHT SOMEONE OR SOMETHING HAMMER AND TONGS
→ GO AT IT HAMMER AND TONGS

hammer (away) at someone to interrogate someone; to ask questions endlessly of someone. (Figurative.)

hammer something **down** to pound something down, making it even with the surrounding area.

hammer something **home** to try extremely hard to make someone understand or realize something.

hammer something **in(to** someone) AND **pound** something **in(to** someone) to teach something to someone intensively, as if one were driving the information in by force.

hammer something **in(to** something) AND **pound** something **in(to** something) to drive something into something as with a hammer.

hand ['hænd] **1.** *n.* the structure at the end of the arm used for grasping; the most distant part of the arm, below the wrist. **2.** *n.* the cards given or dealt to someone in a card game; one session in a game of cards. **3.** *n.* side; direction. (No plural.) **4.** *n.* one of the pointers on a clock or watch. **5.** *tv.* to give something to someone by using one's ①. **6.** the *adj.* use of ① or ④.

→ BE PUTTY IN SOMEONE'S HANDS
→ BITE THE HAND THAT FEEDS ONE
→ BOUND HAND AND FOOT
→ BY A SHOW OF HANDS
→ CAN'T SEE ONE'S HAND IN FRONT OF ONE'S FACE
→ CLOSE AT HAND
→ COME AWAY EMPTY-HANDED
→ DIRTY ONE'S HANDS
→ DO SOMETHING BY HAND
→ EAT OUT OF SOMEONE'S HAND
→ FOLD ONE'S HANDS
→ FORCE SOMEONE'S HAND
→ FROM HAND TO HAND
→ GET ONE'S HANDS DIRTY
→ GET THE UPPER HAND (ON SOMEONE)
→ GO AWAY EMPTY-HANDED
→ HAVE CLEAN HANDS
→ HAVE ONE'S HAND IN THE TILL
→ HAVE ONE'S HANDS FULL (WITH SOMEONE OR SOMETHING)
→ HAVE ONE'S HANDS TIED
→ HAVE SOMEONE OR SOMETHING IN ONE'S HANDS
→ HAVE SOMEONE'S BLOOD ON ONE'S HANDS
→ HAVE SOMETHING AT HAND
→ IN HAND
→ JOIN HANDS
→ KNOW SOMEONE OR SOMETHING LIKE THE BACK OF ONE'S HAND
→ KNOW SOMEONE OR SOMETHING LIKE THE PALM OF ONE'S HAND
→ LIVE FROM HAND TO MOUTH
→ ONE'S HANDS ARE TIED

→ PUT ONE'S HAND TO THE PLOW
→ SHAKE HANDS
→ SHAKE SOMEONE'S HAND
→ SHOW ONE'S HAND
→ SIT ON ITS HANDS
→ SIT ON ONE'S HANDS
→ SOIL ONE'S HANDS
→ TAKE THE LAW INTO ONE'S OWN HANDS
→ TIE SOMEONE'S HANDS
→ TIME HANGS HEAVY ON SOMEONE'S HANDS.
→ WAIT ON SOMEONE HAND AND FOOT
→ WASH ONE'S HANDS OF SOMEONE OR SOMETHING
→ WITH BOTH HANDS TIED BEHIND ONE'S BACK
→ WITH ONE HAND TIED BEHIND ONE'S BACK

hand in glove (with someone) very close to someone.

hand over fist [for money and merchandise to be exchanged] very rapidly.

hand over hand [moving] one hand after the other (again and again).

hand something **down** [for a court] to issue a ruling. (Legal.)

hand something **down from** someone **to** someone to pass something down through many generations.

hand something **down (to** someone) to pass on something to a younger person, often a younger relative.

hand something **off (to** someone) to give a football directly to another player. (Football.)

hand something **out (to** someone) to pass something, usually papers, out to people.

handicap ['hæn di kæp] **1.** *n.* a disability; a disadvantage; something that hinders someone from doing something in the usual way. **2.** *n.* [in sports or games] placing restrictions on a better player in order to make the event more competitive. **3.** *tv.* to prevent someone from doing something in the usual way; to hinder someone.

handkerchief ['hæn kɚ tʃɪf] *n.* a square of soft fabric used to wipe one's nose or face.

handle ['hæn dəl] **1.** *n.* the part of an object that is held on to so that the object can be used, moved, picked up, pushed, pulled, opened, or closed. **2.** *tv.* to feel someone or something with one's hands; to use one's hands on someone or something. **3.** *iv.* [for something] to work in a certain way while being used; [for a vehicle or boat] to be guided, driven, or steered.
→ FLY OFF THE HANDLE
→ GET A HANDLE ON SOMETHING
→ HAVE A HANDLE ON SOMETHING

handle someone **with kid gloves** to be very careful with a touchy person; to deal with someone who is very difficult.

hands down easily and without opposition; indisputably.

handsome ['hæn səm] **1.** *adj.* very attractive; [of a male] very good-looking. (Adv: *handsomely.* Comp: *handsomer;* sup: *handsomest.*) **2.** *adj.* ample; generous; more than enough. (Adv: *handsomely.* Comp: *handsomer;* sup: *handsomest.*)

handwriting ['hænd raɪt ɪŋ] **1.** *n.* writing done by hand with a pen or pencil instead of with a type-writer or computer. (No plural form.) **2.** *n.* one's own style of writing; a sample of one's own handwriting. (No plural form.)
→ SEE THE (HAND)WRITING ON THE WALL

hang ['hæŋ] **1.** *tv., irreg.* to suspend something from a higher place, using a rope, chain, etc. (Past tense and past participle: HUNG.) **2.** *tv., irreg.* to attach something to a wall. **3.** *tv.* to execute a person by suspending the person by the neck. (Past tense and past participle: *hanged* for this sense.) **4.** *iv., irreg.* to be suspended over something; to remain above someplace or thing.
→ GET THE HANG OF SOMETHING
→ HAVE SOMETHING HANGING OVER ONE'S HEAD
→ KEEP SOMEONE OR SOMETHING HANGING IN MIDAIR
→ LEAVE SOMEONE OR SOMETHING HANGING IN MIDAIR
→ TIME HANGS HEAVY ON SOMEONE'S HANDS.

hang (around) AND **hang (out)** to waste time somewhere; to do nothing for a period of time.

hang around (someplace**)** to loiter someplace; to be in a place or in an area, doing nothing in particular.

hang around with someone to spend time doing nothing in particular with someone.

hang back (from someone or something**)** to lag back behind someone or something; to stay back from someone or something, perhaps in avoidance.

hang by a hair AND **hang by a thread** to be in an uncertain position; to depend on something very insubstantial for support.

hang by a thread Go to HANG BY A HAIR.

hang fire to delay or wait; to be delayed.

hang in the balance to be in an undecided state; to be between two equal possibilities.

Hang on! Be prepared for fast or rough movement.

hang on 1. to wait awhile. **2.** to survive awhile. (Figurative.) **3.** to linger or persist.

hang on someone's **every word** to listen carefully to everything someone says.

hang on (to someone or something) AND **hold on (to** someone or something) **1.** to grasp someone or something. **2.** to keep someone or something.

hang one's **hat up** somewhere to take up residence somewhere.

hang (out) Go to HANG (AROUND).

hang out (with someone or something) to associate with someone or a group on a regular basis.

hang someone **in effigy** to hang a dummy or some other figure of a hated person.

hang together 1. [for something or a group of people] to hold together; to remain intact. **2.** [for a story] to flow from element to element and make sense. **3.** [for people] to spend time together.

hang up 1. [for a machine or a computer] to grind to a halt; to stop because of some internal

complication. **2.** to replace the telephone receiver after a call.

hangar ['hæŋ ɚ] *n.* a large building where airplanes are stored and serviced.

hanger ['hæŋ ɚ] *n.* a wooden, metal, or plastic frame for suspending clothing inside a closet.

happen ['hæp ən] *iv.* to occur; to take place.
→ CAN'T WAIT (FOR SOMETHING TO HAPPEN)

happen to do something to do something by chance, without planning to do it; to have the good or bad fortune to do something.

happen to someone or something to be done to someone or something; to be experienced by someone or something.

happen (up)on someone or something to find someone or something, as if by accident.

happiness ['hæp i nəs] *n.* being happy; being glad or joyful. (No plural.)

happy ['hæp i] **1.** *adj.* [of someone or some creature] feeling or showing joy or being in a good mood; [of someone] glad, pleased, or willing. (Adv: *happily.* Comp: *happier;* sup: *happiest.*) **2.** *adj.* causing joy; joyful. (Adv: *happily.* Comp: *happier;* sup: *happiest.*)
→ (AS) HAPPY AS A CLAM
→ HIT A HAPPY MEDIUM
→ STRIKE A HAPPY MEDIUM

harbor ['hɑr bɚ] **1.** *n.* a sheltered port where ships and boats can anchor safely. **2.** *tv.* to keep something in one's mind, especially bad feelings toward someone.

hard ['hɑrd] **1.** *adj.* firm; solid; not soft. (Comp: *harder;* sup: *hardest.*) **2.** *adj.* difficult; not easy to do. (Comp: *harder;* sup: *hardest.*) **3.** *adj.* severe; harsh; demanding. (Comp: *harder;* sup: *hardest.*) **4.** *adj.* forceful; violent; not gentle. (Comp: *harder;* sup: *hardest.*) **5.** *adj.* [of water] having a high mineral content. (Comp: *harder;* sup: *hardest.*) **6.** *adv.* with great force or energy. (Comp: *harder;* sup: *hardest.*)
→ (AS) HARD AS NAILS
→ BETWEEN A ROCK AND A HARD PLACE
→ DRIVE A HARD BARGAIN
→ HIT SOMEONE HARD

hard of hearing [of someone] unable to hear well; [of someone] partially deaf.

hard on someone's **heels** following someone very closely; following very closely to someone's heels.

a **hard-and-fast rule** a strict rule.

hardly ['hɑrd li] *adv.* barely; almost not at all.

hardly have time to think so busy that one can hardly think properly; very busy.

hardware ['hɑrd wɛr] **1.** *n.* tools, nails, screws, door handles, electrical supplies, brackets, buckets, utensils, and similar things used in building and maintenance. (No plural form.) **2.** *n.* computer equipment; the machinery of a computer, as opposed to software programs. (No plural form.)

hare ['hɛr] *n.* an animal, such as the jackrabbit, that is very similar to a rabbit, but larger.
→ (AS) MAD AS A MARCH HARE

harm ['hɑrm] **1.** *n.* mental or physical damage to someone or something. (No plural.) **2.** *tv.* to damage someone or something.

harmful ['hɑrm fʊl] *adj.* causing damage or harm to someone or something. (Adv: *harmfully.*)

harmony ['hɑr mə ni] **1.** *n.* the effect of different musical notes that are played or sung together, creating a pleasant sound. (Plural only for types and instances.) **2.** *n.* agreement; peace. (No plural. Figurative on ①.)

harp ['hɑrp] *n.* a musical instrument having strings attached to a frame of wood.

harp on someone or something to keep talking about someone or something until everyone is tired of hearing about it. (Informal.)

harsh ['hɑrʃ] **1.** *adj.* rough; unpleasant to look at or listen to; unpleasant to touch, taste, or smell. (Adv: *harshly.* Comp: *harsher;* sup: *harshest.*) **2.** *adj.* mean; cruel; severe. (Adv: *harshly.* Comp: *harsher;* sup: *harshest.*)

harvest ['hɑr vəst] **1.** *n.* the gathering of a crop of grain, fiber, fruit, vegetables, etc. **2.** *n.* the total amount of grain, fiber, fruit, or vegetables produced in an area. **3.** *tv.* to collect a crop of grain, fiber, fruit, or vegetables when it is ready.

has ['hæz] **1.** *tv.* the present-tense form of HAVE used for the third-person singular, that is, with *he, she, it,* and singular nouns. **2.** *aux.* the present-tense form of HAVE ⑤ used for the third-person singular, that is, with *he*, *she*, *it*, and singular nouns, in forming the present PERFECT verb form. (Used before the past participle of a verb. Reduced to *'s* in contractions.)

hash something **over (with** someone**)** to discuss something with someone.

hat ['hæt] *n.* an article of clothing shaped to cover the head.
→ AT THE DROP OF A HAT
→ BE OLD HAT
→ EAT ONE'S HAT
→ HANG ONE'S HAT UP SOMEWHERE
→ KEEP SOMETHING UNDER ONE'S HAT
→ PASS THE HAT
→ PULL SOMETHING OUT OF A HAT
→ TALK THROUGH ONE'S HAT
→ TOSS ONE'S HAT INTO THE RING
→ WEAR MORE THAN ONE HAT

hatch ['hætʃ] **1.** *n.* an opening in a wall, ceiling, or floor. **2.** *iv.* [for a baby bird or reptile] to break an eggshell from the inside and come out.
→ COUNT ONE'S CHICKENS BEFORE THEY HATCH

hatchet ['hætʃ ɪt] *n.* a short axe.
→ BURY THE HATCHET

hate ['het] **1.** *n.* intense dislike. (No plural.) **2.** *tv.* to dislike someone or something intensely.
→ ONE'S PET HATE

hate someone's **guts** to hate someone very much. (Informal and rude.)

hate to do something to strongly dislike doing something.

haul ['hɔl] **1.** *tv.* to carry something, using force; to drag something heavy. **2.** *tv.* to carry or bring someone or something by truck or other vehicle. **3.** *n.* an instance of traveling from one place to

another, and the distance, time, or effort involved.
→ OVER THE LONG HAUL
→ OVER THE SHORT HAUL

haul someone **in** [for an officer of the law] to take someone to the police station.

haul someone **over the coals** Go TO RAKE SOMEONE OVER THE COALS.

have ['hæv] **1.** *tv., irreg.* to own something; to possess something; to possess a quality. (Past tense and past participle: HAD; in the present tense, the third-person singular form is HAS.) **2.** *tv., irreg.* to undergo something; [for something] to happen to oneself; to experience something. **3.** *tv., irreg.* to eat or drink something; to consume something. **4.** *tv., irreg.* to cause something to be done; to cause someone or something to do something. **5.** *aux.* a verb that is used to form the PERFECT verb forms, which show that an action is completed. (Used before the past participle of a verb.)
→ AS LUCK WOULD HAVE IT
→ CHICKENS HAVE COME HOME TO ROOST
→ EAT ONE'S CAKE AND HAVE IT TOO
→ HARDLY HAVE TIME TO THINK
→ NOT HAVE A LEG TO STAND ON
→ SHOULD HAVE STOOD IN BED
→ WALLS HAVE EARS.
→ WOULD LIKE (TO HAVE)

have a bee in one's **bonnet** to have an idea or a thought remain in one's mind; to have an obsession.

have a big mouth to be a gossiper; to be a person who tells secrets.

have a bone to pick (with someone**)** to have a matter to discuss with someone; to have something to argue about with someone.

have a chip on one's **shoulder** to be tempting someone to an argument or a fight.

have a (close) brush with something to have a brief contact with something; to have an experience with something.

have a close call Go to HAVE A CLOSE SHAVE.

have a close shave AND **have a close call** to have a narrow escape from something dangerous. (Also with *be*.)

have a familiar ring [for a story or an explanation] to sound familiar.

have a foot in both camps to have an interest in or to support each of two opposing groups of people.

have a frog in one's **throat** to have a feeling of not being able to speak because of a lump in one's throat or as if it were sore. (Also with *get*.)

have a good head on one's **shoulders** to have common sense; to be sensible and intelligent.

have a green thumb to have the ability to grow plants well.

have a handle on something AND **get a handle on** something to have or get control of something; to have or get an understanding of something.

have a head for something have the mental capacity for something.

have a heart to be compassionate; to be generous and forgiving.

have a heart of gold to be generous, sincere, and friendly.

have a heart of stone to be cold, unfeeling, and unfriendly.

have a hold on someone to have a strong and secure influence on someone.

have a keen interest in something to have a strong interest in something; to be very interested in something.

have a look for someone or something Go to TAKE A LOOK FOR SOMEONE OR SOMETHING.

have a lot going (for one**)** to have many things working to one's benefit.

have a low boiling point to anger easily.

have a nose for something to have the talent for finding something.

have a one-track mind to have a mind that thinks entirely or almost entirely about one subject, especially sex.

have a peep AND **take a peep** to look quickly, sometimes through a small hole.

have a price on one's **head** to be wanted by the authorities, who have offered a reward for one's capture.

have a run of something a continuous series of events.

have a run-in with someone to have an unpleasant and troublesome encounter with someone.

have a scrape (with someone or something**)** to come into contact with someone or something; to have a small battle with someone or something.

have a soft spot in one's **heart for** someone or something to be fond of someone or something.

have a sweet tooth to desire to eat many sweet foods—especially candy and pastries. (As if a certain tooth had a craving for sweets.)

have a taste for something a desire for a particular food, drink, or experience.

have a vested interest in something to have a personal or biased interest, often financial, in something.

have a weakness for someone or something to be unable to resist someone or something; to be fond of someone or something; to be (figuratively) powerless against someone or something.

have an ax to grind to have something to complain about.

have an ear for something to have the ability to learn music or languages.

have an in (with someone**)** to have a way to request a special favor from someone; to have influence with someone. (The *in* is a noun.)

have an itch for something to have a desire for something.

have an itch to do something to have a desire to do something.

have an itching palm Go to HAVE AN ITCHY PALM.

have an itchy palm AND **have an itching palm** to be in need of a tip; to tend to ask for tips; to crave

money. (As if placing money in the palm would stop the itching.)

have arrived to reach a position of power, authority, or prominence.

have bearing on something to have an effect or influence on something.

have clean hands to be guiltless. (As if the guilty person would have bloody hands.)

have egg on one's **face** to be embarrassed because of an error that is obvious to everyone.

have eyes bigger than one's **stomach** to have a desire for more food than one could possibly eat.

have eyes in the back of one's **head** to seem to be able to sense what is going on outside of one's range of vision. (Not literal.)

have feet of clay [for a strong person] to have a defect of character.

have foot-in-mouth disease to embarrass oneself through a silly verbal blunder; to put one's foot in one's mouth (not literally) a lot.

have got something to have something; to possess something. (Used only with the present tense of HAVE ⑤, as with *have got* or *has got*.)

have got to do something to be obliged to do something; must do something. (Used only with the present tense of HAVE ⑤, as with *have got to* or *has got to*.)

have had its day to no longer be useful or successful.

have it out (with someone**)** to settle something with someone by fighting or arguing.

have mixed feelings (about someone or something**)** to be uncertain about someone or something.

have money to burn to have lots of money; to have more money than one needs; to have enough money that some can be wasted.

have one's **back to the wall** to be in a defensive position.

have one's **cake and eat it too** AND **eat** one's **cake and have it too** to enjoy both having something and using it up.

have one's **ear to the ground** AND **keep** one's **ear to the ground** to listen carefully, hoping to get warning of something.

have one's **finger in the pie** to be involved in something.

have one's **finger in too many pies** to be involved in too many things; to have too many tasks going to be able to do any of them well.

have one's **hand in the till** to be stealing money from a company or an organization. (The *till* is a cash box or drawer.)

have one's **hands full (with** someone or something**)** to be busy or totally occupied with someone or something.

have one's **hands tied** to be prevented from doing something. (*Figurative.*)

have one's **head in the clouds** to be unaware of what is going on.

have one's **heart in** one's **mouth** to feel strongly emotional about someone or something.

have one's **heart set on** something to be desiring and expecting something.

have one's **nose in a book** to be reading a book; to read books all the time.

have one's **sights trained on** something Go to TRAIN ONE'S SIGHTS ON SOMETHING.

have one's **tail between** one's **legs** to be frightened or to lack bravery.

have one's **words stick in** one's **throat** to be so overcome by emotion that one can hardly speak.

have other fish to fry to have other things to do; to have more important things to do. (*Other* can be replaced by *bigger, better, more important,* etc.)

have someone **dead to rights** to have proved someone unquestionably guilty.

have someone **in** one's **pocket** to have control over someone.

have someone or something **in** one's **hands** to have control of or responsibility for someone or something. (*Have* can be replaced with *leave* or *put.*)

have someone **over** to invite someone as a guest to one's house.

have someone **pegged as** something Go to PEG SOMEONE AS SOMETHING.

have someone's **blood on** one's **hands** to be responsible for someone's death; to be guilty of causing someone's death.

have someone's **eye** Go to CATCH SOMEONE'S EYE.

have something **at hand** Go to HAVE SOMETHING AT ONE'S FINGERTIPS.

have something **at one's fingertips** AND **have** something **at hand** to have something within (one's) reach.

have something **down pat** to have learned or memorized something perfectly.

have something **hanging over** one's **head** to have something bothering or worrying one; to have a deadline worrying one.

have something **in stock** to have merchandise available and ready for sale.

have something **out** to have something, such as a tooth, stone, or tumor, removed surgically.

have something **to spare** to have more than enough of something.

have something **wrapped up** Go to GET SOMETHING SEWED UP.

have the gall to do something to have sufficient arrogance to do something.

have the Midas touch to have the ability to be successful, especially the ability to make money easily. (MIDAS = a legendary king whose touch turned everything to gold.)

have the presence of mind to do something to have the calmness and ability to act sensibly in an emergency or difficult situation.

have the right-of-way to possess the legal right to occupy a particular space on a public roadway.

have the time of one's **life** to have a very good time; to have the most exciting time in one's life.

have to do something to be obligated to do something; must do something.

have to do with someone or something to concern or affect someone or something; to be associated with or related to someone or something.

have too many irons in the fire to be doing too many things at once.

the **have-nots** ['hæv 'nɑts] *n.* people who do not have enough money to live comfortably.

the **haves** ['hævz] *n.* people who have enough money to live comfortably; people who are rich and privileged.

hawk ['hɔk] **1.** *n.* a bird of prey, similar to a falcon, with strong beak and claws, a long tail, and good eyesight. **2.** *tv.* to sell something, especially in the street.
→ WATCH SOMEONE LIKE A HAWK

hay ['he] *n.* grass or plants cut, dried, and used as food for cattle, horses, etc. (No plural.)

haystack ['he stæk] *n.* a large amount of hay that is piled together to dry.
→ LIKE LOOKING FOR A NEEDLE IN A HAYSTACK

hazard a guess to make a guess.

hazard an opinion to give an opinion.

he ['hi] **1.** *pron.* a third-person singular masculine pronoun. (Refers to male creatures. Used as a subject of a sentence or a clause. See also HIM, HIMSELF, and HIS.) **2.** *pron.* a third-person singular pronoun. (Used when the sex of a grammatical subject is unimportant, indeterminate, undetermined, or irrelevant. Objected to by some as actually referring only to males in this sense. See also THEY ②.) **3.** *n.* a male person or creature.

head ['hed] **1.** *n.* the part of the body of humans and animals above the neck, including the face, eyes, nose, mouth, ears, brain, and skull. **2.** *n.* the brain; the mind. **3.** *n.* an individual animal, used especially in counting cows, horses, and sheep. (No plural. Always a singular form preceded by words that tell how many.) **4.** *n.* the leader of a company, country, organization, group, etc.; a chief; someone who is in charge. **5.** *n.* the top, front, or upper part of something, such as a table, a page, a sheet of paper, a line [of people], or a [school] class. **6.** *adj.* primary; chief; foremost. (Prenominal only.) **7.** *tv.* to lead a group of people; to be in charge of a group of people or part of a company. **8.** *iv.* to move in a certain direction.

→ BANG ONE'S HEAD AGAINST A BRICK WALL
→ BEAT ONE'S HEAD AGAINST THE WALL
→ BRING SOMETHING TO A HEAD
→ BURY ONE'S HEAD IN THE SAND
→ CAN'T MAKE HEADS OR TAILS (OUT) OF SOMEONE OR SOMETHING
→ COME TO A HEAD
→ COUNT HEADS
→ DRUM SOMETHING IN(TO SOMEONE'S HEAD)
→ GET ONE'S HEAD ABOVE WATER
→ GET SOMETHING INTO SOMEONE'S THICK HEAD
→ GO OVER SOMEONE'S HEAD
→ GO TO SOMEONE'S HEAD
→ HAVE A GOOD HEAD ON ONE'S SHOULDERS

→ HAVE A HEAD FOR SOMETHING
→ HAVE A PRICE ON ONE'S HEAD
→ HAVE EYES IN THE BACK OF ONE'S HEAD
→ HAVE ONE'S HEAD IN THE CLOUDS
→ HAVE SOMETHING HANGING OVER ONE'S HEAD
→ HIDE ONE'S HEAD IN THE SAND
→ HIT THE NAIL (RIGHT) ON THE HEAD
→ HOLD ONE'S HEAD UP
→ IN OVER ONE'S HEAD
→ KEEP A CIVIL TONGUE (IN ONE'S HEAD)
→ KEEP ONE'S HEAD ABOVE WATER
→ MAKE SOMEONE'S HEAD SPIN
→ MAKE SOMEONE'S HEAD SWIM
→ OFF THE TOP OF ONE'S HEAD
→ OUT OF ONE'S HEAD
→ OVER SOMEONE'S HEAD
→ PER HEAD
→ REAR ITS UGLY HEAD
→ TURN SOMEONE'S HEAD

a **head** AND **per head** a person; an individual.

head and shoulders above someone or something clearly superior to someone or something. (Often with *stand*.)

head back (someplace**)** to start moving back to someplace.

head of cabbage AND **head of lettuce** *n.* the edible, top part of a cabbage or a lettuce plant.

head of lettuce Go to HEAD OF CABBAGE.

head someone or something **off** to intercept and divert someone or something.

head something **up 1.** to get something pointed in the right direction. (Especially a herd of cattle or a group of covered wagons.) **2.** to be in charge of something; to be the head of some organization.

headache ['hɛd ek] **1.** *n.* a pain in the head, especially one that lasts a long time. **2.** *n.* a problem; a bother; a worry. (Figurative on ①.)

heads will roll some people will get into trouble. (Informal. From the use of the guillotine to execute people.)

heal over [for the surface of a wound] to heal.

heal up [for an injury] to heal.

health ['hɛlθ] **1.** *n.* freedom from diseases of the mind or the body. (No plural.) **2.** *n.* vigor; general condition. (No plural. Figurative on ①.) **3.** the *adj.* use of ① or ②.
→ GET A CLEAN BILL OF HEALTH
→ GIVE SOMEONE A CLEAN BILL OF HEALTH
→ IN THE PICTURE OF (GOOD) HEALTH
→ NURSE SOMEONE BACK TO HEALTH

heap ['hip] *n.* a large pile of things; a stack of things piled together.

heap something up to make something into a pile.

heap something (up)on someone or something 1. to pile something up on someone or something. **2.** to give someone too much of something, such as homework, praise, criticism, etc. (Figurative.)

hear ['hɪr] **1.** *iv., irreg.* to be able to sense or experience sounds by means of the ears. (Past tense and past participle: HEARD.) **2.** *tv., irreg.* to sense or receive a certain sound or a certain utterance. **3.** *tv., irreg.* to learn that something has happened. (The object can be a clause with THAT ⑦.) **4.** *tv., irreg.* [for a court of law] to listen to the two sides of a court case. **5.** *tv., irreg.*

to pay attention to someone or something; to listen to someone or something. (The object can be a clause with THAT ⑦.)
→ LIKE TO HEAR ONESELF TALK
→ SO QUIET YOU COULD HEAR A PIN DROP
→ SO STILL YOU COULD HEAR A PIN DROP

hear someone out 1. to hear all of what someone has to say. **2.** to hear someone's side of the story.

heard ['hɚd] past tense and past participle of HEAR.
→ MAKE ONESELF HEARD

hearing ['hɪr ɪŋ] **1.** *n.* the sense that allows one to recognize sound; the ability to hear. (No plural form.) **2.** *n.* an examination of basic evidence in a court of law. **3.** the *adj.* use of ①.
→ HARD OF HEARING

heart ['hɑrt] **1.** *n.* a large, four-chambered muscle that pumps blood throughout the body. **2.** *n.* ① considered as a symbol of the center of a person's emotions, thoughts, and love. (Figurative on ①.) **3.** *n.* the shape ♥. **4.** *n.* [in a deck of playing cards] one card of a group of cards that bears a red ♥.
→ an ACHING HEART
→ BREAK SOMEONE'S HEART
→ CROSS ONE'S HEART (AND HOPE TO DIE)
→ DIE OF A BROKEN HEART
→ DO SOMEONE'S HEART GOOD
→ EAT ONE'S HEART OUT
→ FIND IT IN ONE'S HEART (TO DO SOMETHING)
→ FOLLOW ONE'S HEART
→ FROM THE BOTTOM OF ONE'S HEART
→ GET TO THE HEART OF THE MATTER
→ HAVE A HEART
→ HAVE A HEART OF GOLD

→ HAVE A HEART OF STONE
→ HAVE A SOFT SPOT IN ONE'S HEART
  FOR SOMEONE OR SOMETHING
→ HAVE ONE'S HEART IN ONE'S MOUTH
→ HAVE ONE'S HEART SET ON SOMETHING
→ LOSE HEART
→ ONE'S HEART IS IN ONE'S MOUTH
→ ONE'S HEART IS SET ON SOMETHING
→ OPEN ONE'S HEART (TO SOMEONE)
→ SET ONE'S HEART ON SOMETHING
→ TO ONE'S HEART'S CONTENT
→ WITH ALL ONE'S HEART AND SOUL

the **heart** *n.* the most central, essential, or vital part of something; the core of something. (No plural. Treated as singular. Figurative on HEART ①.)

heartbeat ['hɑrt bit] **1.** *n.* one full pulse of the heart. **2.** *n.* a moment; a second or two.
→ DO SOMETHING IN A HEARTBEAT
→ BE A HEARTBEAT AWAY FROM
  SOMETHING

hearty ['hɑr ti] **1.** *adj.* energetic; vigorous; strong and lively. (Adv: *heartily.* Comp: *heartier;* sup: *heartiest.*) **2.** *adj.* [of a meal] large and satisfying. (Adv: *heartily.* Comp: *heartier;* sup: *heartiest.*)
→ HALE AND HEARTY

heat ['hit] **1.** *n.* hotness; the quality that is felt at a higher temperature. (No plural.) **2.** *n.* hot weather. (No plural.) **3.** *n.* a grouping of contestants in a sporting event. (The winners of different HEATS compete in later HEATS or the final event.) **4.** *tv.* to cause something to become hotter. **5.** *iv.* to become hotter or warmer.
→ IN A DEAD HEAT
→ IN HEAT

heat up 1. to get warmer or hot. **2.** to grow more animated or combative.

heaven ['hɛv ən] *n.* [in certain religions] the place where God resides and where the souls of good people go after death. (Usually associated with the sky. No plural.)
→ IN HEAVEN
→ IN SEVENTH HEAVEN
→ MANNA FROM HEAVEN
→ MOVE HEAVEN AND EARTH TO DO
  SOMETHING

the **heavens** *n.* the sky; space. (Treated as plural.)

heavy ['hɛv i] **1.** *adj.* weighing a lot; of great weight. (Adv: *heavily.* Comp: *heavier;* sup: *heaviest.*) **2.** *adj.* [of sound] strong, deep, and ponderous. (Adv: *heavily.* Comp: *heavier;* sup: *heaviest.*) **3.** *adj.* great in amount; dense; intense; thick. (Adv: *heavily.* Comp: *heavier;* sup: *heaviest.*) **4.** *adj.* serious; requiring a lot of thought to understand. (Adv: *heavily.* Comp: *heavier;* sup: *heaviest.*)
→ TIME HANGS HEAVY ON SOMEONE'S
  HANDS.

hectic ['hɛk tɪk] *adj.* very active; very excited; very busy. (Adv: *hectically* [...ɪk li].)

heed ['hid] *tv.* to pay close attention to something, such as advice.
→ TAKE HEED

heel ['hil] **1.** *n.* the back part of the foot; the part of the foot that bears the weight of the body. **2.** *n.* the part of a shoe or sock that covers the back part of the foot. **3.** *n.* the part of a shoe that supports the back part of the foot.
→ ACHILLES' HEEL
→ COOL ONE'S HEELS
→ DIG IN ONE'S HEELS
→ HARD ON SOMEONE'S HEELS
→ HIGH HEELS

→ KICK UP ONE'S HEELS
→ ON THE HEELS OF SOMETHING
→ SET ONE BACK ON ONE'S HEELS
→ TAKE TO ONE'S HEELS

heels *n.* shoes with a tall HEEL ③, worn by women, usually on formal occasions. (Short for HIGH HEELS. Treated as plural, but not countable. Number is expressed with *pair(s) of heels*.)

height ['haɪt] **1.** *n.* the amount that someone or something is tall; vertical length [of a person or of a vertical object]. (No plural.) **2.** *n.* the length of something from bottom to top; the distance to a higher point from a lower level.
→ AT THE HEIGHT OF SOMETHING

heighten ['haɪt n] **1.** *tv.* to cause something to become more intense or exciting. **2.** *iv.* to become more intense or exciting.

held ['hɛld] past tense and past participle of HOLD.

helicopter ['hɛl ə kɑp tɚ] *n.* an aircraft with large, rotating blades that can lift and hold the aircraft in the air.

he'll ['hil] *cont.* he will.

hell ['hɛl] **1.** *n.* [in certain religions] the place where the devil resides and where the souls of wicked people go after death. (No plural. Sometimes capitalized.) **2.** *n.* suffering, misery, and despair. (Figurative on ①. No plural.) **3.** *interj.* a word used to indicate anger or surprise. (Colloquial.)
→ BEEN TO HELL AND BACK
→ FOR THE HELL OF IT
→ LIKE A BAT OUT OF HELL

hello [hɛ 'lo] **1.** *n.* an act of greeting someone; an act of saying ②. (Plural ends in -s.) **2.** *interj.* a word used in greeting someone or in answering the telephone.
→ DROP IN (TO SAY HELLO)

helm ['hɛlm] *n.* the wheel or lever used to control the direction of a ship. (No plural form.)
→ AT THE HELM (OF SOMETHING)

help ['hɛlp] **1.** *n.* aid; assistance. (No plural. Treated as singular.) **2.** *n.* someone or a group hired to do a job, usually a service job. (No plural. Treated as singular or plural, but not counted.) **3.** *iv.* to give assistance. **4.** *tv.* to give assistance to someone or something; to aid someone or something. **5.** *tv.* to relieve an illness or condition; to ease the discomfort caused by something; to make a sickness or discomfort less severe. **6.** *interj.* a cry used when one needs aid or assistance.
→ CANNOT HELP DOING SOMETHING
→ PITCH IN (AND HELP)
→ PITCH IN (AND HELP) (WITH SOMETHING)

help do something to assist [someone to] do something.

help out someplace to help [with the chores] in a particular place.

help out (with something) to help with a particular chore.

help someone back (to something) to help someone return to something or someplace.

help (someone) do something to assist someone [to] do something.

help someone off with something to help someone take off an article of clothing.

help (someone) out to help someone do something; to help someone with a problem.

hem ['hɛm] **1.** *n.* the folded and sewn edge of a piece of cloth. **2.** *tv.* to make a nice, even edge on a piece of cloth by folding and sewing.

hemisphere ['hɛm əs fɪr] **1.** *n.* half of a sphere; half of a ball. **2.** *n.* one of two halves of the earth.

hen ['hɛn] *n.* a female bird, especially a female chicken.
→ (AS) MAD AS A WET HEN
→ (AS) SCARCE AS HENS' TEETH
→ SCARCER THAN HENS' TEETH

her ['hɚ] **1.** *pron.* an objective form of SHE, referring to females. (Used after prepositions and as the object of verbs.) **2.** *pron.* an objective form of SHE, referring to ships and certain countries. (Also other informal uses.) **3.** *pron.* a possessive form of SHE, referring to females. (Used as a modifier before a noun. Compare this with HERS.)
→ GIVE THE DEVIL HER DUE

herb ['ɚb] *n.* a plant whose seeds or leaves are used for flavoring food or for medicines.

herd ['hɚd] **1.** *n.* a large group of cattle or other similar large animals such as elk, buffalo, zebra, elephants, etc. **2.** *tv.* to cause a large group of people or animals to move together. **3.** *tv.* to take care of cattle, sheep, or other groups of animals. **4.** *iv.* to form into a group; to move as a group.

here ['hɪr] **1.** *adv.* in, at, to, or from the location of the speaker or writer who uses this word. **2.** *adv.* now; at this point in time or in a process. **3.** *adv.* a form that begins a sentence and is followed by a verb, which then is followed by the subject of the sentence. (Often used to point out or offer something. Takes *be, go, stand, rest,* or a similar verb.) **4.** *n.* this place.

Here's to someone or something. an expression used as a toast to someone or something to wish someone or something well.

heritage ['hɛr ɪ tɪdʒ] *n.* the cultural background of a group of people. (No plural.)

hermit ['hɚ mɪt] *n.* someone who moves away from society and who lives alone.

hero ['hɪr o] **1.** *n.* someone who is honored and respected for bravery or courage. (Compare this with HEROINE. Plural ends in *-es.*) **2.** *n.* the main male character in a story, movie, or play. (See also HEROINE. Plural ends in *-es.*)

heroic [hɪ 'ro ɪk] *adj.* courageous; brave; valiant. (Adv: *heroically* [...ɪk li].)

heroine ['hɛr o ɪn] **1.** *n.* a brave and courageous woman; a woman who does heroic actions. (Compare this with HERO.) **2.** *n.* the main female character in a story, movie, or play. (See also HERO.)

hers ['hɚz] *pron.* a possessive form of SHE. (Used in place of a noun. Compare this with HER.)

herself [hɚ 'sɛlf] **1.** *pron.* the reflexive form of SHE. (Used after a verb or a preposition when the subject of the sentence is the same female to which the pronoun

refers.) **2.** *pron.* an emphatic form of SHE. (Follows the nominal that is being emphasized.)
→ BY HERSELF

he's ['hiz] **1.** *cont.* he is. **2.** *cont.* he has. (Where HAS is an auxiliary.)

hid ['hɪd] past tense of HIDE.

hidden ['hɪd n] Past participle of HIDE.

hide ['haɪd] **1.** *tv., irreg.* to place something out of view; to place something so that it cannot be seen; to conceal something. (Past tense: HID; past participle: HIDDEN.) **2.** *iv., irreg.* to place oneself so that one cannot be seen; to conceal oneself. **3.** *n.* the skin of an animal, especially when used to make leather.
→ GO INTO HIDING
→ NEITHER HIDE NOR HAIR

hide one's **head in the sand** Go to BURY ONE'S HEAD IN THE SAND.

hide one's **light under a bushel** to conceal one's good ideas or talents. (A biblical theme.)

hide out (from someone or something**)** to hide oneself so that one cannot be found by someone or something.

hide someone or something **away (**someplace**)** to conceal someone or something somewhere.

high ['haɪ] **1.** *adj.* far above the ground; further above than average; not low. (Comp: *higher*; sup: *highest*.) **2.** *adj.* extending a certain distance upward; at or reaching a particular distance above the ground or above sea level. (Follows the measure of height. Comp: *higher*; sup: *highest*.) **3.** *adj.* great

in power, rank, or importance. (Adv: *highly*. Comp: *higher*; sup: *highest*.) **4.** *adj.* [of heat, number, pitch, price, velocity, intelligence, standards, etc.] great or strong, or greater or stronger than what is normal or average. (Adv: *highly*. Comp: *higher*; sup: *highest*.) **5.** *n.* the top point; a peak. **6.** *adv.* to or at a place that is far up. (Comp: *higher*; sup: *highest*.)
→ (AS) HIGH AS A KITE
→ (AS) HIGH AS THE SKY
→ ACT HIGH-AND-MIGHTY
→ HOLD SOMEONE IN HIGH REGARD
→ HUNT HIGH AND LOW FOR SOMEONE OR SOMETHING
→ LEAVE SOMEONE HIGH AND DRY
→ RUN HIGH
→ SEARCH HIGH AND LOW FOR SOMEONE OR SOMETHING

high heels ['haɪ 'hilz] *n.* women's shoes having long or tall heels. (Treated as plural, but not countable. Can be shortened to HEELS.)

high school ['haɪ skul] **1.** *n.* a school for students who have finished the lower grades of school. **2.** the *adj.* use of ①. (Hyphenated.)

highly ['haɪ li] the *adv.* form of HIGH ③; very much. (Comp: *higher*; sup: *highest*.)

highway ['haɪ we] *n.* a main road—especially one designed for high speed—used to get from one city to another.

hike ['haɪk] **1.** *n.* a long walk, especially in the woods, mountains, etc. **2.** *iv.* to travel or walk as in ①.

hike something **up** to raise something, such as prices, interest rates, a skirt, pants legs, etc.

hiker [ˈhaɪkɚ] *n.* someone who hikes.

hill [ˈhɪl] **1.** *n.* a raised part of the earth's surface, smaller than a mountain. **2.** *n.* a heap or mound of soil, especially one made by an animal.
→ OVER THE HILL

hilltop [ˈhɪl tɑp] *n.* the top of a hill.

him [ˈhɪm] **1.** *pron.* an objective form of HE ①. (The pronoun used to refer to males. Used after prepositions and as the object of verbs.) **2.** *pron.* an objective form of HE ②. (Used when the sex of a grammatical object of a verb or preposition is unimportant, indeterminate, undetermined, or irrelevant. Objected to by some as actually referring only to males in this sense. See also THEM ②.)

himself [hɪm ˈsɛlf] **1.** *pron.* the reflexive form of HE ①. (Used after a verb or a preposition when the subject of the sentence is the same male to which the pronoun refers.) **2.** *pron.* the reflexive form of HE ②. (Used after a verb or a preposition when the sex of the subject of the sentence is unimportant, indeterminate, undetermined, or irrelevant. This sense is objected to by some as actually referring only to males.) **3.** *pron.* an emphatic form of HIM. (Follows the nominal being emphasized.)
→ BY HIMSELF

hind [ˈhaɪnd] *adj.* positioned at the rear or back of something. (Prenominal only.)

hinge [ˈhɪndʒ] *n.* a jointed device that fits two things together so that one of the things, such as a door or gate, can move.

hinge (up)on someone or something to depend on someone or something; to depend on what someone or something does.

hint [ˈhɪnt] **1.** *n.* a clue; a suggestion that helps solve a puzzle or answer a question. **2.** *n.* a small trace; a little bit of something; a small amount. **3.** *tv.* to suggest ①; to provide ①. (The object is a clause with THAT ⑦.)

hip [ˈhɪp] **1.** *n.* the joint that connects the leg with the body; the area on each side of the body, below the waist, where the leg joins the trunk of the body. **2.** *adj.* in style; fashionable. (Older slang. Comp: *hipper*; sup: *hippest*.)
→ SHOOT FROM THE HIP

hippopotami [hɪp ə ˈpɑt ə maɪ] a plural of HIPPOPOTAMUS.

hippopotamus [hɪp ə ˈpɑt ə məs] *n., irreg.* a large, round-shaped African mammal that lives in and near rivers, having thick skin and very little hair. (Plural: *hippopotamuses* or HIPPOPOTAMI.)

hire [ˈhaɪɚ] *tv.* to employ someone at a job; to pay someone to do work.
→ NOT FOR HIRE

hire someone **away (from** someone or something**)** [for one] to get someone to quit working for someone or something and begin working for one.

his [ˈhɪz] **1.** *pron.* the possessive form of HE, referring to a male who has already been mentioned. (Comes before a noun.) **2.** *pron.* the possessive form of HE, referring to a male who has already been mentioned. (Used in place of a noun.) **3.** *pron.* the possessive form of HE, referring to a person who has already been mentioned. (Used when the sex of the person referred to is unimportant, indeterminate, undetermined, or irrelevant. Objected to by some as referring only to males in this sense. See also THEIR ②.) **4.** *pron.* the possessive form of HE, referring to a person who has already been mentioned. (Used in place of a noun. Used when the sex of the person referred to is unimportant, indeterminate, undetermined, or irrelevant. Objected to by some as actually referring only to males in this sense.)

hiss ['hɪs] **1.** *n.* the sound that a snake makes; a long *s* sound. **2.** *iv.* to make ①.

history ['hɪs tə ri] **1.** *n.* the study of events that have happened. (No plural.) **2.** *n.* a record of events that have happened. **3.** *n.* background; facts about the past of someone or something.
→ GO DOWN IN HISTORY

hit ['hɪt] **1.** *tv., irreg.* to strike someone or something; to contact someone or something violently or with force. (Past tense and past participle: *hit*.) **2.** *tv., irreg.* to reach something. **3.** *n.* someone or something that is very successful. **4.** *n.* [in baseball] a play where the batter HITS as in ① the ball with a bat and is able to get to a base safely. **5.** *adj.* [of music or performances] popular. (Prenominal only.)

→ MAKE A HIT (WITH SOMEONE OR SOMETHING)

hit a happy medium Go to STRIKE A HAPPY MEDIUM.

hit a plateau to reach a higher level of activity, sales, production, output, etc., and then stop and remain unchanged.

hit a snag to run into a problem.

hit a sour note Go to STRIKE A SOUR NOTE.

hit back (at someone or something) 1. to strike someone or something back. **2.** to retaliate against someone or something; to get even with someone or something for doing something wrong.

hit bottom to reach the lowest or worst point.

hit home AND **strike home** to really make sense; [for a comment] to make a very good point.

hit it off (with someone) to start a good and friendly relationship with someone from the first meeting.

hit someone hard to affect someone's emotions strongly.

hit (someone) like a ton of bricks to surprise, startle, or shock someone.

hit someone (right) between the eyes to become completely apparent; to surprise or impress someone.

hit someone (up) for something to ask someone for the loan of money or for some other favor. (Colloquial.)

hit something off to begin something; to launch an event.

hit the bull's-eye to achieve the goal perfectly.

hit the nail (right) on the head to do exactly the right thing; to do something in the most effective and efficient way.

hit the spot to be exactly right; to be refreshing.

hit (up)on someone or something **1.** to discover someone or something. **2.** to strike or pound on someone or something. (Colloquial.)

hitch a ride Go to THUMB A RIDE.

hive ['haɪv] *n.* the box, container, or structure that bees live in. (See also BEEHIVE.)

a **hive of activity** the location where things are very busy.

hives *n.* any one of various skin diseases characterized by a rash. (Treated as singular or plural, but not countable.)

hobby ['hɑb i] *n.* an activity that is done in one's spare time; an activity that one likes to do.

hobo ['ho bo] *n.* a tramp; someone who travels from city to city looking for food or work. (Usually male. Plural ends in -s or -es.)

Hobson's choice the choice between taking what is offered and getting nothing at all. (From the name of a stable owner in the seventeenth century who offered customers the hire of the horse nearest the door.)

hockey ['hɑk i] *n.* a game, played on ice, where skaters try to hit a rubber disk into a goal area. (No plural.)

hoe ['ho] **1.** *n.* a garden tool consisting of a small blade attached to a long handle, used to remove weeds or to break up soil. **2.** *tv.* to use ① on something; to remove weeds or break up soil with ①.
→ a TOUGH ROW TO HOE

hog ['hɔg] **1.** *n.* a full-grown pig, especially one raised for food or to produce young. **2.** *n.* someone who is very greedy or messy. (Figurative on ①.) **3.** *tv.* to take more than one's fair share of something. (Informal.)
→ ROAD HOG

hoist ['hoɪst] **1.** *n.* a device for lifting heavy things. **2.** *tv.* to raise something using ropes or chains.

hold ['hold] **1.** *tv., irreg.* to keep someone or something in one's arms or hands. (Past tense and past participle: HELD.) **2.** *tv., irreg.* to support the weight of someone or something; to bear the weight of someone or something. **3.** *tv., irreg.* to grasp something so it remains in a certain position. **4.** *tv., irreg.* to reserve something; to set something aside, waiting for further action. **5.** *tv., irreg.* to contain something; to have enough room for something. **6.** *tv., irreg.* to cause an event to take place. **7.** *tv., irreg.* to retain a certain position or condition. **8.** *tv., irreg.* to restrain someone or something; to keep someone or something under control. **9.** *iv., irreg.* to withstand a strain; not to break under pressure. **10.** *iv., irreg.* to remain connected to a telephone line while one's call has been temporarily suspended—so the caller or the person who was called can

talk on another telephone line.
11. *n.* a grasp; a grip. **12.** *n.* a good or secure grasp of something.
13. *n.* the place in a ship or plane where cargo is stored.
→ CAN'T HOLD A CANDLE TO SOMEONE
→ DON'T HOLD YOUR BREATH.
→ HAVE A HOLD ON SOMEONE
→ LEAVE SOMEONE HOLDING THE BABY
→ LEAVE SOMEONE HOLDING THE BAG
→ PUT A HOLD ON SOMETHING

hold back (on something) to withhold something; to give only a limited amount.

hold forth (on someone or something) to speak at great length about someone or something.

hold off ((from) doing something) to avoid doing something; to postpone doing something.

hold on 1. to wait. (Often a command.) **2.** to be patient. (Often a command.)

hold on (to someone or something) Go to HANG ON (TO SOMEONE OR SOMETHING).

hold one's ground Go to STAND ONE'S GROUND.

hold one's head up to have self-respect; to retain or display one's dignity.

hold one's own to do as well as anyone else.

hold one's peace to remain silent.

hold one's temper Go to KEEP ONE'S TEMPER.

hold one's tongue to refrain from speaking; to refrain from saying something unpleasant.

hold out to endure; to last; to survive.

hold out (against someone or something) to continue one's defense against someone or something.

hold out (for someone or something) to insist on getting someone or something; to refuse to accept less than someone or something. (Informal.)

hold out the olive branch to offer to end a dispute and be friendly; to offer reconciliation. (The olive branch is a symbol of peace and reconciliation. A biblical reference.)

hold someone **hostage** to keep someone as a hostage.

hold someone **in high regard** to have very great respect for someone or something; to admire someone or something greatly.

hold someone or something **down 1.** to keep someone, something, or some creature down. **2.** to prevent someone or something from advancing.

hold someone or something **off 1.** to make someone or something wait. **2.** AND **keep** someone or something **off** to resist and attack by someone or something.

hold someone or something **out (of** something) **1.** to keep someone or something out of something. **2.** to set someone or something aside from the rest; to prevent someone or a group from participating.

hold someone or something **over** to keep a performer or performance for more performances. (Because the performance is a success.)

hold someone or something **up**
1. to keep someone or something upright. **2.** to rob someone or a group. **3.** to delay someone or something.

hold someone's **attention** to keep someone's attention; to keep someone interested.

hold something **out (to** someone**)** to offer something to someone.

hold the fort to take care of a place, such as a store or one's home.

hold true [for something] to be true; (for something) to remain true.

hold up (for someone or something**)** to wait; to stop and wait for someone.

hold up (on someone or something**)** to delay or postpone further action on someone or something.

hold up one's **end (of the bargain)** to do one's part as agreed; to attend to one's responsibilities as agreed.

hold water to be able to be proved; to be correct or true.

holder ['hold ə˞] *n.* something that holds something; something that keeps something in a certain position.

holdup ['hold əp] **1.** *n.* a robbery, especially one committed with a gun; a stickup. **2.** *n.* a delay; the reason that something is not moving properly.

hole ['hol] *n.* an opening made in or through a solid object; an opening in the surface of something.
→ a SQUARE PEG IN A ROUND HOLE
→ IN THE HOLE

→ MONEY BURNS A HOLE IN SOMEONE'S POCKET.
→ OUT OF THE HOLE
→ POKE A HOLE IN SOMETHING
→ POKE A HOLE THROUGH SOMETHING
→ PUNCH A HOLE IN SOMETHING

a **hole in one 1.** an instance of hitting a golf ball into a hole in only one try. (From the game of golf.) **2.** an instance of succeeding the first time.

holiday ['hɑl ə de] **1.** *n.* a period of time when most businesses and schools are closed in honor of someone or something. **2.** *n.* a holy day; a religious celebration.

holier-than-thou excessively pious; acting as though one is more virtuous than other people.

hollow ['hɑl o] **1.** *n.* an open space inside an object; a cavity. **2.** *n.* a small valley; a sunken area of land. **3.** *adj.* having an open space inside; not solid. (Adv: *hollowly.* Comp: *hollower;* sup: *hollowest.*) **4.** *adj.* sunken. (Adv: *hollowly.* Comp: *hollower;* sup: *hollowest.*)

hollow something **out** to make the inside of something hollow.

holster ['hol stə˞] *n.* a fabric or leather case for a gun, worn on the body or attached to a saddle.

holy ['hol i] *adj.* sacred; associated with divine matters. (Comp: *holier;* sup: *holiest.*)

homage ['ɑm ɪdʒ] praise, respect, and honor.
→ PAY HOMAGE TO SOMEONE

home ['hom] **1.** *n.* the place where one lives; one's house or apartment. **2.** *n.* the place where someone was born; the place that someone comes from; the place where someone grew up. **3.** *n.* an institution or building where people who need special care live. **4.** *n.* a place where something is found, based, or located; a place where something originated or was invented. **5.** the *adj.* use of ①, ②, ③, or ④. **6.** *adv.* at ① or ②; to ① or ②.

→ CHICKENS HAVE COME HOME TO ROOST
→ COME HOME (TO ROOST)
→ EAT SOMEONE OUT OF HOUSE AND HOME
→ FUNERAL HOME
→ HAMMER SOMETHING HOME
→ HIT HOME
→ KEEP THE HOME FIRES BURNING
→ MAKE ONESELF AT HOME
→ STRIKE HOME

home in (on someone or something) to aim directly at someone or something.

home office ['hom 'ɔf ɪs] **1.** *n.* the central office of a company. **2.** *n.* an office in one's home.

home on(to something) to aim directly at something; to fix some type of receiver on a signal source.

homemaker ['hom mek ɚ] *n.* a person who manages a home, especially a married woman who manages her home and, possibly, children.

homeowner ['hom o nɚ] *n.* someone who owns a home.

homesick ['hom sɪk] *adj.* sad and depressed because one is away from one's home.

homework ['hom wɚk] **1.** *n.* schoolwork that is to be completed at home or elsewhere outside the school building. (No plural.) **2.** *n.* preparation that

should be done before a meeting or discussion. (Figurative on ①. No plural.)

honest ['ɑn əst] **1.** *adj.* always telling the truth; not lying; able to be trusted. (Adv: *honestly*.) **2.** *adj.* obtained fairly and legally; not stolen. (Adv: *honestly*.) **3.** *adj.* sincere; appearing fair and ①. (Adv: *honestly*.)

honesty ['ɑn ɪs ti] *n.* the quality of being honest; truthfulness. (No plural.)

honey ['hʌn i] *n.* a sweet, sticky substance made by bees. (Plural only for types and instances.)

honeymoon ['hʌn i mun] **1.** *n.* the vacation that two newly married people take after the wedding. **2.** *n.* a calm period of good business or political relations, especially right after someone new has come to power.

The honeymoon is over. a phrase said when the early, pleasant beginning of something has ended.

honk ['hɔŋk] **1.** *n.* the sound made by a horn or a goose. **2.** *iv.* to make the sound of a horn or a goose. **3.** *tv.* to sound a horn; to cause a horn to make a noise.

honor ['ɑn ɚ] **1.** *n.* the respect or regard shown to someone or something. (No plural.) **2.** *n.* character and integrity; honesty and fairness; a way of being that earns trust. (No plural.) **3.** *n.* a pleasure; a privilege. **4.** *tv.* to hold someone in high regard; to respect someone. **5.** *tv.* to make a payment as agreed; for a bank to accept a

check and pay out the money that the check was written for.
→ DO THE HONORS
→ GUEST OF HONOR
→ ON ONE'S HONOR

honor someone's **check** to accept someone's personal check.

hood ['hʊd] **1.** *n.* a covering for the head and neck, sometimes attached to a coat and sometimes also covering the face. **2.** *n.* the metal panel that covers the top of the front of a car.

hoof ['hʊf, 'huf] *n., irreg.* the hard part on the bottom of the foot of a horse, deer, and certain other animals. (Plural: HOOVES.)

hook ['hʊk] **1.** *n.* a bent or curved piece of plastic, wood, wire, or metal, used to catch, pull, or hold something. **2.** *n.* [in boxing] a short blow given while one's elbow is bent. **3.** *tv.* to catch and pull something with ①.
→ GET (SOMEONE) OFF THE HOOK
→ GET OFF THE HOOK
→ LET SOMEONE OFF (THE HOOK)

hook in(to something) to connect into something.

hook someone or something **up (to** someone or something) AND **hook** someone or something **up (with** someone or something) to attach someone or something to someone or something.

hook someone or something **up (with** someone or something) Go to HOOK SOMEONE OR SOMETHING UP (TO SOMEONE OR SOMETHING).

hook something **into** something to connect something to something.

hook something **up** to set something up and get it working—

such as electricity, gas, water, telephone lines, etc.

hoot ['hut] **1.** *n.* the noise that an owl makes. **2.** *iv.* to make ①; to make a noise like ①.

hooves ['huvz] plural of HOOF.

hop ['hɑp] **1.** *n.* a small movement upward, like a jump. **2.** *n.* an airplane flight, especially a short one. **3.** *iv.* to jump up and down; to jump forward a small distance. **4.** *iv.* [for frogs, rabbits, kangaroos, etc.] to move by jumping.

hop in something to get into a car, truck, van, or taxi quickly to make a quick or short trip.

hop on something to board a plane, train, bus, or bicycle to make a quick trip.

hope ['hop] **1.** *n.* the happy feeling that something one wants to happen will actually happen. (No plural.) **2.** *n.* something that is desired; something that one wants to happen; an expectation. **3.** *tv.* to feel happy about and wish for something that one wants to happen in the future. (The object is a clause with THAT ⑦.)
→ CROSS ONE'S HEART (AND HOPE TO DIE)

hope against all hope to have hope even when the situation appears to be hopeless.

hope to do something to feel happy about and wish to do something in the future.

horizon [hə 'raɪ zən] *n.* the line in the distance where the sky seems to meet the earth.
→ ON THE HORIZON

horizontal [hor ə 'zɑn təl] *adj.* flat; parallel to flat ground; not up and down. (Adv: *horizontally.*)

horn ['horn] **1.** *n.* a hard, usually pointed growth on the heads of cattle, goats, antelope, sheep, etc. **2.** *n.* the hard substance that an animal's hoof or HORN as in ① is made of. (No plural.) **3.** *n.* a device that makes noise, as in a car or other vehicle. **4.** *n.* one of the brass musical instruments, such as the trumpet, the cornet, the tuba, the French horn, and the trombone, played by blowing air through a shaped tube. (Often in compounds.)
→ BLOW ONE'S OWN HORN
→ LOCK HORNS (WITH SOMEONE)
→ ON THE HORNS OF A DILEMMA
→ TAKE THE BULL BY THE HORNS
→ TOOT ONE'S OWN HORN

horn in (on someone**)** to attempt to displace someone.

hornet ['hor nɪt] *n.* a large kind of stinging wasp.
→ (AS) MAD AS A HORNET
→ STIR UP A HORNET'S NEST

horrible ['hor ə bəl] **1.** *adj.* causing horror or terror. (Adv: *horribly.*) **2.** *adj.* awful; bad. (Adv: *horribly.*)

horrify ['hor ə faɪ] *tv.* to frighten someone very badly; to terrify someone.

horror ['hor ɚ] **1.** *n.* intense dread or fear; fright. (Plural only for types and instances.) **2.** *n.* someone or something that causes fear or fright; an experience of ①.
→ IN HORROR

horse ['hors] *n.* an animal, larger than a donkey, that is used for carrying people and pulling heavy things, especially on farms.

→ BEAT A DEAD HORSE
→ DARK HORSE
→ EAT LIKE A HORSE
→ PUT THE CART BEFORE THE HORSE
→ STRAIGHT FROM THE HORSE'S MOUTH
→ WORK LIKE A HORSE

a **horse of a different color** See a HORSE OF ANOTHER COLOR.

a **horse of another color** and a **horse of a different color** another matter altogether.

horse sense common sense; practical thinking.

hose ['hoz] **1.** *n.* a flexible tube used to direct water or some other liquid. (Treated as singular. Plural: *hoses.*) **2.** *n.* men's socks, especially to go with formal clothing. (No plural. Treated as plural, but not countable. Number is expressed with *pair(s) of hose.*) **3.** *n.* women's long, sheer stockings, made of silk or nylon. (No plural. Treated as plural, but not countable. Number is expressed with *pair(s) of hose.*) **4.** *n.* PANTYHOSE. (No plural. Treated as plural, but not countable.)

hospital ['hɑs pɪt əl] *n.* a building where medical care for serious diseases and illnesses is provided.

host ['host] **1.** *n.* someone who receives and welcomes guests. (Male or female. Sometimes *hostess* is used for a female.) **2.** *n.* the person arranging a party or gathering, especially where food is served. (Male or female. Sometimes *hostess* is used for a female.) **3.** *n.* someone who introduces people on a television show; someone who has a talk show on television. **4.** *n.* a large number of people or things. **5.** *tv.* to be ③ on a television show. **6.** *tv.* to be ① or ② at a party.

hostage ['hɑs tɪdʒ] **1.** *n.* someone or something held by force, to be released only when stated demands are met. **2.** the *adj.* use of ①.
→ HOLD SOMEONE HOSTAGE
→ TAKE SOMEONE HOSTAGE

hot ['hɑt] **1.** *adj.* having a high temperature; not cold or warm. (Adv: *hotly.* Comp: *hotter;* sup: *hottest.*) **2.** *adj.* [of food] very spicy, causing a burning feeling in the mouth. (Adv: *hotly.* Comp: *hotter;* sup: *hottest.*) **3.** *adj.* very intense; excited or angry. (Figurative on ①. Adv: *hotly.* Comp: *hotter;* sup: *hottest.*) **4.** *adj.* currently popular. (Informal. Comp: *hotter;* sup: *hottest.*)
→ PIPING HOT
→ SELL LIKE HOT CAKES
→ STRIKE WHILE THE IRON IS HOT

hot on something enthusiastic about something; very much interested in something; knowledgeable about something. (Informal.)

hot under the collar very angry.

hotel [ho 'tɛl] *n.* a building where people can rent a place to stay while away from home on business or vacation.

hour ['aʊ ɚ] **1.** *n.* a unit of time measurement equal to 60 minutes or ¼₄ of a day. **2.** *n.* a period of time set aside for some activity. **3.** *n.* the distance that can be traveled in ①.
→ AT THE ELEVENTH HOUR
→ KEEP LATE HOURS
→ OFFICE HOURS
→ ON THE HOUR

hourly ['aʊ ɚ li] **1.** *adj.* happening every hour; happening once an hour. **2.** *adv.* every hour; once an hour.

house 1. ['haʊs] *n., irreg.* a building where a person or a family lives; a home. (Plural: ['haʊ zəz] or ['haʊ səz].) **2.** ['haʊs] *n.* a household; all the people who live in ①. (No plural.) **3.** ['haʊs] *n., irreg.* a legislature; a legislative body. **4.** ['haʊs] *n., irreg.* the part of a theater where the audience sits. **5.** ['haʊz] *tv.* to provide shelter to someone or some creature.
→ BRING THE HOUSE DOWN
→ EAT SOMEONE OUT OF HOUSE AND HOME
→ ON THE HOUSE
→ TREE HOUSE

house pet ['haʊs pet] *n.* a dog, cat, bird, fish, or other animal kept in a house as a PET.

housebreak ['haʊs brek] *tv., irreg.* to train a pet not to defecate or urinate in the house, or in the case of a cat, outside its special place. (Past tense: HOUSEBROKE; past participle: HOUSEBROKEN.)

housebroke ['haʊs brok] past tense of HOUSEBREAK.

housebroken ['haʊs brok ən] past participle of HOUSEBREAK.

household ['haʊs hold] **1.** *n.* the group of people who live in a house or apartment. **2.** *adj.* found in ①; associated with ①.

housekeeper ['haʊs kip ɚ] **1.** *n.* someone who is paid to manage household chores. **2.** *n.* someone who manages the cleaning in a hotel, resort, hospital, or large building. **3.** *n.* a person who is paid to clean someone's house. (Euphemistic.)

houseplant ['haʊs plænt] *n.* a plant usually grown indoors.

housework ['haʊs wɝk] *n.* cooking, cleaning, washing, and other household tasks. (No plural.)

how [haʊ] **1.** *interrog.* in what way?; by what means? **2.** *interrog.* to what extent?; to what degree? **3.** *interrog.* in what condition? **4.** *conj.* the way in which; the manner in which.

how many [haʊ 'mɛn i] *interrog.* in what number(s)?

how much [haʊ 'mʌtʃ] *interrog.* in what amount?

however [haʊ 'ɛv ɝ] **1.** *adv.* but; nevertheless; in spite of something. **2.** *adv.* no matter how. (Followed by an adjective or adverb.) **3.** *conj.* in whatever way; by whatever means.

howl [haʊl] **1.** *n.* a long wail, as with the cry of a wolf or the sound of a high wind. **2.** *iv.* to make ①.

huddle ['hʌd l] **1.** *n.* a group of people crowded together. **2.** *n.* [in football] a group of players close together, planning the next play. **3.** *iv.* [for a number of people] to stand closely together in a small space, especially to keep warm. **4.** *iv.* [for a creature] to curl up somewhere; to bring one's arms and legs close to the body, as if to keep warm.

huddle (up) (together) to bunch up together.

hue [hju] *n.* color; a variety, shade, or intensity of a color.

hue and cry a loud public protest or opposition.

huff and puff to breath very hard; to pant as one exerts effort.

hug ['hʌg] **1.** *n.* an act of holding someone or something in one's arms in a friendly or loving way. **2.** *tv.* to hold someone as in ①. **3.** *tv.* to stay close to a curb, railing, wall, or some other object as one moves along.

huge ['hjudʒ] **1.** *adj.* [of size] very large or enormous. (Adv: *hugely.* Comp: *huger;* sup: *hugest.*) **2.** *adj.* of a notable extent; [of extent, degree, or amount] notably large. (Adv: *hugely.* Comp: *huger;* sup: *hugest.*)

hum ['hʌm] **1.** *n.* a long, vibrating sound, like a long "mmmm-mmm"; a low murmur; a quiet buzzing sound. (No plural.) **2.** *iv.* to make a long, vibrating sound, like a long "mmmmmmmmm"; to sing with one's mouth closed. **3.** *tv.* to sing musical notes with one's mouth closed, as in ②.

human ['hju mən] **1.** *n.* a person; a HUMAN BEING. **2.** the *adj.* use of ①. (Adv: *humanly.*) **3.** *adj.* showing feelings that people normally show. (Adv: *humanly.*)
→ EVERYTHING HUMANLY POSSIBLE
→ the MILK OF HUMAN KINDNESS

human being ['hju mən 'bi ɪŋ] *n.* a person; a human creature, especially considering special human characteristics, such as intelligence, kindness, sympathy, etc. (The same as a HUMAN.)

human race *n.* all humans as a group of people. (No plural.)

humble ['hʌm bəl] **1.** *adj.* aware of one's faults; modest. (Adv: *humbly.* Comp: *humbler;* sup: *humblest.*) **2.** *adj.* simple; lowly; not elegant. (Adv: *humbly.* Comp: *humbler;* sup: *humblest.*) **3.** *tv.* to lower the position of someone; to cause someone to become ①.
→ EAT HUMBLE PIE

humid ['hju mɪd] *adj.* [of weather] damp; [of air] containing much moisture. (Adv: *humidly.*)

humor ['hju mɚ] **1.** *n.* the quality of being funny. (No plural.) **2.** *tv.* to tolerate someone who behaves oddly; to accept someone who has strange whims or desires.
→ SENSE OF HUMOR

humorous ['hju mə rəs] *adj.* funny; amusing; having humor. (Adv: *humorously.*)

hump ['hʌmp] *n.* a large, rounded bump or swelling.
→ OVER THE HUMP

hunch ['hʌntʃ] *n.* a guess based on how one feels.

hunch up to squeeze or pull the parts of one's body together.

hundred ['hʌn drəd] **1.** *n.* the number 100; the number between 99 and 101. (Additional forms as with *two hundred, three hundred, four hundred,* etc.) **2.** *n.* 100 people or things.
→ ONE IN A HUNDRED

hung ['hʌŋ] **1.** a past tense and past participle of HANG. **2.** *adj.* [of a jury] unable to reach a decision; [of a jury] not having a majority.

hunger ['hʌŋ gɚ] **1.** *n.* a general lack of food. (No plural.) **2.** *n.* the feeling of a need for something. (Figurative on ①. No plural.)

hunger for something to have a strong desire for something.

hungry ['hʌŋ gri] *adj.* wanting food; lacking food; having an empty stomach. (Adv: *hungrily.* Comp: *hungrier;* sup: *hungriest.*)
→ (AS) HUNGRY AS A BEAR

hungry for someone or something desiring someone or something.

hunk ['hʌŋk] *n.* a large, solid amount of something.

hunt ['hʌnt] **1.** *tv.* to search for and kill animals for food or for sport. **2.** *iv.* to search for and kill animals as in ①.

hunt for someone or something to search for someone or something.

hunt high and low for someone or something AND **search high and low for** someone or something to look carefully in every possible place for someone or something.

hunt someone or something **down 1.** to chase and catch someone or something. **2.** to locate someone or something.

hunt someone or something **out** to find someone or something even if concealed.

hunt someone or something **up** to seek someone or something.

hunt through something to search through the contents of something; to search among things.

hunter ['hʌn tɚ] *n.* someone who hunts; someone who searches for and kills animals for food or sport.

hurl ['hɚl] **1.** *tv.* to throw someone or something with force. **2.** *tv.* to shout something negative, such as an insult or bad words.

hurl an insult (at someone**)** to direct an insult at someone; to say something insulting directly to someone.

hurl someone or something **down** to throw or push someone or something downward to the ground.

hurry ['hɚ i] **1.** *iv.* to move quickly or briskly. **2.** *tv.* to cause someone or something to move quickly or briskly. **3.** *n.* a rush; an effort to be fast or faster.

hurry away AND **hurry off** to leave in a hurry.

hurry back (to someone or something**)** to return to someone or something immediately or as fast as possible.

hurry off Go to HURRY AWAY.

hurry on Go to HURRY UP.

hurry someone or something **in(to** something**)** to make someone or something go into something fast.

hurry someone or something **up** to make someone or something go or work faster.

hurry up AND **hurry on** to move faster.

hurt ['hɚt] **1.** *n.* pain of the body or emotions; an ache. (Plural only for types and instances.) **2.** *tv., irreg.* to injure a part of the body; to harm one's mental processes or emotional well-being. (Past tense and past participle: hurt.) **3.** *tv., irreg.* to have a bad effect on some-

one or something; to be bad for someone or something. **4.** *tv., irreg.* to cause pain in something; to give someone pain. **5.** *iv., irreg.* to feel pain.
→ CRY BEFORE ONE IS HURT

husband ['hʌz bənd] *n.* a married man; the man that a woman is married to.

hush ['hʌʃ] **1.** *n.* silence; quiet; calm. (No plural.) **2.** *tv.* to cause someone or something to be calm and quiet. **3.** *iv.* to become calm and quiet.

hush money money paid as a bribe to persuade someone to remain silent and not reveal certain information.

hush someone or something **up** to make someone or something be quiet.

hush something **up** to keep something from public knowledge.

hush up to be quiet; to get quiet; to stop talking.

husky ['hʌs ki] **1.** *adj.* [of a voice] low sounding as if the speaker has a sore throat. (Adv: huskily. Comp: huskier; sup: huskiest.) **2.** *adj.* big and strong; muscular. (Adv: huskily. Comp: huskier; sup: huskiest.) **3.** *n.* a kind of dog that pulls sleds in the far north.

hut ['hʌt] *n.* a small shelter; a humble dwelling.

hutch ['hʌtʃ] **1.** *n.* a cage for rabbits or other small animals. **2.** *n.* a cupboard or cabinet with shelves.

hyena [haɪ 'i nə] *n.* a wild, doglike animal of Africa that eats meat and has a loud cry that sounds like laughter.

hymn ['hɪm] *n.* a religious song of praise meant to be sung by worshipers.

hype ['haɪp] **1.** *n.* an extreme amount of publicity; exaggerated praise used for publicity. (No plural.) **2.** *tv.* to provide ① for someone or something.

hyphen ['haɪ fən] *n.* the mark of punctuation (-). (It is placed between the parts of some compound words, between the words in certain phrases, or between syllables where a word has been split between two lines of print.)

hypnotism ['hɪp nə tɪz əm] **1.** *n.* hypnotizing people as a method of exploring and influencing the mind. (No plural.) **2.** *n.* the process of hypnotizing someone. (No plural.)

hypnotize ['hɪp nə taɪz] *tv.* to place someone in a sleeplike condition.

I [ˈaɪ] *pron.* the first-person singular pronoun—in writing, it refers to the writer, and in speaking, it refers to the speaker. (Used as the subject of a sentence or a clause. Compare this with ME.)

ice [ˈaɪs] **1.** *n.* frozen water. (No plural. Number is expressed with *piece(s)* or *cube(s) of ice.*) **2.** *tv.* to cover a cake with icing or frosting. (See also ICING.)
→ BREAK THE ICE
→ ON THIN ICE
→ PUT SOMETHING ON ICE
→ SKATE ON THIN ICE

ice cream [ˈaɪs ˈkrim] **1.** *n.* a frozen dessert or snack food made from cream or milk and some kind of fruit or other flavoring. (No plural.) **2.** the *adj.* use of ①. (Hyphenated.)

ice cube [ˈaɪs kjub] *n.* a small cube of ice, used to make drinks and liquids cold.

ice over [for water] to freeze and develop a covering of ice.

ice skate [ˈaɪs(s) sket] **1.** *n.* a boot with a thin blade on the bottom that allows one to glide on top of ice. **2.** *iv.* to glide across ice while wearing a pair of ①. (Hyphenated. Can be shortened to SKATE.)

ice something down to cool something with ice.

ice up to become icy.

iceberg [ˈaɪs bɚg] *n.* an enormous piece of ice floating in the sea.

icicle [ˈaɪs sɪ kəl] *n.* a pointed spike of ice that hangs from something such as a tree branch.

icing [ˈaɪ sɪŋ] *n.* cake frosting; a sweet coating for cakes, cookies, and other desserts. (No plural.)

icy [ˈaɪ si] **1.** *adj.* covered with or made of ice. (Adv: *icily.* Comp: *icier;* sup: *iciest.*) **2.** *adj.* very cold; freezing cold. (Adv: *icily.* Comp: *icier;* sup: *iciest.*)

I'd [ˈaɪd] **1.** *cont.* I would. **2.** *cont.* I had. (Where HAD is an auxiliary.)

idea [aɪ ˈdi ə] **1.** *n.* a thought produced by the mind; an opinion. **2.** *n.* a picture of something produced by the mind; a mental picture. **3.** *n.* a suggestion; a plan.
→ FLIRT WITH THE IDEA OF DOING SOMETHING

ideal [aɪ ˈdil] *adj.* perfect; perfectly suitable. (Adv: *ideally.*)

the **ideal** *n.* the best example of something; the perfect type. (No plural. Treated as singular.)

ideals *n.* high moral standards; strong moral beliefs.

identical [aɪ ˈdɛn tɪ kəl] *adj.* equal; exactly alike. (Adv: *identically* […ɪk li].)

identical to someone or something exactly the same as someone or something.

identification [aɪ dɛn tə fə ˈke ʃən] **1.** *n.* identifying someone or something; the condition of being identified. (Plural only for types and instances.) **2.** *n.* some kind of document that identifies someone; something that proves who someone is. (No plural.)

identify [aɪ ˈdɛn tə faɪ] **1.** *tv.* to state who or what someone or something is; to allow the identification of someone or something. **2.** *tv.* to reveal someone's identity.

identify someone or something **with** someone or something to associate people and things, in any combination.

identity [aɪ 'dɛn tə ti] *n.* who or what a certain person or thing is. (No plural form.)
→ a CASE OF MISTAKEN IDENTITY

idiom ['ɪd i əm] **1.** *n.* a phrase whose meaning is different from the combined literal meanings of the separate words that make up the phrase. **2.** *n.* a mode of expression or design.

idiot ['ɪd i ət] *n.* a foolish person; a stupid person.

idle something **away** to waste one's time in idleness; to waste a period of time, such as an afternoon, evening, or one's life.

if ['ɪf] **1.** *conj.* in the event [that something is the case]; on the condition [that something is the case]. **2.** *conj.* whether. (Often introduces an indirect question.) **3.** *conj.* although; even though.

if not otherwise; if that does not happen; if that is not the case; if that is not so.

if so if that is the case; if that is so; if that happens.

if worst comes to worst in the worst possible situation; if things really get bad.

ignorant ['ɪg nə rənt] **1.** *adj.* without knowledge; without information; uninformed. (Adv: *ignorantly.*) **2.** *adj.* caused by a lack of

knowledge; resulting from a lack of knowledge. (Adv: *ignorantly.*)
→ PLAY IGNORANT

ignore [ɪg 'nɔr] *tv.* to pay no attention to someone or something.

I'll ['aɪl] *cont.* I will.

ill ['ɪl] **1.** *adj.* sick; not well; not healthy. **2.** *adv.* badly. (Before a participle or certain adjectives. Usually hyphenated.) **3.** *n.* harm. (No plural.)
→ FALL ILL
→ SPEAK ILL OF SOMEONE

ill will ['ɪl 'wɪl] *n.* angry feelings or bad intentions. (No plural. Treated as singular.)

ill-disposed to doing something not friendly; not favorable; not well disposed.

illegal [ɪ 'li gəl] *adj.* not legal; against the law. (Adv: *illegally.*)

ill-gotten gains money or other possessions acquired in a dishonest or illegal fashion.

illness ['ɪl nəs] **1.** *n.* a sickness; a disease. **2.** *n.* a period of being sick.

ills *n.* troubles.

illusion [ɪ 'lu ʒən] **1.** *n.* a vision of something that is not really there; a false image. **2.** *n.* a false belief; something that seems to be true but is not true.

I'm ['aɪm] *cont.* I am.

image ['ɪm ɪdʒ] **1.** *n.* that which is seen in a mirror or similar surface. **2.** *n.* a sculpture, painting, or other form of art that represents someone or something; a picture or photograph of someone or something. **3.** *n.* a picture of something in one's mind; a mental picture. **4.** *n.* the opinion that people have about a certain person or thing; someone's or something's reputation.

imagery ['ɪm ɪdʒ ri] *n.* words, music, or pictures that represent or create images, often making one think about situations or feelings. (No plural. Treated as singular.)

imaginary [ɪ 'mædʒ ə nɛr i] *adj.* existing only in the mind; not real. (Adv: *imaginarily* [ɪ mædʒ ə 'nɛr ə li].)

imagination [ɪ mædʒ ə 'ne ʃən] **1.** *n.* the part of the mind that produces thoughts and images that are not real or not experienced; the part of the mind that imagines things. (No plural.) **2.** *n.* the ability to think of new and interesting ideas; the ability to imagine something. (No plural.)

imagine [ɪ 'mædʒ ɪn] **1.** *tv.* to think of someone or something; to form an image of someone or something in one's mind. (The object can be a clause with THAT ⑦.) **2.** *tv.* to think something; to believe something; to suppose something; to guess something. (The object is a clause with THAT ⑦.)

imitate ['ɪm ə tet] **1.** *tv.* to attempt to copy the style, behavior, or success of someone whom one admires or wants to be like. **2.** *tv.* to copy the behavior, speech, and movement of someone for amusement.

imitation [ɪm ə 'te ʃən] **1.** *n.* copying someone's actions or deeds; copying something. (No plural.) **2.** *n.* a copy; a duplicate. **3.** *n.* an act of imitating someone or something. **4.** *adj.* fake; artificial; resembling something.

immaculate [ɪ 'mæk jə lɪt] *adj.* pure; absolutely clean; spotless. (Adv: *immaculately.*)

immaterial [ɪm ə 'tɪr i əl] *adj.* not relevant; having nothing to do with something. (Adv: *immaterially.*)

immediate [ɪ 'mid i ɪt] **1.** *adj.* happening now; happening at once. (Adv: *immediately.*) **2.** *adj.* closest to someone or something in space or time; next to someone or something. (Adv: *immediately.*)

immediate occupancy [of an apartment or house] ready to be moved into at this moment.

immemorial [ɪm mə 'mor i əl] [since a time] so long ago that no one can remember the details, origin, date, issues, etc.
→ SINCE TIME IMMEMORIAL

immense [ɪ 'mɛns] *adj.* very large; huge; enormous. (Adv: *immensely.*)

immerse oneself **in** something [ɪ 'mɚs...] to become deeply involved with something; to become absorbed in something.

immerse someone or something **in** something [ɪ 'mɚs...] to put someone or something into a liquid; to put someone or something underwater.

immersion [ɪ 'mɚ ʒən] **1.** *n.* placing something under water or in a liquid. (Plural only for types and instances.) **2.** *n.* being completely involved in something. (Figurative on ①. No plural.)

immigrate ['ɪm ə gret] *iv.* to come into a new country to live.

immodest [ɪ 'mɑd əst] **1.** *adj.* not modest; revealing; shameless. (Adv: *immodestly.*) **2.** *adj.* not modest about oneself; often bragging. (Adv: *immodestly.*)

immoral [ɪ 'mɔr əl] *adj.* without morals; not moral; breaking moral rules. (Adv: *immorally.*)

immortal [ɪ 'mɔr təl] **1.** *adj.* everlasting; lasting forever; never dying; living forever. (Adv: *immortally.*) **2.** *adj.* continuing to be remembered forever; never forgotten. (Adv: *immortally.*)

immune (to something) [ɪ 'mjun …] **1.** protected against a certain disease, either naturally or through medication. **2.** not in danger of being affected by something; secure from the danger of something.

immunize someone **against** something to vaccinate someone against some disease; to do a medical procedure that causes a resistance or immunity to a disease to develop in a person.

impact 1. ['ɪm pækt] *n.* the crash of objects striking one another with force. **2.** ['ɪm pækt] *n.* the influence or effect of someone or something. (Figurative on ①.) **3.** [ɪm 'pækt] *tv.* to crash into something.
→ UPON IMPACT

impasse ['ɪm pæs] *n.* a place where movement or progress is blocked by something; a deadlock. (No plural form.)
→ REACH AN IMPASSE

impatient [ɪm 'pe ʃənt] *adj.* not patient; not able to wait for someone or something. (Adv: *impatiently.*)

implant something **in(to)** someone or something to embed something into someone or something.

implicate someone **in** something to say that someone is involved in something.

imply [ɪm 'plaɪ] *tv.* to suggest something; to indicate something without actually saying it. (The object is a clause with THAT ⑦.)

impolite [ɪm pə 'laɪt] *adj.* rude; not polite; not courteous. (Adv: *impolitely.*)

import 1. [ɪm 'port] *tv.* to bring in (to one country) a product from a foreign country. **2.** ['ɪm port] *n.* a product that is brought into one country from another country.

importance [ɪm 'port ns] **1.** *n.* the condition of being important. (No plural.) **2.** *n.* the relative position or rank of someone or something. (No plural.)

important [ɪm 'port nt] *adj.* having a great effect, value, or influence. (Adv: *importantly.*)

impose something **(up)on** someone to force something on someone.

impose (up)on someone to make a bothersome request of someone.

impress someone **with** someone or something to awe someone with someone or something.

impress something **(up)on** someone to make someone fully aware of something.

imprint something **into** something
Go to IMPRINT SOMETHING ON(TO) SOMETHING.

imprint something **on(to)** something **1.** to print something onto something. **2.** AND **imprint** something **into** something to record something firmly in the memory of someone. **3.** AND **imprint** something **into** something to make a permanent record of something in an animal's brain.

imprison someone **in** something to lock someone up in something.

improve (up)on something to make something better.

improvise on something [for a musician] to create a new piece of music on an existing musical theme.

impulse ['ɪm pəls] **1.** *n.* a short burst of electrical energy. **2.** *n.* the sudden desire to do something; a whim. (Figurative on ①.)
→ ON IMPULSE

impure [ɪm 'pjʊr] **1.** *adj.* not pure; dirty; mixed with other things. (Adv: *impurely.*) **2.** *adj.* not morally pure. (Adv: *impurely.*)

in [ɪn] **1.** *prep.* inside something; within something; surrounded by something else. **2.** *prep.* into something; entering into a space; going through a boundary and to a position that is surrounded by something else. **3.** *prep.* at some point during a certain time period. **4.** *prep.* after a certain period of time. **5.** *prep.* with something or using something, especially a language or a way of writing or expressing something. **6.** *adv.* inward; indoors; going into something; in a way that someone or something will be in a position that is surrounded by something else. **7.** *adv.* at home; at one's office; available.

in a dead heat finishing a race at exactly the same time; tied. (Here, *dead* means "exact" or "total.")

in a flash quickly; immediately.

in a huff in an angry or offended manner.

in a little bit in a small amount of time.

in a mad rush in a hurry; in a busy rush.

in a nutshell [of news or information] in a (figuratively) very small container like a NUTSHELL; stated in just a few words.

in a pinch if absolutely necessary; if there is no other alternative.

in a rut Go to (STUCK) IN A RUT.

in a (tight) spot caught in a problem; in a difficult position.

in a tizzy an excited and confused condition; a fuss.

in a vicious circle in a situation in which the solution of one problem leads to a second problem, and the solution of the second problem brings back the first problem, etc.

in a world of one's **own** aloof; detached; self-centered.

in addition (to something**)** additionally; further; moreover; as an additional thing or person.

in advance [of something given, paid, or provided] before it is due.

in agreement in harmony; agreeing.

in back of someone or something behind someone or something.

in bad faith without sincerity; with bad or dishonest intent; with duplicity.

in bad taste AND **in poor taste** rude; vulgar; obscene.

in between located in the middle of two things.

in black and white in writing or printing; made official by being written or printed.

in bloom with many flowers; at the peak of blooming.

in blossom with many flowers; at the peak of blooming.

in broad daylight publicly visible in the daytime.

in bulk in large quantities or amounts, rather than smaller, more convenient quantities or amounts.

in case in the event [that] something happens; preparing for something that may happen.

in contempt (of court) showing disrespect for a judge or courtroom procedures.

in creation Go to ON EARTH.

in custody (of someone or something**)** AND **in** someone's or something's **custody** the condition of being kept guarded by police.

in debt having debts; having much debt; owing money.

in deep water in a dangerous or vulnerable situation; in a serious situation; in trouble.

in denial in a state of refusing to believe something that is true.

in detail with lots of details; giving all the details.

in disguise hidden behind a disguise; looking like something else.

in earnest [done] with good and honest intentions.

in effect 1. in existence; applicable. **2.** producing a particular effect; effectively.

in essence basically; essentially.

in existence now existing; currently and actually being.

in fact truthfully; actually.

in fashion fitting in well with the clothing that has been designed for a particular season of a particular year.

in fine feather in good humor; in good health.

in flight while flying.

in full swing in progress; operating or running without restraint.

in general referring to the entire class being discussed, without being specific; speaking broadly of the entire range of possibilities; in most cases or situations.

in good condition Go to IN GOOD SHAPE.

in good shape AND **in good condition** physically and functionally sound and sturdy. (Used for both people and things.)

in hand controlled; under control.

in heat [of animals] in a period of sexual excitement; in estrus.

in heaven in a state of absolute bliss or happiness.

in horror with intense shock or disgust.

in ink written or signed with a pen that uses ink.

in its entirety AND **in their entirety** in a state of completeness.

in jeopardy in danger; at risk; at hazard.

in labor [of a woman] experiencing the pains and exertion of childbirth.

in less than no time very quickly.

in many respects Go to IN SOME RESPECTS.

in memory of someone to continue the good memories of someone; in honor of a deceased person.

in midair in a point high in the air.

in mint condition in perfect condition.

in name only nominally; not actual, only by terminology.

in need (of something) [of someone or some creature] requiring something.

in neutral with the shift lever of a vehicle in the position where the motor is running but is not powering the wheels or other moving parts.

in no mood to do something not to feel like doing something; to wish not to do something.

in nothing flat in exactly no time at all.

in one ear and out the other [for something to be] ignored; [for something to be] unheard or unheeded.

in one fell swoop Go to AT ONE FELL SWOOP.

in one's birthday suit naked; nude.

in one's blood Go to IN THE BLOOD.

in one's mind's eye in one's mind.

in one's or **its prime** at one's or its peak or best time.

in one's right mind sane; rational and sensible. (Often in the negative.)

in one's second childhood being interested in people or things that normally interest children.

in one's spare time in one's extra time; in the time not reserved for doing something else.

in over one's head with more difficulties than one can manage.

in park [of an automobile transmission] having the gears locked so the automobile cannot move.

in pencil written or signed with a pencil.

in person [with someone] actually present in a place rather than appearing in a film, on a television screen, or through a radio broadcast.

in poor taste Go to IN BAD TASTE.

in print [for a book] to be available for sale. (Compare this with OUT OF PRINT.)

in proportion AND **out of proportion** showing the right or wrong proportion relative to something else.

in public in a place or way so that other people can see or know about something.

in rags in worn-out and torn clothing.

in reality viewing things realistically; really; actually.

in receipt of something in a state of having received something.

in recent memory the period of time in which things that can be remembered happened.

in return by way of giving something back; as a way of paying someone back for something; as part of an exchange.

in round figures Go to IN ROUND NUMBERS.

in round numbers AND **in round figures** as an estimated number; as a figure that has been rounded off to the closest whole number.

in ruin in a state of having been destroyed.

in season 1. currently available for selling. (Some foods and other things are available only at certain seasons.) **2.** legally able to be caught or hunted. **3.** [of a dog] in estrus. (See also IN HEAT.)

in secret secretly.

in session [of a court, congress, or other organization] operating or functioning.

in seventh heaven in a very happy state.

in shape [of someone] in good physical condition.

in short order very quickly.

in short supply scarce.

in sight able to be seen.

in some respects AND **in many respects** with regard to some or many details. (Here RESPECTS = aspects.)

in someone's or something's custody Go to IN CUSTODY (OF SOMEONE OR SOMETHING).

in someone's (own) (best) interests to someone's own advantage; as a benefit to oneself. (Compare this with IN THE INTEREST(S) OF SOMETHING.)

in someone's prayers [of someone] remembered and called by name when someone prays.

in spite of someone or something without regard to someone or something; even though another course had been prescribed; ignoring a warning.

in stock readily available, as with goods in a store.

in storage in a place where things are stored or kept.

in surgery involved in surgery.

in tandem in single file.

in tatters in torn pieces of cloth.

in terms of something relating to something; with regard to something.

in the affirmative in the form of an answer that means yes.

in the air everywhere; all about. (Also used literally.)

in the bargain in addition to what was agreed on.

in the black not in debt; in a financially profitable condition.

in the blood AND **in one's blood** built into one's personality or character.

in the cards in the future.

in the context of something under the circumstances in which something has happened.

in the doghouse in trouble; in (someone's) disfavor.

in the doldrums sluggish; inactive; in low spirits.

in the flesh bodily or physically present; in person.

in the forefront (of something**)** Go to AT THE FOREFRONT (OF SOMETHING).

in the gutter [for a person to be] in a bad state, mentally and physically.

in the hole in debt.

in the interest(s) of something in order to advance or improve something.

in the interim (between things**)** in the meantime; in the time between the ending of something and the beginning of something else.

in the know knowledgeable.

in the lap of luxury in luxurious surroundings.

in the line of duty as part of one's expected duties.

in the long run over a long period of time; ultimately.

in the meantime the period of time between two things; the period of time between now and when something is supposed to happen.

in the money wealthy; having succeeded financially.

in the mood for something AND **in the mood to** do something having the proper state of mind for a particular situation or for doing something.

in the mood to do something Go to IN THE MOOD FOR SOMETHING.

in the neighborhood of something Go to (SOMEWHERE) IN THE NEIGHBORHOOD OF SOMETHING.

in the nick of time just in time; at the last possible instant; just before it's too late.

in the nude in a state of nudity.

in the picture of (good) health in a very healthy condition.

in the pink (of condition) in very good health; in very good condition, physically or emotionally.

in the prime of life in the best and most productive period of one's life.

in the public eye publicly; visible to all; conspicuous.

in the rear located in the space or area behind someone or something.

in the red in debt.

in the right on the moral or legal side of an issue; on the right side of an issue.

in the right place at the right time in the location where something is to happen exactly when it happens. (Usually about something good.)

in the same boat in the same situation; having the same problem.

in the same breath [stated or said] almost at the same time; as part of the same thought or conversation.

in the twinkling of an eye very quickly.

in the wind about to happen.

in the world Go to ON EARTH.

in the wrong on the wrong or illegal side of an issue; guilty or in error.

in the wrong place at the wrong time in the location where something is to happen exactly when it happens. (Usually about something bad.)

in their entirety Go to IN ITS ENTIRETY.

in theory according to a theory; theoretically.

in time within the proper time; before the deadline; before the time limit; within the allotted time.

in times past long ago; in previous times.

in top form 1. [of someone or some creature] in very good physical condition. **2.** able to make witty remarks and clever statements quickly and easily.

in tow being towed [by someone]; closely following; under someone's control.

in transit while in the process of being transported.

in trouble in danger; at risk.

in tune AND **out of tune** in or out of a state where musical notes are at their proper intervals so that none are flat or sharp.

in two shakes of a lamb's tail in a very short time; very quickly.

in unison […'ju nə sən] **1.** acting as one; together and at the same time. **2.** [of musical notes, instru-ments, or voices] having the same pitch.

in vain futile(ly); without having the result one wanted.

inaccurate [ɪn 'æk jə rɪt] *adj.* not accurate; incorrect. (Adv: *inaccurately.*)

inactive [ɪn 'æk tɪv] **1.** *adj.* not active; not moving. (Adv: *inactively.*) **2.** *adj.* [of someone] not or no longer working actively or being actively involved. (Adv: *inactively.*) **3.** *adj.* having no effect; [of a chemical] not reacting. (Adv: *inactively.*)

inadequate [ɪn 'æd ə kwɪt] *adj.* not adequate; not enough; not good enough. (Adv: *inadequately.*)

incarcerate someone **in** something to imprison someone in something.

inch ['ɪntʃ] **1.** *n.* a unit of measurement of distance, equal to $1/12$ of a foot or approximately 2.54 centimeters. **2.** *iv.* to move very slowly; to move a distance equal to ① at a time.
→ EVERY INCH A SOMETHING
→ EVERY INCH THE SOMETHING
→ WITHIN AN INCH OF ONE'S LIFE

inch by inch one inch at a time; little by little.

incline 1. ['ɪn klaɪn] *n.* a slant; a slope; a surface that is on an angle to flat ground. **2.** [ɪn 'klaɪn] *iv.* to slant; to slope.

incline toward someone or something **1.** to lean or slant toward someone or something. **2.** to favor or "lean" toward choosing someone or something.

inclined to do something to tend to do something; to "lean" toward doing something.

include [ɪn 'klud] **1.** *tv.* [for something] to contain something or to have something among its parts. **2.** *tv.* [for someone] to cause someone or something to be a part of something; to add something to something else.

include someone **in (**something**)** to invite someone to participate in something.

income ['ɪn kəm] *n.* the amount of money received as wages, interest, or similar payments; money received in exchange for goods or services.

income tax ['ɪn kəm tæks] *n.* a federal, state, or local tax on income that has been earned.

incorporate someone or something **in(to)** something to plan to include someone or something in something; to combine someone or something into something.

incorrect [ɪn kə 'rɛkt] *adj.* not correct; wrong; false. (Adv: *incorrectly.*)

increase 1. ['ɪn kris] *n.* growth; becoming larger. (Plural only for types and instances.) **2.** [ɪn 'kris] *iv.* to become larger, faster, or more powerful; to become larger in number or amount. **3.** [ɪn 'kris] *tv.* to cause something to become larger, faster, or more powerful; to cause something to become larger in number or amount.

incubator ['ɪŋ kjə bet ɚ] **1.** *n.* a container that keeps eggs warm until they hatch. **2.** *n.* a special container or device in which babies that are born too early are kept for warmth and care.

indeed [ɪn 'did] **1.** *adv.* very much so; quite. **2.** *adv.* in fact; actually. **3.** *interj.* Amazing!

indent [ɪn 'dɛnt] *tv.* [in writing or typing] to begin a line a few spaces farther from the edge or margin than the other lines, as at the beginning of a paragraph.

indentation [ɪn dɛn 'te ʃən] **1.** *n.* a notch; a dent; a cut. **2.** *n.* indenting lines of type or writing. (Plural only for types and instances.)

independence [ɪn dɪ 'pɛn dəns] *n.* freedom from someone or some government; liberty. (No plural.)

independent [ɪn dɪ 'pɛn dənt] **1.** *adj.* not dependent on someone or something; not controlled by others; not ruled by other people or countries. (Adv: *independently.*) **2.** *adj.* not needing the support of others; self-supporting. (Adv: *independently.*) **3.** *adj.* separate; distinct from other things. (Adv: *independently.*) **4.** *n.* a politician or a voter who does not belong to a political party.

index ['ɪn dɛks] **1.** *n., irreg.* an alphabetical list of topics showing where each topic can be found in the main part of a book, report, magazine, journal, etc. (Plural: *indexes* or INDICES.) **2.** *n., irreg.* a scale where prices or amounts of certain things are compared with the prices or amounts of those same things at an earlier date. **3.** *tv.* to locate important topics and list them and their locations, as in ①.

indicate ['ɪn də ket] **1.** *tv.* to point something out verbally; to state a fact. (The object is a clause with THAT ⑦.) **2.** *tv.* to make something known; to draw someone's attention to something. (The object can be a clause with THAT ⑦.) **3.** *tv.* [for a meter, chart, signal] to show specific information. (The object can be a clause with THAT ⑦.)

indices ['ɪn dɪ siz] a plural of INDEX.

indigestion [ɪn də 'dʒɛs tʃən] *n.* an upset stomach; the digestion of food that causes pain. (No plural.)

individual [ɪn də 'vɪ dʒu əl] **1.** *n.* a person; one person. **2.** *adj.* separate; single. (Adv: *individually*.)

indoor ['ɪn dor] *adj.* inside a building; kept within walls and under a roof. (Prenominal only.)

indoors [ɪn 'dorz] *adv.* in or into a building.

industry ['ɪn də stri] **1.** *n.* the production of goods; the manufacture of products. (No plural.) **2.** *n.* the business activity concerning a specific kind of product or service. **3.** *n.* hard work or labor.

inedible [ɪn 'ɛd ə bəl] *adj.* not able to be eaten; not good for eating. (Adv: *inedibly*.)

inf. an abbreviation of INFINITIVE FORM.

infant ['ɪn fənt] **1.** *n.* a baby; a young child. **2.** the *adj.* use of ①.

infection [ɪn 'fɛk ʃən] **1.** *n.* the entrance and growth of disease-producing organisms in the body. (Plural only for types and instances.) **2.** *n.* a disease caused by ①.

inferior [ɪn 'fɪr i ɚ] **1.** *adj.* lower in amount, rank, power, quality, or strength than someone or something else. (Adv: *inferiorly*.) **2.** *n.* someone who has a lower-ranking job than someone else.

inferno [ɪn 'fɚ no] **1.** *n.* a large, fierce fire. (Plural ends in -s.) **2.** *n.* a place that is very hot. (Figurative on ①. Plural ends in -s.)

infinitive form [ɪn 'fɪn ə tɪv 'form] *n.* a form of a verb—preceded by *to*—that does not show tense, number, or person. (Abbreviated INF. here. Can be shortened to *infinitive*.)

inflammable [ɪn 'flæm ə bəl] *adj.* able to catch fire; FLAMMABLE; not fireproof. (The opposite is NONFLAMMABLE. Adv: *inflammably*. This *in* shows emphasis, not negativeness.)

inflation [ɪn 'fle ʃən] **1.** *n.* the process of putting air or gas into something; blowing something up. (No plural.) **2.** *n.* an economic condition in which too much money is available for purchasing too few goods. (No plural.)

influence ['ɪn flu əns] **1.** *n.* the power or ability to cause certain results or to affect what happens. (Plural only for types and instances.) **2.** *n.* a cause of some behavior. **3.** *tv.* to affect someone or something.
→ UNDER THE INFLUENCE OF SOMETHING

influenza [ɪn flu 'ɛn zə] *n.* the flu; an easily spread sickness caused by a virus. (No plural.)

informal [ɪn 'form əl] **1.** *adj.* not formal, official, or final. (Adv: *informally*.) **2.** *adj.* [of words, language, or speech] used every day but a little more relaxed than more formal speech. (Adv: *informally*.) **3.** *adj.* [of dress] not formal; casual. (Adv: *informally*.)

information [ɪn fɚ 'me ʃən] *n.* news; knowledge about something; facts. (No plural. Number is expressed by *piece(s)* or *bit(s)* of *information*.)
→ A MINE OF INFORMATION

ingredient [ɪn 'grid i ənt] *n.* something that is part of a mixture.

inhale [ɪn 'hel] **1.** *iv.* to breathe in. **2.** *tv.* to breathe something in.

inherit [ɪn 'hɛr ɪt] **1.** *tv.* to receive the assets of a person when the person dies. **2.** *tv.* to receive a characteristic or feature from one's parents or ancestors.

inject [ɪn 'dʒɛkt] **1.** *tv.* to put a liquid into a living body through a hollow needle. **2.** *tv.* to introduce a fluid into something under pressure.

injection [ɪn 'dʒɛk ʃən] *n.* injecting something. (Plural only for types and instances.)

injure ['ɪn dʒɚ] *tv.* to harm someone or something; to damage someone or something.

injury ['ɪn dʒə ri] *n.* physical or mental damage or harm; a specific instance of damage or harm.
→ ADD INSULT TO INJURY

ink [ɪŋk] **1.** *n.* a colored liquid used for writing or printing. (Plural only for types and instances.) **2.** *n.* a liquid that is injected into the water by an octopus—and by some other sea animals—to confuse pursuers. (No plural.)
→ IN INK

inn [ɪn] *n.* a small hotel; a place that offers rooms to rent for travelers.

inner ['ɪn ɚ] *adj.* on the inside; nearer to the center; further inside.

inning ['ɪn ɪŋ] *n.* [in baseball] a period of playing time that ends after the two teams have received three outs each during their turns batting.

innocent ['ɪn ə sənt] **1.** *adj.* free from guilt or sin; not guilty. (Adv: *innocently*.) **2.** *adj.* harmless; not meant to cause harm. (Adv: *innocently*.) **3.** *adj.* too trusting; not recognizing things that are evil; inexperienced. (Adv: *innocently*.)
→ (AS) INNOCENT AS A LAMB
→ FIND SOMEONE INNOCENT
→ PLAY INNOCENT

inoculate someone **against** something to immunize someone against a disease.

input ['ɪn pʊt] **1.** *n.* addition; the act of putting something into something. (No plural.) **2.** *n.* advice; opinions; ideas or suggestions. (Informal. No plural.) **3.** *n.* information; data; information that is put into a computer. (No plural.) **4.** *n.* an electronic signal that is fed into a circuit. **5.** *tv., irreg.* to put data into a computer. (Past tense and past participle: *inputted* or *input*.)

inquire [ɪn 'kwaɪɚ] *iv.* to ask someone about something. (Also spelled *enquire*.)

inquiry [ɪn 'kwaɪɚ i] **1.** *n.* a question. (Also spelled *enquiry*.) **2.** *n.*

an investigation; a search for truth; a search for an answer.

the **ins and outs of** something the details of something. (Informal.)

insane [ɪn 'sen] **1.** *adj.* crazy; not sane. (Adv: *insanely*.) **2.** *adj.* owing to insanity; done because of insanity. (Adv: *insanely*.) **3.** *adj.* very stupid; very foolish; very idiotic. (Informal. Adv: *insanely*.)

insanity [ɪn 'sæn ə ti] *n.* the state or condition of being insane. (No plural.)

inscribe something **on(to)** something to write or engrave certain information on something. (Emphasis is on the message that is inscribed.)

inscribe something **with** something to engrave something with a message.

insect ['ɪn sɛkt] **1.** *n.* a small creature with wings and six legs. **2.** *n.* a bug; any creature similar to ①.

inside 1. ['ɪn 'saɪd] *n.* the interior of a building or an object; the part of an object that is within something. **2.** [ɪn 'saɪd, 'ɪn saɪd] *adj.* interior; in, of, or about ①. **3.** [ɪn 'saɪd] *adv.* in or into a room or building; in or into an object. **4.** [ɪn 'saɪd, 'ɪn saɪd] *prep.* within a room or building; within an object; within the interior; in an interior position.
 → BOTTLE SOMETHING UP (INSIDE (SOMEONE))
 → GET THE INSIDE TRACK
 → KNOW SOMETHING INSIDE OUT

insight ['ɪn saɪt] **1.** *n.* wisdom; the ability to observe and identify things that are important. (No plural.) **2.** *n.* a statement showing

that one has observed and identified something important.

insist (up)on something to demand something.

inspect [ɪn 'spɛkt] *tv.* to examine someone or something carefully.

inspection [ɪn 'spɛk ʃən] *n.* study; inspecting and reviewing. (Plural only for types and instances.)

instance ['ɪn stəns] *n.* an example; a case; an occurrence.
 → FOR INSTANCE

instant ['ɪn stənt] **1.** *n.* one moment in time; a very short amount of time. **2.** *adj.* immediate; without delay. (Adv: *instantly*.) **3.** *adj.* [of food or drink] easily and quickly prepared.

instead [ɪn 'stɛd] *adv.* in place of something; as another choice.

instead of someone or something in place of someone or something; as a substitute for someone or something.

instill something **in(to)** something to add something to a situation.

instinct ['ɪn stɪŋkt] *n.* an ability someone or some creature is born with to act or respond in a particular way.

institution [ɪn stɪ 'tu ʃən] **1.** *n.* an organization that serves a special purpose. **2.** *n.* an established tradition; a habit; a custom.

instruct [ɪn 'strʌkt] *tv.* to teach someone something; to educate someone about something.

instruct someone **to** do something to order or request someone to do something.

instruction [ɪn 'strʌk ʃən] **1.** *n.* education; teaching. (No plural.) **2.** *n.* an order or set of orders; a direction or set of directions. (Usually plural.)

instructor [ɪn 'strʌk tɚ] *n.* a teacher; someone who instructs people about something.

instrument ['ɪn strə mənt] **1.** *n.* a thing that is used to help someone do something; a tool; a device. **2.** *n.* something that shows a measurement. **3.** *n.* an object that produces musical notes when played.

insult [ɪn 'sʌlt] **1.** *n.* an offensive remark; a rude statement that offends someone. **2.** *tv.* to offend someone; to say something rude or offensive to someone.
→ ADD INSULT TO INJURY
→ HURL AN INSULT (AT SOMEONE)

insurance [ɪn 'ʃɚ əns] **1.** *n.* a contract that pays a sum of money in the case of a loss or injury. (No plural. Number is expressed with INSURANCE POLICY or INSURANCE POLICIES.) **2.** *n.* something that protects against a loss or an injury. (No plural.) **3.** *n.* the business of writing and selling ①. (No plural.) **4.** the *adj.* use of ①, ②, or ③.

insurance policy [ɪn 'ʃɚ əns 'pɑl ə si] *n.* the document or contract that states the protections offered by insurance.

insure [ɪn 'ʃɚ] **1.** *tv.* to purchase insurance for someone or something. (Compare this with ENSURE.) **2.** *tv.* [for an insurance company] to sell insurance on someone or something.

intelligence [ɪn 'tɛl ɪ dʒəns] **1.** *n.* the level of someone's ability to learn and understand. (No plural.) **2.** *n.* information about an enemy and the enemy's plans. (No plural.) **3.** *n.* a department within a military service that gathers ②. (No plural.)

intelligent [ɪn 'tɛl ə dʒənt] *adj.* smart; able to learn and understand things well. (Adv: *intelligently*.)

intensity [ɪn 'tɛn sə ti] *n.* the degree or amount of power or strength. (Plural only for types and instances.)

intent on doing something determined to do something.

intention [ɪn 'tɛn ʃən] *n.* a purpose; a plan.

intercourse ['ɪn tɚ kors] *n.* copulation, usually human copulation. (Short for SEXUAL INTERCOURSE.)
→ SEXUAL INTERCOURSE

interest ['ɪn trəst] **1.** *n.* the attention or concern shown toward someone or something. (No plural.) **2.** *n.* something that causes ①; something that attracts one's curiosity or attention as in ⑤. **3.** *n.* the money—usually a percentage of the amount borrowed—that a lender charges to someone who borrows money. (No plural.) **4.** *n.* the money—usually a percentage of the amount held—that a bank or other financial institution pays for holding someone's money for a period of time. (No plural.) **5.** *tv.* to capture the attention or curiosity of someone or something.
→ HAVE A KEEN INTEREST IN SOMETHING

→ HAVE A VESTED INTEREST IN SOMETHING
→ IN SOMEONE'S (OWN) (BEST) INTERESTS
→ IN THE INTEREST(S) OF SOMETHING
→ OF INTEREST (TO SOMEONE)
→ PIQUE SOMEONE'S INTEREST

interesting ['ɪn trəs tɪŋ] *adj.* causing interest or curiosity; worthy of interest; keeping someone's interest. (Adv: *interestingly.*)

interestingly ['ɪn trəs tɪŋ li] **1.** *adv.* in a way that causes or keeps someone's interest. **2.** *adv.* strangely; curiously.

interfere [ɪn tɚ 'fɪr] *iv.* to get involved [with something that is private or restricted].

interfere with someone or something to create an interruption; to disturb someone; to disturb the operation of something.

interference [ɪn tɚ 'fɪr əns] **1.** *n.* interfering; serving as a problem; getting involved and making oneself a bother. (No plural.) **2.** *n.* an electronic disturbance that prevents the clear reception of a radio or television signal. (No plural.)

interim *n.* the time in between events; the meantime; the meanwhile; an interval.
→ IN THE INTERIM (BETWEEN THINGS)

interior [ɪn 'tɪr i ɚ] **1.** *n.* a part or surface that is within something; a part or surface that is inside of something. **2.** *n.* the area within something; the space that is inside something. **3.** the *adj.* use of ① or ②.

interj. an abbreviation of INTERJECTION.

interjection [ɪn tɚ 'dʒɛk ʃən] *n.* a word, expression, or phrase that is

used to express something with force or emotion. (Abbreviated *interj.* here.)

intermediate [ɪn tɚ 'mid i ɪt] *adj.* between two stages, levels, sizes, weights, etc. (Adv: *intermediately.*)

intermission [ɪn tɚ 'mɪ ʃən] *n.* a pause between the parts of a play, movie, opera, or other performance.

international [ɪn tɚ 'næʃ ə nəl] **1.** *adj.* of or about two or more countries; between two countries; among three or more countries. (Adv: *internationally.*) **2.** *adj.* global; in all nations. (Adv: *internationally.*)

Internet ['ɪn tɚ nɛt] *n.* a digital system of high-speed global communication and data transfer. (No plural. Not a proper noun, but usually capitalized. Can be shortened to NET.)

interrog. an abbreviation of INTERROGATIVE.

interrogative [ɪn tə 'rɑg ə tɪv] *n.* a word or expression used to ask a question. (WHO, WHAT, WHEN, WHERE, WHY, and HOW are the most common INTERROGATIVES. Abbreviated *interrog.* here.)

interrupt [ɪn tə 'rʌpt] **1.** *iv.* to break into a conversation; to start talking while someone else is talking. **2.** *tv.* to stop the flow or movement of something; to stop something temporarily.

interruption [ɪn tə 'rʌp ʃən] **1.** *n.* interrupting; stopping and interfering in a conversation or an activity. **2.** *n.* a break in the flow of something.

intersection [ɪn tɚ ˈsɛk ʃən] **1.** *n.* a junction of two or more roads, streets, highways, etc.; a place where roads or streets come together or cross. **2.** *n.* the point at which two or more things join.

interval [ˈɪn tɚ vəl] **1.** *n.* a period of time between two events. **2.** *n.* the distance between two points in a series of points. **3.** *n.* the distance between two musical tones.
→ AT REGULAR INTERVALS

intervene in something to get involved in something.

interview [ˈɪn tɚ vju] **1.** *n.* a meeting between an employer and a job seeker, where the employer asks questions of the job seeker. **2.** *n.* a meeting where a reporter asks questions of someone. **3.** *tv.* to ask questions of someone, possibly about employment; to make direct inquiries of someone. **4.** *tv.* to ask questions of someone for a television or radio program, a newspaper or magazine article, etc.

intestine [ɪn ˈtɛs tɪn] *n.* the tube or channel between the stomach and the rectum. (Often plural with the same meaning.)

into [ˈɪn tu] **1.** *prep.* to the inner part of something; to the interior of something. **2.** *prep.* up against someone or something. **3.** *prep.* interested in something. (Informal.)

in(to) a jam in(to) a difficult situation.

into being into existence.

into someone's **clutches** in(to) the control of someone who has power or authority over someone else.

intransitive verb [ɪn ˈtræn sə tɪv ˈvɚb] *n.* a verb not taking a direct object. (Abbreviated *iv.* here.)

introduce [ɪn trə ˈdus] *tv.* to establish something; to bring something into use; to make something known or familiar to someone.

introduce someone **(to** someone**)** to present someone to someone else when they meet for the first time.

introduce someone **to** something to show someone something for the first time.

introduction [ɪn trə ˈdʌk ʃən] **1.** *n.* an instance of presenting one person to another person. **2.** *n.* making the availability of something known to people. **3.** *n.* the part of a book, chapter, or lecture that comes at the beginning and explains its purpose. **4.** *n.* the basic and important information about a subject.

intrude (up)on someone or something to encroach on someone or something or on matters that concern only someone or something.

intrusion [ɪn ˈtru ʒən] **1.** *n.* entering into a situation where one is not wanted; a visit that is not welcome. **2.** *n.* breaking into a house or other building.

invasion [ɪn ˈve ʒən] **1.** *n.* a military attack. **2.** *n.* the attack and spread of something bad or dangerous. (Figurative on ①.)

an **invasion of privacy** an intrusion that results in the loss of someone's privacy.

invent [ɪn 'vɛnt] **1.** *tv.* to create something that has never been made before. **2.** *tv.* to make up a story, an excuse, or a lie. (Figurative on ①.)

invention [ɪn 'vɛn ʃən] **1.** *n.* the creation of a new device; the production of a new machine or a new process. (No plural.) **2.** *n.* a new device; something that has been created for the first time.

inventor [ɪn 'vɛn tɚ] *n.* someone who INVENTS ① something; someone who has invented something.

inventory ['ɪn vən tor i] **1.** *n.* goods and supplies on hand or stored in a warehouse; stock waiting to be sold. (No plural form.) **2.** *n.* a list showing the number of each item that has been packed, received, shipped, etc.
→ TAKE INVENTORY

invest in someone or something to put resources into someone or something in hopes of increasing the value of the person or thing.

invest someone **with** something to endow someone with something, such as power or privilege.

invest (someone's**) time in** something to put one's time, effort, or energy into a project.

invest (something **in** someone or something to give something such as money or guidance to someone or something.

investment [ɪn 'vɛst mənt] *n.* money that is assigned to a project, stocks, a bank account, etc., with the hope and expectation of profit.

investor [ɪn 'vɛs tɚ] *n.* someone who puts money into an investment.

invitation [ɪn vɪ 'te ʃən] *n.* a written, printed, or spoken statement asking someone to attend an event or to do something.

invite someone **in(to** someplace**)** to bid or request someone to enter a place.

invite someone **out** to ask someone out on a date.

invite someone **over (for** something**)** to bid or request someone to come to one's house for something, such as a meal, party, chat, cards, etc.

invoice ['ɪn vɔɪs] **1.** *n.* a bill; a document showing how much money is owed for goods or services. **2.** *tv.* to present someone or a business firm with ①.

irk [ɝk] *tv.* to annoy, upset, or irritate someone.

iron ['aɪɚn] **1.** *n.* an element that is a common metal, used to make steel. (No plural.) **2.** *n.* a small device with a flat metal bottom, heated and used to press the wrinkles out of cloth. **3.** *adj.* made from ①. **4.** *tv.* to smooth the wrinkles out of clothes with ②.
→ HAVE TOO MANY IRONS IN THE FIRE
→ STRIKE WHILE THE IRON IS HOT

iron something **out 1.** to use an iron to make cloth flat or smooth. **2.** to ease a problem; to smooth out a problem. (Figurative. Here *problem* is synonymous with *wrinkle*.)

irony ['aɪ rə ni] **1.** *n.* using words in a funny or sarcastic way to create a meaning opposite from their combined literal meaning in a funny or sarcastic way. (No plural.) **2.** *n.* an event that has the opposite result of what was planned or expected.

irradiate [ɪ 'red i et] *tv.* to treat something with radiation; to treat food with radiation to keep it from spoiling.

irreg. an abbreviation of IRREGULAR ④.

irregular [ɪr 'rɛg jə lɚ] **1.** *adj.* not regular; oddly shaped; uneven. (Adv: *irregularly.*) **2.** *adj.* happening at differing intervals of time; not happening regularly. (Adv: *irregularly.*) **3.** *adj.* different from what is normal, and therefore unacceptable. (Euphemistic.) **4.** *adj.* [of the form of a noun, verb, adjective, or adverb] not regular in the way it changes form, such as with the plural, past tense, comparative, or superlative. (Abbreviated *irreg.* here. Adv: *irregularly.*)

irritate ['ɪr ɪ tet] **1.** *tv.* to cause a part of the body to become red or swollen. **2.** *tv.* to bother or annoy someone or something.

irritation [ɪr ɪ 'te ʃən] **1.** *n.* a bother; something that irritates. **2.** *n.* the condition of being sore or itchy; soreness or tenderness of skin or other body tissues. (Plural only for types and instances.)

is [ɪz] *iv.* a form of BE, used in the present tense of the third-person singular, that is, with *he, she, it,* and singular nouns. (Reduced to *'s* in contractions.)

island ['aɪ lənd] **1.** *n.* a piece of land surrounded by water and smaller than a continent. **2.** *n.* something that is completely surrounded by something else. (Figurative on ①.)
→ DESERT ISLAND

isle ['aɪl] *n.* an island.

isn't ['ɪz ənt] *cont.* is not.

isolate ['aɪ sə let] *tv.* to keep someone or something separate from other people or things; to separate someone or something from other people or things.

isolation [aɪ sə 'le ʃən] *n.* the state of being isolated; keeping someone or something away from other people or things. (No plural.)

issue ['ɪ ʃu] **1.** *n.* one of a set of publications that are available regularly. **2.** *n.* the number of stamps or magazines printed at one time. **3.** *n.* a topic; the topic being discussed; a concern. **4.** *tv.* to assign something to someone; to supply something to someone. **5.** *tv.* to speak or utter a command; to deliver or publish a written command or order. **6.** *tv.* to publish a magazine, bulletin, newsletter, or newspaper.

issue a call for something to make an invitation or request for something.

it [ɪt] **1.** *pron.* a form referring to something that is not human; a form referring to a plant, an animal, or something that is not living. (However, IT is sometimes used to refer to a baby or a small child. See also ITS and ITSELF. The plural is THEY.) **2.** *pron.* a form used as the subject of a sentence where there is no real actor or doer. (Usually with the verb BE, but with others also.) **3.** *n.* the player who must find or chase everyone else in various children's games.

itch ['ɪtʃ] **1.** *n.* a feeling on the skin that makes one want to scratch. **2.** *iv.* [for the skin] to have ①.
→ HAVE AN ITCH FOR SOMETHING
→ HAVE AN ITCHING PALM
→ HAVE AN ITCH TO DO SOMETHING

itchy ['ɪtʃ i] *adj.* with the feeling of itching; constantly itching. (Comp: *itchier*; sup: *itchiest*.)
→ HAVE AN ITCHY PALM

it'd ['ɪt ɪd] **1.** *cont.* it would. **2.** *cont.* it had, where HAD is an auxiliary.

item ['aɪ təm] *n.* one thing that is part of a list or a series; a unit; a piece of information; a piece of news.

it'll ['ɪt əl] *cont.* it will.

it's ['ɪts] **1.** *cont.* it is. (Compare this with ITS.) **2.** *cont.* it has. (This HAS is an auxiliary. Compare this with ITS.)

its ['ɪts] *pron.* the possessive form of IT; belonging to it. (Compare this with IT's.)

itself [ɪt 'sɛlf] **1.** *pron.* the reflexive form of IT. **2.** *pron.* an emphatic form of IT. (Follows the nominal that is being emphasized.)
→ BLOW ITSELF OUT
→ BURN (ITSELF) OUT
→ BY ITSELF
→ an END IN ITSELF
→ LEND ONESELF OR ITSELF TO something
→ SPEAKS FOR ITSELF

iv. an abbreviation of INTRANSITIVE VERB.

I've ['aɪv] *cont.* I have. (This HAVE is an auxiliary.)

ivory ['aɪ vri] **1.** *n.* the hard, white substance of which an elephant's tusk is made. (No plural.) **2.** *n.* the color of ①. **3.** the *adj.* use of ① or ②.
→ LIVE IN AN IVORY TOWER

ivy ['aɪv i] *n.* a plant that holds onto walls, trees, etc., and climbs as it grows. (Plural only for types and instances.)

jack ['dʒæk] **1.** *n.* a device used to lift heavy things off the ground, especially to push up a car wheel in order to change a tire. **2.** *n.* [in a deck of playing cards] a card that has a picture of a young man on it and is signified by the letter *J*.

jack something **up** to push something up with a JACK.

jacket ['dʒæk ɪt] **1.** *n.* a light coat; the light coat that is part of a suit. **2.** *n.* a covering for a book or a sound recording.
→ LIFE JACKET

jack-of-all-trades someone who can do several different jobs instead of specializing in one.

jail ['dʒel] **1.** *n.* a building where criminals are locked up or where people are locked up while waiting for a trial. **2.** *tv.* to put someone in ①; to order someone to spend time in ①.

jam ['dʒæm] **1.** *n.* a sweet food made by boiling fruit and sugar until it is thick. (Plural only for types and instances.) **2.** *tv.* to cause something to become stuck; to force something to fit someplace. **3.** *iv.* to become stuck; to be unable to work properly because something is stuck; to be unable to move because something is stuck.
→ IN(TO) A JAM
→ TRAFFIC JAM

janitor ['dʒæn ɪ tɚ] *n.* someone who cleans and takes care of a building.

January ['dʒæn ju ɛr i] Go to MONTH.

jar ['dʒɑr] **1.** *n.* a container with a wide, circular top, usually made of glass or clay, and usually without handles. **2.** *n.* the contents of ①. **3.** *tv.* to hit (lightly) or shake someone or something.

jaw ['dʒɔ] **1.** *n.* the upper or lower bones that form the mouth and support the teeth. **2.** *n.* one of the two parts of a device that holds something tight, such as a vise or pliers.

jawbone ['dʒɔ bon] *n.* the upper or especially, the lower bones that form the mouth and support the teeth.

jazz ['dʒæz] **1.** *n.* a style of music characterized by its rhythms, harmony, and the creative ways its players work together while it is being played. (No plural.) **2.** the *adj.* use of ①.

jazz something **up** to make something more exciting or livelier.

jealous ['dʒɛl əs] *adj.* not liking anyone who, one believes, might try to take away one's things or the people one loves. (Adv: *jealously.*)

jealousy ['dʒɛl ə si] *n.* the condition of being jealous; not liking someone who has something one wants. (No plural.)

jeans ['dʒinz] *n.* a pair of cloth pants, often dark blue, made of sturdy material. (Treated as plural. Number is expressed by *pair(s) of jeans.*)

jelly ['dʒɛl i] **1.** *n.* a soft food that is made by boiling fruit juice and sugar together and is often spread on bread. (Plural only for types and instances.) **2.** *adj.* made with ①.

jeopardy ['dʒɛp ɚ di] *phr.* a state of risk or hazard.
→ IN JEOPARDY

jerk ['dʒɚk] **1.** *n.* a sudden push or pull of the muscles; a movement made when something starts or stops quickly. **2.** *tv.* to push or pull someone or something suddenly. **3.** *iv.* to move with ①; make a movement like ①.

jerk something **away (from** someone or something) to grab something away or pull something back from someone or some creature.

jerk something **off ((of)** someone or something) to grab something off someone or something.

jerk something **out (of** someone or something) to pull something out of someone or something, quickly.

jerk something **up 1.** to pull something up quickly. **2.** to lift up something, such as ears, quickly.

jet ['dʒɛt] **1.** *n.* a stream of air, water, steam, or another fluid that is shot out from a small opening at high pressure. **2.** *n.* an airplane that moves at high speed using engines similar to a rocket. (Short for JET PLANE.) **3.** *iv.* [for water, steam, or another fluid] to form a stream by being forced out of a small opening under pressure. **4.** *iv.* to travel by ②. **5.** *tv.* to cause water, steam, or another fluid to form a stream by forcing it out of a small opening under pressure.

jet engine ['dʒɛt 'ɛn dʒən] *n.* an engine powered by JET PROPULSION.

jet plane ['dʒɛt 'plen] *n.* a high-speed plane; a plane that has one or more jet engines. (Can be shortened to JET.)

jet propulsion ['dʒɛt prə 'pʌl ʃən] *n.* a means of pushing something forward by forcing a jet out of the back. (No plural.)

jet-black ['dʒɛt 'blæk] *adj.* deep, shiny black in color.

jewel ['dʒu əl] *n.* a gem; a valuable stone; a piece of jewelry.

jeweler ['dʒu (ə) lɚ] *n.* someone who deals in watches, valuable gems, and precious metals.

jewelry ['dʒu (ə)l ri] *n.* objects usually made of valuable metals or stones, such as rings, earrings, necklaces, bracelets, and pins. (No plural. Treated as singular. Number is expressed with *piece(s) of jewelry*.)

jiggle ['dʒɪg əl] **1.** *tv.* to move someone or something up and down or from side to side. **2.** *iv.* to move up and down or from side to side.

jingle ['dʒɪŋ gəl] **1.** *n.* the ringing noise of metal objects gently hitting together; the noise of a small bell being struck. **2.** *n.* a tune or song used in advertising. **3.** *tv.* to make ringing noises by hitting metal objects together. **4.** *iv.* [for metal objects] to make noises when struck together; [for a small bell] to make a noise when shaken.

job ['dʒɑb] **1.** *n.* a career; an occupation; regular employment. **2.** *n.* a task; a duty; a responsibility; a piece of work. **3.** *n.* the performance or result of one's work.

→ FALL DOWN ON THE JOB

job lot a mixed collection of varying quality. (Informal.)

jockey for position to try to push or work one's way into an advantageous position at the expense of others.

jockey someone or something **into position** to manage to get someone or something into a chosen position.

jog ['dʒɑg] **1.** *n.* a slow, gentle run usually done for exercise; a [human] trot. **2.** *n.* a bend to the right or the left; something that causes a line not to be straight. **3.** *iv.* to exercise by running slowly.

jog someone's **memory** to stimulate someone's memory to recall something.

jogger ['dʒɑg ɚ] *n.* someone who exercises by jogging.

Johnny-come-lately someone who joins in (something) after it is already under way.

Johnny-on-the-spot someone who is in the right place at the right time.

join ['dʒɔɪn] **1.** *iv.* to come together; to connect; to unite. **2.** *tv.* to connect someone or something to someone or something else; to unite people or things into a single unit. **3.** *tv.* to enroll in a club, class, the military, or some other organization; to become a member of an organization.

join hands [for people] to hold hands so that each person is holding the hands of two other people; [for two people] to hold each other's hands.

Join the club! an expression indicating that the person spoken to is in the same, or a similar, unfortunate state as the speaker. (Informal.)

join the fray AND **jump into the fray** to join the fight or argument.

join up to become part of some organization.

join ((up) with someone or something**)** to bring oneself into association with someone or something.

joint ['dʒɔɪnt] **1.** *n.* a place where two things, especially bones, join. **2.** *adj.* (Adv: *jointly.*) done or owned together; joined; united.
→ PUT SOMEONE'S NOSE OUT OF JOINT

joke ['dʒok] **1.** *n.* something said or done to make people laugh, especially a short story told to make people laugh. **2.** *tv.* to say something in a teasing or playful manner; to say something that is meant to be funny. (The object is a clause with THAT ⑦.) **3.** *iv.* to tell ①; to kid or tease [someone]; to say or do things that are meant to be funny.
→ ALL JOKING ASIDE
→ CRACK A JOKE
→ NO JOKE
→ PLAY A JOKE ON SOMEONE
→ a STANDING JOKE

jolt someone **out of** something to startle someone out of a period of relaxation or distraction.

jot something **down** to make a note of something.

journal ['dʒɚ nl] **1.** *n.* a diary; a book where one writes down one's feelings, thoughts, or activities.

2. *n.* a magazine, periodical, or scholarly publication.

journey ['dʒɚn i] **1.** *n.* a trip; a voyage. **2.** *iv.* to travel.

joy ['dʒɔɪ] **1.** *n.* extreme pleasure or happiness. (No plural.) **2.** *n.* someone or something that causes extreme pleasure or happiness.
→ BURST WITH JOY
→ LEAP FOR JOY

joyful ['dʒɔɪ fəl] **1.** *adj.* [of someone] full of joy; extremely happy; very glad. (Adv: *joyfully*.) **2.** *adj.* [for something] causing joy; causing extreme happiness.

joyous ['dʒɔɪ əs] *adj.* full of joy; extremely happy; very glad. (Adv: *joyously*.)

judge ['dʒʌdʒ] **1.** *n.* an official who hears and settles cases in a court of law and who presides over trials. **2.** *n.* someone who helps decide the winner of a contest or competition. **3.** *tv.* to hear and settle a case in a court of law; to preside over a trial in a court of law. **4.** *tv.* to help decide the winner of a contest or competition. **5.** *tv.* to state an opinion about someone or something; to evaluate someone or something. **6.** *tv.* to estimate something; to make a guess that something will happen. (The object is a clause with THAT ⑦.)
→ (AS) SOBER AS A JUDGE

judgment ['dʒʌdʒ mənt] **1.** *n.* the ability to make the proper decisions; the ability to judge. (No plural.) **2.** *n.* the result of judging; the decision made by a judge or a jury. **3.** *n.* an opinion. (No plural.)

juggle ['dʒʌg əl] **1.** *tv.* to keep three or more objects moving through the air by catching and throwing them in a circle. **2.** *tv.* to deal with several things at the same time. **3.** *iv.* to toss objects in the air as in ①.

juice ['dʒus] *n.* the liquid part of fruit, vegetables, or meat. (Plural only for types and instances.)
→ STEW IN ONE'S OWN JUICE

July [dʒə 'laɪ] Go to MONTH.

jumbo ['dʒʌm bo] *adj.* extra large; larger than regular.

jump ['dʒʌmp] **1.** *iv.* to leap up; to spring up; to push off the ground with one's legs. **2.** *iv.* to move suddenly, as if surprised or scared. **3.** *iv.* to go up sharply; to increase sharply; to rise sharply. (Figurative on ①.) **4.** *tv.* to start a car by connecting its battery to another car's battery. **5.** *n.* a leap off the ground; a leap off the ground and over, through, or across something. **6.** *n.* a sudden rise; an increase. (Figurative on ⑤.)
→ GET THE JUMP ON SOMEONE

jump in((to) something) to leap into something, such as water, a bed, a problem, etc.

jump into the fray Go to JOIN THE FRAY.

jump off ((of) something) to leap off something.

jump off the deep end Go to GO OFF THE DEEP END.

jump off the deep end (over someone or something) to get deeply involved with someone or something. (Often refers to romantic involvement.)

jump on the bandwagon Go to GET ON THE BANDWAGON.

jump out of one's **skin** to react strongly to a shock or surprise.

jump out of something to leap from something.

jump over something to leap over or across something.

jump the gun to start before the starting signal.

jump the track 1. [for something] to fall or jump off its rails or guides. (Usually said about a train.) **2.** to change suddenly from one thing, thought, plan, or activity to another.

jump to conclusions to move too quickly to a conclusion; to form a conclusion from too little evidence. (Idiomatic.)

jump up (on someone or something) to leap upward onto someone or something.

jumping-off point a point or place from which to begin a venture.

junction ['dʒʌŋk ʃən] *n.* a place where two or more things come together, especially the place where roads or train tracks come together or cross.

June ['dʒun] Go to MONTH.

jungle ['dʒʌŋ gəl] *n.* a tropical forest of thick, lush plant growth, usually near the equator.

junior ['dʒun jɚ] **1.** *n.* someone who is younger or who has a lower rank or position than someone else. **2.** *n.* a student in the third year of high school (11th grade) or the third year of college. **3.** *adj.* of or about someone who is younger or who has a lower rank or position. **4.** *adj.* of or about the third year of high school or college. (Prenominal only.)

junk ['dʒʌŋk] **1.** *n.* things that are worthless; things that should be thrown away. (No plural.) **2.** *tv.* to throw something away.

jury ['dʒɚ i] **1.** *n.* a group of people who listen to evidence at a trial in a court of law and make a decision about the truth of the facts of the case. **2.** the *adj.* use of ①.

just ['dʒʌst] **1.** *adj.* fair; not biased; honest; right; in accordance with the law. (Adv: *justly.*) **2.** *adj.* as someone deserves; appropriate. (Adv: *justly.*) **3.** *adv.* only. **4.** *adv.* barely; by a small amount. **5.** *adv.* exactly [the right amount and no more].
→ GET ONE'S JUST DESERTS
→ GET ONE'S JUST REWARD(S)
→ STOP (JUST) SHORT (OF SOMETHING)

Just a minute! Wait only a short time!; Wait a short period of time!

just so 1. in perfect order; neat and tidy. **2. Just so!** Precisely right!; Quite right!

just what the doctor ordered exactly what is required, especially for health or comfort.

justice ['dʒʌs tɪs] **1.** *n.* the quality or condition of being just; fairness, especially in a court of law. (No plural.) **2.** *n.* the administration of law; the practice of law within the court system. (No plural.) **3.** *n.* a judge. (Also a title and term of address.)
→ a TRAVESTY OF JUSTICE
→ MISCARRIAGE OF JUSTICE
→ POETIC JUSTICE

justify ['dʒʌs tɪ faɪ] *tv.* to explain why one did something; to give a good reason for something.

jut out (from something**)** to stick outward or project from something.

jut out (into something**)** to stick outward or project into an area.

jut out (over someone or something**)** to stick out or project over someone or something.

juvenile ['dʒu və naɪl] **1.** *n.* a child [from a legal point of view]. **2.** *n.* a young animal. **3.** *adj.* youthful; for young people.

K

kangaroo [kæŋ gə 'ru] *n.* a large animal of Australia that hops on its hind legs. (Plural ends in *-s.*)

keel ['kil] *n.* the main beam along the bottom of a boat or ship on which the frame is built.

keel over to fall over; to capsize.

keen ['kin] **1.** *adj.* [of a cutting edge] sharp. (Adv: *keenly.* Comp: *keener;* sup: *keenest.*) **2.** *adj.* [of a sense of taste, vision, hearing, touch, or smell] very sensitive or sharp. (Figurative on ①. Adv: *keenly.* Comp: *keener;* sup: *keenest.*)

keen on doing something willing or eager to do something.

keep ['kip] **1.** *tv., irreg.* to cause someone or something to remain somewhere. (Past tense and past participle: KEPT.) **2.** *tv., irreg.* to have something for a period of time; to continue to have something. **3.** *iv.* to continue to do something.

keep a civil tongue (in one's **head)** to speak decently and politely. (Also with *have.*)

keep a close rein on someone or something Go to KEEP A TIGHT REIN ON SOMEONE OR SOMETHING.

keep a secret to know a secret and not tell anyone.

keep a stiff upper lip to be cool and unmoved by disturbing events. (Also with *have.*)

keep a straight face to make one's face stay free from laughter.

keep a tight rein on someone or something AND **keep a close**

rein on someone or something to watch and control someone or something closely.

keep after someone **(about** something**)** to nag someone about something.

keep an eye out (for someone or something**)** to watch for the arrival or appearance of someone or something. (Also with *have.* The *an* can be replaced by *one's.*)

keep at someone **(about** something**)** to harass someone about something.

keep at something to continue to do something; to continue to try to do something.

keep away (from someone or something**)** to avoid someone or something; to maintain a physical distance from someone or something.

keep back (from someone or something**)** to continue to stay in a position away from someone or something.

keep body and soul together to feed, clothe, and house oneself.

keep from doing something to avoid doing something; to refrain from doing something.

keep late hours to stay up or stay out until very late; to work late.

keep off ((of) something**)** to remain off something; not to trespass on something.

keep on an even keel to remain cool and calm.

keep on someone **(about** something) to nag someone about something.

keep on (something) to work to remain mounted on something, such as a horse, bicycle, etc.

keep on something to pay close attention to something.

keep one's **ear to the ground** Go to HAVE ONE'S EAR TO THE GROUND.

keep one's **eye on a ball 1.** to watch or follow the ball carefully, especially when one is playing a ball game; to follow the details of a ball game very carefully. **2.** to remain alert to the events occurring around one.

keep one's **feet on the ground** to remain sensible and able to function reasonably.

keep one's **head above water** to stay ahead of one's responsibilities.

keep one's **nose to the grindstone** to keep busy continuously over a period of time.

keep one's **opinions to** oneself to stop mentioning one's own opinions, especially when they disagree with someone else's.

keep one's **temper** AND **hold** one's **temper** not to get angry; to hold back an expression of anger.

keep one's **weather eye open** to watch for something (to happen); to be on the alert (for something); to be on guard.

keep one's **word** to uphold one's promise.

keep (oneself) **to** oneself to remain private; not to mix with other people very much.

keep out (of something) **1.** to remain uninvolved with something. **2.** to remain outside something or someplace.

keep someone **at** something to make sure someone continues to work at something.

keep someone **back 1.** to hold a child back in school. **2.** to keep someone from advancing in life.

keep someone **down** to prevent someone from advancing or succeeding.

keep someone **from** doing something to prevent someone from doing something.

keep someone **in stitches** to cause someone to laugh loud and hard, over and over. (Also with *have.*)

keep someone **on** to retain someone in employment longer than is required or was planned.

keep someone or something **back** to hold someone or something in reserve.

keep someone or something **hanging in midair** to maintain someone or something in a state of waiting before reaching an ending or completion.

keep someone or something **in mind** AND **bear** someone or something **in mind** to remember and think about someone or something.

keep someone or something **off** Go to HOLD SOMEONE OR SOMETHING OFF.

keep someone or something **out (of** something) **1.** to prevent someone or something from getting into something or some place.

2. to keep the subject of someone or something out of a discussion.

keep someone **posted** to keep someone informed (of what is happening); to keep someone up-to-date.

keep someone **up 1.** to hold someone upright. **2.** to prevent someone from going to bed or going to sleep.

keep something **on** to continue to wear an article of clothing.

keep something **on an even keel** to keep something in a steady and untroubled state.

keep something **to** oneself to keep something a secret.

keep something **under** one's **hat** to keep something a secret; to keep something in one's mind (only).

keep something **under wraps** to keep something concealed (until some future time).

keep something **up 1.** to hold or prop something up. **2.** to continue doing something. **3.** to maintain something in good order.

keep the home fires burning to keep things going at one's home or other central location, maintaining a routine.

keep the wolf from the door to maintain oneself at a minimal level; to keep from starving, freezing, etc.

keep up (with the Joneses) to stay financially even with one's peers; to try hard to get the same amount of material goods that one's friends and neighbors have.

keep up (with the times) to stay in fashion; to keep up with the news; to be contemporary or modern.

keeper ['kip ɚ] *n.* someone who keeps someone or something; a protector; a guard; someone who cares for animals in a zoo. (See also ZOOKEEPER.)

keepsake ['kip sek] *n.* something that is kept to remind the owner of someone or something; a memento.

keg ['kɛg] **1.** *n.* a small wooden barrel, especially one that holds 100 pounds of nails. **2.** *n.* a small metal barrel, especially one that holds beer.
→ SITTING ON A POWDER KEG

kennel ['kɛn əl] *n.* a place where dogs are kept.

kept ['kɛpt] past tense and past participle of KEEP.

ketchup AND **catsup** ['kɛtʃ əp, 'kɛt səp] *n.* a thick liquid, made from tomatoes, that is put on food for flavoring. (Plural only for types and instances.)

kettle ['kɛt əl] *n.* a large cooking pot; a pot for heating liquids.
→ A FINE KETTLE OF FISH
→ THE POT CALLING THE KETTLE BLACK

key ['ki] **1.** *n.* a device that unlocks or locks a lock; something that unlocks something that is locked. **2.** *n.* something that gives access to an answer or a solution; something that provides the answers or solutions for something. (Figurative on ①.) **3.** *n.* a part of a machine or instrument that is pressed down to make something happen, as on a computer keyboard, a typewriter, or a piano. **4.** *n.* a musical scale that begins on a particular note; a set of related musical notes. **5.** *adj.* important; essential; basic.

keyboard ['ki bord] **1.** *n.* a row of keys that make a certain musical sound when pressed. **2.** *n.* an electronic device that creates music. **3.** *n.* the rows of keys standing for letters, symbols, and numbers as found on typewriters, computers, etc.

keynote ['ki not] *adj.* [of a speech or a speaker] primary or main. (Prenominal only.)

keypad ['ki pæd] **1.** *n.* [on a computer] a special, separate set of number keys arranged as on a calculator. **2.** *n.* any small control panel having an arrangement of push buttons, as found on a telephone or a calculator.

kick ['kɪk] **1.** *tv.* to strike someone or something with the foot, usually the toe of a shoe or boot. **2.** *iv.* to move one's legs back and forth as if KICKING something as in ①. **3.** *n.* an act of striking someone or something with the foot, as in ①.

kick back (at someone or something**)** to kick at someone or something in revenge.

kick something **back (to** someone or something**)** to move something back to someone, something, or someplace by kicking.

kick something **down** to break down something by kicking.

kick something **in** to break through something by kicking.

kick something **out (of** something**)** to move something out of something or someplace by kicking.

kick up a fuss AND **kick up a row; kick up a storm** to become

a nuisance; to misbehave and disturb (someone). (*Row* rhymes with *cow*.)

kick up a row Go to KICK UP A FUSS.

kick up a storm Go to KICK UP A FUSS.

kick up one's **heels** to celebrate; to act free or liberated.

kid ['kɪd] **1.** *n.* a child; a youngster. (Informal.) **2.** *n.* a baby goat. **3.** *n.* the skin of ②. (No plural.) **4.** *tv.* to tease someone; to joke with someone; to trick someone. **5.** *adj.* [of a brother or sister] younger. (Informal. Prenominal only.)
→ HANDLE SOMEONE WITH KID GLOVES

kid stuff Go to KID'S STUFF.

kidney ['kɪd ni] **1.** *n.* one of the two organs that separate waste and water from the bloodstream, creating urine. **2.** the *adj.* use of ①.

kid's stuff AND **kid stuff** a very easy task.

kill ['kɪl] **1.** *tv.* to cause the death of someone or something directly. **2.** *tv.* to end something; to cause something to end. (Figurative on ①.) **3.** *iv.* to cause death. **4.** *n.* an animal that is hunted and KILLED as in ①. (No plural.)

kill someone or something **off** to kill all of a group of people or creatures.

kill the fatted calf to prepare an elaborate banquet (in someone's honor).

kill the goose that laid the golden egg to destroy the source of one's good fortune.

kill time to waste time.

kill two birds with one stone to solve two problems with one solution; to achieve two good results from one action.

killed outright killed immediately.

killer ['kɪl ɚ] *n.* someone or something that kills; someone or something that causes death.

kilogram ['kɪl ə græm] *n.* a metric unit of weight, equal to 1,000 grams or about 2.2 pounds.

kilometer [kɪ 'lɑm ə tɚ] *n.* a metric unit of distance, equal to 1,000 meters or about ⅝ of a mile.

kilowatt ['kɪl ə wɑt] *n.* a metric unit of electrical power, equal to 1,000 watts per hour.

kin ['kɪn] *n.* family; relatives. (No plural form. Treated as plural.)
→ SOMEONE'S NEXT OF KIN

kind ['kaɪnd] **1.** *n.* a sort; a type; a variety. **2.** *adj.* thoughtful; helpful. (Adv: *kindly.* Comp: *kinder;* sup: *kindest.*)
→ TWO OF A KIND

kindergarten ['kɪn dɚ gɑrd n] *n.* the grade before first grade, usually for children between the ages of 4 and 6.

kindness ['kaɪnnəs] *n.* the quality of being kind; politeness and caring.
→ DO SOMEONE A KINDNESS
→ the MILK OF HUMAN KINDNESS

king ['kɪŋ] **1.** *n.* the male ruler of a nation where the head of the country inherits his office from a previous ruler. **2.** *n.* a playing card with a picture of ① on it. **3.** *n.* a playing piece in chess that can move one space in any direction.
→ FIT FOR A KING

kingdom ['kɪŋ dəm] **1.** *n.* a country ruled by a king or queen. **2.** *n.* one

of three kinds of life forms—such as the animal or plant KINGDOM.

kiss ['kɪs] **1.** *n.* a touching of one's lips to someone or something, especially someone else's lips. **2.** *tv.* to touch one's lips to someone or something, especially someone else's lips. **3.** *iv.* [for two people] to KISS each other on the lips, as in ②.

kiss and make up to forgive (someone) and be friends again. (Also used literally.)

the **kiss of death** an act that puts an end to someone or something.

kiss something **good-bye** to anticipate or experience the loss of something.

kit ['kɪt] **1.** *n.* a container or carrying device that holds tools, equipment, or supplies for a specific purpose. **2.** *n.* the parts and instructions needed to build a particular thing, such as a model airplane.
→ FIRST-AID KIT

kitchen ['kɪtʃ ən] **1.** *n.* a room where food is stored and cooked. **2.** the *adj.* use of ①.
→ EVERYTHING BUT THE KITCHEN SINK

kite ['kaɪt] *n.* a small wooden frame covered with cloth, paper, or plastic and attached to a long string—flown in the wind for amusement.
→ (AS) HIGH AS A KITE

kitten ['kɪt n] *n.* a baby cat; a young cat.
→ (AS) WEAK AS A KITTEN

knee ['ni] **1.** *n.* the front part of the joint in the middle of the leg. **2.** *n.* the part of a pants leg that covers ①.

kneecap ['ni kæp] *n.* the flat bone at the front of the knee.

kneel ['nil] *iv., irreg.* to put the weight of one's body on one or both knees. (Past tense and past participle: *kneeled* or KNELT.)

kneel down (before someone or something**)** to show respect by getting down on one's knees in the presence of someone or something.

knelt ['nɛlt] a past tense and past participle of KNEEL.

knew ['nu] past tense of KNOW.

knew it was coming AND **(had) known it was coming** to have known in advance that something was to happen.

knife ['naɪf] **1.** *n., irreg.* a long, flat utensil or tool that has a handle and a sharp edge used for cutting. (Plural: KNIVES.) **2.** *tv.* to stab someone or something.

knit ['nɪt] *tv.* to make a fabric or clothing by using long needles to loop yarn or thread together.

knit one's **brow** to wrinkle one's brow, especially by frowning.

knives ['naɪvz] plural of KNIFE.

knock ['nɑk] **1.** *iv.* to hit one's knuckles against something. **2.** *n.* the noise made by rapping or tapping as with ①. **3.** *n.* a sharp hit; a rap; a thump. **4.** *tv.* to hit or bump something and make it move or fall; to hit something against someone or something.

knock it off to stop talking; to be silent. (Usually a rude command.)

knock on wood a phrase said to cancel out imaginary bad luck. (Often said when one has just mentioned something good that one hopes will succeed or continue.)

knock someone **cold 1.** to knock someone out. (Informal.) **2.** to stun someone; to shock someone.

knock someone **for a loop** Go to THROW SOMEONE FOR A LOOP.

knock someone or something **down** to thrust someone or something to the ground by force.

knock someone **out 1.** to knock someone unconscious. **2.** to make someone unconsciousness. **3.** to wear someone out; to exhaust someone.

knock someone **over** to surprise or overwhelm someone. (Figurative.)

knock (up) against someone or something to bump against someone or something.

knot ['nɑt] **1.** *n.* a tight lump made where pieces of rope, cord, hair, string, etc., are tied together. **2.** *n.* a hard circle of wood in a board, where a small branch was joined. **3.** *n.* a unit of speed equal to 1.15 miles per hour, used to measure the movement of ships and wind at sea. **4.** *tv.* to tie something in ①; to fasten something with ①. **5.** *iv.* to become tied or twisted into ①.
→ TIE THE KNOT
→ TIE SOMEONE IN KNOTS

know ['no] **1.** *tv., irreg.* to have met and become familiar with someone. (Past tense: KNEW; past participle: KNOWN.) **2.** *tv., irreg.* to understand something; to have had experience with something. **3.** *tv., irreg.* to recognize someone or something. **4.** *tv., irreg.* to have knowledge about someone or

something; to have information about someone or something. (The object can be a clause with THAT ⑦.)
→ (HAD) KNOWN IT WAS COMING
→ IN THE KNOW
→ LET SOMEONE KNOW (ABOUT SOMETHING)
→ NOT KNOW ONE'S OWN STRENGTH
→ NOT KNOW SOMEONE FROM ADAM
→ NOT KNOW ENOUGH TO COME IN OUT OF THE RAIN

know (all) the tricks of the trade to possess the skills and knowledge necessary to do something.

know better to be wise, experienced, or well taught.

know one's **ABCs** to know the most basic things (like the alphabet) about something.

know someone **by sight** to know the name and recognize the face of someone.

know someone or something **like a book** Go to KNOW SOMEONE OR SOMETHING LIKE THE PALM OF ONE'S HAND.

know someone or something **like the back of** one's **hand** Go to KNOW SOMEONE OR SOMETHING LIKE THE PALM OF ONE'S HAND.

know someone or something **like the palm of** one's **hand** AND **know** someone or something **like the back of** one's **hand; know** someone or something **like a book** to know someone or something very well.

know something **from memory** to have memorized something so that one does not have to consult a written version; to know something well from having seen it very often.

know something **in** one's **bones** Go to FEEL SOMETHING IN ONE'S BONES.

know something **inside out** to know something thoroughly; to know about something thoroughly.

know the ropes to know how to do something.

know the score AND **know what's what** to know the facts; to know the facts about life and its difficulties.

know what's what Go to KNOW THE SCORE.

know when one **is not wanted** to sense when one's presence is not welcome; to know when one is not among friends. (Usually said when someone feels hurt by being ignored by people.)

know which side one's **bread is buttered on** to know what is most advantageous for oneself.

know-how knowledge and skill. (Informal.)

knowledge ['nɑl ɪdʒ] *n.* the information that is known about someone or something. (No plural.)

known ['non] Past participle of KNOW.

known fact something that is generally recognized as a fact.

known quantity someone whose character, personality, and behavior are recognized and understood.

knuckle ['nʌk əl] *n.* the joint between the bones of a finger or the joint between a finger and the hand.

L

lab ['læb] *n.* LABORATORY.

label ['leb əl] **1.** *n.* a small notice bearing important information. **2.** *tv.* to attach ① to something.

labor ['leb ɚ] **1.** *n.* a kind of work, especially hard, physical work. (No plural.) **2.** *n.* workers, especially in contrast to people in management. (No plural. Treated as singular.) **3.** *n.* the work a woman's body does to bring about birth; the contractions of the womb in the process of giving birth. (No plural.) **4.** the *adj.* use of ①, ②, or ③. **5.** *iv.* to work hard.
→ the FRUIT(S) OF ONE'S LABOR(S)
→ IN LABOR
→ ONE'S LABOR(S)

labor of love a task that is either unpaid or badly paid and that one does simply for one's own satisfaction or pleasure to please someone whom one likes or loves.

labor pains ['leb ɚ 'penz] *n.* the (mother's) pains that accompany the birth of a child.

laboratory ['læb rə tor i] **1.** *n.* a room or building that contains scientific equipment for experiments, tests, manufacture, or instruction. (Often shortened to LAB.) **2.** the *adj.* use of ①.

lace ['les] **1.** *n.* a delicate web of cotton or other thread woven into a design or pattern. (No plural.) **2.** *n.* a string used for tying something closed, especially for tying one's shoes closed; a SHOELACE. **3.** *adj.* made of ①.

lace into someone or something to set to work on someone or something; to ATTACK ③ someone or something.

lace something (up) to tie something closed, especially one's shoes, using a string that goes through a series of holes or loops.

lack ['læk] **1.** *n.* a shortage of something; the condition of not having any of something. **2.** *tv.* to need something; not to have enough of something; to be without something.

lacy ['les i] **1.** *adj.* made of lace. (Adv: *lacily.* Comp: *lacier;* sup: *laciest.*) **2.** *adj.* delicate and complex like lace; having a delicate pattern. (Figurative on ①. Adv: *lacily.* Comp: *lacier;* sup: *laciest.*)

ladder ['læd ɚ] *n.* a set of steps attached to two side pieces, used for climbing up to reach something or climbing down from something.
→ AT THE BOTTOM OF THE LADDER

ladies' man a man who likes the company of women and whose company is liked by women, the suggestion being that he likes to flirt with them.

ladle ['led l] **1.** *n.* a large, deep spoon with a long handle, used for serving a liquid from a bowl. **2.** *tv.* to serve a liquid using ①.

lady ['led i] **1.** *n.* a refined woman. (Compare this with GENTLEMAN.) **2.** *n.* a woman. (Also a term of address.)

lady-killer a man who is very popular with women and who likes to flirt and make love with them; a man whom women cannot resist.

lag ['læg] *n.* a delay; the period of time between the end of one event and the start of another.

lag behind (someone or something) to fall behind someone or something; to linger behind someone or something.

laid ['led] past tense and past participle of LAY.
→ KILL THE GOOSE THAT LAID THE GOLDEN EGG

lain ['len] a past participle of LIE ③.

lair ['lɛr] *n.* an animal's shelter; the place where an animal sleeps.

lake ['lek] *n.* a large body of water surrounded by land.

lamb ['læm] **1.** *n.* a young sheep. **2.** *n.* the meat of ① used as food. (No plural.)
→ (AS) INNOCENT AS A LAMB
→ IN TWO SHAKES OF A LAMB'S TAIL
→ LIKE A LAMB TO THE SLAUGHTER
→ LIKE LAMBS TO THE SLAUGHTER

lame ['lem] *adj.* not able to walk properly; limping; crippled. (Adv: *lamely.* Comp: *lamer;* sup: *lamest.*)

lamp ['læmp] **1.** *n.* a device that makes light; an electric light bulb. **2.** *n.* a stand—often ornamental—that holds an electric light bulb.

lamppost ['læmp post] *n.* a post that supports a street light.

lampshade ['læmp ʃed] *n.* a cover that fits over the electric light bulb in a lamp to soften the glare of the light.

land ['lænd] **1.** *n.* the dry, solid part of the earth's surface; the part of the earth's surface that is not cov-

ered with water. (No plural.) **2.** *n.* ground; dirt; soil. (No plural.) **3.** *n.* a portion of ①; an area of ground. (No plural.) **4.** *n.* a country. **5.** *iv.* [for someone or something that is moving or falling through the air] to stop and come to rest somewhere, especially on the ground. **6.** *iv.* [for an airplane] to return to the ground safely. **7.** *tv.* [for a pilot] to return an airplane to the ground safely.
→ DO A LAND-OFFICE BUSINESS
→ LAY OF THE LAND
→ LIVE OFF THE FAT OF THE LAND
→ ON LAND

the land of Nod sleep. (Humorous. From the fact that people sometimes nod when they are falling asleep. This is a pun, because the *land of Nod* is also the name of a place referred to in the Bible.)

land someone with someone or something to give or pass on someone or something unpleasant or unwanted to someone else.

land up somehow or somewhere to finish somehow or somewhere; to come to be in a certain state or place at the end. (Usually in the wrong place or in a bad situation.)

land (up)on someone or something to light or come to rest on someone or something.

landing ['læn dɪŋ] *n.* [an airplane's] coming to earth; [a pilot's] act of bringing a plane to earth.

landing strip *n.* the runway or strip of pavement or earth where a plane leaves and returns to earth, especially if short or privately owned.

landlady ['lænd led i] *n.* a woman who owns and rents out space where people can live, such as houses and apartments; a woman who manages residential rental property. (See also LANDLORD.)

landlord ['lænd lord] *n.* a person or a company that manages and collects rent for houses, apartments, and offices.

landscape ['lænd skep] **1.** *n.* the land and the things visible on it, such as trees, bodies of water, rocks, hills, etc. (Plural only for types and instances.) **2.** *n.* a painting or drawing of the land or other outdoor scenes. **3.** *tv.* to arrange flowers, trees, bushes, hills, rocks, and other objects to make a yard or park look beautiful.

a **landslide victory** a victory by a large margin; a very substantial victory, particularly in an election.

lane ['len] **1.** *n.* a road, path, or route. **2.** *n.* a section of a road wide enough for one line of traffic; a section of a running track wide enough for one person to run; a division of a swimming pool wide enough for one person to swim.

language ['læŋ gwɪdʒ] **1.** *n.* the system of spoken and written symbols used by people to express thoughts, meaning, and emotions. (Plural only for types and instances.) **2.** *n.* any system of symbols used in a computer program. **3.** *n.* a specific style of expression. (No plural.)
→ SIGN LANGUAGE
→ SPEAK THE SAME LANGUAGE

lantern ['læn tən] *n.* a protective case with clear sides, containing a source of light.

lap ['læp] **1.** *n.* the flat surface formed by the tops of the upper legs when someone is sitting. **2.** *n.* one trip around a track; two lengths of a swimming pool. **3.** *iv.* [for water] to move in small waves, making a gently splashing noise.
→ IN THE LAP OF LUXURY

lap over (something**)** [for something] to extend or project over the edge or boundary of something else.

lap something **up 1.** [for an animal] to lick something up. **2.** [for someone] to accept or believe something with enthusiasm. (Figurative.)

lap (up) against something [for waves] to splash gently against something.

lapel [lə 'pɛl] *n.* on a coat or jacket, one of the flaps that is folded back toward the shoulders, just below the collar.

lapse into a coma to go into a coma.

large ['lardʒ] **1.** *adj.* greater in size than average; more than average; big. (Comp: *larger;* sup: *largest.*) **2.** *n.* an object, especially one for sale, that is ① in size.
→ LOOM LARGE

largely ['lardʒ li] *adv.* primarily; mainly.

lash ['læʃ] **1.** *n.* a blow from a whip. **2.** *n.* an EYELASH. **3.** *tv.* to hit someone or something with a whip. **4.** *tv.* to tie someone or something [to something]; to bind someone or something.

last ['læst] **1.** *adj.* final; at the end; after all other people or things. (Adv: *lastly*.) **2.** *adj.* the most recent; nearest in the past; latest. **3.** *adj.* least likely; least appropriate. **4.** *iv.* to continue for a length of time; to remain; to endure.
→ AT LAST
→ AT THE LAST MINUTE
→ BREATHE ONE'S LAST
→ GET THE LAST LAUGH
→ GET THE LAST WORD
→ ON ONE'S OR ITS LAST LEGS
→ PAY ONE'S LAST RESPECTS
→ THAT'S THE LAST STRAW.
→ the VERY LAST

last but not least last in sequence, but not last in importance.

last name ['læst 'nem] one's surname or family name.

the **last (one)** someone or something that is the final one in a sequence.

last something **out** to endure until the end of something.

latch ['lætʃ] **1.** *n.* a device for holding a door or window closed; a lock for a door or window that can be locked and unlocked with a key. **2.** *tv.* to close a door or window so that the LATCH as in ① seizes and holds the door or window closed firmly. **3.** *iv.* [for ①] to seize and hold [something]; [for something] to close firmly with ①.

late ['let] **1.** *adj.* not on time; past the time that something is supposed to happen; past the time that someone or something is to be in a place. (Comp: *later*; sup: *latest*.) **2.** *adj.* far into a certain period of time; toward the end of

a certain period of time. **3.** *adj.* no longer living; dead, especially having died recently; now dead. (Prenominal only.) **4.** *adv.* after the time that something is supposed to happen.
→ KEEP LATE HOURS

late in the day far into a project or activity; too late in a project or activity for action, decisions, etc., to be taken. (Also used literally.)

lately ['let li] *adv.* recently.

later ['let ɚ] *adv.* at a time after the present time; at a future time.

lather ['læð ɚ] **1.** *n.* white foam that is made by mixing soap with water. (No plural.) **2.** *tv.* to cover something with ①.

laugh ['læf] **1.** *iv.* to express pleasure or amusement by making short, happy sounds with the voice. **2.** *n.* the noise that someone makes when amused, as in ①.
→ GET THE LAST LAUGH
→ NO LAUGHING MATTER

laugh out of the other side of one's **mouth** to change sharply from happiness to sadness.

laugh someone or something **down** to cause someone to quit or cause something to end by laughing in ridicule.

laugh something **off** to treat a serious problem lightly by laughing at it.

laugh something **out of court** to dismiss something as ridiculous.

laugh up one's **sleeve** to laugh secretly; to laugh quietly to oneself.

laughter ['læf tɚ] *n.* the sound(s) made when people laugh. (No plural. Treated as singular.)

launch ['lɔntʃ] **1.** *tv.* to set a new boat or ship into the water for the first time. **2.** *tv.* to send a rocket or its cargo into the air. **3.** *tv.* to begin a project; to start carrying out a plan. (Figurative on ①.) **4.** *n.* an instance of sending something as in ① or ②.

launch into something to start doing something.

launching pad ['lɔn tʃɪŋ pæd] *n.* the platform from which rockets are launched.

launder ['lɔn dɚ] *tv.* to wash clothes or fabric; to wash and iron clothes or fabric.

laundry ['lɔn dri] **1.** *n.* clothes that need to be washed; clothes that have just been washed and dried. (No plural.) **2.** *n.* a business where clothes can be taken to be washed. **3.** *n.* a location in a house or apartment building where clothes are washed.

lavatory ['læv ə tor i] **1.** *n.* a sink used for washing one's hands; a wash basin with running water available. **2.** *n.* a bathroom; a room with a toilet. (Euphemistic.)
→ GO TO THE LAVATORY

lavish ['læv ɪʃ] *adj.* in or involving large amounts; grand and excessive. (Adv: *lavishly.*)

law ['lɔ] **1.** *n.* a rule; a statement of obligation within a legal system. **2.** *n.* a principle that describes something that happens as a regularity in mathematics or the natural world. **3.** *n.* the study of the

system of LAWS as in ①. (No plural.)
→ BREAK A LAW
→ BREAK THE LAW
→ LAY DOWN THE LAW
→ TAKE THE LAW INTO ONE'S OWN HANDS

the law *n.* the police force; police officers. (No plural. Treated as singular.)

the law of gravity ['lɔ əv 'græv ə ti] *n.* the fact that gravity pulls things toward the center of the earth. (No plural. Also *law of gravitation.*)

a law unto oneself one who makes one's own laws or rules; one who sets one's own standards of behavior.

lawn ['lɔn] *n.* an area of ground with cut grass; a yard.

lawn mower ['lɔn mo ɚ] *n.* a machine with blades that is used for cutting grass. (Can be shortened to MOWER.)

lawsuit ['lɔ sut] *n.* a claim or complaint brought into a court of law. (Can be shortened to SUIT.)

lawyer ['lɔ jɚ] *n.* someone who is trained in law and is a member of the bar.

lax ['læks] *adj.* loose; not strict; not demanding. (Adv: *laxly.* Comp: *laxer;* sup: *laxest.*)

lay ['le] **1.** a past tense of LIE. **2.** *adj.* not trained in a profession, such as law or medicine; not ordained as a religious leader. **3.** *tv., irreg.* to place something on a surface or in a flat position. (Compare this with ④ and LIE ③. Past tense and past participle: LAID.) **4.** *tv., irreg.* [for a hen] to produce and deposit an egg.

lay a finger on someone or something to touch someone or something, even slightly, even with a finger. (Usually in the negative.)

lay an amount of money **out for** someone or something Go to LAY AN AMOUNT OF MONEY OUT ON SOMEONE OR SOMETHING.

lay an amount of money **out on** someone or something AND **lay** an amount of money **out for** someone or something to spend an amount of money on someone or something.

lay an egg to give a bad performance.

lay down the law 1. to state firmly what the rules are (for something). **2.** to scold someone for misbehaving.

lay it on thick AND **pour it on thick; spread it on thick** to exaggerate praise, excuses, or blame.

lay of the land 1. the arrangement of features on an area of land. **2.** the arrangement or organization of something other than land.

lay off ((from) something) to cease doing something.

lay off ((of) someone or something) to stop doing something to someone or something; to stop bothering someone or something.

lay one's **cards on the table** Go to PUT ONE'S CARDS ON THE TABLE.

lay over (someplace) to wait somewhere between segments of a journey.

lay someone away to bury someone. (Euphemism.)

lay someone off (from something) to put an end to someone's employment at something.

lay something away (for someone) to put something in storage for someone to receive at a later time. (Often said of a purchase that is held until it is paid for.)

lay something in to build up a supply of something.

lay something on the line Go to PUT SOMETHING ON THE LINE.

lay something out to explain something; to go over details of a plan carefully.

lay something to waste Go to LAY WASTE TO SOMETHING.

lay something up 1. to acquire and store something. **2.** [for something] to disable something.

lay waste to something AND **lay something to waste** to destroy something (literally or figuratively).

layer ['le ɚ] *n.* a level; one level of thickness that is placed on a surface.

layer cake ['le ɚ kek] *n.* a cake made of sections of cake placed on top of each other and separated by frosting.

lazy ['lez i] **1.** *adj.* doing almost no work; avoiding work. (Adv: *lazily.* Comp: *lazier;* sup: *laziest.*) **2.** *adj.* moving slowly. (Figurative on ①. Adv: *lazily.* Comp: *lazier;* sup: *laziest.*)

lead 1. ['lɛd] *n.* a heavy, soft, grayish metallic element. (No plural.)

2. ['lid] *n.* a clue; a hint; information that can be used to solve a crime. **3.** ['lid] *n.* the distance or amount by which someone or something is ahead of someone or something else, especially in a race or contest. **4.** ['lid] *n.* the main role in a movie or play. **5.** ['lid] *tv., irreg.* to guide someone or something; to show someone or something the way. (Past tense and past participle: LED.) **6.** ['lid] *tv., irreg.* to be the leader of someone or something; to be in charge of someone or something. **7.** ['lid] *tv., irreg.* to be ahead of another team or other players in a competition. **8.** ['lid] *iv., irreg.* to guide; to show the way.
→ FOLLOW SOMEONE'S LEAD
→ ONE THING LEADS TO ANOTHER.

the **lead** [...'lid] *n.* the front position; the first place.

lead a dog's life AND **live a dog's life** to lead a miserable life.

lead back (to someplace) [for a pathway] to return to a place.

lead down to something [for a pathway or other trail] to run downward to something.

lead off to be the first one to go or leave.

lead off (with someone or something) to begin with someone or something.

lead someone down the garden path to deceive someone.

lead someone on 1. to guide someone onward. **2.** to lead someone to believe something that is not so; to deceive someone.

lead someone on a merry chase to lead someone in a purposeless pursuit.

lead the life of Riley AND **live the life of Riley** to live in luxury.

lead up to something 1. to aim at something; to route movement to something. **2.** to prepare to say something; to lay the groundwork for making a point. **3.** to prepare the way for something; to have something as a consequence.

leader ['lid ɚ] *n.* a ruler; someone who leads or is in charge of a group of people.

leading question a question that suggests the kind of answer that the person who asks it wants to hear.

leaf ['lif] **1.** *n., irreg.* the flat, usually green, part of a tree or plant that is attached to a branch or stem. (Plural: LEAVES.) **2.** *n., irreg.* an extra section that can be placed in the top of a table to make it larger.
→ TAKE A LEAF OUT OF SOMEONE'S BOOK
→ TURN OVER A NEW LEAF

leaf out [for a plant] to open its leaf buds.

leaf through something to look through something, turning the pages.

leafy ['lif i] *adj.* having a lot of leaves; covered with leaves. (Comp: *leafier*; sup: *leafiest*.)

league ['lig] **1.** *n.* a group of people, organizations, or countries that work together because they have a common interest or goal. **2.** *n.* a group of sports teams that play against each other.

leak ['lik] **1.** *n.* an opening in a channel, pipe, tire, container, etc., that allows something to escape. **2.** *n.* an instance of something escaping from an opening as in ①. **3.** *n.* an instance of secret information being revealed secretly. (Figurative on ②.) **4.** *iv.* [for a container] to have an opening as in ① that allows water, air, or something else to escape. **5.** *tv.* [for a container with an opening as in ①] to allow water, air, or something else to escape or enter. **6.** *tv.* to secretly reveal secret information. (Figurative on ⑤.)

leak in(to something**)** [for a fluid] to work its way into something.

leak out [for information] to become known.

leak out (of something**)** [for a fluid] to seep out of something or someplace.

leak something **out** to permit [otherwise secret] information to become publicly known.

leakage ['lik ɪdʒ] **1.** *n.* the process of leaking. (No plural.) **2.** *n.* something that is leaked. (No plural.)

leaky ['lik i] *adj.* tending to leak; likely to leak. (Comp: *leakier*; sup: *leakiest*.)

lean ['lin] **1.** *iv.* to be slanting; to be sloped. **2.** *adj.* [of someone or something] very thin or skinny. (Adv: *leanly.* Comp: *leaner*; sup: *leanest*.) **3.** *adj.* [of meat] having almost no fat. (Adv: *leanly.* Comp: *leaner*; sup: *leanest*.)

lean back (against someone or something**)** to recline backwards, putting weight on someone or something.

lean over 1. to bend over. **2.** to tilt over.

lean toward doing something to tend toward doing something; to favor doing something.

lean toward someone or something **1.** to incline or bend toward someone or something. **2.** to tend to favor [choosing] someone or something.

leap ['lip] **1.** *iv., irreg.* to jump from one place to another. (Past tense and past participle: *leaped* or LEAPT.) **2.** *tv., irreg.* to jump over something. **3.** *n.* a jump; an instance of leaping.
→ BY LEAPS AND BOUNDS

leap for joy to jump up because one is happy; to be very happy. (Usually figurative.)

leapt ['lɛpt] a past tense and past participle of LEAP.

learn ['lɚn] *tv.* to receive knowledge; to gain a particular piece of knowledge. (The object can be a clause with THAT ⑦.)

learn about someone or something AND **learn of** someone or something to be told about something; to receive news or information about someone or something.

learn of someone or something Go to LEARN ABOUT SOMEONE OR SOMETHING.

learn something **from the bottom up** to learn something thoroughly, from the very beginning; to learn all aspects of something, even the most lowly.

lease ['lis] *n.* a rental contract.
→ A NEW LEASE ON LIFE

lease something **(from** someone or some group**)** to rent something from someone or a company.

lease something **(to** someone**)** to rent something to someone.

least ['list] **1.** *adj.* a superlative form of LITTLE; the smallest [amount]. **2.** *adv.* in the smallest amount; to the smallest degree; the opposite of MOST. **3.** *pron.* the smallest amount.
→ LAST BUT NOT LEAST
→ THE LINE OF LEAST RESISTANCE
→ THE PATH OF LEAST RESISTANCE

leather ['lɛð ə·] **1.** *n.* a material made from the skin of an animal, used to make shoes, coats, belts, gloves, etc. (Plural only for types and instances.) **2.** *adj.* made of ①.

leave ['liv] **1.** *iv., irreg.* to go away; to exit from a place. (Past tense and past participle: LEFT.) **2.** *tv., irreg.* to depart from a place. **3.** *tv., irreg.* to depart [from a place], letting someone or something remain in the place. **4.** *tv., irreg.* to depart from and abandon someone, such as a husband or wife. **5.** *tv., irreg.* to cause someone or something to be in a certain condition. **6.** *tv., irreg.* to will something to someone or something; to give something to someone or something after one dies. **7.** *n.* an extended period of time away from one's duties.
→ TAKE IT OR LEAVE IT

leave a bad taste in someone's **mouth** [for someone or something] to leave a bad feeling or memory with someone.

leave a sinking ship Go to DESERT A SINKING SHIP.

leave one **to** one's **fate** to abandon someone to whatever may happen—possibly death or some other unpleasant event.

leave one's **mark on** someone [for someone like a teacher] to affect the behavior and performance of another person.

leave someone **for dead** to abandon someone as being dead. (The abandoned person may actually be alive.)

leave someone **high and dry 1.** to leave someone unsupported and unable to maneuver; to leave someone helpless. **2.** to leave someone without any money at all.

leave someone **holding the baby** to leave someone with the responsibility for something, especially something difficult or unpleasant, often when it was originally someone else's responsibility.

leave someone **holding the bag** to leave someone to take all the blame; to leave someone appearing guilty.

leave someone **in peace** to stop bothering someone; to go away and let someone have peace. (Does not necessarily mean to go away from a person.)

leave someone **in the lurch** to leave someone waiting for or anticipating one's actions.

leave someone or something **hanging in midair** to suspend dealing with someone or something; to leave someone waiting for an ending; to leave something waiting to be finished or continued. (Also used literally.)

leave someone or something **out (of** something) to neglect to include someone or something in something.

leave something **on 1.** to allow something [that can be turned off] to remain on. **2.** to continue to wear some article of clothing.

leave something **up to** someone or something to allow someone or something to make a decision about something.

leaves ['livz] plural of LEAF.

lecture ['lɛk tʃɚ] **1.** *n.* a long talk about a certain subject; a speech. **2.** *n.* a speech that warns or scolds. **3.** *iv.* to give ①; to talk about a certain subject. **4.** *tv.* to talk to people about a certain subject, especially to talk to an audience or a class. **5.** *tv.* to scold someone about something; to give ① to someone.

lecturer ['lɛk tʃɚ ɚ] **1.** *n.* someone who gives a lecture. **2.** *n.* someone who gives lectures; especially someone below the rank of professor or instructor who teaches at a university or college.

led ['lɛd] past tense and past participle of LEAD.

ledge ['lɛdʒ] *n.* a narrow surface that sticks out along a wall or under a window; a shelf.

leer ['lɪr] *n.* a look of sexual desire or interest.

leer at someone to stare at someone with sexual desire or lust.

left ['lɛft] **1.** past tense and past participle of LEAVE. **2.** *n.* the direction to the west when you are facing north. (No plural.) **3.** *adj.*
toward ②; located at ②. **4.** *adv.* toward ②.

→ COME OUT OF LEFT FIELD
→ OUT IN LEFT FIELD

the **Left** *n.* politicians or citizens whose political views are liberal or radical rather than conservative. (No plural. Treated as singular.)

left-hand ['lɛft hænd] *adj.* left; on, to, or at one's left side. (Prenominal only.)

left-handed ['lɛft hæn dɪd] **1.** *adj.* favoring the use of the left hand. (Adv: *left-handed* or *left-handedly*.) **2.** *adj.* designed for people who are ①. **3.** *adv.* [of writing] done with the left hand.

leftover ['lɛft ov ɚ] *adj.* remaining; unused and therefore extra. (Prenominal only.)

leftovers ['lɛft ov ɚz] *n.* portions of food left over from a meal; portions of food remaining after a meal. (Treated as plural. Rarely countable.)

leg ['lɛg] **1.** *n.* one of the two body parts that support a human; one of the four body parts that support most other mammals, or similar parts that support certain other animals, such as insects. **2.** *n.* the part of a piece of clothing that wraps around ①. **3.** *n.* [in furniture or other structures] a vertical piece that supports weight. **4.** *n.* a part of a trip; a part of a distance to be covered.

→ COST AN ARM AND A LEG
→ HAVE ONE'S TAIL BETWEEN ONE'S LEGS
→ NOT HAVE A LEG TO STAND ON
→ ONE'S TAIL IS BETWEEN ONE'S LEGS
→ ON ONE'S OR ITS LAST LEGS
→ PAY AN ARM AND A LEG (FOR SOMETHING)

→ PULL SOMEONE'S LEG
→ STRETCH ONE'S LEGS

legal ['lig əl] **1.** *adj.* lawful; according to the law. (Adv: *legally.*) **2.** *adj.* of or about law. (Adv: *legally.*)

legal tender ['lig əl 'tɛn də˞] *n.* legal money; money that must be accepted as payment.

legend ['lɛdʒ ənd] **1.** *n.* an old and often repeated story; a fable; a myth. **2.** *n.* an explanation of symbols used on a map, plan, chart, etc.

legislate ['lɛdʒ ɪ slet] **1.** *tv.* to make laws. **2.** *tv.* to pass a law about something. (The object can be a clause with THAT ⑦.)

legislate against something to prohibit something; to pass a law against something.

legislate for something to pass a law that tries to make something happen.

legislation [lɛdʒ ɪ 'sle ʃən] **1.** *n.* writing and making laws. (No plural.) **2.** *n.* laws that have been made; a set of laws. (No plural. Number is expressed with *piece(s) of legislation*.)

legislative ['lɛdʒ ɪ sle tɪv] *adj.* of or about making laws or the people who make laws. (Adv: *legislatively.*)

legislator ['lɛdʒ ɪ sle tə˞] *n.* someone who makes laws; a member of a legislature.

legislature ['lɛdʒ ɪ sle tʃə˞] *n.* the group of people who are elected or appointed to make laws.

leisure ['li ʒə˞] **1.** *n.* free time; time that is not spent at work or sleeping; time when one can do what one wants. (No plural.) **2.** the *adj.* use of ①.

lemon ['lɛm ən] **1.** *n.* a sour, yellow citrus fruit. **2.** *n.* a product, such as a car, that does not work properly and cannot be repaired. (Informal.) **3.** *adj.* made or flavored with ①.

lemonade [lɛm ən 'ed] *n.* a drink made from the juice of lemons, sugar, and water. (No plural.)

lend ['lɛnd] **1.** *tv., irreg.* to grant someone permission to use or borrow something for a period of time. (Past tense and past participle: LENT.) **2.** *tv., irreg.* to contribute an effect to something; to add a quality to something. (Figurative on ①.)

lend an ear (to someone**)** to listen to someone.

lend oneself or itself **to** something [for someone or something] to be adaptable to something; [for someone or something] to be useful for something.

length ['lɛŋkθ] **1.** *n.* the measurement of something from end to end; the amount of time that has passed. (The opposite of WIDTH. Plural only for types and instances.) **2.** *n.* a piece of something of a certain or known ①.

lengthen ['lɛŋk θən] **1.** *tv.* to make something longer. **2.** *iv.* to become longer.

lens ['lɛnz] **1.** *n.* a piece of curved glass, or some other clear material, that bends rays of light. **2.** *n.* the clear, curved part of the eye—

located behind the pupil—that focuses light rays on the retina.

lent ['lɛnt] past tense and past participle of LEND.

leopard ['lɛp ɚd] *n.* a large animal in the cat family, typically having yellowish fur with black spots.

less ['lɛs] **1.** *adj.* the comparative form of LITTLE; a smaller amount. (Used with things that are measured in quantities. Compare this with *fewer*, at FEW, which is used with things that can be counted.) **2.** *adv.* to a smaller extent or degree; not as much. **3.** *suffix* a form meaning *without* that can be added to nouns and to adjectives that have come from verbs. (The resulting adjectives can be made into nouns with the *-ness* suffix and into adverbs with the suffix *-ly*.)
→ IN LESS THAN NO TIME

lessen ['lɛs ən] **1.** *iv.* to become less; to decrease in size, amount, or power. **2.** *tv.* to cause something to become less.

the **lesser (of the two)** the smaller one (of two); the one having the least amount.

the **lesser of two evils** the less bad thing, of a pair of bad things.

lesson ['lɛs ən] **1.** *n.* a session of instruction with a teacher; the material to be covered in one session of instruction; something, such as a school assignment, that is to be learned, studied, or prepared. **2.** *n.* something that one learns from an experience; an experience that one learns something from.

let ['lɛt] **1.** *tv., irreg.* to allow someone or something to do something; to allow something to happen. (Past tense and past participle: *let*.) **2.** *tv., irreg.* to rent an apartment or room (to someone).
→ DON'T LET SOMEONE OR SOMETHING GET YOU DOWN.
→ LIVE AND LET LIVE

let down one's **guard** to relax one's efforts or vigilance.

let go of someone or something to release someone or something.

let grass grow under one's **feet** to do nothing; to stand still.

let off steam AND **blow off steam** to release excess energy or anger.

let on (about someone or something**)** to confirm or reveal something about someone or something.

let one's **emotions show** to be emotional, especially when it is not appropriate.

let one's **hair down** to become more intimate and begin to speak frankly.

let out [for an event that includes many people] to end.

let out a sound to make [some kind of a] sound.

let out (with) something **1.** to state or utter something loudly. **2.** to give forth a scream or yell.

let someone **know (about** something**)** to tell someone something; to inform someone of something.

let someone **off (the hook)** to release someone from a responsibility.

let someone **off (with** something) to give someone a light punishment [for doing something].

let someone or something **down** to fail someone or something; to disappoint someone or a group.

let something **out 1.** to reveal something; to tell about a secret or a plan. **2.** to enlarge the waist of an article of clothing.

let something **out (to** someone) to rent something to someone.

let something **pass** to let something go unnoticed or unchallenged.

let something **slide (by)** Go to LET SOMETHING SLIP BY.

let something **slip by** AND **let** something **slide (by) 1.** to forget or miss an important time or date. **2.** to waste a period of time.

let the cat out of the bag AND **spill the beans** to reveal a secret or a surprise by accident.

let the chance slip by to lose the opportunity (to do something).

let up 1. to diminish. **2.** to stop [doing something] altogether.

let up (on someone or something) to reduce the pressure or demands on someone or something.

let's ['lɛts] *cont.* let us; we will [do something]. (A gentle command or request. A response is usually expected.)

letter ['lɛt ɚ] **1.** *n.* a written or printed symbol in an alphabet. **2.** *n.* a written message sent to a person or a group.

letter carrier ['lɛt ɚ kɛr i ɚ] Go to MAIL CARRIER.

lettuce ['lɛt ɪs] *n.* a leafy, green vegetable, often used in salads.

(No plural. Number is expressed with *leaf* or *leaves of lettuce* and *head(s) of lettuce*.)
→ HEAD OF LETTUCE

level ['lɛv əl] **1.** *n.* a flat surface; a horizontal plane. **2.** *n.* one of the floors of a building or other structure. **3.** *n.* a layer; a step or a stage. **4.** *n.* the amount of a measurement; a position on a scale of measurement. **5.** *n.* a tool or device that shows when a surface is exactly horizontal or vertical. **6.** *adj.* [of a surface] exactly horizontal, so every point is the same height. **7.** *adj.* [of a measurement] steady; not changing. (Figurative on ⑥.) **8.** *tv.* to knock down trees, buildings, or other objects until the land is flat; to clear land by knocking down trees or buildings.
→ FIND ONE'S OWN LEVEL
→ ON THE LEVEL
→ SEA LEVEL
→ (STRICTLY) ON THE LEVEL

level off [for variation or fluctuation in the motion of something] to diminish; [for a rate] to stop increasing or decreasing.

level out [for something that was going up and down] to assume a more level course or path.

level something **at** someone to aim a remark at someone; to direct something at someone.

level something **off** to make something level or smooth.

level something **out** to cause something to assume a more level course or path.

lever ['lɛv ɚ] **1.** *n.* a bar of metal or wood, positioned so that it increases one's power in lifting or moving heavy objects. **2.** *n.* a bar or handle that serves as a control device.

liability [laɪ ə 'bɪl ə ti] **1.** *n.* a kind of danger to people that could cause a lawsuit against whoever is responsible for creating the danger. (No plural form.) **2.** *n.* a cost or [monetary] charge; a potential cost; a negative consideration. (No plural form.)
→ ASSUME LIABILITY (FOR SOMETHING)

liar ['laɪ ɚ] *n.* someone who tells lies; someone who does not tell the truth.

liberty ['lɪb ɚ ti] **1.** *n.* the freedom from control; the freedom to think or act for oneself. (No plural.) **2.** *n.* the permission to do something; a right or a privilege that one has been given.

librarian [laɪ 'brɛr i ən] *n.* someone who manages or helps operate a library.

library ['laɪ brɛr i] **1.** *n.* a building or room that has a supply of books or similar materials available for use by a number of people. **2.** *n.* a collection of books, records, videotapes, etc.

license ['laɪ səns] **1.** *n.* a document that proves that someone has official permission to do or own something. **2.** *n.* a freedom to do something. (No plural.) **3.** *tv.* to give or sell someone a ① for something; to authorize someone or something; to permit someone or something.

license plate ['laɪ səns 'plet] *n.* a rectangular panel, showing a car's license number, that is put on the rear and, in some states, the front

of a car. (Can be shortened to PLATE.)

license to do something permission, right, or justification to do something.

lick ['lɪk] **1.** *tv.* to move the tongue along someone or something; to taste something by moving one's tongue along it; to make something wet by moving one's tongue along it. **2.** *n.* the movement of the tongue along the surface of something as in ①. **3.** *n.* a small amount of something that one gets by moving the tongue as in ①.
→ GIVE SOMETHING A LICK AND A PROMISE

lick one's **lips** to show eagerness or pleasure about a future event.

lid ['lɪd] **1.** *n.* a cover for a container, surface, hole, etc. **2.** *n.* the fold of skin over the eye; an EYELID.

lie ['laɪ] **1.** *n.* a statement that is not true and that the speaker knows is not true; a false statement. **2.** *iv.* to say something that is not true; to tell ①. (Past tense and past participle: LIED. Present participle: LYING.) **3.** *iv., irreg.* to be in a flat position; to place oneself in a flat position. (Past tense: LAY; past participle: LAIN. See also LAY. Present participle: LYING.) **4.** *iv., irreg.* to be located; to be in a certain place. **5.** *iv., irreg.* to remain in a place or condition; to stay in a certain condition or position.
→ a PACK OF LIES
→ TAKE SOMETHING LYING DOWN

lie down to recline.

lie fallow 1. [for land] to remain unused. **2.** [for a skill and talent] to remain unused and neglected.

lie in [for a woman] to lie in bed awaiting the birth of her child.

lie through one's **teeth** to lie boldly, obviously, and with no remorse.

lied ['laɪd] past tense and past participle of LIE ②.

life ['laɪf] **1.** *n.* the power that causes plants and animals to exist, in general. (No plural.) **2.** *n., irreg.* an individual instance of ① that can be lived, lost, saved, spent, wasted, etc.; the period of time between the time of one's birth and one's death or between the time of one's birth and the present. (Plural: LIVES.) **3.** *n., irreg.* the activities, experiences, and habits of a person. **4.** *n.* excitement; vigor. (No plural.) **5.** *n.* a kind of living; a quality of living. (No plural.)
→ ALL WALKS OF LIFE
→ CLAIM A LIFE
→ GET THE SHOCK OF ONE'S LIFE
→ HAVE THE TIME OF ONE'S LIFE
→ IN THE PRIME OF LIFE
→ LEAD A DOG'S LIFE
→ LEAD THE LIFE OF RILEY
→ LIVE A DOG'S LIFE
→ LIVE A LIFE OF SOMETHING
→ LIVE THE LIFE OF RILEY
→ MAKE LIFE MISERABLE FOR SOMEONE
→ a MATTER OF LIFE AND DEATH
→ MILESTONE IN SOMEONE'S LIFE
→ a NEW LEASE ON LIFE
→ ONE'S MISSION IN LIFE
→ RUN FOR ONE'S LIFE
→ the SEAMY SIDE OF LIFE
→ WITHIN AN INCH OF ONE'S LIFE

life jacket AND **life preserver; life vest** ['laɪf dʒæk ət, ... prə 'zɚv ɚ, ... vɛst] *n.* a thick jacket without sleeves that floats and will keep the person who wears it from sinking in the water. (See also LIFE-SAVER.)

life of the party the type of person who is lively and helps make a party fun and exciting.

life preserver Go to LIFE JACKET.

life vest Go to LIFE JACKET.

lifeboat ['laɪf bot] *n.* a boat used to carry people away from a sinking ship; a boat used to save people in danger of drowning.

lifeguard ['laɪf gɑrd] *n.* someone who works at a beach or swimming pool to encourage water safety and rescue people from danger in the water.

lifesaver ['laɪf sev ɚ] **1.** *n.* someone or something that saves someone's life. **2.** *n.* something that serves well in an emergency. (Figurative on ①.)

lifetime ['laɪf taɪm] **1.** *n.* the time that a person or animal is living. **2.** *n.* the period of time that something works or can be used. (Figurative on ①.)

lift ['lɪft] **1.** *tv.* to pick someone or something up from the ground; to raise someone or something to a higher level. **2.** *iv.* [for clouds, fog, smoke, smog] to rise or go away. **3.** *n.* a free ride in a car or truck. (Informal.) **4.** *n.* something that makes someone feel happier, stronger, or more awake.

lift off [for a plane or rocket] to move upward, leaving the ground.

lift something off (of) someone or something to raise something and uncover or release someone or something.

light ['laɪt] **1.** *n.* a form of radiation or energy that makes things visible. (No plural.) **2.** *n.* something that produces ①, such as a lamp or a flame. **3.** *n.* something, such as a match, that produces fire. (No plural.) **4.** *n.* the period of time when the sun is in the sky; daytime. (No plural.) **5.** *n.* a traffic signal that uses ② that are red, yellow, and green to control people and vehicles. (Short for TRAFFIC LIGHT.) **6.** *n.* a view; the way that something is seen or thought of. (No plural.) **7.** *adj.* pale in color; not dark or deep; mixed with white. (Adv: *lightly*.) **8.** *adj.* not heavy; not weighing much; easy to carry. (Adv: *lightly*.) **9.** *adj.* not having much force; gentle. (Figurative on ⑧. Adv: *lightly*.) **10.** *iv., irreg.* [for a creature] to land on a surface after flight. (Past tense and past participle: *lighted* or LIT.) **11.** *tv., irreg.* to set something on fire; to cause something to begin to burn.
→ (AS) LIGHT AS A FEATHER
→ BEGIN TO SEE THE LIGHT
→ BRING SOMETHING TO LIGHT
→ COME TO LIGHT
→ GET OFF LIGHTLY
→ HIDE ONE'S LIGHT UNDER A BUSHEL
→ MAKE LIGHT OF SOMETHING
→ OUT LIKE A LIGHT
→ SEE THE LIGHT (AT THE END OF THE TUNNEL)
→ SEE THE LIGHT (OF DAY)
→ TRAFFIC LIGHT

light someone or something **up** to shine lights on someone or something.

light up 1. [for something] to become brighter. **2.** [for someone] to become interested in and responsive to something.

light (up)on someone or something **1.** to land on someone or something; to settle on someone or something. **2.** to arrive at something by chance; to happen upon something. (Figurative. Close to ①.)

lighter ['laɪtɚ] *n.* a device that makes a flame to light cigarettes or cigars.

lighthouse ['laɪt haʊs] *n., irreg.* a tall structure near the sea with a bright light near the top that warns ships away from danger. (Plural: [...haʊ zəz].)

lighting ['laɪt ɪŋ] **1.** *n.* light that makes things and people visible; illumination; the type or quality of light in a room or other place. (No plural.) **2.** *n.* the equipment that directs light, especially for effect in a television or movie studio or on a stage. (No plural.)

lightning ['laɪt nɪŋ] *n.* a flash or streak of light in the sky, especially during a thunderstorm. (No plural. Number is expressed with *bolt(s)* or *flash(es)* of *lightning*.)

lightning bug AND **firefly** ['laɪt nɪŋ bəg, 'faɪr flaɪ] *n.* a type of beetle that is able to fly and to illuminate its body in the dark.

like ['laɪk] **1.** *tv.* to enjoy someone or something; to find someone or something pleasant. **2.** *n.* a desire; something that one enjoys having or doing. **3.** *adj.* similar; same. (Prenominal only.) **4.** *prep.* similar to someone or something; in the same way as someone or something. **5.** *prep.* for instance, the following people or things; such as the following people or things.

6. *conj.* in the same way as someone or something does; similar to the way someone or something is. (Viewed as incorrect by some people.) **7.** *conj.* as though; as if. (Viewed as incorrect by some people.)

like a bat out of hell with great speed and force.

like a bolt out of the blue suddenly and without warning.

like a bump on a log unresponsive; immobile.

like a fish out of water awkward; in a foreign or unaccustomed environment.

like a lamb to the slaughter AND **like lambs to the slaughter** [proceeding] quietly and without seeming to realize or complain about the likely difficulties or dangers of a situation.

like a sitting duck AND **like sitting ducks** unguarded; unsuspecting and unaware.

like a three-ring circus chaotic; exciting and busy.

like lambs to the slaughter Go to LIKE A LAMB TO THE SLAUGHTER.

like looking for a needle in a haystack [of a search] hopeless.

like nothing on earth unique, extraordinary and, surprising. (Informal.)

like sitting ducks Go to LIKE A SITTING DUCK.

like to hear oneself **talk** [for someone] to enjoy one's own talking more than other people enjoy listening to it.

like water off a duck's back easily; without any apparent effect.

likelihood ['laɪk li hʊd] *n.* the chance of being likely; the state of something being probable. (No plural.)

likely ['laɪk li] **1.** *adj.* probable. **2.** *adj.* suitable; apt.
→ (AS) LIKELY AS NOT

likely to do something apt to do something; tending to do something.

lily ['lɪl i] *n.* a flower with large petals that grows from a bulb.
→ GILD THE LILY

limb ['lɪm] **1.** *n.* a large tree branch. **2.** *n.* an arm, leg, or wing.
→ OUT ON A LIMB

lime ['laɪm] **1.** *n.* a small, green citrus fruit. **2.** *n.* a white substance, made by burning a kind of rock, which is used to make plaster, cement, and mortar. (No plural.) **3.** *adj.* made or flavored with ①.

limit ['lɪm ɪt] **1.** *n.* a boundary; the edge; the farthest point of something; the greatest amount allowed or possible. **2.** *tv.* to prevent someone or something from passing a certain point or amount; to restrict something to a certain amount of space or time.
→ GO THE LIMIT
→ The SKY'S THE LIMIT.
→ SPEED LIMIT

limp ['lɪmp] **1.** *n.* an uneven walk; a way of walking where one's foot drags or moves as if it is injured. **2.** *iv.* to walk to somewhere showing ①. **3.** *adj.* not stiff; having no resistance. (Adv: *limply*. Comp: *limper*; sup: *limpest*.)

line ['laɪn] **1.** *n.* a thin mark, straight or curved, made on the surface of something. **2.** *n.* a border; a mark that shows the limit, border, or end of something. **3.** *n.* a wide band; a stripe. **4.** *n.* a string, rope, or cord. (On boats and ships, ropes are called *lines*.) **5.** *n.* a wire, pipe, or cable that carries a public utility company's product, such as electricity, water, gas, telephone, etc. **6.** *n.* a telephone connection. **7.** *n.* a row or series of people standing and waiting for a turn to do something. **8.** *n.* a row of words in printing or writing. **9.** *n.* something that is said by an actor onstage or in a film. **10.** *tv.* to put a lining in something; to cover the inside of something with something else.
→ DRAW THE LINE BETWEEN SOMETHING AND SOMETHING ELSE
→ DROP SOMEONE A LINE
→ DROP SOMEONE A FEW LINES
→ the END OF THE LINE
→ FALL IN(TO) LINE (WITH SOMEONE OR SOMETHING)
→ IN THE LINE OF DUTY
→ LAY SOMETHING ON THE LINE
→ the PARTY LINE
→ PUT SOMETHING ON THE LINE
→ READ BETWEEN THE LINES
→ SIGN ON THE DOTTED LINE
→ STEP OUT OF LINE
→ TOE THE LINE

the **line of least resistance** and the **path of least resistance** the course of action that will cause the least trouble or effort.

line someone or something **up 1.** to put people or things in line. **2.** to schedule someone or something [for something].

line someone or something **up (in something)** to put people or things into some kind of formation, such as a row, column, ranks, etc.

line up to get into a line; [for a number of people or vehicles] to join or form a line.

line up for something to form or get into a line and wait for something.

line up in(to) something to form or get into a line, row, rank, column, etc.

linen ['lɪn ən] **1.** *n.* a fabric made from flax. (No plural form.) **2.** *n.* tablecloths and sheets made of ① or some other fabric; underwear. (Sometimes plural with the same meaning.) **3.** the *adj.* use of ① or ②.
→ AIR ONE'S DIRTY LINEN IN PUBLIC
→ WASH ONE'S DIRTY LINEN IN PUBLIC

linger on (after someone or something**)** AND **stay on (after** someone or something**)** to outlast someone or something; to live longer than someone else or long after an event.

lining ['laɪn ɪŋ] *n.* a fabric or other material put on the inside surface of something for protection, warmth, etc.

link ['lɪŋk] **1.** *n.* one of the loops or circles that make up a chain. **2.** *n.* someone or something that connects someone or something to someone or something else. (Figurative on ①.) **3.** *tv.* to connect someone or something to someone or something else.

link up to someone or something AND **link (up) with** someone or something to join up with some-one or something.

link (up) with someone or something Go to LINK UP TO SOMEONE OR SOMETHING.

lint ['lɪnt] *n.* a tiny piece of thread; a small cluster of threads, dirt, hair, etc. (No plural.)

lion ['laɪ ən] *n.* a large, tan-colored wild animal in the cat family, native to Africa.

the lion's share (of something) the larger share of something.
→ BEARD THE LION IN HIS DEN
→ MOUNTAIN LION

lip ['lɪp] **1.** *n.* one of the two ridges of flesh on the outside of the mouth. **2.** *n.* a rim; an edge, espe-cially a part of an edge of a con-tainer.
→ BUTTON ONE'S LIP
→ KEEP A STIFF UPPER LIP
→ LICK ONE'S LIPS

liquid ['lɪk wɪd] **1.** *n.* a flowing sub-stance, such as water, that is not a gas or a solid. **2.** *n.* the sounds [l] and [r]. **3.** *adj.* in the form of ①. **4.** *adj.* [of an asset that can be] easily converted to cash.

liquor ['lɪk ɚ] **1.** *n.* broth or juices from cooking. (No plural.) **2.** *n.* alcohol for drinking. (Plural only for types and instances.)

list ['lɪst] **1.** *n.* a printed or written series of words, names, or items. **2.** *n.* a slant or tilt to one side, as with a ship. **3.** *tv.* to write things on ①. **4.** *iv.* to lean to one side.
→ ON A WAITING LIST

listen ['lɪs ən] *iv.* to pay attention to a source of sound.

listen in (on someone or some-thing) **1.** to join someone or a group as a listener. **2.** to eavesdrop on someone.

lit ['lɪt] a past tense and past par-ticiple of LIGHT.

liter ['lit ɚ] *n.* a metric unit of liq-uid measurement equal to 1.06 quarts.

literacy ['lɪt ə rə si] *n.* the ability to read and write. (No plural.)

literal ['lɪt ə rəl] **1.** *adj.* [of the meaning of a word or phrase] basic instead of secondary or figu-rative. (Adv: *literally*.) **2.** *adj.* exact, especially pertaining to translations; translating or inter-preting one word at a time. (Adv: *literally*.)

literature ['lɪt ə rə tʃɚ] **1.** *n.* writ-ing considered as art, such as fic-tion, plays, and poetry. (No plural.) **2.** *n.* all the written mate-rial of a specific subject or region. (No plural.) **3.** *n.* information; a brochure or small book that has information about something. (No plural.)

litmus test a question or experi-ment that seeks to determine the state of one important factor.

little ['lɪt əl] **1.** *adj.* small in size. (Comp: *littler*; sup: *littlest*.) **2.** *adj.*, *irreg.* not much. (Without *a*. Comp: LESS; sup: LEAST. Used with items that cannot be counted. Compare this with FEW ①.) **3.** *adj.*, *irreg.* some; a small amount. (With *a*. Comp: LESS; sup: LEAST. Used with items that cannot be counted. Compare this with FEW ②.) **4.** *adv.*, *irreg.* not much; not a lot. (Comp: LESS; sup: LEAST.)
→ PRECIOUS LITTLE

→ TWIST SOMEONE AROUND ONE'S LITTLE FINGER

a **little 1.** *adv.* somewhat; to some degree or in some amount. (Comp: LESS; sup: LEAST.) **2.** *n.* a small amount [of something mentioned before or known from the context]; some. (No plural. Treated as singular. Use *a few* for items that are counted.)

a **little bird told me** learned from a mysterious or secret source.

little by little slowly, a bit at a time.

livable ['lɪv ə bəl] *adj.* suitable to be lived in or with. (Adv: *livably*.)

live 1. ['laɪv] *adj.* not dead; having life. **2.** ['laɪv] *adj.* carrying electricity; electrically charged. (Figurative on ①.) **3.** ['laɪv] *adj.* on the air; not taped; broadcast at the same time something is happening. **4.** ['laɪv] *adv.* while something is really happening; broadcast at the moment that something is happening. **5.** ['lɪv] *iv.* to be; to exist; to be alive; to survive. **6.** ['lɪv] *iv.* to reside at a certain address; to reside in or at a certain place. **7.** ['lɪv] *iv.* to exist in a certain way.

live a dog's life Go to LEAD A DOG'S LIFE.

live a life of something to have a life of a certain quality or style.

live and let live to not interfere with other people's business or preferences.

live beyond one's **means** to spend more money than one can afford.

live by one's **wits** to survive by being clever.

live from hand to mouth to live in poor circumstances.

live in an ivory tower to be aloof from the realities of living.

live off (of) someone or something to obtain one's living or means of survival from someone or something.

live off the fat of the land to grow one's own food; to live on stored-up resources or abundant resources.

live out of a suitcase to live briefly in a place, never unpacking one's luggage.

live something **down** to overcome some embarrassing or troublesome problem or event.

live the life of Riley Go to LEAD THE LIFE OF RILEY.

live through something to endure something; to survive an unpleasant or dangerous time of one's life.

live up to one's **end of the bargain** to carry through on a bargain; to do as was promised in a bargain.

live up to something to be equal to expectations or goals.

live with something to put up with something. (Does not mean "to dwell with.")

live within one's **means** to spend no more money than one has.

live within something **1.** to live within certain boundaries. **2.** to keep one's living costs within a certain amount, especially within one's budget, means, etc.

live without something to survive, lacking something.

333

lively [ˈlaɪv li] *adj.* showing energy or excitement; cheerful; active. (Comp: livelier; sup: liveliest.)

liven something **up** to make something more lively or less dull.

liver [ˈlɪv ɚ] **1.** *n.* an organ, in the body of an animal, that produces fluids used in digestion and performs other important functions. **2.** *n.* a whole ①, eaten as food. **3.** *n.* ①, eaten as food. (No plural.)

lives 1. [ˈlaɪvz] plural of LIFE. **2.** [ˈlɪvz] the third-person singular of LIVE.

livestock [ˈlaɪv stɑk] *n.* animals that are kept on a farm or ranch, usually for the production of food. (No plural. Treated as singular or plural, but not countable.)

living room [ˈlɪv ɪŋ rum] *n.* the main room of a house or apartment, large enough to hold a number of people.

lizard [ˈlɪz ɚd] *n.* a reptile with legs, scaly skin, and a tail.

load [ˈlod] **1.** *n.* something that is carried; a burden; a weight. **2.** *n.* the amount of something that can be carried; one large portion of something for carrying. **3.** *n.* the amount of electricity used by an electrical device. **4.** *tv.* to put bullets into a gun; to put film or videotape into a camera; to install computer software into a computer. **5.** *tv.* to fill something with something.
→ GET A LOAD OFF ONE'S FEET
→ GET A LOAD OFF ONE'S MIND
→ TAKE A LOAD OFF ONE'S FEET

load someone or something **into** something to put someone or something into something.

load up (with something) to take or accumulate a lot of something.

loaf [ˈlof] **1.** *n., irreg.* a mass of bread dough baked in one piece. (Plural: LOAVES.) **2.** *n., irreg.* a mass of food cooked in a shape like ①. (Often part of a compound.) **3.** *iv.* to waste time.

loan [ˈlon] **1.** *n.* something, especially money, that is lent to someone. **2.** *tv.* to lend something to someone; to let someone borrow something. (Some people object to the use of LOAN in this sense rather than LEND, reserving LOAN for the lending of money.)
→ FLOAT A LOAN
→ TAKE OUT A LOAN

loathe [ˈloð] *tv.* to hate someone or something very much.

loaves [ˈlovz] plural of LOAF.

lobby [ˈlɑb i] **1.** *n.* the entrance room of a building. **2.** *tv.* to try to influence someone who makes laws or regulations to vote a certain way.

lobby against something to solicit support against something, such as a piece of legislation or a government regulation.

lobby for something to solicit support for something among the members of a voting body, such as the Congress.

lobster [ˈlɑb stɚ] **1.** *n.* an edible sea animal with six legs and (possibly) two large claws. **2.** *n.* the meat of ① used as food. (No plural.) **3.** *adj.* made or flavored with ②.

local [ˈlok əl] **1.** *adj.* of or about the nearby area. (Adv: *locally*.) **2.** *n.* a bus or train that stops at every station. **3.** *n.* a person who lives in the area that something is in. (Often plural.)

locate [ˈlo ket] **1.** *tv.* to find someone or something; to learn where someone or something is. **2.** *tv.* to place someone or something in a particular place.

location [lo ˈke ʃən] *n.* the place where someone or something is; the place where someone or something is found.
→ ON LOCATION

lock [ˈlak] **1.** *n.* a device on a door opening that prevents the door from being opened without a key. **2.** *n.* a device similar to a ① that controls access to something. **3.** *n.* a part of a canal or river between two heavy, watertight gates where the level of the water can be raised or lowered, allowing boats to move from one level of water to another. **4.** *n.* a small bundle of [head] hair; a strand or curl of hair. **5.** *iv.* not to be able to move.
→ COMBINATION LOCK
→ PICK A LOCK

lock horns (with someone**)** to get into an argument with someone.

lock someone or something **up** to put someone or something into a place that can be secured with a lock; to put someone or something in jail.

lock something **in** to take action to fix a rate or price at a certain figure.

lock something **(up)** to secure something by using a lock so it cannot be opened without a key.

lock, stock, and barrel absolutely every part or item.

locker [ˈlak ɚ] *n.* a cabinet like a tiny closet that can be locked, where clothes and valuables are kept.
→ DAVY JONES'S LOCKER

locomotive [lok ə ˈmot ɪv] **1.** *n.* a train engine. **2.** the *adj.* use of ①.

locust [ˈlok əst] *n.* a kind of insect that travels in large swarms and destroys crops.

lodge [ˈladʒ] **1.** *n.* a small, privately owned cabin for campers, hunters, skiers, and others who like to stay in the country. **2.** *n.* the place where a men's organization meets. **3.** *n.* the structure that beavers build to live in. **4.** *iv.* to become stuck somewhere; to become wedged in something.

lodge a charge against someone to place a charge against someone.

lodge something **against** something to place or prop something against something.

log [ˈlɔg] **1.** *n.* a length of the trunk or main branch of a tree with all of the branches removed. **2.** *n.* a detailed record of a trip written by the captain of a ship, plane, train, etc. **3.** *tv.* to note something in ②.
→ LIKE A BUMP ON A LOG

log off AND **log out** to record one's exit from a computer system. (This action may be recorded, or logged, automatically in the computer's memory.)

log on to sign oneself on to use a computer system. (This action may be recorded, or logged, automatically in the computer's memory.)

log out Go to LOG OFF.

logic ['lɑdʒ ɪk] **1.** *n.* the science of reasoning; the part of philosophy that deals with reason. (No plural.) **2.** *n.* a method of argument or reasoning. (No plural.) **3.** *n.* sense; rational thought; the ability to reason. (No plural.)

logical ['lɑdʒ ɪ kəl] *adj.* making sense; according to the rules of logic. (Adv: *logically* [...ɪk li].)

lollipop ['lɑl i pɑp] *n.* a piece of hard candy on the end of a stick.

lone ['lon] *adj.* only; alone; without others. (Prenominal only. See also ALONE. No comparative or superlative.)

lonely ['lon li] **1.** *adj.* sad because one is alone; lonesome. (Comp: *lonelier;* sup: *loneliest.*) **2.** *adj.* isolated; away from other people. (Comp: *lonelier;* sup: *loneliest.*)

lonesome ['lon səm] *adj.* lonely; sad because one is alone. (Adv: *lonesomely.*)

long ['lɔŋ] **1.** *adj.* great in length or in amount of time. (Comp: *longer;* sup: *longest.*) **2.** *adj.* having a certain length; lasting a certain amount of time. (Follows the measure of length or time. Comp: *longer.*) **3.** *adv.* for a great extent of time before or after the time indicated. **4.** *adj.* seeming to take more time than normal; seeming to be farther than normal. (Comp: *longer;* sup: *longest.*)
→ ALL DAY LONG
→ ALL MONTH LONG
→ ALL NIGHT LONG
→ ALL SUMMER LONG
→ ALL YEAR LONG
→ AS LONG AS
→ IN THE LONG RUN
→ MAKE A LONG STORY SHORT
→ NOT LONG FOR THIS WORLD
→ OVER THE LONG HAUL
→ SO LONG AS

long ago long before this time; much earlier than now.

long distance ['lɔŋ 'dɪs təns] **1.** *n.* telephone service between points that are far apart. (No plural.) **2.** *adj.* covering a great distance; linking people or things that are far apart. (Hyphenated.) **3.** *adv.* in a way that covers a great distance; not locally. (Hyphenated.)

Long time no see. a phrase indicating that one has not seen someone for a long time.

look ['lʊk] **1.** *n.* an act of seeing [someone or something]; an act of trying to see someone or something. **2.** *n.* a manner or style of appearing. **3.** *n.* an expression on the face. **4.** *iv.* to seem; to appear [to be]. **5.** *iv.* to face a certain direction; to be positioned in a certain direction.
→ FARAWAY LOOK
→ FAR-OFF LOOK
→ HAVE A LOOK FOR SOMEONE OR SOMETHING
→ LIKE LOOKING FOR A NEEDLE IN A HAYSTACK
→ TAKE A LOOK FOR SOMEONE OR SOMETHING

look as if butter wouldn't melt in one's **mouth** to appear to be cold and unfeeling (despite any information to the contrary).

look at someone or something to move the eyes to see or examine someone or something.

look away (from someone or something) to turn one's gaze away from someone.

look back (at someone or something) AND **look back (on** someone or something) **1.** to gaze back and try to get a view of someone or something. **2.** to think about someone or something in the past.

look back (on someone or something) Go to LOOK BACK (AT SOMEONE OR SOMETHING).

look daggers at someone to give someone a dirty or angry look.

look down (at someone or something) **1.** to turn one's gaze downward at someone or something. **2.** AND **look down on** someone or something to view someone or something as lowly or unworthy.

look down on someone or something Go to LOOK DOWN (AT SOMEONE OR SOMETHING).

look good on paper to seems fine in theory, but not perhaps in practice; to appear to be a good plan.

look in (on someone or something) to check on someone or something.

look into something **1.** to gaze into the inside of something. **2.** to investigate something.

look like a million dollars to look very good.

look like the cat that swallowed the canary to appear as if one has just had a great success.

look on to be a spectator.

look out to be careful; to think and move fast because something dangerous is about to harm one. (Usually a command.)

look out for someone or something **1.** to be watchful for the appearance of someone or something. **2.** to be alert to the danger posed by someone or something. **3.** to protect or guard someone or something.

look someone or something **over** to examine someone or something.

look someone or something **up** **1.** to seek someone, a group, or something out. **2.** to seek information about someone or something in a book or listing.

look the other way to ignore (something) on purpose. (Also used literally.)

look through something **1.** to gaze through something. **2.** to examine the parts, pages, samples, etc., of something.

look up to show promise of improving.

look up to someone to admire someone.

look (up)on someone or something **as** something to view someone or something as something; to consider someone or something to be something.

loom ['lum] **1.** *n.* a machine used for weaving cloth, blankets, or rugs. **2.** *iv.* to appear somewhere in a threatening or unfriendly way.

loom large to be of great importance, especially when referring to a possible problem, danger, or threat.

loom out of something to appear to come out of or penetrate something.

loom up to appear to rise up [from somewhere]; to take form or definition, usually threateningly.

loop ['lup] *n.* anything that looks like a circular figure formed by a line that curves and possibly crosses itself.
→ KNOCK SOMEONE FOR A LOOP
→ THROW SOMEONE FOR A LOOP

loose ['lus] **1.** *adj.* not tight; having room to move. (Adv: *loosely.* Comp: *looser;* sup: *loosest.*) **2.** *adj.* free; escaped and not confined. **3.** *adj.* not exact. (Figurative on ①. Adv: *loosely.* Comp: *looser;* sup: *loosest.*) **4.** *adj.* [of morals] lax or not restrained. (Adv: *loosely.* Comp: *looser;* sup: *loosest.*) **5.** *adv.* freely.
→ AT LOOSE ENDS
→ BREAK LOOSE (FROM SOMEONE)
→ PLAY FAST AND LOOSE (WITH SOMEONE OR SOMETHING)

loosen someone or something **up 1.** to make someone's muscles and joints move more freely by exercising them. **2.** to make someone or a group more relaxed and friendly.

loosen something **up** to make something less tight.

loosen up to become loose or relaxed.

loot ['lut] **1.** *n.* stolen money or objects. (No plural.) **2.** *tv.* to rob things or places, especially during a war or a riot. **3.** *iv.* to steal [something], especially during a war or riot.

lord it over someone to dominate someone; to direct and control someone.

lose ['luz] **1.** *tv., irreg.* [for someone or something] to "escape" from one's care, ownership, or possession. (Past tense and past participle: LOST.) **2.** *tv., irreg.* to have less of something after doing something or after something happens. **3.** *tv., irreg.* not to win something; not to gain or receive something. **4.** *iv., irreg.* not to win; to be defeated.

lose face to lose status; to become less respectable.

lose heart to lose one's courage or confidence.

lose one's **grip** to lose control over something.

lose one's **temper** to become angry.

lose one's **train of thought** to forget what one was talking or thinking about.

lose oneself in something to have all one's attention taken up by something.

lose out to lose in competition; to lose one's expected reward.

lose out (on something) to miss enjoying something; to miss participating in something.

lose out to someone or something to lose in a competition to someone or something.

loss ['lɔs] **1.** *n.* an instance of losing something. **2.** *n.* the value of something that was lost; how much something lost costs; money that is lost or never earned. **3.** *n.*

the death of someone; the death of a loved one. **4.** *n.* a defeat; the failure to win.
→ CUT ONE'S LOSSES

lost ['lɔst] **1.** past tense and past participle of LOSE. **2.** *adj.* unable to be found. **3.** *adj.* no longer owned; no longer in one's possession. **4.** *adj.* not knowing where one is; not knowing how to get to where one wants to be.
→ MAKE UP FOR LOST TIME

lost in thought busy thinking.

lost on someone having no effect on someone; wasted on someone. (Informal.)

lot ['lɑt] **1.** *n.* a part of the available goods; a group of goods. **2.** *n.* fate; destiny; the kind of life that one has been granted. **3.** *n.* an area of land; a share of land; a piece of property.
→ COVER A LOT OF GROUND
→ DRAW LOTS
→ GET A LOT OF MILEAGE OUT OF SOMETHING
→ HAVE A LOT GOING (FOR ONE)
→ JOB LOT
→ PARKING LOT

a **lot 1.** AND **lots** *n.* many of the people or things already mentioned; much of something already mentioned. (Treated as singular or plural, but not countable.) **2.** *adv.* much; often.

a **lot of** someone or something AND **lots of** someone or something many people or things; much of someone or something.

lotion ['lo ʃən] *n.* a creamy liquid that is rubbed on the body to soothe, add moisture, or clean the skin. (Plural only for types and instances.)

lots of someone or something Go to a LOT OF SOMEONE OR SOMETHING.

loud ['laʊd] **1.** *adj.* [of sound] having much volume or intensity; not quiet. (Adv: *loudly.* Comp: *louder;* sup: *loudest.*) **2.** *adj.* too bright; showy. (Figurative on ①. Adv: *loudly.* Comp: *louder;* sup: *loudest.*) **3.** *adv.* sounding as in ①. (Comp: *louder;* sup: *loudest.*)

lounge around (someplace) to lie about someplace.

love ['lʌv] **1.** *n.* a strong emotion of attraction, care, romance, or desire toward someone. (No plural.) **2.** *n.* a strong interest in something. (No plural.) **3.** *n.* [in tennis] a score of zero. **4.** *tv.* to care deeply for someone romantically. **5.** *tv.* to care deeply for someone; to care very much about someone. **6.** *tv.* to care about or like something very much.
→ FALL IN LOVE (WITH SOMEONE OR SOMETHING)
→ LABOR OF LOVE

love at first sight love established when two people first see one another.

love to do something to enjoy something; to enjoy doing something; to have an interest in doing something.

lovely ['lʌv li] *adj.* beautiful; pretty; attractive. (Comp: *lovelier;* sup: *loveliest.*)

lovely weather for ducks rainy weather.

lover ['lʌv ɚ] **1.** *n.* one of two people who love each other in a romantic way. **2.** *n.* someone whom one loves in a romantic way; a mate to whom one may or may not be married. **3.** *n.* someone who enjoys something; someone who enjoys doing something.

low ['lo] **1.** *adj.* only a little way above the ground or sea level; not high. (Comp: *lower*; sup: *lowest*.) **2.** *adj.* near the bottom of something. (Comp: *lower*; sup: *lowest*.) **3.** *adj.* less than average in amount, power, volume, height, intensity, cost, etc. (Comp: *lower*; sup: *lowest*.) **4.** *adj.* [feeling] weak or unhappy. (Comp: *lower*; sup: *lowest*.) **5.** *adj.* mean; unkind; cruel. (Comp: *lower*; sup: *lowest*.) **6.** *adj.* [of a supply or of strength] inadequate or not enough. (Comp: *lower*; sup: *lowest*.) **7.** *adv.* to or at a position below or near the bottom of something.
→ BURN WITH A LOW BLUE FLAME
→ HAVE A LOW BOILING POINT
→ HUNT HIGH AND LOW FOR SOMEONE OR SOMETHING
→ RUN LOW (ON SOMETHING)
→ SEARCH HIGH AND LOW FOR SOMEONE OR SOMETHING

lower ['lo ɚ] **1.** *iv.* [for something] to go from a high level to a low level. **2.** *tv.* to cause something to go from a high level to a low level; to move something down.

lower one's **sights** to set one's goals lower.

lower one's **voice** to speak more softly.

lower oneself **to** some level to bring oneself down to some lower level or behavior.

lower the boom on someone to scold or punish someone severely; to crack down on someone and become very strict. (Originally nautical.)

lowercase ['lo ɚ 'kes] *adj.* [of a letter or letters] in the smaller size as with *i* in *Bill*: not capitalized. (Compare this with UPPERCASE.)

lowly ['lo li] *adj.* humble; low in rank; simple; meek. (Comp: *lowlier*; sup: *lowliest*.)

loyal ['lɔɪ əl] *adj.* true to one's friends, country, or promises. (Adv: *loyally*.)

loyalty ['lɔɪ əl ti] *n.* the quality of being loyal. (Plural only for types and instances.)

lubrication [lu brə 'ke ʃən] **1.** *n.* applying something that will make things slippery; applying oil or grease. (No plural.) **2.** *n.* something like oil or grease that makes things slippery. (Plural only for types and instances.)

luck ['lʌk] **1.** *n.* random chance; fortune; chance. (No plural.) **2.** *n.* good or bad fortune; success or failure. (No plural.)
→ AS LUCK WOULD HAVE IT
→ OUT OF LUCK
→ PRESS ONE'S LUCK
→ PUSH ONE'S LUCK

lucky ['lʌk i] **1.** *adj.* [of someone] having good luck; fortunate. (Comp: *luckier*; sup: *luckiest*.) **2.** *adj.* causing good luck; bringing good fortune. (Comp: *luckier*; sup: *luckiest*.) **3.** *adj.* showing, having, or being good luck. (Adv: *luckily*. Comp: *luckier*; sup: *luckiest*.)
→ THANK ONE'S LUCKY STARS

lug ['lʌg] **1.** *n.* a small piece that sticks out of something. **2.** *tv.* to carry or move someone or something heavy.

luggage ['lʌg ɪdʒ] *n.* baggage; suit-cases. (No plural. Number is expressed with *piece(s) of luggage*.)

lukewarm ['luk 'wɔrm] **1.** *adj.* slightly warm. **2.** *adj.* without excitement; without enthusiasm. (Figurative on ①. Adv: *luke-warmly.*)

lull ['lʌl] *n.* a quiet moment between long periods of noise or activity; a temporary calm.

the **lull before the storm** a quiet period just before a period of great activity or excitement.

lull someone **into a false sense of security** to lead someone into believing that all is well before attacking or doing something bad.

lull someone **to sleep** to cause someone to fall asleep.

lullaby ['lʌl ə baɪ] *n.* a quiet song that is sung to help someone fall asleep.

lumber ['lʌm bɚ] **1.** *n.* timber, logs, and boards used for building. (No plural.) **2.** *iv.* to move in a heavy or clumsy way.

lump ['lʌmp] *n.* a hard mass of some substance having no specific shape.
→ GET A LUMP IN ONE'S THROAT

lump people or things **together** to think of or treat several people or things as a single group; to think of several people or things as being the same or as being in the same category.

lump sum ['lʌmp 'sʌm] *n.* money paid in a single, general payment.

lunatic fringe the more extreme members of a group.

lunch ['lʌntʃ] **1.** *n.* a meal eaten around noon; a meal eaten in the middle of the day. **2.** *iv.* to eat a meal around noon; to eat ①.

lunch out to eat lunch away from one's home or away from one's place of work.

luncheon ['lʌn tʃən] *n.* a formal meal in the middle of the day. (Fancier than a LUNCH, and usually involving a number of people.)

lunchroom ['lʌntʃ rum] *n.* a room where people in a school, office, or factory eat lunch.

lung ['lʌŋ] *n.* one of a pair of organs in the body that are used when breathing.
→ AT THE TOP OF ONE'S LUNGS

lunge ['lʌndʒ] **1.** *iv.* to move for-ward suddenly with force. **2.** *n.* a sudden forward movement with force.

lurch ['lɚtʃ] **1.** *n.* a sudden move-ment like a jerk or a jump. **2.** *iv.* to move in a way that is out of con-trol; to move without control.
→ LEAVE SOMEONE IN THE LURCH

lure ['lʊr] **1.** *tv.* to try to attract or catch a person or an animal by offering something the person or animal wants; to tempt someone or something. **2.** *n.* someone or something that attracts; some-thing that is used to attract a per-son or animal.

lure someone or something **in(to something)** to attract, tempt, or entice someone or something into something or a place.

lurk ['lɚk] **1.** *iv.* to hang out some-place without being noticed; to be someplace without being noticed.

2. *iv.* to connect to an Internet discussion and just read messages without ever sending any.

lush ['lʌʃ] **1.** *adj.* [of a place] very comfortable; [of a place] richly comfortable. (Adv: *lushly.* Comp: *lusher;* sup: *lushest.*) **2.** *adj.* covered with plants and thick vegetation. (Adv: *lushly.* Comp: *lusher;* sup: *lushest.*)

luxury ['lʌɡ ʒə ri] **1.** *n.* expensive comfort; elegance; the very best of things. (Plural only for types and instances.) **2.** *n.* something that is not necessary but is desired.
→ IN THE LAP OF LUXURY

lying ['laɪ ɪŋ] present participle of LIE.

lynch ['lɪntʃ] *tv.* to capture and hang someone who is thought to have committed a crime. (Outside the legal system.)

lynx ['lɪŋks] *n.* a type of wild cat with a short tail, long legs, and ears that have fluffy fur at the tips.

lyric ['lɪr ɪk] **1.** *adj.* of or about poetry that expresses the feelings of the poet. (Adv: *lyrically* [...ɪk li].) **2.** *n.* a short poem.

lyrics *n.* the words of a song. (Treated as plural.)

M

ma'am ['mæm] *cont.* a polite form of address for a woman. (A contraction of *madam*.)

macaroni [mæk ə 'ron i] *n.* pasta in the shape of curved tubes. (No plural.)

machine [mə 'ʃin] *n.* a device created to do some kind of work.

machinery [mə 'ʃin (ə) ri] *n.* machines and parts of machines, in general. (No plural.)

mad ['mæd] **1.** *adj.* crazy; insane; mentally ill. (Adv: *madly*. Comp: *madder*; sup: *maddest*.) **2.** *adj.* angry; upset. (Comp: *madder*; sup: *maddest*. Not prenominal.)
→ (AS) MAD AS A HORNET
→ (AS) MAD AS A MARCH HARE
→ (AS) MAD AS A WET HEN
→ IN A MAD RUSH
→ STEAMING (MAD)

mad about someone or something AND **mad for** someone or something having a strong interest in someone or something; very enthusiastic about someone or something.

mad for someone or something Go to MAD ABOUT SOMEONE OR SOMETHING.

made ['med] past tense and past participle of MAKE.

made to measure [of clothing] made especially to fit the measurements of a particular person.

magazine [mæg ə 'zin] *n.* a booklet that is published at regular intervals of time.

magic ['mædʒ ɪk] **1.** *n.* sorcery or the use of special, unnatural, or evil powers. (No plural.) **2.** *n.* the art of performing tricks that use

illusion to fool an audience. (No plural.) **3.** *n.* a special quality or power that lures or interests people. (Figurative on ①. No plural.) **4.** the *adj.* use of ①, ②, or ③. (Adv: *magically* [...ɪk li].)

magical ['mædʒ ɪ kəl] **1.** *adj.* having or using MAGIC ①. (Adv: *magically* [...ɪk li].) **2.** *adj.* exciting and interesting; romantic. (Adv: *magically* [...ɪk li].)

magician [mə 'dʒɪ ʃən] **1.** *n.* someone who practices magic or sorcery. **2.** *n.* a performer who entertains by creating illusions.

magnet ['mæg nət] **1.** *n.* an iron or steel object that draws other iron or steel objects toward it. **2.** *n.* someone or something that people or things are attracted toward. (Informal. Figurative on ①.)

magnetic [mæg 'nɛt ɪk] **1.** *adj.* able to draw or attract iron or steel in the way that a magnet does. (Adv: *magnetically* [...ɪk li].) **2.** *adj.* able to be affected or harmed by magnetism. (Adv: *magnetically* [...ɪk li].) **3.** *adj.* [of someone's personality] attracting or drawing people [to oneself].

magnetism ['mæg nə tɪz əm] **1.** *n.* the physical laws of how magnets attract metal. (No plural.) **2.** *n.* a charm or attraction that draws people toward someone. (Figurative on ①. No plural.)

maid ['med] *n.* a woman who is paid to cook, clean, and do other work around the house.

maiden voyage the first voyage of a ship or boat.

mail ['mel] **1.** *n.* letters and packages that are delivered by the post office. (No plural. Number is expressed with *piece(s) of mail*.) **2.** *tv.* to send (someone) a letter or package by ①.
→ BY RETURN MAIL

the **mail** *n.* the postal system. (Treated as singular.)

mail carrier AND **letter carrier** ['mel kɛr ɪ ɚ, 'lɛt ɚ kɛr ɪ ɚ] *n.* someone who works for the postal system and picks up and delivers mail.

mailbox ['mel bɑks] **1.** *n.* a place where mail is put so it can be picked up and taken to the post office and then delivered. **2.** *n.* a container into which a mail carrier delivers mail. **3.** *n.* the electronic version of ②, where e-mail is received.

main ['men] **1.** *adj.* most important; primary; chief. (Prenominal only. Adv: *mainly*.) **2.** *n.* an important pipe that carries water, sewage, gas, etc.

maintain [men 'ten] **1.** *tv.* to continue something as before; to keep doing something. **2.** *tv.* to take care of something; to make sure that something works properly. **3.** *tv.* to support someone or something, especially with money. **4.** *tv.* to assert an opinion; to defend one's opinion and continue to assert it when someone argues against it. (The object can be a clause with THAT ⑦.)

maintenance ['men tə nəns] *n.* keeping equipment and supplies in good condition. (No plural.)

majesty ['mædʒ ə sti] *n.* dignity; greatness and importance, especially of royalty. (No plural.)

major ['me dʒɚ] **1.** *adj.* large in size or amount; great; important; serious. **2.** *adj.* primary; more important. (Prenominal only.) **3.** *n.* an officer in the army, air force, or marines who is above a captain and below a lieutenant colonel. (Sometimes a term of address. Capitalized when written as a proper noun.) **4.** *n.* a student's primary area of study. **5.** *n.* someone whose ④ is in a certain subject.

major in something to specialize in a certain subject in school.

majority [mə 'dʒɔr ə ti] **1.** *n.* those people who are part of the largest group or division of people, considered as a single group. (No plural. Treated as singular.) **2.** *n.* [in a group] a number of people or things equal to more than half of the whole group, considered as individuals. (No plural.) **3.** *n.* the largest number of votes; a number of votes equal to a specific proportion of all the votes. (No plural.)

make ['mek] **1.** *tv., irreg.* to bring something into being; to put something together from other parts; to form something; to build something; to produce something. (Past tense and past participle: MADE.) **2.** *tv., irreg.* to cause someone or something to be in a certain condition. **3.** *tv., irreg.* to cause someone or something [to] do something; to force someone or something [to] do something. **4.** *tv., irreg.* to assign someone to a job; to appoint someone to a posi-

tion. **5.** *tv., irreg.* to earn money; to acquire something. **6.** *tv., irreg.* to arrive at a place; to arrive at a place in time for something; to reach something; to manage to get to something. **7.** *tv., irreg.* to become something; to assume a certain status or job. **8.** *n.* a brand; a certain style or kind.
→ CAN'T MAKE HEADS OR TAILS (OUT) OF SOMEONE OR SOMETHING
→ KISS AND MAKE UP
→ WHAT MAKES SOMEONE TICK

make a bed AND **make someone's bed** to fix the sheets of a bed that has been slept in.

make a beeline for someone or something to head straight toward someone or something.

make a check out (to someone or something**)** to write a check to be paid to someone or a group.

make a clean breast of something to confess something.

make a face to twist one's face into a strange expression in order to show one's dislike, ridicule, etc., or in order to make someone laugh.

make a friend AND **make friends** to establish a link of friendship with someone.

make a go of it to make something work out all right.

make a great show of something to make something obvious; to do something in a showy fashion.

make a hit (with someone or something**)** to please someone or something.

make a long story short to bring a story to an end.

make a nuisance of oneself to be a constant bother.

make a reservation AND **make reservations** to reserve a seat, as in an airplane, restaurant, or theater, in advance; to reserve a room, as in a hotel, in advance.

make a run for it to run fast to get away or get somewhere.

make a silk purse out of a sow's ear to create something of value out of something of no value.

make allowances for something to keep something in mind when making a decision or policy; to allow for the possibility of something.

make arrangements to prepare a plan or plans; to create a scheme in advance.

make cracks (about someone or something**)** to ridicule or make jokes about someone or something.

make fast work of someone or something Go to MAKE SHORT WORK OF SOMEONE OR SOMETHING.

make friends Go to MAKE A FRIEND.

make good money to earn a large amount of money. (Here, *good* means plentiful.)

make life miserable for someone to make someone unhappy over a long period of time.

make light of something to treat something as if it were unimportant or humorous.

make merry to have fun; to have an enjoyable time.

make mincemeat of someone **1.** to defeat someone completely.

(Informal.) **2.** to scold or punish someone severely.

make mischief to cause trouble.

make off with someone or something to leave and take away someone or something.

make oneself **at home** to make oneself comfortable as if one were in one's own home.

make oneself **clear** to give a clear explanation or clear orders.

make oneself **heard** to speak loudly so that one will be heard above the noise.

make (out) after someone or something to run after someone or something; to start out after someone or something.

make (out) for someone or something to run toward someone, something, or someplace.

make out (with someone or something**)** to manage satisfactorily with someone or something.

make over someone or something to pay a lot of attention to someone or something.

make overtures to give hints about something; to present or suggest ideas.

make reservations Go to MAKE A RESERVATION.

make short work of someone or something AND **make fast work of** someone or something to finish with someone or something quickly.

make someone or something **over** to convert someone or something into a new or different person or thing.

make someone or something **tick** to cause someone or something to run or function. (Originally the kind of thing that would be said about a clock or a watch.)

make someone **the scapegoat for** something to make someone take the blame for something.

make someone **up** to put makeup on someone, including oneself.

make someone's **bed** Go to MAKE A BED.

make someone's **blood boil** to make someone very angry.

make someone's **blood run cold** to shock or horrify someone.

make someone's **hair stand on end** to cause someone to be very frightened.

make someone's **head spin** Go to MAKE SOMEONE'S HEAD SWIM.

make someone's **head swim** AND **make** someone's **head spin 1.** to make someone dizzy or disoriented. **2.** to confuse or overwhelm someone.

make someone's **mouth water** to make someone hungry (for something); to cause someone to salivate.

make something **from scratch** to make something by starting with the basic ingredients.

make something **off (of)** someone or something to make money from someone or something.

make something **out** to see, read, or hear something well enough to understand it.

make something **up 1.** to invent a story or tale; to fabricate something, such as a story or a lie. **2.** to redo something; to do something that one has failed to do in the past.

make something **up out of whole cloth** to create a story or a lie from no facts at all.

make something **worth** someone's **while** to make something profitable enough for someone to do.

make the feathers fly Go to MAKE THE FUR FLY.

make the fur fly AND **make the feathers fly** to cause a fight or an argument.

make the grade to be satisfactory; to be what is expected.

make up for lost time to do much of something; to do something fast.

make up something to form or constitute something; to be a part of something.

make up (with someone**)** to reconcile with someone; to end a disagreement (with someone).

make use of someone or something to use or utilize someone or something.

makeup ['mek əp] **1.** *n.* substances applied to the face to improve its appearance. (No plural. Treated as singular.) **2.** *n.* the contents of something; the parts or substances that form something. (No plural. Treated as singular.) **3.** the *adj.* use of ①.

male ['mel] **1.** *adj.* of or about men or boys; of or about animals of the sex that is, at maturity, capable of causing a female to become preg-

nant. **2.** *adj.* [of an electrical or electronic connector] having short metal rods to be inserted into or between electrical contacts. **3.** *n.* a human or animal that is ①.

malice ['mæl ɪs] *n.* the desire to harm someone or something; the desire to do something evil. (No plural.)

mall ['mɔl] **1.** *n.* a large building with many stores inside; a shopping center. **2.** *n.* a wide, formal walkway, usually lined with trees.

mallet ['mæl ət] *n.* a tool shaped like a hammer with a large head.

mammal ['mæm əl] *n.* one of a large class of warm-blooded animals whose females are able to produce milk to feed their young.

man ['mæn] **1.** *n., irreg.* an adult male person. (Plural: MEN.) **2.** *n.* the human race; all people. (No plural. Treated as singular.) **3.** *n., irreg.* a strong and brave human male. **4.** *tv.* to provide a business or organization with one's services or labor.
→ BE A MARKED MAN
→ LADIES' MAN
→ ODD MAN OUT
→ YOUNG MAN

a **man about town** a fashionable man who leads a sophisticated life.

the **man in the street** the ordinary person.

manage ['mæn ɪdʒ] *tv.* to be in charge of someone or something; to guide someone or something.

manage to do something to be able to do something, even though there are problems.

manager ['mæn ɪ dʒɚ] *n.* someone who manages or controls someone or something.

maniac ['men i æk] **1.** *n.* someone who has a dangerous, sometimes violent, mental illness. **2.** *n.* someone who is wild, foolish, and too eager. (Figurative on ①.)

mankind ['mæn 'kaɪnd] *n.* the human race; all people. (No plural. Treated as singular.)

manna from heaven unexpected help or comfort; an unanticipated benefit or advantage.

manner ['mæn ɚ] *n.* a method; a style; a way of doing something; a way of being.

mannerism ['mæn ə rɪz əm] *n.* a gesture or movement of a certain person; a habit or trait of a certain person.

manners *n.* the elements of proper and polite behavior.

mansion ['mæn ʃən] *n.* a very large house; a large, elegant house.

mantel ['mæn təl] *n.* the frame around a fireplace, and especially the shelf above the fireplace.

mantle ['mæn təl] *n.* something that completely covers or weighs down someone or something, such as a heavy coat.

man-to-man AND **woman-to-woman** speaking frankly and directly, one person to another.

manual ['mæn j(u)əl] **1.** *n.* a book that explains how to do or use something; an instruction book; a book of information about something. **2.** *adj.* of or about the hand or hands. (Adv: *manually*.)

manufacture [mæn jə 'fæk tʃɚ] **1.** *n.* the science and business of making products in factories or industry. (No plural.) **2.** *tv.* to make something in large amounts in a factory or by using machines.

manufacturer [mæn jə 'fæk tʃɚ ɚ] *n.* a person, business, or company that manufactures products.

manuscript ['mæn jə skrɪpt] **1.** *n.* a book or text that is written by hand. **2.** *n.* the original copy of a book or article that is sent to a publisher.

many ['men i] **1.** *adj., irreg.* numerous; of a large number. (See also MORE and MOST for the comparative and superlative. MANY is used with things that can be counted. Compare this with MUCH.) **2.** *pron.* a large number of people; a large number of people or things already referred to.
→ HAVE TOO MANY IRONS IN THE FIRE
→ HOW MANY
→ IN MANY RESPECTS

map ['mæp] **1.** *n.* a drawing that shows certain features of the earth's surface; a sketch or drawing that shows locations or the relations between things or places. **2.** *tv.* to draw ①.

map something out to plot something out carefully, usually on paper.

marble ['mɑr bəl] **1.** *n.* a kind of stone that can be cut, shaped, and polished. (Plural only for types and instances.) **2.** *n.* a small, solid ball of colored glass, used in MARBLES. **3.** *adj.* made of ①.

marbles *n.* a game that involves directing one MARBLE ② into a group of them.

march ['mɑrtʃ] **1.** *iv.* to walk in rigid steps, in the manner of a soldier. **2.** *iv.* to walk someplace with a certain goal in mind; to walk someplace for a certain reason. **3.** *tv.* to force someone to move or walk. **4.** *n.* an act of walking in a line, like soldiers. **5.** *n.* a demonstration or protest where people are walking with signs or chanting. **6.** *n.* music that has a strong beat and is used in parades or while soldiers MARCH as in ①. **7.** Go to MONTH. (Capitalized.)
→ (AS) MAD AS A March HARE
→ STEAL A MARCH (ON SOMEONE)

march on [for time] to continue.

march to a different drummer to believe in a different set of principles; to be unconventional in one's values.

margarine ['mɑr dʒə rɪn] *n.* a food made from animal or vegetable fats, used in place of butter; a spread for bread. (Plural only for types and instances.)

margin ['mɑr dʒɪn] **1.** *n.* the space between the edge of a text and the edge of the page. **2.** *n.* an extra amount; the amount that is more than what is needed.

marine [mə 'rin] **1.** *adj.* of or about salt water and the creatures that live in salt water. **2.** *adj.* of, about, from, or concerning the sea. **3.** *adj.* of or about ships and shipping on the sea. **4.** *n.* someone who is a member of the U.S. Marine Corps, a branch of the United States military services that serves on land and sea and in the air.

mark ['mɑrk] **1.** *n.* a spot; a stain; a dent; something that spoils a clear or clean surface. **2.** *n.* a line or figure made by a pencil, crayon, pen, or other writing device. **3.** *n.* something that is a sign of something; something that stands for something else. **4.** *iv.* to draw or make ①. **5.** *tv.* to put a spot on something; to stain something; to spoil an otherwise clear or clean surface with ①. **6.** *tv.* to indicate something; to show something; to symbolize or represent something; to stand for something.
→ BE A MARKED MAN
→ LEAVE ONE'S MARK ON SOMEONE
→ PUNCTUATION MARK
→ QUESTION MARK
→ QUOTATION MARKS
→ TOE THE MARK
→ WIDE OF THE MARK

mark something **down 1.** to reduce the price of something. **2.** to write something down on paper.

mark something **up 1.** to make marks all over something. **2.** to raise the price of something. **3.** to raise the wholesale price of an item to the retail level.

market ['mɑr kɪt] **1.** *n.* a place or building where people gather to buy and sell things. **2.** *n.* the business, building, or system through which company shares are traded. (Short for STOCK MARKET.) **3.** *n.* an area or country where a product is needed or used; a certain group of people for which a product is needed or by which a product is used. **4.** *n.* the demand for a certain product. **5.** *tv.* to advertise a

product; to promote a product; to make a plan for selling a product.
→ a DRUG ON THE MARKET
→ ON THE MARKET
→ STOCK MARKET

marketplace ['mɑr kɪt ples] **1.** *n.* a place, usually outside, where things are bought and sold. **2.** *n.* trade; buying and selling. (No plural.)

markup ['mɑrk əp] *n.* a price increase; the amount a price is raised.

marriage ['mɛr ɪdʒ] **1.** *n.* the religious or legal union of a husband and a wife. **2.** *n.* the ceremony that joins a man and a woman in ①; a wedding.

marry ['mɛr i] **1.** *iv.* to unite with someone in a marriage. **2.** *tv.* to unite two people in a marriage; to perform a wedding ceremony. **3.** *tv.* to take someone as a husband or a wife.
→ GET MARRIED

marsh ['mɑrʃ] *n.* a low area of land sometimes covered with water.

marshmallow ['mɑrʃ mɛl o] *n.* a soft, spongy candy made from sugar. (Originally made from the roots of a flower called the *marsh mallow*.)

marvel ['mɑr vəl] *n.* someone or something that is amazing or surprising.

masculine ['mæs kjə lɪn] **1.** *adj.* having features usually associated with a male; manly. (Adv: *masculinely*.) **2.** *adj.* a grammar term describing a certain class of nouns, some of which refer to males. (See also GENDER.)

mash ['mæʃ] *tv.* to crush something until it is a soft paste; to beat something into a pulp or paste.

mash something **up** to crush something into a paste or pieces.

mask ['mæsk] **1.** *n.* a covering that disguises the face. **2.** *n.* a covering that protects the face, eyes, nose, or mouth. **3.** *tv.* to conceal something; to hide something; to put ② on someone or something.

mass ['mæs] **1.** *n.* an amount of something with no specific shape; a lump; a heap. **2.** *n.* the scientific term for the amount of matter that makes up an object. (No plural.) **3.** *adj.* suitable for many people or things; involving many people or things. (Prenominal only.) **4.** *n.* a Christian church service with communion. (Capitalized.)

massive ['mæs ɪv] *adj.* very large; enormous; powerful. (Adv: *massively*.)

mast ['mæst] *n.* [on a ship] an upright beam or pole to which sails are attached.
→ AT HALF-MAST

master ['mæst ɚ] **1.** *n.* a person who has authority over people, animals, or things; a man who has authority over people, animals, or things. **2.** *n.* someone who is very skilled at something. **3.** *n.* an original page or document that copies are made from. **4.** the *adj.* use of ①, ②, or ③. (Prenominal only.) **5.** *adj.* primary; main; chief; controlling everything else. (Prenominal only.) **6.** *adj.* of professional standing or quality. (Prenominal only.) **7.** *tv.* to become skilled in something; to learn how to do something well; to gain control of an ability.

mat ['mæt] **1.** *n.* a piece of material for covering part of a floor, especially in front of a door. **2.** *n.* a piece of thick, padded material used to cushion falls in certain sports. **3.** *n.* a tangled mass of hair, weeds, strings, or other things.

match ['mætʃ] **1.** *n.* a sporting event; a competition. **2.** *n.* someone or something that is the equal of or just like someone or something else; two people or things that are equal or alike. **3.** *n.* a thin stick with a chemical substance on one end, which, when struck against a hard surface, creates fire. **4.** *tv.* [for something] to be exactly like something else; to fit something exactly; to go with something well. **5.** *iv.* to be exactly alike; to go together well; to fit together well.
→ MEET ONE'S MATCH
→ STRIKE A MATCH
→ WHOLE SHOOTING MATCH

match up [for people or things] to match, be equal, or complementary.

mate ['met] **1.** *n.* the sexual partner of a living creature. **2.** *n.* a spouse; a husband or a wife. **3.** *n.* one of a pair. **4.** *n.* a friend or colleague; a person who shares someplace or activity with someone. **5.** *iv.* to have sex; to breed. (Used primarily of animals.) **6.** *tv.* to bring a male and female animal together so that breeding will result.

material [mə'tɪr i əl] **1.** *n.* a substance that an object is made of; a substance that can be used to

make things. **2.** *n.* cloth; fabric. (No plural.) **3.** *n.* information, knowledge, experience, or imagination used to develop a story, movie, book, program, etc. (No plural.) **4.** *adj.* of or about the physical world. (Adv: *materially.*) **5.** *adj.* of importance or relevance. (Adv: *materially.*)

maternal [mə'tɚ nəl] **1.** *adj.* of or about mothers or motherhood. (Adv: *maternally.*) **2.** *adj.* related through the mother's side of the family. (Adv: *maternally.*)

math ['mæθ] **1.** *n.* MATHEMATICS. (No plural. Treated as singular.) **2.** the *adj.* use of ①.

mathematic [mæθ ə 'mæt ɪk] *adj.* having the exactness or precision of mathematics. (See also MATHEMATICS.)

mathematics [mæθ ə 'mæt ɪks] *n.* the science that studies the properties and relationships of numbers and shapes. (Treated as singular.)

matter ['mæt ɚ] **1.** *n.* anything that takes up space. (No plural.) **2.** *n.* a certain kind of substance. (No plural.) **3.** *n.* a concern; an issue; an affair. **4.** *iv.* to be important; to have meaning.
→ the CRUX OF THE MATTER
→ GET TO THE HEART OF THE MATTER
→ GRAY MATTER
→ NO LAUGHING MATTER
→ SUBJECT MATTER

a **matter of life and death** a matter of great urgency; an issue that will decide between living and dying. (Usually an exaggeration. Sometimes humorous.)

a **matter of opinion** the issue of how good or bad someone or something is.

mattress ['mæ trɪs] *n.* a large, rectangular pad that is used to sleep on.

mature [mə 'tʃʊr] **1.** *adj.* [of someone] adult or fully grown; [of fruit or vegetables] ripe or ready to eat. (Adv: *maturely*.) **2.** *adj.* characteristic of an adult; sensible; responsible. (Adv: *maturely*.) **3.** *tv.* to cause someone or something to become ① or ②. **4.** *iv.* to become ①. **5.** *iv.* [for a bond] to reach full value; [for a payment] to be due.

maturity [mə 'tʃʊr ə ti] **1.** *n.* the state of being mature or developed; the degree to which someone or something is mature. (No plural.) **2.** *n.* human wisdom; adult thinking. (No plural.) **3.** *n.* the date when an amount of money becomes due and must be paid.

maximum ['mæk sə məm] **1.** *n.* the highest amount or degree possible; the upper limit or boundary. **2.** *adj.* greatest; highest; most.

may ['me] **1.** *aux.* be allowed to do something; have permission to do something. (Often CAN is used in place of MAY, even though, in standard English, CAN refers to ability, and MAY refers to permission. See also MIGHT.) **2.** *aux.* be possible. (See also MIGHT.) **3.** *aux.* a form used to extend a wish or express a hope; let it be that.... **4.** Go to MONTH. (Capitalized.)
→ COME WHAT MAY

maybe ['me bi] *adv.* perhaps; possibly yes, possibly no.

mayonnaise [me ə 'nez] *n.* a creamy sauce for salads and sandwiches; a sauce made from eggs, oil, and vinegar. (No plural.)

mayor ['me ɚ] *n.* the elected leader of a city, town, or village.

maze ['mez] **1.** *n.* a network of connected passages, arranged so that it is hard to get from one place to another because most of the paths are blocked. **2.** *n.* something that is as confusing as ①. (Figurative on ①.)

me ['mi] **1.** *pron.* the objective form of I, the first-person singular pronoun. (Used after prepositions and transitive verbs and as an indirect object.) **2.** *pron.* a first-person singular form. (Used after a shortened form of BE to refer to the speaker or writer. Usually, either "It's me" or the more formal "It is I." Rarely, if ever, "It's I" or "It is me.")

meadow ['mɛd o] *n.* an area of grass-covered land; an area of land where cows, sheep, or goats can eat.

meal ['mil] **1.** *n.* a regular occasion where food is eaten, especially breakfast, lunch, or dinner. **2.** *n.* the food that is eaten at ①. **3.** *n.* crushed grain; flour. (Plural only for types and instances.)
→ SQUARE MEAL

mealy-mouthed not frank or direct. (Informal.)

mean ['min] **1.** *adj.* cruel; not kind; selfish. (Adv: *meanly*. Comp: *meaner*; sup: *meanest*.) **2.** *adj.* average. (Prenominal only.) **3.** *n.* an average; the average of a group of numbers. **4.** *tv., irreg.* [for language] to represent, indicate, or express something; [for someone] to indicate, express, or intend something by words or actions. (Past tense and past participle: MEANT.) **5.** *tv., irreg.* [for something] to indicate or signal something. **6.** *iv., irreg.* to intend to do something.

mean (for someone**) to** do something to intend (for someone) to do something.

meaning ['min ɪŋ] *n.* the sense of a word, statement, or symbol; what a word, statement, or symbol means.

means ['minz] *n.* one's [financial] ability to accomplish something.
→ BEYOND ONE'S MEANS
→ LIVE BEYOND ONE'S MEANS
→ LIVE WITHIN ONE'S MEANS

meant ['mɛnt] past tense and past participle of MEAN.

meant to be destined to exist or happen.

meant to be something destined or fated to be something.

meantime ['min taɪm] the period of time between two things; the period of time between now and when something is supposed to happen.
→ IN THE MEANTIME

measles ['mi zəlz] *n.* an easily spread disease common in children, characterized by fever and red spots on the skin. (Treated as singular or plural, but not countable. Often preceded by *the.*)

measure ['mɛ ʒɚ] **1.** *n.* a unit in a system that determines the amount of something. **2.** *n.* one of the series of groups of musical

notes that makes up a piece of music. **3.** *n.* the extent, amount, or quantity of something. **4.** *n.* a course of action; a plan. **5.** *n.* a law; a proposed law; a resolution. **6.** *tv.* to determine the size, extent, amount, degree, etc., of something. **7.** *iv.* to be a certain size, extent, amount, degree, etc.
→ MADE TO MEASURE

measure something **off 1.** to determine the length of something. **2.** to distribute something in measured portions.

measure up (to someone or something**)** to compare well to someone or something.

measurement ['mɛ ʒɚ mənt] **1.** *n.* a system of measuring. (No plural.) **2.** *n.* the process of measuring. (No plural.) **3.** *n.* the size, length, weight, or amount of something, as determined by measuring.

meat ['mit] **1.** *n.* the flesh of animals used as food. (Plural only for types and instances.) **2.** *n.* the main idea or content of something. (Figurative on ①. No plural.)

meatloaf ['mit lof] **1.** *n.* a dish of chopped meat shaped like a loaf of bread and baked. (Plural only for types and instances.) **2.** *n.* a unit or loaf of ①.

medal ['mɛd l] *n.* a small piece of metal—usually flat and having a design or words on it—that is given to someone as an honor.

medallion [mə 'dæl jən] **1.** *n.* a large medal. **2.** *n.* a large design or decorative element; a decorative element resembling a large coin or medal.

meddle in something ['mɛd l...] to interfere in someone's business; to involve oneself in someone's business when one is not wanted.

meddle with something ['mɛd l...] to play with and interfere with something.

media ['mid i ə] **1.** *n.* the Latin plural of MEDIUM ①. (Although it is a Latin plural, MEDIA can be treated as singular or plural in English. Not countable.) **2.** *n.* the Latin plural of MEDIUM ②. (Often treated as singular. Not countable.) **3.** *n.* the Latin plural of MEDIUM ③. (Often treated as singular. Not countable.)

mediator ['mid i et ɚ] *n.* someone who helps negotiate the settlement of a disagreement.

medical ['mɛd ə kəl] *adj.* of or about medicine or the study and practice of medicine. (Adv: *medically* [...ɪk li].)

medicate ['mɛd ə ket] *tv.* to put medicine on or in someone or something; to treat someone or something with medicine or drugs.

medication [mɛd ə 'ke ʃən] **1.** *n.* the use or application of medicine. (No plural.) **2.** *n.* a kind of medicine; a dose of medicine.

medicine ['mɛd ə sən] **1.** *n.* the science and study of preventing, identifying, and curing diseases in the body. (No plural.) **2.** *n.* something that is used to treat a disease, especially something that is taken by the mouth or injected into the body. (Plural only for types and instances.)
→ a DOSE OF ONE'S OWN MEDICINE
→ TAKE ONE'S MEDICINE

medieval [mid i 'i vəl] *adj.* of or about the Middle Ages in Europe, from about A.D. 500 to 1450. (Adv: *medievally*.)

mediocre [mi di 'o kɚ] *adj.* only average; halfway between good and bad; just acceptable.

medium ['mid i əm] **1.** *n., irreg.* a channel or pathway for sending information—such as newspapers, radio, television, print advertising, etc. (The Latin plural is MEDIA, and the English plural is *mediums*.) **2.** *n., irreg.* a substance in which organisms such as bacteria can be grown and kept alive. (Rarely used in the singular. Plural: MEDIA.) **3.** *n., irreg.* the [different kinds of] materials used by an artist. (The Latin plural is MEDIA, and the English plural is *mediums*.) **4.** *n.* the middle size of an object for sale that comes in different sizes. (Plural: *mediums*.)
→ HIT A HAPPY MEDIUM
→ STRIKE A HAPPY MEDIUM

meek ['mik] *adj.* letting others do as they want; not protesting. (Adv: *meekly*. Comp: *meeker*; sup: *meekest*.)

meet ['mit] **1.** *tv., irreg.* to come together with someone either by chance or on purpose; to encounter someone. (Past tense and past participle: MET.) **2.** *tv., irreg.* [for something] to touch someone or something; to come into contact with someone or something. **3.** *tv., irreg.* to be

introduced to someone. **4.** *iv.,*
irreg. to come together; to join; to
connect; to make contact; to
touch.

meet one's **death** AND **meet** one's
end to die.

meet one's **end** Go to MEET ONE'S
DEATH.

meet one's **match** to encounter
one's equal.

meet someone **halfway** to compromise with someone.

meeting ['mit ɪŋ] **1.** *n.* a group of
people who have come together
for a specific reason. **2.** *n.* an
instance of people coming
together, perhaps by accident.
→ CALL A MEETING TO ORDER

a **meeting of minds** the establishment of agreement; complete
agreement.

megabyte ['mɛg ə baɪt] *n.* a unit
consisting of about one million
BYTES. (The abbreviation is *MB,*
and the word can be shortened to
meg.)

mellow ['mɛl o] **1.** *adj.* [of colors,
sounds, textures, or tastes that are]
soft, deep, relaxing, or muted.
(Adv: *mellowly.* Comp: *mellower;*
sup: *mellowest.*) **2.** *adj.* relaxed
and quiet. (Informal. Figurative on ①.
Adv: *mellowly.* Comp: *mellower;*
sup: *mellowest.*) **3.** *tv.* to cause
someone or a group to become ②.
4. *iv.* to become ②.

melody ['mɛl ə di] *n.* the series of
notes that make up the tune of a
song; a song; a tune.

melon ['mɛl ən] **1.** *n.* one of a family of large round or oval fruits
with thick rinds and juicy, edible

insides. **2.** *n.* the edible part of ①;
① used as food. (No plural. Number is expressed with *piece(s)* or
slice(s) of melon.)

melt ['mɛlt] **1.** *iv.* [for a solid] to
become liquid; to turn into a liq-
uid. **2.** *tv.* to cause something solid
to become liquid; to cause something solid to turn into a liquid.
3. *tv.* to cause something to disappear or fade. (Figurative on ②.)
4. *n.* an instance of turning into a
liquid as in ①.
→ LOOK AS IF BUTTER WOULDN'T MELT
IN ONE'S MOUTH

melt down 1. [for something fro-
zen] to melt. **2.** [for a nuclear
reactor] to become hot enough to
melt through its container.

melt in one's **mouth** to taste very
good; [for food] to be very rich
and satisfying.

melt into something to melt and
change into a different physical
state.

melt something **down** to cause
something frozen to become a liquid; to cause something solid to
melt.

melt something **into** something to
cause something to change its
physical state through melting.

member ['mɛm bɚ] *n.* someone
who belongs to a group or an
organization.

membership ['mɛm bɚ ʃɪp] **1.** *n.*
the connection between one person and an organization to which
the person belongs. (Plural only
for types and instances.) **2.** *n.* all
of the members of a group or
organization. (No plural.)

memento AND **momento** [mə'mɛn to] *n.* a souvenir; something that reminds one of someone else or of a place that one has been to.

memo ['mɛm o] *n.* a note or announcement, especially in an office. (A shortened form of the word *memorandum*. Plural ends in -s.)

memorable ['mɛm ə rə bəl] *adj.* worth remembering; easy to remember. (Adv: *memorably.*)

memorial [mə'mor i əl] **1.** *adj.* [of something] used to remind someone of a person, thing, place, or event. (Prenominal only.) **2.** *n.* something that is a reminder of an event in the past or of a person no longer living.

memory ['mɛm ə ri] **1.** *n.* the brain or mind, thought of as a place where ideas, words, images, and past events reside. (No plural.) **2.** *n.* the functioning or quality of ①; the ability of ① to function. **3.** *n.* an instance of remembering a past event, experience, person, or sensation; someone or something that is remembered. **4.** *n.* the part of a computer where information is kept until it is needed. (No plural.)
→ IN MEMORY OF SOMEONE
→ IN RECENT MEMORY
→ JOG SOMEONE'S MEMORY
→ KNOW SOMETHING FROM MEMORY

men ['mɛn] plural of MAN.
→ SEPARATE THE MEN FROM THE BOYS

menace ['mɛn ɪs] **1.** *n.* a threat; someone or something that threatens harm, violence, or danger. **2.** *tv.* to threaten someone or something with harm, violence, or danger.

mend ['mɛnd] **1.** *tv.* to fix something; to repair something. **2.** *iv.* to become healthy; to become well.
→ ON THE MEND

mend (one's) fences to restore good relations (with someone).

mend one's ways to improve one's behavior.

menstrual ['mɛn str(u)əl] *adj.* associated with menstruation. (Adv: *menstrually.*)

menstrual period ['mɛn str(u)əl 'pɪr ɪ əd] *n.* the time during which a woman menstruates. (Can be shortened to PERIOD.)

menstruate ['mɛn stru et] *iv.* to experience menstruation; to have a menstrual period.

menstruation [mɛn stru 'e ʃən] *n.* the monthly process in sexually mature women who are not pregnant in which the lining of the uterus is shed. (No plural.)

mental ['mɛn təl] **1.** *adj.* of or about the mind; done by the mind. (Adv: *mentally.*) **2.** *adj.* of or about illness of the mind.

mention ['mɛn ʃən] **1.** *tv.* to say or write something; to tell about something briefly. (The object can be a clause with THAT ⑦.) **2.** *tv.* to refer to someone or something. **3.** *n.* an instance of saying or writing something as in ②; a brief statement; a reference.
→ NOT WORTH MENTIONING

mention something in passing to mention something casually; to mention something while talking about something else.

menu ['mɛn ju] **1.** *n.* a list of food and drink available at a restaurant. **2.** *n.* a list of options or functions available in a computer program. (Figurative on ①.)

meow [mi 'aʊ] **1.** *n.* the sound a cat makes. **2.** *iv.* [for a cat] to make its characteristic sound.

merchandise ['mɚ tʃ ən daɪs] *n.* products for sale or trade; things that are for sale. (No plural. Treated as singular.)

merchant ['mɚ tʃ ənt] *n.* someone who buys and sells products in order to make money; a retailer.

mercury ['mɚ kjə ri] **1.** *n.* a silver-gray element that is liquid at room temperature. (No plural.) **2.** *n.* the closest planet to the sun in our solar system. (Capitalized.)

mercy ['mɚ si] *n.* kindness; pity; compassion. (No plural except when referring to *God's mercies*.)
→ THROW ONESELF AT THE MERCY OF THE COURT
→ THROW ONESELF ON THE MERCY OF THE COURT

mere ['mɪr] *adj.* only; nothing more than. (Prenominal only. Adv: MERELY. Comp: none; sup: *merest*.)

merely ['mɪr li] *adv.* this only; only this and nothing else; just.

merge ['mɚdʒ] **1.** *iv.* to join with something else. **2.** *iv.* to enter the flow of traffic. **3.** *tv.* to cause two or more things to come together and become one.

merger ['mɚdʒ ɚ] *n.* an act or process of joining two organizations into one.

merit ['mɛr ɪt] **1.** *n.* worth; value. (No plural.) **2.** *n.* a good point; a

virtue. (Usually plural.) **3.** *tv.* to deserve something; to be worthy of something.

merry ['mɛr i] *adj.* happy; cheerful; joyful. (Adv: *merrily*. Comp: *merrier*; sup: *merriest*.)
→ LEAD SOMEONE ON A MERRY CHASE
→ MAKE MERRY

mesh ['mɛʃ] *n.* material that is woven in such a way that there are holes between the threads or wires. (Plural only for types and instances.)

mesh together to fit together.

mesh with something to fit with something.

mess ['mɛs] **1.** *n.* something or someplace that is dirty or untidy. **2.** *n.* a group of things that are not in order; a situation that is not organized; confusion. **3.** *n.* [in the military services] a meal, eaten by a group.

mess someone or something **up** **1.** to put someone or something into disarray; to make someone or something dirty or untidy. **2.** to interfere with someone or something; to misuse or abuse someone or something.

message ['mɛs ɪdʒ] **1.** *n.* a communication between two or more people; a piece of written or spoken information for someone. **2.** *n.* the moral of a story; a lesson that is to be learned from a story.
→ GET THE MESSAGE

messenger ['mɛs ən dʒɚ] *n.* someone who delivers messages, documents, parcels, or flowers.

messy ['mɛs i] *adj.* dirty or not organized; not clean and tidy.

(Adv: *messily.* Comp: *messier;* sup: *messiest.*)

met ['mɛt] past tense and past participle of MEET.

metal ['mɛt əl] **1.** *n.* a solid mineral substance that can be cast or beaten into different shapes. (Plural only for types and instances.) **2.** *adj.* made from ①.

metallic [mə 'tæl ɪk] *adj.* associated with metal; made of metal.

meter ['mit ɚ] **1.** *n.* the basic unit of the measurement of length in the metric system, equal to 39.37 inches. **2.** *n.* a device that measures and displays the amount of something that is used. **3.** *n.* the rhythms caused by accents in poetry and music. (Plural only for types and instances.) **4.** *tv.* to measure the flow of something with ②.

method ['mɛθ əd] *n.* a way of doing something; a system; a procedure.

metric ['mɛ trɪk] *adj.* of or about the system of measurement based on the meter. (Adv: *metrically* […ɪk li].)

mice ['maɪs] a plural of MOUSE.

microphone ['maɪ krə fon] *n.* a device that changes sound waves into electrical waves so that the sound can be broadcast, recorded, or made louder. (Can be shortened to MIKE.)

microscope ['maɪ krə skop] *n.* a device that makes very small objects appear much larger.

midair ['mɪd 'ɛr] *adj.* in the air; not touching the ground.
→ IN MIDAIR

→ KEEP SOMEONE OR SOMETHING HANGING IN MIDAIR
→ LEAVE SOMEONE OR SOMETHING HANGING IN MIDAIR

midday 1. ['mɪd 'de] *n.* noon; the middle of the day. (No plural.) **2.** ['mɪd de] *adj.* happening in the middle of the day; happening at noon. (Prenominal only.)

middle ['mɪd l] **1.** *n.* a place or time halfway between two ends or sides; the center. **2.** *n.* the area of the waist; halfway along the body of a human or other creature. **3.** *adj.* central; at the same distance from either end; halfway between the beginning and the end. (Prenominal only.)
→ PLAY BOTH ENDS (AGAINST THE MIDDLE)
→ SMACK-DAB IN THE MIDDLE

middle-of-the-road halfway between two extremes, especially political extremes.

midnight ['mɪd naɪt] **1.** *n.* 12:00 at night; twelve o'clock at night. **2.** *adj.* happening at ①; beginning at ①. (Prenominal only.)
→ BURN THE MIDNIGHT OIL

Midwest ['mɪd 'wɛst] **1.** *n.* the middle part of the United States. (No plural.) **2.** the *adj.* use of ①.

might ['maɪt] **1.** *n.* power; strength. (No plural.) **2.** *aux.* a form that expresses possibility. (See also MAY and COULD.) **3.** *aux.* a form expressing permission. (See also MAY and COULD.)

mighty ['maɪt i] *adj.* powerful; strong; very great. (Adv: *mightily.* Comp: *mightier;* sup: *mightiest.*)
→ ACT HIGH-AND-MIGHTY

mike ['maɪk] *n.* a device for converting sounds to electronic audio signals. (Short for MICROPHONE.)

mild ['maɪld] **1.** *adj.* gentle or calm; not extreme, powerful, or severe. (Adv: *mildly.* Comp: *milder;* sup: *mildest.*) **2.** *adj.* [of food] plain and not spicy. (Adv: *mildly.* Comp: *milder;* sup: *mildest.*) **3.** *adj.* light; not severe or harsh. (Adv: *mildly.* Comp: *milder;* sup: *mildest.*)

mile ['maɪl] *n.* a unit of measurement of length, equal to 5,280 feet or about 1.6 kilometers.
→ BE A MILLION MILES AWAY
→ GO THE EXTRA MILE
→ MISS (SOMETHING) BY A MILE
→ NAUTICAL MILE
→ STAND OUT A MILE
→ STICK OUT A MILE

mileage ['maɪl ɪdʒ] **1.** *n.* a distance expressed in miles. (Plural only for types and instances.) **2.** *n.* the total number of miles that can be traveled using one gallon of gasoline. (No plural.)
→ GET A LOT OF MILEAGE OUT OF SOMETHING

milestone in someone's **life** a very important event or point in one's life. (From the stone at the side of a road showing the distance to or from a place.)

military ['mɪl ə tɛr i] *adj.* having to do with the armed forces. (Adv: *militarily* [mɪl ə 'tɛr ə li].)

the **military** *n.* the armed forces; the army. (Treated as singular.)

militia [mə 'lɪʃ ə] *n.* a group of citizens who are not part of the professional army but who are trained as soldiers.

milk ['mɪlk] **1.** *n.* the white liquid made by female mammals to feed their young. (Usually refers to cows' milk used as food. No plural.) **2.** *n.* a white liquid from certain plants. (No plural.) **3.** *tv.* to take ① from an animal.
→ CRY OVER SPILLED MILK

the **milk of human kindness** the natural kindness and sympathy shown to others.

milk someone **for** something to pressure someone into giving information or money.

mill ['mɪl] **1.** *n.* a building containing the machinery needed to turn grain into meal. **2.** *n.* a machine or device that crushes grains, seeds, or coffee beans.
→ BEEN THROUGH THE MILL

milligram ['mɪl ə græm] *n.* a unit of measurement of weight; one one-thousandth (1/1000) of a gram.

millimeter ['mɪl ə mit ɚ] *n.* a unit of measurement of length; one one-thousandth (1/1000) of a meter.

million ['mɪl jən] **1.** *n.* the number 1,000,000. (Additional numbers are formed as with *two million, three million, four million,* etc.) **2.** *adj.* 1,000,000; consisting of 1,000,000 things; having 1,000,000 things.
→ BE A MILLION MILES AWAY
→ FEEL LIKE A MILLION (DOLLARS)
→ LOOK LIKE A MILLION DOLLARS
→ ONE IN A MILLION

millionaire [mɪl jə 'nɛr] *n.* someone who has $1,000,000 in assets after debt is subtracted.

a **millstone about** one's **neck** a continual burden or handicap.

mincemeat [ˈmɪns mit] **1.** *n.* a mixture of fruit, spices, and sometimes chopped meat, as a filling for pies. (No plural form.) **2.** the *adj.* use of ①.
→ MAKE MINCEMEAT OF SOMEONE

mind [ˈmaɪnd] **1.** *n.* the part of humans that thinks and has feelings. **2.** *n.* the center of intelligence and memory; the imagination; the creative part of humans. **3.** *tv.* to care for someone or something; to tend to someone or something. **4.** *tv.* to be opposed to something; to care if someone does something. **5.** *iv.* to be opposed [to something]; to object.
→ BEAR SOMEONE OR SOMETHING IN MIND
→ BOGGLE SOMEONE'S MIND
→ ENTER ONE'S MIND
→ GET A LOAD OFF ONE'S MIND
→ GIVE SOMEONE A PIECE OF ONE'S MIND
→ HAVE A ONE-TRACK MIND
→ HAVE THE PRESENCE OF MIND TO DO SOMETHING
→ IN ONE'S MIND'S EYE
→ IN ONE'S RIGHT MIND
→ KEEP SOMEONE OR SOMETHING IN MIND
→ A MEETING OF MINDS
→ ON ONE'S MIND
→ OUT OF ONE'S MIND
→ PUT ONE'S MIND TO SOMETHING
→ SLIP ONE'S MIND

mind one's **own business** to attend only to the things that concern one.

mind one's **p's and q's 1.** to mind one's manners; to pay attention to small details of behavior. **2.** to pay attention to small details of behavior.

mind you a phrase indicating that something should be taken into consideration.

mine [ˈmaɪn] **1.** *n.* an opening into the earth from which precious metals, minerals, or gems are recovered. **2.** *n.* a source of something in large amounts; someone, something, or someplace that supplies large amounts of something. (Figurative on ①.) **3.** *n.* a bomb that is placed under the surface of the soil or water and explodes when it is touched. **4.** *tv.* to remove precious metals, minerals, or gems from the earth. **5.** *tv.* to place bombs under the surface of the soil or water at a particular location. **6.** *pron.* the first-person singular possessive pronoun. (Used in place of a noun.)
→ BACK TO THE SALT MINES
→ YOUR GUESS IS AS GOOD AS MINE.

a **mine of information** someone or something that is full of information.

mineral [ˈmɪn (ə) rəl] **1.** *n.* one of many kinds of crystallike substances dug from the earth; a substance that is gotten by mining. **2.** *n.* an element that plants and animals need in order to function properly. **3.** the *adj.* use of ①.

minimal [ˈmɪn ə məl] *adj.* smallest possible [amount]. (Adv: *minimally*.)

minimum [ˈmɪn ə məm] **1.** *n.* the least amount or degree possible; the smallest amount or degree possible. **2.** *adj.* minimal; smallest; lowest; least.

minister [ˈmɪn ɪ stɚ] **1.** *n.* a pastor; a preacher; the leader of a Christian church. **2.** *n.* [in many countries] someone who is the head of a government department.

mink ['mɪŋk] **1.** *n., irreg.* a small, long, furry animal similar to the weasel or ferret. (Plural: *mink* or *minks*.) **2.** *n.* the fur of ①. (No plural.) **3.** *n.* a coat made from ②. **4.** *adj.* made from ②.

minnow ['mɪn o] *n.* a kind of very small, thin fish that lives in fresh water.

minor ['maɪn ɚ] **1.** *adj.* small in size or amount; not serious; not very important. **2.** the *adj.* use of ①. **3.** *n.* a student's secondary area of study. **4.** *n.* someone who is younger than the legal age of responsibility.

mint ['mɪnt] **1.** *n.* a small plant with leaves that have a fresh, strong flavor, and the leaves themselves. (No plural.) **2.** *n.* a candy that is flavored with ①. **3.** *n.* a building where the government makes coins and paper money. **4.** *adj.* tasting like ①; flavored with ①. **5.** *adj.* perfect; in excellent condition. **6.** *tv.* to make something, especially coins, from metal.
→ IN MINT CONDITION

minus ['maɪn əs] **1.** *prep.* reduced by some amount; decreased by some amount; made less by some amount; with something omitted or subtracted. (Symbolized by (−).) **2.** *adj.* below zero; less than zero; [of a number] negative. (Precedes the amount. Symbolized by (−).) **3.** *adj.* [of a school letter grade] less than the full grade. (Follows the letter. Symbolized by (−).) **4.** *n.* a negative factor; a lack.

minute 1. ['mɪn ɪt] *n.* a unit of the measurement of time, equal to 60 seconds or 1/60 hour. **2.** [maɪ 'nut] *adj.* very small. (Adv: *minutely*.)
→ AT THE LAST MINUTE
→ EVERY MINUTE COUNTS
→ JUST A MINUTE

minutes ['mɪn ɪts] *n.* a written account of what happened at a meeting. (Treated as plural, but not countable.)

miracle ['mɪr ə kəl] **1.** *n.* a remarkable event that cannot be explained by the laws of nature. **2.** *n.* an unexpected, lucky event. (Figurative on ①.)

miraculous [mɪ 'ræk jə ləs] **1.** *adj.* not able to be explained by the laws of science or nature. (Adv: *miraculously*.) **2.** *adj.* unexpectedly excellent. (Figurative on ①. Adv: *miraculously*.)

mirage [mɪ 'rɑʒ] *n.* an image of something that does not really exist, especially an image of water in the desert; something that fools one's vision.

mirror ['mɪr ɚ] **1.** *n.* a piece of polished glass, treated in a way that makes it reflect images perfectly. **2.** *n.* someone or something that shows what someone or something thinks, looks like, acts like, or is. (Figurative on ①.) **3.** *tv.* to show something as though it were seen in ①; to represent something.

mirth ['mɚθ] *n.* fun and laughter. (No plural.)

miscarriage of justice a wrong or mistaken decision, especially one made in a court of law.

mischief ['mɪs tʃɪf] **1.** *n.* playful trouble; slightly bad tricks or deeds. (No plural.) **2.** *n.* some-

one—usually a child—who is a source of trouble or problems.
→ MAKE MISCHIEF

misconduct ['mɪs 'kɑn dəkt] *n.* bad behavior; behavior that is not good or moral. (No plural.)

miser ['maɪz ɚ] *n.* someone who is very selfish and has a lot of money.

miserable ['mɪz ə rə bəl] **1.** *adj.* unhappy; very sad; depressed. (Adv: *miserably.*) **2.** *adj.* unpleasant; depressing. (Adv: *miserably.*) **3.** *adj.* poor; squalid; wretched. (Adv: *miserably.*)
→ MAKE LIFE MISERABLE FOR SOMEONE

misfit ['mɪs fɪt] *n.* someone who does not seem to belong with other people or fit a situation.

misfortune [mɪs 'for tʃən] *n.* bad luck; bad fortune. (Plural only for types and instances.)

mishap ['mɪs hæp] *n.* an unlucky event or accident; bad luck; an unfortunate accident.

misjudge [mɪs 'dʒʌdʒ] *tv.* to make the wrong judgment about someone or something.

mislaid [mɪs 'led] past tense and past participle of MISLAY.

mislay [mɪs 'le] *tv., irreg.* to put something in a location that is later forgotten. (Past tense and past participle: MISLAID.)

mismanage [mɪs 'mæn ɪdʒ] *tv.* to manage someone or something badly; to deal with someone or something badly.

misplace [mɪs 'ples] *tv.* to put something someplace and then forget where it is.

miss ['mɪs] **1.** *tv.* to fail to hit, catch, meet, or reach someone or something. **2.** *tv.* to fail to locate or observe people or things that are where they are meant to be. **3.** *tv.* to notice the absence of someone or something. **4.** *tv.* to feel sad about the loss, departure, or absence of someone or something. **5.** *tv.* to avoid or escape something; to avoid doing something. **6.** *tv.* to lack something; to fail to acquire or experience something that is available. **7.** *n.* a failure to hit, reach, catch, or do something. **8.** *n.* a polite form of address for girls and young women. **9.** *n.* a title for a girl or unmarried woman. (Capitalized when written as a proper noun.)

miss out (on something) not to do something because one is unaware of the opportunity; to fail to or neglect to take part in something.

miss (something) **by a mile** to fail to hit something by a great distance.

miss the point to fail to understand the point, purpose, or intent of something.

mission ['mɪ ʃən] **1.** *n.* a journey to a place to do an important task. **2.** *n.* a specific task or duty; a specific aim or objective.
→ ONE'S MISSION IN LIFE

misspell [mɪs 'spɛl] *tv.* to spell something wrongly.

mist ['mɪst] **1.** *n.* a light spray of water or other liquid; a small cloud formed by spraying water or other liquid. **2.** *tv.* to spray someone or something with water or other liquid; to cover something with ① or water vapor.

mist over Go to MIST UP.

mist up AND **mist over** [for something] to acquire a coating of mist.

mistake [mɪ 'stek] **1.** *n.* an error; something that is wrong; something that is not correct. **2.** *tv., irreg.* to have the wrong idea about something. (Past tense: MISTOOK; past participle: MISTAKEN.)

mistake someone or something **for** someone or something to think that one thing or person is another; to confuse one thing or person with another.

mistaken [mɪ 'stek ən] Past participle of MISTAKE.
→ a CASE OF MISTAKEN IDENTITY

mister ['mɪs tɚ] *n.* a title for an adult male; a form of address for men. (The abbreviation, MR., is used in writing.)

mistook [mɪs 'tʊk] past tense of MISTAKE.

mistreat [mɪs 'trit] *tv.* to treat someone or something badly; to abuse someone or something.

mistrust [mɪs 'trʌst] **1.** *tv.* not to trust someone or something; to doubt someone or something. **2.** *n.* lack of trust; doubts about someone or something; distrust. (No plural.)

misty ['mɪs ti] *adj.* [of a surface] covered with mist; [of air] filled with mist. (Adv: *mistily.* Comp: *mistier;* sup: *mistiest.*)

misunderstand [mɪs ən dɚ 'stænd] *tv., irreg.* to understand someone or something incorrectly. (Past tense and past participle: MIS-UNDERSTOOD.)

misunderstood [mɪs ən dɚ 'stʊd] past tense and past participle of MISUNDERSTAND.

misuse 1. [mɪs 'jus] *n.* incorrect use; improper use; using something wrongly. (No plural.)
2. [mɪs 'juz] *tv.* to use something the wrong way; to use something for a purpose for which it was not meant to be used.

mitten ['mɪt n] *n.* a piece of clothing for one's hand, without separate parts for each finger but with a separate area for the thumb.

mix ['mɪks] **1.** *n.* a mixture; a combination of different people or things. **2.** *n.* a combination of different foods that is ready to be cooked or used in cooking. **3.** *tv.* to combine or blend different things so that they form one thing. **4.** *tv.* to do two things at the same time. **5.** *iv.* to be friendly and comfortable with other people; to be with other people.
→ HAVE MIXED FEELINGS (ABOUT SOMEONE OR SOMETHING)

mix in (with someone or something**)** to mix or combine with people or substances.

mix someone or something **in(to** something**)** to combine someone or something into something.

mix someone **up** to confuse someone.

mix someone **up with** someone to confuse one person with another.

mix something **up (with** something**) 1.** to mix or stir something with a mixing or stirring device. **2.** to confuse something with something else.

mixed ['mɪkst] **1.** *adj.* combined; blended. **2.** *adj.* [of the thoughts or feelings that someone has about someone or something] combining very different things, such as liking and disliking. **3.** *adj.* having both males and females; for both sexes.

a **mixed bag** a varied collection of people or things.

mixture ['mɪks tʃɚ] *n.* a combination or blend of different people or things.

moan ['mon] **1.** *n.* a deep, long cry of sadness, suffering, pain, or grief. **2.** *iv.* to make a deep, long cry of sadness, suffering, pain, or grief.

mob ['mɑb] **1.** *n.* a large group of people crowded around someone or something. **2.** *tv.* [for a large group of people] to crowd around someone or something.

mobile 1. ['mob əl] *adj.* able to move easily; able to be moved easily; movable. **2.** ['mo bil] *n.* a hanging arrangement of balanced objects that move with air currents. (Refers to decorations, works of art, or devices to entertain infants.)

mock ['mɑk] **1.** *tv.* to make fun of someone; to laugh at or ridicule someone, especially by copying how that person speaks or acts. **2.** *tv.* to copy or imitate someone or something. **3.** *adj.* not real.

mockery ['mɑk ə ri] *n.* something that is a poor substitute for the real thing or person.

mockingbird ['mɑk ɪŋ bɚd] *n.* a bird native to the Americas, so called because it imitates the calls or songs of other birds.

mode ['mod] **1.** *n.* a way of doing something; a method; a manner. **2.** *n.* a feature of a verb that shows whether it is a statement, command, or wish; MOOD ②.

model ['mɑd l] **1.** *n.* a copy of an object, usually made smaller than the original. **2.** *n.* someone or something that is the perfect example of something; someone or something that is to be copied or imitated; a standard. **3.** *n.* someone who is paid to wear and show off clothing that is available for sale. **4.** *n.* someone who poses for artists and photographers. **5.** *n.* one style of a certain product in a series of styles. **6.** *adj.* perfect; worthy of imitation; regarded as the perfect example. (Prenominal only.) **7.** *adj.* built to a smaller scale than normal. (Prenominal only.) **8.** *iv.* to work as ③ or ④. **9.** *tv.* [for ③] to wear and show off clothing.

modem ['mod əm] *n.* a device that connects a computer with a telephone line or a television cable system so that information can be sent or received over that line.

moderate 1. ['mɑd ə rɪt] *adj.* not extreme; in the center; average or medium. (Adv: *moderately.*) **2.** ['mɑd ə rɪt] *n.* someone whose political or social views are not extreme. **3.** ['mɑd ə ret] *tv.* to reduce something; to cause something to be less strong. **4.** ['mɑd ə ret] *tv.* to lead a discussion; to lead a meeting.

moderation [mɑd ə 'reɪ ʃən] *n.* being moderate; [doing things] within reasonable limits. (No plural.)

modern ['mɑd ɚn] *adj.* up-to-date; new; of or about the present or very recent time. (Adv: *modernly*.)

modest ['mɑd ɪst] **1.** *adj.* shy; humble; not bragging about oneself. (Adv: *modestly*.) **2.** *adj.* not excessive; moderate; not large. (Adv: *modestly*.) **3.** *adj.* decent; not revealing too much of one's body. (Adv: *modestly*.)

moist ['mɔɪst] *adj.* damp; a little bit wet. (Adv: *moistly*. Comp: *moister*; sup: *moistest*.)

moisten ['mɔɪ sən] *tv.* to make something moist; to make something damp.

moisture ['mɔɪs tʃɚ] *n.* wetness; water in the air; vapor. (No plural.)

molasses [mə 'læs ɪz] *n.* a sweet, dark, sticky liquid made in the process of making sugar. (This is singular. No plural.)

mold ['mold] **1.** *n.* a fuzzy or slimy growth that forms on animal or plant matter. (Plural only for types and instances.) **2.** *n.* a hollow object that has a certain shape. (Certain liquids—such as clay, resin, cement, rubber, etc.—are poured into it, and when the liquid hardens, it will have the same shape as the mold.) **3.** *n.* something that was shaped by or made in ②. **4.** *tv.* to shape something; to form something into a certain shape; to shape something using ②. **5.** *iv.* to be covered with ①.

→ CAST IN THE SAME MOLD

mole ['mol] *n.* a small, furry mammal that lives underground, eats worms and bugs, and cannot see well.

molecule ['mɑl ə kjul] *n.* the smallest part into which a chemical compound can be divided without changing its chemical composition.

molt ['molt] **1.** *tv.* [for an animal] to shed feathers, skin, or fur. **2.** *iv.* [for animals] to shed [something], as with ①.

molten ['molt n] *adj.* melted; made into liquid. (Adv: *moltenly*.)

mom ['mɑm] *n.* mother. (Informal. Also a term of address. Capitalized when written as a proper noun.)

moment ['mo mənt] **1.** *n.* an instant in time; a brief period of time. **2.** *n.* a certain point in time.
→ the BIG MOMENT
→ EVERY MOMENT COUNTS
→ NOT A MOMENT TO SPARE
→ ON THE SPUR OF THE MOMENT
→ WITHOUT A MOMENT TO SPARE

the moment everyone has been waiting for Go to the BIG MOMENT.

moment of truth the point at which someone has to face the reality of a situation.

momento [mə 'mɛn to] Go to MEMENTO.

momentum [mo 'mɛn təm] *n.* the force and speed of movement or progress. (No plural.)

monarch ['mɑn ɑrk] *n.* a king or a queen.

Monday ['mʌn de] Go to DAY.

monetary ['mɑn ə tɛr i] *adj.* of or about money. (Adv: *monetarily* [mɑn ə 'tɛr ə li].)

money ['mʌn i] **1.** *n.* currency; coins and bills issued by a government. (No plural.) **2.** *n.* wealth; riches. (No plural.)
→ FORK MONEY OUT (FOR SOMETHING)
→ HAVE MONEY TO BURN
→ HUSH MONEY
→ IN THE MONEY
→ LAY AN AMOUNT OF MONEY OUT FOR SOMEONE OR SOMETHING
→ LAY AN AMOUNT OF MONEY OUT ON SOMEONE OR SOMETHING
→ MAKE GOOD MONEY
→ POUR MONEY DOWN THE DRAIN
→ PUT YOUR MONEY WHERE YOUR MOUTH IS!
→ THROW GOOD MONEY AFTER BAD

Money burns a hole in someone's **pocket.** a phrase meaning that someone spends as much money as possible, and that having money makes a person want to spend it.

Money is no object. It does not matter how much something costs.

Money talks. Money gives one power and influence to help get things done or to get one's own way.

monitor ['mɑn ə tɚ] **1.** *n.* a device that looks somewhat like a television set and is used to display computer information. **2.** *n.* a measuring device that keeps a record of something. **3.** *tv.* to watch, listen to, or keep a record of something.

monk ['mʌŋk] *n.* a man who devotes his life to religion as part of an all-male religious organization.

monkey ['mʌŋ ki] *n.* a small, hairy primate with a long tail.

monkey around to fool around; to behave badly.

monkey business peculiar or out-of-the-ordinary activities, especially mischievous or illegal ones.

monopoly [mə 'nɑp ə li] **1.** *n.* the condition existing when someone or something has complete control over something. **2.** *n.* a business that is the only provider of a service or product. **3.** *n.* the right to be the only provider of a service or product, as authorized by a government.

monster ['mɑn stɚ] *n.* a large creature that scares people.

monstrosity [mɑn 'strɑs ə ti] *n.* someone or something that is huge and very ugly.

month ['mʌnθ] **1.** *n.* one of the 12 divisions of a year. (The months of the year, in order, are JANUARY, FEBRUARY, MARCH, APRIL, MAY, JUNE, JULY, AUGUST, SEPTEMBER, OCTOBER, NOVEMBER, DECEMBER.) **2.** *n.* a period of about 30 or 31 days; a period of four weeks.
→ ALL MONTH LONG

monthly ['mʌnθ li] **1.** *adj.* happening every month; happening once a month. **2.** *adv.* every month; once a month.

months running Go to DAYS RUNNING.

monument ['mɑn jə mənt] **1.** *n.* a structure that is built in memory of a person or event. **2.** *n.* something that preserves the memory of a person, culture, or event. (Figurative on ①.)

mood ['mud] **1.** *n.* a state of mind; the way one is feeling. **2.** *n.* a feature of a verb that shows whether it is a statement, a command, or a wish; MODE ②.
→ IN NO MOOD TO DO SOMETHING
→ IN THE MOOD FOR SOMETHING
→ IN THE MOOD TO DO SOMETHING

moon ['mun] **1.** *n.* a large natural satellite that orbits around a planet. **2.** *n.* the natural satellite that orbits around the earth.
→ ASK FOR THE MOON
→ ONCE IN A BLUE MOON
→ PROMISE SOMEONE THE MOON
→ PROMISE THE MOON (TO SOMEONE)

moonlight ['mun laɪt] **1.** *n.* the light from a moon. (No plural.) **2.** *adj.* done at night, while the moon is shining; happening while the moon is shining. (Prenominal only.) **3.** *iv.* to have a second job in the evening or at night in addition to the job one has during the day. (Past tense and past participle: *moonlighted.*)

moose ['mus] *n., irreg.* a northern animal—similar to a large deer—the males of which have wide, flat horns on their heads. (Plural: *moose.* See also ELK ②.)

mop ['mɑp] *n.* a group of thick, heavy strings or a sponge, attached to a pole, used wet or dry for cleaning floors.

mop something **down** to clean a surface with a mop.

mop something **off** to wipe the liquid off something.

mop something **up** to clean something with a mop, a towel, a sponge, etc.

mop up to clean up [liquid or dirt] with a mop, a towel, a sponge, etc.

moral ['mɔr əl] **1.** *adj.* of or about good and bad, according to society's standards of right and wrong. (Adv: *morally.*) **2.** *adj.* showing or representing good behavior and values. (Adv: *morally.*) **3.** *n.* the lesson that can be learned from a story.

moral support ['mɔr əl sə 'pɔrt] *n.* help that is mental or psychological rather than physical or monetary.

morale [mə 'ræl] *n.* confidence; the amount of confidence felt by a person or group of people. (No plural.)

morality [mə 'ræl ə ti] *n.* the goodness or rightness of someone's behavior; good behavior measured by society's standards of right and wrong. (No plural.)

morals *n.* a person's MORAL ① principles of behavior, especially concerning sex. (Treated as plural, but not countable.)

more ['mɔr] **1.** *adj.* the comparative form of MUCH or MANY; a greater amount or number. (Prenominal only.) **2.** *pron.* the comparative form of MUCH or MANY; a greater amount or number. **3.** *n.* an additional amount or number. (No plural.) **4.** *adv.* a word used to form the comparative form of some adjectives and adverbs; to a greater extent. **5.** *adv.* of a greater amount.
→ BITE OFF MORE THAN ONE CAN CHEW
→ WEAR MORE THAN ONE HAT

more and more an increasing amount; additional amounts.

more than one **can bear** AND
more than one **can take; more
than one** can **stand** more of
something, such as trouble or
something bad, than a person can
endure.

more than one **can stand** Go to
MORE THAN ONE CAN BEAR.

more than one **can take** Go to
MORE THAN ONE CAN BEAR.

morning ['mor nɪŋ] **1.** *n.* the period
of the day from midnight to noon.
2. *n.* dawn; sunrise. **3.** *adj.* happening during ①. (Prenominal
only.)
→ FIRST THING (IN THE MORNING)

the **morning after (the night
before)** the morning after a night
spent drinking, when one has a
hangover.

mornings *adv.* every MORNING ①.

morsel ['mor səl] *n.* a small piece of
something, especially food.

mortal ['mor təl] **1.** *n.* a human
being; someone or something that
must die; someone or something
that will not live forever. **2.** *adj.*
unable to live forever; having to
die at some time. (Adv: *mortally*.)

mortar ['mor tɚ] **1.** *n.* a kind of
cement that binds bricks or stones
to each other, especially when a
wall is being built. (Plural only for
types and instances.) **2.** *n.* a short,
wide cannon that shoots shells in a
high arc. **3.** *n.* a hard bowl used to
hold substances being ground into
powder.

mortgage ['mor gɪdʒ] **1.** *n.* an
agreement by which a borrower
grants a lender the ownership of
an asset in exchange for a loan of

money, thus protecting the loan
with the asset. (When the loan is
repaid, the ownership of the property is returned to the borrower. If
the borrower is unable to pay the
loan, the asset then belongs to the
lender.) **2.** *tv.* to use an asset to
secure a loan.

mosquito [mə 'skit o] *n.* a small
insect, the female of which sucks
blood from warm-blooded creatures. (Plural ends in *-s* or *-es*.)

moss ['mɔs] *n.* a small, soft green
plant without flowers that grows
in masses on rocks and other surfaces. (Plural only for types and
instances.)

most ['most] **1.** *adj.* the superlative
form of MUCH or MANY; the greatest
amount or number. (Prenominal
only.) **2.** *adj.* over half; almost all.
(Prenominal only. Adv: *mostly*.)
3. *n.* over half or almost all of a
certain group of things or people;
over half or almost all of something. (No plural. Treated as singular or plural, but not countable.)
4. *adv.* a word used to form the
superlative form of some adjectives and adverbs; to the greatest
extent. (Usually with *the*.) **5.** *adv.*
very. (Used for emphasis.)

mostly ['most li] **1.** *adv.* more than
half; for the most part. **2.** *adv.*
most of the time; usually.

motel [mo 'tɛl] *n.* a hotel for people
traveling by car; a hotel alongside a
highway.

moth ['mɔθ] *n., irreg.* a small insect
with large, broad wings and
antennae, similar to a butterfly,
but usually not as colorful. (Plural:
['mɔðz].)

mothball [ˈmɔθ bɔl] *n.* a small ball made of a substance that keeps moths away from clothes.

mother [ˈmʌð ɚ] **1.** *n.* a female who has given birth to a child or offspring. **2.** *n.* a term of address used with one's own ①. (Capitalized when written as a proper noun.) **3.** *adj.* [of one's language or country] native. (Prenominal only.) **4.** *tv.* to take care of someone in the manner of ①.
→ TIED TO ONE'S MOTHER'S APRON STRINGS

motherhood [ˈmʌð ɚ hʊd] *n.* the state of being a mother. (No plural.)

motion [ˈmo ʃən] **1.** *n.* movement; moving. (Plural only for types and instances.) **2.** *n.* a formal proposal that something be done, made during a meeting. **3.** *tv.* to direct someone by moving a part of one's body, usually the hands. **4.** *iv.* to point or indicate by moving a part of one's body, usually the hands.
→ GO THROUGH THE MOTIONS
→ SLOW MOTION
→ TABLE A MOTION

motion picture [ˈmo ʃən ˈpɪk tʃɚ] *n.* a movie; a film; a story on film.

motion someone **aside** to give a hand signal to someone to move aside.

motion someone **away from** someone or something to give a hand signal to someone to move away from someone or something.

motive [ˈmot ɪv] *n.* a reason for doing something; something—such as an idea, a need, or a way of thinking—that causes a person to do something.

motor [ˈmot ɚ] *n.* an engine; a machine that changes some kind of fuel into power that can lift, turn, or move things.

motorboat [ˈmot ɚ bot] *n.* a boat that is powered by a motor or engine.

motorcycle [ˈmot ɚ saɪ kəl] *n.* a vehicle that has two wheels and a frame larger and heavier than a bicycle, and that is powered by a motor.

motorist [ˈmot ə rɪst] *n.* someone who drives a car.

motto [ˈmat o] *n.* a short statement that expresses a belief or a rule of behavior. (Plural ends in *-s* or *-es*.)

mound [maʊnd] *n.* a small hill or pile.

mount [maʊnt] **1.** *n.* a support; an object that something is attached to or hung from. **2.** *n.* a (particular) mountain. (Abbreviated *Mt.*) **3.** *tv.* to get on an animal or vehicle that one must ride with one leg on either side of the animal or vehicle. **4.** *tv.* to climb something; to go up something. **5.** *tv.* to hang something to a fixed support; to attach something to a fixed support.

mount up 1. to get up on a horse. **2.** [for something] to increase in amount or extent.

mountain [ˈmaʊnt n] **1.** *n.* a very tall mass of land that pushes up from the surface of the earth; a very tall hill. **2.** *n.* a very tall pile of something; a very large amount of something. (Figurative on ①.)

mountain lion [ˈmaʊnt n ˈlaɪ ən] *n.* a large, American wild animal in the cat family, also called the *panther* or the *cougar*.

mountain range ['maʊnt n 'rendʒ] *n.* a row or line of mountains.

mourn ['morn] **1.** *tv.* to feel sorrow or sadness about the death or loss of someone or something. (E.g., to *mourn the death of someone.*) **2.** *tv.* to feel sorrow or sadness about someone who has died. (E.g., to *mourn someone.*) **3.** *iv.* to feel sorrow or sadness, especially about someone's death. (E.g., to *mourn because of a death.*)

mourner ['mor nɚ] *n.* someone who mourns; someone who attends a funeral.

mouse ['maʊs] **1.** *n., irreg.* a small, furry rodent with tiny eyes and a long tail, like a rat but smaller. (Plural: MICE.) **2.** *n., irreg.* a device that can be moved around by one hand to control the movements of a pointer on a computer screen. (Plural: MICE or *mouses.*)
→ (AS) POOR AS A CHURCH MOUSE
→ (AS) QUIET AS A MOUSE
→ PLAY CAT AND MOUSE (WITH SOMEONE)

mousetrap ['maʊs træp] *n.* a simple device that is used to trap mice that are indoor pests.

mousse ['mus] *n.* a rich, creamy dessert made from cream, eggs, and fruit or chocolate. (Plural only for types and instances.)

mouth 1. ['maʊθ] *n., irreg.* the opening on the faces of animals where food and air enter the body. (Plural: ['maʊðz].) **2.** ['maʊθ] *n., irreg.* an opening of something; the entrance to something. (Figurative on ①.) **3.** ['maʊθ] *n., irreg.*

the place where a river joins a lake, sea, or ocean. **4.** ['maʊð] *tv.* to move ① as if one were speaking but without producing actual speech.
→ BORN WITH A SILVER SPOON IN ONE'S MOUTH
→ BY WORD OF MOUTH
→ DOWN IN THE MOUTH
→ FOAM AT THE MOUTH
→ HAVE A BIG MOUTH
→ HAVE FOOT-IN-MOUTH DISEASE
→ HAVE ONE'S HEART IN ONE'S MOUTH
→ LAUGH OUT OF THE OTHER SIDE OF ONE'S MOUTH
→ LEAVE A BAD TASTE IN SOMEONE'S MOUTH
→ LIVE FROM HAND TO MOUTH
→ LOOK AS IF BUTTER WOULDN'T MELT IN ONE'S MOUTH
→ MAKE SOMEONE'S MOUTH WATER
→ MELT IN ONE'S MOUTH
→ NOT OPEN ONE'S MOUTH
→ ONE'S HEART IS IN ONE'S MOUTH
→ PUT ONE'S FOOT IN ONE'S MOUTH
→ PUT WORDS INTO SOMEONE'S MOUTH
→ PUT YOUR MONEY WHERE YOUR MOUTH IS!
→ STICK ONE'S FOOT IN ONE'S MOUTH
→ STRAIGHT FROM THE HORSE'S MOUTH
→ TAKE THE WORDS (RIGHT) OUT OF ONE'S MOUTH

mouthpiece ['maʊθ pis] **1.** *n.* the part of a musical instrument that is blown into; the part of a musical instrument that is put on or between one's lips. **2.** *n.* the part of a machine or device that is placed on or next to someone or something's mouth.

mouthwash ['maʊθ waʃ] *n.* a liquid that is used to rinse one's mouth in order to make the breath smell better or to kill germs in the mouth.

move ['muv] **1.** *iv.* to go to a different time or space; to change posi-

tion in time or space. **2.** *iv.* to be in motion. **3.** *iv.* to change where one lives or works. **4.** *tv.* to transport someone or something to a different time or space; to cause someone or something to change position. **5.** *tv.* to cause someone or something to remain in motion. **6.** *tv.* to affect someone's emotions or feelings. **7.** *tv.* to formally make a suggestion at a meeting; to formally propose something. (The object is a clause with THAT ⑦.) **8.** *n.* an instance of changing position as in ①; a movement. **9.** *n.* the act of going to a new house to live. **10.** *n.* one step in a plan; an action that has a specific result. **11.** *n.* a player's turn in a game.
→ ON THE MOVE
→ PRIME MOVER

move away (from someone or something) **1.** to withdraw from someone or something. **2.** to move, with one's entire household, to another residence.

move back (from someone or something) to move back and away from someone or something. (Often a command.)

move heaven and earth to do something to make a major effort to do something.

move in (for something) to get closer for some purpose, such as a kill.

move in (on someone or something) **1.** to move closer to someone or something; to make advances or aggressive movements toward someone or something. (Both literal and figurative senses.) **2.** to attempt to take over

or dominate someone or something.

move in(to something) **1.** [for someone] to come to reside in something or someplace. **2.** to enter something or someplace. **3.** to begin a new line of activity.

move off (from someone or something) to move away from someone or something.

move on to continue moving; to travel on; to move away and not stop.

move on something to do something about something.

move on (to something) to change to a different subject or activity.

move out (of someplace) **1.** to leave a place; to begin to depart. **2.** to leave a place of residence permanently.

move someone **up** to advance or promote someone.

move up (in the world) to advance (oneself) and become successful.

move up (to something) to advance to something; to purchase a better quality of something.

movement ['muv mənt] **1.** *n.* moving; changing position in time or space. (Plural only for types and instances.) **2.** *n.* a division of a symphony or other classical work of music. **3.** *n.* a common social or political goal and the people who work together to promote it.
→ BOWEL MOVEMENT

movie ['muv i] **1.** *n.* a film; a motion picture; a story on film. **2.** the *adj.* use of ①.

mow ['mo] *tv., irreg.* to cut grass. (Past participle: *mowed* or MOWN.)

mow someone or something **down** to cut, knock, or shoot someone or something down.

mower ['mo ɚ] *n.* a machine used to cut grass evenly. (Short for LAWN MOWER.)
→ LAWN MOWER

mown ['mon] a past participle of MOW.

Mr. ['mɪst ɚ] *n.* a title for an adult male. (The abbreviation of MISTER.)

Mrs. ['mɪs əz] *n.* a title for a married woman.

Ms. ['mɪz] *n.* a title for an adult female.

much ['mʌtʃ] **1.** *adv., irreg.* to a great extent; to a great degree; a lot. (Comp: MORE; sup: MOST.) **2.** *adj., irreg.* a lot; to quite an extent or degree. (Comp: MORE; sup: MOST.) **3.** *n.* a large extent; a large degree; a large amount. (No plural.)
→ HOW MUCH
→ TAKE TOO MUCH ON

mucus ['mju kəs] *n.* the slimy substance secreted by the body to protect and moisten certain tissues. (No plural.)

mud ['mʌd] *n.* a mixture of dirt and water; very wet soil. (No plural.)
→ (AS) CLEAR AS MUD

muddle through (something**)** to manage to get through something awkwardly.

muddy ['mʌd i] **1.** *adj.* covered with mud. (Adv: *muddily.* Comp: *muddier;* sup: *muddiest.*) **2.** *adj.*

not clear; cloudy. (Said especially of colors or liquids. Figurative on ①. Adv: *muddily.* Comp: *muddier;* sup: *muddiest.*)

muffler ['mʌf lɚ] **1.** *n.* part of the exhaust system of a car that softens the noises of the engine. **2.** *n.* a scarf that can be wrapped around the neck for warmth.

mug ['mʌg] **1.** *n.* a drinking cup with a handle. **2.** *n.* the contents of ①. **3.** *tv.* to attack and rob someone.

mugger ['mʌg ɚ] *n.* someone who attacks and robs people on the street.

muggy ['mʌg i] *adj.* hot and humid. (Adv: *muggily.* Comp: *muggier;* sup: *muggiest.*)

mulch ['mʌltʃ] **1.** *n.* plant matter or other material spread on plants to protect them and to retain the moisture in the soil. (Plural only for types and instances.) **2.** *tv.* to spread ① around plants in a garden.

mule ['mjul] *n.* the offspring of one horse and one donkey.
→ (AS) STUBBORN AS A MULE

mull something **over** to think over something; to ponder something.

multiple ['mʌl tə pəl] **1.** *adj.* involving many parts; consisting of many parts. (Adv: *multiply* ['mʌl tə pli].) **2.** *n.* a number that can be divided by another number without a remainder; a number that can be divided evenly by another number.

multiply ['mʌl tə plaɪ] **1.** *tv.* to increase something. **2.** *iv.* to reproduce; to have offspring; to breed. **3.** *iv.* to increase.

multiply a number **by** a number to add an amount to itself the number of times shown by another number; to perform multiplication.

multiply by something to use the arithmetic process of multiplication to expand numerically a certain number of times.

munch ['mʌntʃ] *tv.* to eat a crisp food that makes a noise; to eat something noisily.

munch on something to eat something; to chew on something.

municipal [mju 'nɪs ə pəl] *adj.* of, for, or serving a city, town, or village. (Adv: *municipally.*)

mural ['mjʊr əl] *n.* a picture or scene that is painted on the surface of a wall.

murder ['mɚ dɚ] **1.** *n.* the killing of a human, done on purpose and against the law. **2.** *tv.* to kill someone on purpose and against the law.
→ BE MURDER ON SOMETHING
→ CRY BLOODY MURDER
→ SCREAM BLOODY MURDER

murderer ['mɚ dɚ ɚ] *n.* someone who kills someone else; someone who is found guilty of murder.

murmur ['mɚ mɚ] **1.** *n.* a low, quiet sound. **2.** *n.* an irregular sound made by the heart, caused by defects in the heart. **3.** *iv.* to make low, quiet sounds; to speak very quietly. **4.** *tv.* to say something very quietly. (The object can be a clause with THAT ⑦.)

muscle ['mʌs əl] **1.** *n.* a group of long tissues in the body that can be shortened to make parts of the body move. **2.** *n.* strength; power. (No plural. Figurative on ①.)

muscle in (on someone or something**)** to interfere with someone or something; to intrude on someone or something.

muscle someone **out (of** something**)** to force someone out of something; to push someone out of something.

muscular ['mʌs kjə lɚ] **1.** *adj.* in or of the muscles. **2.** *adj.* having muscles that are strong and well developed. (Adv: *muscularly.*)

museum [mju 'zi əm] *n.* a building where art or things of or about science, history, or some other subject are placed on display for the public to see and learn about.

mushroom ['mʌʃ rum] **1.** *n.* a kind of fungus that is often used as food. **2.** *iv.* to grow very quickly or suddenly.

mushroom into something to grow suddenly into something large or important.

mushy ['mʌʃ i] *adj.* soft and pulpy. (Adv: *mushily.* Comp: *mushier;* sup: *mushiest.*)

music ['mju zɪk] **1.** *n.* the sounds of the voice or of instruments making pleasant tones in a series or a series of groups. (No plural in standard English. Number is expressed with *piece(s) of music.*) **2.** *n.* a piece of paper that shows the notes of a particular song or melody. (No plural.)
→ FACE THE MUSIC

→ SET SOMETHING TO MUSIC

musical ['mju zɪ kəl] **1.** *adj.* causing music to be made; producing notes or tones. (Adv: *musically* [...ɪk li].) **2.** *adj.* of or about music. (Adv: *musically* [...ɪk li].) **3.** *n.* a play or movie in which the actors sing songs, usually as a way of moving the story forward.

musician [mju 'zɪ ʃən] *n.* someone who plays a musical instrument; someone who writes music; someone who is in a band or an orchestra.

muss something **(up)** ['mʌs...] to make something messy, especially one's hair; to move someone's hair out of place.

mussel ['mʌs əl] *n.* a kind of shellfish, usually having very dark shells, that can be eaten as food.

must ['mʌst] **1.** *aux.* a form showing a requirement to do something; [to] have to [do something]. (Uses *had to* for a past tense.) **2.** *aux.* a form indicating probability or likelihood. (Uses the form *has to have* plus the past participle or *must have* plus the past participle for a past tense.) **3.** *n.* something that is necessary or essential.

must not *aux.* a form that indicates what one is not allowed to do.

mustache ['mʌs tæʃ] *n.* hair that grows on the upper lip.

mustard ['mʌs tɚd] **1.** *n.* a plant with a bright yellow flower. (No plural.) **2.** *n.* a seasoning or sauce made from the powdered seeds of ①, water or vinegar, and spices.

(Plural only for types and instances.)

muster (up) one's **courage** to build up one's courage; to call or bring forth one's courage.

mustn't ['mʌs ənt] *cont.* must not. (Indicates what one is not allowed to do or what one may not do.)

musty ['mʌs ti] *adj.* smelling old and stale; smelling like mold. (Adv: *mustily.* Comp: *mustier;* sup: *mustiest.*)

mutual ['mju tʃu əl] **1.** *adj.* shared by two or more people; equally felt or done by each person toward the other. (Adv: *mutually.*) **2.** *adj.* common to two or more people; known to two or more people. (Adv: *mutually.*)

mutual fund ['mju tʃu əl 'fʌnd] *n.* an investment in which a large number of people own shares of investments in many assets. (Can be shortened to FUND.)

muzzle ['mʌz əl] **1.** *n.* [in certain animals] the part of the face that sticks out. **2.** *n.* a cover put over the mouth of an animal so that it will not bite someone or something. **3.** *n.* the front end of a gun; the barrel of a gun. **4.** *tv.* to put ② on an animal.

my ['maɪ] **1.** *pron.* the first-person singular possessive pronoun. (Describes people or things belonging to the speaker or writer. Used as a modifier before a noun. Compare this with MINE ⑥.) **2.** *interj.* a word used to show surprise.

myself [maɪ 'sɛlf] **1.** *pron.* the first-person singular reflexive pronoun.

2. *pron.* ① used to emphasize the speaker or the writer as subject of the sentence.
→ BY MYSELF

mystery ['mɪs tə ri] **1.** *n.* the quality of not being explained, known, or understood; the quality of being hidden or secret. (Plural only for types and instances.) **2.** *n.* a book that involves a crime or murder that is solved in the story. **3.** the *adj.* use of ①.

myth ['mɪθ] **1.** *n.* a fable; a story that explains a mystery of nature or tells how something came into existence. **2.** *n.* someone or something that is imaginary or invented; something that is not based in fact. (Figurative on ①.)

mythical ['mɪθ ə kəl] *adj.* imaginary; [of a character, story, or situation] invented. (Adv: *mythically* […ɪk li].)

mythology [mɪθ 'ɑl ə dʒi] **1.** *n.* the study of myths. (Plural only for types and instances.) **2.** *n.* a collection of myths about someone, something, or some culture.

N

n. an abbreviation of NOMINAL.

nag ['næg] **1.** *tv.* to continue to bother someone; to demand, by complaining all the time, that someone do something. **2.** *iv.* to continue to be a bother and a pest by making demands.

nag at someone **(about** someone or something**)** to pester someone about someone or something.

nail ['nel] **1.** *n.* a thin rod of metal, pointed on one end. **2.** *n.* one of the hard, flat tips at the ends of fingers and toes. **3.** *tv.* to attach or secure something with ①.
→ (AS) HARD AS NAILS
→ BITE ONE'S NAILS
→ FIGHT SOMEONE OR SOMETHING TOOTH AND NAIL
→ GO AT IT TOOTH AND NAIL
→ HIT THE NAIL (RIGHT) ON THE HEAD

nail in someone's or something's **coffin** something that will harm or destroy someone or something.

nail someone **down (on** something**)** Go to PIN SOMEONE DOWN (ON SOMETHING).

nail something **up 1.** to put something up, as on a wall, by nailing. **2.** to nail something closed; to use nails to secure something from intruders.

naked ['nek əd] *adj.* nude; wearing no clothes.
→ WITH THE NAKED EYE

name ['nem] **1.** *n.* the word that indicates someone, something, or someplace. **2.** *n.* [someone's] fame or reputation. **3.** *n.* someone who is famous or important. **4.** *tv.* to give or apply a NAME as in ① to someone, something, or someplace. **5.** *tv.* to state or recite the ① of someone or something. **6.** *tv.* to appoint someone; to choose someone or something.
→ DROP NAMES
→ DROP SOMEONE'S NAME
→ DROP THE NAME OF SOMEONE
→ FIRST NAME
→ IN NAME ONLY
→ WORTHY OF THE NAME

nap ['næp] **1.** *iv.* to sleep for a short period of time, especially during the day. **2.** *n.* a short amount of sleep, especially during the day. **3.** *n.* the upright threads of a carpet or of a piece of material, such as velvet. (No plural.)
→ CATCH SOMEONE NAPPING
→ TAKE A NAP

nape ['nep] *n.* the back [of the neck].
→ BY THE NAPE OF THE NECK

napkin ['næp kɪn] *n.* a square of fabric or paper used for protecting one's clothes and keeping tidy at meals.

narrate ['nɛr et] **1.** *tv.* to tell a story. **2.** *iv.* to tell about events that are being shown in a film, a slide show, on television, or in some other performance setting.

narrow ['nɛr o] **1.** *adj.* not wide; short from side to side in comparison with the length of something from one end to the other. (Adv: *narrowly.* Comp: *narrower;* sup: *narrowest.*) **2.** *adj.* limited; not broad. (Figurative on ①. Adv: *narrowly.* Comp: *narrower;* sup: *narrowest.*) **3.** *tv.* to cause something to become ①. **4.** *iv.* to become ①. **5.** *iv.* to become ②.

narrow something **down (to** people or things**)** to reduce a list of possibilities from many to a selected few.

nasal ['nez əl] **1.** *adj.* of or about the nose. (Adv: *nasally.*) **2.** *adj.* of the quality of sound heard when making the speech sounds [m], [n], or [ŋ]. (Adv: *nasally.*) **3.** *n.* a speech sound, such as [m] or [n], made by opening the passage to the nose at the back of the throat.

nasty ['næs ti] **1.** *adj.* mean; angry; unpleasant. (Adv: *nastily.* Comp: *nastier;* sup: *nastiest.*) **2.** *adj.* dirty-minded; offensive to one's morals. (Adv: *nastily.* Comp: *nastier;* sup: *nastiest.*) **3.** *adj.* very serious; bad; dangerous. (Adv: *nastily.* Comp: *nastier;* sup: *nastiest.*) **4.** *adj.* not pleasant to see, hear, smell, taste, or touch. (Adv: *nastily.* Comp: *nastier;* sup: *nastiest.*)

nation ['ne ʃən] **1.** *n.* a country; a country that governs itself. **2.** *n.* the people of a country; a group of people who are ruled by the same government.

national ['næʃ ə nəl] **1.** *adj.* of or about a nation; belonging to a nation; throughout a nation. (Adv: *nationally.*) **2.** *n.* a citizen of a specific nation or a particular group of nations.

nationality [næʃ ə 'næl ə ti] *n.* the status that arises from having citizenship in a particular country or being born in a particular country.

native ['ne tɪv] **1.** *n.* something that comes from a certain country or region. **2.** *n.* someone born in a particular place. **3.** *adj.* born or raised in a certain country or region; belonging to a certain country or region. (Adv: *natively.*)

Native American ['ne tɪv ə 'mɛr ə kən] **1.** *n.* a person belonging to one of the groups of people that lived in North America when the Europeans arrived; an American Indian. (Often capitalized, but sometimes seen as *native American.*) **2.** the *adj.* use of ①.

native to someplace originating in or existing naturally in a certain country or region.

natural ['nætʃ ə rəl] **1.** *adj.* made by nature; existing in nature; not artificial; not made by people; not affected by people. (Adv: *naturally.*) **2.** *adj.* existing since birth; not learned. (Adv: *naturally.*) **3.** *n.* someone who is thought of as perfect for a certain job; someone who does something very well, especially through inborn ability. **4.** *n.* a musical note that is not a sharp or a flat; one of the white keys on the piano.

nature ['ne tʃɚ] **1.** *n.* everything in the world except the material products of human work and thought: people, animals, plants, rocks, land, water, the weather, etc. (No plural.) **2.** *n.* land that has not been affected by humans. (No plural.) **3.** *n.* [someone's or something's] character; the essential qualities of someone or something; what something or someone really is.
→ CALL OF NATURE
→ SECOND NATURE TO SOMEONE

nausea ['nɔ zi ə] *n.* a feeling of sickness; the feeling that one has to vomit. (No plural.)

nauseous ['nɔ ʃəs, 'nɔ zi əs] **1.** *adj.* causing nausea; sickening; causing someone to feel sick. (Adv: *nauseously*.) **2.** *adj.* experiencing nausea; sickened. (Adv: *nauseously*.)

nautical ['nɔt ɪ kəl] *adj.* of or about ships, shipping, or sailors. (Adv: *nautically* [...ɪk li].)

nautical mile ['nɔt ɪ kəl 'maɪl] *n.* a measurement of distance at sea equal to about 1.15 miles on land.

naval ['ne vəl] *adj.* of or about a navy.

navel ['ne vəl] *n.* the depression in the center of the belly where a baby is attached to its mother until shortly after birth.

navigate ['næv ə get] **1.** *tv.* to steer a ship, airplane, or other vehicle in some direction. **2.** *tv.* to travel or follow a route on the water, over land, or in the air. **3.** *iv.* to determine the proper direction or route.

navigation [næv ə 'ge ʃən] *n.* the rules, skills, and science of navigating. (No plural.)

navy ['ne vi] *n.* the branch of the military that deals with protecting the sea or fighting at sea.

near ['nɪr] **1.** *prep.* at a place that is not far away from someone or something; at a time that is not far away from something. **2.** *adj.* close in distance, time, relationship, or effect. (Comp: *nearer;* sup: *nearest.*) **3.** *adv.* at or to a place that is not far away; at or to a time that is not too distant. (Comp: *nearer;* sup: *nearest.*) **4.** *tv.* to come closer to someone or something; to approach someone or something.

5. *iv.* to come closer in time or space; to approach.
→ DRAW NEAR
→ DRAW NEAR (TO SOMEONE OR SOMETHING)

nearby ['nɪr 'baɪ] **1.** *adv.* near; close; not far away. **2.** *adj.* near; close; not far away.

nearly ['nɪr li] *adv.* almost; not quite.

neat ['nit] *adj.* clean; tidy; orderly. (Adv: *neatly.* Comp: *neater;* sup: *neatest.*)

necessary ['nɛs ə sɛr i] *adj.* required; needed. (Adv: *necessarily* [nɛs ə 'sɛr ə li].)
→ DEEM IT (TO BE) NECESSARY
→ DEEM THAT IT IS NECESSARY

necessity [nə 'sɛs ə ti] **1.** *n.* the quality of being necessary or needed. (No plural.) **2.** *n.* something that is required; something that is needed or necessary.

neck ['nɛk] **1.** *n.* the narrow part of the body that connects the head to the rest of the body; the outside of the throat. **2.** *n.* the narrowest part of something; something narrow that connects two things. (Figurative on ①.)
→ BREAK ONE'S NECK (TO DO SOMETHING)
→ BREATHE DOWN SOMEONE'S NECK
→ A MILLSTONE ABOUT ONE'S NECK
→ BY THE NAPE OF THE NECK
→ RISK ONE'S NECK (TO DO SOMETHING)
→ STICK ONE'S NECK OUT
→ UP TO ONE'S NECK (IN SOMETHING)
→ A YOKE AROUND SOMEONE'S NECK

neck and neck exactly even, especially in a race or a contest.

necklace ['nɛk ləs] *n.* a decorative band, chain, or similar object that is worn around the neck.

necktie ['nɛk taɪ] *n.* a specially made strip of decorative cloth, typically worn under the collar of a man's shirt. (Also a TIE. Originally served the purpose of keeping the collar closed.)

need ['nid] **1.** *n.* something that is required or necessary; something that must be done or had; a requirement. **2.** *tv.* to require something; to have to have something; to want something for a certain reason.
→ IN NEED (OF SOMETHING)

need something **yesterday** to require something in a very big hurry. (Informal.)

need to do something to have to do something.

needle ['nid əl] **1.** *n.* a thin, pointed spike of metal having a narrow slit that thread fits through, used for sewing. **2.** *n.* a thin, hollow, pointed spike of metal used for injecting and removing body fluids. **3.** *n.* a thin, pointed spike used to show a position on a scale or meter. **4.** *n.* the part of a record player that "rides" on a (vinyl) record as it is played. **5.** *n.* a long, thin, sharply pointed leaf of a pine tree. **6.** *n.* a long, thin, sharp thorn as found on a cactus. **7.** *tv.* to annoy someone.
→ LIKE LOOKING FOR A NEEDLE IN A HAYSTACK
→ ON PINS AND NEEDLES
→ PINS AND NEEDLES

needlework ['nid əl wɚk] *n.* crafts that are done with a needle, such as sewing. (No plural.)

needy ['nid i] *adj.* [of someone] very poor; [of someone] needing the basic things in life. (Adv: *needily.* Comp: *needier*; sup: *neediest.*)

the **needy** *n.* people who are poor. (No plural. Treated as plural, but not countable.)

negative ['nɛg ə tɪv] **1.** *adj.* meaning "not" or "no"; expressing "not" or "no"; showing refusal or denial. (Adv: *negatively.*) **2.** *adj.* not positive; the opposite of positive; lacking something that makes a thing positive; not good. (Adv: *negatively.*) **3.** *adj.* less than zero; minus; below the number zero. **4.** *adj.* cynical; not having hope; having a sad or gloomy outlook. (Adv: *negatively.*) **5.** *adj.* showing that a certain disease or condition is not present. (Adv: *negatively.*) **6.** *adj.* [of some part of an electrical circuit] lower in electrical charge than other points in the same circuit, allowing electrical energy to flow from other parts of the circuit. (Adv: *negatively.*) **7.** *n.* a word or statement that means "not" or "no." **8.** *n.* a piece of film (for photography). **9.** *n.* a quality or factor that is ②.

neglect [nɪ 'glɛkt] **1.** *tv.* not to take care of someone or something; not to pay attention to someone or something; to ignore someone or something. **2.** *n.* the lack of taking care of someone or something; a lack of paying attention to someone or something. (No plural.)

neglect to do something to forget to do something; to fail to do something.

negotiate [nə 'go ʃi et] **1.** *iv.* to discuss the matters that need to be settled before reaching an agreement. **2.** *tv.* to make an agreement through discussions as in ①. **3.** *tv.* to move around or through a difficult route successfully.

neighbor ['ne bɚ] **1.** *n.* someone who lives very close by. **2.** *n.* someone who is sitting or standing next to oneself.
→ NEXT-DOOR NEIGHBOR

neighborhood ['ne bɚ hʊd] **1.** *n.* a specific area within a larger city or town where people live. **2.** *n.* the people who live in a certain area of the city.
→ (SOMEWHERE) IN THE NEIGHBORHOOD OF SOMETHING
→ IN THE NEIGHBORHOOD OF SOMETHING

neither ['ni ðɚ] **1.** *adj.* not EITHER; not one person or thing nor the other; not either of two people or things. **2.** *pron.* not EITHER; not either one (of two people or things). (Treated as singular.) **3.** *conj.* not. (Used before a sequence of two words or phrases connected by NOR.)

neither does someone [someone does] not either.

neither fish nor fowl not any recognizable thing.

neither hide nor hair no sign or indication (of someone or something.)

nephew ['nef ju] *n.* the son of one's brother or sister; the son of one's spouse's brother or sister.

nerve ['nɚv] **1.** *n.* a fiber in the body that carries messages to and from the brain. **2.** *n.* courage; bravery. (No plural.)
→ GET ON SOMEONE'S NERVES
→ GET UP ENOUGH NERVE (TO DO SOMETHING)

→ GRATE ON SOMEONE('S NERVES)
→ OF ALL THE NERVE

ness [nəs] *suffix* a form that can be added freely to adjectives to create a noun with a parallel meaning.

nest ['nest] **1.** *n.* a structure made of twigs that is built by a bird as a shelter for its eggs and that is typically rounded and bowl-shaped. **2.** *n.* a place where certain animals live with their young. **3.** *iv.* to build or live in ① or ②.
→ FEATHER ONE'S (OWN) NEST
→ FOUL ONE'S OWN NEST
→ STIR UP A HORNET'S NEST

nestle down (in something**)** to settle down in something; to snuggle into something, such as a bed.

nestle (up) against someone or something AND **nestle up (to** someone or something**)** to lie close to someone or something; to cuddle up to someone or something.

nestle up (to someone or something**)** Go to NESTLE (UP) AGAINST SOMEONE OR SOMETHING.

net ['net] **1.** *n.* a piece of mesh fabric—made of string, wire, or cord and sometimes attached to something—that is typically used to catch, trap, or block something. **2.** *n.* a system for fast electronic communication connecting people, businesses, and institutions. (Short for INTERNET. Usually capitalized.) **3.** *adj.* remaining after all factors have been considered, deducted, or added, as with weight, income, cost, effect, results, outcome, etc.

network ['net wɚk] **1.** *n.* a pattern of crossing lines, paths, or similar structures; a system of lines, paths, or similar structures that are connected together. **2.** *n.* a group of computers connected to each other and the systems that connect them. **3.** *n.* a group of radio or television stations that broadcast the same programs. **4.** *n.* a collection of friends or business contacts. **5.** *iv.* to make social and business contacts; to talk with people in one's area of business or interest.

neurotic [nʊ ˈrɑt ɪk] **1.** *adj.* of or about a mild psychological problem or illness, such as having obsessions or irrational fears; affected by such a problem or illness. (Adv: *neurotically* [...ɪk li].) **2.** *n.* someone who has irrational fears or obsessions or some other mild psychological problem or illness.

neuter [ˈnut ɚ] **1.** *adj.* neither masculine nor feminine; not having a SEX ③. **2.** *adj.* [of a class of words] not masculine or feminine.

neutral [ˈnu trəl] **1.** *adj.* not joining with either side in a war, conflict, or argument. (Adv: *neutrally*.) **2.** *adj.* at neither extreme; in the middle of a scale. (Adv: *neutrally*.)
→ IN NEUTRAL

never [ˈnɛv ɚ] *adv.* not ever; at no time.
→ GO AND NEVER DARKEN ONE'S DOOR AGAIN

new [ˈnu] **1.** *adj.* recently done, made, bought, acquired, discovered, or built; not existing or known of before. (Adv: *newly*. Comp: *newer*; sup: *newest*. See also NEWS.) **2.** *adj.* the more recent of two or more things. (Comp:

newer; sup: *newest*.) **3.** *adj.* not familiar; strange; unknown. (Adv: *newly*. Comp: *newer*; sup: *newest*.) **4.** *adj.* different; changed. (Adv: *newly*. Comp: *newer*; sup: *newest*.) **5.** *adj.* beginning again; starting over. (Adv: *newly*. Comp: *newer*; sup: *newest*.)
→ BREAK NEW GROUND
→ FEEL LIKE A NEW PERSON
→ RING IN THE NEW YEAR
→ TURN OVER A NEW LEAF

new blood Go to FRESH BLOOD.

a **new lease on life** a renewed and revitalized outlook on life; a new start in living.

a **new one on** someone something that one has not heard before and that one is not ready to believe. (Informal. The *someone* is often *me*.)

newcomer [ˈnu kəm ɚ] *n.* someone who has recently arrived at a certain place.

newly [ˈnu li] *adv.* recently; as of late; just.

newlywed [ˈnu li wɛd] *n.* someone who has recently married.

news [ˈnuz] **1.** *n.* information, particularly current information about a person or a recent event. (Treated as singular. No other singular form in this sense.) **2.** *n.* a television or radio program where information about recent events is broadcast. (Treated as singular. No other singular form in this sense.)
→ BREAK THE NEWS (TO SOMEONE)

newspaper [ˈnuz pe pɚ] *n.* a daily or weekly publication consisting of news, articles, and advertisements printed on large sheets of paper.

newt ['nut] *n.* a small amphibian with four legs and a tail.

next ['nɛkst] **1.** *adj.* following; nearest in sequence after; soonest after. **2.** *adj.* located in the nearest position to something; [of someone or something] beside someone or something [else]. **3.** *adv.* at the soonest time after now; in the nearest place or position after this one.
→ SOMEONE'S NEXT OF KIN

next door ['nɛks 'dor] in or at the house or apartment next to one's own. (Hyphenated before a nominal.)

next to nothing hardly anything; almost nothing.

next to someone or something very near to someone or something; beside someone or something.

next-door neighbor ['nɛks dor 'ne bɚ] *n.* the person living in the house or apartment closest to one's own.

nice ['naɪs] **1.** *adj.* pleasant; agreeable; enjoyable. (Adv: *nicely.* Comp: *nicer;* sup: *nicest.*) **2.** *adj.* kind; friendly. (Adv: *nicely.* Comp: *nicer;* sup: *nicest.*) **3.** *adj.* good; clever; well done. (Informal. Adv: *nicely.* Comp: *nicer;* sup: *nicest.*)

nice and some quality enough of some quality; adequately; sufficiently.

nick ['nɪk] **1.** *n.* a small dent or chip on the surface of something. **2.** *tv.* to put or cause a small dent or chip on the surface of something.
→ IN THE NICK OF TIME

nickel ['nɪk əl] **1.** *n.* a metallic element that does not rust easily. (No plural.) **2.** *n.* a U.S. coin worth five cents.

nickname ['nɪk nem] **1.** *n.* a secondary, familiar, or intimate name for someone or something. **2.** *tv.* to give someone, something, or someplace a NICKNAME as in ①.

niece ['nis] *n.* the daughter of one's brother or sister; the daughter of one's spouse's brother or sister.

night ['naɪt] **1.** *n.* the time between sunset and sunrise; the darkness between sunset and sunrise; nighttime. (No plural.) **2.** *n.* the period of time between sunset and midnight. **3.** *n.* a specific ① or ② when something happens or is planned. **4.** *n.* a unit of measure based on the number of NIGHTS ① but also including the period of time between NIGHTS ①. (E.g., stay at a hotel *for seven nights.*) **5.** *adj.* happening during ① or ②.
→ ALL NIGHT LONG
→ (AS) DIFFERENT AS NIGHT AND DAY
→ BY NIGHT
→ the MORNING AFTER (THE NIGHT BEFORE)
→ SHIPS THAT PASS IN THE NIGHT

night owl ['naɪt aʊl] *n.* someone who stays up late at night; someone who works at night.

nightclub ['naɪt kləb] *n.* a bar or club open at night where there is entertainment, dancing, performances, etc.

nightgown ['naɪt gaʊn] *n.* an item of clothing like a dress, usually for women, that is worn in bed.

nightlife ['naɪt laɪf] *n.* entertainment and social activities that take place during the night. (No plural.)

nightmare ['naɪt mɛr] **1.** *n.* a frightening dream. **2.** *n.* a real event that is frightening or awful. (Figurative on ①.)

nights *adv.* every night; during every night; only at night.

nighttime ['naɪt taɪm] **1.** *n.* the time during the night; the time from after sunset until sunrise. (No plural.) **2.** the *adj.* use of ①.

nine ['naɪn] 9. Go to FOUR.
→ ON CLOUD NINE

nine days' wonder something that is of interest to people only for a short time.

nineteen ['naɪn 'tin] 19. Go to FOUR.

nineteenth ['naɪn 'tinθ] 19th. Go to FOURTH.

ninetieth ['naɪn ti əθ] 90th. Go to FOURTH.

ninety ['naɪn ti] 90. Go to FORTY.

ninth ['naɪnθ] 9th. Go to FOURTH.

nip ['nɪp] **1.** *tv.* to pinch or bite someone or something. **2.** *tv.* to remove something by pinching or biting.

nip and tuck [of two people or things moving] almost even; almost tied.

nip something **in the bud** to put an end to something at an early stage.

nitwit ['nɪt wɪt] *n.* an idiot; someone who is foolish or stupid.

nix ['nɪks] *tv.* to put a stop to something; to end something; to reject something.

no ['no] **1.** *adj.* not any; not a; not one; not any amount of. **2.** *adv.* a word that is used as an answer to show that one does not agree.

3. *adv.* a word that is used to stress a negative statement. **4.** *n.* a negative answer. (Plural ends in *-s* or *-es*.)

no (ifs, ands, or) buts about it absolutely no discussion, dissension, or doubt about something.

no joke a serious matter. (Informal.)

no laughing matter a serious matter.

no point in doing something no purpose in doing something.

no skin off someone's **nose** Go to NO SKIN OFF SOMEONE'S TEETH.

no skin off someone's **teeth** AND **no skin off** someone's **nose** no difficulty for someone; no concern of someone.

no spring chicken no longer young.

nobility [no 'bɪl ə ti] *n.* dignity; the quality of being noble. (No plural.)

noble ['nob əl] **1.** *adj.* refined; moral; showing dignity. (Adv: *nobly.* Comp: *nobler;* sup: *noblest.*) **2.** the *adj.* use of ①. (Adv: *nobly.* Comp: *nobler;* sup: *noblest.*) **3.** *adj.* [of a chemical element] not able to mix with other elements; [of a chemical element] not able to react with other elements. **4.** *n.* a member of the nobility.

nobody ['no bad i] **1.** *pron.* no person; no one; not anybody. (No plural.) **2.** *n.* someone who is not important; someone who has no power.

nobody's fool a sensible and wise person who is not easily deceived.

nod ['nɑd] **1.** *n.* a quick downward or up-and-down movement of the head, usually to show agreement. **2.** *tv.* to express something by moving one's head as in ④. **3.** *tv.* to move one's head in agreement as in ④. **4.** *iv.* to move one's head down, or up and down, quickly, especially to show agreement or approval, or as a greeting. **5.** *iv.* to let one's head jerk down as one begins to fall asleep. **6.** *iv.* [for one's head] to jerk down as one begins to fall asleep while sitting or standing.
→ GET THE NOD
→ the LAND OF NOD

nod off to fall asleep. (Informal.)

noise ['nɔɪz] *n.* annoying or unwanted sound. (Plural only for types and instances.)

noisy ['nɔɪz i] *adj.* [of a sound or of someone or something making sounds] loud; [of someone or something] making much noise. (Adv: *noisily.* Comp: *noisier;* sup: *noisiest.*)

nominal ['nɑm ə nəl] **1.** *n.* a noun or expression that can serve as the subject of a sentence, the direct or indirect object of a verb, or the object of a preposition. (Abbreviated *n.* here.) **2.** *adj.* functioning as ①. (Adv: *nominally.*) **3.** *adj.* in name only; in theory, but not in reality. (Adv: *nominally.*) **4.** *adj.* [of a fee or charge] very small, especially as compared with what something is worth. (Adv: *nominally.*)

none ['nʌn] **1.** *pron.* not one; not any; no person; no thing. **2.** *pron.* not one part; no part.

none of someone's **business** not of someone's concern.

none other than someone the very person.

none the wiser not knowing any more.

none the worse for wear no worse because of use or effort.

none too not very; not at all.

nonflammable [nɑn 'flæm ə bəl] *adj.* difficult to burn; impossible to burn; not flammable. (Adv: *nonflammably.*)

nonprofit [nɑn 'prɑf ɪt] *adj.* not making a profit; not organized or established for the purpose of making money.

nonsense ['nɑn sɛns] *n.* something that does not make sense; something that is foolish. (No plural.)
→ STUFF AND NONSENSE

nonstop [nɑn 'stɑp] **1.** *adj.* without stopping or pausing; continuous. **2.** *adv.* without stopping; continuously.

noodle ['nud l] *n.* a strip or piece of pasta.

noon ['nun] *n.* the time in the middle of the day between morning and afternoon; 12:00 in the daytime; midday. (No plural.)

noonday ['nun de] *adj.* happening at noon; happening in the middle of the day. (Prenominal only.)

noontime ['nun tɑɪm] **1.** *n.* noon; the middle of the day. (No plural.) **2.** *adj.* happening at noon; happening in the middle of the day. (Prenominal only.)

noose ['nus] *n.* a loop tied at the end of a rope, used to trap or hang someone or something.

nor ['nor] *conj.* a word used to connect a series of persons or things that are not options or possibilities.

nor does someone someone does not either; neither does someone.

the **norm** [...'norm] *n.* the normal or expected amount, quality, or way. (No plural.)

normal ['nor məl] **1.** *adj.* regular; typical; usual; expected. (Adv: *normally.*) **2.** *adj.* sane; not sick in the mind. (Adv: *normally.*)

north ['norθ] **1.** *n.* the direction to the left of someone or something facing the rising sun. (No plural.) **2.** *n.* the northern part of a region, country, or planet. (No plural form. Capitalized when referring to a specific region of the United States.) **3.** *adj.* at ①; in ②; on the side toward ①; facing toward ①. **4.** *adj.* from ①. (Used especially to describe wind.) **5.** *adv.* toward ①; into the northern part of something.

north pole ['norθ 'pol] **1.** *n.* the point in the Arctic that is as far north as it is possible to go. **2.** *n.* the actual location of ①. (Capitalized.)

northeast [norθ 'ist] **1.** *n.* a direction halfway between north and east. (No plural.) **2.** *n.* an area in the northeastern part of a city, region, or country. (No plural. Capitalized when referring to a specific region of the United States.) **3.** *adj.* in ②; toward ①;

facing ①. **4.** *adj.* [of wind] blowing from ①. **5.** *adv.* toward ①.

northeastern [norθ 'ist ərn] *adj.* in the northeast; toward the northeast; facing northeast.

northern ['nor ðərn] **1.** *adj.* in the north; toward the north; facing the north. **2.** *adj.* [of wind] blowing from the north.

northwest [norθ 'wɛst] **1.** *n.* a direction halfway between north and west. (No plural.) **2.** *n.* an area in the northwestern part of a country. (No plural. Capitalized when referring to a region of the United States.) **3.** *adj.* in ②; toward ①; facing ①. **4.** *adj.* [of wind] blowing from ①. **5.** *adv.* toward ①.

northwestern [norθ 'wɛs tərn] *adj.* in the northwest; toward the northwest; facing northwest.

nose ['noz] **1.** *n.* the structure between the mouth and the eyes in humans, being the organ used for smelling and breathing, and a similar structure in other animals. **2.** *n.* the sense of smell; ① used for smelling something. **3.** *n.* the front end of an airplane, a rocket, a ship, or some other similar thing. (Figurative on ①.)
→ (AS) PLAIN AS THE NOSE ON ONE'S FACE
→ BLOW ONE'S NOSE
→ CAN'T SEE BEYOND THE END OF ONE'S NOSE
→ COUNT NOSES
→ CUT OFF ONE'S NOSE TO SPITE ONE'S FACE
→ HAVE A NOSE FOR SOMETHING
→ HAVE ONE'S NOSE IN A BOOK
→ KEEP ONE'S NOSE TO THE GRINDSTONE
→ NO SKIN OFF SOMEONE'S NOSE

→ NOT SEE FURTHER THAN THE END OF ONE'S NOSE
→ PAY THROUGH THE NOSE (FOR SOMETHING)
→ POKE ONE'S NOSE IN(TO SOMETHING)
→ PUT ONE'S NOSE TO THE GRINDSTONE
→ PUT SOMEONE'S NOSE OUT OF JOINT
→ RIGHT UNDER SOMEONE'S NOSE
→ RUB SOMEONE'S NOSE IN SOMETHING
→ RUNNY NOSE
→ STICK ONE'S NOSE IN(TO SOMETHING)
→ THUMB ONE'S NOSE AT SOMEONE OR SOMETHING
→ TURN ONE'S NOSE UP AT SOMEONE OR SOMETHING
→ UNDER SOMEONE'S (VERY) NOSE
→ WIN BY A NOSE

nose someone or something **out** to defeat someone or something by a narrow margin. (Alludes to a horse winning a race "by a nose.")

nosedive ['noz daɪv] **1.** *n.* a sudden drop or decline, especially the sudden fall of an airplane with the nose pointing downward. **2.** *iv.* to plunge with the nose pointing downward. **3.** *iv.* [for a measurement] to decline or drop suddenly. (Figurative on ②.)
→ GO INTO A NOSEDIVE
→ TAKE A NOSEDIVE

nostril ['nɑs trəl] *n.* one of the two outside holes of the nose.

nosy ['noz i] *adj.* trying to find out (private) things about people or things; snooping; prying. (Adv: *nosily*. Comp: *nosier*; sup: *nosiest*.)

not ['nɑt] **1.** *adv.* a negative particle used with verbs, adverbs, participles, prepositions, nominals, and adjectives. (Contracted to *n't*.) **2.** *adv.* a negative particle that stands for a part of a sentence that is being refused, denied, or negated.

not a moment to spare AND **without a moment to spare** in a very big hurry.

not able to see the forest for the trees allowing many details of a problem to obscure the problem as a whole.

not able to stomach someone or something AND **cannot stomach** someone or something not to be able to put up with someone or something; not to be able to tolerate or endure someone or something.

not agree with someone [for food] to be unacceptable to someone and make the person sick.

not at all not to any extent or degree; not in any way. (Always in the negative or questions.)

not born yesterday experienced; knowledgeable in the ways of the world.

not carry weight (with someone) [for someone] to have no influence with someone; [for something] to have no significance for someone.

not for hire [of a taxi] not available to take new passengers.

not for publication not to be talked about openly; secret.

not give it another thought not to worry about something anymore.

not have a leg to stand on [for a person's argument or a case] to have no support.

not hold water to make no sense; to be illogical. (Said of ideas, arguments, etc., not people. It means that the idea has holes in it.)

not know enough to come in out of the rain to be very stupid.

not know one's **own strength** not to realize how destructive or harmful one's strength can be. (Present tense only.)

not know someone **from Adam** not to know someone at all.

not long for this world to be about to die.

not one's **place** not one's role to do something.

not open one's **mouth** AND **not utter a word** to say nothing at all; not to say anything; not to tell something (to anyone).

not see further than the end of one's **nose** to care only about what is actually present or obvious; not to care about the future or about what is happening elsewhere or to other people.

not set foot somewhere to stay out of or away from somewhere; not to go somewhere.

not show one's **face** not to appear (somewhere).

not sleep a wink not to sleep at all; to be sleepless; not to close one's eyes in sleep even as long as it takes to blink.

not someone's **cup of tea** not something one prefers.

not tell a soul not to reveal something to anyone.

not up to scratch not adequate.

not utter a word Go to NOT OPEN ONE'S MOUTH.

not worth mentioning 1. not important enough to require a comment. **2.** [of an error or wrong] not worth apologizing for.

not worth the trouble not important enough to require a comment.

notation [no'teʃən] *n.* a set of signs or symbols that is used to represent something.

notch ['natʃ] **1.** *n.* a V-shaped cut in a surface, made for a specific reason. **2.** *n.* a degree of quality or quantity. (Figurative on ①.) **3.** *tv.* to make a V-shaped cut for a specific reason.

note ['not] **1.** *n.* a short written message. **2.** *n.* a comment on the bottom of a page or at the end of a book that explains, clarifies, or provides the source of something in the text. (See also FOOTNOTE.) **3.** *n.* a piece of paper money; a bill. **4.** *n.* the written symbol for a specific musical tone. **5.** *n.* a specific musical tone; one sound made by singing or playing a musical instrument. **6.** *n.* a sign of something; a hint of something. **7.** *tv.* to write something as a short message. (The object can be a clause with THAT ⑦.) **8.** *tv.* to remark about something; to state something; to observe something. (The object is a clause with THAT ⑦.) **9.** *tv.* to pay attention to something; to remember something. (The object can be a clause with THAT ⑦.)
→ HIT A SOUR NOTE
→ SOMEONE OF NOTE
→ STRIKE A SOUR NOTE

notebook ['notbʊk] *n.* a book in which notes are written.

notepaper ['not pe pɚ] *n.* paper that notes, such as thank-you notes, are written on. (Plural only for types and instances.)

notes *n.* information that is written down by someone while listening to a lecture or reading a book.

nothing ['nʌθ ɪŋ] **1.** *pron.* not one thing; not a thing; not anything. (No plural. Treated as singular.) **2.** *n.* something that is without meaning; something that is not significant or important; not anything that is significant or important. (No plural. Treated as singular.) **3.** *n.* zero; no amount. (No plural.)
→ IN NOTHING FLAT
→ LIKE NOTHING ON EARTH
→ NEXT TO NOTHING
→ SWEET NOTHINGS
→ WANT FOR NOTHING

nothing but only; just.

nothing but skin and bones AND **all skin and bones** very thin or emaciated.

nothing short of something more or less the same as something bad; as bad as something.

notice ['not ɪs] **1.** *tv.* to see, hear, taste, or smell someone or something; to be aware of someone or something. (The object can be a clause with THAT ⑦.) **2.** *n.* an announcement; a sign that warns or informs; a warning. **3.** *n.* attention; a state of awareness [about something]. (No plural.)
→ SIT UP AND TAKE NOTICE

noticeable ['not ɪs ə bəl] *adj.* able to be seen; easily seen; easily noticed. (Adv: *noticeably.*)

notify ['not ə faɪ] *tv.* to inform someone about something; to tell someone officially about something.

notion ['no ʃən] **1.** *n.* an opinion; a belief. **2.** *n.* a whim; an intention.

noun ['naʊn] *n.* a word that refers to a person, place, thing, or idea. (See also NOMINAL.)

nourish ['nɚ ɪʃ] **1.** *tv.* to feed someone or something; to give someone or something the things necessary for life and health. **2.** *tv.* to encourage something; to support something as it develops. (Figurative on ①. Used especially with feelings and emotions.)

novel ['nav əl] **1.** *n.* a relatively long, written story. **2.** *adj.* new; original; not known before.

novelty ['nav əl ti] **1.** *n.* the quality of being novel; the quality of being new or original. (Plural only for types and instances.) **2.** *n.* a small item, often inexpensive and usually interesting or amusing. **3.** the *adj.* use of ① or ②. (Prenominal only.)

November [no 'vɛm bɚ] Go to MONTH.

novice ['nav ɪs] **1.** *n.* someone who is new at a job or responsibility. **2.** *n.* someone who has just joined a religious order and will become a monk or a nun. **3.** *adj.* [of someone] new to a task or activity. (Prenominal only.)

now ['naʊ] **1.** *adv.* at this moment; at this point in time; immediately. **2.** *adv.* in these days; in modern times; in present times. **3.** *adv.* a word used for emphasis, to get someone's attention, with commands, and to move on to the next topic. **4.** *n.* the present; this time. (No plural.)

now and then sometimes; occasionally.

nowhere ['no ʌɛr] *adv.* at no place; to or toward no place; not to or at any place.
→ COME FROM NOWHERE

nowhere near not nearly.

nuclear ['nu kli ɚ] *adj.* of or about the nucleus of an atom or the energy created by splitting or fusing the nuclei of atoms.

nuclei ['nu kli ɑɪ] plural of NUCLEUS.

nucleus ['nu kli əs] **1.** *n., irreg.* the center of something; the core of something. (Plural: NUCLEI.) **2.** *n., irreg.* the core of an atom, consisting of protons and neutrons. **3.** *n., irreg.* the control center of a living cell.

nude ['nud] **1.** *adj.* naked; not wearing any clothes. **2.** *n.* someone who is not wearing any clothes; a statue or a painting of someone who is not wearing any clothes.
→ IN THE NUDE

nuisance ['nu səns] *n.* a bother; someone or something that is annoying.
→ MAKE A NUISANCE OF ONESELF

numb ['nʌm] **1.** *adj.* unable to feel anything; unable to sense anything. (Adv: *numbly* ['nʌm li]. Comp: *number* ['nʌm ɚ]; sup: *numbest* ['nʌm əst].) **2.** *tv.* to cause someone or something to be unable to feel anything.

number ['nʌm bɚ] **1.** *n.* a symbol or a word that expresses an amount; a symbol or a word that shows how many; a digit or series of digits that has an assigned significance. **2.** *n.* a specific ① that identifies someone or something in a series. (Also appears as the symbol (#).) **3.** *n.* a song; a piece of music. **4.** *n.* a grammatical category showing whether one or more than one person or thing is being referred to. (Plural only for types and instances.) **5.** *tv.* to assign something a ①. (Refers especially to things in a series.) **6.** *tv.* to reach a total of a certain amount; to be a certain amount.
→ CARDINAL NUMBER
→ DIVIDE A NUMBER BY A NUMBER
→ DIVIDE A NUMBER INTO A NUMBER
→ DIVIDE BY A NUMBER
→ GO INTO A NUMBER
→ IN ROUND NUMBERS
→ MULTIPLY A NUMBER BY A NUMBER
→ ONE'S DAYS ARE NUMBERED
→ ORDINAL NUMBER

a **number of** people or things some people or things, in an indefinite amount. (NUMBER is treated as plural, but not countable.)

number off (by something**)** to say a number in a specified sequence when it is one's turn.

number someone **off** to assign numbers or positions in a sequence to a group of people.

numeral ['num ə rəl] *n.* the symbol or figure that represents a number.
→ ARABIC NUMERAL
→ CARDINAL NUMERAL
→ ORDINAL NUMERAL
→ ROMAN NUMERAL

numerous ['num ə rəs] *adj.* many; several; a lot. (Adv: *numerously*.)

nun ['nʌn] *n.* a woman who is a member of a religious order.

nurse ['nɚs] **1.** *n.* someone, usually a woman, trained to provide medical care, often under the supervision of a physician. **2.** *n.* a woman who raises other people's children; a woman who helps a family raise its children. **3.** *tv.* to feed a baby milk from one's breast. **4.** *tv.* [for anyone] to treat a disease or a sick person. **5.** *iv.* [for a female mammal] to feed a baby mammal as in ③. **6.** *iv.* [for a baby mammal] to suck or take milk from a female mammal.

nurse someone **back to health** [for anyone] to provide medical care that will restore someone to good health.

nurse someone **through (something)** to care for a sick person during the worst part of a sickness or recovery.

nursery ['nɚs (ə) ri] **1.** *n.* a room for babies in a hospital or residence. **2.** *n.* a place where children are watched while their parents are busy at something else. **3.** *n.* a place where plants are grown and sold.

nut ['nʌt] **1.** *n.* a hard, woody shell containing an edible part. **2.** *n.* the edible part of ①, used as food. **3.** *n.* someone who is crazy, insane, or foolish. (Slang.)
→ EVERYTHING FROM SOUP TO NUTS

nutrition [nu 'trɪ ʃən] *n.* the science of providing people with information about healthy food. (No plural.)

nuts and bolts (of something) the basic facts about something; the practical details of something.

nutshell ['nʌt ʃɛl] *n.* the hard, woody shell around the edible part of a nut.
→ IN A NUTSHELL

nutty ['nʌt i] **1.** *adj.* tasting like a nut; made from nuts. (Adv: *nuttily.* Comp: *nuttier;* sup: *nuttiest.*) **2.** *adj.* crazy; insane. (Slang. Adv: *nuttily.* Comp: *nuttier;* sup: *nuttiest.*)

nuzzle up to someone or something to nestle against someone or something, especially if leading with the nose or face.

nylon ['naɪ lɑn] **1.** *n.* a very strong but light, often flexible fiber made from chemicals, that is used especially to make clothes and fabric. (No plural.) **2.** *adj.* made from ①.

o

oak ['ok] **1.** *n.* a kind of strong tree that produces an edible nut. **2.** *n.* wood from ①. (Plural only for types and instances.) **3.** *adj.* made from ②.

oar ['or] *n.* a long pole with one wide, flat end—similar to a paddle—used to steer and row boats.
→ PUT IN ONE'S OAR

oases [o 'e siz] plural of OASIS.

oasis [o 'e sɪs] **1.** *n., irreg.* a place in a desert that has water and trees. (Plural: OASES.) **2.** *n., irreg.* a place that is free of problems or difficulties. (Figurative on ①.)

oat ['ot] **1.** *n.* a cereal grain used as food for humans and cattle. **2.** *n.* a single grain of ①. **3.** *adj.* made of ①.
→ SOW ONE'S WILD OATS

oath ['oθ] *n., irreg.* a promise that one will speak only the truth; a promise that one will do something. (Plural: ['oðz].)
→ TAKE AN OATH
→ UNDER OATH

oatmeal ['ot mil] **1.** *n.* crushed oats. (No plural.) **2.** *n.* cooked ①, usually eaten with milk and sugar. (No plural.) **3.** *adj.* made with crushed oats.

oats *n.* a cereal grain used as food for humans and cattle. (Treated as plural, but not countable.)

obedience [o 'bid i əns] *n.* the condition of being obedient. (No plural.)

obedient [o 'bid i ənt] *adj.* obeying; willingly following orders. (Adv: *obediently.*)

obey [o 'be] **1.** *tv.* to yield to someone and do as one has been instructed; to follow instructions, commands, or rules. **2.** *iv.* to do as one is told.

object 1. ['ab dʒɛkt] *n.* a thing; something that can be seen or touched. **2.** ['ab dʒɛkt] *n.* a goal; an aim; someone or something that a thought or an action is directed toward. **3.** ['ab dʒɛkt] *n.* a noun or nominal that is affected by the action or condition of a verb, a noun or nominal within a prepositional phrase.
→ MONEY IS NO OBJECT.

object (to something) [əb 'dʒɛkt…] to oppose something; to argue against something; to make an objection about something.

objection [əb 'dʒɛk ʃən] *n.* a stated reason for not wanting to do something.

oblige [ə 'blaɪdʒ] *iv.* to do something nice for someone; to do someone a favor.

oblige someone **to** do something to require someone to do something.

oblong ['ab lɔŋ] *adj.* [especially of a circle or a rectangle] long and a little narrow. (Adv: *oblongly.*)

obnoxious [əb 'nak ʃəs] *adj.* very annoying; very irritating. (Adv: *obnoxiously.*)

oboe ['o bo] *n.* a musical instrument that has a long, thin wooden body and a mouthpiece holding a double reed.

obscure [əb 'skjur] **1.** *adj.* [of reasoning or explanation] hard to understand or not clearly stated. (Adv: *obscurely*.) **2.** *adj*. not well known; not famous. (Adv: *obscurely*.) **3.** *adj*. hard to see; hidden, especially by darkness. (Adv: *obscurely*.) **4.** *tv*. to make something hard to see; to keep something from view; to dim or darken something. **5.** *tv*. to make something difficult to understand; to cloud one's meaning. (Figurative on ④.)

observe [əb 'zɚv] **1.** *tv*. to watch something; to see something; to notice something. **2.** *tv*. to obey a law or custom; to pay attention to a law or custom. (The object can be a clause with THAT ⑦.) **3.** *tv*. to celebrate a holiday. **4.** *tv*. to make a comment or a remark; to state something. (The object is a clause with THAT ⑦.)

obsessed [əb 'sɛst] *adj*. thinking about someone or something too much, as if one were forced to do so.

obsessed with someone or something always thinking about a person, a thought, or an activity.

obstruct [əb 'strʌkt] *tv*. to get in the way of someone or something; to block someone or something.

obstruction [əb 'strʌk ʃən] *n*. something that is in the way; something that is blocking the way.

obtain [əb 'ten] *tv*. to get something; to gain possession of something; to come to own something.

obvious ['ɑb vi əs] *adj*. easily recognized; easily seen or understood; plain; clear. (Adv: *obviously*.)

occasion [ə 'ke ʒən] **1.** *n*. a time when something happens; a time when something occurs; an instance. **2.** *n*. a special event.

occasional [ə 'ke ʒə nəl] *adj*. happening from time to time; happening once in a while; not happening all the time or regularly. (Adv: *occasionally*.)

occult [ə 'kʌlt] *adj*. hidden from regular knowledge; filled with mystery.

the **occult** *n*. things that are hidden from regular knowledge or experience, including magic and other secret things. (No plural. Treated as singular.)

occupancy ['ɑk jə pən si] **1.** *n*. occupying a house, building, or other piece of property. (No plural.) **2.** *n*. the number of people that a room or building is allowed to hold. (No plural.)
→ IMMEDIATE OCCUPANCY

occupant ['ɑk jə pənt] *n*. someone who lives in a certain place; a business that occupies a certain building or space.

occupation [ɑk jə 'pe ʃən] **1.** *n*. a job; a career; what one does for a living. **2.** *n*. taking or keeping possession of a region or a country.

occupy ['ɑk jə paɪ] **1.** *tv*. to use or consume time by doing something. **2.** *tv*. to keep someone busy doing something. **3.** *tv*. to be in a certain place; to take up the space in a certain place; to live in a certain place; to have one's business in a certain place. **4.** *tv*. to move into and take control of another country.

occur [ə 'kɚ] **1.** *iv.* to happen; to take place. **2.** *iv.* to be; to exist; to be found.

occur to someone to come to someone's mind; [for a thought] to enter into someone's mind.

occurrence [ə 'kɚ əns] *n.* an event; something that happens; an incident.

the **occurrence of** something the existence of something; the appearance or happening of something in a particular place.

ocean ['o ʃən] *n.* a large body of salt water that covers ¾ of the earth's surface, or one of that body's four divisions: the Arctic Ocean, the Atlantic Ocean, the Indian Ocean, and the Pacific Ocean.

an **ocean of** someone or something Go to OCEANS OF SOMEONE OR SOMETHING.

oceans of someone or something AND an **ocean of** someone or something a very large number of people or things.

o'clock [ə 'klɑk] *adv.* a word used to indicate the time of day. (It follows a number from 1 to 12 and means that it is that time exactly, or zero minutes past the hour. Literally, *of the clock*.)

octagon ['ɑk tə ɡɑn] *n.* a flat figure or shape with eight sides.

octave ['ɑk tɪv] *n.* a musical interval of two notes where the higher note is twelve half tones above the lower note; [on a piano] the first and eighth key in a row of eight white keys.

October [ɑk 'to bɚ] Go to MONTH.

octopi ['ɑk tə paɪ] a plural of OCTOPUS.

octopus ['ɑk tə pəs] *n., irreg.* a boneless sea creature with eight legs. (Greek for "eight-footed." The English plural is *octopuses* or OCTOPI.)

odd ['ɑd] **1.** *adj.* strange; different; unusual; out of place. (Adv: *oddly.* Comp: *odder;* sup: *oddest.*) **2.** *adj.* not even; [of a number] not able to be divided by two without an amount (one) being left over. **3.** *adj.* not regular; [of occasions or events] random; occasional. (Prenominal only. Comp: *odder;* sup: *oddest.*)

odd man out an unusual or atypical person or thing.

oddity ['ɑd ə ti] **1.** *n.* the state of being unusual or strange. (No plural.) **2.** *n.* something that is odd; something that is unusual or strange.

the **odds are against one** one's chances are slim; there is little chance of one succeeding; the situation is not favorable to one.

odor ['o dɚ] *n.* a smell; a scent; an aroma.

of [əv] **1.** *prep.* belonging to someone; owned by someone; closely associated with someone. (Takes a nominal in the possessive form. Pronouns that can follow OF in this sense are *mine, yours, his, hers, ours,* and *theirs.*) **2.** *prep.* connected to someone or something; relating to someone or something; associated with someone or something; representing someone or something; being a portion or part from something. **3.** *prep.* made from something. **4.** *prep.* containing something; including someone or something; having people or things as the members or parts. **5.** *prep.* a preposition expressing a measurement or an amount. **6.** *prep.* a preposition linking a type of location to the name of a location. **7.** *prep.* referring to someone or something; about someone or something; concerning someone or something. **8.** *prep.* having a certain quality or aspect. **9.** *prep.* before a certain hour.

of all the nerve how shocking; how dare (someone). (The speaker is exclaiming that someone is being very insolent or rude.)

of interest (to someone**)** interesting to someone.

of the first water of the finest quality. (Originally a measurement of the quality of a pearl.)

off ['ɔf] **1.** *prep.* away from someone or something; not on someone or something. (① through ④ are often *off of*, a construction objected to by some.) **2.** *prep.* less than something; deducted from something. **3.** *prep.* leading away from a place or path; turning from a place or path; connecting to a place or path. **4.** *prep.* in or over the water near land. **5.** *adj.* stopped; not being used; causing something not to function or operate, especially by stopping the flow of electricity. (Not prenominal.) **6.** *adj.* wrong; not accurate. (Not prenominal.) **7.** *adj.* can-

celed. (Not prenominal.) **8.** *adj.* [of a time period] free of work. (Not prenominal.)

off base unrealistic; inexact; wrong.

off campus not located within the campus of a college or university.

off duty not working at one's job.

off the air [relating to radio or television stations and programs] not broadcasting or being broadcast.

off the record unofficial; informal.

off the subject not concerned with the subject being discussed.

off the top of one's **head** [to state something] rapidly and without having to think or remember.

off to a running start with a good, fast beginning.

off-color 1. not the exact color (that one wants). **2.** rude, vulgar, or impolite.

offend [ə 'fɛnd] *tv.* to shock someone, especially through one's actions, attitude, or behavior.

offense 1. [ə 'fɛns] *n.* the breaking of a law; a crime; an illegal act. **2.** [ə 'fɛns] *n.* something that is shocking or disgusting. **3.** ['ɔ fɛns] *n.* a way of attacking; an attack.

offensive 1. [ə 'fɛn sɪv] *adj.* shocking; annoying; offending someone. (Adv: *offensively*.) **2.** ['ɔ fɛn sɪv] *adj.* of or about attacking. (Adv: *offensively*.) **3.** [ə 'fɛn sɪv] *n.* an attack.

offer ['ɔf ɚ] **1.** *tv.* to present something that can be taken or refused.

2. *tv.* to propose a price for something that is being sold. **3.** *n.* something that is OFFERED as in ①. **4.** *n.* a price or amount that is OFFERED as in ②.

offer to do something to indicate that one is willing to do something.

offering ['ɔf ɚ ɪŋ] *n.* something that is offered, especially to a church, to a charity, or as part of a religious ceremony.

office ['ɔf ɪs] **1.** *n.* a room—usually assigned to one person—where business is done. **2.** *n.* the combined workplaces of a number of people. **3.** *n.* a position of power and responsibility, especially in a government or an organization.
→ DO A LAND-OFFICE BUSINESS
→ HOME OFFICE
→ POST OFFICE

office hours ['ɔf ɪs ɑʊ ɚz] *n.* the times when an office is open. (Treated as singular or plural. Rarely singular.)

officer ['ɔ fə sɚ] *n.* someone in a position of authority, especially in the military, the government, or some other organization.
→ POLICE OFFICER

official [ə 'fɪ ʃəl] **1.** *n.* an officer; someone in a position of authority. **2.** *adj.* of or about the power, authority, and responsibility of an office or an officer. (Adv: *officially.*)

offshore ['ɔf 'ʃɔr] *adj.* located or occurring in, on, or over the water away from the shore.

offspring ['ɔf sprɪŋ] *n.* [a person's] child or children; [an animal's] young. (No plural. Treated as singular or plural.)

offstage ['ɔf 'stedʒ] **1.** *adj.* next to the visible part of the stage of a theater, but not visible to the audience. **2.** *adv.* at, to, or toward the area next to the visible part of the stage.

often ['ɔf ən] *adv.* frequently; happening many times.

oh ['o] *interj.* a form expressing surprise or other feelings.

oil ['ɔɪl] **1.** *n.* a slick, greasy liquid that does not dissolve in water. (Plural only for types and instances.) **2.** *tv.* to put lubrication on something using ①; to make something slippery by putting ① on it; to put ① on something.
→ BURN THE MIDNIGHT OIL
→ POUR OIL ON TROUBLED WATER

oilcan ['ɔɪl kæn] *n.* a can that is used to apply oil as lubrication.

oily ['ɔɪl i] *adj.* made of oil; containing oil; soaked with oil. (Comp: *oilier*; sup: *oiliest*.)

oink ['ɔɪŋk] **1.** *n.* the sound made by a pig. **2.** *iv.* to make the sound of a pig.

ointment ['ɔɪnt mənt] *n.* a substance that is put on the skin to heal it, soothe it, or soften it.
→ FLY IN THE OINTMENT

okay AND **OK** [o 'ke] **1.** *adv.* all right; adequately. **2.** *adv.* to a degree of intensity below "very good" but above "poor." **3.** *adj.* just good, but not excellent. **4.** *interj.* a word used to confirm that one understands something. **5.** *n.* approval. **6.** *tv.* to approve something.

old ['old] **1.** *adj.* having been alive for a long time; not recently born; not young. (Comp: *older;* sup: *oldest.*) **2.** *adj.* having existed for a long time; not recently made; not new. (Comp: *older;* sup: *oldest.*) **3.** *adj.* of a certain age. (Follows the age. Comp: *older.*) **4.** *adj.* previous; former. (Comp: *older;* sup: *oldest.*)
→ (AS) COMFORTABLE AS AN OLD SHOE
→ BE OLD HAT
→ A CHIP OFF THE OLD BLOCK
→ FROM THE OLD SCHOOL
→ the GOOD OLD DAYS
→ RIPE OLD AGE

old age ['old 'edʒ] **1.** *n.* the period when one is old. (No plural.) **2.** *adj.* of or about ①. (Hyphenated.)

old-fashioned ['old 'fæʃ ənd] *adj.* belonging to the style, actions, behavior, or rules of the past. (Adv: *old-fashionedly.*)

olive ['ɑ lɪv] **1.** *n.* a tree grown in warm climates for its fruit. **2.** *n.* the fruit of ①, used for food.
→ HOLD OUT THE OLIVE BRANCH

omelet ['ɑm lɪt] *n.* a dish made of beaten eggs, cooked flat and folded over, sometimes stuffed with other foods.

omission [o 'mɪʃ ən] **1.** *n.* not listing or not including someone or something; omitting someone or something. **2.** *n.* something that has been left out; something that has been omitted.

omit [o 'mɪt] *tv.* to leave someone or something out; to forget to list or include something.

on ['ɔn] **1.** *prep.* above and supported by someone or something; covering or partially covering someone or something; touching the surface of someone or something. **2.** *prep.* traveling by [plane, train, boat, bus, motorcycle, bicycle, etc.]. (But one travels *in* an automobile.) **3.** *prep.* near something; at the edge of [a body of water]. **4.** *prep.* about someone or something. **5.** *prep.* [happening] at a specific time, identified by the date or the day. **6.** *prep.* as a member or part of some group. **7.** *adj.* operating; turned on as in ⑨. **8.** *adj.* still happening; not canceled; continuing as scheduled. **9.** *adv.* so that something operates; so that something has the power to operate.

on a bias AND **on the bias** on a diagonal line; on a diagonal pathway or direction.

on a fool's errand involved in a useless journey or task.

on a shoestring with a very small amount of money.

on a waiting list [for someone's name to be] on a list of people waiting for an opportunity to do something.

on active duty in battle or ready to go into battle. (Military.)

on all fours on one's hands and knees.

on Broadway located in the Broadway (New York City) theater district; currently performing or being performed in the Broadway theater district.

on campus located within the campus of a college or university.

on cloud nine very happy.

on consignment [of goods] having been placed in a store for sale, without transferring the title of the goods to the operator of the store.

on credit using credit; buying something using credit.

on duty at work; currently doing one's work.

on earth AND **in creation; in the world** of all things, places, or people; out of all the possibilities; given all options. (Used after *who, what, when, where,* or *how* to express surprise or amazement.)

on fire burning; being burned with flames.

on foot [running or walking] using the FEET.

on impulse after having had an impulse or thought.

on land on the soil; on the land and not at sea.

on location in a place, located far from a movie studio, where a movie is filmed.

on one's feet 1. standing up; standing on one's feet. **2.** well and healthy, especially after an illness.

on one's honor on one's solemn oath; [promised] sincerely, speaking as an honorable person.

on one's last legs AND **on its last legs** almost completely worn-out, exhausted, or broken down; close to dying or ending.

on one's mind occupying one's thoughts; currently being thought about.

on one's person [of something] carried with one.

on one's toes alert.

on patrol Go to (OUT) ON PATROL.

on pins and needles anxious; waiting eagerly and nervously.

on probation 1. serving a period of probation. **2.** serving a trial period.

on purpose [doing something] in a way that is meant or planned; not an accident.

on sale available for purchase at a reduced price.

on second thought having given something more thought; having reconsidered something.

on someone's doorstep Go to AT SOMEONE'S DOORSTEP.

on someone's say-so on someone's authority; with someone's permission.

on someone's shoulders [serving as a burden] on someone. (Usually with *responsibility. On* can be replaced with *upon.*)

on standby waiting for one's turn, especially describing travelers who wait near a train, plane, or bus, hoping that a seat will become available.

on target on schedule; exactly as predicted.

on the air [relating to a radio, television station] broadcasting; [relating to a radio or television program] being broadcast. (Compare this with OFF THE AIR.)

on the average generally; usually.

on the bench 1. directing a session of court. (Said of a judge.) **2.** sitting, waiting for a chance to play in a game. (In team sports such as basketball, football, and soccer.)

on the bias Go to ON A BIAS.

on the block 1. on a city block. **2.** on sale at auction; on the auction block.

on the borderline in an uncertain position between two statuses; undecided.

on the button exactly right; in exactly the right place; at exactly the right time.

on the contrary in opposition to what has just been said.

on the defensive overly ready to defend oneself.

on the dot at exactly the right time.

on the go busy; moving about busily.

on the heels of something soon after something.

on the horizon soon to happen.

on the horns of a dilemma having to decide between two things, people, etc.; balanced between one choice and another.

on the hour at the beginning of the hour or of each hour; precisely when the numbered hour begins—for example, at 3:00, not 3:08 or 3:30.

on the house [something that is] given away free by a merchant.

on the level Go to (STRICTLY) ON THE LEVEL.

on the market available for sale; offered for sale.

on the mend getting well; healing.

on the move moving; happening busily.

on the off chance because of a slight possibility [that something may happen or might be the case]; just in case.

on the QT quietly; secretly.

on the right track following the right set of assumptions.

on the spot 1. at exactly the right place; at exactly the right time. **2.** in trouble; in a difficult situation.

on the spur of the moment suddenly; spontaneously.

on the tip of one's **tongue** about to be said; almost remembered.

on the wagon not drinking alcohol; no longer drinking alcohol. (Refers to a "water wagon.")

on the wrong track going the wrong way; following the wrong set of assumptions.

on thin ice in a risky situation.

on tiptoe standing or walking on the front part of the feet (the balls of the feet) with no weight put on the heels. (This is done to gain height or to walk quietly.)

on top victorious over something; famous or notorious for something.

on top of the world feeling wonderful; glorious; ecstatic.

on trial being tried in court.

on vacation taking a trip; taking time off from work.

once ['wʌns] **1.** *adv.* one time. **2.** *adv.* at a time in the past; formerly.

once in a blue moon very rarely.

oncoming ['ɔn kəm ɪŋ] *adj.* coming toward [oneself]; approaching.

one ['wʌn] **1.** 1. Go to FOUR. **2.** *n.* a BILL ③ or NOTE ③ worth a single dollar. **3.** *adj.* happening on or at a particular time. (Prenominal only.) **4.** *adj.* united; together; joined. (Not prenominal.) **5.** *pron.* a person or thing that is referred to. **6.** *pron.* you; anybody; a person.
→ the LAST (ONE)
→ AS ONE
→ AT ONE FELL SWOOP
→ GO IN ONE EAR AND OUT THE OTHER
→ HAVE A ONE-TRACK MIND
→ a HOLE IN ONE
→ IN ONE EAR AND OUT THE OTHER
→ IN ONE FELL SWOOP
→ KILL TWO BIRDS WITH ONE STONE
→ a NEW ONE ON SOMEONE
→ SIX OF ONE AND HALF A DOZEN OF THE OTHER
→ WEAR MORE THAN ONE HAT
→ WITH ONE HAND TIED BEHIND ONE'S BACK

one in a hundred Go to ONE IN A THOUSAND.

one in a million Go to ONE IN A THOUSAND.

one in a thousand AND **one in a hundred; one in a million** unique; one of a very few.

One thing leads to another. One event sets things up for another event and so on.

one thing or person **after another** a series of people or things that seems without limit.

one's **back is to the wall** one is in a defensive position.

One's bark is worse than one's **bite.** Although one appears threatening, one will not actually do much damage.

one's **better half** one's spouse. (Usually refers to a wife.)

one's **days are numbered** one faces death or dismissal.

one's **deepest sympathy** one's very sincere sympathy.

one's **ears are red** one has red ears from embarrassment.

One's eyes are bigger than one's **stomach.** One has taken or asked for more food than one can eat.

one's **fair share** the amount of something that one is due relative to what other people are receiving.

one's **folks** *n.* relatives, especially one's own parents. (Treated as plural, but not countable.)

one's **hands are tied** one is prevented from doing something.

one's **heart is in** one's **mouth** [for one] to feel strongly emotional.

one's **heart is set on** something one desires and expects something.

one's **labor(s)** *n.* one's work or the product of one's work; effort. (Singular or plural with the same meaning, but not countable.)

one's **mission in life** one's purpose for living; the reason for which one lives on the earth.

one's **number is up** one's time to die—or to suffer some other unpleasantness—has come.

one's **pet hate** something that is disliked intensely and is a constant or repeated annoyance.

one's **pet peeve** a frequent annoyance to someone; one's "favorite" or most-often encountered annoyance.

one's **tail is between** one's **legs** one is acting frightened or cowed.

one's **way** *n.* one's desire; one's wish. (No plural.)

one's **wits** *n.* one's intelligence; one's control of one's thinking, understanding, temper, and actions.

one's **word** *n.* someone's promise; someone's pledge. (No plural.)

one's **words stick in** one's **throat** to find it difficult to speak because of emotion.

oneself [wən 'sɛlf] *pron.* the reflexive form of the pronoun ONE ⑥. (Used when *one* is the subject of the sentence.)

onion ['ʌn jən] **1.** *n.* a plant with a large, round edible bulb and thin green stalks. **2.** *n.* the edible bulb of ①, sometimes sliced or chopped. **3.** *adj.* made with or flavored with ②.

only ['on li] **1.** *adj.* sole; single. **2.** *adv.* [this and] nothing more. **3.** *conj.* except that.

onset ['ɔn sɛt] *n.* the beginning of something; the start of something.

onstage [ɔn 'stedʒ] **1.** *adj.* located or happening on a part of a stage that an audience can see. **2.** *adv.* on, to, or toward a part of the stage that an audience can see.

onto ['ɔn tu] *prep.* to a position that is on something.

onward ['ɔn wɚd] *adv.* further in space or time; forward in space or time.

ooze ['uz] **1.** *n.* mud; slime; a thick liquid. (No plural.) **2.** *iv.* to flow slowly, like mud or a very thick liquid; to seep out of a hole slowly.

opaque [o 'pek] **1.** *adj.* not able to be seen through; not allowing light to pass through; not clear. (Adv: *opaquely.*) **2.** *adj.* hard to understand. (Figurative on ①. Adv: *opaquely.*)

open ['o pən] **1.** *adj.* not shut; not closed; not sealed. **2.** *adj.* allowing customers to enter; ready for business. **3.** *adj.* not decided. **4.** *adj.* available; free and not restricted. (Adv: *openly.*) **5.** *adj.* sincere; honest about one's feelings. (Adv: *openly.*) **6.** *tv.* to cause something to become ①; to allow a place to be entered into or exited from. **7.** *tv.* to establish the beginning of something; to cause something to start. **8.** *iv.* to be accessible; to become ready for business or use.
→ BE (OUT) IN THE OPEN
→ KEEP ONE'S WEATHER EYE OPEN
→ NOT OPEN ONE'S MOUTH
→ PRY SOMETHING OPEN

open a can of worms to uncover a set of problems; to create unnecessary complications.

open a conversation to start a conversation.

an **open book** someone or something that is easy to understand.

open for business [of a shop, store, restaurant, etc.] operating and ready to do business.

open one's **heart (to** someone**)** to reveal one's private thoughts to someone.

open (out) on(to) something [for a building's doors] to exit toward something.

open secret something that is supposed to be a secret but is known to a great many people.

open something **up 1.** to open something that was closed. **2.** to begin working on something for which there are paper records, such as a case, investigation, file, etc.

open something **up (to** someone**)** to make something available to someone; to permit someone to join something or participate in something.

open to something agreeable to hear or learn about new ideas or suggestions.

open up (to someone**) 1.** to tell [everything] to someone; to confess to someone. **2.** [for opportunities] to become available to someone. (Figurative.)

open up (to someone or something**) 1.** [for doors] to become open to someone, something, or some creature can enter; to open for someone or something. **2.** [for someone] to become more accepting of someone or something.

an **open-and-shut case** something, usually a legal case or a problem, that is simple and straightforward.

opener ['o pə nɚ] *n.* someone or something that opens something.

opening ['o pə nɪŋ] **1.** *n.* a way into a container, compartment, or room; a way through a wall or barrier. **2.** *n.* something that is available; a job that is available. **3.** *n.* an opportunity to do something or say something. (Figurative on ①.)

4. *adj.* at the beginning; the first; the earliest.

opening gambit an opening movement or statement that is made to secure a position that is to one's advantage.

opera ['ɑ prə] **1.** *n.* the branch of theater or music in which lengthy performances include solo and choral singing, orchestra music, and sometimes dance. (No plural.) **2.** *n.* a presentation or performance of a musical production as in ①.

operate ['ɑp ə ret] **1.** *iv.* [for a machine or device] to work or function. **2.** *iv.* to perform surgery; to perform an operation. **3.** *tv.* to cause something to work or function; to direct or manage something.

operate on someone or something to perform surgery on a certain part of the body or on someone or something.

operation [ɑ pə 're ʃən] **1.** *n.* surgery; a medical procedure where something is done to the body, usually involving cutting. **2.** *n.* the way something works; the way something is used.

operator ['ɑp ə ret ɚ] **1.** *n.* someone who operates a machine. **2.** *n.* someone who handles telephone calls; the person one talks to when one dials "0" on a telephone.

opinion [ə 'pɪn jən] **1.** *n.* thoughts, ideas, or attitudes concerning someone or something. (Plural only for types and instances.) **2.** *n.* advice from a professional or an expert.

→ FORM AN OPINION
→ HAZARD AN OPINION
→ KEEP ONE'S OPINIONS TO ONESELF
→ A MATTER OF OPINION

opossum [ə 'pɑs əm] *n.* a small, gray, furry animal with a hairless, flexible tail.

opponent [ə 'pon ənt] *n.* someone who is on the opposite side in a contest, fight, or argument.

opportunity [ɑp ɚ 'tu nə ti] *n.* a good chance for doing something; a favorable time for doing something.

oppose [ə 'poz] *tv.* to be against someone or something; to fight against someone or something; to argue against someone or something. (Often passive.)

opposite ['ɑp ə sɪt] **1.** *adj.* completely different in at least one major respect. (Adv: *oppositely.*) **2.** *adj.* of or about a location that is the farthest point away within a defined area. (Adv: *oppositely.*) **3.** *prep.* across from someone or something; facing someone or something. **4.** *n.* someone or something that is OPPOSITE as in ① as compared to someone or something else.

opposite sex ['ɑp ə sət 'sɛks] *n.* [from the point of view of a female] a male; [from the point of view of a male] a female.

opposition [ɑp ə 'zɪ ʃən] **1.** *n.* a state of being against someone or something; resistance. (No plural.) **2.** *n.* the people who are against something. (No plural.)

oppress [ə 'prɛs] *tv.* to rule someone or a group of people harshly or cruelly; to keep someone from succeeding.

optic ['ɑp tɪk] *adj.* of or about the eye or vision. (Adv: *optically* […ɪk li].)

optical ['ɑp tɪ kəl] *adj.* of or about the eye or vision. (Adv: *optically* […ɪk li].)

option ['ɑp ʃən] *n.* a choice; something [else] that is available for choosing.

or ['or] **1.** *conj.* a word used in a list of items to show a choice or difference. **2.** *conj.* otherwise; if not. **3.** *conj.* that is to say.

or else or suffer the consequences.

oral ['or əl] **1.** *adj.* of or about the mouth. (Adv: *orally.*) **2.** *adj.* spoken. (Adv: *orally.*)

orange ['or ɪndʒ] **1.** *n.* a color of the rainbow between red and yellow, and the color of ②. (Plural only for types and instances.) **2.** *n.* a round, juicy citrus fruit—of the color ①—that grows on a tree. **3.** *adj.* of the color ①. **4.** *adj.* made with ②; flavored with ②.

orbit ['or bɪt] **1.** *n.* a pathway around a planet or a star, such as that taken by a planet, a moon, or a rocket. **2.** *tv.* to move in a circle around a star or planet. **3.** *iv.* to move in a circle around a star or planet.

orchard ['or tʃɚd] *n.* a farm of fruit or nut trees.

orchestra ['or kə strə] *n.* a group of several musicians and the instruments they play, usually including strings.

orchid ['or kɪd] *n.* a flower with unusually shaped and brightly colored petals.

ordain [or 'den] **1.** *tv.* to confer the status of being a priest or a minister on someone. **2.** *tv.* to order something; to make something a law. (The object can be a clause with THAT ⑦.)

ordeal [or 'dil] *n.* a very difficult experience.

order ['or dɚ] **1.** *n.* the sequence in which a series of things is arranged. **2.** *n.* a state of everything being in its proper place. (No plural.) **3.** *n.* a state of being able to be used; condition. (No plural. See also OUT OF ORDER.) **4.** *n.* a state wherein people are following rules and behaving properly. (No plural.) **5.** *n.* a command. **6.** *n.* a request for certain goods or services. **7.** *n.* one serving of a kind of food. **8.** *tv.* to request goods or services. **9.** *tv.* to request a serving of food or a full meal. **10.** *tv.* to arrange someone or something into a certain sequence.
→ CALL A MEETING TO ORDER
→ FOLLOW ORDERS
→ IN SHORT ORDER
→ JUST WHAT THE DOCTOR ORDERED
→ OUT OF ORDER
→ PLACE AN ORDER

the **order of the day** something necessary or usual at a certain time.

order someone **in(to** something**)** to command someone to get into something.

order something **in** to have something, usually food, brought into one's house or place of business.

orderly ['or dɚ li] **1.** *adj.* neat; in order. **2.** *n.* a hospital worker who assists doctors and nurses in caring for patients.

ordinal number Go to ORDINAL NUMERAL.

ordinal numeral AND **ordinal number** ['or dɪ nəl 'nu mə rəl, 'or dɪ nəl 'nʌm bɚ] *n.* the number used to show rank or position in a series, such as *first, second, third,* etc. (See also CARDINAL NUMERAL.)

ordinary ['ord n ner i] *adj.* usual; common; typical; regular. (Adv: *ordinarily* [ord n 'ner ə li].)

organ ['or gən] **1.** *n.* a part of an animal that performs a specific function. **2.** *n.* a musical instrument with keyboards that control the air flow into many pipes of different lengths, each sounding a different note. (Also **pipe organ**.)

organism ['or gə nɪz əm] *n.* a plant or an animal; a living thing.

organization [or gə nə 'ze ʃən] *n.* a group of people, such as those in a club or society; a company; a department of government.

organize ['or gə naɪz] **1.** *tv.* to arrange different parts in a way so that they work properly; to arrange different parts into a system. **2.** *tv.* to form an organization or meeting.

origin ['or ə dʒən] *n.* the starting point; something that other things develop from.

original [ə 'rɪdʒ ə nəl] **1.** *adj.* not copied or based on something else. **2.** *adj.* first; earliest. (Adv: *originally*.) **3.** *n.* something that copies are made from; the first example of something that other examples are based on.

originate [ə'rɪdʒ ə net] **1.** *tv.* to cause something to exist; to found something; to establish something, such as an organization. **2.** *iv.* to start; to begin.

orphan ['or fən] **1.** *n.* a young child whose parents are dead or missing. **2.** *tv.* to cause someone to become ①. (Typically passive.)

ostrich ['as trɪtʃ] *n.* a large bird that runs very quickly but cannot fly.

other ['ʌð ɚ] **1.** *pron.* the second of two people or things; the remaining person or things. **2.** the *adj.* use of ①. **3.** *adj.* more of the same or similar kind of thing or people.
→ EVERY OTHER PERSON OR THING
→ GO IN ONE EAR AND OUT THE OTHER
→ HAVE OTHER FISH TO FRY
→ IN ONE EAR AND OUT THE OTHER
→ LAUGH OUT OF THE OTHER SIDE OF ONE'S MOUTH
→ LOOK THE OTHER WAY
→ NONE OTHER THAN SOMEONE
→ SIX OF ONE AND HALF A DOZEN OF THE OTHER
→ THERE ARE PLENTY OF OTHER FISH IN THE SEA.
→ TURN THE OTHER CHEEK
→ WITH EVERY (OTHER) BREATH

the **other side of the tracks** the poorer part of a town, often near the railroad tracks. (Especially with *from the* or *live on the*.)

otherwise ['ʌð ɚ waɪz] **1.** *conj.* or else; or it is that. **2.** *adv.* in another way; in a different way; differently. **3.** *adv.* in every regard except [this one]; in every way except [this one].

otter ['at ɚ] **1.** *n.* a long, thin, furry animal that lives in and near water, and eats fish. **2.** *n.* the skin and fur of ①. (No plural.) **3.** *adj.* made from ②.

ought to do something ['ɔt...] have to do something; obliged to do something.

ought to happen AND **ought to** be somehow ['ɔt...] likely to happen; should happen; likely to be somehow.

ounce ['aʊns] **1.** *n.* a unit of measurement of weight equal to ¹⁄₁₆ of a pound or about 28 grams. **2.** *n.* a unit of measurement of liquid equal to ¹⁄₁₆ of a pint or ⅛ of a cup.

our ['aɚ] *pron.* the first-person plural possessive pronoun including the speaker or writer. (Used as a modifier before a noun.)

ours *pron.* the first-person plural possessive pronoun. (Used in place of a noun.)

ourselves ['aɚ 'sɛlvz] **1.** *pron.* the first-person plural reflexive pronoun. **2.** *pron.* a form used to emphasize WE.
→ BY OURSELVES

oust ['aʊst] *tv.* to get rid of someone or something; to remove someone or something by force.

out ['aʊt] **1.** *adv.* away from a place; not in a place; not in the usual condition; not at the usual position; to a point beyond a limit. **2.** *adv.* in the open air; into the open air; outside; not inside. **3.** *adj.* not at the usual position; to a point beyond a limit; not at home; not at work. (Not prenomi-

nal.) **4.** *adj.* no longer in style; old-fashioned. (Not prenominal.)
5. *adj.* not a possible choice. (Not prenominal. Informal.) **6.** *adj.* no longer burning; no longer giving off light. (Not prenominal.) **7.** *adj.* not working; not functioning properly. (Not prenominal.)
8. *adj.* [in baseball, of someone] no longer permitted to play in a particular turn. (Not prenominal.)
9. *adj.* used up; no longer having more of a substance. (Not prenominal.) **10.** *adj.* unconscious; not aware; not awake. (Not prenominal.)

out and about able to go out and travel around; well enough to go out.

out cold AND **out like a light** unconscious; deeply asleep.

out in left field offbeat; unusual and eccentric.

out like a light Go to OUT COLD.

out of a clear blue sky AND **out of the blue** suddenly; without warning.

out of all proportion of an exaggerated proportion; of an unrealistic proportion compared with something else.

out of circulation [of someone] not interacting socially with other people.

out of control not manageable; not restrained; disorderly.

out of earshot too far from the source of a sound to hear the sound.

out of gas tired; exhausted; worn-out.

out of luck without good luck; having bad fortune.

out of one's **element** not in a natural or comfortable situation.

out of one's **head** Go to OUT OF ONE'S MIND.

out of one's **mind** AND **out of** one's **head; out of** one's **senses** silly and senseless; crazy; irrational.

out of one's **senses** Go to OUT OF ONE'S MIND.

out of order 1. not following correct procedure in a meeting. **2.** not working; not functioning; broken.

out of practice performing poorly due to a lack of practice.

out of print [for a book] to be no longer available for sale. (Compare this with IN PRINT.)

out of proportion Go to IN PROPORTION.

out of season 1. not now available for sale. **2.** not now legally able to be hunted or caught.

out of service inoperable; not currently operating; OUT OF ORDER.

out of spite with the desire to harm someone or something.

out of the blue Go to OUT OF A CLEAR BLUE SKY.

out of the corner of one's **eye** [seeing something] at a glance; glimpsing (something).

out of the frying pan into the fire from a bad situation to a worse situation.

out of the hole out of debt.

out of the question not possible; not permitted.

out of the red out of debt.

out of the running no longer being considered; eliminated from a contest.

out of the woods past a critical phase; out of the unknown.

out of thin air apparently out of nowhere; as if from nothing.

out of this world wonderful; extraordinary.

out of tune Go to IN TUNE.

out of tune (with someone or something**) 1.** not in musical harmony with someone or something. **2.** not in (figurative) harmony or agreement with someone or something.

out of turn not at the proper time; not in the proper order.

out on a limb in a dangerous position; taking a chance.

(out) on patrol away from a central location, watching over a distant area.

out on the town celebrating at one or more places in a town.

out to lunch 1. eating lunch outside the office. **2.** unalert; uninformed.

outcast ['aʊt kæst] *n.* someone who has been rejected, abandoned, or deserted.

outcome ['aʊt kəm] *n.* the final result; the effect of something.

outcry ['aʊt kraɪ] **1.** *n.* a strong protest; an uproar. **2.** *n.* a loud cry.

outdoor [aʊt 'dor] *adj.* not inside; not in a building; used or done OUTDOORS.

outdoors [aʊt 'dorz] *adv.* in or into the open air; not inside a building.

outer ['aʊ tɚ] **1.** *adj.* farther away from the center. **2.** *adj.* exterior; on the outside.

outer space ['aʊ tɚ 'spes] *n.* the universe beyond the atmosphere of earth. (No plural.)

outgrew [aʊt 'gru] past tense of OUTGROW.

outgrow [aʊt 'gro] **1.** *tv., irreg.* to no longer fit into one's clothes because one has grown. (Past tense: OUTGREW; past participle: OUTGROWN.) **2.** *tv., irreg.* to become too mature to do certain things meant for younger children. (Figurative on ①.) **3.** *tv., irreg.* to grow to be taller or to grow faster than someone else.

outgrown [aʊt 'gron] Past participle of OUTGROW.

outlaw ['aʊt lɔ] **1.** *tv.* to make something illegal; to declare that something is against the law. **2.** *n.* a criminal.

outlay ['aʊt le] *n.* money spent for a certain reason; time or energy spent for a certain reason.

outlet ['aʊt lɛt] **1.** *n.* the socket in a wall where something can be plugged in for electrical power. **2.** *n.* a way out for something. **3.** *n.* a way to let one's feelings out; a way to use one's creativity. (Figurative on ②.)

outline ['aʊt laɪn] **1.** *n.* the shape of someone or something; the border of someone or something. **2.** *n.* a list of the main topics of a speech or text; a plan. **3.** *tv.* to draw the shape of someone or something; to draw the border of someone or something. **4.** *tv.* to list the main topics of a speech or text. **5.** *tv.* to describe a plan.

outlive [ɑʊt ˈlɪv] *tv.* to live longer than someone else; to work, function, or last longer than something else.

outlook [ˈɑʊt lʊk] **1.** *n.* an imagined view of the future course that something may take. (No plural.) **2.** *n.* a way of looking at things that happen.

output [ˈɑʊt pʊt] **1.** *n.* the amount of something that is made; production. (No plural.) **2.** *n.* something that is produced. (No plural.) **3.** *n.* the energy that is produced by a machine. (No plural.) **4.** *n.* information that is produced by a computer. (No plural.)

outrage [ˈɑʊt redʒ] **1.** *n.* a very cruel or horrible deed. **2.** *n.* anger caused by a very cruel or horrible action. (No plural.) **3.** *tv.* to anger someone greatly by doing a very cruel or horrible deed.

outright [ˈɑʊt rɑɪt] **1.** *adj.* complete; direct; openly and without delay. **2.** *adj.* [of money given] without limitations. **3.** *adv.* without limitations.
→ KILLED OUTRIGHT

outside [ˈɑʊt ˈsɑɪd] **1.** *n.* the part of something that faces away from the center of something; the surface of something that is out. (Also plural with the same meaning, but not countable.) **2.** *adj.* on ①; external; not inside a building. **3.** *adj.* farther from the center than something else. **4.** *adj.* not

associated with the inner group. (Prenominal only.) **5.** *adv.* to or toward ①; on or at ①; in or into the outdoors. **6.** *prep.* past the limit of something; beyond something; on or toward the exterior of something.
→ AT THE OUTSIDE
→ FALL OUTSIDE SOMETHING
→ STEP OUTSIDE

outward [ˈɑʊt wɚd] **1.** *adv.* away; away from someplace; toward the outside. **2.** *adj.* of or about one's appearance instead of one's feelings or thoughts. (Adv: *outwardly.*)

outweigh [ɑʊt ˈwe] **1.** *tv.* to weigh more than someone or something else. **2.** *tv.* to be more important than someone or something else. (Figurative on ①.)

outwit [ɑʊt ˈwɪt] *tv.* to be more clever than someone and therefore win at something.

oval [ˈo vəl] **1.** *adj.* shaped like an egg; almost shaped like a circle, but flatter. (Adv: *ovally.*) **2.** *n.* a shape like that of an egg; the shape of a flattened circle.

oven [ˈʌv ən] **1.** *n.* an appliance or enclosed space within an appliance that can be heated to cook food. **2.** *n.* an appliance that is heated to dry and harden pottery or other objects.

over [ˈo vɚ] **1.** *prep.* above someone or something; higher than someone or something. **2.** *prep.* on someone or something; covering someone or something. **3.** *prep.* across something; from one side of something to the other; above and to the other side of something. **4.** *prep.* off and down from something. **5.** *prep.* during something; throughout some period of time. **6.** *prep.* more than a certain measurement; greater than something. (Some people prefer *more than* to OVER in this sense.) **7.** *prep.* with something noisy in the background. **8.** *prep.* from [the radio, the Internet, or a telephone]. **9.** *prep.* covering the surface of someone or something. **10.** *adv.* at some other place; on the other side of something. **11.** *adv.* down; so that a surface faces down. **12.** *adv.* again. **13.** *prefix* too; too much. (Usually in a compound.) **14.** *adj.* done; finished; at the end. (Not prenominal.)

over again Go to (ALL) OVER AGAIN.

over someone's **head** too difficult or clever for someone to understand.

over the hill old; too old to do something.

over the hump past the difficult part.

over the long haul for a relatively long period of time.

over the short haul for the immediate future.

over the top to or at a point where one has achieved more than one's goal.

over there Go to (WAY) OVER THERE.

overate [o vɚ 'et] past tense of OVEREAT.

overboard ['ov ɚ bord] *adv.* [falling, dropping, or being thrown] from a boat or ship into the water.
→ GO OVERBOARD

overcame [o vɚ 'kem] past tense of OVERCOME.

overcharge [o vɚ 'tʃɑrdʒ] *tv.* to charge someone more money for something than it really costs.

overcoat ['o vɚ kot] *n.* a heavy coat that is worn over other clothes.

overcome [o vɚ 'kʌm] **1.** *tv., irreg.* to defeat someone or something; to fight and win against someone or something. (Past tense: OVERCAME; past participle: *overcome*.) **2.** *tv., irreg.* to cause someone to become helpless, especially because of emotion.

overdose [o vɚ dos] **1.** *n.* a large dose of a drug that causes someone to faint or die. **2.** *iv.* to become unconscious or die because one has taken too many drugs or too much medicine.

overeat [o vɚ 'it] *iv., irreg.* to eat too much. (Past tense: OVERATE; past participle: OVEREATEN.)

overeaten [o vɚ 'it n] past participle of OVEREAT.

overhead 1. ['o vɚ hɛd] *n.* the costs of running a business; business expenses. (No plural. Treated as singular.) **2.** ['o vɚ hɛd] the *adj.* use of ①. **3.** ['o vɚ hɛd] *adj.* above one's head. (Prenominal only.) **4.** ['o vɚ 'hɛd] *adv.* above one's head; in the air; passing through the air.

overheat [o vɚ 'hit] **1.** *iv.* to become too hot; to break or stop working because of being worked too hard. **2.** *tv.* to cause something to become too hot.

overkill ['o vɚ ˌkɪl] *n.* the condition of having or doing more than is necessary. (No plural.)

overlap 1. [o vɚ 'læp] *iv.* [for parts of two or more things] to happen at the same time. **2.** [o vɚ 'læp] *iv.* [for parts of two or more things] to cover the same space. **3.** [o vɚ 'læp] *tv.* [for something] to partially cover something [else]. **4.** [o vɚ 'læp] *tv.* [for something] to begin before something else finishes; to place the beginning of something over the end of something else. **5.** ['o vɚ ˌlæp] *n.* the extra part of something that extends over something else. (No plural.) **6.** ['o vɚ ˌlæp] *n.* the amount by which something extends over something else. (No plural.)

overlook 1. ['o vɚ ˌlʊk] *n.* a high place that provides a good view of a lower place. **2.** [o vɚ 'lʊk] *tv.* to forget or neglect something. **3.** [o vɚ 'lʊk] *tv.* to ignore something.

overnight 1. ['o vɚ ˌnaɪt] *adj.* done during the night; lasting through the night. **2.** [o vɚ 'naɪt] *adv.* through the night; during the night. **3.** [o vɚ 'naɪt] *adv.* in just one night.

oversaw [o vɚ 'sɔ] past tense of OVERSEE.

overseas [o vɚ 'siz] **1.** *adv.* across the sea; on the other side of the ocean. **2.** *adj.* done, used, or about a place on the other side of the ocean.

oversee [o vɚ 'si] *tv., irreg.* to supervise someone or something; to watch over someone or something so that something is done

properly. (Past tense: OVERSAW; past participle: OVERSEEN.)

overseen [o vɚ 'sin] past participle of OVERSEE.

oversight ['o vɚ ˌsaɪt] *n.* something that is not noticed or thought of.

oversleep [o vɚ 'slip] *iv., irreg.* to sleep longer than one wanted to; to sleep too long. (Past tense and past participle: OVERSLEPT.)

overslept [o vɚ 'slɛpt] past tense and past participle of OVERSLEEP.

overthrew [o vɚ 'θru] past tense of OVERTHROW.

overthrow [o vɚ 'θro] *tv., irreg.* to remove someone or something from power; to seize power from a government. (Past tense: OVERTHREW; past participle: OVERTHROWN.)

overthrown [o vɚ 'θron] Past participle of OVERTHROW.

overtime ['o vɚ ˌtaɪm] **1.** *n.* time at work past the time when one normally finishes. (No plural.) **2.** *n.* money earned by working past the time when one normally finishes. (No plural.) **3.** *n.* [in a sporting event] an extra amount of playing time allowed in order to break a tie score. (No plural.) **4.** *adv.* past the hours when one normally finishes. **5.** *adj.* of or about working extra as in ①.

overture ['o vɚ ˌtʃɚ] **1.** *n.* the piece of music at the beginning of an opera, symphony, ballet, etc., that introduces key melodies and themes. **2.** *n.* the communication of an intention to make an offer of something.
→ MAKE OVERTURES

owe ['o] **1.** *tv.* to be in debt for a sum of money; to have to pay someone for something. **2.** *tv.* to be obliged to give someone something.

owing to something because of something; due to the fact of something.

owl ['aʊl] *n.* a bird that has large eyes that face the front and a short, curved beak, and is active at night.
→ (AS) WISE AS AN OWL
→ NIGHT OWL

own ['on] **1.** *tv.* to possess something; to have something as a belonging. **2.** *adj.* belonging to oneself or itself. **3.** *adj.* a form indicating something already mentioned as belonging to oneself or itself.
→ AFRAID OF ONE'S OWN SHADOW
→ BLOW ONE'S OWN HORN
→ COME INTO ONE'S OWN
→ COME INTO ITS OWN
→ CUT ONE'S (OWN) THROAT
→ DIG ONE'S OWN GRAVE
→ A DOSE OF ONE'S OWN MEDICINE
→ FEATHER ONE'S (OWN) NEST
→ FIND ONE'S OWN LEVEL
→ FOUL ONE'S OWN NEST
→ HOLD ONE'S OWN
→ IN A WORLD OF ONE'S OWN
→ IN SOMEONE'S (OWN) (BEST) INTERESTS
→ MIND ONE'S OWN BUSINESS
→ NOT KNOW ONE'S OWN STRENGTH
→ PADDLE ONE'S OWN CANOE
→ SIGN ONE'S OWN DEATH WARRANT
→ STAND ON ONE'S OWN TWO FEET

→ STEW IN ONE'S OWN JUICE
→ TAKE THE LAW INTO ONE'S OWN HANDS
→ TELL ITS OWN STORY
→ TELL ITS OWN TALE
→ TOOT ONE'S OWN HORN
→ UNDER ONE'S OWN STEAM

own up to someone to confess or admit something to someone.

own up to something to admit something; to confess to something.

owner ['o nɚ] *n.* someone who owns something.

ownership ['o nɚ ʃɪp] *n.* the state of being an owner; the right one has to own something. (No plural.)

ox ['ɑks] *n., irreg.* an adult male of a kind of cattle. (An ox has been made unable to breed. Plural: OXEN.)
→ (AS) STRONG AS AN OX

oxen ['ɑk sən] plural of ox.

oxygen ['ɑks ɪ dʒən] *n.* a gas that makes up about 20 percent of the air we breathe. (No plural.)

oyster ['ɔɪs tɚ] **1.** *n.* a small sea creature that lives between two hinged shells and sometimes produces pearls. **2.** *n.* ① used as food.

ozone ['o zon] *n.* a kind of oxygen produced when an electrical spark, such as lightning, passes through the air. (No plural.)

P

pace ['pes] **1.** *n.* the speed at which someone or something moves. (No plural.) **2.** *n.* a distance of one step when running or walking. **3.** *iv.* to walk back and forth slowly and regularly.
→ AT A SNAIL'S PACE
→ a CHANGE OF PACE
→ PUT ONE THROUGH ONE'S PACES
→ PUT SOMETHING THROUGH ITS PACES

pace something **out 1.** to deal with a problem by pacing around. **2.** to measure a distance by counting the number of strides taken while walking.

pack ['pæk] **1.** *n.* a group of things that have been placed together—in a case, for example—so they can be carried. **2.** *n.* a group of animals that live, hunt, and travel together. **3.** *tv.* to fill a container completely. **4.** *tv.* to gather, assemble, and arrange things and place them in a space or container.
→ SEND SOMEONE PACKING

a **pack of lies** a series of lies.

pack something **up (in** something**)** to prepare something to be transported by placing it into a container.

pack up to prepare one's belongings to be transported by placing them into a container; to gather one's things together for one's departure.

package ['pæk ɪdʒ] **1.** *n.* a group of things that are wrapped together or boxed; a container in which goods are sold or shipped. **2.** *n.* a parcel, especially one that is wrapped in paper or something similar. **3.** *tv.* to place something

in a container, especially to make it available for sale.

packed (in) like sardines packed very tightly.

pact ['pækt] *n.* an agreement; a treaty.

pad ['pæd] **1.** *n.* a small cushion or mass of soft material used to protect something, make something comfortable, absorb fluid, or give something a certain shape. **2.** *n.* a tablet of paper; a stack of pieces of paper that are glued together along one edge. **3.** *iv.* to walk softly and very quietly. **4.** *tv.* to make a movie, book, program, etc., longer by adding extra words, longer pauses, extra performance material, etc.
→ LAUNCHING PAD

pad the bill to put unnecessary items on a bill to make the total cost higher.

paddle ['pæd l] **1.** *n.* a kind of oar used to steer and move a canoe or other small boat. **2.** *n.* a round or long flat object used to spank someone. **3.** *tv.* to move a canoe with ①. **4.** *tv.* to spank someone with ② or with the hand. **5.** *iv.* to propel [something] with ①.

paddle one's **own canoe** to do something by oneself; to be alone.

pagan ['pe gən] **1.** *n.* someone whose religion is not Christianity, Islam, or Judaism; someone who has no religion. **2.** *adj.* of, by, for, or about ①.

page ['pedʒ] **1.** *n.* one sheet of paper in a book. **2.** *n.* one side of one sheet of paper in a book. **3.** *n.*

411

a sheet of paper suitable for writing or printing or having writing or printing. **4.** *n.* a signal that someone has a waiting message or telephone call, especially a beep from a pager. **5.** *tv.* to alert someone that a message or telephone call is waiting.

pager ['pe dʒɚ] *n.* an electronic device that makes a signal to alert someone to a waiting message or telephone call.

paid ['ped] **1.** past tense and past participle of PAY. **2.** *adj.* hired; employed; receiving money.

pail ['pel] **1.** *n.* a bucket; a container without a lid and with a curved handle that connects to opposite sides of the rim. **2.** *n.* the contents of ①.

pain ['pen] *n.* hurt or ache caused by injury, sickness, or mental distress. (Plural only for types and instances.)
→ BE RACKED WITH PAIN
→ LABOR PAINS
→ SHARE SOMEONE'S PAIN

painkiller ['pen kɪl ɚ] *n.* a type of a medicine or drug that ends or relieves pain.

paint ['pent] **1.** *n.* a colored liquid that is spread on a surface to give the surface color and protection and that gets hard when it dries. (Plural only for types and instances.) **2.** *tv.* to cover something with ①, using a brush or something similar. **3.** *tv.* to make a picture of someone or something using ①. **4.** *iv.* to cover walls or other objects with ①. **5.** *iv.* to make pictures with ①.

paint over something to cover something up with a layer of paint.

paint something **out** to cover something up or obliterate something by applying a layer of paint.

paint the town red to have a wild celebration during a night on the town.

paintbrush ['pent ˈbrʌʃ] *n.* a brush used to apply paint to a surface.

painting ['pen tɪŋ] **1.** *n.* the art and study of making pictures with paint. (No plural.) **2.** *n.* a picture that is made with paint.

pair ['pɛr] **1.** *n.* a set of two similar or matching things; two people or two things. **2.** *n.* [in card games] two cards with the same number or value. **3.** *tv.* to sort or order people or things into sets of two.

pair up (with someone) to join with someone to make a pair.

pajama *adj.* of, by, for, or about PAJAMAS.

pajamas [pə ˈdʒɑ məz] *n.* clothes worn in bed or worn at night before one goes to bed. (Treated as plural. Number is expressed by *pair(s) of pajamas*.)

pal ['pæl] *n.* a friend; a chum. (Informal.)

pal around (with someone) to associate with someone as a good friend.

palace ['pæl ɪs] *n.* a very large, luxurious house, especially one where a king, queen, or important political leader lives or once lived.

pale ['pel] **1.** *adj.* having a lighter color than usual; faded. (Adv:

palely. Comp: *paler;* sup: *palest.*)
2. *iv.* to become lighter in color; to whiten or weaken in color; to fade.
3. *iv.* [for someone] to become ①
and appear faint. **4.** *iv.* [for something] to appear to be weak or inadequate.
→ BEYOND THE PALE

palm ['pɑm] **1.** *n.* the front of the hand between the wrist and the bottom of the fingers. **2.** *n.* a tree with a long trunk and long, pointed leaves at the top, attached to a hard stem. (Short for PALM TREE.) **3.** *tv.* to hide something in one's ①.
→ HAVE AN ITCHING PALM
→ HAVE AN ITCHY PALM
→ KNOW SOMEONE OR SOMETHING LIKE THE PALM OF ONE'S HAND

palm something **off (on** someone**)** to try to get something accepted as good.

palm tree ['pɑm tri] *n.* a tree with a long trunk that has no branches and long, pointed leaves attached to a hard stem. (Can be shortened to PALM.)

pan ['pæn] **1.** *n.* a wide, shallow vessel used for cooking. **2.** *tv.* to give a bad review about a movie, book, or play; to criticize something harshly. **3.** *iv.* [for a camera] to move while filming, traveling over a scene as one's eyes might move.
→ A FLASH IN THE PAN
→ OUT OF THE FRYING PAN INTO THE FIRE

pancake ['pæn kek] *n.* a thin, round cake made of flour, eggs, and milk that is cooked on both sides.
→ (AS) FLAT AS A PANCAKE

pane ['pen] *n.* a section of glass in a window or door.

panel ['pæn əl] **1.** *n.* a thin, flat square or rectangular section of hard material. **2.** *n.* a group of people who are selected to talk about something or judge someone or something. **3.** *tv.* to cover the walls of a room with ①.

panic ['pæn ɪk] **1.** *n.* a fear that is out of control; a sense of terror. (No plural.) **2.** *iv., irreg.* to feel ①; to experience fear that is frantic and out of control. (Past tense and past participle: PANICKED. Present participle: *panicking.*) **3.** *tv., irreg.* to cause someone or some creature to experience ①.

panicked ['pæn ɪkt] past tense and past participle of PANIC.

pant ['pænt] **1.** *iv.* to make quick, shallow breaths, as an overheated dog does. **2.** *n.* a gasp; a quick, shallow breath.

panties *n.* a pair of women's underpants. (Treated as plural. Number is expressed with *pair(s) of panties.* Also countable.)

pantry ['pæn tri] *n.* a small room near a kitchen, where pots, pans, dishes, silverware, tablecloths, food, and other kitchen items are kept.

pants *n.* trousers; clothing worn below the waist, having a separate tube, hole, or compartment for each leg. (Treated as plural. Number is expressed with *pair(s) of pants.* Also countable.)
→ BY THE SEAT OF ONE'S PANTS

pantyhose ['pæn ti hoz] *n.* a garment that is made of sheer stockings extending from a pair of panties. (No plural. Treated as plural, but not countable. Number is expressed with *pair(s) of pantyhose*.)

paper ['pe pɚ] **1.** *n.* processed fiber and other substances, pressed into sheets, used for writing, printing, drawing on, and other things. (No plural. Number is usually expressed with *piece(s)* or *sheet(s) of paper*.) **2.** *n.* WALLPAPER; decorated paper that is glued to walls. (No plural.) **3.** *n.* a newspaper. **4.** *n.* an article; an essay. **5.** *adj.* made from ①. **6.** *tv.* to cover something with wallpaper.
→ GET SOMETHING DOWN (ON PAPER)
→ LOOK GOOD ON PAPER
→ PUT SOMETHING ON PAPER
→ TOILET PAPER

paper clip ['pe pɚ 'klɪp] *n.* a device made of bent wire that can hold a few sheets of paper together.

papers 1. *n.* documents; sheets of PAPER ① in groups or stacks, bearing information. (Treated as plural, but not countable.) **2.** *n.* documents that prove who one is; one's passport or visa, carried while visiting a foreign country. (Treated as plural, but not countable.)

paperweight ['pe pɚ wet] *n.* a heavy object placed on a stack of papers to keep them from blowing away.

par ['pɑr] *n.* [in golf] the normal number of strokes that it takes to get the golf ball from the tee into the hole. (No plural form. A number may follow PAR.)
→ ABOVE PAR
→ BELOW PAR

→ UP TO PAR

parachute ['pɛr ə ʃut] **1.** *n.* a large bowl-shaped piece of fabric attached to and supporting someone who jumps from an airplane or some other very high place. **2.** *iv.* to drift downward, wearing a parachute.

parade [pə 'red] **1.** *n.* a public event where people march or ride down a street with people watching from both sides. **2.** *iv.* to march somewhere in ①. **3.** *tv.* to make someone march in front of people.

parade someone or something **out** to bring or march someone or some creature out in public.

paradise ['pɛr ə daɪs] **1.** *n.* heaven. (No plural.) **2.** *n.* somewhere on earth that seems as lovely and wonderful as ①. (No plural.)
→ a FOOL'S PARADISE

a **paradise on earth** a place on earth that is as lovely as paradise.

paragraph ['pɛr ə græf] *n.* a sentence or group of sentences usually related some way in meaning.

parallel ['pɛr ə lɛl] **1.** *adj.* [lines or plane surfaces] at the same distance apart or at an equal distance apart everywhere. **2.** *adj.* similar; like [a situation]; analogous. **3.** *tv.* to go or be on a route or in a direction that is beside something else as in ①. (E.g., a road that *parallels the railroad tracks*.)

paraphrase ['pɛr ə frez] **1.** *n.* something that someone has said or has written in a different way. **2.** *tv.* to restate something as in ①.

parasite ['pɛr ə saɪt] **1.** *n.* a plant or animal completely dependent on another species of plant or animal for food or support. (PARASITES on humans and animals cause diseases or health disorders.) **2.** *n.* someone who depends on other people for food and shelter; a useless person who is supported by other people. (Figurative on ①.)

parcel ['pɑr səl] **1.** *n.* a package, especially one that is mailed or delivered; something that is wrapped up. **2.** *n.* an amount of land that is sold as a unit.
→ PART AND PARCEL

parcel post ['pɑr səl 'post] **1.** *n.* a class of mail in the postal system limited to small parcels. (No plural.) **2.** *adv.* by way of ①.

pardon ['pɑr dn] **1.** *n.* forgiving someone. (Plural only for types and instances.) **2.** *n.* an act that keeps someone from being punished under the law. **3.** *tv.* to forgive someone; to excuse someone. **4.** *tv.* to release someone from jail; to order that someone not be executed; to keep someone from being punished.

parent ['pɛr ənt] **1.** *n.* the father or the mother of a living creature. **2.** *n.* a business that owns another business; the main office of one or more businesses or other organizations. **3.** *adj.* serving as a ②.

parentheses [pə 'rɛn θə siz] plural of PARENTHESIS.

parenthesis [pə 'rɛn θə sɪs] *n., irreg.* either of the pair of symbols "(" and ")" used to enclose information of secondary importance in writing or printing. (Plural: PARENTHESES.)

park ['pɑrk] **1.** *n.* a piece of land set aside by a city, state, county, or nation for use by the public, usually having trees, grass, and other natural features. **2.** *tv.* to stop a car or other vehicle and leave it in a certain place for a period of time. **3.** *iv.* to leave a car or other vehicle in a certain place for a period of time.
→ IN PARK

parking lot ['pɑr kɪŋ lɑt] *n.* an area of paved land used to park cars on.

parlor ['pɑr lɚ] **1.** *n.* a living room; a place in a home where guests can sit and talk. (Old-fashioned.) **2.** *n.* a store that sells a certain product or service, such as hair care, ice cream, or funerals.

parrot ['pɛr ət] **1.** *n.* a kind of tropical bird, often brightly colored, that can copy human speech. **2.** *tv.* to repeat someone else's words or ideas without thinking. (Figurative on ①. The object can be a clause with THAT ⑦.)

parsley ['pɑrs li] *n.* an herb used in cooking to add flavor to food or as a decoration. (No plural. Number is expressed with *sprig(s) of parsley*.)

part ['pɑrt] **1.** *n.* one piece of the whole; one section of the entire amount. **2.** *n.* one of a set of equal divisions. **3.** *n.* an actor's role in a play or movie. **4.** *n.* the line between two sections of hair on the head, established when combing it. **5.** *tv.* to make a pathway or an opening through a group of people or things. **6.** *tv.* to separate

one's hair along a line, especially when combing it into two sides. **7.** *iv.* to divide or separate, making an opening.
→ TAKE SOMEONE'S PART

part and parcel an essential part; something that is unavoidably included as part of something else.

part of speech ['pɑrt əv 'spitʃ] *n.* one of the classes or divisions of words that reflect grammatical usage, such as NOUN, VERB, ADJECTIVE, etc.

part someone's **hair** to come very close to someone.

partial to someone or something favoring or preferring someone or something.

participate (in something) [pɑr 'tɪs ə pet…] to be one of a group of people or things doing or involved in something.

participation [pɑr tɪs ə 'pe ʃən] *n.* joining in and doing something with other people. (No plural.)

participle ['pɑrt ə sɪp əl] *n.* either the *present participle* (the -*ing* form) or the *past participle*.

particle ['pɑrt ɪ kəl] **1.** *n.* a small piece of something. **2.** *n.* a kind of short, basic word or a part of a word—such as a conjunction, article, or preposition—that affects the meaning of another word. **3.** *n.* a basic unit of matter, such as a proton, neutron, or electron.

particular [pɑr 'tɪk jə lɚ] **1.** *adj.* specific; distinct [from others]. (Adv: *particularly.*) **2.** *adj.* unusual; noticeable; worth noticing. (Adv: *particularly.*) **3.** *adj.* hard to please. (Adv: *particularly.*)

the **particulars of** something specific details about something.

partner ['pɑrt nɚ] **1.** *n.* someone with whom one shares a business; one of the owners of a business. **2.** *n.* someone who shares an activity with someone else.

part-time ['pɑrt 'taɪm] **1.** *adj.* for only part of the time and not full-time. **2.** *adv.* [working] only part of the workweek; not as full-time.

party ['pɑr ti] **1.** *n.* a social gathering of people; a gathering of people who are having fun. **2.** *n.* a group of people who are together for a specific reason. **3.** *n.* a group of people united with a common goal or with common ideas, especially in politics. **4.** *n.* a person. **5.** the *adj.* use of ① or ③. **6.** *iv.* to celebrate; to have fun with other people. (Informal.)
→ LIFE OF THE PARTY
→ the RESPONSIBLE PARTY

the **party line** the official ideas and attitudes that are adopted by the leaders of a particular group and that the other members are expected to accept.

The **party's over.** a phrase said when a happy or fortunate time has come to an end. (Informal.)

pass ['pæs] **1.** *tv.* to reach someone or something and go beyond. **2.** *tv.* to succeed in a [school] course or examination; to have a medical examination where no problems are discovered. **3.** *tv.* to use up a period of time [doing something]; to occupy a period of time [doing something]. **4.** *tv.* to approve or

agree to something, such as a motion, law, or regulation, by means of a vote. **5.** *tv.* to hand something over to someone; to give something to someone. **6.** *tv.* to throw a ball to someone in a game. **7.** *iv.* to reach and go beyond. **8.** *iv.* to meet the requirements for successfully completing a [school] course. **9.** *iv.* [for a motion or law] to be approved by means of a vote. **10.** *iv.* [for time] to progress or proceed. **11.** *n.* a ticket or document showing that one is allowed to go somewhere. **12.** *n.* the transfer of a ball or something similar in various sports. **13.** *n.* a narrow road or pathway, especially through mountains.
→ COME TO PASS
→ LET SOMETHING PASS
→ MENTION SOMETHING IN PASSING
→ SHIPS THAT PASS IN THE NIGHT

pass away to die. (Euphemistic.)

pass on to die. (Euphemistic.)

pass on (to someone or something**)** to leave the person or thing being dealt with and move on to another person or thing.

pass out to faint; to become unconscious.

pass over (someone or something**)** **1.** to skip over someone or something; to fail to select someone or something. **2.** to pass above someone or something.

pass someone or something **up** **1.** to fail to select someone or something. **2.** to travel past someone or something.

pass something **along (to** someone**) 1.** to give or hand

something to someone. **2.** to relay some information to someone.

pass something **back (to** someone**)** to return something by hand to someone.

pass something **down (to** someone**)** AND **pass** something **on (to** someone**) 1.** to send something down a line of people to someone. (Each person hands it to the next.) **2.** to will something to someone.

pass something **on (to** someone**)** Go to PASS SOMETHING DOWN (TO SOMEONE).

pass something **out (to** someone**)** to distribute something to someone.

pass something **over (to** someone**)** to send something to someone farther down in a line of people. (Each person hands it to the next.)

pass the buck to pass the blame for something to someone else; to give the responsibility for something to someone else.

pass the hat to attempt to collect money for some charitable project.

passable [ˈpæs ə bəl] **1.** *adj.* able to be crossed or passed through; able to be traveled over. **2.** *adj.* [a motion or proposition] likely to get enough votes to pass. **3.** *adj.* only adequate; fair; okay. (Adv: *passably.*)

passage [ˈpæs ɪdʒ] **1.** *n.* a path or hallway. **2.** *n.* the progress or movement of time. (No plural.) **3.** *n.* the approval of a law or motion, usually by a vote. (No plural.) **4.** *n.* a short section of a piece of music, a speech, or a written work.

passbook ['pæs bʊk] *n.* a book for keeping track of one's savings account in a bank.

passenger ['pæs ən dʒɚ] *n.* someone who is riding in a vehicle but is not driving it.

passion ['pæʃ ən] **1.** *n.* strong romantic and sexual feeling. (Plural only for types and instances.) **2.** *n.* a very strong interest in something.

passive ['pæs ɪv] **1.** *adj.* not resisting; not active; letting others take charge or control a situation. (The opposite of ACTIVE. Adv: *passively*.) **2.** *adj.* of or about a grammatical state where the verb acts on the subject of the sentence. (The opposite of ACTIVE. Adv: *passively*.) **3.** *n.* a verb phrase that is ②.

passport ['pæs pɔrt] *n.* a document shaped like a small book, showing what country one is a citizen of. (It is needed to enter certain countries.)

a **passport to** something something that allows something good to happen; something that allows entrance to something else.

password ['pæs wɚd] *n.* a secret word, phrase, or set of symbols that allows someone access to something.

past ['pæst] **1.** *n.* a time that has gone by; things that have happened; history. (No plural.) **2.** *adj.* most recent; occurring in the time just before this time. **3.** *adj.* occurring or completed at some previous time. **4.** the *adj.* use of ①.

5. *adv.* by; toward or alongside someone or something and then beyond. **6.** *prep.* farther [in space, time, ability, or quality] than someone or something; beyond [in space, time, ability, or quality] someone or something.
→ BRUSH PAST SOMEONE OR SOMETHING
→ IN TIMES PAST
→ SKIP PAST SOMEONE OR SOMETHING

past tense ['pæst 'tɛns] *n.* the tense of a verb or AUXILIARY VERB that indicates an event or a state that has existed at a previous time.

pasta ['pɑs tə] *n.* a food prepared by mixing flour, water, and sometimes egg to make a dough or paste, and then shaping it into different forms; noodles. (Plural only for types and instances.)

paste ['pest] **1.** *n.* a soft mixture that is easily spread. (Plural only for types and instances.) **2.** *n.* a soft mixture that causes objects to stick together. (Plural only for types and instances.) **3.** *tv.* to cause something to stick to something else with ②.

paste something **up 1.** to repair something with paste. **2.** to assemble a complicated page of material by pasting the parts together.

pastime ['pæs tɑɪm] *n.* an activity that one enjoys; an enjoyable activity that is done to pass the time.

pastor ['pæs tɚ] *n.* a minister in a Christian church.

pastry ['pe stri] **1.** *n.* rich dough that is made with flour and butter or fat and is baked. (Plural only for types and instances.) **2.** *n.* baked foods, typically sweet, usually made with ①. (Plural only for types and instances. Number is expressed with *piece(s) of pastry*.) **3.** *n.* a piece or item of ②; a sweet roll, small cake, or other sweetened, baked food, often with fruit or with a sweet coating or filling.

pasture ['pæs tʃɚ] *n.* a field of grass, especially one where animals eat.
→ PUT SOMEONE OR SOMETHING OUT TO PASTURE

pat ['pæt] **1.** *n.* a gentle tap, especially with the palm of one's hand. **2.** *tv.* to touch or tap someone or something gently a few times, especially with the palm of the hand. **3.** *adj.* perfectly, as if rehearsed or from memory. (Adv: *patly*.)
→ HAVE SOMETHING DOWN PAT

patch ['pætʃ] **1.** *n.* a piece of cloth or other material used to repair a hole or a tear or to cover something. **2.** *n.* a small area of land. **3.** *n.* a small area on a surface that is different from the area around it.

patch something **together (with something)** to use something to repair something hastily or temporarily.

patch something **up** to repair something in a hurry; to make something temporarily serviceable again.

patent ['pæt nt] **1.** *n.* the exclusive right, registered with the government, to benefit from the ownership of a process or invention. **2.** *tv.* to seek and gain ① on something.

path ['pæθ] **1.** *n., irreg.* a track or trail along the earth. (Plural: ['pæðz] or ['pæθs].) **2.** *n., irreg.* the route someone or something takes to achieve a result. (Figurative on ①.)
→ BEAT A PATH TO SOMEONE'S DOOR
→ LEAD SOMEONE DOWN THE GARDEN PATH

the **path of least resistance** See the LINE OF LEAST RESISTANCE.

pathway ['pæθ we] *n.* a PATH ① or ②.

patience ['pe ʃəns] *n.* the quality of being patient and not becoming anxious or annoyed. (No plural.)
→ RUN OUT OF PATIENCE
→ TRY SOMEONE'S PATIENCE

patient ['pe ʃənt] **1.** *adj.* able to wait for something to happen without complaining or becoming anxious or annoyed. (Adv: *patiently*.) **2.** *n.* someone who is getting medical help from a doctor, nurse, or hospital.

patio ['pæt i o] *n.* a paved surface connected to one's house where one can relax, gather with others, barbecue food, etc. (From Spanish. Plural ends in -s.)

patrol [pə 'trol] **1.** *tv.* to watch over an area by walking or driving around. **2.** *iv.* to watch over [an area] by walking or driving around. **3.** *n.* people who watch over an area as in ①.
→ ON PATROL
→ (OUT) ON PATROL

patronize ['pe trə naɪz] **1.** *tv.* to be a regular customer of a store, restaurant, hotel, or other business. **2.** *tv.* to act as if one is superior to someone else.

patter ['pæt ɚ] **1.** *n.* a series of quick tapping sounds. (No plural.) **2.** *iv.* [for falling rain] to make quick tapping sounds as it strikes something.

pattern ['pæt ɚn] **1.** *n.* a design; an arrangement of shapes and colors, especially one that is repeated. **2.** *n.* a repeated element in a series of events. **3.** *n.* a printed or drawn outline of the parts of a garment or something that is to be built.

patty ['pæt i] *n.* a thin, flat disk of ground or mashed food, especially one formed of ground meat.

pause ['pɔz] **1.** *n.* a brief delay; a moment in which someone or something stops talking, moving, or working. **2.** *iv.* to stop for a moment; to stop moving or talking for a moment.

pave ['pev] *tv.* to build or cover a road, street, driveway, highway, etc., with cement, concrete, or some other hard surface.

pavement ['pev mənt] *n.* a flat surface of concrete, cement, or some other hard material covering an area, especially covering a street or sidewalk. (No plural.)
→ POUND THE PAVEMENT

paw ['pɔ] **1.** *n.* the foot of a clawed animal. **2.** *tv.* to handle someone or something with hands or ①.

pay ['pe] **1.** *tv., irreg.* to give money (to someone) in exchange for a product or a service or to settle a debt. (E.g., to *pay twelve dollars.* Past tense and past participle: PAID.) **2.** *tv., irreg.* to give someone an amount of money in exchange for a product or service or to settle a debt. (E.g., to *pay someone.*)

3. *tv., irreg.* to settle a bill or a debt. **4.** *tv., irreg.* [for something] to yield a certain amount of money or a certain benefit. **5.** *n.* wages; salary; the amount of money that one earns from a job. (No plural. Treated as singular.) **6.** *adj.* requiring money in order to be used.
→ ROB PETER TO PAY PAUL
→ THERE WILL BE THE DEVIL TO PAY.

pay a call on someone to visit someone.

pay a visit to someone or something Go to PAY (SOMEONE OR SOMETHING) A VISIT.

pay an arm and a leg (for something**)** AND **pay through the nose (for** something**)** to pay too much money for something.

pay (for something**)** to transfer money in exchange for a product or service.

pay for something to be punished for something.

pay homage to someone to praise, respect, and honor someone.

pay off to yield profits; to result in benefits.

pay one's **debt (to society)** to serve a sentence for a crime, usually in prison.

pay one's **dues** to have earned one's right to something through hard work or suffering.

pay one's **last respects** to attend the wake or funeral of someone; to approach the coffin containing someone in a final act of respect.

pay someone back 1. to return money that was borrowed from a person. **2.** to get even with someone [for doing something]. (Figurative.)

pay (someone or something**) a visit** AND **pay a visit to** someone or something to visit someone or something.

pay someone **respect** to honor someone; to have and show respect for someone.

pay something **down 1.** to make a deposit of money on a purchase. **2.** to reduce a bill by paying part of it, usually periodically.

pay something **in(to** something**)** to pay an amount of money into an account.

pay something **off** to pay the total amount of a bill; to settle an account by paying the total sum.

pay something **out** to unravel or unwind wire or rope as it is needed.

pay something **out (for** someone or something**)** to disburse money for something or something.

pay something **out (to** someone**)** to pay money to someone.

pay something **up** to pay all of whatever is due; to complete all the payments on something.

pay through the nose (for something**)** Go to PAY AN ARM AND A LEG (FOR SOMETHING).

pay to do something to be beneficial to do something; to be profitable.

payday ['pe de] *n.* the day on which a company pays its workers.

payment ['pe mənt] **1.** *n.* transferring money [to someone]. (Plural only for types and instances.) **2.** *n.*

an amount of money paid or to be paid; something that is paid [to someone or something].

payroll ['pe rol] *n.* the list of a company's employees and their salaries.

pea ['pi] **1.** *n.* a small, round, green vegetable that grows in a pod on a vinelike plant. **2.** *n.* the plant that ① grows on. (No singular in this sense. Number is expressed with *pea plant(s)*.)
→ (AS) THICK AS PEA SOUP

peace ['pis] **1.** *n.* a condition where there is no war or fighting; a time when there is order and harmony. (No plural.) **2.** *n.* silence; freedom from anxiety. (No plural.)
→ AT PEACE
→ HOLD ONE'S PEACE
→ LEAVE SOMEONE IN PEACE
→ REST IN PEACE

peaceful ['pis fʊl] **1.** *adj.* without war or fighting; not at war; orderly. (Adv: *peacefully.*) **2.** *adj.* happy and calm; free from anxiety. (Adv: *peacefully.*)

peach ['pitʃ] **1.** *n.* a soft, sweet, juicy, round fruit with a fuzzy skin, yellow-orange pulp, and a large pit in the middle. **2.** *adj.* made with ①; tasting like ①.

peacock ['pi kɑk] **1.** *n.* a large male peafowl having a large, beautifully colored tail that fans out. **2.** *n.* any peafowl.
→ (AS) PROUD AS A PEACOCK

peafowl ['pi faʊl] *n., irreg.* a large bird from Southeast Asia, the males of which have large, showy tails. (Plural: *peafowl* or *peafowls.*)

peahen ['pi hɛn] *n.* a female peafowl.

peak ['pik] **1.** *n.* the top of something, especially a mountain; the highest point of something. **2.** *n.* the maximum amount of effort or accomplishment. **3.** *iv.* to form or rise to ①. **4.** *iv.* to reach ②.

peal ['pil] **1.** *n.* the [loud], ringing sound that bells make. **2.** *n.* a long, loud sound, such as with laughter. **3.** *iv.* to ring loudly; to sound loudly.

peal out [for bells or voices] to sound forth musically.

peanut ['pi nət] **1.** *n.* a plant with seed pods that grow underground. **2.** *n.* the nutmeat of ①; the nutmeat and shell of ①.

peanut butter ['pi nət bət ɚ] **1.** *n.* an edible paste made from crushed peanuts. (No plural.) **2.** *adj.* made with ①. (Hyphenated.)

pear ['per] *n.* a yellow, brown, or green fruit that is rounded at the bottom and narrower toward the top.

pearl ['pɚl] *n.* a hard, white, round substance formed inside an oyster, usually used in jewelry.
→ CAST (ONE'S) PEARLS BEFORE SWINE

pebble ['pɛb əl] *n.* a small stone.

pecan [pɪ 'kɑn] **1.** *n.* a tall tree native to the southern United States and Mexico. **2.** *n.* the edible part of ①; the nutmeat and shell of ①. **3.** *n.* the wood of ①. (Plural only for types and instances.) **4.** *adj.* made with ②. **5.** *adj.* made from ③.

pedal ['pɛd l] **1.** *n.* a device that controls something and is operated with the feet. **2.** *tv.* to ride a

bicycle. **3.** *iv.* to ride [a bicycle] somewhere.

pedestal ['pɛd ə stəl] *n.* a base that supports a statue, vase, column, etc.

peek ['pik] **1.** *n.* a quick, sly look; a quick look at something that one is not supposed to look at. **2.** *iv.* to look quickly at something that one is not supposed to look at.

peek in (on someone or something**)** to glance quickly into a place to see someone or something.

peel ['pil] **1.** *n.* the outer skin of certain fruits and vegetables. (No plural. See also PEELING.) **2.** *tv.* to remove ①. **3.** *tv.* to remove an outer layer from something. (Figurative on ②.) **4.** *iv.* [for an outer layer] to come off.

peel something **off from** something Go to PEEL SOMETHING OFF ((OF) SOMETHING).

peel something **off ((of)** something**)** AND **peel** something **off from** something to remove the outside surface layer from something.

peeling ['pi lɪŋ] *n.* a part of something, especially fruits and vegetables, that has been peeled off. (Often plural.)

peep ['pip] **1.** *n.* a high noise, such as that made by a baby chicken or other birds. **2.** *iv.* to have a quick look at something, especially in secret; a peek. **3.** *iv.* to make a noise, as with ①.
→ HAVE A PEEP
→ TAKE A PEEP

peer in(to something) to stare into something; to look deep into something.

peer out at someone or something to stare out at someone or something.

peeve ['piv] *n.* something that irritates or annoys someone.
→ ONE'S PET PEEVE

peg ['pɛg] **1.** *n.* a thick wooden or plastic pin used to hold objects together. **2.** *tv.* to attach something to something with ①.
→ HAVE SOMEONE PEGGED AS SOMETHING
→ A SQUARE PEG IN A ROUND HOLE

peg someone **as** something AND **have** someone **pegged as** something to think of someone in a certain way.

pelican ['pɛl ɪ kən] *n.* a bird that lives on or near the water and that has a bill with a large scoop on the lower part.

pellet ['pɛl ɪt] *n.* a hard, small ball of something, such as ice, wax, dirt, or metal.

pelt down (on someone or something) [for something] to fall down on someone or something.

pen ['pɛn] **1.** *n.* a thin writing instrument that uses ink. **2.** *n.* a confined area where certain animals are kept. **3.** *tv.* to write something, usually with ①.

pen someone or something **in (**someplace) to confine someone or some creature in a pen.

pen someone or something **up** to confine someone or something to a pen.

penalty ['pɛn əl ti] *n.* a punishment for breaking a rule or law.

pencil ['pɛn səl] **1.** *n.* a thin writing instrument with a pointed core made of a soft black material. **2.** *tv.* to write something with ①.
→ IN PENCIL

pencil sharpener ['pɛn səl 'ʃɑr pə nɚ] *n.* a machine or device that sharpens things, usually pencils.

pencil someone or something **in** to write something or someone's name on a list with a pencil. (Implies that the writing is not final.)

penny ['pɛn i] *n.* a cent; $1/100$ of a dollar in the United States and various other nations.
→ COST A PRETTY PENNY

pension ['pɛn ʃən] *n.* money that is paid to a former employee, from retirement until death, or some other period of time, to replace a salary.

penthouse ['pɛnt haʊs] *n., irreg.* a special apartment on the top floor of a building. (Plural: [...haʊ zəz].)

people ['pip əl] **1.** *n.* persons. (No plural. Treated as a plural. Used as a plural of PERSON.) **2.** *n.* a specific group of ①; a race or ethnic group of ①. (Singular or plural with the same meaning.)
→ NARROW SOMETHING DOWN (TO PEOPLE OR THINGS)
→ SPLIT PEOPLE UP

pep ['pɛp] *n.* energy; vigor. (No plural.)

pepper ['pɛp ɚ] **1.** *n.* a vegetable, often green or red, that is mostly hollow and often very hot and spicy. **2.** *n.* the dried berries of various plants, usually ground, used to season food. (Usually black in the United States and white in Europe. Plural only for types and instances.) **3.** *tv.* to sprinkle ② on food as a seasoning. **4.** *tv.* [for many tiny things] to strike something lightly.

peppy ['pɛp i] *adj.* full of energy; active; excited. (Adv: *peppily.* Comp: *peppier;* sup: *peppiest.*)

per head Go to a HEAD.

perceive [pɚ 'siv] *tv.* to be aware of someone or something with one's mind; to be aware of someone or something through one's senses.

percent [pɚ 'sɛnt] *n.* a one-hundredth part. (No plural. Usually expressed with a number ranging from 0 through 100. Also expressed as (%).)

percentage [pɚ 'sɛn tɪdʒ] *n.* a part that is less than the whole amount.

perch ['pɚtʃ] **1.** *n.* a branch or rod that a bird grasps with its feet when it is at rest. **2.** *n.* a place to sit that is high off the floor or ground; a high ledge. (Figurative on ①.) **3.** *n., irreg.* any one of several species of edible fish. (Plural: *perch,* except when referring to a number of species.) **4.** *iv.* to sit on top of something; to stand on top of something, as does a bird.

perfect 1. ['pɚ fɪkt] *adj.* being the best; completely correct; without flaws. (Adv: *perfectly.*) **2.** ['pɚ fɪkt] *adj.* exactly suitable; exactly what is needed. (Adv: *perfectly.*) **3.** ['pɚ fɪkt] *adj.* complete; total. (Adv: *perfectly.*) **4.** ['pɚ fɪkt] *n.* a grammatical construction showing a completed action or condition; a form of the verb that shows

that something was completed, is completed, or will be completed. (In English, it consists of the past participle of the verb that follows a form of HAVE ⑤. No plural.) **5.** [pɚ 'fɛkt] *tv.* to make something without flaws as in ①.

perfection [pɚ 'fɛk ʃən] **1.** *n.* the condition of being perfect. (No plural.) **2.** *n.* becoming perfect; making something perfect. (No plural.)
→ COOK SOMETHING TO PERFECTION

perform [pɚ 'form] **1.** *tv.* to do something; to do an action. **2.** *tv.* to present a play, sing a song, play a piece of music, do a dance, etc., for an audience. **3.** *iv.* to act, sing, dance, or play music, especially in front of people. **4.** *iv.* to function; to do what is expected or has been assigned.

performance [pɚ 'for məns] **1.** *n.* a presentation of a play, a piece of music, a song, a dance, etc. **2.** *n.* the quality of performing or functioning; how well someone or something performs. (Plural only for types and instances.)

performer [pɚ 'for mɚ] *n.* someone who performs, such as an actor, a singer, a musician, a dancer.

perfume 1. ['pɚ fjum, pɚ 'fjum] *n.* a mixture of pleasant-smelling natural or artificial oils and alcohol that is put on people's skin. (Plural only for types and instances.) **2.** [pɚ 'fjum] *tv.* to place a pleasant-smelling substance on someone; to add a pleasant-smelling substance to the air in a room.

perhaps [pɚ 'hæps] *adv.* maybe; possibly; maybe yes, maybe no.

period ['pɪr i əd] **1.** *n.* a punctuation mark (.) used at the end of a sentence or at the end of an abbreviation. **2.** *n.* a certain length of time, including certain times in history. **3.** *n.* a section or part of certain games, such as basketball. **4.** *n.* a division of the school day. **5.** *n.* the time during the month when a woman menstruates. (Short for MENSTRUAL PERIOD.) **6.** *adj.* [of art, architecture, crafts, or literature] having to do with a certain time in history.
→ MENSTRUAL PERIOD

perish ['per ɪʃ] **1.** *iv.* to die. **2.** *iv.* [for something] to go away or fade away.

Perish the thought. Do not even consider thinking of something. (Literary.)

perjury ['pɚ dʒə ri] *n.* lying in court after one has taken an oath promising not to lie. (No plural.)

perk up to be invigorated; to become more active.

permanent ['pɚ mə nənt] **1.** *adj.* intended or designed to last forever or for a long time; not temporary. (Adv: *permanently.*) **2.** *n.* a type of hair treatment where the hair is caused to stay in a particular arrangement for a long time. (From *permanent wave.*)

permission [pɚ 'mɪ ʃən] *n.* consent; agreement that something may be done. (No plural.)

permit 1. ['pɚ mɪt] *n.* an official document that allows someone to do something. **2.** [pɚ 'mɪt] *tv.* to allow someone to do something; to let someone do something.
→ WEATHER PERMITTING

permit someone **out (of** something**)** to allow someone to go out of something or someplace.

persist [pɚ 'sɪst] **1.** *iv.* to continue to do something; not to give up, even if the task is difficult or if one faces opposition. **2.** *iv.* to continue to exist.

persist in doing something to continue doing something.

persist with something to continue the state of something; to extend an action or state.

person ['pɚ sən] **1.** *n.* a human being; a man, a woman, a boy, or a girl. (PEOPLE is sometimes used as the plural.) **2.** *n.* a grammar term, used to show the relationship of the speaker or writer to the receiver of the message.
→ EVERY OTHER PERSON OR THING
→ FEEL LIKE A NEW PERSON
→ IN PERSON
→ ON ONE'S PERSON

personal ['pɚ sən əl] **1.** *adj.* of or about the private affairs of a particular person; belonging to or used by a particular person. (Adv: *personally.*) **2.** *adj.* done by a certain person, instead of by someone else. (Adv: *personally.*)
→ TAKE SOMETHING PERSONALLY

personality [pɚ sə 'næl ə ti] **1.** *n.* aspects of one's thinking and behavior that make one different from everyone else. **2.** *n.* someone who is well known; a famous person.

personnel [pɚ sə 'nɛl] *n.* the people who work for a company or organization. (No plural.)

perspective on something a way of looking at a situation and determining what is important.

perspire [pɚ 'spaɪɚ] *iv.* to sweat.

persuade [pɚ 'swed] *tv.* to use argument or discussion to cause someone to do or think something.

persuasion [pɚ 'swe ʒən] *n.* efforts to persuade someone of something. (No plural.)
→ BE OF THE PERSUASION THAT SOMETHING IS SO

pertain to someone or something [pɚ 'ten…] to have to do with someone or something; to be relevant to someone or something.

pesky ['pɛs ki] *adj.* being a PEST ① or ②; irritating; annoying; troublesome. (Adv: *peskily.* Comp: *peskier;* sup: *peskiest.*)

pest ['pɛst] **1.** *n.* any animal or insect that destroys crops, spreads disease, or enters people's homes. **2.** *n.* someone or something that causes trouble; someone or something that is a nuisance.

pester ['pɛs tɚ] *tv.* to bother someone; to annoy someone.

pet ['pɛt] **1.** *n.* an animal that is kept in one's home or yard as a companion. **2.** *adj.* [of an animal] kept as ①. (Prenominal only.) **3.** *adj.* special; particular; favorite. (Prenominal only.) **4.** *tv.* to stroke or pat someone or some creature.
→ BE THE TEACHER'S PET
→ HOUSE PET
→ ONE'S PET HATE
→ ONE'S PET PEEVE

petal ['pɛt əl] *n.* one of the colored sections of the blossom of a flower.

petite [pə 'tit] **1.** *adj.* [of a woman] small; [of a woman] short. (From French. Adv: *petitely.*) **2.** *adj.* [of a clothing size or range of sizes] fitting women who are ①.

petition [pə 'tɪ ʃən] **1.** *n.* a document signed by many people who are demanding something from someone. **2.** *tv.* to request something formally of a government or of an authority, often through the use of ①. (The object can be a clause with THAT ⑦.)

petroleum [pə 'tro li əm] *n.* oil that is pumped from under the ground, used to make gasoline and other substances. (No plural.)

phantom ['fæn təm] **1.** *n.* a ghost; an image or memory that is "seen" by the mind in a dream or in a vision, but is not real. **2.** *adj.* like a ghost; unreal; apparent, but not real.

phase ['fez] **1.** *n.* a stage in the development of someone or something; a stage in a sequence of events. **2.** *n.* any of the stages of the appearance of the moon as seen from earth.

philosophy [fɪ 'lɑs ə fi] **1.** *n.* the science and study of the meaning of truth, knowledge, reality, and existence. (No plural.) **2.** *n.* the way one looks at life; the principles one uses to live one's life. (Plural only for types and instances.)

phobia ['fob i ə] *n.* an unreasonable fear; a strong dread. (Also in combinations, such as *claustrophobia, hydrophobia.*)

phone ['fon] **1.** *n.* a TELEPHONE. **2.** *tv.* to call someone by ①; to TELEPHONE someone.

phone call ['fon kɔl] *n.* a message or a conversation using the telephone. (Shortened from TELEPHONE CALL. Can be shortened to CALL.)

photo ['fo to] *n.* a photograph; a snapshot; a picture made by a camera.

photograph ['fo tə græf] **1.** *n.* a picture made by a camera; a photo; a snapshot. (Can be shortened to PHOTO.) **2.** *tv.* to take a picture, with a camera, of someone or something.

photographer [fə 'tɑ grə fɚ] *n.* someone who takes pictures with a camera, especially for a living.

photography [fə 'tɑ grə fi] *n.* the science, study, art, or act of taking a picture with a camera. (No plural.)

phr. an abbreviation of PHRASE ① and ②.

phrase ['frez] **1.** *n.* a group of words that functions as a unit of grammar within a sentence. (Abbreviated *phr.* here.) **2.** *n.* an expression usually including several words. **3.** *n.* a series of notes that is a part of a piece of music. **4.** *tv.* to put communication into words. **5.** *tv.* to perform music, grouping into a series the notes that belong to ③.

physical ['fɪz ɪ kəl] **1.** *adj.* of or about the body; of the body. (Adv: *physically* [...ɪk li].) **2.** *adj.* of or about the laws of nature; of or

about the study of physics. **3.** *adj.* of or about real objects; of or about matter. (Adv: *physically* [...ɪk li].) **4.** *n.* a thorough examination by a doctor. (Short for PHYSICAL EXAMINATION.)

physical examination ['fɪz ɪ kəl ɪg zæm ə 'ne ʃən] *n.* an examination of someone's body and health by a doctor. (Can be shortened to PHYSICAL.)

physician [fɪ 'zɪ ʃən] *n.* a medical doctor.

physics ['fɪz ɪks] *n.* the science and study of the properties of and relationships between matter and energy. (Treated as singular.)

pianist ['pi ə nɪst] *n.* someone who plays the piano, especially a professional piano player.

piano [pi 'æ no] *n.* a large musical instrument in which small, soft hammers connected to a keyboard strike tuned metal strings. (Plural ends in -s.)

pick ['pɪk] **1.** *n.* a tool that is a heavy, pointed metal bar attached to a handle, used for breaking apart ice, rocks, and other objects. **2.** *n.* a choice; a selection. (Plural only for types and instances.) **3.** *tv.* to choose a particular person or thing. **4.** *tv.* to remove something from someplace, especially using one's fingers or a pointed tool. **5.** *tv.* to gather or harvest flowers, fruit, cotton, peas, beans, etc.
→ HAVE A BONE TO PICK (WITH SOMEONE)

pick a lock to open a lock without using a key.

pick and choose to choose very carefully from a number of possibilities; to be selective.

pick at something to eat something a little bit at a time, without interest.

the **pick of** something the best of the group.

pick someone or something **out (for** someone or something**)** to choose someone or something to serve as someone or something.

pick someone or something **out (of** something**) 1.** to lift or pull someone or something out of something. **2.** to select someone or something out of an offering of selections.

pick someone or something **up 1.** to grasp and raise someone or something; to lift someone or something. **2.** to collect someone or something; to stop at a place and gather, obtain, or secure someone or something. **3.** to acquire someone or something.

pick something **out** to select or choose something, such as an item of clothing.

pick up to increase, as with business, wind, activity, etc.

pick up (after someone or something**)** to tidy up after someone or a group.

pick up the tab to pay the bill.

pickle ['pɪk əl] **1.** n. a cucumber—whole, sliced, chopped, or in sections—that has been preserved in salt water or vinegar. **2.** tv. to preserve food, especially vegetables, in salt water or vinegar.

picnic ['pɪk nɪk] **1.** n. a meal prepared to be eaten informally outdoors. **2.** iv., irreg. to have ①. (Past tense and past participle: PICNICKED. Present participle: PICNICKING.) **3.** adj. used for ①.

picnicked ['pɪk nɪkt] past tense and past participle of PICNIC.

picnicking ['pɪk nɪk ɪŋ] present participle of PICNIC.

picture ['pɪk tʃɚ] **1.** n. a drawing, a painting, or a photograph; an image of someone or something. **2.** n. a movie; a MOTION PICTURE. **3.** n. the image on a television screen. **4.** tv. to think of someone or something; to make a mental image of someone or something; to imagine something. **5.** tv. to show someone or something in ①.
→ (AS) PRETTY AS A PICTURE
→ IN THE PICTURE OF (GOOD) HEALTH
→ MOTION PICTURE

the **picture of** something the perfect example of something; an exact image of something.

pie ['paɪ] **1.** n. a kind of food that has a crust of pastry or something similar and is filled with meat, fruit, or some sweet substance. (The crust can be on the bottom or on both the bottom and top. Plural only for types and instances.) **2.** n. a single, complete, round unit of ①.
→ (AS) EASY AS (APPLE) PIE
→ EAT HUMBLE PIE
→ HAVE ONE'S FINGER IN THE PIE
→ HAVE ONE'S FINGER IN TOO MANY PIES
→ A PIECE OF THE PIE

pie in the sky a future reward, especially one that is not likely to be granted.

piece ['pis] **1.** *n.* a part of something; a part broken off of or removed from something; an object that is put together with other objects to make something. **2.** *n.* an example of something, especially of an art or craft, such as music. **3.** *n.* [in games such as chess or checkers that are played on a special board] an object that is placed on the board and, typically, moved to different places on the board according to the rules of the particular game.
→ FALL TO PIECES
→ GIVE SOMEONE A PIECE OF ONE'S MIND
→ VILLAIN OF THE PIECE

a **piece of the pie** AND a **slice of the cake** a share of something.

piece something **together** to fit something together; to assemble the pieces of something, such as a puzzle or something puzzling, and make sense of it.

piecrust ['paɪ krəst] *n.* a piece of pastry found on the bottom and often the top of a pie.

pier ['pɪr] *n.* a dock; a structure like a bridge that extends into the water from the shore, supported by posts or columns.

pierce ['pɪrs] *tv.* to make a hole through someone or something; to cause something to go through something else.

a **piercing scream** a very loud and shrill scream.

pig ['pɪg] **1.** *n.* a farm animal with short legs and a curled tail, raised for food, especially bacon, ham, and pork. (Thought of as greedy and messy.) **2.** *n.* someone who eats a lot of food. (Figurative on

①.) **3.** *n.* someone who is dirty or messy. (Figurative on ①.)
→ GUINEA PIG
→ SERVE AS A GUINEA PIG

pigeon ['pɪdʒ ən] *n.* a bird, commonly found in cities, with short legs and a heavy body, whose head bobs as it walks.

pigment ['pɪg mənt] *n.* a substance that causes paint, skin, dye, or plant tissue to have a certain color. (Plural only for types and instances.)

pile ['paɪl] **1.** *n.* a mound, stack, or heap of something, such as clothing, leaves, dirt. **2.** *n.* a beam of wood or steel that is driven into the ground to support a building, bridge, or other structure. **3.** *tv.* to place or form things or matter into a shape like ①.

pile in(to something) to climb into something in a disorderly fashion.

pile off (something) to get down off something; to climb down off something.

pile on((to) someone or something) to make a heap of people on someone or something.

pile out (of something) to climb out of something, such as a car.

pile someone **in(to** something) to bunch people into something in a disorderly fashion.

pile something **up** to make something into a heap.

pile up 1. to gather or accumulate. **2.** [for a number of vehicles] to crash together.

pilgrim ['pɪl grɪm] **1.** *n.* someone who travels, especially to a holy place, as a religious act. **2.** *n.* one of the settlers of Plymouth Colony in 1620. (Capitalized.)

pill ['pɪl] *n.* a small, formed mass containing vitamins, medicine, or some other drug that is swallowed.

pillar ['pɪl ɚ] *n.* a column; a strong upright structure used to support something or as decoration.
→ FROM PILLAR TO POST

a **pillar of strength** AND a **pillar of support** someone or something that provides support as a pillar does.

a **pillar of support** Go to a PILLAR OF STRENGTH.

pillow ['pɪl o] *n.* a cloth bag filled with feathers or a similar soft material, typically used to support one's head while sleeping, or for decoration.

pillowcase ['pɪl o kes] *n.* a fabric cover for a pillow.

pilot ['paɪ lət] **1.** *n.* someone who flies a plane; someone who guides a boat along a channel. **2.** *tv.* to fly an airplane; to guide a boat through a channel. **3.** *adj.* experimental; serving as a test.

pilot someone or something **through** (something) to guide or steer someone or something through something, especially through a waterway.

pilot something **in(to** something) to steer or guide something into something. (Usually refers to steering a ship.)

pilot something **out (of** something) to steer or guide something out of something. (Usually refers to steering a ship.)

pimple ['pɪm pəl] *n.* a small, round infection on the skin.
→ GET GOOSE PIMPLES

pin ['pɪn] **1.** *n.* a thin, stiff, pointed wire occurring in a variety of forms, such as with a flat top, a plastic end, a safety cover on the end, etc. (The simple ① is also called a *straight pin*.) **2.** *n.* a piece of jewelry that is attached to clothing with a variety of ①. **3.** *tv.* to attach something to something else with some variety of ①. **4.** *tv.* to press someone or something against something.
→ ON PINS AND NEEDLES
→ SO QUIET YOU COULD HEAR A PIN DROP
→ SO STILL YOU COULD HEAR A PIN DROP

pin someone **down (on** something) AND **nail** someone **down (on** something) to demand and receive a firm answer from someone to some question.

pin something **up** to raise something and hold it up with pins.

pinch ['pɪntʃ] **1.** *n.* an act of squeezing a fold of skin, usually causing pain. **2.** *n.* a small amount of something, such as a spice, that can be held between one's first finger and one's thumb. **3.** *tv.* to squeeze or hold something, such as a fold of flesh, between two surfaces.
→ FEEL THE PINCH
→ IN A PINCH
→ TAKE SOMETHING WITH A PINCH OF SALT

pinch something **back** to pinch off a bit of the top of a plant so it will branch and grow more strongly.

pine [ˈpaɪn] **1.** *n.* a kind of tree that has long, thin, sharp needles for leaves. **2.** *n.* wood from ①. (Plural only for types and instances.) **3.** *adj.* made from ②; composed of ②.

pine for someone or something to suffer because one does not have or has lost someone or something.

pineapple [ˈpaɪn æp əl] **1.** *n.* a large, juicy tropical fruit that is yellow on the inside and has a very rough skin. **2.** *n.* the edible part of ①. (No plural.) **3.** *adj.* made from ②; containing or flavored with ②.

pink [ˈpɪŋk] **1.** *n.* the color of red mixed with white; a light, pale red. (Plural only for types and instances.) **2.** the *adj.* use of ①. (Comp: *pinker*; sup: *pinkest*.) → IN THE PINK (OF CONDITION)

pins and needles a tingling feeling in some part of one's body. (Compare this with ON PINS AND NEEDLES.)

pint [ˈpaɪnt] **1.** *n.* a unit of liquid measure, equal to half a quart or ⅛ of a gallon or 16 fluid ounces. **2.** *n.* a unit of dry measure, equal to half a quart or 1/64 of a bushel. **3.** the *adj.* use of ① or ②.

pioneer [paɪ ə ˈnɪr] **1.** *n.* someone who is one of the first of a particular group of people to settle a new area. (From the point of view of the particular group.) **2.** *n.* someone who is one of the first to investigate an area of science that has never been examined; someone who is one of the first people to do something, preparing the way for other people to do the same. **3.** *tv.* to prepare the way for other people to do something; to help develop something for other people.

pipe [ˈpaɪp] **1.** *n.* a hollow tube that is used to carry a fluid from one place to another. **2.** *n.* a tube connected to a small bowl, used to smoke tobacco.

pipe dream a wish or an idea that is impossible to achieve or carry out. (From the dreams or visions induced by the smoking of an opium pipe.)

pipe up (with something**)** to interject a comment; to interrupt with a comment.

piping hot [of food] extremely hot.

pique someone's **curiosity** AND **pique** someone's **interest** to arouse interest; to arouse curiosity.

pique someone's **interest** Go to PIQUE SOMEONE'S CURIOSITY.

pirate [ˈpaɪ rət] **1.** *n.* someone who robs ships at sea. **2.** *tv.* to steal or capture something, especially while at sea. **3.** *tv.* to take something; to use something when one does not have the right to use it. (Figurative on ②.) **4.** *tv.* to duplicate and sell copies of books, records, videos, and software without the permission of the original publisher. (Figurative on ②.)

piss [ˈpɪs] **1.** *iv.* to urinate. (Potentially offensive. The topic and the word are not heard in polite company. Use with caution.) **2.** *n.* urine. (Offensive as with ①.)

pissed off [ˈpɪst ˈɔf] *adj.* angry. (Not often heard in polite company, but its use is increasing.)

pistol ['pɪs təl] *n.* a small gun that can be held and shot with one hand.

piston ['pɪs tən] *n.* a solid cylinder that is moved up and down inside a tube by some force, such as that found in an engine.

pit ['pɪt] **1.** *n.* a large hole in the ground. **2.** *n.* a large, hard seed at the center of some kinds of fruit. **3.** *tv.* to remove ② from fruit.

pit someone or something **against** someone or something to place someone or something in competition with someone or something else.

pitch ['pɪtʃ] **1.** *tv.* to toss something toward someone or something. **2.** *tv.* [in baseball] to toss or throw a ball toward the batter. **3.** *tv.* to toss or throw someone or something. **4.** *iv.* [in baseball] to throw a baseball toward a batter. **5.** *iv.* [for a ship] to plunge up and down; [for the front of a ship] to rise and fall in rough water. **6.** *n.* [in baseball] the movement of the ball from the pitcher toward the batter or the throw that moves the ball toward the batter. **7.** *n.* slope; the amount that something is slanted. (Plural only for types and instances.) **8.** *n.* the measure of the highness or lowness of a sound. (Plural only for types and instances.) **9.** *n.* the standard number of vibrations each second that makes a certain tone; the standard musical sound for a given note. **10.** *n.* tar.

pitch a tent to erect a tent at a campsite.

pitch black very black; as black as pitch (tar).

pitch camp to set up or arrange a campsite.

pitch in (and help) to get busy and help with something.

pitch in (and help) (with something**)** to join in and help someone with something.

pitch someone **a curve** Go to THROW SOMEONE A CURVE.

pitch someone or something **out ((of)** something**)** to throw someone or something out of something or someplace.

pitch-dark very dark; as dark as pitch (tar).

pitcher ['pɪtʃ ɚ] **1.** *n.* the baseball player who pitches the baseball toward the other team's players who then may strike it with the bat. **2.** *n.* a tall container with a handle, used for serving liquids. **3.** *n.* the contents of ②.

pity ['pɪt i] **1.** *n.* a feeling of sorrow caused by seeing or learning about the suffering of other people; sympathy. (No plural.) **2.** *tv.* to be sorry for someone or something; to feel ① for someone or something.

pizza ['pit sə] *n.* a food made of a baked disk of dough covered with spicy tomato sauce, cheese, and perhaps other foods. (Plural only for types and instances.)

place ['ples] **1.** *n.* a position in space; a location; a certain area. **2.** *n.* a house or apartment; a location where one lives. **3.** *n.* a position in relation to other positions in a numbered series. **4.** *tv.* to put

something in a certain position; to put something on a certain surface. **5.** *tv.* to remember when and where one has met someone or something in the past.
→ BETWEEN A ROCK AND A HARD PLACE
→ FALL IN(TO) PLACE
→ FEEL OUT OF PLACE
→ IN THE RIGHT PLACE AT THE RIGHT TIME
→ IN THE WRONG PLACE AT THE WRONG TIME
→ NOT ONE'S PLACE
→ SOMEPLACE

place an order to submit an order.

place of business a place where business is done; a factory or office.

plague ['pleg] *n.* a disease that kills people and is quickly spread. (No plural. Treated as singular.)

plague someone **with** something ['pleg…] to annoy someone with repeated questions, problems, etc.

plaid ['plæd] **1.** *n.* a design of stripes that cross each other at right angles. **2.** the *adj.* use of ①.

plain ['plen] **1.** *n.* a flat area of land; a prairie. (Often plural with the same meaning, but not countable.) **2.** *adj.* obvious; easy to see or understand. (Adv: *plainly.* Comp: *plainer;* sup: *plainest.*) **3.** *adj.* simple; not complex; not decorated. (Adv: *plainly.* Comp: *plainer;* sup: *plainest.*) **4.** *adj.* not attractive; average looking. (Adv: *plainly.* Comp: *plainer;* sup: *plainest.*) **5.** *adv.* simply; clearly; obviously. (Colloquial.)
→ (AS) PLAIN AS DAY
→ (AS) PLAIN AS THE NOSE ON ONE'S FACE

plaintiff ['plen tɪf] *n.* someone who sues someone else; someone who brings a lawsuit against someone else; someone who charges a defendant with doing wrong.

plan ['plæn] **1.** *n.* the ideas for a future action or event; a detailed schedule for doing something. **2.** *n.* a program or structure that provides a benefit to workers. **3.** *tv.* to make ① for an event. **4.** *iv.* to arrange [something] in advance.

plan something **out** to make thorough plans for something.

plan to do something to make a plan for doing something in the future; to mean to do something.

plane ['plen] **1.** *n.* a flat surface. **2.** *n.* an airplane. **3.** *n.* a tool equipped with a blade that is scraped over wood to make it flat or smooth. **4.** *tv.* to make something flat or smooth by using ③.
→ JET PLANE

plane something **down** to smooth something down with a PLANE ③.

planet ['plæn ɪt] *n.* a huge sphere of matter that circles a single star in a permanent orbit.

plank ['plæŋk] **1.** *n.* a board; a long, thin, narrow, flat piece of wood. **2.** *n.* an issue or policy that a political party officially supports. (A figurative ① in the party PLATFORM ③.)

plans *n.* a set of drawings of a house or building before it is built, used to help someone build the building. (Treated as plural.)

plant ['plænt] **1.** *n.* a stationary living thing that makes its own food using sunlight and material from the soil or other substance that supports it. **2.** *n.* a factory. **3.** *tv.* to put a seed or a small ① in the ground so that it will grow; to place [the seeds or young ① of] a crop into the soil. **4.** *tv.* to place someone or something firmly in position. (Figurative on ③.)

plaster ['plæs tɚ] **1.** *n.* a mixture of lime, water, and sand, which hardens when it dries. (Plural only for types and instances.) **2.** *tv.* to apply ① to something.

plastic ['plæs tɪk] **1.** *n.* an artificial material, made from a variety of chemicals, that can be formed into different shapes. (Plural only for types and instances.) **2.** *adj.* made of ①. **3.** *adj.* [of something] easily molded or shaped. (Adv: *plastically* [...ɪk li].)

plate ['plet] **1.** *n.* an almost flat, round dish for holding food. **2.** *n.* a sheet of metal or glass. **3.** *n.* a metal plate that goes on the back of a vehicle showing the license number of the vehicle. (Short for LICENSE PLATE.) **4.** *tv.* to give one sort of metal a thin outer layer of a more valuable metal.
→ LICENSE PLATE

plateau [plæ 'to] **1.** *n.* a flat area of land that is raised up higher than the surrounding land. **2.** *iv.* [for a number or a measurement] to reach a higher level and then remain unchanged.
→ HIT A PLATEAU

platform ['plæt fɔrm] **1.** *n.* a flat structure that is higher than the area around it, especially one that people can occupy standing or sit-

ting. **2.** *n.* the flat surface next to a railroad track where people get on and off trains. **3.** *n.* a formal statement of the ideas and policies of a political party. (See also PLANK ②.)

platter ['plæt ɚ] **1.** *n.* a large plate used for serving food. **2.** *n.* the contents of ①.

play ['ple] **1.** *n.* fun; recreation; something that is done for fun or amusement. (No plural.) **2.** *n.* one movement or action in a game or sport. **3.** *n.* a piece of writing that is written as a series of lines that people say, for performance in a theater. **4.** *n.* a performance of ③. **5.** *iv.* [for a sound-making device] to operate or reproduce sounds that have been recorded. **6.** *iv.* to perform on the stage or in public; to perform. **7.** *iv.* [for a performance] to be performed; [for a movie] to be shown. **8.** *iv.* to take one's turn in a game; to lay down a card in a card game. **9.** *iv.* to perform [on a musical instrument as in ⑬]. **10.** *iv.* to have fun; to amuse oneself; to be active in a sport or game. **11.** *tv.* to perform a role in the theater or in a movie. **12.** *tv.* to take part in a certain game, sport, or activity; to participate in a certain game, sport, or activity. **13.** *tv.* to make music with a musical instrument; to perform a particular piece of music on an instrument. (E.g., to *play a song.*) **14.** *tv.* to perform on a musical instrument. (E.g., to *play a violin.*) **15.** *tv.* [for an electronic device] to process tapes, records, or CDs in a way that produces the sounds or pictures that have been recorded. **16.** *tv.* [for someone] to

cause an electronic device to produce sounds and pictures as in ⑮.
→ BE CHILD'S PLAY
→ FOUL PLAY

play a joke on someone to make a joke that tricks someone.

play a trick on someone to do a TRICK that affects someone.

play along (with someone or something) **1.** to play a musical instrument with someone or a group. **2.** to pretend to cooperate with someone or something in a joke.

play ball (with someone) to cooperate with someone.

play both ends (against the middle) to scheme in a way that pits two sides against each other for one's own gain.

play by ear Go to PLAY SOMETHING BY EAR.

play cat and mouse (with someone) to capture and release someone over and over.

play fast and loose (with someone or something) to act carelessly, thoughtlessly, and irresponsibly toward someone or something.

play ignorant to pretend to be ignorant [of something].

play innocent to pretend to be innocent and not concerned.

play it safe to be or act safe; to do something safely.

play one's **cards close to** one's **vest** Go to PLAY ONE'S CARDS CLOSE TO THE CHEST.

play one's **cards close to the chest** AND **play** one's **cards close to** one's **vest** [for some-

one] to work or negotiate in a careful and private manner.

play out to run out; to finish.

play second fiddle (to someone) to be in a subordinate position to someone.

play someone or something **up** to emphasize someone or something; to support or praise someone or something.

play something **back (to** someone) to play a recording to someone.

play something **by ear 1.** to be able to play a piece of music after just listening to it a few times, without looking at the notes. **2.** AND **play by ear** to play a musical instrument well, without formal training.

play something **through** to play all of something, such as a piece of music or a record.

play (the) devil's advocate to put forward arguments against, or objections to, a proposition, which one may actually agree with, purely to test the validity of the proposition.

play the field to date many different people rather than dating just one person.

play the fool to act in a silly manner in order to amuse other people.

play to the gallery to perform in a manner that will get the strong approval of the audience; to perform in a manner that will get the approval of the lower elements in the audience.

play up to someone to flatter someone; to try to gain influence with someone.

play (up)on something **1.** to make music on a musical instrument. **2.** to exploit something—including a word—for some purpose; to develop something for some purpose.

play with fire to take a big risk.

played out (Informal.) **1.** exhausted. **2.** no longer of interest or influence.

player ['ple ɚ] **1.** *n.* someone who plays a game or sport. **2.** *n.* someone who plays a particular musical instrument. **3.** *n.* something that plays a recording. (Compare this with RECORDER ③.)
→ CASSETTE PLAYER

playful ['ple ful] **1.** *adj.* liking to play; full of fun. (Adv: *playfully*.) **2.** *adj.* funny; humorous; not serious. (Adv: *playfully*.)

playground ['ple graʊnd] **1.** *n.* an outdoor place for children to play. **2.** the *adj.* use of ①.

plaything ['ple θɪŋ] *n.* a toy; something that is played with.

plea ['pli] **1.** *n.* a request; an appeal. **2.** *n.* a statement in court in which one declares that one is guilty or innocent.

plead ['plid] **1.** *tv., irreg.* to declare in court that one is guilty or not guilty before the trial actually begins. (Past tense and past participle: *pleaded* or PLED.) **2.** *tv., irreg.* to claim something as an excuse. (The object can be a clause with THAT ⑦. Past tense and past participle: *pleaded* or PLED.)

plead for something to beg for something; to ask for something.

pleasant ['plɛz ənt] **1.** *adj.* [of something] bringing or causing enjoyment and pleasure. (Adv: *pleasantly*.) **2.** *adj.* [of someone] friendly and nice. (Adv: *pleasantly*.)

please ['pliz] **1.** *adv.* a word used to make requests or commands more polite. **2.** *tv.* to cause someone to be happy or satisfied.
→ AIM TO PLEASE

please yourself AND **suit yourself** to do what one wishes. (Informal.)

pleasure ['plɛʒ ɚ] *n.* a feeling of happiness because of something that one likes; enjoyment; a pleasing feeling or emotion. (Plural only for types and instances.)

pled ['plɛd] a past tense and past participle of PLEAD.

pledge ['plɛdʒ] **1.** *n.* a promise; a vow; a statement that one will do something. **2.** *tv.* to promise something. (The object can be a clause with THAT ⑦.)

pledge to do something to vow or promise to do something.

plentiful ['plɛn tɪ ful] *adj.* having enough or more than enough; ample. (Adv: *plentifully*.)

plenty ['plɛn ti] **1.** *n.* a full supply; more than enough. (No plural.) **2.** *adj.* enough; almost too much. (Not prenominal.)
→ THERE ARE PLENTY OF OTHER FISH IN THE SEA.

plenty of something lots of something; an abundance of something; enough of something.

pliers ['plaɪ ɚz] *n.* a tool with rough jaws, used to grasp objects. (Usually treated as plural. Number is expressed with *pair(s) of pliers*. Also countable.)

plot ['plɑt] **1.** *n.* the story of a movie, book, opera, television show, play, etc. **2.** *n.* a secret plan to do something wrong or illegal. **3.** *n.* a small garden or part of a garden; a small area of land. **4.** *iv.* to plan in secret. **5.** *iv.* to make plans to do something, especially secretly. **6.** *tv.* to plan in secret to do something. **7.** *tv.* to determine the position of something on a map, chart, or graph.
→ BREW A PLOT

plot something **out** to map something out; to outline a plan for something.

The **plot thickens.** a phrase said when things are becoming more complicated or interesting.

plotter ['plɑt ɚ] *n.* a machine that marks points, lines, or curves on a graph.

plow ['plaʊ] **1.** *n.* a farm tool made of a heavy metal blade used to break up and turn over soil. **2.** *n.* a large, curved blade in front of a vehicle that is used to move snow off a road or path. **3.** *n.* a vehicle equipped with ②. **4.** *iv.* to use ①. **5.** *tv.* to cut into land, making rows for planting crops, with ①. **6.** *tv.* to clear a road or path of snow with ②.
→ PUT ONE'S HAND TO THE PLOW

plow something **back into** something to put something, such as a profit, back into an investment.

plow something **in** to work something into the soil by plowing.

plow something **under (something)** to push something under the surface of the soil or of water.

plow through something to work through something laboriously.

pluck ['plʌk] **1.** *tv.* to remove the feathers from a bird; to remove hairs from the body of a person or an animal. **2.** *tv.* to clean a bird of its feathers. **3.** *tv.* to pull something from someplace.

pluck something **off ((of) someone or something)** to pick something off someone or something.

pluck something **out (of something)** to snatch something out of something.

pluck up someone's **courage** to bolster someone's, including one's own, courage.

plug ['plʌg] **1.** *n.* a small device for closing a hole, drain, or other opening. **2.** *n.* the connector that is pushed into an electric receptacle. (Short for ELECTRIC PLUG.) **3.** *n.* a statement made while speaking on television or radio that encourages people to buy something or do something. **4.** *tv.* to mention a product and to encourage people to buy it.
→ ELECTRIC PLUG

plug away (at someone or something) to keep working at someone or something.

plug something **in(to something)** to connect something to something else, usually by connecting wires together with a plug and socket.

plug something **up** to fill up a hole; to block a hole or opening.

plum ['plʌm] **1.** *n.* a fruit with a smooth skin and a soft, sweet, juicy pulp with a large pit. **2.** *n.* a deep purple color. **3.** *adj.* deep purple in color.

plumber ['plʌmɚ] *n.* someone who is trained to install and repair sewer pipes, water pipes, and fixtures such as sinks, toilets, bathtubs, and drains.

plumbing ['plʌmɪŋ] **1.** *n.* the work that a plumber does. (No plural.) **2.** *n.* water pipes, sewer pipes, gas pipes, and related fixtures. (No plural.)

plume ['plum] **1.** *n.* a feather, especially a bright, colorful one. **2.** *n.* something that looks like a feather, especially a cloud of smoke or a jet of water.

plump ['plʌmp] *adj.* a little fat or swollen.

plump something **up** to pat or shake something like a pillow into a fuller shape.

plunge ['plʌndʒ] **1.** *n.* a dive; a jump into water. **2.** *iv.* to dive into a liquid.

plunge in(to something) to dive or rush into something; to immerse oneself in something.

plunge something **in(to** someone or something) to drive or stab something into someone or something.

plural ['plɚ əl] **1.** *n.* a form of a word that refers to more than one thing or person. **2.** the *adj.* use of ①.

plus ['plʌs] **1.** *prep.* in addition to someone or something; added to someone or something. (Symbolized by (+).) **2.** *conj.* and also. **3.** *adj.* above zero; [marking a number] greater than zero. (Symbolized as (+).) **4.** *n.* an advantage; an extra.

ply ['plaɪ] **1.** *n.* a layer of something. (Hyphenated after a number.) **2.** *tv.* to work doing one's job, especially at one's trade.

plywood ['plaɪ wʊd] *n.* a wooden panel made of several thin sheets of wood that are glued together. (No plural.)

pocket ['pak ɪt] **1.** *n.* a small cloth bag that is sewn into clothing and is used to hold things, such as a wallet or keys. **2.** *n.* a small amount of something that is separated from other amounts of it; an isolated amount of something. **3.** *adj.* small enough to fit in ①; meant to be put in ①. **4.** *tv.* to put something in one's ①. **5.** *tv.* to steal something by putting it in one's ①.
→ HAVE SOMEONE IN ONE'S POCKET
→ MONEY BURNS A HOLE IN SOMEONE'S POCKET.

pod ['pad] *n.* a long, soft, narrow shell that holds the seeds of certain plants, such as peas and beans.

poem ['po əm] *n.* a piece of writing in a form that sometimes rhymes and often has a rhythm, usually expressing feelings, emotions, or imagination.

poet ['po ɪt] *n.* someone who writes poetry.

poetic [po 'ɛt ɪk] **1.** *adj.* [of thoughts] expressed as a poem. (Adv: *poetically* [...ɪk li].) **2.** the *adj.* form of POETRY.

poetic justice the appropriate but chance receiving of rewards or punishments by those deserving them.

poetry ['po ə tri] **1.** *n.* a poem; poems; a collection of poems. (No plural. Treated as singular.) **2.** *n.* the art of writing poems. (No plural.)

point ['pɔɪnt] **1.** *n.* the sharp end of something. **2.** *n.* the main idea of something; the purpose of something. **3.** *n.* one idea, argument, or statement in a series of ideas, arguments, or statements. **4.** *n.* a certain position in space or moment in time; a certain degree or position of something. **5.** *n.* [in geometry] the place where two lines cross each other. **6.** *n.* a dot; a DECIMAL POINT. **7.** *n.* a feature, trait, or ability of someone or something. **8.** *n.* a unit of scoring in a game. **9.** *n.* a helpful hint; a piece of advice. **10.** *tv.* to aim someone at someone or something; to direct someone to someone or something. **11.** *iv.* to indicate the location of someone or something by directing one's finger toward the location. **12.** *iv.* to be facing in a certain direction.
→ CASE IN POINT
→ COME TO THE POINT
→ DECIMAL POINT
→ EXCLAMATION POINT
→ GET TO THE POINT
→ HAVE A LOW BOILING POINT
→ JUMPING-OFF POINT
→ MISS THE POINT
→ NO POINT IN DOING SOMETHING

point of view a way of thinking about something; [someone's] viewpoint; an attitude or expression of self-interest.

point someone or something **out** to identify someone or something in a group; to select someone or something from a group.

point the finger at someone to blame someone; to identify someone as the guilty person.

poised for something ready for something; in the right position and waiting for something.

poised to do something ready to do something; in the right position to do something.

poison ['pɔɪ zən] **1.** *n.* a substance that can injure or kill a living creature, especially if eaten, drunk, breathed in, or absorbed through the skin. (Plural only for types and instances.) **2.** *tv.* to kill or harm someone or something with ①. **3.** *tv.* to put ① in something, especially food, in order to kill or harm someone or something. **4.** *tv.* to have a harmful effect on someone or something; to corrupt someone or something. (Figurative on ②.)

poke ['pok] **1.** *n.* a push with one's finger, fist, or elbow, or with a blunt object. **2.** *tv.* to push someone or something with one's finger, fist, or elbow, or with a blunt object.

poke a hole in something AND **poke a hole through** something to make a hole by pushing something through something.

poke a hole through something
Go to POKE A HOLE IN SOMETHING.

poke fun (at someone**)** to make fun of someone; to ridicule someone.

poke one's **nose in(to** something**)** AND **stick** one's **nose in(to** something**)** to interfere with something; to be nosy about something.

poke out (of something**)** to stick out of something; to extend out of something.

poke something **in(to** something**)** to stick or cram something into something.

poker ['pok ɚ] **1.** *n.* a long, narrow metal rod that is used to move logs or coal in a fire. **2.** *n.* a card game where players win by having cards with the highest value. (No plural.)

polar ['po lɚ] *adj.* of or about the areas near the north or south pole.

pole ['pol] **1.** *n.* a long, thin, solid tube of wood, steel, plastic, or other material. **2.** *n.* one of the two places where the imaginary axis on which a planet spins meets the surface of the planet—at the north and south ends of the planet. **3.** *n.* either side of a magnet; either end of a magnet; one of the two strongest points of a magnet that either pulls or pushes metal objects.
→ BE POLES APART
→ NORTH POLE
→ SOUTH POLE

police [pə 'lis] **1.** *tv.* to patrol an area; to control, regulate, or protect an area. **2.** *tv.* to regulate or control people, their behavior, or their actions.

the **police** *n.* people who have the authority to maintain law and order by arresting people who break the law. (No plural. Treated as plural, but not countable. Number is expressed with POLICE OFFICER(S).)

police officer [pə 'lis ɔ fə sɚ] *n.* a member of a police department; a policeman; a policewoman.

policeman [pə 'lis mən] *n., irreg.* a police officer; a male member of a police force. (Plural: POLICEMEN or POLICE OFFICERS.)

policemen [pə 'lis mən] plural of POLICEMAN.

policewoman [pə 'lis wʊm ən] *n., irreg.* a female police officer; a female member of a police force. (Plural: POLICEWOMEN or POLICE OFFICERS.)

policewomen [pə 'lis wɪm ən] plural of POLICEWOMAN.

policy ['pɑl ə si] *n.* a plan of action used by management or government; a regulation.
→ INSURANCE POLICY

polish ['pɑl ɪʃ] **1.** *n.* a substance that is used to make something shiny. (Plural only for types and instances.) **2.** *tv.* to make a surface shiny or glossy, especially by rubbing it. **3.** *tv.* to improve something; to make something better or perfect; to refine something. (Figurative on ②.)

Polish ['po lɪʃ] *adj.* of or about Poland; describing a person born in Poland.

polish something **off** to eat, consume, exhaust, or complete all of something.

polish something **up** to rub something until it shines.

polite [pə 'laɪt] *adj.* courteous; having good behavior; having good manners; doing things in a helpful and kind way. (Adv: *politely.*)

political [pə 'lɪ tɪ kəl] *adj.* of or about politics, politicians, or government. (Adv: *politically* [...ɪk li].)

politician [pɑl ə 'tɪ ʃən] *n.* a person whose business is politics, especially someone holding or seeking a government office.

politics ['pɑl ə tɪks] **1.** *n.* the business or operation of government; the study of the management of government. (Treated as singular or plural, but not countable.) **2.** *n.* someone's beliefs about political issues. (Treated as singular or plural, but not countable.)

poll ['pol] **1.** *n.* a survey that determines the popular opinion about an issue. **2.** *tv.* to ask someone questions as part of a survey.

pollen ['pɑl ən] *n.* a yellow powder made by flowers that is part of the process of making seeds. (Plural only for types and instances.)

polls *n.* the places where people vote. (Treated as plural.)

pollute [pə 'lut] **1.** *tv.* to cause something to become dirty or impure. **2.** *iv.* to make something dirty or impure.

pompous ['pɑmp əs] *adj.* arrogant; too formal; too grand. (Adv: *pompously.*)

pond ['pɑnd] *n.* a small body of water; a body of water smaller than a lake.

→ A BIG FROG IN A SMALL POND

ponder ['pɑn dɚ] **1.** *iv.* to think carefully; to consider. **2.** *tv.* to think about something carefully; to consider something.

ponder (up)on something to think on something; to consider something.

ponderous ['pɑn dɚ əs] *adj.* slow and awkward, especially because of being large or heavy. (Adv: *ponderously.*)

pony ['pon i] *n.* a small horse.

ponytail ['pon i tel] *n.* a bunch of hair pulled toward the back of the head and tied.

poodle ['pud l] *n.* a kind of dog that has very curly fur.

pool ['pul] **1.** *n.* a puddle of water or other liquid. **2.** *n.* a game played with a number of hard balls on a felt-covered table having six pockets and raised sides. **3.** *tv.* to put money or things together for common use.
→ SWIMMING POOL

poor ['por] **1.** *adj.* not rich; having very little money; not owning many things. (Comp: *poorer*; sup: *poorest.*) **2.** *adj.* below a certain level of quality; inferior in operation or function. (Adv: *poorly.* Comp: *poorer*; sup: *poorest.*) **3.** *adj.* worthy of pity or sympathy.
→ (AS) POOR AS A CHURCH MOUSE
→ IN POOR TASTE

the **poor** *n.* people who are POOR ①. (No plural. Treated as plural, but not countable.)

pop ['pɑp] **1.** *n.* a quick, loud noise, like an explosion. **2.** *n.* father. (Informal. Also a term of address.

Capitalized when written as a proper noun.) **3.** *n.* popular music. (No plural.) **4.** *n.* SODA POP. (Informal. No plural.) **5.** *adj.* popular; well liked; favored. **6.** *iv.* to make a sound as in ①; [for something with air in it] to burst suddenly. **7.** *tv.* to cause something to make ①; to cause something with air in it to burst suddenly.
→ SODA POP

pop out (of something**)** to jump out of something; to burst out of something.

pop something **in(to** something**)** to fit, snap, or press something into place in something.

pop something **on((to)** something**)** to snap something onto something.

pop something **out (of** something**)** to release something from something so that it jumps or bursts out, possibly with a popping sound.

pop the question to ask someone to marry one.

pop up (someplace**)** to appear suddenly and unexpectedly someplace.

popcorn ['pɑp kɔrn] **1.** *n.* seeds of various kinds of corn that explode into a soft, white, fluffy mass when heated. (Plural only for types and instances.) **2.** *n.* exploded and puffed-up kernels of ① eaten as food. (No plural. Treated as singular.)

poplar ['pɑp lɚ] **1.** *n.* a kind of tall, thin tree that grows quickly. **2.** *n.* wood from ①. (Plural only for

types and instances.) **3.** *adj.* made from ②.

poppy ['pɑp i] *n.* a flowering herb with large red blossoms.

popular ['pɑp jə lɚ] *adj.* liked by many people; favored by many people; well liked. (Adv: *popularly.*)

populate ['pɑp jə let] *tv.* [for living creatures] to occupy an area. (Usually passive.)

population [pɑp jə 'le ʃən] **1.** *n.* the living creatures of one kind that live in a certain area. **2.** *n.* the number of people or creatures living in a certain place. (No plural.)

porch ['pɔrtʃ] *n.* a covered structure built in front of a house, usually at a doorway.

porcupine ['pɔr kjə pɑɪn] *n.* a large rodent covered with sharp needles or spines that it uses to defend itself.

pore ['pɔr] *n.* a tiny opening in the skin of plants and animals.

pore over something to study something closely; to look over something thoroughly.

pork ['pɔrk] *n.* the meat of a pig, eaten as food. (No plural.)

porpoise ['pɔr pəs] *n.* a mammal that lives in the sea, swimming in groups.

port ['pɔrt] **1.** *n.* a city on an ocean, sea, or lake that has a harbor where ships can be loaded and unloaded. **2.** *n.* a harbor. **3.** *adj.* on, at, or toward the left side of a ship or aircraft when one is facing the front of the ship or aircraft.

porter ['pɔr tɚ] *n.* someone who carries luggage for other people, especially at a hotel, airport, or train station.

portrait ['pɔr trɪt] *n.* a painting, especially of a person or a person's face.

pose ['poz] **1.** *n.* a certain way that someone sits or stands, especially when one is getting one's picture taken or painted. **2.** *iv.* to sit or stand in a certain way when someone is taking or painting one's picture. **3.** *tv.* to place someone or something, as in ①.
→ STRIKE A POSE

pose a question to ask a question; to imply the need for asking a question.

pose as someone or something to pretend to be someone; to pretend to have some role.

posh ['pɑʃ] *adj.* very lavish; elegant; full of style. (Adv: *poshly.* Comp: *posher;* sup: *poshest.*)

position [pə 'zɪ ʃən] **1.** *n.* the place where someone or something is or where someone or something belongs. **2.** *n.* the way that someone or something is placed or situated. **3.** *n.* a point of view; an opinion; the way someone thinks about a certain subject or issue. **4.** *n.* a job. **5.** *tv.* to put someone or something in a certain place.
→ JOCKEY FOR POSITION
→ JOCKEY SOMEONE OR SOMETHING INTO POSITION

possess [pə 'zɛs] **1.** *tv.* to have something; to own something. **2.** *tv.* to influence someone or something completely; [for someone or something, especially an evil spirit or the devil] to control someone or something completely.

possession [pə 'zɛ ʃən] **1.** *n.* ownership. (No plural.) **2.** *n.* a belonging; something that belongs to someone; something that is owned by someone.

possessive [pə 'zɛs ɪv] **1.** *adj.* selfish; unwilling to share. (Adv: *possessively.*) **2.** *adj.* [of a word] showing possession or belonging [to someone or something]. (Adv: *possessively.*) **3.** *n.* the form of a word that shows possession.

possible ['pɑs ə bəl] *adj.* able to be done; able to exist; able to happen; able to be true, but not necessarily true. (Adv: *possibly.*)
→ (AS) SOON AS POSSIBLE
→ EVERYTHING HUMANLY POSSIBLE

post ['post] **1.** *n.* an upright, thick length of wood, steel, or other material. **2.** *n.* a job; a position in a company or a government. **3.** *tv.* to place a written notice where people can see it. **4.** *tv.* to mail something; to send something by mail.
→ FROM PILLAR TO POST
→ KEEP SOMEONE POSTED
→ PARCEL POST

post office ['post ɔf ɪs] *n.* a government building where mail is taken, sorted, and sent to the proper addresses, and where other postal business can be taken care of.

postage ['pos tɪdʒ] **1.** *n.* the cost of sending something through the mail, usually paid for with stamps. (No plural.) **2.** *n.* the stamp or stamps that are placed on something that is mailed. (No plural.

Number is expressed with *postage stamp(s)*.)

postal ['pos təl] *adj.* of or about mail or the post office.

postcard ['post kɑrd] *n.* a card that is thicker than paper, sometimes has a picture on one side of it, and is used to mail someone a short letter, especially when one is traveling.

poster ['pos tɚ] *n.* a large sheet of thick paper carrying a message or a picture.

postmaster ['post mæ stɚ] *n.* someone who is in charge of a post office; the head of a post office.

posture ['pɑs tʃɚ] **1.** *n.* the way that one sits, stands, or moves; the position of the body. (Plural only for types and instances.) **2.** *iv.* to sit or stand in a certain way; to strike a pose.

pot ['pɑt] **1.** *n.* a large, deep, round container, usually used to cook or hold food or liquid. **2.** *n.* a round container that holds soil and a flower or plant. **3.** *n.* the contents of ① or ②. **4.** *tv.* to put a plant in soil in ②.
→ GO TO POT

the **pot calling the kettle black** [an instance of] someone with a fault accusing someone else of having the same fault.

potato [pə 'te to] **1.** *n.* a vegetable root shaped like a large egg. (Plural ends in *-es*.) **2.** *n.* the plant that produces ①. (Plural ends in *-es*.) **3.** *adj.* made of or with ①.

potato chip [pə 'te to tʃɪp]] *n.* a thin slice of potato, fried until it is very crisp. (Often plural. Can be shortened to CHIP.)

potent ['pot nt] **1.** *adj.* powerful; having a strong effect. (Adv: *potently*.) **2.** *adj.* [of a male] able to copulate. (Adv: *potently*.)

pottery ['pɑt ə ri] **1.** *n.* dishes, bowls, vases, and other objects that are made from baked clay. (No plural.) **2.** *n.* the craft or art of making objects out of clay and baking them so that the clay hardens. (No plural.)

pouch ['paʊtʃ] *n.* a small bag that is used to hold a small amount of something.

poultry ['pol tri] *n.* chickens, ducks, geese, and other birds that are used as meat or for providing eggs for humans to eat. (No plural.)

pounce (up)on someone or something to spring or swoop upon someone or something; to seize someone or something.

pound ['paʊnd] **1.** *n.* a unit of measure of weight, equal to 16 ounces or about 0.454 kilogram. **2.** *n.* the basic unit of money in the United Kingdom. (Symbolized as £.) **3.** *n.* a place where stray animals are kept. **4.** *tv.* to hit someone or something very hard again and again; to beat something into a certain shape by hitting it very hard again and again. **5.** *iv.* [for the heart or blood pressure] to beat very hard.

pound a beat to walk a route. (Usually said of a police patrol officer.)

pound away (at someone or something**)** to hammer or batter constantly on someone or something.

pound something **down** to hammer, flatten, or batter something.

pound something **in(to** someone**)** Go to HAMMER SOMETHING IN(TO SOMEONE).

pound something **in(to** something**)** Go to HAMMER SOMETHING IN(TO SOMETHING).

pound the pavement to walk through the streets, looking for a job.

pour ['por] **1.** *iv.* to flow from a place; to come out of a place quickly and continuously. **2.** *tv.* to cause something to pour out of a place quickly and continuously.

pour cold water on something AND **dash cold water on** something; **throw cold water on** something to discourage doing something; to reduce enthusiasm for something.

pour it on thick Go to LAY IT ON THICK.

pour money down the drain to waste money.

pour oil on troubled water to calm things down.

pour out (of something**)** [for someone or something] to stream or gush out of something or someplace.

pour something **off ((of)** something**)** to spill liquid off the top of something.

pouring rain very heavy rain.

poverty ['pɑv ɚ ti] *n.* the lack of the necessities for life. (No plural.)

powder ['pɑʊ dɚ] **1.** *n.* a substance that consists of tiny particles. (Plural only for types and instances.) **2.** *tv.* to cover or dust something with ① or a substance that has been crushed or ground into ①.
→ SITTING ON A POWDER KEG

power ['pɑʊ ɚ] **1.** *n.* the ability to do something; strength. (Plural only for types and instances. Typically singular or plural with the same meaning.) **2.** *n.* the authority to do something; control. (Plural only for types and instances. Singular or plural with the same meaning.) **3.** *n.* the number of times that a number is multiplied by itself. **4.** *tv.* to supply energy to a machine or other device that uses energy.

power something **up** to start something, such as an engine.

power up to start an engine.

powerful ['pɑʊ ɚ fʊl] *adj.* having a lot of power, energy, or force; full of strength or influence. (Adv: *powerfully*.)

the **powers that be** the people who are in authority.

practical ['præk tɪ kəl] **1.** *adj.* useful; able to be used; of or about actions and results, as opposed to ideas or theories. (Adv: *practically* [...ɪk li].) **2.** *adj.* sensible; having common sense. (Adv: *practically* [...ɪk li].)

practice ['præk tɪs] **1.** *n.* doing an action many times so that one will do it better and better. (No plural.) **2.** *n.* a custom; a tradition; the way something is usually done; a habit. **3.** *n.* the business of a doc-

tor or a lawyer. **4.** *iv.* to rehearse. **5.** *tv.* to work at a skill over and over in order to become better at it. **6.** *tv.* to do something; to make a habit of something. **7.** *tv.* to work in medicine or law.
→ OUT OF PRACTICE

practice what you preach to do what you advise other people to do.

prairie ['prɛr i] *n.* a very large area of land that is covered with different kinds of grasses and other plants.

praise ['prez] **1.** *n.* saying that someone or something is good; the use of words to express satisfaction or a favorable judgment. (Singular or plural with the same meaning, but not countable.) **2.** *tv.* to express satisfaction with someone or something; to talk about the good things someone or something does or how good someone or something is. **3.** *tv.* to worship someone or God with words or songs.
→ DAMN SOMEONE OR SOMETHING WITH FAINT PRAISE
→ SING SOMEONE'S PRAISES

prank ['præŋk] *n.* a trick or joke that is played on someone.

prankster ['præŋk stɚ] *n.* someone who plays a trick or joke on someone.

pray ['pre] **1.** *iv.* to give thanks to God; to say a prayer to God; to ask God or some religious being or figure for something. **2.** *tv.* to PRAY as in ①, asking that something will happen the way one wants. (The object is a clause with THAT ⑦.)

pray for something to ask God for something.

prayer ['prɛr] **1.** *n.* communication with God or some other religious being or figure. **2.** *n.* the words one uses when worshiping or praying to God.
→ IN SOMEONE'S PRAYERS

preach ['pritʃ] **1.** *iv.* to give a sermon; to talk about something religious. **2.** *tv.* to deliver a sermon; to deliver a particular message through a sermon. (The object can be a clause with THAT ⑦.)
→ PRACTICE WHAT YOU PREACH

preacher ['pritʃ ɚ] *n.* someone who preaches; the leader of a church; a minister. (Less formal than MINISTER.)

precious ['prɛʃ əs] **1.** *adj.* very valuable; worth a lot of money. (Adv: *preciously.*) **2.** *adj.* very much loved; very dear to someone; cherished. (Figurative on ①. Adv: *preciously.*) **3.** *adj.* charming and cute. (Adv: *preciously.*)

precious few AND **precious little** very few; very little. (Informal.)

precious little Go to PRECIOUS FEW.

precise [prɪ 'saɪs] *adj.* exact; carefully and accurately detailed. (Adv: *precisely.*)

precision [prɪ 'sɪ ʒən] *n.* accuracy; the quality of being precise; doing something precisely. (No plural.)

predict [prɪ 'dɪkt] *tv.* to say that something is going to happen before it happens; to prophesy that something will happen. (The object can be a clause with THAT ⑦.)

prediction [prɪ'dɪk ʃən] *n.* a statement made about something that is going to happen in the future; a prophecy.

preface ['prɛf ɪs] **1.** *n.* an introduction to a speech or to something that is written. **2.** *tv.* to begin a speech or written piece with an introduction.

prefer [prɪ'fɚ] *tv.* to like someone or something better than one likes someone or something else. (The object can be a clause with THAT ⑦.)

prefer to do something to want to do something more than one wants to do something else; to like to do one thing more than doing another thing.

preferable ['prɛf ə rə bəl] *adj.* more preferred; more desirable. (Adv: *preferably.*)

preference ['prɛf ə rəns] **1.** *n.* special attention that is given to certain people or things; favor. (No plural.) **2.** *n.* someone or something that is preferred over someone or something else.

prefix ['pri fɪks] *n.* a letter or a group of letters at the beginning of a word that usually changes the meaning of the word.

pregnant ['prɛg nənt] *adj.* [of a woman or female creature] carrying developing offspring within.

prehistoric [pri hɪ 'stɔr ɪk] *adj.* happening before history was first recorded. (Adv: *prehistorically* […ɪk li].)

prejudice ['prɛdʒ ə dɪs] **1.** *n.* opinion formed about someone or something before learning all the facts. (Plural only for types and instances.) **2.** *tv.* to cause someone to have ①.

prelude ['pre lud] *n.* an introduction, especially a short piece of music that comes before a longer work of music.

prelude to something an act or event that comes before and signals another act or event.

premier [prɪ'mɪr] **1.** *adj.* best; most respected. (Prenominal only.) **2.** *n.* the prime minister of a country.

premiere [prɪ'mɪr] **1.** *n.* the first performance or presentation of a play, film, symphony, etc. **2.** *iv.* [for a play, film, symphony, etc.] to be performed for the first time.

premium ['prim i əm] **1.** *n.* a regular payment to an insurance company for some kind of protection. **2.** *n.* an additional cost in addition to the regular cost. **3.** *n.* a small prize or reward that is given to someone to buy something or use a service. **4.** *adj.* of high quality; costing more; of greater value. → AT A PREMIUM

prenominal [pri 'nɑm ə nəl] *adj.* [of an adjective] occurring before the noun it modifies. (Adv: *prenominally.*)

prep. an abbreviation of PREPOSITION.

prepaid [pri 'ped] past tense and past participle of PREPAY.

prepare [prɪ'pɛr] **1.** *tv.* to make something ready for someone or something; to make something ready for use. **2.** *iv.* to make oneself ready to do something.

prepay [pri 'pe] *tv., irreg.* to pay some amount before it is due; to pay for something in advance; to pay for something before one receives it. (Past tense and past participle: PREPAID.)

preposition [prɛp ə 'zɪ ʃən] *n.* a word that is used to show the relationship of one word or phrase to another word or phrase. (Abbreviated *prep.* here.)

preschool ['pri skul] *n.* a school for small children before they are old enough to go to kindergarten.

prescribe [pri 'skraɪb] **1.** *tv.* [for a physician] to recommend or order that a certain medication be sold to and taken by a patient. **2.** *tv.* [for a doctor] to advise a patient to do something to become or stay healthy. (The object can be a clause with THAT ⑦.) **3.** *tv.* to state something as a law; to establish something as a law. (The object can be a clause with THAT ⑦.)

prescription [pri 'skrɪp ʃən] **1.** *n.* ordering or prescribing something, especially medicine or medical treatment. **2.** *n.* an order to do something or take medicine, especially a written order for medicine given to a patient by a doctor. **3.** *n.* the actual medicine that is ordered by ②.
→ REFILL A PRESCRIPTION

presence ['prɛz əns] **1.** *n.* the state of being present; being in the same place as someone or something else. (No plural.) **2.** *n.* the power or influence one has in a group of people or in an institution. **3.** *n.* something that can be felt or sensed but not seen, such as a spirit.
→ GRACE SOMEONE OR SOMETHING WITH ONE'S PRESENCE
→ HAVE THE PRESENCE OF MIND TO DO SOMETHING

present 1. ['prɛz ənt] *adj.* being in the same room or place as someone or something else; not absent. **2.** ['prɛz ənt] *adj.* now; at this time; happening now. (Adv: *presently.*) **3.** ['prɛz ənt] *n.* now; this time; this moment in time. (No plural.) **4.** ['prɛz ənt] *n.* a gift; something that is given to someone else. **5.** ['prɛz ənt] *n.* the state of a verb that indicates that something is happening now. (Short for PRESENT TENSE.) **6.** [pri 'zɛnt] *tv.* to give something to someone, especially as part of a ceremony. **7.** [pri 'zɛnt] *tv.* to make something available for the public to see; to bring something to someone's attention. **8.** [pri 'zɛnt] *tv.* to introduce someone to someone else.

present tense ['prɛz ənt 'tɛns] *n.* a verb tense showing that something is happening now, at the present time. (No plural. Can be shortened to PRESENT.)

presentation [prɛz ən 'te ʃən] **1.** *n.* the way that something is shown to other people; the manner or style in which something is shown to other people. (No plural.) **2.** *n.* a session of showing or explaining something to other people. **3.** *n.* the ceremony of giving something to someone else.

present-day ['prɛz ənt 'de] *adj.* current; happening now; of or about the present time.

presently ['prɛz ənt li] **1.** *adv.* now; at this time. **2.** *adv.* soon. (Formal.)

preservation [prɛ zɚ 'veɪ ʃən] *n.* the process of preserving something; keeping something safe or in good condition. (No plural.)

preserve [prɪ 'zɚv] **1.** *tv.* to keep someone or something alive, healthy, safe, or in good condition. **2.** *tv.* to do something or add something to something to keep it from spoiling or decaying. **3.** *n.* an area of land where plants and animals are protected.
→ LIFE PRESERVER

preserves *n.* fruit cooked in sugar and sealed in a jar. (Treated as plural, but not countable.)

preside [prɪ 'zaɪd] *iv.* to be in charge of a meeting or a business; to be in control.

preside over something to oversee something, such as a meeting.

president ['prɛz ə dənt] **1.** *n.* the leader of the government of a republic, including the leader of the government of the United States of America. **2.** *n.* the leader or head officer of an organization, club, company, university, etc. **3.** *n.* the office and position of power occupied by ① or ②.
→ VICE PRESIDENT

presidential [prɛz ə 'dɛn ʃəl] *adj.* of or about a president; associated with a president. (Adv: *presidentially*.)

press ['prɛs] **1.** *n.* a machine that prints letters and pictures on paper for newspapers, magazines, books, etc. (Short for PRINTING

PRESS.) **2.** *n.* the coverage of an action or event by newspapers and other media. (No plural.) **3.** *tv.* to push something against something else; to push something with force; to weigh down heavily on something. **4.** *tv.* to move a hot iron over wrinkled clothing or fabric in order to make it smooth. **5.** *iv.* to push against something else; to push with force; to weigh down heavily; to push forward.
→ PRINTING PRESS

the **press** *n.* newspapers and, sometimes, radio and television; the mass media. (No plural. Treated as singular.)

press against someone or something to push or bear upon someone or something.

press down on someone or something to push down on someone or something.

press on something to push or depress something, such as a button, catch, snap, etc.

press one's **luck** Go to PUSH ONE'S LUCK.

press someone **to the wall** Go to PUSH SOMEONE TO THE WALL.

press something **against** someone or something to push or force something against someone or something.

press something **in(to** something) **1.** to force something into something, such as a mold. **2.** to force or drive something into the surface of something.

press something **on(to** something) to put pressure on something and

449

cause it to stick to the surface of something.

press something out (of something) to squeeze something out of something by applying pressure.

press (up)on someone or something to put pressure on someone or something.

pressure ['prɛʃ ɚ] **1.** *n.* the effect of a force or a weight that is pushed against someone or something. (No plural.) **2.** *n.* strong influence; strong persuasion. (Figurative on ①.)
→ UNDER (SOME) PRESSURE

presume (up)on someone or something to take unwelcome advantage of someone or something.

pretend [prɪ 'tɛnd] **1.** *iv.* to act [as if something were so]. **2.** *iv.* to act as if one were doing something; to try to look as if one were doing something. **3.** *tv.* to act as if something were so; to play by acting as if something were so. (The object is a clause with THAT ⑦.)

pretty ['prɪt i] **1.** *adj.* attractive; pleasing; beautiful. (Adv: *prettily.* Comp: *prettier;* sup: *prettiest.*) **2.** *adv.* rather; quite; very.
→ (AS) PRETTY AS A PICTURE
→ COST A PRETTY PENNY

pretzel ['prɛt səl] *n.* a salted, baked stick of bread, often twisted in the shape of a loose knot.

prevail (up)on someone or something **(to** do something**)** to appeal to someone or a group to do something.

prevent someone **from** doing something [prɪ 'vɛnt…] not to

allow someone to do something; to keep someone from doing something.

preventable [prɪ 'vɛnt ə bəl] *adj.* able to be prevented. (Adv: *preventably.*)

prevention [prɪ 'vɛn ʃən] *n.* preventing something. (No plural.)

preview ['pri vju] **1.** *n.* an opportunity to see something before it is available to the public. **2.** *iv.* [for something] to be shown as ①. **3.** *tv.* to watch or listen to something as ①.

previous ['pri vi əs] *adj.* earlier; happening before something else; coming before. (Adv: *previously.*)

prey ['pre] **1.** *n.* an animal that is hunted, killed, or eaten by another animal. (No plural. Compare this with PRAY.) **2.** *n.* someone who is a victim of someone else. (No plural. Figurative on ①.)
→ BIRD OF PREY

prey on some creature to hunt and kill certain animals for food.

prey (up)on someone or something to take advantage of someone or something.

price ['praɪs] **1.** *n.* the amount of money that something costs; the amount of money that something will be sold for. **2.** *tv.* to determine how much something will cost; to set the amount of money that something will cost.
→ HAVE A PRICE ON ONE'S HEAD
→ QUOTE A PRICE

prick up one's **ears** to listen more closely.

pride ['praɪd] **1.** *n.* the pleasure that one feels when one does

something well; the feeling one has when one does something good. (No plural.) **2.** *n.* someone or something for which one has ①. (No plural.) **3.** *n.* a good opinion of oneself; too high an opinion of oneself. (No plural.)
→ TAKE PRIDE IN SOMETHING

priest ['prist] *n.* someone who is trained to perform religious duties. (In the United States, especially in the Roman Catholic, Orthodox Catholic, and Episcopal churches.)

prim ['prɪm] *adj.* very proper; very formal; very exact; very precise; easily shocked by rude or rough behavior. (Adv: *primly.* Comp: *primmer;* sup: *primmest.*)

primary ['praɪ mɛr i] **1.** *adj.* the most important; chief; main; principal. (Adv: *primarily* [praɪ 'mɛr ə li].) **2.** *n.* an election that is held to determine who will represent a political party in the election for a political office.

primary color ['praɪ mɛr i 'kʌl ɚ] *n.* one of the basic colors: red, blue, and yellow. (Other colors can be made by mixing two or three of these together.)

primary school ['praɪ mɛr ɪ 'skul] *n.* a school having only the earliest grades.

prime ['praɪm] **1.** *adj.* [of a state or condition] best or excellent; of the highest quality. **2.** *adj.* most important; chief; first in time, order, or importance. **3.** *tv.* to add water or liquid to a pump to replace the air that is inside so that the pump is able to draw fluid. **4.** *tv.* to make someone or some-

thing ready for something. **5.** *tv.* to cover a surface with primer before painting it.
→ IN ONE'S OR ITS PRIME
→ IN THE PRIME OF LIFE

prime mover the force that sets something going; someone or something that starts something off.

primer ['praɪm ɚ] *n.* a liquid that is spread over wood before one covers the wood with paint. (Plural only for types and instances.)

primitive ['prɪm ə tɪv] **1.** *adj.* early in the development of something; early in the history of humans. (Adv: *primitively.*) **2.** *adj.* very simple; not complicated. (Adv: *primitively.*)

primp ['prɪmp] *iv.* to dress and get ready for a social event very carefully.

prince ['prɪns] **1.** *n.* the son or grandson of a king or a queen. **2.** *n.* the husband of a woman who inherits the throne and becomes queen.

princely ['prɪns li] **1.** *adj.* like a prince; having great charm and manners. **2.** *adj.* elegant; refined; noble. (Figurative on ①.)

princess ['prɪns ɛs] **1.** *n.* the daughter or granddaughter of a king or queen. **2.** *n.* the wife of a prince.

principal ['prɪns ə pəl] **1.** *n.* the head of an elementary, middle, or high school. (Compare this with PRINCIPLE.) **2.** *n.* an amount of borrowed money on which the borrower must pay interest. **3.** *n.* the most important or major person in a group. **4.** *adj.* main; chief; primary; most important. (Adv: *principally* ['prɪn ə pli].)

principle ['prɪn ə pəl] **1.** *n.* obedience to ② and ③; honor. (No plural. Compare this with PRINCIPAL.) **2.** *n.* a general or fundamental law or rule. **3.** *n.* a rule of behavior or conduct.

print ['prɪnt] **1.** *tv.* to make letters of the alphabet by hand so that each letter is separate. **2.** *tv.* to put words or pictures on a blank piece of paper, one page at a time, using some kind of machine. **3.** *tv.* to publish a book, magazine, or newspaper using a printing press or a computer printer. **4.** *tv.* to publish something that is written in a book, newspaper, magazine, etc. **5.** *tv.* to make a photograph from film. **6.** *tv.* to cause a computer to PRINT something as in ②. **7.** *iv.* to make letters of the alphabet so that each letter is separate. **8.** *iv.* to make books, magazines, newspapers, etc., with a printing press. **9.** *iv.* [for a computer printer] to operate as in ②. **10.** *n.* fabric that has a pattern on it. **11.** *n.* a photograph that is made from film; a photograph. **12.** *n.* a FINGERPRINT.
→ IN PRINT
→ OUT OF PRINT
→ SMALL PRINT

print something **out 1.** to write something out by drawing letters. **2.** to use a computer printer to print something.

print something **up** to set something in type and print it; to print something by any process.

printer ['prɪn tɚ] **1.** *n.* a business or person that prints books, magazines, and other materials. **2.** *n.* a machine that causes computer information to be put onto paper.

printing ['prɪn tɪŋ] **1.** *n.* letters or words that are printed by hand; letters that are put on paper so that the letters are separate and distinct. (No plural.) **2.** *n.* letters that are put on a page by a press or a computer. (No plural.) **3.** *n.* all the copies of a book printed by machine at one time.

printing press ['prɪn tɪŋ 'prɛs] *n.* a machine used to print text and pictures on paper. (Can be shortened to PRESS.)

printout ['prɪnt aʊt] *n.* a copy of information from a computer, printed on paper.

prison ['prɪz ən] **1.** *n.* a building that criminals are kept in; a large jail. **2.** *n.* a place where someone is not allowed to leave; a place where someone has no freedom. (Figurative on ①.)

prisoner ['prɪz nɚ] **1.** *n.* someone who is kept in a prison. **2.** *n.* someone or a creature that is not free to go. (Figurative on ①.)

pristine ['prɪs tin] *adj.* as fresh and clean as when it was new; spotless. (Adv: *pristinely*.)

privacy ['praɪv ə si] *n.* a state of being away from other people or away from the attention of the public. (No plural.)
→ an INVASION OF PRIVACY

private ['praɪv ɪt] **1.** *adj.* not shared among everyone; meant only for a small number of people;

not public. (Adv: *privately*.) **2.** *adj.* individual; concerning only one person. (Adv: *privately*.) **3.** *adj.* secluded; isolated; quiet; away from other people. (Adv: *privately*.) **4.** *adj.* not owned, controlled, or managed by the government. (Adv: *privately*.)

privilege ['prɪv (ə) lɪdʒ] *n.* special rights; special and honored status. (Plural only for types and instances.)

privy to something ['prɪv i...] uniquely knowledgeable about something.

prize ['praɪz] **1.** *n.* an award that is given to a winner; an award that is given to someone who does well in a competition. **2.** *tv.* to consider something to be worth very much; to place a great value on something.

pro ['pro] *n.* a PROFESSIONAL; having great skill or training. (Plural ends in -*s*.)

probable ['prɑb ə bəl] *adj.* having a great chance of happening; likely to happen; likely to be true. (Adv: *probably*.)

probably ['prɑb ə bli] *adv.* very likely; likely to happen or likely to be true.

probation [pro 'be ʃən] **1.** *n.* a situation where an offender remains out of jail and just under observation as long as no further crimes are committed. (No plural form.) **2.** *n.* a trial period. (Figurative on ①. No plural form.)
→ ON PROBATION

probe ['prob] **1.** *n.* a complete examination or detailed search for facts. **2.** *n.* a thin rod with a rounded end that is used to examine the inside of a hole, wound, or cavity. **3.** *n.* a rocket or satellite that is sent into space to relay information about space or other planets to scientists on earth. **4.** *tv.* to examine a hole, wound, or cavity, using ② or a similar object. **5.** *iv.* to examine; to search.

problem ['prɑb ləm] **1.** *n.* a question that must be answered; a difficulty. **2.** *n.* a question put forward for solving, as in a school exercise or test. **3.** *adj.* difficult to deal with; difficult to work with; causing difficulty.

procedure [prə 'si dʒɚ] *n.* the way that something is done; the way that a process is done; a method.

proceed [prə 'sid] *iv.* to begin to do something.

proceeds ['pro sidz] *n.* money that is collected or received from someone or something. (Treated as plural, but not countable.)

process ['prɑ sɛs] **1.** *n.* a series of actions; a set of procedures used to do, make, achieve, prepare, or develop something. **2.** *tv.* to do a series of actions to something; to prepare, achieve, or develop something.

proclaim [prə 'klem] *tv.* to declare something officially; to make something public knowledge. (The object can be a clause with THAT ⑦.)

procure [pro 'kjʊr] *tv.* to get something by work or effort.

produce 1. ['pro dus] *n.* food or food products that are farmed or grown; fruits and vegetables. (No plural.) **2.** [prə 'dus] *tv.* to grow something; to create something. **3.** [prə 'dus] *tv.* to cause something to be; to create a result. **4.** [prə 'dus] *tv.* to make something from parts or materials. **5.** [prə 'dus] *tv.* to coordinate and organize the details involved in making or presenting a movie, play, or other performance. **6.** [prə 'dus] *iv.* to do what is expected or required, especially in terms of business goals.

producer [prə 'dus ər] **1.** *n.* someone or something that produces something. **2.** *n.* someone who coordinates and organizes the details involved in making or presenting a movie, television show, play, or other performance.

product ['prɑ dəkt] **1.** *n.* something that is produced; something that is made, created, or grown. **2.** *n.* someone or something that is the result of certain conditions; a result. **3.** *n.* the number that is determined by multiplying two or more numbers together.

production [prə 'dʌk ʃən] **1.** *n.* producing something; making something. (No plural.) **2.** *n.* the amount of or rate of ① . (No plural.) **3.** *n.* a movie, television show, play, or other performance.

profess [prə 'fɛs] *tv.* to declare something; to claim something. (The object can be a clause with THAT ⑦ .)

profession [prə 'fɛ ʃən] **1.** *n.* a job or career, especially one that requires education or training.

2. *n.* all or most of the people who work in a certain ① .

professional [prə 'fɛʃ ə nəl] **1.** the *adj.* form of PROFESSION ① . (Adv: *professionally*.) **2.** *adj.* showing the skill and standards of ③ . (Adv: *professionally*.) **3.** *n.* someone who works in a profession. (Shortened to PRO informally.)

professor [prə 'fɛs ər] *n.* someone who holds a faculty position in a university or college. (Also a term of address.)

profile ['pro faɪl] **1.** *n.* a side view of someone or something, especially of someone's face. **2.** *n.* a short description of someone or something.

profit ['prɑf ɪt] **1.** *n.* the amount of money made by a person or business after all expenses are paid. **2.** *tv.* to benefit someone or something.

profit from something to benefit from something.

program ['pro græm] **1.** *n.* a broadcast show, such as on radio or television. **2.** *n.* a booklet provided to members of an audience, giving information about the performance. **3.** *n.* a schedule of the parts of a performance. **4.** *n.* a set of coded instructions given to a computer.

programmer ['pro græm ər] *n.* someone who writes a computer program.

progress 1. ['prɑ grɛs] *n.* the movement made toward a result or goal. (No plural.) **2.** ['prɑ grɛs] *n.* the improvement that someone or something makes when moving

toward a goal. (No plural.)
3. [prə 'grɛs] *iv.* to move forward; to advance. **4.** [prə 'grɛs] *iv.* to develop; to become better.

prohibit [pro 'hɪb ɪt] *tv.* to forbid something.

prohibition [pro ə 'bɪ ʃən] **1.** *n.* forbidding or not allowing something. (Plural only for types and instances.) **2.** *n.* the period of time in U.S. history when it was illegal to make, sell, or transport alcohol. (Capitalized. No plural.)

project 1. ['prɑ dʒɛkt] *n.* an assignment or task that must be planned, researched, and executed. **2.** [prə 'dʒɛkt] *tv.* to cast a light onto something. **3.** [prə 'dʒɛkt] *tv.* to make one's voice or words louder and carry farther. **4.** [prə 'dʒɛkt] *tv.* to forecast something; to estimate something. **5.** [prə 'dʒɛkt] *iv.* to be louder when speaking. **6.** [prə 'dʒɛkt] *iv.* to stick out; to extend from a surface.

projection [prə 'dʒɛk ʃən] **1.** *n.* something that sticks out or projects. **2.** *n.* a prediction; an estimate of a future state.

projector [prə 'dʒɛk tɚ] *n.* a machine that casts an image on a screen, wall, etc. (The image may have been recorded on film or digitally on tape.)

prolong [pro 'lɔŋ] *tv.* to cause something to last longer than it normally would; to lengthen the time it takes to do something.

prominent ['prɑm ə nənt] **1.** *adj.* famous; well known; respected. (Adv: *prominently*.) **2.** *adj.* notice-able; easy to see. (Adv: *prominently*.)

promise ['prɑm ɪs] **1.** *n.* a sign that someone will be successful or do good work. (No plural.) **2.** *n.* a pledge to do something. **3.** *tv.* to pledge to do something; to vow that one will do something. (The object is a clause with THAT ⑦.) **4.** *tv.* to cause someone to expect something.
→ GIVE SOMETHING A LICK AND A PROMISE

promise someone **the moon** Go to PROMISE THE MOON (TO SOMEONE).

promise the moon (to someone**)** AND **promise** someone **the moon** to make extravagant promises to someone.

promise to do something to make a promise that one will do something.

promote [prə 'mot] **1.** *tv.* to work for the acceptance of someone or something through advertising and other public contacts. **2.** *tv.* to raise someone to a new and higher level in employment or schooling.

promotion [prə 'mo ʃən] **1.** *n.* the movement of someone to a higher level of employment or schooling. (Plural only for types and instances.) **2.** *n.* advertising and other activity intended to sell something. (No plural.)

prompt ['prɑmpt] **1.** *adj.* doing something, such as arriving, at the right time; on time. (Adv: *promptly*.) **2.** *tv.* to encourage or cause someone to do something. **3.** *tv.* to give someone a quiet reminder of what is to be said next. (Especially in stage performances.) **4.** *n.* a symbol on a computer screen that shows that the computer is ready to receive information.

pron. an abbreviation of PRONOUN.

prone to doing something likely to [do] something; apt to do something.

pronoun ['pro naʊn] *n.* a word that takes the place of a noun or nominal and refers to someone or something already mentioned. (Abbreviated *pron.* here.)
→ REFLEXIVE (PRONOUN)

pronounce [prə 'naʊns] **1.** *tv.* to speak the sound of a letter or a word; to make the sound of a letter or a word. **2.** *tv.* to declare something about someone or something officially.

pronunciation [prə nən si 'e ʃən] *n.* the way a letter, group of letters, or a word sounds when spoken; the way someone says things. (Plural only for types and instances.)

proof ['pruf] **1.** *n.* something that shows that something is definitely true. (No plural.) **2.** *n.* a printed copy of something that is checked for mistakes before the final copy is printed; a first or sample version of a photograph. **3.** *tv.* to proofread something.

proofread ['pruf rid] **1.** *tv., irreg.* to read something very carefully to look for mistakes. (Past tense and past participle: *proofread* ['pruf rɛd].) **2.** *iv., irreg.* to read very carefully to look for mistakes.

prop ['prɑp] *n.* an object that is used in a play or in a movie by an actor.

prop someone or something **up** to support someone or something; to prevent someone or something from falling.

propaganda [prɑp ə 'gæn də] *n.* information that tries to influence or change how people think. (No plural.)

propeller [pro 'pɛl ɚ] *n.* a set of blades that rotate very fast in air or water, used to push or move a boat or an airplane.

proper ['prɑp ɚ] **1.** *adj.* right; suitable; correct; appropriate. (Adv: *properly.*) **2.** *adj.* [in grammar, of a noun] referring to a person or place. (Such nouns are capitalized.) **3.** *adj.* referring to a particular place itself, and not an area outside of that place. (Not prenominal. Adv: *properly.*)

properly ['prɑp ɚ li] **1.** *adv.* in the right way; suitably; appropriately; according to what is expected. **2.** *adv.* strictly.

property ['prɑp ɚ ti] **1.** *n.* something that is owned. (No plural.) **2.** *n.* an amount of land and any structures that have been built on it. (No plural.)

prophecy ['prɑf ə si] *n.* the ability to foresee the future. (Plural only for types and instances.)

prophesy ['prɑf ə saɪ] *tv.* to predict what will happen in the future; to say that something is going to happen. (The object can be a clause with THAT ⑦.)

prophet ['prɑf ɪt] **1.** *n.* someone who has the talent of being able to see into the future. **2.** *n.* [in some religions] a person chosen to speak for God.

proportion [prə 'pɔr ʃən] **1.** *n.* the relationship between the sizes of different parts of someone or something. **2.** *tv.* to adjust the amount, degree, or size of something in comparison to something else.
→ BLOW SOMETHING OUT OF (ALL) PROPORTION
→ IN PROPORTION
→ OUT OF PROPORTION

proposal [prə 'poz əl] **1.** *n.* a suggestion; a plan. **2.** *n.* an offer of marriage made to someone.

propose [prə 'poz] *tv.* to suggest something; to say something so that it is considered. (The object can be a clause with THAT ⑦.)

propose a toast to make a TOAST ②, before drinking.

propose (to someone) to ask someone to marry one.

proposition [prɑp ə 'zɪ ʃən] **1.** *n.* a proposal; something that is being considered; a suggestion. **2.** *n.* a statement; a statement that is to be proved either true or false.

propulsion [prə 'pʌl ʃən] *n.* a force that causes something to move forward. (No plural form.)
→ JET PROPULSION

prose ['proz] *n.* the usual form of written language; writing that is not in verse. (No plural.)

prosper ['prɑs pɚ] *iv.* to become successful; to earn enough money so that one can live well; to thrive.

prosperity [prɑs 'pɛr ə ti] *n.* the condition of being prosperous; success; monetary success. (No plural.)

prosperous ['prɑs pə rəs] *adj.* thriving; earning or having enough money so that one can live well. (Adv: *prosperously*.)

protect [prə 'tɛkt] *tv.* to keep someone or something safe; to guard someone or something.

protection [prə 'tɛk ʃən] *n.* keeping someone or something safe; the quality offered by someone or something that protects. (Plural only for types and instances.)

protective [prə 'tɛk tɪv] *adj.* protecting someone or something; giving protection; defending; keeping someone or something safe. (Adv: *protectively*.)

protein ['pro tin] *n.* one of many chemical substances important to the cells of all living plants and animals. (Usually thought of in terms of food.)

protest 1. ['pro tɛst] *n.* a group of people displaying opposition or anger. **2.** ['pro tɛst] *n.* a complaint. **3.** [prə 'tɛst] *tv.* to complain about something; to show disapproval of something. (The object can be a clause with THAT ⑦.) **4.** [prə 'tɛst] *iv.* to complain about something.
→ a RIPPLE OF PROTEST

proton ['pro tɑn] *n.* a particle in the NUCLEUS ② of an atom that carries a positive electrical charge.

prototype ['pro tə taɪp] *n.* the original example of something from which later examples are developed.

proud ['praʊd] **1.** *adj.* showing or feeling pride; having a good opinion about oneself and what one has accomplished. (Adv: *proudly.* Comp: *prouder;* sup: *proudest.*) **2.** *adj.* causing someone to feel pride. (Adv: *proudly.* Comp: *prouder;* sup: *proudest.*) **3.** *adj.* having too high an opinion about oneself; arrogant. (Adv: *proudly.* Comp: *prouder;* sup: *proudest.*)
→ **(AS) PROUD AS A PEACOCK**

prove ['pruv] *tv., irreg.* to provide proof of something; to be the proof of something. (Past participle: *proved* or **PROVEN**. The object can be a clause with **THAT** ⑦.)

prove to be something to be shown to be someone or something; to be found to be someone or something.

proven ['pruv ən] a past participle of **PROVE**.

provide [prə 'vaɪd] **1.** *tv.* to furnish or supply someone or something with something. **2.** *tv.* to state or tell something.

provide for someone to support someone by earning enough money to supply the person with food, clothing, and shelter.

provide for something to allow something to occur or to be supplied.

provided that something **is the case** on the condition that something is the case; only if something is the case.

province ['pra vɪns] **1.** *n.* one of the main divisions of a country,

such as Canada, similar to a state. **2.** *n.* an area of study, knowledge, or activity.

provincial [prə 'vɪn ʃəl] **1.** *adj.* of or about a province or provinces of a country. (Adv: *provincially.*) **2.** *adj.* of limited, local experience; rural in attitude and outlook. (Usually derogatory. Adv: *provincially.*)

provision [prə 'vɪ ʒən] **1.** *n.* a condition; a detail or statement. **2.** *n.* an arrangement that is made ahead of time. (Often plural.)

provisions *n.* food and supplies needed for everyday living. (Treated as plural, but not countable.)

provoke [prə 'vok] **1.** *tv.* to make someone angry; to irritate someone. **2.** *tv.* to cause an action to start or to happen. (Usually leading to negative results.)

prowl ['praʊl] *iv.* to sneak around quietly, like an animal hunting for food or a thief looking for something to steal.

prowler ['praʊl ɚ] *n.* a thief; a burglar who sneaks about in the night.

prude ['prud] *n.* someone who is easily offended or shocked; someone who is overly modest or proper.

prudence ['prud ns] *n.* wisdom; care in thought and action; thoughtful judgment. (No plural.)

prudent ['prud nt] *adj.* wise; thinking carefully before one does something. (Adv: *prudently.*)

prudish ['prud ɪʃ] *adj.* too easily shocked or offended; too modest. (*Adv: prudishly.*)

prune ['prun] **1.** *n.* a dried plum, eaten as food. **2.** *iv.* to remove extra branches or leaves from a plant; to trim a tree, flower, bush, or shrub so that it has a nice, even shape. **3.** *tv.* to make a plant look nice by removing extra branches or leaves.

prune something **off ((of)** something) to cut something off something.

pry ['praɪ] *iv.* to be too curious; to ask personal questions about things that should not concern one.

pry into something to snoop into something; to try to learn about someone else's private matters.

pry something **off ((of)** something) to use a lever to get something off something.

pry something **open** to open something with a tool by using force.

pry something **up** to raise something, as with a lever.

psychiatrist [sɪ 'kaɪ ə trɪst] *n.* a doctor who treats people who have sicknesses of the mind.

psychiatry [sɪ 'kaɪ ə tri] *n.* the science of treating people who have sicknesses of the mind. (No plural.)

psychological [saɪ kə 'ladʒ ɪ kəl] **1.** the *adj.* form of PSYCHOLOGY ①. (*Adv: psychologically* […ɪk li].) **2.** the *adj.* form of PSYCHOLOGY ②. (*Adv: psychologically* […ɪk li].)

psychologist [saɪ 'kal ə dʒɪst] *n.* someone who is trained in psychology; a specialist in behavior.

psychology [saɪ 'kal ə dʒi] **1.** *n.* the study and science of the mind and the behavior of individuals. (No plural.) **2.** *n.* the way people behave, think, and feel; the way a person behaves, thinks, and feels. (No plural.)

public ['pʌb lɪk] *adj.* available to everyone; available to people in general; not restricted; not private. (*Adv: publicly.*)
→ AIR ONE'S DIRTY LINEN IN PUBLIC
→ IN PUBLIC
→ IN THE PUBLIC EYE
→ WASH ONE'S DIRTY LINEN IN PUBLIC

the **public** *n.* people in general. (No plural.)

public school ['pʌb lɪk 'skul] *n.* a school that is paid for by the government through taxes and that is available to all local children.

publication [pʌb lə 'ke ʃən] **1.** *n.* making information in written form, such as in a book, magazine, or newspaper, available to the public. (No plural.) **2.** *n.* any written document that is published.
→ NOT FOR PUBLICATION

publicity [pʌb 'lɪs ə ti] *n.* information that is brought to everyone's attention. (No plural.)

publicly ['pʌb lɪk li] *adv.* [done] in public; [done] where people can see.

publish ['pʌb lɪʃ] **1.** *tv.* to assemble, print, and sell books, magazines, newspapers, or other printed materials. **2.** *tv.* to make something well known.

publisher [ˈpʌb lɪ ʃɚ] *n.* someone or a company that assembles, prints, and makes written materials available for sale.

pudding [ˈpʊd ɪŋ] *n.* a soft, sweet, creamy food, usually eaten as a dessert. (Plural only for types and instances.)

puddle [ˈpʌd l] *n.* a collection of water or other liquid on the ground or the surface of something.

puff [ˈpʌf] **1.** *n.* a short blast of air, smoke, steam, gas, etc., that is blown out from something. **2.** *tv.* to blow air, steam, smoke, etc., out a little bit at a time. **3.** *iv.* to pull smoke from a cigarette or a cigar with small breaths. **4.** *iv.* to breathe when one is out of breath; to breathe with short, quick breaths.
→ HUFF AND PUFF

puff out to swell out.

puff someone or something **up** to boost or promote someone or something.

puff something **out** to cause something to swell out or expand outward.

puff up (into something) to assume a larger shape by filling up with air or water; to swell up into something.

pull [ˈpʊl] **1.** *tv.* to move someone or something in one direction. **2.** *tv.* to drag someone or something behind oneself; to move someone or something behind oneself while one is moving. **3.** *n.* a tug.

pull in(to someplace) to drive into someplace.

pull off (something) to steer or turn a vehicle off the road.

pull out all the stops to use all one's energy and effort in order to achieve something. (From the stops of a pipe organ. The more that are pulled out, the louder it gets.)

pull out (of something) **1.** to withdraw from something. **2.** to drive out of something, such as a driveway, parking space, garage, etc.

pull someone **in(to** something) to get someone involved in something.

pull someone or something **up** to drag or haul someone or something upward or to an upright position.

pull someone's **leg** to kid, fool, or trick someone.

pull someone's or something's **teeth** to reduce the power of someone or something; to make someone or something less of a threat.

pull something **down** to tear something down; to raze something, such as a building.

pull something **off ((of)** something) to pull, tow, tug, or drag something off something else.

pull something **out** to withdraw something.

pull something **out of a hat** AND **pull** something **out of thin air** to produce something as if by magic.

pull something **out of thin air** Go TO PULL SOMETHING OUT OF A HAT.

pull something **up (out of** something**)** to draw something up out of something.

pull the rug out (from under someone**)** to make someone ineffective.

pull the wool over someone's **eyes** to deceive someone.

pull through (something**)** to survive something.

pull up (someplace**)** to arrive at a place in a vehicle; [for a vehicle] to arrive someplace.

pull up stakes to move to another place. (As if one were pulling up tent stakes.)

pulp [ˈpʌlp] **1.** *n.* the soft part inside a fruit, vegetable, or plant. (No plural.) **2.** *n.* any soft, partially solid, wet substance. (No plural.) **3.** *tv.* to make ② from something.

pulpit [ˈpʊl pɪt] *n.* a raised platform that a preacher, priest, minister, etc., stands on when preaching.

pulse [ˈpʌls] **1.** *n.* the rhythm of the flow of blood through one's body, caused by the beating of the heart. (No plural.) **2.** *n.* a rhythm with a regular beat; a movement of something with regular stops and starts. **3.** *iv.* to beat regularly, like the beating of the heart; to beat in rhythm.
→ TAKE SOMEONE'S PULSE

pump [ˈpʌmp] **1.** *n.* a device that forces air, liquid, or gas through a tube or pipe. **2.** *tv.* to force air, liquid, or gas through a tube or pipe.

pump something **in(to** someone or something**)** to try to force something, such as a gas, liquid, information, or money into someone or something.

pump something **out** to empty something by pumping.

pump something **out (of** someone or something**)** to remove something from someone or something by force or suction.

pumpkin [ˈpʌmp kɪn] **1.** *n.* a large, round, heavy orange fruit that grows on a vine. **2.** *adj.* made with ①.

punch [ˈpʌntʃ] **1.** *n.* a sweet drink made by mixing many different things, usually including some kind of fruit juice. (No plural.) **2.** *n.* a tool or machine that pierces holes through objects or that stamps designs on objects. **3.** *n.* a quick, powerful hit. **4.** *n.* impact; effective power; strength. (Figurative on ③.) **5.** *tv.* to hit someone or something powerfully with one's fist.

punch a hole in something to make a hole in something with something.

punch in to record one's arrival at one's workplace at a certain time.

punch out to record that one has left one's workplace at a certain time.

punch something **out (of** something**)** to press on something and make it pop out of something.

punch something **up** to register a figure on a cash register.

punctuation [pəŋk tʃu ˈe ʃən] *n.* the use of PUNCTUATION MARKS to make writing easier to understand. (No plural.)

punctuation mark [pəŋk tʃu 'e ʃən mark] *n.* a symbol used to make writing easier to understand, such as the period (.), the comma (,), the colon (:), the question mark (?), the exclamation point (!), and the hyphen (-), among others.

puncture ['pʌnk tʃɚ] **1.** *n.* a hole in the surface of something made by a sharp or pointed object. **2.** *tv.* to make a hole in the surface of something by using a sharp or pointed object.

punish ['pʌn ɪʃ] **1.** *tv.* to give someone a penalty for doing something wrong. **2.** *tv.* to use or handle something roughly. (Figurative on ①.)

punishment ['pʌn ɪʃ mənt] **1.** *n.* punishing; the practice of giving penalties for doing something wrong. (No plural.) **2.** *n.* rough treatment. (Figurative on ①. No plural.)
→ a GLUTTON FOR PUNISHMENT

punk ['pʌnk] **1.** *n.* a young criminal; a young person who gets into trouble a lot. **2.** *n.* a loud, harsh style of music first made popular in the late 1970s by young people. (No plural.) **3.** the *adj.* use of ① or ②.

puny ['pju ni] *adj.* smaller and weaker than average. (Adv: *punily.* Comp: *punier;* sup: *puniest.*)

pup ['pʌp] *n.* a young dog; a PUPPY; the young of certain animals, including the seal.

pupil ['pju pəl] **1.** *n.* a student; someone who studies in school; someone who is taught by a teacher. **2.** *n.* the round, black opening in the middle of the colored part of the eye that allows light into the eye.

puppy ['pʌp i] *n.* a young dog.

purchase ['pɚ tʃəs] **1.** *n.* an instance of buying something. **2.** *n.* something that is bought. **3.** *tv.* to buy something.

purchaser ['pɚ tʃə sɚ] *n.* a buyer; someone who buys something.

pure ['pjʊr] **1.** *adj.* completely made from only one thing; not mixed with anything. (Adv: *purely.* Comp: *purer;* sup: *purest.*) **2.** *adj.* [of a color] clear and not cloudy. (Adv: *purely.* Comp: *purer;* sup: *purest.*) **3.** *adj.* mere; absolute; nothing but. (Adv: *purely.* Comp: *purer;* sup: *purest.*) **4.** *adj.* without sin; without evil. (Adv: *purely.* Comp: *purer;* sup: *purest.*) **5.** *adj.* not having had sex. (Adv: *purely.* Comp: *purer;* sup: *purest.*)

purge ['pɚdʒ] **1.** *n.* an instance of forcing unwanted people to leave a government, university, society, or other group. **2.** *tv.* to make something clean by getting rid of what is dirty; to clean something out. **3.** *tv.* to destroy records or files.

purity ['pjʊr ə ti] *n.* the quality of being pure; the degree to which something is pure. (No plural.)

purple ['pɚ pəl] **1.** *n.* the color made by mixing blue and red; the color of ripe grapes that are not green or red. (Plural only for types and instances.) **2.** *adj.* of the color ①.

purpose ['pɚ pəs] *n.* an intention; the reason that someone does something; a kind of goal.

→ ON PURPOSE

purse ['pɚs] **1.** *n.* a bag used, especially by women, to hold money and other personal items. **2.** *n.* an amount of money that is offered as a prize.
→ CONTROL THE PURSE STRINGS
→ MAKE A SILK PURSE OUT OF A SOW'S EAR

pursue [pɚ 'su] **1.** *tv.* to chase someone or something; to follow and attempt to catch someone or something. **2.** *tv.* to continue to work toward something; to seek something. **3.** *tv.* to follow a plan of action.

pursuit [pɚ 'sut] **1.** *n.* pursuing someone or something; chasing after someone or something. (No plural.) **2.** *n.* a hobby or job that fills one's time.

push ['puʃ] **1.** *iv.* to force movement in a certain direction. **2.** *tv.* to apply pressure to something, as if to move it. **3.** *tv.* to move something or someone by applying pressure. **4.** *n.* a shove; a powerful movement that causes something to move. (No plural.)

push ahead to move forward or advance with force or effort; to move by using pressure.

push off to go away.

push one's **luck** AND **press** one's **luck** to expect continued good fortune; to expect to continue to escape bad luck.

push (oneself**) away (from** something**)** to move oneself back and away from something.

push out to spread out; to expand outward.

push someone or something **out (of** something**)** to force someone or something out of something.

push someone or something **up** to raise or lift someone or something.

push someone **to the wall** AND **press** someone **to the wall** to force someone into a position where there is only one choice to make; to put someone in a defensive position.

push something **off on(to)** someone to place one's task onto another person; to make someone else do an unwanted job.

push through something **or** someplace to force [one's way] through a crowded place.

put ['pʊt] **1.** *tv., irreg.* to place something in a certain position; to cause something to be in a certain place or position; to move something to a certain place or position. (Past tense and past participle: *put*.) **2.** *tv., irreg.* to express something; to say something in a certain way.
→ STAY PUT

put a bee in someone's **bonnet** Go to HAVE A BEE IN ONE'S BONNET.

put a cap on something to put a limit on something.

put a hold on something to place a restriction on something showing it is reserved, delayed, or inactivated.

put a spin on something to interpret an event to make it seem favorable or beneficial to oneself.

put a stop to something to make something end; to stop something.

put all one's **eggs in one basket** to risk everything at once.

put in a good word (for someone**)** to say something (to someone) in support of someone else.

put in one's **oar** to give help; to interfere by giving advice; to add one's assistance to the general effort.

put in one's **two cents(' worth)** to add one's comments (to something). (Implies that one's comments may not be of great value but need to be stated anyway.)

put on to pretend; to deceive.

put on a brave face to try to appear happy or satisfied when faced with misfortune or danger.

put on one's **thinking cap** to start thinking in a serious manner.

put one through one's **paces** to make one demonstrate what one can do; to make one do one's job thoroughly.

put one's **best foot forward** to act or appear at one's best; to try to make a good impression.

put one's **cards on the table** AND **lay** one's **cards on the table** to reveal everything; to be open and honest with someone.

put one's **foot in it** Go to PUT ONE'S FOOT IN ONE'S MOUTH.

put one's **foot in** one's **mouth** AND **put** one's **foot in it; stick** one's **foot in** one's **mouth** to say something that one regrets; unintentionally to say something stupid, insulting, or hurtful.

put one's **hand to the plow** to begin to do a big and important task; to undertake a major effort.

put one's **mind to** something to give one's complete attention to something.

put one's **nose to the grindstone** to keep busy doing one's work.

put one's **shoulder to the wheel** to get busy.

put oneself out to inconvenience oneself.

put out to generate lots of something. (Colloquial.)

put some teeth into something to increase the power of something.

put someone **off 1.** to delay action with someone. **2.** to repel someone.

put someone **on** to tease or deceive someone.

put someone or some creature **to sleep 1.** to kill someone or some creature. (Euphemistic.) **2.** to cause someone or some creature to sleep, perhaps through drugs or anesthesia.

put someone or something **out to pasture** to retire someone or something. (Originally said of a horse that was too old to work.)

put someone or something **over** to succeed in making someone or something be accepted.

put someone **out** to annoy or irritate someone.

put someone **through the wringer** to give someone a difficult time. (As one squeezes water from clothing in an old-fashioned wringer washing machine.)

put someone **to bed** to help someone—usually a child—get into a bed.

put someone **to shame** to make someone ashamed; to embarrass someone, especially by outdoing someone.

put someone **to sleep** to bore someone.

put someone **to the test** to test someone; to see what someone can achieve.

put someone **up (for** something**)** to nominate or offer someone for some office or task.

put someone's **eye out** to puncture or harm someone's eye and destroy its ability to see.

put someone's **nose out of joint** to offend someone; to cause someone to feel slighted or insulted.

put something **across (to** someone**)** to make something clear to someone.

put something **down** to take the life of a creature mercifully.

put something **off (until** something**)** to postpone or delay something until something happens or until some future time.

put something **on** to dress in an article of clothing.

put something **on ice** AND **put** something **on the back burner** to delay or postpone something; to put something on hold.

put something **on paper** to write something down; to write or type an agreement on paper.

put something **on the back burner** Go to PUT SOMETHING ON ICE.

put something **on the cuff** to buy something on credit; to add to one's credit balance. (As if one were making a note of the purchase on one's shirt cuff.)

put something **on the line** AND **lay** something **on the line 1.** to speak very firmly and directly about something. **2.** to put something at risk; to risk losing something.

put something **through its paces** to demonstrate how well something operates; to demonstrate all the things something can do.

put something **to bed** to complete work on something and send it on to the next step in production, especially in publishing.

put something **up (for sale)** to offer something for sale.

put the cart before the horse to have or do things in the wrong order; to have things confused and mixed up.

put two and two together to figure something out from the information available.

put up a (brave) front to appear to be brave (even if one is not).

put upon someone to make use of someone to an unreasonable degree; to take advantage of someone for one's own benefit. (Typically passive.)

put words into someone's **mouth** to speak for another person without permission.

Put your money where your mouth is! a command to stop talking and make a bet.

putty ['pʌt i] *n.* a soft, oily substance used to seal pipe connections, to seal the edges of glass in window frames, and to fill uneven surfaces. (No plural form.)
→ BE PUTTY IN SOMEONE'S HANDS

puzzle ['pʌz əl] **1.** *n.* something that confuses people; a problem that is confusing or difficult to solve. **2.** *n.* something similar to ① that people try to understand or solve for entertainment. **3.** *tv.* to confuse someone.

puzzle something **out** to figure something out.

pyramid ['pɪr ə mɪd] **1.** *n.* a four-sided structure with sides that are shaped like triangles and meet at one point on top. **2.** *n.* one of a group of large Egyptian tombs—shaped like ①—in which Egyptian kings and queens were once buried.

python ['paɪ θən] *n.* a large snake found in tropical areas of Asia, southeast India, Africa, and Australia that uses its powerful muscles to constrict and kill its prey.

quack [ˈkwæk] **1.** *iv.* to make the characteristic noise of a duck. **2.** *n.* the noise that a duck makes. **3.** *n.* someone who claims to be a doctor but who is not trained to be a doctor.

quaint [ˈkwent] *adj.* strange in an interesting or funny way; charming in an old-fashioned way. (Adv: *quaintly.* Comp: *quainter;* sup: *quaintest.*)

quake [ˈkwek] **1.** *n.* a shaking of the earth; an EARTHQUAKE. (Short for EARTHQUAKE.) **2.** *iv.* to shake; to tremble.

quake in one's **boots** Go to SHAKE IN ONE'S BOOTS.

qualify [ˈkwɑl ə faɪ] **1.** *tv.* to limit something; to restrict something; to narrow the meaning of something. **2.** *iv.* to meet the requirements for something.

quality [ˈkwɑl ɪ ti] **1.** *n.* a characteristic property of someone or something. **2.** *n.* a degree or level of excellence. (No plural.) **3.** *adj.* of ② that is good.

quantity [ˈkwɑn tə ti] *n.* an amount; a certain number of something that can be counted or measured.
→ KNOWN QUANTITY

quarantine [ˈkwɑr ən tin] **1.** *tv.* to isolate a living thing that has a disease or has been around another creature with a disease. **2.** *n.* a period of isolation of living things that have an illness or have been exposed to an illness. (Plural only for types and instances.)

quarrel [ˈkwɑr əl] **1.** *n.* an angry argument; an angry disagreement. **2.** *iv.* to argue with someone angrily; for two or more people to argue angrily.

quarrel (with someone**) (about** someone or something**)** to have an argument with someone about the subject of someone or something.

quarrel (with someone**) (over** someone or something**)** to have an argument with someone about who is going to have someone or something.

quarry [ˈkwɑr i] **1.** *n.* a place where marble, granite, and other kinds of stone are removed from the earth. **2.** *n.* the object of a hunt or search. **3.** *tv.* to remove stone from ①.

quart [ˈkwɔrt] *n.* a unit of measure of liquids, equal to one-fourth gallon, 32 ounces, or about 0.95 liter.

quarter [ˈkwɔr tɚ] **1.** *n.* one-fourth of something; one of four equal parts; one of four parts. **2.** *n.* a coin equal to 25 cents or one-fourth of a dollar. **3.** *n.* fifteen minutes; one-fourth of an hour. (Limited to *quarter to, quarter till, quarter of, quarter after,* and *quarter past.* No plural.) **4.** *n.* three months; one-fourth of a year. **5.** *n.* one of the four periods in professional football, basketball, and other games. **6.** *n.* a neighborhood; a section of a town; a district. **7.** *n.* a period equal to one-third of the school or academic year. **8.** *tv.* to divide something into four parts; to cut something into four parts; to split something into four parts. **9.** *tv.* to give someone, especially soldiers, a place to stay or live.

quarters *n.* the place where someone lives. (Treated as plural.)

queasy ['kwiz i] *adj.* feeling sick, nauseated, or uneasy. (Adv: *queasily.* Comp: *queasier;* sup: *queasiest.*)

queen ['kwin] **1.** *n.* the female ruler of a country or the wife of a king. **2.** *n.* the sole egg-laying female in a colony or hive of certain species of insects, such as bees, termites, or ants. **3.** *n.* a playing card that has a picture of ① on it. **4.** *n.* a chess piece that can move any number of spaces in a straight line in any direction.

queer ['kwɪr] *adj.* odd; strange; unusual; weird. (Adv: *queerly.* Comp: *queerer;* sup: *queerest.*)

quell ['kwɛl] *tv.* to calm or put an end to chaos, confusion, or some other problem.

quench ['kwɛntʃ] **1.** *tv.* to put out a fire by using water. **2.** *tv.* to ease or eliminate one's thirst by drinking something.

quest ['kwɛst] *n.* a search for someone or something.

question ['kwɛs tʃən] **1.** *n.* an inquiry; a speech utterance used to make an inquiry. **2.** *n.* a doubt; a concern; something that one is not sure about. (No plural.) **3.** *n.* a matter to be considered; a problem for solving. **4.** *tv.* to ask ① of

someone. **5.** *tv.* to doubt something; to express one's doubts or concerns about something.
→ BEG THE QUESTION
→ FIELD QUESTIONS
→ LEADING QUESTION
→ OUT OF THE QUESTION
→ POP THE QUESTION
→ POSE A QUESTION

question mark ['kwɛs tʃən mɑrk] *n.* a punctuation mark (?) that is written at the end of a question.

questionable ['kwɛs tʃə nə bəl] **1.** *adj.* in doubt; inviting questions or scrutiny. (Adv: *questionably.*) **2.** *adj.* possibly not honest or true. (Adv: *questionably.*)

questionnaire [kwɛs tʃə 'nɛr] *n.* a printed set of questions.

quick ['kwɪk] **1.** *adj.* fast; rapid; swift. (Adv: *quickly.* Comp: *quicker;* sup: *quickest.*) **2.** *adj.* lasting only for a short period of time; beginning and ending in a short period of time. (Adv: *quickly.* Comp: *quicker;* sup: *quickest.*) **3.** *adj.* able to understand or learn things in a short amount of time. (Adv: *quickly.* Comp: *quicker;* sup: *quickest.*) **4.** *n.* the flesh under one's fingernails or toenails. (No plural.) **5.** *adv.* very rapidly; with great speed. (Colloquial. Comp: *quicker;* sup: *quickest.*)
→ (AS) QUICK AS A WINK
→ CUT SOMEONE TO THE QUICK

quick on the draw Go to QUICK ON THE TRIGGER.

quick on the trigger AND **quick on the draw 1.** quick to draw a gun and shoot. **2.** quick to respond to anything.

quicken ['kwɪk ən] **1.** *iv.* to become faster; to move more quickly; to do something more quickly; to increase the speed of something. **2.** *tv.* to cause something to become faster; to cause something to occur more quickly.

quickness ['kwɪk nəs] *n.* the quality of being quick. (No plural.)

quicksand ['kwɪk sænd] *n.* wet sand, often under water, into which living creatures can sink. (No plural.)

quiet ['kwaɪ ɪt] **1.** *adj.* not loud; making only a small amount of sound. (Adv: *quietly.* Comp: *quieter;* sup: *quietest.*) **2.** *adj.* [of a person] shy and not talkative. (Adv: *quietly.* Comp: *quieter;* sup: *quietest.*) **3.** *adj.* not active; not moving; calm; still. (Adv: *quietly.* Comp: *quieter;* sup: *quietest.*) **4.** *adj.* peaceful; restful. (Adv: *quietly.* Comp: *quieter;* sup: *quietest.*) **5.** *tv.* to cause someone or something to become ①. **6.** *n.* silence. (No plural.)
→ (AS) QUIET AS A MOUSE
→ SO QUIET YOU COULD HEAR A PIN DROP

quiet down to become quiet; to become less noisy.

quiet someone or something **down** to make someone or some creature quieter.

quilt ['kwɪlt] **1.** *n.* a bed covering made from a soft pad between two layers of decorative cloth, stitched together. **2.** *iv.* to work at making ①.

quip ['kwɪp] *n.* a clever, witty, or sarcastic remark.

quirk ['kwɚk] *n.* a strange habit; a strange characteristic.

quit ['kwɪt] **1.** *tv., irreg.* to stop doing something. (Past tense and past participle: *quit.*) **2.** *tv., irreg.* to leave a job; to resign from a job. **3.** *iv., irreg.* [for someone or something] to cease [doing something].
→ CALL IT QUITS

quit on someone **1.** [for something] to quit while someone is using it. **2.** [for one] to leave one's job, usually suddenly or unannounced.

quite ['kwaɪt] *adv.* very; rather; completely.

quiz ['kwɪz] **1.** *n.* a small test; an informal test. (Plural: *quizzes.*) **2.** *tv.* to test someone on or about something; to ask someone questions about someone or something.

quota ['kwot ə] *n.* a required amount of something; a required number of things or people.

quotation [kwo 'te ʃən] *n.* a statement that was said or written, used again by someone else; a statement that is quoted from someone or from someone's writing.

quotation marks [kwo 'te ʃən marks] *n.* the marks (" ") and (' '), called *double quotation marks* and *single quotation marks,* respectively, used to enclose actual speech in writing or printing.

quote ['kwot] **1.** *tv.* to use a quotation; to repeat part of something that someone else has said or written, at the same time telling who said or wrote it. **2.** *tv.* to cite someone or a written source as the origin of a quotation. **3.** *n.* a quotation; a statement that was said or written by someone else.

4. *n.* an estimate of the price of something.

quote a price to name or state the charge for doing or supplying something.

rabbi ['ræb ɑɪ] *n.* the leader of a Jewish synagogue; a Jewish religious leader. (Also a term of address. Capitalized when written as a proper noun.)

rabbit ['ræb ət] *n.* a small animal with soft fur, long ears, and a fluffy tail.

race ['res] **1.** *n.* a contest that has to do with speed; a contest that has to do with how fast people, animals, or machines can move. **2.** *n.* a political election, and the time during the campaign leading up to the election. **3.** *n.* the physical differences among humans that have to do with dividing people into different groups, especially groups based on the color of skin. (Plural only for types and instances.) **4.** *iv.* to run rapidly, as if in a race; to move or operate very fast. **5.** *tv.* to cause someone or something to take part in ①. **6.** *tv.* to cause an engine to run very rapidly. **7.** *tv.* to compete against someone to reach a specific goal.
→ HUMAN RACE
→ RAT RACE

race with someone or something to enter a speed contest with someone or something.

racetrack ['res træk] *n.* the place, usually a large oval, where a race takes place, and the stadium or arena that contains it.

racial ['reʃ əl] *adj.* of or about RACE ③. (Adv: *racially.*)

racism ['res ɪz əm] *n.* prejudice, hatred, or violence shown against someone of a particular race. (No plural.)

racist ['res ɪst] **1.** *n.* someone who believes one race is better than another. **2.** *adj.* exhibiting racism; showing prejudice against someone's race.

rack ['ræk] *n.* a frame with shelves, rods, hooks, or pegs that is used to hang things from or put things on.
→ BE RACKED WITH PAIN
→ GO TO RACK AND RUIN

rack one's **brain(s)** to try very hard to think of something.

rack something **up 1.** to place something onto or into its rack. **2.** to accumulate a number of things, particularly a score, a win, etc.

racket ['ræk ət] **1.** AND **racquet** *n.* a device used to hit a ball or something similar back and forth, usually over a net. **2.** *n.* a dishonest or illegal activity, such as fraud, done to make money.

racquet ['ræk ət] Go to RACKET.

radar ['re dɑr] *n.* a device that uses radio waves to detect an object, usually a car or an aircraft, and to determine that object's location, distance, and speed. (An acronym for *radio detecting and ranging.* No plural.)

radiate ['re di et] *tv.* to cause something to spread out in all directions from a center point; to give off rays of something such as heat or light.

radiate from something **1.** [for rays] to come from something.

2. to extend outward from a central point.

radiation [re di 'e ʃən] **1.** *n.* the release of heat, light, or other energy. (No plural.) **2.** *n.* radioactive particles and energy used in medical treatment. (No plural.)

radical ['ræd ɪ kəl] **1.** *adj.* complete and thorough; extreme. (Adv: *radically* […ɪk li].) **2.** *adj.* [of someone] favoring extreme change. (Adv: *radically* […ɪk li].) **3.** *n.* someone who favors complete change; someone who favors extreme change.

radii ['re di ɑɪ] a plural of RADIUS.

radio ['re di o] **1.** *n.* the sending and receiving of sound through the air by using electromagnetic waves. (No plural.) **2.** *n.* a device that is used to receive electromagnetic waves and turn them into sound. (Plural ends in -s.) **3.** the *adj.* use of ① or ②. **4.** *tv.* to send a message by ①. **5.** *tv.* to send [a message] to someone using ②. **6.** *iv.* to use ② to send a message.

radioactive [re di o 'æk tɪv] *adj.* of or about an element, or its compounds, that releases energy as the result of naturally occurring changes in the nuclear structure of the atoms of the element. (Adv: *radioactively*.)

radius ['re di əs] **1.** *n., irreg.* the distance from the center of a circle to any point on the circle. (Plural: RADII or *radiuses*.) **2.** *n., irreg.* a line that goes from the center of a circle to any point on the circle.

raffle ['ræf əl] *n.* a way of raising money where people buy tickets to win items or prizes that have been donated. (The winning ticket is chosen at random.)

raffle something off to make an item available in a raffle.

raft ['ræft] **1.** *n.* boards or logs that are tied together so they will float on water; a rubber boat that is filled with air and floats on water. **2.** *iv.* to travel across water on ①.

rafter ['ræf tɚ] *n.* one of a series of parallel boards or beams that support a roof.

rag ['ræg] *n.* a piece of cloth, especially one that has no value or is used for cleaning.
→ FROM RAGS TO RICHES
→ IN RAGS

rage ['redʒ] **1.** *n.* extreme, violent anger. **2.** *iv.* to show extreme, violent anger toward something.

rage through something **1.** [for a fire] to burn rapidly through an area or a building. **2.** [for someone] to move rapidly through some sequence or process, as if in a rage.

ragged ['ræg əd] *adj.* torn; [of cloth] torn or damaged. (Adv: *raggedly*.)
→ RUN SOMEONE RAGGED

raid ['red] **1.** *n.* a surprise attack, especially by police or soldiers. **2.** *tv.* to enter someone's property or space and attack quickly, suddenly, and by surprise.

rail ['rel] **1.** *n.* a thick strip of wood or metal, usually used to support or guide someone or something. **2.** *n.* one of a pair of metal strips on which a train travels.

rail at someone **(about** something**)** to complain loudly or violently to someone about something.

railing ['rel ɪŋ] *n.* a thick strip, rail, or tube of wood or metal that people can hold on to for support, usually found on a staircase.

railroad ['rel rod] **1.** *n.* two parallel metal rails on which a train travels. **2.** *n.* a network or system of train tracks, train stations, and trains. **3.** *n.* a business that operates trains. **4.** *tv.* to move something quickly and forcefully; to force someone to do something quickly. **5.** the *adj.* use of ①, ②, or ③.

railroad someone **into** something to force someone into doing something in great haste.

railroad something **through (**something**)** to force something through some organization or legislative body without due consideration.

railway ['rel we] **1.** *n.* a railroad; a railroad of a short length. **2.** the *adj.* use of ①.

rain ['ren] **1.** *n.* water that falls down from the sky in drops. (No plural.) **2.** *n.* an instance or period of ①. (The plural usually indicates a season of RAIN that occurs annually.) **3.** *iv.* [for drops of water] to fall from the sky. (The subject must be ɪt.) **4.** *tv.* to cause something to fall from the sky like ①.
→ POURING RAIN

rain cats and dogs to rain very hard.

rain down on someone or something to fall or drop down on someone or something like rain.

rain in on someone or something [for rain] to enter a window or other opening and get someone or something wet.

rain or shine whether it rains or the sun shines; no matter what.

rain something **down (on** someone or something**)** to pour something, such as criticism or praise, onto someone or something.

rain something **out** [for rain] to force the cancellation of an outdoor event.

rainbow ['ren bo] **1.** *n.* an arch of different colors of light that appears in the sky, caused by rays of sunlight passing through rain or mist. **2.** *adj.* consisting of the colors of the rainbow; from the group of colors of the rainbow.

raincoat ['ren kot] *n.* a waterproof coat that people wear when it rains to keep their clothes dry.

raindrop ['ren drɑp] *n.* one drop of rain.

rainfall ['ren fɔl] **1.** *n.* the drops of rain that fall when it rains; a period of falling rain. (No plural.) **2.** *n.* the amount of rain that falls in a certain place over a certain length of time. (No plural.)

rainstorm ['ren storm] *n.* a storm that has a large amount of rain.

rainy ['re ni] *adj.* having a lot of rain. (Adv: *rainily.* Comp: *rainier;* sup: *rainiest.*)
→ SAVE SOMETHING FOR A RAINY DAY

raise ['rez] **1.** *tv.* to lift someone or something; to move someone

or something to a higher level; to move someone or something upward; to cause someone or something to rise. (Compare this with RISE.) **2.** *tv.* to increase the amount of something; to increase the degree of something; to increase the force of something. **3.** *tv.* to cause plants to grow; to breed animals. **4.** *tv.* to bring up a child; to rear a child. **5.** *tv.* to collect or gather a certain amount of money. **6.** *tv.* to bring up a subject or issue; to mention something; to address a subject or an issue; to begin talking about something. **7.** *n.* an increase in one's salary; an increase in the amount of money one earns at a job.
→ CAUSE (SOME) EYEBROWS TO RAISE

raise one's **sights** to set higher goals for oneself.

raise some eyebrows to shock or surprise people mildly (by doing or saying something).

raise someone or something **up** to lift someone or something up.

raise up to lift oneself up; to get up or begin to get up.

raisin ['re zɪn] *n.* a dried grape, eaten as food.

rake ['rek] **1.** *n.* a tool that has a long handle that is attached to a row of curved metal or plastic "fingers," used to collect fallen leaves, loose grass, etc. **2.** *tv.* to collect something, especially leaves, hay, grass, or other objects on the ground, using ① or something similar. **3.** *tv.* to smooth or clean something by using ①. **4.** *iv.* to use ①; to scrape with ①.

rake someone **over the coals** AND **haul** someone **over the coals** to give someone a severe scolding.

rake something **off ((of)** something) to remove something from something by raking.

rake something **out** to clean something by raking.

rake something **out (of** something) to clean something out of something by raking.

rake something **up 1.** to gather and clean up something with a rake. **2.** to clean something up by raking. **3.** to uncover something unpleasant and remind people about it.

rally ['ræl i] **1.** *tv.* to bring people together for a certain reason or cause. **2.** *n.* a large meeting, especially a large political meeting, held for a special reason.

rally (a)round someone or something to come together to support someone or something.

ram ['ræm] **1.** *n.* a male sheep. **2.** *n.* a heavy pole or beam, the end of which is thrust against something. **3.** *tv.* to hit someone or something; to crash into someone or something.

ram something **through (**something**) 1.** to force something through something. **2.** to force something through a process of study and decision, usually not allowing due consideration.

ram through something to crash or pound through something.

ramble on to go on and on aimlessly; to wander about aimlessly.

(Usually figurative. As with a road, a speaker, a speech, etc.)

ramble on (about someone or something) [for someone] to talk endlessly and aimlessly about someone or something.

rampage ['ræm pedʒ] *n.* a period of wild, angry, or violent behavior.
→ GO ON A RAMPAGE

rampant ['ræm pənt] *adj.* growing, moving, or spreading out of control. (Adv: *rampantly.*)
→ RUN RAMPANT

ran ['ræn] past tense of RUN.

ranch ['ræntʃ] *n.* a very large farm where cattle or other animals are raised.

rancher ['ræntʃ ɚ] *n.* someone who works on a ranch; someone who owns a ranch.

random ['ræn dəm] *adj.* selected by chance. (Adv: *randomly.*)
→ AT RANDOM

rang ['ræŋ] past tense of RING.

range ['rendʒ] **1.** *n.* the area between two extremes; the choices, possibilities, or selections available. **2.** *n.* the distance that something can operate or be used in, especially the distance that someone can see or hear, that a weapon can fire, or that something can travel without needing more fuel. (No plural.) **3.** *n.* a field where cattle or other animals can walk about and look for food. (No plural.) **4.** *n.* a stove with one or more ovens attached. **5.** *iv.* to vary between two limits or extremes; to be located between an upper limit and a lower limit.
→ MOUNTAIN RANGE

range from something **to** something to vary from one thing to another.

rank ['ræŋk] **1.** *n.* one level in a series of levels; one level on a scale of authority, value, or importance. **2.** *iv.* to occupy a certain position on a scale of authority, value, or importance; to be on a list in a certain position. **3.** *tv.* to place someone or something on a list in its proper order or place. **4.** *adj.* smelling or tasting very bad or unpleasant. (Adv: *rankly.*) **5.** *adj.* [of vegetation] growing thickly or coarsely.
→ CLOSE RANKS

rant (at someone) **about** someone or something to talk in a loud, violent way, about someone or something.

rap ['ræp] **1.** *n.* a style of music where the words of the song are spoken in a strong rhythm instead of being sung. (No plural.) **2.** *n.* the sound made by a quick, strong knock or hit.

rap at something to hit or knock on something quickly.

rap on something [for someone] to hit something quickly and sharply, making a knocking sound.

rap something **out (on** something) to tap out the rhythm of something on something.

rap with someone to talk; to chat.

rape ['rep] **1.** *n.* the act and crime of forcing someone to have sex. **2.** *tv.* to force someone to have sex.

rapid ['ræp ɪd] *adj.* quick; swift; moving fast; done quickly; happening quickly. (Adv: *rapidly.*)

rapidity [rə'pɪd ə ti] *n.* quickness; speed. (No plural.)

rapids *n.* the part of a river where the water moves very fast and is very active. (Treated as plural.)

rapture ['ræp tʃɚ] *n.* a feeling or expression of complete joy or delight. (No plural.)

rare ['rɛr] **1.** *adj.* not common; not often found, seen, or done. (Adv: *rarely.* Comp: *rarer;* sup: *rarest.*) **2.** *adj.* [of meat] cooked only a little. (Comp: *rarer;* sup: *rarest.*)

rarin' to go extremely eager to act or do something. (Informal.)

rash ['ræʃ] **1.** *n.* a disease or condition of the skin, making it red, itchy, and bumpy. **2.** *adj.* not thinking about something carefully or long enough; done without careful thought. (Adv: *rashly.* Comp: *rasher;* sup: *rashest.*)

raspberry ['ræz bɛr i] **1.** *n.* a small, sweet, usually red or purple fruit that grows on a bush, and the bush itself. **2.** *adj.* made or flavored with ①.

rat ['ræt] **1.** *n.* a small rodent with a long tail. **2.** *n.* someone who is mean, worthless, not honest, or not loyal. (Figurative on ①.)

rat race a fierce struggle for success, especially in one's career or business.

rate ['ret] **1.** *n.* the relation of an amount to another amount, such as speed in relation to time. **2.** *n.* a price [for each unit of something]. **3.** *tv.* to assign a value or rank to someone or something. **4.** *tv.* to deserve something; to be worthy of something.

rather ['ræð ɚ] **1.** *adv.* instead; on the contrary. **2.** *adv.* to an extent; to a degree; too; very; quite.
→ WOULD RATHER DO SOMETHING

ratify ['ræt ə faɪ] *tv.* to approve something officially; to make something be valid officially.

rational ['ræʃ ə nəl] **1.** *adj.* using the mind or the brain; sensible; reasonable; logical. (Adv: *rationally.*) **2.** *adj.* able to use sense or reason; aware. (Adv: *rationally.*)

rationale [ræʃ ə 'næl] *n.* a reason; the reason for doing something; reasoning or explanation. (No plural.)

rattle ['ræt əl] **1.** *n.* a noise-making device, usually a toy for babies, consisting of a small container with bits of hard material inside. **2.** *n.* the noise made when a number of small things tap against something, as with ①. **3.** *iv.* to make a quick set of short noises. **4.** *tv.* to cause something to make a quick set of short noises.

rattle around in something **1.** to make a rattling noise inside something. **2.** to ride about in a vehicle that rattles. **3.** to live in a place that is much too big. (Figurative.)

rattle something **off** to recite something with ease; to recite a list quickly and easily.

rattlesnake ['ræt əl snek] *n.* a venomous snake with hard rings of skin on its tail that make a rattling sound when it shakes its tail.

rave about someone or something ['rev…] to praise or curse someone or something in a very excited or wild way; to praise someone or something.

ravished with delight made very happy or delighted; filled with happiness or delight.

raw ['rɔ] **1.** *adj.* not cooked. (Comp: *rawer;* sup: *rawest.*) **2.** *adj.* [of something that has been] rubbed until sore; having a layer of skin rubbed off. (Adv: *rawly.* Comp: *rawer;* sup: *rawest.*)

ray ['re] *n.* a beam of something that comes from a source, especially a beam of light, heat, or radiation.

raze ['rez] *tv.* to tear down a building completely.

razor ['re zɚ] **1.** *n.* a tool that holds a sharp blade that is used to shave whiskers or hair. **2.** the *adj.* use of ①.

reach ['ritʃ] **1.** *tv.* to arrive at someplace; to get to someplace. **2.** *tv.* to get hold of someone by some means of communication; to contact someone. **3.** *tv.* to stretch out to a certain place in space or time; to extend to a certain place in space or time. **4.** *tv.* to affect or influence someone; to make someone else understand something. **5.** *tv.* to total a certain amount. **6.** *iv.* to extend all the way. **7.** *n.* the distance that someone or something is able to stretch or extend; the range or capacity of someone or something.

reach a compromise to achieve a compromise; to make a compromise.

reach an agreement to achieve an agreement; to make an agreement.

reach an impasse to progress to the point that a barrier stops further progress.

reach back (in)to something to extend back into a particular period in time.

reach down to extend downward.

reach first base (with someone or something) Go to GET TO FIRST BASE (WITH SOMEONE OR SOMETHING).

reach for someone or something to move or stretch to touch or get something.

reach in(to something) to stick one's hand into something to grasp something.

reach out 1. to extend one's grasp outward. **2.** to enlarge one's circle of friends and experiences.

reach out (after someone or something) to extend one's grasp to someone or something.

reach out into something to extend one's grasp out into something, such as the darkness.

reach out to someone **1.** to offer someone a helping hand. **2.** to seek someone's help and support.

react [ri 'ækt] **1.** *iv.* to show a response [to something]; to make a response [to someone or something]. **2.** *iv.* [for a chemical] to do something when it touches another substance; [for two chemicals] to do something when they are brought together.

reaction [ri 'æk ʃən] **1.** *n.* a response to someone or something; an action that is done in response to someone or something; a feeling that is felt in

response to someone or something. **2.** *n.* the result of a chemical touching another substance; the result when two chemicals are brought together.
→ GUT REACTION

read 1. ['rid] *tv., irreg.* to understand what is meant by written words; to get meaning from written words. (Past tense and past participle: *read* ['rɛd].) **2.** ['rid] *tv., irreg.* to say written words out loud. **3.** ['rid] *iv., irreg.* to be able to understand writing and printing. **4.** ['rid] *iv., irreg.* to say written words aloud.

read between the lines to infer something (from something else); to try to understand what is meant by something that is not written clearly or openly.

read someone **like a book** to understand someone very well.

read someone **out (for** something**)** to chastise someone verbally for doing something wrong.

read someone **out of** something to make a case for the removal of someone from something.

read someone **the riot act** to give someone a severe scolding.

read something **back (to** someone**)** to read back some information to the person who has just given it.

read something **in((to)** something**)** to make inferences as one reads something; to imagine that additional messages, ideas, or biases are present in something that one is reading.

read something **off** to read aloud a list.

read something **over** to read something, concentrating on form as well as content.

read through something to look through some reading material.

read up (on someone or something**)** to study about someone or something by reading.

readily ['rɛd ə li] **1.** *adv.* without difficulty or problems; easily. **2.** *adv.* without delay or doubt; eagerly.

readiness ['rɛd i nəs] *n.* the state of being ready; the state of being prepared. (No plural.)

reading ['rid ɪŋ] **1.** *n.* something written that is meant to be read. **2.** *n.* a measurement shown on a meter or other similar device. **3.** the *adj.* use of ① or ②.

readjust [ri ə 'dʒʌst] *tv.* to adjust something again; to put something back where it belongs.

readjust to someone or something to get used to someone or something again.

readjustment [ri ə 'dʒʌst mənt] **1.** *n.* the process of getting used to something again. (No plural.) **2.** *n.* an act of readjusting something; a movement or change that is made when putting something back where it belongs.

ready ['rɛd i] **1.** *adj.* [of something] able to be used right now. (Comp: *readier*; sup: *readiest*.) **2.** *tv.* to prepare something for use.

ready to do something [of someone or some creature] prepared and eager to do something.

real ['ril] **1.** *adj.* existing; actual; true. (Adv: *really.*) **2.** *adj.* genuine; not fake. (Adv: *really.*) **3.** *adv.* really; very; extremely. (Colloquial.)

real estate ['ril ə stet] **1.** *n.* land, with all the buildings on it. (No plural.) **2.** *n.* the business of dealing in ①. (No plural.) **3.** the *adj.* use of ① or ②. (Hyphenated before a nominal.)

realism ['ri ə lɪz əm] *n.* the point of view concerned with reality in life and art. (No plural.)

realistic [ri ə 'lɪs tɪk] **1.** *adj.* appearing or seeming to be real or authentic. (Adv: *realistically* […ɪk li].) **2.** *adj.* accepting life as it really is; practical. (Adv: *realistically* […ɪk li].)

reality [ri 'æl ə ti] *n.* everything that is real; something that is real; that which exists. (Plural only for types and instances.)
→ IN REALITY

realization [ri əl ə 'ze ʃən] *n.* an understanding that something exists or has happened.

realize ['ri ə laɪz] **1.** *tv.* to understand something; to be aware of something. (The object can be a clause with THAT ⑦.) **2.** *tv.* to make something real; to cause something to exist.

really ['ri (ə) li] **1.** *adv.* actually; truly; in reality. **2.** *adv.* very; completely.

reappear [ri ə 'pɪr] **1.** *iv.* to appear again. **2.** *iv.* to occur again.

rear ['rɪr] **1.** *n.* the part of the body one sits on. (Euphemistic.) **2.** *adj.* in back; hind. **3.** *tv.* to raise offspring. **4.** *iv.* to rise up, especially for a horse to stand on its back legs.
→ AT THE REAR OF SOMETHING
→ BRING UP THE REAR
→ IN THE REAR

rear back 1. [for a horse] to pull back onto its hind legs in an effort to move backwards rapidly. **2.** [for a person] to pull back and stand up or sit up straighter.

rear its ugly head [for something unpleasant] to appear or become obvious after lying hidden.

rear up 1. [for a horse] to lean back on its hind legs and raise its front part up, assuming a threatening posture or avoiding something on the ground such as a snake. **2.** [for something, especially a problem] to rise up suddenly. (Figurative.)

rearrange [ri ə 'rendʒ] *tv.* to arrange something again or in a different way, especially to place people or things in a different order or in different positions with respect to each other.

rearrangement [ri ə 'rendʒ mənt] *n.* creating a new or different arrangement; changing the way that people or things are ordered or positioned with respect to each other. (No plural.)

reason ['ri zən] **1.** *n.* the power or ability to think, understand, and form opinions and conclusions from facts. (No plural.) **2.** *n.* a cause; a motive; an explanation; a rationale. **3.** *iv.* to think; to be able to think; to use the power or ability to think, understand, and form opinions and conclusions. **4.** *tv.* to have an opinion or conclusion

479

based on ①. (The object is a clause with THAT ⑦.)

reason something **out** to figure something out; to plan a reasonable course of action.

reason with someone to persuade someone by using reason; to argue with someone by using reason.

reasonable ['ri zə nə bəl] **1.** *adj.* sensible; making sense; according to reason. (Adv: *reasonably*.) **2.** *adj.* not expensive; having an acceptable cost. (Adv: *reasonably*.)

reasoning ['ri zə nɪŋ] *n.* the process or ability of thinking and forming conclusions from facts and evidence. (No plural.)

reassure [ri ə 'ʃʊr] *tv.* to restore someone's courage or confidence.

rebel 1. ['rɛb əl] *n.* someone who fights or resists power, authority, or government. **2.** [rɪ 'bɛl] to fight or resist power, authority, or government.

rebel against someone or something [rɪ 'bɛl…] to fight against a person, power, laws, rules, authority, or government.

rebellion [rɪ 'bɛl jən] *n.* rebelling; challenging authority. (Plural only for types and instances.)

rebirth [ri 'bɚθ] *n.* seeming to be born again. (No plural.)

rebound 1. ['ri baʊnd] *n.* the return movement of something that bounced off something. **2.** [rɪ 'baʊnd] *iv.* to bounce back after hitting something. **3.** [rɪ 'baʊnd] *iv.* to recover. (Figurative on ②.)

rebuild [ri 'bɪld] *tv., irreg.* to build something again. (Past tense and past participle: REBUILT.)

rebuilt [ri 'bɪlt] past tense and past participle of REBUILD.

receipt [rɪ 'sit] **1.** *n.* a state of having been received. (No plural.) **2.** *n.* a document that proves that something has been received or paid for.
→ IN RECEIPT OF SOMETHING

receipts *n.* money that a business receives from customers; money that is collected by a business or at a performance. (Treated as plural, but not countable.)

receive [rɪ 'siv] **1.** *tv.* to get something; to take something that is given. **2.** *tv.* to accept someone as a member of a group or organization; to welcome someone as a visitor.

receiver [rɪ 'siv ɚ] **1.** *n.* someone or something that receives something. **2.** *n.* the part of a telephone that one holds while one is talking. **3.** *n.* a radio or television set; something that receives broadcast signals.

recent ['ri sənt] *adj.* happening only a short time ago; having existed for only a short time; not long ago. (Adv: *recently*.)
→ IN RECENT MEMORY

receptacle [rɪ 'sɛp tə kəl] **1.** *n.* a container designed to receive something. **2.** *n.* a place to plug in an electric cord. (Short for ELECTRIC RECEPTACLE.)
→ ELECTRIC RECEPTACLE

reception [rɪ 'sɛp ʃən] **1.** *n.* receiving or welcoming someone. **2.** *n.* the quality of broadcast signals that are received by a television set, a radio, or other receiver. (No plural.) **3.** *n.* a party, gathering, or celebration where people are welcomed.

recess 1. ['ri sɛs] *n.* a period of time during the school day when the children are allowed to play, usually outside. **2.** ['ri sɛs] *n.* a period of time during the workday when someone stops working for a few minutes and takes a break; a BREAK ②. **3.** ['ri sɛs] *n.* a space cut or built into a wall; a space that is set back from a wall. **4.** [rɪ 'sɛs] *iv.* to take a break; to stop working for a short time.

recipe ['rɛs ə pi] **1.** *n.* a set of directions for making something to eat. **2.** *n.* a set of directions for preparing or causing anything. (Figurative on ①.)

recipient [rɪ 'sɪp i ənt] *n.* someone who or something that receives something.

recital [rɪ 'saɪt əl] **1.** *n.* the telling of a story; a verbal account of something. **2.** *n.* a concert or performance, often by a single performer playing an instrument, singing, or reading poetry.

recite [rɪ 'saɪt] *tv.* to verbally deliver an answer in school; to repeat something, such as a poem, from memory.

recite something **chapter and verse** to give detailed information; to quote something in great detail, especially some source of authority.

reckless ['rɛk ləs] *adj.* careless; not concerned about safety or danger. (Adv: *recklessly.*)

recklessness ['rɛk ləs nəs] *n.* being reckless; taking risks on purpose. (No plural.)

reclaim [rɪ 'klem] **1.** *tv.* to save or reuse something that would otherwise be thrown away. **2.** *tv.* to demand or claim the return of something that has been given away or taken away.

recognition [rɛk ɪg 'nɪʃ ən] **1.** *n.* realization. (No plural.) **2.** *n.* acknowledgment of the existence of someone or something. (No plural.) **3.** *n.* acknowledgment of service or excellence. (No plural.)

recognizable ['rɛk ɪg naɪz ə bəl] *adj.* in adequate amount or degree to be noticed or identified. (Adv: *recognizably.*)

recognize ['rɛk ɪg naɪz] **1.** *tv.* to identify someone or something. **2.** *tv.* to make an acknowledgment that something exists. (The object can be a clause with THAT ⑦.) **3.** *tv.* to give someone the right to speak, especially at a meeting.

recommend [rɛk ə 'mɛnd] **1.** *tv.* to suggest [making] a particular choice from a range of choices. **2.** *tv.* to suggest a particular course of action. (The object can be a clause with THAT ⑦.)

recommendation [rɛk ə mɛn 'de ʃən] *n.* a suggestion of which selection someone should choose from a range of choices; someone or something that is recommended.

reconcile oneself **to** something to grow to feel comfortable with an undesirable or challenging situation.

reconsider [ri kən 'sɪd ɚ] **1.** *tv.* to consider something again; to think about something again. **2.** *iv.* to consider again; to think about again.

record 1. ['rɛk ɚd] *n.* a written account of facts or information about someone or something. **2.** ['rɛk ɚd] *n.* a flat plastic disk that has sound stored on it and is played on a machine that makes the recorded sounds able to be heard. **3.** ['rɛk ɚd] *n.* the most extreme example of something; the highest, lowest, fastest, slowest, longest, shortest, or any other extreme example of something. **4.** [rɪ 'kord] *tv.* to write down information about someone or something so that other people will be able to read the information. **5.** [rɪ 'kord] *tv.* to store sound on audiotape or to store images on film or videotape; to put a sound or an image into a permanent form.

record something **on** something to make a record of something on the surface of something.

recorded [rɪ 'kor dɪd] **1.** *adj.* written down; having information about someone or something written down; known. **2.** *adj.* stored on cassette, film, or videotape; stored in a permanent form.

recorder [rɪ 'kor dɚ] **1.** *n.* someone who writes down and stores information. **2.** *n.* a musical instrument, consisting of a hollow tube of wood that has holes down one side. **3.** *n.* a machine that records sounds or images and usually is able to play the sounds and images back.

→ BREAK A RECORD
→ CASSETTE RECORDER
→ FOR THE RECORD
→ OFF THE RECORD

recording [rɪ 'kor dɪŋ] *n.* a record; music, speech, or other sound that has been recorded.

recount 1. ['ri kaʊnt] *n.* another counting; a second count; another count, especially in an election when the votes are counted for a second time because the first count is thought to be faulty. **2.** [ri 'kaʊnt] *tv.* to tell a story; to tell the story of something that happened. **3.** ['ri 'kaʊnt] *tv.* to count something again.

recount something **to** someone to tell something to someone; to narrate a series of events, in order.

recover [ri 'kʌv ɚ] **1.** *iv.* to get better after a sickness or injury; to return to good health. **2.** *tv.* to get something back that went away or was lost, stolen, or taken away. **3.** *tv.* to reclaim something; to pull out something useful from something that is not useful.

recovery [ri 'kʌv ə ri] **1.** *n.* the process of getting something back that went away or was lost, stolen, or taken; receiving someone or something that went away or was lost, stolen, or taken. (No plural.) **2.** *n.* the return to someone's or something's regular condition, especially the return of good health after sickness or injury or the return of a good economy after a bad period of time. (No plural.)

recreation [rɛk ri 'e ʃən] *n.* amusement; play; activities that are done for pleasure, enjoyment, or fun. (No plural.)

recreational [rɛk ri 'e ʃə nəl] *adj.* of or about RECREATION. (Adv: *recreationally.*)

recruit [rɪ 'krut] **1.** *tv.* to cause or persuade someone to become a new member of a group, or organization such as the military. **2.** *n.* someone who has just joined a group or organization, especially the military.

recruit someone **into** something to seek out and bring someone into something.

rectangle ['rɛk tæŋ gəl] *n.* a four-sided figure with four right angles, having opposite sides that are parallel and the same length.

rectangular [rɛk 'tæŋ gjə lɚ] *adj.* shaped like a RECTANGLE. (Adv: *rectangularly.*)

rectify ['rɛk tə faɪ] *tv.* to make something right; to correct something.

rectum ['rɛk təm] *n.* the end of the lower intestine, through which waste passes.

recuperate from something to recover from something; to be cured or to heal after something.

recur [ri 'kɚ] *iv.* to repeat; to happen again; to continue to happen.

recycle [ri 'saɪk əl] **1.** *tv.* to change glass, plastic, paper, or other material into a form that can be used again; to recover a resource; to

find a further use for something that might otherwise be wasted. **2.** *tv.* to collect or set aside used glass, plastic, paper, or other material so that it can be made into something useful. **3.** *iv.* to collect and set aside [trash] as in ②.

recycled [ri 'saɪk əld] *adj.* made from a substance that has already been used.

red ['rɛd] **1.** *n.* the color of blood and the traffic signal that means stop. (Plural only for types and instances.) **2.** the *adj.* use of ①. (Adv: *redly.* Comp: *redder;* sup: *reddest.*) **3.** *adj.* [of hair] copper colored or rusty orange. (Comp: *redder;* sup: *reddest.*)

→ GET THE RED-CARPET TREATMENT
→ GIVE SOMEONE THE RED-CARPET TREATMENT
→ IN THE RED
→ ONE'S EARS ARE RED
→ OUT OF THE RED
→ PAINT THE TOWN RED
→ ROLL OUT THE RED CARPET FOR SOMEONE

red tape overly strict attention to the wording and details of rules and regulations, especially by government or public departments. (From the color of the tape used by government departments to tie up bundles of documents.)

redbird ['rɛd bɚd] *n.* any of various birds having red feathers.

redden ['rɛd n] **1.** *iv.* to become red; to turn red. **2.** *tv.* to cause someone or something to become red; to cause someone or something to turn red.

reddish ['rɛd ɪʃ] *adj.* having some of the qualities of the color red. (Adv: *reddishly.*)

redeem [rɪ 'dim] **1.** *tv.* to convert something to cash, especially to convert a coupon, token, ticket, or other thing that is not money but represents money. **2.** *tv.* to do something that restores other people's good opinion of oneself. (Takes a reflexive object.)

redeeming [rɪ 'dim ɪŋ] *adj.* making up for other faults or problems.

redevelop [ri dɪ 'vɛl əp] **1.** *tv.* to develop something again. **2.** *tv.* to build in an area again; to construct buildings in an area again.

redhead ['rɛd hɛd] *n.* someone who has red hair.

redid ['ri 'dɪd] past tense of REDO.

redirect [ri dɪ 'rɛkt] *tv.* to direct or send someone or something to a different place; to send someone or something in a different direction.

redness ['rɛd nəs] *n.* being red; the condition of having the color red. (No plural.)

redo [ri 'du] *tv., irreg.* to do something again; to do something over. (Past tense: REDID; past participle: REDONE.)

redone [ri 'dʌn] Past participle of REDO.

redouble [ri 'dʌb əl] **1.** *tv.* to double the amount of something; to increase the amount of something. **2.** *iv.* to double; to increase.

reduce [rɪ 'dus] **1.** *tv.* to make something smaller or less important; to decrease something. **2.** *iv.* to lose [weight].

reduced to something brought into a certain poorer condition or state.

reduction [rɪ 'dʌk ʃən] **1.** *n.* making something smaller; reducing something. **2.** *n.* the amount by which something is made smaller.

redundant [rɪ 'dʌn dənt] *adj.* extra; not needed; doing the same thing as someone or something else. (Adv: *redundantly.*)

redwood ['rɛd wʊd] **1.** *n.* a tall evergreen tree, found in the western United States, that lives to be very old. **2.** *n.* the wood of ①. (Plural only for types and instances.) **3.** the *adj.* use of ① or ②.

reed ['rid] **1.** *n.* a tall grasslike plant with hollow stems that grows in marshes and other wet places. **2.** *n.* a thin piece of wood in the mouthpiece of woodwind instruments like clarinets, saxophones, and oboes or a similar metal piece in harmonicas, accordions, and pipe organs. **3.** the *adj.* use of ① or ②.

reef ['rif] *n.* a ridge of rocks, sand, or coral that extends from the bottom of a sea or ocean to or almost to the surface of the water.

reek ['rik] *iv.* to smell very bad.

reel ['ril] **1.** *n.* a round frame around which string, thread, yarn, fishing line, film, audiotape, videotape, or other long materials are wound. **2.** *iv.* to twist or turn, as when struck by a powerful blow.

reel something **in** to pull something inward, toward oneself by using a REEL ①.

reel something **off** to recite a list or sequence of words, rapidly, from memory.

reel under something **1.** to stagger under the weight of something. **2.** to stagger because of a blow. **3.** to suffer because of a burden. (Figurative.)

reelect [ˈri ə ˈlɛkt] *tv.* to elect someone again.

reelection [ri ə ˈlɛk ʃən] *n.* the election of someone to the same position for another term.

reestablish [ri ə ˈstæb lɪʃ] *tv.* to establish something again.

refer someone **back to** someone or something to suggest that someone go back to someone or something, such as a source.

refer someone **to** someone or something [rɪ ˈfɚ...] to direct someone to use someone or something for help or information; to direct someone to go to someone or something for help or information.

refer something **back (to** someone or something) to send something back to someone or a group for action.

refer to someone or something [rɪ ˈfɚ...] **1.** to use someone or something for help or information; to go to someone or something for help or information. **2.** to have to do with someone or something; to apply to someone or something; to be related to someone or something.

referee [rɛf ə ˈri] **1.** *n.* someone who judges the playing of sports events; an umpire. **2.** *tv.* to judge the playing of a sports event. **3.** *iv.* to serve as ①.

reference [ˈrɛf (ə) rəns] **1.** *n.* words that refer to something else; something that has to do with something else; something that relates to something else. **2.** *n.* something, such as a book, that is used for help or information; someone or something that provides information about something. **3.** *n.* a statement that someone writes about someone else for that other person's use when applying for something; a statement about someone or someone's character.

refill a prescription to obtain or sell a subsequent set of doses of a medicine upon a doctor's orders.

refine [rɪ ˈfaɪn] **1.** *tv.* to make something purer. **2.** *tv.* to make something more detailed, rational, or effective.

refined [rɪ ˈfaɪnd] **1.** *adj.* made purer; pure; having impure substances removed. **2.** *adj.* elegant; very proper and civilized. (Adv: *refinedly.*)

refinish [ri ˈfɪn ɪʃ] *tv.* to remove an old paint or varnish finish and apply a new one.

reflect [rɪ ˈflɛkt] **1.** *tv.* to show an image in the manner of a mirror. **2.** *tv.* to throw back heat, light, sound, or energy; to bounce back heat, light, sound, or energy. **3.** *tv.* [for something] to show or reveal a personal characteristic of someone.

reflect off something to be reflected away from something;

[for light] to bounce off something.

reflect on something to think deeply or carefully; to ponder; to examine one's thoughts.

reflection [rɪ 'flɛk ʃən] **1.** *n.* a reflected glare; reflected light. **2.** *n.* something, especially an image, that is reflected.

reflexive (pronoun) [rɪ 'flɛks ɪv…] *n.* a form used as an object of a verb or preposition that is identical to the subject. (Reflexive pronouns are MYSELF, OURSELVES, YOURSELF, YOURSELVES, HERSELF, HIMSELF, ITSELF, THEMSELVES, ONESELF.)

reflexive (verb) [rɪ 'flɛks ɪv…] *n.* a verb or verb construction that uses a reflexive pronoun. (Some verbs *must* have a reflexive object; others *can* have a reflexive object.)

reform [ri 'form] **1.** *tv.* to change someone or something for the better; to make someone or something better; to improve someone or something. **2.** *iv.* to improve; to become better; to change for the better. **3.** *n.* a planned improvement; a change that gets rid of past flaws or errors.

reformer [ri 'for mɚ] *n.* someone who reforms and improves people or things.

refrain from something to hold back from doing something; to choose not to do something as planned.

refresh [rɪ 'frɛʃ] **1.** *tv.* to make someone feel better or fresher. **2.** *tv.* to bring something into memory; to restore something to someone's memory.

refreshed [rɪ 'frɛʃt] *adj.* made to feel fresh again; made to feel better because of food, drink, sleep, etc.

refreshing [rɪ 'frɛʃ ɪŋ] *adj.* new and exciting; giving the feeling of being fresh. (Adv: *refreshingly.*)

refreshments [rɪ 'frɛʃ mənts] *n.* food or drink that satisfies one's thirst or hunger.

refrigerate [rɪ 'frɪdʒ ə ret] *tv.* to put something in a refrigerator; to keep something cold.

refrigerator [rɪ 'frɪdʒ ə ret ɚ] *n.* an appliance into which food is placed to keep it cold.

refund 1. ['ri fənd] *n.* the money that is given back when someone returns a product to a store. **2.** [rɪ 'fʌnd] *tv.* to give someone money back when a product is returned.

refuse 1. [rɪ 'fjuz] *tv.* not to accept something; to reject something. **2.** [rɪ 'fjuz] *tv.* to deny someone something; not to allow someone to have something. **3.** ['rɛf jus] *n.* garbage; trash; things that are thrown away. (No plural.)

refuse (to do something) [rɪ 'fjuz…] to decline to do something.

regain something **from** someone or something to take back possession of one's property or right from someone or something.

regard [rɪ 'gɑrd] **1.** *tv.* to think of someone or something in a certain way. **2.** *n.* respect; esteem. (No plural.)
→ HOLD SOMEONE IN HIGH REGARD
→ WITH REGARD TO SOMEONE OR SOMETHING

regardless of something without considering something; at any rate; whatever is done; whatever option is chosen.

region ['ri dʒən] **1.** *n.* an area of land that has a common social, cultural, economic, political, or natural feature throughout it; sometimes a political division of a country. **2.** *n.* a part; an area that has a common feature throughout it.

regional ['ridʒ ə nəl] *adj.* of or about a REGION. (Adv: *regionally.*)

register ['rɛdʒ ɪ stɚ] **1.** *n.* a machine in a store that cashiers use to keep track of money taken in or paid out. (Short for *cash register.*) **2.** *n.* the book that a list or record of something is kept in. **3.** *tv.* to show something such as a feeling or an attitude; to express something. **4.** *iv.* to put one's name and perhaps other information on an official list.

registered ['rɛdʒ ɪ stɚd] *adj.* listed as in REGISTER (4); approved by the government; enrolled.

registration [rɛdʒ ɪ 'stre ʃən] **1.** *n.* the process of registering; the condition of being registered. (No plural.) **2.** *n.* the time when people choose and reserve classes at a school, college, or university. (No plural.)

regret [rɪ 'grɛt] **1.** *n.* sorrow; the feeling of being sad or sorry about something that one has done. (No plural.) **2.** *n.* something that one is sorry about; something that causes sorrow. **3.** *tv.* to feel sad or sorry about having or not having done something; to feel ① about having

or not having done something. (The object can be a clause with THAT ⑦.)

regretful [rɪ 'grɛt fʊl] *adj.* full of regret; feeling sad or sorry about something. (Adv: *regretfully.*)

regular ['rɛg jə lɚ] **1.** *adj.* usual; typical; normal. (Adv: *regularly.*) **2.** *adj.* not changing; even in size, shape, or speed; uniform. (Adv: *regularly.*) **3.** *adj.* [in grammar] following the usual pattern, especially concerning verb forms. (Adv: *regularly.*)
→ (AS) REGULAR AS CLOCKWORK
→ AT REGULAR INTERVALS

regularity [rɛg jə 'lɛr ə ti] *n.* the quality of being regular. (Plural only for types and instances.)

regulate ['rɛg jə let] **1.** *tv.* to control someone or something by a rule or system; to limit someone or something by a rule or system. **2.** *tv.* to fix or adjust something so that it will work at a certain level or standard.

regulation [rɛg jə 'le ʃən] **1.** *n.* the control or order caused by rules, laws, principles, or systems. (Plural only for types and instances.) **2.** *adj.* according to a rule, law, system, or standard; suitable according to a rule, law, system, or standard; standard.

rehearsal [rɪ 'hɚs əl] **1.** *n.* a practice performance of a play, opera, concert, etc., devoted to perfecting the performance for an audience. **2.** the *adj.* use of ①.

rehearse [rɪ 'hɚs] **1.** *tv.* to practice a part in a play, concert, dance, or performance before performing it for the public; [for performers] to practice performing. **2.** *tv.* to cause a group of performers to practice; to cause performers to practice something that is to be performed. **3.** *iv.* to practice [a role, play, piece of music, etc.].

reign ['ren] **1.** *iv.* to rule, especially as king, queen, emperor, or empress. **2.** *iv.* to be the current winner of a contest or holder of a title. **3.** *n.* the period of the rule of a king, queen, emperor, empress, as in ①.

rein ['ren] *n.* one of a pair of long straps attached to either side of the bridle of a horse, mule, donkey, etc. (Used to control the direction of movement of the animal.)
→ KEEP A CLOSE REIN ON SOMEONE OR SOMETHING
→ KEEP A TIGHT REIN ON SOMEONE OR SOMETHING

reinforce [ri ɪn 'fors] *tv.* to make something stronger, more able to resist wear, or longer lasting by adding something to it.

reject 1. [rɪ 'dʒɛkt] *tv.* to refuse to take or accept someone or something. **2.** ['ri dʒɛkt] *n.* someone or something that has been refused as in ①.

rejection [rɪ 'dʒɛk ʃən] *n.* refusal to accept someone or something. (No plural.)

rejoice [ri 'dʒɔɪs] *iv.* to be very happy [about something]; to celebrate [something] joyfully.

rejoicing [ri 'dʒɔɪs ɪŋ] *n.* great joy or happiness expressed by one or more people. (No plural.)

relate [rɪ 'let] *tv.* to tell a story; to tell what was heard. (The object can be a clause with THAT ⑦.)

relate to someone to feel a bond of some type with someone because of shared experiences.

related [rɪ 'let ɪd] **1.** *adj.* connected. (Adv: *relatedly.*) **2.** *adj.* part of the same family; in the same family.

related to someone connected to someone as a relative.

related to something linked or connected to something.

relation [rɪ 'le ʃən] **1.** *n.* someone who is a member of one's family; a relative. **2.** *n.* a connection between two or more things; relationship.

relationship [rɪ 'le ʃən ʃɪp] **1.** *n.* a personal, romantic, business, or social connection between two people. **2.** *n.* a connection between two or more things.

relative ['rɛl ə tɪv] **1.** *n.* someone who is a member of one's family. **2.** *adj.* compared to something else; having meaning only as compared with something else. (Adv: *relatively.*)

relative clause ['rɛl ə tɪv 'klɔz] *n.* a clause that refers or is compared to someone or something. (Also called a *subordinate clause.*)

relax [rɪ 'læks] **1.** *iv.* to become less tight, less stiff, less firm, less tense, or more loose. **2.** *iv.* to become less worried, less busy with work, or less active; to rest, be calm, or slow down. **3.** *tv.* to cause something to become less tight, less stiff, less firm, or less tense. **4.** *tv.* to cause something to become less strict, less harsh, or less severe. **5.** *tv.* to cause someone to become less worried, less busy with work, or less active; to cause someone to rest, be calm, or slow down.

relaxation [rɪ læk 'se ʃən] **1.** *n.* rest, especially after work or busy activity. (No plural.) **2.** *n.* the lessening of tightness, stiffness, tenseness, or firmness; the release of tension from something tight, stiff, tense, or firm. (No plural.) **3.** *n.* making something less severe; the easing of strict rules. (No plural.)

relaxing [rɪ 'læk sɪŋ] *adj.* calming; soothing; restful; making one feel less tense, tight, stiff, or firm. (Adv: *relaxingly.*)

relay [rɪ 'le] *tv.* to receive something and give it to someone else; to receive something and transfer it to something else or move it further along in a process.

release [rɪ 'lis] **1.** *tv.* to let someone or something free; to let someone or something go; to let someone or something loose. **2.** *tv.* to make a book, a movie, information, or a publication available to the public. **3.** *n.* an act of letting someone or something go; an act of setting someone or something free.

relevant ['rɛl ə vənt] *adj.* connected to something; of or about the subject being discussed. (Adv: *relevantly.*)

reliance on someone or something trust in and dependence on someone or something.

relief [rɪ 'lif] **1.** *n.* the feeling that is felt when pain, a burden, a strain, or a problem is eased. (No plural.) **2.** *n.* something that eases pain, a

burden, a strain, or a problem. (No plural.) **3.** *n.* money, clothing, food, or other aid that is made available to help poor people or to help people who are victims of a disaster. (No plural.)

relieve [rɪ 'liv] **1.** *tv.* to ease or get rid of pain, anxiety, or strain. **2.** *tv.* to begin working at a job as a replacement so that the person who was working can have some time to relax.

relieve someone **(of** something**)** to remove fear or anxiety from someone.

relieve someone or some creature **of** something to ease someone's or some creature's burden by removing something.

religion [rɪ 'lɪdʒ ən] *n.* belief in or worship of one or more gods or spirits. (Plural only for types and instances.)
→ CHRISTIAN RELIGION

religious [rɪ 'lɪdʒ əs] **1.** the *adj.* form of RELIGION. (Adv: *religiously.*) **2.** *adj.* believing in or worshiping one or more gods or spirits. (Adv: *religiously.*)

religious about doing something strict about doing something; conscientious about doing something.

relish ['rɛl ɪʃ] **1.** *tv.* to enjoy something very much. **2.** *n.* a mixture of chopped pickled cucumbers or other pickled vegetables. (No plural form.)
→ WITH RELISH

relocate someone or something **(to** someplace**)** [ri 'lo ket…] to move someone or something to a different place.

489

relocate (to someplace**)** [ri 'lo ket...] to move to a different place; to move to a different house or to transfer to a different job site, especially in a different city.

reluctant to do something not wanting to do something; unwilling to do something.

rely (up)on someone or something [ri 'lɑɪ...] to depend on someone or something; to trust that someone will do something; to trust that something will happen.

remain [ri 'men] **1.** *iv.* to stay in someplace; to continue to be in a certain place; to be left over after other parts or things are taken. **2.** *iv.* to continue to be something or act in a particular manner.

remain up to stay awake and out of bed.

remain within (something**)** to stay inside something or someplace.

remainder [ri 'men dɚ] **1.** *n.* the part of something that is left over after part of it is taken. **2.** *n.* the number that is left over after a number is divided into another one.

remaining [ri 'men ɪŋ] *adj.* yet to happen; yet to occur; not yet done or taken care of; not yet taken away; not yet happening; not yet occurring.

remains 1. *n.* things that are left behind. (Treated as plural, but not countable.) **2.** *n.* a corpse; a dead body. (Treated as plural.)

remark [ri 'mɑrk] **1.** *n.* a comment; a statement; something that is said or written about something. **2.** *tv.* to say something; to comment about something; to state an opinion. (The object can be a clause with THAT ⑦.)

remark (up)on someone or something to comment on someone or something.

remarkable [ri 'mɑrk ə bəl] *adj.* worth mentioning; worth talking about; noticeable; unusual. (Adv: *remarkably*.)

remedy ['rɛm ə di] **1.** *n.* a treatment; a cure; something that makes someone become healthy again. **2.** *n.* making bad conditions good or better; the correction of a problem. (Figurative on ①.) **3.** *tv.* to make bad conditions good or better; to correct a problem; to fix something that is wrong or bad.

remember [ri 'mɛm bɚ] **1.** *tv.* to bring back the thought of someone or something into one's mind, memory, or imagination; to think about someone or something again. (The object can be a clause with THAT ⑦.) **2.** *tv.* not to forget someone or something; to keep someone or something in one's mind. (The object can be a clause with THAT ⑦.) **3.** *iv.* to bring [someone or something] back into one's mind, memory, or imagination.

remind [ri 'mɑɪnd] *tv.* to tell someone about something again; to cause someone to remember someone or something.

reminder [ri 'mɑɪn dɚ] *n.* something that reminds someone about something.

reminiscent of someone or something reminding someone about someone or something; seeming like or suggesting someone or something.

remodel [rɪ 'mɑd l] *tv.* to decorate something in a new way; to construct something in a new way; to change a structure or room so that it looks more modern.

remote [rɪ 'mot] **1.** *adj.* far away in space or time; far off; not near; distant; isolated; secluded; not near other things or places. (Adv: *remotely.* Comp: *remoter;* sup: *remotest.*) **2.** *adj.* [of a possibility] very small. (Figurative on ①. Adv: *remotely.* Comp: *remoter;* sup: *remotest.*) **3.** *n.* an electronic device used to control audio and video equipment. (Short for REMOTE CONTROL.)

remote control [rɪ 'mot kən 'trol] *n.* a device that is held in the hand and used to operate a machine or appliance from a distance. (Can be shortened to REMOTE.)

remove [rɪ 'muv] **1.** *tv.* to take something away from a place; to get rid of something. **2.** *tv.* to take off something, especially a piece of clothing.

rend something **from** someone or something to tear something from someone or something.

renew [rɪ 'nu] **1.** *tv.* to cause someone or something to become like new again; to restore someone or something. **2.** *tv.* to cause something that was no longer valid or effective to become useful again; to cause something to be valid for a longer period of time.

renounce [rɪ 'naʊns] *tv.* to give up something; to state formally that one is giving up something, especially a claim or a right.

renovate ['rɛn ə vet] *tv.* to fix up something so that it is in good condition; to restore something to a good condition; to repair a structure.

rent ['rɛnt] **1.** *n.* the money paid for the use of something, especially for the use of a place to live. (No plural.) **2.** *iv.* to live in an apartment that one does not own, but for which one pays ① to the owner.

rent something **(from** someone**)** to get the right to use something (from someone) by paying rent.

rent something **(out) (to** someone**)** to provide something that other people pay money to use.

rental ['rɛn təl] **1.** *adj.* [of an apartment, office space, equipment, or other thing] rented or available to be rented. **2.** *n.* the amount of money that is paid as rent for something. (No plural.)

rented ['rɛn təd] *adj.* occupied or used for a fee, rather than owned.

reorganization [ri or gə nə 'ze ʃən] *n.* reorganizing something; organizing something in a different way, especially so that it works or operates better; the condition of having been reorganized.

reorganize [ri 'or gə naɪz] **1.** *tv.* to organize something in a different way, especially so that it works or operates better. **2.** *tv.* to reform a business, especially after it has gone bankrupt.

repaid [rɪ 'ped] past tense and past participle of REPAY.

repair [rɪ 'pɛr] **1.** *tv.* to fix something; to mend something; to cause something to work again. **2.** *n.* work that will fix or restore something. (Singular or plural with the same meaning.)

repairable [rɪ 'pɛr ə bəl] *adj.* able to be repaired; able to be fixed. (Adv: *repairably.*)

repay [rɪ 'pe] *tv., irreg.* to pay someone back for something; to pay someone for an amount that is owed. (Past tense and past participle: REPAID.)

repayment [rɪ 'pe mənt] *n.* paying back something to someone. (No plural.)

repeat [rɪ 'pit] **1.** *tv.* to do or say something again. **2.** *tv.* to say something that someone else has just said to find out if has been correctly understood. **3.** *tv.* to say something that one has learned.

repeated [rɪ 'pit ɪd] *adj.* previously done or said and being done or said again; done or said more than one time. (Adv: *repeatedly.*)

repetition [rɛp ɪ 'tɪ ʃən] *n.* repeating something. (Plural only for types and instances.)

replace [rɪ 'ples] **1.** *tv.* to take the place of someone or something else. **2.** *tv.* to exchange something for another thing that is more useful or newer. **3.** *tv.* to return something to the place where it belongs; to put something back where it belongs.

replacement [rɪ 'ples mənt] **1.** *n.* replacing someone or something.

(No plural.) **2.** *n.* someone or something that takes the place of someone or something else. **3.** *adj.* used to replace someone or something else.

replay 1. ['ri ple] *n.* something that is played again; an event that is done over; a film clip that is played over, often in slow motion so one can see fast action better. **2.** ['ri 'ple] *tv.* to play something again, especially a game or a piece of film.

reply [rɪ 'plɑɪ] **1.** *iv.* to answer. **2.** *tv.* to say or write something as an answer. (The object is a clause with THAT ⑦.) **3.** *n.* an answer; something that is said or written when answering a question.

report [rɪ 'pɔrt] **1.** *n.* an account that gives information about something. **2.** *n.* the noise made when a shot is fired. **3.** *tv.* to describe news; to provide news. (The object can be a clause with THAT ⑦.)

report back (on someone or something**)** to return with information or an explanation about someone or something.

report back (to someone or something**) 1.** to go back to someone or something and present oneself. **2.** to present information or an explanation to someone or something.

report for something to present oneself for something.

report someone or something **to** someone or something to tell of someone's errors or something that someone did wrong to some-one or something.

report to someone **or** someplace to go to someplace; to present oneself to someone at someplace.

reporter [rɪ ˈpor tɚ] *n.* someone who provides a newspaper, maga-zine, radio station, or television station with news; someone who reports news or information.

repossess [ri pə ˈzɛs] *tv.* [for a company] to take back something purchased on credit when the pur-chaser fails to make payments on time.

represent [rɛp rɪ ˈzɛnt] **1.** *tv.* to portray someone or something; to express something. **2.** *tv.* to act on behalf of someone else; to speak for someone else.

reproach [rɪ ˈprotʃ] **1.** *n.* blame; criticism. (No plural form.) **2.** *tv.* to blame or criticize someone.
→ ABOVE REPROACH

reproduce [ri prə ˈdus] **1.** *tv.* to make a copy of something. **2.** *tv.* to create something again; to do something in the way it has already been done. **3.** *iv.* to have offspring.

reproduction [ri prə ˈdʌk ʃən] **1.** *n.* the process of making a copy of something. (No plural.) **2.** *n.* creating offspring; reproducing. (No plural.) **3.** *n.* a copy of some-thing, especially of a work of art or a book.

reproductive [ri prə ˈdʌk tɪv] *adj.* of or about REPRODUCTION ②. (Adv: *reproductively.*)

reptile [ˈrɛp taɪl] *n.* a class of ani-mals whose temperature is the

same as the surrounding air, including dinosaurs, lizards, snakes, turtles, tortoises, alliga-tors, and crocodiles.

republic [rɪ ˈpʌb lɪk] **1.** *n.* a nation where the people are governed by officials whom they elect. **2.** *n.* a system of government in which the people elect officials to repre-sent them.

reputation [rɛp jə ˈte ʃən] *n.* the basis for the good or bad opinion that people have about someone or something.

request [rɪ ˈkwɛst] **1.** *tv.* to ask for something politely. (The object can be a clause with THAT ⑦.) **2.** *n.* a polite demand; an instance of asking for something.

require [rɪ ˈkwaɪɚ] **1.** *tv.* to demand a particular qualification or skill. **2.** *tv.* to demand that someone do something. (The object can be a clause with THAT ⑦.)

required [rɪ ˈkwaɪɚd] *adj.* demanded and needed; ordered; necessary.

requirement [rɪ ˈkwaɪɚ mənt] *n.* something that must be done; something that is required; some-thing that is necessary.

rerun [ˈri rən] *n.* a television pro-gram that is not new; a television program that has been on televi-sion before.

rescue [ˈrɛs kju] **1.** *tv.* to save someone or something that is in danger. **2.** *n.* an instance of saving someone or something from danger.

research 1. [ˈri sɚtʃ, rɪ ˈsɚtʃ] *n.*
study and examination; the collecting of information. (No plural.) **2.** [rɪ ˈsɚtʃ] *tv.* to collect
information about something in
great detail.

resemble [rɪ ˈzɛm bəl] *tv.* to look
like someone or something; to be
like someone or something.

resent [rɪ ˈzɛnt] *tv.* to feel bitter
toward someone about something;
to feel insulted by someone about
something. (The object can be a
clause with THAT ⑦.)

resentful [rɪ ˈzɛnt fʊl] *adj.* full of
anger or bitter feelings about
someone or something; feeling
that one has been insulted; showing anger or bitter feelings. (Adv:
resentfully.)

reservation [rɛz ɚ ˈve ʃən] **1.** *n.* a
doubt about something; a concern;
something that stops someone
from accepting something. **2.** *n.* a
previous claim on the use of
something at a specific time, such
as a room in a hotel, a table at a
restaurant, or a seat in a theater,
on an airplane, or at a concert.
→ MAKE RESERVATIONS

reserve [rɪ ˈzɚv] **1.** *tv.* to schedule
the use of something at a certain
time; to record a claim for the
future use of something at a certain time. **2.** *tv.* to save something
for future use. **3.** *n.* something
that is saved for future use.

reserved [rɪ ˈzɚvd] **1.** *adj.* saved
for a certain person or certain reason; scheduled to be used by
someone at a certain time. **2.** *adj.*
quiet; keeping to oneself; not talk-

ing about oneself. (Adv: *reservedly*
[rɪ ˈzɚv əd li].)

reserves *n.* troops or soldiers that
are prepared to be called to war.
(Treated as plural, but not countable.)

residence [ˈrɛz ə dəns] **1.** *n.* the
period of time that someone lives
in a certain place. (No plural.
Number is expressed with
period(s) of residence.) **2.** *n.* a
house or an apartment; the place
where someone lives.

resident [ˈrɛz ə dənt] **1.** *n.* a person
who lives in a certain house or
apartment. **2.** *n.* a person who
lives in a certain city, state, or
country. **3.** *n.* a doctor who works
full time at a hospital in order to
get advanced medical training.
4. *adj.* living in or working at a
certain place.

residential [rɛz ə ˈdɛn ʃəl] *adj.* of
or about residences; of or about
homes or apartments rather than
offices, farms, or factories. (Adv:
residentially.)

resign [rɪ ˈzaɪn] *tv.* to quit a position or office.

resign from something to give up
or leave a job, office, committee,
or task.

resign oneself **to** something to
cause oneself to accept something
without complaining; to cause
oneself to yield to something.

resignation [rɛz ɪg ˈne ʃən] **1.** *n.*
voluntarily leaving a job, office,
committee, or task. (Plural only
for types and instances.) **2.** *n.* a
formal statement or document

made by someone who is leaving a job.

resist [rɪ 'zɪst] **1.** *tv.* to oppose something; to refuse to accept something. **2.** *tv.* to keep from doing something; to prevent something from happening; to stop something from happening. (Takes a verb with *-ing*.) **3.** *tv.* to be undamaged by something; to be able to withstand something.

resistance [rɪ 'zɪs təns] *n.* resisting someone or something; the ability to resist someone or something. (No plural.)
→ the LINE OF LEAST RESISTANCE
→ the PATH OF LEAST RESISTANCE

resource ['ri sors] *n.* someone or something that one can go to for help, information, support, or supplies.

resourceful [ri 'sors fʊl] *adj.* able to think of different ways to solve a problem. (Adv: *resourcefully.*)

respect [rɪ 'spɛkt] **1.** *n.* the honor, admiration, or esteem that one feels for someone or something. (No plural.) **2.** *n.* the polite behavior one shows to someone whom one honors or admires. (No plural.) **3.** *tv.* to honor, admire, or esteem someone or something.
→ PAY ONE'S LAST RESPECTS
→ PAY SOMEONE RESPECT
→ WITH RESPECT TO SOMEONE OR SOMETHING

respectable [rɪ 'spɛk tə bəl] *adj.* worthy of respect; deserving respect; deserving honor and acceptance; admirable. (Adv: *respectably.*)

respond [rɪ 'spɑnd] *tv.* to answer a question; to give an answer; to say

something as a response. (The object is a clause with THAT ⑦.)

respond (to someone or something**)** to answer someone or something; to reply to someone or something; to react to someone or something.

response [rɪ 'spɑns] **1.** *n.* an answer; a reply; something that is said or done to answer a question. **2.** *n.* a reaction; something that is done when something happens.
→ GUT RESPONSE

responsibility [rɪ spɑn sə 'bɪl ə ti] **1.** *n.* the authority for something; the duty to take care of someone or something. (Plural only for types and instances.) **2.** *n.* accountability for something wrong or bad; blame for causing something bad or, sometimes, credit for causing something good. (No plural.) **3.** *n.* the quality of being responsible. (No plural.) **4.** *n.* someone or something that one is responsible for.

responsible [rɪ 'spɑn sə bəl] *adj.* reliable; able to do something without being told what to do. (Adv: *responsibly.*)

responsible for someone or something having the job of taking care of someone or something.

the **responsible party** the person or organization responsible or liable for something.

rest ['rɛst] **1.** *n.* sleep. (No plural.) **2.** *n.* relaxation; a period of calm or quiet after work or activity. (No plural.) **3.** *iv.* to relax after work or activity. **4.** *iv.* to remain somewhere. **5.** *tv.* to cause someone or an animal to relax.

→ AT REST

the **rest** *n.* the remainder [of something]; the things that are left over. (Singular form. Treated like a singular or plural, but not countable.)

rest in peace to lie dead peacefully for eternity.

rest up (for something**)** to relax and rest in advance of doing something tiring.

rest up (from something**)** to recover or recuperate from something tiring.

rest (up)on something to lie on something; to relax on something.

restaurant ['rɛs tə rɑnt] *n.* a place where one buys and eats a meal, which is usually served at a table.

restful ['rɛst fʊl] *adj.* causing one to feel rested; peaceful; calm; quiet. (Adv: *restfully.*)

restore [rɪ 'stor] *tv.* to return something to its original or regular condition; to put something back.

restrain [rɪ 'stren] *tv.* to prevent someone or something from moving or doing something.

restrict [rɪ 'strɪkt] *tv.* to limit what someone or something can do; to make something—such as one's rights, one's movement, one's speech—less than it was.

restriction [rɪ 'strɪk ʃən] *n.* a condition that limits action or movement; a rule against doing something; a regulation.

restroom ['rɛst rum] *n.* a room with a toilet, especially in a public building. (A euphemism.)

result [rɪ 'zʌlt] **1.** *n.* the outcome of an event; something that is caused by something else. **2.** *n.* the answer to a math problem; a solution.

result from something to be an effect of something; to be caused by something.

result in something to lead to a particular result.

resulting [rɪ 'zʌl tɪŋ] *adj.* happening because of something else; being a result.

résumé ['rɛz u me] *n.* a document that lists one's education, work history, and other important information.

resume [rɪ 'zum] **1.** *tv.* to do something again after having stopped for a time. **2.** *iv.* to begin again after having stopped for a time.

retail ['ri tel] *adj.* [of a store] selling products to consumers directly.

retail for an amount [for a product] to be available for purchase for a certain price in a retail store.

retailer ['ri tel ɚ] *n.* a shopkeeper; someone or a business that sells products directly to consumers.

retain [rɪ 'ten] **1.** *tv.* to keep something; to continue to have something. **2.** *tv.* to hire a lawyer.

retake 1. ['ri tek] *n.* an act of filming a part of a movie or television show again. **2.** ['ri 'tek] *tv., irreg.* to take a picture again or to film a part of a movie or television show again. (Past tense: RETOOK; past participle: RETAKEN.)

retaken ['ri tek ən] Past participle of RETAKE.

retaliate against someone or something to take revenge against someone or something.

retire [rɪ 'taɪɚ] **1.** *iv.* to stop working permanently and live on the money one has saved. **2.** *iv.* to go to bed. **3.** *tv.* to cause something to no longer be used; to remove something from use. **4.** *tv.* to pay a debt; to finish paying a debt.

retire from something to withdraw from something; to stop working permanently.

retire someone or something **from** something to stop using someone or something for a particular purpose permanently.

retire to someplace **1.** to quit work and move somewhere. **2.** to go to a different place; to go to a place away from other people.

retired [rɪ 'taɪɚd] *adj.* having quit working permanently.

retirement [rɪ 'taɪɚ mənt] *n.* the period of time in one's life after one has stopped work permanently. (No plural.)

retook ['ri 'tʊk] past tense of RETAKE.

retreat [rɪ 'trit] **1.** *iv.* to go back, especially because one cannot fight or go forward. **2.** *n.* an act of going back, especially during a battle, because one cannot fight or move forward. **3.** *n.* a quiet, isolated place; a place that one can go to for quiet, rest, or safety.

return [rɪ 'tɚn] **1.** *iv.* to go back or come back to a previous time, location, position, or condition. **2.** *tv.* to give something back to the person it came from; to put something back in the place it came from. **3.** *tv.* to cause someone or something to go back or come back to a previous time, location, position, or condition. **4.** *n.* an act of coming back or going back as in ①. **5.** *n.* a set of tax forms. (Short for TAX RETURN.)
→ BY RETURN MAIL
→ IN RETURN
→ TAX RETURN

return(s) *n.* the amount of money that is made from a business.

reunion [ri 'jun jən] *n.* a party or gathering of people who are coming together again, especially of people who have not seen each other in a long time.

reunite [ri ju 'naɪt] **1.** *tv.* to bring people or things together again; to unite people or things again. **2.** *iv.* to bring together again; to come together again; to unite again.

rev something **up** to race an engine by giving it lots of gas briefly and repeatedly.

rev up to increase in amount or activity.

reveal [rɪ 'vil] **1.** *tv.* to allow or cause something to be seen. **2.** *tv.* to make information known; to tell a piece of information. (The object can be a clause with THAT ⑦.)

revealing [rɪ 'vil ɪŋ] **1.** *adj.* allowing or causing something to be seen; showing something, especially skin. (Adv: *revealingly.*) **2.** *adj.* giving much information; allowing concealed information to be seen or known. (Adv: *revealingly.*)

revenge [rɪ 'vɛndʒ] *n.* harm done to a person as punishment for a bad deed the person has done to oneself. (No plural.)

revenge oneself **(up)on** someone or something to get revenge against someone or something.

revenue ['rɛv ə nu] **1.** *n.* income; money that is made from a business or an investment. (Usually singular.) **2.** *n.* money that is collected by the government from taxes. (Either singular or plural with the same meaning, but not countable.)

reverberate through something [for sound] to roll through or pass through a space.

reverberate with something to echo or resound with something.

The **Reverend** someone *n.* the title for a minister.

reverse [rɪ 'vɚs] **1.** *tv.* to cause something to go or operate backwards. **2.** *tv.* to cause something to move the opposite way; to turn something the other way; to turn something upside down; to turn something inside out. **3.** *iv.* to go or move backwards; to move in the opposite direction. **4.** *n.* the opposite. **5.** *n.* the back of something; the back side.

review [rɪ 'vju] **1.** *tv.* to examine something again. **2.** *tv.* to study information again, especially before a test. **3.** *tv.* to write or prepare a written evaluation of a play, movie, book, dance, or other work of art. **4.** *iv.* to study again. **5.** *n.* a formal examination or inspection. **6.** *n.* an essay that evaluates a book, play, movie, dance, or other work.

revise [rɪ 'vaɪz] *tv.* to make something current or up-to-date; to change something to include different information.

revised [rɪ 'vaɪzd] *adj.* updated; made current; changed to include new information.

revision [rɪ 'vɪʒ ən] **1.** *n.* a change—usually an improvement—made to a document or a manuscript. **2.** *n.* a document that has been revised.

revival [rɪ 'vaɪ vəl] **1.** *n.* reviving someone or something; the process of returning life or energy to someone. **2.** *n.* a new production of a play or musical that has been done before; something that has been revived. (Figurative on ①.)

revive [rɪ 'vaɪv] **1.** *tv.* to cause someone to return to a conscious state, with normal breathing and heart activity. **2.** *tv.* to bring something back into use; to bring something back into style. **3.** *iv.* to return to a conscious state, as in ①.

revolt [rɪ 'volt] **1.** *iv.* to fight against authority or the government. **2.** *tv.* to cause someone to feel sick with disgust; to offend someone strongly. **3.** *n.* a rebellion; a riot; an instance of fighting as in ① against authority.

revolting [rɪ 'vol tɪŋ] *adj.* sickening; very offensive. (Adv: *revoltingly.*)

revolution [rɛv ə 'lu ʃən] **1.** *n.* an act of seizing a government by force and replacing it with new rulers. **2.** *n.* a complete change. (Figurative on ①.) **3.** *n.* the circular or rotating movement made by an object going around a fixed object or position.

revolve [rɪ 'valv] *iv.* [for someone or something] to turn [around an axis].

revolve around something to move in a circle or oval around a point; to orbit around something.

reward [rɪ 'word] **1.** *n.* something, especially money, given to someone who has done something good. **2.** *tv.* to give someone ①.
→ GET ONE'S JUST REWARD(S)

rewarding [rɪ 'wor dɪŋ] *adj.* satisfying; beneficial; valuable. (Adv: *rewardingly.*)

rewind [ri 'waɪnd] **1.** *tv., irreg.* to cause something, especially an audiotape, videotape, or film, to wind backward. (Past tense and past participle: REWOUND.) **2.** *iv., irreg.* [for something that winds around an object, such as an audiotape, videotape, or film] to run backward. **3.** *n.* a button or device that causes a reverse movement as in ②.

rewound [ri 'waʊnd] past tense and past participle of REWIND.

rewrite 1. [ri 'raɪt] *tv., irreg.* to revise something that has been written. (Past tense: REWROTE; past participle: REWRITTEN.) **2.** ['ri raɪt] *n.* a copy of writing that has been revised.

rewritten ['ri 'rɪt n] **1.** Past participle of REWRITE. **2.** *adj.* written in a different way; revised.

rewrote ['ri 'rot] past tense of REWRITE.

rhinoceros [rɑɪ 'nɑs ə rəs] *n., irreg.* a large animal of Africa and South Asia that has one or two large horns on its nose. (Plural: *rhinoceros* or *rhinoceroses.*)

rhyme ['raɪm] **1.** *n.* a state existing where two or more words end in similar or identical sounds. (No plural.) **2.** *iv.* [for a word or phrase] to end with the same sound or sounds as another word or phrase; [for a poem] to include words or phrases ending with the same sound or sounds, especially at the ends of pairs of lines.

rhythm ['rɪð əm] *n.* beats that occur in a pattern, such as in music. (Plural only for types and instances.)

rib ['rɪb] **1.** *n.* one of the several pairs of bones that are attached to the backbone and curve around to the front of the chest. **2.** *n.* meat that contains ①, eaten as food.

ribbon ['rɪb ən] **1.** *n.* a narrow band of fabric or material, often used as a decoration. **2.** *n.* a special kind of ①, coated with ink, used in a typewriter or computer printer; a special, thin strip of plastic film used in an electric typewriter.

rice ['raɪs] **1.** *n.* a grasslike plant that produces edible seeds. (Plural only for types and instances.) **2.** *n.* the edible grain of ①. (No plural. Number is expressed with *grain(s) of rice.*)

rich ['rɪtʃ] **1.** *adj.* having a lot of money; wealthy; not poor. (Adv: *richly.* Comp: *richer;* sup: *richest.*)

2. *adj.* [for food] having a lot of cream, butter, or other fats. (Adv: *richly.* Comp: *richer;* sup: *richest.*) **3.** *adj.* [of soil] good for growing plants; fertile. (Adv: *richly.* Comp: *richer;* sup: *richest.*) **4.** *adj.* [of a color] vivid or deep. (Adv: *richly.* Comp: *richer;* sup: *richest.*) **5.** *adj.* plentiful; causing or yielding plenty, benefit, or value.
→ STRIKE IT RICH

the **rich** *n.* people who are RICH ①. (No plural. Treated as plural, but not countable.)

rich in something having valuable resources, characteristics, traditions, or history.

rich with something having a lot of something; not lacking something.

riches *n.* wealth; an ample amount of anything good, especially money and property. (Treated as plural, but not countable.)
→ FROM RAGS TO RICHES

ricochet off something ['rɪk ə ʃe...] [for some rapidly moving object, such as a bullet] to bounce off something at an angle.

rid ['rɪd] **1.** *tv., irreg.* to free something or a place of something. (Past tense and past participle: *rid.*) **2.** *tv., irreg.* to make oneself free of someone or something. (Takes a reflexive object.)
→ GET RID OF SOMEONE OR SOMETHING

ridden ['rɪd n] **1.** Past participle of RIDE. **2.** *adj.* burdened with something; full of something. (Only in combinations.)

riddle ['rɪd l] **1.** *n.* a puzzling question whose answer usually requires one to think in an unusual or clever way. **2.** *n.* someone or something that is difficult to understand; someone or something that is puzzling. (Figurative on ①.)

ride ['raɪd] **1.** *tv., irreg.* to sit on or in something that moves; to be a passenger on or in a vehicle that moves or travels. (Past tense: RODE; past participle: RIDDEN. With HORSE, DONKEY, ELEPHANT, and other animals. With TRAIN, BICYCLE, ELEVATOR, MOTORCYCLE, TROLLEY but *ride in* a CAR, TAXI, TRUCK, or Jeep.) **2.** *tv., irreg.* to travel along on something. **3.** *n.* a journey using a vehicle or an animal. **4.** *n.* a kind of entertainment in which people travel in some kind of vehicle to experience interesting sights and sounds, thrills, or learning.
→ GO ALONG FOR THE RIDE
→ HITCH A RIDE
→ THUMB A RIDE

ride away to depart, riding a bike, another vehicle, or an animal.

ride off to depart, riding something such as a horse or a bicycle.

ride on to continue to ride, traveling onward.

ride someone or something **down** to chase down someone or some creature while riding on a horse.

ride something **down** to ride on something that is going down, such as an elevator.

ride something **out** to endure something; to remain with something to its termination.

ride the gravy train to live in luxury.

ride up (on someone) **1.** [for someone on a horse] to approach someone, riding. **2.** [for clothing, especially underpants] to keep moving higher on one's body.

ride (up)on someone or something to use someone or something as a beast of burden.

ridge ['rɪdʒ] **1.** *n.* a long, narrow hill or mountain. **2.** *n.* a long, narrow, raised part of something. **3.** *n.* the line where two surfaces slanted upward meet, as with the top edge of a roof.

ridicule ['rɪd ə kjul] **1.** *tv.* to make fun of someone or something; to mock someone or something. **2.** *n.* laughter or mockery directed at someone or something, especially in a cruel way. (No plural.)

ridiculous [rɪ ˈdɪk jə ləs] *adj.* deserving to be laughed at or mocked; deserving ridicule. (Adv: *ridiculously.*)

riding for a fall risking failure or an accident, usually due to over-confidence.

rifle ['raɪ fʊl] **1.** *n.* a gun with a long barrel. **2.** *tv.* to search an area thoroughly, stealing valuable things.

rifle through something to ransack something; to search through something looking for something to steal.

rig someone or something **out (in** something**)** to decorate or dress someone or something in something.

rig something **up** to prepare something, perhaps on short notice or without the proper materials.

right ['raɪt] **1.** *adj.* the opposite of LEFT; to the east when someone or something faces north. (Only prenominal.) **2.** *adj.* correct; true; not wrong; not false. (Adv: *rightly.*) **3.** *adj.* morally good; according to the law or social standards. (Adv: *rightly.*) **4.** *adj.* proper; suitable; being good for a situation. **5.** *adv.* toward the side described in ①. **6.** *adv.* correctly; not wrongly. **7.** *adv.* properly; suitably; in a way that is good for a situation. **8.** *adv.* directly; straight. **9.** *n.* that which is correct, proper, or good. (No plural.) **10.** *tv.* to cause something to be upright; to fix something that is leaning or has fallen, so that it is standing up again.

→ GET RIGHT ON SOMETHING
→ GIVE ONE'S RIGHT ARM (FOR SOMEONE OR SOMETHING)
→ HAVE THE RIGHT-OF-WAY
→ HIT SOMEONE (RIGHT) BETWEEN THE EYES
→ HIT THE NAIL (RIGHT) ON THE HEAD
→ IN ONE'S RIGHT MIND
→ IN THE RIGHT
→ IN THE RIGHT PLACE AT THE RIGHT TIME
→ ON THE RIGHT TRACK
→ SAIL (RIGHT) THROUGH SOMETHING
→ SERVE SOMEONE RIGHT
→ STEP RIGHT UP
→ TAKE THE WORDS (RIGHT) OUT OF ONE'S MOUTH

right angle ['raɪt 'æŋ gəl] *n.* an angle whose sides join at 90 degrees.

right off the bat immediately; first thing.

right under someone's **nose** Go to UNDER SOMEONE'S (VERY) NOSE.

right-handed ['raɪt hæn dɪd] **1.** *adj.* able to use the right hand better than the left; using the right hand to write with. (Adv: *right-*

handed(ly).) **2.** *adj.* made to be
used by the right hand.

right(s) *n.* something that is due a
person according to civil or moral
law. (*Right* is singular; *rights* is
plural.)
→ HAVE SOMEONE DEAD TO RIGHTS

rigid ['rɪdʒ ɪd] **1.** *adj.* stiff; not
bending; hard to bend; not flexi-
ble. (Adv: *rigidly*.) **2.** *adj.* stubborn
and determined. (Figurative on
① . Adv: *rigidly*.)

rigorous ['rɪg ə rəs] **1.** *adj.* harsh;
strict; severe; demanding. (Adv:
rigorously.) **2.** *adj.* thorough; exact;
according to strict scientific standards; scientifically accurate.
(Adv: *rigorously*.)

rim ['rɪm] **1.** *n.* the edge of something, especially of something that
is circular. **2.** *n.* the part of a wheel
that a tire is put around.

ring ['rɪŋ] **1.** *n.* something made
from a circle of material; a circular
band. **2.** *n.* a piece of jewelry made
from a circle of metal that is usually worn around a person's finger.
3. *n.* a circle. **4.** *n.* a group of people or things that are in a circle.
5. *n.* an enclosed place where boxing and wrestling matches, cir-
cuses, or other forms of entertainment take place. **6.** *n.* the sound
made by a bell or a chime. (No
plural.) **7.** *n.* a group of criminals,
especially ones who work together
as an illegal business. **8.** *tv., irreg.*
to cause a bell to ring. (Past tense:
RANG; past participle: RUNG.) **9.** *iv.,
irreg.* to make a noise like a bell;
[for a bell] to produce a noise.
→ EARS ARE RINGING
→ GIVE SOMEONE A RING

→ HAVE A FAMILIAR RING
→ LIKE A THREE-RING CIRCUS
→ TOSS ONE'S HAT INTO THE RING

ring down the curtain (on something**)** AND **bring down the curtain (on** something**)** to bring
something to an end; to declare
something to be at an end.

ring in the new year to celebrate
the beginning of the new year, at
midnight on December 31. (As if
ringing church bells to celebrate
the new year.)

ring someone **back** to call someone
back on the telephone.

ring someone **up** to call someone
on the telephone. (Chiefly British.)

ring something **up (on** a cash register**)** to record the amount of a sale
on a cash register.

ring true to sound or seem true or
likely. (From testing the quality of
metal or glass by striking it and
listening to the noise made.)

rinse ['rɪns] *n.* an act of washing
with clean water, either for cleaning or to remove soap.

rinse someone or something **down**
to wash or clean someone or
something with water or another
fluid.

rinse someone or something **off** to
wash or clean someone or something by flushing with water or
another fluid.

rinse something **(off)** to wash
something with clean water without using soap.

rinse something **out 1.** to clean
cloth or clothing partially by
immersing it in water and squeez-

ing it out. **2.** to launder something delicate, such as feminine underwear, using a mild soap. **3.** to clean the inside of a container partially by flushing it out with water.

rinse something **out (of** something**)** to remove something from something by flushing it with water.

riot ['raɪ ət] **1.** *n.* a violent, uncontrolled disturbance by a crowd of angry people; a large, violent protest. **2.** *iv.* to participate in ①; to be part of ①.
→ READ SOMEONE THE RIOT ACT

rip ['rɪp] **1.** *n.* a tear; a gash; a ragged cut. **2.** *tv.* to tear something apart; to tear something off; to cause something to come apart by pulling on it. **3.** *iv.* to become torn; to be torn apart.

rip into someone or something **1.** to attack someone or something. **2.** to criticize or censure someone or something severely.

rip off [for something] to tear or peel off.

rip someone or something **up** to tear someone or something into bits; to mutilate someone or something. (See also RIP SOMETHING UP.)

rip something **down** to tear something down. (Refers to something that has been posted or mounted.)

rip something **off ((of)** someone or something**)** to tear something away from someone or something.

rip something **out (of** someone or something**)** to tear something out of someone or something.

rip something **up** to take something up by force and remove it. (Usually refers to something on the floor or ground, such as carpeting or pavement.)

ripe ['raɪp] *adj.* ready to be eaten or used; having developed enough so that it can be eaten or used; ready. (Adv: *ripely.* Comp: *riper;* sup: *ripest.*)
→ WHEN THE TIME IS RIPE

ripe old age a very old age.

ripen ['raɪ pən] *iv.* to become ripe.

a **ripple of excitement** a series of quiet but excited murmurs.

a **ripple of protest** a few quiet remarks protesting something; a small amount of subdued protest.

rise ['raɪz] **1.** *iv., irreg.* to go upward; to move upward; to go to a higher level. (Past tense: ROSE; past participle: RISEN. Compare this with RAISE.) **2.** *iv., irreg.* to wake up and get out of bed. **3.** *iv., irreg.* [for the sun, moon, stars, and other objects in space] to appear to come up past the horizon. **4.** *iv., irreg.* [of dough] to become higher and lighter.

rise and shine to get out of bed and be lively and energetic. (Informal. Often a command.)

rise up 1. to come up; to stand up. **2.** to get up from lying down.

rise (up) against someone or something to challenge someone or something; to rebel against someone or something.

risen ['rɪz ən] Past participle of RISE.

rising ['raɪ zɪŋ] **1.** *adj.* going higher; moving higher; going to a higher level; increasing in amount, strength, or intensity. **2.** *adj.* coming up above the horizon; moving above the horizon.

risk ['rɪsk] **1.** *n.* a danger; a chance of harm or loss; a possibility of harm or loss. **2.** *tv.* to expose someone or something to loss, harm, or death.
→ AT RISK

risk one's **neck (to** do something**)** to risk physical harm in order to accomplish something.

risky ['rɪsk i] *adj.* dangerous; having a possibility of harm or loss; not safe. (Adv: *riskily.* Comp: *riskier;* sup: *riskiest.*)

rival ['raɪv əl] **1.** *n.* a person or team that one works or plays against; someone against whom one competes or plays. **2.** the *adj.* use of ①. **3.** *tv.* to be as good as someone or something else; to equal someone or something else.

river ['rɪv ɚ] *n.* a large natural passage of fresh water that flows into a larger passage or body of water.

rivet someone's **attention** to keep someone's attention fixed [on something].

rivet something **on(to)** something to attach something to something with metal pegs.

road ['rod] **1.** *n.* a path or way that people can drive cars and other vehicles on to get from one place to another. **2.** *n.* a way to reach something or to achieve some result; a way of being or acting that leads to something. (Figurative on ①.)
→ the END OF THE ROAD

road hog someone who drives carelessly and selfishly.

roam ['rom] **1.** *tv.* to travel someplace with no definite destination in mind; to wander someplace. **2.** *iv.* to travel around with no specific goal; to wander.

roar ['ror] **1.** *n.* a very loud, deep noise. **2.** *iv.* to make ①. **3.** *iv.* to laugh very hard and very long because someone or something is very funny.

roar something **out** to say something in a loud roar.

roast ['rost] **1.** *tv.* to cook something by using dry heat; to bake; to cook in an oven; to prepare something by using heat. (Most meats and vegetables are roasted. Bread and ham are baked. Potatoes are either roasted or baked.) **2.** *iv.* to become cooked by using dry heat; to become cooked over fire. **3.** *n.* meat that is suitable for cooking in dry heat; meat that has been cooked with dry heat.

rob ['rɑb] *tv.* to steal something from someone; to take something from someone by force.

rob Peter to pay Paul to take from one person or source just to give to another, so one still has not gained anything oneself.

rob the cradle to marry or date someone who is much younger than oneself.

robber ['rɑb ɚ] *n.* someone who robs people or places; a thief.

robbery ['rɑb (ə) ri] *n.* stealing something that belongs to someone else; theft.
→ DAYLIGHT ROBBERY

robe ['rob] **1.** *n.* a long, one-piece garment, especially worn to show one's rank or position. **2.** *n.* a BATHROBE.

robin [ˈrɑb ən] *n.* a songbird with orange feathers on its breast.

robot [ˈro bɑt] *n.* a machine that does the work of a human and often moves like or looks like a human.

rock [ˈrɑk] **1.** *n.* the mineral substances of which a planet is made. (No plural.) **2.** *n.* a stone; a hard piece of earth; a piece of mineral. **3.** *adj.* made of ①; consisting of ① or ②. **4.** *iv.* to move back and forth; to move from side to side; to sway. **5.** *tv.* to move something back and forth or from side to side.
→ BETWEEN A ROCK AND A HARD PLACE

rock the boat to cause trouble where none is welcome; to disturb a situation that is otherwise stable and satisfactory. (Often negative.)

rocker [ˈrɑk ɚ] Go to ROCKING CHAIR.

rocket [ˈrɑk ət] **1.** *n.* a device used to travel through space or to carry weapons through the air. **2.** *iv.* to travel by ①.

rocking chair AND **rocker** [ˈrɑk ɪŋ ˈtʃɛr, ˈrɑk ɚ] *n.* a chair whose legs are set into two curved pieces of wood so that it can rock back and forth.

rod [ˈrɑd] *n.* a long, narrow cylinder of wood, metal, plastic, or other material.

rode [ˈrod] past tense of RIDE.

rodent [ˈrod nt] *n.* a member of a group of mammals with large, strong, sharp front teeth.

rodeo [ˈro di o] *n.* an event that includes contests involving roping cattle and riding horses or bulls. (Plural ends in *-s*.)

role [ˈrol] **1.** *n.* a part in a play or movie; the part that an actor plays in a play or movie. **2.** *n.* the duty someone has in a group or organization.

roll [ˈrol] **1.** *n.* a small loaf of bread made for one person; a small, round piece of bread for one person. **2.** *n.* a unit of something that has been formed into a tube. **3.** *iv.* to move forward by turning over and over; for a ball to move forward along a surface. **4.** *iv.* to move on wheels. **5.** *tv.* to move something forward by turning it over and over; to move a ball forward along a surface. **6.** *tv.* to move something on wheels; to cause something to move on wheels. **7.** *tv.* to cause something to form the shape of a tube or cylinder.
→ CALL (THE) ROLL
→ CLASS ROLL
→ HEADS WILL ROLL
→ TAKE (THE) ROLL

roll about to move about, turning or rotating, as a wheel or a ball.

roll away to move away by rotating, turning, or moving on wheels.

roll back [for something] to return by rotating, turning, or moving on wheels.

roll by 1. to pass by, rotating, as a wheel or a ball; to move past, rolling on wheels. **2.** to move past, as if rolling.

roll down to move downward, rotating as a wheel or a ball, or to move downward on wheels.

roll down something to move downward or along something, rotating as a wheel or a ball, or to move downward on wheels.

roll in to come in large numbers or amounts. (Informal.)

roll off (someone or something) to flow or fall off someone or something. (Both literal and figurative.)

roll on 1. [for something] to continue rolling. **2.** [for something] to be applied by rolling. **3.** to move on slowly and evenly. (Figurative.)

roll out the red carpet for someone to provide special treatment for someone.

roll over to turn over; to rotate once.

roll something **away** to cause something to move away, rotating, by turning, or moving on wheels.

roll something **back 1.** to return something to someone by rotating it, as with a wheel or a ball, or moving it back on wheels. **2.** to reduce prices.

roll something **down 1.** to move something down, making it rotate like a wheel or a ball, or moving it on wheels. **2.** to crank down something, such as a car window.

roll something **off ((of)** someone or something) to cause something to roll away, off someone or something.

roll something **on(to** something) to apply something, or a coat of a substance, by rolling a device covered with the substance on the thing to be coated.

roll something **out 1.** to bring or take something out by rolling it; to push something out on wheels. **2.** to flatten something by rolling it.

roll something **up** to coil or rotate something into a coil or roll of something.

roller skate ['rol ɚ sket] **1.** n. a special shoe or boot that is fitted with wheels underneath. **2.** iv. to move on ①. (Hyphenated.)

rolling in something having large amounts of something, usually money. (Informal.)

Roman Catholic ['ro mən 'kæθ (ə) lɪk] **1.** n. a follower of the Christian religion that is based in Rome and governed by the Pope. **2.** the adj. use of ①.

Roman numeral ['rom ən 'num ə rəl] n. the form of numbers made from letters, such as I, II, III, IV, V.

romance [ro 'mæns] **1.** n. an interest in love and adventure. (No plural.) **2.** n. a love story. **3.** n. a love experience with someone. **4.** n. a group of languages that includes French, Italian, Spanish, Portuguese, and Romanian. (Capitalized.) **5.** tv. to treat someone in a romantic way; to show someone love. **6.** the adj. use of ①, ②, ③, or ④. (Capitalized with ④.)

romantic [ro 'mæn tɪk] **1.** adj. full of love and adventure; of or about a love experience; of or about love. (Adv: romantically [...ɪk li].) **2.** adj. causing romance; used to create a feeling of romance. (Adv: romantically [...ɪk li].)

romp through something to run through something fast and playfully.

roof ['ruf, 'rʊf] **1.** *n.* the outside covering of the top of a building, vehicle, or other enclosed space. **2.** *n.* the top part of the inside of something, such as the mouth or a cave. **3.** *tv.* to put ① over something; to build ①.
→ GO THROUGH THE ROOF

room ['rum] **1.** *n.* a part of a building that is separated from other parts of the building by a wall with a door in it. **2.** *n.* space that is or could be taken up by someone or something.
→ DINING ROOM
→ EMERGENCY ROOM
→ LIVING ROOM

room together [for two or more people] to share a room, as in a college dormitory.

room with someone to live with someone; to rent a room or an apartment with someone; to be someone's roommate.

roommate ['rum met] *n.* someone with whom one shares an apartment or room.

roomy ['rum i] *adj.* having plenty of room; having a lot of space; having a comfortable amount of space; not crowded. (Adv: *roomily.* Comp: *roomier;* sup: *roomiest.*)

roost ['rust] **1.** *n.* a place, such as a nest or branch, where birds rest or sleep. **2.** *iv.* to occupy ① for rest or sleep.
→ CHICKENS HAVE COME HOME TO ROOST
→ COME HOME (TO ROOST)
→ RULE THE ROOST

rooster ['rust ɚ] *n.* an adult male chicken.

root 1. ['rut, 'rʊt] *n.* the part of a plant that is under the ground, taking water from the soil and supporting the plant. **2.** ['rut, 'rʊt] *n.* the part of a strand of hair that is under the surface of the skin. (Figurative on ①.) **3.** ['rut, 'rʊt] *n.* the origin of something; the source of something; something that causes something else. **4.** ['rut, 'rʊt] *n.* the form of a word that other words are made from. **5.** ['rut, 'rʊt] *tv.* to cause a plant to grow ①. **6.** ['rut] *iv.* to cheer for someone; to provide encouragement for someone or a team, especially for someone or a team in a contest or sports event.

root around (for something) to search through something, looking for something.

root someone or something **out (of** something) to seek and remove someone or something from something or someplace; to seek to discover and bring someone or something to light.

root something **up** [for a pig] to find something in the ground by digging with its nose.

rooted in something based on something; connected to a source or cause.

rooted to the spot unable to move because of fear or surprise.

rope ['rop] **1.** *n.* a strong, thick cord made by twisting smaller cords together. (Plural only for types and instances.) **2.** *tv.* to

catch someone or something by swinging a loop of ①.
→ AT THE END OF ONE'S ROPE
→ KNOW THE ROPES
→ SHOW SOMEONE THE ROPES
→ SKIP ROPE

rope someone **in(to** something**)** to persuade or trick someone into doing something.

rope someone or something **up** to tie someone or some creature up with a rope.

rope something **off** to isolate something with a rope barrier.

rose ['roz] **1.** past tense of RISE. **2.** *n.* a bright, sweet-smelling flower that grows on a plant having thorns. **3.** *n.* the bush that ② grows on.

Rosh Hashanah ['raʃ hə 'ʃa nə] *n.* a holiday in the Jewish religion marking the Jewish New Year.

rosy ['roz i] **1.** *adj.* pink; rose-colored. (Adv: *rosily.* Comp: *rosier;* sup: *rosiest.*) **2.** *adj.* full of hope; optimistic. (Adv: *rosily.* Comp: *rosier;* sup: *rosiest.*)

rot ['rat] **1.** *n.* decay; something that is rotten. (No plural.) **2.** *iv.* to decay; [for plant or animal material] to lose its form because of bacteria. **3.** *tv.* to cause something to decay.

rot off to rot or decompose and fall off.

rot out to decompose and fall out.

rotate ['ro tet] **1.** *iv.* to move in a circle around a fixed point; to move around the center of something in a circle. **2.** *iv.* to go in sequence; to occur in order or in sequence. **3.** *tv.* to move some-

thing in a circle around a fixed point; to cause something to revolve; to move something around an axis.

rotten ['rat n] **1.** *adj.* decayed; spoiled. (Adv: *rottenly.*) **2.** *adj.* very bad; evil; nasty. (Adv: *rottenly.*)

rough ['rʌf] **1.** *adj.* not smooth; not even; having a surface that is uneven or bumpy. (Adv: *roughly.* Comp: *rougher;* sup: *roughest.*) **2.** *adj.* using force; harsh; violent. (Adv: *roughly.* Comp: *rougher;* sup: *roughest.*) **3.** *adj.* coarse; not delicate; not refined. (Adv: *roughly.* Comp: *rougher;* sup: *roughest.*) **4.** *adj.* hard; difficult; severe; not easy. (Comp: *rougher;* sup: *roughest.*) **5.** *adj.* not in final form; not finished; not exact; not detailed; approximate. (Adv: *roughly.* Comp: *rougher;* sup: *roughest.*)
→ a DIAMOND IN THE ROUGH

rough it to live in simple or uncomfortable conditions.

rough someone **up** to treat someone roughly; to beat or harm someone.

rough something **in** to construct or draw something initially, temporarily, or crudely.

rough something **out** to make a rough sketch of something.

rough something **up** to scrape or rub something in a way that makes it rough.

round ['raʊnd] **1.** *adj.* shaped like a circle; circular; curved. (Adv: *roundly.* Comp: *rounder;* sup: *roundest.*) **2.** *adj.* shaped like a

ball; spherical; curved. (Adv: *roundly*. Comp: *rounder;* sup: *roundest*.) **3.** *n.* the bullet or shell for a single shot from a gun. **4.** *n.* a song that people begin singing at different times so that the words and music of the different parts overlap. **5.** *prep.* AROUND. (Informal. ROUND can be used informally for any of the preposition sense listed under AROUND.) **6.** *adv.* AROUND. (Informal.)
→ IN ROUND FIGURES
→ IN ROUND NUMBERS
→ a SQUARE PEG IN A ROUND HOLE

round down to something to ignore or discard a fractional part of a number.

round someone or something **up** to locate and gather someone or something.

round something **down (to** something) Go to ROUND SOMETHING OFF (TO SOMETHING).

round something **off (to** something) AND **round** something **up (to** something); **round** something **down (to** something) to express a number in the nearest whole amount or nearest group of 1, 10, 100, 1,000, ¹⁄₁₀, ¹⁄₁₀₀, ¹⁄₁₀₀₀, etc.

round something **off (with** something) to finish something with something else; to complement something with something.

round something **out** to complete or add to something.

round something **up (to** something) Go to ROUND SOMETHING OFF (TO SOMETHING).

route ['rut, 'raʊt] **1.** *n.* a road; a path; the way one travels; the way

something is sent. **2.** *tv.* to send something by a particular ①.

routine [ru'tin] **1.** *n.* a regular habit; something that is done regularly. (Plural only for types and instances.) **2.** *n.* a piece of entertainment; a skit; a sequence of actions in a performance. **3.** *adj.* normal; as a habit; as usually done. (Adv: *routinely*.)

row 1. ['ro] *n.* a series of people or things in a line; a line of people or things. **2.** ['ro] *n.* a line of seats in a theater, church, auditorium, classroom, or other place where people sit in a line. **3.** ['raʊ] *n.* a quarrel; an argument. **4.** ['ro] *iv.* to move through water in a boat by using oars. **5.** ['ro] *tv.* to move a boat by using oars.
→ GET ONE'S DUCKS IN A ROW
→ KICK UP A ROW
→ a TOUGH ROW TO HOE

rowboat ['ro bot] *n.* a small boat that is moved by using oars.

royal ['rɔɪ əl] **1.** *adj.* belonging to kings, queens, princes, princesses, etc.; of or about kings, queens, princes, princesses, etc. (Adv: *royally*.) **2.** *adj.* elegant; fit for royalty. (Figurative on ①. Adv: *royally*.)

the **royal treatment** very good treatment; very good and thoughtful care of a person.

royalty ['rɔɪ əl ti] **1.** *n.* the rank and power of kings, queens, princes, princesses, etc. (No plural.) **2.** *n.* people who have attained ①. (No plural.) **3.** *n.* money earned from the publication of a copyright holder's work.

rub ['rʌb] *tv.* to push or slide against something with something else.

rub against something to push or slide against something.

rub (away) at something to chafe or scrape something repeatedly.

rub elbows with someone AND **rub shoulders with** someone to associate with someone; to work closely with someone.

rub off ((of) something) [for something] to become detached from something because of rubbing or scraping.

rub off on(to) someone [for a characteristic] to transfer from one person to another.

rub off on(to) someone or something [for something, such as paint] to become transferred to someone or something through the contact of rubbing.

rub salt in a wound to deliberately make someone's unhappiness, shame, or misfortune worse.

rub shoulders with someone Go to RUB ELBOWS WITH SOMEONE.

rub someone or something **down** to stroke or smooth someone or some creature, for muscular well-being.

rub someone **the wrong way** Go to RUB SOMEONE'S FUR THE WRONG WAY.

rub someone's **fur the wrong way** AND **rub** someone **the wrong way** to irritate someone.

rub someone's **nose in** something to remind one of something one has done wrong; to remind some-

one of something bad or unfortunate that has happened.

rub something **away** to remove something by chafing or rubbing.

rub something **in(to** something) to cause something to penetrate a surface by rubbing it against the surface.

rub something **off ((of) something)** to remove something from something by rubbing.

rub something **out** to obliterate something by rubbing.

rub (up) against someone or something to bump or scrape against someone or something.

rubber ['rʌb ɚ] **1.** *n.* a waterproof material that goes back to its original shape when stretched or pressed. (No plural.) **2.** *adj.* made from ①.

rubber band ['rʌb ɚ 'bænd] *n.* a thin strip of rubber formed in a circle.

rubbish ['rʌb ɪʃ] *n.* trash; garbage; things that are thrown away. (No plural.)

rudder ['rʌd ɚ] *n.* a blade at the back of a ship or airplane that can be moved back and forth to control direction.

rude ['rud] **1.** *adj.* not polite; not well mannered; not courteous. (Adv: *rudely.* Comp: *ruder;* sup: *rudest.*) **2.** *adj.* simple; not complex; primitive; coarse; rough; made without complex tools. (Adv: *rudely.* Comp: *ruder;* sup: *rudest.*)

rudeness ['rud nəs] *n.* not being polite; bad manners; bad behavior. (No plural.)

ruffle its **feathers** [for a bird] to point its feathers outward.

ruffle someone's **feathers** to upset or annoy someone.

rug ['rʌg] *n.* a carpet; a thick piece of woven fabric that is used to cover a floor.
→ (AS) SNUG AS A BUG IN A RUG
→ PULL THE RUG OUT (FROM UNDER SOMEONE)

rugged ['rʌg əd] **1.** *adj.* [of a trail] rough and jagged. (Adv: *ruggedly.*) **2.** *adj.* [of something] strong and lasting a long time; [of something] not easily broken. (Adv: *ruggedly.*) **3.** *adj.* [of someone] sturdy and strong. (Adv: *ruggedly.*)

ruin ['ru ɪn] **1.** *tv.* to destroy someone or something completely; to make something worthless. **2.** *n.* the remaining part of an old building. (Often plural.) **3.** *n.* a great amount of destruction. (No plural.)
→ GO TO RACK AND RUIN
→ GO TO WRACK AND RUIN
→ IN RUIN

the **ruin of** someone or something the cause of someone's or something's destruction; a failure.

ruined ['ru ɪnd] *adj.* destroyed; completely damaged; made worthless.

rule ['rul] **1.** *n.* a statement that says what one is or is not allowed to do; a regulation. **2.** *n.* government; the control of someone in authority. (No plural.) **3.** *tv.* to decide something officially. (The object is a clause with THAT ⑦.) **4.** *tv.* to govern a country or its people.
→ GOLDEN RULE
→ a HARD-AND-FAST RULE

rule against someone or something to give a judgment against someone or something.

rule for someone or something Go to RULE IN FAVOR OF SOMEONE OR SOMETHING.

rule in favor of someone or something AND **rule for** someone or something [for a judge or deliberating body] to award a decision to someone or something or to make a decision favoring someone or something.

rule of thumb a general principle developed through practical rather than scientific means. (From the use of one's thumb to make quick and rough measurements.)

rule on something to give a decision or judgment about something.

rule someone or something **out** to eliminate someone or something from consideration.

rule the roost to be the boss or manager, especially at home.

ruler ['rul ɚ] **1.** *n.* someone who rules; someone, such as a king or queen, who runs a government. **2.** *n.* a straight strip of wood, plastic, metal, or other material that has marks on it that show measurement.

rumble ['rʌm bəl] **1.** *n.* a low vibrating sound, like the sound of thunder. **2.** *iv.* to make a low vibrating sound, like the sound of thunder.

rummage through something to toss things about while searching through something.

rumor ['rum ɚ] *n.* news about someone or something that may or may not be true; information that is passed from person to person about someone and that may or may not be true.

rump ['rʌmp] **1.** *n.* the rear part of a person or an animal; the buttocks. **2.** *n.* meat from the rear part of an animal, used as food. (No plural. Number is expressed with *rump roast(s)*.)

a **rump session** a meeting held after a larger meeting.

rumple someone or something **up** to bring disorder to someone['s clothing] or something.

run ['rʌn] **1.** *iv., irreg.* to move quickly in such a way that both feet are off the ground during each stride. (Past tense: RAN; past participle: *run*.) **2.** *iv., irreg.* to work; to be working; to function; to be in operation. **3.** *iv., irreg.* to extend to a certain length or distance; to reach a certain distance or time. **4.** *iv., irreg.* to flow; [for liquids] to move. **5.** *iv., irreg.* [for a liquid color] to spread, flow, or bleed. **6.** *iv., irreg.* to move quickly as a form of exercise or as a sport. **7.** *iv., irreg.* [for one's nose] to drip fluid. **8.** *tv., irreg.* to extend something to a certain length or distance; to cause something to reach a certain distance or time. **9.** *tv., irreg.* to control, own, or manage a business. **10.** *tv., irreg.* to publish something in a newspaper or magazine. **11.** *n.* an instance of RUN-NING as in ①. **12.** *n.* a trip; a journey.
→ DRY RUN
→ HAVE A RUN-IN WITH SOMEONE
→ HAVE A RUN OF SOMETHING
→ IN THE LONG RUN

→ MAKE A RUN FOR IT
→ MAKE SOMEONE'S BLOOD RUN COLD

run a fever AND **run a temperature** to have a body temperature higher than normal; to have a fever.

run a taut ship Go to RUN A TIGHT SHIP.

run a temperature Go to RUN A FEVER.

run a tight ship AND **run a taut ship** to run a ship or an organization in an orderly and disciplined manner. (*Taut* and *tight* mean the same thing. *Taut* is correct nautical use.)

run across someone or something Go to COME ACROSS SOMEONE OR SOMETHING.

run an errand to perform an errand.

run (around) in circles to run around frantically and without a purpose; to be in a state of chaos.

run around with someone to go places with someone; to socialize with someone.

run away (from someone or something**)** to flee someone or something.

run down 1. to come down, running; to go down, running. (See also RUN-DOWN.) **2.** [for something] to lose power and stop working. **3.** to become worn or dilapidated.

run down to someone or something to come or go down to someone or something, rapidly.

run for it to try to escape by running. (Informal.)

run for one's **life** to run away to save one's life.

run for something to be a candidate for an office in an election.

run high [for feelings] to be in a state of excitement or anger.

run in the family [for a characteristic] to appear in all (or most) members of a family.

run into a stone wall to come to a barrier against further progress. (Also used literally.)

run in(to something) **1.** [for a liquid] to flow into something or a place. **2.** to enter something or a place on foot, running. **3.** to stop by a place for a quick visit or to make a purchase quickly.

run low (on something) to near the end of a supply of something.

run off 1. to flee. **2.** to have diarrhea. **3.** [for a fluid] to drain away from a flat area.

run off with someone or something **1.** to take someone or something away, possibly running. **2.** to capture and take away someone or something; to steal someone or something.

run on 1. to continue running. **2.** to continue on for a long time.

run out of gas 1. to use up all one's gasoline. **2.** to become worn-out; to become exhausted.

run out of patience to become annoyed after being patient for a while.

run out (of something) **1.** to leave something or a place, running. **2.** to use all of something and have none left.

run out of time to have used up most of the time available; to have no time left.

run out on someone to depart and leave someone behind.

run over 1. to come by for a quick visit. **2.** to flow or spill over.

run over someone or something to drive, steer, or travel so as to pass over someone or something causing injury or damage.

run over (something) to exceed a limit.

run over something **with** someone to review something with someone.

run rampant to run, develop, or grow out of control.

run someone or something **down 1.** to criticize or deride someone or something. **2.** to collide with and knock down someone or something. **3.** to hunt for and locate someone or something.

run someone or something **in(to** something) to take or drive someone or something into something or someplace.

run someone or something **off** to drive someone or something away from something.

run someone or something **out (of** something) to chase someone or something out of something or someplace.

run someone or something **to earth** to find something after a search. (From chasing a fox into its hole during a hunt.)

run someone **ragged** to force someone to work hard and fast; to keep someone or something busy to the point of exhaustion.

run something **down** to use something having batteries, a motor, or an engine until it has no more power and stops.

run something **in(to** something**)** to guide or route something, such as a wire or a pipe, into something or a place.

run something **off 1.** to duplicate something, using a mechanical duplicating machine. **2.** to get rid of something, such as fat or energy, by running.

run something **out (of** something**)** to drive or steer something out of something or someplace.

run something **up 1.** to raise or hoist something, such as a flag. **2.** to cause something to go higher, such as the price of stocks or goods. **3.** to stitch something together quickly. **4.** to accumulate debt.

run the gamut to cover the range [from one thing to another].

run to seed AND **go to seed** to become worn-out and uncared for. (Said especially of a lawn that needs care.)

run to something **1.** to be sufficient for something; to have enough money for something. **2.** to amount to a certain amount of money.

the **runaround** ['rʌn ə raʊnd] *n.* confusion and frustration resulting from being sent to different people or places to accomplish something. (No plural form.)
→ GET THE RUNAROUND

→ GIVE SOMEONE THE RUNAROUND

run-down ['rʌn 'daʊn] **1.** *adj.* in poor health. **2.** *adj.* [of something] in bad condition owing to neglect.

rung ['rʌŋ] **1.** Past participle of RING. **2.** *n.* one of the poles or boards forming a step of a ladder.

running ['rʌn ɪŋ] **1.** *n.* the activity of someone who runs for sport, health, or pleasure. (No plural.) **2.** the *adj.* use of ①. **3.** *adj.* [of talk] continuous. (Figurative on ②.)
→ DAYS RUNNING
→ MONTHS RUNNING
→ OFF TO A RUNNING START
→ OUT OF THE RUNNING
→ WEEKS RUNNING
→ YEARS RUNNING

runny ['rʌn i] *adj.* [of eggs] not completely cooked and still somewhat liquid. (Comp: *runnier;* sup: *runniest.*)

runny nose *n.* a person's nose that is dripping due to a cold, the flu, etc.

run-of-the-mill [rən əv ðə 'mɪl] *adj.* average; ordinary; typical; normal; regular.

runway ['rʌn we] *n.* a landing strip for an airplane; a track that an airplane takes off from and lands on.

rural ['rʊr əl] *adj.* in the country; not like the city; not urban or suburban. (Adv: *rurally.*)

rush ['rʌʃ] **1.** *n.* hurry; haste; movement in a fast and urgent manner. (No plural.) **2.** *n.* a very sudden movement or flow.
→ IN A MAD RUSH

rush in(to something**) 1.** to run or hurry into a thing or a place. **2.** to begin doing something without the proper preparation.

rush off (from someplace**)** to hurry away from someplace.

a **rush on** something a large, sudden demand for something.

rush out (of something**)** to exit in a hurry.

rush someone or something **in(to** something**)** to lead or carry someone or something into something or someplace hurriedly.

rush someone or something **out (of** something**)** to lead or guide someone or something out of something or someplace hurriedly.

rush something **off (to** someone or something**)** to send something quickly to someone or something.

rush something **through (**something**)** to move something through some process or office in a hurry.

rush through something to hurry to get something finished; to race through something.

rust ['rʌst] **1.** *n.* a dark red or dark orange layer that forms on iron or steel when it is exposed to air or water. (No plural.) **2.** *iv.* to acquire a coating of ①. **3.** *tv.* to cause something to be covered with ①.

rustle ['rʌs əl] **1.** *n.* a soft noise, like the sound that leaves make when they are blown by the wind or the sound made when objects are rubbed together. (No plural.) **2.** *iv.* [for objects] to make a soft noise when rubbed together or blown by the wind. **3.** *tv.* to cause objects to make a noise as in ②. **4.** *tv.* to steal cattle.

rustle something **up** to manage to prepare a meal, perhaps on short notice. (Folksy.)

rusty ['rʌs ti] **1.** *adj.* covered with rust; rusted. (Adv: *rustily.* Comp: *rustier;* sup: *rustiest.*) **2.** *adj.* [of a skill or knowledge] poor or lacking because it has been unused for so long a time. (Adv: *rustily.* Comp: *rustier;* sup: *rustiest.*)

rut ['rʌt] *n.* a deep track that a wheel makes in soft ground; a groove.
→ IN A RUT
→ (STUCK) IN A RUT

ruthless ['ruθ ləs] *adj.* without pity; without mercy; cruel; evil. (Adv: *ruthlessly.*)

rye ['raɪ] **1.** *n.* a tall grass that is farmed for its light brown grain. (No plural.) **2.** *n.* grain from ①. (No plural. Number is expressed with *grain(s) of rye.*) **3.** *adj.* made from ②.

S

sack ['sæk] **1.** *n.* a bag or pouch made of paper, cloth, etc. **2.** *n.* the contents of ①.

sacred ['se krɪd] *adj.* holy; blessed. (Adv: *sacredly.*)

sacred cow something that is regarded by some people with such respect and veneration that they do not like it being criticized by anyone in any way.

sacrifice ['sæ krə faɪs] **1.** *n.* giving up something; not having something that is wanted or needed. (Plural only for types and instances.) **2.** *n.* something that is offered to a god or spirit. **3.** *tv.* to take the life of a creature as in ②. **4.** *tv.* to give up something of value [for someone else's benefit].

sad ['sæd] **1.** *adj.* not happy; feeling sorrow. (Adv: *sadly.* Comp: *sadder;* sup: *saddest.*) **2.** *adj.* unfortunate; [of something] not bringing pleasure. (Adv: *sadly.* Comp: *sadder;* sup: *saddest.*)

sadden ['sæd n] **1.** *iv.* to become sad. **2.** *tv.* to cause someone to become sad.

saddle ['sæd l] **1.** *n.* a leather seat that fits on the back of a horse or other animal that carries people. **2.** *n.* a bicycle or motorcycle seat. **3.** *tv.* to place ① on a horse or a similar animal.

saddle someone **with** something to give someone something undesirable, annoying, or difficult to deal with. (Informal.)

sadness ['sæd nəs] *n.* sorrow; having feelings of gloom or depres-

sion; a lack of happiness. (No plural.)

safe ['sef] **1.** *n.* a solid, sturdy, steel or iron box—with a strong lock—that money, jewelry, papers, or other valuable objects are kept in for protection. **2.** *adj.* not dangerous; not risky; not causing or creating danger. (Adv: *safely.* Comp: *safer;* sup: *safest.*) **3.** *adj.* protected; secure. (Adv: *safely.* Comp: *safer;* sup: *safest.*)
→ PLAY IT SAFE
→ TO BE ON THE SAFE SIDE
→ TO BE SAFE

safe and sound safe and whole or healthy.

safeguard ['sef gɑrd] **1.** *n.* something that protects someone or something from danger. **2.** *tv.* to protect someone or something from danger; to keep someone or something safe.

safekeeping ['sef 'kip ɪŋ] *n.* keeping someone or something safe; a place or state where something is safe. (No plural.)
→ FOR SAFEKEEPING

safety ['sef ti] **1.** *n.* the state of being safe; freedom from harm or danger. (No plural.) **2.** the *adj.* use of ①.

safety belt ['sef ti bɛlt] *n.* a seat belt; a set of straps that extend across one's lap from the top of one's shoulder across the body to the opposite hip.

safe(ty)-deposit box ['sef (ti) də 'paz ət 'baks] *n.* a metal box that is used for holding valuable items and is locked in a large safe or vault.

sag ['sæg] *iv.* to bend, hang, or curve downward.

sage advice very good and wise advice.

said ['sɛd] past tense and past participle of SAY.

sail ['sel] **1.** *n.* a sheet of cloth that is stretched on a mast of a ship to catch the energy of the wind. **2.** *iv.* to travel by boat or ship on the water. **3.** *iv.* [for a ship or boat] to travel on the water. **4.** *iv.* to glide through the air the way a boat moves through water. **5.** *tv.* to steer a boat or ship on the water. **6.** *tv.* to cause something to glide through the air.
→ SMOOTH SAILING

sail into someone or something **1.** to crash into someone or something with a boat or ship. **2.** to crash into someone or something.

sail (right) through something **1.** to travel through something in a boat or ship. **2.** to go through something very quickly and easily. (Figurative.)

sailboat ['sel bot] *n.* a boat that has at least one sail and that moves by the power of the wind.

sailor ['se lɚ] **1.** *n.* someone who works on a boat or a ship. **2.** *n.* someone who is in the navy.

sake ['sek] [someone's] benefit, demands, or welfare.
→ FOR SOMEONE'S OR SOMETHING'S SAKE
→ FOR THE SAKE OF SOMEONE OR SOMETHING

salad ['sæl əd] *n.* a dish of mixed vegetables, especially lettuce, or other food mixed with vegetables, usually with a sauce called *salad dressing.*
→ TOSS A SALAD

salary ['sæl (ə) ri] *n.* the amount of money that someone is paid for working. (Compare to WAGE.)

sale ['sel] **1.** *n.* the exchange of a product or service for money; an act of selling. **2.** *n.* a special event where products or services are sold for less money than normal.
→ FOR SALE
→ ON SALE
→ PUT SOMETHING UP (FOR SALE)

sales *n.* the amount of products or services sold during a certain period of time. (Treated as plural, but not countable.)

salesclerk ['selz klɚk] *n.* someone who works in a store, helping customers and selling products.

salesman ['selz mən] *n., irreg.* someone whose job is selling things; a man whose job is selling things. (Plural: SALESMEN.)

salesmen ['selz mən] plural of SALESMAN.

salespeople ['selz pi pəl] a plural of SALESPERSON.

salesperson ['selz pɚ sən] *n., irreg.* someone whose job is selling things. (Plural: SALESPEOPLE or *salespersons.*)

saleswoman ['selz wʊ mən] *n., irreg.* a woman whose job is selling things. (Plural: SALESWOMEN.)

saleswomen ['selz wɪ mən] plural of SALESWOMAN.

salmon ['sæm ən] **1.** *n., irreg.* a large food fish with soft, pale pink flesh. (Plural: *salmon*.) **2.** *n.* the meat of ①. (No plural.)

salt ['sɔlt] **1.** *n.* a white substance used to season or preserve food and to melt snow and ice. (No plural.) **2.** *n.* a chemical substance made by combining an acid with a metal. (Plural only for types and instances.) **3.** *tv.* to season something by putting ① on it. **4.** *tv.* to cover something with ①.
→ BACK TO THE SALT MINES
→ RUB SALT IN A WOUND
→ TAKE SOMETHING WITH A GRAIN OF SALT
→ TAKE SOMETHING WITH A PINCH OF SALT
→ WORTH ONE'S SALT

salt of the earth the most worthy of people; a very good or worthy person.

salt something **away 1.** to store and preserve food by salting it. **2.** to store something; to place something in reserve. (Figurative.)

salt water ['sɔlt 'wɑt ɚ] **1.** *n.* water with a high salt content, such as that found in the oceans. (No plural.) **2. saltwater** the *adj.* use of ①.

salted ['sɔl tɪd] *adj.* [of food] having salt added.

salty ['sɔl ti] *adj.* tasting like salt; having salt. (Adv: *saltily.* Comp: *saltier*; sup: *saltiest*.)

salute [sə 'lut] **1.** *tv.* to show respect for someone by bringing the right hand to one's head. **2.** *n.* an act of moving the hand to the head as in ①.

same ['sem] **1.** *adj.* not different; being the identical person or thing. **2.** *adj.* being exactly like someone or something else; not different from someone or something else; alike.
→ AMOUNT TO THE SAME THING (AS SOMETHING)
→ BY THE SAME TOKEN
→ CAST IN THE SAME MOLD
→ CUT FROM THE SAME CLOTH
→ IN THE SAME BOAT
→ IN THE SAME BREATH
→ SPEAK THE SAME LANGUAGE
→ TARRED WITH THE SAME BRUSH

the **same as** someone or something identical to someone or something.

sameness ['sem nəs] *n.* the quality of being the same; the degree of being very similar to someone or something. (No plural.)

sample ['sæm pəl] **1.** *n.* a small portion of something that shows what the rest of it is like. **2.** *tv.* to take, try, or taste a small portion of something.

sanctuary ['sæŋk tʃu ɛr i] **1.** *n.* a sacred or holy building; a holy place of worship. **2.** *n.* a place of safety or preservation, especially for birds and other wild animals.

sand ['sænd] **1.** *n.* very tiny particles of rock or seashells, such as are found on beaches and in deserts. (Plural only for types and instances.) **2.** *tv.* to rub something with sandpaper to make it smooth; to smooth something with sandpaper. **3.** *tv.* to put or sprinkle ① on a surface, such as an icy street.
→ BURY ONE'S HEAD IN THE SAND
→ HIDE ONE'S HEAD IN THE SAND

sandpaper ['sænd pe pɚ] *n.* a paper lightly coated with sand particles, used to polish or smooth a surface. (Plural only for types and instances.)

the **sands of time** the accumulated tiny amounts of time; time represented by the sand in an hourglass.

sandwich ['sænd wɪtʃ] **1.** *n.* two pieces of bread with some kind of food in between. **2.** *tv.* to put someone or something tightly between or among other persons or objects.

sane ['sen] **1.** *adj.* having a healthy mind; not crazy. (Adv: *sanely.* Comp: *saner;* sup: *sanest.*) **2.** *adj.* rational; sensible; having or showing common sense. (Adv: *sanely.* Comp: *saner;* sup: *sanest.*)

sang ['sæŋ] past tense of SING.

sanitary ['sæn ə ter i] **1.** *adj.* very clean; not dangerous to one's health. (Adv: *sanitarily.*) **2.** *adj.* used for the disposal of waste that is harmful to health.

sanitation [sæn ə 'te ʃən] *n.* the study and practice of preserving the health of the public, especially concerning the removal of waste. (No plural.)

sanity ['sæn ə ti] *n.* sound mental health. (No plural.)

sank ['sæŋk] a past tense of SINK.

sap ['sæp] **1.** *n.* a fluid in a tree that carries important nutrients to its parts. (No plural.) **2.** *tv.* to take away someone's or something's strength or energy.

sarcasm ['sɑr kæz əm] *n.* the use of words that have the opposite meaning from what is said. (No plural.)

sarcastic [sɑr 'kæs tɪk] *adj.* using sarcasm; using irony; mocking. (Adv: *sarcastically* [...ɪk li].)

sardine [sɑr 'din] *n.* a small, edible fish, usually sold in flat cans.
→ PACKED (IN) LIKE SARDINES

sat ['sæt] past tense and past participle of SIT.

Satan ['set n] *n.* the devil.

satellite ['sæt ə laɪt] **1.** *n.* a natural body of rock and minerals that orbits around a planet; a moon. **2.** *n.* a spacecraft that orbits a planet. **3.** *adj.* dependent on something else that has more power.

satin ['sæt n] **1.** *n.* a soft, silky, smooth cloth that is shiny on one side. (Plural only for types and instances.) **2.** *adj.* made from ①.

satisfaction [sæt ɪs 'fæk ʃən] *n.* a feeling that one is content; fulfillment. (Plural only for types and instances.)

satisfactory [sæt ɪs 'fæk tə ri] *adj.* adequate; meeting certain needs or requirements. (Adv: *satisfactorily.*)

satisfy ['sæt ɪs faɪ] **1.** *tv.* to make someone content; to please someone; to make someone happy with something. **2.** *tv.* to meet or fulfill certain needs or requirements.

Saturday ['sæt ɚ de] Go to DAY.

sauce ['sɔs] *n.* a liquid that is put on food to add flavor. (Plural only for types and instances.)

saucer ['sɔ sɚ] *n.* a small dish that cups are set on.

sausage ['sɔ sɪdʒ] **1.** *n.* a food made of chopped meat mixed with spices (in the United States). (No plural.) **2.** *n.* a food made of ① stuffed into a thin tube of animal intestine or artificial material and made into segments. **3.** *adj.* made with ①.

savage ['sæv ɪdʒ] **1.** *adj.* wild; not tamed; not civilized; primitive. (Adv: *savagely.*) **2.** *adj.* fierce; ready to fight; violent; vicious. (Adv: *savagely.*) **3.** *n.* someone who is wild, not tamed, and not civilized.

save ['sev] **1.** *tv.* to make someone or something safe from harm or danger; to rescue someone or something. **2.** *tv.* to keep a supply of something, especially money, for future use; to place something aside, especially money, for future use. **3.** *tv.* not to spend something; not to use something; to reserve something. **4.** *tv.* to cause something to be unnecessary (for someone); to prevent the need (for someone) to do something.
→ SCRIMP AND SAVE

save something **for a rainy day** to reserve something—usually money—for some future need.

save something **up (for** something**)** to accumulate an amount of money for the purchase of something.

save the day to produce a good result when a bad result was expected.

save up (for something**)** to accumulate something for some purpose.

saved by the bell rescued from a difficult or dangerous situation just in time by something that brings the situation to a sudden end.

savings ['sev ɪŋz] *n.* money that is saved for future use; money that is set aside, especially in a bank account, for future use. (Treated as plural, but not countable.)

savings account ['sev ɪŋz ə 'kaʊnt] *n.* a bank account that is intended for saving money over a long period of time.

saw ['sɔ] **1.** past tense of SEE. **2.** *n.* a cutting tool with a thin blade that is notched with tiny, sharp teeth. **3.** *iv., irreg.* to cut with ②. (Past tense: *sawed;* past participle: *sawed* or SAWN.) **4.** *tv., irreg.* to cut something with ②.

sawn ['sɔn] a past participle of SAW.

say ['se] **1.** *tv., irreg.* to pronounce words; to speak words. (Past tense and past participle: SAID.) **2.** *tv., irreg.* to state something; to declare something; to express something in words. (The object can be a clause with THAT ⑦.) **3.** *n.* a role of authority or influence [in making a decision]. (No plural.)
→ DROP IN (TO SAY HELLO)
→ ON SOMEONE'S SAY-SO

say grace to say a prayer of gratitude before a meal.

scale ['skel] **1.** *n.* a series of numbers at different levels, used for measuring something. **2.** *n.* the relation between a measurement on a map or design compared to the actual measurement it corresponds to. **3.** *n.* a series of musical notes, from low notes to high notes or from high notes to low notes. **4.** *n.* the size or extent of something, especially as compared to something else or an average. (No plural.) **5.** *n.* a device that measures how much something weighs. (Singular or plural with the same meaning.) **6.** *n.* one of

the small, thin pieces of hardened skin on the bodies of most fish and snakes. **7.** *n.* a flake of something, especially dead skin. **8.** *tv.* to climb something. **9.** *tv.* to remove ⑥ from a fish.
→ TIP THE SCALES AT SOMETHING

scale something **down** to make something smaller by a certain amount.

scalp ['skælp] *n.* the skin and any hair growing on it on the top and back of the head.

scan ['skæn] **1.** *tv.* to examine something closely and carefully, as though one were searching for something. **2.** *tv.* to look through something quickly and carelessly; to glance at something; to read through something quickly. **3.** *tv.* to put a picture or a text into a computer file by placing the picture or book on a scanner.

scandal ['skæn dəl] *n.* an event that causes disgrace; an instance of actions that are not legal, moral, or ethical and that become known by other people.

scanner ['skæn ɚ] *n.* a machine that converts a page of a book or a picture to an image that can be stored, viewed, or changed on a computer.

scapegoat ['skep got] **1.** *n.* someone who is blamed for the mistakes of others; someone who takes the blame for the mistakes of others. **2.** *tv.* to blame someone for the mistakes of others.
→ MAKE SOMEONE THE SCAPEGOAT FOR SOMETHING

scar ['skɑr] **1.** *n.* a mark that is left on the surface of something, such

as skin, that has been torn, cut, burned, or otherwise damaged. **2.** *tv.* to cause someone or something to have ①.

scarce ['skɛrs] *adj.* rare; hard to find. (Adv: *scarcely.* Comp: *scarcer;* sup: *scarcest.*)
→ (AS) SCARCE AS HENS' TEETH

scarcer than hens' teeth Go to (AS) SCARCE AS HENS' TEETH.

scare ['skɛr] **1.** *tv.* to cause someone to feel fear or fright; to cause someone to be afraid. **2.** *n.* a bad fright; an instance of being afraid; a feeling of fear.

scare someone or something **off** to frighten someone or some creature away.

scared ['skɛrd] *adj.* feeling fright; filled with fear.

scarf ['skɑrf] *n., irreg.* a long strip of cloth that is wrapped around the neck or face for decoration or to keep warm when it is cold. (Plural: SCARVES.)

scarves ['skɑrvz] plural of SCARF.

scary ['skɛr i] *adj.* causing fear; filling one with fear; causing one to be afraid. (Adv: *scarily.* Comp: *scarier;* sup: *scariest.*)

scatter ['skæt ɚ] **1.** *tv.* to cause each person or thing in a group to move in a different direction. **2.** *tv.* to spread things—such as seeds, papers, ashes, etc.—over a wide area by throwing them. **3.** *iv.* [for each person or thing in a group] to move in a different direction.

scene ['sin] **1.** *n.* all that can be seen from one place. **2.** *n.* the place where something happens; a setting. **3.** *n.* a division of an act of

a play; an incident in a movie or play. **4.** *n.* a display of emotion or action, especially an angry or violent action.
→ ARRIVE (UP)ON THE SCENE (OF SOMETHING)
→ BURST ONTO THE SCENE
→ BURST (UP)ON THE SCENE

scenery ['sin (ə) ri] **1.** *n.* the natural surroundings—trees, mountains, valleys—of an area. (No plural.) **2.** *n.* the things that are built or bought and put on a stage to represent the place where the action of a play takes place. (No plural.)
→ A CHANGE OF SCENERY

scent ['sɛnt] **1.** *n.* a smell; an aroma; an odor; the way someone or something smells. **2.** *tv.* to sense the smell of someone or something.

schedule ['skɛ dʒəl] **1.** *n.* a list showing the times that events are supposed to happen. **2.** *tv.* to put someone or something on ①.
→ AHEAD OF SCHEDULE
→ BEHIND SCHEDULE

scheme ['skim] **1.** *n.* a plan; a method for doing something; a way of doing something, possibly dishonestly. **2.** *iv.* to plot; to make plans, especially dishonest ones.

scheme against someone or something to plot or conspire against someone or something.

scholar ['skɑl ɚ] **1.** *n.* someone who studies a subject thoroughly. **2.** *n.* a student; a pupil. **3.** *n.* someone who has a scholarship.

scholarly ['skɑl ɚ li] **1.** *adj.* concerning scholarship and school-

work. **2.** *adj.* having a lot of knowledge about a certain subject.

scholarship ['skɑl ɚ ʃɪp] **1.** *n.* knowledge that a person receives by studying; evidence of one's knowledge. (No plural.) **2.** *n.* a sum of money given by an organization to a student for school fees or other expenses related to studying.

school ['skul] **1.** *n.* a building for education and instruction. **2.** *n.* all the people who work at or attend a school; all the people who teach or study at a school. **3.** *n.* a group of fish that swim together. **4.** *n.* the education system; participation in the education system. (No plural.)
→ FROM THE OLD SCHOOL
→ GRAMMAR SCHOOL
→ HIGH SCHOOL
→ PRIMARY SCHOOL
→ PUBLIC SCHOOL
→ TELL TALES OUT OF SCHOOL

school of thought a particular philosophy or way of thinking about something.

schoolchild ['skul tʃaɪld] *n., irreg.* a child of school age, especially a child in grades kindergarten through eighth grade; a child who attends school. (Plural: SCHOOLCHILDREN.)

schoolchildren ['skul tʃɪl drɪn] plural of SCHOOLCHILD.

schoolroom ['skul rum] *n.* a room in a school building, especially one where students are taught.

schoolteacher ['skul titʃ ɚ] *n.* someone who teaches in a school.

schoolwork ['skul wɚk] *n.* work that a student must do for a class; the assigned projects that a student must do. (No plural. See also HOMEWORK.)

science ['saɪ əns] **1.** *n.* a system of knowledge obtained by testing and proving facts that describe the way something acts, functions, or exists. (No plural.) **2.** *n.* a kind of study that results in a system of knowledge obtained by testing and proving facts that describe the way something acts, functions, or exists.

scientific [saɪ ən 'tɪf ɪk] **1.** *adj.* using the laws or facts of a science. (Adv: *scientifically* [...ɪk li].) **2.** *adj.* of or about science. (Adv: *scientifically* [...ɪk li].)

scientist ['saɪ ən tɪst] *n.* someone who is skilled in a science; someone who works in a science.

scissors ['sɪz ɚz] *n.* a set of two sharp blades that have handles on one end and are connected in the middle. (Treated as singular or plural. Number is expressed with *pair(s) of scissors.*)

scold ['skold] **1.** *tv.* to speak angrily to someone who has done something wrong. **2.** *n.* someone who speaks as in ①.

scolding ['skol dɪŋ] *n.* speaking angrily to someone as punishment.

scoop ['skup] **1.** *n.* a shovellike utensil or tool. **2.** *n.* the contents of ①.

scope ['skop] *n.* the range of something; the limit of something; the extent of something. (No plural.)

score ['skor] **1.** *n.* the number of points that a person or team has received in a game or contest; the number of points that a person has received on a test. **2.** *n.* a written piece of music for instruments or voices. **3.** *n.* a group of twenty things. **4.** *tv.* to earn one or more points in a game or contest. **5.** *tv.* to cut lines or grooves into a surface; to cut a surface with a series of lines. **6.** *tv.* to earn a certain number of points on a test. **7.** *iv.* to achieve [a level of performance in academic grades]. **8.** *iv.* to earn [a point in a game or contest].
→ KNOW THE SCORE

scour something **off ((of)** something**)** to clean something off something by rubbing with a rough object.

scour something **out** to clean something out by rubbing with a rough object.

scout around (for someone or something**)** to look around for someone or something.

scout someone or something **up** to search for and find someone or something.

scowl ['skaʊl] **1.** *n.* a frown; an angry look. **2.** *iv.* to look angry; to frown.

scrap ['skræp] **1.** *n.* a small piece of something, especially a small piece of something that is left over from a larger piece, especially of food or cloth. **2.** *n.* material, such as metal, that can be reused. (No plural.) **3.** *tv.* to throw something away that is no longer wanted, needed, or able to be used.

scrape ['skrep] **1.** *tv.* to damage something by rubbing a sharp or rough object against it. **2.** *tv.* to remove something by rubbing

with a sharp or rough object. **3.** *iv.* to rub with force against something else. **4.** *n.* damage or injury to an object or the skin caused by rubbing something sharp or rough against it. **5.** *n.* the sound that is made when a rough object rubs hard against something else.
→ BOW AND SCRAPE
→ HAVE A SCRAPE (WITH SOMEONE OR SOMETHING)

scrape by (on something) AND **scrape by (with something)** to manage just to survive with something.

scrape by (something) to manage just to move by something.

scrape by (with something) Go to SCRAPE BY (ON SOMETHING).

scrape something away (from something) to scratch or rasp something off something.

scrape something off ((of) someone or something) to rub or stroke something off someone or something.

scrape something out to empty something by scraping.

scrape something out (of something) to remove something by scraping.

scrape the bottom of the barrel to select from among the worst; to choose from what remains.

scrape through (something) 1. to move through something, scraping or rubbing the sides. **2.** to survive something just barely; to pass a test just barely.

scratch ['skrætʃ] **1.** *tv.* to damage an object's surface by causing a sharp object to cut or tear

in it; to make a cut or tear in the surface of something with a sharp object. **2.** *tv.* to remove something from the surface of something using a sharp object to cut or tear into it. **3.** *tv.* to rub a location of the body that itches with one's fingers, fingernails, or a sharp object. **4.** *iv.* to rub [a part of the body that itches]. **5.** *n.* a cut, tear, or damage as in ①.
→ MAKE SOMETHING FROM SCRATCH
→ NOT UP TO SCRATCH
→ START FROM SCRATCH

scratch someone or something out to mark off or cross out the name of someone or something.

scratch someone or something up to damage or mar someone or something by scratching.

scratch the surface to just begin to find out about something; to examine only the superficial aspects of something.

scream ['skrim] **1.** *iv.* [for someone] to make a very loud noise, especially when hurt, afraid, excited, surprised, or filled with emotion. **2.** *iv.* to speak very loudly; to talk in a very loud voice. **3.** *tv.* to say something in a very loud voice. (The object can be a clause with THAT ⑦.) **4.** *n.* a very loud noise, especially made by someone who is hurt, afraid, excited, surprised, or filled with emotion.
→ a PIERCING SCREAM

scream bloody murder Go to CRY BLOODY MURDER.

screen ['skrin] **1.** *n.* a mesh made of thin wires crossing each other. **2.** *n.* a piece of cloth stretched over a frame, used to block, protect, or separate someone or something from someone or something else. **3.** *n.* a large white surface that movies are projected onto. **4.** *n.* the glass part of a television set or computer monitor on which images are seen. **5.** *tv.* to determine if someone will be allowed to speak or meet with someone else. **6.** *tv.* to show a movie; to make a movie available to the public.

screw ['skru] **1.** *n.* a piece of metal, similar to a nail, having a sharp RIDGE ② wrapped around its shaft. (A screw has a flat or rounded head that has a single groove or two crossed grooves.) **2.** *tv.* to fasten something to something else with ①. **3.** *tv.* to twist ① into wood or metal with a screwdriver. **4.** *tv.* to turn the lid, cap, or top of a container to close it tightly.

screw something **down** to secure something to the floor or a base by the use of screws.

screw up one's **courage** to build up one's courage.

screwdriver ['skru draɪ vɚ] *n.* a common tool used to tighten and loosen screws.

scribble ['skrɪb əl] **1.** *tv.* to draw or write something quickly or in a messy way, especially so that it is hard to recognize or read. (The object can be a clause with THAT ⑦.) **2.** *iv.* to draw or write quickly or in a messy way so that the result is hard to recognize or read. **3.** *n.* marks or words that are hard to recognize or read because they

were drawn or written quickly or in a messy way.

scrimp and save to be very thrifty; to live on very little money, often in order to save up for something.

script ['skrɪpt] **1.** *n.* a document containing the words of a play, movie, or speech. **2.** *n.* a way of writing in which the letters of a word are joined together.

scripture ['skrɪp tʃɚ] *n.* holy writings; one or more holy writings. (Plural only for types and instances. Singular or plural with the same meaning.)

scrub ['skrʌb] **1.** *tv.* to clean or wash the surface of someone or something by rubbing. **2.** *tv.* to remove something from something by rubbing. **3.** *iv.* to clean or wash [oneself] by rubbing, usually with a stiff brush, cloth, or sponge. **4.** *n.* an area of small trees and low bushes; a collection of small trees and bushes. (No plural.)

scrub someone or something **down** to clean someone or something thoroughly by rubbing.

scrub someone or something **off** to clean someone or something by rubbing.

scrub something **off ((of)** something) to clean something off something by scrubbing.

scrub something **out** to clean out the inside of something by rubbing or brushing.

scrub something **out (of** something) to clean something out of something by scrubbing.

scrub up 1. to clean oneself up. **2.** to clean oneself, especially one's hands and arms, as a preparation for performing a surgical procedure. (A special use of ①.)

scrutinize ['skrut n aɪz] *tv.* to examine someone or something closely; to look at something very closely; to inspect someone or something.

scrutiny ['skrut n i] *n.* a close examination; an inspection; looking at something closely. (No plural.)
→ UNDER SCRUTINY

scuba ['sku bə] **1.** *iv.* to dive and explore underwater. (Past tense and past participle: *scubaed*.) **2.** the *adj.* use of ①.

scuba diver ['sku bə 'daɪ vɚ] *n.* someone who does SCUBA DIVING.

scuba (diving) *n.* diving or exploring underwater with a tank that contains air, allowing a diver to breathe, and that can be carried or worn on the back. (No plural. An acronym for *self-contained underwater breathing apparatus*.)

scuff ['skʌf] **1.** *tv.* to make scratches in the surface of something clean and smooth; to make marks on the surface of something clean and smooth. **2.** *iv.* to walk somewhere without picking up one's feet; to slide one's feet along as one walks.

sculptor ['skʌlp tɚ] *n.* an artist who makes art out of clay, stone, metal, or other solid materials.

sculpture ['skʌlp tʃɚ] **1.** *n.* the art of making art from clay, stone, metal, or another solid material.

(No plural.) **2.** *n.* a piece of art that is made out of clay, stone, metal, or another solid material. (Often singular with a plural meaning.)

sea ['si] **1.** *n.* a large body of salt water that is smaller than an ocean. **2.** *n.* one of the large bodies of salt water that cover almost three-fourths of the earth's surface; an ocean.
→ AT SEA
→ AT SEA (ABOUT SOMETHING)
→ BETWEEN THE DEVIL AND THE DEEP BLUE SEA
→ THERE ARE PLENTY OF OTHER FISH IN THE SEA.

sea level ['si lɛv əl] *n.* the horizontal level at the surface of the oceans, which is considered zero.

seafood ['si fud] *n.* animals from the sea, including fish, shellfish, and octopus, that are eaten as food. (No plural.)

seal ['sil] **1.** *n.* a large animal that has thick, coarse fur, lives in and near the sea, and has flat legs. **2.** *n.* an official mark or design of a government, business, organization, or person that is printed or stamped on objects for identification. (A signature usually serves as a seal for an individual.) **3.** *n.* a piece of wax, metal, or other material that has the mark or design of a government, business, organization, or person printed or stamped on it. **4.** *n.* something that causes an opening in an object to remain closed; something that prevents an opening from being opened secretly. **5.** *tv.* to close something tightly; to fasten something tightly, often with

glue or pressure. **6.** *tv.* to fill cracks in an object with a substance so that air, water, or other things cannot pass through the cracks.
→ SIGNED, SEALED, AND DELIVERED

seal something **off (from** someone or something**)** to make something inaccessible to someone or something.

seam ['sim] **1.** *n.* the line of thread where two pieces of cloth have been sewn together. **2.** *n.* the line where two edges of anything meet.
→ BURST AT THE SEAMS
→ COME APART AT THE SEAMS

the **seamy side of life** the most unpleasant or roughest aspect of life. (Informal. A reference to the inside of a garment, where the seams show.)

search ['sɝtʃ] **1.** *iv.* to look carefully, trying to find someone or something. **2.** *tv.* to examine someone or something closely to try to find something. **3.** *n.* an attempt to find someone or something.

search high and low for someone or something Go to HIGH AND LOW FOR SOMEONE OR SOMETHING.

search something **with a fine-tooth comb** Go to GO OVER SOMETHING WITH A FINE-TOOTH COMB.

seashell ['si ʃɛl] *n.* a shell of an animal that lives in the sea; a hard, protective covering made by an animal that lives in the sea, such as an oyster.

seashore ['si ʃor] *n.* the land that borders the sea; the shore that runs along a sea.

seasick ['si sɪk] *adj.* being sick while on a boat or a ship because of the movement of the sea.

seaside ['si saɪd] **1.** *n.* the land that borders a sea; the seashore. (No plural.) **2.** *adj.* located on the seashore; at the side of the sea.

season ['siz ən] **1.** *n.* one of the four times of the year: winter, spring, summer, and fall. **2.** *n.* a period of time marked by a certain kind of weather, an activity, or condition. **3.** *tv.* to add spices to food to make it taste better or different.
→ IN SEASON
→ OUT OF SEASON

seasonal ['siz ə nəl] the *adj.* form of SEASON ②. (Adv: *seasonally.*)

seasoning ['siz (ə) nɪŋ] *n.* a spice; an herb; something that is added to food to make it taste better or different.

seat ['sit] **1.** *n.* something that is used for sitting on; a place where someone can sit. **2.** *n.* the part of a pair of pants that one sits on. **3.** *n.* the part of the body that one sits on; the behind; the buttocks. **4.** *n.* a place where someone is a member, such as in Congress or on a stock exchange. **5.** *tv.* to provide someone with ①; to lead someone to ①; to help someone sit down. **6.** *tv.* to have a certain number of places to sit; to have room for a certain number of seated people.
→ BY THE SEAT OF ONE'S PANTS
→ SHOW ONE TO ONE'S SEAT
→ SHOW SOMEONE TO A SEAT
→ TAKE A BACKSEAT (TO SOMEONE)

seat belt ['sit bɛlt] *n.* a strap that buckles across one's lap, as in a car

527

or an airplane. (See also SAFETY BELT.)

seated ['sit ɪd] *adj.* sitting down in or on something.

seating ['sit ɪŋ] **1.** *n.* a particular arrangement of seats. (No plural.) **2.** *n.* the number of seats that are available in a place. (No plural.)

seawater ['si wɔt ɚ] *n.* salt water as found in the sea.

seaweed ['si wid] *n.* a plant that grows in or at the edge of the sea. (Plural only for types and instances.)

seclude [sɪ 'klud] *tv.* to keep someone away from other people; to keep something away from other things or places.

secluded [sɪ 'klud ɪd] *adj.* private; remote; set apart from other places; kept away from other places or people. (Adv: *secludedly.*)

seclusion [sɪ 'klu ʒən] *n.* the condition of being private and hidden; a place away from other people. (No plural.)

second ['sɛk ənd] **1.** *n.* a basic unit of the measurement of time; 1/60 of a minute; 1/3600 of an hour. **2.** *n.* a moment; a very short period of time. **3.** *n.* a unit of measurement of an angle equal to 1/60 of a minute or 1/3600 of a degree. **4.** *n.* someone or something that comes after the first [one] as in ⑤. **5.** *adj.* coming, happening, or being immediately after the first. (Adv: *secondly.*) **6.** *adv.* in a position that is immediately after the first position.
→ COME OFF SECOND BEST
→ GET ONE'S SECOND WIND
→ GET SECOND THOUGHTS ABOUT SOMEONE OR SOMETHING
→ IN ONE'S SECOND CHILDHOOD
→ ON SECOND THOUGHT
→ PLAY SECOND FIDDLE (TO SOMEONE)

second nature to someone easy and natural for someone.

secondary ['sɛk ən dɛr i] **1.** *adj.* second in importance; not primary. (Adv: *secondarily.*) **2.** *adj.* [of the education of students] from the 6th to 12th or from the 9th to 12th grades, depending on the school district.

secondhand ['sɛk ənd 'hænd] **1.** *adj.* [of goods] already used by someone else; not new. **2.** *adj.* [of stores] selling used products. **3.** *adj.* not experienced directly but heard from another person. **4.** *adv.* learned from someone else.

second-rate not of the best quality; inferior.

seconds *n.* an additional serving of food. (Treated as plural.)

secrecy ['si krɪ si] *n.* the quality of being secret; keeping something a secret. (No plural.)

secret ['si krɪt] **1.** *n.* information known by a small number of people, especially people who have promised not to tell anyone else. **2.** *n.* a mystery; something that cannot be explained. **3.** *adj.* known only by a small number of people who have promised not to tell anyone else. (Adv: *secretly.*) **4.** *adj.* working at a job without others knowing what one does; doing something without others knowing what one is doing. (Adv: *secretly.*)
→ CARRY A SECRET TO THE GRAVE

→ IN SECRET
→ KEEP A SECRET
→ OPEN SECRET
→ TAKE A SECRET TO ONE'S GRAVE

secretary ['sɛk rɪ tɛr i] **1.** *n.* someone who is employed to type letters, answer telephones, organize schedules and meetings, and do other office work. **2.** *n.* someone who keeps a written record of the things that are discussed at the official meetings of an organization. **3.** *n.* someone who is in charge of a department of the United States government. **4.** *n.* a writing desk with drawers and shelves.

secrete [sɪ 'krit] **1.** *tv.* [for a part of a plant or an animal] to produce and release a fluid. **2.** *tv.* to hide something; to put something in a place where others cannot see it or find it.

secretion [sɪ 'kri ʃən] *n.* a fluid that is produced and released by a part of a plant or an animal, such as sap or mucus. (Singular or plural with the same meaning, but not countable.)

secretive ['si krə tɪv] *adj.* tending to do things secretly; tending not to do things publicly or openly. (Adv: *secretively*.)

secretly ['si krət li] *adv.* without being known or seen by others.

section ['sɛk ʃən] **1.** *n.* a separate part of a larger group, place, or thing; a division. **2.** *n.* a unit of measurement of land equal to one square mile or 640 acres. **3.** *tv.* to divide something into separate parts as in ①.

secure [sɪ 'kjʊr] **1.** *adj.* safe from danger, harm, loss, injury, or theft. (Adv: *securely*.) **2.** *tv.* to safely fasten or close something. **3.** *tv.* to obtain something.

security [sɪ 'kjʊr ə ti] **1.** *n.* the state of being or feeling safe from danger, harm, loss, injury, or theft. (No plural.) **2.** *n.* an office or department concerned with the protection of people and property. (No plural.) **3.** *n.* property that is promised to a bank or lender when money is borrowed. (If the money is not paid back, then the bank or lender will be given the property. No plural.) **4.** *n.* a monetary asset or debt agreement, such as a stock or a bond. **5.** the *adj.* use of ①, ②, ③, or ④.

→ LULL SOMEONE INTO A FALSE SENSE OF
   SECURITY
→ SOCIAL SECURITY

security against something something that keeps something safe against potential loss; something that protects something against a loss; a protection.

sedan [sɪ 'dæn] *n.* a car with four doors, a front seat and a backseat, a fixed roof, and room for at least four people.

sedate [sɪ 'det] **1.** *adj.* quiet; calm; relaxed; not excited; not moved by excitement. (Adv: *sedately*.) **2.** *tv.* to give someone or an animal a drug that causes relaxation.

sedative ['sɛd ə tɪv] **1.** *n.* a drug or medicine that causes one to sleep or relax. **2.** the *adj.* use of ①.

sedentary ['sɛd n tɛr i] **1.** *adj.* [of a creature] not very active and keeping still most of the time. (Adv:

sedentarily [sɛd n 'tɛr ə li].) **2.** *adj.*
[of activity] not requiring a lot of
movement. (Adv: *sedentarily* [sɛd
n 'tɛr ə li].)

see ['si] **1.** *iv., irreg.* to sense or
experience with the eyes. (Past
tense: saw; past participle: seen.)
2. *tv., irreg.* to observe someone or
something by the use of the eyes;
to sense or experience someone or
something with the eyes. **3.** *tv.,
irreg.* to understand something; to
comprehend something. (The
object can be a clause with that
⑦.) **4.** *tv., irreg.* to learn something by reading or through direct
observation. (The object can be a
clause with that ⑦.) **5.** *tv., irreg.*
to visit someone; to stop by the
place where someone lives. **6.** *tv.,
irreg.* to meet with someone for an
appointment. **7.** *tv., irreg.* to date
someone; to have a romantic relationship with someone.
→ begin to see daylight
→ begin to see the light
→ can't see beyond the end of one's
 nose
→ can't see one's hand in front of
 one's face
→ long time no see.
→ not able to see the forest for
 the trees
→ not see further than the end of
 one's nose
→ wait-and-see attitude

see double to see two of everything instead of one.

see eye to eye (about something)
and **see eye to eye on** something to view something in the
same way (as someone else).

see eye to eye on something Go
to see eye to eye (about something).

see someone **off** to accompany one
to the point of departure for a trip
and say good-bye.

see someone or something **as**
something to consider someone or
something the same as something.

see someone **to** someplace to
escort someone to a place; to make
sure that someone gets to someplace safely; to accompany someone to a place.

see something **through** to stay
with a project all the way to its
completion.

see stars to see flashing lights after
receiving a blow to the head.

**see the (hand)writing on the
wall** to know that something is
certain to happen.

**see the light (at the end of the
tunnel)** to foresee an end to one's
problems after a long period of
time.

see the light (of day) to come to
the end of a very busy time.

see things to imagine one sees
someone or something that is not
there.

see through someone or something
to recognize the deception
involved with someone or something.

see (to it) that something **is done**
to make sure of something; to
make certain of something; to be
certain to do something.

see to someone or something to
tend to or care for someone or
something.

seed ['sid] **1.** *n.* a part of a plant
that a new plant will grow from if

it is fertilized. **2.** *tv.* to plant crops on an area of land by scattering ①.
→ GO TO SEED
→ RUN TO SEED

seedling ['sid lɪŋ] *n.* a young plant or tree that is newly grown from a seed.

seedy ['si di] **1.** *adj.* having a lot of seeds. (Comp: *seedier;* sup: *seediest.*) **2.** *adj.* run-down; shabby. (Adv: *seedily.* Comp: *seedier;* sup: *seediest.*)

seeing that something **is the case** considering that something is the case; since something is the case.

seek ['sik] *tv., irreg.* to try to find someone or something; to look for someone or something. (Past tense and past participle: SOUGHT.)

seek to do something to try to do something; to attempt to do something; to pledge oneself to do something.

seem ['sim] *iv.* to appear to be a certain way; to give the impression of being a certain way.

seen ['sin] past participle of SEE.

seep ['sip] *iv.* [for a liquid] to pass through something slowly; to leak.

seep in(to something**)** [for a fluid] to trickle or leak (out of something) into something.

seep out (of something**)** [for a fluid] to trickle or leak out of something.

seep through something [for a fluid] to permeate something and escape.

segment ['sɛg mənt] **1.** *n.* a part of something; a part of something that can be easily separated. **2.** *tv.*

to separate something into parts; to divide something into parts.

segregate ['sɛ grɪ get] **1.** *tv.* to separate someone or a group of people from other people; to isolate someone or a group of people. **2.** *tv.* to separate people of one race from people of another race.

segregated ['sɛ grɪ get ɪd] *adj.* [of human races] separated by law or other forces. (Adv: *segregatedly.*)

segregation [sɛ grɪ 'ge ʃən] **1.** *n.* the state existing in a segregated society; the state of races being separated by law or other causes. (No plural.) **2.** *n.* the separation of someone or something from other people or things. (No plural.)

seize ['siz] **1.** *tv.* to grab, take, and hold on to someone or something. **2.** *tv.* to take control of something by force or by authority; to capture something by force or by authority.

seize onto someone or something to grab onto someone or something.

seize up to freeze or halt; [of a machine with moving parts] to jam and stop suddenly.

seize (up)on something **1.** to grasp something tightly. **2.** to take hold of something, such as a plan, idea, etc. (Figurative.)

seizure ['si ʒɚ] **1.** *n.* an act of seizing someone or something. **2.** *n.* a sudden attack of a sickness; a convulsion caused by a sudden attack of a sickness.

seldom ['sɛl dəm] *adv.* almost never; rarely.

531

select [sə 'lɛkt] **1.** *tv.* to pick someone or something from a group of
choices. **2.** *adj.* specifically chosen;
exclusive; specially chosen. (Adv:
selectly.)

selection [sə 'lɛk ʃən] **1.** *n.* a
choice; someone or something
that is chosen; someone or something that is selected. **2.** *n.* a variety of things to choose from,
especially in a store.

selective [sə 'lɛk tɪv] *adj.* choosing
carefully; making careful choices.
(Adv: *selectively.*)

self ['sɛlf] *n.* a reference to a person
as an individual or being. (Usually
in compounds. See also MYSELF,
YOURSELF, HERSELF, HIMSELF, ITSELF,
ONESELF, OURSELVES, YOURSELVES,
THEMSELVES. No plural.)

self-addressed ['sɛlf ə 'drɛst] *adj.*
addressed to oneself.

self-centered ['sɛlf 'sɛn tə-d] *adj.*
selfish; often thinking only of oneself instead of anyone else. (Adv:
self-centeredly.)

self-confidence [sɛlf 'kɑn fɪ dəns]
n. the belief that one is able to do
something; confidence in one's
own ability. (No plural.)

self-conscious [sɛlf 'kɑn ʃəs] *adj.*
aware that one is being seen by
other people, especially when one
is shy or embarrassed around
other people. (Adv: *self-con-
sciously.*)

self-contained [sɛlf kən 'tend]
adj. containing within itself everything that is necessary.

self-control [sɛlf kən 'trol] *n.* the
control of one's own actions or
feelings. (No plural.)

self-discipline ['sɛlf 'dɪs ə plɪn] *n.*
the discipline needed to control
one's feelings and actions. (No plural.)

self-employed [sɛlf ɛm 'plɔɪd] *adj.*
working for one's own business;
not working for other people.

self-esteem [sɛlf ə 'stim] *n.* the
good opinion one has of oneself;
the respect one shows for oneself.
(No plural.)

self-help ['sɛlf 'hɛlp] **1.** *n.* helping
oneself without the help of others.
(No plural.) **2.** *adj.* [of books or
techniques] showing people how
to help themselves without the
help of others.

selfish ['sɛl fɪʃ] *adj.* too concerned
with oneself; too concerned with
what one wants instead of what
other people want; showing more
care for oneself than for other
people. (Adv: *selfishly.*)

selfishness ['sɛl fɪʃ nəs] *n.* the
state of being too greedy and concerned with oneself. (No plural.)

self-reliant [sɛlf rɪ 'laɪ ənt] *adj.*
able to get along or do something
without the help of others. (Adv:
self-reliantly.)

self-respect [sɛlf rɪ 'spɛkt] *n.* the
respect and pride one has for oneself. (No plural.)

self-service ['sɛlf 'sə- vɪs] **1.** *n.* the
system by which one must serve
oneself in a store or business. (No
plural.) **2.** the *adj.* use of ①.

sell ['sɛl] **1.** *tv., irreg.* to transfer a
product in exchange for money; to
transfer a product to someone in
exchange for money. (Past tense
and past participle: SOLD.) **2.** *tv.,*

irreg. to make something available for purchase. **3.** *tv., irreg.* to cause something to be more likely to be used or bought.

sell for some amount to be offered for sale for an amount of money; to be sold for an amount of money.

sell like hot cakes [for something] to be sold very fast.

sell out (to someone) **1.** to sell everything to someone. **2.** to betray someone or something to someone.

sell someone **a bill of goods** to get someone to believe something that is not true.

sell someone or something **out** to betray someone or something.

sell someone or something **short** to underestimate someone or something; to fail to see the good qualities of someone or something.

sell something **off** to sell all of something.

seller ['sɛl ɚ] *n.* someone who sells something for money.

semester [sɪ 'mɛs tɚ] *n.* half of a school year; a term; a 16-week to 18-week period of classes.

semicircle ['sɛm ɪ sɚk əl] *n.* half of a circle; a shape like half of a circle.

semicolon ['sɛm ɪ ko lən] *n.* a punctuation mark (;) that shows separation between two clauses, indicating more of a pause than a comma but less of a pause than a period. (It is also used to separate items in a list if any of the items uses a comma so that the reader is not confused.)

seminar ['sɛm ə nɑr] **1.** *n.* one of the meetings of a type of (college) course that meets regularly with a professor to discuss theories, studies, or research. **2.** *n.* a meeting where a speaker, or panel of speakers, talks and information or ideas about a particular topic is exchanged.

senate ['sɛn ət] **1.** *n.* the smaller of the two groups of people who are elected to make the federal laws in the United States. **2.** *n.* the professors who are the governing body at certain schools and universities.

senator ['sɛn ə tɚ] *n.* someone who is a member of a senate.

send ['sɛnd] *tv., irreg.* to cause someone or something to be transported or to go from one place to another. (Past tense and past participle: SENT.)

send away (for something) to order something to be brought or sent from some distance.

send for someone or something to request that someone come or that something be brought.

send off for something to dispatch an order for something to a distant place.

send one **about** one's **business** to send someone away, usually in an unfriendly way.

send out (for someone or something) to send an order by messenger, telephone, cable, or fax that someone or something is to come or be delivered.

send someone **in for** someone to send someone into a game as a replacement for someone else.

send someone **in(to** something**)** to make someone go into something or someplace.

send someone **into** something to cause someone to be in a certain state or condition.

send someone **off** to participate in saying good-bye to someone who is leaving.

send someone **off (to** something**)** to send someone away to something or someplace, especially away on a journey; to be present when someone sets out on a journey to something or someplace.

send someone **out (for** someone or something**)** to send someone out to search for someone or something.

send someone **over ((to)** someplace**)** to order someone to go to someplace.

send someone **packing** to send someone away; to dismiss someone, possibly rudely.

send someone **to the showers** to send a player out of a game and off the field, court, etc. (Figurative and literal.)

send something **by** something **1.** to send something by a particular carrier. **2.** to deliver something to something or someplace. (Informal.)

send something **off (to** someone or something**)** to send something to someone, something, or someplace.

senile [ˈsi naɪl] *adj.* tending to forget things or be confused because of advancing age. (Adv: *senilely.*)

senility [sə ˈnɪl ə ti] *n.* a state of confusion and loss of memory associated with old age. (No plural.)

senior [ˈsin jɚ] **1.** *adj.* [of people] older; [of employees] having served an employer longer than most other employees. **2.** *adj.* higher in rank or position. **3.** *adj.* of or for students in the fourth year of high school or college. **4.** *adj.* for very old or elderly people; serving elderly people. **5.** *n.* an older person; a SENIOR CITIZEN. **6.** *n.* a student in the fourth year of high school (12th grade) or the fourth year of college.

senior citizen [ˈsin jɚ ˈsɪt ə zən] *n.* someone who is 65 years old or older.

seniority [sin ˈjor ə ti] *n.* the quality of having been employed at one's place of work for a relatively longer period of time than someone else. (No plural.)

sensation [sɛn ˈse ʃən] **1.** *n.* the use of the senses; the ability to see, hear, touch, taste, or smell. **2.** *n.* an awareness of someone or something because of sight, sound, touch, taste, or smell. **3.** *n.* a vague feeling of awareness; a general feeling in the mind. **4.** *n.* someone or something that causes people to become very excited or interested.

sensational [sɛn ˈse ʃə nəl] **1.** *adj.* very exciting or interesting; attracting a lot of attention. (Adv: *sensationally.*) **2.** *adj.* exaggerated and designed to excite and appeal to a mass audience. (Adv: *sensationally.*)

sense ['sɛns] **1.** *n.* each of the abilities allowing creatures to see, hear, touch, taste, or smell. **2.** *n.* a special feeling or sensation, especially one that cannot be described. (No plural.) **3.** *n.* the ability to understand or appreciate something. (No plural. See also SENSE OF HUMOR.) **4.** *n.* good judgment; the ability to make good decisions. (No plural.) **5.** *n.* the meaning or definition of something; a meaning. **6.** *n.* a belief shared by a group of people. **7.** *tv.* to be aware of something with the help of ①. (The object can be a clause with THAT ⑦.) **8.** *tv.* to determine something; to have a feeling about a situation. (The object can be a clause with THAT ⑦.)
→ COME TO ONE'S SENSES
→ COMMON SENSE
→ LULL SOMEONE INTO A FALSE SENSE OF SECURITY
→ OUT OF ONE'S SENSES
→ SIXTH SENSE

sense of humor [sɛns əv 'hju mɚ] *n.* the ability to laugh at things that are funny; the ability to see the funny aspects of a situation. (No plural.)

senseless ['sɛns ləs] **1.** *adj.* without reason; having no purpose; stupid; foolish. (Adv: *senselessly.*) **2.** *adj.* unconscious. (Adv: *senselessly.*)

sensible ['sɛn sə bəl] **1.** *adj.* representing or showing common sense; wise. (Adv: *sensibly.*) **2.** *adj.* practical instead of stylish. (Adv: *sensibly.*)

sensitive ['sɛn sə tɪv] **1.** *adj.* able to feel the effect of something, especially light, sound, smell, taste, or texture; easily affected or harmed by something. (Adv: *sensitively.*) **2.** *adj.* easily offended; [of someone] easily affected by something. (Figurative on ①. Adv: *sensitively.*) **3.** *adj.* easily able to sense a small change in something.

sensitivity [sɛn sə 'tɪv ɪ ti] **1.** *n.* the ability to sense or perceive something. (No plural.) **2.** *n.* the tendency to perceive or imagine even the smallest offense. (Sometimes plural with the same meaning.)

sensory ['sɛn sə ri] *adj.* of the senses; of the ability to see, hear, taste, touch, or smell.

sensual ['sɛn ʃu əl] *adj.* providing pleasure to the body; concerning the pleasures of eating, drinking, sex, etc. (Adv: *sensually.*)

sensuous [sɛn 'ʃu əs] *adj.* affecting the senses; experienced through the senses. (Adv: *sensuously.*)

sent ['sɛnt] past tense and past participle of SEND.

sentence ['sɛn ns] **1.** *n.* a group of words that forms an independent thought, usually including at least a subject and a verb. **2.** *n.* the punishment given to a criminal by a judge in a court of law. **3.** *tv.* [for a judge] to assign a punishment to a criminal.

sentiment ['sɛn tə mənt] *n.* a tender feeling or emotion. (No plural.)

sentimental [sɛn tə 'mɛn təl] *adj.* having tender feelings or emotions, often sad or romantic ones. (Adv: *sentimentally.*)

sentiments *n.* a written or spoken expression of SENTIMENT. (Treated as plural.)

separable ['sɛp ɚ ə bəl] *adj.* able to be separated; able to be divided. (Adv: *separably.*)

separate 1. ['sɛp rət] *adj.* not together; not joined; apart; single; individual. (Adv: *separately.*) **2.** ['sɛp ə ret] *tv.* to be between two or more people or things; to keep two or more people or things apart. **3.** ['sɛp ə ret] *tv.* to cause two or more people or things to be apart. **4.** ['sɛp ə ret] *iv.* to break apart; to divide; to split. **5.** ['sɛp ə ret] *iv.* [for a husband and wife] to stop living together, often as a trial before beginning to divorce each other.

separate something **out (of** something**)** to remove something out from something.

separate the men from the boys to separate the competent from those who are less competent.

separate the sheep from the goats to divide people into two groups according to whether they meet a certain standard.

separated ['sɛp ə ret ɪd] *adj.* [of a married couple] no longer living together but not divorced.

separation [sɛp ə 're ʃən] **1.** *n.* the state of being separated. (Plural only for types and instances.) **2.** *n.* a period of time when two people who are married no longer live together but have not yet divorced.

September [sɛp 'tɛm bɚ] Go to MONTH.

sequence ['si kwəns] **1.** *n.* the order in which a group of people or things are placed; the order in which a series of events happen. **2.** *tv.* to put people or things into ①.

sequester [sɪ 'kwɛs tɚ] *tv.* to keep someone apart from other people, especially to isolate members of a jury from the public during a trial.

serenade [sɛr ə 'ned] **1.** *n.* a song sung to someone; a love song. **2.** *tv.* to sing a romantic song to someone; to play a romantic piece of music for someone.

serene [sə 'rin] *adj.* quiet; calm; peaceful. (Adv: *serenely.*)

serenity [sə 'rɛn ɪ ti] *n.* the quality of being serene. (No plural.)

serial ['sɪr i əl] **1.** *n.* a story that is presented in separate parts. **2.** the *adj.* use of ①. (Adv: *serially.*)

series ['sɪr iz] **1.** *n.* a group of similar things that happen or appear one after the other in a certain order; a group of similar things that are arranged in a row. (Treated as singular.) **2.** *n.* a set of television programs that is broadcast one at a time, usually once per week.

serious ['sɪr i əs] **1.** *adj.* stern; not humorous or playful. (Adv: *seriously.*) **2.** *adj.* important; not minor. (Adv: *seriously.*)

seriousness ['sɪr i əs nəs] *n.* importance; gravity; a state of being SERIOUS ① or ②. (No plural.)

sermon ['sɚ mən] **1.** *n.* a speech about religion or morals, especially one given by a member of the clergy. **2.** *n.* a long speech by someone who is giving advice or who is scolding someone else. (Figurative on ①.)

serpent ['sɚ pənt] *n.* a snake.

servant ['sɚ vənt] *n.* someone who serves a person, the public, or God, especially someone who is paid to work for someone else in that person's house.

serve ['sɚv] **1.** *tv.* to provide someone with a service. **2.** *tv.* to bring (previously ordered) food to someone, as in a restaurant. **3.** *tv.* to provide a useful service or function. **4.** *iv.* to perform military service. **5.** *iv.* to begin a play in a sport like tennis by hitting the ball toward the other player.
→ FIRST COME, FIRST SERVED

serve as a guinea pig [for someone] to be experimented on; to allow some sort of test to be performed on one.

serve someone right [for an act or event] to punish someone fairly (for having done something wrong).

serve something up to distribute or deliver food for people to eat.

serve time to spend a certain amount of time in jail.

serve under someone or something to carry out one's responsibility under the direction or in the employment of someone.

server ['sɚ vɚ] **1.** *n.* a utensil used to serve certain foods. **2.** *n.* a WAITRESS; a WAITER.

service ['sɚ vɪs] **1.** *n.* the work that someone does for the benefit of someone; work done by servants,

clerks, food servers, taxi drivers, etc. (No plural. See ③.) **2.** *n.* the repair of a machine or device; maintenance. (No plural.) **3.** *n.* the benefit provided by a company or organization that fulfills the needs of people but does not usually manufacture products. (This includes *electric service, natural gas service, telephone service, water service, sewer service, message service, diaper service, lawn-care service,* etc.) **4.** *n.* a religious meeting or ceremony. **5.** *tv.* to repair or adjust something mechanical or electronic.
→ OUT OF SERVICE

the **service** *n.* a military duty; serving [one's country in] a military organization.

services *n.* work that is done to help someone, especially the work done by a professional person. (Treated as plural, but not countable.)

serving ['sɚ vɪŋ] *n.* the amount of food or drink that is usually served to one person.

session ['sɛ ʃən] *n.* a period of time during which a meeting is held or an activity is pursued.
→ IN SESSION
→ a RUMP SESSION

set ['sɛt] **1.** *tv., irreg.* to put someone or something on a surface; to place someone or something somewhere. (Past tense and past participle: SET.) **2.** *tv., irreg.* to move someone or something into a certain position. **3.** *tv., irreg.* to join the ends of a broken bone and place them in the proper position. **4.** *tv., irreg.* to determine or estab-

lish a value, a standard, a time, an amount, etc. **5.** *tv., irreg.* to adjust a machine so that it works correctly; to adjust something so that it will show the correct measurement, time, amount, etc. **6.** *iv., irreg.* [for a liquid] to take a certain shape; to become shaped; [for concrete or plaster] to get hard. **7.** *iv., irreg.* [for the sun] to drop below the horizon at night; to sink out of sight. **8.** *n.* a collection of related things; a group of things that are found or belong together. **9.** *n.* the location of the performing area for a play, TV show, or movie. **10.** *adj.* ready. (Not prenominal.) **11.** *adj.* established; determined in advance; arranged.
→ HAVE ONE'S HEART SET ON SOMETHING
→ NOT SET FOOT SOMEWHERE
→ ONE'S HEART IS SET ON SOMETHING
→ TELEVISION SET

set a trap to adjust and prepare a trap to catch a person or an animal.

set foot somewhere to go or enter somewhere. (Often in the negative.)

set great store by someone or something to have positive expectations for someone or something; to have high hopes for someone or something.

set in to begin; to become fixed for a period of time.

set off (for something**)** to leave for something or someplace.

set off on something to begin on a journey or expedition.

set one (back) on one's **feet** AND **set one on** one's **feet again** to reestablish someone; to help

someone become active and productive again.

set one **back on** one's **heels** to surprise, shock, or overwhelm someone.

set one **on** one's **feet again** Go to SET ONE (BACK) ON ONE'S FEET.

set one's **heart on** something to become determined about something.

set one's **sights on** something to select something as one's goal.

set out (on something**)** to begin a journey; to begin a project.

set out to do something to begin to do something; to intend to do something.

set someone **down (on(to)** something**)** to place a person one is carrying or lifting onto something.

set someone **off 1.** to cause someone to become very angry; to ignite someone's anger. **2.** to cause someone to start talking or lecturing about a particular subject.

set someone or something **free** to release someone or something; to allow someone or something to leave, go away, depart, or escape.

set someone or something **up** to place someone or something in a vertical or standing position.

set someone **straight** to make certain that someone understands something exactly. (Often said in anger or domination.)

set someone **up (for** something**) 1.** to arrange a situation so that someone is the target of a deception. **2.** to make someone become part of a joke.

set someone's **teeth on edge**
1. [for a sour or bitter taste] to irritate one's mouth and make it feel strange. **2.** [for a person or a noise] to be irritating or get on someone's nerves.

set something **down (on** something) **1.** to place something on the surface of something. **2.** to write something on paper. **3.** to land an airplane on something.

set something **down to** something to blame something on something else; to regard something as the cause of something.

set something **in(to** something) to put something into its place.

set something **off 1.** to ignite something, such as fireworks. **2.** to cause something to begin. **3.** to make something distinct or outstanding.

set something **to music** to incorporate words into a piece of music; to write a piece of music to incorporate a set of words.

set something **up** to arrange the time and place of a meeting, appointment, interview, etc.

set something **up (for** something) to arrange something for a particular time or event.

set something **(up)on** something to place something on the surface of something.

set the table to arrange a table with plates, glasses, knives, forks, etc., for a meal.

set the world on fire to do exciting things that bring fame and glory to one. (Frequently negative.)

set type to arrange type for printing, now usually on a computer.

setback ['sɛt bæk] *n.* something that causes something to change for the worse.

settle ['sɛt əl] **1.** *tv.* to decide something, especially an argument; to resolve something. **2.** *tv.* to pay a bill or account. **3.** *tv.* to place oneself in a comfortable position. (Takes a reflexive object.) **4.** *tv.* to occupy land or a town and live there, often as a pioneer. **5.** *tv.* to cause something to be calm, still, or less active. **6.** *iv.* to sink, especially into the ground or to the bottom of something.

settle down 1. to become calm. **2.** to get quiet. **3.** to abandon a free lifestyle and take up a more stable and disciplined one.

settle down somewhere to establish a residence somewhere.

settle in(to something) **1.** to become accustomed to something, such as a new home, job, status, etc. **2.** to get comfortable in something.

settle someone **down** to make someone become quiet.

settle (something) **(out of court)** to end a disagreement and reach an agreement without having to go through a court of justice.

settle up with someone to pay someone what one owes; to pay one one's share of something.

settlement ['sɛt əl mənt] **1.** *n.* the establishing of towns or communities in new areas. (No plural.) **2.** *n.* a town established by people who have moved to an area where there was no town before. **3.** *n.* an agreement that ends an argument, disagreement, or fight.

settler ['sɛt lɚ, 'sɛt l ɚ] *n.* a pioneer; someone who is one of the first people to live in a location.

setup ['sɛt əp] *n.* an arrangement; the way something is arranged or organized.

seven ['sɛv ən] 7. Go to FOUR.
→ AT SIXES AND SEVENS

seventeen ['sɛv ən 'tin] 17. Go to FOUR.

seventeenth [sɛv ən 'tinθ] 17th. Go to FOURTH.

seventh ['sɛv ənθ] 7th. Go to FOURTH.
→ IN SEVENTH HEAVEN

seventieth ['sɛv ən ti əθ] 70th. Go to FOURTH.

seventy ['sɛv ən ti] 70. Go to FORTY.

sever ['sɛv ɚ] *tv.* to cut through something; to cut something apart.

sever ties with someone to end a relationship or agreement suddenly.

several ['sɛv (ə) rəl] **1.** *adj.* some; a few, but not many. **2.** *n.* some people or things; a few people or things. (No plural.)

severe [sə 'vɪr] **1.** *adj.* harsh; strict; not gentle. (Adv: *severely.* Comp: *severer;* sup: *severest.*) **2.** *adj.* strong; violent; causing harm; not mild. (Adv: *severely.* Comp: *severer;* sup: *severest.*)

severed ['sɛv ɚd] *adj.* cut off; cut from; separated.

severity [sɪ 'vɛr ɪ ti] *n.* the quality of being severe. (No plural.)

sew ['so] **1.** *tv., irreg.* to attach two pieces of material together or to attach something to a piece of material by making stitches using a needle and thread. (Past tense: *sewed;* past participle: *sewed* or SEWN.) **2.** *iv., irreg.* to attach with stitches using a needle and thread.
→ GET SOMETHING SEWED UP

sewage ['su ɪdʒ] *n.* water and human waste that is carried away by sewers from homes and businesses. (No plural.)

sewer 1. ['su ɚ] *n.* a pipe that carries waste away from homes and businesses. **2.** ['so ɚ] *n.* someone who sews.

sewing ['so ɪŋ] **1.** *n.* the work that is done with a needle and thread; the stitches made in material with a needle and thread. (No plural.) **2.** *n.* a piece of clothing or material that is being sewed. (No plural.) **3.** the *adj.* use of ① or ②.

sewn ['son] a past participle of SEW.

sex ['sɛks] **1.** *n.* human sexual responses and activity. (No plural.) **2.** *n.* copulation; sexual arousal leading to copulation; the urge to copulate; the subject of copulation. (No plural.) **3.** *n.* the state of being male or female. **4.** the *adj.* use of ①.
→ OPPOSITE SEX

sexism ['sɛks ɪz əm] *n.* the belief that men are better than women; discrimination against women because they are women. (No plural.)

sexist ['sɛk sɪst] **1.** *n.* someone, usually a male, who practices SEXISM. **2.** the *adj.* use of ①. (Adv: *sexistly.*)

sexual ['sɛk ʃu əl] **1.** *adj.* of or about copulation or reproduction and the associated feelings and urges. (Adv: *sexually.*) **2.** *adj.* requiring two creatures or organisms for reproduction.

sexual intercourse ['sɛk ʃu əl 'ɪn tɚ kɔrs] *n.* copulation; an act involving the genitals of two people for the purpose of creating pleasure or the production of offspring. (No plural. Can be shortened to INTERCOURSE.)

sexuality [sɛk ʃu 'æl ə ti] *n.* human sexual matters and feelings; the involvement or interest a person has in sex. (No plural.)

sexually ['sɛk ʃu (ə) li] *adv.* in a sexual manner; in a way that concerns sex.

sexy ['sɛk si] *adj.* of or about sex appeal; causing an interest in sex; sexually exciting. (Comp: *sexier;* sup: *sexiest.*)

shabby ['ʃæb i] *adj.* having a messy appearance; looking run-down or worn-out. (Adv: *shabbily.* Comp: *shabbier;* sup: *shabbiest.*)

shack ['ʃæk] *n.* a small house, hut, or shed that has been built quickly or poorly.

shade ['ʃed] **1.** *n.* a place that is not directly exposed to sunlight because an object between that place and the sun blocks the sunlight. (No plural.) **2.** *n.* a variety of a color; the lightness or darkness of a color. **3.** *n.* a slight amount of a quality. **4.** *n.* a device that can be rolled down over a window so that light will not get in or so that people cannot see in. (Short for WIN-DOW SHADE.) **5.** *tv.* to prevent light from reaching an area; to make something darker or harder to see by blocking light. **6.** *tv.* to make something darker by painting or drawing on it with a darker color. → WINDOW SHADE

shades of someone or something reminders of someone or something; things reminiscent of someone or something.

shading ['ʃed ɪŋ] *n.* the use of darker colors in paintings and drawings to make shadows and darker areas. (No plural.)

shadow ['ʃæd o] **1.** *n.* the patch of shade created by someone or something blocking light. **2.** *n.* a slight suggestion; a trace. (Figurative on ①.)

shadow of itself Go to SHADOW OF ONESELF.

shadow of oneself AND **shadow of** itself someone or something that is not as strong, healthy, full, or lively as before.

shady ['ʃe di] **1.** *adj.* in the shade; blocked from direct exposure to light; shaded. (Comp: *shadier;* sup: *shadiest.*) **2.** *adj.* not honest; always making schemes and deceiving people. (Comp: *shadier;* sup: *shadiest.*)

shaft ['ʃæft] **1.** *n.* a rod or pole, such as part of an arrow. **2.** *n.* a pole that is used as a handle, such as with an axe or a golf club. **3.** *n.* a ray [of light]. **4.** *n.* a long, narrow passage, often vertical.

shaggy ['ʃæg i] *adj.* covered with long, thick, messy hair; [of hair] long, thick, and messy. (Adv: *shag-*

gily. Comp: *shaggier;* sup: *shaggiest.*)

shaggy-dog story a kind of funny story that relies on its length and a sudden, ridiculous ending for its humor.

shake ['ʃek] **1.** *iv., irreg.* [for something large] to move up and down, back and forth, or side to side many times very quickly. (Past tense: SHOOK; past participle: SHAKEN.) **2.** *iv., irreg.* [for someone] to move as in ① or seem less secure. **3.** *tv., irreg.* to cause someone or something to move up and down, back and forth, or side to side many times very quickly.
→ IN TWO SHAKES OF A LAMB'S TAIL

shake hands AND **shake** someone's **hand** to take someone's hand and move it up and down as a greeting or to mark an agreement.

shake in one's **boots** AND **quake in** one's **boots** to be afraid; to shake from fear.

shake someone's **hand** Go to SHAKE HANDS.

shake something **down** Go to SHAKE SOMETHING OUT.

shake something **out 1.** to clean something of dirt or crumbs by shaking. **2.** AND **shake** something **down** to test something to find out what the problems are. (Figurative.)

shake something **up 1.** to mix something by shaking. **2.** to upset an organization or group of people by some administrative action.

shaken ['ʃek ən] **1.** Past participle of SHAKE. **2.** *adj.* greatly upset; disturbed; bothered.

shaker ['ʃek ɚ] *n.* a small container that has a few tiny holes on one end from which salt or pepper or sometimes other spices, is spread on food by shaking.

shake-up ['ʃek əp] *n.* a large change in the arrangement of an organization, including the movement, firing, or addition of people who have important jobs.

shaky ['ʃe ki] **1.** *adj.* shaking a small amount; not steady. (Comp: *shakier;* sup: *shakiest.*) **2.** *adj.* risky; not certain; not able to be relied on. (Comp: *shakier;* sup: *shakiest.*)

shall ['ʃæl] **1.** *aux.* a form used with *I* and *we* to indicate something in the future. (Formal. See also WILL and SHOULD DO SOMETHING.) **2.** *aux.* a form used with *you, he, she, it, they,* and names of people or things to indicate something one must do, a command, or a promise. (Formal. See also WILL and SHOULD DO SOMETHING.) **3.** *aux.* a verb form used with *I* and *we* in questions that ask the hearer or reader to decide something concerning the speaker or writer. (Formal. See also WILL and SHOULD DO SOMETHING.)

shallow ['ʃæl o] **1.** *adj.* not deep; having only a small distance from the top of something to the bottom, especially used to describe water. (Adv: *shallowly.* Comp: *shallower;* sup: *shallowest.*) **2.** *adj.* [of thoughts] trivial; not having deep, important thoughts. (Figu-

rative on ①. Adv: *shallowly.*
Comp: *shallower;* sup: *shallowest.*)

shame ['ʃem] **1.** *n.* a feeling that
someone has done something
wrong or bad; a bad feeling of
guilt. (No plural.) **2.** *n.* an unfortunate situation. (No plural.) **3.** *n.*
disgrace; loss of honor. (No plural.) **4.** *tv.* to cause someone to feel
①.
→ PUT SOMEONE TO SHAME

shameful ['ʃem fʊl] *adj.* causing or
deserving shame or disgrace.
(Adv: *shamefully.*)

shameless ['ʃem ləs] *adj.* without
shame, especially when one should
feel shame; not modest. (Adv:
shamelessly.)

shampoo [ʃæm 'pu] **1.** *n.* a liquid
soap used for washing hair. (Plural
only for types and instances.
Plural ends in -*s.*) **2.** *n.* a washing
of one's own or someone else's hair
with ①. (Plural ends in -*s.*) **3.** *tv.*
to wash someone's hair with ①.
4. *iv.* to wash [hair] with ①.

shape ['ʃep] **1.** *n.* a form; a figure; a
mass; an object. **2.** *n.* condition; a
state of being—good or bad. (No
plural.) **3.** *tv.* to cause something
to have a certain form; to form
something.
→ IN GOOD SHAPE
→ IN SHAPE
→ TAKE SHAPE

shape someone **up 1.** to cause
someone to get into good physical
condition. **2.** to cause someone to
become productive, efficient,
competent, etc.

shape up 1. to get into good physical condition. **2.** to become productive, efficient, competent, etc.

shape up or ship out to either
improve one's performance or
one's behavior or quit and leave.

shapeless ['ʃep ləs] *adj.* without a
shape; having no definite form.
(Adv: *shapelessly.*)

shapely ['ʃep li] *adj.* having an
attractive body; attractive in
shape. (Especially used to describe
women. Comp: *shapelier;* sup:
shapeliest.)

share ['ʃɛr] **1.** *n.* one person's part
of something that belongs to more
than one person; a portion. **2.** *n.* a
unit of STOCK ③; a unit into which
the capital of a company or business is divided, and that is owned
by a person or corporation. **3.** *tv.*
to use something together with
another person or other people; to
own something together with
another person or other people.
4. *tv.* to divide something between
two or among three or more people so that each person has a portion of it. **5.** *iv.* to use together
with another person or other people; to own together with another
person or other people.
→ the LION'S SHARE (OF SOMETHING)
→ ONE'S FAIR SHARE

share someone's **pain** to understand and sympathize with someone's pain or emotional
discomfort.

share someone's **sorrow** to feel
someone else's emotional pain.

shared ['ʃɛrd] *adj.* belonging to
two or more people; divided
among two or more people.

shark ['ʃɑrk] *n.* a large, dangerous
fish with a pointed fin on its back
and long, sharp teeth.

sharp ['ʃɑrp] **1.** *adj.* having an edge that cuts things easily or having a point that pierces things easily; not dull. (Adv: *sharply.* Comp: *sharper;* sup: *sharpest.*) **2.** *adj.* having a sudden change in direction; turning at a narrow angle. (Adv: *sharply.* Comp: *sharper;* sup: *sharpest.*) **3.** *adj.* intelligent; smart; able to learn things quickly; aware. (Adv: *sharply.* Comp: *sharper;* sup: *sharpest.*) **4.** *adj.* feeling like a sting, bite, or cut; causing a stinging, biting, or cutting feeling. (Adv: *sharply.* Comp: *sharper;* sup: *sharpest.*) **5.** *adj.* distinct; clear; easily seen or heard. (Adv: *sharply.* Comp: *sharper;* sup: *sharpest.*) **6.** *adj.* [of speech or language] bitterly negative. (Adv: *sharply.* Comp: *sharper;* sup: *sharpest.*) **7.** *adj.* slightly higher in tone. (Comp: *sharper;* sup: *sharpest.*) **8.** *adj.* excellent looking. (Adv: *sharply.* Comp: *sharper;* sup: *sharpest.*) **9.** *n.* a tone that is half a step higher than the next lowest natural tone. **10.** *adv.* exactly at a stated time.

sharpen ['ʃɑr pən] *tv.* to cause something to become sharp.
→ PENCIL SHARPENER

shatter ['ʃæt ɚ] **1.** *iv.* to break into many tiny pieces. **2.** *tv.* to break something into many tiny pieces.

shave ['ʃev] **1.** *tv., irreg.* to remove someone's or something's hair with a sharp blade; to scrape off hair by moving a razor over the skin. (Past tense: *shaved;* past participle: *shaved* or SHAVEN.) **2.** *tv., irreg.* to cut a thin slice from something. **3.** *iv., irreg.* to move a razor over one's skin to remove

hair. **4.** *n.* an instance of removing hair from the face or body by using a razor.
→ HAVE A CLOSE SHAVE

shaven ['ʃev ən] a past participle of SHAVE.

she ['ʃi] **1.** *pron.* the third-person feminine singular pronoun. (Refers to female persons or creatures. Used as the subject of a sentence or a clause. See also HER, HERSELF, and HERS.) **2.** *pron.* the third-person feminine singular pronoun. (Informal. Used to refer to certain objects, such as ships and cars.) **3.** *n.* a female.

shear ['ʃɪr] **1.** *tv., irreg.* to cut or remove something with SHEARS or scissors, especially wool from a sheep. (Past participle: *sheared* or SHORN.) **2.** *tv., irreg.* to trim a sheep totally, removing its wool.

shears *n.* large scissors; a heavy pair of scissors used for cutting thick materials. (Treated as plural. Number is usually expressed with *pair(s) of shears.*)

sheath ['ʃiθ] *n., irreg.* a covering for the blade of a knife or sword. (Plural: ['ʃiðz].)

she'd ['ʃid] **1.** *cont.* she had, where HAD is an auxiliary. **2.** *cont.* she would.

shed ['ʃɛd] **1.** *n.* a small building, usually used for storage. **2.** *iv., irreg.* to release or lose hair, or skin in the case of a reptile. (Past tense and past participle: *shed.*) **3.** *tv., irreg.* [for an animal] to lose skin or hair. **4.** *tv., irreg.* to release a fluid, especially tears or blood. **5.** *tv., irreg.* to rid oneself of a burden or something embarrassing. (Figurative on ③.) **6.** *tv., irreg.* to remove clothing.

shed crocodile tears to shed false tears; to pretend that one is crying.

sheep ['ʃip] *n., irreg.* an animal that grows wool on its body and is raised on farms for its wool and meat. (Plural: *sheep.*)
→ SEPARATE THE SHEEP FROM THE GOATS
→ a WOLF IN SHEEP'S CLOTHING

sheepish ['ʃip ɪʃ] *adj.* weak; timid; easily scared; shy; easily embarrassed. (Adv: *sheepishly.*)

sheer ['ʃɪr] **1.** *adj.* complete; utter. (Comp: *sheerer;* sup: *sheerest.*) **2.** *adj.* transparent; very thin; easy to see through. (Adv: *sheerly.* Comp: *sheerer;* sup: *sheerest.*) **3.** *adj.* straight up and down; vertical but not slanting or sloping. (Adv: *sheerly.* Comp: *sheerer;* sup: *sheerest.*)

sheet ['ʃit] **1.** *n.* a large, thin piece of fabric that is used in pairs on beds. (People sleep between SHEETS.) **2.** *n.* a thin, flat piece of something, such as paper, metal, glass, ice, etc., usually rectangular.

shelf ['ʃɛlf] *n., irreg.* a horizontal, flat piece of wood, metal, etc., that is put against or attached to a wall or is found in bookcases or other furniture. (Plural: SHELVES.)

she'll ['ʃil] *cont.* she will.

shell ['ʃɛl] **1.** *n.* the hard covering on the outside of seeds, nuts, eggs, and shellfish. **2.** *n.* an exploding object that is shot out of a large gun. **3.** *tv.* to free something from ① [by removing ①]. **4.** *tv.* to attack people or a place with SHELLS as in ②.

shellfish ['ʃɛl fɪʃ] **1.** *n., irreg.* an animal that lives in the water and has a shell, including clams, crabs, lobsters, and oysters. (Plural: *shellfish.*) **2.** *n.* the meat of ①. (No plural.)

shelter ['ʃɛl tɚ] **1.** *n.* protection from the weather, danger, or harm. (No plural.) **2.** *n.* a place or structure where one can find ①. **3.** *tv.* to protect someone or something from the weather, danger, or harm.

sheltered ['ʃɛl tɚd] *adj.* [of an area] protected, especially from the weather.

shelve ['ʃɛlv] **1.** *tv.* to place something on a shelf. **2.** *tv.* to delay something until a later time. (Figurative on ①.)

shelves ['ʃɛlvz] plural of SHELF.

shelving ['ʃɛl vɪŋ] *n.* shelves; a set of shelves. (No plural.)

shepherd ['ʃɛp ɚd] **1.** *n.* someone who raises and protects sheep. **2.** *tv.* to guide someone in the way that a shepherd leads sheep. (Figurative on ①.)

sherbet ['ʃɚ bət] *n.* a sweet, frozen dessert usually made of or flavored with fruit juice. (Plural only for types and instances.)

sheriff ['ʃɛr ɪf] *n.* the most important officer elected to enforce the law in a U.S. county.

she's ['ʃiz] **1.** *cont.* she is. **2.** *cont.* she has, where HAS is an auxiliary.

shield ['ʃild] **1.** *n.* a cover for something (such as a part of a machine) that protects someone from being hurt. **2.** *n.* a large piece of metal or wood carried in front of the body to protect it during fighting. **3.** *tv.* to protect someone or something from someone or something; to keep someone or something safe from someone or something.

shift ['ʃɪft] **1.** *n.* a change in policy, position, opinion, or behavior. **2.** *n.* a period during which a worker completes a day at work, such as day shift, night shift, afternoon shift. (In a workplace that operates more than 8 hours per day.) **3.** *tv.* to change the position of someone or something. **4.** *iv.* to experience changes in behavior or opinion.

shift out of something to change out of a particular mode, time, gear, attitude, etc.

shimmer ['ʃɪmɚ] **1.** *iv.* to shine with small waves of light; to shine with reflected light that moves slightly. **2.** *n.* a gleam or glow that seems to move back and forth slightly.

shin ['ʃɪn] *n.* the front of the leg between the knee and the ankle.

shine ['ʃaɪn] **1.** *iv., irreg.* to be bright with light; to reflect light. (Past tense and past participle: *shined* or SHONE.) **2.** *iv.* to do very well; to excel; to be excellent. (Figurative on ①.) **3.** *tv., irreg.* to direct a beam or source of light in a certain direction. (Past tense and past participle: *shined* or SHONE.) **4.** *tv.* to polish something; to cause something to become shiny. **5.** *n.* the brightness of a surface that has been polished.
→ RAIN OR SHINE
→ RISE AND SHINE

shine out 1. to shine or radiate light; to shine forth. **2.** [for a characteristic] to make itself very evident.

shine something **up** to polish something.

shine something **(up)on** someone or something to cast a beam of light onto someone or something.

shine through (something**) 1.** [for rays of light] to penetrate something. **2.** [for something that was obscured or hidden] to become visible or evident.

shine up to someone to flatter someone; to try to get into someone's favor.

shingle ['ʃɪŋ gəl] *n.* a thin panel of wood or another material used to cover a roof in overlapping rows.

shingles *n.* a severe, painful disease of the nerves, causing blisters to form on the skin. (Treated as singular or plural, but not countable.)

shiny ['ʃaɪ ni] *adj.* bright; polished; reflecting a lot of light. (Adv: *shinily.* Comp: *shinier;* sup: *shiniest.*)

ship ['ʃɪp] **1.** *n.* a large boat that travels on water and carries people and cargo. **2.** *tv.* to send something from one place to another by train, truck, plane, or ①.
→ DESERT A SINKING SHIP
→ LEAVE A SINKING SHIP
→ RUN A TAUT SHIP
→ RUN A TIGHT SHIP
→ SHAPE UP OR SHIP OUT

shipment ['ʃɪp mənt] *n.* a load of goods or products ready to be shipped, being shipped, or just received.

shipping [ˈʃɪp ɪŋ] **1.** *n.* the activity or business of delivering products by ship, train, plane, or truck. (No plural.) **2.** *n.* the cost of transporting something. (No plural.) **3.** the *adj.* use of ① or ②.

ships that pass in the night people who meet each other briefly by chance and who are unlikely to meet again.

shipwreck [ˈʃɪp rɛk] **1.** *n.* the destruction of a ship caused by running into something. **2.** *n.* the remains of a ship that has undergone ①. **3.** *tv.* to cause someone to be harmed or stranded owing to ①.

shirt [ˈʃɚt] *n.* a piece of clothing worn above the waist, worn either next to the skin or over an undershirt, and sometimes worn beneath a sweater, jacket, vest, or coat.
→ GIVE SOMEONE THE SHIRT OFF ONE'S BACK

shit [ˈʃɪt] **1.** *n.* dung; feces. (All senses are taboo in polite company. Use only with caution.) **2.** *n.* something poor in quality; junk. **3.** *n.* nonsense; bullshit. **4.** *exclam.* a general expression of disgust. (Usually SHIT! Potentially offensive. Use only with caution.)

shiver [ˈʃɪv ɚ] **1.** *iv.* [for a living creature] to shake a little bit, especially because of cold, sickness, or fear. **2.** *n.* a slight shaking movement, especially because of cold, sickness, or fear.

shock [ˈʃɑk] **1.** *n.* a sudden surprise, especially one that is violent or disturbing. **2.** *n.* a weakened condition of the body caused by a violent or disturbing event. (No plural.) **3.** *n.* a strong, violent force, especially that caused by an earthquake or bomb. **4.** *n.* the passing of electricity through someone's body. **5.** *tv.* to surprise someone, especially in a disturbing or violent way. **6.** *tv.* to offend someone; to disgust someone. **7.** *tv.* to give someone or some creature electricity as in ④.
→ GET THE SHOCK OF ONE'S LIFE

shocking [ˈʃɑk ɪŋ] *adj.* causing surprise, especially in a disturbing or violent way; offensive; causing disgust. (Adv: *shockingly*.)

shoddy [ˈʃɑd i] *adj.* done carelessly; poorly made or done. (Adv: *shoddily*. Comp: *shoddier*; sup: *shoddiest*.)

shoe [ˈʃu] *n.* an outer covering for one's foot, usually having a firm base, but less sturdy than a boot.
→ (AS) COMFORTABLE AS AN OLD SHOE
→ FILL SOMEONE'S SHOES

shoelace [ˈʃu les] *n.* a fabric band or string that is put through the holes on top of a shoe or boot and tied.

shoestring [ˈʃu strɪŋ] *n.* a cord or string used in tightening the shoe to the foot.
→ GET ALONG (ON A SHOESTRING)
→ ON A SHOESTRING

shone [ˈʃon] a past tense and past participle of SHINE.

shook [ˈʃʊk] past tense of SHAKE.

shoot [ˈʃut] **1.** *tv., irreg.* to fire a gun or similar weapon. (Past tense and past participle: SHOT.) **2.** *tv., irreg.* [for a weapon] to send something, such as a bullet or arrow, with great force. **3.** *tv.,*

547

irreg. to send something forward as though from a weapon; to thrust something forward. (Figurative ②.) **4.** *tv., irreg.* to strike someone or some creature with something, such as a bullet or an arrow, that has been sent from a weapon. **5.** *iv., irreg.* to discharge [a weapon]. **6.** *iv., irreg.* to move somewhere very quickly. **7.** *iv., irreg.* to fire guns as a hobby, as for target practice. **8.** *n.* a new bud or stem that sprouts from the ground or from an older part of a plant; a bit of new plant growth.

shoot for something to try to do something; to attempt to do something; to aim toward a goal.

shoot from the hip to speak directly and frankly.

shoot up to grow rapidly.

shooting ['ʃut ɪŋ] **1.** *n.* the sport or skill of hitting targets by firing a gun at them. (No plural.) **2.** *n.* an act of murder, attempted murder, or other harm using a gun.
→ WHOLE SHOOTING MATCH

shop ['ʃap] **1.** *n.* a small store, especially one where a single class of products is sold. **2.** *n.* a place where things are built or repaired. **3.** *iv.* to go to a store to buy things. **4.** *tv.* to visit a particular store, mall, or area in order to buy things.
→ a BULL IN A CHINA SHOP
→ TALK SHOP

shopkeeper ['ʃap kip ɚ] *n.* someone who owns or manages a shop.

shoplift ['ʃap lɪft] **1.** *tv.* to steal merchandise from a shop or store. **2.** *iv.* to steal [something] as in ①.

shoplifter ['ʃap lɪft ɚ] *n.* someone who steals merchandise from a shop or store.

shopping ['ʃap ɪŋ] *n.* buying things; searching for the right thing to purchase. (No plural.)

shopworn ['ʃap worn] *adj.* ruined or damaged from being on display in a store.

shore ['ʃor] *n.* the land along the edge of a body of water.

shore something **up** to support something that is weak; to prop something up.

shoreline ['ʃor laɪn] *n.* the land along the edge of a body of water, especially of an ocean, lake, or sea; the line where the land meets the water.

shorn ['ʃorn] a past participle of SHEAR.

short ['ʃort] **1.** *adj.* not tall; less than average height from top to bottom. (Comp: *shorter;* sup: *shortest.*) **2.** *adj.* not long; less than average length from side to side. (Comp: *shorter;* sup: *shortest.*) **3.** *adj.* not long in time; less than average duration; happening only for a small amount of time; brief. (Comp: *shorter;* sup: *shortest.*) **4.** *adj.* not having enough of something; lacking enough of something. (Comp: *shorter;* sup: *shortest.*) **5.** *adv.* not close enough; not far enough; not enough. **6.** *n.* a flaw in an electrical circuit that allows electricity to go where it should not go. (Short for SHORT CIRCUIT.)
→ CAUGHT SHORT
→ CUT SOMEONE OR SOMETHING (OFF) SHORT

→ END UP WITH THE SHORT END OF
    THE STICK
→ FALL SHORT (OF SOMETHING)
→ GET THE SHORT END OF THE STICK
→ IN SHORT ORDER
→ IN SHORT SUPPLY
→ MAKE A LONG STORY SHORT
→ MAKE SHORT WORK OF SOMEONE OR
    SOMETHING
→ NOTHING SHORT OF SOMETHING
→ OVER THE SHORT HAUL
→ SELL SOMEONE OR SOMETHING SHORT
→ STOP (JUST) SHORT (OF SOMETHING)

short circuit ['ʃɔrt 'sɚ kət] **1.** *n.* a fault in an electrical circuit where the circuit is completed before the electricity has traveled the entire path that it was meant to travel. (Can be shortened to SHORT.) **2.** *tv.* to cause ①. (Hyphenated.) **3.** *iv.* for an electrical circuit to be completed before the electricity has traveled the entire path that it was meant to travel. (Hyphenated.)

short for something a shortened form [of a word or phrase].

short out [for an electrical circuit] to go out because of a short circuit.

shortage ['ʃɔr tɪdʒ] **1.** *n.* a lack; a state of not having enough of something. **2.** *n.* the amount by which something is SHORT ④; the amount of something that is needed in order to have enough.

shortchange ['ʃɔrt 'tʃendʒ] *tv.* to give less than is due someone; to give someone less CHANGE ③ than is due.

shortcoming ['ʃɔrt kəm ɪŋ] *n.* a fault; a flaw; a defect.

shortcut ['ʃɔrt kət] *n.* a path that is shorter, more direct, or quicker to travel than a different or more established route.

shorten ['ʃɔrt n] **1.** *iv.* to become shorter. **2.** *tv.* to cause something to become shorter.

shortening ['ʃɔrt nɪŋ] **1.** *n.* causing something to become shorter. (No plural.) **2.** *n.* butter or some other kind of oily substance, used in frying and baking foods. (Plural only for types and instances.)

short-lived ['ʃɔrt 'lɪvd] *adj.* not lasting very long.

shorts 1. *n.* a pair of pants whose legs end about at the knees. (Treated as plural. Number is expressed with *pair(s) of shorts.* Also countable.) **2.** *n.* underpants for men and boys. (Treated as plural. Number is expressed with *pair(s) of shorts.* Also countable.)

shortsighted ['ʃɔrt 'saɪt ɪd] **1.** *adj.* not able to see things clearly in the distance; able to see things that are near but not able to see things that are far away. (Adv: *shortsightedly.*) **2.** *adj.* acting without considering what will happen in the future. (Figurative on ①. Adv: *shortsightedly.*)

short-staffed ['ʃɔrt 'stæft] *adj.* not having enough people to do a job properly; not having enough employees to run a business properly; needing more people in order to do a job properly.

short-tempered ['ʃɔrt 'tɛm pɚd] *adj.* easily made angry.

short-term ['ʃɔrt 'tɚm] *adj.* only for a short period of time; not permanent; temporary.

shot [ˈʃɑt] **1.** past tense and past participle of SHOOT. **2.** *n.* the firing of a weapon; the shooting of a gun or other weapon. **3.** *n.* someone who shoots in a particular way, such as good or bad. **4.** *n.* an injection of medicine, a vaccine, or a drug. **5.** *n.* in a game, a ball or similar object that is aimed and sent toward a goal in order to score a point. **6.** *n.* a photograph or a length of film or video.
→ GIVE SOMETHING A SHOT
→ TAKE A SHOT AT SOMETHING

a **shot in the arm** a boost; something that gives someone energy.

shotgun wedding a forced wedding.

should be something [ˈʃʊd...] *aux.* OUGHT TO BE SOMEHOW. (Indicating that something is expected.)

should do something [ˈʃʊd...] *aux.* OUGHT TO DO SOMETHING. (Indicating that something must be done.)

should have stood in bed should have stayed in bed. (Has nothing to do with standing up.)

shoulder [ˈʃol dɚ] **1.** *n.* one of two parts of the body where an arm connects with the top of the chest below the neck. **2.** *n.* the dirt or pavement along the side of a road. **3.** *tv.* to have responsibility for something; to take responsibility for something.
→ CARRY THE WEIGHT OF THE WORLD ON ONE'S SHOULDERS
→ HAVE A CHIP ON ONE'S SHOULDER
→ HAVE A GOOD HEAD ON ONE'S SHOULDERS
→ HEAD AND SHOULDERS ABOVE SOMEONE OR SOMETHING
→ ON SOMEONE'S SHOULDERS
→ PUT ONE'S SHOULDER TO THE WHEEL

→ RUB SHOULDERS WITH SOMEONE

shoulder to shoulder side by side; with a shared purpose.

shouldn't [ˈʃʊd nt] *cont.* should not.

should've [ˈʃʊd əv] *cont.* should have, where HAVE is an auxiliary.

shout [ˈʃaʊt] **1.** *iv.* to speak, laugh, or make spoken noises loudly. **2.** *tv.* to speak something loudly; to say something by shouting. (The object can be a clause with THAT ⑦.) **3.** *n.* a loud utterance; a loud cry.
→ ALL OVER BUT THE SHOUTING

shout someone **down** to stop someone from speaking by shouting, yelling, or jeering.

shove [ˈʃʌv] **1.** *iv.* to push with force. **2.** *tv.* to push someone or something with force in some direction. **3.** *n.* a push made with force.

shove off (for something**) 1.** to begin a journey to something or someplace by pushing a boat or ship out onto the water. **2.** to depart for something or someplace, using any form of transportation.

shove one's **way** somewhere to make a path through a crowd by pushing.

shovel [ˈʃʌv əl] **1.** *n.* a tool—having a wide, flat blade attached to a handle—used to lift, move, or remove earth or loose objects. **2.** *iv.* to work by using ①; to move, lift, or remove [something] by using ①. **3.** *tv.* to move, lift, or remove something by using ①. **4.** *tv.* to clear something with ①.

show ['ʃo] **1.** *tv., irreg.* to cause someone to see something; to put something in someone's sight. (Past tense: *showed;* past participle: SHOWN or *showed*.) **2.** *tv., irreg.* to reveal something; to let something be known. (The object can be a clause with THAT ⑦.) **3.** *tv., irreg.* to lead someone; to guide someone to a place. **4.** *tv., irreg.* to prove something; to make something clear. (The object can be a clause with THAT ⑦.) **5.** *tv., irreg.* to display or deliver a kind of treatment, such as sympathy, to someone. **6.** *tv., irreg.* to reveal a condition or illness. **7.** *tv., irreg.* [for a movie theater] to present a movie. **8.** *iv., irreg.* [for a condition] to appear or be visible; to be noticeable. **9.** *iv., irreg.* [for a play or a film] to be presented or displayed. **10.** *n.* a movie, television program, or theater performance. **11.** *n.* a grand spectacle; a noticeable display. **12.** *n.* something that is put on display for the public. **13.** *n.* a display of something, such as raised hands, regard, praise, etc.
→ BY A SHOW OF HANDS
→ LET ONE'S EMOTIONS SHOW
→ MAKE A GREAT SHOW OF SOMETHING
→ NOT SHOW ONE'S FACE
→ STEAL THE SHOW
→ TALK SHOW

show off (to someone**)** to attempt to get attention from someone by one's actions and speech.

show one **to** one's **seat** Go to SHOW SOMEONE TO A SEAT.

show one's **hand** to reveal one's intentions to someone. (From card games.)

show one's **(true) colors** to show what one is really like or what one is really thinking.

show someone **around (**something**)** to give someone a brief tour of something or someplace; to lead someone in an examination of something or someplace.

show someone or something **off (to** someone**)** to show someone or something to someone proudly.

show someone **out (of** something**)** to usher, lead, or escort someone out of something or someplace.

show someone **the ropes** to tell or show someone how something is to be done.

show someone **through (**something**)** to give someone a tour of something or someplace.

show someone **to a seat** AND **show** one **to** one's **seat** to lead or direct someone to a place to sit.

show something **off** to put someone or something on display.

shower ['ʃaʊ ɚ] **1.** *n.* a device [part of the plumbing] that sprays water onto someone who is bathing. **2.** *n.* a bath using ①. **3.** *n.* the place or compartment where one bathes. **4.** *n.* a brief fall of rain, snow, or other liquids in drops. **5.** *n.* a party for a woman who is about to get married or have a baby. **6.** *iv.* to rain; to fall like rain. **7.** *iv.* to wash under ①.
→ SEND SOMEONE TO THE SHOWERS

showing ['ʃo ɪŋ] **1.** *n.* a display of something. **2.** *n.* a display of one's success or lack of success.

shown ['ʃon] a past participle of SHOW.

showroom ['ʃo rum] *n.* a room where products that are available for purchase are displayed.

showy ['ʃo i] *adj.* very noticeable; designed to get attention. (Adv: *showily.* Comp: *showier;* sup: *showiest.*)

shrank ['ʃræŋk] past tense of SHRINK.

shred ['ʃred] **1.** *n.* a very small piece of something; a scrap of something; a fragment. **2.** *tv.* to rip or cut something into scraps or small pieces; to make something into bits by rubbing against a rough or sharp surface.

shredded ['ʃred əd] *adj.* ripped or cut into shreds; made into shreds by rubbing against a rough or sharp object.

shrewd ['ʃrud] *adj.* clever and intelligent; showing good judgment and common sense. (Adv: *shrewdly.* Comp: *shrewder;* sup: *shrewdest.*)

shrewdness ['ʃrud nəs] *n.* the quality of being shrewd. (No plural.)

shriek ['ʃrik] *n.* a loud, shrill, high-pitched scream or sound.

shrill ['ʃrɪl] *adj.* high-pitched and irritating; annoying or loud to the point of causing pain. (Adv: *shrilly.* Comp: *shriller;* sup: *shrillest.*)

shrimp ['ʃrɪmp] **1.** *n., irreg.* a shellfish, about the size and shape of a finger, with a thin body, commonly eaten as food. (Plural: *shrimp* or *shrimps.*) **2.** the *adj.* use of ①.

shrink ['ʃrɪŋk] **1.** *iv., irreg.* to become smaller in size. (Past tense: SHRANK; past participle: SHRUNK or SHRUNKEN. SHRUNK is usually used with auxiliary verbs, and SHRUNKEN is usually used as an adjective.) **2.** *tv., irreg.* to cause someone or something to become smaller in size.

shrink up to shrivel; to recede.

shrivel ['ʃrɪv əl] **1.** *iv.* to become wrinkled while drying up; to wither. **2.** *tv.* to cause someone or something to wither.

shrivel up to contract; to shrink.

shrub ['ʃrʌb] *n.* a plant similar to a very small tree that has many stems coming from the ground; a bush.

shrubbery ['ʃrʌb (ə) ri] *n.* a group of shrubs; shrubs in general. (No plural.)

shrug ['ʃrʌg] **1.** *n.* the lifting of one's shoulders to indicate doubt or a lack of caring or interest. **2.** *tv.* to lift one's shoulders as in ①. **3.** *iv.* to gesture with ①.

shrug something off to ignore something; to dismiss something.

shrunk ['ʃrʌŋk] a past tense and past participle of SHRINK.

shrunken ['ʃrʌŋ kən] a past participle of SHRINK.

shudder ['ʃʌd ɚ] **1.** *iv.* to shake with fear, cold, or disgust. **2.** *n.* a brief, uncontrolled shaking of the body because of fear or disgust.

shuffle ['ʃʌf əl] **1.** *iv.* to walk without picking up one's feet; to walk in a way that one's feet never leave the ground. **2.** *iv.* to mix up [playing cards so that they are] in a different order. **3.** *tv.* to move one's feet without picking them up from the ground. **4.** *tv.* to mix up playing cards so that they are not in any specific order.

shun [ˈʃʌn] *tv.* to avoid someone or something; to stay away from someone or something.

shut [ˈʃʌt] **1.** *tv., irreg.* to close something, such as a door, window, or drawer. (Past tense and past participle: *shut.*) **2.** *tv., irreg.* to close something, such as a door, an eye, or the mouth. **3.** *iv., irreg.* to become closed. **4.** *adj.* closed; moved into a closed position. (Not prenominal.)
→ an OPEN-AND-SHUT CASE

shut off to stop operating; to turn off.

shut someone or something **down** to close a business permanently; to force someone who runs a business to close permanently.

shut someone **up** to cause someone to stop talking or making noise.

shut something **down** to turn something off.

shut up to be quiet. (Slang. Rude.)

shutdown [ˈʃʌt daʊn] *n.* an instance of closing a factory or other place of industry, business, or government for a period of time.

shut-in [ˈʃʌt ɪn] *n.* someone who is not able or not allowed to go outside because of sickness.

shutter [ˈʃʌt ɚ] **1.** *n.* one of a pair of doors or panels that can be closed over the outside of a window. **2.** *n.* a device in a camera that opens and shuts quickly behind the lens in order to allow the proper amount of light when someone takes a picture.

shuttle [ˈʃʌt əl] *n.* a bus or an airplane making regular trips back and forth between two places.

shuttle between places to travel back and forth between two places.

shuttle someone or something **from** person to person AND **shuttle** someone or something **from** place to place to move or pass someone or something from person to person; to move or pass someone or something from place to place.

shuttle someone or something **from** place to place Go to SHUTTLE SOMEONE OR SOMETHING FROM PERSON TO PERSON.

shy [ˈʃaɪ] **1.** *adj.* nervous around other people; not likely to talk around other people; timid; reserved. (Adv: *shyly.* Comp: *shier, shyer;* sup: *shiest, shyest.*) **2.** *adj.* not quite reaching a stated amount; almost having enough of something, but not quite. (Not prenominal. Comp: *shier, shyer;* sup: *shiest, shyest.*)

shy away from someone or something to draw away from someone or something that is frightening or startling; to avoid dealing with someone or something.

shyness [ˈʃaɪ nəs] *n.* the quality of being shy; the quality of being timid or nervous around other people. (No plural.)

sibling ['sɪb lɪŋ] *n.* a brother or sister.

sick ['sɪk] **1.** *adj.* not healthy; ill; having a disease. (Comp: *sicker;* sup: *sickest.*) **2.** *adj.* having an upset stomach and feeling like one has to vomit. (Comp: *sicker;* sup: *sickest.*)
→ (AS) SICK AS A DOG

sick (and tired) of someone or something weary of and disgusted with someone or something, especially something that one must do again and again or someone or something that one must deal with repeatedly.

sicken ['sɪk ən] **1.** *tv.* to cause someone or some creature to become sick. **2.** *tv.* to disgust someone. **3.** *iv.* to become sick; to become ill. **4.** *iv.* to become disgusted [with something].

sickening ['sɪk (ə) nɪŋ] *adj.* causing disgust; disgusting; nauseating. (Adv: *sickeningly.*)

sickness ['sɪk nəs] *n.* the condition of being sick; illness; disease.

side ['saɪd] **1.** *n.* one of the flat surfaces of an object shaped like a box, not including the top or the bottom. **2.** *n.* any of the flat surfaces of a three-dimensional object. **3.** *n.* either surface of something that is thin and flat. **4.** *n.* a particular surface of something. **5.** *n.* the shore along either edge of a river. **6.** *n.* a position or area that is to the right, left, or a certain direction from a central or reference point. **7.** *n.* the entire left or right part of a body. **8.** *n.* a group of people that opposes another group, including sports teams, countries at war, or groups involved with political or social causes. **9.** *adj.* [of a location] at, toward, or beside something.
→ BE A THORN IN SOMEONE'S SIDE
→ BE ON THE SAFE SIDE
→ CHOOSE UP SIDES
→ COME OVER (TO OUR SIDE)
→ FROM SIDE TO SIDE
→ GET OUT OF THE WRONG SIDE OF THE BED
→ GET UP ON THE WRONG SIDE OF THE BED
→ KNOW WHICH SIDE ONE'S BREAD IS BUTTERED ON
→ LAUGH OUT OF THE OTHER SIDE OF ONE'S MOUTH
→ the OTHER SIDE OF THE TRACKS
→ the SEAMY SIDE OF LIFE

side street ['saɪd strit] *n.* a residential street that is not a main street.

sideline ['saɪd laɪn] **1.** *n.* an activity done in addition to one's primary interest or work. **2.** *tv.* to prevent a player from playing in a sporting event.

sidelines *n.* the line along the side of something, especially the line at the boundary of the playing area of a sport. (Treated as plural.)

sidestep ['saɪd stɛp] **1.** *tv.* to avoid injury or a crash by stepping to the side. **2.** *tv.* to avoid or evade something. (Figurative on ①.)

sideswipe ['saɪd swaɪp] *tv.* to hit something along its side; to hit something with one's side.

sidetrack ['saɪd træk] **1.** *tv.* to move a train from a main track to a minor one that runs parallel to the main track. **2.** *tv.* to cause someone to change from the main topic of conversation. (Figurative on ①.) **3.** *tv.* to cause the subject

of a conversation or speech to shift away from the original subject.
→ GET SIDETRACKED

sidewalk ['saɪd wɔk] *n.* a paved path, usually along the side of a street, for people to walk on.

sideways ['saɪd wez] **1.** *adj.* to or from a side. **2.** *adv.* to, on, or from a side or both sides; positioned with the side or edge toward the front.

siege ['sidʒ] *n.* the surrounding of a city, fort, or other place by people who are trying to capture it; an attack.

sift ['sɪft] *tv.* to separate small pieces from larger pieces by shaking the smaller ones through a tool containing a screen.

sift something **out (of** something**)** to get rid of something in something else by sifting.

sift through something to look among a group of things closely.

sigh ['saɪ] **1.** *iv.* to breathe out slowly and noisily, especially to indicate that one is bored, relieved, sad, or tired. **2.** *n.* the sound of breathing out as in ①.

sight ['saɪt] **1.** *n.* the ability to see; the power to see; vision. (No plural.) **2.** *n.* something that is seen; something in one's range of vision; a view. **3.** *n.* something that is worth seeing. (Often plural.) **4.** *n.* something that looks funny or strange. (No plural.) **5.** *tv.* to see someone or something for the first time, especially when one is looking for that person or thing.
→ BUY SOMETHING SIGHT UNSEEN
→ HAVE ONE'S SIGHTS TRAINED ON SOMETHING

→ IN SIGHT
→ KNOW SOMEONE BY SIGHT
→ LOVE AT FIRST SIGHT
→ LOWER ONE'S SIGHTS
→ RAISE ONE'S SIGHTS
→ SET ONE'S SIGHTS ON SOMETHING
→ TRAIN ONE'S SIGHTS ON SOMETHING

sighted ['saɪt ɪd] *adj.* [of someone] able to see; [of someone] not blind.

sightless ['saɪt ləs] *adj.* unable to see; without sight; blind. (Adv: *sightlessly.*)

sightseeing ['saɪt si ɪŋ] *n.* visiting famous or interesting places, especially when one is on vacation. (No plural.)

sign ['saɪn] **1.** *n.* a mark that represents something; a mark that indicates something. **2.** *n.* something that indicates something else. **3.** *n.* a flat object that has information printed on it, placed where everyone can see it. **4.** *n.* a gesture used to communicate. **5.** *tv.* to write one's name [somewhere]. **6.** *tv.* to mark or write on something with one's name. **7.** *tv.* to communicate something by using SIGN LANGUAGE.

sign in to indicate that one has arrived somewhere and at what time by signing a piece of paper or a list.

sign language ['saɪn læŋ gwɪdʒ] *n.* a visual form of communication where the hands assume specific positions that represent words or letters in a language. (No plural.)

sign off 1. [for a broadcaster] to announce the end of programming for the day; [for an amateur radio operator] to announce the end of a transmission. **2.** to quit doing what one has been doing and leave, go to bed, etc. (Figurative.)

sign off on something to sign a paper, indicating that one has finished with something or agrees with the state of something.

sign on to announce the beginning of a broadcast transmission.

sign on the dotted line to place one's signature on a contract or other important paper.

sign one's **own death warrant** to do something that ensures the failure of one's endeavors.

sign out to indicate in writing that one is leaving or going out temporarily.

sign someone **in** to record that someone has arrived somewhere and at what time by recording the information on a paper or a list.

sign someone **out (of** someplace) to make a record of someone's departure from someplace.

sign someone **up (for** something) to record the agreement of someone to participate in something.

sign someone **up (with** someone or something) to record the agreement of someone to join a group of people or an organization.

sign something **away** to sign a paper in which one gives away one's rights to something.

sign something **in** to record that something has been received at a particular time by recording the information on a paper or a list.

sign something **out (of** someplace) to make a record of the borrowing of something from someplace.

sign something **over (to** someone) to sign a paper granting the rights to or ownership of something to a specific person.

sign up (for something) to record one's agreement to participate in something.

signal ['sɪg nəl] **1.** *n.* something that conveys a message by affecting one of the senses; a sound, light, movement, etc., that conveys a message. **2.** *n.* the waves sent by a radio or television transmitter. **3.** *tv.* to indicate something. (The object can be a clause with THAT ⑦.)

signal to someone **to** do something [for someone] to give someone a command or instruction using a signal.

signature ['sɪg nə tʃɚ] *n.* a person's name, handwritten by the person.

signed ['saɪnd] *adj.* marked with someone's signature.

signed, sealed, and delivered formally and officially signed; [for a formal document to be] executed.

significance [sɪg 'nɪf ə kəns] *n.* importance; meaning. (No plural.)

significant [sɪg 'nɪf ə kənt] *adj.* important; having meaning. (Adv: *significantly*.)

signify ['sɪg nə faɪ] *tv.* to mean something; to indicate something; to be a sign of something. (The object can be a clause with THAT ⑦.)

silence ['saɪ ləns] **1.** *n.* absolute quiet; the absence of all sound. (No plural.) **2.** *n.* the absence of comments about something. (No plural.) **3.** *tv.* to cause someone to be quiet; to cause someone to stop talking or to stop making noise.

silent ['saɪ lənt] **1.** *adj.* quiet; not speaking or making noise; done without making noise. (Adv: *silently.*) **2.** *adj.* [of a (spelling) letter] not pronounced; not representing a sound. (Adv: *silently.*)

silk ['sɪlk] **1.** *n.* a smooth, fine thread that is created by a silkworm when making its cocoon. (No plural.) **2.** *n.* cloth woven from ①. (Plural only for types and instances.) **3.** *adj.* made of ②.
→ MAKE A SILK PURSE OUT OF A SOW'S EAR

silkworm ['sɪlk wərm] *n.* a creature that makes a cocoon of silk.

silky ['sɪl ki] *adj.* like silk; soft and smooth; [of cloth] soft and shimmering. (Adv: *silkily.* Comp: *silkier;* sup: *silkiest.*)

sill ['sɪl] *n.* the bottom ledge of a window or door frame.
→ WINDOWSILL

silly ['sɪl i] *adj.* foolish; not sensible. (Comp: *sillier;* sup: *silliest.*)

silly season the time of year, usually in the summer, when there is a lack of important news and newspapers contain articles about unimportant or trivial things instead.

silver ['sɪl vər] **1.** *n.* a bright, white, valuable metallic element, which in its pure form is soft and easily shaped. (No plural.) **2.** *n.* coins, rather than paper money. (From a time when major U.S. coins were made of ①. No plural.) **3.** *adj.* made of ①.
→ BORN WITH A SILVER SPOON IN ONE'S MOUTH

silverware ['sɪl vər wɛr] **1.** *n.* eating or serving utensils that are made from or plated with silver. (No plural.) **2.** *n.* knives, forks, and spoons made of steel, nickel, or metals other than silver. (No plural.)

silvery ['sɪl və ri] *adj.* looking like silver.

similar ['sɪm ə lər] *adj.* resembling something else, but not exactly the same. (Adv: *similarly.*)

similarity [sɪm ə 'lɛr ɪ ti] *n.* a way or an aspect in which someone or something is like or resembles someone or something else.

simmer ['sɪm ər] **1.** *tv.* to boil something gently; to cook something at or just below its boiling point. **2.** *iv.* to boil gently; to cook at or just below the boiling point. **3.** *iv.* to be angry without letting other people know that one is angry. (Figurative on ②.) **4.** *iv.* [for a situation] to be currently somewhat calm but progressing toward violence.

simple ['sɪm pəl] **1.** *adj.* easy; not complicated; not complex. (Adv: *simply.* Comp: *simpler;* sup: *simplest.*) **2.** *adj.* plain; not complicated; not fancy. (Adv: *simply.* Comp: *simpler;* sup: *simplest.*)

simplicity [sɪm 'plɪs ɪ ti] *n.* the quality of being simple or not complicated. (No plural.)

simplify ['sɪm plə faɪ] *tv.* to make something simpler; to make something easier to do or understand; to make something clearer.

simplistic [sɪm 'plɪs tɪk] *adj.* too simple; having been simplified too much. (Adv: *simplistically* [...ɪk li].)

simply ['sɪm pli] **1.** *adv.* easily; without difficulty. **2.** *adv.* merely; only. **3.** *adv.* absolutely; completely; very.

simulate ['sɪm jə let] *tv.* to show the nature or effects of something, allowing the observer to learn about it without experiencing it.

simulation [sɪm jə 'le ʃən] **1.** *n.* a demonstration of the nature or effects of an event without anyone really experiencing it. **2.** *n.* something that has been simulated.

simultaneous [saɪ məl 'te ni əs] *adj.* happening or existing at the same time. (Adv: *simultaneously.*)

sin ['sɪn] **1.** *n.* evil; something that is wicked or wrong; an act that is in opposition to a religious or moral principle. (Plural only for types and instances.) **2.** *iv.* to break a religious or moral principle.

since ['sɪns] **1.** *conj.* from a certain time in the past until now. **2.** *conj.* because. **3.** *prep.* from a certain time in the past until now. **4.** *adv.* from a certain time in the past until now.

since time immemorial since a very long time ago.

sincere [sɪn 'sɪr] *adj.* honest; real; genuine; true. (Adv: *sincerely.* Comp: *sincerer*; sup: *sincerest*.)

sincerely [sɪn 'sɪr li] **1.** *adv.* honestly; really; genuinely; truly.

2. *adv.* a word used as a polite way to finish a letter, before one's signature.

sincerity [sɪn 'sɛr ɪ ti] *n.* the quality of being sincere; honesty. (No plural.)

sinful ['sɪn fʊl] **1.** *adj.* full of sin; having committed a sin. (Adv: *sinfully.*) **2.** *adj.* wicked; bad; evil; leading people into sin. (Adv: *sinfully.*)

sing ['sɪŋ] **1.** *iv., irreg.* to make music with one's voice, uttering a melody with words. (Past tense: SANG; past participle: SUNG.) **2.** *tv., irreg.* to make music as in ①.

sing out to sing more loudly.

sing someone's **praises** to praise someone highly and enthusiastically.

sing something **out** to sing or announce something loudly.

singe ['sɪndʒ] *tv.* to burn something slightly; to burn the edge or end of something.

single ['sɪŋ gəl] **1.** *adj.* one and only one. (Adv: *singly.*) **2.** *adj.* individual; meant for one thing or person. (Adv: *singly.*) **3.** *adj.* not married. (Adv: *singly.*) **4.** *adj.* having only one part; not double; not multiple. (Adv: *singly.*) **5.** *n.* something that is meant for one person. **6.** *n.* a $1 bill. **7.** *n.* someone who is not married.

single someone or something **out (for** something) to choose or pick someone or something for something; to select an eligible person or thing for something.

single-minded ['sɪŋ gəl 'maɪn dɪd] *adj.* having only one purpose. (Adv: *single-mindedly.*)

singular ['sɪŋ gjə lɚ] **1.** *adj.* referring to only one person or thing; the opposite of PLURAL. **2.** *adj.* unusual; exceptional; remarkable. (Adv: *singularly.*) **3.** *n.* the form of a noun that refers to only one person or thing; the opposite of PLURAL.

sink ['sɪŋk] **1.** *iv., irreg.* to go beneath a surface; to fall beneath a surface. (Past tense: SANK or SUNK; past participle: SUNK.) **2.** *iv., irreg.* to become smaller in number; to decrease. **3.** *iv., irreg.* [for someone] to collapse or fall to the ground because of weakness, fear, respect, etc. **4.** *tv., irreg.* to cause something to go lower and lower beneath the surface of water or some other liquid. **5.** *n.* a permanent hollow bowl or basin, especially in a kitchen or bathroom, for washing dishes, one's hands or face, etc.
→ DESERT A SINKING SHIP
→ EVERYTHING BUT THE KITCHEN SINK
→ LEAVE A SINKING SHIP

sink back (into something**)** to lean back and relax in something, such as a soft chair.

sink down to sink or submerge.

sink in(to someone or something**)** to penetrate someone or something. (Used figuratively in reference to someone's brain or thinking.)

sink one's **teeth into** something **1.** to take a bite of some kind of food, usually a special kind of food. **2.** to get a chance to do, learn, or control something.

sink or swim either fail or succeed.

sink something **in((to)** someone or something**) 1.** to drive or push something into someone or something. **2.** to invest time or money in someone or something. (Sometimes implying that it was wasted.)

sinking ['sɪŋ kɪŋ] *adj.* going further downward into a liquid.

sinner ['sɪn ɚ] *n.* someone who sins.

sinus ['saɪ nəs] **1.** *n.* one of a number of spaces inside the bones of the face that are connected to the outside air by way of the nose. **2.** the *adj.* use of ①.

sip ['sɪp] **1.** *tv.* to drink something a little bit at a time. **2.** *n.* a small drink of something; a little taste of something liquid.

siphon AND **syphon** ['saɪ fən] *n.* a tube that has one end in a container of liquid and, through pressure and gravity, pulls the liquid downward into another container placed at a lower level.

siphon something **(off)** to remove liquid from a container by using a siphon.

sir ['sɚ] *n.* a word used to address a male politely.

siren ['saɪ rən] *n.* a device that makes a loud noise of warning, such as that found on police cars, fire trucks, and ambulances.

sissy ['sɪs i] *n.* a weak and shy boy; a boy who behaves like a girl. (Derogatory.)

sister ['sɪs tɚ] **1.** *n.* a female sibling; a daughter of one's mother or
father. **2.** *n.* a nun. (Also a term of
address. Capitalized when written
as a proper noun.)

sit ['sɪt] **1.** *iv., irreg.* to be in a position where the upper part of the
body is straight, and the buttocks
are supported by a chair, a seat,
the floor, or some other surface.
(Past tense and past participle:
SAT.) **2.** *iv., irreg.* [for something]
to be in a certain position; to be in
a place. **3.** *iv., irreg.* [for an ani-
mal] to be positioned with the
back end resting on a surface.
4. *tv., irreg.* to make someone SIT
as in ① in a location.
→ LIKE A SITTING DUCK

sit around to relax sitting; to waste
time sitting.

sit around (somewhere) to sit
somewhere and relax or do nothing; to sit idly somewhere.

sit at someone's feet to admire
someone greatly; to be influenced
by someone's teaching; to be
taught by someone.

sit back to push oneself back in
one's seat; to lean against the back
of one's seat.

sit down to be seated; to sit on
something, such as a chair.

sit in (for someone) to act as a substitute for someone.

sit in (on something) to attend
something as a visitor; to act as a
temporary participant in something.

sit on its **hands** [for an audience]
to refuse to applaud.

sit on one's **hands** to do nothing;
to fail to help.

sit on the fence not to take sides
in a dispute; not to make a clear
choice between two possibilities.

sit (something) out to elect not to
participate in something.

sit through something to remain
seated and in attendance for all of
something.

sit tight to wait; to wait patiently.
(Does not necessarily refer to sitting.)

sit up 1. to rise from a lying to a
sitting position. **2.** to sit straighter
in one's seat; to hold one's posture
more upright while seated.

sit up and take notice to become
alert and pay attention.

sit up with someone to remain
awake and attend someone
throughout the night.

site ['saɪt] *n.* a location where
something is, or was happening,
has happened, or will happen.

sitting on a powder keg in a
risky or explosive situation; in a
situation where something serious
or dangerous may happen at any
time.

sitting target someone or something in a position that is easily
attacked.

situate ['sɪt ʃu et] *tv.* to place
something; to have or make a
place for something.

situation [sɪt ʃu 'e ʃən] *n.* a condition; the circumstances of an
event; a state of affairs.

six ['sɪks] 6. Go to FOUR.
→ AT SIXES AND SEVENS

six of one and half a dozen of the other about the same one way or another.

six-pack ['sɪks pæk] *n.* a package of six things, especially six cans of beer or soft drinks.

sixteen ['sɪks 'tin] 16. Go to FOUR.

sixteenth ['sɪks 'tinθ] 16th. Go to FOURTH.

sixth ['sɪksθ] 6th. Go to FOURTH.

sixth sense a supposed power to know or feel things that are not perceptible by the five senses of sight, hearing, smell, taste, and touch.

sixtieth ['sɪks ti əθ] 60th. Go to FOURTH.

sixty ['sɪks ti] 60. Go to FORTY.

sizable ['saɪz ə bəl] *adj.* large; rather large; much. (Adv: *sizably.*)

size ['saɪz] **1.** *n.* the degree to which someone or something is large or small. (No plural.) **2.** *n.* one measurement in a series of measurements, used to describe ① of a product one wants, such as an article of clothing, a portion of food or drink, certain hardware, etc.

size someone or something **up** to scrutinize someone or something and form a judgment.

sizzle ['sɪz əl] **1.** *n.* the hissing noise made when frying fat or frying food in fat. (No plural.) **2.** *iv.* [for fat or cooking oil] to make a hissing noise when it is fried; to sound like fat when it fries.

sizzling ['sɪz lɪŋ] **1.** *adj.* frying; making the noise that fat does when it is heated. **2.** *adj.* very hot.

skate ['sket] **1.** *n.* an ICE SKATE; a ROLLER SKATE. **2.** *iv.* to move (over a surface) while wearing ICE SKATES or ROLLER SKATES.
→ ICE SKATE
→ ROLLER SKATE

skate on thin ice to be in a risky situation.

skater ['sket ɚ] *n.* someone who ice-skates or roller-skates.

skeleton ['skɛl ə tən] **1.** *n.* the bones of a person or an animal, usually connected in their proper arrangement. **2.** *n.* an outline; the basic structure that supports something. (Figurative on ①.)

skeleton in the closet a hidden and shocking secret; a secret fact about oneself.

skeptic ['skɛp tɪk] *n.* someone who doubts faith, claims, theories, or facts; someone who questions the truth of something, especially religion.

skeptical ['skɛp tɪ kəl] *adj.* doubting; questioning; finding something hard to believe. (Adv: *skeptically* [...ɪk li].)

skepticism ['skɛp tə sɪz əm] *n.* doubt; the condition of being skeptical; skeptical attitude or behavior. (No plural.)

sketch ['skɛtʃ] **1.** *n.* a simple drawing; a rough drawing that is quickly made. **2.** *n.* a brief description; an outline. **3.** *n.* a short skit; a very short play that is usually funny. **4.** *tv.* to draw someone or something roughly and quickly; to make a quick drawing. **5.** *iv.* to draw roughly and quickly.
→ THUMBNAIL SKETCH

sketchy ['skɛtʃ i] *adj.* not complete; without details. (Adv: *sketchily.* Comp: *sketchier;* sup: *sketchiest.*)

ski ['ski] **1.** *n.* one of two long, narrow, thin strips of wood or plastic used to travel on the surface of snow or water. **2.** *iv.* to move on the surface of snow or water on a pair of ①.

skid ['skɪd] **1.** *iv.* [for a wheel of a vehicle] to continue to move over a surface after the brakes have been applied. **2.** *iv.* to slip forward or sideways while moving. **3.** *n.* a forward or sideways slipping movement as with ① or ②.

skier ['ski ɚ] *n.* someone who skis on water or snow.

skiing ['ski ɪŋ] *n.* the sport or activity of moving over snow or water on skis. (No plural.)

skill ['skɪl] *n.* the ability to do something well, especially because of talent, experience, or practice.

skilled ['skɪld] *adj.* having skill; experienced.

skillet ['skɪl ət] *n.* a shallow pan used for frying foods.

skillful ['skɪl fʊl] *adj.* having skill; experienced; able to do something very well. (Adv: *skillfully.*)

skim ['skɪm] **1.** *tv.* to remove something from the surface of a liquid. **2.** *tv.* to glide over the surface of something; to go over the surface of something quickly. **3.** *tv.* to scan reading material; to read something quickly.

skim over something **1.** to glide over the surface of something, without touching it. **2.** to read

something quickly but not carefully.

skim through something to go through something hastily; to read through something hastily.

skin ['skɪn] **1.** *n.* the outer covering of humans and most animals; the outer covering of many fruits and vegetables. (Plural only for types and instances.) **2.** *tv.* to remove the skin from something.
→ ALL SKIN AND BONES
→ BY THE SKIN OF ONE'S TEETH
→ GET UNDER SOMEONE'S SKIN
→ JUMP OUT OF ONE'S SKIN
→ NO SKIN OFF SOMEONE'S NOSE
→ NO SKIN OFF SOMEONE'S TEETH
→ NOTHING BUT SKIN AND BONES

skinny ['skɪn i] *adj.* very thin; without much fat. (Comp: *skinnier;* sup: *skinniest.*)

skip ['skɪp] **1.** *iv.* to move so that one takes a step with one foot, hops on that foot, takes a step with the second foot, and then hops on the second foot, repeatedly. **2.** *tv.* to pass someone or something over; to omit something. **3.** *tv.* to avoid attending a school class or other event and go someplace else.

skip about AND **skip around** to move in a random order; to be random in doing things.

skip around Go to SKIP ABOUT.

skip over someone or something Go to SKIP PAST SOMEONE OR SOMETHING.

skip past someone or something AND **skip over** someone or something to pass over someone or something.

skip rope to jump over an arc of rope that is passed beneath one's feet then over one's head, repeatedly.

skirmish ['skɚ mɪʃ] *n.* a small battle or argument.

skirt ['skɚt] **1.** *n.* an item of women's clothing that wraps around the waist and hangs down, without separate sections for each leg. **2.** *tv.* to move along the edge of something; to not move through the center of something. **3.** *tv.* to evade an issue, topic, or question; to fail to address an issue, topic, or question.

skit ['skɪt] *n.* a short performance that is usually funny or that addresses a certain topic.

skull ['skʌl] *n.* the bones of the head; the bones that protect the brain.
→ GET SOMETHING THROUGH SOMEONE'S THICK SKULL

skunk ['skʌŋk] *n.* a small animal that has black fur with a white stripe down its back and a bushy tail, and that releases a very bad smell when attacked or frightened.

sky ['skaɪ] *n.* the space above the earth; the air above the earth. (Sometimes plural.)
→ (AS) HIGH AS THE SKY
→ OUT OF A CLEAR BLUE SKY
→ PIE IN THE SKY

skydive ['skaɪ daɪv] **1.** *iv.* to jump from an airplane, fall through the air, and then open a parachute. (Past tense and past participle: *skydived.*) **2.** *n.* an instance of jumping from an airplane as in ①.

skylight ['skaɪ laɪt] *n.* a window in the roof or ceiling of a building.

The **sky's the limit.** There is no limit to the success that can be achieved or the money that can be gained or spent.

skyscraper ['skaɪ skre pɚ] *n.* a very tall building.

slab ['slæb] *n.* a thick slice of something; a thick, flat piece of something.

slack ['slæk] **1.** *adj.* loose; not tight; not taut. (Adv: *slackly.* Comp: *slacker;* sup: *slackest.*) **2.** *adj.* not strict; relaxed. (Figurative on ①. Adv: *slackly.* Comp: *slacker;* sup: *slackest.*) **3.** *adj.* not active; not busy. (Adv: *slackly.* Comp: *slacker;* sup: *slackest.*) **4.** *n.* looseness; a part of something that is not pulled tight.

slack off to be lazy; to work only when absolutely necessary; to wane or decline; to decrease in intensity.

slacken ['slæk ən] *iv.* to reduce, especially in speed or tightness; to become slower or looser.

slacks *n.* pants; trousers. (Treated as plural. Number is expressed with *pair(s) of slacks.* Also countable. Rarely singular.)

slain ['slen] past participle of SLAY.

slam ['slæm] **1.** *tv.* to shut something noisily and with force. **2.** *tv.* to insult or criticize someone or something very strongly. (Informal.) **3.** *iv.* [for something] to shut very noisily and with force. **4.** *n.* a loud and violent closing or crash.

slam into someone or something to run into someone or something very forcefully; to crash into someone or something with great force.

slam someone or something **against** someone or something to shove someone or something against someone or something.

slander ['slæn dɚ] **1.** *n.* a spoken or written lie that is meant to hurt someone's reputation; something false that is said in order to hurt someone's reputation. (No plural.) **2.** *tv.* to damage someone's reputation by lying about that person.

slanderous ['slæn dɚ əs] *adj.* understood or intended to be slander. (Adv: *slanderously.*)

slang ['slæŋ] **1.** *n.* words or expressions that are not expected in formal, educational, or business settings. (Not usually plural.) **2.** the *adj.* use of ①.

slant ['slænt] **1.** *n.* a slope; an angle. (No plural.) **2.** *iv.* to slope; to angle; to move at an angle; to rise or fall while moving in a certain direction. **3.** *tv.* to cause something to be angled; to cause something to move at an angle. **4.** *tv.* to express something in a way that favors one point of view over another.

slap ['slæp] **1.** *tv.* to hit someone or something with one's open hand; to hit someone or something with something flat. **2.** *tv.* to put something on a surface carelessly and with force. **3.** *n.* a hit with one's open hand or with something flat. **4.** *n.* the noise made when someone or something is hit with someone's open hand or with something flat.

slap in the face an insult; an act that causes disappointment or discouragement.

slap something **on** to dress in something hastily.

slap something **on(to** someone or something) to place something onto someone or something by slapping.

slap something **together** to make up something very quickly.

slash ['slæʃ] **1.** *tv.* to cut something violently with a sharp object, using large, sweeping movements. **2.** *tv.* to reduce numbers or amounts greatly. **3.** *n.* a cut made by a violent movement as in ①; a gash. **4.** *n.* the (/) symbol; the (\) symbol.

slate ['slet] **1.** *n.* a rock that splits easily into flat, thin layers. (No plural.) **2.** *n.* a group of candidates offered by a political party in an election. (No plural of ①.) **3.** *adj.* made of ①.
→ START (OFF) WITH A CLEAN SLATE

slaughter ['slɔ tɚ] **1.** *tv.* to kill and cut up an animal for food. **2.** *tv.* to kill living creatures ruthlessly.
→ LIKE A LAMB TO THE SLAUGHTER
→ LIKE LAMBS TO THE SLAUGHTER

slave ['slev] *n.* someone who is owned by someone else; someone who is the property of someone else.
→ BE A SLAVE TO SOMETHING

slavery ['slev (ə) ri] *n.* the ownership of slaves. (No plural.)

slay ['sle] *tv., irreg.* to kill someone or some animal; to murder someone. (Past tense: SLEW; past participle: SLAIN.)

slaying ['sle ɪŋ] *n.* a murder; the killing of someone or some animal.

sleazy ['sli zi] *adj.* cheap and crude; having a bad reputation. (Adv: *sleazily.* Comp: *sleazier;* sup: *sleaziest.*)

sled ['slɛd] **1.** *n.* a flat platform attached to long, thin blades that move easily over snow. **2.** *iv.* to ride somewhere on ①; to play with ①; to travel by ①.

sleek ['slik] **1.** *adj.* smooth and shiny. (Especially used to describe hair or fur—of people or animals—that is healthy or well cared for. Adv: *sleekly.* Comp: *sleeker;* sup: *sleekest.*) **2.** *adj.* having neat, smooth lines; stylish. (Adv: *sleekly.* Comp: *sleeker;* sup: *sleekest.*)

sleep ['slip] **1.** *n.* the period of rest when the mind is not conscious; the period of rest when the body is not awake. (No plural.) **2.** *iv.,* *irreg.* not to be awake; to rest the body and mind in an unconscious condition. (Past tense and past participle: SLEPT.) **3.** *tv., irreg.* to provide space for a certain number of people to SLEEP as in ②; to have enough space for a certain number of people to SLEEP as in ②.
→ DOZE OFF (TO SLEEP)
→ LULL SOMEONE TO SLEEP
→ NOT SLEEP A WINK
→ PUT SOMEONE OR SOME CREATURE TO SLEEP
→ PUT SOMEONE TO SLEEP

sleep in to remain in bed, sleeping past one's normal time of arising.

sleep like a log to sleep very soundly.

sleep on something to think about something overnight; to weigh a decision overnight.

sleep something **off** to sleep away the effect of alcohol or drugs.

sleep through something to remain sleeping through some event.

sleepless ['slip ləs] *adj.* without sleep; unable to sleep. (Adv: *sleeplessly.*)

sleepwalk ['slip wɔk] *iv.* to walk while sleeping.

sleepwalker ['slip wɔk ɚ] *n.* someone who walks around while sleeping.

sleepy ['slip i] *adj.* tired; drowsy; needing to sleep. (Adv: *sleepily.* Comp: *sleepier;* sup: *sleepiest.*)

sleet ['slit] **1.** *n.* partly frozen rain; partly frozen rain mixed with snow or hail. (No plural.) **2.** *iv.* [for ①] to fall from the sky.

sleeve ['sliv] *n.* the part of an item of clothing that covers the arm.
→ LAUGH UP ONE'S SLEEVE

sleeveless ['sliv ləs] *adj.* without sleeves. (Adv: *sleevelessly.*)

sleigh ['sle] *n.* a large sled; a platform or carriage—usually pulled by horses or dogs—attached to long, metal blades for traveling over snow.

slender ['slɛn dɚ] *adj.* slim; thin, in a pleasant or graceful way. (Adv: *slenderly.* Comp: *slenderer;* sup: *slenderest.*)

slept ['slɛpt] past tense and past participle of SLEEP.

slew ['slu] **1.** past tense of SLAY. **2.** *n.* a large amount of something. (Informal.)

slice ['slaɪs] **1.** *n.* a thin, flat piece that is cut from something. **2.** *n.* a part; a portion; a share. **3.** *tv.* to cut a thin, flat piece from something; to cut something into thin, flat pieces.

slice in(to something**)** to cut into something, usually with a knife or something similar.

a **slice of the cake** Go to a PIECE OF THE PIE.

slice something **off** to cut something off with slicing motions.

slice through something to cut through something with slicing motions.

slick ['slɪk] **1.** *adj.* wet and slippery; oily and slippery; icy and slippery. (Adv: *slickly.* Comp: *slicker;* sup: *slickest.*) **2.** *adj.* clever; sly; shrewd. (Informal. Adv: *slickly.* Comp: *slicker;* sup: *slickest.*) **3.** *adj.* attractive or nicely designed, but without much content or meaning; shallow. (Adv: *slickly.* Comp: *slicker;* sup: *slickest.*)

slid ['slɪd] past tense and past participle of SLIDE.

slide ['slaɪd] **1.** *iv., irreg.* to move or glide along a smooth surface; to move down a surface; to move without resistance. (Past tense and past participle: SLID.) **2.** *iv., irreg.* to move backward or forward on a groove or track. **3.** *tv., irreg.* to cause someone or something to glide along a smooth surface or on a track; to cause someone or something to move or glide along a smooth surface. **4.** *tv., irreg.* to move something quietly, especially without anyone else noticing. **5.** *n.* a downward movement; a decline. **6.** *n.* a small, square frame with a picture on a piece of film in the center, the image of which can be projected onto a screen. **7.** *n.* a small, thin, rectangular piece of glass that small objects are placed on so that they can be examined under a microscope.
→ LET SOMETHING SLIDE (BY)

slide out of something to slip or glide out of something without much effort.

slide something **in(to** something**)** to insert something into something effortlessly.

slide something **out (of** something**)** to cause something to slip or glide out of something without much effort.

slight ['slaɪt] **1.** *adj.* not very large; not very important. (Adv: *slightly.* Comp: *slighter;* sup: *slightest.*) **2.** *adj.* frail; delicate; not strong. (Adv: *slightly.* Comp: *slighter;* sup: *slightest.*) **3.** *tv.* to neglect mentioning someone or something; to insult a person by ignoring the person's presence or accomplishments. **4.** *n.* the insult of treating someone as unimportant; the lack of attention paid to someone or something.

slightly ['slaɪt li] *adv.* a little; to a small degree.

slim ['slɪm] **1.** *adj.* thin; slender. (Adv: *slimly.* Comp: *slimmer;* sup: *slimmest.*) **2.** *adj.* small in amount or quality; slight. (Adv: *slimly.* Comp: *slimmer;* sup: *slimmest.*)

slim down to become thinner; to become narrower.

slim someone **down** to cause someone to lose weight.

slime ['slaɪm] *n.* a soft, sticky, unpleasant fluid; filth. (No plural.)

slimy [ˈslaɪ mi] *adj.* covered with slime; like slime; filthy. (Adv: *slimily.* Comp: *slimier;* sup: *slimiest.*)

sling [ˈslɪŋ] **1.** *tv., irreg.* to throw something with force; to hurl something; to fling something. (Past tense and past participle: SLUNG.) **2.** *tv., irreg.* to hang or suspend something from something or between two things. (Informal.) **3.** *n.* a strip of cloth that is used to support an injured arm by being looped around the neck.

slip [ˈslɪp] **1.** *iv.* to fall accidentally while moving or being moved; to slide from a place or position. **2.** *iv.* to move or happen quietly, quickly, smoothly, easily, secretly, or without being noticed. **3.** *iv.* to grow worse; to lower; to diminish; to decline. **4.** *n.* an accidental fall as in ①. **5.** *n.* a mistake; an error; something that was done wrong.
→ LET SOMETHING SLIP BY
→ LET THE CHANCE SLIP BY

slip in(to something) to slide or glide into something, such as clothing, a sleeping bag, a tight place, etc.

slip of the tongue an error in speaking in which a word is pronounced incorrectly, or in which the speaker says something unintentionally.

slip off ((of) someone or something) to fall away from or off someone or something.

slip off (to someplace) to sneak away to someplace.

slip one's **mind** [for something that was to be remembered] to be forgotten.

slip out (of something) **1.** to sneak out of a place unnoticed. **2.** to slide out of an article of clothing.

slip something **off** to let an item of clothing slide off one's body; to remove an item of clothing.

slip something **on** to put on an article of clothing, possibly in haste or casually.

slip through someone's **fingers** to get away from someone; for someone to lose track (of something or someone).

slip up to make an error.

slip up on something to make an error in doing something.

slipper [ˈslɪp ɚ] *n.* a foot covering that one wears indoors and that can be taken on and off easily; a shoe made of light materials.

slippery [ˈslɪp (ə) ri] **1.** *adj.* allowing people or things to slip. **2.** *adj.* hard to catch or hold; likely to slip out of one's hands.
→ (AS) SLIPPERY AS AN EEL

slit [ˈslɪt] **1.** *n.* a straight, narrow cut or opening. **2.** *tv., irreg.* to cut or tear something in a straight line so that there is a narrow opening. (Past tense and past participle: *slit.*)

sliver [ˈslɪv ɚ] *n.* a small, thin, sharp piece or stick of something.

slogan [ˈslo gən] *n.* a motto; a unique word or phrase used in advertising or politics.

slope [ˈslop] **1.** *n.* the slanted side of a mountain or hill. **2.** *n.* the amount that a line or surface SLOPES as in ③. (No plural.) **3.** *iv.* to lean, be set, or be formed at an angle. **4.** *tv.* to cause something to be at an angle; to cause something not to be level or straight up and down.

sloping ['slop ɪŋ] *adj.* at an angle; not flat or straight up and down. (Adv: *slopingly.*)

sloppy ['slɑp i] **1.** *adj.* muddy; rainy; very wet as the result of bad weather. (Adv: *sloppily.* Comp: *sloppier;* sup: *sloppiest.*) **2.** *adj.* messy; not tidy; careless. (Adv: *sloppily.* Comp: *sloppier;* sup: *sloppiest.*)

slot ['slɑt] **1.** *n.* a narrow opening in an object or machine. **2.** *n.* a place on a list or schedule. **3.** *tv.* to place someone or something on a list or schedule.

slouch ['slaʊtʃ] *iv.* to sit, stand, or move without holding one's body erect.

slouch down to sag, slump, or droop down.

slouch over to lean or crumple and fall to one side; [for someone] to collapse in a sitting position.

slovenly ['slʌv ən li] *adj.* [of someone] dirty or messy in appearance.

slow ['slo] **1.** *adj.* not fast; not quick; taking a long time; taking more time than average; moving with less speed than average. (Adv: *slowly.* See also ④. Comp: *slower;* sup: *slowest.*) **2.** *adj.* behind schedule; happening later than the time something is supposed to happen. (Comp: *slower;* sup: *slowest.*) **3.** *adj.* boring; dull; without much action or interest. (Adv: *slowly.* Comp: *slower;* sup: *slowest.*) **4.** *adv.* at the pace described in ①. (Comp: *slower;* sup: *slowest.*) **5.** *iv.*

to become ①; to become slower; to move slower. **6.** *tv.* to cause something to become ①; to cause something to move slower.

slow down to decrease speed; to go slower.

slow going the rate of speed when one is making little progress.

slow motion ['slo 'mo ʃən] **1.** *n.* movement in a film or video image that appears slower than in real life. (No plural.) **2.** the *adj.* use of ①. (Hyphenated.)

slow someone or something **down** to cause someone or something to decrease speed or go slower.

slow up to go slower; to go more slowly in order for someone or something to catch up.

slower and slower at a decreasing rate of speed; slow and then even slower.

slug ['slʌg] **1.** *n.* a small, slimy creature, similar to a snail but without a shell. **2.** *n.* a hit or blow, especially with a closed fist. **3.** *tv.* to hit someone or something using one's closed fist.

sluggish ['slʌg ɪʃ] *adj.* moving slowly or without energy; not very active. (Adv: *sluggishly.*)

slum ['slʌm] *n.* a neighborhood where most of the people live in poverty.

slumber ['slʌm bɚ] **1.** *iv.* to sleep. **2.** *n.* sleep; deep rest.

slump ['slʌmp] **1.** *n.* a financial collapse; a sudden fall or decline. **2.** *iv.* to sink; to slouch. **3.** *iv.* [for a value] to sink lower. (Figurative on ②.)

slump over 1. [for someone] to collapse and fall over in a sitting position. **2.** to fall over heavily; to collapse and droop from an upright position.

slung ['slʌŋ] past tense and past participle of SLING.

slur ['slɚ] **1.** *tv.* to say something in a way that is not clear; to pronounce something in a way that is not clear. **2.** *n.* an insult.

slush ['slʌʃ] *n.* a mixture of snow and water; snow that has started to melt. (No plural.)

sly ['slaɪ] *adj.* sneaky; clever; able to do things secretly. (Adv: *slyly.* Comp: *slyer;* sup: *slyest.*)

smack ['smæk] **1.** *tv.* to hit someone or something, especially noisily; to strike someone or something noisily, as with an open hand or a flat object. **2.** *n.* the sound made when something is smacked as in ①.

smack-dab in the middle exactly in the middle.

small ['smɔl] **1.** *adj.* not large; less than average size or weight. (Comp: *smaller;* sup: *smallest.*) **2.** *adj.* little; slight; not a lot; having less than an average amount of something. (Comp: *smaller;* sup: *smallest.*) **3.** *adj.* [of letters] lowercase; [of letters] not capital.
→ a BIG FROG IN A SMALL POND
→ THANKFUL FOR SMALL BLESSINGS

small fry 1. *n.* a child; children. (Treated as singular or plural.) **2.** *adj.* unimportant; an unimportant person or thing; unimportant people or things.

small print *n.* the part of a document that is not easily noticed, often because of the smallness of the print, and that often contains important information.

small talk ['smɔl tɔk] *n.* unimportant conversation; conversation about things that are not important. (No plural.)

small-time *adj.* small; on a small scale.

smart ['smɑrt] **1.** *adj.* intelligent; not stupid; able to learn things quickly. (Comp: *smarter;* sup: *smartest.*) **2.** *adj.* showing a current style; in style; in fashion; trendy. (Adv: *smartly.* Comp: *smarter;* sup: *smartest.*) **3.** *iv.* to sting; to feel sharp pain; to cause sharp pain.
→ (AS) SMART AS A FOX

smash ['smæʃ] **1.** *tv.* to break something into tiny pieces noisily or violently. **2.** *iv.* to break into tiny pieces noisily or violently.

smash into something to bump or crash into something.

smash out of something to break [one's way] out of something.

smash something **in** to crush something inward; to make something collapse inward by striking it.

smash something **up** to break something up into pieces; to destroy something.

smash through something to break [one's way] through some sort of barrier.

smear ['smɪr] **1.** *tv.* to spread something on a surface, especially in a careless or messy fashion. **2.** *tv.* to ruin someone's reputation; to make someone look bad; to say bad things about someone. **3.** *n.* a stain; a mark made by wiping something on a surface.

a **smear campaign (against someone)** a campaign aimed at damaging someone's reputation by making accusations and spreading rumors.

smell ['smɛl] **1.** *n.* odor; something in the air, sensed with one's nose. (Plural only for types and instances.) **2.** *tv.* to sense something with the nose; to sense an odor or scent; to sense something that has an odor or scent. **3.** *iv.* to have a certain quality of scent or odor. **4.** *iv.* to stink; to have a bad smell.

smelly ['smɛl i] *adj.* having a bad or strong odor. (Comp: *smellier;* sup: *smelliest.*)

smile ['smaɪl] **1.** *n.* a facial expression where the ends of the mouth are turned up, indicating happiness, amusement, or a good mood. **2.** *iv.* to have ① on one's face; to look happy or pleased.
→ CRACK A SMILE

smile on someone or something to be favorable to someone or something.

smiling ['smaɪl ɪŋ] *adj.* having a smile; happy; cheerful. (Adv: *smilingly.*)

smock ['smɑk] *n.* a light covering that one wears over one's clothes to protect them from becoming dirty while working, especially as worn by a doctor, nurse, painter, etc.

smog ['smɑg] *n.* smoke and fog that are trapped in the air; a mixture of fumes and smoke that are trapped like fog over a place. (A combination of *smoke* and *fog.* No plural.)

smoke ['smok] **1.** *n.* a cloud of gas that can be seen in the air when something burns. (No plural.) **2.** *n.* an act or session of burning tobacco and inhaling the ①. (Informal.) **3.** *iv.* to give off ①; to release ① into the air. **4.** *iv.* to inhale and then exhale ① from burning tobacco. **5.** *tv.* to inhale ① of burning cigarettes, tobacco, etc., into the lungs. **6.** *tv.* to preserve food by exposing it to ① from burning wood.
→ GO UP IN SMOKE

smoking ['smok ɪŋ] **1.** *adj.* giving off smoke. **2.** *adj.* a word used to indicate that smoking is permitted.

smoky ['smok i] **1.** *adj.* [of air] full of smoke; tasting or smelling like smoke. (Comp: *smokier;* sup: *smokiest.*) **2.** *adj.* giving off more smoke than normal or expected. (Adv: *smokily.* Comp: *smokier;* sup: *smokiest.*)

smolder ['smol dɚ] *iv.* [for wood or other fibers] to burn or give off smoke without having a flame.

smoldering ['smol dɚ ɪŋ] *adj.* burning or giving off smoke without having a flame. (Adv: *smolderingly.*)

smooth ['smuð] **1.** *adj.* having an even surface; having a surface without bumps; not rough. (Adv: *smoothly.* Comp: *smoother;* sup: *smoothest.*) **2.** *adj.* gentle; not rough; calm; not harsh. (Adv:

smoothly. Comp: *smoother;* sup: *smoothest.*) **3.** *adj.* without lumps; having an even texture. (Adv: *smoothly.* Comp: *smoother;* sup: *smoothest.*) **4.** *tv.* to cause something to become ①; to cause something to become smoother.

smooth sailing progress made without any difficulty; an easy situation.

smooth something **down** to make something flat or smooth by pressing.

smooth something **out 1.** to flatten something or make it even by smoothing or pressing it. **2.** to polish and refine something. (Figurative.)

smother ['smʌð ɚ] **1.** *iv.* to die because one cannot get enough oxygen, especially because something is covering one's mouth; to suffocate. **2.** *tv.* to kill a living creature by preventing it from breathing. **3.** *tv.* to cover something with a thick layer of something.

smudge ['smʌdʒ] **1.** *n.* a dirty mark or stain; a smear. **2.** *tv.* to dirty something with a mark.

smug ['smʌg] *adj.* confident and pleased with oneself and one's abilities; too satisfied with oneself. (Adv: *smugly.* Comp: *smugger;* sup: *smuggest.*)

smuggle ['smʌg əl] *tv.* to bring something into or take something out of a country illegally.

smuggler ['smʌg lɚ] *n.* a criminal who brings something into or takes things from a country illegally.

smuggling ['smʌg lɪŋ] *n.* the illegal business of bringing something into or taking things out of a country. (No plural.)

snack ['snæk] **1.** *n.* food that is eaten between meals; a small amount of food. **2.** *iv.* to eat a small amount of food between meals.

snag ['snæg] **1.** *n.* a thread that is pulled away from where it belongs in a fabric. **2.** *n.* something that gets in the way; something that causes a problem in a plan or procedure. **3.** *tv.* to catch a piece of clothing or material by a thread.
→ HIT A SNAG

snail ['snel] *n.* a small, soft creature that has no limbs, has two small feelers, and lives in a hard, round shell.
→ AT A SNAIL'S PACE

snake ['snek] **1.** *n.* a long, thin reptile that has no limbs. **2.** *iv.* to move in twists and turns; to curve like ①. **3.** *tv.* to move something in twists and turns; to bend something into curves like the curves of ①.

snap ['snæp] **1.** *iv.* [for something] to make a sharp, popping sound, usually by breaking. **2.** *iv.* [for something that is pulled tight or is under pressure] to break suddenly. **3.** *tv.* to break something that is pulled tight or is under pressure. **4.** *tv.* to take a picture with a camera. **5.** *tv.* to close ⑧. **6.** *n.* the noise made when something SNAPS as in ① or ②; a quick, sudden, popping sound. **7.** *n.* a sudden breaking of something; the breaking of something that is pulled tight or is under pressure. **8.** *n.* a metallic or plastic fastener that closes firmly when pressed.

snap back (after something) to return to normal after an accident or similar event.

snap back (at someone) to give a sharp or angry response to someone.

snapshot ['snæp ʃɑt] *n.* a photograph; a picture taken with a camera.

snare ['snɛr] **1.** *tv.* to trap someone or something; to catch someone or something in a trap. **2.** *n.* a trap for catching animals.

snarl ['snɑrl] **1.** *iv.* to growl. **2.** *iv.* to become tangled. **3.** *n.* an angry growl.

snarling ['snɑr lɪŋ] *adj.* growling angrily.

snatch ['snætʃ] *tv.* to grab someone or something suddenly; to steal something or kidnap someone.

sneak ['snik] **1.** *iv., irreg.* to move quietly and secretly; to move without being noticed. (Past tense and past participle: *sneaked* or **SNUCK**.) **2.** *tv., irreg.* to obtain or take something, such as a taste, a look, a peek, a touch, etc., quietly and secretly.

sneak in(to someplace) to enter a place quietly and in secret, perhaps without a ticket or permission.

sneak out (of someplace) to go out of a place quietly and in secret.

sneak up on someone or something to approach someone or something quietly and in secret.

sneaker ['snik ɚ] *n.* one of a pair of gym shoes or tennis shoes; one of a pair of comfortable, casual canvas shoes with rubber soles.

sneaky ['snik i] *adj.* doing something dishonest or wrong, quietly and secretly. (*Adv: sneakily.* Comp: *sneakier;* sup: *sneakiest.*)

sneer ['snɪr] **1.** *iv.* to show contempt by the look on one's face. **2.** *n.* a look of contempt.

sneeze ['sniz] **1.** *n.* a sudden and uncontrollable burst of air and mucus that is pushed out of the nose and mouth. **2.** *iv.* to make ①.

snicker ['snɪk ɚ] **1.** *iv.* to laugh; to laugh at someone or something. **2.** *n.* a laugh; a small laugh.

sniff ['snɪf] **1.** *iv.* to breathe in through the nose in small, quick puffs that can be heard. **2.** *iv.* to become aware of a smell by SNIFFING as in ①. **3.** *n.* a small, quick breath made through the nose, made especially when smelling something.

snip ['snɪp] **1.** *tv.* to clip something; to cut something with scissors in short strokes; to cut something up into tiny pieces. **2.** *n.* a short cutting movement; a short stroke made with scissors.

snob ['snɑb] *n.* someone who displays arrogance; someone who acts superior to others.

snobbish ['snɑb ɪʃ] *adj.* arrogant; thinking that one is better than others. (*Adv: snobbishly.*)

snoop ['snup] *iv.* to sneak; to pry; to search through something without the owner's permission.

snoop around (something) to look around in a place, trying to find out something secret or learn about someone else's affairs.

snooze ['snuz] **1.** *iv.* to sleep; to nap. **2.** *n.* sleep; a nap. (Informal.)

snore ['snɔr] *iv.* to breathe loudly while sleeping, especially to pass air through the nose so that it vibrates and makes a loud noise.

snow ['sno] **1.** *n.* water vapor that has frozen into small white flakes that fall from the sky. (No plural.) **2.** *n.* an instance of ① falling from the sky; a coating of ① on the ground. **3.** *iv.* [for ①] to fall from the sky.
→ (AS) WHITE AS THE DRIVEN SNOW

snow blower ['sno blo ɚ] *n.* a machine that clears snow from walks and pavements.

snow someone or something in [for heavy snowfall] to block someone or something in a place.

snowball ['sno bɔl] **1.** *n.* a ball of snowflakes that have been pressed together. **2.** *iv.* to grow at a rapidly increasing rate. (Figurative on ①.)

snowbank ['sno bæŋk] *n.* a big, long mound of snow.

snowbound ['sno baʊnd] *adj.* not able to leave home or travel because there is too much snow.

snowdrift ['sno drɪft] *n.* a ridge of snow shaped by wind blowing it along the ground.

snowflake ['sno flek] *n.* one individual piece of snow; a drop of water that freezes and falls from the sky as snow.

snowman ['sno mæn] *n., irreg.* a mass of snow that has been shaped like a person. (Plural: SNOWMEN.)

snowmen ['sno mɛn] plural of SNOWMAN.

snowplow ['sno plaʊ] *n.* a tractor or other vehicle with a large scoop or blade in front to clear snow from roads, driveways, and other surfaces.

snowstorm ['sno stɔrm] *n.* a storm with lots of snow; a blizzard.

snuck ['snʌk] a past tense and past participle of SNEAK.

snug ['snʌg] **1.** *adj.* warm; cozy; comfortable. (Adv: *snugly.* Comp: *snugger;* sup: *snuggest.*) **2.** *adj.* too tight; fitting too closely. (Adv: *snugly.* Comp: *snugger;* sup: *snuggest.*)
→ (AS) SNUG AS A BUG IN A RUG

snuggle ['snʌg əl] *iv.* to cuddle; to press against someone for warmth or to show affection.

so ['so] **1.** *adv.* to a certain degree; to such a high degree; very. **2.** *adv.* in such a way; in that way; in this way. **3.** *adv.* also; too; as well. (Comes before the verbs BE, DO, or HAVE. In negative constructions, use NEITHER or *not either.*) **4.** *conj.* in order that; with the result that. **5.** *conj.* therefore; hence; consequently. **6.** *interj.* a mild exclamation of surprise or indignation. **7.** *adj.* true. (Not prenominal.)

so long as Go to AS LONG AS.

so quiet you could hear a pin drop Go to SO STILL YOU COULD HEAR A PIN DROP.

so soon early; before the regular time; ahead of schedule.

so still you could hear a pin drop AND **so quiet you could hear a pin drop** very quiet.

soak ['sok] **1.** *iv.* to remain in [a container of] liquid for a period of time. **2.** *tv.* to cause something to become or remain completely wet. **3.** *n.* a period of time spent in [a container of] liquid.

soak in(to something) [for moisture] to penetrate something.

soak something **off ((of)** something) to remove something, such as a label or surface soil, from something by soaking it in a liquid.

soak something **out (of** something) to remove something, such as a stain, from something by soaking in a liquid.

soak through something [for liquid] to work its way through something, such as cloth or paper.

soap ['sop] **1.** *n.* a substance that helps clean objects being washed. (Plural only for types and instances.) **2.** *tv.* to clean someone or something with ①; to cover someone or something with ① while washing.

soap opera ['sop ɑp rə] *n.* a daily or weekly television drama that usually revolves around the lives and problems of people in a certain family, town, or place of work.

soap someone or something **down** to cover someone or something thoroughly with soap or suds.

soapy ['so pi] *adj.* covered with soap. (Adv: *soapily.* Comp: *soapier;* sup: *soapiest.*)

soar ['sor] **1.** *iv.* to fly; to fly upward; to glide. **2.** *iv.* to increase suddenly and in a large amount; to go up suddenly and in a large amount. (Figurative on ①.)

sob ['sɑb] **1.** *iv.* to cry while breathing short, quick breaths. **2.** *n.* a short, quick sound made while one is crying.

sober ['sob ɚ] **1.** *adj.* not drunk; not having been drinking alcohol. (Adv: *soberly.* Comp: *soberer;* sup: *soberest.*) **2.** *adj.* very serious; with dignity. (Adv: *soberly.* Comp: *soberer;* sup: *soberest.*)
→ (AS) SOBER AS A JUDGE

sober someone **up 1.** to take actions that will cause a drunken person to become sober. **2.** to cause someone to face reality.

sober up to return to being sober after a drunken state.

soccer ['sɑk ɚ] *n.* a sport played by two teams of eleven people who move a round ball about a field. (In Europe, soccer is called *football.* No plural.)

social ['so ʃəl] **1.** *adj.* of or about friendship or interaction with other people. (Adv: *socially.*) **2.** *adj.* living together or forming groups in an organized way. (Adv: *socially.*)

social security ['so ʃəl sə 'kjɚ ə ti] **1.** *n.* a pension system operated by the government, making payments to people who have retired or to families of workers who have died. (No plural. Often capitalized.) **2.** the *adj.* use of ①.

society [sə 'sɑɪ ə ti] **1.** *n.* all people; all humans. (No plural.) **2.** *n.* all

people in a certain culture during a certain period of time. **3.** *n.* an organization whose members have similar interests or goals; a club. **4.** *n.* the upper-class people of a community; the community of people assumed to have good manners; people who are thought to be in an exclusive or desirable social class. (No plural.)
→ PAY ONE'S DEBT (TO SOCIETY)

sociology [so si 'al ə dʒi] *n.* the study of the functioning and organization of human society. (No plural.)

sock ['sak] *n.* a fabric covering for the foot, usually worn inside a shoe.

socket ['sak ət] *n.* **1.** one of a number of types of opening that something round fits into. **2.** an opening into which an electrical plug is put.

sod ['sad] *n.* turf; a piece of ground held together by the roots of grass. (No plural.)

soda ['so də] **1.** *n.* a soft drink; a drink with lots of little bubbles, usually sweetly flavored. (Short for SODA POP.) **2.** *n.* water containing lots of little bubbles, having little or no flavor. (Short for SODA WATER.)

soda pop ['so də pap] *n.* a SOFT DRINK; a bubbly drink that has no alcohol and is usually flavored and sweet. (Can be shortened to SODA or POP.)

soda water ['so də wɑ tə] *n.* water that has thousands of tiny bubbles in it. (Can be shortened to SODA.)

sofa ['so fə] *n.* a couch; a seat that is wide enough for more than one or two people.

soft ['sɔft] **1.** *adj.* not hard; yielding to pressure; less hard than average. (Adv: *softly.* Comp: *softer;* sup: *softest.*) **2.** *adj.* delicate; smooth; calm; not rough; not coarse; not harsh; gently affecting the senses. (Adv: *softly.* Comp: *softer;* sup: *softest.*) **3.** *adj.* not strong or strict; weak or lax. (Adv: *softly.* Comp: *softer;* sup: *softest.*) **4.** *adj.* [of water] lacking certain minerals and able to make lather from soap easily. (Comp: *softer;* sup: *softest.*) **5.** *adj.* [of a letter] pronounced like the *c* in *cent* rather than the *c* of *cold.* **6.** *adj.* quiet; not loud. (Adv: *softly.* See also ⑦. Comp: *softer;* sup: *softest.*) **7.** *adv.* quietly; not as loudly. (Comp: *softer;* sup: *softest.*)

soft drink ['sɔft drɪŋk] *n.* a carbonated drink without alcohol; POP; SODA; SODA POP; any refreshing drink that is a substitute for a drink containing alcohol.

softball ['sɔft bɔl] **1.** *n.* a game that is similar to baseball but uses a bigger, softer ball. (No plural.) **2.** *n.* a ball that is like a baseball but is bigger and somewhat softer. **3.** the *adj.* use of ①.
→ (AS) SOFT AS A BABY'S BOTTOM
→ HAVE A SOFT SPOT IN ONE'S HEART FOR SOMEONE OR SOMETHING

software ['sɔft wɛr] *n.* one or more computer programs meant to be used or stored on a computer. (No plural.)

soggy ['sɔg i] *adj.* moist; wet; soaked. (Adv: *soggily.* Comp: *soggier;* sup: *soggiest.*)

soil ['sɔɪl] **1.** *n.* the ground; the top layer of dirt that plants grow in. (Plural only for types and instances.) **2.** *tv.* to make something dirty.

soil one's **diaper(s)** [for a baby] to excrete waste into its diaper.

soil one's **hands** Go to GET ONE'S HANDS DIRTY.

soiled ['sɔɪld] *adj.* dirtied; made dirty.

sold ['sold] past tense and past participle of SELL.

sold out [of a product] completely sold with no more items remaining; [of a store] having no more of a particular product.

soldier ['sol dʒɚ] *n.* someone who serves or fights in an army, especially one who is not an officer.

sole ['sol] **1.** *adj.* only; [the] only [one]. (Adv: *solely.*) **2.** *n.* the bottom surface of the foot; the bottom part of a shoe, boot, or other piece of footwear. **3.** *n., irreg.* a flat, edible fish. (Plural: *sole.*) **4.** *n.* the edible flesh of ③. (No plural.) **5.** *tv.* to put a new SOLE as in ② on a shoe or boot.

solid ['sɑl ɪd] **1.** *n.* something that is hard and does not allow its shape to be changed easily; something that is not a liquid and not a gas. **2.** *adj.* not liquid or gas; having a shape that does not change on its own to fit a container. (Adv: *solidly.*) **3.** *adj.* not hollow; having an inside that is full of something. (Adv: *solidly.*) **4.** *adj.* [of a period

of time] continuous and not interrupted. (Adv: *solidly.* Before or after a noun.) **5.** *adj.* sturdy; well made; dependable; able to be relied on; strong; not likely to break, collapse, or fail. (Adv: *solidly.*)

solids *n.* food that is SOLID ② and not liquid. (Treated as plural.)

solo ['so lo] **1.** *n.* a musical piece performed by one person; a piece of music written primarily for one singer or one instrument. (Plural ends in -s.) **2.** *adj.* done alone; done without help. **3.** *adv.* without help; alone. **4.** *iv.* to perform by oneself; to do something by oneself.

solution [sə 'lu ʃən] **1.** *n.* an answer to a problem or question; a way to fix a problem. **2.** *n.* a liquid that has a solid or gas dissolved in it; a mixture of a liquid and a solid or gas that has been dissolved in the liquid.

solve ['sɑlv] *tv.* to find the answer to a question or a problem.

some ['sʌm] **1.** *adj.* [of a person or creature] unnamed or unknown. **2.** *adj.* a few; more than one, but not many. (Use ANY in negative statements or questions.) **3.** *adj.* [of something] excellent, exciting, or extreme. (Informal. Always stressed.) **4.** *n.* a number of people or things; a few people or things, but less than many. (No plural.)

somebody ['sʌm bɑd i] **1.** *pron.* some person; someone; a certain unnamed person. (Compare this with ANYBODY.) **2.** *n.* a famous or important person rather than just nobody. (Compare this with ANY-BODY.)

someday ['sʌm de] *adv.* at some time in the future.

somehow ['sʌm haʊ] *adv.* in some way; in some manner; in a way that is not yet known.

someone ['sʌm wən] *pron.* somebody; some person; a person; a certain unnamed person. (Compare this with ANYONE.)

someone **of note** a person who is famous.

someone's **affections** someone's expressions of love or caring.

someone's **attentions** someone's caring or attention that indicates a romantic interest.

someone's **next of kin** someone's closest living relative or relatives.

someone's **travels** *n.* [someone's] journeys or visits to other places, especially over a long period of time.

someone's **treat** *n.* someone's act of kindness in paying for someone else's meal or entertainment.

someplace ['sʌm ples] *adv.* SOME-WHERE; at, in, or to someplace. (Informal. SOMEWHERE is preferred by some people. Compare this with ANYPLACE.)

something ['sʌm θɪŋ] **1.** *pron.* some thing; a certain thing that is not known or named. (Compare this with ANYTHING.) **2.** *n.* a thing that is more than nothing. (Compare this with ANYTHING. No plural.) **3.** *adv.* somewhat; in some way. (E.g., *look something alike.*)

something **is the case** something is so; a condition is true; something is an actual event or state.

sometime ['sʌm taɪm] *adv.* at some point in time that is not known or stated.

sometimes *adv.* now and then; occasionally; from time to time.

somewhat ['sʌm ʍət] *adj.* rather; slightly; to some degree; kind of.

somewhere ['sʌm ʍɛr] *adv.* at, in, or to someplace. (Compare this with ANYWHERE.)

(somewhere) in the neighbor-hood of something approximately a particular measurement.

son ['sʌn] *n.* someone's male child; the male child of a parent. (Also used as a term of address by an older person to any boy or young man.)

song ['sɔŋ] **1.** *n.* a story or words that are set to music; words that are sung. **2.** *n.* singing; the art, practice, or action of singing. (No plural.) **3.** *n.* the musical noise that birds make.
→ BUY SOMETHING FOR A SONG
→ FOLK SONG
→ GO INTO ONE'S SONG AND DANCE ABOUT SOMETHING
→ SWAN SONG

songbird ['sɔŋ bɚd] *n.* any common bird with a characteristic song.

soon ['sun] *adv.* in a short period of time; before long; shortly. (Comp: *sooner;* sup: *soonest.*)
→ AS SOON AS
→ (AS) SOON AS POSSIBLE
→ SO SOON

soothe ['suð] **1.** *tv.* to calm someone or something; to comfort someone or something; to ease pain or discomfort. **2.** *iv.* to be a comfort; to be a relief.

soothing ['suð ɪŋ] *adj.* comforting; calming; relieving. (Adv: *soothingly.*)

soprano [sə 'præn o] **1.** *n.* someone, usually a woman, who sings the highest musical notes. (Plural ends in *-s.*) **2.** the *adj.* use of ①.

the **soprano** *n.* the musical part written for SOPRANO ①; the notes usually sung by SOPRANO ①. (No plural. Treated as singular.)

sorcerer ['sɔrs ə rɚ] *n.* a male magician who contacts evil spirits.

sorcery ['sɔr sə ri] *n.* magic practiced with the help of evil spirits. (No plural.)

sore ['sɔr] **1.** *adj.* in a state of hurting; painful; aching. (Adv: *sorely.* Comp: *sorer;* sup: *sorest.*) **2.** *n.* a painful infection or injury on the skin.

sorrow ['sɑr o] **1.** *n.* sadness; grief. **2.** *n.* a cause of sadness, grief, or misfortune.
→ DROWN ONE'S SORROWS
→ SHARE SOMEONE'S SORROW

sorry ['sɑr i] **1.** *adj.* expressing an apology. (Not prenominal. Comp: *sorrier;* sup: *sorriest.*) **2.** *adj.* sad; feeling pity; wishing that something had happened differently. (Not prenominal. Comp: *sorrier;* sup: *sorriest.*) **3.** *adj.* regretful; wishing that one had acted differently. (Not prenominal. Comp: *sorrier;* sup: *sorriest.*) **4.** *adj.* not adequate or acceptable. (Only prenominal. Comp: *sorrier;* sup: *sorriest.*)

sort ['sɔrt] **1.** *n.* a kind; a category; a group of similar persons, things, or qualities. **2.** *tv.* to put things in a particular order; to arrange things by category; to separate things by category.

sort something **out 1.** to sort something; to arrange according to class or category. **2.** to study a problem and figure it out.

sought ['sɔt] past tense and past participle of SEEK.

soul ['sol] **1.** *n.* the part of a human that is said to be separate from the body (and that some religions believe never dies); the part of the body that controls emotion and thought; the spirit. **2.** *n.* a person; a human being. **3.** *n.* the force or spirit that gives something depth or meaning. (Figurative on ①.)
→ EVERY LIVING SOUL
→ KEEP BODY AND SOUL TOGETHER
→ NOT TELL A SOUL
→ WITH ALL ONE'S HEART AND SOUL

sound ['sɑʊnd] **1.** *n.* a property of vibrating air that can stimulate the ears and be heard. (No plural.) **2.** *n.* a noise; vibrations that stimulate the ears. **3.** *n.* a narrow channel of water that connects two larger bodies of water. **4.** *tv.* to cause something to make a noise; to cause something to be heard. **5.** *iv.* to make a characteristic noise. **6.** *iv.* to be heard in a certain way. **7.** *adj.* [of sleep] deep. (Adv: *soundly.*) **8.** *adj.* healthy; not damaged or injured; in good condition. **9.** *adj.* strong; sturdy; safe. (Adv: *soundly.* Comp: *sounder;* sup: *soundest.*) **10.** *adj.* sane; logical; reasonable; well reasoned; using good sense or judgment.

(Adv: *soundly*. Comp: *sounder;* sup: *soundest*.)
→ LET OUT A SOUND
→ SAFE AND SOUND

sound like something to seem like something.

sound off to call out one's name or one's number in a sequence.

sound off (about something**)** to complain loudly about something; to make a fuss over something.

soup ['sup] *n.* a liquid food that is made by boiling meat, fish, vegetables, or other foods. (Plural only for types and instances.)
→ (AS) EASY AS DUCK SOUP
→ (AS) THICK AS PEA SOUP
→ EVERYTHING FROM SOUP TO NUTS

sour ['saʊ ɚ] **1.** *adj.* tasting like an acid; having a taste like lemons; not sweet, salty, or bitter. (Adv: *sourly*. Comp: *sourer;* sup: *sourest*.) **2.** *adj.* [of milk] spoiled. (Adv: *sourly*. Comp: *sourer;* sup: *sourest*.) **3.** *adj.* unpleasant; disagreeable. (Adv: *sourly*. Comp: *sourer;* sup: *sourest*.) **4.** *iv.* [for milk] to become ②.
→ HIT A SOUR NOTE
→ STRIKE A SOUR NOTE

source ['sors] *n.* the origin of something; the place where something comes from.

south ['saʊθ] **1.** *n.* the direction to the right of someone or something facing east. (No plural.) **2.** *n.* the part of a region, country, or planet located toward ①. (No plural. Capitalized when referring to a region of the United States.) **3.** *adj.* to ①; toward ①; facing ①, located in ②. **4.** *adj.* coming from

①, especially used to describe wind. **5.** *adv.* toward ①.

south pole ['saʊθ 'pol] **1.** *n.* the point in the Antarctic that is as far south as it is possible to go. **2.** *n.* the actual location of ①. (Capitalized.)

southeast [saʊθ 'ist] **1.** *n.* the direction halfway between south and east. (No plural.) **2.** *n.* an area in the southeast part of a region or country. (Capitalized when referring to a region of the United States.) **3.** *adj.* located in the ②; toward ①; facing ①. **4.** *adj.* from ①, especially describing wind. **5.** *adv.* toward ①.

southeastern [saʊθ 'is tɚn] *adj.* in the southeast; toward the southeast; facing the southeast.

southern ['sʌð ɚn] **1.** *adj.* in the south; toward the south; facing south. **2.** *adj.* from the SOUTH ①, especially describing wind. **3.** *adj.* concerning the society and culture of the American South. (Often capitalized.)

southerner ['sʌð ɚ nɚ] *n.* someone who lives in the southern part of a country, especially someone from the southern United States. (Sometimes capitalized.)

southwest [saʊθ 'wɛst] **1.** *n.* the direction halfway between south and west. (No plural.) **2.** *n.* the southwestern part of a region or a country. (No plural. Capitalized when referring to a region of the United States.) **3.** *adj.* located in ①; toward ①; facing ①. **4.** *adj.* from ①, especially describing wind. **5.** *adv.* toward ①.

southwestern [sɑʊθ 'wɛs tə˞n] *adj.* in the southwest; toward the southwest; facing the southwest.

souvenir [su və 'nɪr] *n.* something that reminds one of someplace, someone, or one's travels; a keepsake.

sow 1. ['so] *tv., irreg.* to drop or toss seed on the ground; to plant crops by scattering seed on the ground. (Past participle: SOWN or *sowed*.) **2.** ['so] *iv., irreg.* to plant [crops] by scattering seed on the ground. **3.** ['sɑʊ] *n.* a female pig.
→ MAKE A SILK PURSE OUT OF A SOW'S EAR

sow one's **wild oats** to do wild and foolish things in one's youth.

sown ['son] a past participle of SOW.

space ['spes] **1.** *n.* every location in existence in the universe. (No plural.) **2.** *n.* OUTER SPACE; every place past the air surrounding the earth. (No plural.) **3.** *n.* a place or area that has length, width, and depth; a place where there is room for someone or something to be. (No plural.) **4.** *n.* a blank line or empty box on a piece of paper where something is to be written. **5.** *n.* an empty place between two words in a written or printed line. **6.** *tv.* to place things with distance between them.
→ OUTER SPACE

spacecraft AND **spaceship** ['spes kræft, 'spes ʃɪp] *n., irreg.* a rocket or vehicle that travels in space. (Plural: *spacecraft* and *spaceships*.)

spaceship Go to SPACECRAFT.

spade ['sped] **1.** *n.* a tool, similar to a small shovel, used for digging.

2. *n.* the black symbol (♠) found on playing cards; one of the four suits found on playing cards. **3.** *tv.* to dig something with ①.
→ CALL A SPADE A SPADE

spaghetti [spə 'gɛt i] *n.* long, thin, (often dried) sticks made of a flour and water mixture, which are boiled and then eaten as food; long sticks of pasta. (No plural.)

spare ['spɛr] **1.** *adj.* surplus; extra; free; not needed. **2.** *adj.* extra; saved in case of emergency; reserved for emergency use; kept for emergency use. **3.** *n.* something that is extra and not immediately needed. **4.** *n.* an extra tire that is kept in a vehicle in case a tire loses its air. **5.** *tv.* not to permit someone to undergo punishment or execution. **6.** *tv.* to be able to give time, money, or energy.
→ HAVE SOMETHING TO SPARE
→ IN ONE'S SPARE TIME
→ NOT A MOMENT TO SPARE
→ WITHOUT A MOMENT TO SPARE

spare someone something to exempt someone from having to listen to or experience something.

sparrow ['spɛr o] *n.* a common, small, brown bird.

sparse ['spɑrs] *adj.* scattered; not having many people or things in a certain area; not dense; having a very small amount of people or things in an area. (Adv: *sparsely*. Comp: *sparser*; sup: *sparsest*.)

spat ['spæt] **1.** a past tense and past participle of SPIT. **2.** *n.* an argument; a quarrel; a disagreement.

speak ['spik] **1.** *tv., irreg.* to say something; to utter something; to express one's thoughts in words.

(Past tense: SPOKE; past participle: SPOKEN.) **2.** *tv., irreg.* to use a language; to know how to talk in a language. **3.** *iv., irreg.* to talk; to say words.

speak for themselves Go to SPEAKS FOR ITSELF.

speak ill of someone to say something bad about someone.

speak of the devil a phrase said when someone whose name has just been mentioned appears or is heard from.

speak out to speak loudly; to speak to be heard.

speak out (about someone or something**)** to express oneself about someone or something; to tell what one knows about someone or something.

speak out (against someone or something**)** to speak negatively and publicly about someone or something; to reveal something negative, in speech, about someone or something.

speak the same language [for people] to have similar ideas, tastes, etc.

speak up to speak loudly.

speak up for someone or something to speak in favor of someone or something; to come forward and express favorable things about someone or something.

speak with a forked tongue to tell lies; to try to deceive someone.

speaker ['spik ɚ] **1.** *n.* someone who speaks; someone who makes speeches; someone who speaks a particular language. **2.** *n.* the Speaker of the U.S. House of Rep-

resentatives; the presiding officer in the U.S. House of Representatives; the representative of the majority party in the House who has the most seniority. (Capitalized.) **3.** *n.* a device that reproduces sound, as found in a stereo, television, computer, etc.

speaks for itself AND **speak for themselves** to have an obvious meaning; not to need explaining; to need no explanation.

special ['spɛ ʃəl] **1.** *adj.* not ordinary; not regular; set apart from other things, especially for a particular purpose or reason. (Adv: *specially*.) **2.** *n.* something that is set apart from other things, especially for a particular purpose or reason; a unique offering. **3.** *n.* the offering of something for sale at a price that is ①.

specific [spə 'sɪf ɪk] *adj.* particular; certain; definite; precise; exact. (Adv: *specifically* […ɪk li].)

specifics *n.* the details and facts of a matter. (Treated as singular.)

spectacle ['spɛk tə kəl] *n.* something to be viewed; something to be seen; a display; a scene.

spectacles *n.* EYEGLASSES. (Old-fashioned. Treated as plural. Number is expressed with *pair(s) of spectacles*.)

spectator ['spɛk te tɚ] *n.* someone who watches something but does not take part in it.

speculation [spɛk jə 'le ʃən] **1.** *n.* guessing; trying to determine something, especially without knowing all of the facts. (Plural only for types and instances.) **2.** *n.*

an investment in a risky business venture.

sped ['spɛd] past tense and past participle of SPEED.

speech ['spitʃ] **1.** *n.* the production of words by talking. (No plural.) **2.** *n.* a lecture; a formal talk to a group of listeners.
→ PART OF SPEECH

speed ['spid] **1.** *iv., irreg.* to move fast; to go fast, especially to go faster than the legal limit. (Past tense and past participle: SPED.) **2.** *tv., irreg.* to cause something to go or move fast; to cause something to go or move faster. **3.** *n.* the rate at which someone or something moves or does something during a period of time. (Plural only for types and instances.) **4.** *n.* rapid movement; the quickness with which someone or something moves. (No plural.)

speed limit ['spid lɪm ət] *n.* the legal maximum speed that a vehicle is permitted to travel; the fastest speed that a driver can operate a vehicle under the law on a particular road.

speed someone or something **up** to cause someone or something to move faster.

speed up to go faster.

speedboat ['spid bot] *n.* a small boat that has a powerful engine that can be driven at high speeds, especially for pleasure on lakes and rivers.

spell ['spɛl] **1.** *tv., irreg.* to say or write the letters of a word in the right order. (Past tense and past participle: *spelled* or, less fre-

quently, SPELT.) **2.** *tv., irreg.* [for letters] to signify a word. **3.** *iv., irreg.* to know how to say or write the letters of many words; to be able to SPELL words as in ①.

spelt ['spɛlt] a past tense and past participle of SPELL.

spend ['spɛnd] **1.** *tv., irreg.* to pay an amount of money for something that one buys. (Past tense and past participle: SPENT.) **2.** *tv., irreg.* to pass time; to use time or energy; to consume energy.

spendthrift ['spɛnd θrɪft] *n.* someone who wastes money; someone who spends too much money.

spent ['spɛnt] **1.** past tense and past participle of SPEND. **2.** *adj.* exhausted.

sphere ['sfir] **1.** *n.* a perfectly round object; a globe; a ball. **2.** *n.* the area or domain where someone or something has an influence or an effect; the place or environment in which someone or something exists or acts.

spherical ['sfɛr ɪ kəl] *adj.* shaped like a sphere. (Adv: *spherically* [...ɪk li].)

spice ['spɑɪs] **1.** *n.* an herb or other vegetable fiber or seed that tastes or smells unique and is used to give extra flavor to food. **2.** *n.* something that adds excitement or flavor. (Figurative on ①. No plural.) **3.** *tv.* to season or flavor food with ①.

spice something **up 1.** to make some food more spicy. **2.** to make something more interesting, lively, or sexy. (Figurative.)

spicy ['spaɪs i] **1.** *adj.* flavored with spices; seasoned with spices; having a sharp flavor. (Adv: *spicily.* Comp: *spicier;* sup: *spiciest.*) **2.** *adj.* somewhat vulgar; slightly sexually oriented. (Adv: *spicily.* Comp: *spicier;* sup: *spiciest.*)

spider ['spaɪ dɚ] *n.* a small creature with eight legs whose body produces a silk thread that it uses to make a web, which is then used to trap insects, which it eats.

spike ['spaɪk] **1.** *n.* a large, thick, metal nail that comes to a sharp point. **2.** *n.* a pointed metal or plastic object on the bottom of a shoe that gives the wearer extra traction. (Also called a *cleat.*) **3.** *n.* a sharp peak on a graph; an increase that can be represented as a peak on a graph.

spill ['spɪl] **1.** *tv., irreg.* to cause something, especially a liquid, to pour from a container by accident; to cause something, especially a liquid, to fall. (Past tense and past participle: *spilled* or, less frequently, SPILT.) **2.** *iv., irreg.* [for something, especially a liquid] to fall or be poured from a container by accident. **3.** *n.* something, especially a liquid, that has fallen or been poured from a container by accident. **4.** *n.* a fall from something.
→ CRY OVER SPILLED MILK

spill the beans Go to LET THE CAT OUT OF THE BAG.

spilt ['spɪlt] a past tense and past participle of SPILL.

spin ['spɪn] **1.** *iv., irreg.* to turn around in circles quickly. (Past tense and past participle: SPUN. *Spinned* is often heard.) **2.** *iv., irreg.* to rotate on an axis. **3.** *iv., irreg.* [for one's surroundings] to seem to revolve. **4.** *iv., irreg.* to pull and twist, making thread or yarn from wool, cotton, or other fibers. **5.** *tv., irreg.* to cause someone or something to turn around in circles quickly. **6.** *tv., irreg.* to pull and twist fibers into thread or yarn. **7.** *tv., irreg.* [for a spider] to make a web. **8.** *tv., irreg.* to create a tale, story, or lie. **9.** *n.* a short trip in or on a vehicle.
→ MAKE SOMEONE'S HEAD SPIN
→ PUT A SPIN ON SOMETHING

spin a yarn to tell a tale.

spin off [for something] to part and fly away from something that is spinning; [for something] to detach or break loose from something.

spinach ['spɪn ɪtʃ] **1.** *n.* a leafy, green vegetable. (No plural.) **2.** *adj.* made of or with ①.

spine ['spaɪn] **1.** *n.* the column of bones and the nerves within it that are at the center of the back of humans and certain other animals. **2.** *n.* any long, narrow, stiff thing that provides support, such as the side of a cover of a book where the pages are attached. (Figurative on ①.) **3.** *n.* a stiff, pointed growth as found on certain plants and animals, providing protection.

spire ['spaɪɚ] *n.* the top part of a steeple; the top part of a structure on top of a building that comes to a point.

spirit ['spɪr ɪt] **1.** *n.* the part of a human that is separate from the body (and that some religions believe never dies); the part of the body that controls emotion and intellect; the soul. **2.** *n.* a being that does not have a body; a ghost. **3.** *n.* the driving force of something; something that provides energy or force to something; zeal. (Figurative on ①. No plural.)

spirits *n.* strong drink containing alcohol.

spit ['spɪt] **1.** *iv., irreg.* to expel the natural fluid from one's mouth; to push fluid out of one's mouth. (Past tense and past participle: *spit* or SPAT.) **2.** *tv., irreg.* to expel something from one's mouth; to push something out of one's mouth. **3.** *n.* fluid or mucus that comes from someone's mouth. (No plural.) **4.** *n.* a thin rod with a sharp end that food is pushed onto so that it can be roasted over a fire.

spite ['spaɪt] *n.* a desire to annoy someone else or get revenge; malice. (No plural.)
→ CUT OFF ONE'S NOSE TO SPITE ONE'S FACE
→ IN SPITE OF SOMEONE OR SOMETHING
→ OUT OF SPITE

splash ['splæʃ] **1.** *iv.* [for liquid] to scatter in many drops; [for liquid] to fall and spread in waves. **2.** *tv.* to cause a liquid to scatter in many drops or waves. **3.** *n.* an instance of a liquid scattering as in ①, and the sound that goes with it.

splatter ['splæt ɚ] **1.** *iv.* to splash, especially in a careless, clumsy, or messy way. **2.** *tv.* to splash a liquid, especially in a careless, clumsy, or messy way.

spleen ['splin] *n.* an organ in the body, near the stomach, that filters the blood and destroys old, used blood cells.
→ VENT ONE'S SPLEEN ON SOMEONE OR SOMETHING

splendid ['splɛn dɪd] *adj.* excellent; very good; brilliant; wonderful; super. (Adv: *splendidly.*)

splice ['splaɪs] **1.** *tv.* to fasten the ends of two pieces of something together by weaving, taping, or otherwise connecting them. **2.** *n.* a joint or connection that has been made by weaving, taping, or otherwise connecting the ends of two pieces of something.

splint ['splɪnt] *n.* a flat object that is secured to a person's finger, toe, or limb in order to give support or to keep a broken bone in place.

splinter ['splɪn tɚ] **1.** *n.* a sliver; a thin, sharp broken-off piece of wood, glass, or some other material. **2.** *adj.* [of a group of people] separated from a larger group of people. (Prenominal only.) **3.** *iv.* to separate from a larger object or group; to break into smaller pieces or groups. **4.** *tv.* to break something into ①.

split ['splɪt] **1.** *tv., irreg.* to separate something into sections, layers, or groups; to divide something into sections, layers, or groups. (Past tense and past participle: *split.*) **2.** *tv., irreg.* to cut something along its length. **3.** *tv., irreg.* to share something among members of a group; to divide something among members of a group. **4.** *iv., irreg.* [for people or things] to separate into sections, layers, or groups. **5.** *iv., irreg.* [for something] to break or tear open along its length.

6. *n.* the crack, cut, or break made by breaking or cutting something, as in ②. **7.** *n.* a separation within a group. **8.** *adj.* separated; divided; cut from end to end.
→ VOTE A SPLIT TICKET

split off (from something**)** to separate away from something; to sever connection with and separate from something.

split people up to separate two or more people.

split someone or something **up (into** something**)** to divide people or things up into something, such as groups.

split something **off ((of)** something**)** to sever connection with something and separate.

split the difference to divide the difference between two amounts (with someone else).

spoil ['spɔɪl] **1.** *iv.* to become rotten; to rot; to decay. **2.** *tv.* to ruin something; to destroy something; to make something so that it can no longer be used. **3.** *tv.* to treat someone too well; to raise a child without discipline.

spoke ['spok] past tense of SPEAK.

spoken ['spok ən] Past participle of SPEAK.

sponge ['spʌndʒ] **1.** *n.* any of a group of small animals that live in the water, attach themselves to underwater objects, and form a soft, flexible skeleton. **2.** *n.* the soft skeleton of ① used for cleaning or the absorption of liquids, or an artificial substance having the same qualities.
→ THROW IN THE SPONGE

sponge someone or something **down** to remove the [excess] moisture from someone or something.

sponge something **away** to absorb, wipe up, or wipe away something.

sponsor ['spɑn sɚ] **1.** *n.* someone or an organization that supports and guides another person or organization. **2.** *n.* someone who assumes responsibility for creating or developing something. **3.** *n.* a business that advertises during a radio or television program. **4.** *tv.* to support someone or an organization, usually with money, often for the sake of publicity.

spool ['spul] *n.* something that thread, film, wire, etc., can be wound around.

spoon ['spun] **1.** *n.* a utensil that is made of a small, shallow oval bowl at the end of a handle, used for serving food, stirring drinks, and eating liquids and soft foods. **2.** *tv.* to move something to a place with ①.
→ BORN WITH A SILVER SPOON IN ONE'S MOUTH

spoon-feed someone to treat someone with too much care or help; to teach someone with methods that are too easy and do not stimulate the learner to independent thinking.

sport ['sport] **1.** *n.* competition and physical activity as found in games and some outdoor activities. (No plural.) **2.** *n.* a particular game involving physical activity and competition.

a sporting chance a reasonably good chance.

sports car ['sports kɑr] *n.* a kind of expensive, stylish, small car, which can go very fast.

sportsman ['sports mən] *n., irreg.* a man who participates in sports events or various outdoor activities. (Plural: SPORTSMEN.)

sportsmen ['sports mən] plural of SPORTSMAN.

sporty ['spor ti] *adj.* stylish; in fashion. (Adv: *sportily.* Comp: *sportier;* sup: *sportiest.*)

spot ['spɑt] **1.** *n.* a part (typically round) of a surface that is a different color from the rest of the surface. **2.** *n.* a mark, as might be left by blood, paint, food, etc.; a dirty mark. **3.** *n.* a specific location; a place; a position. **4.** *tv.* to recognize someone or something; to happen to see someone or something.
→ HAVE A SOFT SPOT IN ONE'S HEART FOR SOMEONE OR SOMETHING
→ HIT THE SPOT
→ IN A (TIGHT) SPOT
→ ON THE SPOT
→ ROOTED TO THE SPOT

spotless ['spɑt ləs] *adj.* totally clean; without spots. (Adv: *spotlessly.*)

spotlight ['spɑt laɪt] **1.** *n.* a spot or disk of strong, bright light. **2.** *n.* a lamp that produces a circle of strong, bright light. **3.** *n.* something that is the focus of public attention. **4.** *tv.* to place someone or something in the focus of attention.
→ STEAL THE SPOTLIGHT

spouse ['spaʊs] *n.* a husband; a wife.

spout ['spaʊt] **1.** *n.* the opening of something from which a liquid comes out. **2.** *tv.* to push out something, especially a liquid; to force a liquid out, especially through a narrow pipe or tube. **3.** *iv.* to flow into, out of, from, through, down, or onto someone or something.

sprain ['spreɪn] **1.** *tv.* to twist a joint in the body in a way that causes injury or pain. **2.** *n.* a joint that has been twisted in a way that causes injury or pain.

sprang ['spræŋ] past tense of SPRING.

spray ['spreɪ] **1.** *tv.* to direct a stream of small drops of liquid onto a surface. **2.** *tv.* to coat a surface with a stream of small drops of liquid. **3.** *n.* liquid that is pushed through the air in small drops, especially under pressure.

spread ['sprɛd] **1.** *iv., irreg.* to move outward; to become longer, wider, or broader; to extend to a larger or to the largest area possible; to expand. (Past tense and past participle: *spread.*) **2.** *iv., irreg.* to be passed on to many people. **3.** *tv., irreg.* to pass along something to many people. **4.** *tv., irreg.* to stretch something out; to cause something to become longer, wider, or broader. **5.** *tv., irreg.* to apply something onto something else by moving it around, making an even layer.

spread it on thick Go to LAY IT ON THICK.

spread like wildfire to spread rapidly and without control.

spread oneself **too thin** to do so many things that one can do none of them well; to spread one's efforts or attention too widely.

spread out to separate and distribute over a wide area.

spread something **on(to** something**)** to distribute a coating of something onto something.

spread something **out** to open, unfold, or lay something over a wider area.

spree ['spri] **1.** *n.* a session of wild drinking, spending, or partying. **2.** *n.* a period of activity and action.

spring ['sprɪŋ] **1.** *n.* the season of the year between winter and summer. **2.** *n.* a natural source of water from the ground; a place where water comes out of the earth. **3.** *n.* a metal coil; a metal object that is wound in the shape of a coil. **4.** *iv., irreg.* to jump; to leap. (Past tense: SPRANG or SPRUNG; past participle: SPRUNG.) **5.** *iv., irreg.* [for ③] to fail and lose its elastic property. **6.** the *adj.* use of ①.
→ NO SPRING CHICKEN

spring up to appear or develop suddenly; to sprout, as with a seedling.

sprout ['spraʊt] **1.** *iv.* [for a plant] to bud; [for a plant] to start growing leaves, flowers, or buds; [for a plant] to grow from a seed. **2.** *tv.* to grow something, such as a leaf or branch. **3.** *n.* new growth; a new bud, leaf, flower, or stem.

spruce ['sprus] **1.** *n.* a type of pine tree having short needles. **2.** *n.* the wood of ①. (No plural.)

spruce someone or something **up** **1.** to tidy up and groom someone or something. **2.** to refurbish or renew someone or something.

spruce up to make oneself or a place neat or clean.

sprung ['sprʌŋ] Past participle of SPRING; a past tense of SPRING.

spun ['spʌn] past tense and past participle of SPIN.

spur ['spɚ] **1.** *n.* a sharp object worn on the heel of a boot, used to make a horse that one is riding go faster. **2.** *n.* a highway or railroad track that branches from the main one. **3.** *tv.* to poke a horse with ①.
→ ON THE SPUR OF THE MOMENT

spy ['spaɪ] **1.** *n.* someone whose job is to secretly watch other people, organizations, or governments in order to learn information. **2.** *tv.* to see something; to discover something by sight; to secretly watch other people, organizations, or governments in order to learn information.

squad ['skwɑd] *n.* a group of people who work together or who have been trained together for a job; a group of 11 soldiers and a leader who work together.

square ['skwɛr] **1.** *n.* a shape made with four sides that are the same length and four right angles. **2.** *n.* a four-sided area in a city surrounded by streets or buildings. **3.** *n.* an L-shaped or T-shaped tool, used for drawing and measuring right angles. **4.** *n.* a number that is the product of a number multiplied by itself. **5.** *adj.* shaped like ①. (Adv: *squarely.*) **6.** *adj.* forming a right angle; forming a 90-degree angle. (Adv: *squarely.*) **7.** *adj.* [of an area] roughly equal in size and shape to ① that has sides of the requested or demanded length. (Follows the measurement of length.) **8.** *adj.* [of an area shaped like ①] having four sides of a certain length. (A square inch is the area measured by a square that is one inch long and one inch wide. Adv: *squarely.*) **9.** *adj.* having no debts; having settled all debts. **10.** *tv.* to multiply a number by itself. **11.** *tv.* to make something ⑥.

square deal a fair and honest transaction; fair treatment. (Informal.)

square meal *n.* a meal that is complete and balanced.

a **square peg in a round hole** a misfit; someone who does not seem to belong in a situation.

square up to someone or something to face someone or something bravely; to tackle someone or something.

square up with someone to pay someone what one owes; to pay one's share of something to someone. (Informal.)

squash something **down** to crush something down; to pack something down.

squat ['skwɑt] **1.** *iv.* to crouch; to rest, sitting with one's feet on the ground and one's legs bent under one's body. **2.** *adj.* shorter or

thicker than normal or expected. (Adv: *squatly.* Comp: *squatter;* sup: *squattest.*)

squawk ['skwɔk] **1.** *n.* a loud, harsh noise, especially one made by a bird. **2.** *iv.* to make a loud, harsh noise.

squeak ['skwik] **1.** *n.* a short, soft, high-pitched noise. **2.** *iv.* to make a short, soft, high-pitched noise.

squeak by (someone or something) **1.** to manage just to squeeze past someone or something. **2.** to manage just to get past a barrier represented by a person or thing, such as a teacher or an examination.

squeak something **through** to manage just to get something accepted or approved.

squeak through (something) **1.** to manage just to squeeze through an opening. **2.** to manage just to get past a barrier, such as an examination or interview.

squeal ['skwil] **1.** *n.* a loud, shrill noise or cry. **2.** *iv.* to make ①.

squeeze ['skwiz] **1.** *tv.* to press something with force. **2.** *tv.* to force the liquid from something by pressing it.

squeeze someone or something **up** to press people or things close together.

squeeze (themselves) **up** [for people] to press themselves closely together.

squint ['skwɪnt] **1.** *tv.* to close one's eyes almost all the way when looking at someone or something. **2.** *iv.* to have one's eyes almost closed because the light is so bright.

squirm ['skwɚm] *iv.* to move around uncomfortably; to writhe.

squirm out (of something) **1.** to crawl or wiggle out of something. **2.** to escape doing something; to escape the responsibility for having done something.

squirrel ['skwɚ əl] *n.* a rodent that lives in trees and has a large, bushy tail.

squirt ['skwɚt] **1.** *tv.* to force liquid through the air in a stream; to cause liquid to stream through the air. **2.** *tv.* to hit someone or something with a stream of liquid. **3.** *n.* a short stream of liquid that is sent through the air.

stab ['stæb] **1.** *tv.* to thrust a pointed object into someone or something. **2.** *n.* a thrust of a pointed object. **3.** *n.* a sharp, painful feeling.

stab someone **in the back** to betray someone.

stabilize ['steb ə laɪz] **1.** *tv.* to make something steady; to fix something in place; to keep something from moving or changing. **2.** *iv.* to become steady; to be fixed in place.

stable ['steb əl] **1.** *adj.* unlikely to fall, move, or shake; steady; firm. (Adv: *stably.*) **2.** *adj.* not likely to change; constant; permanent. (Adv: *stably.*) **3.** *n.* a building where horses are kept.

stack ['stæk] **1.** *n.* an orderly pile of something; a neat pile of something. **2.** *tv.* to place things in a neat, orderly pile; to arrange things into a neat, orderly pile.

stack something **up** to make a stack of some things.

stack up [for something] to accumulate, as in stacks. (Often used in reference to vehicular traffic.)

stadium ['sted i əm] *n.* a playing field surrounded by rows of seats for spectators.

staff ['stæf] **1.** *n.* the workers who operate and manage an organization. (Plural but treat as singular.) **2.** *n.* a large, heavy stick used for support; a large cane. **3.** *tv.* to provide something with enough workers so that a job can be done properly. **4.** *tv.* [for workers] to provide services for a task.

stage ['stedʒ] **1.** *n.* a period of development; one part of a process. **2.** *n.* the floor, usually raised, in a theater where performers perform. **3.** *tv.* to produce a play at a theater; to put on a play. **4.** *tv.* to plan and do something that attracts public attention.
→ AT THIS STAGE (OF THE GAME)

the **stage** *n.* theater; the business of producing and acting in live theater. (No plural. Treated as singular.)

stain ['sten] **1.** *tv.* to change or add to the color of something; to make something dirty by changing its color. **2.** *tv.* to coat a wooden surface with a liquid that gives it a color. **3.** *tv.* to color tissue or an organism so it can be observed or identified. **4.** *iv.* [for a substance] to have the ability to change the color of something permanently. **5.** *n.* a mark, spot, or flaw. **6.** *n.* a liquid that is used to give color to wood. (Plural only for types and instances.)

stair ['stɛr] *n.* a step or series of steps that go from one level to another. (Usually plural.)

staircase ['stɛr kes] *n.* a set of stairs that allows one to go from one level of a building to another; a stairway.

stairway ['stɛr we] *n.* a set of stairs that allow one to go from one level of a building to another; a staircase.

stake ['stek] *n.* a pointed piece of wood or plastic that is driven into the ground.
→ BURN SOMEONE AT THE STAKE
→ PULL UP STAKES

stake someone **out (on** someone**)** to assign someone to watch someone or to spy on someone.

stake something **off** to mark out the boundaries of an area of land with stakes.

stakes *n.* the amount of money bet in a game; the amount of risk involved in some activity. (Treated as plural, but not countable.)

stale ['stel] *adj.* no longer fresh. (Adv: *stalely.* Comp: *staler;* sup: *stalest.*)

stalk ['stɔk] **1.** *n.* the main stem of a plant, which is connected to the roots, and from which leaves grow. **2.** *tv.* to pursue or approach an animal or a person without being seen or heard.

stalk in(to someplace**)** to stride into a place, perhaps indignantly.

stalk out of someplace to stride out of a place indignantly.

stall ['stɔl] **1.** *n.* a small, enclosed space. **2.** *n.* a space within a barn or stable for one animal, especially a horse. **3.** *n.* a booth in a market, or in a building with an open wall in front, where products are sold. **4.** *iv.* [for a vehicle] to stop because of engine trouble. **5.** *iv.* to wait a while so that one has more time; to evade something by taking extra time.

stall someone or something **off** to cause someone or something to wait; to hold someone or something off; to postpone the action of someone or something.

stammer something **out** to manage to say something, but only one word at a time.

stamp ['stæmp] **1.** *n.* a square of paper issued by the government that must be attached to certain documents to make them official or to indicate that a fee or tax has been paid, especially as used for postage. **2.** *n.* a tool that prints a design (a picture or words) onto a surface. **3.** *n.* the design that is printed onto a surface by ②. **4.** *tv.* to mark an object with ②, usually to make it official or to make an acknowledgment that a fee has been paid or that requirements have been met. **5.** *tv.* to put ① on an envelope. **6.** *tv.* to hit something or make something flat by bringing down one's foot on it with force. **7.** *iv.* to walk heavily somewhere; to walk with heavy steps.

stampede [stæm 'pid] **1.** *n.* a sudden rush of frightened horses or cattle. **2.** *n.* a sudden rush of excited, angry, or impatient people. (Figurative on ①.) **3.** *iv.* to rush as part of a large crowd of people or creatures. **4.** *tv.* to cause ① or ②.

stampede out of someplace [for a crowd of people or creatures] to move rapidly out of a place, as if in panic.

stand ['stænd] **1.** *iv., irreg.* to be in a normal or typical vertical position. (Past tense and past participle: STOOD.) **2.** *iv., irreg.* to be a particular height when in a vertical position on one's feet. **3.** *iv., irreg.* to be in a particular location. **4.** *iv., irreg.* [for a law] to remain in force. **5.** *tv., irreg.* to move someone or something to a vertical position. **6.** *tv., irreg.* to withstand something; to endure something; to put up with something. **7.** *n.* the position one takes on an issue. **8.** *n.* a base, frame, or piece of furniture that supports something. **9.** *n.* the place where a witness sits in a court of law. (Short for WITNESS STAND.)
→ MAKE SOMEONE'S HAIR STAND ON END
→ MORE THAN ONE CAN STAND
→ NOT HAVE A LEG TO STAND ON
→ TAKE THE STAND
→ WITNESS STAND

stand around to wait around, standing; to loiter.

stand aside 1. to step aside; to get out of the way. **2.** to withdraw and ignore something; to remain passive while something happens.

stand back (from someone or something**)** to stand or move well away and to the rear of someone or something.

stand by to wait in a state of readiness.

stand corrected to admit that one has been wrong.

stand down to step down, particularly from the witness stand in a courtroom.

stand in (for someone**)** to represent someone; to substitute for someone.

stand on one's **own two feet** to be independent and self-sufficient, rather than being supported by someone else.

stand one's **ground** AND **hold** one's **ground** to defend and demand one's rights; to resist an attack.

stand out a mile Go to STICK OUT A MILE.

stand out (from someone or something**)** to be prominent when compared to someone or something.

stand up 1. to arise from a sitting or reclining position. **2.** to be in a standing position. **3.** to wear well; to remain sound and intact. **4.** [for a statement] to remain believable. (Figurative.)

stand up against someone or something to challenge or confront someone or something.

stand up and be counted to state one's support (for someone or something).

standard ['stæn dəd] **1.** *n.* something against which something else is tested or measured; something that is the basis of a comparison. **2.** *n.* a degree of quality or excellence. **3.** *adj.* ordinary; conforming to a certain degree or amount; normal. (Adv: *standardly*.) **4.** *adj.* correct and acceptable according to the formal rules of a language. (Adv: *standardly*.)

standby ['stænd baɪ] **1.** *n.* an extra thing or person, nearby and ready. (Plural: *standbys*.) **2.** *n.* a person traveling ON STANDBY. (Plural: *standbys*.) **3.** *adv.* traveling when one is not able to reserve a seat and must travel as ②.
→ ON STANDBY

a **standing joke** a subject that regularly and over a period of time causes amusement whenever it is mentioned.

standstill ['stænd 'stɪl] *n.* a complete stop; a condition in which nothing is moving. (No plural form.)
→ COME TO A STANDSTILL

stank ['stæŋk] a past tense of STINK.

staple ['step əl] **1.** *n.* a small, thin, U-shaped piece of wire that fastens papers together, or that fastens things to a surface. **2.** *n.* any one of the most basic foods. **3.** *tv.* to fasten papers together or to attach something to something else with ①.

stapler ['step lɚ] *n.* a machine that drives staples through paper or into objects.

star ['star] **1.** *n.* a large object in space, such as the sun, that creates its own heat and light. **2.** *n.* a celebrity; a famous entertainer. **3.** *n.* a figure that has five or more points that radiate from a center point. **4.** *n.* ③ used as a mark of a degree of quality. **5.** *tv.* [for a

movie, play, or television show] to feature a particular performer. **6.** *iv.* [for a performer] to appear as a major performer in a movie, play, or television show. **7.** *adj.* most outstanding; most excellent; best.
→ GET STARS IN ONE'S EYES
→ SEE STARS
→ THANK ONE'S LUCKY STARS

starch ['startʃ] **1.** *n.* a white food substance that is part of potatoes, rice, and other grains. (Plural only for types and instances.) **2.** *n.* a substance used to stiffen cloth. (Plural only for types and instances.) **3.** *n.* a food that contains ①. **4.** *tv.* to stiffen fabric or clothing by coating it with or soaking it in ②.

stare ['stɛr] *n.* a long, direct look at someone or something with one's eyes wide open.

stare (at someone or something**)** to look directly at someone or something with one's eyes wide open, as though in fear, shock, surprise, wonder, or stupidity.

stare someone **down** to pressure someone to capitulate, back down, or yield by staring.

stare someone **in the face** [for something] to be very obvious to someone; [for something] to be very easy for someone to see or understand. (Informal.)

start ['start] **1.** *n.* the beginning point of something; the time or place where something begins. **2.** *n.* a shock that may bump, jerk, or jolt the body. **3.** *tv.* to begin a process; to begin doing something; to cause something to oper-

ate, work, or move. **4.** *tv.* to originate something. **5.** *iv.* to begin a movement; to begin a journey; to begin a process; to begin at the lower limit of something. **6.** *iv.* to move or jerk suddenly, as though one were surprised or scared; to be startled.
→ FROM START TO FINISH
→ GET OFF TO A FLYING START
→ OFF TO A RUNNING START

start from scratch to start from the beginning; to start from nothing.

start off to begin; to set out on a journey.

start off (by doing something) to begin a process by doing a particular thing first.

start off (on something) **1.** to begin a series or sequence. **2.** to begin a journey.

start (off) with a clean slate to start out again; to ignore the past and start over again.

start out to begin.

start out as something to begin one's career as something.

start over to begin again.

start someone **off (on** something) to cause someone to begin on a task or job.

start something **up** to start something, such as an engine or a motor.

start up to begin; to begin running, as with an engine.

startle ['stɑrt əl] *tv.* to cause someone to move or jump suddenly because of fear or surprise.

starvation [stɑr 've ʃən] *n.* suffering and possibly death caused by not having food. (No plural.)

starve ['stɑrv] **1.** *iv.* to die because of a lack of food; to die because one does not or cannot eat. **2.** *tv.* to cause someone or some creature to die of hunger.

starving ['stɑr vɪŋ] **1.** *adj.* very hungry. **2.** *adj.* dying from a lack of food.

stash ['stæʃ] *tv.* to hide something somewhere secretly for future use.

state ['stet] **1.** *n.* the condition that someone or something is in. **2.** *n.* the government of a country. (No plural.) **3.** *n.* a division of government within a country or a republic. **4.** the *adj.* use of ②. **5.** the *adj.* use of ③. **6.** *tv.* to express something; to say something. (The object can be a clause with THAT ⑦.)

state trooper ['stet 'tru pɚ] *n.* a state police officer. (Can be shortened to TROOPER.)

statement ['stet mənt] **1.** *n.* something that is said; something that is stated. **2.** *n.* a list showing the status of an account during a period of time.

stateroom ['stet rum] *n.* a private cabin on a ship or train.

static ['stæt ɪk] **1.** *n.* the buzzing noise made when a radio or television station is not tuned in properly or when there is electronic interference. (No plural.) **2.** *adj.* [of electricity] not flowing in an electrical current; tiny electric sparks as found indoors in cold, dry weather. **3.** *adj.* not changing;

stable; steady. (Adv: *statically* [...ɪk li].)

station [ˈste ʃən] **1.** *n.* the building or platform where a train or bus stops to let people on and off. **2.** *n.* a building where workers in a particular service work. **3.** *n.* the specific location where a worker is assigned to work. **4.** *n.* the building or offices from which a television or radio broadcast is transmitted. **5.** *tv.* to place someone at a location for work; to assign someone to a location for work.
→ (AS) BUSY AS GRAND CENTRAL STATION

stationary [ˈste ʃə nɛr i] *adj.* remaining in place; not moving; standing still. (Compare this with STATIONERY.)

stationery [ˈste ʃə nɛr i] *n.* writing paper; writing supplies, including paper, pen, ink, envelopes, etc. (No plural. Compare this with STATIONARY.)

statue [ˈstæ tʃu] *n.* a sculpture of someone or an animal, made of stone, clay, wood, plaster, etc.

status [ˈstæt əs] *n.* someone's position within society or business; rank.

status quo [ˈstæt əs ˈkwo] *n.* the way things are; the current state of affairs. (No plural. Latin for "the state in which.")

stay [ˈste] **1.** *iv.* to remain in a place or position; to continue to be in a place or position. **2.** *iv.* to live in a place for a while, especially as a guest. **3.** *iv.* to continue being in a certain condition; to remain in a certain condition. **4.** *n.* a visit; a period of time when one visits someplace or when one is a guest someplace; a period of time that one lives someplace.

stay away (from someone or something**)** to avoid someone or something.

stay back (from something**)** to keep one's distance from someone or something.

stay on (after someone or something**)** Go to LINGER ON (AFTER SOMEONE OR SOMETHING).

stay out (of something**) 1.** to keep out of something or someplace. **2.** to remain uninvolved in some piece of business.

stay put not to move; to stay where one is. (Informal.)

stay up (for something**)** to remain awake and out of bed for some nighttime event.

steady [ˈstɛd i] **1.** *adj.* not changing in condition, place, or position; firm. (Adv: *steadily.* Comp: *steadier;* sup: *steadiest.*) **2.** *adj.* moving at an even, smooth pace; not moving in jerks and bursts. (Adv: *steadily.* Comp: *steadier;* sup: *steadiest.*) **3.** *adj.* calm; not excited; not upset. (Adv: *steadily.* Comp: *steadier;* sup: *steadiest.*) **4.** *tv.* to cause something to be stable and not changing.

steak [ˈstek] *n.* a slice or slab of a particular meat or fish, eaten as food. (A STEAK is beef unless stated otherwise.)

steal [ˈstil] **1.** *tv., irreg.* to take something that does not belong to one without paying for it or without permission. (Past tense: STOLE;

past participle: STOLEN.) **2.** *tv.*, *irreg.* [in baseball] to reach the next base before the pitcher throws the ball to the batter.

steal a base to advance from one base to another in baseball without the help of a hit or an error.

steal a march (on someone) to get some sort of an advantage over someone without being noticed.

steal away to sneak away quietly.

steal someone's **thunder** to lessen someone's force or authority. (Not literal.)

steal the show Go to STEAL THE SPOTLIGHT.

steal the spotlight AND **steal the show** to give the best performance in a show, play, or some other event.

steam ['stim] **1.** *n.* the gas that water is changed into when it is boiled. (No plural.) **2.** *adj.* powered by ①; containing or using ①. **3.** *tv.* to cook something in ①. **4.** *tv.* to subject someone or something to ① or very hot water vapor. **5.** *iv.* to give off ①. **6.** *iv.* [for food] to cook in ①.
→ BLOW OFF STEAM
→ FULL STEAM AHEAD
→ LET OFF STEAM
→ STEAMING (MAD)
→ UNDER ONE'S OWN STEAM

steam something **off ((of)** something) to loosen and remove something by an application of steam.

steam something **out (of** something) to remove something from something else, through an application of steam.

steam something **up** to cause something to be covered with water vapor due to the presence of steam.

steam up to become covered with a film of steam or water vapor.

steamer ['stim ɚ] **1.** *n.* a ship that is powered by a steam engine. **2.** *n.* an enclosed pot or pan that uses steam to cook food.

steaming (mad) very angry; very mad; very upset.

steel ['stil] **1.** *n.* a very hard substance made of iron, carbon, and other metals, used in constructing tools, machines, and buildings. (No plural.) **2.** *adj.* made of ①.

steep ['stip] **1.** *adj.* slanted at a sharp angle, one that is almost straight up and down. (Adv: *steeply.* Comp: *steeper;* sup: *steepest.*) **2.** *iv.* [for something, such as tea] to soak in hot liquid for a period of time. **3.** *tv.* to soak something in liquid; to immerse something.

steeple ['stip əl] *n.* a tower on the roof of a church or other building, especially a tower that ends in a point.

steer ['stɪr] **1.** *tv.* to cause something to go in a certain direction; to guide someone or something to go in a certain direction. **2.** *tv.* to guide someone toward or away from a course of action. (Figurative on ①.) **3.** *iv.* to aim in a certain direction.

steering wheel ['stɪr ɪŋ wil] *n.* the wheel that a driver or pilot turns to control the direction of a vehicle. (Can be shortened to WHEEL.)

stem ['stɛm] **1.** *n.* the main part of a plant above the ground, which is connected to the roots below the ground, and from which leaves or flowers grow. **2.** *n.* the part of a word that suffixes and prefixes are added to.
→ FROM STEM TO STERN

step ['stɛp] **1.** *n.* the movement made by putting one foot in front of the other while walking. **2.** *n.* the distance traveled by a single ①. **3.** *n.* a flat surface that one places one's foot on when going up or down stairs or a ladder. **4.** *n.* an action in a series of actions in a particular order. **5.** *iv.* to move as in ① in a certain direction.
→ FALL IN(TO STEP)
→ WATCH ONE'S STEP

step aside to move out of someone's path; to step out of the way.

step back (from someone or something**)** to move back from someone or something; to move back so as to provide space around someone or something.

step on it Go to STEP ON THE GAS.

step on someone's **toes** AND **tread on** someone's **toes** to interfere with or offend someone.

step on the gas AND **step on it** to hurry up.

step out into something to go out from a place into a different set of conditions.

step out of line to misbehave; to do something offensive.

step out (of something**)** to go out of a place.

step out (on someone**)** to be unfaithful to a spouse or lover.

step outside 1. to go outside, as if to get some fresh air. **2.** to go outside to fight or settle an argument.

step over (to) someplace to move to a place a few steps away.

step right up to come right to where the speaker is; to come forward to the person speaking. (Used by people selling things.)

step something **up 1.** to make something go more active. **2.** to make something go or run faster.

step up to increase.

step up to something to walk to something, especially a counter or a bar.

stereo ['stɛr i o] **1.** *adj.* [of sound or electronic equipment making sound] coming from two or more speakers in a way that gives realistic effect. **2.** *n.* an electronic device that produces sound coming from two or more sources, providing realistic sound reproduction. (Plural ends in *-s.*)

stern ['stɚn] **1.** *adj.* strict; rigid in discipline. (Adv: *sternly.* Comp: *sterner;* sup: *sternest.*) **2.** *n.* the rear part of a boat or ship.
→ FROM STEM TO STERN

stew ['stu] **1.** *n.* a thick soup of vegetables and often meat cooked slowly in their own juices. (Plural only for types and instances.) **2.** *tv.* to cook something slowly in water and its own juices. **3.** *iv.* [for food] to cook slowly in water and its own juices.

stew in one's **own juice** to be left alone to suffer one's anger or disappointment.

stick [ˈstɪk] **1.** *n.* a small branch; a thin length of wood from a tree. **2.** *n.* a thin piece of wood used for a special purpose. **3.** *tv., irreg.* to attach something to something else with glue, tape, or something else adhesive. (Past tense and past participle: STUCK.) **4.** *tv., irreg.* to put something in a certain position. (Informal.) **5.** *iv., irreg.* to remain attached to something with glue, tape, or something else adhesive.
→ END UP WITH THE SHORT END OF THE STICK
→ GET THE SHORT END OF THE STICK
→ HAVE ONE'S WORDS STICK IN ONE'S THROAT
→ ONE'S WORDS STICK IN ONE'S THROAT

stick around to remain in the general area; to stay in a place. (Colloquial.)

stick one's **foot in** one's **mouth**
Go to PUT ONE'S FOOT IN ONE'S MOUTH.

stick one's **neck out** to take a risk.

stick one's **nose in(to** something**)**
Go to POKE ONE'S NOSE IN(TO SOMETHING).

stick out to project outward.

stick out a mile AND **stand out a mile** to be very obvious. (Informal.)

stick out (from someone or something**)** to project outward from someone or something.

stick out (of someone or something**)** to project from someone or something.

stick someone or something **up** to rob someone or a business establishment. (Presumably with the aid of a gun.)

stick something **down** to fasten something down, as with glue or paste.

stick something **in(to** someone or something**)** to insert something into someone or something.

stick something **out 1.** to cause something to project outward. **2.** to endure something; to stay with something. (The *something* is usually *it*.)

stick to one's **guns** to remain firm in one's convictions; to stand up for one's rights.

stick together 1. [for things] to hold or adhere to one another. **2.** [for people] to remain in one another's company. (Figurative.)

sticky [ˈstɪki] **1.** *adj.* adhesive. (Comp: *stickier*; sup: *stickiest*.) **2.** *adj.* hot and humid; causing one to sweat. (Comp: *stickier*; sup: *stickiest*.) **3.** *adj.* awkward. (Comp: *stickier*; sup: *stickiest*.)

stiff [ˈstɪf] **1.** *adj.* rigid; not flexible; hard to bend. (Adv: *stiffly.* Comp: *stiffer*; sup: *stiffest*.) **2.** *adj.* firm; almost solid; not fluid. (Adv: *stiffly.* Comp: *stiffer*; sup: *stiffest*.) **3.** *adj.* harsh; severe. (Informal. Comp: *stiffer*; sup: *stiffest*.) **4.** *adj.* very formal; not relaxed. (Adv: *stiffly.* Comp: *stiffer*; sup: *stiffest*.)
→ KEEP A STIFF UPPER LIP

stiffen [ˈstɪf ən] *iv.* to become stiff.

still [ˈstɪl] **1.** *adj.* not moving; at rest. (Comp: *stiller*; sup: *stillest*.) **2.** *adj.* quiet; not talking; not making noise. (Not prenominal.) **3.** *adv.* at a time past what was expected. **4.** *adv.* EVEN ④; yet [more]. (Comes after the adjec-

tive. Used with comparisons to make them stronger.)
→ SO STILL YOU COULD HEAR A PIN DROP

stimulant [ˈstɪm jə lənt] *n.* something, especially a drug or chemical, that keeps someone awake or causes someone to be more active.

stimulate [ˈstɪm jə let] *tv.* to excite someone or something; to cause someone or something to be active or excited.

sting [ˈstɪŋ] **1.** *tv., irreg.* to pierce the skin of someone or something with something sharp; [for a bee, wasp, hornet, etc.] to pierce the skin with a stinger and inject a substance that causes a burning pain. (Past tense and past participle: STUNG.) **2.** *tv., irreg.* to cause someone to feel a tingling or burning pain. **3.** *iv., irreg.* to be able to pierce skin as with ①. **4.** *iv., irreg.* [for something] to hurt sharply. **5.** *n.* the piercing of the skin as with ① and the pain that accompanies it. **6.** *n.* a tingling or burning pain.

stinger [ˈstɪŋ ɚ] *n.* the stinging organ of bees, hornets, etc.

stink [ˈstɪŋk] **1.** *n.* a terrible smell; a very bad smell. **2.** *iv., irreg.* to smell bad. (Past tense: STANK or STUNK; past participle: STUNK.)

stir [ˈstɚ] **1.** *tv.* to mix something with one's hand or with an object. **2.** *tv.* to excite someone or an emotion; to cause someone to feel emotion or passion. **3.** *iv.* to change position; to move about. **4.** *n.* an exciting event; something that disturbs the usual order of things.

stir someone **up** to get someone excited; to get someone angry.

stir something **up 1.** to mix something by stirring. **2.** to create or cause trouble.

stir up a hornet's nest to create trouble or difficulties.

stitch [ˈstɪtʃ] **1.** *n.* one movement of a threaded needle through a fabric while sewing. **2.** *n.* the thread that is seen after one movement of a threaded needle through a fabric while sewing. **3.** *n.* a small amount of clothing. (No plural. Usually in negative constructions.) **4.** *n.* a sharp pain. **5.** *tv.* to sew something; to sew things together.
→ KEEP SOMEONE IN STITCHES

stitch something **up** to sew something together; to mend a tear or ripped seam.

stock [ˈstɑk] **1.** *n.* a supply of something to be used or sold. (Plural only for types and instances.) **2.** *n.* a heavy broth made by cooking meats, usually with vegetables, for a long time— used to prepare sauce or soup. (Plural only for types and instances.) **3.** *n.* the total assets of a company divided into equal shares that are usually bought and sold in a STOCK MARKET. (No plural.) **4.** *n.* [a group of] shares of ③ of a specific company. **5.** *tv.* [for a store] to arrange to have ① of a product available for sale. **6.** *adj.* [of a response that seems] trite, rehearsed, and not sincere.
→ HAVE SOMETHING IN STOCK
→ IN STOCK
→ LOCK, STOCK, AND BARREL

stock market ['stɑk mɑr kət] **1.** *n.* a market for the business of buying and selling STOCKS in general. **2.** *n.* some sort of measure of the general value of all the stocks at any one time. (Can be shortened to MARKET.)

stock up (on something**)** to build up a supply of something in particular.

stocking ['stɑk ɪŋ] *n.* a long, knitted or woven sock.

stockpile ['stɑk paɪl] **1.** *n.* a large amount of something that is stored for future use or in case of an emergency. **2.** *tv.* to store a large amount of something for future use or in case of an emergency.

stole ['stol] past tense of STEAL.

stolen ['stol ən] **1.** Past participle of STEAL. **2.** *adj.* taken without the owner's permission or knowledge.

stomach ['stʌm ək] **1.** *n.* the organ of the body in which food is digested. **2.** *n.* the front of the body below the chest and above the waist.
→ CANNOT STOMACH SOMEONE OR SOMETHING
→ HAVE EYES BIGGER THAN ONE'S STOMACH
→ NOT ABLE TO STOMACH SOMEONE OR SOMETHING
→ ONE'S EYES ARE BIGGER THAN ONE'S STOMACH.
→ TURN SOMEONE'S STOMACH

stone ['ston] **1.** *n.* the hard material of which rocks are made. (Plural only for types and instances.) **2.** *n.* a rock; a chunk of ①. **3.** *n.* a jewel; a gem. **4.** *n.* a small, hard object that forms in parts of the body, such as the kid-ney, and causes a lot of pain as it passes through the organ. **5.** *adj.* made of ①. **6.** *tv.* to throw STONES ② at someone or something, often as punishment or torment.
→ CAST THE FIRST STONE
→ HAVE A HEART OF STONE
→ KILL TWO BIRDS WITH ONE STONE
→ RUN INTO A STONE WALL

a **stone's throw away** a short distance; a relatively short distance.

stood ['stʊd] past tense and past participle of STAND.
→ SHOULD HAVE STOOD IN BED

stool ['stul] **1.** *n.* a tall seat that usually has no support for one's back or arms. **2.** *n.* feces; waste matter that is expelled from the body. (Plural only for types and instances.)
→ FALL BETWEEN TWO STOOLS

stoop ['stup] **1.** *n.* a small porch at the door of a house. **2.** *n.* a bent posture, as if one is carrying a heavy weight on one's shoulders. **3.** *iv.* to bend down; to bend forward; to hold one's head and shoulders downward in front of one's body.

stoop down to bend, dip, duck, or squat down.

stoop over to bend over.

stop ['stɑp] **1.** *tv.* to end movement, progress, an activity, or an existence. **2.** *iv.* to move, progress, act, or function no longer; to cease. **3.** *iv.* to stay for a period of time. **4.** *n.* a short visit; a short stay. **5.** *n.* a place where a bus, train, or other vehicle STOPS as in ③ to let passengers get on and off the vehicle. **6.** *n.* a consonant that is made by ending the flow of the breath and suddenly releasing it.

→ COME TO A STOP

→ PULL OUT ALL THE STOPS

→ PUT A STOP TO SOMETHING

stop by (someplace) to go to a place and stop and then continue.

stop in (someplace) to pay a brief visit to a place.

stop (just) short (of something) not to go as far as something; to stop before something.

stop over (someplace) to stay briefly at a place while on the way to another place.

stop something up (with something) to plug something with something.

stop up [for something] to become clogged up.

stoplight ['stɑp lɑɪt] *n.* a traffic signal that has colored lights that indicate whether drivers should stop or go.

stopover ['stɑp ov ɚ] *n.* a place where one stops briefly during a journey, especially a stop at an airport between the city where one took off and the city that one is going to.

stoppage ['stɑp ɪdʒ] *n.* an organized strike; the organized stopping of work, such as during a disagreement between labor and management.

stopwatch ['stɑp wɑtʃ] *n.* a watch that can be started or stopped at any moment, used to determine how long something lasts.

storage ['stor ɪdʒ] **1.** *n.* keeping or storing [things]. (No plural.) **2.** *n.* a place for storing things. (No plural.)

→ IN STORAGE

store ['stor] **1.** *n.* a shop where goods or products are sold. **2.** *n.* a supply of something. **3.** *tv.* to keep something someplace so that it can be used later.

→ DEPARTMENT STORE

→ GROCERY (STORE)

→ SET GREAT STORE BY SOMEONE OR SOMETHING

storekeeper ['stor kip ɚ] *n.* someone who owns or manages a store.

storeroom ['stor rum] *n.* a room where things are stored.

stork ['stork] *n.* a large bird with a long, sharp beak and a long neck.

storm ['storm] **1.** *n.* a period of severe weather with very strong winds, heavy rain or snow, and sometimes thunder and lightning. **2.** *n.* a violent attack or burst of anger. (Figurative on ①.) **3.** *tv.* to attack something with force. **4.** *iv.* [for the weather] to be severe, with strong winds, heavy rain or snow, and sometimes thunder and lightning.

→ EYE OF THE STORM

→ KICK UP A STORM

→ the LULL BEFORE THE STORM

→ TAKE SOMEONE OR SOMETHING BY STORM

storm door ['storm dor] *n.* a second door, outside the regular door, that keeps cold, wind, snow, or rain from entering.

storm in(to someplace) to burst into something or someplace angrily.

A **storm is brewing. 1.** There is going to be a storm. **2.** There is going to be trouble.

storm out (of someplace**)** to leave or burst out of someplace angrily.

storm window ['storm wɪn do] *n.* a second window, placed outside a regular window, that keeps cold, wind, snow, or rain from entering a room or building.

story ['stor i] **1.** *n.* an account of something that has happened. **2.** *n.* a tale; an account that is fiction, told or written for entertainment or amusement. **3.** *n.* a lie. **4.** *n.* a news report; an article of news. **5.** *n.* one level of a building; one layer from floor to ceiling in a building. (In the United States, the floor on ground level is the first story.)
→ COCK-AND-BULL STORY
→ MAKE A LONG STORY SHORT
→ SHAGGY-DOG STORY
→ TALL STORY
→ TELL ITS OWN STORY

stout ['staʊt] *adj.* wide; fat; weighing too much. (Adv: *stoutly.* Comp: *stouter;* sup: *stoutest.*)

stove ['stoʊv] *n.* an appliance that usually contains an oven and has burners on the top, used for cooking.

straight ['stret] **1.** *adj.* not bent or curved; direct; continuing in the same direction. (Adv: *straightly.* Comp: *straighter;* sup: *straightest.*) **2.** *adj.* honest; sincere; telling the truth. (Adv: *straightly.* Comp: *straighter;* sup: *straightest.*) **3.** *adj.* without an interruption; continuous. (E.g., *5 straight hours; five hours straight.*) **4.** *adv.* [going] directly to a place without making a detour]. **5.** *adv.* [moving] in a line that is ①; without turning. **6.** *adv.* upright.

→ GET SOMETHING STRAIGHT
→ GET THE FACTS STRAIGHT
→ KEEP A STRAIGHT FACE
→ SET SOMEONE STRAIGHT
→ VOTE A STRAIGHT TICKET

straight from the horse's mouth from an authoritative or dependable source.

straight from the shoulder [spoken] sincerely and frankly.

straight out frankly; directly. (Informal.)

straighten out 1. to become straight. **2.** to improve one's behavior or attitude.

straighten someone out 1. to make someone's body straight or orderly. **2.** to scold someone about an issue; to cause someone to behave better.

straighten something out to bring order to something that is crooked or disorderly.

straighten something up to make something less messy.

straighten up 1. to sit or stand more vertically. **2.** to behave better.

strain ['stren] **1.** *tv.* to stretch or pull something, especially as much as possible or in a way that causes injury. **2.** *tv.* to separate liquid from something solid by pouring it through a filter. **3.** *tv.* to place something under a burden; to place tension on something. (Figurative on ①.) **4.** *iv.* to stretch tightly; to work hard and carry a heavy load. **5.** *iv.* to use a lot of effort to do something. **6.** *n.* a burden or problem that causes someone distress. **7.** *n.* an injury to a muscle caused by stretching it or pulling it too hard. **8.** *n.* a variety of plant, bacterium, or virus.

strand ['strænd] **1.** *n.* one thread of a rope; one wire of a cable; a thread; a fiber. **2.** *tv.* to cause someone or something to be stuck or held at a location.

strange ['strendʒ] **1.** *adj.* unusual; odd; peculiar; not normal or usual. (Adv: *strangely.* Comp: *stranger;* sup: *strangest.*) **2.** *adj.* not familiar; not usually experienced. (Adv: *strangely.* Comp: *stranger;* sup: *strangest.*)

stranger ['strendʒ ɚ] *n.* someone who is not known to oneself; someone who is not familiar to oneself.

a **stranger to** something or someplace someone who is new to an area or place.

strap ['stræp] **1.** *n.* a strong, narrow strip of material used to secure something. **2.** *tv.* to secure someone or something with a strong, narrow strip of leather or other material.

straw ['strɔ] **1.** *n.* dried stalks of the plants on which grain grows. (No plural. Number is expressed with *piece(s) of straw.*) **2.** *n.* a plastic or paper tube used for drinking a liquid by sucking. **3.** *adj.* made of ①; containing ①.
→ THAT'S THE LAST STRAW.
→ THAT'S THE STRAW THAT BROKE THE CAMEL'S BACK.

strawberry ['strɔ bɛr i] **1.** *n.* a small, soft, red fruit that has tiny seeds on its surface. **2.** *adj.* made with or flavored with ①.

stray ['stre] **1.** *adj.* wandering. **2.** *adj.* occurring or arriving by

chance. **3.** *iv.* to wander; to become lost; to leave the main path or topic. **4.** *n.* an animal that is lost; an animal that wanders around and has no home.

streak ['strik] **1.** *n.* a long, thin line or stripe. **2.** *n.* a period of time during which something is constant; a period of time during which something is not interrupted. **3.** *tv.* to mark something with long, thin lines or stripes. **4.** *iv.* to flow or race along in long, thin lines or stripes. **5.** *iv.* to run or move somewhere very fast.
→ TALK A BLUE STREAK

stream ['strim] **1.** *n.* a small river. **2.** *n.* a steady flow of something, especially something liquid. **3.** *iv.* to flow somewhere steadily and in large amounts.

stream down (on someone or something**)** [for a liquid or light] to flow downward onto someone or something.

stream in(to something**)** to flow or rush into something.

streamer ['strim ɚ] *n.* a very long, thin strip of paper or ribbon used as a decoration during a ceremony, parade, or celebration.

street ['strit] *n.* a road, usually one in a city or a town that has buildings or parks beside it. (Abbreviated *St.* in addresses.)
→ the MAN IN THE STREET
→ SIDE STREET

streetlight ['strit laɪt] *n.* a light, usually on a pole, that lights a street when it is dark outside.

strength ['strɛŋkθ] **1.** *n.* the quality of being strong. (No plural.) **2.** *n.* a virtue; a good feature of

someone or something. (Figurative on ①.)
→ NOT KNOW ONE'S OWN STRENGTH
→ a PILLAR OF STRENGTH
→ a TOWER OF STRENGTH

stress ['strɛs] **1.** *n.* the pressure caused by something that is heavy; strain. (No plural.) **2.** *n.* the mental pressure caused by something that is difficult or demanding; mental tension. (Figurative on ①.) **3.** *n.* emphasis placed on a syllable when speaking by saying it louder or in a different tone. (Plural only for types and instances.) **4.** *n.* emphasis. (No plural.) **5.** *tv.* to place ③ on a syllable when speaking. **6.** *tv.* to place emphasis or focus on something. (The object can be a clause with THAT ⑦.)

stretch ['strɛtʃ] **1.** *tv.* to extend something. **2.** *iv.* to be elastic; to be able to be pulled without breaking. **3.** *n.* a continuous area of land. **4.** *n.* a continuous period of time.
→ AT A STRETCH

stretch one's **legs** to walk around after sitting or lying down for a time.

stretch out 1. to become wider; to become longer; to lengthen. **2.** [for something] to spread one's arms and legs out over time or space. **3.** to lie down on a bed and spread out to nap or sleep.

stretch someone or something **out** to extend or draw out someone or something.

stretch something **out (to** someone or something**)** to reach something out to someone or something.

stretcher ['strɛtʃɚ] *n.* a device like a light bed or cot, used to carry someone who is sick or dead.

strict ['strɪkt] **1.** *adj.* [of rules or discipline] severe, harsh, or demanding. (Adv: *strictly.* Comp: *stricter;* sup: *strictest.*) **2.** *adj.* absolute; exact. (Adv: *strictly.* Comp: *stricter;* sup: *strictest.*)

(strictly) on the level honest; dependably open and fair.

stridden ['strɪd n] Past participle of STRIDE.

stride ['straɪd] **1.** *n.* the length of one's step while walking. **2.** *n.* a long step made while walking. **3.** *iv., irreg.* to walk by taking long steps. (Past tense: STRODE; past participle: STRIDDEN. The past participle is rarely used.)
→ TAKE SOMETHING IN STRIDE

strife ['straɪf] *n.* fighting; a bitter struggle; a heated argument or battle. (No plural.)

strike ['straɪk] **1.** *tv., irreg.* to hit someone or something; to hit something against something; to crash into something. (Past tense and past participle: STRUCK.) **2.** *tv., irreg.* to attack someone or something. **3.** *tv., irreg.* to light a match; to cause something to burn with fire. **4.** *tv., irreg.* to discover something underneath the ground by digging or drilling. **5.** *iv., irreg.* [for a group of workers] to refuse to work until their demands are met. **6.** *iv., irreg.* to attack. **7.** *iv., irreg.* to make contact; to have a negative effect [on someone or something]. **8.** *iv., irreg.* [for a clock] to make a sound like a bell to tell what time it is. **9.** *n.* the

state that exists when workers refuse to work during a labor dispute. **10.** *n.* [in baseball] a penalty given to a player who swings the bat and misses the ball, who hits the ball foul, or who does not swing the bat when the umpire thinks that the ball went by the batter in a location that the batter could have hit it. **11.** *n.* [in bowling] an instance of knocking over all the pins at once.
→ BE (OUT) ON STRIKE
→ GET TWO STRIKES AGAINST ONE
→ GO (OUT) ON STRIKE

strike a balance (between two things**)** to find a satisfactory compromise between two extremes.

strike a chord (with someone**)** to cause someone to remember something; to remind someone or something; to be familiar.

strike a happy medium AND **hit a happy medium** to find a compromise position; to arrive at a position halfway between two unacceptable extremes.

strike a match to light a match.

strike a pose to position oneself in a certain posture.

strike a sour note AND **hit a sour note** to signify something unpleasant.

strike back (at someone or something**)** to return the blows of someone or something; to return the attack of someone or something.

strike for something to conduct a work stoppage in order to gain something.

strike home Go to HIT HOME.

strike it rich to acquire wealth suddenly.

strike out 1. [for a baseball player] to accumulate three strikes, ending that turn at bat. **2.** to have a series of failures. (Figurative.)

strike out (at someone or something**)** to hit at someone or something with the intention of threatening or doing harm.

strike someone **as** something [for a thought or behavior] to affect someone a certain way.

strike someone **funny** to seem funny to someone.

strike someone's **fancy** to appeal to someone.

strike something **down** [for a court] to invalidate a law.

strike up a friendship to become friends (with someone).

strike while the iron is hot to do something at the best possible time, while there is an appropriate opportunity.

string ['strɪŋ] **1.** *n.* a thin rope or a thick thread, especially used for tying something, binding something, or suspending something in the air. (No plural.) **2.** *n.* a length of ① or thread. **3.** *n.* a wire or cord that is stretched tight and is used to produce sound in certain musical instruments. **4.** *n.* a cord used to form the tightly pulled "net" found in a tennis racket and similar sports equipment. **5.** *n.* a number of people or things in a row. **6.** *tv., irreg.* to put ③ or ④ on a guitar, violin, tennis racket, etc. (Past tense and past participle: STRUNG.) **7.** *tv., irreg.* to place some-

thing on ②. (E.g., *to string beads*.)
8. *tv., irreg.* to stretch something
that is like ① from one place to
another.
→ CONTROL THE PURSE STRINGS
→ TIED TO ONE'S MOTHER'S APRON
 STRINGS
→ WITH NO STRINGS ATTACHED
→ WITHOUT ANY STRINGS ATTACHED

string someone **along** to maintain
someone's attention or interest,
probably insincerely.

strings *n.* the musical instruments
whose sounds are made by rubbing a bow across STRINGS as in
STRING ③; the people who play the
instruments having STRINGS as in
STRING ③. (Treated as plural.)

strip ['strɪp] **1.** *n.* a long, flat piece
of something. **2.** *tv.* to undress
someone; to remove someone's
clothes; to remove something's
covering. **3.** *tv.* to make something
empty or bare. **4.** *iv.* to take off
one's clothes; to undress.
→ COMIC STRIP

strip down to remove one's clothing.

stripe ['straɪp] **1.** *n.* a long band of
color or texture; a wide line; a
wide line of something that is different from what is around it.
2. *tv.* to mark something with ①;
to put ① on something.

strode ['strod] past tense of STRIDE.

stroll ['strol] **1.** *n.* a pleasant walk.
2. *iv.* to go for a pleasant walk.

strong ['strɔŋ] **1.** *adj.* having
strength in the mind or body; having power in the mind or the
body; using strength. (Adv:
strongly. Comp: *stronger;* sup:
strongest.) **2.** *adj.* able to last; able

to withstand something; not easily
broken; sturdy. (Adv: *strongly.*
Comp: *stronger;* sup: *strongest.*)
3. *adj.* [of a taste, smell, or color]
intense. (Adv: *strongly.* Comp:
stronger; sup: *strongest.*) **4.** *adj.*
having a certain number [of peo-
ple]. (Follows a specific number.)
→ (AS) STRONG AS AN OX

struck ['strʌk] past tense and past
participle of STRIKE.

structure ['strʌk tʃɚ] **1.** *n.* the way
that something is put together; the
way that something is built; the
way that something or some creature is arranged. (No plural.) **2.** *n.*
a building. **3.** *n.* something that is
made from different parts. **4.** *tv.* to
arrange something so that it has a
certain form; to form something
in a certain way; to make something from different parts.

struggle ['strʌg əl] **1.** *iv.* to work
hard for or against something; to
fight for or against something,
using a lot of effort or energy. **2.** *n.*
a hard fight for or against something; a difficult effort for or
against something.

struggle through (something**)** to
get through something in the best
way possible.

strung ['strʌŋ] past tense and past
participle of STRING.

strut ['strʌt] *iv.* to walk somewhere
arrogantly; to walk somewhere as
though one were more important
than one is.

stub ['stʌb] **1.** *tv.* to hurt a toe by
hitting it against something. **2.** *n.* a
short end of something that
remains after the rest of it is taken
or used.

stubborn ['stʌb ɚn] *adj.* not will-ing to do something that someone else wants; not yielding; not giving in. (Adv: *stubbornly.*)
→ (AS) STUBBORN AS A MULE

stuck ['stʌk] past tense and past participle of STICK.

(stuck) in a rut remaining in an established way of living that never changes.

stuck in traffic to be caught in a traffic jam.

student ['stud nt] *n.* someone who studies or learns, especially at a school; a pupil.

study ['stʌd i] **1.** *tv.* to spend time learning information about some-thing by reading, researching, observing, or experimenting. **2.** *tv.* to examine something closely; to scrutinize something; to observe something closely. **3.** *iv.* to be a student; to read, research, observe, or experiment in order to learn about something. **4.** *n.* the work or effort involved in learning. (The same meaning in singular and plu-ral, but not countable.) **5.** *n.* an examination of something, as with ②. **6.** *n.* a room where someone works as in ③.

stuff ['stʌf] **1.** *n.* any substance that things are made of; the mate-rial that anything is made of. (No plural.) **2.** *n.* things; unnamed objects; belongings; possessions. (No plural.) **3.** *tv.* to fill something with a substance; to pack some-thing into a space or container until there is no room left. **4.** *tv.* to fill the inside of a dead animal with a material that preserves it

and maintains its shape so that it can be displayed.
→ KID'S STUFF

stuff and nonsense nonsense.

stuff the ballot box to put dis-honest ballots into a ballot box; to cheat in counting the votes in an election.

stumble ['stʌm bəl] **1.** *iv.* to trip; to fall over something; to almost fall while one is moving; to walk in a clumsy way. **2.** *iv.* to speak in a clumsy way; to make mistakes while speaking; to trip on one's words. (Figurative on ①.)

stumble through something to get through a sequence of something awkwardly and clumsily.

stumbling block something that prevents or obstructs progress.

stump ['stʌmp] **1.** *n.* the part of something that remains when the other part has been cut off, broken off, removed, or used. **2.** *tv.* to puzzle someone; to confuse some-one.

stun ['stʌn] **1.** *tv.* to surprise some-one completely; to amaze some-one; to shock someone. **2.** *tv.* to cause someone or something to become unconscious, by a blow or by electrical shock.

stung ['stʌŋ] past tense and past participle of STING.

stunk ['stʌŋk] a past tense of STINK; past participle of STINK.

stupid ['stu pɪd] **1.** *adj.* not intelli-gent; not smart. (Adv: *stupidly.* Comp: *stupider;* sup: *stupidest.*) **2.** *adj.* silly; foolish. (Adv: *stupidly.* Comp: *stupider;* sup: *stupidest.*) **3.** *adj.* [of something] annoying;

[of something] causing anger or irritation. (Comp: *stupider;* sup: *stupidest.*)

stupidity [stu ˈpɪd ɪ ti] **1.** *n.* a lack of intelligence. (No plural.) **2.** *n.* the condition of being stupid, incorrect, or not appropriate. (No plural.)

sturdy [ˈstɚ di] *adj.* strong; firm; not easily knocked over. (Adv: *sturdily.* Comp: *sturdier;* sup: *sturdiest.*)

style [ˈstaɪl] **1.** *n.* a way in which something is made, designed, done, said, or written. **2.** *n.* a particular design or theme in clothing or products at a particular period of time. **3.** *n.* the manner in which someone behaves. **4.** *tv.* to design or form something in a certain way.
→ CRAMP SOMEONE'S STYLE

stylish [ˈstaɪ lɪʃ] *adj.* in the current fashion; in style; current; up-to-date. (Adv: *stylishly.*)

sub [ˈsʌb] **1.** *n.* a sealed boat that can remain still or travel underwater. (Short for SUBMARINE.) **2.** *n.* someone or something serving in the place of someone or something else. (Short for SUBSTITUTE.)

subdue [səb ˈdu] **1.** *tv.* to bring someone or something under one's control. **2.** *tv.* to make someone or something less noticeable; to soften the strength or intensity of something.

subject [ˈsʌb dʒɪkt] **1.** *n.* a topic; something that is discussed, examined, or researched. **2.** *n.* a course; something that is studied; a particular field of knowledge. **3.** *n.* someone or something used in an experiment. **4.** *n.* someone who is ruled by a government or a ruler. **5.** *n.* a person, object, or scene that is painted or photographed. **6.** *n.* the noun or noun phrase representing the person or thing that performs the action in an active sentence, or that is the receiver of an action in a passive sentence.
→ CHANGE THE SUBJECT
→ DROP THE SUBJECT
→ OFF THE SUBJECT

subject matter [ˈsʌb dʒɛk ˈmæt ɚ] *n.* content; the subject that a piece of writing or speech deals with.

subject to something **1.** likely to have something, such as a physical disorder. **2.** tentative, depending on something; vulnerable to something.

subjective [səb ˈdʒɛk tɪv] *adj.* of or about what someone thinks about something instead of the actual facts about something. (Adv: *subjectively.*)

sublime [sə ˈblaɪm] *adj.* supreme; wonderful; grand; inspiring. (Adv: *sublimely.*)

submarine [ˈsʌb mə rin] **1.** *n.* a ship that can travel completely underwater, used especially in war and for research. (Can be shortened to SUB.) **2.** *n.* a large sandwich; a sandwich made with two long pieces of bread. (Usually SUB.)

submerge [səb ˈmɚdʒ] **1.** *tv.* to put something under the surface of a liquid; to immerse something in water. **2.** *iv.* to go underwater; to go under the surface of a liquid.

submit someone **to** something [səb 'mɪt...] to make someone suffer through or endure something.

submit something **to** someone or something [səb 'mɪt...] to offer something to someone or a group for review and analysis; to present something to someone or a group for review and analysis.

subscription [səb 'skrɪp ʃən] *n.* an order for a series of issues of a magazine or newspaper.

subsist on something to exist on something; to stay alive on something.

subsoil ['sʌb sɔɪl] *n.* the layer of soil that lies below the surface soil of the earth. (No plural.)

substance ['sʌb stəns] **1.** *n.* the material that something is made of; matter. **2.** *n.* the essence; the important part of something. (No plural.)

substitute ['sʌb stɪ tut] **1.** *iv.* to be put in someone or something else's place as a replacement. **2.** *n.* a replacement; someone or something that is put in someone or something else's place. (Can be shortened to **SUB**.)

substitute someone or something **for** someone or something to replace someone or something with someone or something else; to exchange someone or something for someone or something else.

substitution [səb stɪ 'tu ʃən] **1.** *n.* the replacement of someone or something with someone or something else. (Plural only for types and instances.) **2.** *n.* someone or

something that has been substituted as in ①.

subtract [səb 'trækt] **1.** *tv.* to take a part of something away; to take a quantity away [from another quantity]; to reduce something by a certain amount. (See also **MINUS**.) **2.** *iv.* to lessen or reduce [something] as in ①.

subtraction [səb 'træk ʃən] *n.* the reduction of something by a certain amount; the reduction of a quantity by another quantity. (Plural only for types and instances.)

suburb ['sʌ bəb] *n.* a city, town, or village that is next to or near a large city.

suburban [sə 'bə bən] *adj.* of or about the suburbs.

subway ['sʌb we] *n.* an underground electric train that provides transportation in large cities.

succeed [sək 'sid] **1.** *iv.* to be successful; to reach a goal. **2.** *tv.* to follow someone or something into a job or office.

success [sək 'sɛs] **1.** *n.* accomplishment; achievement. (Plural only for types and instances.) **2.** *n.* someone or something that is successful, especially someone or something that has become famous, important, or rich.

successful [sək 'sɛs fʊl] *adj.* showing evidence of having accomplished something or having reached a high status. (Adv: *successfully*.)

succumb to something to yield to something, especially a temptation, fatal disease, a human weakness, etc.

such ['sʌtʃ] *adj.* so great; so much. → AS SUCH

such as 1. of a particular kind; of the sort that is. **2.** for example.

suck ['sʌk] *tv.* to pull liquid into one's mouth by putting one's lips around something and drawing the liquid in; to pull something into one's mouth with one's lips. → TEACH ONE'S GRANDMOTHER TO SUCK EGGS

suck something up to pick something up by suction, as with a vacuum cleaner or through a straw.

sudden ['sʌd n] *adj.* unexpected; happening without warning. (Adv: *suddenly.*)

suddenly ['sʌd n li] *adv.* unexpectedly; without warning.

suds ['sʌdz] *n.* bubbles formed by soap mixing with water; lather; froth. (Treated as plural, but not countable.)

sue ['su] **1.** *iv.* to start a lawsuit; to file a claim against someone or something in court. **2.** *tv.* to bring a lawsuit against someone or something; to file a claim against someone or something in court.

suffer ['sʌf ɚ] **1.** *tv.* to experience physical or emotional pain because of illness or emotional loss. **2.** *iv.* to feel physical or emotional pain. **3.** *iv.* to worsen; to decline in quality.

suffix ['sʌf ɪks] *n.* a form added to the end of a word that changes or modifies the meaning or function of the word.

suffocate ['sʌf ə ket] **1.** *tv.* to kill someone or a creature by preventing it from getting the oxygen that is needed. **2.** *iv.* to die because one is unable to get the oxygen that is needed.

sugar ['ʃʊg ɚ] **1.** *n.* a sweet substance, usually in crystal form, that is made from certain plants and used to sweeten food and drinks. (No plural.) **2.** *n.* a sweet substance that is found naturally in many foods. (Plural only for types and instances.)

suggest [səg 'dʒɛst] **1.** *tv.* to propose something that will be considered; to express something that one thinks should be considered; to offer something as an option. (The object can be a clause with THAT ⑦.) **2.** *tv.* to bring something to one's mind; to cause something to be thought of in a certain way; to cause something to be a reminder to someone. (The object can be a clause with THAT ⑦.)

suggestion [səg 'dʒɛs tʃən] **1.** *n.* a hint; a trace; something that reminds someone of someone or something. (No plural.) **2.** *n.* a proposal to be considered; an expression of something that one thinks should be considered; the offering of an option; something that is suggested.

suggestive of something reminiscent of something; seeming to suggest something.

suicide ['su ə saɪd] **1.** *n.* killing oneself on purpose. (No plural.) **2.** *n.* someone who has committed ①.

suit ['sut] **1.** *n.* a set of formal clothes, consisting of a jacket, pants, and sometimes a vest, made from the same material. **2.** *n.* a set of things, such as clothing or armor, that are worn together. **3.** *n.* a statement of claims against someone or a business, brought to a court of law. (Short for LAWSUIT.) **4.** *n.* one of the four different sets of cards found in a deck of playing cards: clubs, hearts, spades, and diamonds. **5.** *tv.* to meet the requirements of someone or something. **6.** *tv.* to look good with something; to look good on someone; to match someone.
→ IN ONE'S BIRTHDAY SUIT

suit someone **to a T** AND **fit** someone **to a T** to be very appropriate for someone.

suit yourself Go to PLEASE YOURSELF.

suitable ['su tə bəl] *adj.* right or proper for the situation. (Adv: *suitably.*)

suitcase ['sut kes] *n.* a piece of luggage used for carrying clothing and other personal items while traveling.
→ LIVE OUT OF A SUITCASE

sullen ['sʌl ən] *adj.* being silent and looking angry and irritated because one is in a bad mood. (Adv: *sullenly.*)

sum ['sʌm] **1.** *n.* the total of two or more amounts. **2.** *n.* an amount of money.
→ LUMP SUM

sum (something**) up** to give a summary of something.

summarize ['sʌm ə raɪz] *tv.* to express the main ideas of something.

summary ['sʌm ə ri] *n.* the main ideas of something; a short statement about the important points of a longer speech or text.

summer ['sʌm ɚ] **1.** *n.* one of the seasons of the year, after spring and before autumn. **2.** the *adj.* use of ①.
→ ALL SUMMER LONG

summertime ['sʌm ɚ taɪm] *n.* summer; the season of summer. (No plural.)

summit ['sʌm ət] **1.** *n.* the highest point of something, especially a mountain. **2.** *n.* a meeting involving very important people, especially leaders of governments. (Figurative on ①.)

sun ['sʌn] **1.** *n.* a star; a star that gives light and warmth to a planet; a star that is orbited by a planet. **2.** the SUN (listed below); the star at the center of our solar system; the star that shines on the earth. **3.** *tv.* to expose oneself to the light of ②; to "bathe" oneself in sunlight. (Takes a reflexive object.) **4.** *iv.* to absorb the rays of ②; to "bathe" in the light of ②.

the sun 1. *n.* the star that gives light and warmth to earth; the star that earth orbits. (No plural. Treated as singular. Often capitalized.) **2.** *n.* sunlight; light and warmth that is radiated by ①. (No plural. Treated as singular.)

sunbeam ['sʌn bim] *n.* a ray of sunlight; a beam of sunlight.

sunblock ['sʌn blɑk] Go to SUN-SCREEN.

sunburn ['sʌn bɚn] **1.** *n.* redness and soreness of skin that has been exposed too long to sunlight. (Plural only for types and instances.) **2.** *iv.* [for one's skin] to acquire ①.

sundae ['sʌn de] *n.* a dessert made with ice cream and flavored sauces or toppings.

Sunday ['sʌn de] Go to DAY.

sung ['sʌŋ] Past participle of SING.

sunglasses ['sʌn glæs ɪz] *n.* glasses with dark lenses that are worn to protect the eyes from bright sunlight. (Treated as plural. Number is expressed with *pair(s) of sunglasses.*)

sunk ['sʌŋk] a past tense of SINK; past participle of SINK.

sunlight ['sʌn laɪt] *n.* the light that is given off by the sun. (No plural.)

sunny ['sʌn i] *adj.* with bright sunshine. (Comp: *sunnier;* sup: *sunniest.*)

sunrise ['sʌn raɪz] *n.* the time of day when the sun appears to be moving above the horizon in the east.

sunscreen AND **sunblock** ['sʌn skrin, 'sʌn blɑk] *n.* lotion or cream containing a chemical substance that helps prevent sun damage to the skin. (Plural only for types and instances.)

sunset ['sʌn sɛt] *n.* the time of day when the sun appears to be moving below the horizon in the west.

sunshine ['sʌn ʃaɪn] *n.* sunlight; light from the sun. (No plural.)

super ['sup ɚ] **1.** *adj.* excellent; wonderful; great; marvelous; fabulous. **2.** *adj.* extra large.

superb [sə 'pɚb] *adj.* very good; excellent; of the best quality. (Adv: *superbly.*)

superior [sə 'pɪr i ɚ] **1.** *n.* someone who has a higher rank or position in relationship to someone else. **2.** *adj.* very good; above average; better than something else. (Adv: *superiorly.*)

superiority [sə pɪr i 'ɔr i ti] *n.* the condition of being superior to someone or something else. (No plural.)

superlative [sə 'pɚl ə tɪv] **1.** *n.* the form of an adjective or adverb, usually created with *most* or *-est,* that indicates the highest degree of comparison of that adjective or adverb. **2.** *adj.* having the highest quality. (Adv: *superlatively.*)

supermarket ['su pɚ mɑr kɪt] *n.* a large, food store that stocks several kinds of each item, allowing customers a wide choice.

supervise ['su pɚ vaɪz] *tv.* to direct a worker or a group of workers; to direct something; to oversee someone or something.

supervision [su pɚ 'vɪ ʒən] *n.* paying attention to or watching over [someone or something]. (No plural.)

supper ['sʌp ɚ] *n.* the meal eaten in the evening. (See also DINNER.)

suppertime ['sʌp ɚ taɪm] *n.* the time when supper is eaten. (No plural.)

supply [sə 'plaɪ] **1.** *tv.* to give someone something that is needed or wanted; to give something to someone who needs or wants it. **2.** *n.* an amount of something that

is available; an allotment of something. (Sometimes plural.)
→ IN SHORT SUPPLY

support ['sə 'pɔrt] **1.** *tv.* to provide someone with money, shelter, clothing, and food. **2.** *tv.* to bear the weight of something; to keep something vertical or in place so that it doesn't fall. **3.** *tv.* to give someone or something one's encouragement or favor; to show someone or something approval or favor. **4.** *n.* providing someone with money, shelter, food, and clothing. (No plural.) **5.** *n.* the strength and structure needed to bear the weight of someone or something. (No plural.) **6.** *n.* something that carries the weight of something; a beam; a prop. **7.** *n.* encouragement. (No plural.)
→ MORAL SUPPORT
→ A PILLAR OF SUPPORT

suppose [sə 'poz] *tv.* to consider or imagine that something is or will be true. (The object is a clause with THAT ⑦.)

supposed to do something expected or intended to do something; obliged or allowed to do something.

supreme [sə 'prim] **1.** *adj.* having total authority; having total power; having the highest rank; being the most important. (Adv: *supremely.*) **2.** *adj.* of the highest quality. (Adv: *supremely.*)

sure ['ʃʊr] **1.** *adj.* certain; confident or knowing that something is the case. (Adv: *surely.* Comp: *surer;* sup: *surest.*) **2.** *adv.* certainly. (Informal.) **3.** *adv.* [in response to a yes-or-no question] yes. (Informal.)

surely ['ʃʊr li] *adv.* certainly; without doubt; definitely.

surf ['səf] *n.* waves of water hitting the beach. (No plural.)

surface ['sə fəs] **1.** *n.* the outside of something; the outside layer of something. **2.** *n.* the top of a liquid. **3.** *iv.* [for something underwater] to go up to or above the ② of the water.
→ SCRATCH THE SURFACE

surge ['sədʒ] **1.** *n.* a sudden, powerful burst of electricity. **2.** *n.* a strong forward movement.

surge in(to something) to burst or gush into something or someplace.

surge out (of something) to burst forth or gush out of something or someplace.

surge up to rush or gush upwards.

surgeon ['sə dʒən] *n.* a physician who performs surgery.

surgery ['sə dʒə ri] **1.** *n.* the science and practice of curing sickness and treating injury by performing an OPERATION ①. (No plural.) **2.** *n.* using ① in treating illness and disease.
→ IN SURGERY

surname ['sə nem] *n.* the family name; [in the United States] the last name. (Compare this with FIRST NAME.)

surplus ['sə pləs] **1.** *n.* an amount of something that is more than what is needed; an extra amount; an excess. **2.** *the adj.* use of ①.

surprise [sə 'praɪz] **1.** *n.* something that is not expected; something that happens without

warning. **2.** *n.* the feeling that is caused by something unexpected happening. (No plural.) **3.** *tv.* to cause someone to feel ② by doing something or saying something unexpected. **4.** *tv.* to attack someone or something without warning. **5.** *adj.* unexpected; without warning.
→ COME AS NO SURPRISE
→ TAKE SOMEONE BY SURPRISE

surrender [sə 'rɛn dɚ] **1.** *iv.* to give up, especially when one has lost a battle, argument, or fight; to yield to a force that one has fought against. **2.** *tv.* to give someone or something up to someone; to yield someone or something to someone else. **3.** *n.* giving up as in ①. (No plural.)

surround [sə 'raʊnd] *tv.* to enclose someone or something on all sides; to be on all sides of someone or something.

survey 1. ['sɚ ve] *n.* a set of questions used to collect people's opinions and evidence of their attitudes. **2.** ['sɚ ve] *n.* a document containing ①. **3.** ['sɚ ve] *n.* an examination or study of the condition, contents, or details of something. **4.** ['sɚ ve] *n.* a description or analysis of a subject of study. **5.** ['sɚ ve] *n.* the measurement of land so that accurate maps can be made or so that the legal description of property boundaries is exact. **6.** ['sɚ ve] *tv.* to collect people's opinions on an issue; to ask people for their opinions on an issue. **7.** [sɚ 've] *tv.* to examine or study the condition, contents, or details of something. **8.** [sɚ 've] *tv.* to measure part of

the surface of the earth—or a similar area—exactly, so that accurate maps or legal descriptions can be made.

survive [sɚ 'vaɪv] **1.** *iv.* to remain alive even after a threat to one's life; to live a very long life. **2.** *tv.* to endure someone or something and remain alive or functioning. **3.** *tv.* to outlive someone; to live longer than someone.

survivor [sɚ 'vaɪv ɚ] *n.* someone who remains alive; someone who did not die while others died.

susceptible to something **1.** easily persuaded by something; easily influenced by something. **2.** likely to contract a sickness; likely to become sick.

suspect 1. ['sʌs pɛkt] *n.* someone who is thought to have committed a crime. **2.** ['sʌs pɛkt] *adj.* causing questioning or doubt. (Adv: *suspectly.*) **3.** [sə 'spɛkt] *tv.* to consider something to be likely or true. (The object can be a clause with THAT ⑦.)

suspend [sə 'spɛnd] **1.** *tv.* to hang something from something else; to cause something to hang down from something else above it. **2.** *tv.* to delay something; to stop something for a period of time. **3.** *tv.* to prevent someone from working at a job, attending classes, etc., for a period of time, as a punishment. **4.** *tv.* to cause something to float in the air or in a liquid.

suspense [sə 'spɛns] *n.* an anxious, scary, or uncertain feeling that is caused by not knowing what is going to happen next. (No plural.)

suspicion [sə'spɪʃən] **1.** *n.* an uneasy feeling in which one suspects something. (No plural form.) **2.** *n.* a suspicious idea, as in ①, about someone or something.
→ UNDER A CLOUD (OF SUSPICION)

sustain [sə'sten] **1.** *tv.* to nourish and care for living plants and creatures. **2.** *tv.* to keep something moving, going, or working; to prolong something. **3.** *tv.* to suffer an injury; to have an injury.

swallow ['swɑl o] **1.** *tv.* to cause food or drink to go down one's throat and into the stomach. **2.** *tv.* to believe something without question; to believe something that one is told, even if it is a lie; to accept something that one is told. (Figurative on ①. Informal.) **3.** *iv.* to take [something] into the body by way of the throat. **4.** *n.* the amount of something that can be taken into the mouth and sent down the throat. **5.** *n.* a kind of small songbird.
→ LOOK LIKE THE CAT THAT SWALLOWED THE CANARY

swallow someone or something **up 1.** to eat or gobble up someone or something. **2.** to engulf or contain someone or something. (Figurative.)

swallow something **down** to swallow something.

swam ['swæm] past tense of SWIM.

swamp ['swɑmp] **1.** *n.* an area of very wet, muddy ground, sometimes covered with water. **2.** *tv.* to flood something, especially a boat.

swan ['swɑn] *n.* a large, white bird that lives near the water and has a long, curving neck.

swan song the last work or performance of a playwright, musician, actor, etc., before death or retirement.

swap ['swɑp] **1.** *iv.* to exchange; to trade. **2.** *n.* an exchange; a trade.

swap someone or something **for** someone or something to exchange something for something else; to trade something for something else; to exchange someone for someone else; to trade someone for someone else.

swarm ['swɔrm] *n.* a large number of people or animals, especially bees or other insects, that move together in a densely packed group.

swat ['swɑt] **1.** *tv.* to hit someone or something hard. **2.** *n.* a hard hit; a sharp blow.

sway ['swe] **1.** *iv.* to bend or swing back and forth; to bend to one side and then the other; to move back and forth. **2.** *tv.* to cause someone or something to bend or move back and forth; to bend or move someone or something back and forth. **3.** *tv.* to change someone's opinion or judgment; to influence someone. (Figurative on ②.)

swear ['swɛr] **1.** *iv., irreg.* to curse; to say bad words angrily. (Past tense: SWORE; past participle: SWORN.) **2.** *tv.* to promise or vow something.

swear at someone or something to curse at someone or something present.

swear by someone or something **1.** to utter an oath on someone or something. **2.** to announce one's full faith and trust in someone or something.

swear someone **in** [for an officer of the court] to cause someone to pledge to tell the truth or perform the duties required by law; to cause someone to take an oath.

swear someone **in (as** something**)** to administer an oath to someone who then becomes something.

swear to do something to vow to do something; to make a pledge to do something.

sweat ['swɛt] **1.** *n.* the moisture that comes out of the body through pores in the skin. (No plural.) **2.** *n.* hard work; labor; something that causes ①. (No plural.) **3.** *iv., irreg.* [for moisture] to come out of the body through pores in the skin. (Past tense and past participle: *sweat* or *sweated*.) **4.** *iv.* to work very hard; to labor.
→ BREAK OUT IN A COLD SWEAT
→ BY THE SWEAT OF ONE'S BROW

sweater ['swɛt ɚ] *n.* a warm piece of clothing worn above the waist, usually woven or knitted from wool or cotton.

sweatpants ['swɛt pænts] *n.* warm pants, usually with a soft or fluffy inside layer. (Treated as plural. Number is expressed with *pair(s) of sweatpants*.)

sweatshirt ['swɛt ʃɚt] *n.* a warm, long-sleeved shirt, usually with a soft or fluffy inside layer.

sweaty ['swɛt i] **1.** *adj.* covered with sweat. (Adv: *sweatily*. Comp: *sweatier*; sup: *sweatiest*.) **2.** *adj.* causing sweat, especially because of hot, humid weather or hard

work. (Comp: *sweatier*; sup: *sweatiest*.)

sweep ['swip] **1.** *tv., irreg.* to clean a floor by passing a broom over it; to clean a surface by moving a broom or brush over it to push the dirt away. (Past tense and past participle: SWEPT.) **2.** *iv., irreg.* to clean as in ①. **3.** *n.* a smooth, flowing motion, especially in a curve; a swinging movement.

sweep out of someplace to move or leave in a very noticeable or theatrical way.

sweep something **off ((of)** something**)** to clean something by sweeping.

sweep something **out** to clean something out by sweeping.

sweep something **under the carpet** AND **brush** something **under the carpet** to try to hide something unpleasant, shameful, etc., from the attention of others.

sweep something **up 1.** to clean up and remove something, such as dirt, by sweeping. **2.** to clean up someplace by sweeping. **3.** to arrange something, such as hair, into a curve or wave.

sweep up to clean up by sweeping.

sweet ['swit] **1.** *adj.* tasting like sugar; like sugar or honey. (Adv: *sweetly*. Comp: *sweeter*; sup: *sweetest*.) **2.** *adj.* pleasant; pleasing; having personal charm. (Adv: *sweetly*. Comp: *sweeter*; sup: *sweetest*.)
→ HAVE A SWEET TOOTH
→ TAKE THE BITTER WITH THE SWEET

sweet nothings affectionate but unimportant or meaningless words spoken to a loved one.

sweet tooth ['swit tuθ] *n.* a liking for chocolate, chocolate, or other sweet foods. (Always singular.)

sweeten ['swit n] *tv.* to cause something to become sweet; to add sugar to something.

sweets *n.* candy; pieces of something made with sugar or honey. (Treated as plural.)

swell ['swɛl] **1.** *iv., irreg.* to grow larger; to grow fuller; to rise or grow past the regular amount. (Past tense: *swelled;* past participle: *swelled* or SWOLLEN.) **2.** *iv., irreg.* to increase in size, amount, or intensity. **3.** *tv., irreg.* to cause someone or something to grow larger or fuller; to increase something in size, amount, or intensity. **4.** *n.* the rise and fall of waves.

swell up to enlarge; to inflate; to bulge out.

swelter ['swɛl tɚ] *iv.* to suffer in very hot weather.

swept ['swɛpt] past tense and past participle of SWEEP.

swift ['swɪft] *adj.* rapid; quick; moving or passing fast. (Adv: *swiftly.* Comp: *swifter;* sup: *swiftest.*)

swim ['swɪm] **1.** *iv., irreg.* [for someone] to travel through water by moving arms and legs; [for an animal] to travel through water by moving paws, legs, fins, tail, etc. (Past tense: SWAM; past participle: SWUM.) **2.** *iv., irreg.* [for something] to seem to spin or revolve, owing to one's illness or the loss of one's ability to properly perceive. **3.** *n.* an instance of traveling

through the water by moving one's arms and legs.
→ BE SWIMMING IN SOMETHING
→ MAKE SOMEONE'S HEAD SWIM
→ SINK OR SWIM
→ SWIMMING POOL

swim against the current Go to SWIM AGAINST THE TIDE.

swim against the tide AND **swim against the current** to do the opposite of everyone else; to go against the trend.

swimming pool ['swɪm ɪŋ 'pʊl] *n.* a container or tank that holds water for people to swim or play in. (Can be shortened to POOL.)

swimsuit ['swɪm sut] *n.* a piece of clothing worn for sunning or swimming; the clothing worn by someone who swims.

swindle ['swɪn dəl] **1.** *tv.* to cheat someone, especially to cheat someone out of money. **2.** *n.* cheating; cheating people out of their money.

swine ['swɑɪn] **1.** *n., irreg.* a hog or a pig. (Plural: *swine.*) **2.** *n., irreg.* someone who is disgusting, unpleasant, or contemptible. (Figurative on ①.)
→ CAST (ONE'S) PEARLS BEFORE SWINE

swing ['swɪŋ] **1.** *tv., irreg.* to move something in a sweeping or curved pattern. (Past tense and past participle: SWUNG.) **2.** *tv., irreg.* to move something in a sweeping or circular movement. **3.** *iv., irreg.* to move in a sweeping or curved pattern. **4.** *iv., irreg.* to move while hanging from a fixed point. **5.** *iv., irreg.* to turn suddenly or quickly. **6.** *iv., irreg.* to play on ⑧; to move one's body through the air on a ⑧.

7. *n.* a change; a variation. **8.** *n.* a seat that hangs on ropes or chains, which moves people, usually children, back and forth.
→ GET INTO THE SWING OF THINGS
→ IN FULL SWING

swish something **off ((of)** someone or something) to brush something off someone or something.

switch ['swɪtʃ] **1.** *n.* a lever that turns electricity on and off. **2.** *n.* a change from one thing to another. **3.** *n.* a thin, flexible stick that is cut from a tree. **4.** *tv.* to change something; to swap or exchange things.
→ ASLEEP AT THE SWITCH

switch back (to something) **1.** to return to using or doing something. **2.** [for a road] to reverse upon itself.

switch off 1. [for something] to turn itself off. **2.** [for someone] to stop paying attention. (Figurative.)

switch someone or something **off** to cause someone or something to be quiet or stop doing something.

switch something **back (to** something) to return something to the way it was.

switch something **on** to cause something electrical to start functioning or operating by using a switch.

switch something **on** AND **switch** something **off** to close or open an electric circuit; to turn something on or off.

switchboard ['swɪtʃ bord] *n.* a control panel that an operator uses to connect telephone calls to the proper person.

swollen ['swol ən] **1.** Past participle of SWELL. **2.** *adj.* puffed up; having gotten bigger; growing in size. (Adv: *swollenly.*)

swoop ['swup] *n.* a dive through the air.
→ AT ONE FELL SWOOP
→ IN ONE FELL SWOOP

swoop down (up)on someone or something to dive or plunge downward on someone or something. (Both literal and figurative uses.)

sword ['sord] *n.* a heavy metal weapon with a long, usually sharp blade attached to a handle.
→ CROSS SWORDS (WITH SOMEONE)

swore ['swor] past tense of SWEAR.

sworn ['sworn] Past participle of SWEAR.

swum ['swʌm] past participle of SWIM.

swung ['swʌŋ] past tense and past participle of SWING.

syllable ['sɪl ə bəl] *n.* an uninterrupted segment of speech consisting of a vowel possibly with consonants on one or both sides.

symbol ['sɪm bəl] **1.** *n.* something that represents something else; something that stands for something else. **2.** *n.* a letter, number, or shape that represents a quantity, chemical element, mathematical operation, or other function.

symmetry ['sɪm ə tri] *n.* the arrangement of the opposite sides of something so that they look exactly alike. (No plural.)

sympathy ['sɪm pə θi] *n.* kind feelings for someone having problems and sorrows.
→ ONE'S DEEPEST SYMPATHY

symphony ['sɪm fə ni] *n.* a long piece of music written for an orchestra.

symptom ['sɪmp təm] *n.* a sign, feeling, or problem that is evidence of the existence of something, especially of an illness.

synagogue AND **synagog** ['sɪn ə gɑg] *n.* a building for worship in the Jewish religion.

synonym ['sɪ nə nɪm] *n.* a word that has the same or almost the same meaning as another word.

syphon ['sɑɪ fən] Go to SIPHON.

syringe [sə 'rɪndʒ] *n.* a device from which liquids are pushed out or into which liquids are pulled, usually through a long, thin needle.

syrup ['sɪr əp] *n.* a thick, sweet liquid eaten as food or used to deliver medication. (Plural only for types and instances.)

system ['sɪs təm] **1.** *n.* a group of things that work together to form a network; a group of things arranged in a particular way that function as one thing. **2.** *n.* a method of arrangement; a plan.

systematic [sɪs tə 'mæt ɪk] *adj.* organized and structured; based on a system or plan. (Adv: *systematically* [...ɪk li].)

T

tab ['tæb] **1.** *n.* a small flap that sticks out from the edge of a sheet of paper, cardboard, or something similar. **2.** *n.* a bill that is presented to a customer for payment.
→ PICK UP THE TAB

table ['teb əl] **1.** *n.* an item of furniture whose top is a raised, flat surface supported by legs. **2.** *n.* a chart of numbers, facts, or data presented in columns or rows.
→ CLEAR THE TABLE
→ LAY ONE'S CARDS ON THE TABLE
→ PUT ONE'S CARDS ON THE TABLE
→ SET THE TABLE
→ UNDER THE TABLE

table a motion to postpone the discussion of something during a meeting.

table of contents ['teb əl əv 'kɑn tɛnts] *n.* a list at the beginning of a book, showing what is in the book and the page number of each part.

tablecloth ['teb əl klɔθ] *n.* a piece of fabric that covers the top of a table and hangs over the sides, for decoration or protection of the table's surface.

tablet ['tæb lət] **1.** *n.* a pad of paper; blank sheets of paper that are bound together along the top or side. **2.** *n.* a pill; a small, hard piece of medicine, drugs, or vitamins that a person swallows.

tack ['tæk] **1.** *n.* a small, thin nail with a large head. (See also THUMB-TACK.) **2.** *n.* a course of action that is different from an earlier one; an attempt to do something after earlier attempts have not worked. **3.** *n.* the direction that a ship trav-

els as the result of the wind and the way that its sails are arranged.
→ GET DOWN TO BRASS TACKS

tackle ['tæk əl] **1.** *tv.* to run after, dive onto, and throw a person to the ground, especially in the game of football. **2.** *tv.* to undertake a duty or a problem; to start working on something difficult. (Figurative on ①.) **3.** *n.* equipment used for fishing. (No plural.)

tact ['tækt] *n.* the ability to deal with people without offending them. (No plural.)

tactful ['tækt fʊl] *adj.* showing or having tact. (Adv: *tactfully.*)

tactic ['tæk tɪk] *n.* a skillful way of doing something in order to reach a goal. (Often plural.)

tag ['tæg] **1.** *n.* a small label that has information about the object that it is attached to. **2.** *n.* a game in which a players run around trying to touch someone else, who then runs to touch another person. (No plural.) **3.** *tv.* to put ① on something or some creature. **4.** *tv.* to touch someone, especially in ②.

tag along to go along with or follow someone, often when uninvited or unwanted. (Informal.)

tail ['tel] **1.** *n.* the part of an animal that hangs off from its back, as an extension of the spine. **2.** *n.* the rear part of something; the last part of something. (Figurative on ①.)
→ CAN'T MAKE HEADS OR TAILS (OUT) OF SOMEONE OR SOMETHING
→ HAVE ONE'S TAIL BETWEEN ONE'S LEGS

→ IN TWO SHAKES OF A LAMB'S TAIL
→ ONE'S TAIL IS BETWEEN ONE'S LEGS

the **tail wagging the dog** [a situation in which] a small part [is] controlling the whole thing.

tailor ['te lɚ] **1.** *n.* someone who makes or repairs clothes. **2.** *tv.* to make or repair an item of clothing so that it fits a certain person.

tailspin *n.* a sudden spinning or period of confusion.
→ GO INTO A TAILSPIN

take ['tek] **1.** *tv., irreg.* to get or obtain something by one's own action. (Past tense: TOOK; past participle: TAKEN.) **2.** *tv., irreg.* to accept something that is offered. **3.** *tv., irreg.* to capture something; to win something. **4.** *tv., irreg.* to eat or swallow something, such as medicine. **5.** *tv., irreg.* to use something on a regular basis; to require something as a habit. **6.** *tv., irreg.* to transport someone or something somewhere. **7.** *tv., irreg.* to use a form of transportation, especially public transportation. **8.** *tv., irreg.* to lead someone or something; to guide someone or something. **9.** *tv., irreg.* to record something; to make a picture with a camera. **10.** *tv., irreg.* to interpret something in a certain way. **11.** *tv., irreg.* to observe the measurement of something. **12.** *tv., irreg.* to suffer something; to endure something; to accept something. **13.** *tv., irreg.* to use up time; to consume time; to require that an amount of time be spent [doing something].
→ AS A DUCK TAKES TO WATER
→ MORE THAN ONE CAN TAKE
→ SIT UP AND TAKE NOTICE
→ THAT TAKES CARE OF THAT.

take a backseat (to someone**)** to give control to someone.

take a course (in something**)** to enroll in a course and do the required work.

take a leaf out of someone's **book** to behave or to do something in the way that someone else would. (A *leaf* is a page.)

take a load off one's **feet** Go to GET A LOAD OFF ONE'S FEET.

take a look for someone or something AND **have a look for** someone or something to make a visual search for someone or something; to look for someone or something.

take a nap to sleep for a period of time during the day.

take a nosedive Go to GO INTO A NOSEDIVE.

take a peep Go to HAVE A PEEP.

take a secret to one's **grave** Go to CARRY A SECRET TO THE GRAVE.

take a shot at something Go to GIVE SOMETHING A SHOT.

take a vacation to go somewhere for a vacation; to stop work to have a vacation.

take advantage of someone to use someone unfairly for one's own benefit.

take advantage of something to make good use of something; to benefit from something; to benefit from an opportunity.

take an oath to make an OATH; to promise something as with an OATH.

take attendance to make a record of persons attending something.

take care of someone or something **1.** to deal with someone or something; to handle or manage someone or something. **2.** to provide care for someone or something.

take cold Go to CATCH COLD.

take forty winks to take a nap; to go to sleep.

take heed ['tek 'hid] to be careful; to take care and watch for danger.

take inventory to make an inventory list.

take it or leave it to accept something the way it is or not have it at all.

take off 1. to take flight. **2.** [for someone] to leave. (Colloquial.) **3.** to become active and exciting. (Colloquial.)

take off from something to take flight from something or someplace.

take one's **cue from** someone to use someone else's behavior or reactions as a guide to one's own.

take one's **death (of cold)** Go to CATCH ONE'S DEATH (OF COLD).

take one's **medicine** to accept the punishment that one deserves. (Also used literally.)

take out a loan to get a loan of money, especially from a bank.

take out after someone or something to set out chasing or running after someone or something.

take over (from someone**)** to assume the role or job of someone else.

take pride in something to do something with pride; to have pride for or about something.

take shape [for something, such as plans, writing, ideas, arguments, etc.] to become organized and specific.

take someone **by surprise** to startle someone; to surprise someone with something unexpected.

take someone **hostage** to kidnap or seize someone to be a hostage.

take someone **in 1.** to give someone shelter. **2.** to deceive someone.

take someone or something **at face value** to accept someone or something as actually being the way the person or thing appears to be.

take someone or something **away** to remove someone or something.

take someone or something **by storm** to overwhelm someone or something; to attract a great deal of attention from someone or something.

take someone or something **for granted** to accept someone or something—without gratitude.

take someone or something **off (something)** to remove someone or something from the surface of something else.

take someone or something **on** to agree to deal with someone or something; to begin to handle someone or something.

take someone or something **out (of something)** to carry, lead, or guide someone or something out of something or someplace.

take someone **under** one's **wing(s)** to take over the responsibility of caring for a person.

take someone's **breath away** to overwhelm someone with beauty or grandeur.

take someone's **part** to take someone's side in an argument; to support someone in an argument.

take someone's **pulse** to measure the frequency of the beats of the heart.

take something **apart** to break something to pieces.

take something **down (in something)** to write something down in something, such as a notebook.

take something **in 1.** to reduce the size of a garment. **2.** to bring something or a creature into shelter. **3.** to view and study something; to attend something involving viewing. **4.** to receive money as payment or proceeds. **5.** to receive something into the mind, usually visually.

take something **in stride** to accept something as natural or expected.

take something **lying down** to endure something unpleasant without fighting back.

take something **off** to remove something, such as an article of clothing.

take something **on faith** to accept or believe something on the basis of little or no evidence.

take something **on the chin** to experience and endure a direct blow or assault.

take something **over 1.** to assume responsibility for a task. **2.** to acquire all of an asset or a problem.

take something **personally** to interpret a remark as if it were mean or critical about oneself.

take something **up 1.** [for someone or a group] to decide to discuss a particular topic. **2.** to raise something, such as the height of a hem. **3.** to continue with something after an interruption. **4.** to begin something; to start to acquire a skill in something.

take something **with a grain of salt** Go to TAKE SOMETHING WITH A PINCH OF SALT.

take something **with a pinch of salt** AND **take** something **with a grain of salt** to listen to a story or an explanation with considerable doubt.

take the bitter with the sweet to accept the bad things along with the good things.

take the bull by the horns to meet a challenge directly.

take the law into one's **own hands** to attempt to administer the law oneself; to act as a judge and jury for someone who has done something wrong.

take (the) roll Go to CALL (THE) ROLL.

take the stand to go to and sit in the witness chair on the witness stand in a courtroom in preparation to testify.

take the words (right) out of one's **mouth** [for someone else] to say what one was about to say oneself.

take to one's **heels** to run away.

take too much on to accept too many tasks; to accept a task that is too big a burden for one.

take up one's **abode** somewhere to settle down and live somewhere. (Literary.)

taken ['tek ən] past participle of TAKE.

takeoff ['tek ɔf] *n.* [an airplane's] leaving the ground and flying.

tale ['tel] **1.** *n.* a story. **2.** *n.* a lie.
→ TALL TALE
→ TELL ITS OWN TALE
→ TELL TALES OUT OF SCHOOL

talent ['tæl ənt] **1.** *n.* a special skill; a natural ability. **2.** *n.* people who have a special skill or a natural ability, especially singers or actors; people employed or seeking employment in the entertainment industry. (No plural. Treated as singular.)

talk ['tɔk] **1.** *iv.* to communicate by speaking; to say words. **2.** *iv.* to speak with someone; to have a conversation with someone. **3.** *n.* the production of words; speech. (No plural.) **4.** *n.* a conversation; a chat with someone. **5.** *n.* a speech; a lecture. **6.** *n.* gossip; rumors. (No plural.)
→ LIKE TO HEAR ONESELF TALK
→ MONEY TALKS.
→ SMALL TALK

talk a blue streak to say a lot and talk very rapidly.

talk around something to talk, but avoid talking directly about the subject.

talk back (to someone**)** to challenge verbally a parent, an older person, or one's superior.

talk in circles to talk in a confusing or roundabout manner.

talk of the town the subject of gossip; someone or something that everyone is talking about.

talk oneself **out** to talk until one can talk no more.

talk shop to talk about business matters at a social event (where business talk is not welcome).

talk show ['tɔk ʃo] **1.** *n.* a radio or television program devoted to conversation and opinion by different people. **2.** the *adj.* use of ①. (Hyphenated.)

talk someone **into** something to convince someone to do something through discussion.

talk something **out** to settle something by discussion.

talk something **up** to promote or advertise something by saying good things about it to as many people as possible.

talk through one's **hat** to talk nonsense; to brag and boast.

talk until one **is blue in the face** to talk until one is exhausted.

talks *n.* conversations held for the purpose of negotiating something.

tall ['tɔl] **1.** *adj.* great in height; of a greater height than average; not short. (E.g., *the tree is tall; the tall tree.* Comp: *taller;* sup: *tallest.*) **2.** *adj.* extending a certain distance upward; reaching a certain distance above the ground. (E.g., *the tree is 30 feet tall.* Comp: *taller;* sup: *tallest.*)

tall story AND **tall tale** a story that is difficult or impossible to believe; a lie.

tall tale Go to TALL STORY.

tally ['tæl i] *n.* a score; a mark used to keep track of the number of something being counted; the number of points or votes someone or something has received.

tally something **(up)** to count the number of votes or points that someone or something has received.

tally (with an amount) [for an amount] to match another amount; [for two amounts] to be equal.

tame ['tem] **1.** *adj.* not in a natural, wild state; living with people; being gentle rather than fierce. (Adv: *tamely.* Comp: *tamer;* sup: *tamest.*) **2.** *adj.* not shocking; not wild; not exciting; dull. (Figurative on ①. Adv: *tamely.* Comp: *tamer;* sup: *tamest.*)

tan ['tæn] **1.** *iv.* [especially of people with fair skin] to permit one's skin to darken by being outdoors in sunlight or by exposing oneself to artificial sunlight. **2.** *tv.* to change the skin of an animal into leather by soaking it in a special chemical. **3.** *n.* darkness of the skin from exposure to sunlight as in ①. **4.** *n.* a light brown color. **5.** *adj.* light brown in color. (Comp: *tanner;* sup: *tannest.*)

tandem ['tæn dəm] *adj.* [of two or more people or things] in sequence, one behind another. (Adv: *tandemly.*)
→ IN TANDEM

tangent ['tæn dʒənt] *n.* a line that touches a circle at only one point.
→ GO OFF ON A TANGENT

tangerine [tæn dʒə 'rin] **1.** *n.* a small, orange citrus fruit; a kind of orange whose peel is easy to remove. **2.** the *adj.* use of ①.

tangle ['tæŋ gəl] **1.** *n.* a twisted clump of hair, string, chain, rope, limbs, etc. **2.** *n.* an argument; a disagreement. **3.** *iv.* [for strands] to become twisted together. **4.** *tv.* to twist strands together; to snarl something.

tank ['tæŋk] **1.** *n.* a container for storing air or liquid. (See also FISH TANK.) **2.** *n.* a large vehicle, used by the military, that moves on heavy belts wrapped around a set of wheels.

tantrum ['tæn trəm] *n.* a bad display of temper and emotion. (Short for TEMPER TANTRUM.)
→ TEMPER TANTRUM

tap ['tæp] **1.** *n.* a slight pressure or a very light blow made by something. **2.** *n.* a device that controls the flow of a gas or a liquid from a pipe or a barrel; a faucet. **3.** *tv.* to touch someone or something gently a number of times, especially with the tip of one's finger. **4.** *tv.* to cut something open so that liquid will flow out; to pierce something, such as a barrel, so that liquid will flow out.

tape ['tep] **1.** *n.* a paper or plastic strip with one side that is sticky, used to stick something to something else. (Plural only for types and instances.) **2.** *n.* a magnetic strip of plastic onto which sound or images can be recorded. (No

plural.) **3.** *n.* a reel or cassette of ②; something recorded on a reel or cassette of ②. **4.** *tv.* to stick something to something else with ①; to seal something with ①. **5.** *tv.* to fix something that is torn by placing ① over the tear. **6.** *tv.* to record sound or images onto ②. **7.** *iv.* to make a sound or video recording; to record.
→ RED TAPE

taper off to slacken off gradually; to cease something gradually; to reduce gradually.

tar ['tɑr] **1.** *n.* a black substance similar to very thick oil, used to preserve or waterproof objects. (No plural.) **2.** *tv.* to cover something with ①; to preserve or waterproof something with ①.

tardy ['tɑr di] *adj.* late; not prompt; not on time. (Adv: *tardily.* Comp: *tardier;* sup: *tardiest.*)

target ['tɑr gət] **1.** *n.* someone or something that someone tries to hit or shoot when using a weapon. **2.** someone who is ridiculed, blamed, or made fun of. (Figurative on ①.) **3.** *n.* a goal that one would like to reach; an aim. (Figurative on ①.) **4.** *tv.* to establish something as a goal. **5.** *tv.* to focus on someone, something, or someplace; to give something, someone, or someplace the greatest amount of thought or effort.
→ ON TARGET
→ SITTING TARGET

tariff ['tɛr ɪf] **1.** *n.* a tax that a government charges on products entering or leaving a country. **2.** *n.* the cost of a service, such as the service provided by a utility.

tarred with the same brush having the same faults or bad points as someone else.

task ['tæsk] *n.* a duty; an errand; a responsibility; a chore; an item of work that someone must do, especially a difficult one.

task force ['tæsk fors] *n.* a group of people who are given a certain task, such as a military group that has a certain mission.

taste ['test] **1.** *n.* the ability to sense or experience sweetness, saltiness, bitterness, or sourness with one's tongue. (No plural.) **2.** *n.* a particular flavor as experienced through ①. **3.** *n.* a small sample of food or drink. **4.** *n.* the quality of one's choice or selection in beauty, fashion, or art; the ability to judge what is suitable or fitting. (Plural only for types and instances.) **5.** *tv.* to sense or experience flavor with one's tongue. **6.** *tv.* to put something in one's mouth or on one's tongue so that one can know its flavor; to eat a very small amount of something so one can know its flavor. **7.** *tv.* to experience something for a short while. **8.** *iv.* [for a food] to have a particular flavor.
→ HAVE A TASTE FOR SOMETHING
→ IN BAD TASTE
→ IN POOR TASTE
→ LEAVE A BAD TASTE IN SOMEONE'S MOUTH

a **taste of** something **1.** a TASTE ③ taken in order to sample something. **2.** a limited experience of something; a sample.

tasteless ['test ləs] **1.** *adj.* having no TASTE ②; having no flavor; bland. (Adv: *tastelessly.*) **2.** *adj.*

showing poor TASTE ④; offensive; rude. (Adv: *tastelessly.*)

tasty ['tes ti] *adj.* full of flavor; delicious. (Adv: *tastily.* Comp: *tastier;* sup: *tastiest.*)

tatter ['tæt ɚ] *tv.* to tear a piece of cloth; to fray something.
→ IN TATTERS

taught ['tɔt] past tense and past participle of TEACH.

taunt ['tɔnt] **1.** *tv.* to tease someone; to make fun of someone; to ridicule someone; to provoke someone by saying something unkind. **2.** *n.* an unkind remark that is made to tease or ridicule someone.

taut ['tɔt] *adj.* pulled tight; having no slack; stretched. (Adv: *tautly.* Comp: *tauter;* sup: *tautest.*)
→ RUN A TAUT SHIP

tax ['tæks] **1.** *n.* money charged by a government to pay for the cost of the government and its services. **2.** *tv.* to make someone pay ①. **3.** *tv.* to charge ① on something; to burden something with ①. **4.** *tv.* to burden someone or something; to place a strain on someone or something. (Figurative on ③.)
→ INCOME TAX

tax bracket ['tæks bræk ət] *n.* one of a series of federal income-tax rates and the levels of income associated with that rate.

tax return ['tæks rɪ tɚn] *n.* a form, filled out by someone required to pay taxes, showing the amount of tax that is owed.

taxi ['tæk si] **1.** *n.* a CAB, a TAXICAB. (Short for TAXICAB.) **2.** *iv.* [for an airplane] to move on the ground.

taxicab ['tæk si kæb] *n.* a car that, along with its driver, can be hired for short trips. (Can be shortened to TAXI or CAB.)

tea ['ti] **1.** *n.* the leaves of a bush grown in Asia that are dried and then soaked in boiling water to make a refreshing drink. (Plural only for types and instances.) **2.** *n.* a drink made from ①. (No plural.) **3.** *n.* a drink, like ②, made by soaking dried herbs or other plants in boiling water. (No plural.)
→ NOT SOMEONE'S CUP OF TEA

teach ['titʃ] **1.** *tv., irreg.* to provide instruction in a particular subject. (Past tense and past participle: TAUGHT.) **2.** *tv., irreg.* to instruct someone in how to do something. **3.** *iv., irreg.* to work as a teacher.

teach one's **grandmother to suck eggs** to try to tell or show someone more knowledgeable or experienced than oneself how to do something.

teacher ['titʃ ɚ] *n.* someone who teaches people something; someone who instructs people in a subject.
→ BE THE TEACHER'S PET

team ['tim] **1.** *n.* a group of players who form one side in a game or sport. **2.** *n.* a group of people who work together. **3.** *n.* two or more animals that work together to pull a vehicle or piece of farming equipment.

team up against someone or something to join with someone else against someone or something.

team up (with someone**)** to join with one or more persons; to collaborate with two or more persons.

teammate ['tim met] *n.* a member of a team that one is a part of; another person on one's team.

teamwork ['tim wɚk] *n.* the action of working together as a team. (No plural.)

teapot ['ti pɑt] *n.* a container with a handle and a spout, used to hold and pour tea.
→ A TEMPEST IN A TEAPOT

tear 1. ['tɪr] *n.* a drop of liquid that falls from one's eye when one cries. **2.** ['tɛr] *n.* a rip; a place in a piece of cloth or paper that is ripped. **3.** ['tɛr] *tv., irreg.* to make a hole or a rip in something, especially by pulling it; to pull something into pieces. (Past tense: TORE; past participle: TORN.) **4.** ['tɛr] *iv., irreg.* to be ripped apart. **5.** ['tɛr] *iv., irreg.* to move somewhere very quickly. **6.** ['tɪr] *iv.* to begin to cry; to have tears form in one's eyes. (Past tense and past participle: *teared* ['tird].)
→ BLINK BACK ONE'S TEARS
→ BREAK OUT IN TEARS
→ BREAK (OUT) INTO TEARS
→ SHED CROCODILE TEARS

tear away (from someone or something**)** to leave someone or something, running or moving very fast.

tear down something to race down something very fast.

tear off (from someone or something**)** to leave someone or something in a great hurry.

tear one's **hair (out)** to be anxious, frustrated, or angry.

tear (oneself) away (from someone or something**)** to force oneself to leave someone or something.

tear out (of someplace**)** to leave a place in a great hurry.

tear someone or something **down** to criticize someone or something without mercy.

tear someone **up** to cause someone to grieve greatly.

tear something **away (from** someone or something**) 1.** to peel something from someone or something. **2.** to snatch something away from someone or something.

tear something **down** to raze or demolish something; to destroy something such as a building.

tear something **off ((of)** someone or something**)** to peel or rip something off someone or something.

tear something **out (of** something**)** to remove something from something by ripping or tearing.

teardrop ['tɪr drɑp] *n.* one tear; one drop of liquid that falls from one's eye.

tease ['tiz] **1.** *tv.* to taunt someone; to make fun of someone. **2.** *tv.* to flirt with someone, especially with sexual hints. **3.** *tv.* to separate strands of hair; to comb strands of hair apart. **4.** *iv.* to taunt [someone or something]; to annoy on purpose. **5.** *n.* someone who flirts with someone else as in ②.

technician [tɛk 'nɪ ʃən] *n.* someone who works in the field of industrial or mechanical sciences; someone who works in a laboratory, performing tests.

technique [tɛk 'nik] **1.** *n.* a special method of doing something. **2.** *n.* the skill involved in creating or performing art; the way that art is performed, displayed, or exhibited—showing the artist's skill. (No plural.)

technology [tɛk 'nɑl ə dʒi] *n.* the science and study of the mechanical and industrial sciences. (Plural only for types and instances.)

teen ['tin] **1.** *n.* a teenager. **2.** the *adj.* use of ①.

teenage ['tin edʒ] *adj.* of, for, or about teenagers; of the ages from 13 through 19.

teenager ['tin edʒ ɚ] *n.* someone whose age is between 13 and 19.

teens *n.* the numbers 13–19 or 10–19. (When referring to age, it refers to the period of someone's life from the age of 13 through the age of 19.)

teeth ['tiθ] plural of TOOTH.
 → ARMED TO THE TEETH
 → (AS) SCARCE AS HENS' TEETH
 → BY THE SKIN OF ONE'S TEETH
 → FLY IN THE TEETH OF SOMEONE OR SOMETHING
 → GET ONE'S TEETH INTO SOMETHING
 → GNASH ONE'S TEETH
 → GRIT ONE'S TEETH
 → LIE THROUGH ONE'S TEETH
 → NO SKIN OFF SOMEONE'S TEETH
 → PULL SOMEONE'S OR SOMETHING'S TEETH
 → PUT SOME TEETH INTO SOMETHING
 → SCARCER THAN HENS' TEETH
 → SET SOMEONE'S TEETH ON EDGE
 → SINK ONE'S TEETH INTO SOMETHING

teething troubles 1. a baby's difficulties and pain experienced during the growth of its first set of teeth. **2.** difficulties and problems experienced in the early stages of a project, activity, etc.

telegram ['tɛl ə græm] *n.* a message sent by telegraph.

telegraph ['tɛl ə græf] **1.** *n.* a machine that sends messages in electrical code over electrical wires. **2.** *tv.* to send a message by using ①. (E.g., *telegraphed his response.*) **3.** *tv.* to send [a message] to someone by using ①. (E.g., *telegraphed John with his response.*)

telephone ['tɛl ə fon] **1.** *n.* a device that transmits sound by converting it into electrical signals; a PHONE. **2.** *tv.* to call someone by using ①. **3.** *iv.* to make a call with ①.
 → CELL(ULAR) TELEPHONE

telephone call ['tɛl ə fon 'kɔl] *n.* a message or a conversation using the telephone; an instance of someone contacting someone by telephone. (Can be shortened to CALL or PHONE CALL.)

telescope ['tɛl ə skop] **1.** *n.* a device that makes distant objects, especially objects that are in the sky, look larger so that one can see them better. **2.** *iv.* to become shorter or longer by having one part slide over another as with ①. **3.** *tv.* to make something shorter or longer by sliding one part of it over another.

television ['tɛl ə vɪʒ ən] **1.** *n.* the transmission of an electronic signal containing sounds and images. (No plural. Can be shortened to

TV.) **2.** *n.* the business of producing ① or the programs that are transmitted on ①. (No plural. Can be shortened to TV.) **3.** *n.* an electronic device that converts electronic signals into sounds and images. (Short for TELEVISION SET.) **4.** the *adj.* use of ①, ②, or ③.

television set ['θɛl ə vɪʒ ən 'sɛt] *n.* an electronic device that turns a television signal into images and sound. (Can be shortened to TELE-VISION or TV.)

tell ['tɛl] **1.** *tv., irreg.* to express something in words. (Past tense and past participle: TOLD.) **2.** *tv., irreg.* to inform someone [of something]. **3.** *tv., irreg.* to signal information [to someone]. **4.** *tv., irreg.* to reveal a secret. **5.** *iv., irreg.* to reveal [a secret]. **6.** *iv., irreg.* to try to make trouble for a person by saying (to an authority) what that person has done.
→ NOT TELL A SOUL

tell its own story AND **tell its own tale** [for the state of something] to indicate clearly what has happened.

tell its own tale Go to TELL ITS OWN STORY.

tell one **to** one's **face** to tell (something) to someone directly.

tell someone **where to get off** to rebuke someone; to put one in one's place.

tell tales out of school to tell secrets or spread rumors.

teller ['tɛl ɚ] *n.* someone who works at a bank, receiving and giving out money.

temper ['tɛm pɚ] **1.** *n.* mood; the condition of one's mind, especially in regard to anger. (No plural.) **2.** *n.* an angry mood; the potential of being angry. (No plural.) **3.** *tv.* to soften something; to lessen the force or impact of something; to make something more moderate.
→ HOLD ONE'S TEMPER
→ KEEP ONE'S TEMPER
→ LOSE ONE'S TEMPER

temper tantrum ['tɛm pɚ 'tæn trəm] *n.* a burst of anger; a display of temper like that of a child. (Can be shortened to TANTRUM.)

temperature ['tɛm pɚ ə tʃɚ] **1.** *n.* the degree of how cold or hot something is. **2.** *n.* the degree of the heat of one's blood, especially when it is above average; a fever.
→ RUN A TEMPERATURE

tempest ['tɛmp əst] *n.* a violent storm.

a **tempest in a teapot** an uproar about practically nothing.

temple ['tɛm pəl] **1.** *n.* a building used for worship and ceremonies. **2.** *n.* a Jewish house of worship. **3.** *n.* the flat part on the side of the head between the eye and the ear and above the cheekbone.

temporary ['tɛm pə rɛr i] *adj.* for a limited time; not permanent. (Adv: *temporarily* [tɛm pə 'rɛr ə li].)

tempt ['tɛmpt] *tv.* to arouse someone's desire; to make someone want something.

temptation [tɛmp 'te ʃən] **1.** *n.* desire; an instance of being tempted. (No plural.) **2.** *n.* someone or something that tempts a person.

tempted (to do something) ['temp tɪd] wanting to do something, especially something that one should not do.

ten ['ten] **1.** 10. Go to FOUR. **2.** *n.* a $10 bill.

tend ['tend] *tv.* to take care of something.

tend to do something to be likely to do something; to be inclined to do something.

tend to someone or something to mind someone or something; to take care of someone or something.

tendency ['ten dən si] *n.* the likelihood that someone or something will do something naturally.

tender ['ten dɚ] **1.** *adj.* soft; not tough; easy to chew. (Adv: *tenderly*.) **2.** *adj.* sore; sore when touched; painful. (Adv: *tenderly*.) **3.** *adj.* kind; gentle; showing love or affection. (Adv: *tenderly*.) **4.** *tv.* to offer something formally or legally, such as to offer money in payment of a debt.
→ LEGAL TENDER

tennis ['ten ɪs] *n.* a sport played by two people or two pairs of people who use rackets to hit a small ball from one side of the playing area, over a net, to the other side of the playing area. (No plural.)

tense ['tens] **1.** *adj.* taut; not loose; not relaxed. (Adv: *tensely*. Comp: *tenser*; sup: *tensest*.) **2.** *adj.* nervous; not relaxed. (Adv: *tensely*. Comp: *tenser*; sup: *tensest*.) **3.** *tv.* to tighten something, such as a muscle; to stiffen something; to make something taut. **4.** *n.* a qual-

ity of a verb that indicates the time that the action or state it expresses takes place.
→ PAST TENSE
→ PRESENT TENSE

tense up (for something) to become rigid or firm; to become anxious and ready for something. (Both literal and figurative uses.)

tension ['ten ʃən] **1.** *n.* the degree of tightness of something that is stretched. (Plural only for types and instances.) **2.** *n.* an anxious or nervous feeling; hidden anxiety or anger.

tent ['tent] *n.* a temporary shelter made of fabric supported by poles and ropes.
→ PITCH A TENT

tenth ['tentθ] 10th. Go to FOURTH.

term ['tɚm] **1.** *n.* the length of time that something lasts; a particular period of time. **2.** *n.* a division of a school year; a quarter or semester. **3.** *n.* an expression used in a particular field; a word.
→ COME TO TERMS WITH SOMEONE OR SOMETHING
→ a CONTRADICTION IN TERMS
→ IN TERMS OF SOMETHING

terminal ['tɚ mə nəl] **1.** *adj.* happening at the end of something; at the end; last. (Adv: *terminally*.) **2.** *adj.* resulting in death; causing death; not able to be cured. (Adv: *terminally*.) **3.** *n.* a building that passengers enter and leave from, especially at an airport, bus station, or train station. **4.** *n.* something that makes an electrical connection; the place where current enters or leaves a battery or a circuit. **5.** *n.* a computer device consisting of a keyboard and a screen that displays the information sent to and from a computer.

termite ['tɚ maɪt] *n.* an insect, similar to an ant, that eats wood, causing great damage to wooden objects and structures.

terms 1. *n.* requirements; details; provisions. **2.** *n.* charges; fees and requirements.

terrace ['tɛr əs] **1.** *n.* a flat area connected to or next to the side of a house or apartment; a balcony or patio. **2.** *n.* a flat area of land that has been cut into the side of a hill or mountain.

terrain [tə 'ren] *n.* the physical features of an area of land.

terrible ['tɛr ə bəl] *adj.* awful; horrible; extremely bad. (Adv: *terribly*.)

terribly ['tɛr ə bli] **1.** *adv.* badly; horribly; awfully. **2.** *adv.* very; extremely.

terrier ['tɛr i ɚ] *n.* one of a group of breeds of small dogs, originally bred to be used in hunting.

terrific [tə 'rɪf ɪk] **1.** *adj.* great; wonderful; super; excellent. (Adv: *terrifically* […ɪk li].) **2.** *adj.* extreme[ly bad]. (Adv: *terrifically* […ɪk li].)

terrify ['tɛr ə faɪ] *tv.* to scare someone or something greatly.

territory ['tɛr ə tor i] **1.** *n.* land; area. (No plural.) **2.** *n.* an area of land controlled by a specific government, especially a government that is far away. **3.** *n.* an area of land that is dominated by an animal or group of animals.

terror ['tɛr ɚ] **1.** *n.* extreme fear. (Plural only for types and

instances.) **2.** *n.* someone or something that causes extreme fear.

terrorism ['tɛr ɚ ɪz əm] *n.* the use of violence and terror to achieve political goals. (No plural.)

terrorist ['tɛr ɚ ɪst] *n.* someone who practices terrorism.

test ['tɛst] **1.** *n.* a series of questions or activities that determine someone's knowledge or skill; a school examination. **2.** *n.* an experiment; an action that is done to see how something works. **3.** *tv.* to determine someone's knowledge or skill by evaluating answers to questions or performance of activities. **4.** *tv.* to subject something to ② in order to measure its condition or see how it works.
→ the ACID TEST
→ LITMUS TEST
→ PUT SOMEONE TO THE TEST

test out (of something**)** to score high enough on a special test that one does not need to take a particular school course.

test something **out** to try something out; to test something to see if it works.

testimony ['tɛs tə mo ni] *n.* the statements of a witness, especially in a court of law. (Not usually plural. Treated as singular.)

text ['tɛkst] **1.** *n.* the main words in a book or article, not the pictures, tables, graphs, indexes, etc. (No plural.) **2.** *n.* the words of a speech in written form. **3.** *n.* a book used by students in school or college. (Short for TEXTBOOK.)

textbook ['tɛkst bʊk] **1.** *n.* a book, designed for student use, that is used as a standard source of information about a specific subject. (Can be shortened to TEXT.) **2.** *adj.* [of possible examples] the best and most typical.

texture ['tɛks tʃɚ] **1.** *n.* the evenness or smoothness—or unevenness or roughness—of something. **2.** *n.* the appearance of having ①, such as with a design on paper or in art.

than ['ðæn] *conj.* as compared with someone or something; in comparison with someone or something. (Used before the second item of a comparison.)

thank ['θæŋk] *tv.* to show someone gratitude by saying "thank you"; to express gratitude for something that has been given or done.

thank one's **lucky stars** to be thankful for one's luck.

Thank you. 1. *interj.* a polite expression that is used by the receiver of an action or gift, along with "yes" or "no" in response to a question, or to show gratitude. **2.** *n.* an expression of gratitude. (See also THANKS.) **3.** the *adj.* use of ①. (Hyphenated.)

thankful ['θæŋk fʊl] *adj.* grateful; showing thanks; expressing thanks. (Adv: *thankfully.*)

thankful for small blessings grateful for any benefits or advantages one has, especially in a generally difficult situation.

thanks 1. *interj.* a polite expression that is used by the receiver of an action or gift, along with "yes" or "no" in response to a question, or to show gratitude. (Less formal than THANK YOU.) **2.** *n.* gratitude.

(Treated as plural, but not countable.)

→ a VOTE OF THANKS

Thanksgiving [θæŋks 'gɪv ɪŋ] *n.* a holiday celebrated in the United States and Canada as an expression of individual and national gratitude. (THANKSGIVING is held on the fourth Thursday in November in the United States.)

that ['ðæt] **1.** *adj.* a form referring to someone or something already mentioned or someone or something of which both the speaker and hearer are aware. (Prenominal only. With plural nouns, use THOSE.) **2.** *adj.* a form referring to someone or something further away or the furthest away from the speaker. (Used in contrast with THIS. Prenominal only. With plural nouns, use THOSE.) **3.** *pron.* a form standing for someone or something already referred to or someone or something of which both the speaker and hearer are aware. (Plural: THOSE.) **4.** *pron.* a form standing for someone or something that is further away or the furthest away from the speaker. (Used in contrast with THIS. Plural: THOSE.) **5.** *pron.* which. (Used to connect sentences, clauses, and phrases with noun phrases. Only used with *restrictive clauses.* See WHICH for an explanation. Sometimes means "when" or "where" if it follows a noun phrase referring to a time or place.) **6.** *pron.* who; whom. (Used to connect sentences, phrases, or clauses with noun phrases. Only where WHO or WHOM would be appropriate.) **7.** *pron.* a form used to connect a verb with a clause that is the object of the verb. (Only certain verbs use THAT in this way. This THAT can be omitted.) **8.** *adv.* so; to such a degree. (E.g., [gesturing] *he is that big.*)

That takes care of that. That is settled.

that's [ˈðæts] **1.** *cont.* that is. **2.** *cont.* that has, where HAS is an auxiliary.

That's the last straw. AND **That's the straw that broke the camel's back.** That is the final difficulty or problem that makes the burden too great or that makes the task too difficult, because many problems or difficulties have already preceded it.

That's the straw that broke the camel's back. Go to THAT'S THE LAST STRAW.

That's the ticket. That is exactly what is needed.

thaw [ˈθɔ] **1.** *iv.* [for ice] to melt; [for something frozen] to no longer be frozen; [for the weather] to be warm enough to melt ice or snow. **2.** *iv.* to become less formal; to relax. (Figurative on ①.) **3.** *tv.* to melt something; to cause something to no longer be frozen. **4.** *n.* a condition in which the weather has become warm enough to melt ice or snow.

thaw out to warm up after being frozen.

thaw someone or something **out** to raise the temperature of someone or something above freezing.

the [ðə, ði] **1.** *article* a certain one; certain ones. (The definite article.

Used before nouns or noun phrases to show that a definite thing, person, or group of people or things is being referred to. Pronounced [ˈði] when emphasized or before vowel sounds.) **2.** *article* a form showing a general category. (Used before a noun that is used in a general sense.) **3.** *article* a form indicating the special or specific one, the one that is being talked about. (Used before some names and titles.)

theater AND **theatre** [ˈθiə tɚ] **1.** *n.* a building where movies are shown or where plays are performed. (The spelling *theatre* is used especially for buildings where plays are performed, and much less often for buildings where movies are shown.) **2.** *n.* the business of producing plays for the stage; the study of drama, performance, and acting. (No plural.)

theft [ˈθɛft] *n.* stealing; taking someone else's property without permission. (Plural only for types and instances.)

their [ˈðɛɚ] **1.** *pron.* the possessive form of THEY; belonging to people, animals, or things that have already been mentioned. (Used only as a modifier before a noun.) **2.** *pron.* ① standing for HIS ③; belonging to a person who has already been mentioned. (Used to refer to a preceding noun or pronoun, the sexual reference of which is unimportant, indeterminate, undetermined, or irrelevant. Adopted as a replacement for HIS ③ by those who see HIS ③ as referring to males only. Objected to by some as an unnecessary violation of grammatical number when used for singular nouns.)

theirs *pron.* the possessive form of THEY; belonging to people, animals, or things that have already been mentioned.

them ['ðɛm] **1.** *pron.* the objective form of THEY. (Used to refer to people, animals, and things. Used after prepositions and as the object of verbs.) **2.** *pron.* a form standing for HIM ②, referring to a person already mentioned. (Used to refer to a noun or pronoun, the sexual reference of which is unimportant, indeterminate, undetermined, or irrelevant. Adopted as a replacement for HIM ② by those who see HIM ② as referring to males only. Objected to by some as an unnecessary violation of grammatical number when used for singular nouns.)

theme ['θim] **1.** *n.* a subject of a speech or a text; a topic. **2.** *n.* a melody that is used to identify a certain program, movie, character, or emotion. **3.** *n.* the main melody of a piece of music. **4.** *n.* a visual or decorative concept that connects several parts of something. **5.** *adj.* of or about a piece of music that is readily identified with someone or something.

themselves [ðɛm 'sɛlvz] **1.** *pron.* the reflexive form of THEY, used after a verb or a preposition when the subject of the sentence refers to the same people, animals, or things that the pronoun refers to. **2.** *pron.* the reflexive form of THEY used after THEY or a plural noun phrase as an intensifier.
→ BY THEMSELVES
→ SPEAK FOR THEMSELVES

then ['ðɛn] **1.** *adv.* at that time. **2.** *adv.* next; following; after that. **3.** *adv.* therefore; in that case; so.

theology [θi 'ɑl ə dʒi] *n.* the study and science of religion. (Plural only for types and instances.)

theory ['θɪr i] *n.* knowledge of a science or an art, as opposed to the actual practice of a science or an art; the principles on which a science or an art are based. (Plural only for types and instances.)
→ IN THEORY

there ['ðɛɚ] **1.** *adv.* to or toward that place; at that place; in that place; in that respect; at that point in time; at that point during a process. (Compare this with THEY'RE and THEIR.) **2.** *adv.* a form that begins a sentence or clause and is followed by a verb, which is then followed by the subject of the sentence. (The verb is usually BE—for example, *there is, there are*—but it can also be *go, come, stand, rest,* or another verb. In questions, the verb is placed before *there*.) **3.** *pron.* a particular place or location.

There are plenty of other fish in the sea. There are many other choices, especially regarding the choice of a mate or a date.

There will be the devil to pay. There will be lots of trouble.

there's ['ðɛɚz] **1.** *cont.* there has, where HAS is an auxiliary. **2.** *cont.* there is.

thermometer [θɚ 'mɑm ə tɚ] *n.* a device that measures the temperature of someone or something.

these ['ðiz] plural of THIS.

they ['ðe] **1.** *pron.* the third-person plural subject pronoun; the plural of HE, SHE, or IT. **2.** *pron.* the third-person plural subject pronoun used as a singular. (Used to refer to a preceding noun or pronoun, the sexual reference of which is unimportant, indeterminate, undetermined, or irrelevant. Adopted as a replacement for HE ② by those who see HE ② as referring to males only. Objected to by some as an unnecessary violation of grammatical number when used for singular nouns.) **3.** *pron.* people in general; a group of people.

they'd ['ðed] **1.** *cont.* they would. **2.** *cont.* they had, where HAD is an auxiliary.

they'll ['ðel] *cont.* they will.

they're ['ðeɚ] *cont.* they are. (Compare this with THERE, THEIR.)

they've ['ðev] *cont.* they have, where HAVE is an auxiliary.

thick ['θɪk] **1.** *adj.* not thin; having a greater than average distance between two opposite sides; having a lot of space between two opposite sides. (E.g., *a thick board.* Adv: *thickly.* Comp: *thicker;* sup: *thickest.*) **2.** *adj.* measuring a certain distance between two opposite sides; having a certain depth or width. (E.g., *two feet thick.* Comp: *thicker.* No superlative.) **3.** *adj.* dense; with very little space between things. (Adv: *thickly.*

Comp: *thicker;* sup: *thickest.*) **4.** *adj.* not pouring easily, like glue or molasses; being liquid but not flowing easily. (Adv: *thickly.* Comp: *thicker;* sup: *thickest.*) **5.** *adj.* [of air] not clear; [of air] full of water vapor, smoke, or fog. (Comp: *thicker;* sup: *thickest.*) **6.** *adj.* [of an accent or manner of speaking] showing where the speaker is from.
→ (AS) THICK AS PEA SOUP
→ (AS) THICK AS THIEVES
→ GET SOMETHING INTO SOMEONE'S THICK HEAD
→ GET SOMETHING THROUGH SOMEONE'S THICK SKULL
→ LAY IT ON THICK
→ POUR IT ON THICK
→ SPREAD IT ON THICK
→ THROUGH THICK AND THIN

thick and fast in large numbers or amounts and at a rapid rate.

thicken ['θɪk ən] **1.** *tv.* to cause something to become thicker. **2.** *iv.* [for a liquid] to become thicker.
→ The PLOT THICKENS.

thick-skinned not easily upset or hurt; insensitive to offense.

thief ['θif] *n., irreg.* someone who steals things. (Plural: THIEVES.)

thieves ['θivz] plural of THIEF.
→ (AS) THICK AS THIEVES

thigh ['θaɪ] *n.* [in humans and many animals] the part of the leg between the hip and the knee.

thin ['θɪn] **1.** *adj.* not thick; having less than the average distance between two opposite sides; having very little space between two opposite sides. (Adv: *thinly.* Comp: *thinner;* sup: *thinnest.*) **2.** *adj.* not fat; slender; slim; not having much

fat on one's body. (Adv: *thinly.*
Comp: *thinner;* sup: *thinnest.*)
3. *adj.* not dense; spread out. (Adv:
thinly. Comp: *thinner;* sup:
thinnest.) **4.** *adj.* not thick; [of a
liquid] containing a lot of water;
flowing easily. (Adv: *thinly.* Comp:
thinner; sup: *thinnest.*) **5.** *tv.* to
make something runnier or ④.
→ ON THIN ICE
→ OUT OF THIN AIR
→ PULL SOMETHING OUT OF THIN AIR
→ SKATE ON THIN ICE
→ SPREAD ONESELF TOO THIN
→ THROUGH THICK AND THIN
→ VANISH INTO THIN AIR

thin down to become thinner or
slimmer.

thin on top balding. (Informal.)

thin out to spread out; to become
less dense.

thin something out to make something less dense; to scatter something.

thing ['θɪŋ] **1.** *n.* any object; an
object whose name is not known;
an object whose name is not
important. **2.** *n.* an event; an
action; a deed; a statement; an
idea.
→ AMOUNT TO THE SAME THING (AS
SOMETHING)
→ FIRST THING (IN THE MORNING)
→ FIRST THINGS FIRST.
→ GET INTO THE SWING OF THINGS
→ ONE THING LEADS TO ANOTHER.
→ SEE THINGS
→ the VERY THING

think ['θɪŋk] **1.** *iv., irreg.* to use
one's mind; to have thoughts or
opinions; to form ideas in the
mind. (Past tense and past participle: THOUGHT.) **2.** *iv., irreg.* to be
able to use one's mind; to have the
ability to use one's mind. **3.** *tv.,*
irreg. to have a certain belief or
opinion; to believe something.
(The object can be a clause with
THAT ⑦.)
→ COME TO THINK OF IT
→ HARDLY HAVE TIME TO THINK
→ PUT ONE'S THINKING CAP
→ WISHFUL THINKING

think back (on someone or something**)** to think about someone or
something as a memory from the
past.

think back (to something**)** to
remember something in the past.

think better of something to
reconsider something; to think
again and decide not to do something.

think on one's **feet** to think while
one is talking.

think something out to go through
something in one's mind; to think
through something.

think something over to think
about something and whether one
will choose to do it.

think something through to consider something carefully and try
to settle it in one's mind.

think something up to invent something.

think the world of someone or
something to be very fond of
someone or something.

thin-skinned easily upset or hurt;
sensitive.

third ['θɚd] 3rd. Go to FOURTH.

thirdly ['θɚd li] *adv.* in the third
place; as a third point of discussion.

thirst ['θɚst] *n.* the feeling caused by having nothing to drink; the need to drink. (No plural.)

a **thirst for** something a craving or desire for something.

thirsty ['θɚs ti] *adj.* needing to drink; having had nothing to drink; having thirst. (Adv: *thirstily.* Comp: *thirstier*; sup: *thirstiest.*)

thirsty for something craving or desiring something.

thirteen ['θɚt 'tin] 13. Go to FOUR.

thirteenth ['θɚt 'tinθ] 13th. Go to FOURTH.

thirtieth ['θɚt i əθ] 30th. Go to FOURTH.

thirty ['θɚt i] 30. Go to FORTY.

this ['ðɪs] **1.** *adj.* a form referring to a thing or person that has already been referred to or is obvious and present; a form referring to an object that one is pointing to or otherwise indicating. (Prenominal only. Use THESE with plural nouns.) **2.** *adj.* a form introducing a thing or person new to the conversation. (Colloquial. Prenominal only. Use THESE with plural nouns.) **3.** *adj.* a form referring to the thing, person, or point in time that is closer or the closest to the speaker. (Used in contrast with THAT. Prenominal only. Use THESE with plural nouns.) **4.** *pron.* a form standing for a thing or person that has already been mentioned or is obvious and present. (Plural: THESE.) **5.** *pron.* a form standing for the thing, person, or point in time that is closer or the closest to the speaker. (Used in contrast with THAT. Plural:

THESE.) **6.** *adv.* to the indicated degree. (E.g., [gesturing] *he is this big.*)

thorn ['θorn] *n.* a sharp, pointed growth on a plant.
→ BE A THORN IN SOMEONE'S SIDE

thorough ['θɚ o] *adj.* complete; done with great attention and in great detail. (Adv: *thoroughly.*)

those ['ðoz] **1.** plural of THAT. **2.** *pron.* the people [who do something]. **3.** *adj.* a form referring to people or things already mentioned or people or things of which both the speaker and hearer are aware. (Prenominal only. With singular nouns, use THAT.) **4.** *adj.* a form referring to people or things farther away or the farthest away from the speaker. (Used in contrast with THESE. Prenominal only. With singular nouns, use THAT.)

though ['ðo] **1.** *conj.* in spite of something; in spite of the fact that; although. **2.** *adv.* however.
→ AS THOUGH

thought ['θɔt] **1.** past tense and past participle of THINK. **2.** *n.* thinking; attention; time taken to think about an idea. (No plural.) **3.** *n.* an idea; an opinion; something that one thinks.
→ FOOD FOR THOUGHT
→ GET SECOND THOUGHTS ABOUT SOMEONE OR SOMETHING
→ LOSE ONE'S TRAIN OF THOUGHT
→ LOST IN THOUGHT
→ NOT GIVE IT ANOTHER THOUGHT
→ ON SECOND THOUGHT
→ PERISH THE THOUGHT.
→ SCHOOL OF THOUGHT

thousand ['θaʊ zənd] **1.** *n.* 1,000; the number between 999 and 1,001. (Additional numbers

formed as with *two thousand, three thousand, four thousand,* etc.) **2.** *n.* a group of 1,000 people or things.
→ ONE IN A THOUSAND

thousandth ['θaʊ zəndθ] 1,000th. Go to FOURTH.

thrash something **out** to discuss something thoroughly and solve any problems.

thread ['θrɛd] **1.** *n.* fine string, made of twisted strands of cotton, silk, or other fiber, that is used to sew pieces of cloth together or is woven to make cloth. (Plural only for types and instances.) **2.** *n.* a very thin strand of something; a length of ①. **3.** *n.* a theme or idea that links parts of an argument or a story. (Figurative on ②.) **4.** *n.* the raised ridge that wraps around the length of a screw or a bolt. (Usually plural, but not countable.) **5.** *tv.* to pass ① through something, usually a needle. **6.** *tv.* to place something on ① or on string, wire, etc.
→ HANG BY A THREAD

thread one's **way through** something to make a path for oneself through a crowded area; to move slowly through a crowded area.

thread through something to travel through a crowded area; to travel through an area where there are many obstacles.

threat ['θrɛt] **1.** *n.* a warning; a statement or action that indicates that someone is going to hurt or punish someone in a certain way. **2.** *n.* a sign of danger; a sign that something harmful or dangerous is going to happen.

threaten ['θrɛt n] **1.** *tv.* to express a threat against someone. (The object can be a clause with THAT ⑦.) **2.** *iv.* to be a threat; to be an indication of danger.

threaten to do something [for someone or something] to make a threat to do something.

three ['θri] 3. Go to FOUR.
→ LIKE A THREE-RING CIRCUS
→ TWO'S COMPANY(, THREE'S A CROWD).

threw ['θru] past tense of THROW.

thrift ['θrɪft] *n.* the careful use of money and things; the habit of not wasting money or things. (No plural.)

thrifty ['θrɪf ti] the *adj.* form of THRIFT.

thrill ['θrɪl] **1.** *n.* an intense feeling of emotion, especially excitement, enjoyment, or fear. **2.** *tv.* to cause someone to feel full of emotion, especially excitement, enjoyment, or fear.

thrive ['θraɪv] **1.** *iv., irreg.* to grow and survive; to develop in a very healthy way. (Past tense: THROVE or *thrived;* past participle: *thrived* or THRIVEN.) **2.** *iv., irreg.* to be successful; to become very rich.

thriven ['θrɪv ən] a past participle of THRIVE.

throat ['θrot] **1.** *n.* the front of the neck. **2.** *n.* the inside of the neck, where food and air pass.
→ CUT ONE'S (OWN) THROAT
→ GET A LUMP IN ONE'S THROAT
→ HAVE A FROG IN ONE'S THROAT
→ HAVE ONE'S WORDS STICK IN ONE'S THROAT
→ ONE'S WORDS STICK IN ONE'S THROAT

throb ['θrɑb] **1.** *iv.* to beat strongly and quickly, as with the beating of the heart or some other pulse. **2.** *iv.* to have a pain that occurs with each heartbeat. **3.** *n.* one beat in a series of strong, quick beats.

throne ['θron] **1.** *n.* the chair that a king, queen, or other ruler or important person sits on. **2.** *n.* the position held by a king, queen, or other ruler or important person.

throng in(to something**)** [for a crowd] to swarm into something or someplace.

throng out (of something**)** [for a crowd] to swarm out of something or someplace.

through ['θru] **1.** *prep.* from the outside of one end of something, into it, to the other end of it, and out of the other side of it. **2.** *prep.* because of something; on account of something. **3.** *prep.* moving throughout or within something. **4.** *prep.* during the entire time from beginning to end; during the entire way from start to finish. **5.** *adv.* in one side and out the other. **6.** *adv.* from beginning to end; from start to finish. **7.** *adj.* finished; done.

through thick and thin through good times and bad times.

throughout [θru 'aʊt] *prep.* in every part of something; during every moment of something.

throve ['θrov] a past tense of THRIVE.

throw ['θro] **1.** *tv., irreg.* to send something through the air; to hurl something; to cause something to move through the air. (Past tense:

THREW; past participle: THROWN.) **2.** *tv., irreg.* to put someone or something someplace carelessly, with force, or in a hurry. **3.** *tv., irreg.* [for an animal] to cause a rider to fall off. **4.** *tv., irreg.* to move a switch in order to start or stop the flow of electricity. **5.** *tv., irreg.* to cause someone to be in a certain condition, especially a confused one.
→ a STONE'S THROW AWAY

throw caution to the wind to become very careless.

throw cold water on something Go to POUR COLD WATER ON SOMETHING.

throw good money after bad to waste additional money after having wasted money once before.

throw in the sponge Go to THROW IN THE TOWEL.

throw in the towel AND **throw in the sponge** to quit (doing something).

throw oneself **at** someone's **feet** to bow down humbly at someone's feet.

throw oneself **at the mercy of the court** Go to THROW ONESELF ON THE MERCY OF THE COURT.

throw oneself **on the mercy of the court** AND **throw** oneself **at the mercy of the court** to plead for mercy from a judge in a courtroom.

throw someone **a curve** AND **pitch** someone **a curve 1.** to pitch a curveball to someone in baseball. **2.** to confuse someone by doing something unexpected.

throw someone **for a loop** AND **knock** someone **for a loop** to confuse or shock someone.

throw someone **over (for** someone **else)** to break up with a lover in favor of someone else.

throw someone **to the wolves** to sacrifice someone to something or some fate.

throw something **into the bargain** to include something in a deal.

throw something **off** to cast something, such as a coat, off one's body.

throw something **together** to assemble or create something in a hurry.

throw something **up 1.** to build or erect something in a hurry. **2.** to vomit something.

throw up to vomit.

thrown ['θron] past participle of THROW.

thrust ['θrʌst] **1.** *tv., irreg.* to push someone or something forward with force; to push someone or something in a certain direction with force. (Past tense and past participle: *thrust*.) **2.** *tv., irreg.* to drive a sharp object at or into someone or something. **3.** *iv., irreg.* to move forward with force; to lunge, especially with a sharp object. **4.** *n.* a forceful movement in a certain direction; a lunge; a stab.

thrust out to stick out; to stab outward; to protrude outward.

thrust someone or something **back** to push someone or something backward and away.

thud ['θʌd] *n.* the dull sound of something heavy falling onto, or hitting, something firm but unbreakable.

thumb ['θʌm] **1.** *n.* the first and shortest finger on the hand, separate from the other four, having two knuckles instead of three. **2.** *n.* the part of a glove or mitten that covers ①.
→ ALL THUMBS
→ GET SOMEONE UNDER ONE'S THUMB
→ HAVE A GREEN THUMB
→ RULE OF THUMB
→ TWIDDLE ONE'S THUMBS

thumb a ride AND **hitch a ride** to get a ride from a passing motorist; to make a sign with one's thumb that indicates to passing drivers that one is begging for a ride.

thumb one's **nose at** someone or something to (figuratively or literally) make a rude gesture of disgust with one's thumb and nose at someone or something.

thumbnail ['θʌm nel] *n.* the nail on one's thumb.

thumbnail sketch small; short; brief.

thumbtack ['θʌm tæk] **1.** *n.* a tack with a large, flat head that is pressed with one's thumb to drive the pointed part into a surface. (See also TACK.) **2.** *tv.* to attach something to a surface with ①.

thump ['θʌmp] **1.** *n.* the sound made by hitting someone or something with something hard or against something hard. **2.** *tv.* to hit someone or something with something hard; to hit someone or something against something hard.

thunder ['θʌn dɚ] **1.** *n.* the loud noise that follows lightning. (No plural.) **2.** *n.* any loud noise or explosion that sounds like ①. **3.** *iv.* [for weather conditions] to make ①. **4.** *iv.* to make a noise like ①; to walk or move, making noise like ①.
→ STEAL SOMEONE'S THUNDER

thundershower ['θʌn dɚ ʃaʊ ɚ] *n.* rain with thunder and lightning.

thunderstorm ['θʌn dɚ storm] *n.* a storm with thunder and lightning.

Thursday ['θɚz de] Go to DAY.

thus ['ðʌs] *adv.* therefore; for this reason; for these reasons; as a result.

tick ['tɪk] **1.** *n.* the short, quiet sound made by a watch or a clock. **2.** *n.* a small, flat insect that attaches to the skin of animals and sucks their blood. **3.** *n.* a mark that is made when counting something or checking something. **4.** *iv.* [for a clock, watch, or other timepiece] to make a short, quiet sound each second.
→ (AS) FULL AS A TICK
→ (AS) TIGHT AS A TICK
→ MAKE SOMEONE OR SOMETHING TICK
→ WHAT MAKES SOMEONE TICK

ticket ['tɪk ɪt] **1.** *n.* a piece of paper that shows that its owner has paid for transportation or for entrance into a place. **2.** *n.* a piece of paper that is given as a receipt when one leaves something at a repair shop, cleaners, or other business so that one can get the item back. **3.** *n.* a piece of paper that is given to someone who has broken a traffic or parking law, requiring that per-son to pay a fine or appear in court.
→ THAT'S THE TICKET.
→ VOTE A SPLIT TICKET
→ VOTE A STRAIGHT TICKET

tickle ['tɪk əl] **1.** *tv.* to touch a person's body in a way that causes him or her to laugh. **2.** *tv.* to amuse someone. (Figurative on ①.) **3.** *iv.* to cause a feeling that causes someone to laugh. **4.** *n.* an itchy feeling; a feeling that one needs to scratch, cough, or sneeze.

tickle someone's **fancy** to interest someone; to make someone curious.

ticklish ['tɪk lɪʃ] **1.** *adj.* sensitive to tickling; likely to laugh when tickled. (Adv: *ticklishly*.) **2.** *adj.* difficult; hard to answer; delicate; requiring careful thought or action. (Figurative on ①. Adv: *ticklishly*.)

tide ['taɪd] *n.* the rise and fall of the ocean, caused by the pull of the sun and the moon.

tide someone **over (until** something**)** to supply someone [with something] until a certain time or until something happens.
→ SWIM AGAINST THE TIDE
→ TURN THE TIDE

tidy ['taɪ di] **1.** *adj.* very neat; orderly; not messy. (Adv: *tidily*. Comp: *tidier;* sup: *tidiest*.) **2.** *tv.* to make something ①.

tidy something **up** to clean something up; to make something more orderly.

tidy up to clean up [oneself or a place].

tie ['taɪ] **1.** *tv.* to form string, rope, cord, or thread into a knot or bow,

often as a way to connect it to something or to join two pieces or ends together. (Present participle: *tying*.) **2.** *tv.* to join someone in occupying the same position in a list that ranks a group of things; to have the same score as the opposite player or team. **3.** *iv.* [for two teams] to have the same score; to occupy the same position as someone else in a list that ranks a group of things. **4.** *n.* a NECKTIE; a strip of cloth that is looped around the neck and TIED as in ① so there is a knot at the neck and the two ends hang down in front of one's shirt. **5.** *n.* a result of a game where both teams or players have the same score; a ranking where two or more people or things have the same rank.
→ HAVE ONE'S HANDS TIED
→ ONE'S HANDS ARE TIED
→ SEVER TIES WITH SOMEONE
→ WITH BOTH HANDS TIED BEHIND ONE'S BACK
→ WITH ONE HAND TIED BEHIND ONE'S BACK

tie in (with someone or something**)** to join with someone or something; to connect with someone or something.

tie in(to something**)** to fasten or connect to something.

tie someone **down (to** someone or something**)** to encumber someone with someone or something; to make someone responsible to or for someone or something.

tie someone **in knots** to make someone anxious or upset.

tie someone or something **down** to fasten someone or something down by tying or binding.

tie someone or something **in(to** something**)** to seek to establish a connection between someone or something and some event or occurrence.

tie someone or something **up** to keep someone or something busy or occupied.

tie someone's **hands** to prevent someone from doing something.

tie something **back** to bind or fasten something back out of the way.

tie something **(up)** to fasten something with string, rope, cord, or thread.

tie the knot to get married.

tied to one's **mother's apron strings** dominated by one's mother; dependent on one's mother.

tiger ['taɪ gɚ] *n.* a large, fierce animal that is a member of the cat family and has orange or yellow fur with black stripes.

tight ['taɪt] **1.** *adj.* not loose; having no extra room on the sides or around the edges; fitting closely. (Adv: *tightly.* Comp: *tighter;* sup: *tightest.*) **2.** *adj.* [of a schedule] having no extra time; having no appointments available. (Figurative on ①). Adv: *tightly.* Comp: *tighter;* sup: *tightest.*) **3.** *adj.* closely held; firmly fastened; fixed. (Adv: *tightly.* Comp: *tighter;* sup: *tightest.*) **4.** *adj.* stretched; taut. (Adv: *tightly.* Comp: *tighter;* sup: *tightest.*) **5.** *adv.* in a manner that is ①; firmly; closely. (Comp: *tighter;* sup: *tightest.*)
→ (AS) TIGHT AS A TICK
→ IN A (TIGHT) SPOT

→ KEEP A TIGHT REIN ON SOMEONE OR SOMETHING
→ RUN A TIGHT SHIP
→ SIT TIGHT

tighten ['taɪt n] **1.** *tv.* to make something tight; to make something tighter. **2.** *iv.* to become tight; to become tighter.

tighten one's **belt** to manage to spend less money.

tighten something **up** to make something tighter.

tighten up 1. [for something] to get tighter. **2.** [for someone or a group] to become miserly.

tightrope ['taɪt rop] *n.* a rope or cable that is stretched tight, high above the ground, and on which acrobats perform.
→ WALK A TIGHTROPE

tights *n.* a garment that is worn below the waist and fits closely against one's body, generally worn by women and dancers; panty-hose. (Treated as plural. Number is expressed with *pair(s) of tights.*)

tile ['taɪl] **1.** *n.* baked clay or ceramic material formed into useful shapes for construction and decoration. (Plural only for types and instances.) **2.** *n.* a thin, formed piece of ① used for covering floors, walls, roofs, and other surfaces in buildings and houses. **3.** *n.* a square of soft material that absorbs sound and provides decoration, used in the construction of ceilings. **4.** *tv.* to cover a surface with ② or a similar substance. **5.** *iv.* to work by covering surfaces with ②.

till ['tɪl] **1.** *tv.* to plow land; to prepare soil for planting. **2.** *n.* the

drawer in a cash register or counter where money is kept in a place of business. **3.** *prep.* UNTIL; up to a certain time; during a period of time up to a certain time. **4.** *conj.* UNTIL; up to a certain time. **5.** *conj.* UNTIL; before.
→ HAVE ONE'S HAND IN THE TILL

tilt ['tɪlt] **1.** *tv.* to turn something to its side; to slant something. **2.** *iv.* to be turned to the side; to be tipped; to slant; to slope.

tilt at windmills to fight battles with imaginary enemies; to fight against unimportant enemies or issues. (As with the fictional character Don Quixote, who attacked windmills, imagining them to be enemies.)

timber ['tɪm bɚ] **1.** *n.* trees that are growing; a forest; woods. (No plural.) **2.** *n.* a thick length of wood.

time ['taɪm] **1.** *n.* every moment that ever was, is now, and ever will be; a continuous state of being from the past, through now, and into the future. (No plural.) **2.** *n.* a period of ①; a period of ① between two events. (No plural.) **3.** *n.* the amount of ① that it takes to do something. (No plural.) **4.** *n.* an exact moment in the passage of ①; some moment in the passage of ①. **5.** *n.* the appropriate moment, day, week, etc., to do something. (No plural.) **6.** *n.* an occasion of doing something; an instance of something being done. **7.** *tv.* to measure the existence of something that is happening; to measure how long or how fast it takes someone to do something. **8.** *tv.* to determine the best ④ for

doing something, and do it then.
9. *tv.* to set or arrange something so that it does something at a certain TIME as in ④.
→ AHEAD OF ONE'S TIME
→ GET TIME TO CATCH ONE'S BREATH
→ HARDLY HAVE TIME TO THINK
→ HAVE THE TIME OF ONE'S LIFE
→ IN ONE'S SPARE TIME
→ IN LESS THAN NO TIME
→ IN THE NICK OF TIME
→ IN THE RIGHT PLACE AT THE RIGHT TIME
→ IN THE WRONG PLACE AT THE WRONG TIME
→ IN TIME
→ IN TIMES PAST
→ INVEST (SOMEONE'S) TIME IN SOMETHING
→ KEEP UP (WITH THE TIMES)
→ KILL TIME
→ LONG TIME NO SEE.
→ MAKE UP FOR LOST TIME
→ RUN OUT OF TIME
→ the SANDS OF TIME
→ SERVE TIME
→ SINCE TIME IMMEMORIAL
→ WHEN THE TIME IS RIPE

time flies time passes very quickly. (From the Latin *tempus fugit*.)

Time hangs heavy on someone's **hands.** Time seems to go slowly when one has nothing to do.

time in to record one's arrival time.

time off a period of time during which one does not have to work; free time.

time out to record one's departure time.

time someone **in** to record someone's arrival time.

time someone **out** to record someone's departure time.

time was (when) there was a time when; at a time in the past.

timepiece ['taɪm pis] *n.* a device, especially a clock or a watch, that keeps track of time.

timer ['taɪm ɚ] *n.* someone or something that records time, especially a device that can be set to indicate when a certain amount of time has passed.

times 1. *n.* periods of time and the events that occurred during them. **2.** *prep.* multiplied by a number. (Represented by the symbol (×).)

timid ['tɪm ɪd] *adj.* full of fear; easily scared. (Adv: *timidly.* Comp: *timider;* sup: *timidest.*)

tin ['tɪn] **1.** *n.* a metal that is mixed with other metals to make bronze and is used as a coating for steel so that the steel doesn't rust. (No plural.) **2.** *n.* a can or a container made of ① or plated with ①, or a modern steel can containing no ①. (Usually limited to containers that hold cookies, crackers, and sardines. CAN is used more frequently.) **3.** *adj.* made of or coated with ①.

tinge ['tɪndʒ] **1.** *n.* a very small amount of something, such as a color or an emotion. **2.** *tv.* to add to or improve something with a small amount of something.

tingle ['tɪŋ gəl] **1.** *n.* a light prickly or stinging feeling, as though one received a small shock or thrill. **2.** *iv.* to experience a light stinging feeling, as though one has received a small shock or thrill.

tinker (around) (with something**)** to meddle with something; to play with something, trying to get it to work or work better.

tinkle ['tɪŋ kəl] **1.** *n.* a short, quiet, high-pitched ring or clinking sound something like a soft jingle. **2.** *iv.* to ring in a short, quiet, high-pitched way.

tint ['tɪnt] **1.** *n.* a color; a weakened shade of a color. **2.** *tv.* to color something slightly; to give a small amount of color to something; to dye hair with ①.

tinted ['tɪn təd] *adj.* slightly colored.

tiny ['taɪ ni] *adj.* very small. (Adv: *tinily.* Comp: *tinier;* sup: *tiniest.*)

tip ['tɪp] **1.** *n.* the very end part of an object; the top of an object. **2.** *n.* money that is given to someone for a service. **3.** *n.* a hint; a suggestion; a piece of advice. **4.** *tv.* to lean something to the side; to cause something to slant. **5.** *tv.* to give someone money for a service; to leave someone ②. (E.g., *tip the porter.*) **6.** *tv.* to give a certain sum or percentage of money in gratitude for service. (E.g., *tip 15 percent for good service.*) **7.** *iv.* to lean to the side; to slant. **8.** *iv.* to give people money for their services.
→ ON THE TIP OF ONE'S TONGUE

tip someone **off (about** someone or something) AND **tip** someone **off (on** someone or something) to give someone a valuable piece of news about someone or something.

tip someone **off (on** someone or something) Go to TIP SOMEONE OFF (ABOUT SOMEONE OR SOMETHING).

tip something **over** to cause something to fall over.

tip the scales at something to weigh some amount.

tiptoe ['tɪp to] **1.** *n.* the tips of the toes, referring to walking on the toes. **2.** *iv.* to walk on the tips of one's toes; to walk very quietly or lightly.
→ ON TIPTOE

tire ['taɪɚ] *n.* a circular structure of rubber that surrounds a wheel and is filled with air.
→ FLAT TIRE

tire of someone or something to become impatient with someone or something.

tire (out) to become weary or exhausted.

tire someone **out** to cause someone to become exhausted, sleepy, or weary.

tired ['taɪɚd] **1.** *adj.* sleepy; wanting to sleep; exhausted. (Adv: *tiredly.*) **2.** *adj.* impatient with someone or something; annoyed with someone or something. (Adv: *tiredly.*)
→ SICK (AND TIRED) OF SOMEONE OR SOMETHING

tiring ['taɪr ɪŋ] *adj.* causing one to become tired, especially because it requires a lot of energy, patience, or attention; exhausting. (Adv: *tiringly.*)

tissue ['tɪʃ ju] **1.** *n.* a very soft piece of paper that is used to wipe the skin or for blowing the nose. **2.** *n.* a part of a plant or an animal that is made of many cells having the same function; the group of cells in a plant or animal that form a particular organ. (Plural only for types and instances.)

title ['taɪt əl] **1.** *n.* the name of a book, movie, song, play, picture, or poem. **2.** *n.* a word, often abbreviated, that is placed before a person's name, indicating rank, profession, or social position. **3.** *n.* the official name of a job or position. **4.** *n.* an official document showing that someone owns something. (Compare this with DEED ②.) **5.** *tv.* to give something ①.

tizzy ['tɪz i] an excited and confused condition; a fuss.
→ IN A TIZZY

to [tu, tə] **1.** *prep.* in the direction of someone or something; toward someone or something; in the direction of a place, position, or condition; toward and reaching a place to which one is going. **2.** *prep.* as far as some time, place, thing, or person; until; through. (Often indicated with a hyphen or short dash, as in "1997–1999.") **3.** *prep.* a form that marks the indirect object of a verb, showing the action of a verb toward someone or something. **4.** *prep.* for each; in each; included in each. **5.** *prep.* as far as someone or something; against someone or something. **6.** *prep.* before a certain time. **7.** the marker of the infinitive form of verbs. (This use of TO is often considered to be a preposition, but it has none of the qualities of a preposition.)

to one's **heart's content** as much as one wants.

to the ends of the earth everywhere possible, even to the remotest and most inaccessible points on the earth.

to wit namely; that is; that is to say.

toad ['tod] *n.* a small animal similar to a frog, but which lives mostly on land.

toast ['tost] **1.** *n.* sliced bread that has been browned by heat. (No plural. Number is expressed with *piece(s)* or *slice(s) of toast.*) **2.** *n.* a statement made before an invitation for everyone present to take a drink in approval or agreement. **3.** *tv.* to brown a slice of bread by heating it; to brown something by heating it. **4.** *tv.* to warm something, especially marshmallows, over a fire. **5.** *tv.* to honor someone or something by taking a drink; to drink to the honor of someone or something.
→ PROPOSE A TOAST

toaster ['tos tɚ] *n.* an electrical appliance that toasts bread.

tobacco [tə 'bæk o] *n.* a plant whose leaves are dried to be smoked in cigars, cigarettes, or pipes or to be chewed. (Plural only for types and instances.)

toboggan [tə 'bag ən] **1.** *n.* a long sled without blades. **2.** *iv.* to ride on ①; to go down hills on ①.

today [tə 'de] **1.** *n.* this day; the current day. **2.** *n.* in this period of time. **3.** *adv.* in the current age or general time period. **4.** *adv.* on this day.

toe ['to] **1.** *n.* one of the fingerlike projections on the front of the foot; one of the digits on one's foot. **2.** *n.* the part of a shoe, boot, sock, or other piece of footwear

that covers or encloses one or
more ①.
→ ON ONE'S TOES
→ STEP ON SOMEONE'S TOES
→ TREAD ON SOMEONE'S TOES

toe the line Go to TOE THE MARK.

toe the mark AND **toe the line** to
do what one is expected to do; to
follow the rules.

toenail ['toʊ nel] *n.* the thin, hard
plate that covers the front part of
the end of the toe.

together [tə 'gɛ ðɚ] **1.** *adv.* as one
group of people or things. **2.** *adv.*
at the same time; simultaneously.
→ BAND TOGETHER (AGAINST SOMEONE OR
    SOMETHING)
→ BLEND SOMETHING TOGETHER (WITH
    SOMETHING)
→ CROWD TOGETHER
→ DRAW SOME PEOPLE TOGETHER
→ FLOCK TOGETHER
→ HANG TOGETHER
→ HUDDLE (UP) (TOGETHER)
→ KEEP BODY AND SOUL TOGETHER
→ LUMP PEOPLE OR THINGS TOGETHER
→ MESH TOGETHER
→ PATCH SOMETHING TOGETHER (WITH
    SOMETHING)
→ PIECE SOMETHING TOGETHER
→ PUT TWO AND TWO TOGETHER
→ ROOM TOGETHER
→ SLAP SOMETHING TOGETHER
→ STICK TOGETHER
→ THROW SOMETHING TOGETHER
→ TOSS SOMETHING TOGETHER

toil ['toɪl] **1.** *n.* hard work; hard
labor; work that requires a lot of
physical energy or effort. (Plural
only for types and instances.) **2.** *iv.*
to work hard; to labor; to do work
that requires a lot of physical
energy or effort.

toilet ['toɪ lət] **1.** *n.* a bathroom; a
room that has ②; a restroom. **2.** *n.*
a strong, ceramic bowl, connected

to a drain and having a seat
attached to it, into which one
expels urine or feces.
→ GO TO THE TOILET

toilet paper ['toɪ lət pe pɚ] *n.* very
thin, usually soft paper that is
used to cleanse the affected areas
of one's body after one has used
the toilet. (No plural.)

token ['tok ən] **1.** *n.* a sign of
something; a reminder of something; visible proof of something;
evidence of something. **2.** *n.* a
small piece of metal, similar to a
coin, that is used instead of
money. **3.** *adj.* only serving as a
symbol of something; done solely
for the way it will appear to others.
→ BY THE SAME TOKEN

told ['told] past tense and past participle of TELL.
→ A LITTLE BIRD TOLD ME

tolerant ['tɑl ə rənt] *adj.* willing to
allow others to do something or to
live the way they want to. (Adv:
tolerantly.)

tolerate ['tɑl ə ret] *tv.* to endure
someone or something; to manage
to accept someone or something.

toll ['tol] **1.** *n.* a fee paid for the
privilege of doing something,
especially traveling on certain
routes. **2.** *n.* the extra charge for
certain telephone calls that are not
local. **3.** *iv.* [for a bell] to ring
slowly and repeatedly. **4.** *tv.* to ring
a bell slowly and repeatedly.

tomato [tə 'me to] **1.** *n.* a round,
soft red fruit that grows on a vine
and is eaten as food. (Plural ends
in -*es.*) **2.** *adj.* made or flavored
with ①.

tomb ['tum] *n.* an enclosure in which someone is buried, especially a structure that is above ground level.

tombstone ['tum ston] *n.* a grave marker; a large slab of stone at a grave that shows who is buried at that place and when that person was alive.

tomorrow [tə 'mɑr o] **1.** *n.* the day after today. (Usually singular.) **2.** *n.* the future. (No plural.) **3.** *adv.* during ①; at some time during ①.

ton ['tʌn] *n.* a unit of measure of weight equal to 2,000 pounds. (Also called a *short ton;* used in the United States and Canada.)
→ HIT (SOMEONE) LIKE A TON OF BRICKS

tone ['ton] **1.** *n.* a sound as it relates to its quality, intensity, or pitch. **2.** *n.* a quality of one's voice that reveals one's feelings or attitude. **3.** *n.* a style, character, or mood of an event or circumstance. **4.** *n.* firmness of the muscles. (No plural.)
→ DIAL TONE

tone something **down** to cause something to have less of an impact on the senses of sight or sound; to lessen the impact of something prepared for public performance or consumption.

tongs ['tɔŋz] *n.* a tool or utensil that has two arms joined by a hinge or spring and is used for holding or moving something. (Treated as plural. Number is expressed with *pair(s) of tongs.*)
→ FIGHT SOMEONE OR SOMETHING HAMMER AND TONGS
→ GO AT IT HAMMER AND TONGS

tongue ['tʌŋ] **1.** *n.* the long, typically pink, movable organ in the mouth, used for tasting, managing food, and, in humans, speaking. **2.** *n.* the ① of an animal, eaten as food. (No plural.) **3.** *n.* a language. **4.** *n.* the flap of material that is part of a shoe and fits under the laces. **5.** *n.* a flame; a pointed section of fire.
→ BITE ONE'S TONGUE
→ CAUSE (SOME) TONGUES TO WAG
→ HOLD ONE'S TONGUE
→ KEEP A CIVIL TONGUE (IN ONE'S HEAD)
→ ON THE TIP OF ONE'S TONGUE
→ SLIP OF THE TONGUE
→ SPEAK WITH A FORKED TONGUE

tongue-in-cheek insincere; joking.

tonic ['tɑn ɪk] **1.** *n.* a remedy; something that is good for one's health; something that provides strength. **2.** *n.* a kind of flavored soda water that is somewhat bitter.

tonight [tə 'naɪt] **1.** *n.* this evening; this night. **2.** *adv.* during ①; at some time during ①.

tonsil ['tɑn səl] *n.* one of two small organs in the very back of the mouth at the side of the throat.

too ['tu] **1.** *adv.* as well; also; in addition. **2.** *adv.* more than enough; more than is desired; beyond what is desired. **3.** *adv.* very; extremely. **4.** *adv.* a form used after BE, WILL, DO, HAVE, CAN, SHOULD, WOULD, and COULD to strengthen them in response to a negative statement.

too good to be true almost unbelievable; so good as to be unbelievable.

took ['tʊk] Past participle of TAKE.

tool ['tul] **1.** *n.* anything that helps someone work; an instrument that is used to help someone do work. **2.** *n.* someone who is used by someone else, especially in an unfair way. (Figurative on ①.)

tool something **up** to equip a factory or production line with tools and machines.

tool up to become equipped with tools.

toolshed ['tul ʃɛd] *n.* a small building where gardening tools are stored.

toot ['tut] **1.** *n.* a short blast of a horn or a whistle. **2.** *tv.* to cause a horn or whistle to make a short noise.

toot one's **own horn** AND **blow** one's **own horn** to boast about oneself; to praise oneself.

tooth ['tuθ] **1.** *n., irreg.* one of the hard, usually white, bony objects in the mouth, used for biting and chewing while eating. (Plural: TEETH.) **2.** *n., irreg.* something shaped like ①, especially a small pointed object on a wheel that is part of a machine, the "fingers" of a rake, or the points along the length of a comb or saw.
→ FIGHT SOMEONE OR SOMETHING TOOTH AND NAIL
→ GO AT IT TOOTH AND NAIL
→ GO OVER SOMETHING WITH A FINE-TOOTH COMB
→ HAVE A SWEET TOOTH
→ SEARCH SOMETHING WITH A FINE-TOOTH COMB
→ SWEET TOOTH

toothache ['tuθ ek] *n.* a pain in or around a tooth.

toothbrush ['tuθ brəʃ] *n.* a small brush that is used for cleaning the teeth.

toothpaste ['tuθ pest] *n.* a paste that is placed on a toothbrush and is used for cleaning the teeth. (Plural only for types and instances.)

toothpick ['tuθ pɪk] *n.* a small, thin piece of wood that is used to remove pieces of food from between one's teeth.

top ['tɑp] **1.** *n.* the highest part of something; the upper part of something; the peak of something; the upper surface of something. **2.** *n.* the highest position; the highest rank; the most successful position; the most important position. **3.** *n.* a cover; a cap; a lid. **4.** *n.* a piece of clothing worn above the waist, especially on women. **5.** *adj.* on or at the highest part of something. **6.** *adj.* first; best; most important. **7.** *adj.* greatest; strongest; at the highest intensity. **8.** *tv.* to place something on the highest part of something; to place something on something else.
→ AT THE TOP OF ONE'S LUNGS
→ AT THE TOP OF ONE'S VOICE
→ FROM THE TOP
→ FROM TOP TO BOTTOM
→ IN TOP FORM
→ OFF THE TOP OF ONE'S HEAD
→ ON TOP
→ ON TOP OF THE WORLD
→ OVER THE TOP
→ THIN ON TOP

top something **off (with** something) **1.** to celebrate an end to a task with an event. **2.** to complete the top of something, such as a building.

topic ['tɑp ɪk] *n.* the subject of something that is being written or talked about.

topple over [for something very tall] to fall over.

torch ['tɔrtʃ] **1.** *n.* a large stick or club whose upper end is on fire. **2.** *n.* a machine that makes a very hot flame, used to cut or join together pieces of metal by melting them. **3.** *tv.* to set something on fire; to destroy something with fire.
→ CARRY A TORCH (FOR SOMEONE)
→ CARRY THE TORCH

tore ['tɔr] a past tense of TEAR.

torment 1. ['tɔr mɛnt] *n.* a severe emotional or physical pain; agony. (Plural only for types and instances.) **2.** [tɔr 'mɛnt] *tv.* to cause someone severe pain or agony; to cause someone to suffer.

torn ['tɔrn] **1.** a past participle of TEAR. **2.** *adj.* having a tear; ripped.

torn between something **and** something **else** troubled by a choice or dilemma.

tornado [tɔr 'ne do] *n.* a violent wind that spins in circles very fast and can cause a great amount of damage. (Plural ends in -s or -es.)

torpedo [tɔr 'pi do] **1.** *n.* an explosive device that is fired underwater from a submarine or ship toward another submarine or ship. (Plural ends in -es.) **2.** *tv.* to attack something with ①; to explode something by firing ① at it.

tortoise ['tɔr təs] *n.* a turtle, especially one that only lives on land.

torture ['tɔr tʃɚ] **1.** *n.* the inflicting of pain in a cruel way. (No

plural.) **2.** *tv.* to cause someone to suffer pain in a cruel way.

toss ['tɔs] **1.** *tv.* to throw something lightly or gently; to throw something carelessly. **2.** *tv.* to lift and throw something upward; to cause something to move as if it had been thrown. **3.** *tv.* to flip a coin into the air in order to decide a choice based on which side of the coin appears when it falls; to roll dice. **4.** *iv.* to turn; to move restlessly. **5.** *iv.* to be thrown, especially by water; to be moved with force. **6.** *n.* an instance of throwing something.

toss a salad to mix the lettuce and vegetables of a salad together with dressing.

toss one's **hat into the ring** to state that one is running for an elective office.

toss something **together** to assemble something hastily.

total ['tot əl] **1.** *n.* the whole amount; the sum; the number obtained by adding other numbers together. **2.** *adj.* whole; complete; entire. (Adv: *totally*.) **3.** *tv.* to calculate ①. **4.** *tv.* to come to a certain amount; to reach a certain amount.
→ GRAND TOTAL

total something **up** to add up the total of something.

totally ['tot ə li] *adv.* completely; entirely.

tote ['tot] *tv.* to carry something.

touch ['tʌtʃ] **1.** *tv.* to place one's finger, hand, or some other body part on someone or something. **2.** *tv.* to place one object against

another; to place one object on another. **3.** *tv.* to border something; to share a border with something. **4.** *tv.* to make contact with something; to have no space between two or more objects. (No actual movement is involved.) **5.** *tv.* to handle something; to use something. (Especially in negative constructions.) **6.** *iv.* [for people or things] to make contact or be in contact. **7.** *tv.* to affect someone, especially in a sad way. **8.** *n.* an instance of placing one's finger or hand on someone or something. **9.** *n.* someone's handling or gentle pressure as sensed by the person being TOUCHED as in ①. (No plural.) **10.** *n.* a detail that improves something or adds to something. **11.** *n.* a small amount of something; a little bit of something. **12.** *n.* a special or unique skill or style; evidence of one's skill or style.
→ HAVE THE MIDAS TOUCH

touch down [for an airplane] to come in contact with the ground.

touch someone **for** something to ask someone for a loan of something, usually a sum of money. (Informal.)

touch someone or something **off** to ignite or excite someone or something.

touch something **up** to fix up the minor flaws in something.

touch (up)on something to mention something; to discuss something briefly.

touchy ['tʌtʃ i] *adj.* easily angered; easily upset; irritable; too sensi-

tive. (Adv: *touchily.* Comp: *touchier*; sup: *touchiest.*)

tough ['tʌf] **1.** *adj.* not tender; difficult to chew. (Comp: *tougher*; sup: *toughest.*) **2.** *adj.* hard to do; difficult; not easy. (Comp: *tougher*; sup: *toughest.*) **3.** *adj.* strong and determined; not weak. (Adv: *toughly.* Comp: *tougher*; sup: *toughest.*) **4.** *adj.* stubborn; not likely to have a change of mind. (Adv: *toughly.* Comp: *tougher*; sup: *toughest.*) **5.** *adj.* rough; violent; dangerous. (Adv: *toughly.* Comp: *tougher*; sup: *toughest.*) **6.** *adj.* unfortunate; unlucky. (Informal. Comp: *tougher*; sup: *toughest.*) **7.** *n.* a criminal; someone who is violent or dangerous.

a **tough act to follow** a presentation or performance of such high quality that one will have difficulty maintaining the same standard of quality in one's own presentation or performance.

a **tough row to hoe** a difficult task to undertake.

tough something **out** to endure something; to endure the difficulty of something to the very end.

toughen someone or something **up** to cause someone or something to become stronger, more uncompromising, or more severe.

toughen up to become tougher, stronger, or more severe.

tour ['tʊ ɚ] **1.** *n.* a trip in which several places of interest are visited; a trip in which one visits an interesting place. **2.** *tv.* to travel through a place; to move through a place for entertainment. **3.** *tv.*

[for a performance and its performers] to visit or travel to many places in order to be seen. **4.** *iv.* to travel around from place to place in order to be seen.

tourism ['tʊɚ ɪz əm] **1.** *n.* travel; visiting interesting places, especially for a vacation. (No plural.) **2.** *n.* the business of attracting and serving tourists. (No plural.)

tourist ['tʊɚ ɪst] **1.** *n.* someone who travels for pleasure. **2.** the *adj.* use of ①.

tournament ['tʊɚ nə mənt] *n.* a contest involving several people or teams who play several games in such a way that the winner of one game plays the winner of another game until there is only one champion remaining.

tow ['to] **1.** *tv.* to pull something with a rope or chain. **2.** *n.* an instance of pulling something with a rope or chain.
→ IN TOW

tow someone or something **away** to pull something, such as a car or a boat, away with another car, boat, etc. (The *someone* refers to the property of someone, not the person.)

tow someone or something **in(to** something)** to pull something, such as a car or a truck, into something, such as a garage. (The *someone* refers to the property of someone, not the person.)

tow someone or something **out (of someplace)** to pull something, such as a car, out of something, such as a ditch. (The *someone* refers to the property of someone, not the person.)

toward(s) ['tord(z)] **1.** *prep.* [facing] in a certain direction; facing someone. **2.** *prep.* about or in relation to or about someone or something. **3.** *prep.* just before a certain time. **4.** *prep.* as a payment to someone or something.

towel ['tɑʊ əl] *n.* a piece of cloth or paper that is used to take away moisture from a surface.
→ THROW IN THE TOWEL

tower ['tɑʊ ɚ] *n.* a tall building or structure; a tall part of a building or structure.
→ LIVE IN AN IVORY TOWER

a **tower of strength** a person who can always be depended on to provide support and encouragement, especially in times of trouble.

town ['tɑʊn] **1.** *n.* an area where people live that is smaller than a city but larger than a village. **2.** *n.* the part of a city where businesses, stores, and markets are found. (No plural.) **3.** *n.* a city. **4.** *n.* all the people who live in ①. **5.** the *adj.* use of ①, ②, or ③.
→ GO TO TOWN
→ A MAN ABOUT TOWN
→ OUT ON THE TOWN
→ PAINT THE TOWN RED
→ TALK OF THE TOWN

toy ['tɔɪ] **1.** *n.* something that is made to amuse a child. **2.** *adj.* made to be played with.

trace ['tres] **1.** *n.* a very small amount of something. **2.** *tv.* to draw or copy the outline of something by putting a thin piece of paper on top of it and then drawing over the lines one sees through the thin paper. **3.** *tv.* to follow the path of something's growth, development, or history. **4.** *tv.* to seek the origin of something.

track ['træk] **1.** *n.* the marks made by a vehicle, person, or animal traveling from place to place. **2.** *n.* a pair of parallel metal rails that trains travel on. **3.** *n.* a trail; a path; a rough road. **4.** *n.* a circular pathway used for running or racing. **5.** *n.* a group of sports activities including running, jumping, and other tests of individual endurance and strength. (No plural.) **6.** *tv.* to follow the trail of a person or other creature.
→ DROP IN ONE'S TRACKS
→ GET THE INSIDE TRACK
→ HAVE A ONE-TRACK MIND
→ JUMP THE TRACK
→ ON THE RIGHT TRACK
→ ON THE WRONG TRACK
→ the OTHER SIDE OF THE TRACKS

track someone or something **down** to search and find where someone or something is.

track something **in(to someplace)** to bring something, such as mud, into a place on the bottom of one's feet.

track something **up** to mess a place up by spreading around something dirty or messy with one's feet.

traction ['træk ʃən] *n.* the grip of a wheel or shoe on a surface that allows the wheel or shoe to apply energy to the surface in order to move ahead. (No plural.)

tractor ['træk tɚ] *n.* a motor vehicle with large, thick tires, used for pulling farm equipment in fields.

trade ['tred] **1.** *n.* the business of buying and selling products. (No plural.) **2.** *n.* a particular business.

3. *n.* a job that utilizes a skill. **4.** *n.* the exchange of someone or something for someone or something else. **5.** *tv.* to exchange someone or something for someone or something else. **6.** *iv.* to exchange; to swap.
→ KNOW (ALL) THE TRICKS OF THE TRADE

trade something **in (for** something**)** AND **trade** something **in (on** something**)** to return something, such as a car, to a place where that item is sold as partial payment on a new item.

trade something **in (on** something**)** Go to TRADE SOMETHING IN (FOR SOMETHING).

trade something **off 1.** to get rid of something in an exchange. **2.** to sacrifice something in an exchange.

trademark ['tred mɑrk] **1.** *n.* a word, name, or symbol—used and owned by a manufacturer—that identifies a product. **2.** *n.* a mark or feature that is associated with a certain person or thing. (Figurative on ①.) **3.** *tv.* [for a manufacturer] to protect ① by registering it with the government.

trader ['tred ɚ] *n.* a merchant; someone who buys and sells things as a business.

tradition [trə 'dɪ ʃən] *n.* the way that something has been done from generation to generation. (Plural only for types and instances.)

traditional [trə 'dɪ ʃ ə nəl] *adj.* relating to tradition. (Adv: *traditionally*.)

traffic ['træf ɪk] **1.** *n.* vehicles and their movement—or slowness of movement—on land, on water, or in the air. (No plural.) **2.** *n.* the process of buying and selling. (No plural.)
→ STUCK IN TRAFFIC

traffic jam ['træf ɪk dʒæm] *n.* a situation in which vehicles on a road have stopped or slowed down because there are too many of them.

traffic light ['træf ɪk laɪt] *n.* a signal, usually found at intersections, used to control traffic by a system of lights. (Can be shortened to LIGHT.)

tragedy ['træ dʒə di] **1.** *n.* a serious play that has a sad ending. **2.** *n.* a disaster; a sad, unfortunate, or terrible event.

tragic ['træ dʒɪk] **1.** *adj.* of or about serious plays with sad endings. (Adv: *tragically* [...ɪk li].) **2.** *adj.* sad; terrible; unfortunate. (Adv: *tragically* [...ɪk li].)

trail ['trel] **1.** *n.* the marks made by a vehicle, person, or animal as it travels from place to place; the scent left by a person or animal as it travels from place to place. (See also TRACK.) **2.** *n.* a path through an area that a car cannot travel over; a path for walking, biking, etc. **3.** *tv.* to follow someone or an animal by its scent, footprints, or other clues that the person or animal leaves behind. **4.** *tv.* to leave something dirty on a surface by walking or dragging something across it.

train ['tren] **1.** *n.* a line of railroad cars pulled by an engine. **2.** *tv.* to teach someone a skill; to give someone the knowledge needed to do a job. **3.** *iv.* to prepare [oneself] for a job, contest, or a performance.
→ HAVE ONE'S SIGHTS TRAINED ON SOMETHING
→ LOSE ONE'S TRAIN OF THOUGHT
→ RIDE THE GRAVY TRAIN

train one's **sights on** something AND **have** one's **sights trained on** something to have something as a goal; to direct something or oneself toward a goal. (The same as SET ONE'S SIGHTS ON SOMETHING.)

traitor ['tret ɚ] *n.* one who betrays one's country or leader.

tramp ['træmp] **1.** *n.* someone who lives by begging; a male who lives on the streets and does not have a home. **2.** *n.* the sound of someone marching. (No plural.) **3.** *iv.* to walk heavily and steadily.

transaction [træn 'zæk ʃən] *n.* a business deal; an agreement or negotiation that has been completed.

transfer ['træns fɚ] **1.** *n.* the movement of something from one place to another place. (No plural.) **2.** *n.* a ticket that allows someone to get off one vehicle, usually a bus, and get on another one without paying a second fare. **3.** *iv.* to move from one vehicle to another; to get off one vehicle and get on another one. **4.** *iv.* to move from one site to another site. **5.** *tv.* to move something from one place to another place. **6.** *tv.* to cause someone to move from one job site to another job site.

transform [træns 'form] *tv.* to change something's or someone's shape, form, nature, or appearance.

transfusion [træns 'fju ʒən] *n.* the process of transferring blood from one person to another.

transistor [træn 'zɪs tɚ] *n.* a small electrical device that controls the flow of current in electronic circuits.

transit ['træn zɪt] *n.* transportation; movement of people or goods. (No plural.)
→ IN TRANSIT

transitive verb ['træn sə tɪv 'vɚb] *n.* a verb that is used with a DIRECT OBJECT; a verb that requires a DIRECT OBJECT. (Abbreviated *tv.* here.)

translate ['træn slet] **1.** *tv.* to change something written or spoken from one language to another. **2.** *iv.* to change [something written or spoken in one language] to another language.

translation [trænz 'le ʃən] *n.* changing a message in one language into an equivalent message in another language; changing a sequence of symbols in one code into another code. (Plural only for types and instances.)
→ FREE TRANSLATION

translator ['trænz le tɚ] *n.* someone who translates sentences of one language into another.

transmit [trænz 'mɪt] *tv.* to send information by way of electricity or radio waves.

transmitter ['trænz mɪt ɚ] *n.* a piece of electronic equipment that transmits electromagnetic waves, as for radio or television.

transparent [trænz 'pɛr ənt] **1.** *adj.* clear and able to be seen through. (Adv: *transparently.*) **2.** *adj.* obvious; easily recognized; [of something meant to deceive] easy to figure out. (Figurative on ①. Adv: *transparently.*)

transport ['trænz port] **1.** *n.* carrying people or things from one place to another. (No plural.) **2.** *tv.* to carry someone or something from one place to another.

transportation [trænz pɚ 'te ʃən] **1.** *n.* the system of moving people and goods from one place to another. (No plural.) **2.** *n.* moving people or goods from one place to another. (No plural.)

trap ['træp] **1.** *n.* a device used to catch animals or people. **2.** *n.* a bend in a drain pipe in which water rests in order to prevent harmful gases from the sewer from going into a building. **3.** *tv.* to catch someone or something in ①. **4.** *tv.* to prevent someone or something from escaping, leaving, or getting out.
→ SET A TRAP

trapper ['træp ɚ] *n.* someone who traps animals, skins them, and sells the fur.

trash ['træʃ] **1.** *n.* things that are thrown away; rubbish; refuse. (No plural.) **2.** *tv.* to throw something away. (Slang.)

trauma ['trɔ mə] **1.** *n.* an emotional shock; an emotional response to a shock. **2.** *n.* an injury; a wound; damage to the body.

travel ['træv əl] **1.** *iv.* to visit [places other than where one lives]; to journey. **2.** *iv.* to move through space; to move across a distance. **3.** *tv.* to move on a path or route as one makes a journey. **4.** *tv.* to move over a specific distance as one makes a journey. **5.** *n.* going to and visiting places other than where one lives. (No plural. See also SOMEONE'S TRAVELS.) **6.** the *adj.* use of ⑤.

traveler ['træv lɚ] *n.* someone who travels; someone who goes on trips or journeys.

a **travesty of justice** a miscarriage of justice; an act of the legal system that is an insult to the system of justice.

tray ['tre] *n.* a flat panel with a slightly raised rim, used to carry things, especially food.

tread on someone's **toes** Go to STEP ON SOMEONE'S TOES.

treasure ['trɛ ʒɚ] **1.** *n.* valuable objects, especially ones that are stored; someone or something that is highly valued. **2.** *tv.* to value someone or something highly.

treasurer ['trɛ ʒɚ ɚ] *n.* someone who is in charge of the money of an organization or unit of government.

treasury ['trɛ ʒə ri] **1.** *n.* the money that is owned by an organization or unit of government. **2.** *n.* the department of a government in charge of spending and saving public money.

treat ['trit] **1.** *n.* a bit of tasty food, such as candy or ice cream. **2.** *n.* something that is pleasing. **3.** *tv.* to

handle or consider someone or something in a certain way. **4.** *tv.* to try to cure something.
→ DUTCH TREAT
→ SOMEONE'S TREAT

treatment ['trit mənt] **1.** *n.* the way someone or something is dealt with. (No plural.) **2.** *n.* the method by which someone tries to cure someone. **3.** *n.* the way in which a story or script is presented.
→ GET THE RED-CARPET TREATMENT
→ GIVE SOMEONE THE RED-CARPET TREATMENT
→ the ROYAL TREATMENT

treaty ['trit i] *n.* a formal agreement between two or more nations.

tree ['tri] **1.** *n.* a tall plant whose stem and branches are made of wood, and that often has leaves growing from the branches. **2.** *n.* a diagram that represents the relationship between different levels or positions of power by expressing them as branches at different levels.
→ BARK UP THE WRONG TREE
→ NOT ABLE TO SEE THE FOREST FOR THE TREES
→ PALM TREE

tree house ['tri haʊs] *n., irreg.* a platform or structure built in a tree for children to play in. (Plural: [...haʊ zəz].)

treetop ['tri tɑp] *n.* the top of a tree.

trek ['trɛk] **1.** *n.* a long journey, often done walking. **2.** *iv.* to travel on a long journey, often on foot.

tremendous [trɪ 'mɛn dəs] **1.** *adj.* huge; enormous; very large; immense. (Adv: *tremendously*.)

2. *adj.* wonderful; excellent; superb. (Adv: *tremendously.*)

trial [ˈtraɪl] **1.** *n.* the examination of evidence in a court of law by a judge or jury to settle a legal question, such as guilt or innocence. **2.** *n.* an experiment; a test to see if something works; a test to see if something provides a benefit. **3.** *n.* a difficult ordeal; a problem; a disease and the problems it causes. **4.** *adj.* concerning the first test or an early attempt to get results. **5.** the *adj.* use of ①, ②, or ③.
→ ON TRIAL

triangle [ˈtraɪ æŋ gəl] **1.** *n.* a figure that has three sides and three angles. **2.** *n.* a flat, three-sided object with three sides, used for drawing lines and angles. **3.** *n.* a metallic musical instrument in the shape of ①, that is struck with a small rod to make a ringing noise.

tribe [ˈtraɪb] *n.* a group of people having the same customs, religion, language, and culture; a local division of a larger ethnic group.

tribute [ˈtrɪb jut] *n.* a show of respect or honor.

trick [ˈtrɪk] **1.** *n.* something that is done to deceive someone. **2.** *adj.* made to be used in ①; intended to deceive.
→ BAG OF TRICKS
→ KNOW (ALL) THE TRICKS OF THE TRADE
→ PLAY A TRICK ON SOMEONE
→ USE EVERY TRICK IN THE BOOK

trick someone **into** something to deceive someone into doing something.

trick someone **out of** something AND **trick** something **out of** someone to get something from someone by deception.

trick something **out of** someone
Go to TRICK SOMEONE OUT OF SOMETHING.

tricky [ˈtrɪk i] **1.** *adj.* difficult to do; puzzling; hard to deal with. (Adv: *trickily.* Comp: *trickier;* sup: *trickiest.*) **2.** *adj.* full of tricks; clever and good at deceiving people. (Adv: *trickily.* Comp: *trickier;* sup: *trickiest.*)

tricycle [ˈtraɪ sɪk əl] *n.* a small vehicle with three wheels, two in back and one in front, made for young children to ride on.

trigger [ˈtrɪg ɚ] **1.** *n.* the small lever on a gun, used to fire the gun. **2.** *n.* something that causes something else to happen. (Figurative on ①.) **3.** *tv.* to cause something to happen; to cause something that starts a sequence of events.
→ QUICK ON THE TRIGGER

trigger something **off** to set something off, such as an explosion.

trillion [ˈtrɪl jən] **1.** *n.* the number 1,000,000,000,000. (Additional numbers formed as with *two trillion, three trillion, four trillion,* etc.) **2.** *n.* a group or collection of 1,000,000,000,000 people or things. **3.** *adj.* consisting of 1,000,000,000,000 things.

trillionth [ˈtrɪl jənθ] 1,000,000,000,000th. Go to FOURTH.

trilogy [ˈtrɪl ə dʒi] *n.* a set of three books, plays, movies, etc., that share a common theme or characters and events.

trim [ˈtrɪm] **1.** *tv.* to make something neat by cutting; to cut something neatly. **2.** *tv.* to reduce something; to decrease something. **3.** *tv.* to decorate something. **4.** *adj.* [of someone] thin and of the proper weight. (Adv: *trimly.* Comp: *trimmer;* sup: *trimmest.*) **5.** *n.* the wood around a door or window or along the floor.

trim something **away (from** something**)** to cut something away (from something).

trim something **off ((of)** someone or something**)** to cut something off someone or something.

trio [ˈtri o] **1.** *n.* a group of three, especially a group of three performers. (Plural ends in *-s.*) **2.** *n.* a piece of music written for three instruments or three voices. (Plural ends in *-s.*)

trip [ˈtrɪp] **1.** *n.* a journey between two places; a journey from one place to another. **2.** *iv.* to stumble; to fall over something; to hit one's foot against someone or something, causing a loss of balance. **3.** *tv.* to cause someone to fall; to cause someone to stumble and lose balance. **4.** *tv.* to release a lever or a switch, thus causing something to function.

trip someone **up 1.** to cause someone to trip; to tangle someone's feet. **2.** to cause someone to become confused and awkward, especially when talking or reasoning.

tripod [ˈtraɪ pɑd] *n.* a support or stand that has three legs, especially one that supports a camera.

trite [ˈtraɪt] *adj.* [of an expression] shallow and simple-minded. (Adv: *tritely.* Comp: *triter;* sup: *tritest.*)

triumph [ˈtraɪ əmf] **1.** *n.* celebration; the glory of victory; a victory. (Plural only for types and instances.) **2.** *iv.* to win; to be very successful.

trivial [ˈtrɪv i əl] *adj.* not important; not significant. (Adv: *trivially.*)

trolley [ˈtrɑ li] *n.* a vehicle that is operated by electricity and runs along a track in the street.

trombone [trɑm ˈbon] *n.* a brass musical instrument, played by blowing air into one end with tensed lips, while moving a long sliding part into different positions.

troop [ˈtrup] **1.** *n.* a group of people or animals, especially a group of soldiers. **2.** *iv.* to walk or move as a group.

trooper [ˈtrup ɚ] *n.* an officer in the state police, usually the highway patrol. (Short for STATE TROOPER.)
→ STATE TROOPER

troops *n.* soldiers. (Treated as plural, but not countable.)

trophy [ˈtro fi] **1.** *n.* something that is taken from a battle or a hunt as a symbol of one's success. **2.** *n.* a small statue or prize that is given to the winner of an event or contest.

tropic [ˈtrɑp ɪk] **1.** *n.* one of two imaginary circles around the earth, 23.45 degrees north and south of the equator. **2.** *adj.* TROPICAL; hot and humid.

tropical ['trɑp ɪ kəl] *adj.* of or about the tropics; of or about the weather conditions of the tropics; found in the tropics. (Adv: *tropically* [...ɪk li].)

the **tropics** *n.* the area between the two TROPICS ①; the areas of the earth near the equator. (Treated as singular or plural.)

trot ['trɑt] **1.** *n.* the movement of a horse between a walk and a gallop; the movement of a human between a walk and a run. **2.** *iv.* to move faster than walking, but not as fast as running.

trot someone or something **out** to bring out and display someone or something. (Figurative.)

trot something **out** to mention something regularly or habitually, without giving it much thought.

trouble ['trʌb əl] **1.** *n.* worry; difficulty; anxiety. **2.** *n.* annoyance; bother. **3.** *n.* a sickness; a health problem. **4.** *n.* someone or something that causes worry, difficulty, anxiety, irritation, bother, or problems. **5.** *tv.* to worry someone; to cause someone difficulty or anxiety. **6.** *tv.* to bother or delay someone with an inquiry. **7.** *tv.* to cause someone to feel pain.
→ ASK FOR TROUBLE
→ DROWN ONE'S TROUBLES
→ FISH IN TROUBLED WATERS
→ IN TROUBLE
→ NOT WORTH THE TROUBLE
→ POUR OIL ON TROUBLED WATER
→ TEETHING TROUBLES

troublesome ['trʌb əl səm] *adj.* causing trouble; causing problems. (Adv: *troublesomely.*)

trousers ['traʊ zɚz] *n.* pants; a piece of clothing worn below the waist, having a separate tube, hole, or compartment for each leg and extending to the ankles. (Treated as plural. Number is expressed with *pair(s) of trousers.* Rarely singular.)

trout ['traʊt] **1.** *n., irreg.* a freshwater fish commonly eaten as food. (Plural: *trout.*) **2.** *n.* the flesh of ①, eaten as food. (No plural.)

trowel ['traʊ əl] **1.** *n.* a tool used to apply and smooth mortar or plaster. **2.** *n.* a tool used in gardening for digging small holes and planting individual plants.

truant ['tru ənt] **1.** *adj.* absent from school without permission. (Adv: *truantly.*) **2.** *n.* someone who is absent from school without permission.

truce ['trus] *n.* an agreement to stop fighting.

truck ['trʌk] **1.** *n.* a large motor vehicle designed to carry objects or cargo rather than people. **2.** the *adj.* use of ①. **3.** *tv.* to transport something by ①.

true ['tru] **1.** *adj.* being a fact; actual; real; not false. (Adv: *truly.* Comp: *truer;* sup: *truest.*) **2.** *adj.* sincere; genuine; not fake; not artificial. (Adv: *truly.* Comp: *truer;* sup: *truest.*) **3.** *adj.* properly fitted; at the proper angle. (Adv: *truly.* Comp: *truer;* sup: *truest.*)
→ COME TRUE
→ A DREAM COME TRUE
→ HOLD TRUE
→ RING TRUE
→ SHOW ONE'S (TRUE) COLORS
→ TOO GOOD TO BE TRUE

true to one's **word** keeping one's promise.

truly ['tru li] *adv.* really; honestly; genuinely.

trumpet ['trʌmp ɪt] **1.** *n.* a brass musical instrument on which different notes are produced by blowing air into one end while pressing different combinations of three valves. **2.** *iv.* [for an elephant] to make a characteristic elephant noise.

trunk ['trʌŋk] **1.** *n.* the main stem of a tree. **2.** *n.* the body of a human without its head, arms, or legs. **3.** *n.* a large, sturdy box for transporting or storing clothes or other objects. **4.** *n.* the long, tube-shaped nose of an elephant.

trunks *n.* a swimming suit for men. (Treated as plural. Number is expressed with *pair(s) of trunks.*)

trust ['trʌst] **1.** *n.* a strong belief in the honesty of someone or something. (No plural.) **2.** *tv.* to believe in the honesty of someone or something. **3.** *tv.* to hope something. (The object is a clause with THAT ⑦.)

truth ['truθ] **1.** *n.* the quality of being true or a fact. (No plural.) **2.** *n.* a fact; a true state.
→ the GOSPEL TRUTH
→ a GRAIN OF TRUTH
→ MOMENT OF TRUTH

truthful ['truθ fʊl] **1.** *adj.* [of a statement] able to be proven as true. (Adv: *truthfully.*) **2.** *adj.* regularly telling the truth; honest. (Adv: *truthfully.*)

try ['traɪ] **1.** *iv.* to make an attempt. **2.** *tv.* to use something to see if one likes it; to test something to see if it works well. **3.** *tv.* [for a judge or jury] to hear a [legal] case in a court of law. (E.g., *try a case.*) **4.** *tv.* [for a judge or jury] to subject an accused person to a trial in a court of law. (E.g., *try someone for a crime.*) **5.** *n.* an attempt; an effort to do something.

try one's **wings (out)** to try to do something one has recently become qualified to do.

try out (for something**)** to audition for a part in some performance or other activity requiring skill.

try someone's **patience** to do something annoying that may cause someone to lose patience; to cause someone to be annoyed.

try something **out on** someone to see how someone responds to something or some idea.

try to do something to attempt to do something.

tsar Go to CZAR.

T-shirt ['ti ʃɚt] *n.* a light, cotton shirt with short sleeves and no collar.

tub ['tʌb] **1.** *n.* a large, round or oval container with a flat bottom. **2.** *n.* a BATHTUB.

tuba ['tub ə] *n.* a large brass instrument that makes very low notes. (TUBAS are also sometimes made of lighter-weight material.)

tube ['tub] **1.** *n.* a hollow pipe used for holding or conveying something. **2.** *n.* a soft container that holds paste, such as toothpaste, icing, or medicine.
→ DOWN THE TUBE

tuck ['tʌk] *n.* a fold that is sewn shut to make an item of clothing shorter or fit tighter.
→ NIP AND TUCK

tuck something **in((to)** something**)** to fold or stuff something into something else.

Tuesday ['tjuz de] Go to DAY.

tug ['tʌg] *n.* a hard pull; a yank.

tug at someone or something AND **tug on** someone or something to pull at someone or something with force.

tug on someone or something Go to TUG AT SOMEONE OR SOMETHING.

tulip ['tu ləp] *n.* a flower with a bright, colorful, cup-shaped bloom.

tumble ['tʌm bəl] **1.** *n.* a fall. **2.** *iv.* to fall over; to fall accidentally; to fall helplessly.

tumble out of something to fall, topple, or drop out of something.

tumble over (something**)** to fall over the edge of something.

tummy ['tʌm i] *n.* the stomach or belly. (Informal; used especially with children.)

tumor ['tu mɚ] *n.* a group or cluster of diseased cells in a body that grow independently of the surrounding tissue or structure.

tuna (fish) ['tu nə 'fɪʃh] **1.** *n.,* *irreg.* a large ocean fish, commonly used for food. (Plural: *tuna* or *tunas*.) **2** *n., irreg.* the flesh of a ①, eaten as food. (No plural.) **3.** the *adj.* use of ① or ②. (Hyphenated.)

tune ['tun] **1.** *n.* a melody; a piece of music or a song. **2.** *tv.* to adjust a musical instrument so that its tones are at the proper intervals from each other. **3.** *tv.* to adjust something so that it works properly.
→ CAN'T CARRY A TUNE
→ DANCE TO ANOTHER TUNE
→ IN TUNE
→ OUT OF TUNE
→ OUT OF TUNE (WITH SOMEONE OR SOMETHING)

tunnel ['tʌn əl] **1.** *n.* a passage that is underground, underwater, or through a mountain. **2.** *iv.* to make a passage that goes underground, underwater, or through a mountain.
→ SEE THE LIGHT (AT THE END OF THE TUNNEL)

turbine ['tɚ bɪn] *n.* a large engine or motor that is powered by pressure from wind, water, or some other liquid or gas.

turd ['tɚd] *n.* a lump of fecal material. (Potentially offensive. Use only with care. Colloquial.)

turf ['tɚf] **1.** *n.* the surface of soil with plants or grass growing on it. (No plural.) **2.** *n.* the area that is controlled by a person or group of people. (Usually singular.)

turkey ['tɚ ki] **1.** *n.* a large fowl that is often raised for its meat. **2.** *n.* the meat of ① used as food. (No plural.) **3.** *adj.* made with ②.

turn ['tɚn] **1.** *tv.* to move something around in a circle or an arc; to cause something to move in a circle or an arc. **2.** *tv.* to aim a moving object or vehicle in a different direction. **3.** *tv.* to change the position of something, such as an electrical switch, lever, or handle. **4.** *tv.* to reach a certain age.

5. *iv.* to go in a different direction; to change direction. **6.** *iv.* to change position by moving in a circle or an arc; to change position to face a different direction. **7.** *iv.* to change, especially in form, state, color, or quality; to become some form, state, color, or quality. **8.** *n.* the movement of something that is going in a circle. **9.** *n.* a change in direction. **10.** *n.* a change in a situation; a change in circumstances. **11.** *n.* a chance to do something, especially when two or more people alternate an action.

→ DO SOMEONE A GOOD TURN

→ OUT OF TURN

turn a blind eye to someone or something to ignore something and pretend one does not see it.

turn a deaf ear (to something**)** to ignore what someone says; to ignore a cry for help.

turn about Go to TURN AROUND.

turn against someone or something to attack, defy, or revolt against someone or something.

turn around AND **turn about** to reverse; to face the opposite direction; to change direction of motion.

turn back (from someplace**)** to stop one's journey and return.

turn in((to) someplace**)** to walk or steer one's vehicle into a place.

turn into something to change to a particular condition or state; to become something.

turn off [for something] to go off; to switch off.

turn on [for something] to switch on and start running.

turn on a dime to turn in a very tight turn.

turn one's **nose up at** someone or something to sneer at someone or something; to reject someone or something.

turn out (for something**)** [for people, especially an audience, to leave home] to attend some event.

turn over a new leaf to start again with the intention of doing better; to begin again, ignoring past errors.

turn over in one's **grave** [for a dead person] to be shocked or horrified. (Figurative.)

turn someone **down** to issue a refusal to someone.

turn someone or something **back** to cause someone or something to stop and go back; to cause someone or something to retreat.

turn someone or something **over to** someone or something to release or assign someone or something to someone or something else; to transfer or deliver someone or something to someone or something else.

turn someone or something **up** **1.** to increase the volume of a device emitting the sound of someone or something. **2.** to discover or locate someone or something.

turn someone **out** **1.** to train or produce someone with certain skills or talents. **2.** to force someone to leave a place.

turn someone's **head** to make someone conceited.

turn someone's **stomach** to make someone (figuratively or literally) ill.

turn something **down 1.** to bend or fold something down. **2.** to decrease the volume of something. **3.** to reject something.

turn something **on** to switch on something to make it run.

turn something **out 1.** to manufacture or produce something in great numbers. **2.** to turn off a light.

turn something **to good account** to use something in such a way that it is to one's advantage; to make good use of a situation, experience, etc.

turn something **to one's advantage** to make an advantage for oneself out of something that might otherwise be a disadvantage.

turn something **up 1.** to bend or fold something up. **2.** to turn playing cards face up.

turn the other cheek to ignore abuse or an insult directed at one. (Biblical.)

turn the tide to cause a reversal in the direction of events; to cause a reversal in public opinion.

turn to to start working; to start doing one's job.

turn up 1. [for part of something] to point upward. **2.** to happen.

turn up (somewhere) [for someone or something] to appear in a place.

turtle ['tɔt əl] *n.* a reptile with a round body that is protected by a thick, hard, rounded shell.

tusk ['tʌsk] *n.* a very long, pointed tooth that projects from the face of some kinds of animals.

tutor ['tut ɚ] **1.** *n.* someone who is employed as a private teacher; a teacher who gives private lessons. **2.** *tv.* to teach someone privately. **3.** *iv.* to work as ①.

tuxedo [tək 'si do] *n.* a man's outfit for very formal occasions, including a black jacket, a white shirt, a black bow tie, and pants. (Plural ends in -*s*.)

tv. an abbreviation of TRANSITIVE VERB.

TV ['ti 'vi] an abbreviation of TELEVISION, TELEVISION SET.

tweed ['twid] **1.** *n.* a rough wool fabric. **2.** *adj.* made of ①.

twelfth ['twɛlfθ] 12th. Go to FOURTH.

twelve ['twɛlv] 12. Go to FOUR.

twentieth ['twɛn ti əθ] 20th. Go to FOURTH.

twenty ['twɛn ti] 20. Go to FORTY.

twice ['twaɪs] **1.** *adv.* two times; on two occasions. **2.** *adv.* two times as much; double.

twiddle one's **thumbs** to fill up time by playing with one's fingers.

twig ['twɪg] *n.* a small branch.

twilight ['twaɪ laɪt] **1.** *n.* the time of day after the sun sets and before the sky is completely dark. (No plural.) **2.** *n.* the dim light at ①.

twin ['twɪn] **1.** *n.* one of two children born at the same time from the same mother; one of two offspring born at the same time from the same mother. **2.** *n.* one of two things that are part of a matched set. **3.** *adj.* [of two offspring] born at the same time from the same mother. **4.** *adj.* forming a pair of two things that are similar or matching.

twine [ˈtwaɪn] *n.* strong string made of two or more strands that are twisted together. (Plural only for types and instances.)

twinkle [ˈtwɪŋ kəl] **1.** *iv.* to alternate between shining brightly and not so brightly; to flicker; to sparkle. **2.** *n.* a light that alternates between shining brightly and dimly; a flicker.
→ IN THE TWINKLING OF AN EYE

twirl [ˈtwɚl] **1.** *tv.* to spin something; to move something in circles. **2.** *iv.* to spin; to turn in circles. **3.** *n.* a spin; a circular movement.

twist [ˈtwɪst] **1.** *tv.* to turn something; to rotate something in an arc. **2.** *tv.* to injure a body part by turning it sharply. **3.** *tv.* to bend and turn part of something to change its shape. **4.** *iv.* to curve; to bend; to change shape or direction; to turn one part of a length of something while keeping the other part in place. **5.** *n.* a curve; a state resulting when one part of a length has been turned while the other part stays in one place. **6.** *n.* the movement of twisting as in ①.

twist someone **around** one's **little finger** to manipulate and control someone.

twist someone's **arm** to force or persuade someone.

twist someone's **words (around)** to restate someone's words inaccurately when quoting them or trying to understand them.

two [ˈtu] 2. Go to FOUR.
→ FALL BETWEEN TWO STOOLS
→ GET TWO STRIKES AGAINST ONE
→ IN TWO SHAKES OF A LAMB'S TAIL
→ KILL TWO BIRDS WITH ONE STONE
→ the LESSER (OF THE TWO)
→ the LESSER OF TWO EVILS
→ PUT IN ONE'S TWO CENTS(' WORTH)
→ PUT TWO AND TWO TOGETHER
→ STAND ON ONE'S OWN TWO FEET
→ STRIKE A BALANCE (BETWEEN TWO THINGS)
→ TWO'S COMPANY(, THREE'S A CROWD).

two of a kind people or things that are the same type or similar in character, attitude, etc.

Two's company(, three's a crowd). a saying meaning that two people want to be alone and a third person would be in the way.

type [ˈtaɪp] **1.** *n.* a kind, sort, or category; a group of related people or things. **2.** *n.* a block of wood or metal, with the raised shape of a letter or number on it, used in printing. (No plural.) **3.** *n.* a style or kind of print, especially the shape or darkness that printed letters have. (No plural.) **4.** *tv.* to write something using a keyboard. **5.** *iv.* to use a keyboard.
→ SET TYPE

type something **up** to type a new version of a handwritten document.

typewriter [ˈtaɪp raɪ tɚ] *n.* a machine for printing letters onto paper.

typical [ˈtɪp ɪ kəl] *adj.* average; usual; ordinary; regular; having the main qualities of a type of something. (Adv: *typically* [...ɪk li].)

typo ['taɪp o] *n.* an error made in printing or typing. (Plural ends in -*s*. Short for *typographical error*.)

tyranny ['tɪr ə ni] *n.* the cruel and unfair use of government power. (No plural.)

tyrant ['taɪ rənt] *n.* a ruler who is cruel and unfair.

U

ugly [ˈʌg li] **1.** *adj.* not pleasant to look at; not attractive. (Comp: *uglier*; sup: *ugliest*.) **2.** *adj.* not pleasant; menacing. (Comp: *uglier*; sup: *ugliest*.)
→ REAR ITS UGLY HEAD

ultimate [ˈʌl tə mət] *adj.* final. (Adv: *ultimately*.)

the **ultimate** *n.* the best thing or person; the most superior thing or person. (Informal. No plural. Treated as singular.)

ultimately [ˈʌl tə mət li] *adv.* in the end; at the final decision about an issue.

umbrella [əm ˈbrɛl ə] *n.* a dome-shaped wire frame connected to a handle and covered with water-proof fabric, used as protection against the rain.

umpire [ˈʌm paɪɚ] **1.** *n.* a referee; someone who enforces the rules of certain sports; someone who judges the plays in certain sports. **2.** *iv.* to act as ①. **3.** *tv.* to referee a game; to judge the plays in certain sports.

unable to do something [ən ˈe bəl…] not able to do something; not having the ability to do something.

unaccustomed to someone or something not used to someone or something.

unafraid [ən ə ˈfred] *adj.* not afraid; brave; without fear.

unanimous [ju ˈnæn ə məs] *adj.* in complete agreement; agreed to by everyone; with everyone saying "yes." (Adv: *unanimously*.)

unarmed [ən ˈɑrmd] *adj.* not armed; not carrying any weapons; without any weapons.

unassisted [ən ə ˈsɪs tɪd] *adj.* without assistance; without help.

unaware [ən ə ˈwɛr] *adj.* not aware; not conscious of someone or something; not knowing of some-one or something.
→ CAUGHT UNAWARE(S)

unbelievable [ən bə ˈliv ə bəl] *adj.* extreme and not able to be believed. (Adv: *unbelievably*.)

unbiased [ən ˈbaɪ əst] *adj.* not biased; fair; not favoring one side over another. (Adv: *unbiasedly*.)

unbreakable [ən ˈbrek ə bəl] *adj.* not able to be broken. (Adv: *unbreakably*.)

uncertain [ən ˈsɚt n] **1.** *adj.* [of a decision] able to change or be changed; not sure. (Adv: *uncer-tainly*.) **2.** *adj.* not known for sure; not yet decided. **3.** *adj.* change-able; not reliable. (Adv: *uncer-tainly*.)

uncle [ˈʌŋ kəl] *n.* the brother of one's father or mother; the hus-band of one's aunt. (Also a term of address. Capitalized when written as a proper noun.)
→ DUTCH UNCLE

unclear [ən ˈklɪr] *adj.* not clear; not understood well. (Adv: *unclearly*.)

uncomfortable [ən ˈkʌmf tə bəl] **1.** *adj.* not comfortable; feeling uneasy. (Adv: *uncomfortably*.) **2.** *adj.* causing discomfort. (Adv: *uncomfortably*.)

unconscious [ən'kɑn ʃəs] **1.** *adj.* not conscious; no longer conscious. (Adv: *unconsciously.*) **2.** *adj.* done without thinking. (Adv: *unconsciously.*) **3.** *n.* the part of one's mind of which one is not aware. (No plural.)

undecided [ən dɪ 'saɪd ɪd] **1.** *adj.* unsure of how one will decide; not having made a decision. (Adv: *undecidedly.*) **2.** *adj.* [of a matter that has] not yet been determined. (Adv: *undecidedly.*)

under ['ʌn dɚ] **1.** *prep.* in or at a place below or beneath someone or something; to or into a place below or beneath someone or something. **2.** *prep.* less than something. **3.** *prep.* affected by the control or influence of someone or something; ranked beneath someone or something. **4.** *adv.* below; below the surface; beneath.

under a cloud (of suspicion) to be suspected of something.

under arrest being or having been arrested and in the care of the police in preparation for the filing of a criminal charge.

under construction in the process of being built or repaired.

under control manageable; restrained and controlled.

under fire while being attacked; during an attack.

under oath bound by an oath; having taken an oath.

under one's **own steam** by one's own power or effort.

under scrutiny being watched or examined closely; with close examination.

under (some) pressure experiencing something that causes an amount of stress or anxiety.

under someone's **(very) nose** AND **right under** someone's **nose 1.** right in front of someone. **2.** in someone's presence.

under the counter [for something to be bought or sold] secretly or illegally.

under the influence of something experiencing the effects of something such as alcohol, drugs, or any controlling power or person.

under the table in secret, as with the giving of a bribe; illegally.

under the weather ill.

under the wire just barely in time or on time.

underclothes ['ʌn dɚ kloð)z] *n.* underwear; underpants and undershirts; the clothing worn next to the skin, usually under other pieces of clothing. (Treated as plural, but not countable.)

underclothing ['ʌn dɚ klo ðɪŋ] *n.* underwear; underclothes. (No plural. Treated as singular.)

undergo [ən dɚ 'go] *tv., irreg.* to experience something, especially something that is difficult. (Past tense: UNDERWENT; past participle: UNDERGONE.)

undergone [ən dɚ 'gɔn] Past participle of UNDERGO.

undergraduate [ən dɚ 'græ dʒu ət] **1.** *n.* a college student who has not yet received a bachelor's degree. **2.** the *adj.* use of ①.

underline ['ʌn dɚ laɪn] **1.** *tv.* to draw a line under a word to give the word emphasis; to emphasize a word by drawing a line under it. **2.** *n.* a line that is drawn under a word to give the word emphasis.

underneath [ən dɚ 'niθ] **1.** *prep.* beneath someone or something; below someone or something; under someone or something. **2.** *adv.* under someone or something that is on top; under someone or something.

underpaid [ən dɚ 'ped] *adj.* not paid as well as one should be; not given enough money for one's work.

underpants [ˈʌn dɚ pænts] *n.* an article of clothing worn next to the skin below the waist, usually under other clothing. (Treated as plural. Number is expressed with *pair(s) of underpants.* Also countable.)

undershirt [ˈʌn dɚ ʃɚt] *n.* a piece of clothing worn above the waist next to the skin, usually under other clothing.

undershorts [ˈʌn dɚ ʃorts] *n.* underpants; a piece of clothing worn below the waist next to the skin, usually under other clothing. (Treated as plural. Number is expressed with *pair(s) of undershorts.*)

underside [ˈʌn dɚ saɪd] *n.* the surface of the bottom part of someone or something.

understand [ən dɚ 'stænd] **1.** *iv.,* *irreg.* to know; to be aware of the meaning of something; to know about something; to be familiar with something. (Past tense and past participle: UNDERSTOOD.) **2.** *tv.,*

irreg. to know something; to know the meaning of something. **3.** *tv.,* *irreg.* to assume something; to believe something. (The object is a clause with THAT ⑦.)

understanding [ən dɚ 'stænd ɪŋ] **1.** *n.* the ability to understand. (No plural.) **2.** *n.* an informal agreement. **3.** *adj.* able to understand; sympathetic.

understood [ən dɚ 'stʊd] past tense and past participle of UNDERSTAND.

undertaker [ˈʌn dɚ te kɚ] *n.* someone who arranges funerals.

underwater [ən dɚ 'wɑ tɚ] **1.** *adj.* under the surface of water. **2.** *adj.* made for use under the water. **3.** *adv.* under the surface of water.

underwear [ˈʌn dɚ wɛr] *n.* underclothing, especially underpants; clothing worn next to the skin, usually under other clothing. (No plural. When this refers to underpants, number is expressed with *pair(s) of underwear.*)

underweight [ˈʌn dɚ wet] *adj.* not weighing as much as one should; weighing too little.

underwent [ən dɚ 'wɛnt] past tense of UNDERGO.

underworld [ˈʌn dɚ wɚld] *n.* the world of crime; criminals and their society.

undid [ən 'dɪd] past tense of UNDO.

undo [ən 'du] **1.** *tv., irreg.* to cancel the effects of something; to cause something to be as though nothing had ever been done to it. (Past tense: UNDID; past participle: UNDONE.) **2.** *tv., irreg.* to untie something; to unfasten something.

undoing [ən 'du ɪŋ] *n.* something that causes failure or ruin. (No plural.)

undone [ən 'dʌn] Past participle of UNDO.

undress [ən 'drɛs] **1.** *tv.* to remove someone's clothes. **2.** *iv.* to take off one's own clothes.

unduly [ən 'du li] *adv.* in an excessive way; in an excessively negative way.

unearth [ən 'ɚθ] **1.** *tv.* to remove something from the ground; to dig something up from the earth. **2.** *tv.* to discover and reveal something; to disclose something; to expose something. (Figurative on ①.)

uneasy [ən 'i zi] *adj.* not comfortable; upset; anxious; worried. (Adv: *uneasily*.)

uneducated [ən 'ɛdʒ ə ket ɪd] *adj.* not educated; not having attended school; not having been taught.

unequal [ən 'i kwəl] *adj.* not equal in size, amount, degree, importance, or worth. (Adv: *unequally*.)

uneven [ən 'i vən] **1.** *adj.* [of a surface] not even; not smooth; rough; bumpy. (Adv: *unevenly*.) **2.** *adj.* [of a process or flow] not constant; varying; irregular. (Adv: *unevenly*.) **3.** *adj.* not equal; unequal. (Adv: *unevenly*.)

unexpected [ən ɛk 'spɛk tɪd] *adj.* not expected; surprising; [of something that happens] not known about before it happens. (Adv: *unexpectedly*.)

unfair [ən 'fɛr] *adj.* not fair; unjust; not right; unequal. (Adv: *unfairly*.)

unfasten [ən 'fæ sən] **1.** *tv.* to open something by removing a fastener; to make something loose by adjusting a fastener. **2.** *iv.* to become loose or open.

unfold [ən 'fold] **1.** *tv.* to spread something out; to open something that is folded. **2.** *iv.* to develop; to become known; to be revealed.

unforeseen [ən for 'sin] *adj.* not anticipated; not foreseen; not known in advance.

unforgettable [ən for 'gɛt ə bəl] *adj.* unable to be forgotten; always remembered. (Adv: *unforgettably*.)

unfortunate [ən 'for tʃə nət] *adj.* not fortunate; not lucky. (Adv: *unfortunately*.)

unfriendly [ən 'frɛnd li] *adj.* not friendly; hostile. (Comp: *unfriendlier*; sup: *unfriendliest*.)

unguarded [ən 'gar dɪd] **1.** *adj.* not guarded; not protected; open to attack. **2.** *adj.* careless, especially in trying to keep secrets. (Adv: *unguardedly*.)

unhappy [ən 'hæp i] *adj.* not happy; sad; not pleased. (Adv: *unhappily*. Comp: *unhappier*; sup: *unhappiest*.)

unhealthy [ən 'hɛl θi] **1.** *adj.* bad for one's health. (Adv: *unhealthily*. Comp: *unhealthier*; sup: *unhealthiest*.) **2.** *adj.* sick; having bad health. (Adv: *unhealthily*. Comp: *unhealthier*; sup: *unhealthiest*.)

unicorn ['ju nə korn] *n.* a mythical creature resembling a horse with a single horn on its forehead.

uniform ['ju nə form] **1.** *n.* the clothes that are worn by all the members of a certain group.

2. *adj.* identical; alike; not varying; having no variation. (Adv: *uniformly.*)

unify ['ju nə faɪ] **1.** *tv.* to unite something or a group; to bring many parts together to make one whole thing. **2.** *iv.* to become united; to be brought together to make one whole thing.

unimportant [ən ɪm 'port nt] *adj.* not important; not significant. (Adv: *unimportantly.*)

union ['jun jən] **1.** *n.* the joining together of two or more people or things. **2.** *n.* the bond between two or more people or things that are joined together. **3.** *n.* an organization whose members work together in support of a common interest, especially an organization of workers in a particular trade. **4.** the *adj.* use of ② or ③.

unique [ju 'nik] *adj.* unlike anything else; having no equal; being the only one of its kind. (No comparative or superlative. Adv: *uniquely.*)

unison ['ju nə sən] *adj.* making one sound; [all] sounding the same octave.
→ IN UNISON

unit ['ju nɪt] **1.** *n.* a single thing or person; one part of a group of people or things. **2.** *n.* a group of things thought of as being one thing. **3.** *n.* an amount of a standard measurement.

unite [ju 'naɪt] **1.** *tv.* to join two or more people or things together; to bring two or more people or things together. **2.** *iv.* to join together; to come together.

unite against someone or something to join against someone or something.

unite people **against** someone or something to cause people to join together against someone or something.

united [ju 'naɪt ɪd] *adj.* brought together; joined together, especially because of a common purpose. (Adv: *unitedly.*)

unity ['ju nə ti] *n.* the condition of being together; the condition of being united. (No plural.)

universal [ju nə 'və səl] **1.** *adj.* shared by every member of a group; of or about everyone; understood by everyone. (Adv: *universally.*) **2.** *n.* a concept that is ①.

universe ['ju nə vəs] *n.* everything that exists in space; all of space and everything that exists in it.

university [ju nə 'və sə ti] *n.* a school for higher education, usually consisting of one or more colleges for undergraduates and usually one or more schools for graduate students.

unjust [ən 'dʒʌst] *adj.* not just; unfair; not right. (Adv: *unjustly.*)

unkind [ən 'kaɪnd] *adj.* not kind; mean; without concern for others. (Adv: *unkindly.* Comp: *unkinder;* sup: *unkindest.*)

unknown [ən 'non] **1.** *adj.* not known; unfamiliar. **2.** *adj.* not famous; not recognized. **3.** *n.* someone who is not (widely) known; something that is not known.

unlawful [ən 'lɔ fʊl] *adj.* not legal; illegal; against the law. (Adv: *unlawfully.*)

unless [ən 'lɛs] *conj.* except under the circumstances that something specific happens. (Followed by a clause.)

unlike [ən 'laɪk] **1.** *adj.* not like someone or something else; not equal; not similar; different. (Prenominal only.) **2.** *prep.* not similar to someone or something; different from someone or something. **3.** *prep.* not characteristic or typical of someone or something.

unlikely [ən 'laɪk li] *adj.* not probable; not likely; likely to fail; not likely to succeed.

unlimited [ən 'lɪm ə tɪd] *adj.* not limited; without limits; not restricted. (Adv: *unlimitedly.*)

unlock [ən 'lɑk] *tv.* to open a lock.

unlucky [ən 'lʌk i] **1.** *adj.* not lucky; not having good luck; unfortunate. (Adv: *unluckily.* Comp: *unluckier;* sup: *unluckiest.*) **2.** *adj.* causing bad luck; causing misfortune. (Adv: *unluckily.* Comp: *unluckier;* sup: *unluckiest.*)

unmentionable [ən 'mɛn ʃə nə bəl] *adj.* not able to be mentioned; not to be mentioned, especially because it would not be polite to do so. (Adv: *unmentionably.*)

unpack [ən 'pæk] **1.** *tv.* to remove objects that have been packed; to remove objects that are in a box or suitcase. **2.** *iv.* to remove objects that have been packed.

unpleasant [ən 'plɛz ənt] *adj.* not pleasant; not pleasing; not nice; not enjoyable. (Adv: *unpleasantly.*)

unpopular [ən 'pɑp jə lɚ] *adj.* not popular; not preferred by many people. (Adv: *unpopularly.*)

unreal [ən 'ril] *adj.* not real; incredible; unbelievable.

unrealistic [ən ri ə 'lɪs tɪk] **1.** *adj.* not realistic; not seeming real; seeming fake. (Adv: *unrealistically* [...ɪk li].) **2.** *adj.* not practical. (Adv: *unrealistically* [...ɪk li].)

unreasonable [ən 'ri zə nə bəl] **1.** *adj.* not reasonable; not sensible; not rational. (Adv: *unreasonably.*) **2.** *adj.* too much; excessive. (Adv: *unreasonably.*)

unrest [ən 'rɛst] *n.* a feeling of not being satisfied; a troubled or uneasy feeling. (No plural.)

unruly [ən 'ru li] **1.** *adj.* badly behaved; not obedient; not paying attention to authority. **2.** *adj.* [of hair] not orderly; [of hair] hard to control.

unsatisfactory [ən sæt ɪs 'fæk tə ri] *adj.* not satisfactory; not good enough; not adequate. (Adv: *unsatisfactorily.*)

unscientific [ən saɪ ən 'tɪf ɪk] *adj.* not scientific; not using principles of science. (Adv: *unscientifically* [...ɪk li].)

unscrew [ən 'skru] **1.** *tv.* to remove something, such as a screw or a lid, by turning it. **2.** *iv.* [for a screw, lid, bolt, etc.] to rotate and become loose.

unseen [ən 'sin] *adj.* not seen; hidden; out of sight.
→ BUY SOMETHING SIGHT UNSEEN

unstable [ən 'ste bəl] **1.** *adj.* not secure; not having proper balance. (Adv: *unstably.*) **2.** *adj.* not steady;

likely to change. (Adv: *unstably*.)
3. *adj.* [of someone] mentally disturbed or troubled. (Adv: *unstably*.)

unsteady [ən 'stɛd i] **1.** *adj.* shaky; not secure. (Adv: *unsteadily*.) **2.** *adj.* not dependable; likely to change. (Adv: *unsteadily*.)

unsure [ən 'ʃʊr] *adj.* not sure; uncertain. (Adv: *unsurely*.)

untidy [ən 'taɪ di] *adj.* not tidy; not clean; messy. (Adv: *untidily*. Comp: *untidier*; sup: *untidiest*.)

untie [ən 'taɪ] **1.** *tv.* to loosen something that is tied; to undo something that is tied. (The present participle is *untying* in both senses of the verb.) **2.** *iv.* to become undone as in ①.

until [ən 'tɪl] **1.** *prep.* up to a certain time; during a period of time up to a certain time; continuing during a period of time and then stopping at a certain time. (See also TILL.) **2.** *conj.* up to a time when something happens; up to a time when a certain condition is met. (Followed by a clause.) **3.** *conj.* before. (Used with a negative construction in the main clause.)
→ PUT SOMETHING OFF (UNTIL SOMETHING)
→ TALK UNTIL ONE IS BLUE IN THE FACE
→ TIDE SOMEONE OVER (UNTIL SOMETHING)

untimely [ən 'taɪm li] **1.** *adj.* not timely; happening too soon; happening too early. **2.** *adj.* not suitable; not appropriate; at the wrong time.
→ COME TO AN UNTIMELY END

unto [ən tu] *prep.* to someone or something. (Formal or old.)
→ A LAW UNTO ONESELF

untold [ən 'told] **1.** *adj.* not told; not expressed; not revealed. **2.** *adj.* countless; too great to be counted.

untrue [ən 'tru] *adj.* not true; false; incorrect. (Adv: *untruly*.)

untrue (to someone or something**)** not loyal to someone or something; not faithful to someone or something.

unusual [ən 'ju ʒu əl] *adj.* not usual; strange; different; not ordinary. (Adv: *unusually*.)

unwanted [ən 'wɑn tɪd] *adj.* not wanted. (Adv: *unwantedly*.)

unwelcome [ən 'wɛl kəm] *adj.* not welcome; not wanted. (Adv: *unwelcomely*.)

unwholesome [ən 'hol səm] *adj.* not good for one's morals or one's health. (Adv: *unwholesomely*.)

unwind [ən 'waɪnd] **1.** *tv., irreg.* to remove something that is wound around an object. (Past tense and past participle: UNWOUND.) **2.** *iv., irreg.* to relax. **3.** *iv., irreg.* [for something] to become loose and to pull away from an object that it is wound around.

unwise [ən 'waɪz] *adj.* not wise; foolish; silly. (Adv: *unwisely*.)

unwound [ən 'waʊnd] past tense and past participle of UNWIND.

up [ʌp] **1.** *adv.* from a lower level toward a higher level. **2.** *adv.* toward the north; northward; in the north. **3.** *adv.* into a vertical or almost vertical position; in a vertical or almost vertical position. **4.** *adv.* completely; totally. (Used especially with verbs such as *eat, drink, use,* and *finish*.) **5.** *adv.* tightly; into a tight condition;

firmly. (Used especially with verbs such as *roll, curl, fold,* and *wind.*) **6.** *adv.* together; into a condition in which things are together. (Used especially with verbs such as *add, total, count, link, connect,* and *gather.*) **7.** *adj.* over; finished. (Not prenominal.) **8.** *prep.* on or along something to a higher level or position.

up a blind alley at a dead end; on a route that leads nowhere.

up in arms rising up in anger, as if armed with weapons.

up in the air undecided; uncertain.

up to doing something able to do something.

up to one's **ears (in** something) Go to UP TO ONE'S NECK (IN SOMETHING).

up to one's **neck (in** something) AND **up to** one's **ears (in** something) very much involved in something.

up to par as good as the standard or average; up to the standard.

update ['ʌp det] **1.** *n.* something that has new information, especially a news report that has more information. **2.** *tv.* to make something more modern; to make something up-to-date. **3.** *tv.* to provide the latest information; to inform someone of the latest news.

updated [əp 'det ɪd] *adj.* made modern; changed or made to be modern or current.

upgrade someone or something **to** something to raise someone or something to a higher grade or rank.

upkeep ['ʌp kip] **1.** *n.* maintenance; the work required to maintain something. (No plural.) **2.** *n.* the cost of ①. (No plural.)

upon [ə 'pɔn] **1.** *prep.* on the surface of someone or something. **2.** *prep.* at the instant of doing something; on the occasion of something happening; immediately or very soon after something has happened.

upon impact at the place or time of an impact.

upper ['ʌp ɚ] *adj.* the higher of two things; closer to the top of something than to the bottom.
→ GET THE UPPER HAND (ON SOMEONE)
→ KEEP A STIFF UPPER LIP

the **upper crust** the higher levels of society; the upper class.

uppercase ['ʌp ɚ 'kes] *adj.* [of a letter or letters] in the larger size as with *B* in *Bill;* capitalized. (Compare this with LOWERCASE.)

uproar ['ʌp ror] *n.* a loud, noisy, confused activity.

uproot [əp 'rut] **1.** *tv.* to pull up a plant, including its roots. **2.** *tv.* to cause someone to move from where one lives. (Figurative on ①.)

upset 1. [ə 'sɛt] *adj.* worried about something. **2.** [ə 'sɛt] *adj.* [of someone's stomach] feeling bad or sick. **3.** [ə 'sɛt] *tv., irreg.* to knock something over; to tip something over; to turn something over. (Past tense and past participle: *upset.*) **4.** [ə 'sɛt] *tv., irreg.* to defeat someone or something that was expected to win. **5.** [ə 'sɛt] *tv., irreg.* to disturb someone; to bother someone; to make someone worried. **6.** [əp 'sɛt] *tv., irreg.* to make someone's stomach feel bad. **7.** ['əp sɛt] *n.* a surprise victory; the defeat of someone or something by someone or something else that was not expected to win.

upside down ['ʌp saɪd 'daʊn] *adj.* having the top part at the bottom; having the wrong end or side up. (Hyphenated before a nominal.)

upstairs 1. ['ʌp 'stɛrz] *adj.* located on an upper floor; located on a higher floor. **2.** [əp 'stɛrz] *adv.* on or toward the next floor of a building; on or toward an upper floor of a building. **3.** ['ʌp 'stɛrz] *n.* the top floor of a building; the upper floor of a building. (Treated as singular.)

upstream ['ʌp 'strim] *adv.* against the current of a river.

up-to-date ['ʌp tə 'det] *adj.* current; including or based on the latest facts or information.

upward ['ʌp wəd] *adj.* moving UP; climbing; rising; advancing. (Adv: *upwardly*.)

upward(s) *adv.* to or toward a higher position; to or toward a higher level; to or toward the top part of something.

uranium [jə 'ren i əm] *n.* a chemical element used mainly as fuel for nuclear reactors. (No plural.)

urban ['ə bən] *adj.* of or about a city or cities in general; not suburban or rural.

urge ['ə dʒ] **1.** *n.* a strong feeling, desire, or need to do something. **2.** *tv.* to force or encourage some-

one or something to go forward. (The object can be a clause with THAT ⑦.)

urge someone **to** do something to try to persuade someone to do something; to beg someone to do something.

urgent ['ə dʒənt] *adj.* very important; [of something] needing attention before anything else. (Adv: *urgently*.)

urinate ['jʊr ə net] *iv.* to cause or allow urine to flow from the body.

urine ['jʊr ɪn] *n.* a liquid waste product removed by the kidneys and discharged from the body. (No plural.)

urn ['ən] **1.** *n.* a large vase or pot, often used for plants or for ashes from a dead person's remains. **2.** *n.* a large container for holding hot liquids, especially coffee.

us ['ʌs] *pron.* the objective form of WE, referring to a group of people including the speaker or writer.

U.S. Go to U.S.A.

U.S.A. AND **U.S.** ['ju 'ɛs ('e)] the United States of America.

usage ['ju sɪdʒ] *n.* the way words in a language typically occur in speech. (No plural.)

use 1. ['jus] *n.* consuming or operating something; the intended function of something; the purpose of something, especially the purpose of meeting people's needs. (Plural only for types and instances.) **2.** ['juz] *tv.* to employ someone or something for a certain purpose; to put something into service. **3.** ['juz] *tv.* to treat

someone badly or to one's own advantage.
→ MAKE USE OF SOMEONE OR SOMETHING

use every trick in the book to use every method possible.

use something **up** to consume or use all of something.

used ['juzd] *adj.* already owned; not new; secondhand.
→ BE USED TO DOING SOMETHING
→ BE USED TO SOMEONE OR SOMETHING

used to do something ['jus tə...] did something in the past as a matter of habit or custom.

useful ['jus fʊl] *adj.* helpful; able to be used. (Adv: *usefully.*)

useless ['jus ləs] *adj.* not helpful; not able to be used; having no effect; having no purpose. (Adv: *uselessly.*)

usher ['ʌʃ ɚ] **1.** *n.* someone who shows people to their seats in a church, auditorium, theater, or other place where people gather. **2.** *tv.* to guide someone to a seat; to escort someone to a seat.

usher someone or something **in(to someplace)** to escort or lead a person, a group, or something into a place.

usher someone or something **out (of someplace)** to escort or lead someone, a group, or something out of a place.

usual ['ju ʒu wəl] *adj.* ordinary; typical; customary; common; regular. (Adv: *usually.*)
→ AS USUAL

utensil [ju 'tɛn səl] *n.* a tool that helps someone do something, especially a tool that helps someone cook or eat.

utility [ju 'tɪl ə ti] **1.** *n.* a service providing products such as electricity, water, gas, and waste removal to homes and businesses. **2.** *n.* a company that provides a public service. **3.** *adj.* having a basic function; providing for basic service. (Prenominal only.)

utilize ['jut ə laɪz] *tv.* to use something practically; to make use of something; to employ something for a purpose.

utter ['ʌt ɚ] **1.** *tv.* to say something; to express something aloud. **2.** *adj.* complete; total. (Adv: *utterly.*)
→ NOT UTTER A WORD

utterance ['ʌt ə rəns] *n.* speaking; uttering words. (Plural only for types and instances.)

vacancy ['ve kən si] **1.** *n.* a job or position that is not filled; an opening in employment; a job opening. **2.** *n.* an empty room or building that is available for rent.

vacant ['ve kənt] **1.** *adj.* not occupied; not being used; empty; not filled. **2.** *adj.* [of a look on someone's face] blank, showing no thought or intelligence. (Figurative on ①. Adv: *vacantly*.)

vacation [ve 'ke ʃən] *n.* time when one does not have to work or go to school. (Plural only for types and instances.)
→ ON VACATION
→ TAKE A VACATION

vaccination [væk sə 'ne ʃən] *n.* the use of a vaccine to protect people against disease. (Plural only for types and instances.)

vaccine [væk 'sin] *n.* a substance that is given to people in order to protect them from a certain disease.

vacuum ['væk jum] **1.** *n.* a space that is completely empty and does not have any air in it. **2.** *n.* a machine used to suck up dirt from carpets and other floor coverings. (Short for VACUUM CLEANER.) **3.** *adj.* creating or causing ①. **4.** *tv.* to clean a surface by sucking up dirt with ②. **5.** *iv.* to clean by sucking up dirt with ②.

vacuum cleaner ['væk jum klin ɚ] *n.* a machine that cleans carpets or other materials by creating a partial VACUUM ① that sucks up dirt. (Can be shortened to VACUUM.)

vacuum something **up (from something)** to clean something up from something with a vacuum cleaner.

vague ['veg] **1.** *adj.* not precise; not exact. (Adv: *vaguely*. Comp: *vaguer*; sup: *vaguest*.) **2.** *adj.* having no expression on one's face. (Figurative on ①. Adv: *vaguely*. Comp: *vaguer*; sup: *vaguest*.)

vain ['ven] *adj.* having too much pride about how one looks or about what one has done. (Adv: *vainly*. Comp: *vainer*; sup: *vainest*.)
→ IN VAIN

valiant ['væl jənt] *adj.* very brave; very courageous; heroic. (Adv: *valiantly*.)

valid ['væl ɪd] **1.** *adj.* effective; legally usable or acceptable. (Adv: *validly*.) **2.** *adj.* true; able to be defended or proved; based on facts. (Adv: *validly*.)

valley ['væl i] *n.* a low area of land between two high areas of land; a low area of land that is drained by a large river and the smaller rivers that flow into the larger river.

valor ['væl ɚ] *n.* courage. (No plural.)

valuable ['væl jə bəl] **1.** *adj.* worth a lot of money; having a great value. (Adv: *valuably*.) **2.** *adj.* helpful; useful; important. (Adv: *valuably*.)

valuables *n.* items that are VALUABLE ①. (No singular.)

value ['væl ju] **1.** *n.* the amount of money that something is worth. (No plural.) **2.** *n.* something that is actually worth more than the amount one paid for it; a bargain. **3.** *n.* something of great use; benefit. (No plural.) **4.** *n.* an amount that is represented by a sign or symbol. **5.** *tv.* to believe that something is worth a certain amount of money. **6.** *tv.* to think someone or something is valuable; to regard someone or something as useful or worthy; to regard someone or something highly.

→ TAKE SOMEONE OR SOMETHING **AT FACE VALUE**

valve ['vælv] *n.* a flap or other device in a tube that controls the amount of something that passes through the tube.

van ['væn] *n.* a covered motor vehicle that has a large amount of space behind the driver's seat for carrying large objects or extra people.

vandal ['væn dəl] *n.* someone who damages other people's property or public property on purpose.

vandalism ['væn də lɪz əm] *n.* the damaging of other people's property or public property on purpose. (No plural form in this sense.)

vandalize ['væn də laɪz] *tv.* to damage other people's property or public property on purpose.

vanilla [və 'nɪl ə] **1.** *n.* a flavoring made from the bean of a certain tropical plant. (No plural.) **2.** *adj.* flavored with ①; tasting like ①.

vanish ['væn ɪʃ] *iv.* to disappear; to be seen no longer.

vanish into thin air to disappear without leaving a trace.

vanity ['væn ə ti] **1.** *n.* the condition of being vain; the condition of having too much pride about how one looks or what one has done. (No plural.) **2.** *n.* a flat surface on top of a cabinet with drawers, especially such a unit in a bathroom, with a sink included in the top surface.

vapor ['ve pɚ] *n.* a liquid or solid in the form of a gas.

variant ['vɛr i ənt] **1.** *adj.* different; having a particular difference as compared with something standard or the norm. **2.** *n.* a different form of something, especially a different way of spelling a word.

variation [vɛr i 'e ʃən] *n.* (minor) differences; a minor difference. (Plural only for types and instances.)

variety [və 'raɪ ə ti] *n.* differences of choice; diversity. (Plural only for types and instances.)

various ['vɛr i əs] *adj.* different; several; having several kinds of something; having many kinds of something. (Adv: *variously*.)

varnish ['vɑr nɪʃ] **1.** *n.* a clear liquid that is painted onto the surface of objects made from wood to protect the wood and give it a hard, shiny appearance. (Plural only for types and instances.) **2.** *tv.* to paint a surface with ①.

vary ['vɛr i] **1.** *iv.* to change; to be different; to appear or be used in different forms. **2.** *tv.* to change something; to cause something to be different; to make something different.

vase ['ves] *n.* a decorative container, often used for holding flowers.

vast ['væst] *adj.* very large in size or amount; of an immense size or amount. (Adv: *vastly.* Comp: *vaster;* sup: *vastest.*)

vat ['væt] *n.* a large container, used for storing liquid, especially liquor while it is being made.

vault ['vɔlt] **1.** *n.* a secure, locked room where valuable things are kept and protected. **2.** *n.* a leap; a jump made with the help of a pole or one's hands. **3.** *tv.* to jump a certain distance.

veal ['vil] *n.* the meat of a young cow used as food. (No plural.)

vegetable ['vɛdʒ tə bəl] **1.** *n.* a plant that is eaten as food; a part of a plant that is eaten as food. **2.** *adj.* made with or including ①.

vegetarian [vɛdʒ ɪ 'tɛr i ən] **1.** *n.* someone who does not eat the flesh of animals. **2.** *adj.* [of food] made without the flesh of a once-living creature. **3.** *adj.* serving or eating food other than animal tissue.

vegetation [vɛdʒ ɪ 'te ʃən] *n.* plant life; plants in general. (No plural. Treated as singular.)

vehicle ['vi ɪ kəl] *n.* a machine that is used to carry people or things, especially on roads, including cars, buses, trucks, vans, motorcycles, bicycles, sleds, sleighs, and carriages. (But not trains or airplanes.)

vehicular [vi 'hɪk jə lɚ] *adj.* of or about vehicles. (Adv: *vehicularly.*)

veil ['vel] *n.* a piece of cloth used to hide something.

vein ['ven] **1.** *n.* a vessel that carries blood from parts of the body back to the heart. **2.** *n.* a line that forms part of the framework of a leaf or the wing of an insect. **3.** *n.* a layer of coal or metal within a mass of rock.

velocity [və 'lɑs ə ti] *n.* speed, especially the speed of an object moving in a specific direction. (Plural only for types and instances.)

velvet ['vɛl vɪt] **1.** *n.* a soft fabric whose threads are short and close together and stick up on one side of the fabric. (Plural only for types and instances.) **2.** *adj.* made of ①.

vengeance ['vɛn dʒəns] *n.* hurting someone or damaging someone's property as a form of revenge. (No plural form.)
→ WITH A VENGEANCE
→ WREAK VENGEANCE (UP)ON SOMEONE OR SOMETHING

venom ['vɛn əm] **1.** *n.* the poison in the bite or sting of a snake, spider, and other similar creatures. (No plural.) **2.** *n.* extreme hatred. (Figurative on ①. No plural.)

venomous ['vɛn ə məs] **1.** *adj.* full of venom; containing venom. (Adv: *venomously.*) **2.** *adj.* full of extreme hatred. (Figurative on ①. Adv: *venomously.*)

vent ['vɛnt] **1.** *n.* an opening to a passage through which air or other gases can move. **2.** *tv.* to express one's feelings; to make one's feelings known.

vent one's **spleen on** someone or something to get rid of one's feelings of anger by attacking someone or something.

ventilate ['vɛn tɪ let] *tv.* to bring fresh air into a room or an enclosed space; to expose something or someplace to fresh air.

ventilator ['vɛn tɪ le tɚ] **1.** *n.* a fan that moves air into or out of a room or enclosed space. **2.** *n.* a device that supplies air or oxygen to someone who cannot breathe without help.

venture ['vɛn tʃɚ] **1.** *n.* a risky thing to do, especially an action taken in business where one risks one's money in order to gain more money. **2.** *tv.* to risk something; to expose something to danger; to place something in danger. **3.** *iv.* to go into a place that could be dangerous.

verb ['vɚb] *n.* a word that describes what someone or something is or does; a word that expresses being, action, or occurrence.
→ AUXILIARY VERB
→ INTRANSITIVE VERB
→ REFLEXIVE (VERB)
→ TRANSITIVE VERB

verbal ['vɚb əl] **1.** *adj.* expressed in words; oral; spoken, not written. (Adv: *verbally.*) **2.** *adj.* of or about a verb; formed from a verb. (Adv: *verbally.*)

verbal auxiliary ['vɚb əl ɔg 'zɪl jə ri] Go to AUXILIARY VERB.

verdict ['vɚ dɪkt] **1.** *n.* the decision of a judge or a jury at the end of a trial. **2.** *n.* a conclusion; a judgment; an opinion.
→ BRING A VERDICT IN

verse ['vɚs] **1.** *n.* poetry; language as it is used in poetry. (No plural.)

2. *n.* a group of lines in a poem or song. **3.** *n.* a portion of a chapter of a book of the Bible.
→ RECITE SOMETHING CHAPTER AND VERSE

version ['vɚ ʒən] **1.** *n.* one person's account or description of something that has happened. **2.** *n.* a form of something that is different from another form of it, such as being in a different language or medium.

vertical ['vɚ tɪ kəl] *adj.* straight up and down. (Adv: *vertically* [...ɪk li].)

very ['vɛr i] **1.** *adv.* especially; quite; extremely; greatly; to a large degree. (Used to strengthen the meaning of an adjective or another adverb. *Very* is not used with the comparative forms, but is used with superlative forms, following *the*, to strengthen meaning.) **2.** *adj.* same; actual; identical. (Prenominal only.) **3.** *adj.* mere; simple. (Prenominal only.)

the **very last** the end; an absolute end of something.

the **very thing** the exact thing that is required.

vessel ['vɛs əl] **1.** *n.* a container used to hold liquids. **2.** *n.* a large ship or boat.
→ BLOOD VESSEL

vest ['vɛst] *n.* a piece of clothing that has no sleeves and is worn above the waist on top of a shirt and usually under a suit coat or jacket.
→ LIFE VEST
→ PLAY ONE'S CARDS CLOSE TO ONE'S VEST

vet ['vɛt] **1.** *n.* someone who has served in the military, especially during a war. (Short for VETERAN.) **2.** *n.* a doctor who treats only animals. (Short for VETERINARIAN.)

veteran ['vɛt (ə) rən] **1.** *n.* someone who has served in the military, especially during a war. (Can be shortened to VET.) **2.** *n.* someone who has a lot of experience with something. (Figurative on ①.) **3.** *adj.* experienced; having a lot of experience with something.

veterinarian [vɛt (ə) rə 'nɛr i ən] *n.* a doctor who treats only animals. (Can be shortened to VET.)

veto ['vi to] **1.** *n.* an instance of using one's authority to stop a proposed bill from becoming law. (Plural ends in -es.) **2.** *tv.* to stop a bill from becoming law; not to allow something to happen.

vibrate ['vaɪ bret] **1.** *iv.* to move back and forth very quickly; to shake; to quiver. **2.** *tv.* to move something back and forth very quickly; to shake something.

vibration [vaɪ 'bre ʃən] *n.* the motions of moving back and forth very quickly.

vice ['vaɪs] *n.* a bad or immoral habit.

vice president ['vaɪs 'prɛz ə dənt] *n.* someone who is at a rank just lower than president.

vicinity [vɪ 'sɪn ə ti] *n.* a neighborhood; the location around someone or something; the surrounding area.

vicious ['vɪʃ əs] **1.** *adj.* fierce; cruel; likely to cause pain; dangerous.

(Adv: *viciously.*) **2.** *adj.* evil; cruel. (Adv: *viciously.*)
→ IN A VICIOUS CIRCLE

victim ['vɪk təm] *n.* a person or an animal that dies, suffers, or loses something because of someone else's actions, a sickness, an accident, or a natural disaster.

victimize ['vɪk tə maɪz] *tv.* to cause someone to be a victim; to cause someone to suffer.

victor ['vɪk tɚ] *n.* a winner; someone who wins a fight, game, contest, race, etc.

victory ['vɪk tə ri] *n.* winning; achieving success: the success of defeating an enemy or opponent. (Plural only for types and instances.)
→ A LANDSLIDE VICTORY

video ['vɪd i o] **1.** *n.* moving visible images, such as what is recorded on videotape; the visible part of a television program; the display seen on a computer monitor. (No plural.) **2.** *n.* a movie that is available on videotape; motion or action that is recorded on videotape. (Plural ends in -s.) **3.** *n.* a short film or taped version of a song. (Plural ends in -s.) **4.** the *adj.* use of ①, ②, or ③.

videocassette ['vɪd i o kə 'sɛt] *n.* a device that holds videotape, which is put into a video camera or a videocassette recorder to record or play back images.

videotape ['vɪd i o tep] **1.** *n.* a length of plastic tape on which images can be recorded and played back. (No plural.) **2.** *n.* a reel or cassette of ①; a copy of a movie or a television show that is recorded in ①.

view ['vju] **1.** *n.* the way something looks from a place; a scene. **2.** *n.* an opinion; the way someone thinks about something. **3.** *tv.* to examine someone or something; to look at someone or something closely.
→ a BIRD'S-EYE VIEW
→ POINT OF VIEW

viewpoint ['vju pɔɪnt] *n.* an opinion; the way someone thinks about something.

vigil ['vɪdʒ əl] *n.* an act or instance of staying awake during the night to watch something, to pray, or to take care of someone who is sick.

vigilant ['vɪdʒ ə lənt] *adj.* on guard; watchful; watching over someone or something. (Adv: *vigilantly.*)

vigor ['vɪg ɚ] *n.* strength; energy; DRIVE ⑥. (No plural.)

vile ['vaɪl] **1.** *adj.* very bad; very unpleasant; disgusting. (Adv: *vilely.* Comp: *viler;* sup: *vilest.*) **2.** *adj.* evil; wicked; immoral. (Adv: *vilely.* Comp: *viler;* sup: *vilest.*)

village ['vɪl ɪdʒ] **1.** *n.* a small town; a group of houses and businesses in the country or suburbs. **2.** *n.* all the people who live in a particular ①. **3.** the *adj.* use of ① or ②.

villager ['vɪl ɪdʒ ɚ] *n.* someone who lives in a village.

villain ['vɪl ən] *n.* someone who is wicked or evil, especially someone who is the bad person in a story or movie.

villain of the piece someone or something that is responsible for something bad or wrong.

vine ['vaɪn] *n.* a plant that has long, thin stems that crawl along the ground or the sides of an object.
→ DIE ON THE VINE
→ WITHER ON THE VINE

vinegar ['vɪn ɪ gɚ] *n.* a sour liquid made from wine or apple juice, used to flavor or preserve food. (No plural.)

vinyl ['vaɪ nəl] **1.** *n.* a kind of common plastic. (No plural.) **2.** *adj.* made of ①.

viola [vi 'o lə] *n.* a stringed musical instrument that is similar to, but larger than, a violin.

violence ['vaɪ ə ləns] *n.* rough force; actions that hurt or damage people or things. (No plural. Number is expressed with *act(s) of violence.*)

violent ['vaɪ ə lənt] **1.** *adj.* using rough force that can hurt or damage people or things. (Adv: *violently.*) **2.** *adj.* showing violence. (Adv: *violently.*)

violet ['vaɪ ə lɪt] *n.* a small plant that has dark purple flowers with a delicate smell.

violin [vaɪ ə 'lɪn] *n.* a four-stringed musical instrument played with a bow.

violinist [vaɪ ə 'lɪn ɪst] *n.* someone who plays a violin.

viper ['vaɪ pɚ] *n.* a venomous snake, especially one with fangs.

virtual ['vɚ tʃu əl] **1.** *adj.* having an effect as though someone or something were the real person or thing. (Adv: *virtually.*) **2.** *adj.* of or

about interaction on the Internet;
of or about interaction with other
people through computers. (Adv:
virtually.)

virtue ['vɚ tʃu] **1.** *n.* goodness,
especially in behavior or morals.
(No plural.) **2.** *n.* a good moral
behavior or trait; a trait that is valued by society. **3.** *n.* an advantage;
a benefit.
→ BY VIRTUE OF SOMETHING

virus ['vɑɪ rəs] *n.* a living thing so
small it can only be seen under a
microscope. (Viruses cause infec-
tions and diseases in humans, animals, and plants, including
chicken pox, rabies, and the common cold.)

visa ['vi zə] *n.* an official stamp,
signature, or attachment put in a
passport, which allows its owner
to enter a certain country.

vise [vɑɪs] *n.* a machine made of
metal jaws that can be pushed
tightly together, used for clamping
something tightly so that it doesn't
move while someone works on it.

visible ['vɪz ə bəl] *adj.* able to be
seen; not hidden. (Adv: *visibly.*)

vision ['vɪ ʒən] **1.** *n.* the ability to
see; the power of sight. (No plu-
ral.) **2.** *n.* something that is seen or
experienced in a dream, in one's
imagination, or in one's memory.
3. *n.* insight; the ability to understand what something means and
how it will affect the future. (No
plural.)

visit ['vɪz ɪt] **1.** *tv.* to go to a person
or a place for a period of time; to
be with a person as a visitor; to be
at a place as a visitor. **2.** *tv.* to
examine or inspect something as

part of one's job. **3.** *iv.* to be someone's guest; to stay at someone's
house or at a place as a guest or
tourist. **4.** *n.* an act or instance of
someone going or coming to a
place for a period of time in order
to see someone or something,
experience something, or talk with
someone.
→ PAY A VISIT TO SOMEONE OR SOMETHING
→ PAY (SOMEONE OR SOMETHING) A VISIT

visitor ['vɪz ɪ tɚ] *n.* someone who
visits someone or someplace as a
guest or tourist.

visual ['vɪ ʒu əl] *adj.* of or about
vision or seeing. (Adv: *visually.*)

vital ['vɑɪt əl] **1.** *adj.* very important; absolutely necessary; essential. (Adv: *vitally.*) **2.** *adj.* of or
about life; necessary for life. **3.** *adj.*
active; full of life. (Adv: *vitally.*)

vitamin ['vɑɪ tə mɪn] *n.* a chemical
compound that is important for a
person's health and cannot be
made by the body.

vivid ['vɪv ɪd] **1.** *adj.* clear; distinct.
(Adv: *vividly.*) **2.** *adj.* strongly or
brightly colored; deeply colored.
(Adv: *vividly.*)

vocabulary [vo 'kæb jə lɛr i] **1.** *n.*
the words that someone knows;
the words that are part of someone's language. (No plural.) **2.** *n.*
the words used in a certain business, profession, or activity. (No
plural.) **3.** *n.* a list of words with
brief meanings, like those found in
foreign-language dictionaries; a
glossary of words and their meanings. **4.** *n.* all the words of a language. (No plural.)

vocation [vo 'ke ʃən] *n.* an occupation; a trade; a profession.

voice ['vɔɪs] **1.** *n.* the sounds made by a person who is speaking or singing; the sounds made when speaking or singing. **2.** *n.* a medium or channel for representing someone's opinions. **3.** *n.* a grammar term that describes the relation of the subject of a sentence to the verb. **4.** *tv.* to express an opinion by speaking. **5.** *tv.* [in phonetics] to give a certain quality to a sound by vibrating the vocal folds and making the sound of ①.
→ AT THE TOP OF ONE'S VOICE
→ LOWER ONE'S VOICE

void ['vɔɪd] **1.** *adj.* not binding according to the law; having no legal authority; having no legal effect; no longer valid. **2.** *tv.* to cause a law to stop being a law. **3.** *n.* an area that is empty; an empty space; a gap.

volcano [vɑl 'ke no] *n.* a mountain with an opening at the top or on the sides from which steam, gas, molten rock, and ash sometimes are ejected by pressure or force from inside the earth. (Plural ends in -*s* or -*es*.)

volleyball ['vɑl i bɔl] **1.** *n.* a sport where two teams on opposite sides of a net try to hit a large, light ball back and forth over the net without letting the ball touch the ground. (No plural.) **2.** *n.* the ball used to play ①.

volt ['volt] *n.* a unit of measurement of electrical force.

voltage ['vol tɪdʒ] *n.* an amount of an electrical force, measured in volts.

volume ['vɑl jəm] **1.** *n.* a book, especially one book in a series of books. **2.** *n.* the loudness of sound. (Plural only for types and instances.) **3.** *n.* an amount of something. **4.** *n.* the expression of space in three dimensions, determined by multiplying an object's length, width, and depth.

voluntary ['vɑl ən ter i] **1.** *adj.* [done] by one's own choice. (Adv: *voluntarily* [vɑl ən 'ter ə li].) **2.** *adj.* supported by volunteers or gifts.

volunteer [vɑl ən 'tɪr] **1.** *n.* someone who does work for free; someone who agrees to take on a job or task. **2.** *tv.* to offer one's time, help, or energy at no cost; to give one's services for free. **3.** *tv.* to say something without being forced to talk; to say something by one's own choice. **4.** the *adj.* use of ①.

volunteer for something to submit oneself for some task.

vomit ['vɑm ɪt] **1.** *tv.* to throw food up after one has eaten it; to bring something up from the stomach. **2.** *iv.* to throw [something] up from the stomach through the mouth. **3.** *n.* something that has been thrown up from the stomach through the mouth. (No plural.)

vote ['vot] **1.** *n.* a formal or legal expression of one's opinion on an issue, especially on political issues. **2.** *n.* the ①, viewed collectively, of a large number of people who share a certain characteristic or background. (No plural. Treated as singular.) **3.** *iv.* to express one's opinion on an issue by raising one's hand or marking one's choice on a ballot.
→ CAST ONE'S VOTE

the **vote** *n.* the right to VOTE ③. (No plural. Treated as singular.)

vote a split ticket to cast a ballot on which the votes are divided between two or more parties.

vote a straight ticket to cast a ballot on which all the votes are for members of the same political party.

a **vote of confidence** a poll taken to discover whether or not a person, party, etc., still has the support of a majority of the voters.

a **vote of thanks** a speech expressing appreciation and thanks to a speaker, lecturer, organizer, etc., and inviting the audience to applaud.

vote someone or something **down** to defeat someone or something in an election.

voter ['vot ɚ] *n.* someone who has the right to vote in an election.

vow ['vaʊ] **1.** *n.* an oath; a sincere promise. **2.** *tv.* to make ①; to swear that one will do something. (The object can be a clause with THAT ⑦.)

vowel ['vaʊ əl] **1.** *n.* a speech sound that is made without completely closing any parts of the mouth while air passes through it. **2.** *n.* a letter of the alphabet that represents a speech sound that is not a CONSONANT; [in English] the letters *a, e, i, o,* and *u.* **3.** the *adj.* use of ① or ②.

voyage ['vɔɪ ədʒ] *n.* a journey, especially one made over water, through the air, or in space; a journey made on a ship, airplane, or spacecraft.
→ MAIDEN VOYAGE

vulture ['vʌl tʃɚ] *n.* a large bird that lives on the meat of dead animals.

W

waddle ['wɑdl] *iv.* to walk with slow, short steps while moving the body from side to side, as a duck walks.

wade ['wed] **1.** *iv.* to walk through shallow water or mud. **2.** *tv.* to cross a shallow body of water by walking through it.

wade in(to something) 1. to walk into an area covered by water. **2.** to get quickly and directly involved in something.

waffle ['wɑf əl] **1.** *n.* a thick round or square pancake with depressed squares that form a grid. **2.** *iv.* to change one's mind on an issue many times.

wag ['wæg] **1.** *tv.* to move something up and down or from side to side many times. **2.** *iv.* to move up and down or from side to side many times.
→ CAUSE (SOME) TONGUES TO WAG
→ the TAIL WAGGING THE DOG

wage ['wedʒ] **1.** *tv.* to begin and continue a war, battle, or struggle against someone or something. **2.** *n.* payment for work, especially when a certain amount is paid for each hour worked. (Often plural with the same meaning. Compare this with SALARY.)

wager ['we dʒɚ] **1.** *n.* a bet. **2.** *tv.* to risk an amount of money on the outcome of an event. **3.** *tv.* to bet that something will happen; to bet that something is or will be the case. (The object is a clause with THAT ⑦.)

wagon ['wæg ən] **1.** *n.* a strong four-wheeled vehicle with a flat bottom that is pulled by horses, mules, or oxen. **2.** *n.* a small, light four-wheeled cart with a flat bottom that is pulled as a children's toy.
→ FIX SOMEONE'S WAGON
→ ON THE WAGON

wail ['wel] **1.** *n.* a long, loud cry, especially one of pain or sadness. **2.** *iv.* to cry out with a long, loud sound because of pain or sadness. **3.** *tv.* to utter something with a long, loud cry of pain or sadness. (The object can be a clause with THAT ⑦.)

waist ['west] **1.** *n.* the part of the body below the bottom of the ribs and above the hips. **2.** *n.* the part of a piece of clothing that covers ①; the part of a piece of clothing that hangs from ①.

waistline ['west laɪn] *n.* an imaginary line around the body at the smallest part of one's waist, usually where the top hem of a pair of pants or a skirt rests on the body.

wait ['wet] **1.** *iv.* to stay in a place until someone or something else arrives or returns; to stay in a place until something happens. **2.** *n.* a period of time that one waits for someone or something.
→ CAN'T WAIT (FOR SOMETHING TO HAPPEN)
→ CAN'T WAIT (TO DO SOMETHING)
→ the MOMENT EVERYONE HAS BEEN WAITING FOR
→ ON A WAITING LIST

wait for someone or something to anticipate the arrival of someone or something.

wait on someone to serve someone as a waiter or waitress or as a clerk behind a counter.

wait on someone **hand and foot** to serve someone very well, attending to all personal needs.

wait up (for someone or something**) 1.** to slow down and pause for someone or something to catch up. **2.** to delay going to bed for someone or something or until someone or something does something.

wait (up)on someone to pay homage to someone, as with a king or queen or other ruler.

wait-and-see attitude a skeptical attitude; an uncertain attitude where someone will wait to see what happens before reacting.

waiter ['we tɚ] *n.* a man who serves customers at a restaurant.

waiting in the wings ready or prepared to do something, especially to take over someone else's job or position.

waitress ['we trɪs] *n.* a woman who serves customers at a restaurant.

waive ['wev] **1.** *tv.* to give up something, especially a right or a privilege. (Compare this to WAVE.) **2.** *tv.* to allow someone not to have to do something that is usually required; to excuse someone from fulfilling a requirement.

wake ['wek] **1.** *n.* a gathering, shortly before a funeral, of the friends and relatives of someone who has recently died. **2.** *n.* the path on the surface of a body of water caused by a boat or ship traveling through the water. **3.** Go to WAKE (UP).

wake someone or some creature **(up)** to cause someone or some creature to stop sleeping.

wake the dead to be so loud as to wake those who are "sleeping" the most soundly—the DEAD.

wake (up) 1. to stop sleeping. *iv.* (Past tense: *waked* or WOKE; past participle: *waked* or WOKEN.) **2.** *iv.* to become alert; to pay attention. (Usually a command.)

waken ['wek ən] **1.** *iv.* to wake from sleep; to stop sleeping. **2.** *tv.* to wake someone or something from sleep.

walk ['wɔk] **1.** *iv.* to move on foot at a normal speed and in a way that only one foot at a time is on the ground. **2.** *tv.* to move in, on, or through a space as in ①. **3.** *tv.* to exercise an animal, usually a dog, by taking it for ⑤. **4.** *tv.* to go with someone to a certain place. **5.** *n.* an act of WALKING as in ①, especially as exercise or for pleasure; a journey on foot. **6.** *n.* a path; a place where one can WALK ①.
→ ALL WALKS OF LIFE
→ COCK OF THE WALK
→ WITHIN WALKING DISTANCE

walk a tightrope to be in a situation where one must be very cautious.

walk away with something AND **walk off with** something **1.** to steal something. **2.** to win some-thing easily.

walk in on someone or something to interrupt someone or some-thing by entering a place.

walk off to walk away; to leave on foot abruptly.

walk off with something Go to WALK AWAY WITH SOMETHING.

walk on air to be very happy; to feel very good about something.

walk on eggs to be very cautious.

walk out (of something**) 1.** to exit something or someplace. **2.** to exit one's workplace on strike.

walk out (on someone or some-thing**)** to leave or abandon some-one or something in anger, disgust, or aversion.

walk the floor to pace nervously while waiting.

wall ['wɔl] **1.** *n.* the side of a room from the floor to the ceiling; the side of a building from the ground to the roof. **2.** *n.* a large, flat side of anything; anything that looks like ①. **3.** *n.* a thin tissue that encloses a part of the body of a human, plant, or animal.
→ BANG ONE'S HEAD AGAINST A BRICK WALL
→ BEAT ONE'S HEAD AGAINST THE WALL
→ DRIVE SOMEONE TO THE WALL
→ FORCE SOMEONE TO THE WALL
→ GO TO THE WALL
→ HAVE ONE'S BACK TO THE WALL
→ ONE'S BACK IS TO THE WALL
→ PRESS SOMEONE TO THE WALL
→ PUSH SOMEONE TO THE WALL
→ RUN INTO A STONE WALL
→ SEE THE (HAND)WRITING ON THE WALL

wallet ['wɑl ət] *n.* a small, flat case that is used for carrying money, identification, credit cards, etc. (Often made of leather.)

wallpaper ['wɔl pe pɚ] **1.** *n.* paper, usually with a design on it, that is used to cover and decorate walls. (No plural.) **2.** *tv.* to cover a wall with ①. **3.** *iv.* to apply ① to a wall; to put up ①.

Walls have ears. We may be over-heard.

walnut ['wɔl nət] **1.** *n.* the tree that produces a delicious, edible nut. **2.** *n.* the nut of ①; the nut of ① and its shell. **3.** *n.* wood from ①. (Plural only for types and instances.) **4.** *adj.* made with ② or from ③.

waltz ['wɔlts] **1.** *n.* a dance, with three beats to every measure of music, in which couples turn in a circle as they dance around the dance floor. **2.** *n.* music that has three beats to every measure and is written for ① or suitable for ①. **3.** *iv.* to dance ①.

wander ['wɑn dɚ] *iv.* to travel in no specific direction; to roam somewhere.

wane ['wen] **1.** *iv.* to become less important, less strong, less intense, or smaller. **2.** *iv.* [for the moon] to gradually appear to be smaller after a full moon. (Compare this with WAX ④.)

want ['wɑnt] **1.** *tv.* to desire to have someone or something. **2.** *n.* a desire; a need; something that someone would like to have. **3.** *n.* a lack. (No plural.)
→ KNOW WHEN ONE IS NOT WANTED

→ WASTE NOT, WANT NOT.

want for nothing to lack nothing; to have everything one needs or desires.

want in((to) something**)** to want to come into something or some-place.

want out (of something**)** **1.** to desire to get out of something or someplace. **2.** to desire to be relieved of a responsibility.

want someone or something **out of** something to desire that someone or something leave or be removed from something or someplace.

want to do something to desire to do something; to wish to do something.

war ['wɔr] *n.* fighting or conflict between two or more nations, especially involving a military force of one country attacking another country. (Plural only for types and instances.)

ward ['wɔrd] **1.** *n.* someone, especially a child, who is under the protection of the state, the government, a judge, or someone chosen by a court. **2.** *n.* a political division of a city, especially one that is represented by someone in a city council. **3.** *n.* a section of a hospital, usually containing the beds for patients having similar medical conditions.

warden ['wɔrd n] *n.* someone who is in charge of a prison or jail.
→ GAME WARDEN

wardrobe ['wɔr drob] **1.** *n.* a collection of clothes. **2.** *n.* a piece of furniture that looks like a large box with a door, and is used to store clothing.

warehouse ['wɛr haʊs] **1.** *n., irreg.* a place where large amounts of goods are stored before they are sold or used. (Plural: […haʊ zəz].) **2.** *tv.* to store something in ①.

warm ['wɔrm] **1.** *adj.* somewhat hot; not too hot but not cold. (Adv: *warmly.* Comp: *warmer;* sup: *warmest.*) **2.** *adj.* capable of retaining heat. (Adv: *warmly.* Comp: *warmer;* sup: *warmest.*) **3.** *adj.* pleasant; friendly; indicating that one is pleasant or friendly. (Adv: *warmly.* Comp: *warmer;* sup: *warmest.*)

warm oneself **up** to help oneself get physically prepared to perform in an athletic event.

warm someone or something **(up)** to cause someone or something to become warm.

warm the bench [for a player] to remain out of play during a game—seated on a bench.

warm (up) [for the weather or a person] to become warmer or hotter.

warm up (for something**)** to prepare for some kind of performance or competition.

warm up to someone or something to become more fervent and earnest toward someone, something, or a group; to become more responsive and receptive to someone, a group, or something.

warmth ['wɔrmθ] **1.** *n.* a small amount of heat. (No plural.) **2.** *n.*

kindness; pleasantness; friendliness. (No plural.)

warn ['wɔrn] **1.** *tv.* to alert someone to danger; to inform someone about something dangerous or risky. **2.** *tv.* to tell someone not to do something, implying that punishment will follow repeated violations.

warn someone **against** someone or something to advise someone against someone, something, or doing something.

warn someone **away from** someone or something to advise someone to avoid someone or something.

warn someone **off** to advise a person to stay away.

warning ['wɔr nɪŋ] *n.* something that warns; a statement, sign, or threat of danger.

warranty ['wɑr ən ti] *n.* an official guarantee; a written promise from a manufacturer that something will function in the way that it is supposed to.

warrior ['wɔr jɚ] *n.* someone who is trained to fight; a soldier; a fighter.

warship ['wɑr ʃɪp] *n.* a ship equipped with weapons for making war.

wart ['wɔrt] *n.* a hard, ugly bump that swells from the skin, especially on the face, neck, and hands.

warts and all including all faults and disadvantages.

wary ['wɛr i] *adj.* aware; on guard against harm or danger; careful. (Adv: *warily.* Comp: *warier;* sup: *wariest.*)

was ['wʌz, 'wɑz, wəz] *iv.* a past tense of BE used with the first and third persons singular.

wash ['wɑʃ] **1.** *tv.* to clean someone or something with water or some other liquid. **2.** *tv.* to remove dirt through the use of water or some other liquid. **3.** *tv.* [for water] to carry or move something. **4.** *iv.* to clean [oneself or some part of oneself] with water or some other liquid. **5.** *iv.* to be carried or moved by water. **6.** *n.* laundry; clothes that need to be, are being, or have been cleaned as in ①; clothes that are cleaned as in ① together at one time. (No plural.) **7.** *n.* an act or instance of cleaning or being cleaned as in ①, ②, or ④.
→ COME OUT IN THE WASH

wash away to be carried away by water or some other liquid.

wash off ((of) someone or something**)** to be carried off of or away from someone or something by the action of water or another liquid.

wash one's **dirty linen in public** to discuss one's personal problems in public.

wash one's **hands of** someone or something to end one's association with someone or something.

wash someone or something **away** [for a flood of water] to carry someone or something away.

wash someone or something **off** to clean someone or something by washing.

wash something **away** to clean something by scrubbing and flushing away the dirt.

wash something **off ((of)** someone or something**)** to clean something off someone or something.

washcloth ['waʃ kləθ] *n., irreg.* a small cloth used for washing one's body, especially the face. (Plural: ['waʃ kləðz].)

washer ['waʃ ɚ] **1.** *n.* a washing machine; a machine that washes clothing. **2.** *n.* a small, flat circle of metal or rubber, with a hole in the center, that is put under the head of a bolt or screw or between a nut and a bolt to make a tighter seal.

washroom ['waʃ rum] *n.* a bathroom; a restroom; a room with a toilet.

wasn't ['wʌz ənt] *cont.* was not.

wasp [wasp] *n.* a large stinging insect that is similar to a bee but is able to sting again and again.

waste [west] **1.** *tv.* to use something foolishly or wrongly; to use too much of something. **2.** *n.* garbage; trash; something that is not used and is thrown away. (No plural.) **3.** *n.* a poor or foolish use of something; the failure to use all of the parts of something that are able to be used. (No plural.) **4.** *n.* material that is sent out from the body; urine and feces. (Sometimes plural with the same meaning, but not countable.)
→ LAY SOMETHING TO WASTE
→ LAY WASTE TO SOMETHING

Waste not, want not. a saying meaning that if one never wastes anything, one will never be short of anything.

waste one's **breath** to waste one's time talking; to talk in vain.

wastebasket ['west bæs kɪt] *n.* a container that is used to hold trash.

wastepaper ['west pe pɚ] *n.* paper that is not needed and is thrown away or reused. (No plural.)

wastepaper basket ['west pe pɚ 'bæs kət] *n.* a container for receiving wastepaper.

watch ['watʃ] **1.** *tv.* to observe something as it happens; to pay someone or something attention; to look at someone or something to see what happens. **2.** *tv.* to guard someone or something; to protect someone or something. **3.** *iv.* to pay attention to someone or something; to look at someone or something carefully and attentively. **4.** *n.* a device, typically worn on one's wrist, that displays the time.
→ BEAR WATCHING

watch one's **step** to act with care and caution so as not to make a mistake or offend someone.

watch out (for someone or something**)** to keep looking for someone or something.

watch over someone or something to monitor or guard someone or something.

watch someone **like a hawk** to watch someone very carefully.

water ['wɔt ɚ] **1.** *n.* the liquid that forms oceans, lakes, and rivers; the liquid that falls from the sky as rain and is drunk by humans and animals. (No plural.) **2.** *n.* the surface of a body of ①. (E.g., *the water reflected the image of the clouds.* No plural.) **3.** *tv.* to provide a plant with ①; to put ① on the soil around a plant. **4.** *iv.* [for one's eyes] to fill with tears. **5.** *iv.* [for one's mouth] to fill with moisture, especially when one is about to eat or is thinking about eating food.

→ AS A DUCK TAKES TO WATER
→ DASH COLD WATER ON SOMETHING
→ FISH IN TROUBLED WATERS
→ GET ONE'S HEAD ABOVE WATER
→ HOLD WATER
→ IN DEEP WATER
→ KEEP ONE'S HEAD ABOVE WATER
→ LIKE A FISH OUT OF WATER
→ LIKE WATER OFF A DUCK'S BACK
→ MAKE SOMEONE'S MOUTH WATER
→ NOT HOLD WATER
→ OF THE FIRST WATER
→ POUR COLD WATER ON SOMETHING
→ POUR OIL ON TROUBLED WATER
→ SALT WATER
→ SEAWATER
→ SODA WATER
→ THROW COLD WATER ON SOMETHING

water under the bridge something that is past and forgotten.

waterfall ['wɔt ɚ fɔl] *n.* a flow of water off the side of a mountain, rock, or dam.

waterproof ['wɔt ɚ pruf] **1.** *adj.* not allowing water to pass through; able to keep water inside or outside; not leaking water. **2.** *tv.* to cause something to resist water as in ①.

waters *n.* vast amounts of water as found in rivers, oceans, or large lakes.

watertight ['wɔt ɚ taɪt] **1.** *adj.* not allowing water to pass through; able to keep water inside or outside; not leaking water. **2.** *adj.* perfect; [of an agreement or argument] having no mistakes or defects. (Figurative on ①.)

wave ['wev] **1.** *n.* a moving ridge of water made by wind, the tide, or the movement of something through water. **2.** *n.* a ridge in the surface of something. **3.** *n.* a movement of the hand as in ⑥. **4.** *n.* an increase in crime, heat, or cold. **5.** *tv.* to move something, especially one's hand, when greeting someone, trying to get someone's attention, or calling attention to oneself. **6.** *iv.* to greet someone, to get someone's attention, or to call attention to oneself by moving one's hand. **7.** *iv.* to move up and down or back and forth in the air.

wax ['wæks] **1.** *n.* an oily or fatty substance that melts easily when it is warmed but hardens when it is cool, used to make candles, floor polish, and other substances. (Plural only for types and instances.) **2.** *n.* an oily substance that is produced in the ears. (No plural.) **3.** *tv.* to coat or polish a floor with ①. **4.** *tv.* [for the moon] to gradually appear to be brighter and fuller before a full moon. (Compare this with WANE.)

way ['we] **1.** *n.* a manner; the manner in which something is done; a method. **2.** *n.* a habit; a custom; a regular manner in which something is done. (Usually plural.) **3.** *n.* the route to a certain place. (No plural.) **4.** *adv.* far; far away in time or space.

→ ARGUE ONE'S WAY OUT (OF SOMETHING)
→ BUY ONE'S WAY OUT (OF SOMETHING)
→ CUT BOTH WAYS

→ ELBOW (ONE'S WAY) THROUGH
 SOMETHING
→ FIGHT (ONE'S WAY) BACK TO SOMETHING
→ FIGHT ONE'S WAY OUT OF SOMETHING
→ FIGHT (ONE'S WAY) THROUGH
 SOMETHING
→ FIND ONE'S OR ITS WAY SOMEWHERE
→ GET SOMETHING UNDER WAY
→ HAVE THE RIGHT-OF-WAY
→ LOOK THE OTHER WAY
→ MEND ONE'S WAYS
→ ONE'S WAY
→ RUB SOMEONE'S FUR THE WRONG WAY
→ RUB SOMEONE THE WRONG WAY
→ SHOVE ONE'S WAY SOMEWHERE
→ THREAD ONE'S WAY THROUGH
 SOMETHING

(way) over there in a place some distance away.

wayside ['we saɪd] *adj.* along the way, road, or highway.
→ DROP BY THE WAYSIDE
→ FALL BY THE WAYSIDE

we ['wi] **1.** *pron.* the first-person plural subjective pronoun, referring to the speaker or writer—"I"—together with at least one other person. **2.** *pron.* a special use of ① as a first-person singular subjective pronoun, meaning "I, the speaker or writer." (Used by writers and sometimes by royalty.) **3.** *pron.* everyone; all humans.

weak ['wik] **1.** *adj.* lacking power or strength; not strong or powerful. (Adv: *weakly.* Comp: *weaker;* sup: *weakest.*) **2.** *adj.* lacking strong morals; lacking a moral character. (Adv: *weakly.* Comp: *weaker;* sup: *weakest.*) **3.** *adj.* having too much water; diluted. (Adv: *weakly.* Comp: *weaker;* sup: *weakest.*)
→ (AS) WEAK AS A KITTEN

weaken ['wik ən] **1.** *iv.* to become weak. **2.** *tv.* to cause someone or something to become weak.

weakness ['wik nəs] **1.** *n.* the condition of being weak, especially concerning the health of someone's mind or body. (No plural form.) **2.** *n.* a fault; a flaw; something that weakens someone or something.
→ HAVE A WEAKNESS FOR SOMEONE OR
 SOMETHING

wealth ['wɛlθ] *n.* riches; a large amount of money or property. (No plural.)

a **wealth of** something a large amount of something.

wealthy ['wɛl θi] *adj.* rich; having a large amount of money or property. (Adv: *wealthily.* Comp: *wealthier;* sup: *wealthiest.*)

the **wealthy** *n.* people who are wealthy. (No plural. Treated as plural, but not countable.)

wean ['win] *tv.* to cause a child or young animal to begin to eat food other than milk from the mother.

weapon ['wɛp ən] *n.* any object or machine used to hurt someone, to kill someone, or to defend oneself during a fight or an attack.

wear ['wɛr] **1.** *tv., irreg.* to have something on the body, including clothes, glasses, jewelry, perfume, makeup, and similar things. (Past tense: WORE; past participle: WORN.) **2.** *tv., irreg.* to have something on or related to the body kept or held in a particular way. **3.** *tv., irreg.* to damage something gradually because of continued use. **4.** *iv., irreg.* to damage or worsen gradu-

ally. **5.** *n.* gradual damage that is caused because of continued use. (No plural.) **6.** *n.* clothing, especially a collection of clothing available for sale at a store. (Used in combinations such as *resort wear, business wear,* etc. No plural. Treated as singular.)
→ NONE THE WORSE FOR WEAR

wear more than one hat to have more than one set of responsibilities; to hold more than one office.

wear off [for the effects of something] to gradually vanish or go away.

wear out to become worn from use; to become diminished or useless from use.

wear out one's **welcome** to stay too long (at an event to which one has been invited); to visit somewhere too often.

wear someone **down 1.** to exhaust someone. **2.** to reduce someone to submission or agreement by constant nagging.

wear someone **out** to exhaust or annoy someone.

wear something **down** to grind something away; to erode something.

wear something **out** to make something worthless or nonfunctional from use.

wear (up)on someone to diminish someone's energy and resistance; to bore or annoy someone.

weary ['wɪr i] **1.** *adj.* tired; exhausted; fatigued. (Adv: *wearily.* Comp: *wearier;* sup: *weariest.*) **2.** *iv.* to become tired, exhausted, or fatigued.

weather ['wɛð ɚ] **1.** *n.* the condition of the outside air, including the temperature, the amount of moisture in the air, and the presence or absence of rain, snow, wind, clouds, and sunshine. (No plural.) **2.** *tv.* to withstand something (especially bad WEATHER ①) without damage. **3.** *tv.* [for kinds of ①] to damage something. **4.** *iv.* to change because of exposure to ①.
→ FAIR-WEATHER FRIEND
→ KEEP ONE'S WEATHER EYE OPEN
→ LOVELY WEATHER FOR DUCKS
→ UNDER THE WEATHER

weather permitting if the weather allows it.

weave ['wiv] **1.** *tv., irreg.* to make something by crossing threads or strips of material from side to side so that they go over and under threads or strips of material that are stretched up and down. (Past tense: WOVE; past participle: WOVEN.) **2.** *tv., irreg.* to cross threads or strips of material from side to side so that they go over and under threads or strips of material that are stretched up and down. **3.** *tv., irreg.* to make something by combining different things into a whole. (Figurative on ①.) **4.** *iv., irreg.* to move so that one is always changing direction. (Past tense: sometimes *weaved.*)

web ['wɛb] **1.** *n.* a net of thin, silky threads made by spiders in order to trap other insects for food. **2.** *n.* a network; a detailed arrangement of things that cross and connect with each other. (Figurative on ①.) **3.** *n.* the piece of thin skin between the toes of ducks and

other animals that live in or near the water.
→ WORLD WIDE WEB

the **Web** *n.* the WORLD WIDE WEB; a branch of the computer INTERNET.

we'd ['wid] **1.** *cont.* we had, where HAD is an auxiliary. **2.** *cont.* we would.

wed ['wɛd] **1.** *tv., irreg.* to marry someone; to take someone as a husband or wife. (Past tense and past participle: *wedded* or *wed.*) **2.** *tv., irreg.* to cause two people to become married by performing a marriage ceremony. **3.** *iv., irreg.* to become married.

wed(ded) to someone married to someone.

wedded to something mentally attached to something; firmly committed to something.

wedding ['wɛd ɪŋ] **1.** *n.* the ceremony where two people become married to each other; a marriage ceremony. **2.** *n.* a merger or formation of a close association. (Figurative on ①.)
→ SHOTGUN WEDDING

wedge ['wɛdʒ] **1.** *n.* a piece of wood, metal, or other material that is thick at one end and narrows to an edge at the other end. **2.** *n.* any object shaped like ①. **3.** *tv.* to stick someone or something in a tight space between two people or things, especially so that nothing or no one can move.

Wednesday ['wɛnz de] Go to DAY.

weed ['wid] **1.** *n.* a rough plant that grows in a place where it is not wanted. **2.** *tv.* to remove ① from an area of ground, such as a lawn

or garden. **3.** *tv.* to remove a specific kind of ①. **4.** *iv.* to clean or improve [a garden or lawn] by removing ①.

weed someone or something **out** to remove someone or something unwanted or undesirable from a group or collection.

week ['wik] **1.** *n.* a period of seven days. (See a list of days of the week at DAY.) **2.** *n.* a period of seven days beginning on a Sunday and ending on a Saturday. (According to the calendar.) **3.** *n.* the five or six days during which most workers work, especially Monday through Friday.

weekday ['wik de] **1.** *n.* Monday, Tuesday, Wednesday, Thursday, or Friday. **2.** *adj.* happening on ①; of ①. (Prenominal only.)

weekend ['wik ɛnd] **1.** *n.* the period of time from Friday evening to Sunday night. **2.** *adj.* happening at some time between Friday evening and Sunday night. (Prenominal only.)

weeks running Go to DAYS RUNNING.

weep ['wip] **1.** *iv., irreg.* to cry. (Past tense and past participle: WEPT.) **2.** *tv., irreg.* to shed tears; to cry and make tears.

weigh ['we] **1.** *tv.* to use a scale to determine the weight of someone or something. **2.** *tv.* to think carefully and compare different options or alternatives when making a choice or decision. **3.** *iv.* to have a certain weight. **4.** *iv.* to have a particular kind of influence on someone or something.

weight ['wet] **1.** *n.* the degree of heaviness of someone or something or how heavy someone or something is, as measured according to a specific system. (No plural.) **2.** *n.* a heavy object, used for exercising. **3.** *n.* a heavy object, especially one that keeps something in place, holds something down, or balances something. **4.** *n.* a mental burden; something that occupies one's thoughts. (No plural.) **5.** *n.* influence; important factors.
→ CARRY THE WEIGHT OF THE WORLD ON ONE'S SHOULDERS
→ GROAN UNDER THE WEIGHT OF SOMETHING
→ NOT CARRY WEIGHT (WITH SOMEONE)
→ WORTH ITS WEIGHT IN GOLD

weird ['wɪrd] *adj.* very strange; very odd; very unusual. (Adv: *weirdly.* Comp: *weirder;* sup: *weirdest.*)

welcome ['wɛl kəm] **1.** *tv.* to greet someone in a friendly way. **2.** *tv.* to be happy to receive or experience something. (Figurative on ①.) **3.** *n.* the act of greeting or receiving someone or something with pleasure. **4.** *adj.* accepted with pleasure; wanted.
→ WEAR OUT ONE'S WELCOME

welfare ['wɛl fɛr] **1.** *n.* a state of having good health, comfort, and enough money to live satisfactorily. (No plural.) **2.** *n.* money provided by the government for poor people to live on; the system of providing money for poor people to live on. (No plural.)

we'll ['wɪl] *cont.* we will.

well ['wɛl] **1.** *adv., irreg.* in a good way. (Comp: BETTER; sup: BEST.) **2.** *adv.* enough; sufficiently; to a

good degree. **3.** *adv.* completely; thoroughly; fully. **4.** *adj., irreg.* healthy; in good health. (Comp: BETTER.) **5.** *n.* a deep hole that is dug in the ground to reach water, gas, or oil.

well- *adv.* WELL ①, ②, or ③ used in compounds.

well liked ['wɛl 'laɪkt] *adj.* popular; liked by many people. (Hyphenated before a nominal.)

well-fed ['wɛl 'fɛd] *adj.* eating enough good food to be healthy. (Hyphenated only before a nominal.)

well-fixed Go to WELL-HEELED.

well-heeled AND **well-fixed; well-off** wealthy; having a sufficient amount of money.

well-known ['wɛl 'non] *adj.* usually known by many people; [of people] famous. (Hyphenated only before a nominal.)

well-made ['wɛl 'med] *adj.* properly constructed; sturdy; made with skill. (Hyphenated only before a nominal.)

well-off Go to WELL-HEELED.

well-to-do wealthy and of good social position.

went ['wɛnt] past tense of GO.

wept ['wɛpt] past tense and past participle of WEEP.

we're ['wɪr] *cont.* we are.

were ['wɚ] **1.** *iv.* past tense of BE used with plural forms and YOU singular. **2.** *iv.* the form of BE used with all nouns and pronouns to indicate something that is contrary to fact.

weren't ['wɚnt] *cont.* were not.

west [ˈwɛst] **1.** *n.* the direction to the left of someone or something facing north; the direction in which the sun sets. (No plural.) **2.** *n.* the western part of a region or country. (No plural. Capitalized when referring to a region of the United States.) **3.** *adj.* to ①; on the side that is toward ①; facing ①. (Not prenominal.) **4.** *adj.* from ①. (Especially used to describe wind. Not prenominal.) **5.** *adv.* toward ①; into the western part of something.

the West 1. *n.* Western Europe, North America, and South America, as contrasted especially with Eastern Europe, East Asia, and sometimes other parts of Asia. (No plural. Often capitalized.) **2.** *n.* the part of Europe that was not under the influence of the former Soviet Union or ruled under a political and economic system similar to that in the former Soviet Union. (No plural.)

western [ˈwɛs tən] **1.** *adj.* in the west; toward the west; facing the west. **2.** *adj.* from the west. (Especially used to describe wind.) **3.** *n.* a movie, book, or television show about the development of the part of the United States that is in the West during the 1800s. (Sometimes capitalized.)

wet [ˈwɛt] **1.** *adj.* not dry; covered with or soaked with liquid. (Adv: *wetly.* Comp: *wetter;* sup: *wettest.*) **2.** *adj.* [of weather] rainy. (Adv: *wetly.* Comp: *wetter;* sup: *wettest.*) **3.** *adj.* allowing liquor to be sold [legally]. **4.** *tv., irreg.* to make someone or something ①; to cause someone or something to be ①. (Past tense and past participle: *wet, wetted.*) **5.** *tv., irreg.* to urinate on oneself, on something, or in one's own clothes. (Past tense and past participle: usually *wet.*)
→ (AS) MAD AS A WET HEN
→ GET ONE'S FEET WET

wet behind the ears young and inexperienced.

a **wet blanket** a dull or depressing person who spoils other people's enjoyment.

wetness [ˈwɛt nəs] *n.* moisture; liquid that can be felt or seen. (No plural.)

we've [ˈwiv] *cont.* we have, where HAVE is an auxiliary.

whale [ˈʍel] *n.* a very large mammal that lives in the ocean and breathes through an opening on top of its head.

wharf [ˈworf] *n., irreg.* a platform where ships can dock in order to load or unload people or cargo; a pier. (Plural: WHARVES.)

wharves [ˈworvz] plural of WHARF.

what [ˈʍʌt] **1.** *interrog.* a form used as the subject or object of a sentence or clause when asking questions to get more information about someone or something. **2.** *interrog.* a form used before nominals when asking questions to get more information about that noun or nominal. **3.** *pron.* that which; the thing that; the things that. **4.** *interj.* a form showing great surprise.

What about (doing) something? Would you like to do something?

What about (having**) something?**
Would you like to have something?

what makes someone **tick** that
which motivates someone; that
which makes someone behave in a
certain way.

whatever [ʍət ˈɛv ɚ] **1.** *pron.* anything that; everything that. **2.**
pron. no matter what. **3.** *interrog.*
an emphatic form of **WHAT** ①, similar to *What possibly?* **4.** *adj.* any;
no matter what.

what's [ʍʌts] **1.** *cont.* what is.
2. *cont.* what has, where **HAS** is an
auxiliary.

wheat [ˈʍit] **1.** *n.* a kind of cereal
grain grown for its seeds. (No plural.) **2.** *n.* the seed of ①, ground to
make flour. (No plural. Number is
expressed with *grain(s) of wheat*.)
3. *adj.* made from ②.

wheel [ˈʍil] **1.** *n.* a sturdy circular
object that turns around a central
point and is connected to an axle.
2. *n.* the round object used to steer
a vehicle. (Short for **STEERING
WHEEL**.)
→ **PUT ONE'S SHOULDER TO THE WHEEL**
→ **STEERING WHEEL**

wheelbarrow [ˈʍil bɛr o] *n.* an
open container attached to a
frame with one wheel in front and
handles behind to steer it.

wheelchair [ˈʍil tʃɛr] *n.* a chair
that has wheels instead of legs,
usually two large wheels in back
and two small ones in front, for
people who are unable to walk.

when [ˈʍɛn] **1.** *interrog.* at what
time? **2.** *conj.* at the time that; at
that certain time. **3.** *conj.* considering [the fact that]; as.

when the time is ripe at exactly
the right time.

whenever [ʍɛn ˈɛv ɚ] **1.** *conj.* at
any time; at whatever time. **2.** *conj.*
every time; each time. **3.** *interrog.*
when?; at what time? (Used for
emphasis.)

where [ˈʍɛr] **1.** *interrog.* in what
place?; at what place?; in which
location? **2.** *conj.* in that place; at
that place; in that location. **3.** *conj.*
in the case; such that; wherever.

whereas [ʍɛr ˈæz] **1.** *conj.* but;
however; on the other hand; on
the contrary. **2.** *conj.* since;
because. (Used to introduce legal
documents.)

where's [ˈʍɛrz] **1.** *cont.* where has,
where **HAS** is an auxiliary. **2.** *cont.*
where is.

whether [ˈʍɛð ɚ] *conj.* a form used
with some kinds of questions
when more than one answer is
possible; if.

whether or not either if something
is true or if something is not true;
one way or the other.

which [ˈʍɪtʃ] **1.** *interrog.* a form
used in questions to ask about or
distinguish among specific people
or things; what one or ones? (E.g.,
Which students were late? Used
before a noun.) **2.** *adj.* a form used
to distinguish among people or
things already mentioned or
known from the context; what
[one or ones]; the [one or ones].
(Prenominal only.) **3.** *pron.* a form
used to show the differences
among people or things already
mentioned or known from the
context; what one or ones; the one

or ones. (Treated as singular or plural.) **4.** *pron.* a form used after a word, phrase, or clause and serving to introduce extra, incidental, or descriptive information about the word, phrase, or clause rather than information needed to identify it; the one or ones that. (Treated as singular or plural.) **5.** *pron.* a form used after a word or a phrase and serving to introduce special, contrastive, or distinctive information about the word or phrase; the one or ones that. (Treated as singular or plural.)

whiff ['ʍɪf] **1.** *n.* an odor. **2.** *n.* a bit of an odor sensed by the nose.
→ CATCH A WHIFF OF SOMETHING
→ GET A WHIFF OF SOMETHING

while ['ʍaɪl] **1.** *conj.* during that time; during a certain time that; at the same time as that. **2.** *conj.* and, in contrast; although; on the other hand; and; whereas. **3.** *n.* a length of time. (No plural.)

whim ['ʍɪm] *n.* a sudden wish to do something, especially an unreasonable wish.

whimper ['ʍɪm pɚ] **1.** *n.* a small, quiet moan or cry, especially from someone or something that is afraid. **2.** *iv.* to moan quietly, as though one were afraid. **3.** *tv.* to say something while whimpering, as in ②. (The object can be a clause with THAT ⑦.)

whine ['ʍaɪn] **1.** *n.* a cry not made with the mouth open very much; a soft, high-pitched cry. **2.** *iv.* to complain in a sad, annoying, childish voice. **3.** *tv.* to make a complaint in a sad, annoying,

childish voice. (The object can be a clause with THAT ⑦.)

whip ['ʍɪp] **1.** *n.* a long strip of leather, usually attached to a handle, used for hitting people or animals. **2.** *n.* a member of a political party who organizes and manages members of the party serving in a legislative body. **3.** *tv.* to hit or strike someone or an animal with ①. **4.** *tv.* to beat eggs or cream until the mixture bubbles into a froth. **5.** *tv.* to beat an opponent in a contest or game by a wide margin. (Figurative on ③.)

whisk ['ʍɪsk] **1.** *n.* a wire tool for whipping eggs, cream, and other mixtures. **2.** *tv.* to whip eggs, cream, and other mixtures into a froth.

whisker ['ʍɪs kɚ] *n.* a hair that grows from near the mouth of a cat and certain other animals; a hair that is part of a beard.
→ BY A WHISKER

whiskey ['ʍɪs ki] **1.** *n.* a strong alcohol for drinking made from corn, rye, or other grains. (Plural only for types and instances.) **2.** *n.* a glass of ①; a drink of ①.

whisper ['ʍɪs pɚ] **1.** *tv.* to say something with the breath only, not using the full voice. (The object can be a clause with THAT ⑦.) **2.** *iv.* to speak as in ①. **3.** *n.* speaking done with the breath only, not using the voice.

whistle ['ʍɪs əl] **1.** *n.* a small metal or plastic instrument that makes a shrill, high-pitched sound when one blows air into it. **2.** *n.* a shrill, high-pitched sound made by passing air through a small opening

between one's lips or through ①.
3. *tv.* to make a melody with a
shrill, high-pitched sound made
by passing air through one's lips.
4. *iv.* to make a shrill, high-
pitched sound by passing air
through ① or through one's lips.
→ BLOW THE WHISTLE (ON SOMEONE)

whistle for something to expect or
look for something with no hope
of getting it.

white [ˈʍaɪt] **1.** *n.* the color of salt
or milk. (Plural only for types and
instances.) **2.** *n.* someone who has
light-colored skin, usually persons
of European descent. **3.** *n.* the
clear part of an egg, which turns
① when it is cooked. **4.** *adj.* having the color of salt or milk. (Adv:
whitely. Comp: *whiter;* sup:
whitest.) **5.** *adj.* pale. (Comp:
whiter; sup: *whitest.*) **6.** *adj.* [of
people, usually of European
descent or their skin] light-colored. (See also CAUCASIAN. Comp:
whiter; sup: *whitest.*)
→ (AS) WHITE AS THE DRIVEN SNOW
→ IN BLACK AND WHITE

white elephant something that is
useless and either is a nuisance or
is expensive to keep up.

whiten [ˈʍaɪt n] **1.** *tv.* to cause
something to become white; to
make something white. **2.** *iv.* to
turn pale.

whittle [ˈʍɪt əl] **1.** *tv.* to cut pieces
of wood away a little bit at a time
with a knife; to shave off small
strips from a piece of wood. **2.** *tv.*
to carve an object from wood, cutting away small pieces.

whiz [ˈʍɪz] **1.** *iv.* [for something] to
move very quickly through the air
while making a sound as it passes
by someone or something. **2.** *n.* an
expert; someone who is very
skilled at something; someone
who can do something quickly
and very well. (Figurative on ①.)

who [ˈhu] **1.** *interrog.* what or
which person or people? (The possessive form is WHOSE. The objective form is WHOM.) **2.** *pron.* a
person or the people mentioned.
(Standard English requires WHOM
instead of WHO as the object of a
verb or preposition. WHO can be
used in *restrictive* and *nonrestrictive clauses.*)

who'd [ˈhud] **1.** *cont.* who had,
where HAD is an auxiliary. **2.** *cont.*
who would.

whoever [hu ˈɛv ɚ] **1.** *pron.* anyone; any person who. **2.** *interrog.*
who?

whole [ˈhol] **1.** *adj.* made of the
entire amount; consisting of all
parts; not divided; not separated;
complete. (Adv: *wholly.*) **2.** *adj.*
healthy or the feeling of good
health, in the mind or body. **3.** *adj.*
not expressed as a fraction or a
decimal number. **4.** *n.* something
that is complete; something that
has all of its parts; the entire
amount.
→ MAKE SOMETHING UP OUT OF WHOLE
CLOTH

whole shooting match the entire
affair or organization.

wholesale [ˈhol sel] **1.** *adj.* [of
products] sold in large numbers to
people who will sell the products

one at a time to customers. (Compare this with RETAIL.) **2.** *adj.* done on a large scale; in large amounts. (Figurative on ①.) **3.** *adv.* in large quantities as in ① and at a favorable price.

wholesaler ['hol sel ɚ] *n.* someone who buys products from a manufacturer and sells them to store owners.

who'll ['hul] *cont.* who will.

whom ['hum] *pron.* the objective form of WHO. (Not common in informal English. See the comments at WHO.)

whoop it up to enjoy oneself in a lively and noisy manner. (Informal.)

who's ['huz] **1.** *cont.* who has, where HAS is an auxiliary. **2.** *cont.* who is.

whose ['huz] **1.** *pron.* the possessive form of WHO and WHICH. (WHOSE can be used in *restrictive* and *nonrestrictive clauses*.) **2.** *interrog.* a form used in questions to determine the identity of the person who owns, possesses, or is associated with something; of or belonging to whom?

why 1. ['ʍaɪ] *interrog.* for what reason? **2.** ['ʍaɪ] *conj.* the reason that; the reason for which. **3.** ['ʍaɪ] *interj.* a form used to express surprise, dismay, disgust, or some other emotion.

wicked ['wɪk əd] *adj.* evil; very bad; vile. (Adv: *wickedly.*)

wide ['waɪd] **1.** *adj.* not narrow; broad. (Adv: *widely.* Comp: *wider;* sup: *widest.*) **2.** *adj.* being a certain distance from side to side; measured from side to side. (E.g., *a yard wide.* Follows the measurement of width. Comp: *wider.*) **3.** *adj.* large in size, range, or scope. (Adv: *widely.* Comp: *wider;* sup: *widest.*) **4.** *adv.* as far as possible; to the greatest amount or extent.
→ WORLD WIDE WEB

wide of the mark 1. far from the target. **2.** inadequate; far from what is required or expected.

widow ['wɪd o] *n.* a woman whose husband has died, and who has not married again.

widower ['wɪd o ɚ] *n.* a man whose wife has died, and who has not married again.

width ['wɪdθ] *n.* distance, from side to side. (No plural.)

wield ['wild] **1.** *tv.* to hold and use something, especially a weapon. **2.** *tv.* to have and use power, especially as though it were a weapon. (Figurative on ①.)

wiener ['win ɚ] *n.* a beef or pork sausage, often eaten on a long bun.

wife ['waɪf] *n., irreg.* the woman a man is married to. (Plural: WIVES.)

wig ['wɪg] *n.* a head covering simulating one's own hair; a head covering made of real or artificial hair.

wiggle ['wɪg əl] **1.** *iv.* to move back and forth in quick, little movements. **2.** *tv.* to cause something to move back and forth in quick, little movements.

wild ['waɪld] **1.** *adj.* growing or living in nature; not tame; not grown or kept by a human. (Adv: *wildly.*

Comp: *wilder;* sup: *wildest.*) **2.** *adj.* not in control; out of control; lacking control; reckless. (Adv: *wildly.* Comp: *wilder;* sup: *wildest.*)

→ SOW ONE'S WILD OATS

wilderness ['wɪl dɚ nəs] *n.* a large area of land with no human residents. (No plural. Number is expressed with *wilderness area(s).*)

wildfire ['waɪld faɪr] *n.* an uncontrollable fire or flame in the outdoors.

→ SPREAD LIKE WILDFIRE

wildflower ['waɪld flaʊ ɚ] *n.* a flower that is not grown by a person; a flower that grows in nature.

wild-goose chase a worthless hunt or chase; a futile pursuit.

will ['wɪl] **1.** *interrog.* a form used with a verb to indicate politeness by turning a command into a question. (See also WOULD ③.) **2.** *aux.* a form used with a verb to indicate the future tense. (See also SHALL. See WOULD ① for the past-tense form. Reduced to *'ll* in contractions.) **3.** *aux.* a form used with a verb to command someone to do something. **4.** *aux.* can; be able to. **5.** *aux.* a form used to express something that is always true or something that always happens. **6.** *n.* the power one has in one's mind to do what one wants to do; an intention to do something. **7.** *n.* a legal document that details how one's assets will be distributed after one's death. **8.** *tv.* to leave something to someone in one's ⑦.

willing ['wɪl ɪŋ] *adj.* eagerly ready to do something; happily prepared to do something or to be of service. (Adv: *willingly.*)

willow ['wɪl o] *n.* a tree that has many long, thin, drooping branches with long, thin leaves. **2.** *n.* wood from ①. (No plural.) **3.** *adj.* made of or from ②.

willpower ['wɪl paʊ ɚ] *n.* the ability to control one's will. (No plural.)

wilt ['wɪlt] **1.** *iv.* to wither; [for the leaves or branches of a plant] to lose their strength and sag downward. **2.** *iv.* [for someone] to lose energy. (Figurative on ①.) **3.** *tv.* to cause something to wither or sag as in ①.

win ['wɪn] **1.** *tv., irreg.* to receive or achieve first place in a contest or competition. (Past tense and past participle: WON.) **2.** *tv., irreg.* to achieve or earn something through hard work or effort. **3.** *iv., irreg.* to be in first place in a contest or competition; to be the best in a contest. **4.** *n.* a victory; a triumph.

win by a nose to win by the slightest amount of difference. (As in a horse race where one horse wins with only its nose ahead of the horse that comes in second.)

win someone **over** to succeed in gaining the support and sympathy of someone.

win someone **over (to** something) to succeed in making someone accept or favor something.

wind 1. ['wɪnd] *n.* the movement of air; moving air. (Plural with the same meaning, but not countable.) **2.** ['wɪnd] *n.* breath or the ability

to breathe. (No plural.) **3.** ['wɪnd] *tv.* to cause someone to be out of breath; to cause someone to have a hard time breathing. **4.** ['waɪnd] *tv., irreg.* to tighten the spring of a device such as a watch or a clock. (Past tense and past participle: WOUND.) **5.** ['waɪnd] *iv., irreg.* to move in one direction and then another; to move in twists and turns.
→ GET ONE'S SECOND WIND
→ GET WIND OF SOMETHING
→ IN THE WIND
→ THROW CAUTION TO THE WIND

wind down to start running or operating slower.

wind something **on(to** something**)** to coil or wrap something onto something.

wind something **up** to tighten the spring in something, such as a watch or a clock.

wind up (by) doing something to end by doing something [anyway].

winded ['wɪn dɪd] **1.** *adj.* out of breath; gasping for breath. **2.** the past tense and past participle of WIND.

windmill ['wɪnd mɪl] *n.* a structure that uses metal or wooden blades to capture the power of the wind.
→ TILT AT WINDMILLS

window ['wɪn do] **1.** *n.* an opening in a wall or door, usually covered with a sheet of glass, that allows light and air into a place. **2.** *n.* the sheet of glass that covers an opening in a wall or door.
→ STORM WINDOW

window shade ['wɪn do 'ʃed] *n.* a sheet of fabric designed to cover a window to keep the sun out and to

prevent people from seeing in. (Can be shortened to SHADE.)

windowpane ['wɪn do pen] *n.* the sheet of glass that covers an opening in a wall or door.

window-shopping the habit or practice of looking at goods in shop windows or in stores without actually buying anything.

windowsill ['wɪn do sɪl] *n.* the flat ledge at the bottom of a window.

windpipe ['wɪnd paɪp] *n.* the tube in the body that allows air to travel between the mouth and the lungs.

windshield ['wɪnd ʃild] *n.* the large, curved piece of glass in the front of a car, truck, or bus.

windy ['wɪn di] *adj.* having a lot of wind; with a lot of wind. (Comp: *windier*; sup: *windiest*.)

wine ['waɪn] *n.* a drink that contains alcohol and is made from fruit juice, especially the juice of grapes. (Plural only for types and instances.)

wing ['wɪŋ] **1.** *n.* one of the upper limbs of a bird, or a flying mammal, used for flight. **2.** *n.* an extension on the side of an insect's body, used for flight. **3.** *n.* a structure on an airplane that stands out from its body, which allows the airplane to stay in the air during flight. **4.** *n.* a part of a building that is built out from the central or main part of the building. **5.** *tv.* to shoot a bird in the ① without killing it.
→ CLIP SOMEONE'S WINGS
→ TAKE SOMEONE UNDER ONE'S WING(S)
→ TRY ONE'S WINGS (OUT)
→ WAITING IN THE WINGS

wink ['wɪŋk] **1.** *iv.* to shut and open one eye quickly, especially either as a signal or to show amusement or interest. (Compare this with BLINK.) **2.** *n.* an act of shutting and opening one eye quickly, especially either as a signal or to show amusement or interest.
→ (AS) QUICK AS A WINK
→ NOT SLEEP A WINK
→ TAKE FORTY WINKS

winner ['wɪnɚ] *n.* someone or something that wins.

winter ['wɪntɚ] **1.** *n.* one of the four seasons of the year; the season between fall and spring. **2.** *adj.* concerning or associated with ①. **3.** *iv.* to live in a certain place during ①.

wipe ['waɪp] **1.** *tv.* to rub the surface of someone or something with something in order to clean or dry it. **2.** *tv.* to remove some liquid from a surface, using something absorbent.

wipe someone or something **off** to clean someone or something of something by wiping.

wipe something **off ((of)** someone or something) to remove something from someone or something by wiping.

wipe something **up 1.** to clean up a mess by wiping. (E.g., *clean the dirt up.*) **2.** to clean something by wiping. (E.g., *clean the kitchen up.*)

wire ['waɪɚ] **1.** *n.* a thin metal strand; a thread of metal, especially one used to transmit electricity. (No plural.) **2.** *n.* a length or segment of ①. **3.** *n.* a message that is sent by telegram. **4.** *tv.* to send a message or money by telegraph. (The object can be a clause with THAT ⑦.) **5.** *tv.* to install ① in a building for electricity; to install or adjust any kind of ①. **6.** *tv.* to fasten or secure something with ①. **7.** *tv.* to install hidden microphones in a place so that one can record what is said there.
→ DOWN TO THE WIRE
→ UNDER THE WIRE

wisdom ['wɪzdəm] *n.* intelligence, especially intelligence that is a result of experience; the knowledge required to make good decisions; the quality of being wise. (No plural.)

wise ['waɪz] *adj.* able to make good decisions; showing good judgment; intelligent. (Adv: *wisely.* Comp: *wiser;* sup: *wisest.*)
→ (AS) WISE AS AN OWL
→ NONE THE WISER

wish ['wɪʃ] **1.** *n.* a desire for something. **2.** *tv.* to express ①; to hope that something happens. (The object is a clause with THAT ⑦.) **3.** *iv.* to have a desire to do something.

wishful thinking believing that something is true or that something will happen just because one wishes that it were true or would happen.

wit ['wɪt] **1.** *n.* the ability to understand ideas quickly and make intelligent, clever, and funny comments about them. (No plural.) **2.** *n.* someone who has the ability to understand ideas quickly and make intelligent, clever, and funny comments about them.
→ AT ONE'S WIT'S END
→ LIVE BY ONE'S WITS
→ ONE'S WITS

→ TO WIT

witch ['wɪtʃ] **1.** *n.* someone, usually a woman, who has or claims to have magical powers or who practices a pagan religion. **2.** *n.* a mean or ugly woman. (Derogatory.)

with ['wɪθ] **1.** *prep.* among someone or something; including someone or something; in the company of someone or something; in addition to someone or something. **2.** *prep.* by means of something; by using something. **3.** *prep.* showing a quality or characteristic; showing a state or emotion.

with a vengeance with determination and eagerness.

with a will with determination and enthusiasm.

with all one's **heart and soul** very sincerely.

with all the fixings with all the condiments that accompany a certain kind of food.

with both hands tied behind one's **back** Go to WITH ONE HAND TIED BEHIND ONE'S BACK.

with ease without effort.

with every (other) breath [saying something] repeatedly or continually.

with everything (on it) [of a sandwich] ordered with everything available on it, such as ketchup, mustard, onions, cheese, peppers, chili, lettuce, tomato, etc., as appropriate.

with flying colors easily and excellently.

with it (Informal.) **1.** up-to-date; fashionable. **2.** able to think clearly; able to understand things.

with no strings attached AND **without any strings attached** unconditionally; with no obligations.

with one hand tied behind one's **back** AND **with both hands tied behind** one's **back** easily; even with a handicap.

with regard to someone or something concerning someone or something.

with relish with pleasure or enjoyment.

with respect to someone or something of or about someone or something.

with the best will in the world however much one wishes to do something; however hard one tries to do something.

with the naked eye with eyes that are not aided by lenses as found in glasses or a microscope.

wither ['wɪðɚ] **1.** *iv.* to shrivel; to wilt; [for a plant] to turn brown, sag, and dry out. **2.** *tv.* to cause a plant to shrivel, droop, or wilt; to cause a plant to turn brown and dry out.

wither on the vine AND **die on the vine** [for something] to decline or fade away at an early stage of development.

withheld [wɪθ 'hɛld] past tense and past participle of WITHHOLD.

withhold [wɪθ 'hold] *tv., irreg.* to hold or keep something back [from someone or something].

(Past tense and past participle: WITHHELD.)

within [wɪθ 'ɪn] **1.** *prep.* inside someone or something; in or into the inside part of someone or something. **2.** *prep.* not beyond a specific boundary; between certain limits. **3.** *adv.* into the inside of someone or something.

within an inch of one's **life** very close to ending one's life; almost to the point of death.

within walking distance close enough to walk to.

without [wɪθ 'aʊt] *prep.* not including someone or something; lacking someone or something.

without a moment to spare Go to NOT A MOMENT TO SPARE.

without any strings attached Go to WITH NO STRINGS ATTACHED.

without batting an eye without showing alarm or response; without blinking an eyelash.

without doing something avoiding doing something; while avoiding doing something.

withstand [wɪθ 'stænd] *tv., irreg.* to resist someone or something; to oppose someone or something; not to yield to someone or something. (Past tense and past participle: WITHSTOOD.)

withstood [wɪθ 'stʊd] past tense and past participle of WITHSTAND.

witness ['wɪt nəs] **1.** *n.* someone who sees something happen; someone who is in the same place where something happens; a spectator. **2.** *n.* someone who sees the signing of a legal document. **3.** *tv.* to see something happen; to be in the same place where something happens. **4.** *tv.* to sign a legal document as a way of swearing that one has watched another person, who is directly affected by the document, sign it, and thus show that the other person's signature is real.

witness stand ['wɪt nəs 'stænd] *n.* the place where someone gives testimony under oath in court. (Can be shortened to STAND.)

wives ['waɪvz] plural of WIFE.

wizard ['wɪz əd] **1.** *n.* someone, usually a male, who has or claims to have magical powers. **2.** *n.* an expert; someone who is very skilled at something. (Figurative on ①.)

woke ['wok] a past tense of WAKE.

woken ['wok ən] a past participle of WAKE.

wolf ['wʊlf] *n., irreg.* a wild animal related to the dog that eats meat and travels in groups. (Plural: WOLVES.)
→ CRY WOLF
→ KEEP THE WOLF FROM THE DOOR
→ THROW SOMEONE TO THE WOLVES

a **wolf in sheep's clothing** something threatening disguised as something kind.

wolves ['wʊlvz] plural of WOLF.

woman ['wʊm ən] **1.** *n., irreg.* an adult female person; an adult female human being. (Plural: WOMEN.) **2.** the *adj.* use of ①.

woman-to-woman Go to MAN-TO-MAN.

womb ['wum] *n.* the organ in women and certain other mammals where the developing baby is protected and fed until birth.

women ['wɪm ən] plural of WOMAN.

won ['wʌn] past tense and past participle of WIN.

wonder ['wʌn dɚ] **1.** *n.* someone or something that is amazing, surprising, or like a miracle. **2.** *tv.* to wish to know something; to want to know something. **3.** *adj.* very good, helpful, or of great benefit.
→ NINE DAYS' WONDER

wonderful ['wʌn dɚ fʊl] *adj.* very good; amazing; remarkable; marvelous. (Adv: *wonderfully*.)

wonderland ['wʌn dɚ lænd] *n.* an area or place that is wonderful.

won't ['wont] *cont.* will not.

woo ['wu] **1.** *tv.* to court someone with the intention of marrying. **2.** *tv.* to encourage someone or a group to cooperate, join something, or buy something.

wood ['wʊd] **1.** *n.* the hard substance that trees make as they grow. (Plural only for types and instances.) **2.** *n.* a kind or type of ①. **3.** *n.* a small forest; an area where there are many trees. (Usually plural, but not countable. The meaning is the same for the singular and the plural.) **4.** the *adj.* use of ①, ②, or ③.
→ A BABE IN THE WOODS
→ KNOCK ON WOOD
→ OUT OF THE WOODS

wooden ['wʊd n] **1.** *adj.* made of wood. **2.** *adj.* stiff; not easily moved; not moving easily; not flexible. (Figurative on ①. Adv: *woodenly*.)

woodland ['wʊd lænd] *n.* an area of land that is covered with trees. (Singular or plural with the same meaning, but not countable.)

woodpecker ['wʊd pɛk ɚ] *n.* a bird that has a long, sharp beak for piercing holes in trees and a long tongue to catch insects inside the tree.

woodwind ['wʊd wɪnd] *n.* a group of musical instruments, many of which are made of wood or used to be made of wood, and many of which are played by blowing air across a reed.

woodwork ['wʊd wɚk] *n.* something that is made of wood, especially the trim on the inside of a house or building. (No plural.)

woody ['wʊd i] **1.** *adj.* covered with woods; covered with trees. (Comp: *woodier*; sup: *woodiest*.) **2.** *adj.* [of a plant] containing wood. (Comp: *woodier*; sup: *woodiest*.)

wool ['wʊl] **1.** *n.* the soft, curly hair of sheep and goats. (Plural only for types and instances.) **2.** *n.* thread, yarn, or fabric made from ①. (No plural.) **3.** *adj.* made from ②; WOOLEN.
→ PULL THE WOOL OVER SOMEONE'S EYES

woolen ['wʊl ən] *adj.* made of WOOL.

woolgathering daydreaming.

word ['wɚd] **1.** *n.* a speech sound or group of speech sounds that has a particular meaning; a written symbol or a group of written symbols that represent a speech sound or group of speech sounds that has a particular meaning. **2.** *tv.* to

express something by choosing ① carefully.
→ BREAK ONE'S WORD
→ BY WORD OF MOUTH
→ EAT ONE'S WORDS
→ FROM THE WORD GO
→ GET A WORD IN EDGEWISE
→ GET THE FINAL WORD
→ GET THE LAST WORD
→ GET THE WORD
→ GO BACK ON ONE'S WORD
→ HANG ON SOMEONE'S EVERY WORD
→ HAVE ONE'S WORDS STICK IN ONE'S THROAT
→ KEEP ONE'S WORD
→ NOT UTTER A WORD
→ ONE'S WORD
→ ONE'S WORDS STICK IN ONE'S THROAT
→ PUT IN A GOOD WORD (FOR SOMEONE)
→ PUT WORDS INTO SOMEONE'S MOUTH
→ TAKE THE WORDS (RIGHT) OUT OF SOMEONE'S MOUTH
→ TRUE TO ONE'S WORD
→ TWIST SOMEONE'S WORDS (AROUND)

the **word 1.** *n.* an order; a command. (No plural. Treated as singular.) **2.** *n.* news; information. (No plural. Treated as singular.)

wordy ['wɚd i] *adj.* having too many words; using more words than necessary to express something. (Adv: *wordily.* Comp: *wordier;* sup: *wordiest.*)

wore ['wor] past tense of WEAR.

work ['wɚk] **1.** *n.* an activity that requires effort. (No plural.) **2.** *n.* the effort required to do an activity. (No plural.) **3.** *n.* something that is a result of effort or energy; a piece of music or art. **4.** *n.* a job; an occupation; a career; what one does for a living; what a person does to make money. (No plural.) **5.** *n.* the place where one's job is located; the job site. (No plural.) **6.** *iv.* to be employed; to have a

job; to labor; to earn money at a job. **7.** *iv.* to function properly; to operate properly. **8.** *tv.* to cause something to function as intended. **9.** *tv.* to cause someone or something to operate or function; to cause someone or something to be active; to cause something to use energy. **10.** *tv.* to plow or farm land.
→ ALL IN A DAY'S WORK
→ DIRTY WORK
→ GET DOWN TO WORK
→ MAKE FAST WORK OF SOMEONE OR SOMETHING
→ MAKE SHORT WORK OF SOMEONE OR SOMETHING

work away (at something) to continue to work hard or industriously at something.

work like a horse to work very hard.

work on someone **1.** [for a physician] to treat someone; [for a surgeon] to operate on someone. **2.** to try to convince someone of something. **3.** [for something, such as medication] to have the desired effect on someone.

work one's **fingers to the bone** to work very hard.

work out 1. [for something] to turn out all right in the end. **2.** [for someone] to do a program of exercise.

work out for the best to end up in the best possible way.

work something **in(to** something**)** to press, mix, or force a substance into something.

work something **off 1.** to get rid of body fat by doing strenuous work. **2.** to get rid of anger, anxiety, or

energy by doing physical activity.
3. to pay off a debt through work
rather than by money.

work something **up** to prepare
something, perhaps on short
notice.

work up to something **1.** [for
something] to build or progress to
something. (Usually concerning
the weather.) **2.** [for someone] to
lead up to something.

work (up)on something **1.** to
repair or tinker with something.
2. [for something] to have the
desired effect on something.

workbook ['wɚk bʊk] *n.* a textbook for students, often including
pages that assignments can be
written on.

worker ['wɚk ɚ] *n.* someone who
works; someone who is employed.

workout ['wɚk aʊt] *n.* a period of
physical exercise.

the **works** everything.

world ['wɚld] **1.** *n.* the planet
earth. **2.** *n.* the people who live on
the planet earth; the human race.
3. *n.* a planet other than earth,
especially as the source of other
life forms. **4.** *n.* an area of human
activity, thought, or interest.
  → CARRY THE WEIGHT OF THE WORLD
    ON ONE'S SHOULDERS
  → COME DOWN IN THE WORLD
  → COME UP IN THE WORLD
  → DEAD TO THE WORLD
  → IN A WORLD OF ONE'S OWN
  → IN THE WORLD
  → MOVE UP (IN THE WORLD)
  → NOT LONG FOR THIS WORLD
  → ON TOP OF THE WORLD
  → OUT OF THIS WORLD
  → SET THE WORLD ON FIRE

  → THINK THE WORLD OF SOMEONE OR
    SOMETHING
  → WITH THE BEST WILL IN THE WORLD

World Wide Web ['wɚld 'waɪd
'wɛb] *n.* an international network
of data storage, transfer, and its
visual and audio display, designed
to be accessed through a computer
connection. (Abbreviated *WWW*
and the WEB.)

worldwide ['wɚld 'waɪd] *adj.*
found or occurring throughout the
world; involving everyone in the
world.

worm ['wɚm] *n.* any of numerous
small, soft, tube-shaped animals
having no legs or head, including
some that crawl underground and
others that live as parasites in animals or people.
  → OPEN A CAN OF WORMS

worn ['worn] **1.** Past participle of
WEAR. **2.** *adj.* reduced in value or
usefulness owing to wear.

worn-out ['worn 'aʊt] **1.** *adj.* completely reduced in value or usefulness because of wear. **2.** *adj.* very
tired; exhausted.

worry ['wɚ i] **1.** *n.* a feeling of anxiety; a fear of trouble. (Plural only
for types and instances.) **2.** *n.*
someone or something that causes
①. **3.** *tv.* to be anxious that something bad might happen; to suspect, regrettably, that something
bad might happen. (The object is a
clause with THAT ⑦.) **4.** *tv.* to cause
someone to feel anxiety or to fear
trouble.

worse ['wɚs] **1.** *adj.* more bad; less
good; inferior. (The comparative
form of BAD.) **2.** *adv.* in a way that

is ① than some other way. (The comparative form of *badly*.)
→ NONE THE WORSE FOR WEAR
→ ONE'S BARK IS WORSE THAN ONE'S BITE.

worsen ['wɚ·s ən] **1.** *tv.* to make something worse. **2.** *iv.* to become worse. **3.** *iv.* to become more sick.

worship ['wɚ·ʃɪp] **1.** *tv.* to honor someone or something greatly; to adore someone or something. (Past tense and past participle: *worshiped*. Present participle: *worshiping*.) **2.** *iv.* to attend a church service. (Past tense and past participle: *worshiped*. Present participle: *worshiping*.) **3.** *n.* what is done at a church service; the praise and honor of a spirit, ancestor, god, object, or person. (No plural.)

worst ['wɚst] *adj.* most bad; least good; most inferior. (The superlative of BAD.)
→ IF WORST COMES TO WORST

the **worst** *n.* [among three or more] someone or something that is the most bad or least good. (Treated as singular or plural, but not countable.)

worth ['wɚθ] **1.** *n.* the value of something; the amount of money that something could sell for. (No plural.) **2.** *n.* the importance of someone or something; the degree to which something is able to be used. (No plural.) **3.** *n.* the amount of something that can be bought for a specific amount of money. (No plural.)
→ MAKE SOMETHING WORTH SOMEONE'S WHILE
→ NOT WORTH MENTIONING
→ NOT WORTH THE TROUBLE
→ PUT IN ONE'S TWO CENTS(' WORTH)

worth its weight in gold very valuable.

worth one's **salt** worth one's salary.

worth someone's **while** worth someone's time and trouble.

worthless ['wɚθ ləs] *adj.* having no value or importance; useless. (Adv: *worthlessly*.)

worthy ['wɚ ði] *adj.* deserving one's time, energy, or attention; deserving; useful; having value or importance. (Adv: *worthily*. Comp: *worthier*; sup: *worthiest*.)

worthy of the name deserving or good enough to be called something.

would ['wʊd] **1.** *aux.* a form used as the past tense of WILL to express the future from a time in the past, especially in indirect quotations or in constructions where other past-tense verbs are used. (Contraction: -'d.) **2.** *aux.* a form used to express something that happened many times in the past. (Contraction: -'d.) **3.** *aux.* a form used instead of WILL ① to make commands more polite by turning them into questions. (Contraction: -'d. See also WILL ①; using *would* is usually more polite than using *will*.)

would like (to have) to want someone or something; to prefer someone or something.

would rather do something would more willingly do something; would more readily do something; would prefer to do something. (Often -'d *rather*.)

wouldn't ['wʊd nt] *cont.* would not.

would've ['wʊd əv] *cont.* would have, where HAVE is an auxiliary.

wound 1. ['waʊnd] past tense and past participle of WIND ④ and ⑤. **2.** ['wund] *n.* an injury where the skin is torn or punctured. **3.** ['wund] *n.* an injury to one's feelings. (Figurative on ②.) **4.** ['wund] *tv.* to injure someone; to cause someone to have ②.
→ RUB SALT IN A WOUND

wove ['woːv] past tense of WEAVE.

woven ['wo vən] past participle of WEAVE.

wrap ['ræp] *n.* a shawl or a scarf; a coat or cape.
→ GET SOMETHING WRAPPED UP
→ HAVE SOMETHING WRAPPED UP
→ KEEP SOMETHING UNDER WRAPS

wrap someone or something **(up)** ['ræp...] to enclose someone or something in a cover.

wrap something **up** ['ræp] to bring something to an end; to conclude something.

wrath ['ræθ] *n.* severe anger, especially from someone with a lot of power. (No plural.)

wreak vengeance (up)on someone or something to seek and get revenge on someone or a group by harming someone or the group.

wreath ['riθ] *n., irreg.* a decoration of flowers and leaves arranged in a certain shape, especially a circle. (Plural: ['riθs] or ['riðz].)

wreathe ['rið] *tv.* to make a circle around something.

wreck ['rɛk] **1.** *n.* a serious accident, especially where something is destroyed. **2.** *n.* a ruined vehicle that remains after a serious accident. **3.** *n.* someone or something that is a mess. (Figurative on ②.) **4.** *tv.* to destroy something.

wreckage ['rɛk ɪdʒ] *n.* whatever remains after a serious accident or disaster. (No plural. Treated as singular.)

wrench ['rɛntʃ] **1.** *n.* a tool that turns nuts, bolts, pipes, and other objects into or out of position. **2.** *tv.* to twist or pull something with force. **3.** *tv.* to injure a part of the body by twisting it or pulling it.

wrestle ['rɛs əl] **1.** *tv.* to force someone or something loose, down, away, etc., with force. **2.** *iv.* to participate in a sport in which ones wrestles one's opponent down as in ①.

wringer ['rɪŋ ɚ] *n.* an old-fashioned washing machine that removes water from clothes by pressing them as the clothes are passed between two rollers.
→ PUT SOMEONE THROUGH THE WRINGER

wrinkle ['rɪŋ kəl] **1.** *n.* a crease; a small fold or line, such as in clothing that has not been ironed or on the skin of an old person. **2.** *iv.* to become creased; to get small lines in one's skin or on the surface of something. **3.** *tv.* to cause someone's skin or the surface of something to have ①; to cause creases, folds, or lines to form on the surface of someone or something.

wrist ['rɪst] *n.* the part of the body where the hand joins the lower part of the arm.

write [ˈraɪt] **1.** *tv., irreg.* to make words or symbols on a surface with a pen, pencil, chalk, etc. (Past tense: WROTE; past participle: WRITTEN.) **2.** *tv., irreg.* to put thoughts or ideas into writing; to organize words or symbols into meaningful prose. **3.** *iv., irreg.* to mark on a surface with a pen, pencil, chalk, etc., as with ②. **4.** *iv., irreg.* to work by creating the content for books, articles, movies, plays, or other texts; to be an author; to be a writer. **5.** *iv., irreg.* to prepare and send [a letter or note to someone]. (E.g., *Please write when you can.*)

write away to write a lot; to continue writing.

write away for something to send for something in writing, from a distant place.

write off (to someone) **(for** something) to send away a request, in writing, for something.

write someone **in (on** something) to write the name of someone in a special place on a ballot, indicating a vote for the person.

write someone or something **off (as** something) **1.** to give up on turning someone or something into something. **2.** to give up on someone or something as a dead loss, waste of time, hopeless case, etc. **3.** to take a charge against one's taxes.

write someone or something **up** to write a narrative or description about someone or something.

write something **back to** someone to write a letter or E-mail answering someone.

write something **down** to make a note of something; to record something on paper in writing.

write something **in(to** something) **1.** to write information into something. **2.** to include a specific statement or provision in a document, such as a contract or agreement.

write something **off (on** one's taxes) to deduct something from one's federal income taxes.

write something **out** to put thoughts into writing, rather than keeping them in one's memory.

writer [ˈraɪtɚ] *n.* an author who writes for a living; someone who has written something.

writhe [ˈraɪð] *iv.* to twist and turn in pain or as though in pain.

writing [ˈraɪtɪŋ] **1.** *n.* making sentences, words, or letters with a pen, a pencil, chalk, or other writing instrument. (No plural.) **2.** sentences, words, or letters made with a pen, a pencil, chalk, or other writing instrument. (No plural.) **3.** *n.* something that is written; a book, poem, or other document. (Sometimes plural with the same meaning.)

written [ˈrɪt n] **1.** Past participle of WRITE. **2.** *adj.* placed in writing; printed or spelled out in writing.

wrong [ˈrɔŋ] **1.** *adj.* not correct; not true; mistaken; in error. (Adv: *wrongly.*) **2.** *adj.* bad; evil; illegal; immoral; not lawful. (Adv: *wrongly.*) **3.** *adj.* not desired; not wanted; incorrect. (Adv: *wrongly.*) **4.** *adj.* out of order; not working properly; faulty. **5.** *adv.* in a way that is ③. **6.** *n.* a bad, illegal, improper, or immoral action. **7.** *tv.* to treat someone badly or unfairly.

→ BARK UP THE WRONG TREE
→ GET OUT OF THE WRONG SIDE OF THE BED
→ GET UP ON THE WRONG SIDE OF THE BED

→ IN THE WRONG
→ IN THE WRONG PLACE AT THE WRONG TIME
→ ON THE WRONG TRACK
→ RUB SOMEONE'S FUR THE WRONG WAY
→ RUB SOMEONE THE WRONG WAY

wrote ['rot] past tense of WRITE.

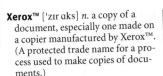

Xerox™ [ˈzɪr ɑks] *n.* a copy of a document, especially one made on a copier manufactured by Xerox™. (A protected trade name for a process used to make copies of documents.)

X-ray [ˈɛks re] **1.** *n.* a ray of energy that can pass through solid or nearly solid matter, such as the body. (Used especially to take pictures of the insides of people or objects.) **2.** *n.* a picture of the inside of a person or an object, made by passing ① through the person or object onto film. **3.** *tv.* to take a picture of the inside of a person or an object using ①.

xylophone [ˈzɑɪ lə fon] *n.* a musical instrument made of a series of wooden bars of different sizes, each of which makes a different note when struck with a small wooden hammer.

Y

yacht ['jɑt] **1.** *n.* a large boat or ship used for pleasure or racing. (Powered by sails, engines, or both.) **2.** *iv.* to travel somewhere on water in ①.

yam ['jæm] **1.** *n.* a vegetable similar to the potato, grown in tropical areas. **2.** *n.* a sweet potato, which is orange and does not taste like a potato.

yank ['jæŋk] **1.** *tv.* to pull someone or something quickly, with force. **2.** *n.* a quick pull; a sharp tug.

yank on something to pull or jerk something, with force.

yard ['jɑrd] **1.** *n.* a unit of measurement of length equal to 36 inches, 3 feet, or about 91.44 centimeters. **2.** *n.* the land that surrounds a house or other dwelling.

yardstick ['jɑrd stɪk] **1.** *n.* a ruler that is 36 inches—that is, one yard—long. **2.** *n.* something that other things are compared with; a standard. (Figurative on ①.)

yarn ['jɑrn] **1.** *n.* thick, soft thread that is used for things like knitting or weaving. (Number is expressed with *ball(s)* or *skein(s) of yarn*.) **2.** *n.* a tale; a story that is not completely true.
→ SPIN A YARN

yawn ['jɔn] **1.** *iv.* to stretch one's mouth open and breathe in and out slowly and deeply, especially when one is tired or bored. **2.** *iv.* [for something like a hole] to have a very wide opening. (Figurative on ①.) **3.** *n.* an act of opening one's mouth, as in ①.

year ['jɪr] **1.** *n.* 12 months; 365.25 days; the time it takes for earth to revolve around the sun. **2.** *n.* a full or partial ① spent doing a certain activity. **3.** *n.* a particular level of study in a school, college, or university.
→ ALL YEAR LONG
→ RING IN THE NEW YEAR

year after year for many years, one after another.

year in, year out year after year; all year long.

yearly ['jɪr li] **1.** *adj.* happening once a year; occurring each year; happening every year. **2.** *adv.* once a year; each year; every year.

years running Go to DAYS RUNNING.

yeast ['jist] *n.* a very small fungus that causes bread to rise and is also used to make alcohol. (Plural only for types and instances.)

yell ['jɛl] **1.** *tv.* to say something loudly; to scream something; to shout something. **2.** *iv.* to speak loudly; to scream; to shout. **3.** *n.* a loud cry; a shout.

yell out to cry out; to shout loudly.

yellow ['jɛl o] **1.** *n.* the color of a ripe lemon or of the yolk of an egg. (Plural only for types and instances.) **2.** the *adj.* use of ①. (Comp: *yellower*; sup: *yellowest*.) **3.** *adj.* timid; scared to do something. (Informal. Comp: *yellower*; sup: *yellowest*.)

yelp ['jɛlp] **1.** *n.* a short, high-pitched bark; a short, high-pitched shout of pain or emotion. **2.** *iv.* to make ①.

yen ['jɛn] **1.** *n.* a strong desire; a strong feeling of wanting something. (No plural.) **2.** *n., irreg.* the basic unit of money in Japan. (Also ¥. Plural: *yen*.)

yes ['jɛs] **1.** *n.* a statement showing that someone agrees with something or gives permission to do something. **2.** *n.* an act of voting showing that one agrees with the proposal. **3.** *adv.* a word showing approval, consent, or willingness. **4.** *adv.* a word emphasizing a positive statement, especially when denying a negative one. (E.g., *Yes, it is!*)

yesterday ['jɛs tɚ de] **1.** *n.* the day before today. **2.** *adv.* on the day before today.
→ NEED SOMETHING YESTERDAY
→ NOT BORN YESTERDAY

yet ['jɛt] **1.** *adv.* up to a certain point in time; by a certain point in time; as of a certain point in time. **2.** *adv.* eventually, even with barriers and delays. **3.** *adv.* still; even; even more. **4.** *adv.* and in spite of that; however; nevertheless. **5.** *conj.* but; however; nevertheless; although.

yield ['jild] **1.** *iv.* to bend, break, or move out of the way because of someone or something that is stronger or more powerful. **2.** *iv.* to surrender to someone or something, especially someone or something that is stronger or more powerful; to submit to someone or something. **3.** *iv.* to allow other traffic or people to have the right of way; to allow another vehicle or person to move first. **4.** *tv.* [for plants or animals] to supply or

produce something such as food. **5.** *n.* the amount of something that is produced.

yield something **to** someone **1.** to give someone else the right to go first, be first, choose, etc. **2.** to give up something to someone.

yoke ['jok] **1.** *n.* a frame of wood that fits around the necks of animals so they can pull something heavy that is attached to the frame. (Compare this with YOLK.) **2.** *tv.* to put ① on oxen or other strong animals.

a **yoke around** someone's **neck** something that oppresses people; a burden.

yolk ['jok] **1.** *n.* the round, yellow part inside an egg. (Compare this with YOKE. E.g., *use four egg yolks.*) **2.** *n.* the substance of ①. (No plural. E.g., *spilled some egg yolk.*)

yonder ['jɑn dɚ] *adv.* over there.

you ['ju] *pron.* the second-person pronoun, singular and plural.

You are welcome. a response to THANK YOU ①.

you'd ['jud] **1.** *cont.* you would. **2.** *cont.* you had, where HAD is an auxiliary.

you'll ['jul] *cont.* you will.

young ['jʌŋ] **1.** *adj.* in the early part of life; not old; having been alive for a short period of time as compared with an average age. (Comp: *younger;* sup: *youngest.*) **2.** *adj.* new; in an early stage of development; recently formed or started. (Comp: *younger;* sup: *youngest.*) **3.** *n.* the offspring of an animal or a human. (No plural. Treated as plural. Countable, but not usually used for one off-spring.)

young lady ['jʌŋ 'led i] *n.* a young girl of any age; a female who is young, relative to the speaker. (Also a term of address.)

young man ['jʌŋ 'mæn] *n.* a boy of any age; a male who is young, relative to the speaker. (Also a term of address.)

young woman ['jʌŋ 'wʊm ən] *n.* a young adult female human; a female who is young, relative to the speaker.

youngster ['jʌŋ stɚ] *n.* a young person; a child.

your ['jʊɚ] *pron.* the possessive form of YOU, the second-person singular and plural pronoun; belonging to the person(s) being spoken or written to. (Used as a modifier before a noun. Compare this with YOU'RE.)

Your guess is as good as mine. Your answer is as likely to be correct as mine is.

you're ['jʊɚ] *cont.* you are. (Compare this with YOUR.)

yours ['jʊɚz] *pron.* the possessive form of YOU, the second-person singular and plural pronoun; the one or ones belonging to the person(s) being spoken or written to. (Used in place of a noun.)

yourself [jʊɚ 'sɛlf] **1.** *pron.* the reflexive form of the singular form of YOU. **2.** *pron.* a strong form of YOU [singular].

yourselves [jʊɚ 'sɛlvz] **1.** *pron.* the reflexive form of the plural of YOU. **2.** *pron.* a strong form of YOU [plural].

youth ['juθ] **1.** *n.* the quality of being young. (No plural.) **2.** *n.* the period of time when one is a child or teenager. (No plural.) **3.** *n.* children or teenagers, as a group. (No plural. Treated as plural, but not countable.) **4.** *n.* someone who is young, especially a male; a child or teenager.

you've ['juv] *cont.* you have, where HAVE is an auxiliary.

yummy ['jʌm i] *adj.* having a good taste; delicious. (Informal. Comp: *yummier;* sup: *yummiest.*)

Z

al ['zil] *n.* a strong passion for a belief or cause; excitement. (No plural.)

bra ['zi brə] *n., irreg.* a horselike mammal that has a whitish hide with dark brown or black stripes. (Plural: *zebra* or *zebras*.)

zenith ['zi nəθ] *n.* the highest possible point.
→ AT THE ZENITH OF SOMETHING

zephyr ['zɛf ɚ] *n.* a gentle wind; a breeze.

zero ['zi ro] **1.** *n.* the number 0. (Plural ends in *-s* or *-es*.) **2.** *n.* nothing. (No plural.)

zero in (on someone or something**)** to aim directly at someone or something.

zero in on something to aim or focus directly on something.

zest ['zɛst] *n.* enjoyment, especially for life; excitement. (No plural.)

zinc ['zɪŋk] *n.* a metallic element. (No plural.)

zip ['zɪp] **1.** *tv.* to open or close something, using a zipper. **2.** *iv.* to move somewhere very quickly. **3.** *n.* energy; vigor. (Informal. No plural.)

zip code ['zɪp kod] *n.* one of the five-digit or nine-digit numbers that is part of the U.S. Postal Service's postal coding system. (An acronym for *Zone Improvement Plan*. Often written *ZIP code*.)

zip something up 1. to close a zipper. **2.** to close a garment by zipping a zipper closed. **3.** to close one's mouth. (Informal. Usually a command: **Zip it up!**)

zipper ['zɪp ɚ] **1.** *n.* a fastener made of two strips of tiny teeth that lock together when a sliding piece is moved over them. **2.** *tv.* to zip something; to open or close something using ①.

zone ['zon] **1.** *n.* an area, especially one that is different in some way from nearby areas. **2.** *tv.* to divide a city into different areas limited only to certain uses; to limit an area to certain uses.

zoo ['zu] *n.* a place where wild animals are kept so that they can be seen by people.

zookeeper ['zu kip ɚ] *n.* someone who takes care of animals at a zoo.

zoom in (on someone or something**) 1.** to move in to take a close-up picture of someone or something, using a special lens. **2.** to focus sharply on a matter related to someone or a problem.